PSYCHOLOGY

for A2 Level

PSYCHOLOGY
for A2 Level

Michael W. Eysenck
and Cara Flanagan

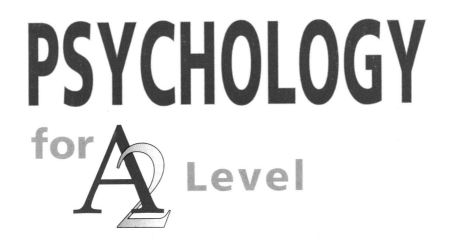

First published 2001 by Psychology Press Ltd
27 Church Road, Hove, East Sussex, BN3 2FA

http://www.psypress.co.uk
http://www.a-levelpsychology.co.uk

Simultaneously published in the USA and Canada
by Taylor & Francis Inc
325 Chestnut Street, Suite 800, Philadelphia, PA 19106

Psychology Press is part of the Taylor & Francis Group

British Library Cataloguing in Publication Data

A catalogue record for this book is available from the British Library

Library of Congress Cataloging in Publication Data

ISBN 1-84169-251-4

Cover design by Hurlock Design, Lewes, East Sussex
Typeset in the UK by Facing Pages, Southwick, West Sussex
Printed and bound in Spain by Book Print S.L.

Dedication

To Christine, Fleur, William, and Juliet
M.W.E.

To Rob, Pip, Jack, and Rosie
C.L.F.

Contents

Acknowledgements

We would like to express our enormous (and sincere) gratitude to those colleagues who have read and offered invaluable advice on various chapters in this book: Evie Bentley, Roz Brody, John Cartwright, Di Dwyer, Paul Humphreys, Matt Jarvis, and Kevin Silber. Also thanks to colleagues whose help was less direct but nonetheless valuable in many different ways: Mike Cardwell, and Liz Hey. Our especial thanks should go to Paul Dukes, Tanya Sagoo, and Mike Forster at Psychology Press who contributed a major part to the production and ultimate success of this book and are nothing short of brilliant.

About the Authors

Michael W. Eysenck is one of the best-known British psychologists. He is Professor of Psychology and head of the psychology department at Royal Holloway University of London, which is one of the leading departments in the United Kingdom. His academic interests lie mainly in cognitive psychology, with much of his research focusing on the role of cognitive factors in anxiety in normal and clinical populations.

He is an author of many titles, and his previous textbooks published by Psychology Press include *Psychology for AS Level* (2000), *Psychology: A Student's Handbook* (2000), *Cognitive Psychology: A Student's Handbook, Fourth Edition* (2000, with Mark Keane), *Simply Psychology* (1996), *Perspectives on Psychology* (1994), *Individual Differences: Normal and Abnormal* (1994), and *Principles of Cognitive Psychology* (1993). He has also written the research monographs *Anxiety and Cognition: A Unified Theory* (1997), and *Anxiety: The Cognitive Perspective* (1992), along with the popular title *Happiness: Facts and Myths* (1990). He is also a keen supporter of Crystal Palace and Wimbledon football clubs.

Cara Flanagan has worked for many years as a GCSE and A-level examiner, team leader, and assessor for various examination boards. She has recently been appointed the Reviser for one of the new psychology specifications and, in that capacity, will be closely involved in setting all the new examination papers. As an experienced examiner, she knows intimately the intricacies of the examination system and what is needed by students to do well in examinations.

Cara has also written extensively for A-level psychology. Her textbooks include, most recently, *Psychology for AS Level* (2000), the *Letts AS Level Revision Guide* (2000), *Early Socialisation* (1999), and *Practicals for Psychology* (1998). She is co-editor of the highly successful Routledge modular series of psychology books. She also contributes regularly to *Psychology Review*, has written various teacher packs, and speaks at student conferences. She looks after three children and a husband, and enjoys walking in the Scottish Highlands where she lives.

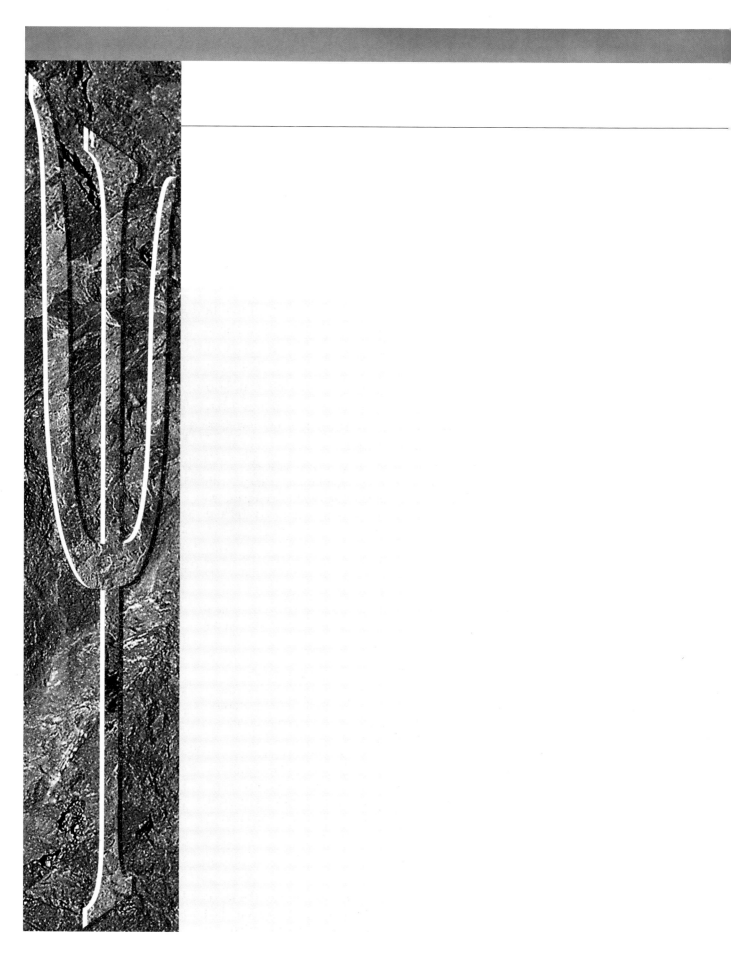

Introduction

Psychology needs no introduction. If you are using this book it is probable that you have completed the first year of your A level studies and are now ready to tackle the last leg—A2 studies. In this half of the AQA A course you have options! You do not have to study all of the material in this book. In fact it is highly unlikely that you would be able to cover all of it in one year. You are now in a position, after your AS studies, to have some idea about what areas of psychology are of interest to you and what areas you find less exciting. This may help in guiding your choices for A2.

There is one area of psychology in this book that is new to you, or at least appears to be new. This is comparative psychology (Part 5), the study of non-human animals with a view to making comparisons with human behaviour. There are elements of comparative psychology that were included in AS, namely the theory of evolution and classical and operant conditioning, so the subject matter is not entirely new.

How A2 Differs From AS

As we have just said, the A2 course contains options, unlike at AS level where the whole AQA A course was compulsory. Aside from this, the two main differences between AS and A2 are:

1. You are a year older than when you started the AS course, and therefore you should be capable of rather more mature thought. Mature thinking is, in part, the outcome of just getting older, but it is also due to your education—your AS studies have enabled you to develop new ideas and new insights. In the second year of study you can use your new knowledge to acquire a deeper understanding of psychology. This is referred to as "synopticity", which we will discuss shortly.
2. The examination for A2 is quite different from the AS examination, and this will direct how you study psychology in the A2 year. You will now have to answer essay questions rather than the questions split into several parts that were used at AS level. You also are required to do a piece of coursework for Unit 6 of the A2 examination.

The A2 Examination

Note that our discussion of the different elements of the examination uses the terms "section" and "unit". These terms do not correspond with the use of "Section" and "Unit" in this textbook, so be aware that the exam papers use a different terminology.

You may recall that the AS examination comprised Units 1–3. The A2 examination consists of:

Unit 4 The options paper (30% of the A2 mark)

Three questions to be answered in 1½ hours. You must select your questions from at least two different sections of the exam paper. Within each section there will be three questions, one drawn from each of the areas listed in brackets.

- Section 1: Social psychology (Social cognition; Relationships; Pro- and anti-social behaviour).
- Section 2: Physiological psychology (Brain and behaviour; Biological rhythms: Sleep and dreaming; Motivation and emotion).
- Section 3: Cognitive psychology (Attention and pattern recognition; Perceptual processes and development; Language and thought).
- Section 4: Developmental psychology (Cognitive development; Social and personality development; Adulthood).
- Section 5: Comparative psychology (Determinants of animal behaviour; Animal cognition; Evolutionary explanations of human behaviour).

Unit 5 The synoptic paper (40% of the A2 mark)

Three questions to be answered in 2 hours, one from each section:

- Section A Individual Differences
  Choose one question from three: Issues in the classification and diagnosis of psychological abnormality; Psychopathology; Treating mental disorders.

- Section B Perspectives: Issues and Debates
  Choose one question from four.
  Two questions set on Issues: Gender bias; Cultural bias; Ethical issues; The use of non-human animals in psychological research.
  Two questions set on Debates: Free will and determinism; Reductionism; Psychology as science; Nature–nurture.

- Section C Perspectives: Approaches
  Choose one question from two. See page 758 for a description of this question.

Unit 6 Coursework

(30% of the A2 mark)

You are required to conduct one piece of coursework, and write a report of your study. This is discussed in Part 8 of this book.

Answering Essay Questions

In the A2 examination you have two kinds of essay questions:

- Unit 4: each to be answered in 30 minutes and marked out of 24.
- Unit 5: each to be answered in 40 minutes, and marked out of 30 and with the addition of synoptic criteria.

We will consider how to answer essay questions in general and then look in particular at the synoptic issue.

Coping with exam stress

Here is a topic that you have already studied: stress. What can psychological research tell us about coping with stress in an examination?

- Increase your sense of control by the use of positive self-statements: "I have spent as much time as I could revising".
- Calm yourself by using some form of relaxation. During the examination have short breaks and think about nice things.
- Social support. Think about people who give you comfort.
- Catharsis. Before the examination go for a run or some other form of physical exercise to relieve pent-up feelings of stress.
- Avoid repression (a form of ego defence) by acknowledging your feelings of worry.
- Write essay plans in the examinations to organise your thoughts and reduce your anxiety about not being able to answer the question.

In addition, there is one really important issue to consider: when one is stressed it is harder to recall material that has been learned in a rote fashion and it is easier to recall things that you understand well. This should encourage you to avoid just learning the facts parrot fashion. Instead you should focus, even when revising, on a more complete *understanding* of what it all means.

Some tips on essay writing

Having marked thousands of examination answers, we are in a position to suggest some of the common problems:

1. Lack of knowledge

Clearly there is no way that you can achieve a good examination mark without the necessary knowledge. Study consistently throughout your course and revise effectively. In your AS book we discussed ways to do this. The A2 year is a chance to start afresh and institute a new system of study and revision throughout the year. Don't leave it until the month before the exam.

2. Effective use of knowledge

When marking an examination answer, it often appears that candidates might have knowledge of relevant research and/or ideas, but simply have not made this clear enough in their answer to attract credit. Always be sure to explain yourself carefully. It is a common misconception that marks are given only for the number of points presented in an answer. This kind of "shopping list" approach does not attract high marks. You must communicate understanding and interpretation. You can demonstrate that you understand the relevance of the material by adding a sentence like "This shows that …" or "One can conclude …". Some other useful phrases are shown in the box on the right.

> **Useful phrases in essays**
>
> So we can see that …
> This would imply …
> One consequence would be …
> One advantage of this is …
> An alternative explanation could be …
> Therefore …
> Not everyone reacts the same way, for example …
> There may be cultural variations …
> This has been applied to ….

Note that there are no "right answers" in psychology—there are only answers that are well informed and well argued. Two students might both get full marks for essays that are entirely different but answer the same question.

3. Anecdotal material

It is tempting to include material such as "My own experience is …" when writing your examination answer. It is likely that your teacher will have used such anecdotes in class to help make the material more understandable and the lessons more lively, but in the examination you will only be credited for *psychologically informed* answers.

4. Answer the question that is set

It would be lovely if the questions in the examination were totally open-ended; if, for example, the question for the pro- and anti-social part of the specification was "Write an essay on pro- and anti-social behaviour". The difficulty with this approach would be that it would not discriminate very well between candidates. Everyone would get good marks because they knew what the question was going to be and could prepare their answer. Therefore the examiner selects certain questions out of a predictable pool of questions, in order to ensure that you have studied more than just one essay-question answer. And you can only be awarded marks for your ability to answer *this* question and not the question you would have liked to answer—no matter how good your other answer may be.

In order to ensure that you answer the question that is set, it is a good idea to deconstruct the question before you begin—just to make sure that you are clear about what is required. This also helps prevent exam nerves taking over and forces you to pause rather than just writing anything that comes into your head. Five minutes of careful thought and planning are well worthwhile.

In order to deconstruct a question you need to be familiar with the AQA A "injunctions" that tell you, the candidate, what to do. The most important ones are set out in the box on the next page. When you open the examination paper, circle the questions that you might possibly answer and in each one underline the key words. For example if the question was:

Do you remember SQ3R? Survey, question, read, recite, and review. Think about applying this to your studies.

How can you use your knowledge about memory and forgetting to devise efficient methods of study and revision?

*How should the "**planning fallacy**" inform your ideas for better studying throughout this year?*

Key terms in bold are explained by the glossary at the back of the book.

In the same way that there are no right answers for students, there are no "right" or "wrong" theories. Freud, Piaget, and Broadbent, for example, did not get it wrong. Their theories continue to be highly influential even though some elements have been criticised.

(a) (Describe) **one** theory of (cognitive development.) **(12 marks)**

(b) (Assess) the extent to which this theory is supported by (psychological studies.)
     (12 marks)

This should help you focus on exactly what is required.

A01 is assessment objective 1: knowledge and understanding of psychological principles, theories, concepts, studies, methods, perspectives, and applications.

A02 is assessment objective 2: analyse and evaluate psychological theories, concepts, studies, methods, principles, perspectives, and applications.

AQA A exam injunctions

AQA A publishes a "Glossary of terms" that defines all the injunctions. The most important ones are included here.

AO1 terms

Describe	Present evidence of what you know.
Outline	Give a summary description in brief form.

Also: consider, define, examine, explain, state

AO2 terms

Evaluate	Make an *informed* judgement of the value (positive or negative) of the topic area, based on systematic analysis.
Criticise	Evaluate the strengths and weaknesses of the topic area.

Also: (critically) analyse, (critically) assess, justify

AO1 and AO2 terms

Discuss	Describe and evaluate with reference to different (contrasting) points of view. You may be asked to discuss with reference to particular criteria.
Critically consider	"Consider" (demonstrate knowledge and understanding) plus "criticise" (evaluate strengths and weaknesses).

Also: compare and contrast, distinguish between

Other terms

Research	Knowledge gained through empirical test (i.e., direct study) or theoretical examination.
Studies	Empirical investigations.
Theory	A complex set of interrelated ideas/assumptions/principles used to explain observed phenomena.
Model	Less complex than a theory, usually comprising a single idea.
Evidence	Empirical or theoretical material.
Findings	The outcome of research.

Also: insights, concepts, methods

---

5. Organise your answer

There is credit to be gained from an organised and well-constructed answer. After deconstructing the question you should note down the key points that you want to cover. This prevents you writing your answer in a disorganised manner, stuffing in everything you think of as you think it. So jot down your ideas first with a view to formulating a co-ordinated answer.

This approach should also prevent you writing "everything you know" about a topic in the hope that something will get credit. If the examiner has to do the work in organising your material, then he or she should get the credit, not you. The ability to be selective is a higher-order skill and one that you should demonstrate in order to get good marks.

"Rules of the game"

The questions in AQA A examinations follow certain rules:

- Only injunctions from the glossary of terms are used.
- AO1 and AO2 are equally balanced in every question (except section C on Unit 5).
- Candidates are guaranteed one question from each subsection of the specification (these subsections are equivalent to the Sections in this book). In the cases of issues and debates there are two questions from these subsections.
- Questions are set from the specification. Make sure you have a copy so that you are familiar with the terms that are used. Anything given as "e.g." is only an example. No question would specifically refer to this. Anything given as "including" is a part of the specification and may be specifically named in a question.
- If a quotation is used in a question, there may be a specific instruction for it to be addressed. You will lose marks in such cases if you do not address the quotation.
- Numbers are specified where appropriate.
- Singular and plural are specified. Make sure you write about studies or factors if that is in the question.

6. Make sure your essay covers both assessment objectives

A common error is for candidates to focus on content rather than skills. Yes, you are being assessed on your knowledge, but you are also being assessed on how you use this knowledge. The two skill clusters are called assessment objective 1 (AO1) and assessment objective 2 (AO2). On all questions there are an equal number of marks for each skill. (12 marks each on Unit 4 and 15 marks each on Unit 5.) Both of these assessment objectives were used at AS level.

AO1 is knowledge and understanding of psychological theories, terminology, concepts, studies, methods, principles, perspectives, and applications, and the ability to communicate this knowledge and understanding of psychology in a clear and effective manner.

AO2 requires you to analyse and evaluate psychological theories, concepts, studies, methods, principles, perspectives, and applications. This includes commentary, assessment, and criticism—remembering that criticism may be positive or negative.

If you are asked to describe research studies, you may evaluate them using theories— this is a way of assessing how we can make sense of the research data, and of considering what is implied by the findings. You may also evaluate research studies with considerations about the methodology and/or ethics in so far as the ethics challenge the findings of the study. Don't overlook points of positive evaluation.

If you are asked to describe theories, you may evaluate them by contrasting them with other theories. Do not simply *describe* another theory but use the other theory as a means of criticism. You may also evaluate a theory by looking at implications and/or applications, and by describing research studies that support or challenge the theory.

> **Evaluation**
>
> Evaluation can be achieved through:
>
> - The use of research studies to provide support for an argument.
> - Providing commentary on research studies, which challenges the findings because of flawed methodology or assumptions.
> - Presenting alternative theories as a contrasting viewpoint.
> - Suggesting useful applications.
> - Considering implications, and/or strengths and weaknesses.

7. Depth and breadth

An excellent answer manages to combine both depth and breadth. That means being able to cover sufficient breadth of ideas while also leaving sufficient time for detail (depth). It is not easy to achieve a good balance between these, but you must bear the trade-off in mind—if you try to cover too much material you will not be able to give enough detail. Therefore you must be selective in the arguments, theories, and/or studies you describe and leave time to elaborate the ones you do include.

One issue to note, in relation to detail, is the question of names and dates. You do not have to know the names and dates of researchers but if you do, it helps in three ways. First, it adds a sense of detail to your essay. Second it helps the examiner identify the particular study or theory you are discussing. Third, it should assist your recall. A name acts like a cue to access an area of memory.

How essays are marked

Psychology A level essays are not marked as right or wrong. There is no "correct" answer. The criteria that are used for assessment have already been mentioned: detail, structure, knowledge, understanding, psychological information, effective use of material, and so on. The examiner reads the essay and then decides which descriptor in the marking allocation best fits the essay. The marking allocation for AQA A Unit 4 (currently in draft form) is summarised in the table on the next page. This table indicates the descriptors for each skill and therefore what you are aiming for:

- AO1: descriptions that are accurate, with evidence of depth and breadth, and are well-structured.
- AO2: a commentary that is informed and coherently elaborated, with arguments that are well-selected and effectively used.

Examiners, when marking, bear in mind the fact that the essay is written by a notional 18-year-old in 30 minutes. An example of how this mark scheme is used is given in the box on page 9.

The Marking Allocation for AQA Specification A (Draft Version)

For Unit 4 assessment objective 1 (AO1)

Band	Marks	Content	Relevance	Organisation and structure	Breadth and depth
3 (Top)	12–11	Accurate and well-detailed		Coherent	Substantial evidence of both, and balance achieved
3 (Bottom)	10–9	Slightly limited, accurate, and well-detailed		Coherent	Evidence of both but imbalanced
2 (Top)	8–7	Limited, accurate, and reasonably detailed		Reasonably constructed	Increasing evidence of breadth and/or depth
2 (Bottom)	6–5	Limited, generally accurate, but lacking in detail		Reasonably constructed	Some evidence of breadth and/or depth
1 (Top)	4–3	Basic, rudimentary, sometimes flawed	Sometimes focused		
1 (Bottom)	2–0	Just discernible; weak/muddled/inaccurate	Wholly or mainly irrelevant		

For Unit 4 assessment objective 2 (AO2)

Band	Marks	Commentary	Use of material	Selection	Elaboration
3 (Top)	12–11	Informed and thorough	Highly effective	Appropriate	Coherent
3 (Bottom)	10–9	Informed	Effective	Appropriate	Coherent
2 (Top)	8–7	Reasonable, but slightly limited	Effective		Evidence of coherent elaboration
2 (Bottom)	6–5	Reasonable, but limited	Reasonably effective		Some evidence of elaboration
1 (Top)	4–3	Minimal, superficial, and rudimentary	Restricted		
1 (Bottom)	2–0	Weak, muddled, and incomplete	Wholly or mainly irrelevant		

For Unit 5 assessment objective 1 (AO1)

Band	Marks	Content	Relevance	Organisation and structure	Breadth and depth	Evidence of different theoretical perspectives and/or methodological approaches
5	15–13	Accurate and well-detailed		Coherent	Substantial evidence of both, and balance achieved	Clear evidence
4	12–10	Slightly limited, accurate, and well-detailed		Coherent	Evidence of both, but imbalanced	Slightly limited
3	9–7	Limited, accurate, and reasonably detailed		Reasonable	Evidence of breadth and/or depth	Limited
2	6–4	Basic, and lacking in detail	Sometimes focused			Little evidence
1	3–0	Weak, muddled understanding	May be irrelevant			Little or none

For Unit 5 assessment objective 2 (AO2)

Band	Marks	Commentary	Use of material	Selection	Elaboration	Critical commentary on the different theoretical perspectives and/or methodological approaches
5	15–13	Informed and thorough	Highly effective	Appropriate	Coherent	Clear
4	12–10	Informed, but slightly limited	Effective		Evidence of coherent elaboration	Slightly limited
3	9–7	Reasonable, but limited	Reasonably effective		Some evidence of elaboration	Limited
2	6–4	Minimal, superficial, and rudimentary	Minimally effective		Little evidence of elaboration	Minimal
1	3–0	Weak, muddled, and incomplete	Not effective			Little or none

A sample essay with examiner's comments

The essay below is a student answer to the question "Describe and evaluate research into factors involved in biological rhythms".   **(24 marks)**

The sentences that are highlighted have been credited as AO2. Examiner's comments have been inserted in brackets.

There are many bodily rhythms. Circannual rhythms last a cycle of a year. Examples of this are migrations of birds and animals, and the mating cycles of animals. This can be shown to be due to environmental factors because birds and animals move towards warmth and food supplies.[First factor identified] *In humans there is a condition known as Seasonal Affective Disorder which is also circannual. It can lead to periods of depression in winter months and can be seen as psychological because the bad winter weather makes people feel depressed. It is also physiological because it has been shown that the absence of sunshine leads to a lower production of melatonin, which makes us feel less happy.*[SAD explained in terms of both psychological and physiological factors. Nice balance and reasonable detail. Good to see use of technical terms.]

Infradian rhythms last over 24 hours, for example the menstrual cycle of women, which lasts 28 days. The physiological effects of the menstrual cycle can be dizziness, and abdominal pains a few days before menstruation. This suggests that it is biological factors that are involved in the bodily rhythm of menstruation. [Interpretation of evidence offered.] *However, there are also psychological effects such as mood swings and irritability.* [Contrasting viewpoint. Could be credited as AO1 but presented in an evaluative sense.] *This shows that both physiological and psychological factors are involved in infradian bodily rhythms.* [Interpretation and commentary] [The second paragraph offers a discussion of the factors that might contribute to the menstrual cycle, an example of a second biological rhythm.]

Circadian rhythms last for 24 hours. Some people have been shown to be "morning" or "evening" types, that is they reach their physical and psychological peak in the morning or evening. There is physiological evidence for this, as people's hormone levels rise and fall through the day, giving rise to changes in mood and aptitude. It is also possible that changes in daylight through the day can affect the person's physiological and psychological state.[Factor explained for circadian rhythm—some people are naturally one type or the other. Could be more explicit and detailed, e.g., what hormone levels rise? But reasonable.] *Research also shows, however, that there are psychological factors which influence whether a person is a "morning" or "evening" type.* [Presented as contrasting view.] *A person's aptitude through the day may influence whether or not they feel better able to do things in the morning or evening, whatever their personal experience and routine is.*[Relevance not entirely clear. In what way is aptitude a biological rhythm? Is the candidate trying to say that aptitude is an alternative explanation? This material has not been effectively used.]

Nocturnal rhythms are those which occur at night, that is sleep cycles. [Fourth biological rhythm.] *Sleep is a very physical state and much research has been conducted into whether the purpose of sleep is for physiological or psychological repair. One theory namely the "Restoration and Repair theory" states that sleep cycles are necessary for the synthesis of neurochemicals which are used up during the body's daytime functioning.* [The candidate appears to be forgetting the title of the essay and writing about the functions of sleep rather than the factors that govern the cycle.] *However more research has been done to disprove this theory, because although we need sleep (lack of sleep leads to dizziness and irritability) when we lose sleep we don't need to catch up on all we've lost. So this shows that the nocturnal body rhythms and sleep cycles are influenced by physiological factors.* [Some attempt to make sense of the material in this paragraph, though better evidence might have been used to identify the physiological factors involved in sleep.]

There are also theories which say that we need sleep for psychological health. [Presenting an alternative view to the previous paragraph.] *Freud believed that we sleep in order to dream, and our dreams are a disguised form of our repressed sexual anxieties and desires. This is supported because our dreams do seem to have meaning but many researchers do not believe that our anxiety and conflict need to be sexual. This indicates that our nocturnal bodily rhythms are also psychological.* [Interpretation]

Sleep cycles follow a pattern which includes five stages, and although they vary in length of time for each person, these are necessary stages that a person needs to follow. [Relevance not clear, detracts from selectivity and organisation. Would have been better omitted.]

Both physiological and psychological factors are involved in bodily rhythms, and this has been shown by research. [Commentary on whole essay but not of great value. Next sentence is more useful.] *It is not clear whether physiological or psychological factors are more important. It is probable that both have a part to play in the function of bodily rhythms. Some researchers tend towards the belief that physiological, psychological and environmental factors are involved in bodily rhythms. This can be seen in Seasonal Affective Disorder where, environmentally, the lack of pleasant weather is a factor, as is the physical lack of melatonin from the sun, and so is the psychological belief that there is nothing to look forward to.* [Repetition of earlier material. In a well-organised essay this would have been saved to use here as an example of interaction between physiological, psychological and environmental factors.] *This is shown in the treatment, which is exposure to more sunshine or extra strong light, though sufferers can be given counselling as well.* [Nice additional point of evaluation in terms of how the knowledge could be applied.]

[Incidentally, the word length of this essay is 664 words, which is a good length essay to be able to write in 30 minutes.]

In determining the mark for this essay, the examiner must ask a number of questions.

AO1: Is it accurate? Yes reasonably. Is it detailed? Again, reasonably. The content may be best described as slightly limited. What about the coherence and structure? Parts could have been omitted but there is a good structure, moving clearly through different biological rhythms. Is there a balance between breadth and depth? The candidate has covered a good range of bodily rhythms and research, and balanced this with a reasonable amount of detail.

Mark for AO1 = band 2 top, 8

Psychological content is *limited*, although *accurate* and *reasonably detailed* at the level of knowledge, description, and understanding. The answer is *reasonably constructed* in terms of its description of research and there is *some evidence of breadth and/or depth*.

The temptation is to go up to band 3 bottom because the essay is slightly limited, rather than limited, but it could not be described as "well-detailed".

AO2: Is the commentary informed? There is some evidence of identifiable research but it tends to be vague. The commentary mainly relies on interpretation rather than any challenge to the data. Contrasting viewpoints are presented but this is repetitive: there are physiological factors and then there are also psychological factors. Is it coherently elaborated? In general it is coherent and points are elaborated. Is the material used effectively? In general yes, but not always. The AO2 material is less effective than the AO1 skills.

Mark for AO2 = band 2 bottom, 6

Evaluation of research is *reasonable* but *limited* in terms of relevant concepts, evidence or applications. The material is used in a *reasonably effective* manner and shows *some* evidence of *elaboration*.

For 7 marks the AO2 material would need to be "slightly limited", "effectively used" and "coherently elaborated". All of these criteria are nearly met, but not quite.

A total of 14 marks would be equivalent to a Grade C.

The synoptic paper

Unit 5 is slightly different from Unit 4. You have a longer time to answer each question and each question is worth more marks (and the whole paper is worth more towards your final A level mark). The reason the questions and paper are worth more is because this paper assesses your understanding of psychology as a whole, as distinct from your knowledge of particular areas.

The mark scheme for this paper is the same as the others, except that there are five bands instead of three, and there is a synoptic criterion (see page 694). In order to receive maximum marks your answer needs to fulfil these criteria:

- AO1: Psychological content is *accurate* and *well-detailed* at the level of knowledge, description, and understanding. The organisation and structure is *coherent*. There is *substantial evidence of breadth and depth* and a *balance* between them is *achieved*. There is *clear* evidence of a range of different theoretical and/or methodological approaches relevant to the question.
- AO2: Psychological content is *informed* and *thorough* in terms of analysis, evaluation, and interpretation of relevant psychological theories, concepts, evidence, or applications. Material has been used in a *highly effective* manner and shows evidence of *appropriate selection* and *coherent elaboration*. There is *clear* commentary on the different theoretical and/or methodological approaches used in the answer.

An essay that would receive 8 marks for each skill cluster would be described as:

- AO1: Psychological content is *limited*, although *accurate* and *reasonably detailed* at the level of knowledge, description, and understanding. The answer is *reasonably* constructed in terms of the psychological content, and there is *evidence of breadth and/or depth*. There is *limited* evidence of a range of different theoretical and/or methodological approaches relevant to the question.
- AO2: Psychological content is *reasonable* but *limited* in terms of analysis, evaluation, and interpretation of relevant psychological theories, concepts, evidence, or applications. Material has been used in a *reasonably effective* manner and shows *some* evidence of *coherent elaboration*. There is *limited* commentary on the different theoretical and/or methodological approaches used in the answer.

Synopticity is defined as an understanding of the breadth of theoretical and methodological approaches in psychology. It is the common threads that run across the specification, and is discussed further in Part 7 of this book.

Deciding Between Options

Most of you may find that your choices in the A2 examination are fixed before you start the course. However if you do have the opportunity to contribute to topic choice then obviously the first thing to think of when selecting the options for Unit 4 is, "What interests me most?"

The second consideration is "What topics would be most useful for my understanding and critical appreciation of the breadth and range of different theoretical perspectives and/or methodological approaches?" This is the synopticity issue. In order to answer questions on Unit 5 you will be able to draw on material from your AS studies. For example, the models of abnormality that formed part of the individual differences module included examples of the main approaches in psychology: biological, psychodynamic, behavioural, and cognitive. The concept of reductionism in psychology was introduced in relation to the learning theory explanation for attachment. And ethical issues formed a central part of the social psychology module.

Approaches in psychology, and issues, such as reductionism and ethics, are examples of the threads that run across the psychology specification, i.e., they are synoptic.

During your A2 year you will gain a deeper understanding of these synoptic issues. However, it might be helpful to focus on certain areas of Unit 4 *because* they contribute to your understanding of synoptic issues. The table below offers some examples of where you might look to develop a deeper understanding of the synoptic topics. This is by no means comprehensive but it should help to organise your thinking about how to address synopticity.

Issues		
Gender bias	**AS**	Role of gender in response to stress
	A2	Gender development (Section 11)
		Moral development (Section 10)
Cultural bias	**AS**	Attachment
		Social influence
	A2	Social perception (Section 1)
		Relationships (Section 2)
Ethical issues	**AS**	Social influence (Ethical issues in psychological research)
	A2	Pro- and anti-social behaviour (Section 3)
		Brain and behaviour (Section 4)
Use of non-human animals	**AS**	Attachment (Harlow's research)
	A2	Sleep (Section 5)
		Comparative psychology (Sections 13, 14, and 15)
Debates		
Free will and determinism	**AS**	Genetic explanations of abnormality
		Obedience (situational determinism)
	A2	Freudian theory (Section 11)
		Evolutionary explanations of human behaviour (Section 15)
		Humanistic and social constructionist approaches (Section 21)
Reductionism	**AS**	Learning theory
	A2	Brain and behaviour (Section 4)
		Attention (Section 7)
		Evolutionary explanations (Sections 13 and 15)
Psychology as science	**AS**	Human memory (use of laboratory experiments)
	A2	Social constructionist approach (Section 21)
		Experimental approach to attention research (Section 7)
Nature–nurture	**AS**	Causes of abnormality
	A2	Perceptual development (Section 8)
		Language acquisition (Section 9)
		Development of intelligence (Section 10)
		Psychopathology (Section 17)
Approaches		
Biological/medical	**AS**	Stress
		Models of abnormality
	A2	Physiological psychology (Sections 4, 5, and 6)
		Biological explanations of mental disorders (Section 17)
		Biological therapies (Section 18)
Behavioural	**AS**	Learning theory as an explanation of attachment
		Models of abnormality
	A2	Explanations of aggression (Section 3)
		Conditioning theory (Section 13)
		Behavioural therapies (Section 18)
Psychodynamic	**AS**	Psychoanalytic theory as an explanation of attachment
		Models of abnormality
	A2	Social and personality development (Section 11)
		Individual differences (Sections 16, 17, and 18)
Cognitive	**AS**	Human memory
		Modes of abnormality
	A2	Social cognition (Section 1)
		Cognitive psychology (Sections 7, 8, and 9)
Evolutionary	**AS**	Attachment theory
	A2	Evolutionary explanations of animal behaviour (Section 13)
		Evolutionary explanations of human behaviour (Section 15)

You should also remember that an appreciation of methodology is part of your synoptic understanding of psychology and this is inherent in *all* areas that you have studied.

SUMMARY

❖   A2 is different from AS because (1) you are more mature and have a grounding in psychology, and (2) the examination requires essay answers and you now have a choice of options.

❖   The AQA A examination consists of three papers: Unit 4 (The options paper, three questions to answer in 1½ hours); Unit 5 (The synoptic paper, three questions to answer in 2 hours); Unit 6 (coursework). Units 4 and 6 are each worth 30% of the A2 mark and Unit 5 is worth 40%.

❖   When answering examination questions, remember to learn the material; use your knowledge effectively; do not use anecdotal material but present psychologically informed answers; organise your answer; ensure that you answer the question that is set; make sure your essay covers both assessment objectives and addresses skills rather than just content; and aim for a balance between depth and breadth.

❖   The synoptic paper (Unit 5) is marked with the addition of the synoptic criterion, which assesses your appreciation of a range of different theoretical and/or methodological approaches relevant to the question. When choosing topics to study for Unit 4, you might consider which topics will be most helpful for the perspectives questions on Unit 5.

FURTHER   READING

The topics in this Introduction are covered in greater depth by P. Humphreys (2001) *Exam success in AQA A psychology* (London: Routledge). The classic book to read as an introduction to psychology is G.A. Miller (1966) *Psychology: The science of mental life* (Harmondsworth, UK: Penguin), which covers the history of psychology and describes some of the main figures.

Two interesting case histories are discussed at length in the following books, giving an in-depth knowledge of many issues in psychology such as ethics and research, privation, language acquisition, gender development, and nature and nurture: The case of Genie is reported by R. Rymer (1993) *Genie: Escape from a silent childhood* (London: Michael Joseph), and an account of the twin boy who lost his penis as the result of a botched circumcision and spent his early life as a girl is given by J. Colapinto (2000) *As nature made him* (London: Quartet Books).

WEB SITES

www.aqa.org.uk
Access to the AQA A specifications for psychology, and other information from the examination board.

www.a-levelpsychology.co.uk
Psychology Press site with useful exam material and book details. Psychology Press is the largest publisher of psychology books in the UK.

An Exercise

Using your knowledge of "the rules of the game" (see page 6), say what is wrong with the following questions:

1. Describe research studies of obedience. (24 marks)

2. (a) Outline **two** research studies on sleep. (6 marks)
    (b) Evaluate these research studies. (12 marks)

3. Discuss Piaget's theory of cognitive development. (24 marks)

4. (a) Consider explanations of forgetting. (12 marks)
    (b) Describe applications of memory research. (12 marks)

5. Describe and discuss two theories of attribution. (24 marks)

6. To what extent can psychologists explain why we sleep? (24 marks)

In the following questions there is something to watch out for, what is it?

7. "If it is nature that is responsible for our intelligence, our aggressiveness and our personality generally, then we must select out those individuals with the best and breed from them."

    With reference to the issues in the above quotation, critically consider the nature–nurture debate in psychology. (30 marks)

8. Describe and evaluate some of the factors that influence gender development. (30 marks)

9. (a) Outline explanations of bystander behaviour. (12 marks)
    (b) Critically assess these explanations with reference to research studies. (12 marks)

Answers: 1. No AO2 injunction. 2. Only 6 marks for AO1, has to be 12 marks. 3. Can't ask for Piaget's theory because it is only an "e.g."on the specification. 4. Both injunctions are AO1. 5. "Discuss" is AO1 and AO2, so the "describe" is not necessary. 6. No injunction. 7. You must address the quotation in your answer. 8. You must discuss more than one factor. 9. In part (a) you must offer a summary description of the explanations not detailed descriptions. In part (b) you must refer to research studies.

Try to generate your own essay questions

A part of the specification is given below. Try to generate your own questions. Some real examples, from past papers, are given at the end.

Specification: Biological rhythms, sleep and dreaming

(a) Biological rhythms. Research studies into circadian, infradian, and ultradian biological rhythms, including the role of endogenous pacemakers and exogenous zeitgebers. The consequences of disrupting biological rhythms (e.g., shift work).

(b) Sleep. Theories and research studies relating to the evolution and functions of sleep, including ecological (e.g., Meddis, Horne) and restoration (e.g., Oswald) accounts. The implications of findings from studies of total and partial sleep deprivation for such theories.

(c) Dreaming. Research findings relating to the nature of dreams (e.g., content, duration, relationship with the stages of sleep). Theories of the functions of dreaming, including neurobiological (e.g., Hobson and McCarley, Crick and Mitchison) and psychological (e.g., Freud, Webb and Cartwright) accounts.

Real questions on biological rhythms:

Describe and evaluate **two** theories of the functions of sleep. (24 marks)
    (January 1997 module paper 5 question 3)

Discuss research into factors involved in bodily rhythms. (24 marks)
    (January 1999 module paper 5 question 3)

(a) Outline the nature of sleep. (6 marks)
(b) Outline **one** theory of the functions of sleep, and evaluate this theory in terms of research studies **and/or** alternative theories. (18 marks)
    (January 2000 module paper 5 question 3)

PART 1

Social Psychology

The word "social" refers to interactions between two or more members of the same species. Social psychologists are interested in the way people affect each other, for example, interpersonal relationships, group behaviour, leadership, conformity, obedience to those in authority, and the influence of the media.

Social psychology differs from sociology in placing greater emphasis on the individual as a separate entity. Sociologists are interested in the structure and functioning of groups, as are many social psychologists. However, social psychologists are also interested in the effects of group processes on the individual members of a social group.

Section 1: Social Cognition pp.16–57

❖ How does our thinking (cognition) affect social behaviour?

❖ How do you know whether someone else is mean or kind?

❖ Is social perception similar to perception of the physical world?

❖ Why do people act in a prejudiced manner?

Section 2: Relationships pp.58–97

❖ Why are we attracted to one person rather than another?

❖ Why do some relationships fade out while others continue?

❖ How does romantic lover differ from companionate love?

❖ Are relationships the same the world over?

Section 3: Pro- and Anti-social Behaviour pp.98–133

❖ Is aggression learned or innate?

❖ Do people ever act altruistically, or are they motivated by selfishness?

❖ How does the media influence our pro- and anti-social behaviour?

1

Social Cognition

The focus of this Section is how we can understand our social world by considering mental processes. We will consider the ways in which we interpret, analyse, and remember information about our world and the people in it.

Attribution of Causality

In our everyday lives, we spend much of our time in the company of other people. It is often important to work out *why* they are behaving in certain ways. For example, suppose that someone you have only just met is very friendly. They may really like you, or they may want something from you, or perhaps they are merely being polite. In order to know the best way of interacting with this person, it is very useful to have a good understanding of the reasons for their apparent friendliness. It is worth emphasising the quite spontaneous and unconscious way that one makes such **attributions**. It is not a deliberate calculation but an involuntary train of thought that you are engaged in all the time.

According to Heider (1958), people are naïve scientists who relate observable behaviour to unobservable causes. This has been called the "**theory of naïve psychology**". Heider suggested that we produce attributions, which are beliefs about the causes of behaviour, and that these attributions are based on two sources of information:

- *Internal attributions*, those based on something within the individual whose behaviour is being observed. For example, you go into a shop to buy a newspaper and the shop assistant does not look you in the face and appears generally gloomy. You assume that she is an unfriendly person. This is an attribution made about the assistant's character, i.e., internal.
- *External attributions*, those based on something outside the individual. In the example just given, you might notice that the shop assistant is extremely friendly to the next customer, which leads you to change your attribution and suspect that it is something about yourself that caused her gloomy behaviour, i.e., something external to the assistant's character.

Internal attributions are often called **dispositional attributions**, whereas external attributions are called **situational attributions**. A dispositional attribution is made when we decide that someone's behaviour is due to their personality or other characteristics. In contrast, a situational attribution is made when someone's behaviour is attributed to the current situation.

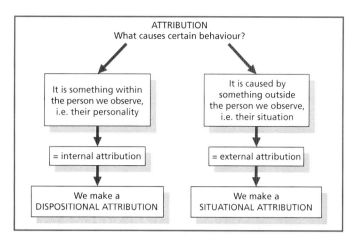

The distinction between dispositional and situational attributions can be seen if we consider the case of an office worker who is working inefficiently. A dispositional attribution would be that he or she is lazy or incompetent. A situational attribution would be that he or she has been asked to do work that is not appropriate to his or her skills.

Attribution Theories

Since Heider's contribution, various theorists have put forward attribution theories based on his ideas. Three of the most important of such theories are discussed next. First, we consider the correspondent inference theory put forward by Jones and Davis (1965). Second, we deal with Kelley's (1967, 1973) attribution theory, and finally, Weiner's three-dimensional model.

Correspondent inference theory

According to correspondent inference theory (Jones & Davis, 1965), we assume that an observed behaviour *corresponds* with some underlying stable characteristic of the person involved. For example, somebody's aggressive behaviour corresponds with the underlying trait of "hostility". Another common example is our assumption that film stars have similar personalities to the roles they play—we assume that the behaviour they are displaying corresponds to underlying character traits.

There are two stages in this process:

If there is no intentionality, no attribution is made.

1. The *attribution of intention*. We decide that effects were intentional if we think that the person knew the consequences of his or her own behaviour, and that he or she had the ability to perform the action required to produce those consequences.
2. The *attribution of disposition*. An observer (the one making attributions) is likely to make dispositional rather than situational attributions about an actor (the one who is observed) when the behaviour:
   - Is *low in social desirability*. For example, if someone is very rude in a social situation, we tend to conclude that he or she is an unpleasant person. On the other hand, if they are conventionally polite, then we do not feel we have learned much about them.
   - Yields *noncommon effects*. If the other person's actions have rare or noncommon effects not shared by other actions, then we infer an underlying disposition. In other words, if the effects produced by one course of action could not be produced by alternative courses of action, we infer a dispositional cause. For example, imagine Karen is deciding between going to work for two advertising agencies: "Hook'em" who promote cigarettes, and "Help'em" who do public service ads. Both companies offer the same pay and work conditions. If she chooses "Help'em" then we would explain her action in terms of disposition because the only noncommon effect (i.e., fact that is not shared) is the work that the companies do. She must have selected the second company because of the work that they do, and this choice is attributed to disposition (Aronson, Wilson, & Akert, 1998).
   - Has *hedonic relevance*, i.e., when the behaviour has specific effects for the perceiver. In the previous example, your attributions would be affected if you worked in the voluntary sector. If Karen choose the "Help'em" agency despite better pay elsewhere you might still attribute her behaviour to disposition because she, like you, values helping other people.

If Arpad tells you he is going to the theatre for the first time ever, would you make a dispositional or situational attribution? What further information might change your attribution?

   - Has *personalism*, when the behaviour is seen as directly intended to benefit or harm the perceiver. For example, when a friend gives you a gift you are likely to attribute her behaviour to internal factors ("She likes me") whereas if a gift is given to someone else you are more likely to attribute it to a situational explanation, such as "It must be his birthday".

NONCOMMON EFFECTS PRINCIPLE: WHICH CAR WILL YOU BUY?

Car A	Car B	Car C
Lead-free petrol	4-star petrol	Diesel
Power steering	Power steering	Power steering
Air bag	Air bag	Air bag
Expensive to service	Cheap to service	Cheap to service

If you buy Car A, we can infer that lead-free petrol is important to you. You will not have made your decision because of the power steering or air bags, as they are common to the other two cars. We might then infer that you also care about the environment.

Evaluation

Jones and Harris (1967) provided support for this model in a study where they presented their American participants with short essays either for or against the Castro government in Cuba. The participants were informed either that the essay writers had chosen which side to support (choice condition), or that they had been told to write a pro- or anti-Castro essay as part of an examination on a political science course (no-choice condition). The participants' task was to estimate the essay writer's real attitudes towards Castro. The participants paid some attention to the situation (whether or not the essay writer had a choice), but less than they should have done. In the no-choice situation they should have concluded nothing about the writer's true attitudes, but in fact participants were greatly influenced by the views expressed by the writer in this condition. This demonstrates that individuals do infer a corresponding underlying attitude on the basis of observable behaviours.

There are a number of criticisms of the correspondent inference explanation for attribution. First, attribution may be more complex in real life. When Jones and Nisbett (1972) gave additional information about the political persuasions of essay writers (this time the essays were either pro- or anti-marijuana), they found that participants did make adjustments. In the choice condition (essayists supposedly had a choice over what they could write) a moderate essay was judged by participants as conforming to the author's opinion, i.e., moderate. However, the same essay was judged as moderately unfavourable if the author had been asked to write a strongly favourable essay. In other words, judgements about the tone of the essay were related to the directions the authors had been given. You might also consider the study by Fein et al. on page 23.

Second, the theory emphasises the importance of intentionality—that actions are the consequence of an individual's intentions. However, many behaviours are not intentional, such as clumsiness or careless behaviour, and this cannot be accounted for within the framework of this theory, because the theory states that only intentional behaviours are given attributions.

In addition, the notion of noncommon effects presumes that people pay attention to non-occurring behaviours whereas other research has not found this (e.g., Nisbett & Ross, 1980). Finally, the theory predicts that actions which are contrary to expectation (e.g., those low in social desirability) produce correspondent inferences, but some behaviours that confirm expectations (e.g., behaviours in line with stereotypes) can also yield correspondent inferences. Therefore a number of the predictions of the theory are not supported in fact.

We think of John Wayne as a hero and all-round nice guy because that is what he was often like in his movies. We are making inferences about his true disposition on the basis of observable behaviours. This is an example of "correspondent inference".

Kelley's attribution theories

Kelley (1967) extended attribution theory in various ways. He argued that the ways in which people make causal attributions depend on the information available to them. When you have a considerable amount of relevant information from several sources, you

Think of a time when someone you did not know acted rudely towards you. What did you think of them?

are able to detect the *covariation* of observed behaviour and its possible causes. For example, if a man is generally unpleasant to you, it may be because he is an unpleasant person or because you are not very likeable. If you have information about how he treats other people, and you know how other people treat you, then you can work out what is happening. This is the covariation model.

In everyday life, we often only have information from a single observation to guide us in making a causal attribution. For example, you see a car knock down and kill a dog. In such cases, you must make use of information about the configuration or arrangement of factors. For example, if there was ice on the road or it was a foggy day, this will increase the chances that you will make a situational attribution of the driver's behaviour. This is the causal schemata model.

Covariation model

According to Kelley (1967), people making causal attributions use the covariation principle. This principle states that "an effect is attributed to a condition that is present when the effect is present, and absent when the effect is absent" (Hewstone & Antaki, 1988, p.115). There are three types of information that we use when deciding why someone has behaved in a given way:

* *Consensus*: the extent to which others in the same situation behave (or have behaved) in the same way.
* *Consistency*: the extent to which the person usually behaves in the way he or she is currently behaving.
* *Distinctiveness*: the extent to which the person's behaviour in the present situation differs from his or her behaviour in the presence of other people.

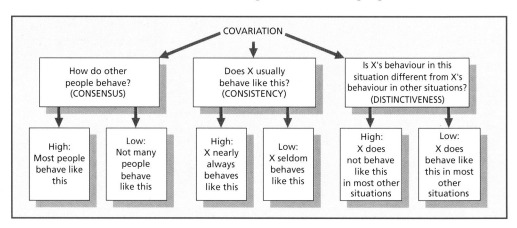

Is the covariation model or the causal schemata model more likely to be relevant to everyday life? Why?

Information about consensus, consistency, and distinctiveness is used to make a dispositional or situational attribution. If someone's behaviour has high consensus, high consistency, and high distinctiveness, then we will probably make a situational attribution. Here is an example: everyone is rude to Bella; Mary has always been rude to Bella in the past; Mary has not been rude to anyone else. Here Mary's behaviour is attributed to the unpleasantness of Bella rather than to her own unpleasantness.

In contrast, we will make a dispositional attribution if someone's behaviour has low consensus, high consistency, and low distinctiveness. Here is an example: only Mary is rude to Susan; Mary has always been rude to Susan in the past; Mary is rude to everyone else. Therefore we attribute Mary's behaviour to her disposition.

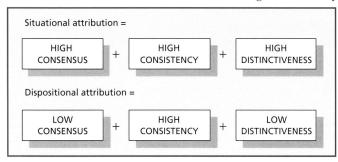

Evaluation of the covariation model. Research has given support to this model. For example, McArthur (1972) gave participants 12 event-depicting sentences that contained information (high or low) about consistency, distinctiveness, and consensus. For example, "Tom always laughs at this comedian" (high consistency), "Tom laughs at all comedians" (low distinctiveness), "Tom laughs at only this comedian" (high distinctiveness), "Everyone laughs at this comedian" (high consensus). Participants attributed external or internal causes as the model predicted.

However, such evidence is taken from highly artificial situations. In real life people use other sources of information. For example, Garland et al. (1975) found that, when participants were given greater choice about the information used to make attributions, some chose things like personality rather than consistency, distinctiveness, and consensus.

In addition, there are alternative ways of explaining the research findings that are simpler. For example, people may simply be attending to the most salient (noticeable) feature of a statement and this explains the basis for their attributions.

The covariation model also assumes that it is possible to make judgements about covariation but in fact it is quite difficult to do this, and we often have only incomplete information on which to base our judgements.

Causal schemata model

Kelley (1973) developed a new model in an attempt to overcome some of the earlier objections. He suggested that observers rely on causal schemata. These operate like equations. We have various mental formulae which tell us how causes interact to produce specific behaviours. In fact these formulae are more properly called **heuristics**—general guidelines or "rules of thumb" that *may* solve a problem but don't guarantee a solution (unlike a formula). The value of such heuristics is that they save a lot of time and effort in the process of interpreting often ambiguous and complex social perceptions.

The phrase "rule of thumb" is often used to describe heuristics. The phrase originated as a means of describing a stick with which to beat one's wife! The phrase means "a rule of general principle based on experience rather than theory".

The two main kinds of causal schemata are:

- *Multiple necessary causes*. This heuristic tells us that two or more behaviours are jointly necessary for a particular cause to be attributed. For example, in order to make an attribution of kindness you need to observe an act of kindness *and* know that the person was not receiving some payment for it. You only label a person as mean if they are mean to you and you observe them being mean to others (otherwise it might be just some grudge against you!).
- *Multiple sufficient causes*. In some cases we favour one particular explanation out of a range of possible explanations. In such cases we may operate a **discounting principle** where an observer selects the most obvious potential cause out of all available possibilities. For instance, when observing a sporting figure advertising a chocolate bar we attribute this behaviour to the likely appearance fee rather than an altruistic desire to help promote the chocolate. Another heuristic is the **augmenting principle** where the observer tends to place greater importance on one causal explanation if the behaviour appears to be "against the odds". For example, if you hear that a person has just passed their A levels you may think they are reasonably bright, but if you heard that in fact they got four grade As this augments the effect. The augmenting principle applies to both multiple necessary and multiple sufficient causes.

Note: Kelley uses the word "schemata" as the plural of "schema", but in later Units you will see "schemas" used instead. "Schemas" has tended to replace "schemata" in recent work, so the two terms have now become interchangeable.

Evaluation of the causal schemata model.   This model has the obvious advantage of explaining how we are able to make attributions when information is incomplete. An especially attractive feature is the use of heuristics to explain how we can make inferences so quickly and easily. However, the model lacks empirical support.

Weiner's three-dimensional model

Weiner (1980) was especially interested in the attributions that people make about their own successes and failures. Such attributions have important consequences for the future. For example, if you attribute your success on a test to hard work then you will continue to work hard, whereas if you attribute the success to luck then there is less reason for you to revise conscientiously in the future. Attitudes to failure are equally important.

Weiner proposed that there are three dimensions of attribution:

- *Locus*: external or internal (E or I).

- *Stability*: stable or unstable (S or U).
- *Controllability*: controllable or uncontrollable (C or U).

Attributions are made using all three dimensions. For example, a person might explain their lateness to school by: "It always takes me a long time to walk to school" (locus: E, stability: S, controllability: C) or "I'm just a born latecomer" (locus: I, stability: S, controllability: U).

Evaluation of the three-dimensional model

One obvious benefit of this model is that it recognises the importance of other dimensions rather than just the internal/external one. A further benefit is that the model has interesting applications such as attribution retraining, which involves teaching people to emphasise internal control. For example, Dweck (1975) retrained 12 children who were experiencing difficulty with failure. One group were told they were taking too long and should try harder, while a second group were given only positive feedback. The first group showed greater persistence and attributed any failures to lack of effort, whereas the second group were more likely to give up, continuing to attribute failure to lack of ability. The model can also be applied to an understanding of depression. Abramson et al. (1978) suggested that depressed individuals tend to attribute failure to themselves (internal) rather than to external factors, and such individuals see these attributions as unchanging (stable) and as global rather than specific. A depressive attributional style can be overcome through retraining (see page 681).

What advice would you give teachers on the basis of the research by Dweck?

The model has a lot of empirical support and has also been tested in a variety of cultural settings. Schuster, Forsterling, and Weiner (1989) worked with participants from Belgium, Germany, India, South Korea, and England. The participants were given the description of an individual who had failed to get a job and they were asked to rate various possible explanations for this failure in terms of stability, controllability, locus, and also universality (does it influence only this or also other outcomes?). The possible explanations were in terms of ability, effort, interest, luck, mood and so on. Schuster et al. found that all groups (except the Indians) were highly consistent in their use of the four categories (stability, controllability, locus, universality) supporting the claim that Weiner's model is valid in non-Western cultures as well.

However, there may be significant individual differences in the way that people use the three dimensions to make attributions, as in the case of depressives. A further drawback is that this model, like all attribution theories, assumes that people make judgements in a logical and rational manner—which may not always be true.

Biases in the Attribution Process

A bias is a prejudice or systematic factor that produces mistakes. It has been found that people make predictable errors when making attributions, and these result in biases for external or internal attributions.

Fundamental attribution error

One of the best known errors or biases is the **fundamental attribution error** (FAE), which is "the tendency to over-emphasise dispositions and to under-emphasise situational factors as causes of behaviour" (Hewstone & Antaki, 1988). In other words, we are biased in the direction of regarding other people's actions as being due to their personality rather than to the situation. For example, interviewers may interpret the nervousness of someone being interviewed for a job as being due to their personality rather than to the stressfulness of the situation.

Can you think of your own example of FAE?

Research evidence

Evidence of the fundamental attribution error was obtained in the study by Jones and Harris (1967), described earlier. This study showed how participants preferred to make internal attributions about the essayists' political opinions even when it was clear that external attributions were more appropriate. In another study Ross et al. (1977) arranged for participants to judge the general knowledge of contestants and questioners in a quiz. The observers knew that the questioners had made up the questions, so clearly they would appear more knowledgeable, yet the observers still rated the questioners as having more general knowledge than the contestants. This indicates a bias in the direction of internal attributions. The questioners, however, did not rate themselves as more superior, so they were able to accommodate the situational cues and make realistic attributions.

In your AS level studies the fundamental attribution bias was used to explain the results of Milgram's (1963) classic obedience studies. When asked to decide how many people would show total obedience in Milgram's situation, we tend to think along the following lines: "Only a psychopath would give massive electric shocks to another person. There aren't many psychopaths about, and so only a tiny percentage of people would be totally obedient." This line of reasoning focuses exclusively on the individual participant's characteristics. In line with the fundamental attribution error, it ignores the relevant situational factors (e.g., the scientific expertise and status of the experimenter; or the insistence of the experimenter that the participant continue to give electric shocks).

Can you use the fundamental attribution error to explain why we might believe that a sports star is actually advertising a product because he likes it instead of attributing his actions to the fee he is earning?

Suppression of true attitudes

There are doubts as to whether the fundamental attribution error is really fundamental. It is hard to believe that people *always* underestimate the importance of situational factors. Suppose that someone had a strong reason for suppressing their true attitudes. Fein, Hilton, and Miller (1990) tested this in a study in which the participants read an essay written by a student called "Rob Taylor" on a controversial topic. Some of the participants were told that Rob had been assigned to write either in favour of or against a particular point of view. Other participants were told that Rob had been allowed to choose what point of view to express. However, the professor who would be evaluating Rob had very strong views on the topic. Finally, they were told that Rob's essay put forward the same views as those held by his professor.

Those participants who thought that Rob had been assigned a point of view made the fundamental attribution error. Thus, they decided that Rob's true attitudes were those expressed in the essay. In contrast, those participants who thought that Rob had a good reason for hiding his true attitudes (i.e., pleasing his professor) concluded that the views he put forward in his essay did not reflect his true attitudes. Thus, we do not make the fundamental attribution error when it is clear that people have a hidden motive for what they are saying or doing.

Are we more likely to assume that this man is sleeping rough because of situational factors (he's been taken ill, forgotten his house keys) or dispositional factors (he can't keep a job, he's drunk and rowdy in accommodation, for example)?

Causal factors

What factors are responsible for the fundamental attribution error? The most important is probably **salience**: someone's behaviour is often more salient or prominent than the situation. McArthur and Post (1977) reported evidence for the importance of salience. Observers watched and listened to a conversation between two people. One of those involved in the conversation was made salient by being illuminated by a bright light, whereas the other was made non-salient by being in a dim light. The behaviour of the person who was made salient was rated as being caused more by disposition and less by the situation than was the behaviour of the non-salient person.

In what other situations might the other person have hidden motives?

It is also likely that the fundamental attribution error will occur in situations where an individual's attention is directed elsewhere, however in situations where an observer has the cognitive time to weigh up attributions then the fundamental attribution error will be less likely. This was demonstrated in the study by Gilbert et al. (see Key Study on the next page).

Reducing the fundamental attribution error

Gilbert, Pelham, and Krull (1988) tried to identify some of the processes involved in the fundamental attribution error. According to their theory, people initially make an automatic dispositional attribution when they observe someone's behaviour. That is sometimes followed by effortful cognitive processing, which may lead them to change their mind and attribute the behaviour to the situation. They tested this theory in a study in which the participants saw a videotape of a woman who was obviously anxious. She was pulling at her hair, shifting in her seat, biting her fingernails, and tapping her fingers. The participants could not hear what the woman was saying, but the topics she was supposed to be discussing were included as subtitles in the videotape. In one condition, the topics were anxiety-provoking (e.g., sexual fantasies; hidden secrets; public humiliation). In the other condition, the topics were fairly neutral (e.g., world travel; fashion trends; ideal holidays). In fact, the participants in both conditions saw exactly the same videotape except for the subtitles.

Half of the participants who watched the videotape were told to memorise the list of topics, whereas the other half simply watched the videotape. After the videotape had been presented, the participants were asked to indicate the extent to which the woman's anxiety was attributable to her disposition. It would seem more reasonable to give a stronger dispositional attribution when the woman was anxious when talking about neutral topics than when she was talking about anxiety-provoking topics, and that is exactly what was found among participants who simply watched the videotape. In contrast, the participants who were given the memory task gave the *same* dispositional attribution regardless of what the woman was talking about. Why did they give a dispositional attribution when the woman was talking about anxiety-provoking topics? According to Gilbert et al. this occurred because these participants were too busy learning the list to engage in the effortful processing needed to produce a situational attribution.

Discussion points

1. Do the findings of Gilbert et al. provide strong support for their theory?

2. Why do you think that people have the fundamental attribution error?

What assumptions do we make about the motives of politicians (such as Gordon Brown, above) when they meet the public?

Why do people possess the fundamental attribution error? According to Gilbert (1995, p.108), there are two main reasons. First, we like to think that life is fair, and using dispositional attributions can help us to preserve that belief:

> *A dispositionist worldview is … a general sense that people do what they do because of the kinds of people they are, and that … whatever happens to them is pretty much their own doing … by and large, we get what we work for, get what we ask for, and get what we deserve.*

Second, we like to think that what happens in our lives is predictable. If the behaviour of other people is determined mainly by their personalities, this makes their future behaviour much more predictable than if their behaviour varied considerably from situation to situation.

Evaluation of the fundamental attribution error

On the positive side, people often exaggerate the importance of disposition and minimise that of the situation as causes of behaviour. Sometimes these effects are extreme, as in the case of our reluctance to attribute obedience to the situation.

On the negative side, the fundamental attribution error may be less important in everyday life than in the laboratory. In everyday life, we realise that many people (e.g., politicians; second-hand car salespeople) have hidden motives that may influence their behaviour in certain situations.

Cultural differences.   The fundamental attribution error may be less common in Asian cultures than in American and European ones. As Moscovici and Hewstone (1983) pointed out, most Western cultures emphasise individualism and the notion that individuals should take responsibility for their own actions. Such cultural norms are very much in line with the fundamental attribution error. In contrast, the emphasis in most Asian cultures is on the group rather than on the individual. Supporting evidence was reported by Miller (1984). Adult Americans and Indian Hindus were asked to explain common events, such as the behaviour of a colleague who stole someone else's idea. The Americans showed a strong tendency to favour dispositional explanations over situational ones (they used dispositional explanations three times as often), whereas the Indian Hindus had the reverse style, they preferred situational explanations twice as much as dispositional ones.

Attributions that are made by people from a collectivist culture tend to be contextualised. Attributions made by people in individualistic cultures tend to be more focused on personal choice.

Why do you think Indian Hindus favour situational explanations?

Actor–observer effect

The second major example of a bias in the attribution process is the **actor–observer effect**. The actor is the person about whom the attributions are being made and the observer is observing and making the attributions. Suppose a mother is discussing with her son why he has done poorly in an examination. The son may argue that the questions were unusually hard, that the marking was unfair, and so on. In contrast, his mother may focus on the child's laziness and general lack of motivation. In more general terms, the son sees his own behaviour as being determined by various external or situational factors, whereas his mother focuses on internal or dispositional factors within her son. The actor–observer effect suggests that the actor tends to make situational attributions whereas an observer tends towards dispositional ones.

Jones and Nisbett (1972) argued that the processes involved in this example operate in numerous circumstances. According to them (1972, p.80) the actor–observer effect arises because

> *there is a pervasive tendency for actors to attribute their actions to situational requirements, whereas observers tend to attribute the same actions to stable personal dispositions.*

Research evidence

Nisbett et al. (1973) carried out various studies on the actor–observer effect. In one study, male college students wrote an essay about why they liked their girlfriends, and another essay about why their best friend liked his girlfriend. When writing about themselves, the students made twice as many situational attributions as dispositional attributions about their girlfriends. In contrast, when writing about their best friend, they used an equal number of situational and dispositional attributions. An explanation was dispositional if it referred in any way to the person doing the choosing ("I need someone I can be relaxed with" or "He likes blondes"). Statements were scored as situational if they referred to the entity being assessed (e.g., "She is a relaxed person to be with" or "She is a good cook").

In another study, Nisbett et al. asked their participants to rate themselves, their best friend, their father, an admired acquaintance, and Walter Cronkite (a well-known American television presenter) on a series of trait adjectives (e.g., tense–calm). They could either pick one of the adjectives or argue that it depended on the situation. The participants were much more inclined to say that the expression of the trait depended on the situation when describing themselves than when describing any of the other people. According to Nisbett et al., people are much more aware of the importance of situational factors in determining their own behaviour than in determining that of others.

Causal factors

Why do actor–observer differences in attribution occur? Such differences may depend on the fact that we possess much more information about ourselves than about other people. This may lead us to be aware of the subtle ways in which our behaviour is influenced by the situation, but unaware that the same is true of others. This explanation

Were there any possible confounding variables in Storms' study?

has not received much support. For example, participants in the study by Nisbett et al. knew much more about their father and their best friend than about an admired acquaintance or Walter Cronkite, but this did not affect their attributions.

Another possible reason for the actor–observer effect stems from the fact that we can see other people but cannot see ourselves. However, we can see the situation, and this may lead us to exaggerate its importance in determining our behaviour. This notion was tested by Storms (1973). Two participants took part in a "get acquainted" conversation, and two additional participants observed them. Two videos were made of the conversations, one from the actor's point of view, and the other from the observer's point of view. Some of the participants made attributions of the actor's behaviour after watching one of the two videos. The usual actor–observer effect was obtained when actors and observers viewed the video made from their own perspective. However, the opposite pattern of results was obtained when actors and observers viewed the video taken from the opposite perspective. When people observed their own behaviour, they tended to attribute it to dispositional rather than to situational factors.

Self-serving bias

The actor–observer effect discussed in the previous paragraphs does not always apply. Actors make more situational attributions about themselves than observers do, but in terms of dispositional attributions there is actually little difference between actors and observers, as we saw earlier in the study by Nisbett et al. (1973). Another limitation of the actor–observer effect is that it does not account for attributions for success—in such cases actors generally attribute their own behaviour to dispositional rather than situational factors. Examples of internal or dispositional explanations would be "I worked very hard" or "I have a lot of ability" and examples of external or situational explanations would be "The task was very difficult" or "I didn't have enough time to prepare". These tendencies to both take the *credit for success* but accept no *blame for failure* are often described as the **self-serving bias**.

Causal factors

There are various reasons why we might have a self-serving bias.

Intentions.   According to the cognitive account (Miller & Ross, 1975), we usually intend to succeed and do not intend to fail. As a result, we put much effort into the attempt to succeed. If our internal intentions and efforts are confirmed by success, then it is understandable that we attribute our behaviour to internal factors. If our intentions and efforts are thwarted and we fail, then we may tend to argue that obstacles in the situation have prevented our behaviour from matching our intentions.

Think of something you have recently been successful in achieving. How did you explain your success? Is there also something you have failed to achieve? How did you explain your failure?

Motivation.   Miller (1976) found that motivational factors play an important role. The participants were given a test of social perceptiveness, and then told on a random basis that they had succeeded or failed. Half of them were told that it was a good test of social skills, whereas the others were told that it was a poor test. Those who believed the test was valid showed much more evidence of a self-serving bias than the others. These findings suggest that the motivation to protect or enhance self-esteem may underlie the self-serving bias.

Depression and low self-esteem.   Further support for the role of self-esteem in the self-serving bias comes from the study of depressed individuals. They often fail to show the self-serving bias. Indeed, as we have already noted they tend to exhibit the opposite pattern of attributing failure to internal factors and success to external factors (e.g., Abramson et al., 1978). Depressed individuals have very low self-esteem, and typically feel there is nothing they can do to boost it. In other words, they do not have enough motivation to show the self-serving bias.

Evaluation of the self-serving bias

There is strong evidence for the self-serving bias. It has the advantage of encouraging us to persevere even when things are going against us. For example, unemployed workers are more likely to find work if they exhibit the self-serving bias, and avoid attributing their failure to obtain a job to their incompetence or lack of skill.

On the negative side, it remains unclear whether the self-serving bias is better explained in motivational terms (enhancing self-esteem) or in cognitive terms (confirmation or non-confirmation of internal intentions and efforts). The self-serving bias is stronger in individualist cultures than in collectivist ones. Kashima and Triandis (1986) asked American and Japanese students to remember detailed information about landscapes shown on slides. Both groups tended to explain their successes in terms of situational factors (e.g., luck) and their failures in terms of task difficulty. However, the Americans were more inclined to explain their successes in terms of high ability than their failures in terms of low ability, whereas the Japanese showed the opposite pattern. Thus, the self-serving bias was more apparent in the American participants.

Extensions of the self-serving bias

The self-handicapping bias is an extension of the self-serving bias and a strategy often used by people. Prior to some major event, like a sports race or an important examination, an individual may offer all sorts of reasons for their possible failure in terms of situational factors, such as saying "I never do well when we have to run in that stadium" or "It doesn't help that I have three exams that week". By doing this the individual is ensuring (or trying to ensure) that others will attribute any failure to situational rather than dispositional factors. In addition, should the individual actually manage to succeed, apparently against very high odds, then their success is greatly enhanced. Definitely a case of a "no lose" situation!

Ingroup bias occurs when we use attributions to increase the status of our **ingroup** and thus our own self-esteem. Duncan (1976) showed white participants a video of a white or black person violently pushing another during a heated conversation. Participants made internal attributions ("violent personality") when the pusher was black and external ones for the white aggressor ("he was provoked"). Such explanations are usefully applied to understanding prejudice.

And finally, there is an intriguing bias called defensive attribution, which is related to the sense of fairness mentioned earlier in relation to the FAE. Whenever there is a major disaster or other incident where individuals are injured or killed, people tend to quickly offer explanations about why this might have occurred. These explanations or attributions are usually constructed in such a way as to make us feel safer. For example, if a person was badly injured in a car accident we "prefer" to explain this as being due to the fact that he or she wasn't wearing a seat-belt or is a careless driver rather than it being due to some circumstances beyond the driver's control. This enhances our own sense of safety because we can ensure that we are wearing our seat-belt and do drive carefully. The greater the consequences of an action, the more that attributions tend to be dispositional rather than situational. Walster (1966) demonstrated this in an experiment where participants were given the details of a car accident and asked to rate the car owner's responsibility. The more serious the consequences of the accident, the more responsibility the owner was assigned.

Think of a recent major disaster. Who was blamed? Does this fit the defensive attribution explanation?

Social Perception

The topic of **social perception** aims to explain how we perceive our social world. The term "perception" is used in the same sense as it is used in sensory perception. We absorb data from the world around us and then we *interpret* this in such a way as to make sense of the data. It is the process of interpretation that we will focus on in this Unit. A variety of explanations have been offered: impression formation, schemas and stereotyping, and social representations.

Impression Formation

When you meet someone for the first time you form an impression of them. This may apply to casual situations, such as meeting a new neighbour in your local pub, or it may be applied to quite formal situations, such as job interviews. Early research into social perception focused on the elements of impression formation.

Asch's configural model

Asch (1946) proposed that impression formation is the result of gathering together a list of traits associated with a person and using these to produce an "impression". Some traits are more *central* than others. For example, if a person was described as "intelligent - skilful - industrious - cold - determined - practical - cautious", the word "cold" may assume more importance in your final impression than the other more *peripheral* traits.

To test the hypothesis that some traits are more important in impression formation than others, Asch gave lists of words like the one above to students and asked them to write a brief characterisation of the person in a few sentences. He also gave his participants a list of 18 pairs of opposites, and asked them to select one adjective from each pair, which they believed best fitted the person. If participants were given the list of words shown in the previous paragraph, with the word "cold" replaced by the word "warm", they judged the person also to be generous, wise, happy, good-natured, humorous, sociable, popular, humane, altruistic, and imaginative. Those participants given the word "cold" selected the opposite traits, in other words, the socially-undesirable traits. If the words "polite" and "blunt" were used instead of warm/cold, there were no significant differences between groups of participants. These are not central traits.

Kelley (1950) repeated this experiment in a more naturalistic setting. He introduced a temporary lecturer to a group of students, saying that their normal lecturer was away.

As a matter of interest, he told them, it would be useful to have some feedback at the end of the talk about the lecturer. For the students' information he provided them each with a short biography of the lecturer. The students did not realise that there was one small difference in the descriptions they were given. One version included the word "warm" and the other used the word "cold". After the lecture the students were asked to assess the lecturer's performance and his personality. Those students who were given the word "warm" rated the lecturer as considerate, informal, sociable, popular, humorous, humane, and better natured. Students given the word "cold" gave the opposite ratings. This was confirmed in the way the students responded to the lecturer, 56% of the "warm" students entered into the discussion at the end compared with 32% of the "cold" students.

When assessing an individual's personality and other attributes, participants go beyond the initial bare terms and integrate them into a rounded, meaningful whole. They automatically make inferences about traits that are not included in the original information. A change of a single word can alter the entire impression formed, but only if the words are central traits. Central traits create a **halo effect**, the tendency for the total impression formed to be unduly influenced by one outstanding trait.

How might physical attractiveness create a halo effect?

Biases in forming impressions

We have seen that central traits can lead to biased first impressions. Asch used his word list approach to investigate other biases. One of them concerns **primacy** and **recency**, as described in the Key Study overleaf. The primacy effect appears to be stronger, possibly because initial traits will form expectations, which then influence how subsequent traits are perceived. There are occasions, however, when the recency effect is stronger, such as if the time interval is increased between the initial and subsequent information.

Asch also looked at the question of trait consistency. Participants who were given the words "kind - wise - honest - calm - strong" selected traits such as "soothing, peaceful, gentle", whereas participants given "cruel - shrewd - unscrupulous - calm - strong" chose "deliberate, silent, impassive". In other words they opted for a "grimmer" side of "calm". This suggests that people do try to maintain some consistency within an impression. It also shows that prior expectancies affect the way the same characteristics might be interpreted, but probably only when subsequent words in the list can be interpreted in more than one way. In other words, the words are ambiguous.

Kenrick and Gutierres (1980) demonstrated a "contrast effect". When an object is contrasted with something even less appealing, in contrast it looks much better. They arranged for male students to rate the potential attractiveness of a blind date before or after watching an episode from *Charlie's Angels* (featuring several attractive girls). Those men who did the rating afterwards gave lower ratings than the ones who did the rating beforehand.

Implicit personality theory

Bruner and Taguiri (1954) suggested that people have their personal "theories" about what personality traits tend to go together. These are in part derived from cultural stereotypes ("dumb" blondes are not intelligent) and also from personal experience. Wrightsman (1964) called these "philosophies of human nature". This has been experimentally demonstrated, for example Rosenberg and Sedlak (1972) found that people assumed that intelligent people are friendly but not self-centred.

What trait do you think goes together with "cuddly"—generous or mean?

Evaluation

Asch's research lacked realism. This artificiality may well have led to results that lacked **ecological validity** and were due to **demand characteristics**. Participants responded to cues in the experiment rather than demonstrating real-life behaviour. For instance, it may be that the words warm/cold stood out from the other words in the list, not because they are central traits, but because they belong to a rather different dimension. Rosenberg et al. (1968) suggest that there are two main dimensions for evaluating people: social and

Primacy and recency

It is said of writers that "you are only as good as your last book", an example of the **recency effect**. Asch (1946) investigated this with respect to impression formation. One set of participants (group A) was given the following stimulus words "intelligent - industrious - impulsive - critical - stubborn - envious". Group B was given the same words but in the reverse order. The effect was to produce two quite different impressions. Group A perceived their target as an able person who possesses certain shortcomings. Group B judged their person as a "problem" whose abilities are hampered by serious difficulties. This demonstrates that word order affects impression formation. It would appear that initial traits have greater weight than subsequent ones (primacy rather than recency).

In a later experiment, Luchins (1957) produced a slightly more realistic stimulus. He gave participants the following story:

Jim left the house to get some stationery. He walked out into the sun-filled street with two of his friends, basking in the sun as he walked. Jim entered the stationery store, which was full of people. Jim talked with an acquaintance while he waited for a clerk to catch his eye. On his way out, he stopped to chat with a school friend who was just coming into the store. Leaving the store, he walked toward school. On his way out he met the girl to whom he had been introduced the night before. They talked for a short while, and then Jim left for school.

Participants were then asked various questions, such as "Do you like him?", "What does he look like?", "Jim was waiting for his turn in the barber shop. The barber overlooked him to call on another customer who had just come in. What did Jim do?" Participants described Jim as an extrovert type: sociable, popular, likeable, happy, athletic, and he would protest if the barber overlooked him.

In contrast, if participants were given a different paragraph about Jim, their responses were affected:

After school Jim left the classroom alone. Leaving the school, he started his long walk home. The street was brilliantly filled with sunshine. Jim walked down the street on the shady side. Coming down the street toward him, he saw the pretty girl whom he had met on the previous evening. Jim crossed the street and entered a candy store. The store was crowded with students, and he noticed a few familiar faces. Jim waited quietly until the counterman caught his eye and then gave his order. Taking his drink, he sat down at a side table. When he had finished his drink he went home.

How are these two accounts of Jim different?

This time they pictured him as an introvert: shy, quiet, unfriendly, unpopular, thin, weak, and someone who would not protest to the barber.

Participants form an impression of Jim's personality on the basis of what information they have. This is not as unreasonable as it may sound. When you first meet someone, you only have a glimpse of their characteristics but you need to build an image of this person for future reference: "Do I trust him?", "Would I like to see her again?", "Will I avoid him next time?" Impressions are a precondition of social life. When you get to know the person better, you might revise this impression, though a bad first impression may prevent that happening.

Some participants were presented with both versions of the "Jim" account merged together but in different orders. There was a strong primacy effect, first impressions count. If, however, a time interval was allowed between reading the two versions, a recency effect was shown.

Interestingly, in these experiments no one said, "How am I to know?" Participants do their best in experiments—but this may well result in demand characteristics which mean that these findings may not generalise to real life.

■ Activity: Both Asch's and Luchins' experiments could be used as the basis for your own investigations.

You could give participants Asch's word lists and ask them to indicate their impressions using the following adjective lists:

generous–ungenerous	humorous–humourless	important–insignificant
wise–shrewd	sociable–unsociable	humane–ruthless
happy–unhappy	popular–unpopular	good looking–unattractive
good natured–irritable	reliable–unreliable	persistent–unstable
serious–frivolous	restrained–talkative	altruistic–self-centred
imaginative–hard-headed	strong–weak	honest–dishonest

Discussion points

1. To what extent do you think that these experiments have ecological validity?

2. How might you explain the fact that there is generally a stronger primacy effect?

intellectual. Warm/cold would be social cues whereas the other traits (intelligent, skilful, industrious, etc.) were intellectual. Participants then selected traits from an adjective checklist, containing mainly social traits. It is more likely that such traits would be affected by warm/cold.

However, an element of the configural model has validity. This is the role of schemas in producing expectations and impressions. Traits, in a sense, act like schemas.

Schema Theory

As we have just seen, a single piece of information about a person may generate a complex set of expectations about that individual. This can be explained using the concept of **schemas**. A schema is a cognitive structure that contains knowledge about a thing, including its attributes and the relations among its attributes (Fiske & Taylor, 1991).

There are many types of schema. We have *person schemas* that represent knowledge about people we know. You have a schema for each person and this schema holds a collection of concepts about that person, and generates expectations. We each have a *self-schema* that is more complex than other-person schemas. Your self-concept contains a variety of self-schemas.

What information would be contained in your self-schema?

Schemas that are about events are called **scripts** (Schank & Abelson, 1977). These guide us when performing commonplace activities, such as going to the cinema or to a football match. These schemas contribute to the meaningfulness of the event. A lack of relevant scripts leads to a sense of disorientation and frustration—just the kind of feeling one gets when visiting a foreign country and trying, for example, to use the public transport system. One simply doesn't know how to go about getting a ticket, how to indicate that you would like the bus to stop, where to sit on the bus, and so on. Our scripts provide us with a collection of expectations about how to behave and what will happen.

We also have *role schemas* that contain information about how particular groups of people are likely to behave; this would include a schema for a doctor or traffic warden. Role schemas also include our expectations about other social groups, and if these expectations are shared rather than personal beliefs they are called **stereotypes**.

Schemas and stereotypes

There is a certain amount of overlap between the concepts of schemas and of stereotypes. Hamilton (1981) suggests that stereotypes are a particular kind of schema, they are concepts relating to identifiable social groups. Andersen and Klatzky (1987) distinguish between social schemas and stereotypes by saying that the former are more complex and the latter are more likely to be culturally determined. Both schemas and stereotypes provide a means of organising information and generating future expectations that simplify our social perceptions. Later we will return to the topic of stereotyp*ing*, or the effects of using stereotypes. In the immediate discussion we will consider the value and limitations of schemas and stereotypes.

The cognitive miser

Schemas and stereotypes are an obvious outcome of our cognitive processes. When processing information we identify important factors, categorise, summarise, build concepts, and store them away for future use. Stereotypes and schemas are especially useful because they allow us to save cognitive energy. They summarise large amounts of information and provide an instant and fairly accurate picture from meagre data. Taylor (1981) used the term cognitive miser to express this tendency to use the least complex and demanding mental processes to produce generally adaptive behaviour. Such simplified cognitive processing depends on the use of heuristics and the process of categorisation.

In what way are schemas an example of "adaptive behaviour"?

The stereotypical image of Italian matriarchs being wonderful cooks has given rise to several advertising campaigns for Italian food products.

The economical nature of stereotypes

Why do we have stereotypes? The main reason seems to be that stereotypes provide a simple and economical way of perceiving the world. Relevant evidence was reported by Macrae, Milne, and Bodenhausen (1994). They asked their participants to perform two tasks at the same time. One task involved forming impressions of a number of imaginary people when given their names and personality traits. The other task involved listening to information presented on a tape followed by a test of comprehension. Half of the participants were given the chance to use stereotypes by being told the job held by each of the imaginary people in the impression-formation task. The idea was that being told that someone was, for example, a used-car salesman or a doctor would activate stereotypical information about the kind of person who has that kind of job. The remaining participants were not given this stereotype-relevant information.

The key finding was that the participants who were able to use stereotypes performed better on both tasks. This suggests strongly that the use of stereotypes saves precious cognitive resources, because they provide a convenient (if inaccurate) summary of a person or object.

Discussion points

1. Do the findings of Macrae et al. really show that stereotypes reduce cognitive processing?

2. Are there other reasons why people have stereotypes?

Heuristics

A schema represents knowledge about a person or event, and heuristics tell us how to use this knowledge. In the last Unit you were introduced to the term "heuristic". These are rules of general principle that tell us the likely relationship between things. Strictly speaking they are not formulae because they do not guarantee a solution to a problem but they offer likely outcomes. A good heuristic must provide a quick and simple way of dealing with large amounts of information, and must be reasonably accurate most of the time. There are various kinds of heuristic.

What would be the prototype of a chair? Are all chairs like this?

Representativeness heuristic.   The **representativeness heuristic** enables us to make judgements about something on the basis of probability. For example, if you observe a woman driving up to a school and dropping off several children you might perceive her as a mother rather than a child-minder just because "mother" is a more likely explanation. The representativeness heuristic helps us decide quickly whether a person belongs to a particular category by matching the characteristics of the person to the characteristics of the typical example, or **prototype**. This explains how stereotypes work. We hold a stereotype of a particular social group (e.g., students walk around holding a pile of books and dressed in jeans and sweatshirts) and anyone who fits that stereotypical image is classed as one of them.

One unfortunate problem with this is that such stereotypes are self-fulfilling. We often do not find out if our representativeness heuristics are right or wrong, and also prefer information that supports their predictions rather than disproves them. This is called a **confirmation bias**. Cohen (1981) demonstrated this in a study where participants were shown a videotape of a woman doing various things, like having dinner with her partner. Participants were told beforehand that the woman was either a waitress or a librarian. Afterwards, the participants were asked to rate the woman on a 37-item trait questionnaire, and also asked to recall features about the woman's appearance and behaviour, using a list of the 18 features. Cohen found 78% accuracy for recall of consistent information compared with 71% recall of inconsistent information. "Consistency" and "inconsistency" were determined by independent raters beforehand, so for a waitress it was more likely that she would eat burgers, drink beer, play a guitar, and go bowling. For a librarian, consistent information included eating roast beef, drinking wine, wearing glasses, and playing golf. The video information was varied in different conditions but you can see that recall was affected by stereotypes and such recall perpetuates stereotypes.

Availability heuristic.   The **availability heuristic** refers to the fact that the choice of category is related to how quickly instances or associations come to mind. You are more likely to judge someone to be an accountant than an actuary because the former is a more "available" category. This makes sense, as objects that are more common are usually easier to think of than those that are not. In one experiment McKelvie (1997) gave participants lists of names and later asked them to recall the names. In one condition the lists contained the names of 26 famous women and 26 nonfamous men. Participants were asked to estimate how many male and female names had been given and they said there were more females. This can be explained in terms of availability of certain information in memory. As a counterbalance, in another condition there were 26 famous male names and 26 nonfamous women. Participants said there were more men's names in this condition.

We also use the availability heuristic when making judgements about ourselves. Schwarz et al. (1981) asked participants to think of six occasions when they had acted assertively; most people found this fairly simple. In another condition another group of participants were asked to think of twelve occasions when they had acted assertively, which proved more difficult. Finally, all participants were asked to give an overall rating to how assertive they were as individuals. The participants who had to give twelve examples would have thought of themselves as *relatively* unassertive because proportionately they were not able to think of as many examples. This prediction was supported by the finding that these participants did rate themselves as less assertive, an example of the availability heuristic in so far as the twelve-occasion group had proportionately fewer instances to bring to mind. (Both the representativeness and availability heuristic are discussed in Section 9, Language and Thought, as they are used to explain aspects of reasoning in general.)

The motivated tactician.   People do not always use heuristics. Sometimes, in the interests of expediency, we behave as cognitive misers, but at other times we possess the capacity to be far more diligent and systematic in our information processing. This approach represents the individual as a "fully engaged thinker" who chooses between alternative information processing strategies on the basis of currently active goals, motives, and needs (Fiske & Taylor, 1991).

This was demonstrated in a study by Harkness, DeBono, and Borgida (1985). Female participants were asked to judge how willing a fictitious person named Tom Ferguson would be to date various other women. Pen-pictures were given for the women, and the participants used fairly simple strategies to decide who he would be most likely to date: for example he would be more likely to date someone with a sense of humour. However, all this changed if the female participants were more highly motivated to make careful judgements. If the participants thought that *they* were taking part in a dating study and that *they* would be dating Tom, they then used more complex strategies to make judgements about Tom, and their judgements were more accurate.

This study has important applications to all areas in psychology because it highlights the difference between being fully engaged and only partially engaged. What can you conclude about the involvement of most participants in psychology experiments?

Categorisation

People also use the process of categorisation to simplify their social perceptions. Categorisation involves matching a person to an existing social category. Although this may be seen as a useful social tool, it has a number of consequences, such as the fact that once a person has been categorised, it is assumed that he or she possesses the characteristics of the group even though such characteristics were never evident during the initial categorisation. There are other important effects.

Social identity and prejudice.   Social identity theory (Tajfel, 1978) proposes that categorisation is an effect of social identity; we perceive ourselves as belonging to a number of categories. These categories can include racial group, nationality, work group, gender, social group, and so on. Thus, for example, an individual may identify herself as a female, as a student, as a member of a netball team, and as a Londoner, all at the same time. Of particular importance, everyone has a number of **social identities**, based on the different groups with which they identify.

Our own group is the **ingroup** and other people belong to **outgroups**. People increase their self-esteem by regarding the groups with which they identify as being superior to all other groups. In a nutshell, the key assumption of social identity theory is that how we feel about ourselves depends on how positively we view the groups with which we identify. This may serve as a basis for intergroup prejudice, as explored in the next Unit.

The illusion of outgroup homogeneity. Perceivers acknowledge greater differentiation between ingroup members and representations of ingroup members are more complex than those of outgroup members, thus confirming existing stereotypes. This so-called **illusion of outgroup homogeneity** was demonstrated by Quattrone and Jones (1980). Students from Princeton University and from Rutgers University in the USA saw a videotape of a student allegedly from their own university or from the other university. The student in the video was deciding whether to wait alone or with other participants while the experimenter fixed a piece of apparatus. The participant students were then asked to estimate the percentage of other students from the same university as the videotaped student who would make the same choice. The participants tended to guess that nearly all of the students from the other university would make the same decision as the videotaped student. However, this was not the case when the student was from the same university as themselves.

Social and cultural stereotyping

Schemas and stereotypes offer a rapid and effortless, if not entirely accurate, way of forming social perceptions. What are the consequences of such cognitive short-cuts? Stereotypes are specifically concerned with our perceptions of other social and cultural groups and therefore can lead to intergroup tensions and prejudice. The process of using stereotypes has been described as **stereotyping**. Taguiri (1969) describes it as the tendency

> to place a person in categories according to some easily and quickly identifiable characteristic such as age, sex, ethnic membership, nationality or occupation, and then to attribute to him qualities believed to be typical of members of that category.

We will now examine the specific effects of social and cultural stereotyping.

Research evidence

Katz and Braly (1933) carried out the first systematic study of stereotyping. They asked students to indicate which characteristics were typical of a series of groups (e.g., Germans; Black Africans; English). There was fairly good agreement that the Germans were efficient and nationalistic, whereas the Black Africans were seen as happy-go-lucky and superstitious. The English were sportsmanlike and intelligent, and the Japanese were also

What characteristics do you think each of these people might possess?

intelligent and industrious. This suggests that, in the 1930s, there were clear racist stereotypes. Gilbert (1951) replicated the study and found that students showed an increased awareness of the undesirability of such statements; some refused point blank to participate and others commented on the inaccurate nature of such statements, although they still produced stereotypical views. However, a further analysis of Gilbert's research (Karlins et al., 1969) suggested that in fact the stereotypes were still very much in existence, though the content had changed since 1933.

The greatest problem with this approach is that the task itself *forced* the participants to produce stereotypes, whether or not they actually thought in a stereotyped way. McCauley and Stitt (1978) used a better method in a study on stereotypes of Germans. They asked their participants a series of questions such as, "What percentage of people in the world generally are efficient?" and "What percentage of Germans are efficient?" The average answer to the former question was 50%, whereas it was 63% to the latter one. Thus, it is nonsense to suppose that most people think all Germans are efficient. In fact, the general feeling is that they are somewhat more efficient than other nationalities. This is a much less extreme form of stereotyping, but it is still stereotyping.

There is also the question of to what extent such stereotypes translate into prejudiced behaviour.

What ethical issues might be important in such research?

Stereotypes and prejudice

People who regard most or all of the members of some outgroup as having the same stereotyped characteristics tend to be prejudiced against that group. How do stereotypes lead to prejudice? Bodenhausen (1988) put forward a cognitive approach. According to this approach, information consistent with our stereotypes is attended to and stored away in memory, whereas information inconsistent with our stereotypes is ignored and/or forgotten.

Bodenhausen (1988) tested his cognitive approach in two studies based on the notion that many Americans are prejudiced against people of Spanish origin. In his first study, American participants were asked to imagine that they were jurors at a trial. The defendant was described to some of them as Carlos Ramirez, a Spanish-sounding name. To others, he was described as Robert Johnson. The participants then read the evidence, and decided how likely it was that the defendant was guilty. Those who knew him as Carlos Ramirez rated him as more guilty than did those who knew him as Robert Johnson. This suggests that stereotypes lead to biased processing of information.

In his second study, Bodenhausen tried to find out more about the processes involved. He argued that stereotypes might lead the participants to *attend* only to information fitting their stereotype, or it might lead them to *distort* the information to make it support their stereotype. In order to prevent selective attention to stereotype-fitting information, Bodenhausen asked the participants to rate each item of evidence immediately in terms of whether it favoured or did not favour the defendant. Carlos Ramirez was no longer rated as more guilty than Robert Johnson. Thus, in the first experiment the stereotypes made participants attend to information fitting the stereotype, and caused them to disregard other items of information. In the second experiment, when they were forced to attend to all information equally, the effects of stereotyping disappeared.

How might you use this information to advise about better courtroom practices?

Illusory correlations

It has been suggested that **illusory correlations** can help explain why stereotypes sometimes lead to prejudice. When two things co-occur people often perceive a relationship where none exists, especially when the two things are unusual or distinctive, such as the presence of a minority ethnic group and a crime being committed. The co-occurrence of two unusual things might lead you to associate the minority group with criminal behaviour, and can explain negative stereotyping of minority groups, possibly leading to prejudiced behaviour.

Chapman (1967) demonstrated illusory correlations in an experiment where students were given lists of things such as lion/tiger, lion/eggs, bacon/eggs, blossoms/notebook, and notebook/tiger. At the end they were asked to recall how often each word was paired with each other word. In fact all pairs had occurred equally frequently but participants reported more of the meaningful pairings (such as eggs/bacon) and more of the distinctive pairings (such as blossoms/notebook). This suggests that people operate two bases for forming illusory correlations: (1) "associative meaning" where one links two things together because they ought to be together, and (2) "paired distinctiveness" where two items are linked because they are both distinctive.

The link between this and prejudice was further demonstrated in a study by Hamilton and Gifford (1976). Participants were asked to recall statements about two groups: A and B. Overall there were more statements given about group A, so that in a sense group B was the minority group. There were also more positive statements than negative statements about either group. However, participants reported that there were more negative statements (minority statements) about the minority group. The link between minority statements and minority groups is an example of paired distinctiveness. Associative meaning may also take place because individuals have preconceptions that certain negative attitudes go with minority groups and therefore tend to make this association because they ought to go together (McArthur & Friedman, 1980).

Influence of stereotypes

Despite the potential effects of stereotypes, people are not always affected by them. Most people are consciously aware of the effects of stereotypes and generally try to control them but what happens is that this breaks down in complex situations. An experimental demonstration of this was produced by Darley and Gross (1983). They showed students a videotape of a primary-age schoolgirl called "Hannah". There were four groups:

- Group 1 saw a video of her in a high-class neighbourhood
- Group 2 saw a video of her in a run-down neighbourhood.
- Groups 3 and 4 saw one of the two videos plus a clip of Hannah doing a test—her performance was ambiguous as sometimes she could do the hard questions and sometimes she couldn't do the easy ones.

Afterwards, the students were asked to estimate Hannah's academic ability. The effect of the stereotypes aroused by the videos was only apparent in groups 3 and 4. It was suggested that this was because the participants in groups 1 and 2 were able to control the effects of stereotypes aroused by the neighbourhood because it was a simple scenario. When they saw the video clips alone they judged Hannah to be "average", thus resisting the stereotype conveyed by her background. When participants were given more information they felt a false sense of rationality and now attempted to make an "educated" judgement, but inevitably one that was affected by stereotypes.

Evaluation

It is often argued that stereotypes are undesirable for two main reasons: (1) they can lead to prejudice; and (2) they represent very oversimplified views of the world, and so are inaccurate and misleading. It is true that negative stereotypes of other groups can be dangerous, and are increasingly regarded as unacceptable. Two obvious examples are sex- and race-based stereotypes. Sexism and racism have caused great damage over the years in terms of both prejudice and discrimination. Laws based on the notion of equal opportunities have been passed in several countries. These laws have had the effect of preventing much of the discrimination that used to exist. However, although active discrimination may have been reduced, there is often much underlying prejudice.

Oversimplification.   In spite of the arguments against stereotypes that have just been put forward, it is not the case that all stereotypes lead to prejudice. Stereotypes are often oversimplified, but they help us to make sense of a very complex world. Even the least prejudiced person probably makes use of several stereotypes every day. For example, Brown (1988) pointed out that most people have stereotypes about night people and day people (those who go to bed early and get up early). We think of night people as being unconventional and rebellious, whereas day people are thought of as self-controlled and responsible.

We all use stereotypes, usually without even thinking about them, e.g., "Essex girl", "trainspotter", "punk". Make a list of some other examples in common use.

A "kernel of truth".   Stereotypes are often inaccurate. However, that is not always the case. For example, Triandis and Vassiliou (1967, p.324) studied people from Greece and from the United States, and came to the following conclusion, "There is a 'kernel of truth' in most stereotypes *when they are elicited from people who have firsthand knowledge of the group being stereotyped.*" McCauley and Stitt (1978) asked various groups of Americans to estimate the percentage of adult Americans in general and the percentage of adult Black Americans who had not completed high school, were born illegitimate, had been the victims of violent crime, and so on. There were differences in the estimates for most of the questions, thus showing the existence of stereotypes. However, McCauley and Stitt compared the estimates against the relevant government statistics. In their answers to about half of the questions, the participants *underestimated* the actual differences between the two groups. These findings provide additional support for the notion that stereotypes often possess a kernel of truth.

Social representations

A third approach to social perception is the explanation offered by **social representations**. Much of our knowledge of the world is not obtained through first-hand experience, but rather is obtained indirectly from social interactions. For example, we may have very definite views about individual members of the royal family even though we have not met them, because we have discussed them with friends. The term "social representations" is often used to refer to such socially derived knowledge. Moscovici (1981, p.181) offered a fuller definition of social representations:

> *a set of concepts, statements and explanations originating in daily life in the course of inter-individual communications. They are the equivalent, in our society, of the myths and belief systems in traditional societies; they might even be said to be the contemporary version of common sense.*

The concept of social representations emphasises the way that we represent *social* knowledge and how this knowledge is unconsciously shaped by *social* groups, i.e., such representations are social in two ways. Social representations are more than schemas because the concept includes social dynamics, i.e., the idea that representations are constantly changing (dynamic).

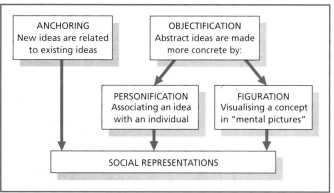

How do we form new social representations? According to Moscovici, two key processes are involved: anchoring and objectification. **Anchoring** refers to the way in which new ideas are related closely to existing knowledge and categories. **Objectification** is the process of making abstract ideas more concrete; it has the advantages of making ideas more understandable and easier to remember. According to Moscovici and Hewstone (1983), objectification can involve either personification or figuration. As they pointed out, most people's social representations about psychoanalysis centre on Sigmund Freud. This is an example of personification. Figuration or visualisation of an abstract idea is involved when we picture the law of gravity in terms of an apple falling on Newton's head.

Why do we rely so heavily on social representations? According to Moscovici (1988, p.215):

> *We derive only a small fraction of our knowledge and information from the simple interaction between ourselves and the facts we encounter in the world. Most knowledge is supplied to us by communication that affects our way of thinking and creates new concepts.*

In other words, the world is so complex that we often need to make use of the views and knowledge of others to make sense of it. In addition, it is easier for members of a group to communicate with each other if they share numerous social representations.

The media often use objectification, e.g., "butter mountain", "millennium bug". List some of your own examples.

Research evidence

Representations of intelligence.   Carugati (1990) found support for some of Moscovici's (1981) ideas in a study on social representations of intelligence among Italian teachers and parents. They regarded intelligence as a gift, which is an example of anchoring a complex concept to what is known. They also used objectification by assuming that individual differences in intelligence can be used to predict future success.

Representations of health.   Herzlich (1973) studied the social representations of health and illness in 80 French people by conducting conversational interviews with them. Most of them regarded health as a pool or reservoir within individuals that can be used up. Illness, on the other hand, lies outside individuals and is influenced by lifestyle. Living in a city can produce illness, whereas living in the countryside preserves the pool of health. Advertisers take account of these social representations. Advertisements for health foods typically show charming rural scenes, even though the products being advertised are mostly manufactured in large factories in towns.

Representations of mental illness.   Jodelet (1991) looked at social representations of mental illness in a French village called Ainay-le-Chateau. This village was chosen because mental patients lived as lodgers in the homes of many of the villagers. Jodelet obtained most of her information from living in the village, but she also carried out in-depth interviews and conducted a large questionnaire survey. Most of the villagers regarded the mental patients as dirty, and notions of dirtiness and contamination loomed large in their social representations of mental illness. Why was this the case? According to Jodelet (1991, pp.143–144):

> *dirtiness seems to siphon off the major part of the negativity of insanity and is a less disturbing manifestation of the illness than others. Dirtiness which is due to illness is unthreatening. That alone makes it worth putting up with.*

Errors of attribution.   Earlier in this Section we saw that, according to the actor–observer effect, people attribute the behaviour of others to their personality, but attribute their own behaviour to the situation. This effect is usually regarded as applying to individuals. However, Guimond, Begin, and Palmer (1989) argued that errors and biases can develop out of social representations. The normal effect was reversed when poor, unemployed people and social science students were asked to provide reasons for poverty. Unemployed people blamed themselves for being poor, whereas the social science students attributed poverty to society and the situation in which poor people find themselves.

What caused this reversal of the normal actor–observer effect? Presumably the poor had learned the social representations of poverty that are common in society, and the social science students had learned the social representations frequently expressed by social scientists. Thus, knowledge of social representations can eliminate the actor–observer effect.

Evaluation

Could you hold a conversation with a friend about "global warming" or "BSE"? Where did your knowledge come from? Do you both have similar beliefs?

Our beliefs and knowledge about the world depend to a large extent on our communications with other people. Moscovici (1985, p.95) was probably right to argue that, "Social representations are the outcome of an unceasing babble and a permanent dialogue between individuals." As a result, groups of people and even entire cultures will often share very similar social representations. The notion of social representations is valuable, because it encourages us to search for the social origins of much of our knowledge.

On the negative side, theoretical accounts of social representations are rather vague. In addition, the processes underlying the formation of social representations have not been studied in detail. One of the criteria for a scientific theory is that it should generate hypotheses that are falsifiable. This has not happened sufficiently with theories of social representation. One of the few clear predictions is that social representations should be shared across a social group. In fact, this is often not the case. In the study by Carugati (1990), parents who were also teachers held the social representation that intelligence is a gift more strongly than parents who were not teachers. The latter group of parents put more emphasis on the view that intelligence is a quality that can be developed by teachers. Galli and Nigro (1987) studied Italian children's social representations of radioactivity shortly after the Chernobyl explosion. The children's representations were very similar, presumably because the explosion had led to considerable discussion about radioactivity and the danger of nuclear power and this led to greater consistency across the group.

Prejudice and Discrimination

Many people regard prejudice and discrimination as meaning the same thing. In fact, there is an important distinction between them. **Prejudice** is an attitude, whereas **discrimination** refers to behaviour or action. If someone dislikes a given minority, but does not allow this dislike to affect their behaviour, then that person shows prejudice but not discrimination. According to Baron and Byrne (1991, p.183), prejudice "is an attitude (usually negative) toward the members of some group, based solely on their membership in that group." In contrast, discrimination usually involves negative actions (e.g., aggression) directed at the members of some group.

Origins and Maintenance of Prejudice and Discrimination

There are several causes of prejudice. However, it can be argued that there are two main categories to which most of these causes belong. First, prejudice may depend on the personality or other characteristics of an individual who is prejudiced. Second, environmental or cultural factors may produce prejudice. For example, a dramatic increase in the level of unemployment within any given country may lead to greater prejudice and discrimination against minority groups within that country. In reality, of course, we may well need to consider both the individual and the social and cultural context in which an individual lives in order to understand prejudice fully.

In what follows, we will initially consider some important approaches to prejudice that have focused on the individual. After that, the emphasis shifts to a consideration of the main social and cultural factors responsible for producing prejudice.

In the early 1960s, during a period of high immigration from the West Indies to the UK, the MP Enoch Powell warned of the dangers of social unrest following the distortion of the labour market. His "rivers of blood" speech was taken by many as a call for repatriation of immigrants, and was quoted by both those for and those against immigration.

Personality explanations: The psychodynamic approach

Sigmund Freud put forward his psychoanalytic theories at the end of the nineteenth century and in the early part of the twentieth century (see Section 11, Social and Personality Development). His views were so influential that they led to a number of psychodynamic theories based loosely on his theories. Two psychodynamic theories of prejudice have been put forward: the frustration–aggression hypothesis, and the theory of the authoritarian personality.

Frustration–aggression hypothesis

Dollard et al. (1939) argued that aggression against individuals and groups is caused by frustration. Frustration leads to the build-up of an unpleasant state of arousal, which is released in the form of aggression. It is often not possible to show aggression or hostility

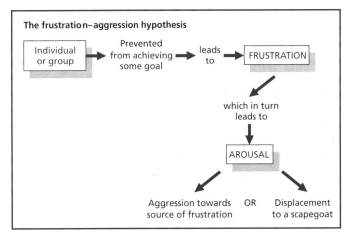

The frustration–aggression hypothesis

towards the source of the frustration, because it is too powerful. This leads to what Freud called *displacement*: the aggression is directed towards a substitute target or scapegoat (e.g., our boss annoys us, so we go home and kick the cat). The frustration–aggression hypothesis in its original form focused on individual levels of frustration, which can vary considerably from one person to another. However, it was later applied to large groups within society as well as to individuals.

There are many historical examples of scapegoating apparently caused by frustration. Massive inflation and very high levels of unemployment in Germany during the 1920s were followed by the rapid growth of anti-Semitism or anti-Jewish prejudice. Hovland and Sears (1940) argued that drops in cotton prices in the United States reflected increased poverty and led to frustration. They also argued that the number of lynchings (killing a person for an alleged offence, without any legal trial) could be taken as a measure of scapegoating. As predicted by the frustration–aggression hypothesis, those years in which the cotton prices were lowest tended to be the ones with the most lynchings in certain areas of America.

Can you think of any similar examples since the Second World War when, as a result of problems such as high unemployment, one group used another as a scapegoat for their frustrations?

Evaluation.   On the positive side, the frustration–aggression hypothesis provides a plausible account of one of the factors causing prejudice. On the negative side, frustration can lead to constructive attempts to remove its source or to a resigned attitude as well as to aggression. In addition, the frustration–aggression hypothesis does not explain why aggression is directed against one particular group (e.g., black people) rather than another (e.g., Jews).

Authoritarian personality

Adorno et al. (1950) focused on individual differences in prejudice. According to them, people with an authoritarian personality are most likely to be prejudiced. The **authoritarian personality** includes the following characteristics:

- Rigid beliefs in conventional values.
- General hostility towards other groups (outgroups).
- Intolerance of ambiguity.
- Submissive attitudes towards authority figures.

Early experiences.   Adorno et al. argued that childhood experiences play a key role in the development of the authoritarian personality. Harsh treatment causes the child to have much hostility towards his or her parents. This hostility remains unconscious, because the child is unwilling to admit to it. This causes motivated forgetting, or what Freud called *repression*. The child seems to idealise his or her parents, and in later life acts in a submissive way towards authority figures. However, there is still much hostility lying below the surface. This hostility is displaced on to non-threatening minority groups, and appears in the form of prejudice. Thus, the key theoretical assumption is as follows: the hostility that harshly treated children find hard to express towards their parents is later redirected towards innocent groups.

E-Scale and F-Scale.   Adorno et al. devised a number of questionnaires relating to their theory. One of these questionnaires was the Ethnocentrism Scale (E-Scale), ethnocentrism being the belief that one's ethnic group is superior to all others. The scale measures prejudice towards a number of minority groups, including black and Jewish people. However, the most important questionnaire was the **F (Fascism) Scale**, which was designed to measure the attitudes of the authoritarian personality. A clearer idea of what the F-Scale measures can be seen by looking at a few items: "Obedience and respect for authority are the most important virtues children should learn"; "Most of our social problems would be solved if we could somehow get rid of the immoral, crooked, and feeble-minded people"; "What the youth needs most is strict discipline, rugged determination, and the will to work for family and country". Respondents indicated agreement or disagreement.

Adorno et al. obtained various kinds of evidence for the validity of the F-Scale. They gave large groups of people a number of tests and clinical interviews as well as the F-Scale. Those who scored high on the F-Scale tended to be more prejudiced than low scorers. For example, the F-Scale correlated +.75 with the Ethnocentrism Scale. As predicted, high scorers on the F-Scale had been treated more harshly than non-authoritarian individuals during childhood.

More evidence was obtained by Milgram (1974). He found that most people are prepared to give very strong electric shocks to another person when ordered to do so by an authority figure. Those with an authoritarian personality are supposed to be submissive to authority, and so they should be especially likely to give powerful electric shocks. As predicted, high scorers on the F-Scale gave stronger shocks than low scorers.

THE NINE PERSONALITY TRAITS OF THE AUTHORITARIAN PERSONALITY, FROM ADORNO ET AL.'S F-SCALE	
Traits	**Description**
Conventionalism	Very conventional, great dislike of change
Authoritarian–submissive	Deferential to authority
Authoritarian–aggressive	Very hostile to people who challenge authority
Anti-inception	Very intolerant of behaviour that is "wrong" in any way
Superstition and stereotype	Believes in fate
Power and "toughness"	Has a dominating and bullying manner
Destructiveness and cynicism	Very hostile towards anyone with whom they disagree
Projectivity	Projects own unconscious impulses on to other people
Sex	Has an exaggerated interest in sexual behaviour that is not regarded as "normal"

Cultural differences.   The work by Adorno et al. (1950) was carried out in America shortly after the end of the Second World War. It seems likely that some features of the authoritarian personality would vary from one culture to another, and from one time period to another. Some relevant evidence has been reported by Peterson et al. (1993). Americans with an authoritarian personality were strong supporters of family values, and believed very much in the American way of life. Thus, for example, they opposed abortion, argued that homelessness is caused by laziness, and wanted drug dealers to be treated very harshly.

A very different picture emerged from a study of the authoritarian personality in Russia by McFarland et al. (1992). Authoritarian Russians tended to favour continuing Communist control of the former Soviet Union, a point of view that is almost the opposite of endorsing the American way of life! The findings suggest that those with an authoritarian personality are very conservative. They dislike change, and want those in authority to punish anyone who poses a threat to the existing order. Thus, the beliefs of authoritarian individuals are coloured by the dominant values in their culture.

Evaluation.   On the positive side, some individuals are more prejudiced than others, and the F-Scale is a reasonable measure of these individual differences. As is predicted by the theory, childhood experiences help to determine whether someone will develop an authoritarian personality. Note, however, that this explanation is one of early socialisation, not Adorno's more Freudian concept of projecting repression on to outgroups (Pennington, 2000).

On the negative side, there are several problems. First, widespread uniformity of prejudice in certain cultural groups (e.g., anti-Jewish prejudice in Nazi Germany) cannot be explained in terms of the authoritarian personality. Billig (1976) suggests that reducing group behaviour to individual personality characteristics ignores the role of group norms and the wider social context. Uniformity of behaviour within a social group must be related to the socio-cultural context and not individual personality characteristics.

Second, Adorno et al. (1950) assumed that the authoritarian personality is associated with extreme right-wing views. Rokeach (1960) suggested that the same rigidity and intolerance equally applied to those with extreme left-wing views. Individuals with extreme left- or right-wing political views have closed minds and exhibit dogmatism.

Third, nearly all of the items on the F-Scale are worded so that agreement with them indicates an authoritarian attitude. As a result, those with an acquiescence response set (a tendency to agree to items regardless of their meaning) seem to be authoritarian. Fourth, Adorno et al. (1950) reported that in-depth interviews with high F-Scale scorers supported

At the same time as research in America found that authoritarian personalities tended to favour strongly the American way of life, authoritarians in Russia were equally committed to the Communist ideals. This photograph of the Russian leader Khrushchev shows him in a typically authoritarian mood.

their theory. However, the interviewers knew in advance the F-Scale scores of those being interviewed, and this may have distorted the findings.

More recent research has been encouraged by the production of a new, more valid scale to measure authoritarianism. Altmeyer (1998) produced a Right Wing Authoritarian Scale (RWA) based on a much narrower conception of authoritarianism. It is concerned with just three components: authoritarian submission, authoritarian aggression, and conventionalism. Research using this scale has found a positive correlation between authoritarianism and prejudice towards, for example, homosexuals and criminals.

Environmental and cultural factors

All of the following explanations share one common characteristic. They suggest that prejudice is the consequence of social groups. This may be due to what goes on within a social group or what goes on between social groups.

The interpersonal approach: Conformity

A fairly straightforward way of explaining prejudice in terms of group processes is to use conformity. You will recall from your AS studies that conformity is the change in behaviour that results from real or imagined group pressure. If you belong to a group that expresses prejudice towards other groups, it is likely that you will conform to this group norm. This is likely to be the result of **normative social influence**, i.e., a desire to be liked by other members of the group and also to avoid being rejected. It may also be the consequence of **informational social influence** if you felt uncertain about what is regarded as correct behaviour.

Research evidence

White southerners in America are regarded as more prejudiced against Blacks than are the Whites in the northern United States. Is this because southerners are generally more prejudiced personalities or is it an effect of different cultural norms? Pettigrew (1959) distributed questionnaires to adults in four northern towns and four southern towns. The participating adults were randomly chosen from town directories. The questionnaire consisted of items from the authoritarianism (F) scale, anti-Semitism (A-S) scale and anti-Negro prejudice (N) scale. Pettigrew found, as he expected, that the levels of prejudice against Negroes were higher in the south but overall levels of prejudice were the same in the north and south. This indicates that the particular *kind* of prejudice may be related to local norms. The same personality type behaves differently depending on the attitude of their culture towards black people. Conformists were conforming to their group norms. An interesting observation from the data was that the white northerners who were most conformist were least prejudiced, whereas the most conformist white southerners were most prejudiced.

Studies in other countries have supported this finding. For example, Bagley and Verma (1979) compared levels of racial discrimination in Britain and Holland. Both countries have similar proportions of black and white residents but Dutch culture disapproves of prejudice more strongly. They found that levels of prejudice are lower in Holland. This suggests that the cultural norm, which is anti-prejudice towards black people, lowers the amount of discrimination.

On the basis of this research would you expect adolescents (who are generally more conformist) to exhibit more or less prejudice than adults?

The intergroup approach: Social identity theory

Social identity theory was put forward by Henri Tajfel (1978, 1981). This theory was described earlier in this Section (see page 33). Social identity leads to categorisation and social comparison. Comparisons are made between groups in order to increase self-esteem, and we all have a need to increase our self-esteem. Ingroup favouritism and outgroup negative bias enhance social and personal esteem, and lead to biased perceptions of in- and outgroup members i.e., prejudice.

Research evidence

Tajfel (1982) demonstrated this in his studies of the minimal group, which showed how social identity can be formed with amazing ease. In one of these studies (1970), 14- and 15-year-old boys estimated the number of dots seen in brief exposures. They were then assigned at random to one of two minimal groups: the over-estimators or the under-estimators. After that, they awarded points (which could be exchanged for money) to other individuals who were identified as belonging to the same group or to the other group. Nearly all the boys awarded more points to members of their own group than to members of the other group, demonstrating the effects of social identity. This study is described in greater detail in the Key Study that follows.

The minimal group experiment

Tajfel (1970) demonstrated how both ingroup favouritism and outgroup negative bias can be created on the basis of only very minimal social identity. In the first experiment eight groups of 14–15-year-old boys took part. The boys were told that the purpose of the experiment was to investigate visual judgements. They were shown slides of dots and for each slide were asked to estimate the number of dots. They were then told whether they were over- or under-estimators (in fact they were randomly assigned to one of these groups).

Each boy was then asked to play a "matrix game" on his own. They were each given a booklet with 18 matrices like the one shown below. For each matrix they should select one column. Their choice of column would determine the number of points (and eventually money) awarded to the two boys identified, but there was no personal gain for the person doing the choosing. The only information they had was about the group membership of the two boys. At the end each boy would receive his total number of points in real money.

Member no. 74 of over-estimators group	12	10	8	6	4	2	0	−1	−5	−9	−13	−17	−21	−25
Member no. 36 of under-estimators group	−25	−21	−17	−13	−9	−5	−1	0	2	4	6	8	10	12

Each boy had to tick one column, for example the one that held the numbers 4 and −9.

If a boy had to make an *inter*group choice (giving points to an over- or an under-estimator), the boys tended to give more money to members of their own group. When the boys had an entirely ingroup (or outgroup) choice to make, they tended towards the point of maximum fairness (this would be 0 and −1 in the example).

This demonstrates that even though the boys had only a minimal sense of social identity they were still awarding points on the basis of ingroup favouritism alone, showing the power of social identity.

In a second experiment the matrices were more complicated. Boys were supposedly assigned group membership on the basis of their expressed preference for the paintings of Klee or Kandinsky (it was again random assignation). The matrices this time enabled Tajfel to assess:

- *Maximum joint profit* (MJP): the largest possible award for two people.
- *Maximum ingroup profit* (MIP): largest possible award to member of the ingroup.
- *Maximum difference* (MD): largest possible difference in gain between a member of ingroup and a member of outgroup, in favour of the former.

An example of one of these matrices is shown below.

Member no. 74 of Klee group	19	18	17	16	15	14	13	12	11	10	9	8	7
Member no. 36 of Kandinsky group	1	3	5	7	9	11	13	15	17	19	21	23	25

In this case, if the boy participating was a member of the Klee group:

- MJP would be a choice of 7 and 25.
- MIP would be 19 and 1.
- MD would be 19 and 1 (favouring the Klee group).

This time Tajfel found that the MJP exerted hardly any effect at all. In other words boys did not make their choices on the basis of trying to give both parties their best joint deal. The MIP and MD exerted a strong effect. Participants always tried to give their ingroup members the best deal at the cost of the outgroup member. In a situation where the choice was between two outgroup members, participants' choices were not as near the MJP as when choosing between two ingroup members. Participants were simply less fair with outgroup members.

This confirmed the ease with which outgroup discrimination could be triggered, based on only minimal social identity. In a later study by Billig and Tajfel (1973) the participants were told that group membership was determined randomly but participants still showed ingroup favouritism. The results may be due to demand characteristics, but in real life we sometimes have little other information to go on.

Discussion points

1. In what way would you suggest that this study lacked ecological validity?

2. According to Tajfel, what are the minimum conditions for creating ethnocentrism?

Ingroup favouritism.   A similar amount of ingroup favouritism was found even when the participants were told they had been put into groups on a random basis (e.g., by the toss of a coin). Ingroup favouritism has also been found when judgements of likeableness/unlikeableness have to be made. The participant's own group is consistently judged as being more likeable than the other group.

There is evidence of ingroup favouritism in the real world. Brown (1978) reported a study of factory workers, who were highly motivated to maintain the wage differentials between their department and others in the same factory. This remained the case, even when this would lead to a reduction in their own earnings.

Why do people discriminate between an ingroup and an outgroup even with minimal groups? Doise (1976) argued that part of what is involved is **categorical differentiation**. The basic idea is that we exaggerate the differences between our group and other groups. We do this because it allows us to simplify and to organise our social worlds.

Self-esteem.   Why do people favour their group over other groups? According to social identity theory, they do this because it increases their sense of social identity and boosts their self-esteem. These notions were tested by Lemyre and Smith (1985). All their participants were put into groups at random. Some were then allowed to give rewards to members of either an ingroup or an outgroup. The other participants had to give rewards either to one of two ingroups or to one of two outgroups. Those participants who were able to discriminate in favour of an ingroup over an outgroup had higher self-esteem than those unable to discriminate in that way.

Further evidence of a link between social identity and self-esteem was reported by Hirt et al. (1992). They studied college students who were very keen fans of their basketball team. When the team was defeated, their self-esteem and feelings of competence were reduced. Those whose sense of social identity is less bound up with a team sometimes use psychological distancing to cope with its defeats. Cialdini et al. (1976) phoned students several days after their college team had lost a game of American football. The students mostly used the pronoun "they" to describe the team's defeat. In contrast, they used the pronoun "we" when their team had won, and they further showed a sense of social identity by wearing college scarves and other college clothing.

However, not all the findings are as supportive of the theory. Brown (1996, p.548) reviewed the evidence, and concluded as follows: "the social-identity hypothesis that self-esteem is an important variable controlling or being controlled by intergroup discrimination cannot be unambiguously sustained." For example, it cannot explain the fact that for some groups social identity leads to *lower* self-esteem because the group is assigned an inferior role. Social identity theory would predict that, in such situations, individuals would not identify with the social group.

Are you a football fan, or fan of a pop group? Do their successes increase your sense of self-esteem?

Evaluation

Group membership and social identity have powerful effects on attitudes towards the self, the ingroup, and outgroups. As predicted by social identity theory, people often develop a sense of social identity because it increases their self-esteem.

The findings from minimal-group studies have been interpreted as indicating the importance of social identity. However, Rabbie, Schot, and Visser (1989) argued that self-interest can also determine behaviour in the minimal-group situation. Some participants were told that they would receive only what outgroup members gave them. These participants showed outgroup favouritism, because self-interest outweighed the sense of social identity.

Another limitation of social identity theory is that it is not applicable to some cultures. Wetherell (1982) compared the attitudes and behaviour of White and Polynesian children in New Zealand. As predicted by social identity theory, the White children tended to discriminate in favour of their group and against the Polynesian children. However, the Polynesian children were co-operative towards the White children, and showed very little ingroup favouritism. In some studies (e.g., Mullen et al., 1992), members of poorly regarded minority groups actually showed favouritism towards more highly regarded outgroups. This is the opposite of what is predicted by social identity theory, and indicates that cultures vary in their beliefs and values.

Why would individuals in a collectivist society be less likely to experience ingroup favouritism?

Finally, it is assumed within the theory that most people have several different social identities. More research needs to be done to find out why some identities come to the surface more readily than others, and to explore the factors that determine which social identity is dominant at any given time.

In terms of being an explanation for prejudice, social identity theory can explain the existence of stereotypes and intergroup attitudes, but it cannot account for the hostility that is associated with prejudice.

The intergroup approach: Realistic conflict theory

According to Sherif (1966), prejudice often results from intergroup conflict. When two groups compete for the same goal, the members of each group tend to become prejudiced against the members of the other group. According to realistic conflict theory, such conflicts of interest cause prejudice.

This theoretical approach developed from the well-known Robber's Cave experiment by Sherif et al. (1961), which is described in the Key Study overleaf. This showed that when competition was added to a pre-existing sense of group identity, hostility was created. The findings were supported by a study in Russia. Andreeva (1984) found that ingroup favouritism and prejudice increased while boys at Pioneer youth camps were engaged in competitive sports. Andreeva also found that prejudice decreased when the boys co-operated in working on agricultural collectives.

The notion that competition always leads to prejudice and intergroup conflict was rejected by Tyerman and Spencer (1983). They argued that competition only has dramatic effects when those involved have not previously formed friendships, as was the case with the boys in the Sherif et al. and Andreeva studies. Tyerman and Spencer observed scouts who already knew each other well as they competed in groups against each other in their annual camp. Competition did not produce the negative effects observed by Sherif et al. (1961). The effects of hostility were also observed in the study by Hovland and Sears (see page 40) but here again there were pre-existing social identities.

People who feel strongly about a particular cause are sometimes likely to experience violent clashes with people who do not share the same values.

Evaluation

Realistic conflict theory offers an explanation for the hostility element of prejudice. It does not explain the origin of prejudiced attitudes but can account for how, when such attitudes exist and there is intergroup conflict, prejudiced behaviour is the result.

The Robber's Cave experiment

Sherif et al. (1961) organised a two-week summer camp for a total of 22 boys at Robber's Cave in the western United States (it had been the hideaway of Jesse James). The boys were assigned to one of two groups, each of which adopted their own name (the Eagles and the Rattlers). The groups soon developed their own identities and group norms, helped to some extent by the fact that they were given caps and T-shirts with their name on to increase this sense of group identity. In one group it became the norm to act tough, not complaining about small injuries, and to swear a lot. The other group swam in the nude and regarded any expression of homesickness as taboo.

> ### KEY STUDY EVALUATION — Sherif et al.
>
> Sherif et al.'s study has been regarded as very important because it showed ordinary boys acting in different ways towards each other depending on the situation. Competition resulted in dislike and hostility, a common goal led to friendship and good feelings. It might be interesting to speculate about whether the results would have been different if all the participants had been girls. It has been argued that while they are growing up girls are rewarded for co-operation, whereas boys are rewarded for competitiveness. It could also be argued that the participants were not a representative group, in that they were not randomly selected especially for the study.

Having created this sense of social identity, the next step was to introduce intergroup competition in order to generate the realistic conflict. The camp counsellors set up a grand tournament, to involve ten sporting events plus cabin cleanliness awards and acting events. The boys were told that whichever group did better in various sporting events and other competitions would receive a trophy, knives, and medals. As a result of this competition, a fight broke out between the members of the two groups, and the Rattlers' flag was burned. Prejudice was shown by the fact that each group regarded its own members as friendly and courageous, whereas the members of the other group were thought to be smart-alecks and liars.

In what way might these findings be culture-specific?

Prejudice was later reduced when the experimenters replaced the competitive situation with a co-operative one in which the success of each group required the co-operation of the other one, such as repairing a broken water cistern and pushing the camp bus that broke down.

Discussion points

1. What comments might you make about the ethics of this study?
2. How important is group conflict as a cause of prejudice?

The intergroup approach: Relative deprivation

Runciman (1966) argued that we can become prejudiced when there is a gap between what we have done and what we expected to be able to do. He used the term **relative deprivation** to refer to such gaps. The key point is that one's feelings of deprivation are judged in terms of what other people might be perceived to have. This exacerbates pre-existing *prejudices* about an *outgroup*, especially at times of economic hardship, and is expressed as aggression towards that group. Runciman drew a distinction between two forms of relative deprivation:

1. *Egotistic deprivation*: this stems from comparisons with other individuals regarded as similar to oneself.
2. *Fraternalistic deprivation*: this is produced by comparisons between groups rather than individuals. The notion that one's own group is being unfairly treated by comparison with some other group often reflects group norms or expectations of what is fair and just.

Martin Luther King, American civil rights leader, was himself well-educated and of a higher socio-economic status than many of the people on whose behalf he campaigned.

We can see the value of the distinction between egotistic and fraternalistic deprivation by considering the leaders of minority groups protesting about the discrimination shown against the group. Such leaders are usually successful individuals who are not egotistically deprived. However, they have a strong sense of fraternalistic or group deprivation. For example, trade union leaders in the United Kingdom who act on behalf of their poorly paid members are usually well-paid and successful individuals. In similar fashion, the most militant Blacks in the United States during the 1960s and 1970s tended to be well-educated and of fairly high socio-economic status (Abeles, 1976).

Support for relative deprivation theory was reported by Vanneman and Pettigrew (1972). Those town dwellers in the United States who had the most extreme racist attitudes reported being the most fraternally deprived.

Evaluation

Runciman's (1966) relative deprivation theory (especially the notion of fraternalistic deprivation) helps us to understand prejudice. It is based on group norms, and explains the fact that prejudice is often found in most members of a given group. In addition, the notion of egotistic deprivation explains why the level of prejudice and hostility is greater in some individuals than in others. However, for the theory to be convincing, we would need to know in more detail the processes involved in producing fraternalistic deprivation.

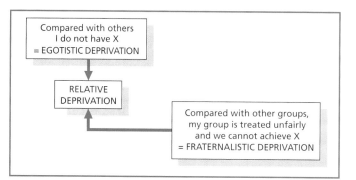

Reduction of Prejudice and Discrimination

Prejudice and discrimination are common in most cultures. It is a matter of considerable importance to find suitable ways for reducing (and ideally eliminating) all forms of prejudice and discrimination. Psychologists have identified various approaches that can be taken, some of which are discussed here. For example, prejudice and discrimination can be reduced if individuals from different groups co-operate to achieve common goals. Alternatively, social contact between groups can also have beneficial effects, especially when attempts are made to blur the boundaries between groups. Finally, there are indications that an effective way of reducing prejudice is to put people on the receiving end of prejudice and discrimination, so that they can experience for themselves how unpleasant it is.

Common goals

It has often been argued that prejudice and discrimination between two groups in conflict can be reduced if they agree to pursue some common or superordinate goal. This was shown by Sherif et al. (1961) in the study discussed earlier. To reduce the conflict between the Rattlers and the Eagles, it was decided that the camp's drinking water should be turned off. In order to restore the supply, the two groups had to combine forces. Several other situations were set up, in which co-operation on a common goal was essential. These situations included rescuing a truck that had got stuck, and pitching tents. As a result of pursuing these common goals, the two groups showed much friendlier attitudes towards each other. In fact, the boys chose as their friends more members of the other group than of their own. However, one should note that if the groups are unsuccessful at the joint task the effects would be counterproductive, i.e., a further emphasis on separate group identities.

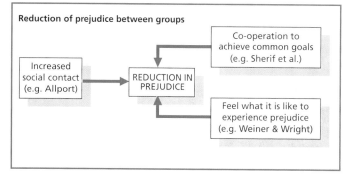

The jigsaw classroom

Aronson and Osherow (1980) tried to reduce prejudice in schools by means of co-operation on common goals. The schools in Austin, Texas had recently been desegregated. This led to concerns about the racial conflict that might result from having black and white children in the same classes. One class of black and white children was divided into small groups for a learning task, for example one group was given the task of finding out about the life of Abraham Lincoln. Within each group, every child was made responsible for learning a different part of the information (e.g., one child had to research Lincoln's early life, and another found out about Lincoln's attitudes towards slavery). Each member of the group then taught what he or she had learned to the other group members so they would all be able to take a test. After that, the children received a mark based on their overall knowledge of the topic. This approach was called the **jigsaw classroom**. The reason

Could raising the competence of low achievers have been made a common goal in the jigsaw classroom?

Having children work in groups with superordinate goals helps reduce racial barriers.

for this was that all the children had a major contribution to make, just as all of the pieces in a jigsaw puzzle are needed to complete it.

The findings with the jigsaw classroom were promising. The children showed higher self-esteem, better school performance, more liking for their classmates, and some reduction in prejudice. However, most of the effects were rather small. There are two likely reasons for this. First, the jigsaw classroom was only used for 45 minutes a day, three days a week, for a six-week period. Second, the groups did not always work in a co-operative way. If the common goals were not achieved, or if the groups co-operating with each other felt they were losing their own identities, then prejudice and discrimination increased rather than decreased (Brown & Wade, 1987). Additional problems were identified by Rosenfield, Stephan, and Lucker (1981). They used the jigsaw classroom technique, and found that minority group members who were low in competence tended to be blamed for slowing down the learning of the more competent students. Their evidence suggested that the jigsaw approach can confirm existing prejudiced attitudes rather than reducing them.

Social contact

According to Allport's (1954) **contact hypothesis**, prejudice can be reduced by increased contact between prejudiced individuals and the groups against which they are prejudiced. There are various reasons why this should be the case. First, stereotypes are based on the assumption that everyone in a given group is very similar, but frequent contact with members of that group disproves that stereotype. Second, interacting with members of another group often makes it clear that the individual is more similar to the prejudiced individual in their attitudes and behaviour than he or she had thought.

CASE STUDY: *New Era Schools Trust*

The New Era Schools Trust (or NEST) runs three boarding schools in South Africa, in Durban, Johannesburg, and Cape Town. The unique aim of all the NEST schools is not only to produce well-educated and personable young people, but also to eliminate any trace of racial prejudice in their students. To achieve this, all races are mixed together from the very first day at school, living and studying alongside each other in a way that is rare even in post-apartheid South Africa. The teachers are similarly multiracial, and there is an equal mix of boys and girls.

Not only are the different races regarded as equal in NEST schools, their cultures are also given equal value. Schools in South Africa have generally taken the view that African culture is irrelevant, and have taught exclusively from a white perspective. At NEST schools the pupils study Xhosa poets as well as Keats, and the lives of Zulu warriors as well as Napoleon. This sense of total equality permeates everything—there are no prefects or top-down discipline, no uniforms or corporal punishment, and everyone takes a hand in doing the chores.

NEST has found that more black parents than white parents wish their children to attend a NEST school. White children tend to have better access to well-equipped schools where they are not required to help clean the dormitories, whereas many black parents are keen for their children to leave the deprivation of the townships to receive their education. This imbalance is lessening, however, as white parents realise what good academic success the NEST schools are achieving. In 1992 their pass rate was 100%, when private white schools and white church schools averaged 90%.

(Based on an article by Prue Leith, *The Times*, May 1993.)

Some research findings support the contact hypothesis. For example, Deutsch and Collins (1951) compared the attitudes of black and white American housewives living close to each other with those of housewives living in segregated housing. Prejudice decreased over time for the housewives living close to each other. After a while, their level of prejudice became much less than that of the housewives in segregated housing.

Social contact on its own is not usually enough. As we saw in the summer camp study of Sherif et al. (1961), social contact between the two groups of boys led to conflict rather than to harmony. Even organising a big feast or a large firework display failed to reduce intergroup hostility. Thus, other factors need to be added to social contact if prejudice is to be reduced. Allport (1954) was well aware that contact on its own is not sufficient to produce large reductions in prejudice. He argued that the groups concerned should be involved in a co-operative activity, and that there should be formal institutional support for integration. In addition, Allport felt that contact would be most effective in reducing prejudice when it involved groups having equal status.

One of the most ambitious attempts to test the contact hypothesis in a thorough way was carried out at Wexler Middle School, as described in the box below.

Wexler Middle School

The contact hypothesis was tested in a study carried out at Wexler Middle School in Waterford in the United States (see Brown, 1986). It involved desegregation, that is, members of different groups attended the same school. A large amount of money was spent on the school to provide it with excellent facilities. It was decided that the numbers of black and white students would be about the same, so that it was not regarded as a white school or a black school. Much was done to make all of the students feel equal, with very little streaming on the basis of ability. Co-operation was increased by having the students work together to buy special equipment they could all use.

The results over the first three years were encouraging. There was much less discrimination, with the behaviour of the black and white students towards each other being friendly. However, while there were many black–white friendships, these friendships rarely extended to visiting each other's houses. In addition, some stereotyped beliefs were still found. Black and white students agreed that black students were tougher and more assertive than white students, whereas white students were cleverer and worked harder than black students.

Discussion points

1. Why were the findings from Wexler Middle School more promising than those from other studies (see later)?

2. Are there ways in which desegregation could be made more effective?

Evaluation

In spite of the success of the study carried out at Wexler Middle School in Waterford, other studies involving desegregation in schools have not worked well. Stephan (1987) reviewed studies on desegregation, and concluded that it often produces increases in white prejudice rather than the desired reduction. In addition, contact between Whites and Blacks rarely had positive effects on the black students. One of the problems is that white and black students in desegregated schools often keep very much within their own group in the playground and at lunchtime. According to Stephan (1987), desegregation is most likely to lead to reduced prejudice when the students are of equal status, there are co-operative one-on-one interactions, members of the two groups have similar beliefs and values, and contact occurs in various situations and with several members of the other group. However, these requirements are not usually met in most desegregated schools.

How could relative deprivation theory be used to explain the lack of success in attempts at desegregation?

The contact hypothesis has been criticised because it seems to focus too much on changing the prejudiced views of the dominant group and not enough on the attitudes of the minority group. In many cases, contact between the dominant and minority groups involves intergroup anxiety (Stephan & Stephan, 1989). The members of the dominant group are anxious to avoid saying or doing anything that could be regarded as prejudiced, whereas the members of the minority group are anxious that they may be victimised or

In November 1989, in Enniskillen, Northern Ireland, an integrated primary school was opened for children of all religions. What do you think motivated the people of Enniskillen to take this unusual step?

negatively evaluated. If contact is to lead to reduced prejudice, it is important to consider ways of reducing intergroup anxiety.

Decategorisation

Brewer and Miller (1984) were in general agreement with the contact hypothesis. However, in their decategorisation theory, they argued that social contact will only reduce prejudice when the boundaries between the conflicting groups become blurred or less rigid. When this happens, members of each group are less likely to think of members of the other group in terms of categories or group membership. Instead, they respond to members of the other group as individuals.

Research by Aronson and Osherow (1980) discussed earlier may show the value of decategorisation. They reduced racial barriers in children by having them work together in groups in the "jigsaw classroom". In general terms, teaching methods that focus on co-operative learning and the removal of group barriers are effective in reducing conflicts and prejudice between groups (Slavin, 1983).

Evaluation

Hewstone and Brown (1986) pointed out that decategorisation often works only in a limited way. Decategorisation and co-operation may be very effective in the situation in which they are used. However, the reduction in prejudice often does not extend to other members of the group or to other situations. The techniques used to produce decategorisation involve treating members of the other group as individuals. As a result, there is likely to be a reduction in prejudice towards those individuals rather than towards the group as a whole.

In order for reduced prejudice to generalise from a given individual to his or her group, it may be important to ensure that the individual's group affiliation is clear. Some interesting relevant evidence was reported by Wilder (1984). Students had a pleasant meeting with a student belonging to a rival college. This led to reduced prejudice towards the rival college when the student was regarded as a typical member of that college. However, there was no reduction when he was regarded as atypical. Thus, it is important that individuals are *representative* of the group to which they belong for a general reduction in prejudice to occur.

Have you ever encountered someone from a "rival" group and been pleasantly surprised by what you found?

Experiencing prejudice

People can be prejudiced because they do not know what it feels like to be on the receiving end of prejudice. It follows that prejudice could be reduced by arranging for people to experience prejudice for themselves. Weiner and Wright (1973) tested this notion. White American children aged 9 or 10 were put at random into an orange or a green group, and wore coloured armbands to identify their group membership. On the first day, the orange children were told that they were cleverer and cleaner than the green children, and they were given privileges that were denied to the orange children.

Elliott (1977) conducted an investigation where she told all her blue-eyed students that they were inferior to the brown-eyed pupils. This was done as an attempt to show them what discrimination feels like. Within a day the blue-eyed children were being subjected to playground taunts from the brown-eyed children, and their classwork appeared to be suffering. Elliott reversed the process and said that in fact it was the brown-eyed pupils who were inferior. Very quickly the children's behaviours also reversed. Afterwards, Elliott told them about what she had done and used this to teach them about prejudice and discrimination. Ten years later, at a class reunion, the children said they thought they were more tolerant of others and actively opposed to prejudice as a consequence of that experiment in class (Elliott, 1990).

The situation was reversed on the second day. On each day, the group that was discriminated against felt inferior, showed reduced self-confidence, and did less well in their schoolwork.

In order to see whether the experience of these children had made them less prejudiced, they were asked whether they wanted to go on a picnic with some black children. Nearly all (96%) of the children agreed. In contrast, only 62% of children who had not been exposed to prejudice agreed to go on the picnic. Thus, experiencing discrimination at first hand can reduce prejudice and discrimination towards other people, though such manipulation raises ethical questions.

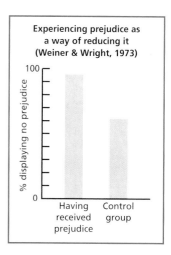

Why do you think some of the control group did not display prejudice?

Self-regulation

Monteith (1993) argued for an approach to prejudice reduction based on **self-regulation**. According to this approach, even individuals who are not generally prejudiced are likely to have negative stereotypes of various kinds stored away in long-term memory. For example, they may have a stereotype based on the notion that French people are arrogant. When they meet a French person, this stereotype will be activated automatically. This may lead them to behave rudely. If they realise that their behaviour is discrepant from their non-prejudiced outlook, then they are likely to experience feelings of guilt and self-criticism. They may also try to identify the situational cues that led them to behave in a prejudiced way.

An implication of this analysis of prejudiced behaviour is that individuals low in prejudice can eliminate it by regular self-regulation of their thoughts and feelings. This requires being more reflective, and thinking about any stereotypes that are activated automatically *before* they can lead to prejudiced behaviour. Monteith (1993) reported evidence that prejudice can be reduced through the development of self-regulatory mechanisms. However, it should be noted that this approach is only likely to reduce prejudice in those who are initially low in prejudice *and* motivated to avoid prejudiced thinking and behaviour. Indeed, Devine (1995, p.509) admitted that the model "does not directly address the experiences of high prejudiced people."

Evaluating the methods of reducing prejudice

Much of the research on methods of reducing prejudice has been disappointing. As we have seen, the most common approach based on the contact hypothesis only seems to succeed when the circumstances in which majority and minority groups meet are carefully controlled. More worryingly, even if contact is found to produce beneficial effects, these effects rarely generalise beyond the contact situation. One reason for these disappointing findings is that producing contact between groups is an *indirect* way of trying to change prejudiced attitudes. In contrast, self-regulation has the advantage of trying to change negative attitudes in a *direct* way.

Other major problems with most attempts to reduce prejudice were identified by Devine (1995, p.500):

Even though several theoretical explanations have been advanced concerning the processes involved in the acquisition of prejudice, there has been a paucity [lack] of research that uses these theories in order to identify the processes involved in the reduction of prejudice. As a consequence ..., prejudice-reduction techniques seemed to have a "hit-or-miss" quality about them; the processes responsible for the technique's successes and failures often were—and remain—unknown.

What recommendations would you make to the head teacher of a secondary school to help reduce prejudice? How would you measure the effectiveness of any changes?

Attempts to reduce prejudice by increasing contact between different groups rarely generalises beyond the contact situation.

Psychological research on prejudice can be used in schools to help reduce prejudice.

SECTION   SUMMARY

Attribution of Causality

❖ Heider proposed that we behave like naïve scientists: we make observations and attribute causes. These attributions are either internal (dispositional) or external (situational). Several theories have been developed to explain this process of attribution.

❖ According to correspondent inference theory (Jones & Davis), we assume that an observed behaviour *corresponds* with some underlying stable characteristic of the actor using an attribution of (1) intention and (2) disposition. Dispositional attributions are more likely if an action is low in social desirability, yields noncommon effects, and has hedonic relevance or personalism. Research has shown that individuals do infer a corresponding underlying attitude on the basis of observable behaviours, but in general the attribution process is more complex in real life. In addition attributions are made when behaviours are not intentional and when behaviours actually confirm expectations rather than being unusual.

❖ Kelley proposed two theories of attribution. The covariation model suggests that we decide whether to make a dispositional or situational attribution of someone else's behaviour on the basis of information about consensus, consistency, and distinctiveness. High consensus, high consistency, and high distinctiveness will probably lead to a situational attribution, whereas a dispositional attribution is likely where there is low consensus, high consistency, and low distinctiveness. Like the previous theory, this model has gained support from rather artificial research studies. Real life is more complex and often insufficient data are available for making covariation judgements. This led Kelley to propose a second model, causal schemata or heuristics, which suggests how causes interact to produce specific behaviours. The two main kinds of causal schemata are multiple necessary causes and multiple sufficient causes, which includes the discounting and augmenting principles. The model can explain how we are able to make inferences so quickly, especially with only ambiguous or partial information, but it lacks empirical support.

❖ Weiner's three-dimensional model is particularly concerned with attributions of success and failure. Attributions are made on three dimensions: locus, stability, and controllability. This model recognises other dimensions besides the internal/external one of the other models. It has interesting applications in attribution retraining and has been used to explain depression. This model has good empirical support including cross-cultural research, however it continues to portray attribution as a logical, rational process.

❖ Biases in the attribution process produce a preference for external or internal attributions. According to the fundamental attribution error (FAE), we tend to attribute the behaviour of others to their disposition or personality rather than to situational factors. There is good research support for this, and the FAE can be used to explain Milgram's obedience studies. However, the FAE may not be that fundamental; we may not be biased if we suspect that others have hidden motives. It may be possible to explain the FAE in terms of salience (disposition is more salient), and as being due to cognitive time pressure. The FAE makes us feel that life is fair and that our lives are predictable. It appears to be less common in collectivist cultures than in individualist cultures.

❖ The actor–observer effect suggests that the actor tends to make situational attributions whereas an observer tends towards dispositional ones. This might happen because we possess much more information about ourselves than about others, but is more likely to be due to the fact that we can see the situation but not ourselves.

❖ The self-serving bias represents our tendency to take the credit for success but accept no blame for failure. This can be explained in terms of cognitive factors (confirmation or non-confirmation of intentions), or motivational factors (enhancing self-esteem). It is stronger in individualist cultures than in collectivist ones. The self-serving bias can be extended to the self-handicapping bias (prior to an important event an individual explains potential failure in situational terms), ingroup bias (self-esteem increased by treating the ingroup favourably), and defensive attribution (the greater the consequences of an action, the more that attributions tend to be dispositional rather than situational).

❖ Social perception involves interpreting data about the social world. Impression formation can be explained by Asch's configural model where some traits, such as warm/cold, are seen as more central than others in determining an overall impression. Research studies, both laboratory and field experiments, show that participants do make inferences about traits that are not included in the original information, in some cases producing a halo effect. There are other biases in impression formation: primacy/recency, the effects of trait inconsistency, and a contrast effect. Implicit personality theory suggests that we each have "theories" about what traits tend to go together. Such theories are in part learned and in part culturally determined. It may be that central traits are not actually central but are social traits that stand out in a list of intellectual traits, and inevitably affect assessment in terms of other social traits.

❖ A schema is a cognitive structure that contains knowledge about a thing, including its attributes and the relations among its attributes. Schemas, like traits, generate a complex set of expectations about that individual. There are person schemas, self-schemas, and schemas about events, called scripts. Role schemas that are shared expectations rather than personal beliefs are called stereotypes. Schemas and stereotypes streamline our cognitive processes and are desirable because we are cognitive misers. This is related to the use of heuristics and categorisation. A heuristic tells us about the likely relationship between things, such as a representativeness heuristic (using prototypes) or an availability heuristic (instances that most quickly come to mind). Such rules of general principle speed up cognitive processing though at some cost to accuracy. However there are occasions when people do not use heuristics (the motivated tactician). Categorisation involves matching a person to an existing social category and is an effect of social identity; we perceive ourselves and others as belonging to certain groups (ingroups and outgroups). This leads to, for example, the illusion of outgroup homogeneity.

❖ Social and cultural stereotyping are the consequences of cognitive short-cuts. Research evidence suggests that people have shared cultural stereotypes, but this may be a demand characteristic of such studies. Better-designed studies indicate less stereotyping. Other research indicates that stereotypes do lead to biased processing of information, as in the case of hypothetical defendants. This is probably because stereotypes make us attend to information fitting the stereotype, and cause us to disregard other items of information. Illusory correlations can also explain why stereotypes sometimes lead to prejudice. Negative stereotyping of minority groups may occur because of perceived relationships when two things that are unusual or distinctive co-occur. Most people do try to control the effect of stereotypes on judgement but, in complex situations this may not be possible. Stereotypes lead to racism and sexism yet they do help us make sense of a very complex world. Stereotypes may be inaccurate but they persist because they contain a "kernel of truth".

❖ Social representations, i.e., socially derived knowledge, are a third approach to social perception. Social representations are more than schemas and may be our only means of acquiring some forms of knowledge. Social representations are formed through anchoring (relating new concepts to existing knowledge) and objectification (making abstract ideas more concrete). Research evidence includes Italian representations of intelligence as a gift, French representations of health as a reservoir that can be emptied, and French representations of some mentally ill patients as "dirty". Social representations can lead to a reversal of the actor–observer effect—attributions are made in line with learned social representations about, e.g., poverty. The notion of social representations is

Social Perception

valuable, because it encourages us to search for the social origins of much of our knowledge. However, theoretical accounts are rather vague and there is evidence that social representations are not always shared across social groups, as the theory would predict.

Prejudice and Discrimination

❖   Prejudice is an attitude, whereas discrimination refers to behaviour or action. Explanations of the origins of prejudice can be divided into personal characteristics or environmental/cultural factors.

❖   The psychodynamic approach is one kind of personality explanation, including the frustration–aggression hypothesis and the authoritarian personality. The frustration–aggression hypothesis suggests that frustration builds up and leads to aggression that is displaced on to a scapegoat. There are many historical examples of this (e.g., anti-Semitism before the Second World War) but the hypothesis does not explain why aggression is directed against one particular group. The authoritarian personality has rigid beliefs, general hostility towards other groups, intolerance of ambiguity, and submissive attitudes towards authority figures. This results from a harsh upbringing where repressed feelings are later expressed as hostility towards minority groups. The authoritarian personality is tested using the F-scale, which has shown that prejudiced individuals are also submissive and obedient. Cross-cultural research shows that authoritarian personalities want to maintain the dominant values in their culture. Problems with this account of prejudice are that it ignores the influence of cultural values, the F-Scale may have a response set, and finally the interviews may have been biased.

❖   There are a variety of explanations that are environmental and cultural factors: both interpersonal and intergroup approaches. Conformity is an example of the interpersonal approach. Individuals adopt group norms and in cultures where the norm is to be prejudiced, then individuals behave in this way.

❖   Social identity theory is an example of the intergroup approach. Social identity leads to categorisation and social comparison, ingroup favouritism and outgroup negative bias, which all enhance social and personal self-esteem, and lead to prejudice. The minimal group experiment demonstrated the ease with which social identities are formed and lead to ingroup favouritism. This appears to extend to the real world. Categorical differentiation allows us to simplify and to organise our social worlds. There is evidence to support the fact that social identity increases self-

esteem. However, self-interest can also determine behaviour in the minimal-group situation, social identity may not apply to all cultures, and the theory cannot predict which one of several identities is selected at any one time. As an explanation for prejudice, social identity theory can explain the existence of stereotypes and intergroup attitudes, but not the hostility that is associated with prejudice.

❖ Realistic conflict theory is a second example of the intergroup approach to explaining the origins and maintenance of prejudice. Intergroup conflict and competition between social groups lead to hostility, as demonstrated in the Robbers' Cave study as well as a study in Russia. However such hostility doesn't appear unless there are pre-existing social identities, so realistic conflict theory offers an explanation for the hostility element of prejudice but not the initial bias.

❖ The third example of the intergroup approach is relative deprivation theory. Perceptions of relative deprivation exacerbate existing prejudices and lead to intergroup hostility. The distinction between egotistic and fraternalistic deprivation is important in understanding the role of minority group leaders who are fraternalistic but not egotistically deprived. Relative deprivation theory is based on group norms and thus explains why prejudice is shared by the group, however some of the processes are unclear, such as what produces fraternalistic deprivation.

❖ Reducing prejudice and discrimination is a matter of considerable importance. The Robbers' Cave experiment showed that the use of common (superordinate) goals is one method of reducing prejudice. The jigsaw classroom pioneered a technique for working towards common goals, however research found rather small effects in terms of prejudice reduction and in some cases it served to confirm existing prejudiced attitudes rather than reducing them, such as when minority group members slowed the team down.

❖ Social contact (contact hypothesis) between groups of equal status can also reduce prejudice by allowing group members to differentiate between individuals in outgroups, thus breaking down stereotypes. This approach has had some success but contact alone is not enough. When attempts are made to desegregate groups, the individuals still stick to their own groups rather than mixing, and intergroup hostility may even be increased. One important aim may be to reduce intergroup anxiety.

❖ Decategorisation theory suggests that increased social contact will work only if the boundaries between conflicting groups are blurred. This permits group members to be seen as individuals. However, decategorisation tends not to generalise beyond the immediate situations except if individuals are seen as representative of their group.

❖ Experiencing prejudice at first hand can reduce prejudice. It may be that people do not know what it feels like to be on the receiving end of prejudice. Experimental evidence supports the value of direct experience, though there are ethical concerns with such manipulation.

❖ The self-regulation approach suggests that people should be more reflective, and think about any stereotypes that are activated automatically before they can lead to prejudiced behaviour. This approach is appropriate for motivated individuals but is unlikely to appeal to highly prejudiced individuals.

FURTHER READING

The topics in this Section are covered in greater depth by D. Pennington (2000) *Social cognition* (London: Routledge), written specifically for the AQA A specification. There are good chapters dealing with the issues discussed in this Section in M. Hewstone, W. Stroebe, and G.M. Stephenson (Eds.) (1996) *Introduction to social psychology (2nd Edn.)* (Oxford: Blackwell). A readable book that deals with social cognition is N. Hayes (1993) *Principles of social psychology* (Hove, UK: Psychology Press). Prejudice and discrimination are discussed in detail by J. Vivian and R. Brown (1994) in A.M. Colman (Ed.), *Companion encyclopaedia of psychology (Vol. 2)* (London: Routledge).

Example Examination Questions

You should spend 30 minutes on each of the questions below, which aim to test the material in this Section.

1. **(a)** Outline **two** theories relating to the attribution of causality. (12 marks)
   (b) Evaluate **one** of these theories, with reference to research studies. (12 marks)

2. Discuss errors and biases in the attribution process (e.g., self-serving bias and the fundamental attribution error). (24 marks)

3. "The way each of us perceives other people is very much influenced by the social and cultural stereotypes that we have."

   With reference to the quotation, discuss social and cultural influences on the perception of the social world. (24 marks)

4. **(a)** Describe the nature of social representations. (12 marks)
   (b) Assess the value of such representations in explaining social perception. (12 marks)

5. Describe and evaluate **one** explanation of the origins of prejudice and/or discrimination. (24 marks)

6. Discuss **two** ways in which prejudice might be reduced. (24 marks)

Examination Tips

Question 1. In part (a) the term "outline" means that you should present your chosen theories as a summary description only. You have no more than 15 minutes to do this so don't lose marks by providing too much detail for one theory and failing to attract marks for your second theory. In part (b) you are required to evaluate only one of the theories. It would be creditworthy to make comparisons with the second theory from part (a), or any other theory, but this must be done explicitly. You are required to use research studies in your evaluation but you are not restricted to these, and therefore you might also consider issues such as culture bias and attribution biases.

Question 2. "Discuss" is an AO1 and AO2 term requiring both a description and an evaluation of the named concepts. Two *examples* are given in the question but they are provided for inspiration only. Evaluation is likely to consist of reference to research studies and a consideration of culture bias. You might also consider applications of this research. The danger may be that you can do more on evaluation and do not maximise your AO1 marks. Make sure you give a full 15 minutes to descriptions. Examples are a good way to add extra detail.

Question 3. In this question, you will lose some marks if you do not engage with the quotation. One way to do this is to start your answer by deconstructing the quotation to guide you in what you will write. Try also to make reference back to the quotation throughout the essay. You must both describe and evaluate social and cultural influences. If you wish you can deal with these separately (where social influences could include social perception generally) or deal with social/cultural as one general issue.

Question 4. Part (a) requires a straightforward description of social representations. Ensure you provide a well-detailed and structured account. In part (b) you should consider how much of social perception can be explained using the concept of social representation. The trick here is to use your knowledge effectively in order to construct an argument in answer to the question, rather than just describing evidence. You might employ useful phrases such as "This suggests that …" or "The point this illustrates is …".

Question 5.   The question requires only one explanation; any other explanations may be used in evaluation as long as they are explicitly presented in this way. For maximum credit you should not merely say "we can evaluate theory x with theory y" and then just describe your second theory; you should continually be aware that the second theory is there by way of contrast (or agreement) and make references back to the first theory. Note that the question asks for origins only, not maintenance or reduction—though the implications of the theory for reduction might be a useful evaluative point.

Question 6.   The question is on reduction and therefore any material on origins would only attract credit if it is made explicitly relevant. You are restricted to two "ways" but could use other ways by way of contrast as long as this is explicit. Each factor should be described in detail (for 6 marks each) and then evaluated by, for example, considering research evidence, the general success of the approach, and a reflection on some of the potential limitations.

WEB SITES

http://www.socialpsychology.org
  Huge, searchable social psychology 'portal' with resources and thousands of links to social psychology-related sites on the internet: see http://www.socialpsychology.org/social.htm#prejudice for links concerning prejudice and discrimination.

http://www.psych.purdue.edu/~esmith/scarch.html
  Social Cognition Paper Archive and Information Center.

http://www.richmond.edu/%7Eallison/glossary.html
  Social psychology glossary.

http://ibs.derby.ac.uk/~garyt/SocialLecture3.html
  Lecture notes and links on attribution theory.

http://www.psy.anu.edu.au/social/socident.htm
  Explanation of social identity theory.

http://www.oklahoma.net/~jnichols/perth.html
  Personality theory and assessment links.

http://buster.cs.yale.edu/implicit/measure3.html
  Test your prejudices about age, race, gender.

http://www.noctrl.edu/~ajomuel/crow/topicprejudice.htm
  Links to prejudice-related topics.

http://aps.psychsociety.com.au/member/racism/index.html
  Detailed paper on Psychological Perspectives on Racism by the Australian Psychological Association, with particular reference to Aboriginal people and immigration.

http://www.inform.umd.edu/EdRes/Topic/Diversity/Reference/divdic.html
  "Diversity Dictionary": glossary of terms related to cultural diversity and different ethnic and social groups.

http://www.apa.org/pi/
  The American Psychological Society's (APA) public information section.

www.a-levelpsychology.co.uk/websites.html
  A continually updated list of useful links, may be found at the Psychology Press A level psychology site.

2

Relationships

This Section looks at various aspects of interpersonal relationships: how they begin and end, and how culture and sub-culture also play a part in this process.

Attraction and the Formation of Relationships

There are several types of interpersonal relationships, ranging from romantic relationships to casual friendships in the workplace. However, we will focus mostly on the formation of romantic relationships as this has been the topic most investigated by psychologists.

Explanations of Interpersonal Attraction

Why are you attracted to one person rather than another? Numerous factors are involved in the formation of interpersonal relationships. It is not possible to consider all the relevant factors here. What has been done instead is to focus on five of the main ones: physical attractiveness, proximity, attitude similarity, demographic similarity, and similarity in personality.

Physical attractiveness

The first thing that we generally notice when meeting a stranger is their physical appearance. This includes how they are dressed and whether they are clean or dirty, and it often includes an assessment of their physical attractiveness. People tend to agree with each other about whether someone is physically attractive. Women whose faces resemble those of young children are often perceived as attractive. For example, photographs of females with relatively large and widely separated eyes, a small nose, and a small chin are regarded as more attractive. However, wide cheekbones and narrow cheeks are also seen as attractive (Cunningham, 1986), and these features are not usually found in young children.

Cunningham also studied physical attractiveness in males. Men having features such as a square jaw, small eyes, and thin lips were regarded as attractive by women. These features can be regarded as indicating maturity, as they are rarely found in children.

Evidence that physically attractive people are thought of as being generally attractive was reported by Brigham (1971). Males and females both argued that physically attractive individuals are poised, sociable, interesting, independent, exciting, and sexually warm.

Can you think of any famous people who are considered attractive, but who do not meet Cunningham's attractiveness criteria?

Joan Collins (top left) fits Cunningham's "attractive female" characteristics—note how her features are similar to the little girl's (top right). Pierce Brosnan (bottom left), however, looks very different from the little boy (bottom right).

This is called the **halo effect**, the tendency for the total impression formed to be unduly influenced by one outstanding trait.

The matching hypothesis

The **matching hypothesis** proposes that we don't seek the most physically attractive person but that we are attracted to individuals who match us in terms of physical attraction. This compromise is necessary because of a fear of rejection (a more attractive person might reject your advances) and/or to achieve a balance between partners.

Walster et al. (1966) tested this by asking students to rate partners who had been randomly selected in terms of their interpersonal attraction, see Key Study on the facing page. This study did not find that attraction was related to matching. The students preferred partners who were more physically attractive, not someone matching with their own attractiveness.

However, subsequent studies have found support for the matching hypothesis. Walster and Walster (1969) did a repeat of the original computer dance but this time the students had met beforehand and this probably meant that they had more time to think about the qualities they were looking for in a partner. As predicted by the matching

Testing the matching hypothesis

Walster et al. (1966) advertised a "computer dance" for students during fresher's week at college. The first 376 male and 376 female volunteers were allowed in at $1.00 each. When the students arrived to sign up for the dance, four independent judges assessed each student's physical attractiveness as a measure of social desirability. The participants were seated upstairs and asked to fill in a lengthy questionnaire, ostensibly for use in the computer pairing. In fact the questionnaire was used to provide data about similarity and the pairing was done randomly (except that no man was assigned to a taller woman). The dance was held two days later, before which the students were given their dates' names. During the dance, participants were asked to complete a questionnaire about the dance and their dates. The more physically attractive students were liked more by their partners than were the less attractive students, a finding that does not support the matching hypothesis.

Physical attractiveness proved to be the most important factor in liking, above such qualities as intelligence and personality. Liking was not affected by how attracted the other person felt towards the participant. Physical attractiveness was also the best predictor of the likelihood that they would see each other again, though it assumed less importance.

Discussion points

1. Does the matching hypothesis seem correct in your experience?
2. Why does physical attractiveness play such an important part in dating behaviour and in relationships?

hypothesis, students expressed the most liking for those who were at the same level of physical attractiveness as themselves.

Murstein (1972) obtained further support for the matching hypothesis. The physical attractiveness of engaged couples and those going out together was judged from photographs. There was a definite tendency for the two people in each couple to be similar in terms of physical attractiveness.

■ Activity: Use photographs of couples from newspapers and magazines to replicate Murstein's study on the matching hypothesis. This will be a correlational study (i.e. non-experimental). Variations on Murstein's study might include looking at dating couples, couples who have been married for 10 years or more, or homosexual couples. You must bear in mind all the related ethical considerations.

Evaluation

Physical attractiveness is of importance in influencing initial attraction for other people. However, some people are much more affected by physical attractiveness than others. Towhey (1979) asked males and females how much they thought they would like a person whose photograph they had seen, and about whom they had read biographical information. The judgements of those scoring high on the Macho Scale (dealing with sexist attitudes, stereotypes, and behaviour) were much influenced by physical attractiveness, whereas those scoring low on the Macho Scale almost ignored physical attractiveness as a factor.

Is physical attractiveness mainly of importance only in the early stages of a relationship? The answer seems to be "no". For example, Murstein and Christy (1976) reported that married couples were significantly more similar than dating couples in physical attractiveness.

The matching hypothesis has been extended to suggest that couples can achieve a match in ways other than physical attractiveness, for example, a good-looking woman

The **matching hypothesis** predicts a match that is not necessarily based on looks alone. In fact, physical attractiveness can be matched with intelligence, as in the case of Marilyn Monroe and Arthur Miller.

Friendships arise and are maintained between people who live close to each other, and who enjoy similar leisure pursuits.

Does the concept of proximity apply to your friends?

may be attracted to a man who lacks *physical* attractiveness but possesses other highly attractive features, such as intelligence or wealth.

Proximity

Proximity or nearness is an important factor in determining our choice of friends. Strong evidence for this was obtained by Festinger, Schachter, and Back (1950). They studied married graduate students who had been assigned randomly to flats in 17 different two-storey buildings. It was found that about two-thirds of their closest friends lived in the same building. Festinger et al. found that close friends who lived in the same building were twice as likely to be living on the same floor as the other floor. If you live on the same floor as someone, you are likely to bump into each other more frequently than if you are on different floors. This study suggests that such increased contact increases the likelihood that relationships form.

The importance of proximity extends to romantic relationships that lead to marriage. Bossard (1932) looked at 5000 marriage licences in Philadelphia. He found there was a clear tendency for those getting married to live close to each other. However, this may be less true today, because people are generally more mobile and travel much more than was the case in the 1930s. Having said that, it is still the case that you have to meet someone before forming a relationship, such as by going to the same college or the same swimming club, and frequency of contact is a starting point. Even internet relationships are formed through a kind of proximity.

Friendships and relationships are more common between individuals living close to each other, but so are antagonistic relationships. Ebbesen, Kjos, and Konecni (1976) found that most of the enemies of residents in apartment blocks in California also lived close by.

Evaluation

It is fairly obvious that proximity will be an important factor in the formation of relationships because proximity determines who you are likely to meet. Kerckhoff and Davis (1962) used the term "filter" to describe how superficial traits are used in the initial selection of friends or partners. We will consider this further at the end of this Unit (see page 69).

Attitude similarity

One of the factors determining interpersonal attraction is attitude similarity. Newcomb (1961) paid students to take part in his study. Initially information was obtained about the beliefs and attitudes of students. He then used this information to assign students to rooms. Some students were given a room with someone of similar attitudes, whereas others were paired with someone having very different attitudes. Friendships were much more likely to develop between students who shared the same beliefs and attitudes than between those who did not (58% and 25%, respectively).

Byrne et al. (1968) found that attitude similarity had much more of an effect on interpersonal attraction when the attitudes were of importance to the individual. They arranged matters so that the other person seemed to have similar attitudes to the participants on either 75% or 25% of the topics. This was done by deliberately providing fake information about the other person. It was only when similarity was related to the topics of most importance to the participants that it affected attraction.

Evaluation

Do you think that preferring similar leisure activities is important in intimate relationships?

Werner and Parmalee (1979) argued that it was not attitude similarity as such that was important. They found that similarity in preference for leisure activities (which is related to attitude similarity) was more important for friendship than was attitude similarity. According to Werner and Parmalee (1979, p.62), "those who play together, stay together."

Demographic similarity

Several studies have considered the effects of demographic variables (e.g., age; sex; social class). It has nearly always been found that those who have similar demographic characteristics are more likely to become friends. For example, Kandel (1978) asked students in secondary school to identify their best friend among the other students. These best friends tended to be of the same age, religion, sex, social class, and ethnic background as the students who nominated them.

Similarity in personality

Reasonable similarity in physical attractiveness, attitudes, and demographic variables is found in friends, engaged couples, and married couples. What about similarity in personality? One possibility is that people who have similar personalities are most likely to become involved with each other ("Birds of a feather flock together"). Another possibility is that dissimilar people are most likely to become friends or to marry ("Opposites attract"). Winch (1958) argued for the latter possibility. He claimed that married couples will be happy if they each have complementary needs. For example, if a domineering person marries someone who is submissive, this may allow both of them to fulfil their needs.

Winch found that married couples who were different in personality were happier than those who were similar. However, most of the evidence indicates that similarity of personality is important, and that people tend to be intimately involved with those who are like themselves. Burgess and Wallin (1953) obtained detailed information from 1000 engaged couples, including information about 42 personality characteristics. There was no evidence for the notion that opposites attract. There was significant within-couple similarity for 14 personality characteristics (e.g., feelings easily hurt; leader of social events).

Evaluation of the five factors

There is much evidence that the formation of interpersonal relationships depends to a large extent on several kinds of similarity. Why is similarity so important? Rubin (1973) suggested various answers. First, if we like those who are similar to us, there is a reasonable chance that they will like us. Second, communication is easier with people who are similar. Third, similar others may confirm the rightness of our attitudes and beliefs. Fourth, it makes sense that if we like ourselves, then we should also like others who resemble us. Fifth, people who are similar to us are likely to enjoy the same activities.

Much research in this area is rather artificial. For example, the importance of physical attractiveness has sometimes been assessed by showing participants photographs of people they have never met, and asking them to indicate how much they would like to go out with them. Of course, physical attractiveness is going to have an enormous influence on the results when no other relevant information is available. Interpersonal relationships are formed over time as two people begin to know each other better, but the processes involved have rarely been studied in the laboratory.

A further limitation of most research is that individual differences have been largely ignored. Some people attach more importance than others to similarity of physical attractiveness, attitudes, and so on, but very little is known about this.

Considering the factors involved in the formation of relationships, what type of person are you likely to form a successful relationship with? Would it be someone like yourself or not?

Theories of Attraction and the Formation of Relationships

Psychologists are interested in formulating theoretical accounts of behaviour, on the basis of research evidence. We have reviewed some of the findings about the factors involved in interpersonal attraction. The next step is to consider how these can be woven into a coherent theory.

One major issue, for any theory, is its ability to account for the enormous diversity of interpersonal relationships between people. For example, it is important to distinguish between romantic relationships, same-sex friendships, opposite-sex friendships, interpersonal relationships in the workplace, and so on. It is obvious from experience that the processes involved in relationship formation differ considerably from one type of interpersonal relationship to another. It is hard to handle such diversity within a single theory. Many theorists have not been as careful as they might have been in indicating the type or types of interpersonal relationship to which their theory is most applicable. In addition they have ignored cultural and sub-cultural diversity, topics which are considered in the final Unit of this Section.

There are two other factors to consider in relation to any theory of interpersonal attraction and relationship formation. First of all, we have already noted the difficulties associated with research in this area. Studying social and interpersonal relationships is a nightmare for experimental psychologists because it is almost impossible for the researcher to *control* any of the important factors that influence the formation, maintenance, and dissolution of relationships except in highly artificial situations. Another problem is that one of the key features of nearly all interpersonal relationships is that they change over time. In order to understand these changes, we need to focus on the *processes* involved. However, these processes typically occur over long periods of time, and are very hard to observe experimentally. Therefore theories of interpersonal attraction and the formation of relationships may be rather poorly supported by research evidence.

Sociobiological theories

One way of considering social relationships is in **sociobiological** or **evolutionary** terms (see Section 13, Determinants of Animal Behaviour). The central idea is that the behaviours we observe around us must be **adaptive**, otherwise individuals possessing those characteristics would not have lived long enough to pass on those characteristics to their offspring. An adaptive behaviour is one that promotes the survival of the individual *and* results in successful reproduction. Therefore behaviours that are related to successful relationship formation leading to reproduction will be likely. If you're not successful at this your genes will die out!

What other characteristics would be considered preferable in a partner according to the sociobiological approach?

One of the implications of the sociobiological approach is that males and females should both seek sexual partners who are most likely to produce healthy children. This could explain why physically healthy partners are generally preferred to unhealthy ones. Men may tend to prefer women who are younger than themselves because younger women are more likely to be fertile (Buss, 1989). There is a detailed discussion of this theory and the research evidence in Section 15, Evolutionary Explanations of Human Behaviour (pages 562–589).

The sociobiological approach has been extended to account for the close relationships that are often found within families. One of the ways in which an individual can help to ensure the survival of his or her genes is by protecting relatives so that they will be able to reproduce. For example, children share 50% of their genes with each of their parents. As a result, there are strong evolutionary reasons why parents should devote considerable efforts to looking after their children. The same considerations apply to our relationships with other relatives, with the level of involvement being determined by the genetic similarity. The term **kin selection** is used to describe the notion that survival of an individual's genes is ensured by helping the survival of close relatives (see Section 13, Determinants of Animal Behaviour, and also later in this Part, pages 113–114).

Some evidence is consistent with the sociobiological approach. Fellner and Marshall (1981) found that 86% of people were willing to be a kidney donor for their children, 67% would do the same for their parents, and 50% would be a kidney donor for their siblings.

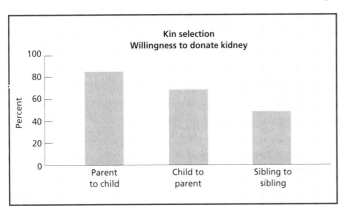

Kin selection
Willingness to donate kidney

Evaluation

Sociobiological theories of relationships help to account for the special nature of the relationships within families, and especially for the enormous amounts of time and resources that most parents devote to their children. However, such theories do not explain most relationships. For example, the notion that romantic relationships have reproduction as their primary goal does not apply to many homosexual relationships, or to heterosexual relationships in which there is no intention to have children.

The greatest limitation of sociobiological theories is that they focus on sexual relationships and ignore non-sexual relationships and friendships with non-relatives. It is hard for such theories to explain why women love their best friend as much as their lover, and like their best friend more (Sternberg & Grajek, 1984). In general terms, sociobiological theories are inadequate to account for interpersonal relationships.

Parents invest a lot of time and resources in their children, which may be explained by biological theories of relationships—the parents' chances of passing on their genes are improved if they can help their children to survive and succeed.

Reinforcement and need satisfaction theory

Reinforcement and need satisfaction theory is based on the notion that a key reason why we form friendships and relationships is because of the rewards or reinforcements that we receive from others. These rewards often consist of approval, smiling, and so on. Foa and Foa (1975) argued that the rewards provided by other people can also include sex, status, love, help, money, and agreement with our opinions. These things may be rewarding because they meet our various social needs. For example, obtaining the approval of others satisfies our need for self-esteem, being comforted satisfies our dependency needs, controlling others meets our needs for dominance, and making love satisfies our sex needs (Argyle, 1988).

Byrne (1971) argued that classical conditioning also plays an important role in determining the effects of reinforcement on interpersonal attraction. He found that positive feelings, or affect, are created when someone expresses similar attitudes to ours, whereas negative affect is produced when someone expresses dissimilar attitudes. Of greatest relevance to his theory, Byrne also found that someone whose picture was present was liked more when the participants listened to someone expressing similar attitudes to their own than when they were listening to dissimilar attitudes. According to Byrne, this resembles the way in which a tone can produce salivation if it is generally followed by the sight of food. (Classical conditioning is described in Section 13, Determinants of Animal Behaviour.)

List the needs that are being met in the following types of relationship: best friend, parent with child, lover.

Research support

Veitch and Griffitt (1976) tested the reinforcement affect model by arranging for single participants to wait in an experimenter's office while the experimenter went on an errand. The radio was left on with music playing and, in the time alone, the participant (a student) heard two news broadcasts. They were either good or bad news. When the experimenter returned the participant was asked to fill in a "Feelings Scale" (to assess their emotional state) and to read a questionnaire supposedly filled in by another student. It was filled in to be either in close agreement or disagreement with attitudes previously expressed by the participant in an earlier questionnaire that had been done in class. The participant filled in an "Interpersonal Judgement Scale" to rate the supposed other student. The participants exposed to the "good" news reported significantly more positive feelings than those who listened to the "bad" news. In addition "good news" participants felt significantly more attracted to the hypothetical other student. The effect was stronger where attitudes were more similar, though it occurred where attitudes were dissimilar. This supports the idea that positive feelings increase the possibilities of interpersonal attraction.

What psychological harm may have been caused in this experiment?

Other research has supported this study, for example, Rabbie and Horowitz (1960) found that strangers expressed greater liking for each other when they were successful in a game-like task than when unsuccessful. However, Duck (1992) criticises these studies because they rely on the rather artificial "bogus stranger" method. There is no actual stranger but only one that is imagined and this may not elicit realistic responses.

Evaluation

We are more attracted to those who provide us with reinforcement than those who do not. For example, individuals who are high on rewardingness (i.e., friendly, co-operative, smiling, warm) are consistently liked more than individuals who are low on rewardingness (Argyle, 1988). However, reinforcement theory does not provide an adequate account of interpersonal attraction for various reasons. First, the theory seems much more relevant to the very earliest stages of attraction than to attraction within an ongoing friendship or relationship. Second, as Argyle pointed out, reinforcement has not been shown to be of much importance in determining the strength of the relationship between parents and their children.

Third, reinforcement theory assumes that people are totally selfish, and only concerned about the rewards they receive. In fact, people are often concerned about other people, and about the rewards that they provide for other people. Fourth, whether or not reinforcement increases interpersonal attraction depends to a large extent on the *context* in which the reinforcement is provided. For example, the need for sexual satisfaction can be fulfilled by a prostitute, but this does not mean that men who resort to prostitutes become attracted to them as people.

Fifth, reinforcement and need satisfaction theories seem of more relevance to the **individualistic** societies of the Western world than to the **collectivistic** societies of the non-Western world (this is discussed further later). More speculatively, these theories may tend to be more applicable to men than to women. In many cultures, there is more emphasis on females than on males learning to be attentive to the needs of others (Lott, 1994).

Based on reinforcement theory, how would you advise someone to behave to make a good impression on, or be liked by, someone they have never met before?

Economic theories: Exchange and equity

An "economic theory" is one that expresses relationships in terms of some distribution of resources or trading of one thing for another.

Social exchange theory

Social exchange theory (e.g., Thibaut & Kelley, 1959) is similar to reinforcement theory, but provides a more plausible account of interpersonal attraction. It is assumed that everyone tries to maximise the rewards (e.g., affection; attention) they obtain from a relationship, and to minimise the costs (e.g., devoting time and effort to the other person; coping with the other person's emotional problems). It is also assumed that if a relationship is to continue, people expect the other person to reward them as much as they reward the other person.

Thibaut and Kelley argued that long-term friendships and relationships go through four stages:

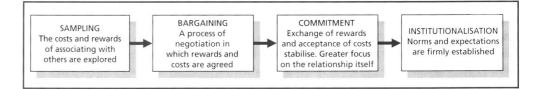

What rewards and costs are associated with the following relationships: best friend, parent with child, lover?

Additional assumptions are sometimes included in social exchange theory. For example, how satisfied individuals are with the rewards and costs of a relationship will depend on what they have come to expect from previous relationships. In other words, they have a **comparison level** (CL) (Thibaut & Kelley, 1959), representing the outcomes they believe they deserve on the basis of past experiences—so if in the past they have had very poor relationships they may expect very little from subsequent ones. In addition, their level of satisfaction will depend on the rewards (e.g., affection; sex) and costs (e.g., arguments; loss of control) that would be involved if they formed a relationship with someone else; this is known as the "comparison level for alternatives" (CLalt).

Equity theory

Some theorists (e.g., Hatfield, Utne, & Traupmann, 1979) have extended exchange theory to include more of an emphasis on fairness or equity. According to equity theory, people expect to receive rewards from a relationship which are proportional to the rewards they provide for the other person. However, it is assumed within the theory that imbalance can be tolerated if the two people involved in a relationship accept the situation. Walster et al. (1978) expressed the main assumptions of equity theory as follows:

1. Individuals try to maximise the rewards they receive and minimise the costs.
2. There is negotiation to produce fairness; for example, one partner may do the shopping every week to compensate for being away playing sport twice a week.
3. If the relationship is unfair or inequitable, it produces distress, especially in the disadvantaged person.
4. The disadvantaged person will try hard to make the relationship more equitable, particularly when it is very inequitable.

Sharing domestic chores may be a result of negotiation in an equitable relationship, in which each partner feels the other takes their share of responsibilities.

Research evidence

Hatfield et al. (1979) asked newlyweds to indicate the extent to which they felt that they were receiving more or less than they should in view of what they were contributing to the marriage. They were also asked to indicate their level of contentment, happiness, anger, and guilt. The under-benefited had the lowest level of overall satisfaction with their marriage, and tended to experience anger. The over-benefited came next (they tended to feel guilty), and those who perceived their marriage as equitable had the highest level of satisfaction. Men who were over-benefited were almost as satisfied as those in an equitable marriage, but over-benefited women were much less satisfied than women with equal benefit (Argyle, 1988).

The finding that those who perceive their marriages as equitable are happiest, and those who perceive themselves as under-benefited are least happy, was replicated by Buunk and VanYperen (1991). However, these findings applied only to those individuals who were high in exchange orientation (i.e., expecting rewards given by one person in a relationship to be followed immediately by rewards given by the other person). Those low in exchange orientation had fairly high marriage satisfaction regardless of whether they were over-benefited, under-benefited, or receiving equal benefit. (See Key Study overleaf for a discussion of communal and exchange couples.)

What could be the cause of gender differences, such as the one between over-benefited males and over-benefited females?

Evaluation

Equity theory seems more plausible than exchange theory. It takes more account of the rewards and costs of the other person as well as of the individual himself or herself. The most obvious criticism of both approaches is that they assume that people are very selfish and self-centred in their friendships and relationships. This assumption may possess some validity in an individualist society such as that of the United States, but is less likely to apply to collectivist societies. Evidence of cultural differences was reported by Gergen, Morse, and Gergen (1980). European students were found to prefer equality in their relationships, with an equal distribution of rewards. In contrast, American students tended to favour equity, based on a constant ratio of rewards to inputs.

One of the more obvious predictions from equity theory is that the future quality of equitable relationships should be greater than that of inequitable ones. However, there are various studies in which there was no association between equity and future quality (see Buunk, 1996).

Much of the research in this area has not proved very informative. Some of the reasons for this were identified by Argyle (1988, p.224):

What is the difference between equity and equality?

Communal and exchange relationships

Several theorists have doubted whether intimate relationships can be understood properly in terms of traditional theories. For example, Clark and Mills (1979) argued that there are two major kinds of relationships:

- *Communal relationships*: the main focus is on giving the other person what he or she needs; these relationships typically involve close friends or family members.
- *Exchange relationships*: the main focus is on the notion that what one puts into the relationship should balance what one receives; these relationships usually involve acquaintances or strangers.

According to Clark and Mills, most romantic relationships are not based on the principle of exchange. Those involved in such relationships are much more concerned about being able to meet the needs of the other person than about exchange or reciprocity.

Clark (1984) presented evidence consistent with this proposed distinction between communal and exchange relationships. Male students located sequences of numbers in a matrix with someone called Paula. Each student was told that he and Paula would receive a joint payment based on their performance, and they must decide how much each of them received. Some participants were told that Paula was single and was taking part in the experiment to make friends. The others were told that Paula was married, and that her husband was going to pick her up. Clark predicted that the former participants would tend to think in terms of a possible communal relationship with Paula, whereas the latter participants would expect an exchange relationship.

The participants found that Paula had already circled some sequences of numbers with a felt-tip pen. What was of interest was whether the participants used a pen of a different colour. It was argued that students looking for an exchange relationship would do so, because it would allow them to be paid on the basis of their contribution. In contrast, those seeking a communal relationship should use a pen of the same colour, because they were mainly concerned about their combined efforts. The findings were as predicted. About 90% of those students who thought Paula was married used a felt-tip pen of a different colour, compared with only 10% of those who thought she was single. Clark also found that pairs of friends were less likely than pairs of strangers to use different-coloured pens.

Fiske (1993) extended the line of theorising proposed by Clark and Mills (1979). According to him, there are four types of relationship:

- Exchange: based on reciprocity.
- Communal: based on catering for the other person's needs.
- Equality matching: based on ensuring that everyone receives the same; for example, giving all of the children in a family an ice cream of the same size.
- Authority: based on the notion that one person's orders are obeyed by others.

Discussion points

1. Does the study by Clark and Mills really show that there is a distinction between exchange and communal relationships?
2. Have social psychologists focused too much on exchange relationships and not enough on communal relationships?

[Exchange] theory has led mainly to very artificial experiments ... Research on real-life relationships has been hampered by the difficulty of scaling rewards.

Notions of exchange and equity are more important between casual acquaintances than they are between people who are close friends or emotionally involved with each other. Happily married couples do not focus on issues of exchange or equity. Murstein, MacDonald, and Cerreto (1977) found that marital adjustment was significantly poorer in those married couples who were concerned about exchange and equity than in those couples who were not. Furthermore there are differences in the behaviour of communal and exchange relationships, as discussed in the Key Study above.

Assessing attitudes through the use of coloured felt-tip pens is quite ingenious, but how valid do you think it is?

Filter theory

As was mentioned previously, Kerckhoff and Davis (1962) argued that relationships go through a series of filters, each of which is essential for the relationship to begin or to continue. The first filter revolves around the fact that we only meet a very small fraction of the people living in our area (a proximity filter). Most of those we do meet will tend to be of similar social class and education to ourselves, and they may also be of the same racial or ethnic group (a similarity filter).

The next filter is based on psychological factors. Kerckhoff and Davis found that the chances of a short-term (under 18-month) relationship becoming more permanent depended most on shared values and beliefs. The fourth filter is complementarity of emotional needs. The ability to satisfy the other person's emotional needs was the best predictor of survival of long-term relationships that were studied over a seven-month period.

Do you think that factors such as social class, ethnicity, education level, and age are important in the formation of relationships?

Evaluation

There is considerable evidence that the factors that are important in the early stages of a relationship differ from those that matter later on (see Brehm, 1992), and this is emphasised within filter theory. Another advantage is that it helps us to make theoretical sense of the wide range of factors that influence the formation and maintenance of interpersonal relationships (see later). The main limitation of filter theory is that its focus is on romantic relationships, and thus it tells us little about the factors influencing the development of friendships.

Maintenance and Dissolution of Relationships

The next step, after the formation of relationships, is to consider how they are maintained and ultimately why some of them fail. Various factors contribute to the maintenance of friendships and relationships. These factors include self-disclosure, commitment, various maintenance strategies, and the following of relationship rules. In contrast, a decline in the level of self-disclosure is typically associated with a reduction in the strength of a relationship. Dissolution tends to be explained in terms of the typical sequence of events that may be followed when a relationship breaks down, as well as the factors that may contribute to such breakdown.

There are a wide variety of different relationships: between friends, between acquaintances, and between relatives especially parents and children. Perhaps the most obvious and important relationship is romantic involvement as in marriage. Much of the psychological research focuses on this kind of relationship, and it will be the focus of the discussion here.

Maintenance of Relationships

Self-disclosure

Sternberg (1986) identified intimacy as a key component of both liking and loving. **Self-disclosure**, which involves revealing personal and sensitive information about oneself to another person, is of fundamental importance in developing and maintaining intimacy. According to Altman and Taylor's (1973) **social penetration theory**, the development of a relationship involves increased self-disclosure on both sides. People who have just met tend to follow the **norm of self-disclosure reciprocity**, according to which they match the level of self-disclosure of the other person. According to Altman and Taylor, the move towards revealing more about oneself should not be done too rapidly, because the other person may feel threatened.

Why is self-disclosure risky in a new relationship?

Think of a time when you were getting to know someone better. What did you spend your time doing? Could it be described as mutual self-disclosure?

Depenetration

As a relationship develops, there is less adherence to the norm of self-disclosure reciprocity. In an intimate relationship, the other person is most likely to respond to hearing sensitive personal information by offering support and understanding rather than by engaging in self-disclosure (Archer, 1979). Problems in maintaining a relationship tend to be associated with what Altman and Taylor (1973) called depenetration. **Depenetration** involves abandoning the habit of intimate self-disclosure to the other person across a wide range of topics. It takes two main forms. One form is simply refusing to reveal intimate information to the other person. The other form is talking intimately about only a few topics; these topics are chosen in order to hurt the other person, and usually involve strong negative feelings (Tolstedt & Stokes, 1984).

Gender differences

It is often argued that women tend to have higher levels of self-disclosure in their various relationships than do men. The relevant evidence from 205 studies was reviewed by Dindia and Allen (1992). On average, women self-disclose more than men with their romantic partners of the opposite sex and with their same-sex friends. However, there was no difference between men and women in their self-disclosure levels to male friends. Most of the sex differences in self-disclosure were not large, but the differences did not seem to have become smaller over the past 30 years or so.

On average, women disclose more personal and sensitive information about themselves to same-sex friends than men do (Dindia & Allen, 1992).

Commitment

Commitment, in the sense of a determination to continue the relationship, increases over time. What are the factors leading to the growth of commitment? Rusbult (1980) put forward an investment model, in which she identified three key factors:

1.   *Satisfaction*: the rewards provided by the relationship.
2.   *Perceived quality of alternatives*: individuals will be more committed to a relationship if there are no other attractive options.
3.   *Investment size*: the more time, effort, money, and so on invested in the relationship, the greater will be the commitment.

Lund (1985) found that the level of commitment depended more on investment size than on satisfaction or rewards. Michaels, Acock, and Edwards (1986) found that commitment to a relationship was stronger when the outcomes received exceeded those anticipated in alternative relationships than when they were smaller. They also found that the extent to which the relationship was equitable did not predict commitment.

Limitations

There are two limitations with Rusbult's approach. First, the three factors she identifies are not truly independent of each other. For example, individuals who are very satisfied with a relationship are more likely to have a large investment in it. Second, most of the research has focused on short-term rather than long-term relationships (Buunk, 1996).

Going for walks together is an example of the kind of maintenance strategy used by couples to maintain their relationship.

Maintenance and repair strategies

Dindia and Baxter (1987) carried out a thorough study of the strategies used by married couples to maintain their marriages. They found evidence for 49 such strategies, which could be divided into maintenance strategies and repair strategies. Maintenance strategies mostly involved joint activities such as going for walks together or talking about the events of the day, and occurred because they were pleasurable. In contrast, repair strategies involved discussing issues or making difficult decisions, and occurred because there were problems within the relationship.

Dindia and Baxter found differences between those who had been married for only a short period of time, and those who had been married much longer. Newlyweds tended to make more use of maintenance strategies than the long-term married, but the reasons for this are not clear. The positive view is that maintenance strategies are less necessary when two people know each other very well. The negative view is that those who have been married for a long time simply take each other for granted and put less effort into everyday joint activities.

Rusbult, Zembrodt, and Iwaniszek (1986) identified four strategies that people use to deal with conflicts in relationships. Each strategy is active or passive, and constructive or destructive.

- *Voice* is the active, constructive strategy, in which people discuss their problems and seek answers to the relationship difficulties.
- *Loyalty* is the passive, constructive strategy, in which people wait and hope that the situation will improve.
- *Neglect* is a passive and destructive strategy, in which individuals ignore their partners or spend less time with them.
- Finally, there is *exit*. This is an active and destructive strategy involving individuals deciding to abandon the relationship.

A stage theory of maintenance

Levinger (1980) proposed that, over time, a relationship becomes progressively more intimate. The five stages in his ABCDE model are:

A: Acquaintance. A relationship starts with mutual attraction. We examined possible factors for this in the last Unit, such as attractiveness and proximity. In some relationships this stage may last indefinitely.

B: Build-up. As a couple engage in self-disclosure they become increasingly interdependent. At this stage participants may be evaluating rewards and costs.

C: Continuation. The relationship, if continuing, becomes consolidated. Partners may make some kind of long-term commitment such as becoming engaged or married, or buying a house together. Their lives become enmeshed by meeting each other's friends and families, and sharing routines and pastimes.

D: Deterioration. Not all relationships reach this stage but for those that do the causes may be a imbalance of costs and rewards, or a high number of risk factors. These are discussed later in this Unit.

E: Ending. Deterioration may lead to the end.

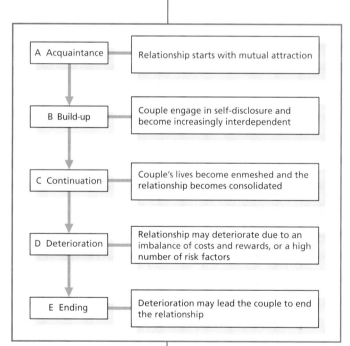

The greatest strength of Levinger's model is that it emphasises the notion that relationships and close friendships change in predictable ways over time. However, Levinger regards the sequence of stages of a relationship as occurring in a fixed order, and so focuses on the similarities among relationships. In fact, there are large differences among couples in the progress of their relationships (Brehm, 1992). As a result, it may be preferable to think in terms of flexible phases rather than fixed stages (Brehm, 1992). Levinger's model provides some answers to *what* and *when* questions, telling us what happens during the course of a relationship and when different stages occur. However, it has little to say about *why* questions: Why do relationships go through this set of fixed stages? Why do relationships initially improve over time and then deteriorate?

This model can provide a useful framework for presenting the facts described in this Unit.

Do all relationships go through all of Levinger's five stages?

What determines the choice of strategy? Rusbult et al. studied lesbian, gay, and heterosexual couples. Individuals with high psychological femininity (warmth, intimacy; concern with interpersonal relations) were much more likely to react constructively to relationship problems than were those with high masculinity (aggressiveness, independence, assertiveness).

VOICE	Active	Constructive	Discuss problems and seek answers	High psychological femininity
LOYALTY	Passive	Constructive	Wait and hope things improve	
NEGLECT	Passive	Destructive	Ignore partner and spend less time with them	High psychological masculinity
EXIT	Active	Destructive	Individual decides to abandon relationship	

Relationship rules

In order to maintain a relationship successfully (whether a romantic relationship, friendship, or whatever), it is necessary for both of the people involved to keep to certain informal relationship rules ("behaviour which it is believed ought or ought not to be performed in each relationship", Argyle, 1988, p.233). Argyle and Henderson (1984) argued that there are four criteria by means of which friendship rules can be identified:

- There should be general agreement that the behaviour indicated in the rule is relevant to friendship.
- The rule should not be applied in the same way to current and former friends.
- Failure to stick to the rule should tend to lead to the abandonment of the friendship.
- The rule should identify some of the ways in which people's behaviour towards close friends and acquaintances differs.

Argyle and Henderson applied these four criteria to a study of friendship rules in England, Italy, Hong Kong, and Japan. They found that there were six rules that seemed to be of major importance to friendships in all four countries. These were:

1. Trust and confide in the other person.
2. Show emotional support.
3. Share news of success.
4. Strive to make the friend happy when with him or her.
5. Volunteer help in time of need.
6. Stand up for a friend in his or her absence.

Can you think of any other rules that operate in your relationships?

Argyle et al. (1986) found that there were some interesting cultural differences in the importance attached to certain rules. For example, participants in Hong Kong and Japan were more likely than those in Britain or in Italy to support rules such as obeying superiors, preserving group harmony, and avoiding loss of face.

Cognitive factors

Duck and Pond (1989) noted that the key factor about routines is the way that partners talk to one another in and about their interactions; relationships are not a string of routines but the cognitions (thoughts) that surround them. Murray and Holmes (1993) argued that an important way in which individuals maintain relationships is by means of "storytelling", in which the partner's faults are regarded as favourably as possible. Their research is described in the Key Study on the facing page. Fincham and Bradbury (1993) argued that the kinds of attributions that married people make about their spouse have an effect on how successfully the marriage is maintained. Husbands and wives who attributed their partner's negative behaviour to *internal* characteristics (e.g., personality) were more dissatisfied with the marriage one year later than were those who attributed it to external factors (e.g., hard work; worries about the family).

An argument? No...he just suddenly felt he needed to get some air.

Cognitive factors in maintenance

Murray and Holmes (1993) argued that an important way in which individuals maintain relationships is by means of storytelling, in which the partner's faults are regarded as favourably as possible. This storytelling occurs even in unpromising circumstances. Murray and Holmes studied individuals who claimed that their relationships involved little conflict, and that conflict is harmful to intimacy. Some of them were then informed that there is strong evidence that conflict is beneficial to the development of intimacy. Finally, the participants were asked to write narratives describing the development of intimacy in their relationship.

What happened? The participants who had been told that conflict is advantageous were much more likely to write narratives in which they argued that conflicts and disagreements were valuable. For example, one participant wrote, "I feel he is facilitating our growth by increasingly being able to tell me when he disagrees with my opinions in all areas", and another wrote, "We've had only three disagreements ... we were able to get to the root of the problem, talk it out, and we managed to emerge from it closer than before." Murray and Holmes (1993, p.719) concluded as follows:

> We suspect that individuals' continued confidence in their partners ... depends on their continued struggle to weave stories that depict potential faults in their partners in the best possible light.

KEY STUDY EVALUATION — Murray and Holmes

The research by Murray and Holmes is important, because most previous researchers had ignored the role of storytelling in maintaining relationships. However, we need to know more of the factors determining when those involved in relationships will make use of storytelling. There is also the issue of whether the participants really believed what they were writing, rather than simply expressing views that they thought the experimenter wanted them to express.

Discussion points

1. What do you think of the storytelling approach to understanding the maintenance of relationships?
2. Are people aware that they are constructing stories about their partner?

What do you think is likely to happen if you tell yourself a story about your partner that emphasises their faults?

Dissolution of Relationships

There are many reasons why relationships come to an end. The reasons that are important in any one case depend on the particular circumstances in which the people concerned find themselves, and on their particular characteristics. Some relationship break-ups are accompanied by bitter recrimination and even violence, whereas others are handled in a more "civilised" way. In spite of these differences, it has been argued that similar processes tend to be involved in the dissolution of all relationships.

Stage models

One approach is to consider the stages of relationship as a means of explaining how relationships break down. An alternative would be to list "risk factors", i.e., those factors that are likely to trigger dissolution.

Lee's stage model

According to Lee (1984), the break-up of relationships should be regarded as a process taking place over a period of time rather than as a single event. More specifically, he argued that there are five stages involved in the process:

- *Dissatisfaction*: one or both of the partners realise that there are real problems within the relationship.
- *Exposure*: the problems identified in the dissatisfaction stage are brought out into the open.
- *Negotiation*: there is much discussion about the issues raised during the exposure stage.
- *Resolution attempts*: both partners try to find ways of solving the problems discussed in the negotiation stage.

How does this model compare with
Levinger's ABCDE model
(on page 71).

• *Termination*: if the resolution attempts are unsuccessful, then the relationship comes
to an end.

Lee identified these five stages on the basis of a study of over 100 premarital romantic
break-ups. The exposure and negotiation stages tended to be the most intense and
exhausting stages in the break-up. One of the key findings was that it tended to
be those relationships that had been the strongest in which it took the longest time
to work through the five stages of dissolution. This makes sense: the more valuable
a relationship has been, the harder (and longer) it is worth fighting for its
continuation.

Duck's phase model

Duck (1982) put forward a somewhat similar stage model of the break-up of relationships.
He identified four phases or stages of break-up, where each phase is triggered by a
threshold:

What is the difference between a
"model" and a "theory"? If you
were asked a question about
"theories of relationships", do you
think you could include these
models?

• Threshold: "I can't stand this any more". *Intrapsychic phase*: this involves thinking
about the negative aspects of one's partner and of the relationship, but not discussing these thoughts with him or her. It corresponds roughly to Lee's dissatisfaction stage.
• Threshold: "I'd be justified in withdrawing". *Dyadic phase*: this phase involves confronting the partner with the negative thoughts from the intrapsychic stage, and
trying to sort out the various problems. It corresponds to Lee's stages of exposure,
negotiation, and resolution attempts.
• Threshold: "I mean it". *Social phase*: this phase involves deciding what to do now
that the relationship is effectively over; it includes thinking of face-saving accounts
of what has happened. It corresponds roughly to Lee's termination stage.
• Threshold: "It's now inevitable". *Grave-dressing phase*: this phase focuses on
communicating a socially acceptable account of the end of the relationship. It is an
important phase in terms of preparing the people
involved for future relationships.

Comparing the two models

There are some important differences between Lee's stage
model and Duck's phase model. Lee's version focuses
mainly on the various processes involved when there is still
some hope that the relationship can be saved, whereas
Duck's model focuses more on the processes involved after
it is clear that the relationship is at an end. It is probable
that a six- or seven-stage model incorporating all of the
processes identified in the two models would provide a
more adequate account of relationship break-ups than
either model on its own.

Both models have some useful practical implications.
They can be used to identify the stage of breakdown
and suggest appropriate ways to attempt to repair the
relationship. The models also suggest how, once a
relationship has broken down, couples may deal with
the end in order to be ready to start afresh in new
relationships. Duck (1994), for example, suggested
that couples in the intrapsychic phase should aim
to re-establish liking for their partner by focusing on
the positive aspects of their relationship rather than
the tendency in this phase to focus on the negative.

Neither model explains why relationships break down
but merely focuses on the sequence of likely events. We will
consider some explanations next.

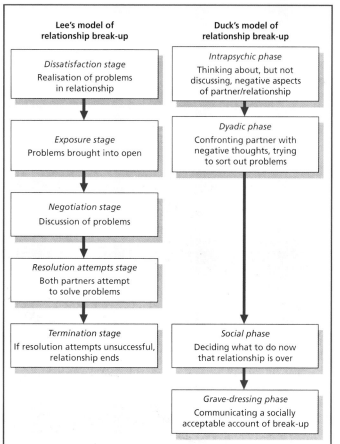

Risk factors

Duck (1992) also considered the findings from longitudinal studies. He identified several factors that seem to make relationships more fragile and liable to dissolution. It is possible to distinguish between *internal* factors (e.g., the personalities of the two people) and *external* factors (e.g., one partner moves to another part of the country; the appearance of a rival; job loss). Duck (1992) suggested that these could be classified as predisposing and precipitating factors.

Predisposing personal factors (internal)

As one gets to know a partner better, one also becomes more aware of their personal characteristics, some of which will be distasteful. For example, your partner may leave dirty clothes lying around or like to eat food with lashings of garlic. For some people such characteristics may trigger the dissolution of the relationship.

There are other personal factors that may be important. Partners' interests or attitudes may change and the things that once held you together now no longer do so. If hobbies change, you may find yourselves spending less time together. Pre-existing differences, such as having different religious or educational backgrounds, may come to be significant. During the initial phases of the relationship one might overlook such differences but they may become progressively more significant.

Marriages where partners come from very different backgrounds in terms of culture, race, or religion are less stable than those where partners come from similar backgrounds. Marriages between partners from lower socio-economic groups and/or lower education levels are more likely to end in divorce. This suggests that these factors predispose the relationship to break down.

Marriages in which the partners are very young (e.g., teenagers) are less likely to last than marriages in which the partners are older. There are likely to be several reasons why age is a factor. Younger people tend to be less mature, they have not yet developed their adult personality, and they are less likely to have either a steady income or full-time employment.

A further personal factor is the inability to conduct a relationship. This may be due to having poor role models (parents who were divorced or who argued all the time) or the fact that one partner has poor social skills.

Precipitating factors (external)

In contrast, Duck identified other factors that are external and that may *precipitate* breakdown. For example, deception, boredom, relocation, conflict, or a better alternative are all factors that may herald the beginning of the end.

Jealousy and infidelity. One especially important factor in the dissolution of a relationship is jealousy. It is triggered by a real or imagined rival, and is a surprisingly common emotion. Eysenck (1990) discussed a study in which 63% of male students and 51% of female students admitted that they were currently jealous.

What factors produce jealousy? Buss et al. (1992) asked students whether they would experience greater distress in response to sexual or to emotional infidelity. Among male students, 60% reported greater distress over a partner's sexual infidelity. In contrast, 83% of the female students said they would be more distressed by emotional infidelity.

The destructive power of jealousy was emphasised by Buss et al. According to them:

The more insecure you are, the more you will be jealous. Jealousy says Abraham Maslow, "practically always breeds further rejection and deeper insecurity." … It is never, then, a function of love but of our insecurities and dependencies. It is the fear of a loss of love and it destroys that very love.

Buss et al. may have overstated their case, but there is some truth in their assertions. Jealousy is typically related to strong feelings of dependence and insecurity about the relationship (Salovey, 1991). It also has the negative effect of reducing the jealous person's level of self-esteem (Mathes, Adams, & Davies, 1985).

Other factors

The factors identified by Duck tell only part of the story. There are successful and stable marriages in which the partners possess all of the vulnerability factors, and there are partners having none of these factors who nevertheless have short-lived marriages. Some of these factors may be more complex than they appear to be. For example, consider the fact that couples with lower educational levels are more likely to divorce. What is important is not really the educational level itself, but rather the reduced prospects of owning their own home and having reasonable full-time jobs, which follow from the low level of education.

Jealousy may be caused by a real rival, but can be just as painful when the jealous partner imagines that he or she has competition.

It is important to note that the data from most longitudinal studies are limited. For example, 75% of the samples used in the longitudinal studies reviewed by Karney and Bradbury (1995) consisted mainly of middle-class white couples. Karney and Bradbury (1995, p.17) identified other limitations:

Nearly half of the studies lack the power to detect small effects, even though the effects in question are likely to be small in many cases. Data have been drawn almost exclusively from self-report surveys and interviews, whereas alternative means of gathering data have yet to be exploited.

Sex differences

A further factor is gender difference. Women are more likely than men to end heterosexual relationships, and initiate about two-thirds of divorce proceedings in many Western

A longitudinal study of marital problems and subsequent divorce

Amato and Rogers (1997) published the results of a study conducted between 1980 and 1992. They investigated the extent to which reports of marital problems in 1980 predicted divorce in the following 12 years. In 1980, telephone interviewers used random-digit dialling to locate a national sample of 2033 married persons aged 55 years and under. Of those contacted, 78% completed the full interview. The analysis was based on individuals for whom information on marital status existed at two or more points in time (that is, 86% of the original 1980 sample). Wives were more likely to report their marital problems than husbands—this was not because husbands had fewer problems but because they tended not to report them.

The main factors that were found to predict divorce were infidelity, spending money foolishly, drinking or drug use or both, jealousy, moodiness, and irritating habits.

Discussion points

1. What theoretical framework might be useful in explaining these findings?
2. How could such evidence be put to practical use?

countries. In general, the partner who initiates the break-up is the one who is less distressed by the ending. However, this tendency is much stronger in men than in women (Franzoi, 1996). Why is this so? According to Franzoi, control and power are more associated with the traditional male role than with the traditional female role. As a result, men find it very hard to cope when their partner renders them powerless and out of control by ending the relationship.

Theories of Maintenance and Dissolution in Relationships

In the last Unit we considered various theories that account for the formation of relationships. These same theories can be related to maintenance and dissolution.

Social exchange theory

Levinger (1976) argued that the chances of a marriage surviving depend on three factors:

1. The attractions of the relationship, such as emotional security and sexual satisfaction.
2. The barriers to leaving the marriage, such as social and financial pressures.
3. The presence of attractive alternatives, such as a more desirable partner.

Divorce is most likely when the marriage has few attractions, there are only weak barriers to leaving the relationship, and there are very attractive alternatives. This is similar to Thibaut and Kelley's (1959) concept of a "comparison level for alternatives" (CLalt). When this is higher than the comparison level (CL) then we are motivated to leave a relationship.

Evaluation

One of the advantages of Levinger's social exchange theory is that it helps to explain why marital dissatisfaction does not strongly predict subsequent divorce (Karney & Bradbury, 1995). For example, married couples who are dissatisfied may not divorce because there are strong barriers to leaving the marriage and no attractive alternatives. The greatest disadvantage of Levinger's social exchange theory is that it does not explain the processes that cause initially successful marriages to become unsuccessful.

How do these theories of maintenance and dissolution differ from models of dissolution described on pages 73–74?

Equity theory

Like exchange theory, equity theory (described on page 67) predicts that when elements of a relationship become unbalanced, one partner will leave. You may recall that equity is slightly different from exchange because there is a sense of *fair* rewards rather than an exchange of rewards. Inequitable relationships lack a sense of fairness and this produces dissatisfaction in one partner. The greater the inequity the more dissatisfied the partner will feel, but also the more motivated the partner should be to try to put things right.

According to Karney and Bradbury (1995), some couples who have enduring vulnerabilities can become stuck in this vicious cycle.

Vulnerability–stress–adaptation model

Karney and Bradbury (1995) put forward a vulnerability–stress–adaptation model of marriage. According to this model, there are three major factors that determine marital quality and stability or duration:

1. Enduring vulnerabilities: these include high neuroticism (a personality dimension concerned with anxiety and depression) and an unhappy childhood.
2. Stressful events: these include short- and long-lasting life events such as illness, unemployment, and poverty.

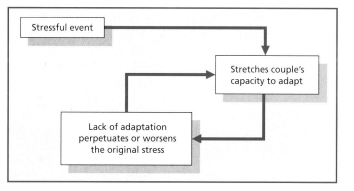

Depressed individuals are likely to create stressful situations in their lives, affecting their relationship with their partner.

3. Adaptive processes: these include constructive and destructive coping strategies to resolve difficulties.

A key assumption of the model is that the three factors all affect each other. The use of adaptive processes is influenced by enduring vulnerabilities and by stressful events. For example, married individuals who are high on neuroticism or whose parents divorced tend to have relatively poor adaptive processes, and the stress created by unemployment is associated with more negative and less constructive interactions with spouses (Aubry, Tefft, & Kingsbury, 1990). In addition, enduring vulnerabilities can play a role in creating stressful events. For example, individuals who are very depressed often create stressful conditions in their lives (Hammen, 1991). Adaptive processes can also create stressful conditions. For example, clinically depressed individuals whose spouses were very critical were more likely to suffer relapses than were individuals with less critical spouses (Hooley et al., 1986).

According to the vulnerability–stress–adaptation model (Karney & Bradbury, 1995, p.24), one of the main ways in which a marriage can disintegrate is through the following vicious cycle:

(a) stressful events challenge a couple's capacity to adapt, (b) which contributes to the perpetuation or worsening of those events, (c) which in turn further challenge and perhaps overwhelm their capacity to adapt.

This vicious cycle is most likely to occur in couples having enduring vulnerabilities.

Evaluation

As we saw earlier, numerous factors are associated with the maintenance or dissolution of marriages. One of the strengths of the vulnerability–stress–adaptation model is the way in which most of these factors can be related directly to the three broad variables of enduring vulnerabilities, stress, and adaptive processes. Another strength of the model is that it shows how these three variables can interact in different ways to reduce marital quality.

The greatest limitation of the vulnerability–stress–adaptation model is its emphasis on marital quality or satisfaction as the major determinant of marital stability. As Levinger (1976) argued, factors *external* to the marriage also affect marital stability. These factors include the barriers to leaving the relationship and the presence of attractive alternatives.

Psychological Explanations of Love

They say that love is what makes the world go round. It certainly is of critical importance in terms of emotional development. In your AS level studies you reviewed theories of attachment, in particular Bowlby's view that secure early attachments lead to healthy adult relationships. Hazan and Shaver's "Love Quiz" demonstrated this link.

What is love? It is an intense feeling of deep affection for another. Psychologists distinguish between liking and loving, and between different kinds of love, most importantly companionate and romantic (passionate) love.

Liking and loving

The best-known attempt to distinguish between liking and loving was made by Rubin (1970), who put forward the Rubin Love Scale and the Rubin Liking Scale. The items on the love scale measure three main factors: (1) desire to help the other person; (2) dependent needs of the other person; and (3) feelings of exclusiveness and absorption. In contrast, the items on the liking scale measure respect for the other person's abilities and similarity of the other person in terms of his or her attitudes and other characteristics.

Rubin's love and liking scales are highly correlated with each other. Sternberg and Grajek (1984) found that liking and loving scores for a lover correlated +0.72, and these

The love quiz

Could it be that early attachment type can be used to explain later styles of adult romantic love? Hazan and Shaver (1987) proposed that the reason adults experience different kinds of romantic relationships is because of their different experiences as infants. To test this hypothesis they devised a "love quiz", a questionnaire that could assess an individual's style of love as well as their attachment type. The quiz consisted of two components:

- A measure of attachment style. A simple adjective checklist of childhood relationships with parents, and parents' relationships with each other.

- The love experience questionnaire which assessed individuals' beliefs about romantic love, such as whether it lasted for ever, whether it was easy to find, how much trust there was in a romantic relationship, and so on.

The love quiz was printed in the *Rocky Mountain News*, a local newspaper, and readers were asked to send in their responses. The researchers analysed the first 620 replies received, from people aged from 14 to 82. Hazan and Shaver used the answers (1) to classify respondents as secure, ambivalent, or avoidant "types" based on their description of their childhood experiences, and (2) to classify them on their adult style of romantic love. Hazan and Shaver found a consistent relationship between attachment "type" and adult style of love:

- Secure types described their love experiences as happy, friendly, and trusting. They emphasised being able to accept their partner regardless of any faults and their relationships tended to be more enduring.
- Anxious ambivalent types experienced love as involving obsession, a desire for reciprocation, emotional highs and lows, and extreme sexual attraction and jealousy. They worried that their partners didn't really love them or might abandon them.
- Avoidant lovers typically feared intimacy, emotional highs and lows, and jealousy. They believed that they did not need love to be happy.

These attachment "types" are based on research by Ainsworth et al. (1978) in the Strange Situation, as discussed in your AS studies.

Discussion points

1. Can you think of another way of explaining the correlation between attachment type and later love relationships?
2. What ethical issues are raised by this research?

The kind of lover you are may be related to the kind of attachment you had as an infant.

scores correlated +0.66 for best friend, +0.73 for one's mother, and +0.81 for one's father. These high correlations mean that Rubin's scales do not discriminate very well between liking and loving.

Rubin did find that women tended to like the men more than the men liked the women. Men tended to love in the context of a sexual relationship whereas women experienced intimacy and attachment in a wider variety of relationships.

Romantic and companionate love

Berscheid and Walster (1978) distinguished between liking, companionate love, and romantic or passionate love. Companionate love is on a continuum with liking—liking that involves more depth of feeling and involvement than simply liking an acquaintance. Romantic love is entirely different. Companionate love develops through mutual rewards, familiarity, steady and positive emotions, and tends to deepen over time, whereas passionate love is based on intense emotions which often become diluted over time, novelty, and a mixture of emotions (joy and anxiety, excitement and deep despair).

Which kind of love is likely to be involved in marriage or long-term relationships?

Sternberg's triangular theory

Sternberg (1986) developed a **triangular theory of love**. According to this theory, love consists of three components: intimacy; passion; and decision/commitment. Sternberg defined them as follows:

The intimacy component refers to feelings of closeness, connectedness, and bondedness in loving relationships … The passion component refers to the drives that lead to romance, physical attraction, sexual consummation, and related phenomena in loving relationships. The decision/commitment component refers to, in the short term, the decision that one loves someone else, and in the long term, the commitment to maintain that love.

The relative importance of these three components differs between short-term and long-term relationships. The passion component is usually the most important in short-term relationships, with the decision/commitment component being the least important. In long-term relationships, on the other hand, the intimacy component is the most important, and the passion component is the least important.

Sternberg argued that there are several kinds of love, consisting of different combinations of the three components. Some of the main kinds of love are as follows:

- Liking or friendship: this involves intimacy but not passion or commitment.
- Romantic love: this involves intimacy and passion, but not commitment.
- Companionate love: this involves intimacy and commitment, but not passion.
- Empty love: this involves commitment, but not passion or intimacy.
- Fatuous love: this involves commitment and passion, but not intimacy.
- Infatuated love: this involves passion but not intimacy or commitment
- Consummate love: this is the strongest form of love, because it involves all three components (commitment, passion, and intimacy).

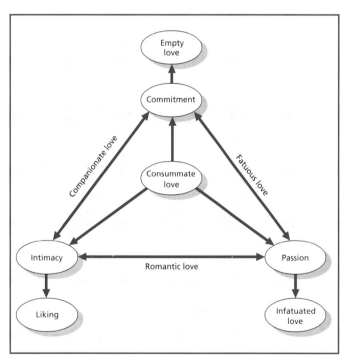

Evaluation

It is possible to use this theory to analyse a relationship and perceive similarities and differences between partners. This may help to sensitise partners to changes they might make in order to make the relationship more satisfactory.

One disadvantage is that some of the components are rather vague. For example, the decision/commitment variable doesn't specify on what basis an individual actually decides to love another person.

Three-factor theory of love

Hatfield and Walster (1981) have described a different approach to understanding love. This approach is related to Schachter and Singer's (1962) cognitive labelling theory of emotion, which suggested that all emotional experiences are the outcome of (1) being in a state of physiological arousal and (2) providing an appropriate label for that arousal (see pages 220–221). For example, if you were walking along a street and a bear jumped out, your likely emotional response would be one of fear. At a physiological (bodily) level you would experience a racing heart and

---

Who do you love?

Who do we tend to love and like the most? Sternberg and Grajek (1984) found that men generally love and like their lover more than their mother, father, sibling closest in age, or their best friend. Women also loved and liked their lover and best friend more than their mother, father, or sibling closest in age. However, women differed from men in that they loved their lover and their best friend of the same sex equally, but liked their best friend more than their lover.

Sternberg and Grajek also found that the amount of love that someone has for one member of their family predicts the amount of love they will have for the other members. For example, people who love their father very much also tend to have high levels of love for their mother and sibling closest in age. However, the amount of love that someone has for their lover or best friend is not predictable from the amount of love they feel for members of their own family.

sweaty palms. These are signs of physiological arousal. However, imagine the same scene except that it is Halloween and where you live there are no bears. If someone jumps out in front of you, you are still likely to experience some physiological arousal but this time you will "label" it as amusement. Dutton and Aron (1974) illustrated this in a study of "Love on a suspension bridge", see the Key Study below.

Love on a suspension bridge

Dutton and Aron (1974) provided evidence that supports the three-factor theory. They arranged for participants to be interviewed about scenic attractions while they were visiting a state park. The interviewer was an attractive woman who approached men either on a high suspension bridge or on a low bridge. The hypothesis was that those participants on the suspension bridge should be in a state of heightened physiological arousal, and in the presence of an attractive woman might mislabel their arousal as sexual attraction. Those men on the low bridge would be less likely to feel sexual attraction because they had less physiological arousal.

In order to assess sexual attraction there was one question on the questionnaire that involved describing a picture, based on the Thematic Apperception Test where it is presumed that an individual's feelings are unconsciously expressed through their interpretation of the picture. The participants' descriptions were later analysed for sexual content thus giving a measure of the amount of attraction that the men felt. Men on the suspension bridge showed greater attraction than those interviewed on a low bridge or when the interviewer was male. This can be explained in terms of greater arousal experienced on the suspension bridge leading to a need to find an appropriate emotional label (attractive female interviewer). If the interviewer is male this "explanation" won't do.

Discussion points

1. Consider the ethics of this research design.

2. To what extent can this research finding explain "passionate love"?

If we apply this concept of cognitive labelling to love, then we see that love is basically a state of physiological arousal. It is labelled as love when an appropriate love-object is present and cultural cues teach you that this emotion is called "love".

Evaluation

This is a plausible account of love and can explain cultural differences. However it may only be relevant to certain love experiences. People often report that they fell in love gradually which would suggest that the label came first. On the other hand this theory could explain "love at first sight". Some criticisms of Schachter and Singer's theory are relevant here. For example, there is the question of whether the spontaneity of many emotional experiences can be explained by cognitive labelling (see also page 221).

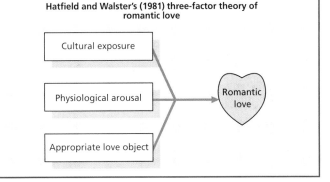

Hatfield and Walster's (1981) three-factor theory of romantic love

Cultural and Sub-cultural Differences in Relationships

Most of the research on interpersonal relationships has been carried out in Western cultures, especially those of the United States and the United Kingdom. The research has also been limited by its focus on heterosexual relationships at the expense of homosexual ones, and because voluntary relationships have been studied rather than obligatory ones. According to postmodern theorists, these limitations are very important. They argue that behaviour and communication need to be understood within the context in which they occur, and this context clearly differs considerably from one culture to another, and across different types of relationship. The crucial point here was made by Moghaddam et al. (1993):

> *The cultural differences in interpersonal relationships remind us that scientists, like everyone else, are socialised within a given culture ... The cultural values and environmental conditions in North America have led Northern American social psychologists to be primarily concerned with first-time acquaintances, friendships, and intimate relationships.*

What sort of methodological and ethical problems are associated with research into sexual behaviour?

We can readily accept that there are large differences in interpersonal relationships between cultures. However, there have also been substantial changes in such relationships within many cultures over the centuries. An American doctor, Celia Mosher, asked her middle-class female patients questions about their sexual lives during the latter part of the nineteenth century. Those who were born in the middle of the century described sex as necessary for reproduction, but did not regard it as pleasurable. Those who were born later in the century, described sex in much more positive terms, and saw sex as closely linked to passionate love (Westen, 1996).

It is important not to regard some types of relationships as better or worse than others. The relationships that individuals form depend on their personal needs and attitudes, the cultural context in which they live, and so on. As far as we can judge, all the various types of relationships are often very satisfying to the individuals concerned, and that is what matters.

The postmodern approach

Those who favour the postmodern approach (e.g., Wood & Duck, 1995) doubt the value of most research on interpersonal relationships. According to the postmodern approach, relationships need to be considered in terms of the context or environment in which they occur. There are various ways in which the available evidence can be interpreted, and it is hard or impossible to establish that one interpretation is preferable to any other.

Social purpose

Lalljee (1981) put forward related ideas. According to him, we need to consider the underlying social purposes of the explanations that people provide for their behaviour. For example, when two people divorce, they typically explain the disintegration of their marriage in different terms. Each of them tends to suggest that it was the unreasonable behaviour of the other person that led to divorce. In view of people's need to justify their own behaviour to other people, it becomes very difficult to establish the truth. The postmodernists go further, and claim that there is no single "truth" that can be discovered. In the study discussed earlier, Murray and Holmes (1993) showed that storytelling about one's relationship can easily be altered to accommodate awkward facts. This suggests that the truth is a flexible notion.

Discourse analysis

Many postmodernists argue that progress can be made in understanding interpersonal relationships by making use of discourse analysis. **Discourse analysis** involves qualitative analysis of people's written or spoken communications; these are often taped under fairly natural conditions. An interesting example of discourse analysis is contained in the work of Gavey (1992). She studied the sexual behaviour of six women who had been forced to have sex. Here is part of what one of the women had to say:

> *He kept saying, just, just let me do this or just let me do that and that will be all. And this could go on for an hour ... So after maybe an hour of me saying "no", and him saying "oh, come on, come on", I'd finally think, "Oh my God ... for a few hours' rest, peace and quiet, I may as well".*

This example shows that discourse analysis can provide striking evidence about the nature of relationships. However, Gavey (1992) and others who have used discourse analysis have often obtained evidence from only a small number of participants. This raises the issue of whether the findings obtained can be generalised to larger populations. There are also issues concerning the validity of the procedure. For example, we might expect someone to describe their sexual experiences rather differently to their partner, to a close friend, to an acquaintance, and to a stranger.

Western and Non-Western Cultures

Individualist and collectivist cultures

Goodwin (1995) argued that a key difference between most Western societies and most Eastern societies is that the former tend to be **individualist**, whereas the latter tend to be **collectivist**. In other words, it is expected in Western societies (especially the United States) that individuals will make their own decisions and take responsibility for their own lives. In Eastern societies, in contrast, it is expected that individuals will regard themselves mainly as part of family and social groups, and that their decisions will be influenced strongly by their obligations to other people. This difference in attitude was summed up by Hsu (1981): "An American asks 'How does my heart feel?' A Chinese asks 'What will other people say?'." As a result, those in individualist Western societies tend to stress the personality of a potential spouse, whereas those in collectivist Eastern societies favour arranged marriages based on social status.

Romantic love

Evidence on love and marriage from India, Pakistan, Thailand, Mexico, Brazil, Hong Kong, the Philippines, Australia, Japan, England, and the United States was reported by Levine et al. (1995). Their key finding was that there was correlation of +0.56 between a society's individualism and the perceived necessity of love for the establishment of a marriage. In other words, there was a fairly strong tendency for members of individualist societies to regard love as more important for marriage than did members of collectivist societies.

Friendships

There is one other important difference between individualist and collectivist societies, which applies to friendships. As Goodwin (1995) pointed out, people in collectivist societies tend to have fewer but closer friendships than do people in individualist societies. For example, Salamon (1977) studied friendship in Japan and in West Germany. Japanese friendships were much more likely to be ones in which there were no barriers between the friends, so that very personal information could be discussed freely. This is known as the *"shin yin"* relationship.

Voluntary and involuntary relationships

In most non-Western cultures, it remains the case that marriages tend to be arranged rather than based on romantic love. Some of the cultural differences in attitudes towards romantic love were studied by Shaver, Wu, and Schwartz (1991). Most Chinese people associate romantic love with sorrow, pain, and unfulfilled affection. In the eyes of Chinese people, the Western view that marriage should be based on romantic love is regarded as unrealistically optimistic.

Evidence from 42 hunter-gatherer societies around the world was reported by Harris (1995; cited in Westen, 1996). There was evidence of romantic love in 26 of these societies. However, only six gave individuals complete freedom of choice of marriage partner, with all the others having arranged marriages or at least giving parents the right of veto.

Are arranged marriages happier or less happy than love marriages? Most of the available evidence indicates that the average level of marital satisfaction is about the same. Yelsma and Athappily (1988) compared Indian arranged marriages with Indian and North American love marriages. In most respects, there were no differences between the two kinds of marriages.

The distinction between individualist and collectivist societies should not be taken too far. Even in societies in which arranged marriages are not the norm, there is often

Evaluation of cross-cultural research

There are several reasons for conducting cross-cultural research—that is, research that looks at the customs and practices of different countries and makes comparisons with our own cultural norms. First of all, such research can tell us about what might be universal in human behaviour. If the same behaviours are observed in many different cultures, all of which have different ways of socialising children, then the behaviour may be due to innate (universal) factors rather than learning. The second reason for conducting cross-cultural research is that it offers us insights into our own behaviour. Insights that we may not otherwise be aware of. Perhaps that is the appeal of watching programmes on the television that show foreign lands and different people.

There are some major weaknesses to cross-cultural research. First of all, any sample of a group of people may well be biased and therefore we may be mistaken in thinking that the observations made of one group of people are representative of that culture. Second, where the observations are made by an outsider, that person's own culture will bias how they interpret the data they observe. Finally, the psychological tools that are used to measure people, such as IQ tests and questionnaires about relationships, are designed in one particular culture and based on assumptions of that culture. They may not have any meaning in another culture.

Therefore cross-cultural research has the potential to be highly informative about human behaviour, but also has many important weaknesses.

Which of Hsu's questions (see page 82) would you consider first when meeting a potential partner? Are they equally important or not?

In many non-Western cultures, arranged marriages are the norm. Evidence suggests that the average level of marital satisfaction is the same in both arranged marriages and those that are not arranged.

some restricted element of choice of marriage partner. In individualist societies, parents often strive to influence the marriage choice of their children.

Permanent and impermanent relationships

The duration of relationships varies considerably between cultures. In some countries divorce is much less tolerated. For example, in China divorce is regarded as shameful and the divorce rate is less than 4% of married couples (Goodwin, 1999) whereas in the United States about 40–50% are divorced (US Bureau of Census, 1992).

Simmel (1971) claims that divorce is higher in individualistic societies because the philosophy is that one should constantly seek the ideal partner. People in individualistic societies are also more reliant on their one partner, rather than on a network of relationships within a community. This individualist/collectivist difference was illustrated in a study of Jewish families in New York (Brodbar-Nemzer, 1986). Over 4000 households were interviewed. Some were more traditionally Jewish—they attended synagogue regularly, had close friends who were Jewish, belonged to Jewish organisations, and contributed to Jewish charities. These families were examples of collectivist sub-cultures, as distinct from those Jewish families who classed themselves as Jewish but were more representative of individualist society. The former group had greater marital stability.

Other Cultural Variations

Physical attributes

It is perhaps natural for us to assume that what is true in our culture about interpersonal relationships is likely to be true in other cultures as well. In fact, this is by no means the case. Consider, for example, the factors influencing whether someone is seen as physically attractive or unattractive. What is regarded as physically attractive is determined to some extent by the current standards of the dominant social group. In the case of the North American culture, light skin is regarded as more attractive than dark skin by a majority of the population. Even African American college students express a preference for lighter skin tones (Bond & Cash, 1992). The study by Anderson et al. (1992) demonstrates the differences in cultural attitudes to female body shape (see Key Study on the facing page).

Marriages with a significant age difference between partners often have the added disadvantage of being more in the public eye.

Relative age: The sociobiological approach

In spite of various cultural differences in standards of physical attractiveness, there are also some important similarities. Buss (1989b) studied 37 cultures around the world, and found that men in all of these cultures preferred women who were younger than themselves, and women preferred men who were older than themselves in all cultures except Spain. Buss also found that the personal qualities of kindness and intelligence were regarded as important in virtually all of the cultures he studied.

There are various possible reasons why men prefer younger women, and women prefer older men. One approach has been put forward by **sociobiologists**, who try to explain human social behaviour in terms of genetic and biological factors. According to sociobiologists (e.g., Buss, 1989), what men and women find attractive in the opposite sex are those features that maximise the probability of producing offspring and so allow their genes to carry over into the next generation. Younger women are preferred to older ones because older women are less likely to be able to have children. In similar fashion, women prefer older men because they are more likely to be able to provide adequately for the needs of their offspring.

Evaluation

The sociobiological approach is inadequate. First, sociobiologists do not provide an explanation of why men and women in nearly all cultures regard kindness and intelligence as being more important than age. Second, the factors determining the choice of marriage partner differ considerably from one culture to another. The

Cross-cultural differences in preference for female body shape

Standards of physical attractiveness vary from one culture to another. Anderson et al. (1992) reported an interesting study on female body size preferences in 54 cultures. They divided these cultures into those with a very reliable food supply, those with a moderately reliable food supply, those with a moderately unreliable food supply, and those with a very unreliable food supply. Preferences for different female body sizes were divided into heavy body, moderate body, and slender body. The findings were as follows:

Preference	Food Supply			
	Very unreliable	Moderately unreliable	Moderately reliable	Very reliable
Heavy body	71%	50%	39%	40%
Moderate body	29%	33%	39%	20%
Slender body	0%	17%	22%	40%

In view of the obsessive focus on slimness in women in Western culture, it comes as a surprise to discover that heavy women are preferred to slender women in the great majority of the cultures studied by Anderson et al., especially those in which the food supply is moderately or very unreliable. How can we explain these cultural differences? Presumably it occurs because heavy women in cultures with unreliable food supplies are better equipped than slender women to survive food shortages, and to provide nourishment for their children. This factor is not relevant in cultures having a very reliable food supply, and in these cultures heavy and slender women were regarded as equally attractive.

KEY STUDY EVALUATION — Anderson et al.

The research by Anderson et al. is important because it shows that there are considerable cultural differences in preferred female body size. However, we need to remember that this study is correlational in nature, and that we cannot establish causes from correlations. Thus, we cannot be sure that cultural differences in preferred female body size actually depend on the reliability of the food supply rather than on other ways in which cultures differ from each other.

Discussion points

1. Why are there such great cultural differences in preferred body shape for women?

2. Are eating disorders likely to be more common in poor countries as they become more affluent?

sociobiologists consistently underestimate the importance of cultural factors in their explanations of social behaviour.

Howard, Blumstein, and Schwartz (1987) tried to explain the preference of men for younger women and of women for older men in social and cultural terms. According to them, women have historically had much lower social status than men. Women who wish to enhance their social status have usually had to do this by marrying an older man of high status. As women were unable to offer high social status because of the structure of society, they needed to offer youth and physical attractiveness instead. Of course, there have been important changes in society in recent years. Far more women than ever before have full-time jobs, and are financially independent from men. It follows from the socio-cultural theory of Howard et al. (1987) that the preference of women for older, high-status men may change as a result. Time will tell.

Monogamy and polygamy

A further apparent cultural difference exists in terms of the kinds of marriages that are acceptable. In some societies it is the norm for one man to have two or more wives. This is a form of polygamy called **polygyny**. There is also serial polygyny, where a male bonds with one female for a while and then moves on to another. Humans are usually regarded as a monogamous by nature (pairs bond once during their lifetime), however studies across different cultures show that in fact humans tend towards polygyny (see pie chart on page 572).

The arguments in favour of polygyny are also sociobiological. It is claimed that males benefit from impregnating many women because this maximises the number of their offspring, especially in a situation where there is plenty of shared care on offer, as in a harem. The women benefit because they gain a man with resources—a man who

attract a harem must have resources. Such a man will either have power or good looks, and in either case the woman's offspring may inherit such characteristics. If the offspring are sons, they may have greater reproductive success, which ensures the continuance of the mother's genes as well (this is called the **sexy sons hypothesis**), so both partners benefit from polygyny.

These sociobiological accounts are described in greater detail in Section 15, Evolutionary Explanations of Human Behaviour.

Sub-cultural Differences in Relationships

A sub-culture is a group of individuals within a culture who share morals, values, and social practices that set them apart from other sub-cultural groups within the larger culture. We might consider historical differences in this context as well as differences between men and women, and social classes.

Gender differences

We have already mentioned certain gender differences in the way men and women perceive and handle relationships, for example women self-disclose more than men with their romantic partners of the opposite sex and with their same-sex friends.

Another way to express gender differences was suggested by Wright (1982) who described male friendships as "side-by-side" whereas women are "face-to-face". Males tend to engage in activities together and thus have instrumental relationships, whereas female relationships involve sharing emotions and are called expressive relationships.

In terms of differences in romantic love, Risavy (1996) assessed gender differences using assessment scales designed to measure satisfaction with a romantic or marital relationship; the categories were based on Lee's (1973) six styles of love: Ludus (game-playing love), Mania (possessive love), Pragma (logical love), Agape (altruistic love), Storge (companionate love), and Eros (romantic love). Risavy found that men were more likely than females to endorse the love style of Agape and women were more likely than men to endorse the love style of Pragma. The results also indicated that older men were more pragmatic in their love styles than younger men, whereas women showed no age differences.

Evaluation

It is possible that such gender differences are innate and related to the different roles of males and females in mating and child-rearing. On the other hand, Duck and Wright (1993) suggest that gender differences have been exaggerated by research studies and do not correspond to real differences. In a re-analysis of some earlier data they did not find an instrumental/expressive dichotomy.

ial class differences

are trends that can be seen in the way that working-class and middle-class people
in relationships. For example, Haskey (1987) reported that divorce rates were four
igher in unskilled manual families than in professional families. Argyle (1994)
tendency for middle-class individuals to have friendships based on shared
and attitudes, and with work colleagues. Working-class friendships tend to be
munity-based and involve mutual helping and activities in social clubs and
n an early age there are social class differences, Newson and Newson (1968)
middle-class mothers interacted with their children more. Erikson et al. (1985)
"high risk" mothers, those who were from a low social class, poorly educated,
chaotic conditions, tended to have insecurely attached children.

it would be foolish to think that these differences extend to all aspects of
For instance, Risavy (1996) in the study just mentioned, found no effect on
ocial class.

Evaluation

The study by Erikson et al. highlights one of the difficulties of making statements about social class and relationships. It is likely that social class is associated with a multitude of other factors, such as education and geographical mobility, each of which may affect the kinds of relationships. However, it may be that there are sub-cultural differences between broad groups of individuals within a society (working-class and middle-class people) and one of the features of the difference is in terms of the way they interact with others.

Historical differences

We noted at the start of this Unit that attitudes towards sex have changed over time. Changes have also taken place in attitudes towards romantic love. It has for some time been the case in most Western societies that choice of marriage partner is based largely on romantic love. This was certainly not the case in earlier times. In the past, issues about property and the relative social standing of the families concerned tended to be more important than the emotional feelings of the bride and bridegroom. The increased emphasis on romantic love as the key ingredient in a successful marriage helps to explain the dramatic increase in the divorce rate. The percentage of marriages in the 1990s that ended in divorce in the United Kingdom is about eight times greater than was the case in the 1940s. In addition, there were much greater legal and social barriers to divorce in the 1940s.

What theory of relationships included "barriers" as an important element in maintenance?

"Understudied" relationships

Understudied relationships provide us with further information about sub-cultural differences. The term "understudied" is used to refer to the fact that certain relationships have been relatively understudied, partly because of their newness and/or fairly recent acceptability.

Gay and lesbian relationships

Most of the research on romantic relationships has concentrated exclusively on heterosexual couples. However, there are millions of people in the world who are involved in homosexual relationships, and such relationships are increasingly being studied.

Why has psychological research mainly focused on heterosexual couples?

Misconceptions.   There are many misconceptions about homosexual relationships, and it is sometimes assumed that such relationships are very different from heterosexual ones. This is not, in fact, the case. As Bee (1994) pointed out:

What sort of practical problems might prevent homosexual couples from cohabiting?

> *Gay partnerships are more like heterosexual relationships than they are different. The urge to form a single, central, committed attachment in early adult life is present in all of us, gay or straight.*

It has often been assumed that homosexual relationships tend to be short-lived and unsatisfactory. In fact, it seems that about 50% of gay men and perhaps 65% of lesbians are in a steady relationship at any one time (Peplau, 1991). Kurdek and Schmitt (1986) measured love for their partner and liking for their partner in married, heterosexual cohabiting, gay, and lesbian couples. The mean level of love was high in all four types of couple, and did not differ significantly among them. The mean level of liking for their partner was also fairly high in all types of couple, but it was somewhat lower for heterosexual cohabiting couples than for any of the other couples.

The assumption that homosexual and heterosexual relationships are basically similar was described by Kitzinger and Coyle (1995) as **liberal humanism**. This approach was a move forward from the view that gays and

In 1996, 175 gay and lesbian couples took part in a formal domestic partners ceremony in San Francisco, similar to the conventional marriage ceremony.

What cross-cultural differences might you expect to find in homosexual relationships?

lesbians are inferior to heterosexuals, and promoted the notion that they should be regarded as individuals rather than as members of a group defined by sexual orientation. It sounds like a reasonable approach, however it continues to equate homosexual relationships with heterosexual ones and ignores the particular difficulties that gays and lesbians have to contend with in terms of the prejudices of society.

Differences between homosexual and heterosexual relationships.   The liberal humanistic view that homosexual relationships closely resemble heterosexual ones is an oversimplification. Homosexual couples are more likely than heterosexual ones to have additional sexual partners outside the relationship. Among couples together for more than 10 years, 22% of wives, 30% of husbands, 43% of lesbians, and 94% of gay men reported having had sex with at least one person other than their partner (Blumstein & Schwartz, 1983).

A major difference between homosexual and heterosexual relationships is that more importance is attached to equality of status and power in homosexual relationships. A lack of power equality was found to be a factor in the ending of lesbian and gay relationships but not of heterosexual marriages (Blumstein & Schwartz, 1983).

Another difference is that homosexuals have to contend with the hostility of society. As Kitzinger and Coyle (1995, p.67) pointed out:

> *Lesbian and gay couples are struggling to build and to maintain relationships in the context of a society that often denies their existence, condemns their sexuality, penalises their partnership and derides their love for each other.*

As a result, cohabitation is much less common in homosexual relationships than heterosexual ones.

Finally, heterosexual married couples typically stay together for longer than any type of unmarried couple, including gay or lesbian couples. One reason for this is undoubtedly that there is more social, cultural, and religious support for married couples than for unmarried ones.

Evaluation

One justification for psychological research is that it enables us to better understand our own behaviour. If you are a heterosexual reader then the earlier Units on relationships may have appealed to you because you used them to understand and explain the relationships in which you have been involved. The same is true for homosexual individuals who have an equal interest in knowing about and understanding homosexual relationships, and this alone justifies such research. Clearly there is a lot of such research remaining to be done before we can understand homosexual relationships.

A second reason for conducting research is for the purpose of real-world application and the HIV crisis provided just such a scenario. In order to plan effective prevention and treatment campaigns it was necessary to have accurate information about the sexual relationships between homosexual men.

"Electronic" friendships

This is clearly a fascinating new area of research for social psychologists, where they can even conduct their studies through participant observation and online questionnaires! The concept of "electronic" relationships refers to all interpersonal contacts through the medium of the internet. The three main sources of contact are e-mail, usenets, and chat rooms.

What particular ethical problems may arise from conducting online research (e.g., informed consent)?

E-mail

E-mail, or electronic mail, is a way of writing a message and, instead of posting it, you send it via the internet to another person's post-box, where it awaits collection by the recipient. This means one can collect an e-mail anywhere one has access to a computer.

How does e-mail differ from other forms of communication? Prior to the age of electronic methods, communication was either face-to-face (corporeal), or phone-to-phone (voice only), or the written word ("snail" mail). When we speak with someone face to face there are a host of channels through which we are communicating aside from the actual words. In fact the nonverbal signals or **paralanguage** may be more important than the words themselves, for example body posture and eye gaze express liking for someone else. On the telephone some of these nonverbal signals are still there, such as pauses and tone of voice. In letters, all such signals have been removed or, if they are included, it is done deliberately. The reason why nonverbal signals tend to have so much power is that many of them are not under conscious control. Certainly some people are able to monitor the way they present themselves and can learn to control nonverbal cues that indicate, for example, uncertainty or dishonesty. But most people don't and therefore we use nonverbal signals as a means of knowing what someone really means, especially the emotional content of their message.

Many people use e-mail as a way of making contact with friends and acquaintances. Issues surrounding e-mail relationships were explored in the recent Tom Hanks film *You've Got Mail*.

For business contacts the lack of paralanguage would appear to make e-mail an ideal form of communication, though there is the difficulty of misunderstandings. You may think you've expressed yourself clearly but another person may take a different meaning from your words. Had the words been spoken, you might have accompanied them with subtle cues that aided interpretation.

For more personal contacts, a new vocabulary and form of language is growing both on e-mail and in chat rooms to communicate nonverbal information (see box below). In Section 9, Language and Thought, we consider the relationship between language and social groups. Language and paralanguage are used as a means of creating a social group identity, for example your accent and dialect identify you as a group member and indicate your desire to belong to that group. This is true of internet communication. Using accepted abbreviations and symbols shows others that you are "one of them".

Nonverbal signals in face-to-face encounters are hard to control. Try making yourself look someone in the eye as you speak with them. What did you feel about doing this?

Internet language

An explosion of terminology has appeared on the internet and in connection with the internet, and various glossaries are published to help users decode these new words. A few new concepts and words are explained here.

Emoticons

Font combinations used as e-mail shortcuts to convey emotions and expressions. For example:

Happy :-)	Devil with grin >:-)	Angel with halo O:-)
Surprised :-0	Sad :-(	Wink (sarcasm) ;-)

Fasgrolia

Stands for the "fast-growing language of abbreviations, initialisms and acronyms". Newsgroups, chat rooms, and e-mail have spawned a rich set of acronyms and initialisms for common phrases. A few of the more common ones are:

FWIW	–	For What It's Worth
IMO	–	In My Opinion; or IMHO - In My Humble Opinion
LOL	–	Laughing Out Loud
BTW	–	By The Way
FYI	–	For Your Information
ROTFL	–	Rolling On The Floor Laughing
RTFM	–	Read The #&!@ing Manual
TIA	–	Thanks In Advance

Also, more technical fasgrolia, such as

CMC is Computer Mediated Communication.
FtF stands for Face-to-Face (communication).
FUD stands for Fear, Uncertainty, and Disinformation.
POTS stands for "Plain Old Telephone Service".

General words to express new behaviours and experiences

Alias: A nickname used in sending e-mail or in online chat rooms

Cybersquatting: The act of registering a popular internet address, usually a company name, with the intent of selling it to its rightful owner.

Digerati: The digital version of literati, it is a reference to a vague crowd of people seen to be knowledgeable, hip, or otherwise in-the-know in regard to the digital revolution.

Internesia: The growing tendency to forget exactly where in cyberspace you saw a particular bit of information.

Flame: A strong opinion or criticism of something, usually as a frank inflammatory statement in an e-mail.

Lurking: Listening in to the discussion on a usenet newsgroup without contributing to the discussion. Lurking is encouraged for beginning users so that they can get acquainted with the form, style, tone, and content of the list.

Netiquette: The informal rules of conduct for internet users. Breaching these rules can result in highly disruptive aggressive behaviour or nasty messages (flames) being sent to your organisation and through the internet.

Virus: A destructive program that has the ability to reproduce itself and infect other programs or disks on your computer.

Usenets

"Usenet" is an umbrella term for more than 14,000 forums or newsgroups, each related to a specific topic. It is an ongoing discussion that you can join and leave and come back to any time you like. You just read what's been posted, post your comment or response, and come back and see what others had to say. Each usenet has a common focus, which might be an interest in sleep research or UFOs, or you might have a disorder such as depression or Parkinson's disease; the list is endless.

There are various counselling and diagnostic services on the net for addressing problems ranging from poor self-esteem and stressful relationships to addictions. Bloom (1998) points to the wide number of serious ethical concerns raised by this. For example, these include confidentiality, validity of data delivered via computer networks, misuse of computer applications by counsellors, lack of counsellor awareness of location-specific factors, and credentialling.

Another kind of usegroup is MUDs. MUD stands for Multi-User Dungeon or Dimension, a usually text-based multi-user simulation environment. Some are purely for fun and flirting, others are used for serious software development, or education purposes. A significant feature of most MUDs is that users can create things that stay after they leave and which other users can interact with in their absence, thus allowing a world to be built gradually and collectively. One user described his MUD experience thus:

I don't care how much people say they are, muds are not just games, they are *real*!!! My mud friends are my best friends, they're the people who like me most in the entire world. Maybe the only people who do … They are my family, they are not just some dumb game …

JennyMUSH: A case of internet abuse

JennyMUSH was set up as a virtual help centre for people who have experienced sexual assault or abuse. The administrator, or "God", was a psychology student with a research interest in this field, and whose university fully supported the JennyMUSH project. Such official support ensures some degree of security for users of the system, but was unable to prevent a single user from being able to subvert the delicate social balance of the system by using both technical and social means to enact anonymously what amounted to virtual rape.

Two weeks after being assigned a character, a user of the system used the MUD's commands to transform him or herself into a virtual manifestation of every other user's fears. This user changed "her" initial virtual gender to male, "his" virtual name to "Daddy", and then used the special "shout" command to send messages to every other user connected to the MUD. He described virtual assaults in graphic and violent terms. At the time at which this began, none of the MUD's administrators, or Wizards, were connected to the system, a fact that may well have been taken into account by the user. For almost half an hour, the user continued to send obscene messages to others. During that time, some of his victims logged out of the system, taking the simplest course to nullify the attack. Those users who did not log off moved their "virtual personae" (i.e., their electronic selves) to the same place (electronically speaking) as that of their attacker. Many pleaded with him to stop, many threatened him, but they were powerless to prevent his attacks.

At the end of that half hour, one of the Wizards connected to the system. He found twelve users connected to the system, all congregated in one place. On transporting himself to that place, he found eleven of those users being obscenely taunted by the twelfth. Quickly realising what was going on, the Wizard took a kind of vengeance on the erring user that is only possible in virtual reality. He took control of the user's virtual manifestation, took away from him the ability to communicate, changed his name to "Vermin" and changed his description to the following: "This is the lowest scum, the most pathetic dismal object which a human being can become."

From E. Reid (1999). *Communities in cyberspace*. In M. Smith & P. Kollock (Eds.) (London: Routledge).

There are adventure MUDs and social MUDs. JennyMUSH is an example of the latter. It was set up as a virtual help centre for people who have experienced sexual assault or abuse. The founder was a psychology student whose field of interest was the treatment of survivors of assault and abuse. However, JennyMUSH is an example of the difficulties of policing usegroups (see the box on the left).

Are the relationships developed in these usegroups shallow, impersonal, and hostile, or are they capable of liberating interpersonal relations from the confines of physical locality and creating opportunities for new, but genuine personal relationships and communities? Parks and Floyd (1996) investigated this by interviewing 176 members of internet newsgroups and their contributors, of whom 61% reported forming a new personal relationship via a newsgroup. Predictors of whether an individual formed such a relationship were frequency and duration of newsgroup participation. Online relationships often reached high levels of relational development and broadened to include interaction in other channels and settings: 98% communicated by direct e-mail; one third telephoned each other, and 28% used the postal system. Furthermore, one third of the newsgroup members who reported a personal relationship met each other in person.

There is no reason to suppose that internet relationships aren't governed by the same factors as offline ones. The Key Study by McKenna and Yael (1999) on the facing page compares internet and face-to-face meetings. In the case of the internet, proximity is determined by frequency of meeting (as mentioned on page 62) rather than face-to-face encounters. Hultin (1993, cited in Dwyer, 2001) found that initially people in usegroups sought out similar individuals, for example in terms of ethnic origin.

The computers that bind: Relationship formation on the internet

McKenna and Yael (1999) conducted a series of studies focusing on the formation and development of relationships between people who met initially on the internet. The research focuses on the personality factors that predispose some people to seek out friends and romantic partners on the internet; the speed with which these relationships develop; the similarities and the differences between internet relationship formation and traditional or "offline" relationship development; and the consequences of Internet relationships for the individuals' real life. Four different methodologies were used for data collection: participant observation, in-depth interviews, a survey conducted with nearly 600 newsgroup users, and two laboratory experiments.

In terms of the first aim McKenna and Yael found that individuals who are socially anxious and lonely are more likely to form intimate relationships with others via the internet. Individuals who feel that they are able to express their "real self" on the internet are more likely to subsequently arrange to speak with or meet partners offline.

Results of the two laboratory experiments reveal that individuals like one another better if they first meet via the Internet than if the first meeting takes place face to face. It is also shown that people tend to present and effectively convey a more idealised version of themselves in internet meetings than they do in face-to-face meetings. The survey and laboratory findings confirm the reports of the majority of those interviewed that internet relationships form more easily and then develop more quickly than traditional relationships, and end up becoming just as real. It appears that people tend, ultimately, to make their internet friends and romantic partners part of their actual, physical, day-to-day social worlds.

Discussion points

1. What is "participant observation" and what limitations are associated with this research method?
2. Why might individuals like each other better if they met on the internet than if they met face to face?

However, like in offline relationships, if significant differences in attitudes and interests were discovered then gradually the exchanges became shorter and less frequent until communication ceased altogether. Cooper and Sportolari (1997) point out that computer-mediated relating reduces the role that physical attributes play in the development of attraction, and enhances other factors such as proximity, rapport, similarity, and mutual self-disclosure, thus promoting erotic connections that stem from emotional intimacy rather than lustful attraction. It allows adult (and teen) men and women more freedom to deviate from typically constraining gender roles that are often automatically activated in face-to-face interactions, which may be a positive consequence. However online relating can lead to destructive results when people act on, or compulsively overindulge in, a speeded-up, eroticised pseudo-intimacy. We will consider such erotic relationships next.

Chat rooms

A chat room is actually a channel over which people can meet and exchange messages in real time. The word "room" is used to promote the metaphor that you are actually speaking with someone as if in the same room.

Chats can take place among a large group, or individuals can go off on their own for private chats. Much of the focus is ultimately on romantic relationships and erotic encounters. Branwyn (1993) quoted by Deuel (1996) explains that "Compu-sex enthusiasts say it's the ultimate safe sex for the 1990s, with no exchange of bodily fluids, no loud smoke-filled clubs, and no morning after."

Cyberaffairs

A romantic or sexual relationship that is initiated through contact on the net is called a "cyberaffair". Griffiths (1999) suggests that there three types of cyberaffair. First, there are relationships between two people who meet on the internet and develop an erotic dialogue purely for sexual arousal. Such individuals may have real-life partners and the cyberaffair may be brief. Second, there are relationships that are more emotional than sexual, and which lead to offline contact, as described in the "Love at first byte" Case

To what extent do you think that self-disclosure forms part of internet relationships? What other explanations for formation, maintenance, and dissolution are equally as relevant in internet relationships as in face-to-face encounters?

Study below. The third kind of cyberaffair is where two people meet offline but maintain their relationship almost exclusively online, possibly because of geographical distance. These people may only meet occasionally but may talk on the internet daily.

Why are such relationships potentially seductive and addictive? Griffiths (2000) offers the following explanations. The internet is easy to access from home or work. It is becoming quite affordable and has always offered anonymity. For some people it offers an emotional and mental escape from real life, and this is especially true for individuals who are shy or feel trapped in unhappy relationships. It is also true for individuals who work long hours and have little opportunity for social life. The key features have been summed up variously as the Triple A Engine (access, affordability, and anonymity) or ACE Model (anonymity, convenience, and escape) (Cooper, 1998; Young, 1999).

Problems with electronic affairs.   There are two major drawbacks. First, as we have seen some individuals may well masquerade as something they are not. The potential havoc this can cause and the persistent sense of mistrust that this engenders in computer-mediated relationships means that many people cannot relax. However, the potential for being something you are not is not necessarily all bad. It might be an interesting experience to try out being a man or being a member of a minority ethnic group to see how others behave towards you. However, encouraging such practice, even with the aim of reducing sexism and racism, might be viewed as ethically unsound.

The second major drawback is that internet relationships encourage vulnerable individuals to be seduced emotionally and sexually, and may replace real-life relationships, which are ultimately more complex and satisfying. Many people do actually end up having a real-time relationship with friends they have met on the net but this is not true of everyone.

One shouldn't forget that many of the problems inherent in internet relationships have always been with us. The telephone was and is used for erotic conversations with strangers. Letters have been used as a means for communicating with penpals, again leading in some cases to marriage as well as life-long friendships. These forms of communication permit anonymity and escape but they lack the immediacy and ease of access that is now available for many people on the internet.

CASE STUDY: *Love at First Byte*

It's a new take on the age-old story. Boy meets girl—but in cyberspace. They make small talk via their computers and find they have lots in common. After months of wishing, wondering and long-distance message-sending, they finally meet face to face. And then, to put the virtual icing on the cake, they fall in love and decide to get married.

On 24 August 1996, John Herbert, 23, of Hertfordshire, and Heather Waller, 25, resident of Buffalo, New York State, will walk down the aisle. So far as written records show, John and Heather are the first people to have conducted a successful courtship by computer.

While agreeing that their romance is hardly Mills and Boon material, John and Heather both maintain that their path to true love was not the soulless, automated journey some people make it out to be.

"For a start, there's a lot of mistrust around on the Web," says John, who had his fingers burnt once before when it turned out that the person with whom he had been conducting an online flirtation was in fact a man pretending to be a woman. "You often get blokes chatting you up just for a laugh," he says, grimacing. "That was why I was so pleased when Heather actually phoned me up. It was reassuring to know that she really was a woman."

Indeed, far from seeing their coming-together as some kind of impersonal, electronic process, both John and Heather view it as a traditional, almost Victorian, romance: a union of souls first, bodies later. There is even a literary dimension, of sorts, in the way they developed their relationship through the written word. "Not many people realise it, but there is quite an art to expressing your feelings on the internet," says

John. The other person gets it straight away. "It's not like talking on the telephone, either. The good part is that there's less financial pressure, because the internet costs only around 85p an hour, so you don't have this feeling that you're burning money.

"The not-so-good part is that when you're on the phone, you can hear the subtleties of expression in the other person's voice. On the internet, you can mean one thing, but the words you actually write can come across as meaning something else."

To cope with this, John has adopted a whole lexicon of symbol and speech patterns which are designed to invest messages with a kind of emotional sub-text. Sarcasm, for example, can read rather coldly, which is why he uses the symbol ;-) (look at it sideways) to show a smiling face winking. Similarly >:-o denotes horned devilment, while :-! conveys tight-lipped frustration and a suppressed swear-word. In addition, he employs a bizarre kind of third-person commentary—e.g., "observes John quizzically", or "shrugs John grumpily"—in order to invest the written word with the right tone.

John and Heather met on the Monochrome system, devised by "Absolute Zero" (aka Dave Brownley), who reserves the right to banish those miscreants who misuse it. John and Heather are now both "staff" members, which means it is their (unpaid) job to patrol given sectors of Monochrome, trimming overlong or out-of-date files and "slapping" users who resort to bad language or tasteless jokes.

Adapted from an article by Christopher Middleton in the *Telegraph* on 10 May 1996

SECTION SUMMARY

❖ Certain factors explain why we form relationships with one person rather than another. Physical attraction is top of the list, and is generalised to other attractive characteristics (the halo effect). According to the matching hypothesis, we are attracted to those who match our own physical attraction. Support for this hypothesis has been obtained in studies of initial attraction and in married couples. Some people may be more influenced by physical attractiveness than others. Matching can be achieved through other attractive characteristics beyond good looks.

❖ The second factor is proximity, which may be physical or psychological. Increased contact has been shown to increase the likelihood of friendships and romantic relationships—and also of antagonistic relationships.

❖ Attitude similarity plays a part in determining interpersonal attraction, as does similarity in preference for leisure activities. Those who are similar in demographic variables (e.g., age, sex, social class) are more likely to become friends. People having similar personalities are also most likely to become involved with each other. Evidence that opposites attract each other was not supported by subsequent research. Similarity is probably important for various reasons. Liking for a similar person is likely to be reciprocated, communication is easier, and it confirms our attitudes. If one likes oneself then one should like someone similar, and partners can share activities. However much of the research is artificial and largely correlational. It tends to ignore individual differences.

❖ Theories of attraction and the formation of relationships offer an account of research evidence, though this is flawed because of its artificial nature.

❖ Sociobiological theories are based on the idea that behaviours that promote reproduction are naturally selected. Men and women should seek partners who will produce healthy offspring who can be cared for, which explains why men prefer young women and women want men with resources. Family relationships can also be explained in terms of kin selection. However, many sexual relationships cannot be explained this way.

❖ According to reinforcement and need satisfaction theory, we are attracted to people who provide us with reward or reinforcement, but we dislike those who punish us. Some of the main rewards are providing help or money, respect or status, sex, and love. This theory is of most relevance to the initial stages of attraction. It assumes that people are very selfish, and it ignores the context in which reinforcement is provided. This explanation is more relevant to individualist societies.

❖ Economic theories suggest that relationships involve some kind of trade. According to social exchange theory, people try to maximise the rewards and minimise the costs of interpersonal relationships. Satisfaction can be expressed in terms of comparison levels as well as a comparison level for alternatives. Equity theory is an extension of exchange theory and emphasises fairness. People expect to receive rewards from a relationship that are proportional to the rewards they provide for the other person. If a relationship lacks fairness (inequity) then the disadvantaged partner strives for greater equity. Equity was found to be associated with happiness in relationships, though this may apply only to exchange couples rather than communal couples.

❖ Equity theory is more plausible than exchange theory, because it takes more account of the other person's rewards and costs. Both approaches apply more to individualist cultures. We would expect to find an association between equity and future quality of a relationship, but research hasn't supported this. Exchange and equity may be more important in casual relationships, in fact marital adjustment may be poorer in exchange couples.

❖ Filter theory proposes that various factors progressively filter out individuals as prospective friends/partners—proximity, similarity, and shared values. The final filter, emotional needs, may be the best predictor of long-term relationships. This emphasises the different factors that are important at different stages of a relationship, but may apply only to romantic relationships.

Maintenance and Dissolution of Relationships

❖ Not all relationships last (are maintained) and those that do last may eventually breakdown (dissolve). Levinger's stage theory outlines the whole process: acquaintance, build-up, continuation, deterioration, and ending.

❖ Social penetration theory suggests that relationships develop as a result of mutual self-disclosure (norm of self-disclosure reciprocity) but this lessens in time as each partner listens to self-disclosures rather than responding with self-disclosure. Depenetration involves abandoning disclosure. Women self-disclose more to women than men.

❖ Commitment can be explained by the investment model: satisfaction, perceived quality of alternatives, and especially investment size, determine commitment. All three factors are interrelated, which lessens the predictive value of the factors.

❖ Many relationships are sustained by maintenance strategies. These are used more during the early stages of a relationship, possibly because they are less necessary when you know someone well. There are also conflict strategies (voice, loyalty, neglect, and exit).

❖ Informal relationship rules are important for maintenance. There seem to be six key friendship rules: trust the other person; show emotional support; share news of success; strive to make the friend happy; offer help in time of need; and stand up for a friend in his or her absence. Cultural similarities and differences have been found.

❖ Cognitive factors are also important in maintenance, such as "storytelling" and attributions made about one's partner's behaviour.

❖ The final stage of a relationship is dissolution. One approach to understanding dissolution is through stage models. Lee identified five stages in the break-up of premarital relationships: dissatisfaction; exposure; negotiation; resolution attempts; and termination. The exposure and negotiation stages are the most intense and exhausting ones. Duck identified four phases: intrapsychic, dyadic, social, and grave-dressing. Lee's model focuses on the processes before break-up becomes inevitable. The two models could be combined. Both models have some useful practical implications but neither offers an explanation of *why* some relationships dissolve.

❖ The question "why" can be answered with reference to predisposing risk factors (e.g., distasteful habits, changes in interests, coming from different backgrounds, being young) and precipitating risk factors (deception, relocation, conflict). Jealousy and infidelity are especially strong precipitating factors. The concept of risk factors is an oversimplification because many relationships are maintained despite such factors. There are also sex differences to consider.

❖ Theories of maintenance and dissolution overlap with those of relationship formation. Social exchange theory suggests that breakdown is likely if there are few attractions, weak barriers to leaving the relationship, and very attractive alternatives. Dissatisfaction plus high barriers does not lead to divorce. Equity theory also predicts that imbalance (due to lack of fairness) leads to breakdown.

❖ The vulnerability–stress–adaptation model suggests that all three factors (vulnerability, stress, adaptation) affect each other and may result in a vicious cycle leading to breakdown. This overlooks the role of external factors in breakdown.

❖ Different kinds of love can be distinguished: liking, companionate love, and romantic love. Rubin measured liking and love and found a high association, though women tended to like the men more than the men liked the women. Men tended to love in the context of a sexual relationship.

❖ Companionate love is on a continuum with liking. According to Sternberg's triangular theory, love consists of three components: intimacy; passion; and decision/commitment. In the short term, passion is usually the most important, with intimacy most important later. The three components combine to produce: liking, romantic love, companionate love, empty love, fatuous love, infatuated love, and consummate love. The three components can be used to analyse a relationship, however some of the components are rather vague.

❖ The three-factor theory of love proposes that physical arousal (factor 1) is interpreted as love as a consequence of cultural cues (factor 2) and the presence of an appropriate love-object (factor 3). This is related to the cognitive labelling theory of emotion. This can explain cultural differences and love at first sight, but can't explain the fact that many people fall in love gradually.

❖ Our understanding of relationships is limited by the narrow scope of research settings, therefore it is important to study other cultures and sub-cultures, an approach suggested by the postmodern approach.

❖ One way that Western and non-Western cultures vary is in terms of individualism versus collectivism. Individualist Western societies stress the personality of a potential spouse, romantic love, voluntary marriages, the quest for an ideal partner, and the reasonableness of divorce; whereas those in collectivist Eastern societies favour arranged marriages based on social status, having fewer but closer friendships, and being less tolerant of divorce. Arranged marriages appear to have high levels of satisfaction and people in collectivist cultures see romantic relationships as unrealistically optimistic. Aside from the individualist/collectivist dimension, there are other cultural differences such as different views on physical attractiveness. Heavy women are overwhelmingly preferred to slender women in cultures having a very unreliable food supply.

❖ However, there are also cultural similarities such as in relative age and polygyny. Both of these can be explained in terms of sociobiological theory. Men benefit by mating with younger women, women benefit by choosing older men with greater resources. This explains the universality of older men marrying younger women, though the situation may be changing, which supports an economic rather than a sociobiological interpretation. Polygyny is found in most societies. It benefits the males because they maximise their reproduction and it benefits the women because their men have power and good looks, characteristics that may be passed on to their sons and maximise the continuation of the mother's genetic line (sexy sons hypothesis).

❖ Sub-cultural variation can be seen in gender, social, and historical differences. Males may conduct more "side-by-side" instrumental relationships whereas women have more "face-to-face" expressive relationships. Men may be more likely to endorse the love style of Agape, whereas women tend towards Pragma. These differences may be innate or they may be the result of socialisation and/or the rather artificial nature of relationship research. There are some social class differences, in terms of divorce rates, the kind of people with whom individuals associate, and also in terms of family interactions, but love style does not appear to be associated with class. Generalisations about social class are likely to be oversimplifications because social class is associated with a multitude of other factors. Historical differences are exemplified by changing attitudes towards sex, different views of the association between romantic love and marriage, and changing divorce rates.

❖ Certain relationships have been relatively understudied. There are many misconceptions about gay and lesbian relationships, for example that homosexual relationships are short-lived and lacking love. The liberal humanistic view is that gay partnerships are more like heterosexual relationships than they are different, though there are differences. For example, homosexual couples are more likely to have additional sexual partners, and to place greater importance on equality of status and power, and homosexual couples also have to contend with the hostility of society. Heterosexual marriages may be more long-lasting because of the social and cultural support for such unions.

❖ Electronic relationships are a fast-growing area of research. E-mail communication lacks nonverbal signals which are important because they are not under conscious

Cultural and Sub-cultural Differences in Relationships

control and communicate important emotional information. New forms of written communication, such as emoticons and fasgrolia, have developed in electronic communications so that messages can have emotional content and also as a means of creating a social group identity. Usenets are communication channels where groups can meet to discuss specific topics, such as exchanging information or offering help and advice. Such groups are open to abuse either from individuals offering help who are not qualified to do so, or from anti-social individuals who take advantage of the medium. Many people derive great satisfaction from usegroups but it has been questioned whether such relationships are shallow or genuine. Research suggests that many relationships formed in this way lead on to more personal contact.

❖ Chat rooms are a particular kind of usenet for the explicit purpose of more personal relationships, such as cyberaffairs. Such affairs may be just for eroticism, though some lead on to real-time romantic encounters. Others use the medium to continue real-time relationships when face-to-face contact is not possible. The appealing nature of such relationships can be explained, for example in terms of the ACE Model (anonymity, convenience, and escape). The danger is that affairs may be founded on untruths and vulnerable individuals may be seduced emotionally and sexually. Cyber relationships may replace real-life relationships which are ultimately more complex and satisfying. Many of these same issues have existed before, for example with penpals.

FURTHER READING

The topics in this Section are covered in greater depth by D. Dwyer (2001) *Relationships (2nd Edn.)* (London: Routledge), written specifically for the AQA A specification. Interpersonal relationships are discussed in an accessible way by N. Hayes (1993) *Principles of social psychology* (Hove, UK: Psychology Press) and also in Chapters 8 and 9 of S.L. Franzoi (1996) *Social psychology* (Madison, USA: Brown & Benchmark). R. Goodwin (1999) *Personal relationships across cultures* (London: Routledge) looks at cultural and sub-cultural variation, and, for electronic relationships, you might look at P. Wallace (1999) *The psychology of the internet* (Cambridge University Press), which is written in a lively and amusing style.

Example Examination Questions

You should spend 30 minutes on each of the questions below, which aim to test the material in this Section.

1. **(a)** Describe **two** research studies relating to interpersonal attraction.   **(12 marks)**
    (b) Evaluate these studies with reference to theories of interpersonal attraction.   **(12 marks)**

2. **(a)** Describe findings from psychological research into the formation of relationships.   **(12 marks)**
    (b) Assess the value of these findings with reference to theories of the formation of relationships.   **(12 marks)**

3. Describe and evaluate psychological research into the maintenance of relationships.   **(24 marks)**

4. Critically consider **two** psychological explanations of love.   **(24 marks)**

5. **(a)** Outline **two** theories of the formation and/or maintenance of interpersonal relationships.   **(12 marks)**
    (b) Assess these theories in terms of their relevance to Western and non-Western cultures.   **(12 marks)**

6. "Psychological research into relationships has tended to focus on romantic heterosexual relationships and ignored all the many other relationships between people, such as friendship and homosexual relationships, as well as those conducted over long distance such as 'electronic' friendships. There is no doubt that this is changing."

    Discuss research into "understudied" relationships.   **(24 marks)**

Examination Tips

Question 1. Note the word "describe" rather than "outline" for part (a) which means detail is important. When describing studies you can use the same guidelines as for AS level: write something about the aims, procedures, findings, and conclusions. Do *not* offer any evaluation of the studies as part (a) is AO1 alone and evaluation will receive no credit and cannot be exported to part (b). You must restrict your description to two studies. In part (b) you may refer to any relevant research studies and draw general conclusions about interpersonal attraction. Part of assessing the value of such studies could include a consideration of the validity of the research—if the methodology is flawed then the study cannot inform us much.

Question 2. Part (a) is AO1 and requires a focus on findings only, i.e., anything that has been found out from research—and remember that "research" includes both studies and theories. Part (b) again requires that you use this evidence to offer commentary about the formation of relationships.

Question 3. This is a straightforward question. You should remember again that "research" refers to studies and/or theories. You may choose to use evidence related to the formation and/or dissolution of relationships but, if you do, ensure that you make this relevant to the question set. Evaluation may involve looking at the implications of the theories, at research evidence that supports the theories (or otherwise), issues of cultural and/or individual variation, and any general commentary that informs us about the value of the theory.

Question 4. It is helpful, when "critically considering" a topic, to include both strengths and weaknesses. The question requires two explanations only but, if you wish to refer to others then ensure that they are explicitly presented as a form of evaluation. Make sure you give a full 15 minutes to evaluation otherwise you are sacrificing important marks.

Question 5. The term "outline" means that you should present your chosen theories as a summary description only. You have no more than 15 minutes to do this so don't lose marks by providing too much detail for one theory and failing to attract many marks for your second theory. In part (b) you are not required to describe research into other cultures but to assess the extent to which the theories presented in part (a) can explain behaviour in all cultures. You may make reference to research studies but must use this material *effectively* to construct an overall argument.

Question 6. In this question you are not required to address the quotation but it is there to encourage you to consider various "understudied" relationships. "Research" may include theories and/or research studies.

WEB SITES

http://www.socialpsychology.org/social.htm#interpersonal
  Links about interpersonal relationships.
http://www.muohio.edu/~psybersite/attraction/
  Article and links about physical attraction.
http://www.mexconnect.com/mex_/culxcomp.html
  Interesting summary of cultural differences between Mexicans and their neighbours in North America.
http://www.culturebytes.com/
  Articles about real-life cross-cultural relationship experiences.
www.a-levelpsychology.co.uk/websites.html
  A continually updated list of useful links, including those printed in this book, may be found at the Psychology Press A level psychology site.

3

Pro- and Anti-social Behaviour

This Section focuses on behaviour such as aggression and altruism. Why do some people behave aggressively whereas others do not? We examine social psychological and sociobiological approaches.

Nature and Causes of Aggression

Aggression involves hurting others on purpose. It has been defined as "any form of behaviour directed towards the goal of harming or injuring another living being who is motivated to avoid such treatment" (Baron & Richardson, 1993). The hurting has to be deliberate. For example, someone who slips on the ice and crashes into someone by accident would not be regarded as behaving aggressively.

Psychologists have identified different types of aggression, for example, person-oriented and instrumental aggression. **Person-oriented aggression** is designed to hurt someone else, and so causing harm is the main goal. In contrast, **instrumental aggression** has as its main goal obtaining some desired reward (e.g., an attractive toy), with aggressive behaviour being used to obtain the reward.

There is also a distinction between proactive and reactive aggression. **Proactive aggression** is aggressive behaviour that is initiated by the individual to achieve some desired outcome (e.g., gaining possession of an object). **Reactive aggression** is an individual's reaction to someone else's aggression.

It is important to note that aggressive behaviour need not involve fighting or other forms of physical attack. Of course, very young children often resort to physical attacks. However, by the age of 4 or 5, children usually have a good command of language, and they make much use of teasing and other forms of verbal aggression. In the research discussed later, aggression is assessed in several ways, such as aggressive play behaviour, willingness to give electric shocks to someone else, and punching and hitting a doll. The key measurement problem is that aggression involves the *intent* to harm someone or something, and it is often hard to know whether participants intended to cause harm.

It is not easy to define aggression. Do you think that the definition offered here covers all aspects of aggression? What about boxing?

The main goal of the aggression in this picture is to obtain a "reward" by stealing the bag, rather than to hurt someone. This is an example of instrumental aggression.

Social Psychological Theories of Aggression

Social learning theory

One of the most influential theories of aggression is that of **social learning** put forward by Albert Bandura (e.g., 1973). According to this approach, most behaviour (including aggressive behaviour) is learned. In the words of Bandura (1973):

> *The specific forms that aggressive behaviour takes, the frequency with which it is displayed, and the specific targets selected for attack are largely determined by social learning factors.*

These three elements of social learning were demonstrated in Bandura's research with children and the Bobo doll (see Key Study on the next page). In this study it was found that exposure to an aggressive model led to imitation of specific acts, generally increased levels of aggression, and aggression was directed at the same target (Bobo doll).

Direct and indirect reinforcement

Identify the three different ways that aggression can be learned.

The essence of social learning theory is that new behaviours are learned indirectly as well as through direct reinforcement (traditional learning theory: classical and operant conditioning). Indirect reinforcement (vicarious reinforcement) results in observational learning. **Vicarious reinforcement** occurs when another person is observed to be rewarded for certain actions and this makes it more likely that an observer will imitate the actions. The imitator is not likely to repeat the behaviour immediately but may, at an appropriate time in the future, reproduce the behaviour. Thus it is said that **observational learning** has taken place and the behaviour may be imitated or **modelled** at a later date. This means that a model must be stored internally, and implies the involvement of cognitive processes. This is a departure from traditional learning theory which rejects the involvement of any cognitive factors in learning.

When aggression is imitated

Individuals are more likely to imitate another's behaviour if:

- The model is similar to themselves, such as being the same gender or similar in age.
- The model is perceived as having desirable characteristics or is admired, as in the case of a rock star or an impressive teacher.
- The individual has low self-esteem.
- The individual is highly dependent on others.
- Reinforcement is direct. Children respond most to direct reward, next to seeing a model in action, and least to a filmed model, especially a cartoon character (Bandura et al., 1963).

Vicarious punishment may also occur, leading to a reduced response. For example, if you see someone else being told off for teasing, then you are less likely to do it. In addition social modelling may reduce the likelihood of a response because a different response has been strengthened. This was demonstrated in a study by Walters and Thomas (1963) who recruited participants for a study on the effects of punishment on learning. The participants worked in pairs, one was supposedly learning a task (this person was actually a confederate of the experimenters). The "true" participant was told to give the learner a shock following each error that was made. After each error, the participant was given the opportunity to select the level of shock to use for the next trial. Prior to the experiment all participants had been shown a film. Those participants who watched a violent scene were found to select higher shock intensities than those who watched a nonviolent movie scene.

Can you think of an occasion when your own behaviour has been disinhibited?

This is an example of **disinhibition**. The participants observed socially unacceptable behaviour in the film and this *weakened* the pro-social behaviours they had previously learned. In other words their tendency to behave pro-socially was disinhibited or

The social learning of aggression

Bandura, Ross, and Ross (1961) carried out a classic study on observational learning or modelling, demonstrating that aggression can be learned via social interactions (i.e., social learning). Young children watched as an adult behaved aggressively towards a Bobo doll. The adult punched the doll and hit it with a hammer. After 10 minutes the children were moved to another room where there were some toys, including a hammer and a Bobo doll. The children had to walk some distance before they got to the room. This was done to create a sense of frustration. Once in the room, they were watched through a one-way mirror and rated for their aggression. The children who had watched a model behaving aggressively were more violent and imitated exactly some of the behaviours they had observed, as compared with children who either had seen no model or watched an adult (model) behaving in a non-aggressive manner.

Bandura (1965) carried out another study on aggressive behaviour towards the Bobo doll. One group of children simply saw a film of an adult model kicking and punching the Bobo doll. A second group saw the same aggressive behaviour performed by the adult model, but this time the model was rewarded by another adult for his aggressive behaviour by being given sweets and a drink. A third group saw the same aggressive behaviour, but the model was punished by another adult, who warned him not to be aggressive in future.

Those children who had seen the model rewarded, and those who had seen the model neither rewarded nor punished, behaved much more aggressively towards the Bobo doll than did those who had seen the model punished. It could be argued that the children who had seen the model being punished remembered less about the model's behaviour than did the other groups of children. However, this was shown not to be the case by Bandura. All the children were rewarded for imitating as much of the model's aggressive behaviour as they could remember. All three groups showed the same good ability to reproduce the model's aggressive behaviour. Thus, the children in all three groups showed comparable levels of observational learning, but those who had seen the model punished were least likely to *apply* this learning to their own behaviour.

KEY STUDY EVALUATION — Bandura

Bandura exaggerated the extent to which children imitate the behaviour of models. Children are very likely to imitate aggressive behaviour towards a doll, but they are much less likely to imitate aggressive behaviour towards another child. Bandura consistently failed to distinguish between real aggression and playfighting, and it is likely that much of the aggressive behaviour observed by Bandura was only playfighting (Durkin, 1995).

The Bobo doll is of interest to young children, because it has a weighted base and so bounces back up when it is knocked down. Its novelty value is important in determining its effectiveness. Cumberbatch (1990) reported that children who were unfamiliar with the doll were five times more likely to imitate aggressive behaviour against it than were children who had played with it before.

Finally, there is the problem of **demand characteristics**. These are the cues used by participants to work out what a study is about. In an experiment, participants try to guess what it is they should be doing. This leads them to search for cues which might help them and they use these cues, or demand characteristics, to direct their behaviour. Because experiments aim to have the same conditions for all participants, all participants will be using the same cues and therefore they all end up behaving in ways that are predictable from the set up of the experiment. As Durkin (1995, p.406) pointed out:

Where else in life does a 5-year-old find a powerful adult actually showing you how to knock hell out of a dummy and then giving you the opportunity to try it out yourself?

The Bobo doll experiment provided cues which "invited" the participants to behave in certain predictable ways.

Discussion points

1. How might the frustration–aggression hypothesis explain these findings?
2. How important do you think observational learning is with respect to producing aggressive behaviour?

Considering the points made in the evaluation of Bandura's work, what conclusions can be reached from this study in terms of aggression?

Adult "models" and children attack the Bobo doll.

unlearned as a result of modelling. This concept of disinhibition is discussed again later when considering the effects of the media.

More research evidence

The development of aggression.   Probably the most important social models for a child are his or her parents. Patterson et al. (1989) looked at the factors in a child's home environment that might be related to the development of aggression. The researchers compared families having at least one highly aggressive child with other families of the same size and socio-economic status who had no problem children. Assessments were made through questionnaires and interviews with children, parents, peers, and teachers, as well as home observations. The key feature of certain families was a "coercive home environment" where little affection was shown, and family members were constantly struggling with each other and using aggressive tactics to cope. Parents rarely used social reinforcement or approval as a means of behaviour control. Instead they used physical punishment, nagging, shouting, and teasing. The children in such families were typically manipulative and difficult to discipline.

Patterson suggested that the coercive home environment may create aggressiveness in three main ways. First, harsh discipline and lack of supervision results in disrupted bonding between parent and child, and lack of identification. Second, the parental behaviours provoked aggressiveness in the children. Finally, the children learned to behave aggressively through modelling; they observed that aggression was a means of resolving disputes. This analysis has useful practical application. It is possible that the way to reduce aggressiveness is to teach parents alternative skills, and give anti-social children social skills training (see page 677).

Video games and aggression.   Another source of evidence in relation to social learning theory is research that has considered the relationship between video games and aggression. A number of studies have examined the differences in children's behaviour after playing an aggressive video game. For example, Cooper and Mackie (1986) observed the free play of 9- and 10-year-old children after they had played aggressive video games, and found that aggressive behaviour increased in girls but not boys. In another study, this time with 4–6-year-olds, aggression levels did increase (Silvern & Williamson, 1987) and the same was true in a study with 7–8-year-olds (Irwin & Gross, 1995). Clearly these data suggest that younger children may be more susceptible than older children, though a self-report study by Griffiths and Hunt (1993) found that older children who played video games reported higher levels of aggression. In this case it could be that aggressive personality was the cause and not the effect of the video games. On the other hand, the study by Griffiths and Hunt was related to long-term aggression and therefore has greater validity. Most of the other studies have just looked at short-term effects, including Bandura's original observational studies.

Cross-cultural evidence.   Finally, we might consider cross-cultural evidence. If aggression is due to social learning then we would expect the different practices in different cultures to produce variations in levels of aggression. Some of the best-known work on cross-cultural differences in aggression is that of the anthropologist Margaret Mead (1935). She compared three New Guinea tribes living fairly close to each other. In one tribe (the Mundugumor), both men and women were very aggressive and quarrelsome in their behaviour. At times, the Mundugumor had been cannibals who killed outsiders in order to eat them. In a second tribe (the Arapesh), both men and women were non-aggressive and co-operative in their treatment of each other and their children. When they were invaded, the Arapesh would hide in inaccessible parts of their territory rather than fight the invader. In the third tribe (the Tchambuli), the men carved and painted, and indulged themselves with elaborate hairdos, whereas the women were relatively aggressive.

It is probable that Mead exaggerated the extent of the gender differences, for example even in the Tchambuli tribe it was the men who did most of the fighting in time of war. The fact that the men were *relatively* more aggressive in each society

It is easy to dismiss the features listed here as not being present in your home environment—at least one of them probably is.

Does cross-cultural evidence suggest that aggression is learned, or not?

suggests that some aspects of aggression are biologically determined; but the fact that some societies are more aggressive than others supports the role of social learning in aggression.

Evaluation

Bandura's social learning approach is an important one. Much aggressive behaviour is learned, and observational learning or modelling is often involved. It has been found that children who watch violent programmes on television are more likely to behave in an aggressive way. These studies (discussed later) are consistent with social learning theory.

Social learning theory can account for cultural and individual variation; it can also explain why we behave aggressively in some situations and not others. When we are rewarded or reinforced for behaving aggressively this is related to specific situations. In other situations we might find that the same behaviour is not rewarded. For example, a child might find it a useful strategy to shout at a friend in the playground, but the same behaviour used in class would be sharply discouraged. The child learns when aggression is appropriate and when it is not. This is called **context-dependent learning**.

In spite of the successes of social learning theory, there are reasons for arguing that Bandura's approach is limited in scope. Aggressive behaviour does not depend only on observational learning. The cross-cultural evidence demonstrated that aspects of aggression are innate. Twin studies have also provided evidence of the importance of genetic factors. For example, McGue, Brown, and Lykken (1992) obtained scores on the aggression scale of the Multi-Dimensional Personality Questionnaire from 54 pairs of identical twins and 79 pairs of fraternal twins. The scores correlated +0.43 for identical twins and +0.30 for fraternal twins. The fact that the correlation was higher for identical twins suggested that genetic factors were of some importance, though it is possible that the twins reared together have learned aggression in their homes.

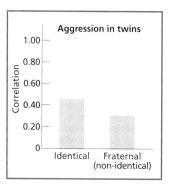

Frustration–aggression hypothesis

Think of occasions when you have behaved aggressively. Many of them probably involved frustrating situations. Dollard et al. (1939) argued in their **frustration–aggression hypothesis** that there are close links between frustration and aggression. In the words of Miller (1941, pp.337–338)

> *the occurrence of aggression always presupposes frustration … Frustration produces instigations to a number of different types of responses, one of which is an instigation to some form of aggression.*

What types of situation do you find frustrating?

Research evidence

Evidence supporting the frustration–aggression hypothesis was reported by Doob and Sears (1939). Participants imagined how they would feel in each of 16 frustrating situations. In one situation, the participants imagined they were waiting for a bus, but the bus driver went past without stopping. Most of the participants reported that they would feel angry in each of the frustrating situations. Of course, anger does not always turn into aggression.

In what other ways do people respond to frustration?

Justified and unjustified frustration.   Most of the evidence indicates that the frustration–aggression hypothesis is oversimplified. For example, Pastore (1952) argued that it is important to distinguish between justified and unjustified frustration. According to him, it is mainly unjustified frustration that produces anger and aggression. Doob and Sears (1939) found strong support for the frustration–aggression hypothesis because their situations involved unjustified frustration. Accordingly, Pastore (1952) produced different versions of the situations used by Doob and Sears (1939) involving justified frustration. For example, the situation with the non-stopping bus was rewritten to indicate that the bus was out of service. As predicted, Pastore (1952) found that justified frustration led to much lower levels of anger than did unjustified frustration.

What would happen to soldiers if they did not behave aggressively?

Situational factors.   Evidence that aggressive behaviour does not always stem from frustration was reported by Zimbardo (1973). In his Stanford prison experiment (which was covered in your AS studies), the mock prisoners did less and less to frustrate the wishes of the mock warders. However, the mock warders behaved in an increasingly aggressive way towards them. In times of war, soldiers often behave aggressively towards the enemy because they are ordered to do so rather than because they are frustrated.

Environmental cues.   Berkowitz and LePage (1967) argued that aggressive behaviour does not depend only on frustration. The presence in the environment of aggressive cues also plays a part in making people behave aggressively, and this notion was tested by Berkowitz and LePage. Male university students received electric shocks from another student, who was a confederate working for the experimenter. They were then given the chance to give electric shocks to the confederate. In one condition, a revolver and a shotgun were close to the shock machine. In another condition, nothing was placed nearby. The presence of the guns increased the average number of shocks that were given from 4.67 to 6.07. This is known as the **weapons effect**. According to Berkowitz (1968, p.22):

> *Guns not only permit violence, they can stimulate it as well. The finger pulls the trigger, but the trigger may also be pulling the finger.*

How might you use this quote to argue against those Americans who believe in the right of every individual to bear arms?

We need to consider a potential problem with the interpretation of the weapons effect. The presence of the guns may lead participants to assume that the experimenter wants them to behave in an aggressive way. If so, then only those participants who were suspicious of the experimenter's intentions would show the weapons effect. In fact, the evidence indicates that suspicious participants do *not* show the weapons effect. This suggests that Berkowitz's interpretation of the weapons effect is probably correct.

Cognitive-neoassociation.   Berkowitz (1989) revised the frustration–aggression hypothesis in his cognitive-neoassociationistic approach. He argued that an aversive or unpleasant event causes negative affect or emotion (e.g., anxiety; anger). This negative affect activates tendencies towards aggression and towards flight. The behaviour we actually display depends on our interpretation of the situation. Suppose someone knocks into you as you are walking along the pavement. This may cause negative feelings and a tendency towards behaving in an aggressive way. However, if you realise that it was a blind person who knocked into you, your aggressive tendencies are likely to be replaced by feelings of guilt.

Could the demand characteristics of Berkowitz's laboratory situation have led participants to guess the true purpose of the study?

According to Berkowitz's (1989) theory, a frustrating situation is one example (but not the only one) of an aversive event. In similar fashion, behaving in an aggressive way is only one of several ways of responding to frustration. This theory is vaguer than the original frustration–aggression hypothesis. However, it is more reasonable than the frustration–aggression hypothesis, and more in line with the available evidence.

Excitation-transfer theory

It may be preferable to describe aggression as the consequence of a generally increased level of arousal or excitation. Zillmann (e.g., 1979) developed an excitation-transfer theory, according to which arousal caused by one stimulus can be transferred and added to the arousal produced by a second stimulus. What is important in determining the emotional reaction to the second stimulus is the way in which the transferred arousal is interpreted. For example, suppose that someone insults you on a very hot day. You might normally ignore the insult. However, because the hot weather has made you more aroused, you may become very aggressive. According to the theory, however, this should *only* happen if you attribute your aroused state to being insulted rather than to the temperature. The notion that the interpretation given to one's arousal level is important resembles the theoretical approach of Schachter and Singer (1962) in their cognitive labelling theory of emotion (see page 220).

The best way to see what is involved in excitation-transfer theory is to consider an experimental example of excitation transfer. In a study by Zillmann, Johnson, and Day (1974), male participants were provoked by a confederate of the experimenter. Half of the participants rested for 6 minutes and then pedalled on a cycling machine for 90 seconds, whereas the other half pedalled first and then rested. Immediately afterwards, all of the participants had the chance to choose the level of shock to be given to the person who had provoked them.

What do you think happened? Zillmann et al. predicted that participants who had just finished cycling would attribute their arousal to the cycling, and so would not behave aggressively towards their provoker. In contrast, those who had just rested for 6 minutes would attribute their arousal to the provocation, and so would behave aggressively by delivering a strong electric shock. The results were in line with these predictions.

> **Relative deprivation theory**
>
> This theory can explain both aggressive and prejudiced behaviour (see page 46). The basic principle is that a sense of having less than one feels entitled to leads to aggression. One's feelings of deprivation are judged in terms of what other people might be perceived to have, i.e., deprivation is relative to the state of others. A sense of relative deprivation exacerbates pre-existing *prejudices* about an *outgroup*, especially at times of economic hardship, and is expressed as aggression towards that group.

What ethical questions are raised by Zillmann et al.'s study?

Evaluation

Unexplained arousal can lead to increased anger and aggression in the way predicted by excitation-transfer theory. However, the theory is rather limited. In real life, we generally know *why* we are aroused, and the theory does not apply to such situations.

Do you think that excitation transfer happens often in everyday life?

Deindividuation

Deindividuation refers to the loss of a sense of personal identity that can occur when we are, for example, in a crowd or wearing a mask. One explanation offered for unruly mob behaviour is that the loss of identity that occurs when you are part of a crowd means that individuals feel less constrained by norms of social behaviour, and more able to behave in an anti-social way.

In Zimbardo's (1973) prison study the guards were deinidividuated because they wore uniforms and were given reflective sunglasses. However the prisoners also wore uniforms and were further deindividuated by having stockings on their heads and being referred to by a number rather than their name. The prisoners didn't behave aggressively but they did conform to the role of being a prisoner (i.e., they were very obedient). This suggests that deindividuation results in high levels of conformity rather than aggression *per se*, as the prison guards were also conforming to a role.

The Ku Klux Klan uniform provides both anonymity and a shared identity for its wearers.

Evaluation

The major difficulty with using deindividuation as an explanation for aggression is the fact that it does not always lead to aggression. There are circumstances where deindividuation may even lead to higher levels of pro-social behaviour. Wearing a nurse's uniform leads to a loss of personal identity and adopting the norms for that uniform. Whereas wearing the uniform of a soldier might lead one to adopt more aggressive behaviours. Deindividuation can increase conformity to certain social norms.

In some crowd situations, deindividuation actually leads to decreased conformity, though it could be argued that individuals are conforming to the norm of the crowd. In other crowd situations, such as a rock concert, the norm would be different and so would the behaviour of the crowd. Deindividuation means one tends to relinquish personal control.

Individuals in a crowd experience a sense of deindividuation and this might explain why mobs act in an unruly way. However, this is not true of all "mobs", such as at a rock concert. Deindividuation is better described as increased conformity.

To one team this looks like a foul; to the other, a justifiable defensive manoeuvre.

Can you think of any recent news items that could be interpreted in different ways according to which side a person supported?

Social constructionism

Most of the theories of aggression we have considered so far are based on the assumption that it is fairly easy to decide whether someone is behaving in an aggressive way. However, social constructionists such as Gergen (1997) argue that matters are more complex than that. According to them, we impose subjective interpretations or constructions on the world around us. An example of people interpreting events in different ways can be seen at almost any football game. Tackles that seem like cynical fouls deserving a sending-off to the supporters of one team are regarded as perfectly fair by the supporters of the other team.

The social constructionist approach as applied to aggression is based on a number of assumptions:

1. Aggressive behaviour is a form of social behaviour, and it is not simply an expression of anger; according to Gergen (1997, p.124), "emotional expressions [of anger] are extended forms of interchange, somewhat like cultural dances."
2. Our interpretation or construction of someone else's behaviour as aggressive or non-aggressive depends on our beliefs and knowledge.
3. Our decision whether to behave aggressively or non-aggressively depends on how we interpret the other person's behaviour towards us.

Research evidence

The first assumption is supported by numerous cases in which an individual behaves aggressively towards someone else some time after being angered by that person. For example, in the days (thankfully past!) when teachers used to cane their students, the caning would often take place days after the student had behaved badly.

The second assumption is supported by the work of Blumenthal et al. (1972). They studied the attitudes of American men towards police and student behaviour during student demonstrations. Students with negative attitudes towards the police judged the behaviour of the police to be violent, whereas the sit-ins and other actions of the students were regarded as nonviolent. In contrast, men with positive attitudes to the police did not regard their assaults on students or their use of firearms as violent. However, they condemned student sit-ins as violent acts deserving arrest.

The study by Blumenthal et al. indicates that aggression is not simply a descriptive concept. It is also an evaluative concept, in that our judgement that someone is behaving aggressively depends on the constructions we place on their behaviour. How do we decide whether someone is behaving aggressively? According to Ferguson and Rule (1983), there are three main criteria:

- Actual harm.
- Intention to harm.
- Norm violation, when the behaviour is perceived as illegitimate and against society's norms.

The norm of reciprocity is of particular importance in deciding whether an act is aggressive. According to the **norm of reciprocity**, if someone has done something to you, then you are justified in behaving in the same way to that person. Evidence that the norm of reciprocity applies to aggressive behaviour was reported by Brown and Tedeschi (1976). Someone who initiated a hostile act against another person was seen as aggressive and unfair. In contrast, someone who attacked another person after having been provoked was regarded as behaving fairly and non-aggressively.

Are there situations where the norm of reciprocity does not apply?

The third assumption of the constructionist approach, that we decide whether to behave aggressively towards someone on the basis of our interpretation of their behaviour, was supported in a study by Ohbuchi and Kambara (1985). They studied how people reacted when harm was done to them. People were more likely to retaliate when they believed that the other person intended to hurt them than when they thought that the other person did not realise the pain he or she had caused.

Support for the third assumption in real-life situations was reported by Marsh et al. (1978). They studied violent attacks by students in schools, and found that these attacks were neither random nor spontaneous. The attacks generally occurred in classes with less effective teachers, because the students interpreted this as a sign that the school authorities had written them off. This interpretation (although mistaken) produced anger and aggression.

Evaluation

One of the most valuable aspects of the constructionist approach is the notion that our interpretation or construction of situations and people's behaviour determines our responses. Such interpretations or constructions depend on our attitudes and beliefs. Thus, we need to distinguish between what actually happens in social situations, and the way in which what happens is perceived and interpreted.

On the negative side, social constructionists seem to exaggerate the differences between different individuals' constructions of what has happened. There are many cases in which nearly everyone would agree that someone is behaving aggressively, for example if a defenceless old woman is suddenly attacked by a mugger and her handbag is stolen.

Some social constructionists such as Gergen go so far as to argue that there is no objective reality at all. According to Gergen (1997, p.119):

Research findings don't have any meaning until they are interpreted, and these interpretations are not demanded by the findings themselves. They result from a process of negotiating meaning within the community.

Effects of environmental stressors on aggressive behaviour

A number of environmental factors have been identified as triggers for aggression. We saw earlier that a gun might be a cue to aggression and Zillmann suggested that temperature might lead to excitation-transfer.

Temperature

Baron and Bell (1976) studied the effects of heat on aggression by seeing how willing participants were to give electric shocks to another person. Temperatures within the range 92–95°F (33–35°C) generally increased the level of aggression. However, extreme heat led to a reduced level of aggression towards another person who had provided a negative evaluation of the participant. In those conditions, the participants were very stressed. If they had given shocks to the other person, they would have had to deal with that person's angry reactions, and they felt unable to deal with the added stress.

Episodes of road rage may result when one driver makes the assumption that another has been deliberately aggressive. In fact, the apparently aggressive driver could be lost, in the wrong lane, driving an unfamiliar car, or in the middle of a row with a passenger, and the offensive behaviour could be completely unintentional.

In a naturalistic study, Baron and Ransberger (1978) showed that incidences of violence could be related to high air temperatures. They used collected data on incidents of group violence in the US as well as the corresponding weather reports. They found that when the temperature was moderately hot, around 84°C, violence was highest; when temperatures got any hotter, aggression declined. This confirms the finding that temperature can act as a stressor leading to the response of aggression.

However, other evidence does not support the notion that aggressive behaviour declines when the heat becomes extreme. Anderson (1989) considered the effects of temperature on various forms of aggressive behaviour, such as assault, rape, and murder.

There was a steady increase in all of these aggressive acts as the temperature rose, with no indication of any reduction in extreme heat.

Noise

Noise levels also act as a stressor and may lead to arousal and frustration. Glass et al. (1969) arranged for 60 undergraduates to complete a number of cognitive tasks, such as word searches, under one of four conditions: loud or soft noise which was played at random (unpredictable) or fixed (predictable intervals). There was also a no-noise condition. During the task physiological arousal was measured using the galvanic skin response (GSR, a measure of autonomic arousal or stress). After the task participants were asked to complete four puzzles. Two of them were insoluble. Frustration (stress) was measured in terms of the length of time that participants persisted at these tasks.

Do you feel that the study by Glass et al. raises any clinical concerns?

Participants did adapt to the noise. In the predictable noise condition, participants made fewer errors, and had lower GSR and higher task persistence than those in the random noise condition. Those in the no-noise condition made even fewer errors. This suggests that random noise has the greatest effect; but even predictable noise creates some stress. Glass et al. suggested that this is because we can "tune out" constant stimuli while still attending at a preconscious level, but unpredictable stimuli require continued attention, and this reduces our ability to cope with stress. Therefore noise is, in itself, a stressor. And such stressors may lead to aggression as described by the frustration–aggression hypothesis.

Crowding and overcrowding

It is often argued that people will tend to behave in an aggressive way when there is severe *overcrowding* which leads to the psychological experience of *crowding*. Evidence supporting this view was reported by Loo (1979), who studied the behaviour of young children in a day nursery. The overall level of aggressive behaviour went up as the number of children in the nursery increased. In similar fashion, there are more acts of aggression and riots in prisons with a high density of prisoners than in those with a low density (McCain et al., 1980).

Studies of other species confirm the link between crowding and aggression. Calhoun (1962) carried out a study in which there was a steady increase in the number of rats living in a large enclosure. Even though the rats were well cared for, they grew more and more aggressive as the enclosure became crowded. The level of aggression finally became so high that some of the young rats were killed, and others were simply eaten. Most of the rats did not become aggressive and did their best to keep out of harm's way but there still was *increasing* aggression, presumably as a consequence of overcrowding.

Freedman (1973) suggests that the physiological arousal of a crowd heightens the mood you are in. In some situations a crowd may be associated with enjoyment, as in a rock concert, or pro-social behaviour, as at a peace gathering. However, if you are not enjoying yourself you might feel stressed, or behave anti-socially.

Do crowds always lead to negative behaviour? The feeling of crowding is likely to heighten the mood people are in rather than always making people feel aggressive.

Negative affect escape model

Baron (1977) has outlined a general theory to incorporate these findings; the negative affect escape model. According to this model unpleasant stimuli (e.g., noise, heat) usually increase aggressive behaviour, because this provides a way of reducing the negative affect. However, if the unpleasant stimuli become very intense, then there is often less aggressive behaviour as people try to escape or simply become passive.

Evaluation

It is not known why laboratory tests of this model tend to support it, whereas data from real-life situations do not (as described earlier). One possibility is that it may be easier to escape from unpleasant stimuli in the laboratory than in real life. Another possibility is that provoking stimuli in real life can be much more intense than in the laboratory. As a result, the high levels of negative affect generated by heat or noise are more likely to trigger aggressive behaviour in real life.

Biological Theories of Aggression

So far in this Unit, we have focused on social psychological explanations of aggression. But we should not ignore the fact that there are other, contrasting explanations—namely, the purely biological explanations of aggression. These may be useful as a means of evaluation though, strictly speaking, they are outside the AQA A specification. Therefore we will deal with them only very briefly.

The physiological approach

One way to explain why men are more aggressive, in general, than women is in terms of the male hormone **testosterone**. Kalat (1998) reports that men aged 15 to 25, who have the highest levels of testosterone, also show the highest levels of violence as measured by crime statistics. Further evidence can be gleaned from the fact that in non-human animals, those males who have been castrated (and thus produce no male hormones) fight least. Female aggression has also been linked to hormones. For example, Floody (1968) reviewed research on pre-menstrual syndrome and found evidence to support the view that during this time of hormonal fluctuation women increase in irritability and hostility, and also are more likely to commit a crime.

The neurotransmitter **serotonin** has also been linked with increased aggression. For example, people with a history of criminal behaviour have been found to have low levels of serotonin (Virkkunen et al., 1987).

A third way of explaining aggression in physiological terms is with reference to brain anatomy. Raine, Buchsbaum, and LaCasse (1997) found significant differences in the brain structure of murderers and normal individuals, such as reduced activity in both sides of the prefrontal cortex and in the amygdala.

One major difficulty with physiological explanations of aggression is that it is difficult to know whether physiological correlates are causes or effects of aggressiveness.

The genetic approach

One classic study in the 1960s (Jacobs et al., 1965) found that a surprising number of men in prison had XYY sex chromosomes instead of the normal XY. The researchers supposed that the extra Y chromosome might make the men more aggressive. Later studies have found that such genetic abnormalities are in fact widespread throughout the general population and therefore can't explain aggression.

More recently, studies have identified genetic trends in twins and families. For example, Brunner et al. (1993) identified a common gene in male members of a Danish family who all exhibited abnormal aggressive behaviour. This potential "gene for aggression" was used as a defence argument in the 1995 trial of Stephen Mobley, who was eventually found guilty of murder despite testimony from his aunt that various members of his family over the last four generations had been inexplicably very violent, aggressive, and criminal.

The evolutionary or ethological perspective

Ethologists and evolutionary psychologists argue that aggression must be understood in terms of its natural function. Animals, especially males, are biologically programmed to fight over resources. One of the classic ethological accounts was from Lorenz (1966). His conclusions were based on observations of non-human animals in their natural environment. He felt that his view was equally applicable to humans because they are governed by the same laws of natural selection. He argued that aggression is a highly adaptive response because an individual who is aggressive controls food, territory, and mating, and thus is the one most likely to survive to reproduce.

In non-human animals aggression does not generally result in harm to the animal towards which the aggression is directed. Any species where aggression leads to death or serious injury will eventually become extinct unless it evolves a form of natural regulation. However, the belief that animals have effective signals to turn off aggression has been challenged by a number of studies. For example, Goodall (1978) noted that appeasement gestures did not stop fighting among a troop of chimpanzees. Parallels between humans and animals may be oversimplified.

Psychoanalytic explanation

Freud proposed that aggression was related to innate instincts, i.e., biological drives. Each individual has a life wish (Eros) and a death wish (Thanatos). The death wish drives us towards self-destruction and, according to Freud, the not always unpleasant wish to return to lifelessness and the mother's womb. The life instinct tries to prevent the death instinct taking over, which results in a redirection of the desire for self-destruction. What would be self-aggression becomes aggression towards others. It is possible for the individual to channel this outward aggression into harmless activity such as sport. This is called catharsis, the release of pent-up energy. Freud felt that it was necessary to release our hostile and destructive impulses regularly otherwise they would result in undesirable behaviour.

Evaluation

Biological explanations of aggression have some practical usefulness in suggesting ways to reduce aggression, though not all of them are desirable (e.g., drugs to counter hormones) or successful (it is not clear whether sport increases or decreases aggression). The biological approach is highly deterministic, as we saw in the suggestion that some criminals might argue that their behaviour was not their fault. Biological explanations also cannot explain cultural variation in aggression.

Altruism and Bystander Behaviour

You must have met some people who were very helpful and co-operative, and others who were aggressive and unpleasant. Psychologists use the terms pro-social behaviour and anti-social behaviour to describe these very different ways of treating other people. **Pro-social behaviour** is behaviour that is of benefit to someone else. It includes actions that are co-operative, affectionate, and helpful to others. In contrast, **anti-social behaviour** is behaviour that harms or injures someone else. In the last Unit we considered aggression. For the most part this is seen as an anti-social behaviour, though this is not always true. There are instances where an aggressive act may serve a pro-social purpose, i.e., acting in a manner that is helpful to others, such as when you push someone away because they were attacking another person. Helping behaviour, such as altruism, would appear to be pro-social but, as we will see, this isn't always true either.

Altruism

The clearest examples of pro-social behaviour involve what is generally called altruism. **Altruism** is voluntary helping behaviour that is costly to the person who is altruistic. It is based on a desire to help someone else rather than on any possible rewards. It has often been assumed that altruism depends on empathy. **Empathy** is the ability to share the emotions of another person, and to understand that person's point of view.

The empathy–altruism hypothesis

Eisenberg et al. (1983) put forward a theory on moral development in children (see Section 10, Cognitive Development). This theory suggested that moral development was linked to the growth of empathy. Batson (e.g., 1987) argued that the same is true of adults. According to his **empathy–altruism hypothesis**, altruistic or unselfish behaviour is motivated mainly by empathy. He claimed that there are two main emotional reactions that occur when we observe someone in distress (adjectives describing each reaction are in brackets):

- *Empathic concern*: a sympathetic focus on the other person's distress, plus the motivation to reduce it (compassionate; soft-hearted; tender).
- *Personal distress*: concern with one's own discomfort, plus the motivation to reduce it (worried; disturbed; alarmed).

Evaluation

The basic assumption of the empathy–altruism hypothesis that altruistic behaviour depends on empathy is supported by most of the evidence obtained by Batson and his colleagues (see the Key Study below). It is also supported by the developmental evidence

Research evidence supporting the empathy–altruism hypothesis

Batson et al. (1981) devised a situation to test the empathy–altruism hypothesis. Female students observed a student called Elaine receiving a number of mild electric shocks. The students were then asked whether they would take the remaining shocks instead of Elaine. Some of the students were told that they were free to leave the experiment if they wanted. The other students were told that they would have to stay and watch Elaine being shocked if they refused to take the shocks themselves. All the students received a placebo drug that actually had no effects and were given misleading information about the drug, so that they would interpret their reactions to Elaine as either empathic concern or personal distress. It must be open to doubt whether all the participants believed this somewhat unlikely story!

Participants who could leave (*interpreted reaction*)		Participants who had to stay (*interpreted reaction*)	
Empathic concern	Personal distress	Empathic concern	Personal distress
Most offered to take shocks	Few offered to take shocks	Most offered to take shocks	Most offered to take shocks, motivated by social disapproval rather than desire to help

Most of the students in the two groups who felt empathic concern offered to take the remaining shocks regardless of whether they could easily escape from the situation. In contrast, most of those who felt personal distress offered to take the shocks when escape was difficult, but far fewer did so when escape was easy. Thus, those feeling personal distress were motivated to help by fear of social disapproval if they did not help, rather than by any real desire to help Elaine.

Batson et al. argued that the students feeling empathic concern helped Elaine for unselfish reasons. However, there are other possibilities. For example, they might have wanted to avoid self-criticism or social disapproval. In order to test this possibility, Batson et al. (1988) carried out a modified version of the 1981 study. Some of the female participants were told that they would only be allowed to help Elaine by taking some of her electric shocks if they did well in a difficult mathematical task. Someone who was motivated to help Elaine only to avoid social disapproval and self-criticism might well offer to help, but then deliberately perform poorly on the mathematical task. This could be regarded as taking the easy way out. Many of those feeling personal distress did just that, and performed at a low level on the mathematical task. However, most of the students feeling empathic concern volunteered to help Elaine and did very well on the mathematical task. Their refusal to take the easy way out suggests that their desire to help was genuine, i.e., they were motivated by empathy–altruism.

KEY STUDY EVALUATION — Batson et al.

Batson et al.'s study was intended to test the empathy–altruism hypothesis. However, mechanisms other than empathy may have played a part, including fear of social disapproval, or even the demand characteristics of the experimental situation. The students might easily have guessed that the experimenter was interested in their level of care for another person and behaved in what they thought was the expected or socially acceptable way.

It might also be interesting to speculate on the reasons why psychologists so often use the inflicting of electric shocks in their experiments, even if the shocks are only simulated. Mild shocks are often used in animal experiments, but their use in human experiments often seems contrived and artificial. How often do people find themselves in such a situation in real life?

Discussion points

1. Does this study seem to provide a good test of the empathy–altruism hypothesis?
2. Do you think that someone needs to experience empathy in order to behave altruistically?

discussed in Section 10, Cognitive Development. That evidence suggests that children's thinking and behaviour become more altruistic as their ability to empathise with others increases.

One limitation of the empathy–altruism hypothesis is that it is hard to be sure that people are offering help for altruistic reasons rather than simply to avoid the disapproval of others, to avoid the feelings of guilt associated with failing to help, or to experience pleasure when the other person has received help. However, Batson and Oleson (1991, p.80) argued that the emerging pattern of findings means that "we must radically revise our views about human nature and the human capacity for caring." That may be overstating matters. As Batson et al. (1983) pointed out, genuine concern for others is often "a fragile flower, easily crushed by egotistic [self-centred] concerns." They provided some evidence for this assertion. Of participants feeling empathic concern, 86% were willing to take Elaine's place when she received mild shocks. However, this figure was reduced dramatically to only 14% when Elaine received painful shocks.

The experimental evidence relating to the empathy–altruism hypothesis is rather limited in some ways. The focus has been on short-term altruistic behaviour that has only a modest effect on the participants' lives. This can be contrasted with real life, in which altruistic behaviour can involve providing almost non-stop care for an ageing relative for several or many years. It is not clear whether the same processes are involved in the two cases.

Empathic joy hypothesis

Smith, Keating, and Stotland (1989) argued that the empathy–altruism hypothesis was inadequate. They put forward an **empathic joy hypothesis**, according to which empathic concern leads people to help a needy person, because this allows them to share in that person's joy at receiving successful help. It is predicted by this hypothesis that those high in empathic concern should be motivated to learn about their successful acts of helping more than about their unsuccessful ones. However, Batson et al. (1991) found that this was not the case. Indeed, it was those *low* in empathic concern who were most interested in hearing about their successful altruistic behaviour. This and other evidence indicates that the empathy–altruism hypothesis is more accurate than the empathic joy hypothesis.

Negative-state relief model

Cialdini et al. (1987) put forward the **negative-state relief model** to explain why empathy leads to helping behaviour. According to this model, a person who experiences empathy for a victim usually feels sad as a result. They help the victim because they want to reduce their own sadness. Thus, empathic concern should not lead to helping behaviour if steps are taken to remove the sadness that is usually found with empathy. The model also includes the notion that helping is most probable when the rewards for helping are high and the costs are low. Thus, people in an unpleasant mood are more likely to help than those in a neutral mood when helping is easy and very rewarding (e.g., it reduces their unpleasant mood).

Research evidence

The negative-state relief model was tested by Cialdini et al. (1987) using the same situation as Batson et al. (1981). The participants were given a placebo drug having no actual effects. However, the experimenters told the participants that the drug would "fix" the participants' mood and prevent it being altered. They predicted that the participants would be less inclined to help the student who was receiving shocks if this would not allow them to reduce their sad feelings. This prediction was supported. Participants feeling empathic concern were less likely to help if they had been given the drug.

Evidence that sadness does not always lead to helping behaviour was reported by Thompson, Cowan, and Rosenhan (1980). When they asked students to imagine the feelings that would be experienced by a friend who was dying, this led to an increase in helping behaviour. However, when they asked the students to imagine their own reactions

Why might the behaviour of carers not be altruistic?

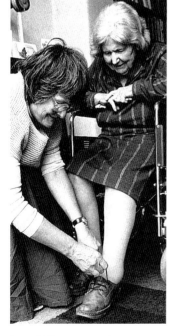

In real life as opposed to experimental situations, altruistic behaviour may involve many years of commitment rather than a brief impulse.

to this situation, there was no increase in helping behaviour. This suggests that people can be so focused on their own emotional state that they fail to help others in need.

Evaluation

One of the reasons why empathic concern leads to altruistic behaviour is because altruistic behaviour reduces the helper's negative emotional state (e.g., sadness). However, the negative-state relief model is rather limited. First, it suggests that empathy only leads to altruistic behaviour for the selfish reason that it makes us feel better. There may be some sense of reward for "doing good" (e.g., when giving blood) but Lerner and Lichtman (1968) demonstrated that self-interest ("egotistic altruism") is not the only factor in human behaviour. In this study participants were to work in pairs, a random number would be drawn to determine which one chose the roles: one would be the "learner" and receive electric shocks, and the other would be a "control". Most of the true participants behaved altruistically and took the role of learner even if they were told that they had won but the other girl was scared, or that she said would leave the experiment unless she was the control, or that the other girl gave the choice to the first participant without drawing. Presumably we behave in this way because we have learned to be altruistic.

Second, Franzoi (1996) reports research evidence that indicates that bad moods are far more likely to increase helping behaviour in adults than in children. However, this is not predicted by the model. Third, the model is limited, because it applies only to mild negative feelings. According to the model, intense negative feelings should not lead to helping behaviour.

Television programmes aimed at raising money for charity, such as the UK's Comic Relief and Children in Need, rely on high levels of empathic concern among those who are watching.

Sociobiological explanation

Sociobiology is an approach to explaining social behaviour in terms of **evolutionary** processes. The theory of evolution proposes that any behaviour which promotes the survival of an individual will be retained in future generations because it is naturally selected (this is the principle of **natural selection**). Individuals who do not possess such adaptive behaviours are likely to die and/or be unsuccessful at reproduction. However, this principle alone cannot explain altruism because an individual who behaves altruistically may die (for example, if they risk their life to help another), thus restricting the individual's reproductive success. Yet there are many examples of altruism in the animal world, such as the partridge that draws a predator away from its nest by pretending that it has a broken wing and walking off in another direction. Batson (1983) tells the story of a red setter and young girl sitting in the back seat of a car when the car burst into flames. The dog jumped out of the car but jumped back in to save the child when he realised she was still in there. This is called the **paradox of altruism**. How can we account for this social behaviour when the theory of evolution would suggest that it would not be naturally selected?

How might you explain why the dog helped the girl?

Kin selection

It is possible to explain this paradox if one uses the **gene** rather than the individual as the basic unit of evolution, which was the contribution of sociobiology. Sociobiologists such as Maynard Smith (1964) used the concept of **kin selection** to describe the idea that a behaviour is adaptive if it promotes the survival of the **gene pool** to which the individual belongs rather than the individual alone. So, if an act of altruism assists the survival and reproduction of kin, then this behaviour is naturally selected.

The closer the kin, the more likely one should be to help. It should also be the case that one would choose to behave in an altruistic way to an individual who has greater reproductive potential. Burnstein, Crandall, and Kitayama (1994) tested these expectations

Could sociobiological explanations account for cultural differences in helping behaviour?

by asking people to say how they would behave in hypothetical life-or-death situations, such as saving someone from a house on fire. People reported that they were much more likely to help relatives than non-relatives, and to aid close kin over distant kin, the young over the old, the healthy over the sick, the wealthy over the poor, and the pre-menopausal woman over the post-menopausal woman. However, when it was a matter of an everyday favour, they gave less weight to kinship and opted to help either the very young or the very old over those of intermediate age, the sick over the healthy, and the poor over the wealthy. This suggests that altruism is driven by different principles from ordinary helpfulness.

Reciprocal altruism

It is also possible to explain altruism in evolutionary terms using the concept of "payback". One animal performs a favour for another with the presumption that, at a later date, this favour will be returned. Trivers (1971) used the term **delayed reciprocal altruism** to refer to this state of affairs. The most obvious problem with delayed reciprocal altruism (or reciprocity as it is also known) is the possibility of cheating. If someone behaves altruistically towards you, but you then refuse to help that person, then you have gained overall but they have lost. Non-human animal examples of delayed reciprocal altruism are discussed in Section 13, Determinants of Animal Behaviour.

Rescue in the Potomac River

Washington, January 14, 1982. There was a hero, name unknown, in today's plane crash into the iced-over waters of the Potomac River just after the jet took off from Washington airport.

To the rescuers in the helicopter, he was only a head in the water, a balding man, perhaps in his mid-50s, with a heavy moustache. He was clinging with five others to the tail section of the Air Florida 737, the only part of the plane still afloat. The helicopter crew threw down a yellow ring life preserver attached to a rope. "He could have gone on the first trip," said the helicopter pilot. "We threw the ring to him first, but he passed it to somebody else," a man who was bleeding badly from a head injury.

"We went back five times, and each time he kept passing the ring to somebody else, including three ladies who were hanging onto the tail section."

Finally, after making several trips and plucking everyone else from the water, the helicopter returned to pick up the man who had put the others first. "We flew back out to get him but he was gone."

Adapted from *New York Times*, 14 January 1982, p.6

Biological versus psychological altruism

It is possible that biological explanations can account for some aspects of human behaviour with regard to altruism, and this is referred to as biological altruism. However, in humans, altruistic behaviour may be more than this. People *think* about their actions. Their behaviour is influenced by personal choice, empathy, morals, and social norms. The behaviour of the bystander who drowned while saving passengers from an aircrash in the Potomac River illustrates all of these characteristic (see the box).

In non-human animals, it is likely that altruistic behaviour is explained in terms of sociobiology, though this doesn't entirely explain the case of the red setter mentioned earlier. This could be an example of reciprocal altruism or mistaken kin identity (the red setter regards the child as kin because of being reared together). It is also possible that non-human animals are capable of empathy.

Bystander Behaviour

Have you ever been in the situation where someone was in trouble and you did nothing? How did you feel? Can you explain why you did not help?

One of the haunting images of our time is that of someone being attacked violently in the middle of a city, with no one being willing to help them. This apparent apathy or reluctance to help was shown very clearly in the case of Kitty Genovese. She was stabbed to death in New York as she returned home from work at 3 o'clock one morning in March 1964. Thirty-nine witnesses watched her murder from their apartments, but none of them intervened. Indeed, only one person called the police. Even that action was only taken after he had asked advice from a friend in another part of the city. This case is described in greater detail on the next page.

The police asked the witnesses why they had done nothing to help Kitty Genovese. According to a report in the *New York Times*:

How would you explain why none of the bystanders helped Kitty Genovese?

> *The police said most persons had told them they had been afraid to call, but had given meaningless answers when asked what they had feared. "We can understand the reticence of people to become involved in an area of violence," Lieutenant Jacobs said, "but when they are in their homes, near phones, why should they be afraid to call the police?"*

CASE STUDY: *The Kitty Genovese Murder*

At approximately 3.20 in the morning on 13 March 1964, 28-year-old Kitty Genovese was returning to her home in a middle-class area of Queens, New York, from her job as a bar manager. She parked her car and started to walk to her second-floor apartment some 30 metres away. She got as far as a streetlight, when a man who was later identified as Winston Mosely grabbed her. She screamed. Lights went on in the nearby apartment building. Kitty yelled, "Oh my God, he stabbed me! Please help me!" A window opened in the apartment building and a man's voice shouted, "Let that girl alone!" Mosely looked up, shrugged, and walked off down the street. As Kitty Genovese struggled to get to her feet, the lights went off in the apartments. The attacker came back some minutes later and renewed the assault by stabbing her again. She again cried out, "I'm dying! I'm dying!" Once again the lights came on and windows opened in many of the nearby apartments. The assailant again left, got into his car and drove away. Kitty staggered to her feet as a city bus drove by. It was now 3.35 am. Mosely returned and found his victim in a doorway at the foot of the stairs. He then raped her and stabbed her for a third time—this time fatally. It was 3.50 when the police received the first call. They responded quickly and were at the scene within two minutes, but Kitty Genovese was already dead.

The only person to call the police, a neighbour of Ms Genovese, revealed that he had phoned only after much thought and after making a call to a friend to ask advice. He said, "I didn't want to get involved." Later it emerged that there were 38 other witnesses to the events over the half-hour period. Many of Kitty's neighbours heard her screams and watched from the windows, but no one came to her aid. The story shocked America and made front-page news across the country. The question people asked was why no one had offered any help, or even called the police earlier when it might have helped. Urban and moral decay, apathy, and indifference were some of the many explanations offered. Two social psychologists, Bibb Latané and John Darley, were unsatisfied with these explanations and began a series of research studies to identify the situational factors that influence whether or not people come to the aid of others. They concluded that an individual is less likely to provide assistance the greater the number of other bystanders present.

Diffusion of responsibility

John Darley and Bibb Latané (1968) were interested in the Kitty Genovese case, and in the whole issue of bystander intervention. They tried to work out why Kitty Genovese was not helped by any of the numerous witnesses who saw her being attacked. According to them, a victim may be in a more fortunate position when there is just one bystander rather than several. In such a situation, responsibility for helping the victim falls firmly on to one person rather than being spread among many. In other words, the witness or bystander has a sense of personal responsibility. If there are many observers of a crime or other incident, there is a **diffusion of responsibility**, in which each person bears only a small portion of the blame for not helping. As a result, there is less feeling of personal responsibility. Darley and Latané demonstrated this in a series of studies that are described in the Key Study on the next page.

A related way of considering what is involved here is to think in terms of social norms or culturally determined expectations of behaviour. One of the key norms in many societies is the **norm of social responsibility**: we should help those who need help. Darley and Latané argued that the norm of social responsibility is strongly activated when only one person observes the fate of a victim. However, it is much less likely to influence behaviour when there are several bystanders.

In the years since the publication of Darley and Latané's (1968) ground-breaking research, several researchers have identified factors other than diffusion of responsibility which determine whether or not a victim will be helped. We will consider some of these factors, and then proceed to discuss some theories of bystander intervention.

Interpreting the situation

Ambiguous situations

In real life, many emergencies have an ambiguous quality about them. For example, someone who collapses in the street may have had a heart attack, or they may simply have had too much to drink. Not surprisingly, the chances of a bystander lending assistance to a victim are much greater if the situation is interpreted as a genuine emergency. Brickman et al. (1982) carried out a study in which the participants heard a bookcase falling on another participant, followed by a scream. When someone else interpreted the situation as an emergency, the participant offered help more quickly than when the other person said there was nothing to worry about.

Demonstrating the diffusion of responsibility

Darley and Latané tested their ideas in various studies. The participants were placed in separate rooms, and told to put on headphones. They were asked to discuss their personal problems, speaking into a microphone and hearing the contributions of others to the discussion over their headphones. They were led to think that there were one, two, three, or six people involved in the discussion. In fact, however, all of the apparent contributions by other participants were tape recordings.

Each participant heard that one of the other people in the discussion was prone to seizures, especially when studying hard or taking examinations. Later on, they heard him say, "I-er-I— uh-I've got one of these-er-seizure-er-er-things coming on and-and-and I could really-er-use some help so if somebody would-er-er-help-er-er-help-er-uh-uh-uh [choking sounds] … I'm gonna die-er-er-I'm … gonna die-er-help-er-er-seizure-er … [choking sounds, silence]."

Of those who thought they were the only person to know that someone was having an epileptic fit, 100% left the room and reported the emergency. However, only 62% of participants responded if they thought that there were five other bystanders who knew about it. Furthermore, those participants who thought they were the only bystander responded much more quickly than did those who thought there were five bystanders: 50% of them responded within 45 seconds of the onset of the fit, whereas none of those who believed there were five other bystanders did so.

Two other interesting findings emerged from the research of Darley and Latané. First, the participants who believed that there were five other bystanders denied that this had had any effect on their behaviour. This suggests that people are not fully aware of the factors determining whether or not they behave in a pro-social or helpful way. Second, those participants who failed to report the emergency were not apathetic or uncaring. Most of them had trembling hands and sweating palms. Indeed, they seemed more emotionally aroused than the participants who did report the emergency.

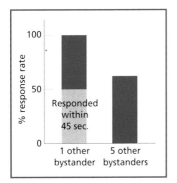

Discussion points

1. Why do you think the findings of Darley and Latané have had so much influence on subsequent research?

2. Should we be concerned about the artificiality of the situation used by Darley and Latané?

Perceived relationships

In many incidents, the perceived relationship between those directly involved can have a major influence on the bystanders' behaviour. Shotland and Straw (1976) arranged for a man and a woman to stage a fight close to onlookers. In one condition, the woman screamed, "I don't know you." In a second condition, she screamed, "I don't know why I ever married you." When the onlookers thought the fight involved strangers, 65% of them intervened, against only 19% when they thought it involved a married couple. This suggests that bystanders are reluctant to become involved in the personal lives of strangers.

It is likely that one of the reasons why none of the bystanders went to the assistance of Kitty Genovese was because they assumed that there was a close relationship between her and her male attacker. Indeed, a housewife who was among the bystanders said, "We thought it was a lovers' quarrel."

Victim characteristics

Most bystanders are influenced by the victim's characteristics. This was shown by Piliavin, Rodin, and Piliavin (1969). They staged incidents in the New York subway, with a male victim staggering forwards and collapsing on the floor. He either carried a black cane and seemed sober, or he smelled of alcohol and carried a bottle of alcohol. Bystanders were much less likely to help when the victim was "drunk" than when he was "ill". Drunks are regarded as responsible for their own plight, and it could be unpleasant to help a smelly drunk who might vomit or become abusive.

Bystander characteristics: Individual differences

What characteristics of bystanders determine the likelihood that they will help a victim?

Skills and expertise

Huston et al. (1981) argued that bystanders who have relevant skills or expertise are most likely to offer help to a victim. For example, suppose that a passenger on a plane collapses suddenly, and one of the stewardesses asks for help. It is reasonable to assume that a doctor is more likely to offer his or her assistance than someone lacking any medical skills. Huston et al. studied the characteristics of bystanders who helped out in dangerous emergencies. There was a strong tendency for helpers to have training in relevant skills such as life-saving, first aid, or self-defence.

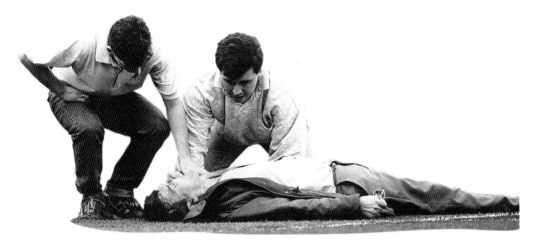

Bystanders who have some relevant skill to offer are more likely to get involved than those who don't know what to do.

Gender differences

Eagly and Crowley (1986) reviewed the literature on gender differences in helping behaviour. They found that men are more likely than women to help when the situation involves some danger, or when there is an audience. Men are more likely to help women than other men, especially when the women are attractive. In contrast, women are equally likely to help men and women.

Personality factors

It might be expected that bystanders with certain personality characteristics (e.g., sociable; warm-hearted; conscientious) would be more likely to help a victim than those with other personality characteristics (e.g., unsociable; reserved; expedient). There is evidence indicating that those who offer help tend to be other-oriented rather than self-oriented (Dovidio, Piliavin, & Clark, 1991). However, the effects of personality are typically rather small, especially when there is obviously an emergency.

Perceived similarity

Bystanders are usually most likely to help a victim if he or she is perceived as similar to themselves. However, there are some exceptions. Gaertner and Dovidio (1977) used a situation in which white participants heard a victim in the next room apparently being struck by a stack of falling chairs. When it was not clear whether or not there was an emergency (there were no screams from the victim), the white participants helped a white victim faster than a black one. The findings were different when the victim screamed, and so there was clearly an emergency. In that case, a black victim was helped as rapidly as a white victim.

What do these findings mean? They suggest that perceived similarity between the bystander and the victim often influences helping behaviour. However, the effects of

There is also evidence that people who have heard of research such as Gaertner and Davidio's study are more likely to intervene and help.

perceived similarity can be wiped out by the demands of the situation if it is clear that there really is an emergency.

Other activities

Do you consider there are any ethical problems with studies like that of Batson et al.? Did the participants give their informed consent to take part?

Bystanders do not only take account of the emergency itself. They also take into account the activity they were involved in when they came upon the emergency. Batson et al. (1978) sent their participants from one building to another to perform a task. On the way, they went past a male student who was slumped on the stairs coughing and groaning. Some of the participants had been told that it was important for them to help the experimenter by performing the task, and that they were to hurry. Only 10% of these participants stopped to help the student. However, if the participants were told that helping the experimenter was not very important, and that there was no hurry, then 80% of them helped the student.

Models of bystander behaviour

How can we make theoretical sense of the various findings on bystander intervention?

The decision model

At any stage in Latané and Darley's model, why might a person answer "no"?

Latané and Darley (1970) put forward a **decision model**. According to this model, bystanders who lend assistance to a victim do so after working their way through a five-step sequence of decisions, producing a "yes" answer at each step. The complete decision-making sequence is as follows:

- Step 1: Is something the matter?
- Step 2: Is the event or incident interpreted as one in which assistance is needed?
- Step 3: Should the bystander accept personal responsibility?
- Step 4: What kind of help should be provided by the bystander?
- Step 5: Should the help worked out at step 4 be carried out?

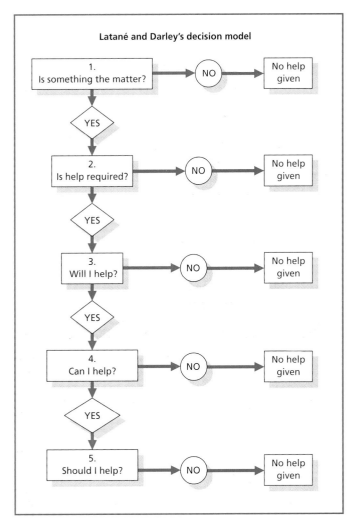

Latané and Darley's decision model

Evaluation

The decision model has two strengths. First, it assumes that there are several different reasons why bystanders do not lend assistance. The experimental evidence that we have discussed provides substantial support for that assumption. Second, the decision model gives a plausible explanation of why it is that bystanders so often fail to help a victim. If bystanders produce a "no" answer at any point in the decision sequence, then help will not be forthcoming.

On the negative side, the model does not provide a detailed account of the processes involved in decision-making. For example, it seems reasonable to assume that bystanders who interpret the situation as an emergency and who also accept personal responsibility would nearly always lend assistance to the unfortunate victim. We need to know more about the processes involved when "yes" decisions at steps 1, 2, and 3 are followed by a "no" decision at steps 4 or 5.

Another limitation of the model is that it de-emphasises the influence of emotional factors on the bystanders' behaviour. Bystanders who are anxious or terrified are unlikely to work carefully through the five decision-making stages contained in the decision model. The model assumes a rather logical sequence of thought.

Arousal/cost–reward model

Piliavin et al. (1981) put forward an **arousal/cost–reward model**. According to this model, there are five steps that bystanders go through before deciding whether or not to assist a victim:

1. Becoming aware of someone's need for help; this depends on attention.
2. Experience of arousal.
3. Interpreting cues and labelling their state of arousal.
4. Working out the rewards and costs associated with different actions.
5. Making a decision and acting on it.

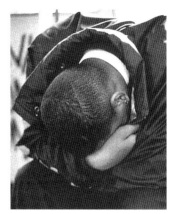

Would you stop to find out what the problem is?

The fourth step is perhaps the most important, and deserves more detailed consideration. Some of the major rewards and costs involved in helping and not helping are as follows:

- Costs of helping: physical harm; delay in carrying out other activities.
- Costs of not helping: ignoring personal responsibility; guilt; criticism from others; ignoring perceived similarity.
- Rewards of helping: praise from victim; satisfaction from having been useful if relevant skills are possessed.
- Rewards of not helping: able to continue with other activities as normal.

Evaluation

The arousal/cost–reward model provides a more complete account than the decision model of the processes involved in determining whether to provide help. As we saw in our review of the literature, bystanders often seem to take account of the potential rewards and costs associated with helping and not helping. It is also probably true that bystanders are generally more likely to think about the possibility of helping when they experience a state of arousal than when they do not.

On the negative side, it is implied by the arousal/cost–reward model that bystanders spend some time considering all of the elements in the situation and the other demands on their time before deciding what to do. In fact, people faced by a sudden emergency often respond impulsively and with very little thought. Even if bystanders do consider the relevant rewards and costs, it is perhaps unlikely that they consider *all* of them. Another problem with the model is that it is not always the case that a bystander needs to experience arousal before helping in an emergency. Someone with much experience of similar emergencies (such as a doctor responding to someone having a heart attack) may respond efficiently without becoming aroused.

Cross-cultural and individual differences

Most of the research we have discussed was carried out in the United States. It is dangerous to assume that what is true in one culture is true in other cultures, and this

---

■ Activity: Complete a table such as this one and rate each situation in order of likelihood of helping.

Devise your own table or use this one to assess the public's views on helping. Compare their responses with Piliavin et al.'s reasons for helping or not helping. Do your results show any sex or age-group differences?

Situation Rating	Costs	Rewards
A pregnant woman drops her shopping bag		
A blind person requests help to cross the road		
There is a car crash on the motorway		
A hitch-hiker is thumbing a lift on a lonely road		

danger is perhaps especially great with respect to altruism. The dominant approach to life in the United States is based on self-interest rather than on any great altruistic concern for others. Darley (1991) described this approach as follows:

In the United States and perhaps in all advanced capitalistic societies, it is generally accepted that the true and basic motive for human action is self-interest. It is the primary motivation.

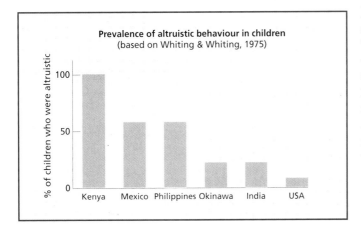

Prevalence of altruistic behaviour in children
(based on Whiting & Whiting, 1975)

Evidence that this selfish approach is not dominant in all cultures was reported by Whiting and Whiting (1975). They considered the behaviour of young children between the ages of 3 and 10 in six cultures (United States; India; Okinawa, an island in southwest Japan; Philippines; Mexico; and Kenya). At one extreme, Whiting and Whiting found that 100% of young children in Kenya were high in altruism. At the other extreme, only 8% of young children in the United States were altruistic. The other cultures were in between the two extremes.

Eisenberg and Mussen (1989) reviewed several studies on cross-cultural differences in altruism. They concluded that there are large differences from one culture to another. In their own words:

Most children reared in Mexican villages, Hopi children on reservations in the Southwest [of America], and youngsters on Israeli kibbutzim are more considerate, kind, and co-operative than their "typical" middle-class American counterparts.

Individualism and collectivism

What do these findings mean? Several factors are involved. First, industrialised societies such as those in most parts of the United States and Okinawa place much emphasis on competition and personal success. This emphasis is likely to reduce co-operation and altruism. Second, the family structure in non-industrialised cultures such as those of Kenya, Mexico, and the Hopi is quite different from that in industrialised cultures. Children in non-industrialised societies are often given major family responsibilities (e.g., caring for young children), and these responsibilities help to develop altruistic behaviour. Third, it is possible that members of non-industrialised and collectivistic societies expect to receive more co-operation and help from others, in which case their behaviour may be less altruistic than it looks (Fijneman, Willemsen, & Poortinga, 1996).

Why might the behaviour of people in collectivist cultures be less altruistic than it first appears?

Individual variation

Apart from cultural differences, there are also important individual differences in altruistic behaviour *within* any given culture. Davis (1983) developed an Interpersonal Reactivity Index. This was designed to measure tendencies towards empathic concern (e.g., warmth; compassion) and towards personal distress (e.g., anxiety; uneasiness). He identified the characteristics of those who watched the annual Jerry Lewis muscular dystrophy telethon in the United States, and then gave their time, effort, and money to helping. As would be expected on Batson's empathy–altruism hypothesis, those who scored high on empathic concern were most likely to watch the programme and to help.

Encouraging altruism

Observational learning

How can people be made more altruistic? According to social learning theory, observational learning from models could be an effective technique. Midlarsky and Bryan (1972) tested this notion in a study involving children observing a model giving valuable tokens to a charity. Ten days later, these children were more likely than other children to donate sweets to the same charity.

The importance of observational learning or modelling in everyday life was shown by Rosenhan (1970). He studied White Americans who had worked wholeheartedly in an altruistic way for the civil rights movement during the 1960s. Most of their parents had set them a good example by behaving in a consistently altruistic way, thus providing altruistic models for their children. Rosenhan also studied White Americans who had been less involved in the civil rights movement. Most of their parents had argued in favour of altruism, but were less likely to have *behaved* in an altruistic way. Thus, most of these parents failed to provide good models of altruistic behaviour. This may explain why their children had only been partly involved in the civil rights movement.

What other factors, apart from modelling, may be the cause of these children's low involvement in the civil rights movement?

Rewards

Another way of trying to increase altruism is by offering rewards for helping. This may be effective with young children who have not yet developed much empathic concern for others. However, rewards or reinforcement can have the opposite effect to that intended with older children. Fabes et al. (1989) promised toys to some children if they sorted coloured paper squares for children who were sick in hospital. Other children were not offered any reward for carrying out the same task. After a while, all of the children were told that they could continue to sort the coloured squares, but that they would not receive any reward for doing so. The children who had been rewarded were less likely to continue to be helpful than those who had not been rewarded. The findings were strongest among those children whose mothers believed in using rewards to make their children behave well.

At what age, according to Eisenberg et al. (1983), would rewards be most effective? See page 409.

Why are rewards so ineffective in producing altruistic behaviour? The main reason is that those who are rewarded for behaving helpfully are motivated by the thought of the reward rather than by the desire to help other people. As a result, removal of the rewards often causes the helpful behaviour to stop.

Social norms

The ways in which individuals behave are influenced greatly by social norms, which are the expected forms of behaviour within any given society. In order to encourage people to behave more altruistically, it may be necessary to alter some of the social norms within Western cultures. Piliavin et al. (1981, p.254) argued that helping behaviour could be increased by means of re-training:

> In our society, we are trained from an early age to see the problems of others as "none of our business"... This tendency saves all of us a great deal of emotional distress, but it contributes ... to the increasing alienation and self-absorption of which we all are currently being accused. We may need more training as busybodies; respect for privacy prevents empathic arousal, and directs one's attention to the costs of intervention, specifically the cost of being thought intrusive.

Passers-by may hesitate to offer help in case it is considered intrusive or patronising.

One way to alter social norms is through media intervention, the topic of the next Unit.

Media Influences on Pro- and Anti-social Behaviour

Explanations of Media Influence

When we use the term the "media" we are referring to any medium of communication: books, newspapers, magazines, music (pop songs) audiotapes, films, videotapes, and television. Most of the research in this area is focused on the last two kinds of media but we should remember that all other forms of media have strong influences. There was a fear, in Victorian times, that penny "novellas" would damage vulnerable minds. The medium has changed but the fear hasn't.

It is highly probable that massive exposure to television programmes (and especially violent ones) affects the beliefs of viewers in various ways, and may also affect their behaviour. In this Unit we will consider the effects of the media on pro-social and anti-social behaviour, but first we might consider general explanations as to how the media exert an influence.

Social learning theory

According to Bandura's social learning theory, one of the factors in media influence will be observational learning or modelling. We learn ways of behaving aggressively or altruistically from observing people on television behaving in this manner, and this behaviour may be imitated subsequently. This is especially likely if the behaviours are reinforced and/or the observer identifies with the characters on television, either because they are similar in terms of gender or age, or because they are admired. This might lead us to question the extent to which we may imitate cartoon characters as we are unlikely to identify with them.

Disinhibition effect

The effect of cartoons may be explained in terms of **disinhibition**. Much of the time we exert conscious control over our behaviour, and feel we should inhibit behaviours that are seen to be anti-social. High levels of violence in the media promote the view that such behaviour is common and acceptable, and this reduces our normal inhibitions about behaving in this way. For example, you watch a scene that shows a son hitting his father when the father says the son must stay home, and this decreases your normal inhibitions about behaving in such a way.

This applies generally to anti-social rather than pro-social behaviour, but we might imagine that where people normally feel inhibited about helping in an emergency situation, portrayal of such behaviour in a television programme might disinhibit us in future. For example, normally we would feel inhibited about stepping in between two lovers having a quarrel, but a programme on television that showed how this may have been helpful might reduce our normal inhibitions, i.e., it would disinhibit us.

How might you use the concept of desensitisation to explain an increase or decrease in pro-social behaviour?

Desensitisation

Desensitisation is a different concept from disinhibition. Here it is suggested that violent acts reduce our responsiveness As Franzoi (1996) pointed out we gradually become less responsive to, and emotionally concerned by, acts of violence, because we have seen so many on television. In a study by Thomas et al. (1977), two groups of children watched a videotape of young children behaving aggressively. Their physiological reactions to this videotape were recorded. Those children who had seen a television programme containing much violence just before watching the videotape became less aroused physiologically than did those who had just watched a programme containing no violence. Such reduced responsiveness may be associated with an increased acceptance of violent behaviour.

Cognitive priming

Another reason why media violence may play a part in producing aggressive behaviour is because of **cognitive priming**. The basic idea is that the aggressive cues presented in violent television programmes lead to aggressive thoughts and feelings. When college students were asked to write down their thoughts while watching violent films (e.g., *The French Connection*), they reported numerous aggressive thoughts, increased anger, and a high level of physiological arousal.

Some of the most convincing evidence for the importance of cognitive priming was reported by Josephson (1987). Some Canadian boys were shown a television programme involving violence in the form of a gun battle, in which the snipers communicated with each other by means of walkie-talkies. The other boys watched a nonviolent programme about a motocross team. After they had watched the television programme, all of the boys played floor hockey. Before the game started, the referee gave the boys instructions either by walkie-talkie or in a tape recording. The boys who watched the violent programme and received instructions by walkie-talkie were more aggressive during the hockey game than were the boys who had watched the same programme but received instructions by tape recording. Thus, the walkie-talkie acted as a cognitive prime or cue to aggression.

The same principle could be applied to pro-social behaviour.

Stereotypes

Another means by which the media influence our behaviour is through the use of **stereotypes**. All media need to communicate a great deal of information in a relatively short time, so they use standard cultural and sub-cultural stereotypes such as foreigners given roles of the "enemy" (using foreign sounding names and/or accents). Men are also more often portrayed as criminals or aggressors. There are positive stereotypes as well, such as overweight people depicted as "jolly", and women portrayed as caring. Mulac et al. (1985) analysed the content of a number of children's programmes, and found strong gender stereotyping: males were more dynamic and female characters had greater socio-intellectual status and aesthetic quality.

These stereotypes can be anti-social in so far as they perpetuate prejudices. They may also be pro-social if they try to break down existing stereotypes.

Counter-stereotypes

One way to deal with the problem of stereotypes is to replace them with **counter-stereotypes**. Thus we see a successful lawyer in a wheelchair (for those who remember *Ironside*), women judges, and single fathers. It does appear that changing stereotypes has had positive consequences. For example, Greenfield (1984) found that *Sesame Street*'s use of ethnic and disabled minorities helped children from minority groups have a greater sense of cultural pride.

Displacement effect

One of the more worrying aspects of television watching is that it replaces an individual's experience of the real world and creates norms that may be unrealistic. The **deviance amplification effect** is an example of this. Programmes that concentrate on disasters or extreme situations are much more popular than those dealing with rather humdrum aspects of life. News programmes, in particular, focus on unusual and often negative events. Gerbner and Gross (1976) found that people who watch a lot of television rate the outside world as being more dangerous and threatening than it actually is.

In 1996 in Britain two children were killed by strangers out of an approximate total of 12,000 children under the age of 19 who died. Does this surprise you? How can the deviance amplification effect explain this?

Stimulation hypothesis

Finally we must remember that the media have enormous potential for education. This may be in terms of providing suitable models for children to imitate but may be most effective when individuals are placed in commonplace situations and methods of resolution are provided. So, for example, an individual is shown behaving anti-socially and the television character deals with the situation in a pro-social manner. One programme on American television, *Freestyle*, aimed to reduce sex-role stereotypes in children by presenting characters who try to engage in behaviours that are nonstereotypical, but the character finds this difficult. Eventually the difficulties are overcome and the character is rewarded for this (Johnston & Ettema, 1986).

However, there is a danger that children will imitate the anti-social behaviour and disregard the resolution! Lovelace and Huston (1983) claim that the most effective way of communicating a pro-social message may be to present the pro-social behaviour without any contrasting conflict or anti-social behaviour. However, the conflict resolution strategy can effectively convey pro-social behaviour if there are a variety of models showing pro-social actions, if the pro-social resolution is given sufficient time and attention, and if viewing conditions are adequate. A third technique, the presentation of unresolved conflict, can be useful in classroom or therapeutic situations where an adult can guide post-viewing discussion and activity, but it has unknown effects in unsupervised circumstances.

Media Influences on Pro-social Behaviour

The effects of television can be positive, and can lead to pro-social behaviour. In the same way that seeing people behaving violently on television can produce violent behaviour in viewers, so seeing people behaving in a caring way can increase caring behaviour.

Research evidence

Which past or present television programmes do you consider to be pro-social?

Increased pro-social or helping behaviour as a result of watching television programmes has been found in children of various ages. Friedrich and Stein (1973) studied American preschool children, who watched episodes of a pro-social television programme called *Mister Rogers' Neighborhood*. These children remembered much of the pro-social information contained in the programmes, and they behaved in a more helpful and co-operative way than did children who watched other television programmes with neutral or aggressive content. They became even more helpful if they role-played pro-social events from the programmes.

Sprafkin, Liebert, and Poulos (1975) studied 6-year-olds. Some of these children watched an episode of *Lassie*, in which a boy was seen to risk his life in order to rescue a puppy from a mine shaft. Other groups of children saw a different episode of *Lassie*, in which no helping was involved, or they saw an episode of a situation comedy called *The Brady Bunch*. After watching the programme, all of the children had the chance to help some distressed puppies. However, to do so they had to stop playing a game in which they might have won a big prize. The children who had watched the rescue from the mine shaft spent an average of over 90 seconds helping the puppies, compared with under 50 seconds by the children who had watched the other programmes. This shows that they imitated specific acts they had seen.

Baran (1979) studied older children between the ages of 8 and 10. These children watched an episode of *The Waltons*, in which there was much emphasis on helping behaviour. These children were then found to behave in a more helpful or pro-social way than other children who had not seen the programme.

Limitations

Duration of effect

Hearold (1986) reviewed more than 100 studies on the effects of pro-social television programmes on children's behaviour. She concluded that such programmes do generally make children behave in more helpful ways. Indeed, the beneficial effects of pro-social programmes on pro-social behaviour were on average almost twice as great as the adverse effects of television violence on aggressive behaviour. However, helping behaviour was usually assessed shortly after watching a pro-social television programme. It is not altogether clear whether pro-social television programmes can have long-term effects on children's pro-social behaviour. In a study by Sagotsky, Wood-Schneider, and Konop (1981), children of 6 and 8 saw co-operative behaviour being modelled. Children of both ages showed an immediate increase in co-operative behaviour. However, only the 8-year-olds continued to show increased co-operation seven weeks later.

Evidence that observational learning from a film can produce beneficial longer-term changes in behaviour was reported by O'Connor (1980). Children who avoided playing with other children were shown a film of children playing happily together. Every child who saw the film played more with other children afterwards, and this effect seemed to last for a long time.

Situation-specificity

Lovelace and Huston (1983) suggested that learning from pro-social programmes is often situation-specific. In order to make the effects more generalised it is necessary to show ordinary people in a variety of everyday situations working together, helping each other, and being sensitive to each other. Dramatic story formats appear better suited than brief didactic scenes for influencing children's behaviour. Discussion with children after viewing and related play can enhance the effects of the TV programme.

Media Influences on Anti-social Behaviour

It has been calculated that the average 16-year-old in Western society has seen about 13,000 violent murders on television, and it seems reasonable to assume that this must have some effect on their behaviour. There is, indeed, a positive relationship between the amount of television violence children have seen and the aggressiveness of their behaviour. However, it is hard to interpret such correlational evidence. It may be that watching violent programmes causes aggressive behaviour. On the other hand, it may be that naturally aggressive children choose to watch more violent programmes than non-aggressive children.

Physical and verbal aggression

One of the more thorough studies of physical and verbal aggression was reported by Leyens et al. (1975). The participants were juvenile delinquents at a school in Belgium. They lived in four dormitories, two of which had high levels of aggressive behaviour and two of which had low levels. During a special Movie Week, boys in two of the dormitories (one high in aggression and the other low) watched only violent films, whereas boys in the other two dormitories watched only nonviolent films.

Can you see any ethical issues in the Leyens et al. study?

There was an increased level of physical aggression among the boys who saw the violent films, but not among those who saw the nonviolent films. The findings were more complex for verbal aggression. This increased among boys in the aggressive dormitory who saw violent films, but it actually decreased among boys from the non-aggressive

---

CASE STUDY: *Movie Violence*

Since its release in 1994, the film *Natural Born Killers* has been surrounded by controversy and has sparked a long-standing debate about the effect of viewing intense violence on the human mind. The film follows the story of Mickey and Mallory Knox, a young couple who go on a killing spree across America, claiming 52 lives at random. Their flippant attitude towards the crimes they commit is portrayed as exciting and thrilling by the media and as a result their murderous behaviour catches the imagination of a generation of young impressionable people who idolise them. The notion of admiring cold-blooded killers may seem to be far-fetched, but alarming similarities have emerged between the reaction to the fictional Mickey and Mallory and other real-life killers. *Natural Born Killers* has been linked to at least a dozen murders, including two cases in France where the defence has blamed the film as providing inspiration for the crime.

In October 1998 the French courts sentenced Florence Rey to 20 years in prison for her part in a shoot-out that left five people dead. She was committing the crime with her boyfriend, Audry Maupin, who was killed in the shoot-out. Publicity material from the film was found in the flat that Rey shared with her boyfriend at the time of the shootings. The press latched on to this and called the pair "France's Natural Born Killers", and as in the film the vulgarity of the multiple murder was lost and replaced by a glamorous image of rebellion that was both enticing and thrilling. Before long, young Parisians were wearing a picture of the convicted woman on their

T-shirts. This was the first time a real-life murderer had been idolised in public.

Stronger links between the film and a murder were discovered in the case of Véronique Herbert and her boyfriend Sébastian Paindavoine who lured their victim into a trap and then stabbed him to death. There was no motive for the attack and Herbert placed the blame on *Natural Born Killers*. She said, "The film coincided with my state of mind. Maybe I muddled up dream and reality. I wanted to eliminate someone, as if by magic … The idea of killing invaded me." In the light of such testimony, can anyone deny the link between the sort of violence depicted in *Natural Born Killers* and Herbert and Paindavoine's gruesome act?

The pro-censorship lobby says the film and subsequent murders provide conclusive evidence that screen violence is rapidly translated into street violence. The image of killing, especially in a fictional world where the characters do not have to live with the consequences of their actions, can become a reality. Such allegations against a film cannot be dismissed and the controversy surrounding the subject matter has been fuelled by the similarities between Mickey and Mallory and the real-life murderers. However, there is an argument against censorship which states that *Natural Born Killers* was intended as a satire on the bloodlust of the media and American society and that it is society that should be held responsible for any acts of violence rather than the film itself.

dormitory who saw violent films. A final finding was that the effects of the violent films on aggression were much stronger shortly after watching them than they were later on. A limitation of this study is that the experimenters did not distinguish clearly between real and pretend aggression.

Longitudinal research

Eron (1982) and Huesmann, Lagerspit, and Eron (1984) reported on a major longitudinal study. First of all, the amount of television watched and levels of aggressiveness were assessed in some young children. Then aggressiveness and the amount of television watched were reassessed in the same participants several years later. One of the key findings was that the amount of television violence watched at a young age predicted the level of later aggressiveness (measured by the number of criminal convictions by the age of 30). This suggests that watching television violence may be one of the causes of aggressive behaviour. In addition, there was evidence that children who were aggressive when young tended to watch more violent television programmes several years later. This suggests that more aggressive individuals choose to watch more violent television programmes.

Absence of television

So far we have considered only studies in which television violence led to increased aggression. However, several studies have found no effect of television on aggression. Of particular interest is evidence obtained in the United States during the early 1950s. The Federal Communications Commission refused to issue any new television licences between the end of 1949 and the middle of 1952. As a result, television arrived in some parts of the United States two or three years before others. According to FBI crime statistics, the level of violent crime was no greater in those areas that had television than in those that did not. Furthermore, the introduction of television into an area did not lead to an increase in violent crime. However, the introduction of television was followed by an increase in the number of thefts (Hennigan et al., 1982). This may have occurred because the advertisements on television made many people more determined to acquire material possessions.

A similar study has recently been carried out on St. Helena in the south Atlantic, which is best known for the fact that Napoleon spent the last few years of his life there. Its inhabitants received television for the first time in 1995, but there is no evidence of any adverse effects on the children. According to Charlton (1998):

The question of whether or not violence depicted in films and on TV leads to violent behaviour is often discussed and was hotly debated in relation to the Oliver Stone film *Natural Born Killers*. The film itself looks at media focus on violence and how it can be glamorised.

Do you think that children from St. Helena would identify with characters in American television programmes? How does this affect the impact of the findings?

> *The argument that watching violent television turns youngsters to violence is not borne out, and this study on St. Helena is the clearest proof yet. The children have watched the same amounts of violence, and in many cases the same programmes, as British children. But they have not gone out and copied what they have seen on TV.*

Some of the evidence consisted of secret videoing of the children playing at school. Charlton reported that "Bad behaviour is virtually unheard of in the playground, and our footage shows that what is viewed is not repeated." What are the factors preventing television violence from influencing the children of St. Helena? According to Charlton (1998): "The main ones are that children are in stable home, school, and community situations. This is why the children on St. Helena appear to be immune to what they are watching."

What characters in television programmes do children imitate today? Does such imitation have negative effects?

Evaluation

It is hard to evaluate the effects of television violence on aggressive behaviour. Many of the studies are limited in scope, focusing only on the short-term effects on behaviour of exposure to a single violent programme. Such studies can tell us little or nothing about the long-term effects of prolonged exposure to violent programmes. The somewhat inconclusive nature of the evidence was summarised as follows by Gunter and McAleer (1990):

> *the measurement of television's effects … .is highly complex … we are still a long way from knowing fully the extent and character of television's influence on children's aggressive behaviour.*

Children are exposed to violent images at an early age and often incorporate them into their play. How well do they distinguish between a play scenario and how they behave in real life?

Wood, Wong, and Chachere (1991) reviewed 28 laboratory and field studies concerned with the effects of media violence on aggression in children and adolescents. It was found in both laboratory and field studies that exposure to media violence led to more aggressive behaviour towards strangers, classmates, and friends. In general, the effects were stronger under laboratory conditions.

Comstock and Paik (1991) reviewed more than 1000 findings on the effects of media violence. There are generally strong short-term effects, especially with respect to minor acts of aggression. In addition, there seem to be rather weaker long-term effects. They concluded that there are five factors that tend to increase the effects of media violence on aggression:

1. Violent behaviour is presented as being an efficient way to get what one wants.
2. The person who is behaving violently is portrayed as similar to the viewer.
3. Violent behaviour is presented in a realistic way rather than, for example, in cartoon form.
4. The suffering of the victims of violence is not shown.
5. The viewer is emotionally excited while watching the violent behaviour.

Bearing in mind Comstock and Paik's five factors, what advice would you give film makers who do not wish to provoke aggression in their audiences?

Individual differences

A key issue is the extent to which all people are affected by violence on television. It may be that people with aggressive personalities are more drawn to such programmes and therefore the observed effects of television violence are an effect rather than a cause of aggressive tendencies. A second explanation is that only certain vulnerable individuals are affected by such violence. Most people can watch violence without significantly increased aggressiveness. However, theories of aggression tell us that some people become predisposed to aggression because of frustration, personality characteristics, or perhaps other environmental factors such as heat. In such circumstances violence on television might lead to increased interpersonal aggression. One particular group of vulnerable individuals are children, who may have as yet unformed personalities and are especially susceptible to the effects of disinhibition, desensitisation, and socially mediated models. This is why, of course, we prefer young people not to watch violence in the media.

Cross-cultural differences

Nearly all research on the effects of media violence has been carried out in the United States or the United Kingdom. As a result, we do not really know whether the findings would be the same in other cultures. One of the few cross-cultural studies was carried out by Huesmann and Eron (1986). They tested children and parents over a period of three years in Finland, Israel, Poland, and Australia. In the first three countries, the amount of television violence that young children had seen predicted their subsequent level of aggression, even when their initial level of aggressiveness was controlled for statistically. However, these findings were not obtained with Australian children. The overall findings suggest that media violence increases aggressive behaviour in most countries.

Other anti-social behaviours

Violence and aggression are not the only anti-social behaviours associated with the media. Prejudice can be inflamed by newspaper and other media reports. Televised role portrayals and inter-racial interactions are sources of vicarious experience and contribute to the development and maintenance of stereotypes, prejudice, and discrimination among children. Limited portrayals of ethnic groups and of inter-ethnic interaction mean that children develop stereotypical views of our society.

Fairchild (1988) suggested a concept for an educational TV programme that would address the concerns emerging from research on the effects of media violence, the portrayal of minorities and women in the media, and the pro-social potential of TV. The pilot TV programme involved an inter-racial and cross-gender team of skilled young adults, cast in counter-stereotypical roles, who travelled to other planets to solve problems of intergroup conflict. To reduce prejudice, the team of protagonists shared equal status and common goals, they co-operated in a fairly intimate context, and they enjoyed successful outcomes. Such programmes might help to encourage a sense of world community, promoting intercultural understanding, and impede the formation of the enemy image! Lofty and pro-social aims indeed.

It is possible that the multi-ethnic nature of *Star Trek* carried a considerable pro-social message about ethnic co-operation and tolerance.

SECTION SUMMARY

Nature and Causes of Aggression

❖ Aggression involves intentional hurt. We can distinguish between person-oriented and instrumental aggression, proactive and reactive aggression.

❖ Bandura's social learning approach suggests that aggression is learned through direct and indirect (vicarious) reinforcement. Indirect reinforcement leads to observational learning and subsequent modelling. The observer learns to imitate specific acts towards a specific model and also learns generally increased levels of aggression. Imitation is more likely if the model is similar and/or possesses desirable characteristics. Modelling is more likely in individuals who have low self-esteem. The more direct the reinforcement, the stronger the influence. Films provide less direct reinforcement than live models. Vicarious punishment leads to a reduced response, and some behaviours may be disinhibited. Research has also shown how children may learn aggression through modelling parents' aggressive coping tactics. Video games increase aggressiveness, especially in younger children. However, it is possible that aggression is a cause rather than an effect of video game playing. Many of the studies have involved only short-term effects. Cross-cultural evidence also supports social learning theory, such as Mead's classic studies of three New Guinea tribes.

❖ Social learning is an important explanation of aggression, and can be used to account for media influence and cultural differences, as well as the context-specific nature of aggressive behaviour. The essence is that aggression is learned through direct and indirect reinforcement, and also influenced by punishment and disinhibition. Some models are more effective than others. Social learning is not the only explanation; for example, biological factors are important in aggression too, as indicated by twin studies.

❖ The frustration–aggression hypothesis suggests that frustration always produces aggression, and aggression always depends on frustration. Research evidence indicates that frustration leads to anger, though this may not turn into aggression. This hypothesis is oversimplified, for example justified frustration leads to less anger than unjustified frustration. Situation can be more important than frustration and environmental cues may trigger aggression, as demonstrated by the weapons effect. The original hypothesis was modified by Berkowitz, in a cognitive-neoassociationistic approach. He argued that an aversive or unpleasant event causes negative feelings that activate tendencies towards aggression and flight. How we then behave depends on our interpretation of the situation.

❖ Excitation-transfer theory suggests that aggression is a consequence of a generally increased level of arousal; again arousal is interpreted using situational cues. This is similar to the cognitive labelling theory of emotion. There is research support for this theory but in real life we generally know *why* we are aroused and don't use situational cues.

❖ When people experience deindividuation they may behave more aggressively, however they may also behave more pro-socially. Deindividuation leads to higher levels of conformity and loss of personal control. Relative deprivation theory can be used to explain aggression as well.

❖ The social constructionist approach considers the question of how we interpret an aggressive behaviour. An individual may not intend to be aggressive but their action might be interpreted in this way, which means aggression is an evaluative rather than a descriptive concept. This is a useful approach because it enables us to distinguish between what actually happens and what interpretation different people place on an event. However, it does suggest that no act is truly aggressive, which may not be realistic.

❖ Environmental factors can act as a cue to aggression, as suggested by both frustration–aggression and excitation-transfer theories. High temperatures have been shown to lead to increased aggression but very high temperatures may not have this effect, possibly because individuals don't feel they can deal with an aggressive response. Research has shown that unpredictable noise may lead to arousal and frustration, which could be translated into aggression. Overcrowding is also associated with increased aggression, in certain situations. It may be more accurate to say that crowding heightens the mood of a crowd.

❖ The negative affect escape model can be used to explain the effect of environmental factors. According to this model unpleasant stimuli usually increase aggressive behaviour, because this provides a way of reducing the negative affect. However, if the negative stimuli become very intense, there is often less aggressive behaviour as people try to escape or simply become passive. But real-life studies do not support this—which may be because in real life passivity is not an option.

❖ As a counterpoint to these explanations we can consider biological explanations. Physiological explanations include the effects of hormones and neurotransmitters, and differences in brain anatomy. Individual differences in aggression may be genetic. Ethologists argue that aggression is adaptive behaviour and Freud suggested it was an innate instinct, a redirection of the our desire for self-destruction which could be rendered harmless through catharsis and sport. Biological explanations are deterministic and cannot account for cultural variation.

Altruism and Bystander Behaviour

❖ Altruism is an example of a pro-social behaviour. The altruist helps another at some cost to themselves and for no reward.

❖ According to the empathy–altruism hypothesis, altruistic or unselfish behaviour in adults is motivated mainly by empathy. When we observe someone in distress, we feel empathic concern and personal distress, and feel motivated to reduce it. The empathic joy model has been proposed as well, however it would predict that those high in empathic concern should be more motivated to learn about their successful acts of helping than about their unsuccessful ones. This is not supported by research. In terms of the empathy–altruism hypothesis, it is hard to know whether people help others for altruistic reasons rather than to avoid feelings of guilt or the disapproval of others. In some situations egotistic concerns clearly govern behaviour. This model may apply to short-term altruistic acts, as in laboratory studies, but not be relevant to long-term altruism.

❖ The negative-state relief model suggests that people help a victim because they want to reduce their own sadness, which is produced by empathic concern. Research evidence supports the prediction that, if you reduce sadness, then participants are less likely to behave altruistically. Other evidence shows that people can be so focused on their own emotional state that they fail to help others in need. The limitations of the model are that it suggests altruism is related to selfishness, it does not explain why children are less affected than adults, nor does it explain why intense negative feelings should not lead to helping behaviour.

❖ Sociobiologists explain altruism as an adaptive behaviour. Within Darwin's theory altruism is a paradox but it can be explained by kin selection where the gene is seen as the unit of natural selection. Altruistic behaviour towards relatives promotes the survival of the gene pool and is naturally selected. People do say that they would be more likely to help relatives in emergency situations but would help non-relatives and people past their reproductive years when performing everyday favours. This suggests that altruism is driven by different principles from ordinary helpfulness. Reciprocal altruism can also be explained in evolutionary terms as long as no one cheats. Human behaviour may be understood in terms of psychological rather than biological altruism.

❖ Bystander behaviour describes situations where an individual observes an emergency and does or does not offer to help. The classic real-life example was the case of Kitty Genovese. Bystanders are often less likely to help a victim if there are many other bystanders, because there is a diffusion of responsibility. A lone person is more likely to respond to the norm of social responsibility. Why else is help not forthcoming? It may be that individuals find it difficult to interpret the situation because it is ambiguous, or because it is not clear what relationship exists between the two people fighting. Help may not be forthcoming if the victim appears to be responsible for their own plight (e.g., is drunk). Help may also be less likely because of characteristics of the potential helper: some individuals have more skills and expertise, and people who offer help tend to be other-oriented rather than self-oriented. People prefer to help others who are similar, though this appears to be less true when there is a clear emergency. Help may be less forthcoming if you have another task on your mind.

❖ The decision model can be used to co-ordinate all these factors: is something the matter, is assistance needed, should I accept personal responsibility, what kind of help is needed, should I do it? This model has the advantage of explaining the variety of different decisions that have to be made and why help is therefore not always forthcoming. On the negative side not all the outcomes are clear and the model doesn't refer to the effects of emotion on decision-making.

❖ The arousal/cost–reward model proposes a different five steps to helping behaviour: (1) becoming aware of the need for help, (2) arousal, (3) interpreting cues, (4) working out the rewards and costs associated with different actions, and (5) making a decision and acting on it. Rewards and costs of helping and not helping are determined by various factors such as praise, physical harm, and public censure. This model has the advantage of including the importance of arousal in the decision to help, but it still suggests that people do not act impulsively.

❖ There are important cross-cultural and individual differences in helping behaviour. In the United States, where much of the research was carried out, behaviour tends to be based on self-interest. Research shows that other cultures, such as in Kenya, are much more altruistic. Industrialised societies place much emphasis on competition, and the family structure in non-industrialised cultures helps to develop altruistic behaviour, though in such societies mutual help means that behaviour may be less altruistic than it looks. There are also individual differences within any culture, such as the fact that some individuals have greater empathy.

❖ The value of understanding altruistic behaviour is to increase it. This might be done through observational learning, offering rewards (though this may be counterproductive), and altering social norms (which may be achieved through media intervention).

❖ The media are any means of communication: books, magazines, films, and television. The most obvious way to explain the potential influence of the media is social learning theory. Individuals model behaviours that they see or read about in the media, especially those that appear to be reinforced, and those of characters with whom they identify.

❖ The disinhibition effect suggests that exposure to certain behaviours in the media reduces our normal inhibitions. This is likely to result in anti-social behaviour but could lead to pro-social behaviour as in reducing our reluctance to intervene in a lovers' quarrel.

❖ Desensitisation occurs when our normal sensitivities are dulled by overexposure.

❖ Cognitive priming acts like the weapons effect—cues in the media may trigger aggressive thoughts, thus increasing arousal and possibly aggressive behaviour.

❖ Stereotypes are inevitable in the media as a means of communicating lots of information very quickly. However they are anti-social because they perpetuate prejudices, though they can also be used pro-socially in the form of counter-stereotypes.

❖ Television may exert an anti-social effect by displacing real-life experiences (a displacement effect). The result may be that people who watch a lot of television see the world as much more deviant than it actually is (the deviance amplification effect).

❖ The media can stimulate thought and pro-social behaviour, especially when demonstrating ways of dealing with anti-social situations (conflict resolution). The danger is that the resolution is overlooked and the anti-social behaviour is imitated. Conflict resolution needs to be given adequate programme time and it is necessary to ensure that observers attend to the resolution.

❖ The pro-social effects of television have been shown in many research studies looking, for instance, at *Mister Rogers' Neighborhood* and *The Waltons*. There are limitations to this evidence, for example the demonstrated effects are fairly short-term though there is some evidence of long-term effects. The pro-social behaviours that are learned may also be quite situation-specific.

❖ Any correlation between amount of violent television watched and aggressive behaviour may be the consequence of a cause or an effect. In one study, physical aggression increased following watching a violent film but verbal aggression only increased in boys who were previously classed as aggressive. In another study the amount of television violence watched at a young age predicted levels of later aggressiveness, a result that may be due to a cause or effect of aggressiveness.

❖ In the United States, areas without television broadcasts in the 1950s did not have lower rates of crime though theft did increase after television reception was available. Observations in St. Helena, where television is relatively new, bear this out. However this is a stable society where children appear to be immune to what they are watching.

Media Influences on Pro- and Anti-social Behaviour

❖ Most studies tell us little about the potential long-term effects. Overall the effects of media violence on aggression may be due to: showing it as being an efficient way to get what one wants, portraying the violent individual as similar to the viewer, showing violent behaviour in a realistic way, not showing the suffering of the victims of violence, and creating emotional excitement in the viewer. Individuals with aggressive personalities will be more drawn to watching violent programmes and probably more affected. Children may be especially vulnerable to influence. Television violence appears to have similar effects in most countries.

❖ Pro- and anti-social behaviour goes beyond helpfulness and aggression; it can include attempts to reduce prejudice and promote world peace.

FURTHER READING

The topics in this Section are covered in greater depth by D. Clarke (2001) *Pro- and antisocial behaviour* (Routledge Modular Series) (London: Routledge), written specifically for the AQA A specification. Other useful sources are F.M. Moghaddam (1998) *Social psychology: Exploring universals across cultures* (New York: W.H. Freeman), and B. Gunter and J. McAleer (1997) *Children and television* (London: Routledge). Chapters 13 and 14 in Hewstone, Stroebe, and Stephenson (1996) *Introduction to social psychology (2nd Edn.)* (Oxford: Blackwell) provide up-to-date coverage of most of the topics discussed in this Section. Chapters 11 and 12 in S.L. Franzoi (1996) *Social psychology* (Chicago: Brown & Benchmark) deal with aggression and pro-social behaviour in detail and in an accessible way. Another useful reference is N. Hayes (1993) *Principles of social psychology* (Hove, UK: Lawrence Erlbaum Associates Ltd).

Example Examination Questions

You should spend 30 minutes on each of the questions below, which aim to test the material in this Section.

1. Describe and evaluate **one** social psychological theory of aggression.   (24 marks)

2. Critically consider research into the effects of **two** environmental stressors on aggressive behaviour.   (24 marks)

3. (a) Outline **two or more** explanations for human altruism.   (12 marks)
    (b) Evaluate these and/or other explanations with reference to research studies.   (12 marks)

4. (a) Outline research evidence relating to bystander behaviour.   (12 marks)
    (b) Assess the effects of cultural differences on pro-social behaviour.   (12 marks)

5. Critically consider **two** research studies relating to media influences on *anti-social* behaviour.   (24 marks)

6. "There is much public interest in the debate about the effects of violence in the media on the behaviour of young children; but why don't people focus more on the potentially pro-social influences?"

    Discuss the above quotation in relation to the pro- and anti-social effects of the media.   (24 marks)

Examination Tips

Question 1.   You must restrict yourself to describing one theory of aggression but may introduce other theories as a means of evaluation as long as this is explicit. It is desirable to do more than just say "I will evaluate my first theory by describing a second theory". True evaluation is achieved through genuinely comparing the theories and highlighting some features of your first theory through contrasts. Further evaluation may be achieved with reference to research studies and consideration of individual and cultural differences. The practical implications of the theory in, for example, reducing aggression are also a form of evaluation.

Question 2. The injunction "critically consider" requires that you describe (AO1) and then criticise this consideration—involving reference to both strengths and limitations. The term "research" refers to either theory or studies. The essay itself focuses on two environmental stressors. Therefore you should identify two stressors such as noise and temperature, and critically consider the research related to each.

Question 3. In part (a) the injunction "outline" requires that you offer no more than a summary description. You will not receive credit for detail in this answer but for breadth. Thus it may be better to offer as many explanations as possible. Note that the essay refers only to altruism and not to bystander behaviour. Any explanations of the latter would only receive credit if they account for altruism (or the lack of it). This must be explicit. Any research studies should be saved for part (b), where the focus should be on using the studies to evaluate the explanations rather than simply describing them. Use of phrases like "This shows that …" and "I would argue that …" should help you be evaluative rather than just descriptive.

Question 4. The emphasis is slightly different in this question, compared to question 3. Again the injunction for part (a) is "outline" but this time it is research evidence you are asked for (which was in part b last time), and also it is bystander behaviour that is the focus. Part (b) requires an assessment of cultural differences. There is a danger again that you will just describe such differences and/or the research studies that have demonstrated such differences. However, credit will be given for the extent to which you use such evidence effectively, in essence answering the question "Are relationships the same the world over?"

Question 5. Again, the injunction "critically consider" requires a description plus an evaluation including reference to strengths and weaknesses. You should identify two research studies only and describe each in terms of aims, procedures, findings, and conclusions. Evaluation can refer to any aspect of the study and may also refer to theories arising from the study (a possible strength). You must restrict yourself to anti-social behaviour, though evaluation might consider the reverse side of the coin— pro-social behaviour.

Question 6. This question requires that you make reference to the quotation in your answer. To maximise your marks you should fully engage with the quotation by making reference to the issues that it raises throughout your answer rather than just reiterating the quotation at the beginning and end. You are asked to discuss both pro- and anti-social effects and therefore need to be selective about the material you use, otherwise you will end up sacrificing depth (detail) for breadth.

WEB SITES

http://www.yorku.ca/dept/psych/classics/Bandura/bobo.htm
The classic study by Bandura et al. (1961) using the Bobo doll.

http://www.noctrl.edu/~ajomuel/crow/topicaggression.htm
Links to aggression-related topics.

http://www.socialpsychology.org/social.htm#prosocial
Links about pro-social behaviour.

http://longman.awl.com/wade/think/critical_17_1.htm
Short essay on bystander apathy.

http://www.chelt.ac.uk/ess/st-helena/faq.html
Questions and answers about the St. Helena research project where the effects of the introduction of television onto an island were documented.

http://www.medialit.org/Violence/indexviol.htm
Many links regarding the debate on the effects of violence in the media.

PART 2

Physiological Psychology

In your AS studies you were introduced to "physiological psychology" through the topic of stress, as an example of a behaviour that can be explained in terms of physiological processes.

"Physiology" refers to bodily processes. Physiological psychologists are interested in how to explain behaviour in terms of bodily processes. They look at topics such as how the nervous system functions, how hormones affect behaviour, and how the different areas of the brain are specialised and related to different behaviours.

Section 4: Brain and Behaviour pp.136–167

❖ What techniques are used by physiological psychologists to find out how the brain works?

❖ Are certain areas of the brain "hard-wired" for specific tasks, such as memory?

❖ Why is the brain divided into two halves (hemispheres)?

❖ Do people with "split brains" have one mind or two?

Section 5: Biological Rhythms—Sleep and Dreaming pp.168–197

❖ Where is your biological clock?

❖ What makes you go to sleep and wake up?

❖ Why do animals need to sleep?

❖ Do dreams have any real meaning?

Section 6: Motivation and Emotion pp.198–227

❖ What causes an organism to act?

❖ What parts of the brain govern motivational and emotional states?

❖ What have motivation and emotion got in common?

❖ Do we smile because we are happy, or are we happy because we smile?

4

Brain and Behaviour

Behaviour is governed by the brain, but how are they connected? A variety of techniques has been developed to investigate brain functioning, both invasive and non-invasive. In this Section, we also look at the research investigating the relationship between different parts of the brain and particular functions, such as language, as well as the phenomenon of split-brain functioning.

Methods of Investigating the Brain

Non-invasive Techniques

As you read about the various non-invasive and invasive techniques that have been used to study the brain, you may find it hard to decide which techniques are the best. In fact, different techniques are designed for different purposes, and are not usually in direct competition. The techniques vary in their spatial and temporal resolution. "Spatial resolution" refers to the fact that some techniques provide information about the neuronal level of functioning of particular neurons, whereas others tell us about activity over the entire brain. "Temporal resolution" relates to time. Some techniques provide information about brain activity on a millisecond-by-millisecond basis, whereas others measure brain activity over much longer time periods such as minutes or hours.

There is no single "best level" of spatial or temporal resolution. High spatial and temporal resolutions are advantageous if a very detailed account of brain functioning is required. In contrast, low spatial and temporal resolutions are more useful if a general view of brain activity is needed.

Electroencephalogram (EEG)

The **electroencephalogram** (EEG) is based on electrical recordings taken from the scalp. It was first used by Hans Berger over 65 years ago. Very small changes in electrical activity within the brain are picked up by **electrodes** placed on the scalp. These changes are shown on a computer screen and can be printed out. The pattern of changes is sometimes referred to as "brain waves".

The EEG has proved useful in many ways. For example, it has been found that there are five stages of sleep, varying in terms of the depth of sleep and the presence or absence of dream activity (see Section 5, Biological Rhythms: Sleep and Dreaming). These stages differ in terms of the EEG record, and EEG research was crucial in identifying these stages. It has also proved useful in the detection of epilepsy, damaged brain tissue, and the

If a neuropsychologist examined the activity of brain cells, would this be high spatial or high temporal resolution?

137

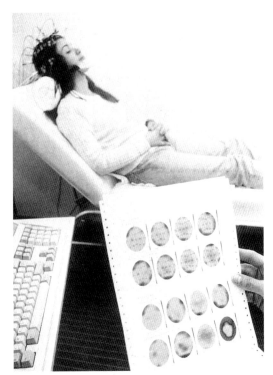

Brain activity recorded using an EEG.

location of tumours, shown by abnormal changes in brain wave patterns. However, the use of EEGs has been largely superseded by the use of brain scans.

The EEG has further been of value in identifying the functions of the two hemispheres of the brain. There is more activity in the left hemisphere than in the right hemisphere when someone is carrying out a language-based task (Kosslyn, 1988). However, the opposite is the case during the performance of a spatial task (Kosslyn, 1988). These findings confirm those from other lines of research, such as studies of brain-damaged patients, another non-invasive technique that relies on natural accidents.

Strengths and limitations of EEGs

The EEG is a rather blunt instrument in two ways. First, it measures electrical activity in several different areas of the brain at once, and so it is hard to work out which parts of the brain are more active, and which are less active. Second, it is an indirect measure of brain activity, because the recording electrodes are on the scalp. The EEG has been compared to trying to hear what people are saying in the next room by putting your ear to the wall.

Evoked potentials

However, EEGs can be used more precisely. Suppose we want to know how the brain responds to a given stimulus (e.g., a tone). This can be assessed by extracting what are known as **evoked potentials** from EEG recordings. A stimulus is presented several times, and the EEG recordings from each presentation are then averaged. This is done to distinguish genuine effects of stimulation from background brain activity.

The value of evoked potentials can be illustrated by considering a study by Loveless (1983). The participants were instructed to listen to the stimuli presented to one ear and to ignore those presented to the other ear. Loveless found differences in evoked potentials between attended and unattended stimuli within about 60 milliseconds of stimulus presentation. Thus, attended and unattended stimuli are processed differently in the brain at a very early stage of processing.

How useful are evoked potentials? They provide fairly detailed information about brain activity over time, but do not reveal precisely which regions of the brain are involved.

Brain scanning

In recent years, various brain scanning techniques have been developed to study cortical functioning. The ones we will consider here are computerised axial tomography (CAT scans), magnetic resonance imaging (MRI scans), functional MRI, positron emission tomography (PET scans), and superconducting quantum interference devices (Squid magnetometry).

CAT scans

In order to produce a **CAT scan**, the individual lies on a table with his or her head in the middle of a doughnut-shaped ring. An X-ray beam then goes through the individual's head from front to back, and the level of radioactivity is detected. The level of radioactivity is lower when the X-rays pass through very dense material. To obtain a fairly full picture, the X-ray emitter and detector are moved around the ring to assess the level of radioactivity from different angles. The several images obtained are then combined by a computer into a composite, three-dimensional picture.

Why has it been so important for scientists and psychologists to determine the locations of various brain functions?

Strengths and limitations.   CAT scans are very useful for detecting tumours, blood clots, and other brain abnormalities. They are also used with accident victims to identify the damaged parts of the brain. However, CAT scans have clear limitations. They do not

The dark patches on these CAT scans (left) show frontal lobe damage in the brain of a 67-year-old man. Compare these with the undamaged brain of a healthy 16-year-old boy (right).

permit precise localisation of brain damage and they cannot show the actual functioning of the brain. They are also very expensive.

MRI scans

MRI scans are similar to CAT scans in some ways, but produce clearer and more detailed pictures. What happens in an MRI scan is that radio waves are used to excite atoms in the brain. This produces magnetic changes, which are detected by an 11-ton magnet surrounding the patient. These changes are then interpreted by a computer and turned into a very precise three-dimensional picture. MRI scans can be used to detect very small brain tumours.

Strengths and limitations.   MRI scans provide more detailed information about the brain than CAT scans. MRI scans can be obtained from numerous different angles, whereas CAT scans can only be obtained in the horizontal plane. However, MRI scans share with CAT scans the limitation of telling us about the structure of the brain rather than about its functions.

Functional MRI

The MRI technology has been applied to the measurement of brain activity to provide **functional MRI** (fMRI). This approach provides three-dimensional images of the brain with areas of high activity clearly indicated so one has a picture of the brain while it is functioning. It is less well known than the PET scan (discussed later), but is more useful. Functional MRI provides more precise spatial information than PET scans, and it also shows changes over much shorter periods of time. The technique is illustrated in the study by Gabrieli et al. (see page 140).

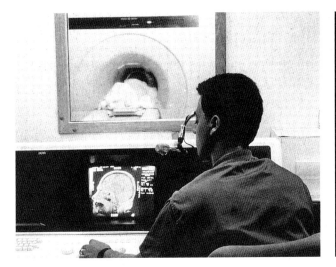

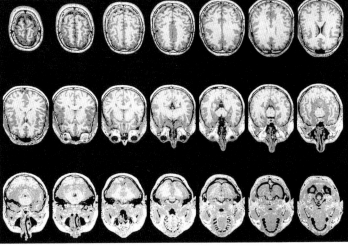

In an MRI scanner, an 11-ton magnet detects magnetic changes in the brain, which are used to generate precise three-dimensional images.

MRI scanning creates "slice" images through the body, useful in detecting brain tumours and cancers. These 21 scans are taken from the top of the head (top left) down to the level of the teeth (lower right).

Strengths and limitations.   Raichle (1994, p.350) argued that fMRI has several advantages over other techniques:

> *The technique has no known biological risk except for the occasional participant who suffers severe claustrophobia in the scanner (the entire body must be inserted into a relatively narrow tube). fMRI provides both anatomical and functional information, which permits an accurate anatomical identification of the regions of activation in each subject. The spatial resolution (i.e., providing information at the neuronal level) is quite good, approaching the 1–2 millimetre range.*
>
> *The main problem with fMRI is that it assesses blood flow, but blood flow follows neuronal activity in the cortex by almost 1 second. As a result, we do not obtain immediate evidence of brain activity.*

Using functional MRI

Gabrieli et al. (1996) used functional MRI to study the parts of the brain involved in the processing of meaning. Their participants were given two tasks to perform: (1) deciding whether words were concrete (referring to objects) or abstract; (2) deciding whether words were in capital letters. Gabrieli et al. argued that the first task involved the processing of meaning, whereas the second one did not.

The key finding was that fMRI indicated that parts of the left prefrontal cortex were more active when the meaning task was being performed. Gabrieli et al. (1996, p.283) concluded that "the process visualised in left inferior pre-frontal cortex may be thought of as a search for meaning". They also found that the words that had been processed for meaning were recalled much better than the words not processed for meaning. This confirms the prediction from levels of processing theory (part of your AS studies).

In general terms, the findings of Gabrieli et al. confirm the value of fMRI as a way of studying cognitive processing. More specifically, their findings suggest that activity in the left prefrontal cortex could be used as an independent measure of whether participants are processing meaning.

Discussion points

1. Some of the limitations with fMRI are discussed in the text. Do these limitations pose problems for the interpretation of the study by Gabrieli et al.?

2. The two tasks used by Gabrieli et al. may have differed in difficulty level as well as in the processing of meaning. Would it be a good idea to repeat their study using different tasks?

What is the feature of fMRI that makes it a functional rather than a structural method?

PET scans

Of all the new methods, the one that has attracted the most media interest is positron emission tomography or the **PET scan**. The technique is based on positrons, which are the sub-atomic particles. A radioactive form of glucose is injected into the body. When part of the cortex becomes active it needs glucose for energy, and the radioactive glucose moves rapidly to that place. A scanning device that looks similar to a CAT scanner measures the positrons emitted from the radioactive glucose. A computer then translates this information into pictures of the activity levels of different parts of the brain. It may sound dangerous to inject a radioactive substance into someone; however, only tiny amounts of radioactivity are involved, too small to be considered a real risk.

The potential value of PET scans can be seen if we consider the work of Tulving (1989) using a related method. He found that the front part of his brain was most active when personal events were being thought about (episodic memory), whereas the back part of his brain was most active when he thought about his general knowledge of the world (semantic memory). These findings suggest that different parts of the brain are involved in thinking about different kinds of information in long-term memory.

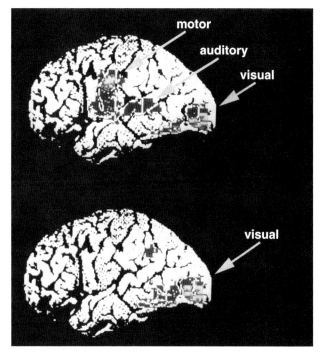

This **PET scan shows active areas of the brain** involved in reading (darker patches). Top: The participant is reading aloud. Active regions of the brain are visual cortex for sight; motor region for speech production; auditory region as the participant hears the sound of their own voice. Bottom: The participant is reading silently, and only the visual cortex is active.

Strengths and limitations.   PET scans show us the brain in action, and so they are an advance on CAT and MRI scans. However, they are more limited than is sometimes realised. They tell us which areas of the brain are active, but they do not identify these areas with precision. Furthermore, PET scans indicate the activity levels in different areas of the brain over a period of 60 seconds or more, but not on a moment-by-moment basis (i.e., poor temporal resolution). Their use also makes assumptions about activity in that it assumes that all relevant activity is coupled with an increase in glucose utilisation.

Squid magnetometry

In last decade or so, a new technique known as **Squid magnetometry** has been developed. Squid stands for superconducting quantum interference device, and it measures very accurately the magnetic field produced when a group of neurons in the brain is active. An important reason for this accuracy is that the skull is completely transparent to magnetic fields, which contrasts with the fact that the bones of the skull reduce the

Maguire et al. (1997) used PET scans to show that taxi drivers' right hippocampus was active when they were recalling routes around London but not when recalling information about landmarks. In a later study, Maguire et al. (2000) actually found that the hippocampus was larger in taxi drivers than in most other people!

BRAIN SCANNING METHODS: A SUMMARY OF STRENGTHS AND LIMITATIONS

	Strengths	Limitations
CAT scan	Can detect damaged parts of the brain in accident victims, as well as tumours and blood clots.	Precise location of damage cannot be determined. Brain function cannot be shown, only structure.
MRI scan	Produces more detailed information and can detect very small tumours.	Brain function cannot be shown, only structure.
Functional MRI	Produces 3D images that provide structural and functional information.	Blood flow follows neuronal activity by about a second. As functional MRI assesses blood flow, it does not give immediate evidence of brain activity.
PET scan	Shows the brain in action and which part is active when different tasks are performed.	Does not provide a moment-by-moment analysis, but shows activity over a 60-second period.
Squid magnetometry	Can produce an accurate image of brain activity because it measures the magnetic field activated neurons.	Extraneous sources of magnetism may interfere with measurements. The Squid has to be kept at extremely low temperatures.

conduction of electrical activity. This means that magnetic signals get through but electrical signals are muffled.

Strengths and limitations.   There are some problems associated with the use of Squid magnetometry. The magnetic field generated by the brain when thinking is about 100 million times weaker than the Earth's magnetic field, and a million times weaker than the magnetic fields around overhead power cables. As a result, it is very hard to prevent irrelevant sources of magnetism from interfering with the measurement of brain activity. Another problem is that superconductivity requires temperatures close to absolute zero, which means that the Squid has to be immersed in liquid helium at four degrees above the absolute zero of –273°C (the equipment, not the person!).

Invasive Techniques
Ablations and lesions

One of the main approaches to finding out the locations of various brain functions is to observe the effects of destroying parts of the brain of a non-human animal. The basic assumption is that whatever abilities are eliminated or greatly impaired after surgery depend on the part of the brain that has been destroyed.

We can draw a distinction between ablations and lesions. **Ablation** involves surgical procedures in which brain tissue is systematically destroyed and often removed. There are various ways in which this can be done. For example, brain tissue can be sucked away through a glass pipette or slender tube attached to a vacuum pump, or it can be removed with a knife, or it can be burned out by inserting electrodes into the brain.

What are some of the problems associated with using studies of non-human animals to draw conclusions about human brain function?

A **lesion** is a wound or injury. When brain lesions are produced surgically, the amount of tissue destroyed is typically less than with ablation. What generally happens is that a hole is drilled in the skull of an anaesthetised animal. An electrode is then inserted through the hole into a specified part of the brain and an electric current is passed through the electrode. The electric current that is used to create a lesion can be either direct current or based on radio frequency.

How is it known that the tip of the electrode is in the correct place? This is usually achieved by using a **stereotaxic** apparatus, which fixes the animal's head and provides the experimenter with precise information about the location of the electrode in three-dimensional space. The stereotaxic apparatus is used in conjunction with a stereotaxic atlas containing detailed drawings of the brain and the distances between different parts.

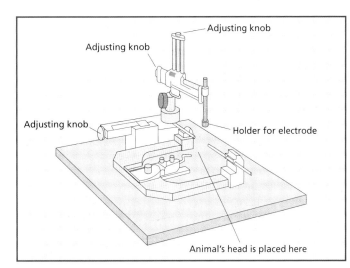

Adjusting knob
Adjusting knob
Adjusting knob
Holder for electrode
Animal's head is placed here

A stereotaxic apparatus, which fixes the animal's head and provides the experimenter with precise information about the location of the electrode in three-dimensional space for the purpose of forming a lesion.

Strengths and limitations

Ablations and lesions can provide very useful information about the functions of different parts of the brain. However, there are various limitations of the surgical approach:

1. It is difficult to interpret the findings because all parts of the brain are interconnected. Suppose, for example, that there are three brain areas A, B, and C adjacent to each other. One particular capacity depends on areas A and C, with information being passed between these two areas through area B. Destruction of area B will stop the animal from showing the capacity, even though that area is not directly involved. By analogy, destroying the plug on your television set will stop the set from working, in spite of the fact that the plug is not responsible for producing television pictures.
2. Surgical destruction of a specific area can lead to fairly widespread reduced functioning in adjacent brain areas. This makes it hard to assess the precise importance of the destroyed area.

3. The reverse can also be true, namely, that if a behavioural function is carried out by more than one region then destruction of only one of them may result in no loss of the function and hence to the false conclusion that that region is not involved in the function. The same sort of problem might arise if there is a rapid recovery of function by it being taken over by another brain region.
4. Researchers sometimes fail to destroy the part or parts of the brain they intended to destroy.
5. There are very serious ethical issues associated with the surgical procedures discussed here. In many countries, a special licence is required before ablations or lesions can be carried out, and there is regular monitoring to ensure that there is adherence to ethical guidelines. It is used much less now than in the past.

Brain damage

We have seen that one way of studying the brain is by causing deliberate damage to part or parts of it, but ablation and lesion techniques are rarely used with humans (except in the occasional instance of psychosurgery, see page 215, and the split-brain operation on page 156). "Natural" incidents where brain damage has occurred can be used instead, where people have been in car accidents, or experienced alcohol abuse, or suffered strokes. The term **cognitive neuropsychology** is used to describe the area of research concerned with trying to understand the workings of the cognitive system by studying brain-damaged patients and the kinds of impairment associated with brain damage. We can use techniques already discussed (e.g., CAT, MRI, functional MRI, PET) to find out exactly which parts of the brain are damaged. Before brain scans were available, one had to wait until a person died so that a post-mortem examination could allow the damaged brain areas to be identified, which limited the amount of knowledge that could be gained from the study of brain damage.

When studying people who have suffered brain damage, how would you determine what their functioning was like before the damage occurred? Why is this important?

Strengths and limitations

Different patients rarely have exactly the same pattern of brain damage. It is often hard to interpret the findings from a series of patients, each of whom differs in terms of brain damage and the pattern of impairment. Moreover, we cannot always know how normal the patient's behaviour was prior to the damage so we can't generalise from such studies to normal behaviour.

Such studies have nevertheless contributed much to our understanding of the functioning of the brain. For example, the studies by Wernicke and Broca, described on pages 153–155, and the split-brain studies by Sperry (see pages 157–158) relied on brain damage that was either natural or deliberate.

Single-unit recording

Single-unit recording is a fine-grain technique developed over 40 years ago to permit study of single neurons. A micro-electrode about one 10,000th of a millimetre in diameter is inserted into the brain to obtain a record of intracellular potentials (electrical charges inside the brain cells). A stereotaxic apparatus (discussed earlier) is used to ensure that the electrode is in the correct position. Single-unit recording is a very sensitive technique, as electrical charges of as little as one-millionth of a volt can be detected.

The best-known application of this technique was by Hubel and Wiesel (1962). They used the single-unit recording technique with cats to study the neurophysiology of vision when visual stimuli were presented. Their findings are discussed in more detail on pages 258–259. In general terms, however, they found that many brain cells respond to very specific aspects of visual stimuli. This discovery influenced many subsequent theories of visual perception.

Strengths and limitations

Since the brain has millions of cells, this method is a very slow way of understanding how the brain works. In addition, since this method involves the destruction of brain tissue

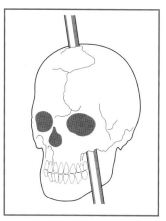

The skull of Phineas Gage shows the hole that was created when an iron rod was forced into his head by an explosion while he was working on a railroad track in the USA in 1848. He survived the injury but experienced a profound change in his personality. The once responsible and mild-mannered man became violent and impulsive. The rod damaged his frontal cortex, supporting the view that this area is responsible for high level control of impulsive behaviour (see Case Study on page 217). This is an example of how naturally occurring brain damage can tell us more about brain function.

(albeit rather small-scale destruction), its use has been limited to non-human animals and such findings are not always applicable to human brain function.

The most important aspect of this method is that it records from *inside* a cell and this is also its biggest limitation as it is impossible to keep the electrode in position for any length of time. Multiple-unit recording uses larger electrodes and records extracellular activity from just a few hundred cells. It is less exact but possibly more reliable.

Penfield and electrical stimulation of the brain

Wilder Penfield (1969) carried out numerous operations on epileptic patients. During these operations, he often stimulated the surface of the brain with a weak electric current. The stimulating electrode sometimes caused the patient to re-experience events from his or her past with great vividness. Penfield (1969, p.165) argued that his findings indicated permanent storage of information: "It is clear that the neuronal action that accompanies each succeeding state of consciousness leaves its permanent imprint on the brain. The imprint, or record, is a trail of facilitation of neuronal connections that can be followed again by an electric current many years later."

Close examination of Penfield's data indicates that his conclusions cannot be accepted. Only 7.7% of his patients showed any evidence of recovery of long-lost memories, and the fact that they were epileptic patients means that we cannot be sure that we would obtain the same findings with other groups of people. Penfield emphasised the vividness and the details of the patients' remembered experiences, but in most cases the recollections were actually rather vague and limited.

From a scientific point of view, it is unfortunate that Penfield did not have any independent verification of the events that his patients claimed to remember during electrical stimulation. There is also an issue as to whether these were true recollections or whether they were merely a synthesis of random firings (in much the same way as argued in the activation-synthesis model of dreaming).

Discussion points

Does Penfield's research raise any ethical concerns?

1. Why do you think psychologists were excited by Penfield's findings?
2. How could we carry out a study that reduces the problems that Penfield encountered?

Electrical stimulation of the brain (ESB)

Electrical stimulation of the brain has shown some results, such as rats learning to press a lever to obtain the reward of a pleasurable electrical stimulus to the hypothalamus. An electrical stimulus differs from a nerve impulse, making it difficult to interpret findings.

Electrical stimulation of the brain simply involves applying a weak electric current to the brain through very small electrodes. The current is lower than the naturally occurring levels of electrical activity in the brain. If this is done carefully, then the brain appears to respond to the current as if it were an actual nerve impulse.

Electrical stimulation by means of electrodes was used by Olds and Milner (1954). They used the technique to demonstrate the "pleasure centre" of the brain. Rats would press a lever several hundred times when rewarded by electrical stimulation of the hypothalamus. In later work, it turned out that self-stimulation effects were most dramatic when the area stimulated was in the medial forebrain bundle in the lateral hypothalamus (Olds & Forbes, 1981).

Strengths and limitations

The main problem with interpreting the findings from studies using electrical stimulation is that an electrical stimulus differs in many ways from nerve impulses. According to Carlson (1994, p.196):

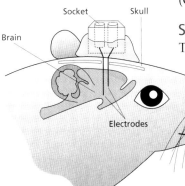

Electrical brain stimulation is probably as natural as attaching ropes to the arms of the members of an orchestra and then shaking all the ropes simultaneously to see what they can play.

More recent methods have attempted to use currents of a more natural level of strength.

Optical dyes

There are various ways in which optical dyes have been used to shed light on cortical functioning, of which the most useful is perhaps the technique developed by Blasdel (1992). Part of the skull of monkeys was removed surgically close to the area of the primary visual cortex. After that, a glass window was placed over the primary visual cortex. An optical dye was then injected into the primary visual cortex. This dye was voltage-sensitive, so that it changed colour when an electrical field passed through it. Visual stimuli were then presented to the monkeys, with those cells that responded to the stimuli changing colour. Video recordings were made so that the pattern of colour changes in the primary visual cortex could be analysed in detail.

One of the ways in which Blasdel used this technique was to compare the responses when a stimulus was presented to only one eye. Some cortical cells responded only to left-eye or right-eye stimulation, whereas others responded equally regardless of the eye to which the stimuli were presented.

Strengths and limitations

One limitation is that this technique can only be used to study the "visible" cortical regions, i.e., those that would be apparent when examining the surface of the brain. One strength is the direct nature of the record obtained.

> **Control versus involvement**
>
> All the methods of studying brain function described here contribute to the debate about the key issue of control versus involvement. When evaluating research we must be aware that it cannot demonstrate for certain whether the part of the brain in question controls a particular behaviour or is merely involved in it.

Localisation of Function in the Cerebral Cortex

What is Localisation?

The brain is responsible for directing and organising our behaviour. Certain areas of the brain are responsible for particular functions, such as vision or language. **Localisation** refers to the extent that any one function is centred on a particular and precise area of the brain. Functions that are not localised are termed "distributed", in other words distributed throughout the brain.

Lashley (1931) studied localisation of function in rats' brains. He trained the rats to learn a maze and then lesioned some parts of their cerebral cortex. Lashley was trying to discover where in the brain memories were stored. To his surprise, what he found was that the effects of a lesion of a given size were very similar in any part of the brain. This led him to put forward the **principle of equipotentiality**, the view that all parts of the **cerebral cortex** had the potential to be equally involved in the storage of memories, i.e., memory is not localised. Lashley's research also led him to propose the principle of **mass action**, according to which the amount of material stored in the cortex is equivalent to the space it occupies. Thus the more cortex you remove, the more severe will be the likely resulting memory deficit. This principle of mass action would suggest that memories are stored throughout the cortex in a distributed fashion. While this may be true for memory in general, it is not true for other functions and it is not true for specific aspects of memory.

How would you explain Lashley's findings?

Anatomical Organisation of the Cerebral Cortex

Before considering the functional organisation of the cerebral cortex (how it is organised by function) we should look briefly at the anatomical organisation (i.e., structured). The human cerebral cortex can be divided up in two main ways. First, it can be divided into four lobes or areas known as the frontal, parietal, temporal, and

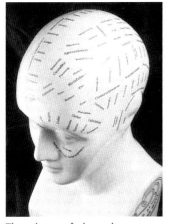

The science of phrenology was popular at the turn of the nineteenth century.

Phrenology

Towards the end of the eighteenth century Franz Joseph Gall, a German physiologist, pioneered the idea that cerebral functions were specialised in particular areas of the brain, i.e., he introduced the notion of localisation. He also created the science of **phrenology**. This "science" was based on the idea that the more a person used certain parts of their brain, the larger those parts became, causing the shape of the skull to be distorted. Gall and his student Surzheim studied vast numbers of skulls and in the end identified 35 faculties that could be identified by their bumps.

However, it was later recognised that the shape of the skull bore little relationship to the brain underneath, thus invalidating the basic premise of phrenology. On the other hand, Gall's ideas about localisation were found to be quite accurate.

occipital. The lobes are anatomical regions named for the bones of the skull lying closest to them. The frontal lobe is at the front of the brain, and the occipital lobe is at the back of the brain. The other two lobes are in the middle of the brain, with the parietal lobe at the top and the temporal lobe below it.

Second, the entire brain is divided into two hemispheres. This has led to a distinction between the left and right cerebral hemispheres. Each of the four lobes is represented in both hemispheres.

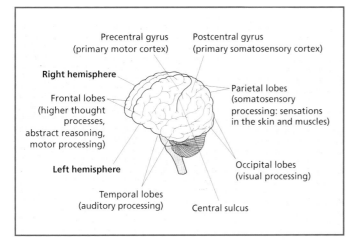

Precentral gyrus (primary motor cortex)
Postcentral gyrus (primary somatosensory cortex)
Right hemisphere
Frontal lobes (higher thought processes, abstract reasoning, motor processing)
Parietal lobes (somatosensory processing: sensations in the skin and muscles)
Left hemisphere
Occipital lobes (visual processing)
Temporal lobes (auditory processing)
Central sulcus

Frontal lobes.   The frontal lobes contain the primary and secondary motor cortex. They are involved in the planning and control of movements. In addition, the frontal lobes are involved in thinking and reasoning and have been linked to aspects of personality.

Parietal lobes.   The parietal lobes contains the primary somatosensory cortex. This area receives information from various senses about temperature, pain, and pressure.

Temporal lobes.   The temporal lobes are involved in auditory processing. The most important form of this processing is speech perception. They are also a major area for the processing of memory information (hence temporal lobe amnesia).

Occipital lobes.   The occipital lobes are mainly concerned with visual processing. If you are struck on the back of the head close to the occipital area, you will see "stars". The occipital lobe plays a key role in vision, but the temporal and parietal lobes are also involved in vision. Indeed, it has been estimated that as much as 50% of the entire cerebral cortex is devoted to visual processing. There is more coverage of the cortical areas involved in visual processing, in Section 8, Perceptual Processes and Development.

What does the phrase "functional organisation" mean?

CASE STUDY: *Computers and the Brain*

Computer technology is developing at a very rapid pace, and it seems now that not only are some computers small enough to fit in your pocket, but the physical movement necessary to interact with the machine may soon be replaced with mental dexterity. Researchers in America have been working on a computer that will be controlled by a person's brain alone. This is not science fiction: the device is being used by a 57-year-old man who is paralysed as a result of a stroke. Tiny implants (glass cones containing miniature electrodes) have been placed in the man's motor cortex, where nerves have been encouraged to grow through them using chemicals extracted from the man's knees. When the nerves grow, they connect to the electrodes, allowing the computer to detect brain signals via a transmitter located just under the man's skull. The man can control the computer cursor just by thinking.

According to Pritchard (1998) this man is now "able to use the system to control a computer cursor to pick phrases on a screen, and communicate with the outside world". At the moment, movement of the cursor is limited to simple up and down, right and left commands, but the benefits to people with severely restricted movement should not be underestimated. This research is just one of the growing number of projects looking at ways in which we can communicate mentally with computers, but what ethical questions might studies like this raise?

Functional Organisation of the Cerebral Cortex

In the anatomical descriptions one can see that each lobe of the cerebral cortex is associated with particular functions. The box on the right summarises this. However, none of the four lobes is devoted exclusively to one function and some functions are represented in more than one lobe. Therefore we can also consider the functional organisation, as distinct from the anatomical organisation, of the cerebral cortex.

It is as well to remember that some motor and sensory functions, as well as other functions, are controlled below the level of the cortex, at a **subcortical** level, for example by the spinal cord—which can explain why it is true that headless chickens do run about!

> ## A summary of the functional organisation of the cerebral cortex
>
> The four lobes of the cerebral cortex differ somewhat in terms of what they do. Robert Sternberg (1995, p.93) provided a good summary of their functions:
>
> higher thought processes, such as abstract reasoning and motor processing, occur in the frontal lobe, somatosensory processing (sensations in the skin and muscles of the body) in the parietal lobe, auditory processing in the temporal lobe, and visual processing in the occipital lobe.

The Primary Motor Area

The control of muscles is extremely complex, which is not surprising when you consider the extent to which animals are capable of often highly precise and highly co-ordinated muscle activities. Muscles are directly controlled by **motor neurons** (a nerve is made up of a collection of neurons). These neurons originate from the spinal column, which means that some of them are very long—the motor neurons that enable you to wiggle your toes are more than a metre in length. From the spinal column the neurons pass up to the **medulla oblongata** in the hindbrain, and finally to the **primary motor cortex** which is located in the frontal lobe of the cerebral cortex.

Penfield and Boldrey (1937) studied the primary motor cortex by applying electrical stimulation to particular regions. They found that stimulation of different regions in this area resulted in twitching of certain body parts and were able to form a topographical map of the primary motor cortex, as shown on page 148. It is perhaps amazing to see that every area of the body has a corresponding representation in the brain. This map shows that some regions of the body are over-represented, such as the fingers and the mouth. When we use the phrase "over-represented" we are not suggesting that there are more neurons than necessary, simply that there are more than one might expect given the size of the physical area. The over-representation, or disproportionate representation, reflects the fact that these areas require and are capable of greater fine motor control.

All regions of the body are represented in the primary motor cortex and for almost all of these motor control is **contralateral**, i.e., the right hemisphere controls the left side of the body and vice versa.

As techniques for studying the brain have become more precise, researchers have discovered that the primary motor cortex consists of many parallel bands of neurons rather than just one band. Each band is topographically organised. Researchers have also found that neurons need to be activated in several adjacent strips in order for a muscle to be activated. This explains why damage to just

The **primary motor area** is responsible for highly co-ordinated movement, such as when an animal or bird goes after its prey, like this mountain lion.

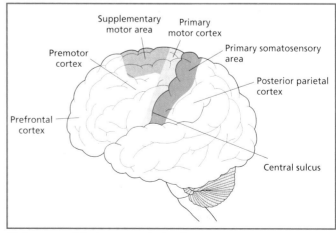

Motor areas of the human cerebral cortex.

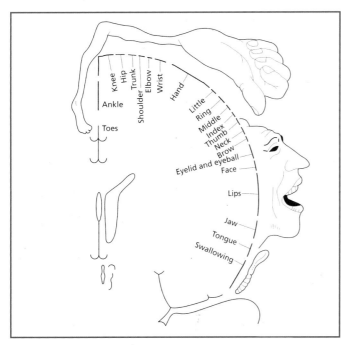

A **cross-section** through the primary motor cortex showing its topographical organisation—how different regions correspond to different parts of the body.

one set of neurons rarely prevents movement in a corresponding body region. However, widespread damage to this area, through a stroke or other brain incident, is likely to result in lasting paralysis.

Initiating movement

When a person wishes to engage in a motor activity, such as writing their name, this activity starts in the frontal lobe, just in front of the primary motor cortex. The first step is to form an intention—an activity that takes place in the prefrontal area.

The next step in this process is co-ordinated by the secondary motor cortex, which lies between the prefrontal area and the primary motor cortex. The secondary motor cortex consists of the supplementary motor area (SMA) and the premotor cortex. The SMA is involved in co-ordinating motor responses. Monkeys with lesions in this area are still able to reach and grasp, but they cannot do this in an organised way (Brinkman, 1984). The premotor cortex is used mainly when sensory information is used to determine motor responses. This was found by Colebatch et al. (1991). PET scans revealed that the premotor cortex was active when the participants made hand movements in time to a metronome, but not when they made the same hand movements without a metronome present. Both the SMA and the premotor cortex exert **bilateral** control in order that you are able to co-ordinate both sides of your body simultaneously.

The third step is that messages are passed to the appropriate areas of the primary motor cortex to activate the actual muscles. This three-step model is called the **hierarchical model**. Supporting evidence has only recently been gathered using sophisticated imagining techniques. For example, Roland (1993) showed that if an individual engages in a rather simple activity such as wiggling a finger, then only the primary motor cortex is active (on the side opposite to the wiggling finger). If the individual engages in a more complex activity, such as touching the ends of each finger with the thumb, then both the SMA and prefrontal cortex show increased activity, as well as the primary motor cortex. Even just imagining doing the task results in SMA and prefrontal activity.

It may be worth noting here that this account focuses only on the role of the cortex in movement. At a subcortical level the cerebellum is very important in organising the sensory information that guides movement.

Responding to sensory stimulation

Motor activity is initiated by intention or sensory activity. Which do you think is more important?

Some motor activity is the direct result of sensory input rather than intention. In this case the posterior parietal cortex provides sensory information to the SMA and the premotor cortex. We will now consider the way that sensory information is processed.

The Primary Sensory Areas

Sensory information is transmitted to the cerebral cortex. Visual information is sent to the **visual cortex**, auditory information is sent to the **auditory cortex**, and information from other body regions (such as that for touch, temperature, pressure, and taste) is transmitted to the **somatosensory area**.

Primary somatosensory area

Why do you think that the primary motor and somatosensory areas lie next to each other?

This is located in the parietal area, just behind (posterior to) the primary motor cortex and, like the primary motor cortex, is a thin strip on which the areas of the body are

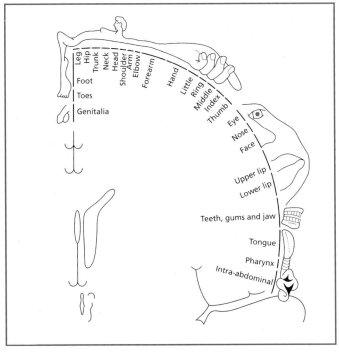

A cross-section through the primary somatosensory cortex showing its topographical organisation.

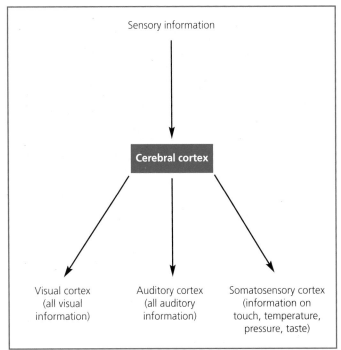

The primary sensory areas.

topographically represented (see figure above left). If a region of this strip is electrically stimulated the result will be the sensation of being touched on the corresponding region of the body. There are contralateral connections in the somatosensory area, as with the primary motor cortex.

The somatosensory cortex, again like the primary motor cortex, has areas that are disproportionately represented and this differs from animal to animal. For example, cats have relatively large inputs from their whiskers and tail. The somatosensory cortex is also divided into strips, each receiving distinct combinations of somatosensory input.

■ Activity: Ask someone else to shut their eyes while you touch them with either one sharp point or two sharp points (about 0.5cm apart when there are two) simultaneously. You can do this either on the person's back or on their index finger. Ask them to say whether one or two points were touched on the skin. Two are easily detected on the finger but only one is detected on the back. This demonstrates the different sensitivities of different parts of the body.

Primary visual area

We have seen that the occipital lobe houses the primary visual cortex. This area of the brain receives electrical signals from both eyes in a contralateral manner (right eye sends information to left visual cortex) and an ipsilateral manner (right eye sends signal to right visual cortex). In fact the right eye does not send all information to the *left visual cortex*, only the information from the right visual field. The information from the right visual field of the left eye also is sent to the *left visual cortex*. The same is true for the left visual fields of both eyes and the right visual cortex.

This is important in depth perception because our two eyes are separated and therefore receive slightly different inputs. The **binocular disparity** that is produced offers useful information for depth perception (see also pages 273 and 293–294). The right hemisphere can compare the inputs from the left and right eye for the right visual field and therefore detect the slight differences that signal depth.

Primary visual cortex

The primary visual cortex is also called visual area 1 (V1) or the striate cortex. V1 is responsible for the early stages of visual perception. Hubel and Wiesel (1979) first identified the cells of V1 by placing microelectrodes in certain brain cells of both cats

Compare the topographical maps for the motor and somatosensory areas. Which parts of the body are given relatively more representation in each area?

and monkeys. The animals' were shown pictures of lines with different orientations so the researchers could determine how the brain reacted to these lines. They recorded the electrical activity of individual cells in the V1 area and demonstrated the existence of simple and complex cells. *Simple cells* respond most to dark bars in a light field, light bars in a dark field, or to straight edges between areas of light and dark. They respond to stimuli of a particular orientation. *Complex cells* resemble simple cells in that they respond to straight-line stimuli that are presented in a particular orientation. However, complex cells respond to larger areas of vision, and a majority of complex cells respond to stimulation of either eye, whereas nearly all simple cortical cells respond only to stimulation of one eye (left or right). There are many more complex cells than simple cells. There are also *hypercomplex cells* that respond to groups of complex cells and detect features such as corners. (See pages 258–259 for further details.)

Subsequent research has found that the situation is more complex than Hubel and Wiesel first described. It seems that the cells of V1 are divided into modules. Each module comprises two long thin box-like areas, one receiving input from the right eye and one receiving input from the same region of the left eye. In each module there is a central core called the **blob**, which is sensitive to colour. The region around the blob (the **inter-blob region**) is sensitive to orientation, as well as some movement and binocular disparity.

Blindsight

The primary visual cortex appears to act as a kind of gateway to later visual processing. After V1, information is passed to at least 30 different cortical areas (Stirling, 2000). This would lead us to expect that patients whose primary visual cortex has been damaged through injury or disease should be unable to see. In fact, what happens is more complex. Such patients report being blind, but some of them are nevertheless able to perform visual tasks. For example, there was the case of DB, who denied that he could see anything in his left visual field. According to Weiskrantz et al. (1974, p.726), in spite of that

> *(a) he could reach for visual stimuli [in his left field] with considerable accuracy; (b) could differentiate the orientation of a vertical line from a horizontal or diagonal line; (c) could differentiate the letters "X" and "O".*

How might one investigate blindsight?

This phenomenon is known as **blindsight**. It probably occurs because some information passes directly from subcortical structures to the secondary visual cortex without going through the primary visual cortex. This allows patients with blindsight to perform simple visual tasks, but is insufficient to produce conscious awareness.

Primary auditory area

The primary auditory area lies in the temporal lobe. Most processing is contralateral (the left ear passes signals to the right auditory cortex) but some processing is ipsilateral (the left ear also sends signals to the left auditory cortex). This contralateral and ipsilateral input means that the sound heard in the right and the left ear can be compared, which is important in identifying the direction of sound because the ear that is further away from the sound will have a slightly delayed input.

Penfield (1969) tested responses to electrical stimulation in this area in conscious human participants, using implanted electrodes. He found that people would think they were hearing the ringing of a doorbell or a sound like a car starting when the primary auditory cortex was stimulated.

The primary auditory cortex is organised in vertical functional columns. All of the neurons within a vertical column respond mainly to sounds of similar frequency. Regions towards the front of the primary auditory cortex respond to higher frequencies, whereas those towards the back respond to lower frequencies. The most common effect of damage to the auditory cortex in humans is word deafness. This involves difficulty in perceiving speech and in identifying any sounds that are presented briefly.

CASE STUDY: *Graham's Blindness*

Thirty-four years ago a child ran in front of a man's car causing a serious accident. The car delivered a near-fatal blow to the back of the driver's neck resulting in brain damage. The driver of the vehicle, known to scientists as "GY" but otherwise known as Graham, has a very unusual brain. Graham is one of the few people in the world who experience "blindsight".

The car accident caused Graham to be totally blind on the right side of his visual field. He sees nothing to the right of his focal point with either eye. However, when cued by experimenters, he can still use that blind field to accomplish tasks you'd think of as requiring sight. Graham can reach out to grab an object, discriminate between lines at different angles to each other, and locate spots of light on a screen—even if he says he sees nothing at all. To him, it usually feels like guesswork. But clearly, even if Graham himself is guessing, his nervous system "knows" what's out there. In other words, Graham sees in his blind field—but unconsciously.

Actually, it's more complicated than that. If a bright light is flashed rapidly enough, Graham does become aware of something, usually "a dark shadow". And when objects or lights move fast enough, Graham experiences a strange sensation he can only describe as something akin to pure movement—motion stripped of form, colour or depth.

Most of us think of sight as a sense that automatically involves and requires consciousness, often of a rich and subjective kind. But blindsight researchers know different. Having studied people like Graham for years, they know that not all visual skills lead to or require consciousness. In fact, the opposite is true, and more and more of these skills are being uncovered all the time. Just after the accident, doctors feared that Graham would die or suffer massive brain damage. Amazingly, however, the impact of the head wound was confined to nerves in the left half of a segment of tissue, called V1, at the back of the brain. V1 is one of the main reception sites in the brain for signals from the retina. It also plays a key role in normal vision—hence Graham's right-sided blindness. Graham knew nothing of his blindsight until the late 1970s when researchers at Imperial College in London, led by the late Keith Ruddock, began testing him. Then, as now, many scientists had a hard time accepting that someone could respond, often with stunning accuracy, to visual stimuli they denied being able to see. Nor were the scientists alone in their doubt. Graham recalls, "For several years, I thought I must be cheating."

But equipment that tracked the direction of his gaze proved he wasn't sneaking a look with his good field. And today, careful experimenters don't even let blindsight participants say what they can and can't see—a subjective account that could be open to bias. Instead, the experimenters measure perception directly by monitoring changes in the pupils of the participants' eyes, which contract slightly in response to visual stimuli. But even if the authenticity of blindsight is now unassailable, researchers are still divided over how to interpret Graham's strange vision. What, in the end, is blindsight really telling us about the nature of visual perception and consciousness? Some researchers have suggested that blindsight is little more than a weak version of normal sight, akin perhaps to peripheral vision.

According to this view, what the participants' brains have lost is not so much the ability to produce visual consciousness as the ability to process basic visual information. Signals from the retina follow the usual pathways through the brain: they just seldom gather the requisite strength. But this explanation is rejected by Larry Weiskrantz, an Oxford psychologist who has done more than anyone to raise the scientific profile of blindsight in the past 25 years. He insists, "Blindsight is not just having weak eyesight." After all, in one visual field Graham is aware and the other he isn't, yet in both fields he can achieve stunning levels of performance. On some tasks, such as detecting a pattern of light and dark stripes, he sometimes does even better in his blind field

than in his normal one. And in a detailed analysis of Graham's blindsight skills it was found to be impossible to simulate his signal detection abilities using a model based on degraded normal vision. This distinction is significant.

If Graham's blindsight is just weakened normal vision, there is no need to argue that what is specifically lacking in his brain is visual consciousness: he simply lacks sight. And if he and similar participants just lack sight, it becomes less obviously crucial for researchers to distinguish visual awareness from basic visual perception in their theories of vision—and more reasonable for them to lump consciousness in with basic perception instead and say that they're both produced by the same brain mechanisms. Instead, according to Weiskrantz and his colleagues, blindsight subjects do not lack the ability to detect things such as wavelengths, but rather visual consciousness itself—the redness of red, and so on. If Weiskrantz is right, anyone who thinks simulating such basic perceptual skills alone on a computer will eventually produce a conscious machine is being rather optimistic. Instead, something else is required. No one knows what this second ingredient is, but Weiskrantz and others believe that brain scans of participants like Graham can at least provide clues. The idea is simple. Put someone like Graham in an fMRI brain scanner—designed to look for brain function rather than structure—and get him to perform a visual task in his blind field. In fact, get him to do the task twice, first in his unconscious seeing mode and then in his conscious seeing mode. Subtract the brain scans and the result should tell you whether—and how—brain activity differs between vision with and vision without awareness.

Of course, there's more to it than that, but experiments like this are now under way in several labs, and so far the results seem to support the idea that aware vision is not just a "more intense" version of unaware vision. In Graham, for example, "conscious seeing" seems to produce a different pattern of brain activation compared with "unconscious seeing". There is more activity at the front of the cortex and less in the lower regions when Graham is aware of something in his blind field. There is activity deep down in a midbrain structure, the superior colliculus.

And that second finding helps to confirm the answer to a different question of how blindsight happens in the brain. If Graham's eyes cannot get signals to the V1 area that is the main reception site for right field vision, how does all that visual information guiding his blindsight "guessing" get into the cortex? The answer is along other, secondary routes that can bypass V1. And one of these goes via the superior colliculus.

Weiskrantz believes this secondary pathway is to some extent operating in all of us, although its activity seems to be more fully developed in people with cortical blindness. In other words, we may not realise it, but we probably all have the pathways used in blindsight. "It would be a waste of effort for the brain to spend time making events conscious that don't really require it," Weiskrantz points out. "There are lots of times in life where we carry out visual discriminations without any awareness at all. It's when we're going on automatic pilot."

After over 20 years of participating in experiments to determine the nature and limitations of his blindsight, Graham would like to know the answer to one question. That is, "If I'm so good at discriminating wavelengths, orientations, shapes and movement in my blind field, why can't I see in it?" Perhaps one day someone will know, but in the meantime they will have to answer another question: What is the nature of consciousness?

Adapted from D. Concar, Out of sight, into mind. *New Scientist*, 5 September 1988.

Association Areas

We have considered how primary motor and sensory functions are localised to particular lobes of the cerebral cortex (frontal includes motor function, parietal includes somatosensory function, temporal includes auditory function, occipital includes visual function). However, these localised functions take up relatively little cortical space in the lobes, leaving large areas of the cortex without an apparently clear function. In fact their function is to associate and integrate information. Originally it was thought that such "**association areas**" only involved links between motor and sensory functions because of the proximity of the association areas to the primary sensory and motor regions. However, later it was found that in reality relatively little sensorimotor integration takes place, and that most association cortex is actually involved in higher-order processing. We will start by looking at motor and sensory association.

Motor and sensory association areas

As we have seen, parts of the frontal lobes are concerned with planning movement and co-ordinating sensory and motor input. These functions are part of the motor association areas of the cortex. There are also motor association areas in the parietal, temporal, and occipital lobes. This is supported by evidence from people with brain damage. People with damage to certain areas of the parietal lobe can describe what they see but have trouble using this information to guide their movements. For example, they would have difficulty reaching out to grasp an object. Individuals with damage to parts of the occipital lobe can't describe the shape and location of objects but can reach out and grasp such objects. This illustrates two different kinds of motor association.

The visual association cortex is concerned with movement, colour perception, object recognition, and shape analysis, among other things. As we have already noted there are more than 30 areas of the cortex involved with this processing. One such area is in the temporal cortex where shape analysis takes place. Individuals with damage to this area may suffer from **visual agnosia**. They can see but fail to be able to recognise objects. For example, Warrington and Taylor (1978) showed patients pictures of a rolled-up umbrella, an open umbrella, and a walking stick and asked them to find a match. They matched the folded umbrella and the walking stick because they looked similar, demonstrating a failure to recognise the function of the objects—the two umbrellas made a better match. Another example of visual agnosia is described in the Case Study below.

CASE STUDY: *The Man Who Mistook His Wife for a Hat*

Mr P was "a musician of distinction, well-known for many years as a singer, and then at the local School of Music, as a teacher. It was here, in relation to his students, that certain strange problems were first observed. Sometimes a student would present himself, and Mr P would not recognise him; or specifically, would not recognise his face. The moment the student spoke, he would be recognised by his voice. Such incidents multiplied, causing embarrassment, perplexity, fear—and, sometimes, comedy."

"At first these odd mistakes were laughed off as jokes, not least by Mr P himself … His musical powers were as dazzling as ever; he did not feel ill … The notion of there being 'something the matter' did not emerge until some three years later, when diabetes developed. Well aware that diabetes could affect his eyes, Mr P consulted an ophthalmologist, who took a careful history, and examined his eyes closely. 'There's nothing the matter with your eyes,' the doctor concluded. 'But there is trouble with the visual parts of your brain. You don't need my help, you must see a neurologist.'"

And so Mr P went to see Oliver Sacks who found him quite normal except for the fact that, when they talked, Mr P faced him with his *ears* rather than his eyes. Another episode alerted Sacks to the problem. He asked Mr P to put his shoe back on.

"'Ach,' he said, 'I had forgotten the shoe', adding *sotto voce*, 'The shoe? The shoe?' He seemed baffled.

He continued to look downwards, though not at the shoe, with an intense but misplaced concentration. Finally his gaze settled on his foot: 'That is my shoe, yes?'

Did he mis-hear? Did he mis-see?

'My eyes,' he explained, and put his hand to his foot. '*This* is my shoe, no?'

'No that is not. That is your foot. *There* is your shoe.'

'Ah! I thought it was my foot.'

Was he joking? Was he mad? Was he blind?"

Oliver Sacks helped Mr P put on his shoe and gave him some further tests. His eyesight was fine, for example he had no difficulty seeing a pin on the floor. But when he was shown a picture of the Sahara desert and asked to describe it, he invented guesthouses, terraces, and tables with parasols. Sacks must have looked aghast but Mr P seemed to think he had done rather well and decided it was time to end the examination. He reached out for his hat, and took hold of his wife's head, and tried to lift it off. He apparently had mistaken his wife's head for his hat.

The condition Mr P suffered from is called visual agnosia and results from brain damage of some kind.

From Oliver Sacks (1985) *The man who mistook his wife for a hat*, Picador.

Thinking and language

The motor association cortex directs intention and planning in relation to movement, as we have seen. The association area in the frontal lobe is also generally involved with intention and planning, as well as problem solving and memory, and so forms part of an animal's general ability to think. The case of Phineas Gage, described on pages 216 and 217, illustrates how frontal lobe damage affects the ability to form intentions and control impulses.

Do you recall which kind of association area accounts for the greatest amount of cortex?

The frontal association area is also involved in language, as are other association areas in the temporal lobe. We will consider two important language association areas, called Broca's area and Wernicke's area, as examples of localisation of function in the cortex. It is worth pointing out, however, that localisation of function is not always as clear cut as it may appear, at least for some regions of cortex.

Broca's area: Speech production

In the 1860s, Paul Broca studied patients suffering from what is now known as Broca's aphasia or expressive aphasia, such as one called "Tan" (see the Case Study below). These patients have great difficulty in speaking, and their spoken language tends to be very slow and lacking in fluency. In contrast, their ability to comprehend speech is relatively good, but typically worse than that of someone without brain damage. Patients with Broca's or expressive aphasia have three kinds of problems with speech production (although there are great individual differences in terms of their relative severity):

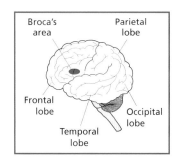

- Anomia: difficulty in finding the right word.
- Agrammatism: difficulty in speaking in a grammatical way.
- Articulation problems: many words are mispronounced.

Broca (1861) argued that expressive aphasia is caused by a lesion in the frontal association cortex, in a region of the brain now known as Broca's area. This is would be an example of a localised function in the cortex.

The term "basal ganglia" applies to a group of structures: the caudate nucleus, the putamen, the globus pallidus, the substantia nigra, and the subthalamic nucleus.

Broca was partially correct, in that Broca's area is definitely involved in expressive aphasia. However, expressive aphasia is generally only found when brain damage extends beyond Broca's area into adjacent parts of the frontal lobe and subcortical white matter (Damasio, 1989). Therefore, the function is not quite as simply localised as first appears.

Why did Broca underestimate the area of brain involved in expressive aphasia? The area affected by brain damage is often larger than the area in which there is obvious tissue damage. For example, PET scans of aphasic patients with subcortical damage to the **basal ganglia** have revealed that there can be impaired functioning of apparently "undamaged" parts of the frontal cortex (Metter, 1991). Further evidence that the basal ganglia can be involved in expressive aphasia was obtained by Damasio, Eslinger, and Adams (1984). Patients with damage to the basal ganglia showed most of the symptoms associated with expressive aphasia.

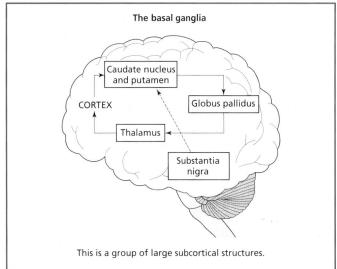

The basal ganglia

This is a group of large subcortical structures.

Wernicke's area: Comprehension

A few years after Broca, Carl Wernicke studied stroke patients who were able to speak, but who had very poor ability to understand language. These patients had suffered damage to a part of the left hemisphere in the middle and back areas of the superior temporal gyrus (a

CASE STUDY: *"Tan"*

Paul Broca's first and most famous neurological patient was "Tan": so-called because the only syllables he could utter were "tan-tan". Broca found that Tan's understanding of speech seemed relatively intact. Broca was curious about why this should be, and when Tan died, Broca performed a post-mortem and found damage in what is now known as Broca's area of the brain. Tan's brain is embalmed and preserved in a museum in Paris, and the damaged area is clearly visible.

Can you think why we have to be careful in interpreting the findings from brain-damaged patients?

little above and behind the left ear). This later came to be known as Wernicke's area. Patients with Wernicke's or receptive aphasia speak fluently but in an almost meaningless way. Try to guess what was being described by a patient with receptive aphasia who was studied by Geschwind (1979): "Mother is away here working her work to get better, but when she's looking the two boys looking in the other part. She's working another time." In fact, the patient was looking at a picture of a woman with two boys behind her stealing biscuits.

As a result, we cannot test the ability of receptive aphasics to understand speech by asking them to respond verbally. One approach is to ask patients with Wernicke's aphasia to point to specified objects, a task that they find very difficult. Perhaps surprisingly, most patients with Wernicke's aphasia do not seem to realise that they have severe language problems.

Patients with Wernicke's aphasia typically have a number of language problems, with the severity of each problem varying from patient to patient:

- Pure word deafness: spoken words cannot be recognised even though non-speech sounds (e.g., a bird's call) are recognised.
- Word comprehension: difficulties in understanding word meanings.
- Thought expression: difficulties in producing meaningful speech that expresses the speaker's thoughts.

Conduction aphasia

We have discussed Broca's area and Wernicke's area separately. However, these two areas are joined by a bridge of nerve fibres called the **arcuate fasciculus**. Damage to this set of nerve fibres produces what is known as **conduction aphasia**. Patients with conduction aphasia are generally able to understand speech and to speak in a fluent and meaningful way. However, they find it very hard to repeat nonwords or unfamiliar words they have heard.

The Wernicke–Geschwind connectionist model for (a) speaking a heard word and (b) speaking a written word.

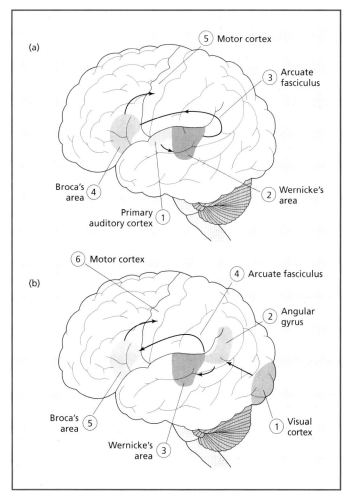

(a)
5 Motor cortex
3 Arcuate fasciculus
Broca's area 4
Primary auditory cortex 1
2 Wernicke's area

(b)
6 Motor cortex
4 Arcuate fasciculus
2 Angular gyrus
Broca's area 5
Wernicke's area 3
1 Visual cortex

The localisation of language

The Wernicke–Geschwind model is an attempt to outline the areas of the cortex involved in language. According to this model, seven areas of the brain are involved in language processing: primary visual cortex, angular gyrus, primary auditory cortex, Wernicke's area, the arcuate fasciculus, Broca's area, and primary motor cortex. Understanding speech involves auditory signals proceeding from the primary auditory cortex to Wernicke's area, whereas reading aloud involves first of all the primary visual cortex, followed by the angular gyrus (which produces an auditory code for each word), followed by Wernicke's area. In speech production, information proceeds from Wernicke's area to the arcuate fasciculus, and then on to Broca's area, followed by the primary motor cortex, and then the speech muscles.

This model is partially correct, but suffers from three main problems. First, some of the relevant brain areas are less important than is suggested by the model. Lesions that destroy all of Broca's area or most of the arcuate fasciculus typically fail to produce permanent speech difficulties (Rasmussen & Milner, 1975), and much of Wernicke's area can be removed without causing any lasting language impairments (Ojemann, 1979). Second, other areas seem to be involved. Only the left hemisphere is included in the Wernicke–Geschwind model, but PET scans of participants performing various language tasks showed much activity in the right hemisphere (Petersen et al., 1989). Third, the model is too neat and tidy. For example, the processes involved in reading familiar words are usually different from those involved in reading unfamiliar words, but this is not allowed for in the model.

Studies of brain-damaged patients have revealed much about the locations of different speech-related functions. However, there is an important limitation of most of the work on brain-damaged patients. All aphasias are syndromes. A syndrome consists of various symptoms found together in numerous patients. Syndrome-based approaches exaggerate the similarities among different patients allegedly suffering from the same syndrome, and often minimise the similarities among patients claimed to have different syndromes. This makes it difficult to claim an accurate link between a syndrome and a location in the brain.

Wernicke's area is part of the auditory association cortex, and so it seems reasonable to assume that this area is involved in pure word deafness or the inability to recognise words. Studies on Wernicke's patients using CAT and MRI scans have provided support for this assumption (Carlson, 1994). However, pure word deafness can also be caused by damage to the primary auditory cortex (which is adjacent to Wernicke's area) or by damage to the axons conveying information from the primary auditory cortex to Wernicke's area.

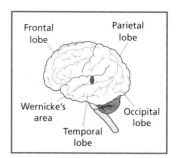

Localised Versus Distributed Function

The concept of localisation is that certain functions are restricted to specific regions of the brain. The findings discussed in this Unit support this idea insofar as there clearly are many functions that are localised.

Earlier in this Section we considered Lashley's ideas that it was the amount of brain tissue, rather than specific locations, which mattered most. It would be difficult to explain his findings if localisation of function is true. The solution to this apparent contradiction lies in the concept of **distributed control**. The fact that there are so many interconnections between different localised functions means that damage to one specific region rarely results in a complete loss of function. This is a compromise between a strict localisation view and Lashley's concept of equipotentiality because it means that there is cortical specialisation but the interconnections mean that no one area has overall control.

This kind of distributed control can be seen in visual processing (remember blindsight) and also in language. It is also well exemplified in memory functions, the behaviour that interested Lashley. Research has indicated many localised cortical and subcortical centres for memory. For example, Tulving (1989) found that when participants were using their episodic memory parts of the frontal cortex were active, whereas semantic memory was associated with a high level of activation in the posterior regions of the cortex. Maguire et al. (1997) found that the right hippocampus (another subcortical structure) was active when taxi drivers were recalling routes around London but not when recalling information about landmarks. The fact that memory is governed by such a vast array of different locations means that it would not make sense to regard this as a localised function, though individual facets of memory may be localised.

Why are some functions more localised than others? This is probably related to the complexity of the system. The more complex a behaviour, the more the function is distributed. In fact, as research into brain activity has progressed we have realised just how complicated—and distributed—most behavioural functions are. This could be because complexity and importance go together; having a function present in many areas would mean that if there was brain damage, only some of the brain, and therefore some of the function, would be lost.

One final point should be made about localisation, which is the question of how much these functions are "hard-wired". The advantage of localised function is that it enables complex systems to function rather than having to be "wired" from scratch in each individual. The disadvantage is that brain damage may result in a permanent loss of the function because it cannot simply start again somewhere else. However, research has progressively shown that the brain and its neurons do have some degree of adaptability. For example, Mogilner et al. (1993) studied individuals with syndactyly, a congenital disorder where the fingers are fused together. Electrical activity was recorded before and after surgery to separate the fingers. Prior to surgery the cortical map of the individuals with syndactyly was quite different from normal brains but after surgery there was clear reorganisation in the brain. This suggests that the cortical mapping of the somatosensory area is not as "hard-wired" as was once thought but that the brain responds to new inputs. This is important research because it provides useful insights into the treatment of individuals who have lost function after nerve damage, suggesting that there is some possibility of recovery.

Given these advantages and disadvantages, what functions are more likely to be localised and/or "hard-wired"?

Lateralisation of Function in the Cerebral Cortex

So far we have discussed the cerebral cortex as if its two **hemispheres** or halves are very similar in their functioning. However, this is by no means the case. There is much hemispheric specialisation, meaning that the two hemispheres differ in their functions. This produces numerous situations in which there is cerebral dominance, with one hemisphere being mainly responsible for processing information in that situation.

The term "**lateralisation**" refers to the fact that one side or hemisphere has a greater role in a particular function ("lateral" means "side"). The term "**hemispheric asymmetry**" is also used to describe this laterality—the fact that the hemispheres are not the same or symmetrical. The two best known examples of hemisphere asymmetry are related to language and **handedness**.

Much of what we know about hemispheric specialisation and cerebral dominance comes from the study of split-brain patients, so we will consider these first. Then we will look at the organisation of language in the brain, handedness, and finally at another hemisphere asymmetry, emotion.

Split-brain Studies

"Split-brain" refers to an operation that is performed to divide the human brain into two quite separate halves. In this operation the **corpus callosum** is cut. The corpus callosum is a collection of about 250 million axons connecting sites in one hemisphere with those in the other. There are two other pathways connecting the two hemispheres, collectively called commissures, but the corpus callosum is far more important in terms of the rapid transmission of information from one hemisphere to another—the brain's own information super-highway!

The split-brain operation has been performed on individuals suffering from severe epilepsy, a condition where electrical activity in the brain causes seizures ("fits"). In most epileptics these can be reasonably well controlled by drugs. In cases where this isn't possible, a potential solution would be to sever the connections between the right and left hemisphere to limit the electrical storm. Indeed, it does work—epileptics suffered less severe seizures after they were operated on.

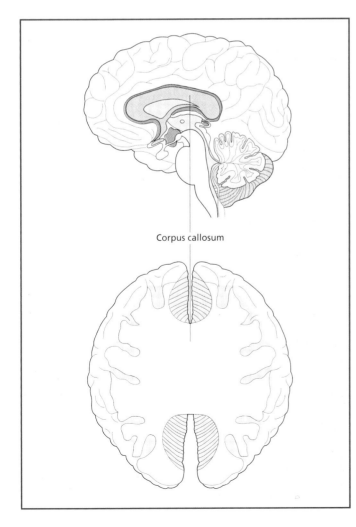

Corpus callosum

One brain, two minds

A press release from Fredric Schiffer of McLean Hospital in Massachusetts on 8 October 1998 described how new evidence supported one of the most important findings of split-brain research: that each hemisphere of the brain has a mind of its own. He studied two split-brain patients whose right and left hemispheres appeared to have distinct opinions and feelings. For instance, Patient A's left brain reported no anger toward bullies who had tormented him during childhood. His right brain, however, was still "extremely" upset by those early experiences. Patient A's two minds were in much closer agreement about less emotional topics. When asked about his perception of himself, Patient B's two minds held different opinions. His right hemisphere perceived him as good; his left hemisphere saw him as inadequate.

Schiffer hypothesises that in many people, as in Patient A, one mind may be less mature and more disturbed by past trauma than the other. This can give rise to feelings of anxiety or depression to self-destructive behaviours, ranging from procrastination to addiction.

Adapted from http://www.mclean.harvard.edu/PublicAffairs/2brain.htm

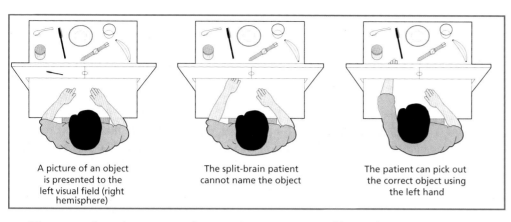

A picture of an object is presented to the left visual field (right hemisphere)

The split-brain patient cannot name the object

The patient can pick out the correct object using the left hand

Why is a split-brain patient unable to name an object presented to the left visual field?

However, there is a cost to these patients in terms of brain functioning. It was not initially realised that cutting the corpus callosum would cause any problems for split-brain patients because when this condition occurs naturally people are able to learn sufficient coping mechanisms to function reasonably well. Psychologists studying split-brain patients have recorded some intriguing data that highlight the differences between the left and right hemispheres and which also raise philosophical questions about the brain and mind. Most of the studies involved presenting visual stimuli in such a way that some information went to the left hemisphere and some information to the right hemisphere. The anatomy of the visual pathways is complex. The fibres from the outer half of each retina go to the same hemisphere, whereas those from the inner half cross over and go to the opposite hemisphere (see illustration on page 275). As a result, information presented to the left half of each retina will proceed only to the left hemisphere, and information presented to the right half of each retina will go only to the right hemisphere. This provides researchers with an exciting opportunity to study what happens in each hemisphere. Roger Sperry has been one of the main figures in this area, conducting studies from the 1950s until his death in 1980. You can read about his findings in the two Key Studies that follow.

Split-brain behaviour

Sperry (1968) studied the behaviour of a group of individuals who suffered from severe epileptic seizures, so severe that their seizures could not be controlled by drugs. A commissurotomy (severing the cerebral commissures and the corpus callosum) was performed to help their epilepsy and this provided an opportunity to study the effects of hemispheric deconnection (split-brain) on behaviour.

The diagram above shows how split-brain patients were tested. The patient covered one eye and was instructed to look at a fixed point in the centre of a projection screen. Slides were projected on to either the right or left of the screen at a very high speed, one picture every 0.1 seconds or faster. Below the screen there was a gap so that the participant could reach objects but not see his or her hands.

The basic findings were:

- If a picture was first shown to the left visual field, the participant did not recognise it when the same picture appeared in the right visual field.
- If visual material appeared in the right visual field, the patient could describe it in speech and writing.
- If visual material appeared to the left visual field the patient could identify the same object with their right hand but not their left hand.
- If visual material was presented to the left visual field the patient consistently *reported* seeing nothing or just a flash of light to their left. However, the participant could point to a matching picture or object with their *right* hand. This confirms that the right hemisphere cannot speak or write (called aphasia and agraphia respectively).

Sperry tried a number of other tests. For example, he flashed two different pictures to the right and left visual fields: $ to the left and ? to the right. Left-handed participants would draw a dollar sign. All participants would *say* that they saw the question mark. If the right-handed

In one study with split-brain patients, the left hemisphere is told (via words on a card to the right visual field) to keep perfectly still, while the right hemisphere (via pictograms to the left visual field) is told to pick up a cup (placed in a position visible by both eyes) with the left hand. As the left hand moves to get the cup, the right hand shoots out to stop it. How can you explain this?

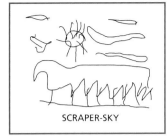

SCRAPER-SKY

A left-hand drawing by a split-brain patient attempting to draw a skyscraper. He saw the word "scraper" in the left visual field and the word "sky" in the right visual field. His left hemisphere controlled his left hand enough to draw sky and his right hemisphere controlled it enough to draw a scraper, but neither hemisphere could combine the two words to make the emergent concept "skyscraper".

patient was asked what he had just drawn he would say the question mark (which was the wrong answer).

Sperry did find that some things stayed the same, for example split-brain patients showed no changes in IQ, nor were their personalities changed. When they watched TV they seemed unaware of the separate visual input. This is likely to be the result of having learned coping strategies. For example, moving their head about so that both left and right visual fields receive all input. A more complex strategy was observed in the laboratory tests. If a participant saw an object in their right visual field (left hemisphere) they could not recognise it with their left hand (right hemisphere) but the patient could say out loud what the object was (language in the left hemisphere) and this could be heard by the right hemisphere because hearing is bilateral. Thus the left hand could now identify the object.

Sperry also found that the right hemisphere is not totally word blind. Some split-brain patients, when shown words to their left visual field, could identify the item with their left hand (right hemisphere). However, they were still not able to say what it was.

The left hand could also sort objects into categories and was better at tasks that involved spatial relationships. Most interestingly, the right hemisphere was more responsive to emotion. If a nude figure was shown in among a series of geometric shapes, the participant typically denied seeing anything (left hemisphere is talking) but at the same time the participant might blush or display a cheeky grin (controlled by right hemisphere).

It also appeared that the right hemisphere sometimes expressed annoyance when "it" heard an error made by the left hemisphere.

Discussion points

1. To what extent do you think that the two halves of the split brain represent two minds?

2. Suggest one ethical concern relevant to this study.

Faces and objects

The following study by Levy, Trevarthen, and Sperry (1972) took advantage of the anatomy of the visual pathways. Split-brain patients were shown faces, in which the left half of one person's face was presented next to the right half of another person's face. These faces were presented very briefly to prevent the eyes moving during presentation. This made sure that information about the right half of the picture went to the left hemisphere, and information about the left half went to the right hemisphere. The patients were asked to say what they had seen. They generally reported seeing the right half of the picture. However, when they were asked to use their fingers to point to what they saw, most of the patients pointed to the left half of the picture. These findings suggest that language is mainly (or exclusively) based in the left hemisphere, whereas the spatial processing involved in pointing to something depends far more on the right hemisphere.

Discussion points

1. Why is this research on split-brain patients regarded as of major importance?

2. Why do we need to be careful when generalising from the performance of split-brain patients to that of other people?

Evaluation of split-brain studies

The findings from split-brain patients are dramatic. The split-brain patients studied by Sperry and others had suffered from severe epilepsy over a period of several years, and epilepsy is normally caused by brain damage. The patients had also been treated with drugs for many

■ Activity: You can test some of Sperry's ideas by doing a simple experiment. Balance a rod on either the right or the left index finger for as long as possible. If right-handed people do this while remaining silent, they can balance the rod longer on the right index finger than on the left. However, if they talk while they try to balance the rod, then the opposite result is obtained: they can now balance the rod longer on the left index finger than on the right. It is as if speaking knocks the rod off the right index finger.

What is happening here? Speech and the right hand are both controlled by the left hemisphere, and so interfere with each other. In contrast, speech and the left hand are controlled by different hemispheres, and so interfere very little with each other.

years and this may have affected their brains. This makes it hard to know whether the ways in which they processed information before the operation were the same as in people with intact brains.

Furthermore, the sample of split-brain patients studied has been rather small and may be influenced by all sorts of other individual differences such as sex, age, IQ, or other abilities. However, the evidence collected from these patients has been confirmed from the study of normal individuals.

Evidence from the study of normal individuals

There are various experimental methods that have been used in normal individuals to study the role of each hemisphere in information processing. For example, there is the divided visual field technique, in which two stimuli are presented at the same time, one to each hemisphere. The stimulus that is detected or reported first provides an indication as to which hemisphere is better able to process information from that kind of stimulus.

The auditory equivalent of the divided visual field technique is the dichotic listening task. Two words or other auditory stimuli are presented at the same time, one to each ear, and the participants are asked to report what they hear. In interpreting the findings from the dichotic listening task, it has to be borne in mind that information presented to the left ear goes to the right hemisphere first, and information from the right ear proceeds initially to the left hemisphere. However, visual or auditory information that goes initially to one hemisphere will go through the corpus callosum and into the other hemisphere within 100 milliseconds or less.

What has emerged from the relevant research? Green (1994, p.69) has provided a useful summary:

In divided field studies, face recognition, pattern recognition, discriminating brightness and colours, depth perception, and perceiving the orientation of lines all produce a right hemisphere advantage. Words, letters, and digits (numbers) produce a left hemisphere advantage. In dichotic listening studies recognition of environmental sounds, and aspects of music such as duration and emotional tone produce a right hemisphere advantage, whereas spoken digits, words, nonsense syllables, backwards speech, and normal speech all produce a left hemisphere advantage.

In essence the left hemisphere is linguistic and the right hemisphere is concerned with visuospatial processing.

Fechner's question

This question concerns the extent to which mind and body are one. If they are, then an individual with a split-brain should have two minds. Sperry and others have argued that split brain patients do have two minds or streams of consciousness. Sperry suggested that it may be less confusing if one thinks of split-brain patients as two rather than one individual. Clearly one hemisphere does not know what the other hemisphere is doing. It is like two separate and rather unco-ordinated individuals.

It is hard to evaluate this claim, but the evidence tends not to support it. If these patients have two minds, then it should be possible to produce a dialogue between the two minds. However, MacKay (1987) argued that this had not happened with any split-brain patients. According to him, "despite all encouragements we found no sign at all of recognition of the other 'half' as a separate person." One of the patients even asked MacKay, "Are you guys trying to make two people out of me?"

The Organisation of Language in the Brain

We have already considered the organisation of language in terms of some of its localised functions: Broca's area is a location for speech production and Wernicke's area is a location for speech comprehension. We have also seen, from the split-brain studies, that language is a lateralised function. In fact hemispheric asymmetry or lateralisation is probably clearest with respect to language.

It has been known for more than 100 years that language in the great majority of right-handed people (about 95%) is based mainly in the left hemisphere. In left-handed people, about 70% have language based in the left hemisphere. The remainder of right- and left-handed people either have language mainly in the right hemisphere, or neither hemisphere is dominant for language.

Some of the most convincing evidence that language in normal individuals is mainly a left-hemisphere function is based on the Wada test, supporting the evidence from split-brain studies. What happens is that an anaesthetic is injected into an artery supplying one hemisphere, and the participant is then asked to read aloud. For over 90% of people,

In what way is language both localised and lateralised?

reading aloud is more disrupted when it is the left hemisphere that is anaesthetised rather than the right hemisphere (Green, 1994).

Not all language functions are governed by the left hemisphere, a point apparent from the split-brain studies. Certain emotional aspects of language are under the control of the right hemisphere. Individuals with damage to the area of the right hemisphere equivalent to Broca's area speak in a monotone; and those with damage to the equivalent to Wernicke's area have problems understanding the emotional tone of speech.

Why is language lateralised?

It appears that this left dominance is innate. Witelson and Pallie (1973) examined the brains of 14 infants who died before the age of 3 months and found that for 12 of them the planum temporale (an area of the temporal lobe associated with language) was twice as large on the left than on the right indicating an inherited hemisphere asymmetry.

One explanation that has been offered for this innate asymmetry is that, if there were two competing language centres—in each hemisphere—this might cause interference when speaking. In fact there is some evidence to support this from studies of stuttering. More stutterers than non-stutterers have been found to have mixed or right-hand dominance for speech. Jones (1966) used sodium amytal to paralyse one hemisphere at a time, in order to establish where patients' speech centres were located so that he could operate on tumours (if they could still talk when the left side was paralysed, the centre must be on the right). He found that all patients with mixed dominance stuttered but if the left hemisphere centres were removed (along with the tumour) their stuttering stopped.

Handedness

Handedness or hand preference appears to be another characteristic that is asymmetrical and innate. Most people have a distinct preference for using their right or left hand, and this preference has even been observed in the womb where unborn babies have shown a distinct preference for sucking either their left or right hand (Stirling, 2000). About 10% of all people are either left handed (dominant right hemisphere) or ambidextrous. Studies of prehistoric cave paintings show that the same percentage were left-handers at that time, again supporting the view that handedness is innate. As we have seen, for some left-handers the whole brain may be reversed so that, for example, the language centres are in the right hemisphere. It is also generally true that left-handers are also left footed and their left visual field is stronger. For such individuals the right side of their brain is dominant; for other left-handers cerebral dominance is described as mixed.

Left-handedness has long been seen as undesirable. In fact the Latin word for "left" is "sinister". Left-handedness is more common among individuals with dyslexia and there is some indication of lower non-verbal IQs in left-handers (Levy, 1969). But perhaps the most intriguing relationship is between handedness, cerebral dominance, and gender.

A classic study by Maccoby and Jacklin (1974) looked at the findings of a number of studies on sex differences, and reported that boys in general have better visuospatial skills (right hemisphere) and girls have better linguistic skills (left hemisphere). Subsequent research has supported this generalisation. For instance, Kimura (1992) found that boys as young as 3 years old find it easier to learn a route from A to B, a visuospatial task. Neurological studies also

---

Social representations and the split brain

The concept of social representations has been applied to the development of scientific ideas. Moscovici (1981) first described social representations as shared beliefs within a social/cultural group that are used to explain social events. Such explanations evolve through, for example, everyday conversations and media reports, eventually becoming regarded as "facts". Scientific ideas are social representations as much as any other kind of knowledge inasmuch as the ideas evolve as they are transmitted from one person to another. Moscovici suggested that initially a scientific theory is largely communicated among specialists but gradually these ideas filter through to the wider public and, in doing so, the concepts and images are applied to other situations. In the end the original ideas may be used to explain things quite different from the original set of facts.

Moscovici and Hewstone (1983) have suggested that this process can be applied to split-brain research. The initial findings were that there are significant differences between the left and right brain: differences in terms of language and spatial processing but also in terms of logic and analysis (left brain) versus emotion or synthesis (right brain). This distinction has been used to support the view that people differ along these dimensions—some people have logical minds (dominant left hemisphere), whereas others have more emotional thought (dominant right hemisphere). It may even be that men are more right brain and women more left brain. Eventually what happens is that a rather limited set of scientific findings becomes transformed into a set of ideological beliefs, for example about innate differences between men and women. Unfortunately such beliefs may be based on flimsy evidence.

support this difference. McGlone (1980) reported that damage to the right hemisphere was more likely to result in impaired visuospatial behaviour in men than in women. It may be that visuospatial control is more bilateral in women, or that women use more linguistically dominated strategies for visuospatial tasks, but either way the findings support a sex difference.

Geschwind and Galaburda (1985) have put forward a hypothesis that can account for this, as well as other facts such as the greater likelihood for boys to suffer from certain disorders such as autism or dyslexia. It is possible that the male **hormone** testosterone may impair the development of the left hemisphere during early pre- and postnatal development which could lead to, for example, dyslexia (linked with left hemisphere damage). Non-human animal studies have shown this effect of testosterone to be true. In addition, testosterone exposure is known to affect the immune system, which explains why boys are more prone to certain illnesses.

Emotion

There has been much interest in the issue of whether various emotions depend more on the left or right hemisphere. The split-brain studies support a right hemisphere advantage for emotion. Gainotti (1972) explored this issue by considering patients who had suffered brain damage to only one hemisphere. Patients with damage to the left hemisphere experienced anxiety and aggression, whereas those with damage to the right hemisphere seemed relatively unemotional and indifferent. These findings led him to conclude that emotional experience depends more on the right hemisphere than on the left one. In similar fashion, some studies have found that in brain-damaged patients the right hemisphere was better than the left hemisphere at perceiving mood (Tompkins & Mateer, 1985).

Additional evidence of the involvement of the right hemisphere was reported by Etcoff et al. (1992). They presented their participants with people who were either lying or telling the truth. Patients with damage to the left hemisphere were better than those with damage to the right hemisphere and non-brain-damaged controls at detecting lying. Presumably they focused on the subtle emotional signs in facial expressions associated with lying that are processed by the right hemisphere, and paid less attention to the misleading use of language by liars that would have been processed by the left hemisphere. Other research has investigated a link between anti-social personality disorder, where individuals lack empathy, and right hemisphere responsiveness (see box on page 216, "Emotion and laterality").

These images have half a smiling face and half a neutral face. If you look at them carefully, can you tell which one looks happier—the one with a smile on the left or the one with a smile on the right? Does your finding fit in with the fact that the right hemisphere is dominant for interpreting emotional expressions?

However, the picture may not be quite so straightforward. Davidson et al. (1990) took EEG recordings of their participants as they watched films designed to produce feelings of pleasure or disgust. Feelings of pleasure were associated with greater activity in the left hemisphere, whereas feelings of disgust led to greater activity in the right hemisphere. They concluded that positive emotions have greater left hemisphere involvement, whereas negative emotions have greater right hemisphere involvement.

Hemispheric Asymmetry: An Overview

Kolb and Whishaw (1990) provided a review of the literature on hemispheric lateralisation. They concluded that there is a left hemisphere dominance for the following functions: words; letters; verbal memory; all language skills; arithmetic; and complex movements. In contrast, there is a right hemisphere dominance for the following functions: faces; emotional expression; nonverbal memory; spatial abilities (e.g., geometry); touch; music; and movement in spatial patterns.

It may be, however, that these two groups of skills can be explained in terms of two general concepts: analytic versus synthetic (or holistic) processing, as found in the research by Bradshaw and Sherlock (1982; see the Key Study below). According to Sperry (1985), the right hemisphere usually processes information in a synthetic fashion (as a whole). In contrast, the left hemisphere processes information in an analytic or logical fashion (bit by bit). For example, the appreciation of a painting may be synthetic when one stands back and takes in the whole picture, or it could be analytic when one studies in detail the techniques that the artist used. (See also the Key Study below.)

The notion that the left hemisphere operates in an analytic way whereas the right hemisphere operates in a synthetic way has a grain of truth about it. However, this is clearly a very oversimplified view, in part because a wide range of different processing activities occur *within* each hemisphere. Kimura (1979) put forward a motor theory that may be an advance on the analytic–synthetic theory. According to Kimura, the left hemisphere is specialised for the control of all precise movements, of which speech is merely one example. As predicted, patients with lesions in the left hemisphere who had impaired speech also had reduced ability to make precise facial movements (Kimura & Watson, 1989).

The basis of hemispheric differences

Do hemispheric differences depend on the type of stimulus presented or on the type of processing that the stimulus receives? This issue was addressed by Bradshaw and Sherlock (1982). They presented their participants with faces made up of squares, triangles, and rectangles. On each trial, the participants had to decide whether a target face had been presented. In one condition, the target was a face in which the features were all close together. In the other condition, the target was a face in which the nose was pointing up.

What did Bradshaw and Sherlock find? The participants were better at detecting the target with the features close together when it was presented to the right hemisphere rather than the left hemisphere. However, the nose target was detected better by the left hemisphere than by the right hemisphere. These findings indicate that hemispheric differences can depend on the type of processing required rather than simply on the type of stimulus. According to Bradshaw and Sherlock, the right hemisphere is good at holistic processing involving the whole stimulus. That is why the closeness of the features was detected more accurately by the right hemisphere. In contrast, the left hemisphere is good at analytic processing, in which a stimulus is processed component by component. That is why the nose target was detected more accurately by the left hemisphere.

Discussion points

1. What important issues were Bradshaw and Sherlock (1982) trying to study?
2. Are there other ways we could test the notion that the right hemisphere engages in holistic processing, whereas the left hemisphere engages in analytic processing?

SECTION   SUMMARY

❖ Several non-invasive and invasive techniques have been devised to study brain functioning. These techniques differ greatly in their spatial and temporal resolution, i.e., how close to the neuronal level the technique is and how often brain activity is sampled (respectively).

❖ The EEG is one of the best known non-invasive techniques. Electrodes on the scalp produce information about brain waves, as used in the study of sleep stages. However, it is an imprecise and indirect measure of brain activity.

❖ Evoked potentials based on EEG recordings provide details of brain activity over time, but not which parts of the brain are most active.

❖ There are various types of brain scans, including CAT scans, MRI scans, functional MRI, and PET scans. In a CAT scan X-rays are passed through an individual's head highlighting denser areas and a three-dimensional picture is composed. This technique is useful for detecting brain tumours, but does not permit precise localisation and does not show active functioning of the brain. MRI scans produce a more detailed picture by detecting magnetic changes to radio waves passed through the brain, but again tell us more about structure than function. PET scans and fMRI show us the brain in action. FMRI provides more spatial information, but not immediate evidence of brain activity. PET scans report regions of brain activity by detecting radioactive glucose. Precise location is poor and PET scans do not indicate brain activity levels on a moment-by-moment basis. Squid magnetometry measures magnetic fields very accurately, but the signal can be affected by irrelevant sources.

❖ Ablations and lesions are examples of invasive techniques. Ablation involves destruction and possibly removal of tissue, whereas lesions are surgical cuts. A stereotaxic apparatus is used to locate the area to be lesioned precisely. These methods were commonly used in brain research; however, it is hard to interpret the findings because of the many interconnections in the brain, which means one can't be certain what region is the main source of a behavioural function; damage to one area may reduce functioning in adjacent areas; many behaviours are governed by more than one region; and destruction may miss the target area. There are serious ethical issues associated with the use of ablation and lesioning.

❖ In humans ablations and lesions are rarely used, for ethical reasons, but "natural" incidents of brain damage can provide valuable information about localisation of functions in the brain. Cognitive neuropsychologists study brain-damaged patients using non-invasive brain scanning techniques in order to understand the workings of the cognitive system. However, it is difficult to interpret data from such studies because each instance is unique and we don't know about the patient's abilities prior to brain damage.

❖ Single-unit recordings have provided detailed information about the responsiveness of individual brain cells, as in Hubel and Wiesel's research. The small-scale destruction involved limits its use mainly to non-human animals, generating data that may not generalise to humans. It is difficult to keep an electrode in position, which may reduce the accuracy of the technique. Multiple-unit recording is s less exact method, but possibly more reliable.

❖ Electrical stimulation of the brain (ESB) aims to produce the same responses as actual nerve impulses and record the effects, as in research on the pleasure centre of the brain. However, ESB is not the same as nervous impulses, although recent attempts have aimed to improve this.

❖ Optical dyes can be used to identify the responses of cells to stimulation because they change colour when electrically stimulated by the brain's natural activity. This can only be used to study the "visible" cortical regions, but it does provide a direct record.

Localisation of Function in the Cerebral Cortex

❖ Localisation of function refers to the notion that any one function is centred on a particular and precise area of the brain. Lashley conducted early research on memory, finding that it was distributed throughout the brain. He described this in his principles of equipotentiality and of mass action.

❖ The cerebral cortex is the outer 2 millimetres of the brain. It is divided anatomically into two hemispheres and each hemisphere is divided into four lobes. The frontal lobes are involved in the planning and control of movements, and in thinking and reasoning. The parietal lobes contain the primary somatosensory cortex. The temporal lobes contain the areas involved in hearing, and the occipital lobes are mainly concerned with visual processing.

❖ The primary motor cortex in the frontal lobe receives input from the motor neurons via the spinal cord and the medulla. All body regions are represented topographically in the primary motor cortex, for almost all of these motor control is contralateral, and there are many parallel bands with the same organisation. Those regions requiring finer motor control are disproportionately represented. The process of initiating movement involves the forming of an intention (prefrontal area), co-ordinating the response (bilateral control in supplementary motor area (SMA) and the premotor cortex), and finally passing messages to the primary motor area which exerts contralateral control over the body's muscles. Some motor activity arises as a response to sensory input rather than direct intention.

❖ The primary sensory areas are the somatosensory area and the visual and auditory cortices. The somatosensory area in the parietal lobe (just behind the primary motor cortex) consists of several topographically organised strips representing different body regions, which are disproportionately represented. The primary visual area (V1) in the occipital lobe receives input from its opposite visual field. Hubel and Wiesel suggested that simple, complex, and hypercomplex cells of V1 respond to lines of particular orientation and detect features such as corners. More recent data describes the cellular organisation in terms of box-like blobs and inter-blob regions, which are sensitive to colour and orientation respectively. V1 acts as a gateway to at least 30 different cortical areas but it apparently can be bypassed, as evidenced by the phenomenon of blindsight. The primary auditory cortex is organised in vertical functional columns, each responding to sounds of similar frequency.

❖ The association cortex is largely involved with higher-order processing of the inputs to the primary sensory and motor regions of the cortex. There are motor association areas in all four lobes of the cortex. Damage to any of these areas results in unique motor problems. There are also visual association areas throughout the brain. Damage to the temporal lobe can result in visual agnosia. The frontal association area is involved in our ability to think, and also in language production (Broca's area). Language comprehension (Wernicke's area) is linked to an area in the association cortex of the temporal lobe. Two aphasias: Broca's (expressive) aphasia and Wernicke's (receptive) aphasia are linked to these areas of the association cortex. The Wernicke–Geschwind model is an attempt to describe the localisation of language. It is likely to be an imperfect model, partly because of difficulties in exactly linking brain regions to specific functions.

❖ The concept of distributed function is a compromise between a strict localisation view and Lashley's concept of equipotentiality. No one area has overall control. Distributed function can be seen in visual processing, language, and memory. Any complex activity is likely to have distributed control. Localisation offers the advantage of a hard-wired system ready for action from birth, but it is susceptible to permanent loss of function if brain damage occurs. Recent research suggests that the brain is more adaptable than was once thought.

❖ Lateralisation describes the fact that the two cerebral hemispheres are asymmetrical. Each hemisphere is specialised in relation to certain functions such as language, handedness, and emotion. One way to study this is using split-brain patients. Some individuals suffering from severe epilepsy have their corpus callosum severed in order to separate the hemispheres and reduce their epileptic "electrical storms". This alleviates their condition and prevents communication between hemispheres, enabling researchers to study the specialised functions of the separate hemispheres. Studies on split-brain patients suggest that language processing occurs in the left hemisphere, and spatial processing and emotion in the right hemisphere. It is possible that split-brain patients are atypical but these behaviours have been confirmed in studies involving normal individuals. The divided visual field technique and the dichotic listening task both produce evidence supporting a right hemisphere advantage for spatial processing, such as face recognition and depth perception, and the processing of sounds. There is a left hemisphere advantage for visual and auditory recognition of letters and digits.

❖ Language is both localised and lateralised. Studies of split-brain patients and using the Wada test with normal individuals show that most people have language centres in the left hemisphere, though the right hemisphere has some linguistic capacity. Left hemisphere language dominance appears to be innate and may be adaptive because competing language centres might cause problems such as stuttering.

❖ Most people are right handed (left hemisphere dominant). Left-handedness is at least partly innate. It may also be related to prenatal impairment due to the male hormone testosterone. Boys are better at right hemisphere tasks (visuospatial processing) and girls show a left hemisphere advantage (language). Left-handers and boys are also more likely to suffer from certain disorders such as dyslexia and autism. Testosterone may affect left hemisphere development and also has been shown to impair the functioning of the immune system. This would explain why boys are more right hemisphere dominant (left hemisphere impaired) and also why they may suffer more from certain illnesses.

❖ Research evidence initially indicated that emotion is more dependent on the right hemisphere. Patients with right hemisphere brain damage tend to be unemotional and indifferent, and less able to perceive a person's mood or tell whether they are lying. However, it may be that positive emotions have greater left hemisphere involvement, whereas negative emotions have greater right hemisphere involvement.

❖ It is possible the right and left hemisphere asymmetry can be explained in terms of two general concepts: analytic versus synthetic (or holistic) processing, rather than in terms of different functions such as language versus visuospatial processing. However, this may be an oversimplified view. Motor theory is one alternative, suggesting that the left hemisphere is specialised for the control of all precise movements.

Lateralisation of Function in the Cerebral Cortex

FURTHER READING

The Routledge Modular Series includes books especially written for the AQA A specification including K. Silber (1999) *The physiological basis of behaviour* (London: Routledge), and J. Stirling (1999) *Cortical functions* (London: Routledge). There is very clear and accessible coverage of cortical functions in J.P.J. Pinel (1997) *Biopsychology (3rd Edn.)* (Boston: Allyn & Bacon), and J.W. Kalat (1998) *Biological psychology (6th Edn.)* (Pacific Grove, CA: Brooks/Cole). Cortical functions are also discussed (but in a more complex way) in N.R. Carlson (1994) *Physiology of behaviour (5th Edn.)* (Boston: Allyn & Bacon). The topics of this Section are also dealt with in S. Green (1994) *Principles of biopsychology* (Hove, UK: Psychology Press).

Example Examination Questions

You should spend 30 minutes on each of the questions below, which aim to test the material in this Section.

1. **(a)** Describe and critically assess **one** invasive method of investigating the brain.   **(12 marks)**
   (b) Describe and critically assess **one** non-invasive method of investigating the brain.   **(12 marks)**

2. **(a)** Describe **one** method of investigating the brain.   **(6 marks)**
   (b) Describe **one** research study that used the method described in (a).   **(6 marks)**
   (c) Assess the value of this research study, with reference to our understanding of functions
       in the cerebral cortex.   **(12 marks)**

3. Discuss the extent to which psychological functions are localised in the
   cerebral cortex.   **(24 marks)**

4. Describe and evaluate research on the functional organisation of the motor area of
   the cerebral cortex.   **(24 marks)**

5. Discuss the organisation of language in the brain, including reference to both localisation
   and lateralisation of function.   **(24 marks)**

6. Describe and assess research into hemisphere asymmetries.   **(24 marks)**

Examination Tips

Question 1. In part (a) you are assessed on both skills: AO1 and AO2; six marks for each, which should guide you in your writing time—slightly more than 6 minutes to describe one invasive method and then the same to evaluate it. Evaluation should be in terms of strengths and limitations. You might use examples of the method either as a means of elaborating your description (AO1) or, if you are explicit that the example is in some way an assessment of the technique it could be AO2. The same applies to part (b) for one non-invasive method. Do not present more than one method in either part as you are wasting valuable time on material that will receive no credit unless it is explicitly given as an evaluation.

Question 2. Both parts (a) and (b) assess AO1. You must ensure that the study described in part (b) is linked to the method in part (a). There is no reason why you can't answer part (b) first. When describing a study you can follow the method you used at AS: cover the aims, procedures, findings, and conclusions. The conclusions may be relevant to part (c) as a means of assessing the value of the study "with reference to our understanding of functions in the cerebral cortex". However the same material is unlikely to receive credit twice unless used in a different way. Reference to other research studies would only be creditworthy if it contributes to assessing the value of the study from part (b). Assessment can further be achieved through criticisms of the method of brain investigation (strengths and weaknesses) and criticisms (positive and negative) of any aspect of the research study.

Question 3. The question concerns localisation only (not lateralisation). The AO1 element of your answer is likely to concern straightforward descriptions of various localised cortical functions. In order to attract a high mark you should avoid a list-like approach and provide sufficient detail for band 3. The AO2 element should focus on the debate between whether the functions you have described are actually distributed rather than localised, and the relative merits of both localised and distributed control. Practical applications of this debate would also be relevant.

Question 4. Note that the term "research" refers to both theories and studies. Evaluation can be of the research itself, or a wider discussion of localised versus distributed control of motor functions, and the practical applications of such research. Make sure you give a full 15 minutes to descriptions. Examples are a good way to add extra detail.

Question 5. You are required to consider both the localisation and lateralisation of language; omission of one will result in a partial performance penalty (automatic loss of 8 marks). Description is straightforward though you should again remember that depth is as important as breadth—be selective in the material you choose to present so that you can provide sufficient detail for a high mark. Evaluation can be achieved by, for example, criticism of any research method, consideration of the adaptive value of lateralisation and of localisation, and practical applications.

Question 6. You may focus exclusively on split-brain research in this question, or you can widen your consideration to other examples of hemispheric asymmetry (e.g., emotion). Assessment should concern issues such as methodology of any research studies, possible ethical or practical issues, and even a consideration of the philosophical issues raised by split-brain research.

WEB SITES

www.brain.com
> News, information and latest research about the brain, with an emphasis on cerebral health and fitness.

http://faculty.washington.edu/chudler/neurok.html or its UK mirror site:
http://www.soton.ac.uk/~jrc3/chudler/neurok.html
> This is a fantastic and very extensive site called "Neuroscience for Kids", which has numerous pages covering the whole of biological psychology. For information specifically about lobes of the brain, have a look at:
> http://faculty.washington.edu/chudler/lobe.html

http://www.med.harvard.edu/AANLIB/
> Harvard University's "Whole Brain Atlas".

http://www.macalester.edu/~psych/whathap/UBNRP/Imaging/
> Methods of monitoring the brain, with useful links.

http://www.lsadc.org/web2/lang____brain.html
> Interesting article about language and the brain (note: four underscore characters in the last part of this address!)

www.ability.org.uk/index1.html
> The official site of the UK Ability organisation, whose slogan is "see the ability, not the disability", with information and links on aphasia, agnosia, and other disabilities.

http://neuro.med.cornell.edu/VL/
> Links to neuroscience institutes, university departments, and societies throughout the world.

http://www.bae.ncsu.edu/bae/research/blanchard/www/465/textbook/imaging/links/
> Medical imaging links.

http://www.biology.about.com/science/biology/library/organs/brain/blcortex.htm
> Anatomy of the cerebral cortex.

http://www.bas.ac.uk/home.htm
> British Aphasia Society.

5

Biological Rhythms: Sleep and Dreaming

There is a wide variety of biological rhythms—periodically recurring features of biological organisms, which are classified by the period of the cycle. In this Section, we explore biological clocks, and the external and internal cues that act as pacemakers for different cycles. Sleep is the most well-known cycle, and we look at some studies of sleep deprivation that attempt to tell us more about the function of sleep; we also discuss the theories explaining the purpose of sleep. Finally, we investigate the theories of dreaming, a behaviour that is little understood: when, what, and why do we dream?

Biological Rhythms

A rhythm is something that is regularly repeated. In living organisms there is a vast array of rhythms: plants open and close daily, people eat several times a day, birds migrate annually, and so on. These rhythms are repeated over different intervals and they are governed by both internal (**endogenous**) and external (**exogenous**) factors. In this Unit we will critically consider research relating to different kinds of rhythm and how these rhythms are determined. We will also consider the consequences of disrupting these rhythms.

Different Kinds of Biological Rhythm

The three main categories are:

- **Circadian rhythm** (from two Latin words meaning "about" and "day"). Most of the biological rhythms possessed by human beings repeat themselves every 24 hours. According to Green (1994), mammals possess about 100 different biological circadian rhythms. For example, temperature in humans varies over the course of the 24-hour day, reaching a peak in the late afternoon and a low point in the early hours of the morning. Other examples of human circadian rhythms are the sleep–waking cycle and the release of hormones from the pituitary gland.
- **Ultradian rhythm**, meaning rhythms of less than one day. A good example of an ultradian rhythm is to be found in sleep. While you are asleep you pass through cycles of lighter and deeper sleep, each cycle lasting about 90 minutes.

- **Infradian rhythm**, meaning greater than 1 day, for example those rhythms repeating once a month. Perhaps the best known example of an infradian rhythm in humans is the menstrual cycle, which typically lasts about 28 days. Those rhythms that repeat once a year are called **circannual rhythms**.

We will consider some circadian and infradian rhythms. An example of an ultradian rhythm, the stages of sleep, is discussed in the next Unit.

The Sleep–Waking Cycle: A Circadian Rhythm

The 24-hour sleep–waking cycle is of particular importance, and is associated with other circadian rhythms. For example, bodily temperature is at its highest about halfway through the waking day (early to late afternoon) and at its lowest halfway through the sleeping part of the day (about 3am). Why is the sleep–waking cycle 24 hours long? One possibility is that it is strongly influenced by *external* events such as the light–dark cycle, and the fact that each dawn follows almost exactly 24 hours after the preceding one. Another possibility is that the sleep–waking cycle is *endogenous*, meaning that it is based on internal biological mechanisms or pacemakers that have a 24-hour periodicity.

As many hormones have circadian rhythms, it is important to note the time a blood sample is taken, as this could affect interpretation of results.

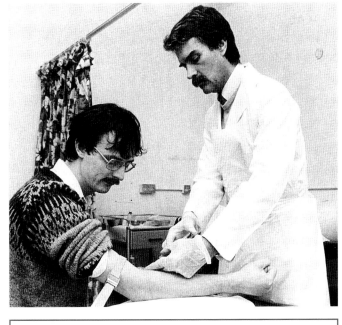

Did you know?

The fact that there are circadian rhythms for many hormones has important applications in medicine. When a doctor takes a sample of blood or urine it is important to record the time of day at which the sample was taken in order to properly assess it. For example, the stress hormone cortisol is at its highest level in the morning. If an early morning sample of urine was tested for cortisol but thought to have been taken later in the day, it might be assumed that the person was highly stressed.

Recent research has also suggested that biorhythms should be considered when prescribing medicines. It seems that the standard practice of taking a drug at regular intervals throughout the day may not only be ineffective, but can also be counterproductive or even harmful. Evidence shows that certain medical illnesses whose symptoms show a circadian rhythm respond better when drugs are co-ordinated with that rhythm (Moore-Ede et al., 1982).

Research studies

How can we decide whether the sleep–waking cycle depends mainly on external or on internal factors? One approach is to study individuals who are removed from the normal light–dark cycle, e.g., by being kept in the dark. Michel Siffre spent 2 months in a dark cave. At first, there was no very clear pattern in his sleep–waking cycle. Later on, however, he developed a sleep–waking cycle of about 25 hours rather than the standard one of 24 hours (Siffre, 1975). This suggests the influence of some internal, **biological clock**.

Other studies have supported this. Wever (1979) discussed studies on participants who spent several weeks or months in a bunker or isolation suite. Most of them settled down to a sleep–waking cycle of about 25 hours, though this is not a universal finding. Folkard (1996) studied one individual who had a 30-hour cycle.

These findings suggest that there is, indeed, an endogenous sleep–waking cycle. However, the fact that there is a discrepancy between the endogenous sleep–waking cycle and the normal sleep–waking cycle indicates that external cues such as changes in light and dark also play a role in **entraining** our biological clock. We will now look, first, at the basis of the endogenous clock and then at external (exogenous) cues.

Endogenous factors: The biological clock

The main pacemaker for endogenous rhythms is the **suprachiasmatic nucleus** (SCN). This is a small group of cells in the **hypothalamus**. It is called "suprachiasmatic" because it lies just above the **optic chiasm**. This location is not surprising because it can then receive input fairly directly from the eye, and therefore the rhythm can be reset by the amount of light entering the eye. The SCN also generates its own rhythms, probably as a result of protein synthesis. It is likely that what happens is that the cells in the SCN produce a protein for a period of hours until the level inhibits further production, again for hours; next, when the protein level drops below another threshold, the SCN starts producing the protein again (Kalat, 1998). This generates the biological rhythm.

This rhythm then affects the sleep–wake cycle via the **pineal gland**. Electrical stimulation of the pineal gland produces the hormone **melatonin,** which makes a person feel sleepy (see the Key Study below); when light levels are low more melatonin is released. Incidentally, in birds and reptiles, as opposed to mammals, light falls directly on the pineal gland, which is located just under the skull.

Evidence to support the functioning of the SCN comes from various studies. Morgan (1995) removed the SCN from hamsters and found that their circadian rhythms disappeared. The rhythms could be re-established by transplanted SCN cells from foetal hamsters. Morgan also transplanted the SCN cells from mutant hamsters (hamsters who had been bred to have shorter cycles than normal) and found that the transplanted hamsters took on the mutant rhythms. Silver et al. (1996) also showed that transplanted SCNs can restore circadian rhythm to an animal whose own SCN has been ablated.

There is also evidence of a second biological clock, again in the SCN. Nearly all participants in the long-term bunker studies showed evidence of two different patterns: one for their sleep–waking cycle and one for their temperature cycle (Wever, 1979).

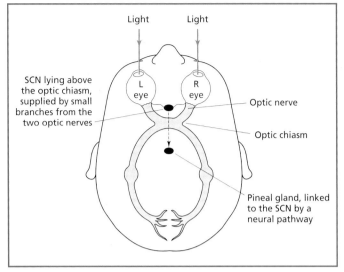

The **visual pathway** in the brain showing the connection to the suprachiasmatic nucleus (SCN) and onward to the pineal gland.

Sleep and melatonin

Some of the strongest evidence of the involvement of melatonin in the sleep–waking cycle was reported by Schochat, Luboshitzky, and Lavie (1997). They made use of the ultra-short sleep–wake paradigm, in which their six male participants spent 29 hours between 7am one day to noon the following day in the sleep laboratory. Throughout that time they spent 7 minutes in every 20 lying down in bed in a completely darkened room trying to sleep. This method allowed Schochat et al. to measure sleep propensity or the tendency to sleep at different times of day. The period of greatest sleep propensity is known as the "sleep gate", and starts in the late evening. Surprisingly, the period of lowest sleep propensity (known as the "wake maintenance zone") occurs in the early evening shortly before the sleep gate.

Schochat et al. measured the levels of melatonin by taking blood samples up to three times an hour during the 29-hour session. The key finding was as follows: "We demonstrated a close and precise temporal relationship between the circadian rhythms of sleep propensity and melatonin; the nocturnal [night] onset of melatonin secretion consistently precedes the nocturnal sleep gate by 100–120 min" (1997, p.367). This close relationship between increased melatonin levels and increased sleep propensity does not prove that they are causally related. However, Schochat et al. discussed other studies that strengthen the argument that melatonin is important in determining sleep propensity. For example, individuals who suffer from insomnia find it much easier to get to sleep when they are given melatonin about 2 hours before bedtime.

The **endogenous mechanisms** involved in regulating bodily rhythms.

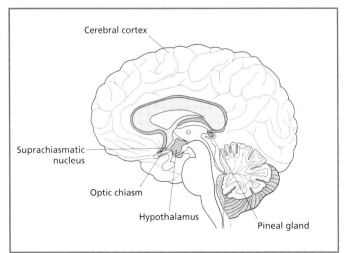

Discussion points

1. What are some of the good features of the study carried out by Schochat et al.?

2. What are the limitations of their approach?

In this area of research, unlike other areas of psychology, single case studies are referred to by their full names rather than initials. Can you explain why that is?

Folkard's (1996) study of Kate Aldcroft found that she developed a 30-hour sleep–wake cycle but a 24-hour temperature cycle. These findings indicate strongly that there are separate internal clocks controlling the sleep–waking cycle and temperature.

Exogenous factors

As we have seen, the SCN also receives direct information from the eye about the level of light. This means the SCN can be controlled internally but also can be reset by external cues. In fact recent evidence shows that humans may receive information about light from elsewhere in the body. Campbell and Murphy (1998) demonstrated that participants given regular light exposure on the backs of their knees had changes in their circadian rhythms in line with the light/dark they were exposed to. However, it is not clear how this information would get to the SCN.

Can you think of anyone whose melatonin cycle differs from the norm?

Light is considered to be the dominant **zeitgeber**, the technical term for an external event that partially controls biological rhythms and literally means "time giver". An interesting study by Miles et al. (1977) documented the problems of a young man who was blind from birth. He had a strong 24.9-hour circadian rhythm despite the fact that he was exposed to a variety of zeitgebers such as clocks and radios. His problems in resetting his biological clock were so great that he had to use stimulants and sedatives to co-ordinate his sleep–wake cycle with the rest of the world. This demonstrates that light really is the dominant time-giver.

However, there is also evidence that shows that, where appropriate, light cues are disregarded. Luce and Segal (1966) pointed out that people who live within the Arctic Circle still sleep for about 7 hours despite the fact that during the summer months the sun never sets. In certain circumstances other external cues take over, such as social customs that dictate when it is time to get up and go to bed. The sleep–wake cycle is more strongly controlled by endogenous factors, but it is important that these cues can be overridden. For example, if you were trapped in a dark cave, your need to stay awake to be able to respond to rescuers would overturn the messages to the SCN that it was dark and therefore time to go to sleep.

Internal and external control

Both endogenous and exogenous signals are important and both cause us difficulties. Think of the difficulties people experience when working shifts. Darkness tells them they should be asleep. Think also of the difficulties related to jet lag—the light tells us we should be awake but our internal clock says it's time for sleep. We will consider the effects of these disruptions later.

There are good reasons why our biorhythms should be sensitive to *both* internal and external control. Without external control animals would not be sensitive to seasonal variations. They would not shed hair in summer or grow extra hair in winter. Some animals sleep at night, possibly because it is safer; other animals hunt at night because they are adapted for this. In either case the animal needs to respond to light cues. Light cues are not likely to be the only cues as far as seasonal variation is concerned. Air temperature would also be important as it would alter the nutritional needs in order to maintain core body temperature. Therefore we can see that responsiveness to external cues enables animals to adapt to environmental conditions, which is vital for survival.

However, if animals were solely at the mercy of environmental cues we would have very irregular biological patterns and this might be life threatening.

How do you evaluate physiological explanations? See the box on page 203.

Indirect effects of circadian rhythms

So far we have focused mainly on a circadian rhythm that is directly related to underlying biological processes. There are other, more psychological rhythms that depend indirectly on basic circadian rhythms. For example, there are fairly consistent patterns of performance on many tasks throughout the day. People tend to peak at certain times of the day.

The classic work in this area was carried out by Blake (1967). He asked naval ratings to perform several tasks at five different times of day (08.00; 10.30; 13.00; 15.30; and 21.00). For most of the tasks, the best performance was obtained at 21.00, with the second-best level of performance occurring at 10.30. However, later studies found that peak performance on most tasks is reached at around midday rather than during the evening (Eysenck, M.W., 1982).

Why might people perform at their best at midday rather than earlier or later in the day? Relevant evidence was obtained by Akerstedt (1977). Self-reported alertness (assessed by questionnaire) was greatest at about noon, as was the level of adrenaline. Adrenaline is a hormone associated with states of high physiological arousal within the **autonomic nervous system** (ANS). However, it should be noted that the notion of physiological arousal is rather vague and imprecise. Furthermore, these are correlational data, and it is hard to be sure that the high level of midday performance *depends* on arousal.

Are you a "morning" or an "evening" person?

After the midday peak there may be a trough. Blake (1967) found that most of his participants showed a clear reduction in performance at 13.00 compared to their performance at 10.30. This reduction in performance occurred shortly after lunch, and is commonly known as the "post-lunch dip". The explanation for this is that the physiological processes involved in digestion make us feel sluggish and reduce our ability to work efficiently. It is also noteworthy that the act of digestion is governed by the **parasympathetic branch** of the ANS, which leads to general relaxation, whereas physiological arousal is an effect of the antagonistic ANS branch, the **sympathetic branch**.

> ■ Activity: Design a questionnaire to measure alertness and distribute it to volunteer participants. Ask them to complete it at regular intervals over several days. Analyse the data to see if there are "morning" and "evening" people, in terms of levels of alertness. What are the methodological problems you may encounter?

The Menstrual Cycle: An Infradian Rhythm

Infradian rhythms are bodily rhythms for which the cycle time is greater than one day. One of the clearest examples of an infradian rhythm is the menstrual cycle in women. (In other mammals the cycle is longer or shorter than the human 28 days, but is still infradian.) This cycle is governed by hormones, an endogenous mechanism. **Hormones** are biochemical substances that are produced by endocrine glands and released into the bloodstream. Small amounts of such hormones have a large effect on target organs such as, in the case of the menstrual cycle, the ovaries and womb. The menstrual cycle is governed by the female hormones oestrogen and progesterone. These hormones cause the lining of the womb to become engorged with blood and one egg to ripen and be released. If the egg is not fertilised, then the lining of the womb is shed. On average this cycle takes 28 days but there are large individual variations, from 20 to 60 days.

This endogenous rhythm can be affected by many external cues. Reinberg (1967) documented the duration of a woman's menstrual cycle during and after she spent 3 months in a cave, with only dim lighting. Her sleep–wake cycle lengthened slightly and her menstrual cycle became shorter during her stay in the cave. It took a further year for her cycle to return to normal. This suggests that light can influence the menstrual cycle, probably by generally affecting the action of the SCN and the circadian cycle which then has implications for the infradian rhythm.

Even more interestingly there is evidence that a woman's menstrual cycle can be entrained by the menstrual cycle of other women; an example of exogenous control, albeit biological. It has been a common observation that women who spend time together, such as girls living in boarding schools and nuns, appear to have synchronised menstrual cycles

Can you think of any evolutionary advantages for synchronised menstrual cycles?

(McClintock, 1971). It is likely that this happens because of **pheromones**, biochemical substances that act like hormones but are released into the air rather than the bloodstream. These pheromones have no smell and are not consciously detectable but they carry messages from one individual to another of the same species. Support for this comes from a study by Russell et al. (1980; see the Key Study below). But why would this happen? One possibility is that there might be an evolutionary advantage for a social group to have synchronised pregnancies so that all the women in the group were breastfeeding at the same time. This would mean that child care could be shared, which would be especially helpful if one mother died (Bentley, 2000). Members of other animal species certainly share feeding though; in fact, wet nursing in humans shows that you can continue to breastfeed even if your child was born much earlier.

The effects of pheromones

Hormones are produced by the endocrine system and distributed in the blood so that their influence can be felt by target organs. Pheromones are biochemical substances, like hormones, but pheromones are released into the air and affect other individuals. Ants produce pheromones as a means of "telling" other ants where to find food. Most mammals use pheromones in sexual attraction, signalling when a female is in her fertile phase. In fact the pheromones of some animals are used to produce perfume. It has also been noted that pheromones may explain why women who live together, such as in boarding schools, have synchronised menstrual cycles.

To test this, Russell et al. (1980) arranged to apply the pheromones of one woman to a group of sexually inactive women. The donor's odour was collected from pads placed under her arms. Once every 24 hours the pads were replaced. The old pad was then dissolved in alcohol to remove any bacteria. Finally, the pad was rubbed on the upper lip of each participant. This was repeated daily for 5 months. Some of the women were in a control group where they received the same treatment but did not receive the odour. Participants did not know which group they were in. A record was kept of the participants' menstrual cycles.

Why was it necessary to use sexually inactive women in this study?

At the end of the experiment four out of the five women in the odour group had menstrual cycles that synchronised to within a day of the odour donor.

Discussion points

1. Can you suggest any other explanations for the findings of this study?

2. What ethical issues might a researcher have to consider when conducting a study such as this?

Another example of the effect of external cues has been found in women who work with men. It has been found that they have much shorter menstrual cycles. McClintock (1971) has suggested that male pheromones may reset a woman's biological clock. One possible explanation is that this would have adaptive value. Women who ovulate more often when men are present are likely to have more offspring and this would increase the genetic strain that has this characteristic response to male presence. At other times a short menstrual cycle would be disadvantageous because of the drain on resources.

Circannual Rhythms

Circannual rhythms are biological rhythms that last for about 1 year before repeating. They are more common in some animal species than in humans, and this is especially true of species that hibernate during the winter. Convincing evidence of a circannual rhythm in the gold-mantled ground squirrel was reported by Pengelley and Fisher (1957). They put a squirrel in a highly controlled environment with artificial light on for 12 hours every day, and a constant temperature of 0°C. Despite the fact that the external cues were unchanging, the squirrel hibernated from October through to the following April, with its body temperature dropping dramatically from 37°C before hibernation to 1°C during hibernation. The circannual rhythm for this squirrel was somewhat less than a year, having about 300 days' duration. It would appear that this circannual rhythm was endogenously controlled.

Migration is another circannual rhythm. In general it is thought that migration is controlled by alterations in day length and/or food supplies, both of which are external cues. However, this can't explain why birds living in the equator travel north because changes at that latitude in daylight and temperature over the year are minimal. It is possible that migration is also endogenously controlled. Gwinner (1986) kept wild birds in a controlled environment for 3 years, maintaining 12 hours of light each day. Nevertheless they showed signs of migratory restlessness, which does support the existence of an endogenous mechanism.

Seasonal affective disorder

Some people suffer from **seasonal affective disorder** (SAD), which resembles a circannual rhythm. The great majority of sufferers from seasonal affective disorder experience severe depression during the winter months, but a few seem to experience depression in the summer instead. The evidence suggests that seasonal affective disorder is related to seasonal variations in the production of melatonin, which is a hormone secreted by the pineal gland (Barlow & Durand, 1995). Melatonin affects production of serotonin, which is implicated in depression (see Section 17, Psychopathology). Melatonin is produced primarily at night, i.e., darkness, and so more is produced during the dark winter months. As would be expected,

A young seasonal affective disorder sufferer receiving phototherapy from a light box on the right of the picture.

seasonal affective disorder is more common in northern latitudes where the winter days are very short. Terman (1988) found that nearly 10% of those living in New Hampshire (a northern part of the United States) suffered from seasonal affective disorder, compared with only 2% in the southern state of Florida.

Phototherapy is recommended for the treatment of seasonal affective disorder (Barlow & Durand, 1995). This involves exposing sufferers to about 2 hours of intense light shortly after they wake up in the morning. It is assumed that this treatment reduces the production of melatonin. However, as Barlow and Durand (1995, p.256) pointed out, the effectiveness of phototherapy "is not yet clear since no controlled studies have been conducted; also the mechanism of action or cause has not been established".

Why is it important to conduct controlled studies?

The Consequences of Disrupting Biological Rhythms

Jet lag can be a problem for airline staff who frequently cross time zones in the course of their work.

In our everyday lives, there is usually no conflict between our endogenously controlled rhythms and external events or zeitgebers. However, there are situations in which there is a real conflict. Probably the two most important examples of such conflict are jet lag and shiftwork.

Jet lag

It is sometimes thought that jet lag occurs because travelling by plane can be time-consuming and tiring. In fact, jet lag occurs only when flying from east to west or from west to east, not from north to south. In other words it is related to changing time zones and depends on a discrepancy between internal and external time. For example, suppose you fly from Scotland to the east coast of the United States. You leave at eleven in the morning British time, and arrive in Boston at five in the afternoon British time. However, the time in Boston is probably midday. As a result of the 5-hour difference, you are likely

to feel very tired by about 8 o'clock in the evening Boston time (which is 1am on your internal "clock").

Klein, Wegman, and Hunt (1972) found that adjustment of the sleep–waking cycle was much faster for westbound flights (going to the States) than for eastbound ones, regardless of whether you were travelling home or going away from home. For eastbound flights, re-adjustment of the sleep–waking cycle took about 1 day per time zone crossed. Thus, for example, it would take about 6 days to recover completely from a flight to Britain from Boston.

Why is it easier to adapt to jet lag when flying in a westerly direction? An important reason is that the day of travel is effectively lengthened when travelling west, whereas it is shortened when travelling east. As the endogenous sleep–waking cycle is about 25 hours, it seems reasonable that it is easier to adapt to a day of more than 24 hours than to one of fewer than 24 hours. This is because phase delay (putting one's internal clock on hold) is easier to adapt to than phase advance.

Is it easier to override endogenous cues for sleep or for waking?

People also generally cope better with staying up later than with getting up earlier, again because phase delay is easier. In other words, we don't like to be woken up when our body clock tells us we should be sleeping, but we can cope with being awake when our body clock says we should be asleep. A study by Schwartz et al. (1995) supported this. They analysed the results of American baseball games where teams had to travel across time zones to play opposing teams on the east or west coast (the time difference is 3 hours). West coast teams who travelled east (phase advance) had significantly fewer wins than east coast teams travelling west—which gives the east coast teams a distinct advantage. (Though, of course, it might simply be that the east coast teams were better.)

What are the dangers with taking melatonin?

One suggestion to combat jet lag is to use melatonin to reset the body clock (see the Case Study below). An alternative is to adopt local eating times and bedtimes as soon as possible, so that these social cues help reset your biological clock.

Shiftwork

What about shiftwork? As they say, there are only two problems with shiftwork: you have to work when you want to be asleep, and you have to sleep when you want to be awake. The effects of shiftwork require serious consideration partly because it is a feature of our industrialised society. We need people in industry, transportation, and health care to work around the clock in order to maintain the systems that underpin our society. It is estimated that approximately 20% of people employed in the United States work in shifts (US Congress, 1991). The second reason to be concerned about shiftwork is that records show that more accidents occur at night—when people are working when they should be asleep. The industrial accidents at Chernobyl, Bhopal, and Three-Mile Island all occurred between

---

CASE STUDY: *Melatonin and Aircrew*

Melatonin is now available in US chemists and some claim it is the cure for jet lag. Jet lag can lead to fatigue, headache, sleep disturbances, irritability, and gastrointestinal disturbances—all with a potentially negative impact on flight safety. Interestingly, reported side-effects of melatonin use include many similar symptoms. Although some researchers claim melatonin is among the safest known substances, no large clinical evaluations have been performed to evaluate long-term effects.

Scientists believe melatonin is crucial for the functioning of our body clock. Studies suggest that treating jet lag with melatonin can not only resolve sleeping problems but also increase the body clock's ability to adjust to a new time zone. However, those in the medical community advise caution. Melatonin is not a universal remedy for everyone who must travel over many time zones. It is thought by some that it should not be used unless the user intends to spend more than 3 days in the new time zone. International aircrews will often cover several time zones, typically flying overnight west to east, spending 24 hours on the ground, then returning during the day (east to west). This cycle is likely to be repeated several times before an extended period of sleep is possible. Melatonin usage to adjust the body clock in these circumstances is viewed by many scientists as inappropriate.

Timing the dose of melatonin is very important. Studies show that resynchronisation of the sleep–waking cycle only occurred if the subjects were allowed to sleep after taking the medication. In those participants unable to sleep after taking melatonin, the circadian rhythm was actually prolonged. More worryingly, melatonin's effect on fine motor and cognitive tasks is unknown and the nature of melatonin's sedative effects are uncertain.

Unfortunately, there are no published clinical studies evaluating flying performance while taking melatonin. The US Armed Forces are actively evaluating melatonin's aeromedical usefulness. Despite ongoing research, no US military service permits the routine use of melatonin by aviators. Significantly, aircrew participating in experimental study groups are not allowed to perform flying duties within 36 hours of using melatonin.

1am and 4am; and most lorry accidents occur between 4am and 7am. Moore-Ede (1993) estimated the cost of shiftworker fatigue in the US to be $77 billion annually as a result of both major accidents and also ongoing medical expenses due to shiftwork-related illnesses.

Would you expect to find that industrial accidents are more likely to occur at certain times of day?

There are ways to lessen the effects of shiftwork by using different work patterns. Monk and Folkard (1983) identified two major types of shiftwork: (1) rapidly rotating shifts, in which the worker only does one or two shifts at a given time before moving to a different work time: (2) slowly rotating shifts, in which the worker changes shifts much less often (e.g., every week or month). There are problems with both shift systems. However, rapidly rotating shifts may be preferable. They allow workers to maintain fairly constant circadian rhythms, whereas slowly rotating shifts can cause harmful effects by causing major changes to individuals' circadian rhythms. On the other hand, research has found that it takes most people about a week before their circadian rhythms have adjusted to a new sleep–wake cycle, so one might expect slowly rotating shifts to be better. Rapid rotation means your rhythms are always disrupted (Hawkins & Armstrong-Esther, 1978). It might help if shiftworkers reset their biological clocks as quickly as possible. Research has shown that it is possible to reset biological clocks using bright lights as a substitute for sunlight to reset the SCN. Dawson and Campbell (1991) exposed workers to a 4-hour pulse of very bright light which appeared to help them work better.

Another way to lessen the effects of shiftwork is by using phase delay rather than phase advance, as we noted in relation to jet lag. It would be better to rotate shifts with the clock rather than against it so one is doing early shifts and then later shifts, then night shifts and then back to early shifts. Czeisler et al. (1982) tested this in a chemical plant in Utah, finding that the workers reported feeling better and much less tired on the job. The management also reported increased productivity and fewer errors.

Sleep

Sleep is an important part of all our lives, generally occupying almost one-third of our time. There are various ways of trying to understand sleep. First of all we can describe it. The most obvious way to do this is in terms of an ultradian rhythm with a number of stages, each of which lasts about 90 minutes, repeated five or six times a night. Second, we can consider the question of what function is served by sleep. What happens when individuals are deprived of sleep? Why do all animals sleep? Why do different animals have different patterns of sleep?

Stages of Sleep: An Ultradian Rhythm

Early investigations discovered two surprising features of sleep. First of all it is not as passive as one might be led to think when watching someone asleep. Individuals are often quite active during sleep. Second, there are different kinds of sleep. Being asleep is not a total loss of consciousness but a descent into reduced consciousness passing through different levels of awareness and different kinds of brain activity.

The notion of different kinds of sleep is described using the concept of "stages". One implication of a "stage theory" is that the stages follow a regular sequence, which is the case with sleep stages. A second implication is that there are qualitative differences between stages. In the case of sleep, each stage is defined by a distinctive pattern of brain activity, i.e., a qualitative and not just a quantitative difference.

The development of the electroencephalograph (or EEG) was crucial in the investigation of sleep because, without it, we had no way of measuring what is going on when someone is asleep. This technique of investigating the brain was described in Section 4, Brain and Behaviour (see page 137). In essence, scalp electrodes are used to obtain a continuous measure of the electrical or brain-wave activity, which is recorded as a trace. Without this method of objective recording, researchers relied on self-reporting, which

What happens to you physiologically and psychologically when you are asleep?

tells us nothing about the physiology of sleep. Other useful physiological measures include eye-movement data from an electro-oculogram or EOG, and muscle movements from an electromyogram or EMG.

There are two main aspects to EEG activity: frequency and amplitude. Frequency is defined as the number of oscillations of EEG activity per second, whereas amplitude is defined as half the distance between the high and low points of an oscillation. In practice, frequency is used more often than amplitude to describe the essence of EEG activity.

- *Stage 1*: A person becomes relaxed and brain waves are synchronised. In simple terms this means that the activity from different parts of the brain is in synchrony, that is, peaks and troughs in the wave pattern occur at the same time. There are characteristic alpha waves (waves having a frequency of between 8 and 12 cycles per second) in the EEG. There is slow eye rolling, and reductions in heart rate, muscle tension, and temperature. This stage can be regarded as a state of drowsiness. The transition from awake beta waves to the alpha waves of stage 1 is often accompanied by a **hypnogogic state**, in which we may experience hallucinatory images.
- *Stage 2*: The EEG waves become slower and larger (theta waves of frequency 4–8Hz), but with short bursts of high-frequency sleep spindles. There is little activity in the EOG. K-complexes are also characteristic of stage 2. These are the brain's response to external stimuli, such as noises in the room. This stage lasts about 20 minutes. It is still quite easy to be awakened at this stage.
- *Stage 3*: Sleep deepens as the brain waves slow down and the person is described as "descending the sleep staircase". The EOG and EMG records are similar to stage 2, but the EEG consists mainly of long, slow delta waves (1–5Hz) with some sleep spindles.

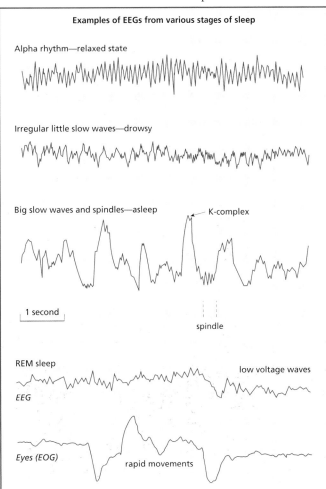

Examples of EEGs from various stages of sleep

Alpha rhythm—relaxed state

Irregular little slow waves—drowsy

Big slow waves and spindles—asleep

K-complex

1 second

spindle

REM sleep

low voltage waves

EEG

Eyes (EOG)

rapid movements

- *Stage 4*: There is a majority of the long, slow delta waves that are present in smaller amounts in the previous stage, and very little activity in the EOG or the EMG. This is a deeper stage of sleep than any of the first three stages, and it is often known as slow-wave sleep (SWS). It is hard to wake someone up at this stage, though personally significant noises, such as your own baby crying, will rouse you. Body temperature drops (which is why you need bed covers). However, there are some physiological activities that start rather than slow down in SWS. For example, growth hormones are secreted at this time. Though this is the deepest stage of sleep it is the time when sleepwalking occurs and also sleeptalking and "night terrors" (a particular kind of nightmare where the dreamer may appear to be awake but terrified).
- *Stage 5*: Rapid eye movement or REM sleep, in which there are rapid eye movements and a very low level of EMG activity, while the brain waves resemble beta activity at around 13–30Hz. REM sleep has been called **paradoxical sleep**, because it is harder to awaken someone from REM sleep than from any of the other stages, even though the EEG indicates that the brain is very active. The body is also paralysed during REM sleep, which may serve the useful function of preventing us from acting out our dreams.

After the sleeper has worked through the first four stages of progressively deeper sleep, he or she reverses the process. Stage 4 sleep is followed by stage 3, and then by stage 2. However, stage 2 is followed by REM sleep (stage 5). After REM sleep, the sleeper starts another cycle, working his or her way through stages 2, 3, and 4, followed by stage 3, then stage 2, and then REM sleep again. A complete sleep cycle or ultradian cycle lasts about 90 minutes. Most sleepers complete about five ultradian cycles during a normal night's sleep, with progressively less SWS and more REM activity as morning approaches.

The proportion of the cycle devoted to REM sleep tends to increase from one cycle to the next.

Evaluation

One point to remember is that the data collected about sleep stages are produced in highly artificial conditions. Participants have to spend the night in a sleep laboratory where they are wired up to various machines and may be woken during the night to report their dreams. It is possible that normal sleep patterns are not always the same as those in laboratory studies.

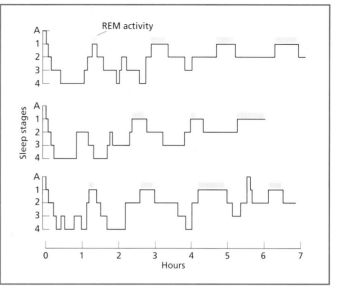

Cyclic variations in EEG during three typical nights' sleep. Note the increased REM activity as the night progresses, and reduced stage 4 sleep.

REM sleep and dreaming

REM sleep is the most interesting stage of sleep. Many people associate REM sleep with dreaming. Aserinsky and Kleitman (1955) first discovered this association, which was further investigated by Dement and Kleitman (1957; see the Key Study on page 188). Dement and Kleitman woke up their participants when they were in REM sleep, and most

---

Sleepwalking

Dreams don't always occur in REM sleep. REM dreaming is accompanied by paralysis, probably to protect the sleeper from acting out their dreams and injuring themselves. People also dream in non-REM (NREM) sleep, but less often, and they are not in a paralysed state. It is possible to act out NREM dreams, which can lead to sleepwalking.

Sleepwalking is more common than one might guess. Thirty per cent of all children between the ages of 5 and 12 have walked in their sleep at least once, and persistent sleepwalking occurs in 1–6% of youngsters. Boys walk in their sleep more often than girls, and the tendency to wander during deep sleep is sometimes inherited from one of the parents.

The typical sleepwalking episode begins about 2 hours after the person goes to sleep, when they suddenly "wake" and abruptly sit up in bed. Although their eyes are wide open, they appear glassy and staring. When asked, sleepwalkers respond with mumbled and slurred single-word speech. The person may perform common acts such as dressing and undressing, opening and closing doors, or turning lights on and off. Sleepwalkers seem to see where they are going since they avoid most objects in their way, but they are unaware of their surroundings. Unfortunately, this means that they cannot tell the difference between their bedroom door and the front door, or the toilet and the wastebasket. The sleepwalker is usually impossible to awaken and does not remember the episode in the morning. The episode typically lasts 5 to 15 minutes and may occur more than once in the same night.

Although sleepwalkers avoid bumping into walls and tripping over furniture, they lack judgement. A sleepwalking child might do something like going to the garage and getting in the car, ready to go to school at 4 o'clock in the morning. Sometimes their lack of judgement can be dangerous. One sleepwalking child climbed a tree and another was found by the police walking down the street in the middle of the night. Therefore, sleepwalkers are in danger of hurting themselves and must be protected from self-injury.

Most children outgrow sleepwalking by the time they are teenagers, but for a small number of individuals the pattern continues into adulthood.

Christian Murphy escaped with cuts and bruises when he fell from his first-floor bedroom window while sleepwalking. His mother's Mercedes that was parked below broke his fall. Once he had landed he got up, still sleepwalking, and set off down the road.

Why do you think there are several stages of sleep?

of them reported that they had just been dreaming. This link offered researchers an objective way to study dreams, or at least it would if REM sleep was the only time when dreams occurred. However, later research has shown that about 30% of sleepers in slow-wave sleep report having been dreaming when woken up (Green, 1994). This is a fairly high percentage, even though it is lower than the 70–75% for those awoken from REM sleep. But it does mean that REM sleep and dreaming are not equivalent. One reason that people think they do not dream in slow-wave sleep is because they are deeply asleep and, by the time they are awake, they have forgotten their dream. On the other hand, of course, it may be the case that 70% of people genuinely do not dream outside of REM sleep.

The dreams reported from REM sleep differ from those from other stages of sleep. Dreams during REM sleep tend to be vivid and detailed, whereas non-REM (NREM) dreams contain much less detail and are less coherent, with vague plots and concerning more commonplace things (McIlveen & Gross, 2000).

Types of sleep

We have seen that REM is one type of sleep, and the term NREM is used to describe the other stages of sleep. REM sleep has also been called paradoxical sleep because of the apparent paradox between being physically paralysed yet mentally active. Meddis (1979) used the terms **active** and **quiet sleep** for REM and NREM sleep respectively, and Horne (1988) referred to **core sleep** to describe those aspects of sleep that are more essential to survival, i.e., if we are deprived of core sleep this does seem to matter whereas other kinds of sleep appear to be less important. Finally there is **micro-sleep**, brief periods of relaxed wakefulness during the day when a person stares blankly into space and temporarily loses awareness. Such periods may permit some restorative functions to take place.

Research Studies of Sleep Deprivation

Considering that we spend almost 200,000 hours asleep in the course of a lifetime, it would seem reasonable to assume that sleep must serve one or more key functions, but it has proved hard to discover these functions. One way of trying to work out *why* we sleep is to deprive people of sleep and see what happens. It could be argued that the kinds of problems and impairments experienced by sleep-deprived individuals are those that sleep is designed to prevent.

People often cope surprisingly well when deprived of sleep. Consider, for example, the case of Peter Tripp. He was a New York disc jockey who took part in a "wakeathon" for charity. He managed to stay awake for 8 days or about 200 hours. He suffered from delusions and hallucinations (e.g., that his desk drawer was on fire). These delusions were so severe that it was hard to test his precise level of psychological functioning. However, it is not clear whether he showed any long-term effects from his wakeathon. One report suggests that he suffered psychological consequences months and even years later, but we do not know to what extent such behaviour was the result of his one bout of sleep deprivation. It should be noted that the whole study lacked adequate control and may relate only to the characteristics of this unique individual.

Horne (1988) discussed the case of Randy Gardner, a 17-year-old student who remained awake for 264 hours or 11 days in 1964. Towards the end of the 11-day period, he suffered from disorganised speech, blurred vision, and a small degree of paranoia (e.g., thinking that other people regarded him as stupid because of his impaired functioning). In view of the fact that Randy Gardner missed out on about 80–90 hours of sleep, he had remarkably few problems. He was clearly less affected than Tripp by sleep deprivation, even though he remained awake for 3 extra days.

After his ordeal was over, Randy Gardner slept for 15 hours. He slept longer than usual for a few nights thereafter, before reverting to his normal sleep pattern. However, he did not recover more than 25% (about 20 hours) of the 80–90 hours of sleep he had missed. If sleep were essential we would expect that he would need to recover it all. He did, however, recover almost 70% of stage 4 deep sleep and 50% of REM sleep, with very small recovery percentages for the other stages of sleep. This suggests that stage 4 and REM sleep are of special importance.

You will note that these are studies of single individuals, because it is difficult to arrange large-scale deprivation experiments over a prolonged period of time—not many people are willing (or have the time) to go without sleep for 11 days! Hüber-Widman (1976) documented the effects of sleep deprivation over time (see the Key Study on page 182)

What are the drawbacks of using case studies to collect evidence?

is also possible to conduct experimental studies with non-human animals. Rechtschaffen et al. (1983) placed two rats at a time on a disc above a water container. The EEG activity of both rats was monitored. One rat was not allowed to sleep, because the disc started to rotate and caused it to fall in the water whenever its EEG activity indicated that it was starting to sleep. In contrast, the other rat was allowed to sleep, because the disc stopped rotating when its EEG indicated sleep. All of the sleep-deprived rats died within 33 days, whereas the rats that were not sleep-deprived seemed in good health.

It is hard to be sure whether findings on rats also apply to humans. However, Lugaressi et al. (1986) studied a 52-year-old man who could hardly sleep at all because of damage to parts of his brain involved in sleep regulation. Not surprisingly, he became absolutely exhausted, and was unable to function normally. Eventually he died, possibly as a result of the sleeplessness, though the anxiety created by his condition may have contributed (as may also have been the case with the rats). The post-mortem examination revealed that he had lesions in those areas of his brain linked with control of sleep.

REM sleep deprivation

We saw in the case of Randy Gardner that he recovered more of his lost REM sleep than most other stages of sleep. Dement (1960) carried out a systematic study of REM and NREM sleep. Some of his participants were deprived of REM sleep over a period of several days, whereas others were deprived of NREM sleep. In general, the effects of REM sleep deprivation were more severe, including increased aggression and poor concentration. Those deprived of REM sleep tried to catch up on the REM sleep they had missed. They started to enter REM sleep 12 times on average during the first night in the laboratory, but this rose to 26 times on the seventh night. When they were free to sleep undisturbed, most of them spent much longer than usual in REM sleep; this is known as a REM rebound effect.

Again research with non-human animals may be an important source of information. Jouvet (1967) used the "flower-pot technique" to test the consequences of REM deprivation in cats and other animals. He placed an upturned flower-pot in a large tank of water. The cats had to sit on the pots and eventually fell asleep. In NREM sleep they were able to remain sitting up, but with loss of muscle tone in REM sleep they slipped into the water and were abruptly awoken. Very soon they woke up as soon as their heads began to nod. In the end the cats died, leading to the conclusion that the lack of REM sleep had been fatal. It is possible, however, that again the stress of the whole experience may have also affected their health.

How do you deprive someone of NREM sleep? If the answer is that you cannot, what does this say about the validity of Dement's research?

Is it possible to study sleep deprivation in humans without encountering ethical difficulties?

Air traffic controllers have to be alert to tiny changes in flashing lights on their screens at all hours of the day or night; as the lights represent aircraft, motivation to be vigilant remains high.

Task performance

There have been more controlled laboratory studies of sleep deprivation in humans than just the case studies described earlier (see Eysenck, M.W., 1982, for a review). Sleep deprivation over the first 3 days or so has few adverse effects on tasks that are complex and interesting. However, sleep-deprived individuals tend to perform poorly on tasks that are monotonous and uninteresting. This is especially the case when these tasks are performed in the early hours of the morning and need to be performed over a longish period of time. A good example is the vigilance task, in which the participants have to detect signals (e.g., faint lights) that are only presented occasionally.

What do these findings mean? According to Wilkinson (1969, p.39), it is "difficult for us to assess the 'real' effect of lost sleep upon subjects' *capacity* as opposed to their *willingness* to perform". Wilkinson and others found that most of the adverse effects of sleep loss

Many people feel that, when they are tired, they can't work at their best. What do psychiatrists suggest to be the reason for this depressed performance?

on performance could be eliminated if attempts were made to motivate the participants (e.g., by providing knowledge of results). It thus appears that poor performance by sleep-deprived individuals is usually due to low motivation rather than to reduced capacity.

Effects over time

It appears that impaired performance on boring tasks is the main problem caused by sleep deprivation over the first 3 nights of sleep loss. During the fourth night of sleep deprivation, there tend to be very short (2–3 second) periods of micro-sleep during which the individual is unresponsive (Hüber-Weidman, 1976; see the Key Study below). In addition, this length of sleep deprivation sometimes produces the so-called "hat phenomenon". In this phenomenon, it feels to the sleep-deprived person as if he or she were wearing a rather small hat that fits very tightly. From the fifth night on, there may be delusions as reported by Peter Tripp, though Randy Gardner did not suffer from these so early on. From the sixth night on, there are more severe problems such as partial loss of a sense of identity and increased difficulty in dealing with other people and the environment. Some of these symptoms were experienced by Randy Gardner. The term sleep-deprivation psychosis has been used to refer to these symptoms (Hüber-Weidman, 1976). However, this is probably an exaggerated description of the actual symptoms.

The effects of sleep deprivation

Hüber-Weidman (1976) reviewed a large number of sleep deprivation studies, and produced a summary of the findings:

- After 1 night of sleep deprivation people report not feeling very comfortable, but it is tolerable.
- Two nights: People feel a much greater urge to sleep, especially when the body temperature rhythm is lowest at 3–5am.
- Three nights: Tasks that involve sustained attention or complex processing become much more difficult, especially when they are boring. If the experimenter offers encouragement or the tasks are made more interesting, then performance is improved. This is again worst in the very early hours.
- Four nights: Micro-sleep periods start to occur while the sleep-deprived person is awake. These last about 3 seconds during which the person stares blankly into space and temporarily loses awareness. They also generally become irritable and confused.
- Five nights: The above effects continue and the person may start to experience delusions. It appears that cognitive abilities, such as problem solving, remain fairly unimpaired.
- Six nights: The person starts to show signs of "sleep deprivation psychosis", which involves a loss of a sense of personal identity, a sense of depersonalisation, and increased difficulty in coping with other people and the environment.

Discussion points

1. What conclusions can you draw from this review of studies about sleep deprivation?

2. What might be the purpose of micro-sleep?

Partial deprivation

What do partial deprivation studies tell us about the purpose of sleep?

Some research studies have looked at the effects of reduced sleep, rather than total deprivation as in the previous studies. Webb and Bonnet (1978) deprived their participants of 2 hours of sleep a night. The participants reported feeling fine. They did, however, go to sleep more quickly the next night and also slept for longer. A further study looked at the possibility of reducing sleep needs. Participants spent 2 months making themselves have gradually less and less sleep. Eventually they were able to have just 4 hours sleep a night without apparent ill effects.

The physiology of sleep

This is an alternative theoretical account of sleep, focusing on the physiological events of sleep rather than the psychological need for sleep.

The typical processes in human sleep are as follows. Darkness causes the *suprachiasmatic nucleus* (the SCN, our "biological clock") to produce *melatonin*, which in turn enhances the production of *serotonin*. This accumulates in the *pons*, a region of the hindbrain. In particular it accumulates in the *raphe nucleus*. When levels of serotonin have risen to an appropriate level this causes the *reticular activating system* (RAS) to shut down. The RAS is involved with levels of arousal or alertness (Moruzzi & Magoun, 1949).

Once a person is asleep, there are further physiological mechanisms that govern the sleep cycle:

1. The *raphe nucleus* (in the RAS) initiates NREM sleep. We know this from various studies. For example, Jouvet (1967) lesioned the raphe system in cats and found this resulted in sleeplessness, concluding that serotonin and the raphe nucleus initiate sleep (called the monoamine hypothesis because serotonin is a monoamine).
2. The *locus coeruleus* (shu-rule-us) produces *noradrenaline*, which leads to onset of REM sleep. The locus coeruleus is inactive during REM sleep and also much of our waking time. It appears to

be involved in the special kind of arousal that helps form memories, which may explain why we do not always remember dreams.

3. The *pons* produces *acetylcholine*, which leads to REM sleep. We know this because drugs that stimulate the production of acetylcholine quickly change NREM to REM sleep (Baghdoyan, Spotts, & Snyder, 1993). The pons also transmits PGO (pons-geniculate-occipital) waves, which lead to REM sleep. As a REM period continues, these PGO waves spread to more of the cerebral cortex. During prolonged periods of REM deprivation, the PGO waves emerge during other stages of sleep besides REM sleep. They may even occur when awake and are associated with strange behaviours such as hallucinations.

The three systems are:

- The serotonergic system of the raphe nuclei. Drugs that block serotonin prevent the onset of REM (Kalat, 1998).
- The noradrenergic system of the locus coeruleus. When noradrenaline levels fall REM sleep is impaired (Jouvet, 1967).
- The acetylcholinergic system of the pons. Drugs that block acetylcholine interfere with the continuation of REM sleep (Kalat, 1998).

Theories of Sleep

Several theories of sleep function have been proposed over the years. However, most of them belong to two broad classes of theory:

1. Recovery or restoration theories.
2. Adaptive or evolutionary theories.

It may help to bear a few facts in mind as you are considering these theories. First, all animals sleep, which suggests that sleep serves some important function. The fact that the part of the brain that governs sleep is the oldest (in an evolutionary sense) also marks sleep out as a fundamental requirement of all animals.

Second, different species have quite different sleep requirements: they either sleep little and often, or for long periods at one time; or they sleep during the day or during the night, or they sleep one hemisphere at a time (as in the case of some dolphins). This suggests that sleep is an evolutionary adaptation to environmental conditions.

Finally, sleep deprivation studies show that there are some physical affects of both NREM and REM deprivation but these may be related to motivation as much as some kind of reduced capacity.

Recovery or restoration theories

An important function of sleep is probably to save energy and to permit the restoration of tissue. This notion is central to various recovery or restoration theories, such as those of Oswald (1980) and Horne (1988). These theories focus on the benefits of sleep for the physiological system. It is also possible that sleep conveys advantages to the psychological system. In other words, sleep may also serve to restore psychological functions.

Physiological restoration
If physiological restoration is the function of sleep then we would expect that:

- Sleep deprivation would have serious effects because physiological restoration was prevented.
- Animals who use more energy, would be likely to need to sleep more.
- More sleep would be likely to be required after periods of physical exertion.

The evidence from sleep deprivation studies suggests some negative effects, as we have seen, especially if an animal is deprived of SWS and/or REM sleep. Oswald (1980) identified SWS as being important in the recovery process, especially as it has been linked with the release of growth hormone and protein synthesis. There is also evidence of essential physiological processing during REM sleep. Stern and Morgane (1974) argue that the normal function of REM sleep is to restore levels of **neurotransmitters** after a day's activities. This is supported by evidence that some people on antidepressants show decreased REM, possibly because the drugs are increasing their neurotransmitter levels. The negative effects of REM rebound (see page 181) also support the view that REM sleep provides a restorative function.

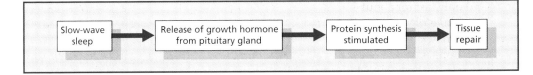

However, it is possible that restoration occurs during waking hours but is less efficient or more resource intensive. Then loss of sleep would have an effect but not necessarily a serious one. So sleep deprivation effects alone are not sufficient evidence.

In terms of animals that use more energy, we should look at the evidence related to small mammals that have comparatively high metabolic rates. Allison and Cicchetti (1976) surveyed 39 mammalian species to work out the amount of time spent in slow-wave sleep (SWS) and in REM sleep. Body weight and metabolic rate were found to be related to amounts of SWS, with smaller mammals having more SWS. In terms of REM sleep, vulnerability to danger (e.g., danger of being preyed upon) was found to be important, with those most vulnerable having less REM sleep than those least vulnerable.

Why do you think small animals need relatively more slow-wave sleep than larger ones?

Evidence of the effects of physical exertion can be found both in natural and laboratory experiments. Shapiro et al. (1981) studied runners who had taken part in an ultra marathon covering 57 miles. These runners slept about an hour and a half longer than normal on the 2 nights after the ultra marathon, and there was an especially large increase in the amount of time devoted to SWS. Researchers also cite the evidence that newborn infants (who experience enormous brain growth) have a very high percentage of their time asleep devoted to REM sleep (Green, 1994). On the other hand, Horne and Minard (1985) tried to exhaust their participants with numerous activities and found that they went to sleep faster but not for longer. It might be imagined that people who take very little exercise would sleep for less time than those who take an average amount of exercise, but there is little or no evidence to support this.

Although studies show that people need extra sleep following extreme exertion, there is no evidence that people who take little or no exercise reduce their sleeping time.

Psychological functions

As was mentioned earlier, one of the possible functions of sleep is to permit restoration of psychological functions. There are various studies in which associations were found between quality of sleep and mood. Naitoh (1975) discussed various studies concerned with the effects of 1 night's sleep deprivation on mood. The effects were consistently negative. Sleep-deprived individuals described themselves as less friendly, relaxed, good-natured, and cheerful than those who had not been sleep-deprived.

Insomniacs (who have persistent problems with sleeping) tend to be more worried and anxious than people who sleep normally. However, it is not clear whether their anxiety is a cause or an effect of sleep deprivation. It is usually assumed that it is more a question of people's worries and concerns disrupting sleep than of disrupted sleep causing worries. This is supported by Berry and

Webb (1983), in a study in which they assessed self-reported anxiety. When people slept well during a given night, their level of anxiety on the following day was lower than when they had slept poorly.

So the evidence supports the view that lack of sleep causes depressed mood and increased anxiety, therefore suggesting that sleep has a role in the recovery of some psychological functions.

Evaluation of recovery theories

There is considerable support for the theory but there are also problems or inconsistencies. The notion that SWS may be related to protein synthesis doesn't make sense when one considers that amino acids, which are the ingredients of proteins, can't be stored in the body and only last for about 4 hours after a meal. This would mean that protein synthesis could only take place in the initial 4 hours of sleep and can't explain why we appear to need more than 4 hours' sleep (Bentley, 2000). Though we might mention the study by Webb and Bonnet (see page 182) that did indeed find that people could be trained to reduce their sleep requirements to 4 hours nightly without apparent ill effects.

Another question is why we need to reduce consciousness during sleep. There is evidence that relaxed wakefulness during which there are rather low levels of energy expenditure could and does provide an opportunity for bodily repair. Horne (1988) put forward a recovery theory resembling that of Oswald (1980) but which emphasised periods of relaxed wakefulness, termed micro-sleep. What evidence supports this position? Horne pointed out that most of Randy Gardner's problems during sleep deprivation were connected with brain processes rather than with other physiological processes in the body. The implication is that sleep is not essential for the repair of bodily tissues, which can happen at other times. The concept of micro-sleep can also explain why people don't always experience symptoms of sleep deprivation when they have had no sleep—they may have had periods of micro-sleep when apparently awake. However, considering that these periods are so brief it is difficult to see how much could be restored.

If restoration was the only function of sleep then we would expect to find consistent effects from sleep deprivation. The apparently inconsistent effects may be due to the fact that only some aspects of sleep provide a physiological and/or psychological restoration function, i.e., core sleep that includes SWS and also REM sleep. The importance of these stages of sleep is supported by the previously discussed sleep-deprivation study on Randy Gardner. After his long period of sleep deprivation, there was much greater recovery of REM sleep and stage 4 slow-wave sleep than of the other stages of sleep. But then why do we have other sleep stages; is it to help us move in and out of core sleep?

We can also argue that if sleep has a restorative function we would expect people who are more active to require more sleep. But we have seen that the evidence does not wholly support this view.

Finally, we can ask why, if sleep is restorative in all animals, there are so many different variations in the way that animals sleep. It may be that sleep serves an adaptive rather than a restorative function.

Do you find that some worries and problems recede after a good night's sleep? Is this valid evidence for the function of sleep?

Adaptive or evolutionary theories

According to various theorists sleep can be regarded as an adaptive behaviour favoured by evolution. The theory of evolution is explained in the box on the next page. Evolutionary theories presume that sleep occurs in all animals because it promotes survival and reproduction, and therefore is naturally selected. Each animal adapts their sleep behaviour to suit their unique environmental demands.

Sleep as protection against predation

Meddis (1975a) proposed that the sleep behaviour shown by any species depends on the need to adapt to environmental threats and dangers. Thus, for example, sleep serves the function of keeping animals fairly immobile and safe from predators during periods of

The principles of evolution

You may recall, from your AS level studies, that evolution is a fact. The *theory* of evolution offers an account of why living species have changed and continue to change. The key principle is survival—animals that survive must have adaptive characteristics that have enabled them to survive. It is likely that sleep is in some way adaptive—otherwise why would all animals sleep?

The essential principles of Darwin's theory of evolution are:

- Environments are always changing, or animals move to new environments.
- Living things are constantly changing. This happens partly because of sexual reproduction where two parents create a new individual by combining their **genes**. It also happens through chance **mutations** of the genes. In both cases new traits are produced.
- Those individuals who possess traits that are best adapted to an environment are more likely to survive to reproduce (it is reproduction rather than survival that matters). Or, to put it another way, those individuals who best "fit" their environment survive (survival of the fittest). Or, to put it still another way, the genes of the individuals with these traits are naturally selected.

The end result is that physical characteristics and behaviours that are adaptive, i.e., help the individual to better fit its environment, are the ones that survive. Those traits that are non-adaptive disappear, as do the individuals with those traits.

time when they cannot engage in feeding and other kinds of behaviour. In the case of those species that depend on vision, it is adaptive for them to sleep during the hours of darkness.

It follows that those species in danger from predators should sleep more of the time than those species that are predators. In fact, however, predators tend to sleep more than those preyed upon (Allison & Cicchetti, 1976). This might seem inconsistent with adaptive theories of sleep. However, species that are in danger from predators might benefit from remaining vigilant most of the time and sleeping relatively little. This seems like an example of having your cake and eating it, in the sense that any pattern of findings can be explained by the adaptive or evolutionary approach! Thus it is not possible to falsify Meddis' theory.

Interesting evidence that the pattern of sleep is often dictated by the environmental threats faced by animals was reported by Pilleri (1979). Dolphins living in the River Indus are in constant danger from debris floating down the river. As a consequence, these dolphins sleep for only a few seconds at a time to protect themselves from the debris.

Hibernation theory

Webb (1982) suggested a different adaptive account, called the hibernation theory. In this version of an evolutionary theory, sleep is seen as adaptive because it is a means of conserving energy in the same way that hibernation enhances survival by reducing physiological demands at a time of year when they would be hard to fulfil. The same principles could be applied to staying awake at night. Any animal that is not nocturnal will be twiddling its thumbs, so to speak, and might as well relax and save energy. The same could be said of nocturnal animals during the day. Animals that don't rest when not engaged in finding food, use more energy and need more food, which may decrease their survival potential.

Evaluation of adaptation theories

Bearing in mind the two theoretical approaches to sleep, explain why human babies sleep a lot.

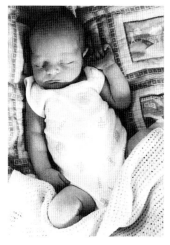

We have already seen that there are problems with the predation theory, in terms of it being non-falsifiable. There are also problems with applying this theory to human sleep. It is possible that when our ancestors were evolving, sleep did provide an adaptive advantage for either or both safety and energy conservation. (This is called the environment of evolutionary adaptation—EEA—the period in human evolution during which time our genes were shaped and selected by natural selection to solve survival problems operating then, roughly between 35,000 and 3 million years ago.) However, one wonders why there hasn't been some move in the direction of less sleep when today there would be enormous advantages for an individual who needed very little sleep—think what you could do if you didn't have to sleep!

Empson (1989) regards these adaptation theories as a "waste of time" because they propose that sleep itself is just wasting time so that the individual is safer and/or using less energy. But deprivation studies do suggest that lack of sleep has distinct consequences so it can't just be a waste of time, as suggested by evolutionary theories.

Recovery or adaptation?

How can we decide between recovery and adaptive theories of sleep function? According to most recovery theories, sleep is absolutely essential to well-being. In contrast, sleep is generally rather less crucial according to adaptive theories. There are no reports of human beings who have managed without sleep. However, there are a few reports of individuals who led normal healthy lives in spite of regularly sleeping for very short periods of time each day (e.g., Meddis, Pearson, & Langford, 1973).

Horne (1988) made the important point that sleep probably serves different purposes in different species. Thus, no single theory of the functions of sleep is likely to be adequate.

On balance, the recovery approach seems to provide a more thorough and well-developed account of sleep. However, it could be argued that these two approaches address somewhat different issues. The recovery approach provides some views on *why* sleep is important, whereas the adaptive approach also focuses on *when* different species sleep.

When two different approaches address different issues within an area of psychology, is it possible to make a true comparison between them?

Dreaming

The Nature of Dreams

Most but not all dreaming takes place during REM (rapid eye movement) sleep. We can thus use the duration of REM sleep during the night as one approximate measure of how long any given individual spends dreaming. It also means we can consider what other physiological activities are taking place simultaneously to try to find out why people (and other animals) dream. The fact that we devote so much time to dreaming (about 700 hours a year) suggests that dreams are likely to fulfil some important function or functions. As we will see, various theorists have tried to identify these functions.

We know that non-human animals have REM sleep—any cat or dog owner will described episodes of twitching in their pet's sleep as if it were chasing rabbits. However, we have no way of finding what their subjective experiences actually are. In humans we can ask people to tell us about their dreams, though again we do not know how many of their dreams are forgotten, or to what extent their recall is distorted by the fact that they were asleep. A classic study by Dement and Kleitman (1957; see the Key Study on the next page) aimed to provide researchers with a way of conducting objective research into dreams.

A photo montage illustrating eye movement during REM sleep.

In fact not all animals have REM sleep. It has not been observed in dolphins nor in the spiny anteater but otherwise appears to be common to all mammals. It is not found in fish, reptiles, and amphibians and only occasionally in some birds of prey. This suggests some link with higher order brain functioning.

Remembering your dreams

Newborn babies spend about 9 hours a day in REM sleep, and adults 2 hours. You may not feel that you spend this amount of time dreaming. One reason is that maybe not all of REM sleep involves dreaming. Another reason is that we forget more than 95% of our dreams. What are these forgotten dreams about? Researchers have obtained some idea by using sleep laboratories, in which sleepers are woken up when the EEG and EOG records indicate that a dream is taking place. This allows the researcher to assess the content of dreams that probably would normally be forgotten, and these tend to be much more ordinary and less strange than the dreams we normally remember (Empson, 1989). This is important, because it shows that the dreams we normally remember are not *representative* or typical of dreams in general. It would thus not be appropriate to produce a general theory of dreaming purely on the basis of the 5% of dreams we normally remember, aside from the problem of subjective recall.

In what way are REM sleep and dreams the same—and how are they different?

An objective method for the study of dreaming

Dement and Kleitman (1957) sought to demonstrate a link between REM activity and dreaming, to facilitate research into dreaming. If one could demonstrate that REM activity was dreaming, then you could investigate the possible functions of dreaming by finding out what else was related to REM activity rather than having to rely on the subjective and unreliable reports of dreamers once they woke up.

If REM sleep is dreaming then we might expect:

- Dreams to be specific to REM sleep.
- The duration of REM activity and the subjective report of dreaming to be similar.
- The movement of the eyes to be related to the visual imagery of the dream. For example, if someone dreamt of playing basketball their eyes would move up and down.

KEY STUDY EVALUATION—Dement and Kleitman

A key criticism of this research is its artificiality. It is quite possible that sleeping in a laboratory would not be entirely representative of normal sleeping, and dreaming, patterns. Furthermore the fact that participants were awoken during the night might affect their behaviour, especially when one considers the effects of REM deprivation (see page 182). Nevertheless this research did provide some useful data about dreaming—although it did not find an exclusive link between REM activity and dreaming.

Nine adults took part in the study. Typically a participant reported to the sleep laboratory just before their usual bedtime and went to bed in a darkened room. Electrodes were attached around the participant's eyes to measure eye movement (EOG), and to the participant's scalp to record brain activity as a measure of depth of sleep (EEG). At various times during the night a bell rang and woke the participants up. They were woken either randomly or during alternations of REM and NREM activity. The participant then spoke into a recording machine by their bed, saying (a) whether they had been dreaming and (b) describing the content of the dream. An experimenter was listening outside the room and, if he had further questions, he would come in and ask the participant about other details. On average participants were awoken six times a night.

Dement and Kleitman found that all participants had REM activity every night. REM periods lasted between 3 and 50 minutes. During that time the eyes were not constantly in motion but there were bursts of activity. Interestingly REM activity occurred at regular intervals for each individual. For one participant they were every 70 minutes, for another every 104 minutes. The average was an REM episode every 92 minutes.

Most dreams were recalled during REM sleep but some dreams were reported when patients were woken from NREM sleep. When participants were awoken during deep sleep they sometimes were rather bewildered and reported that they must have been dreaming, though they couldn't remember the dream. They recalled a mood, such as anxiety or pleasantness, but no specific content.

One way to estimate the length of the dream was in terms of the number of words the participant used to describe the dream. Another way was to ask the participant to estimate the length. Both were positively correlated with the length of REM activity.

There did appear to be some support for a relationship between eye movement and dream activity, for example, when one participant displayed horizontal eye movements (which were quite rare) they dreamt they were watching two people throwing tomatoes at each other.

Discussion points

1. What are the main findings of this study?
2. How could these findings be used to investigate the function of dreams?

One reason why dreams are forgotten may be that during REM sleep a part of the hindbrain—the locus coeruleus—is inactive. This structure may be important for the special kind of arousal that helps us form memories and may explain why we often have only partial recall for our dreams (Chiara, Pompeiano, & Tononi, 1996).

Dreaming and consciousness

Are we conscious when we are dreaming? Empson (1989) identified various differences between dreaming and waking consciousness. First, dreamers typically feel that they have little or no control over their dreams, whereas we nearly always have a sense of conscious control in our waking lives. However, some people have **lucid dreams**, in which they know they are dreaming and can sometimes control the dream content. For example,

LaBerge, Greenleaf, and Kedzierski (1983) studied a woman who was able to create lucid sex dreams that produced orgasms.

Second, dreams often contain elements that would seem illogical or nonsensical in our waking consciousness. For example, dreams sometimes include impossible events or actions (e.g., someone floating above the ground), and they can also include various hallucinations and delusions.

Third, we tend to be totally absorbed by our dream imagery, reflecting what Empson (1989) described as the "singlemindedness of dreams". However, when we are awake, we can usually stand back from our conscious thoughts and avoid becoming dominated by them.

Is it possible that there are different kinds of dreams and different functions?

Theories of the Functions of Dreaming

In what follows, we will be discussing five of the main theories of dreaming. These theories can be divided into two groups: neurobiological theories, which focus on the benefits of dreaming for the brain and nervous system, and psychological theories, which focus on what dreams can do for our psyche.

In considering these theories it is crucial to remember that REM sleep is not the same as dreaming. People don't always report dreams in REM sleep and they dream in NREM sleep. Some theories try to explain the function of REM sleep (and we presume this may explain dreaming) and other theories offer explanations of dreaming in general, in or outside of REM sleep. These are psychological theories.

Neurobiological theories of the functions of dreaming

Activation-synthesis theory

Hobson and McCarley (1977) were impressed by the fact that the brain is as physiologically active during REM (rapid eye movement) sleep as it is during normal waking life. This led them to put forward the activation-synthesis theory of dreaming. According to this theory, during dreaming there are high levels of activation in several parts of the brain, including those areas involved in perception, action, and emotional reactions. This activation is essentially random and is not related to any actual body activity since bodily movements are inhibited during REM sleep. The reason for this is both an output blockade at the top of the spinal column, which prevents commands for action being acted upon, and an input blockade, which inhibits processing of environmental stimuli. However, signals resembling those that normally come from the eyes and ears (but not the nose and mouth) are spontaneously generated within the hindbrain and midbrain structures of the brain. Dreamers generally interpret these internal signals as if they were produced by external stimuli, and this is the experience of dreaming.

How do dreamers react to the high level of random brain activation that occurs during REM sleep? According to Hobson (1988), dreamers try to make sense of it by synthesising or combining the information contained in the bursts of neural activity. As this activity is essentially random, it is often very difficult for dreamers to produce coherent dreams. Indeed, one might wonder how it is possible at all. According to Hobson (1988), "The brain is so inexorably bent upon the quest for meaning that it attributes and even creates meaning when there is little or none in the data it is asked to process."

Research evidence.   There is physiological evidence to support the activation-synthesis theory. Research on cats indicated that there is apparently random firing of cells in cats' brains during REM sleep (Hobson, 1988). This then produces activation in the parts of the brain that are used in visual perception and the control of motor movements, and may be synthesised into a dream.

Hobson (1994) has also provided evidence of how internally generated signals are misinterpreted as external signals. He noted that cortical levels of the neurotransmitters noradrenaline and serotonin are lower during REM sleep than during NREM sleep or

Have you ever had a dream that incorporated external stimuli? When and why might this phenomenon be useful?

This contradictory evidence leads us to question the tendency of researchers to focus on evidence that supports their theory and reject other evidence. Is this in keeping with the aims of scientific research?

waking life. (It is worth noting here that this is contradictory evidence in relation to the restoration theory of sleep—where it is suggested that REM sleep is a time when neurotransmitter levels are replenished.) According to Hobson, these reduced levels of noradrenaline and serotonin prevent the effective use of attentional processes and of the capacity to organise information in a coherent way. This makes it easier for the brain to misinterpret internally generated signals as if they came from external stimuli or from responses. Hobson went on to argue that the problems of attention caused by low levels of noradrenaline and serotonin may also explain why we fail to remember the great majority of our dreams.

Evaluation.   The greatest strength of the activation-synthesis theory is that it is based on detailed information on the physiological activity of the brain during dreaming. The theory can explain why smells and tastes rarely or never appear in our dreams—because only those parts of the brain involved with vision and hearing are activated. The activation-synthesis theory also accounts for the incoherent nature of many dreams. If dreams occur as a result of random activity in the brain, and attentional processes are not functioning effectively, then it is entirely understandable that we often find our dreams hard to understand.

The greatest limitation of the theory is that it does not provide a convincing account of the fact that some dreams possess clear meaning and coherence. It may be true that the brain has a "quest for meaning", but this is hardly a detailed explanation of dream coherence. The theory is also of little value in explaining why it is that so many people have dreams that relate to their present concerns or why many dreams are repetitive. This is puzzling if dreams are based on *random* brain activity. Though it might be that any synthesis that takes place draws on past experiences and therefore becomes meaningful to the dreamer.

We should also remember that activation-synthesis is related to REM activity, but dreaming also takes place at other times though in a different way. It is possible that NREM dreams may be the synthesis of different kinds of brain activity.

Reverse-learning theory

Crick and Mitchison (1983) put forward a challenging approach to dreaming known as reverse-learning or unlearning theory. According to this theory, the main function of dreaming is to get rid of useless information stored in the brain. This information (which they called "parasitic information") uses up valuable space in the cortex, and so dreaming helps to free up some of this space for the storage of more useful information. More specifically, there are neuronal networks in the cortex. According to Crick and Mitchison, these networks are strongly interconnected, and this can lead to overloading. The elimination of unimportant information during dreaming allows the neuronal networks to function more efficiently.

What are the physiological processes involved in dreaming and the elimination of unwanted information? According to Blakemore (1988):

> *Dreams are, quite literally, a kind of shock therapy, in which the cortex is bombarded by barrages of impulses from the brainstem below, while a different mode of synaptic modification ensures that the unwanted elements of each circuit are unlearned.*

The subjective experience of dreaming is a kind of "read out" of the search and destroy activity. As with activation-synthesis theory, dreams are seen as an accidental by-product of a neurobiologically inevitable or necessary process.

Research evidence.   It is hard to test reverse-learning theory. However, Crick and Mitchison (1983) claimed that the size of the cortex in different species of mammals provides support for their theory. The only mammals not having the REM sleep associated with dreaming are dolphins and spiny anteaters. With no REM sleep one might presume that these species are unable to get rid of useless information. According to Crick and Mitchison, these species only manage to function effectively because they have an unusually large cortex for mammals of their size and therefore have no need to jettison unwanted material.

On the other hand, it has been argued that the human cortex is much more highly folded than that of a dolphin or spiny anteater so that it may have just as much capacity. Yet another alternative explanation, put forward by Winson (1997), is that the dolphin and spiny anteater have to perform the clearing up operations while awake, which is why they need a larger cortex to cope with doing this at the same time as the daily processing tasks. Other animals have evolved an alternative strategy (i.e., REM sleep).

Evaluation.   Reverse-learning theory represents an interesting approach to dream function. If dreaming is simply designed to allow us to erase valueless information, then it makes sense that we rarely remember the content of our dreams. As we have seen, we forget about 95% of our dreams, which is entirely consistent with the reverse-learning theory.

However, there are some major problems with the theory. First, dreams are often meaningful or significant (see the evidence related to problem-solving theory), whereas it would be predicted by the theory that they should be relatively meaningless. Second, there is evidence that foetuses engage in something resembling REM sleep. It is hard to believe that they are trying to forget meaningless information before they are even born! Though this is not inconceivable. For example, we know that there are large numbers of neuronal connections being organised during development. If a foetus is, say, trying out new motor programmes, some will be efficacious and some will be erroneous. Dreaming might, therefore, serve the same purpose.

Third, modern connectionist ideas about the brain suggest that we have a vast potential for information storage and there is no need to save space.

Comment on neurobiological theories

We have already noted that both theories see dreams as an accidental by-product of neurobiological processes. The theories have no explanation for why dreams should have meaning beyond the possibility that our cognitive processes have a tendency to impose meaning on any set of data.

One further issue is the question of REM and NREM dreaming. Both theories describe one basic explanation or function for dreams. But why would this apply to several different physiological states (REM and NREM activity)? It might be that other kinds of activity in NREM are also synthesised. We can probably at best conclude that these accounts of dreaming are partial explanations, and may only be related to REM activity.

Is it possible that REM "dreams" are a different process to more coherent "psychological" dreams?

Psychological theories of the functions of dreaming

Psychological theories start from the notion that dreams are psychological rather than physiological experiences, and therefore we would expect them to serve a psychological function. It may be coincidental that many dreams are in REM sleep.

Freud's wish-fulfilment theory

Probably the best-known theory of dreaming was put forward by Sigmund Freud (1900). He claimed that all dreams represent *wish fulfilment*, mainly of repressed desires (e.g., sexual desires). The source of this theory was his own dreams and the descriptions of dreams provided by his patients. In one of his dreams, Freud found himself with a patient, Irma, who was not recovering as well Freud hoped and he blamed himself for this. In his dream Freud met Irma at a party and examined her. In the dream he saw a chemical formula for a drug prescribed by another doctor and realised that this other doctor had used a dirty syringe, and this was the source of Irma's problem. This meant that Freud was no longer to blame for Irma's illness. Freud interpreted this dream as wish fulfilment.

Such wish fulfilments are often unacceptable to the dreamer, leading Freud to describe dreams as "the insanity of the night". This unacceptableness leads the dreamer to produce separate manifest and latent content. The **manifest content** of a dream is what the dreamer actually dreams, whereas the **latent content** is the true meaning of the dream.

How easy is it to test Freud's wish-fulfilment theory? Is this a strength or weakness of the theory?

"Dream-work" transforms a forbidden wish into a non-threatening form, thus reducing anxiety and allowing the dreamer to continue sleeping.

Psychoanalysis can be used to uncover the latent content. Indeed, according to Freud, dream analysis provides a *via regia* or royal road to an understanding of the unconscious mind. An important feature of such dream analysis involves working out the meaning of various dream symbols. Such symbols may be universal, such as poles, guns, and swords representing the penis, and horse-riding and dancing representing sexual intercourse. However, Freud suggested that many symbols were more likely to be personal and he didn't support the idea of "dream dictionaries" based on universal symbols. In one case, he was analysing a patient's dream about a wiggling fish. The patient suggested that this might represent a penis. However, Freud considered this and concluded that in fact the dream represented the patient's mother, who was a passionate astrologer and a Pisces (the astrological sign for a fish). Freud also famously said, with reference to a dream involving a cigar, yet another symbol for the penis, "Sometimes a cigar is only a cigar." In other words, not all dreams are symbolic and many dreams require careful individual rather than universal interpretation.

Is it strange that Freud's theory is associated with dream dictionaries, yet he didn't really subscribe to this view?

Research evidence.   There is evidence that many dreams are relevant to current concerns. Hajek and Belcher (1991) studied the dreams of smokers who were involved in a programme designed to help them stop smoking. Most of the participants reported dreams about smoking during the course of treatment and for a year afterwards. Most of these dreams were what they called dreams of absent-minded transgressions or DAMITS. In these dreams, engaging in smoking was followed by feelings of panic or guilt.

Hajek and Belcher found that dreaming about smoking seemed to help the ex-smokers. Those who had the most dreams about smoking (and about feeling bad about it) were less likely to start smoking again than those who had few such dreams. However, these are correlational findings, and do not show that the dreams were actually useful.

Evaluation.   Freud deserves credit for having put forward the first systematic theory of dream function. In view of the somewhat repressive nature of Austrian society at the end of the nineteenth century, the time of Freud's writing, it is likely that some of the dreams of Freud's patients did represent wish fulfilment in a distorted form.

Freud argued that dreams can provide us with vital information about the unconscious thoughts and feelings of the dreamer. Most later theorists have been unwilling to go that far, but have accepted that dreams can tell us something about the thoughts and feelings of the dreamer. For example, it is claimed within activation-synthesis theory that dreamers have a "quest for meaning" that leads them to interpret the brain's activity in certain ways.

There are various problems with wish-fulfilment theory. First, it is improbable that there is much repression of unacceptable desires in today's liberal and permissive society. Hayes (1994) also pointed that, if dreams have a wish-fulfilment function, then we would expect in our society to find a stronger food and eating content.

Second, some dreams (nightmares) are very frightening, and it is hard to regard them as wish fulfilling even in a distorted way. Third, the latent content of a dream as identified through psychoanalysis generally seems open to question. In other words, dubious methods are used to identify the latent content of a dream. Although some dreams undoubtedly represent wish fulfilment (and not always in a distorted form!), it is unlikely that all dreams can reasonably be regarded as wish fulfilling.

Problem-solving theory

If you have a problem on your mind, one piece of advice is to "sleep on it". This suggestion may not be as absurd as it seems as there are many reports of impressive problem solving during sleep. One of the most famous examples of a valuable dream was reported by the chemist Kekule. He had a dream about a ring of snakes, linked together with the tail of one in the mouth of another. This revealed to him the ring-like atomic structure of benzene molecules, a problem he was working on at the time.

■ Activity: Keep a "dream diary" for 2 weeks, noting down not only the content of your dreams but also any links you notice to events in your waking life. Which of the five theoretical approaches described here provides the best explanation for your dreams, or does each approach address a different aspect?

Webb and Cartwright (1978) proposed that solving work, sex, health, and relationship problems was the purpose of dreaming. Like Freud's wish-fulfilment theory, problem-solving theory also suggests that dreams are a way of coping with problems. Dreams are a way of expressing current concerns. These concerns may relate to the wishes emphasised by Freud, but may also relate to fears (e.g., job insecurity, or health of a loved one). These concerns are often expressed in a symbolic way rather than directly. For example, students who are concerned they may fail a forthcoming examination may dream about falling over a cliff or tripping over something in the street.

However, in problem-solving theory, the manifest content of the dream is the true meaning of the dream rather than there being any latent content, though the dream may rely on metaphor, such as the ring of snakes as a representation of chemicals being linked together in a circular form.

Research evidence.   Webb and Cartwright (1978) described a study where participants were given problems to solve and then allowed to go to sleep. Some were woken whenever they entered REM sleep. Those who had been allowed to sleep uninterrupted were able to provide more realistic solutions to the problems the next day, suggesting that their REM sleep had given them the opportunity to work through the problems.

In another study Cartwright (1984) interviewed women who were undergoing divorce and were either depressed or not depressed, and compared them with a non-depressed married group who had never considered divorce. All 29 participants were studied over a period of 6 nights in a sleep laboratory. The non-depressed divorcing women reported having longer dreams and ones that dealt with marital status issues. Such issues were absent from the dreams of the depressed group. Presumably the depression was associated with an inability to deal with problems and the ability to use dreams in this way helped the individuals to cope better. Hartmann (1973) also found that people who were experiencing various kinds of problems had more REM sleep than the less troubled individuals.

If we dream about personally relevant issues, why is it that we remember only a small fraction of our dreams?

Evaluation.   This appears to be a reasonable account of dreaming and is supported by some research studies. However, there are things that the theory doesn't explain, perhaps most obviously why people and animals have dreams that are not related to the solution of problems! Many dreams are commentaries on life experiences and have no clear meaning. It would also seem to follow from problem-solving theory that it would be useful for us to remember our dreams. It seems puzzling that we remember fewer than 5% of our dreams. There is also the question of why sleep is necessary—we can also solve problems by engaging in another task for a while, as is indicated by the saying "a change is as good as a rest".

The most reasonable conclusion is that problem-solving theory helps to explain some dreams, but does not provide a comprehensive account of all types of dream. Finally, this approach, like all psychological approaches, is uninformative about the physiological processes involved in dreaming.

Survival strategy theory

Winson (1997) has recently put forward a theory of dreams that resembles problem-solving theory. According to Winson:

> REM sleep is the information-processing period when memories and events of the day are juxtaposed [placed close together] with things that happened in the past to form a strategy for survival. What was this or that like? What better actions can I take in a similar situation in the future? All the indications are that REM sleep plays an important part in our survival.

There is some support for this theory in the finding that people who are deprived of REM sleep find it hard to remember the key events of the previous day.

Winson argued that the inhibition against movement found during dreaming is important: "If you didn't have this neural block on activity while you sleep, you would

When awake, our thoughts are highly varied and serve different purposes. Why shouldn't the same be true when we are asleep?

attempt to wake up and act out your dreams. Eye movements are not stopped because they don't interfere with sleeping."

Evaluation. It is hard to evaluate survival strategy theory, because relatively few studies have been designed specifically to test it. However, if dreams are designed to provide a survival strategy, it might be expected that most of them would be remembered. The fact that so few dreams are remembered suggests that many dreams do not provide useful guidance for future action.

S E C T I O N   S U M M A R Y

Biological Rhythms

❖ Biological rhythms are periodically recurring features of biological organisms. Circadian rhythms occur once a day, ultradian rhythms occur less than 1 day, and infradian once a day and include circannual rhythms, which repeat once a year.

❖ The sleep–waking cycle is the most obvious circadian rhythm. Research into the effects of light deprivation (e.g., in a cave) show that circadian rhythms persist in the absence of light and other cues, indicating the existence of an internal (endogenous) biological clock. The fact that these cave residents did not have 24-hour circadian rhythms shows that external (exogenous) cues also play a role in circadian rhythms. The suprachiasmatic nucleus (SCN) in the hypothalamus acts as an endogenous pacemaker, generating its own rhythms. The SCN receives input directly from the eye so it can also be reset by light cues. The SCN sends output to the pineal gland, regulating the production of melatonin. High levels of melatonin are associated with sleepiness.

❖ Light is the dominant zeitgeber but other external cues are important, such as social routines. The circadian rhythms of people living within the Arctic Circle illustrate the influences of internal and external mechanisms. It is adaptive to be able to respond to environmental change, which is why animals are sensitive to these zeitgebers. There are various psychological circadian rhythms, such as task performance. There is evidence for a peak at midday followed by a possible trough after lunch. The peak might be due to high levels of adrenaline, and the trough due to eating lunch.

❖ The menstrual cycle is an example of an infradian rhythm. This cycle is governed endogenously by the release of hormones from the pituitary gland. There is also evidence that the cycle can be affected by exogenous factors, such as light, or by pheromones produced by other women or by men.

❖ Circannual rhythms are also classed as infradian. External cues such as day length and temperature may affect hibernation and migration but there is research evidence to show that endogenous control is also important in, for example, squirrels and wild birds. In humans seasonal affective disorder is an example of a circannual rhythm where some individuals become depressed in relation to seasonal variation, possibly as a result of melatonin level alterations changing daylight hours. Phototherapy is used as a treatment.

❖ When body rhythms are disrupted there may be serious consequences. Jet lag is due to experiencing a discrepancy between internal and external time cues. It is more pronounced when travelling in a easterly direction (phase advance) than westerly (phase delay). Shiftwork also disrupts bodily rhythms. The costs in terms of accidents and health are high. One solution is to use rapidly rotating shifts to reduce the internal/external discrepancy. Other possibilities include slowly rotating shifts to allow the body's natural rhythms to catch up, to use bright lights to reset the biological clock, or to use phase delay changes in shift patterns.

Sleep

❖ Sleep consists of five separate stages. Physiological measures such as the EEG, EOG, and EMG are used to measure physiological activity during sleep. As a person falls asleep their brain waves have progressively reduced frequency and amplitude, and bodily activity also slows down. Of particular importance is stage 4 sleep (which is slow-wave—SWS—and deep). After this stage the sleeper ascends the "sleep staircase" and enters a more active phase, stage 5 or REM sleep, during which most dreaming occurs. Dreams also occur in NREM sleep though these dreams are not as vivid or detailed. The sequence of five stages is repeated during the night with progressively less SWS sleep and more REM activity.

❖ The effects of sleep deprivation should indicate whether sleep is necessary and also indicate what particular functions sleep serves. Case studies of prolonged sleep deprivation show few ill effects, but it is inappropriate to overgeneralise from these studies. Studies of non-human animals have found that sleep deprivation results in death, and this is supported by the case of a man who was unable to sleep and also died. Randy Gardner did show a greater need to recover SWS and REM sleep after his ordeal, and studies of REM deprivation in both humans and animals have shown greater effects from REM deprivation than sleep deprivation in general, and confirmed the REM rebound effect. Controlled laboratory studies suggest that deprivation may affect motivation rather than actual performance. After more than 3 days there are increased periods of micro-sleep and eventually sleep deprivation psychosis. Studies of partial sleep deprivation indicate that people can cope with less sleep.

❖ Restoration theories of sleep, such as those by Oswald and Horne, propose that during sleep physiological recovery takes place of, for example, proteins and neurotransmitters. SWS and REM sleep are likely to be most important in recovery. Support for this view comes from studies of sleep and REM deprivation, from evidence that smaller animals with higher metabolic rates sleep more, and evidence from studies of physical exertion. Psychological restoration may also be a function of sleep. Various studies show that mood and anxiety may be negatively affected by lack of sleep. There are some problems with the restorative account. Can proteins be stored in the body? Why do we have to reduce consciousness when asleep rather than just relaxing. Why do we have other stages of sleep apart from core sleep?

❖ Evolutionary theories of sleep suggest that sleep promotes survival and thus is adaptive and thus naturally selected. Meddis suggested that sleep keeps animals safe at times of danger, such as during the night. Webb suggested that sleep, like hibernation, prevents an animal expending energy unnecessarily. Criticisms focus on the non-falsifiablility of the theory and the question of how much it can explain human sleep. Suggesting, as these theories do, that sleep is a "waste of time" can't explain why some sleep deprivation has harmful consequences.

❖ Recovery or adaptation? It may be that recovery theory explains *why* we sleep, whereas adaptation theory focuses on *when*.

❖ Dreams during REM sleep tend to be more vivid and detailed than those rarer dreams experienced during NREM sleep. Individuals awoken during REM sleep are not always dreaming. Most but not all mammals have REM sleep. Most people have about six episodes of REM activity per night, lasting up to 50 minutes. People forget more than 95% of their dreams and the dreams that are normally remembered tend to be the more unusual ones. There are differences between the consciousness experienced during dreaming and that during waking.

Dreaming

❖ Neurobiological theories of the functions of dreaming suggest that REM activity is the key. According to the activation-synthesis theory of Hobson and McCarley, random electrical activity in the brain during REM sleep is interpreted as meaningful sensory data. The brain imposes meaning (synthesis) and this gives rise to the experience of a dream. The activation-synthesis theory has the advantage of being based on detailed information about brain processes, but the disadvantage that it does not explain adequately the existence of coherent dreams. Crick and Mitchison's reverse-learning or unlearning theory suggests that the main function of dreaming is to eliminate useless information stored in the brain, and so to free up space in the cortex. It is hard in this theory to account for meaningful dreams and to fit in with modern connectionist ideas related to the almost infinite capacity of neural networks.

❖ Psychological theories focus on the psychological benefits gained from dreams, whether they occur during REM sleep or not. According to Freud's wish-fulfilment theory, dreams represent the fulfilment of mainly repressed desires. An individual copes with the repressed information by having dreams that express manifest content (the actual dream) rather than latent content (its true meaning). Latent content can be discovered through dream analysis. Freud's theory may have been appropriate at the time it was written and can explain the fact that dreams often do represent our current concerns, but it is not clear why dreams are not related to other concerns such as food, nor why we have nightmares which could hardly be wish fulfilment.

❖ Webb and Cartwright's problem-solving theory also suggests that dreams are a way of working through matters that are troubling us. Here, dreams only have manifest content though they may use metaphor. There is empirical support for this view, but it doesn't explain why not all dreams are related to problem solving.

❖ Winson's survival strategy theory is again related to problem solving. It proposes that in dreams we combine and re-combine past events to help form strategies for survival. We remember those dreams that suggest adaptive strategies.

FURTHER READING

The topics in this Section are covered in greater depth by E. Bentley (2000) *Awareness: Biorhythms, sleep and dreaming* (London: Routledge), written specifically for the AQA A specification. The topics are also analysed in an accessible way in J.P.J. Pinel (1997) *Biopsychology (3rd Edn.)* (Boston: Allyn & Bacon). A. Alvarez (1995) *An exploration of night life, night language, sleep and dreams* (London: Cape) covers many interesting topics. S. Coren (1996) *Sleep thieves* (New York: The Free Press) offers readable coverage of biological rhythms and sleep.

Example Examination Questions

You should spend 30 minutes on each of the questions below, which aim to test the material in this Section.

1. **(a)** Describe **two** research studies into circadian biological rhythms.   (12 marks)
   (b) Evaluate these studies.   (12 marks)

2. Discuss the role of endogenous factors in bodily rhythms.   (24 marks)

3. "To sleep is to dream." Discuss explanations relating to functions of sleep.   (24 marks)

4. Discuss the implications of findings from studies of total and partial sleep deprivation.   (24 marks)

5. **(a)** Consider neurobiological theories of the function of dreaming.   (12 marks)
   (b) Evaluate these theories in terms of alternative theoretical accounts.   (12 marks)

6. Discuss research findings relating to the nature of dreams.   (24 marks)

Examination Tips

Question 1. In part (a) you should present two research studies following the guidelines used at AS level, i.e., describe their aims, procedure, findings, and conclusions. Any evaluative comments are credited in part (b). Such evaluation may be positive (e.g., other research support, practical applications) or negative (e.g., poor methodology, lack of validity). Description of any other research studies would only receive credit where it offers some insight into (evaluation of) the initial two studies.

Question 2.   It is possible to use virtually everything you know in this essay because external factors can be used as a means of evaluation (as long as they are presented explicitly in this way). Therefore the likely problem in this essay will be lack of selectivity. In order to obtain high marks you need to supply depth and breadth, structure, and coherent elaboration. If you try to include everything you know it is likely to read like a list and lack sufficient detail (AO1 skill) and elaboration (AO2 skill).

Question 3.   You are not required to refer to the quotation in your answer but it is there to suggest a topic that you might consider when discussing the function of sleep. Your temptation might be to present a prepared essay on restoration and evolutionary theories, but you might also consider dreams. "Discuss" is an AO1 and AO2 term (describe and evaluate). Remember that both positive and negative evaluation is creditworthy.

Question 4.   This essay does not require you to describe studies of sleep deprivation but to discuss (describe + evaluate) the implications of these studies. This means that some description would be creditworthy but that AO1 credit will also come from a description of what the studies tell us. AO2 credit will come from the effective use of this material to present a critical argument (e.g., one that considers alternative viewpoints or the implications for theories). If you ignore the "partial sleep" research your final mark will be limited to a ceiling of 16 marks for partial performance.

Question 5.   "Consider" is an AO1 term and therefore in part (a) you are required to describe neurobiological theories. The "two or more" indicates that you could obtain full marks with reference to only two such theories. Part (b) is a straightforward evaluation with some hints about how you might do this.

Question 6.   The focus here is on the findings of research studies, i.e., what have researchers found about the nature of dreams from their studies? You might be tempted to write a list of different studies and their findings, which would be acceptable, but a better answer would use the findings themselves as the backbone of the essay. Evaluation could be in terms of methodological criticisms of the studies or the implications of the findings for theories of the function of dreaming. Remember that REM sleep is not the same as dreaming.

WEB SITES

http://www.websciences.org/sltbr/links.htm
   Useful links on the site of the Society for Light Treatment and Biological Rhythms.

http://www.circadian.com/
   This site includes a useful glossary of terms.

http://www.lboro.ac.uk/departments/hu/groups/sleep/
   A top UK sleep research centre at Loughborough University, UK.

http://www.crhsc.umontreal.ca/dreams/
   Dream and Nightmare Research Laboratory in Canada.

http://www.sleepnet.com/index.shtml
   Large site with lot of information and links about sleep-related issues (including dreams) and sleeping disorders.

http://sawka.com/spiritwatch/lucid.htm
   Papers on lucid dreaming.

http://www.sleephomepages.org/
   Collection of sleep-related portals.

http://www.asdreams.org/
   Association for the Study of Dreams.

6

Motivation and Emotion

What makes us tick? Basic motivational drives, such as hunger and thirst, are common to all animals; higher motives, such as emotion, which is a key element of psychological study, drive other human behaviours. This Section discusses the many theories, based on brain mechanisms, that have arisen to explain these behaviours.

Brain Mechanisms of Motivation

We can only really understand someone else when we begin to appreciate the motivational forces driving their behaviour.

Motivation is highly relevant to the following:

- The *direction* of behaviour: the goal or goals being pursued.
- The *intensity* of behaviour: the amount of effort, concentration, and so on, invested in behaviour.
- The *persistence* of behaviour: the extent to which a goal is pursued until it is reached.

A definition including these ingredients was put forward by Taylor et al. (1982, p.160):

> *Motivation ... is generally conceived of by psychologists in terms of a process, or a series of processes, which somehow starts, steers, sustains and finally stops a goal-directed sequence of behaviour.*

The best examples of motivated behaviour come from the study of primary drives such as hunger and thirst. If someone is very hungry, we would expect their behaviour to be directed towards the goals of finding and eating food, we would expect them to put in much effort, and we would expect them to continue looking for food until they found some.

Hunger and thirst are both regulated by **homeostasis**, a concept introduced in your AS level studies. Homeostasis is a mechanism that regulates some internal characteristic at a fairly constant level in spite of external variability. For example, humans possess a regulatory mechanism that maintains our internal bodily temperature at a given level even when there are very large variations in external temperature. Eating and drinking behaviour both depend on regulatory mechanisms to some extent. Regulatory mechanisms involve a system variable (the characteristic to be regulated), a set point (the ideal value for the system variable), a detector that assesses the actual value of the system

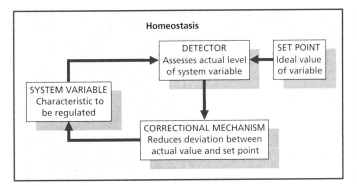

Homeostasis

variable, and a correctional mechanism that reduces any deviation between the actual value and the set point.

Homeostatic behaviours are regulated in the brain by the **hypothalamus**, a small structure at the base of the brain. The hypothalamus produces hormones that trigger emotional and stress responses. The hypothalamus also receives information from sensory receptors both inside and outside the body, and contains specialised receptors that judge if a system variable (such as water or temperature) is too high or too low, and activates appropriate mechanisms to correct this.

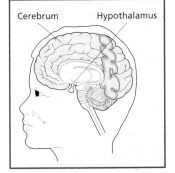

Hunger

What factors determine when we start and stop eating? In affluent parts of the world people generally eat as a consequence of learned social signals, such as mealtimes or because we see food and feel hungry, rather than as a consequence of genuine hunger. Thus much of our eating is not governed by homeostatic mechanisms, though we do have the experience of feeling full and not wanting to eat. What mechanisms in the brain tell us when we are hungry and when we are full?

Cannon and Washburn's experiment with a balloon

When you feel hungry this is often accompanied by hunger pangs, which feel like contractions of the stomach. Is this what they are? Cannon and Washburn (1912) devised an experiment  where Washburn swallowed a balloon that was attached to a tube. The balloon could be inflated via the tube that came out through his mouth. If the balloon was inflated it was possible to detect muscle contractions because they would force air in and out of the tube. The tube was connected to a device that recorded changes in air pressure.

Whenever Washburn detected a hunger pang he pressed a key to record this. The record showed that each time he felt a hunger pang his stomach also contracted, demonstrating a clear relationship and suggesting that the subjective sensation of hunger is controlled by the stomach contractions.

KEY STUDY EVALUATION — Cannon and Washburn

Neat as this explanation is, there are problems. First of all, people who have had their stomach removed still experience hunger pains. Second, cutting the vagus nerve, which sends signals to the brain from the stomach, also has little effect (Pinel, 1997). However, people who have had a leg amputated still think they can feel their leg, so it is possible that the brain is "imagining" the continuing sensory input in both instances, which would support the view that signals from the stomach do play a role in the sensation of hunger.

Discussion points

1. The data in this experiment were collected from one participant. Is it reasonable to generalise from this?
2. Why would it be important for the body to use other cues than hunger pangs when determining hunger?

Hypothalamic theory

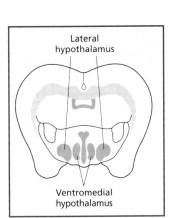

Early research on animals suggested that the hypothalamus plays a major role in regulating eating behaviour. It was claimed (e.g., Anand & Brobeck, 1951) that the lateral nucleus of the hypothalamus (LH) is a feeding centre, which is responsible for initiating food intake. In contrast, the ventromedial nucleus of the hypothalamus (VMH) is a satiety centre, which causes eating to stop.

If this is correct, then a lesion (small cut) in the feeding centre should reduce feeding, whereas a lesion in the satiety centre should lead to increased feeding. Support for the former came from Anand and Brobeck who found that lesions to the lateral nucleus stopped rats from eating, so they lost weight rapidly. Similarly, support for the latter came from Hetherington and Ranson (1942) who observed the effects of lesions to the ventromedial nucleus. The rats started to eat much more than they had done previously, and their weight often doubled as a result.

Hoebel and Teitelbaum (1966) found that lesions to the ventromedial nucleus were followed by two phases: the dynamic phase and the static phase. Rats ate many times the normal amount of food during the dynamic phase, which usually lasted between 4 and 12 weeks. During the subsequent static phase, however, there was no further increase in body weight, with food consumption being regulated to maintain the weight reached at the end of the dynamic phase.

Evaluation

The hypothalamic theory of hunger is no longer accepted because at best it is an oversimplification. Lesions to the lateral hypothalamus lead to reduced drinking as well as to reduced eating, and they also make animals generally unresponsive to stimuli (Pinel, 1997). Therefore, it cannot simply be regarded as a feeding centre.

The ventromedial hypothalamus is not a satiety centre for various reasons. First, lesions to the ventromedial hypothalamus typically damage other related areas so we can't be sure what part of the brain may play a key role. Second, rats with lesions in the ventromedial hypothalamus become obese, i.e., the rats don't stop eating as we would expect, but they do not seem very hungry. For example, lesioned rats are more willing than control rats to eat tasty food, but they will not work as hard as controls to gain access to it (Teitelbaum, 1957). Third, a major effect of lesions to the ventromedial hypothalamus is to increase body fat. Han, Feng, and Kuo (1972) found that lesioned rats gained more body fat than control rats given the same amount of food. Lesioned animals eat a lot because the food they eat goes into body fat and contributes relatively little to their immediate energy needs.

Standardised eating times are the norm, with work and social schedules being planned around them.

Glucostatic theory

The hypothalamic theory did not provide a detailed account of the kinds of information used by the hypothalamus to produce eating behaviour or its cessation. Mayer (1955) put forward the glucostatic theory to fill this gap. According to this theory, there are specialised neurons known as **glucostats**, which measure the level of blood glucose. Glucostats produce high rates of firing when the availability of glucose is low, and these high rates of firing result in hunger.

Where are the glucostats or glucose-sensitive receptors located? They are found in the brain and in the liver (Carlson, 1994). For example, Russek (1971) injected a dog with glucose either into the jugular vein of the neck or directly into the liver. Glucose injected into the jugular vein did not affect the dog's food intake, whereas glucose injected into the liver caused it to stop eating for several hours.

Evaluation

Evidence supporting the glucostatic theory was reviewed by Campfield and Smith (1990). There is generally a decline in blood glucose levels shortly before rats start eating, but this does not prove that falling glucose levels *cause* eating behaviour. However, Campfield and Smith discussed other studies in which a small injection of glucose into rats' veins

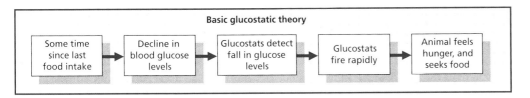

Basic glucostatic theory

Some time since last food intake → Decline in blood glucose levels → Glucostats detect fall in glucose levels → Glucostats fire rapidly → Animal feels hunger, and seeks food

Hunger is obviously an adaptive behaviour (without it we would die), but why are there no homeostatic mechanisms for important vitamins?

delayed eating, provided that this was done when blood glucose levels were going down—which does seem to support a causal role for blood glucose levels. However, Pinel (1997) reports that other research has found that eating behaviour is often unaffected even by large infusions of glucose.

Lipostatic theory

Hunger can be produced by low levels of glucose. Glucose is one of the major nutrients (substances providing nourishment), but there are two others: lipids or fatty acids, and amino acids. According to the lipostatic hypothesis (e.g., Nisbett, 1972), eating behaviour is initiated when the hypothalamus receives information that the levels of lipids or fatty acids are low.

Where are the receptors that detect low levels of lipids or fatty acids? Ritter and Taylor (1990) found that hunger produced by a lack of fatty acids was eliminated by cutting the vagus nerve (the nerve that transmits information from the stomach to the brain) as it enters the abdominal cavity. This suggests that there are lipid-sensitive receptors in or close to the abdominal cavity.

Evaluation

What factors other than social or cultural ones might motivate you to eat?

Lipoprivation (depriving cells of lipids) causes hunger, especially when combined with glucoprivation (depriving cells of glucose). Friedman, Tordoff, and Ramirez (1986) gave rats moderate doses of chemicals producing either lipoprivation or glucoprivation. There was a marked increase in food intake when both chemicals were given together, but much smaller effects when only one chemical was used. This suggests that there must be multiple control over the initiation of eating behaviour.

Cessation of eating

All of the accounts so far have focused on what motivates behaviour to eat. Why do we stop eating? There are social pressures to eat meals of a certain size, but there are also internal physiological processes. Deutsch and Gonzalez (1980) found that the stomach plays an important role. They operated on rats to insert an inflatable cuff that could be

The Prince Regent (later George IV) was a well-known glutton.

used to prevent food from leaving the stomach. When 5 millilitres of the stomach contents were removed artificially, the rats consumed almost exactly 5 millilitres more of the liquid diet in order to compensate for what had been lost.

There is other strong evidence that the gastrointestinal tract plays a role. Receptors in the gastrointestinal tract respond to ingested food by causing the release of peptides. Several of these peptides send satiety signals to the brain and lead to a cessation of eating. Relevant evidence was reported by Gibbs, Young, and Smith (1973). They injected the peptide cholecystokinin into hungry rats, and found that this led to reduced eating. Similar findings have been obtained for several other peptides.

Evaluation of homeostatic theories

It is tempting to assume that we are motivated to eat when our energy level falls significantly below our energy set point or optimal level, and that we stop eating when we have returned to our set point. Some of the theories we have discussed (e.g., the glucostatic and lipostatic theories) are based on those assumptions. However, Pinel (1997) argues that the set-point approach with its homeostatic emphasis is inadequate. When most people in Western societies eat meals, they have no significant physiological or energy deficits (e.g., glucose levels, fat deposits). For most of us, hunger has more to do with social and cultural factors (e.g., expected mealtimes) than it has with basic physiological processes. Positive-incentive theory (described in the Key Study below) offers a combined account of psychological and physiological factors.

Studies on sham feeding provide strong evidence against homeostatic theories. In these studies, animals are operated on so that the food they eat passes along a tube and out of the body rather than going to the stomach. In spite of the fact that the animals (e.g., rats) are not obtaining any energy from their food, they initially eat only the amount of their usual diet that they have been used to eating (Weingarten & Kulikovsky, 1989). Such findings indicate that eating behaviour is only very imperfectly controlled by restoring energy levels.

Another issue is that it would take too long for some of the proposed satiety mechanisms to initiate. We stop eating long before some of them have had time to register.

> ### How do you "evaluate" physiological explanations?
>
> Students and teachers often ask how it is possible to evaluate explanations in this part of the specification. To evaluate means no more than assessing the value of an explanation. This can be done with reference to empirical support for any theory and/or through offering alternative and better explanations. Or even looking at explanations that are weaker. It is also possible to offer explanations that are not physiological, to demonstrate that there are other possibilities. Finally, in order to evaluate an explanation, one might consider situations where the system fails. In other words, does the physiological mechanism always work, or are there occasions when its responses are undesirable or inappropriate?
>
> In addition to "evaluation", the skill cluster AO2 includes "commentary" which means that marks are awarded for any informed comment. The aim is to encourage students to go beyond their knowledge and to offer informed opinions about the value of that knowledge. The term "informed" refers to knowledge drawn from your psychology course rather than commonsense opinion.

> ■ Activity: List the physiological and psychological mechanisms involved in eating behaviour. You may find it helpful to present your answers in a "mind map" format, with "Eating" as the central construct.

Eating disorders

A further way to evaluate theories of hunger is to consider situations where hunger mechanisms have gone wrong. At one extreme there is the disorder of overeating (obesity) and at the other extreme there is undereating or undernourishing (anorexia nervosa or bulimia nervosa). Explanations have been offered for both in terms of hypothalamic or physiological function.

Positive-incentive theory

Positive-incentive theory (e.g., Rolls & Rolls, 1982) is more in line with the evidence for eating behaviour than is the set-point or homeostatic approach. According to positive-incentive theory, hunger levels are determined by the anticipated pleasure of eating. Numerous factors influence the level of anticipated pleasure; they include the anticipated flavour of the food, the length of time since the last meal, the time of day with respect to normal mealtimes, blood glucose levels, and so on. In other words, basic physiological processes and social factors both contribute to our feelings of hunger.

Strong support for positive-incentive theory was reported by Rogers and Blundell (1980). They compared the eating behaviour of rats offered their normal diet and those offered what is known as a cafeteria diet, which consists of a variety of palatable foods. In this study, the rats on a cafeteria diet were offered bread and chocolate in addition to their normal diet.

What were the findings? The rats given the cafeteria diet had an average increase of 84% in their daily calorie intake. After 120 days on their new diet, these rats showed an average increase of 49% in their body weight. These findings (although based only on rats) may help to explain why there has been a dramatic increase in the number of very fat or obese people in the Western world. They suggest that an important part of the explanation is that the ready availability of foods that satisfy our preferences for fatty, sweet, and salty tastes encourages us to eat more than we should, as would be expected on positive-incentive theory. In contrast, set-point or homeostatic theory cannot readily explain why so many people become obese.

Discussion points

1. Consider which aspects of our eating behaviour are explained by positive-incentive theory. For example, the kinds of tastes associated with desserts are very different from those associated with main courses.

2. Do you feel that positive-incentive theory has relevance for your patterns of eating?

Cafeteria diet

What suggestions for dieting might be drawn from this theory?

Obesity

The study of obesity in mice led to the identification of a protein called leptin, which circulates in the blood and signals high fat levels (Halaas et al., 1995). Body fat produces leptin and the body's response to leptin is a reduction in general hunger levels. However further investigation did not find that obese individuals had low leptin levels, so why isn't their hunger decreased? It appears that obese people are insensitive to leptin at the leptin receptor sites. The receptors for leptin are located in the hypothalamus and their task is to inhibit the release of neuropeptide Y (NPY) (Stephens et al., 1995). Normally NPY increases feeding. When NPY is inhibited, hunger is decreased. This indicates an important role for NPY, and one that requires further research.

Anorexia nervosa and bulimia nervosa

It is possible that anorexics have disturbed hypothalamic functioning. Park et al. (1995) studied four females suffering from anorexia nervosa, all of whom had had glandular fever or a similar disease shortly before the onset of the eating disorder. Park et al. argued, rather speculatively, that the physical disease may have influenced the functioning of the hypothalamus, and this caused homeostatic imbalances.

However, altered hypothalamic activity may well not be a cause of anorexia nervosa. It is more likely to occur as a result of the weight loss or the anorexic's emotional distress. In addition, post-mortems have not revealed any lesions in this area of the brain.

Serotonin may be involved in some cases of anorexia and bulimia. Serotonin is a neurotransmitter, which is implicated in a number of behaviours such as arousal, aggressiveness, and sleep. Fava et al. (1989) reported links between anorexic behaviour and changes in the levels of serotonin and also noradrenaline (discussed in your AS level studies). Eating large amounts of starchy foods containing carbohydrates can increase serotonin levels in the brain, and this may improve mood in individuals who have low serotonin levels. This may explain why bulimics like to eat starchy food.

In addition, antidepressants (especially SSRIs—selective serotonin reuptake indicators) have been used successfully on people with eating disorders. This supports the possibility of an underlying neurotransmitter dysfunction.

In your psychology studies, what other effects of serotonin have you learned about?

Thirst

The motivation to drink has also been explained in various ways. Like hunger, there is a complex interaction between the body's physiological systems and the brain's central governing capacity.

Intracellular and extracellular water

The first point to recognise is that our need for water can stem from extracellular loss (loss of water from outside the body cells) or from intracellular loss. This water is contained in the blood that bathes our body's cells, carrying nutrients to the cells and taking away waste products.

About one-third of the water in the human body is found outside cells and so is extracellular, with the remaining two-thirds is inside cells and so intracellular. Rolls, Wood, and Rolls (1980) found in various species that intracellular deficits have more effect on drinking behaviour. When they eliminated the intracellular deficit in water-deprived animals by injections, this reduced the amount of drinking by 75%. In contrast, eliminating the extracellular deficit reduced drinking by only about 15%.

Osmosis (or how water moves in and out of cells)

Water (whether inside or outside cells) contains dissolved substances, of which the most important is salt. Water containing many substances is said to have high osmotic pressure, whereas water containing few substances has low osmotic pressure. The cell membrane is semi-permeable. This means that water can pass through it, but the substances dissolved in the water can't pass through. When there is water on both sides of a semi-permeable membrane, then water on the side having the lower osmotic pressure will pass through to the side having the higher osmotic pressure. This continues until the osmotic pressure is the same on both sides. This process is called **osmosis** and when the semi-permeable membrane is a cell membrane the result is that osmosis pressure inside and outside the cell becomes the same.

Cells need water, and if the osmotic pressure outside the cells is too low, then no water will get through the cell, ultimately causing death.

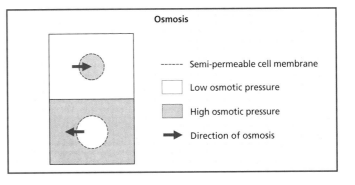

How water deprivation leads to thirst

You may have thought thirst was a simple matter. However there are two different reasons why the body needs water: **osmotic thirst** and **hypovolemic thirst**.

Osmotic thirst

When a person consumes salt this passes through their blood but does not move into the cells because, when water passes through the semi-permeable membrane of the cell (due to osmotic pressure) the substances dissolved in the water remain on the outside. This high level of salt outside the cell then causes water to leave the cells. Changes in osmotic pressure are detected within the lateral preoptic area of the hypothalamus by **osmoreceptors**. This leads to direct and indirect means of restoring balance:

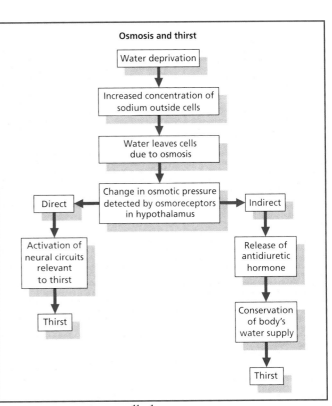

1. Directly by creating a desire for water (i.e., osmotic thirst).
2. Indirectly because antidiuretic hormone is released causing the kidneys to excrete more concentrated urine, conserving the body's water supplies.

Volumetric thirst

Water deprivation also results from a reduction in blood volume (**hypovolumetric thirst**). This might result after a massive blood loss, such as a cut, or a heavy menstrual flow. Note that this explanation of thirst does not involve the brain, and therefore can be presented as an alternative explanation to that of the osmoreceptors in the brain.

Blood-flow receptors detect the reduction in blood volume, and they trigger kidney function directly. Blood pressure receptors, called baroreceptors, in the wall of the heart also detect reduced blood volume, and they affect the functioning of the kidneys by increasing the release of antidiuretic hormone. Antidiuretic hormone reduces the amount of urine produced in the kidneys, and it also leads to the release of the hormone renin. In turn, renin leads to the formation of the peptide hormone angiotensin II in the blood. Angiotensin II produces increased blood pressure and also leads to the release of the hormone aldosterone. Aldosterone leads the kidneys to reabsorb sodium, which has the effect of preventing additional decreases in blood volume.

Cessation of drinking

What causes people to stop drinking water? Considerations of homeostasis and the notion of a set point might lead to the assumption that people keep drinking until the

Even people experiencing severe thirst will stop drinking, and feel that they have had enough to drink, before their body has had a chance to absorb the water they have consumed.

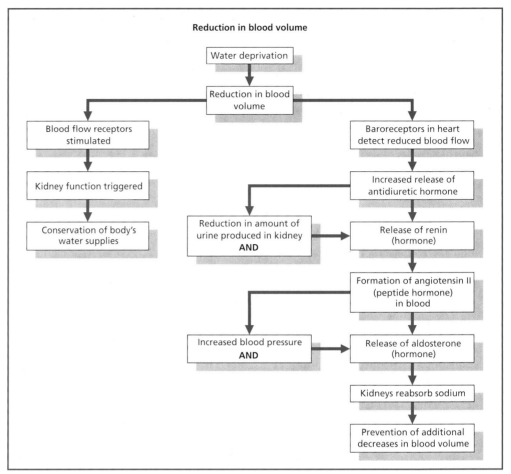

Reduction in blood volume

Water deprivation

↓

Reduction in blood volume

Blood flow receptors stimulated

↓

Kidney function triggered

↓

Conservation of body's water supplies

Baroreceptors in heart detect reduced blood flow

↓

Increased release of antidiuretic hormone

Reduction in amount of urine produced in kidney **AND**

Release of renin (hormone)

Formation of angiotensin II (peptide hormone) in blood

Increased blood pressure **AND**

Release of aldosterone (hormone)

↓

Kidneys reabsorb sodium

↓

Prevention of additional decreases in blood volume

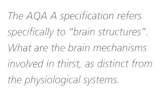

The AQA A specification refers specifically to "brain structures". What are the brain mechanisms involved in thirst, as distinct from the physiological systems.

intracellular and extracellular water levels are restored to normality. However, that cannot be the case. Much drinking in humans occurs in the absence of any significant deficits in water levels or blood volume. In addition, people who do drink in response to fluid deficits generally stop drinking before the water has had time to be absorbed into the body. In fact, there are satiety (satisfaction) receptors in the mouth and in the intestines which cause drinking to stop. These receptors become satiated especially rapidly when the taste of the liquid remains the same; this is known as sensory-specific satiety. Rolls et al. (1980) compared water drinking in rats that were offered either water on its own or flavoured water in which the flavour changed frequently. Rats in the latter group drank almost three times as much water as those in the former group.

Theories of Motivation

Early theories of motivation attached great importance to the notion of **instinct**, which is an innate impulse or motive. According to McDougall (1912), there are numerous instincts. They include food-seeking, sex, curiosity, fear, parental protectiveness, disgust, anger, laughter, self-assertiveness, gregariousness, acquisitiveness, rest, migration, appeal for assistance, comfort, submissiveness, and constructiveness.

McDougall claimed to be able to account for all behaviour by attributing it to the attempt to satisfy one or other of these instincts. However, it does not make much sense to identify so many instincts. It is improbable that constructiveness or submissiveness are fundamental motives. Another problem is that there is a great danger of circular argument. For example, to argue that someone is being self-assertive because of their self-assertiveness instinct does not really explain their behaviour!

Classifying Motives

There have been several attempts since McDougall to classify or categorise our motives. One system is based on the distinction between *internally* and *externally* aroused motives (**intrinsic** and **extrinsic** motives respectively). The motives for food, water, sleep, and eliminating waste products all depend largely on internal factors, whereas motives such as a desire to avoid extreme temperatures or to withdraw from painful stimulation are triggered by external stimuli. However, most motives depend on both internal and external factors. For example, although the goal of eating often involves internal physiological conditions, it is also affected by external stimuli such as the sight of appetising food. Another clear example is sexual motivation. This is affected by sex hormones in the bloodstream, but it is also influenced by external factors such as the availability of an attractive and willing partner.

There are other ways of categorising motives. One way is to categorise them into *cyclic* and *non-cyclic* motives. Cyclic motives are those where the motivational force increases and decreases in a more or less regular way over time. The needs to sleep and to eat are cyclic motives, whereas the motive to avoid painful stimulation is not. Cyclic motives tend to be internally aroused, whereas non-cyclic motives are externally aroused.

Another way of classifying motives is into *primary* or basic, and *secondary* or acquired. Primary motives appear without the necessity for learning, and are found in nearly every member of a species. They include the needs for food, drink, and elimination. Secondary motives are learned, and it is usually assumed that their existence owes much to primary motives. For example, many people regard the acquisition of money as an important goal in its own right. However, the initial importance of money is simply as a way of being able to satisfy primary motives, such as those for food and drink.

We can also classify explanations in terms of whether they are *physiological* or *psychological*.

Physiological Theories of Motivation

Drive theories

Woodworth (1918) introduced the notion of **drives**, by which he meant the motivational forces that cause individuals to be active and to strive for certain goals.

Homeostatic drive theory

One of the first drive theories of motivation was **homeostatic drive theory**. This theory was based on the notion of homeostasis, first described by Cannon (1929), to refer to the processes by which we maintain a reasonably constant internal environment. As we have seen, there are regulatory or homeostatic mechanisms involved in hunger and thirst. Animals are motivated to seek food or liquid in order to return their body to a steady state. Once this occurs the drive is reduced.

However, it is not at all clear that homeostatic drive theory can account for other forms of motivation. Before evaluating homeostatic drive theory, however, we will consider a related type of drive theory.

■ Activity: How would you categorise the possible motives for the following behaviours?

- Studying for exams
- Working for money
- Voluntary work
- Going to a party
- Getting married
- Having children

Can you think of any other motives that are cyclic or non-cyclic?

Extrinsic and intrinsic motives

Extrinsic rewards can destroy intrinsic motivation, an observation that has important implications for teaching and parenting. The following folk tale illustrates how intrinsic motives (in this case, pleasure seeking) are extinguished by extrinsic motives (money), so that when the extrinsic motive is removed, the original motive has disappeared:

Each day the children harassed the old woman. After school they would play outside her window; if she asked them to be quiet, they only called her obscene names and shouted more loudly.

One day as the children approached, she called to them, "I have grown fond of listening to you play, but my hearing isn't what it used to be. If you will play in front of my window, I will pay each of you fifty cents."

The children laughed at the woman's foolish request, but agreed. For a week they collected their payment and raised a tremendous din.

The next week, however, the woman greeted them with a frown. "Times are hard. I can only pay you 25 cents this week." The children complained, but agreed to her offer. Three days later, the woman met them again. "Times are hard. I can only pay you ten cents," she told them.

"Ten cents? That's not enough," they said. And they left her in peace.

From Forsyth (1987) *Social psychology*, Brooks-Colen, p.158

A study by Lepper et al. (1973) supported the point made in this story. Lepper et al. asked 55 preschool children to draw a picture, telling some of them that they would receive a certificate for good drawing. So there was an "expected reward" and an "unexpected reward" group. At the end both groups of children were given a certificate. There was also a no-certificate group. Some weeks later the children were again asked to draw a picture; they found that the no-certificate group was most willing to do a drawing, followed by those who had not expected the certificate. This supports the view that it is more valuable for children to be allowed to develop their own, internal sense of control rather than offering external, financial incentives. So tell your parents you don't want to be given £50 for passing your A levels!

Drive-reduction theory

Hull (1943) put forward drive-reduction theory, in which he argued that there is an important distinction between needs and drives. Needs are essentially physiological in nature; they include hunger, water, and so on. In contrast, drives are less physiological and more psychological, and they are based on needs. So this theory is both physiological and psychological.

Hull's approach was called drive-reduction theory because it was assumed that behaviour is motivated by the attempt to reduce one or more drives. Drive reduction is reinforcing or rewarding. According to the principles of **operant conditioning**, anything that is rewarding is more likely to be repeated and a rewarded behaviour is repeated (learned), so that animals and humans learn to behave in ways that produce drive reduction. For example, if a young child learns that eating biscuits from a jar in the kitchen reduces hunger drive, then he or she will show an increased tendency to return to the biscuit jar when hungry.

Dollard and Miller (1950) used drive reduction theory to explain attachment behaviour (as we considered in your AS level studies). Hunger and thirst are both primary drives. According to Dollard and Miller, the mother (or person doing the feeding) in providing food and water reduces the infant's primary drives. Therefore the mother becomes a **secondary reinforcer**. From then on the infant seeks to be with this person because the person is now a source of reward in themselves. The infant has thus become attached. This explanation of attachment has been criticised because research has shown that infants do not become most attached to the person who feeds them (e.g., Harlow, 1959).

Food-seeking or curiosity?

A central assumption in drive-reduction theory was that an individual's behaviour in a given situation is determined by drive or motivation, and by what he or she has learned (habits). This led Hull to produce an equation which suggested that the tendency to respond = drive x habit. He later added further assumptions about the role of incentives and other factors. However, he still maintained that behaviour depends mainly on a combination of motivation (drive) and learning (habit).

Evaluation of homeostatic drive theories

Homeostatic drive theory can account for some aspects of hunger and thirst. However, the whole drive theory approach is inadequate. Why is this so? First, there are many exceptions to the notion that all behaviour is directed towards drive reduction. Much human and animal behaviour is based on curiosity, and it is hard to regard curiosity as involving the reduction of either a drive or a need. Animals have been found to be motivated by a desire for pleasure. For example, in a classic experiment Olds and Milner (1954) found that rats who received electrical stimulation of a particular part of the brain (the "pleasure centre" in the hypothalamus) in return for pressing a lever repeated this behaviour thousands of times an hour for several hours. Again, no physiological need is reduced by this behaviour. Unless, of course, all animals are innately hedonistic.

Second, the theoretical approach was based largely on studies with other species, especially rats. It is possible (if unlikely) that rats, dogs, and other species are largely motivated to reduce physiological needs and drives. However, it is improbable that this is true of humans. For example, the humanistic psychologist Maslow argued that humans are motivated in part by love and belonging needs, aesthetic or artistic needs, and the need for self-actualisation (see later in this Unit). Whether or not one agrees with the humanistic approach, the forces that motivate humans are much more numerous than those included in drive theories.

Third, there is very little recognition in drive theories that cognitive factors play an important role in human motivation. Some theorists (e.g., Locke, 1968) have argued that motivation depends in large measure on the goals we set. For example, someone who is firmly committed to obtaining a B grade in A level psychology is likely to be more

Attachment between an infant and caregiver has been explained in terms of drive-reduction theory: the caregiver reduces the infant's primary drives, thus becoming a secondary reinforcer.

If one of our drives is anxiety, and we are motivated to reduce it, what types of behaviour would this explain?

motivated (and will work harder) than someone who is only concerned about passing. This aspect of motivation was ignored by Cannon and by Hull.

Optimum level of arousal

An alternative, physiological explanation can be presented in terms of general levels of arousal. The concept of arousal refers to the state of being ready to respond. A moderate level of arousal is necessary for normal functioning. Too little arousal and an animal is likely to be overtaken by environmental events (such as a pouncing lion). Too much arousal and the body's resources become depleted (as you have seen in your AS level studies of stress and the GAS model).

The **optimum level of arousal** (OLA) theory is similar to the homeostatic drive model because it suggests that the animal has a drive to return to an optimum state— moderate arousal. OLA has the advantage of being able to explain those behaviours that didn't fit into the homeostatic model, such as curiosity. Hebb (1958) noted that monkeys will do puzzles despite receiving no external reward. Thus they are not motivated by a reward but by their need to be moderately aroused. Interestingly, this explanation can be applied to animals in zoos that become bored, leading in some cases to severe psychological disturbance. In recent years zoos have recognised this and given animals toys to play with.

In an examination, what is your ideal state of arousal?

Too much arousal can lead to sensory overload, as has been found in studies of urban living. Ludwig (1975) suggests that this could explain many of the disorders in our highly urbanised society. There are individual differences in the degree to which individuals cope with, and seek arousal. Zuckerman (1979) identified "sensation-seekers", people who have a high OLA and engage in activities that produce a thrill, such as rollercoasters or bungee jumping. According to Eysenck (1963) the personality traits of extraversion and introversion are linked to arousal. He suggested that extroverts have lower cortical arousal than introverts and therefore seek excitement to enhance their arousal levels.

Optimum levels of arousal are good for performance. The **Yerkes–Dodson law** (1908) describes the *curvilinear* relationship between arousal and performance (see below). When arousal is very low or very high, performance is poor. Performance is highest at a medium level of arousal. This relationship applies in many different behaviours and has research support. For example, Davis and Harvey (1992) found that major league baseball players performed less well in the closing stages of a game if the pressure was too great.

Evaluation

OLA has been used to explain why animals seek to explore their environment and why they "play". Both of these behaviours are important in cognitive development, and to explain them just in terms of arousal perhaps ignores the primary motive for the behaviour.

A further problem with this theory is that, like drive-reduction theory, it is not possible to define optimum levels of arousal except in terms of the behaviour itself. If an animal

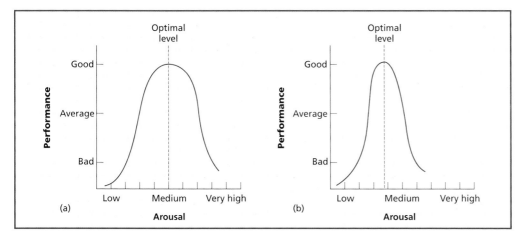

The Yerkes–Dodson law; (a) a simple task and (b) a complicated task.

seeks arousal then its current level must be too low, and vice versa. It is difficult, therefore, to determine what the behaviour of an optimally aroused animal should look like. This means it isn't necessary to have a concept of optimum arousal.

Psychological Theories of Motivation

Drive-reduction theory was both physiological and psychological, but there are other theories that contain a greater psychological emphasis.

Need-press theory

Murray (1938) argued in his need-press theory that we have 20 manifest needs. These include dominance, achievement, affiliation, play, sex, aggression, and nurturance. Each need has a desired or intended effect, and feelings and actions associated with it. For example, the dominance need involves the desire to control or influence other people, feelings of confidence, and actions designed to influence and persuade others. In order to understand someone's behaviour, we have to take account of **press**, which consists of those features of the environment relevant to need-satisfaction. For example, the need for dominance can only be satisfied when there are other people around who are willing to be influenced.

If there is no "press", what happens to behaviour?

How can needs be measured? The Thematic Apperception Test (TAT) was developed by Murray (Morgan & Murray, 1935). It consists of a number of pictures (e.g., a young man turned away from an older woman). The individual taking the test is told to say what is happening in the picture, what led up to the situation, and what will happen subsequently. These stories are usually interpreted in a rather flexible and subjective fashion to identify the individual's underlying motives and conflicts. Murray (1938, p.529) developed the Thematic Apperception Test as part of "an attempt to discover the covert (inhibited) and unconscious (partially repressed) tendencies of normal persons".

Need for achievement

McClelland, who worked with Murray, developed a measure of need for achievement (nAch) based on the ways the TAT pictures were interpreted. Need for achievement was defined as a need to do things better or to surpass standards of excellence. Those who score highly on need for achievement tend to prefer moderately difficult tasks (which provide a challenge) to ones that are either very easy or very hard (Koestner & McClelland, 1990). They also prefer work activities where they are responsible for the outcome. Koestner and McClelland (1990) suggest that societies with a high nAch have higher levels of productivity than those with a low nAch. A survey of children's books published in 40 countries between 1925 and 1950 indicated a positive correlation between nAch and economic progress.

Is it possible to claim that high nAch causes economic progress?

McClelland et al. (1953) also carried out an interesting cross-cultural study on need for achievement. They collected the folk tales of eight Native American cultures and rated them for achievement motivation. They also rated the cultures for the amount of training in independence received by the children. The level of need for achievement was much higher in cultures that encouraged independence.

Evaluation

The approach to motivation adopted by Murray and by McClelland is concerned with important needs. Need for achievement has been found to predict job success, and to account for some of the differences among cultures. On the negative side, the Thematic Apperception Test and the measures of need for achievement developed by McClelland have fairly low reliability and validity. Thus, they do not measure needs consistently (reliability) and do not predict behaviour very accurately (validity). Many of the needs identified by Murray have not been studied in detail, and so it is hard to evaluate the overall success of the need-press theory.

How do you think the need for achievement might relate to individualistic and collectivistic cultures?

Humanistic theories of motivation

According to the humanistic psychologist Abraham Maslow (1954, 1970), most theories of motivation are very limited. They deal with basic physiological needs such as hunger and thirst, or with the need to avoid anxiety. However, such theories generally omit many important needs relating to personal growth. Maslow addressed these issues by putting forward a theory based on a **hierarchy of needs**. Physiological needs or requirements, including those for food and drink, are at the lowest level of the hierarchy, with safety needs immediately above them. In the middle of the hierarchy are needs for affection and intimacy. Above that level, there is the need for esteem, with the need for self-actualisation (or fulfilling one's potential) at the top of the hierarchy (see diagram).

Maslow regarded all the needs towards the bottom of the hierarchy as deficiency needs, because they are designed to reduce inadequacies or deficiencies. Needs towards the top of the hierarchy (e.g., self-actualisation) represent growth needs, and are designed to promote personal growth. The key notion of self-actualisation was described as follows by Maslow (1954):

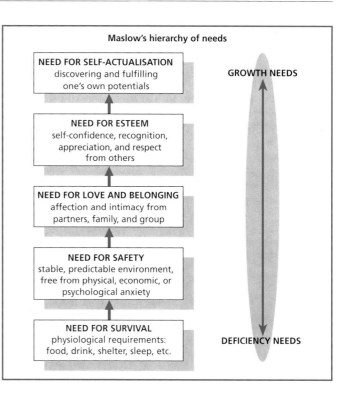

Maslow's hierarchy of needs

NEED FOR SELF-ACTUALISATION
discovering and fulfilling one's own potentials

NEED FOR ESTEEM
self-confidence, recognition, appreciation, and respect from others

NEED FOR LOVE AND BELONGING
affection and intimacy from partners, family, and group

NEED FOR SAFETY
stable, predictable environment, free from physical, economic, or psychological anxiety

NEED FOR SURVIVAL
physiological requirements: food, drink, shelter, sleep, etc.

GROWTH NEEDS

DEFICIENCY NEEDS

> *A musician must make music, an artist must paint, a poet must write, if he is to be ultimately at peace with himself. What a man can be, he must be. This need we may call self-actualisation.*

According to Maslow (1954, 1970), people only focus on their growth needs after their deficiency needs have been met. An implication of this view is that fewer people manage to satisfy their growth needs than to satisfy their deficiency needs. Maslow (1970) estimated that Americans satisfy about 85% of their physiological needs, 70% of their safety needs, 50% of their belongingness and love needs, 40% of their self-esteem needs, and only 10% of their self-actualisation needs.

Aronoff (1967) found that most West Indian fishermen had their security and esteem needs met, and this enabled them to handle an income and lifestyle that was less predictable than cane cutting.

Research study

Aronoff (1967) tested the prediction that higher needs will only emerge when lower needs are satisfied. He compared fishermen and cane cutters in the British West Indies. Fishermen worked on their own. They generally earned more than cane cutters, who worked in groups. Cane cutting was a more secure job, because the rewards fluctuated much less than for fishermen, and because cane cutters were paid even when unwell. According to Maslow's theory, it should be mainly those whose security and esteem needs were met who chose the more challenging and responsible job of fisherman. This prediction was confirmed by Aronoff (1967).

Evaluation

The greatest strength of Maslow's approach to motivation is that it is more comprehensive than other approaches. More specifically, the needs for self-actualisation and for esteem seem very important, but were not included in most earlier theories of motivation. However, the notion of

The humanistic approach in psychology

The humanistic approach to psychology was developed mainly by Carl Rogers and Abraham Maslow in the United States during the 1950s. According to Cartwright (1979, pp.5–6), humanistic psychology

> is concerned with topics that are meaningful to human beings, focusing especially upon subjective experience and the unique, unpredictable events in individual human lives.

Humanistic psychology has forced many psychologists to question some of their basic beliefs. Humanistic psychologists differ from most other psychologists in focusing on conscious experience rather than on behaviour; on personal responsibility and free will rather than on determinism; and on discussion of experience rather than on use of the experimental method. Humanistic psychologists also emphasise the importance of the individual's striving towards personal growth and fulfilment. Whether or not the views of humanistic psychologists are valid, they have certainly succeeded in offering an alternative point of view.

Can you name some people who, in your opinion, have become self-actualised?

self-actualisation is vague, and it has proved hard to develop good ways of measuring it. Maslow may have been overly optimistic in his assumption that everyone has the potential to become a self-actualiser. The fact that the average British person spends 25 hours a week watching television suggests that there are many people whose motivation for personal growth is not enormous! (Apologies to any reader who avidly watches television.)

The notion that self-actualised people are creative, self-accepting, and have excellent interpersonal relations ignores the fact that many people possess only some of those characteristics. For example, the artist van Gogh was outstandingly creative, but he was so lacking in self-acceptance that he committed suicide. There are numerous examples of very creative individuals whose personal and emotional lives were disaster areas—should they be regarded as self-actualised or not? The hierarchy of needs assumes that self-actualisation is at the top, but for some individuals this is not the case. It is also not the case in all cultures. Not all societies see self-centred goals as the ultimate in human behaviour, for example **collectivistic** cultures strive for the greater good of the community rather than focusing on individual achievement.

Humanistic psychologists argue that self-actualisation occurs mainly because of needs within the individual rather than because of the beneficial impact of the environment. However, the environment often helps the process of self-actualisation. For example, most Western societies provide their citizens with many years of schooling, training opportunities for those with special skills, part-time courses, and so on. It is probable that self-actualisation depends on external (environmental) as well as internal (need) factors.

Goal-setting theory

Why do people work? This is a question of critical interest to the management of any workforce. Many theories that focus on motivation to work are concerned with external or extrinsic incentives. One example of this is **goal-setting theory**.

How does motivation in humans differ from motivation in other species? Humans are often motivated by long-term goals (e.g., passing examinations), whereas other species typically focus on short-term goals (e.g., finding food). This aspect of human motivation was recognised by Locke (1968, p.159). According to his goal-setting theory, the key factor in motivation is the goal. Locke (1968) defined the goal as "what the individual is consciously trying to do". The goal that someone has set himself or herself can be assessed by direct questioning.

How does goal setting relate to performance? According to Locke (1968, p.162), there is a straightforward relationship between goal difficulty and performance: "the harder the goal the higher the level of performance". This happens because people try harder when difficult goals are set (see the Key Study on the next page).

Goal theory has also been applied to the effects of incentive on performance. According to Locke et al. (1968, p.104), "Incentives such as money should affect action only if and to the extent that they affect the individual's goals and intentions." Support for this hypothesis was obtained by Farr (1976) in a study on speed of card sorting. Providing financial incentives led to the setting of much higher goals and to increased sorting speed.

Research support

Locke et al. (1981) reviewed the evidence on goal theory. Goal setting had led to improved performance in about 90% of studies, especially under the following conditions:

- Goal commitment: individuals accept the goal that has been set.
- Feedback: information about progress towards goals is provided.

Harder goals do improve performance

Evidence supporting goal theory was reported by Latham and Yukl (1975). They divided workers whose job was cutting and transporting wood into three categories:

1. Workers simply instructed to "do your best" (do-your-best groups).
2. Groups assigned to a specific hard goal in terms of hundreds of cubic feet of wood per week (assigned groups).
3. Groups in which everyone participated in setting a specific hard production goal (participative groups).

Latham and Yukl found that the do-your-best groups set the easiest goals, and so were predicted to have the poorest performance. In contrast, the participative groups set the hardest goals, and so should have performed the best. As predicted, the do-your-best groups averaged 46 cubic feet of wood per hour; the assigned groups averaged 53 cubic feet; and the participative groups averaged 56 cubic feet. These differences may not seem very large. However, the work performance of the participative groups was almost 22% greater than that of the do-your-best groups, and any company would be delighted to increase the productivity of its workers by 22%!

Discussion points

1. Why do you think goal-setting theory is perhaps the most widely used theory in the workplace?
2. What do you think are the weaknesses of Locke's approach? (See the text for some ideas.)

- Rewards: goal attainment is rewarded.
- Ability: individuals have sufficient ability to attain the goal.
- Support: management or others provide encouragement.

How does Locke et al.'s list of five conditions relate to your own experience of short-term and long-term goals (e.g., studying psychology)?

Evaluation

Goal setting and goal commitment are often important in determining the level of performance, as predicted by goal theory. Goal theory also sheds some light on individual differences in motivation and performance: highly motivated workers set higher goals and are more committed to them than are poorly motivated workers.

However, Locke's goal theory is rather limited. For example, an individual's goal level is seen as corresponding to his or her conscious intentions, but people's motivational forces are not always open to conscious awareness. Another limitation is that goal theory ignores some potential disadvantages of setting high goals and being committed to those goals. These disadvantages include various negative emotional states such as anxiety, stress, and frustration. Another limitation is that major motivating forces such as hunger and thirst are not considered.

Conclusion

Motivation is both one of the most important and the least understood areas in psychology. The physiological and psychological approaches to motivation tell us more about *how* motivation occurs than *why*. It is easy to be impressed by the detailed physiological processes involved, and to lose sight of the ways in which motivation depends on the psychological, social, and cultural context. Equally, the more psychological approach sometimes ignores basic, physiological needs.

Theories of motivation have important real-world applications, for example in personnel selection. However, it has proved very hard to devise valid measures that will predict how hard someone will work. What is generally of most value is the individual's work record so far, on the basis that the past often predicts the future. It is disappointing that theories of motivation do not allow us to improve on that simple approach.

More recently, the growth of sport psychology has also looked to theories of motivation. A winning athlete or team relies on continuing drive to win, especially in the jaws of defeat. And nowhere is motivation more important—especially to you the

How would theories of motivation inform the process of personnel selection?

■ Activity: List the motivation theories covered in this Unit. Next to each theory say what advice would be given to someone who is studying for exams to improve their motivation.

reader—than in the desire to do well in academic studies! Think what advice you should give yourself about motivation to work on the basis of the theories you have read here.

Emotion

The study of emotion is of great importance within psychology. However, like all "big concepts", it is not easy to define. According to Drever (1964, p.82), emotion involves:

bodily changes of a widespread character—in breathing, pulse, gland secretion, etc.—and, on the mental side, a state of excitement or perturbation, marked by a strong feeling.

We can go beyond Drever's definition to identify the following components of emotion:

- *Cognitive* (thinking). Emotions are usually directed towards people or objects (e.g., we are in an anxious emotional state because the situation is dangerous), and we know the situation is dangerous rather than harmless as a result of thinking.
- *Physiological*. There are generally a number of bodily changes involved in emotion. Many of them (such as increased heart rate, increased blood pressure, increased respiration rate, sweating) occur because of arousal in the sympathetic division of the **autonomic nervous system** or hormonal activity within the **endocrine system** (see the AS book for details of the autonomic nervous system).
- *Experiential*. This is the feeling that is experienced, which can only be assessed in the human species.
- *Expressive*. This is facial expression and other aspects of nonverbal behaviour such as bodily posture. Emotions are inferred from these expressions.
- *Behavioural*. This is the pattern of behaviour (e.g., fight or flight) produced by an emotional state.

Think of a recent emotional experience. Which of these components were present?

Brain Systems in Emotion

Papez circuit

Many parts of the brain are involved in emotion. The first systematic attempt to identify the key brain systems involved in emotion was made by Papez (1937). He studied cases of rabies, a disease that typically produces high levels of aggression. This increased aggression seemed to be associated with damage to the hippocampus. Papez combined this information with findings from studies of brain-damaged individuals to propose the **Papez circuit** as the basis of emotion. This circuit consists of a loop running from the hippocampus to the hypothalamus and from there to the anterior thalamus. The circuit continues via the cingulate gyrus and the entorhinal cortex back to the hippocampus.

Evaluation

The Papez circuit is oversimplified. For example, there seem to be subtle differences in the functions of different parts of it. Flynn (1976) studied the effects of electrical stimulation of various parts of the hypothalamus in cats. Cats responded with a quiet, biting attack when one area was stimulated, but with an affective (emotional) attack involving claws and hissing when another area was stimulated. (Bard, 1929, had called this **sham rage**, a kind of cool aggression which was displayed in cats whose cerebral cortex had been ablated.)

The Papez circuit.

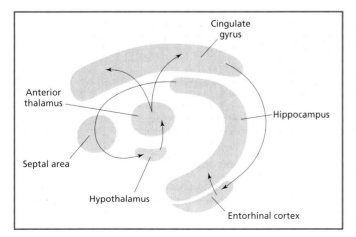

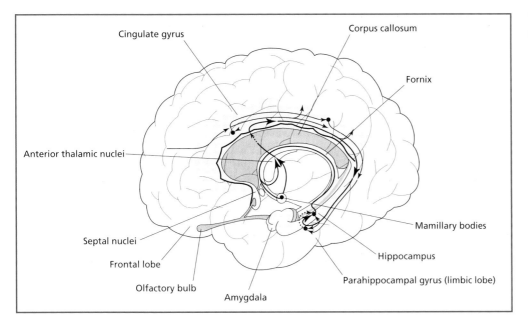

The Papez–MacLean limbic system.

Papez–MacLean limbic model

MacLean (1949) suggested some improvements, calling his model the Papez–MacLean **limbic model**. This model differed from the original Papez circuit in that the role of the cingulate gyrus was reduced, and there was increased emphasis on the role of the amygdala and the hippocampus. Part of the reason for this emphasis on the amygdala came from the work of Klüver and Bucy (1939). Monkeys with their anterior temporal lobe removed became less aggressive, showed little fear, tended to put objects in their mouths, and engaged in more sexual activity. This pattern of behaviour is known as the **Klüver–Bucy syndrome**, and depends mostly on damage to the amygdala, which lies within the temporal lobe. In humans, the damage can be due to tumours or head injuries.

The role of the amygdala

More is now known about the role of the amygdala in emotion. According to LeDoux (1989), the amygdala is the brain's "emotional computer", and is involved in assessing the emotional significance of stimuli. LeDoux discussed evidence based on studies of monkeys in which the neurons connecting the amygdala with either vision or hearing were lesioned or cut. The monkeys could still see and hear stimuli, but they were no longer able to assess the emotional importance of those stimuli.

What ethical considerations should be made in relation to such research?

Two brain circuits

LeDoux (1995) has put forward a modified version of the limbic theory of emotion. According to him, information about emotional stimuli is relayed to the thalamus. After that, two rather separate brain circuits are involved. First, there is a rapid emotional response based on information passing from the thalamus to the amygdala, which often leads to autonomic and endocrine changes. These changes are then interpreted by the cortex. Second, there is a slower emotional response based on the direct transmission of information from the thalamus to the cortex.

What happens when there is a conflict between the emotional reactions generated by the two brain circuits? An example might be the experience that many people have in a dentist's waiting room: "I feel very anxious even though there is nothing to be frightened about." In such cases, the first circuit based on the amygdala is indicating

Amygdalotomies

As a result of work such as that of Klüver and Bucy (1939), "psychosurgeons" in the United States carried out numerous operations on criminals serving jail sentences. Many of these operations were amygdalotomies, in which parts of the amygdala were destroyed. This was done by putting fine wire electrodes into the amygdala through a small hole drilled in the skull, and then passing strong electric currents through the electrodes. These amygdalotomies generally reduced fear and anger in those operated on, but they often had very unfortunate side-effects. For example, Thomas R was a 34-year-old engineer who suffered delusions and became unable to work after surgery. He was found on one occasion walking about with his head covered by bags, rags, and newspapers. He justified this behaviour by saying that he was frightened that other bits of his brain might be destroyed. Thankfully, amygdalotomy is very rarely carried out nowadays.

Emotion and laterality

In Section 4, Brain and Behaviour, we considered lateralisation of function in the cerebral cortex. Research has demonstrated that certain aspects of emotion are controlled by the right hemisphere (see page 161). For example, individuals with right hemisphere brain damage behave in a relatively unemotional fashion. If the damage is in part of the temporal lobe, individuals may speak in a monotone and/or have problems understanding the emotional tone of speech. Other research has found that people with right hemisphere brain damage, when asked to identify emotional expressions, can recognise happy expressions but have difficulty with sad or fearful expressions (Adolphs et al., 1996).

In the split-brain studies it was shown that patients are able to develop a complex strategy for dealing with information presented to the right hemisphere, for example if they are asked to say what they are holding in their left hand. The signals from the left hand go to the right hemisphere, but language is usually controlled by the left hemisphere. Patients might just give any answer—but the answer is "heard" by the right "emotional" hemisphere and this hemisphere can instruct the face to cringe. This is detected by the left hemisphere, which will guess again!

This laterality might explain anti-social personality disorder, a condition in which individuals lack appropriate emotional responses and lack empathy. Day and Wong (1996) tested the time taken for participants to respond to negative emotional words that were presented to either the left or right hemisphere (words presented to the left visual field are processed by the right hemisphere, and vice versa). The study found that normal participants were faster with the words to the right hemisphere whereas participants classed as anti-social performed equally with both hemispheres, suggesting that their right hemisphere was not as well developed as normal.

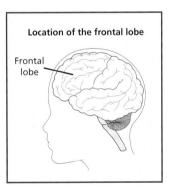

Location of the frontal lobe

Frontal lobe

a high level of anxiety, whereas the second circuit based on a direct link between the thalamus and the cortex is not.

Evaluation of the role of the limbic system

It is clear that the limbic system is involved in emotion. However, limbic theories of emotion are limited in various ways. First, most of the evidence is based on a few emotions such as fear and anger or rage. The role of the limbic system in other emotions (e.g., love or grief) is less clear. Second, most studies have been carried out on other species. The brain systems involved in human emotion are probably more complicated than those involved in emotion in other species. Third, and related to the second point, humans have a larger area of cortex and much more developed cognitive systems than other species. This is important in emotion. For example, we can become anxious merely by thinking about some unpleasant future events (e.g., sitting examinations), which is presumably much less true of other species. It is an advantage of LeDoux's (1995) theory that it focuses more than previous theories on the role of the **cortex** in emotion and therefore can explain human emotions.

Frontal lobes

The frontal lobes are also involved in emotion. This was perhaps first suspected as a result of a terrible injury sustained by a dynamite worker called Phineas Gage (see Case Study on page 217, and diagram on page 143). He was ramming a charge of dynamite into a hole with a steel rod when there was an explosion, and the steel rod was driven through his orbitofrontal cortex and the top of his head. He turned from a hard-working and serious man into someone who was rather childish and unconcerned. Thus, the accident seemed to have reduced his experience of emotion.

About a hundred years later, Jacobsen, Wolfe, and Jackson (1935) removed the frontal lobes of a chimpanzee called Becky. Jacobsen et al. (1935, pp.9–10) described how, before the operation, when Becky made an error "she immediately flew into a temper tantrum, rolled on the floor, defaecated and urinated". After the operation, she "showed no evidence of emotional disturbance". A Portuguese neuropsychiatrist, Egas Moniz, was impressed by these findings and sought to apply them to the treatment of human mental disorders. He developed frontal lobotomies to destroy parts of the frontal lobes or to cut them off from the rest of the brain. Frontal lobotomies were carried out on tens of thousands of people, and were successful in reducing anxiety, obsessions, and compulsions. As a result, Moniz was awarded the Nobel Prize in 1949.

However, the operation produced very serious side-effects. The patients typically failed to experience normal emotions any more, and most were unemployable after surgery. In view of these side-effects, frontal lobotomies are no longer carried out. In a strange twist to the tale, Moniz was shot by one of his patients, and spent the rest of his life in a wheelchair. (See page 664 for more on lobotomies.)

Evaluation

The frontal lobes seem to play a role in deciding on the personal meaning of situations and in producing the appropriate emotional reactions. They are connected to the other brain systems we have discussed, because outputs from the frontal lobes go to the amygdala, the hippocampus, and the hypothalamus. The fact that several areas of the brain are known to be involved in emotion reminds us that emotions depend on the integrated functioning of the brain rather than solely on certain small parts of it (i.e., distributed rather than localised function. That fact alone should have suggested to Moniz and others that frontal lobotomies were unlikely to prove very effective. In

Facial expressions associated with emotion are generally recognised across cultures, suggesting that the expressive aspect of emotion is innate.

addition, such operations raise major ethical issues, because it is very hard to justify changing someone's personality so dramatically.

Theories of Emotion

James–Lange theory

The first major theory of emotion was put forward independently in the United States by William James and in Denmark by Carl Lange. For obvious reasons, it came to be known as the James–Lange theory. According to the theory, the following states are involved in producing emotion:

- There is an emotional stimulus (e.g., a car coming rapidly towards you as you are crossing the road).
- This produces bodily changes (e.g., arousal in the autonomic nervous system).
- Feedback from the bodily changes leads to the experience of emotion (e.g., fear or anxiety).

These three stages can be seen in the following example taken from James (1890): "I see a bear, I run away, I feel afraid." Stage 1 is seeing the bear, running away is stage 2, and feeling afraid is stage 3.

> **CASE STUDY:** *Phineas Gage*
>
> The link between emotional state and brain function was famously demonstrated in the case of Phineas Gage, a construction foreman on the American railroad who, on 13 September 1848, was involved in a gruesome accident (Rylander, 1948). An explosive charge went off accidentally, and a metal spike 3 feet long and 1 inch thick was driven through Gage's head, entering at his cheek and passing out through the top of his skull. Amazingly, Gage survived his injuries, and his memory, attention, and cognitive processes appeared to be largely unaffected. However, his personality was so badly changed that his employers refused to take him back into work. They wrote that "the balance between his intellectual faculties and animal propensities seems to have been destroyed". Before the accident, Gage had been a well-balanced, civilised, and conscientious man, but now he was "fitful, irreverent, indulging at times in the grossest profanity [swearing] ... impatient of restraint or advice when it conflicts with his desires ... A child in his intellectual capability and manifestations, he has the animal passions of a strong man." Poor Gage was so changed that his friends said he was "no longer Gage", and it is reported that he eventually became an exhibit in a circus, probably the only means of earning a living open to him at the time.
>
> Gage is discussed on page 216.

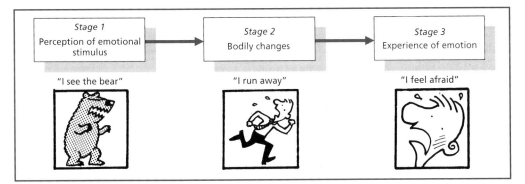

Stage 1 Perception of emotional stimulus	→	Stage 2 Bodily changes	→	Stage 3 Experience of emotion
"I see the bear"		"I run away"		"I feel afraid"

■ Activity: Running on the spot

White, Fishbein, and Rutstein (1981) lent support to the James–Lange theory with a study where participants were asked to run on the spot and then rate video pictures of women. Those who ran for 120 seconds rated the video pictures as more attractive than those who ran for only 15 seconds. This suggests a link between the amount of arousal and the depth of emotional experience! Try the experiment for yourself.

One of Hohmann's patient's described his emotional experiences as lacking physiological arousal. How might this be understood within the framework of LeDoux's two brain circuits (see page 215)?

Research evidence

One prediction from the James–Lange theory would be that individuals with no physiological experiences should be unable to have emotional experiences. Evidence supporting this prediction was reported by Hohmann (1966). He studied 25 paralysed patients who had suffered damage to the spinal cord, that greatly restricted their awareness of physiological arousal. For those patients with the least ability to experience arousal, there was a large reduction in their emotional experiences of anger, grief, and sexual excitement. In the words of one patient, "Sometimes I act angry when I see some injustice. I yell and cuss and raise hell ... but it just doesn't have the heat to it that it used to. It's a kind of mental anger."

Later research has generally not confirmed the findings of Hohmann (1966). Bermond et al. (1991) found that most patients with spinal damage reported *increased* intensity of emotions. They even reported that the bodily symptoms of emotion were as great as before they were injured. These findings suggest that feedback from bodily changes is *not* needed for emotion to be experienced. This is supported by the Valins effect (see the Key Study below).

The Valins effect

KEY STUDY EVALUATION — Valins

It might be worth considering the fact that noise itself can be arousing so that heartbeat sounds might lead to physiological arousal. To control for this Valins had a second condition where participants heard the same sounds but were not told that the heartbeats were their own. In this condition there was no relation between increased heartbeat sounds and attractiveness ratings.

Valins (1966) asked whether the state of physiological arousal is necessary for an emotional experience. To assess this he arranged for some volunteer participants—introductory psychology students—to look at slides of semi-nude women. The students were told that the study concerned physiological reactions to sexually oriented stimuli. Their reactions to the slides were being recorded and they were led to believe that they were hearing an amplified version of their heartbeat while looking at the slides.

Participants were given false feedback when they were told that the sounds they heard were their own heartbeat. In fact, they heard a tape where the heartbeats were either increased or decreased for particular "critical" slides.

The perceived attractiveness of each slide was measured by asking the participants to rate the slides for attractiveness. At the end of the experiment participants were asked if there were any slides they would like to keep, providing an additional measure of attractiveness. Finally, 4 weeks later, participants were asked to rate a set of photos including the experimental ones.

The slides accompanied by supposedly increased heartbeat were rated as more attractive on all occasions. This suggests that subjective emotional states exist without any real physiological change, in contrast to the predictions from the James–Lange theory. In addition, this study shows that people are relatively unaware of their actual physiological state, otherwise the tape recordings would not have been believed.

Discussion points

1. Can you think of an alternative way to explain these findings?

2. Is deception acceptable in this study?

What are the physiological responses associated with adrenaline?

A second prediction arising from the James–Lange theory, is that the emotion we experience should depend on the specific bodily changes. Thus, each emotion should have its own pattern of bodily changes. There is some support for this view. Smiling is associated with happiness, crying with misery, and running away with fear. Ax (1953) compared the physiological responses to fear and to anger. Fear was created by telling the participants that they might receive an unpleasant electric shock, and anger was created by having a technician make a series of rude and unkind remarks. The physiological responses of fear were similar to those produced by the hormone adrenaline, whereas the responses of anger were like those produced by a combination of adrenaline and noradrenaline. Schwartz et al. (1981) also found physiological "signatures" for certain

Turn the corners of your mouth upwards so that you look as if you're smiling. Do you think the picture is funny? According to the study by Laird (1974) you should—he asked participants to relax and contract certain facial muscles. Cartoons viewed when participants were "smiling" were rated as funnier than those when they were "frowning". Participants were amused because they were smiling, not smiling because they are amused.

primary emotions: happiness, sadness, anger, and fear. Participants were asked to close their eyes and imagine scenes from the past or future that would evoke these emotions. They were told to try to recreate both the feelings and the sensations associated with the scene. Schwartz et al. found that heart rate and blood pressure were lowest during happiness and highest during anger. Sadness had a higher heart rate than happiness, but lower blood pressure.

Evaluation

As predicted by the James–Lange theory, physiological changes can occur before we experience emotion. However, the theory is inadequate in various ways. First, we often experience emotion before the bodily changes have occurred, rather than afterwards as the theory predicts. In other words, emotions can be triggered directly by an emotional stimulus rather than indirectly via bodily changes.

Second, the assumption that there is a distinctive pattern of bodily changes associated with every emotional state is only partially correct. Many different emotional states are associated with a broadly similar state of arousal of the autonomic system, suggesting that the rich variety of emotional experience cannot depend solely on bodily changes.

Third, the theory states that an emotional stimulus produces a series of bodily changes. However, very little is said about how this happens. It was only later theorists (e.g., Lazarus, 1966) who considered in detail how the ways in which the situation is interpreted produce physiological changes and emotional experiences.

Finally, it is possible to experience arousal but with no accompanying emotional experience. For example if you run up the stairs, you do not (usually) have a sense of happiness or sadness. Cannon cited research by Marañon (1924) to support this. The participants were injected with adrenaline, a drug whose effects are similar to those of a naturally occurring state of arousal. When they were asked how they felt, 71% simply reported their physical symptoms with no emotional experience. Most of the remaining participants reported "as if" emotion, i.e., an emotion lacking its normal intensity. Why did almost none of the participants report true emotions? Presumably because physiological arousal alone is not sufficient for an emotional experience.

Cannon–Bard theory

The Cannon–Bard theory was put forward as an alternative to the James–Lange theory. When someone is put in an emotional situation, a part of the brain known as the thalamus

Would the pattern of arousal of an athlete's autonomic nervous system before a race indicate a single emotional state?

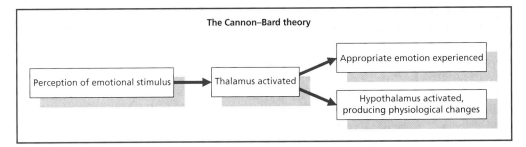

The Cannon–Bard theory

Perception of emotional stimulus → Thalamus activated → Appropriate emotion experienced

→ Hypothalamus activated, producing physiological changes

Scary funfair rides can cause emotional arousal.

is activated. This is followed by two separate and simultaneous effects: (1) the appropriate emotional state is experienced, and (2) another part of the brain (the hypothalamus) is activated, producing physiological changes, such as arousal in the sympathetic division of the autonomic nervous system.

According to the Cannon–Bard theory, our feelings are not determined by the level of physiological arousal. As a result, this theory has no problem with the fact that our experience of emotion can occur before the relevant bodily changes have taken place. However, it does have problems with Hohmann's (1966) findings on patients with damage to the spinal cord. If perception of the bodily changes in emotion has no effect on emotional experience, it is hard to explain why such patients show much reduced emotionality. However, as we have seen, it has proved hard to repeat Hohmann's findings (e.g., Bermond et al., 1991).

Evaluation

There is some accord between this theory and LeDoux's altered version of limbic theory (see page 215), which proposed that there were two brain circuits for emotion: the rapid emotional response related to physiological changes, and the slower emotional response involving higher order processing.

However, the Cannon–Bard theory is limited in a number of ways. First, the evidence generally suggests that the experienced intensity of emotional states depends in part on the level of physiological arousal (e.g., White, Fishbein, & Rutstein, 1981) and this isn't explained by this theory. Second, perhaps more importantly, the theory tells us nothing about how we decide whether a given situation is emotional. This is an important omission, because there are many ambiguous situations (e.g., hearing a noise outside in the middle of the night) that can be interpreted as being emotional or non-emotional. These limitations were addressed in cognitive labelling theory, to which we now turn.

Cognitive labelling theory

Schachter and Singer (1962) started the modern era in emotion research with their very influential **cognitive labelling theory**. It was one of the first theories of emotion to focus on cognitive factors. Their main proposal was that there are two factors, both of which are essential for emotions to be experienced:

- High physiological arousal.
- A cognitive interpretation of (or *label* for) that arousal.

According to Schachter and Singer (1962), an emotional state will not be experienced if either of these two crucial factors is missing. The study by Marañon (1924), described on page 219, can be explained using this theory. The participants interpreted (or labelled) their state of arousal as having been produced by the drug, and so didn't need to attach an emotional label to it. Schachter and Singer (1962) carried out an expanded version of Marañon's study (see the Key Study on the next page).

Evaluation

Schachter and Singer (1962) were right to argue that cognitive processes are important in determining *whether* emotion will be experienced, and in determining *which* emotion will

The wonder drug Suproxin

Schachter and Singer (1962) enlisted volunteers for a study that ostensibly aimed to test the effects of the vitamin compound "Suproxin" on vision. In fact, the participants were injected with either adrenaline (to produce arousal) or a salt-based solution having no effect on arousal. (Note that in the study the term epinephrine is used because Americans use this term instead of the word adrenaline.)

Some of the participants were correctly informed about the effects of the drug (epinephrine informed). Others were misinformed (told the injection would have mild effects only) or uninformed (told there would be no side-effects). This meant that participants who had the arousal either had an explanation for it (they knew that arousal would be a side-effect of the drug) or had no expectation that they might feel aroused.

After the injection, the participants were put in a situation designed to produce either euphoria (joy) or anger. This was done by putting them in the same room as someone (a confederate) who acted in a joyful way (making paper planes and playing paper basketball) or in an angry way (reacting to a very personal questionnaire that the confederate had been asked to complete). The intention here was to provide a "label", either joy or anger, for the participant to give to his state of arousal.

Which groups were the most emotional? It should have been those groups who were given adrenaline (and so were very aroused), but who would not interpret the arousal as having been produced by the drug. Thus, it was predicted that the misinformed and uninformed groups given adrenaline should have been most emotional. The findings broadly supported the predictions, but many of the effects were rather small.

KEY STUDY EVALUATION — Schachter and Singer

There have been a host of criticisms made of this study. First of all is the issue of whether it is reasonable to compare arousal states created by drugs with real-life emotions. In any case, adrenaline does not have the same effect on all people.

A second area of criticism concerns the selective reporting of the findings. In the final analysis the researchers excluded some of the participants who had not reported any physiological sensations. If their data had been included the results would have been even less significant.

Third, subsequent studies have failed to replicate these findings. For example, Marshall and Zimbardo (1979) found that large doses of adrenaline reduced (rather than increased) their participants' happiness in the euphoria or joy condition. Perhaps a high level of arousal is generally regarded as unpleasant. However, there was support from a study by Dutton and Aron (1974) where participants met a female interviewer on a suspension bridge (high fear, high arousal) or a low bridge. High arousal participants were more likely to make contact afterwards, suggesting that they mislabelled their arousal as attraction when in the presence of a female interviewer.

Another study also supported the original one and offered an explanation for its rather weak findings. One of the reasons why the study by Schachter and Singer (1962) did not produce strong effects may be because those given the salt-based solution may have become physiologically aroused by being put into an emotional situation. If so, they would have had the high arousal and emotional labels, which together produce an emotional state. Schachter and Wheeler (1962) argued that the way to stop people becoming aroused was to give them a depressant drug that reduces arousal. In this later study the participants were given a depressant, or adrenaline, or a substance having no effects, and were told in each case that the drug had no side-effects. They then watched a slapstick film called *The Good Humour Man*. As predicted, those given adrenaline (and thus aroused) found the film the funniest, whereas those given the depressant (and thus de-aroused) found it least funny.

Discussion points

1. How does the approach adopted by Schachter and Singer differ from those of previous theorists?

2. What are the weaknesses with this research and this theoretical approach? (See the text for some ideas.)

be experienced. Their cognitive labelling theory led several other theorists to develop cognitive approaches to emotion, such as cognitive appraisal theory described next, and so their theory has been very influential.

The theory can explain how emotions are learned and can also explain why emotional intensity tends to be greater when the level of physiological arousal is high, as demonstrated by the study by White et al. (1981; see the Activity on page 218).

On the negative side, we have noted in the Key Study Evaluation above that the research evidence isn't entirely clear, casting doubt on the validity of the theory. It is also questionable as to whether the spontaneity of many emotional experiences can be explained by cognitive labelling.

Lazarus' cognitive appraisal theory

Most theorists nowadays no longer accept cognitive labelling theory as an adequate account of emotion. However, it is fairly generally accepted that Schachter and Singer (1962) were right to emphasise the role of cognitive processes in emotion. One of the most influential cognitive approaches to emotion subsequently put forward was by Lazarus

What ethical issues might concern psychologists today if a researcher suggested replicating the experiment by Schachter and Singer?

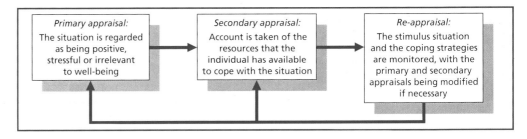

(1982, 1991). According to Lazarus (1982, p.1021), "Cognitive appraisal (of meaning or significance) underlies and is an integral feature of all emotional states."

According to Lazarus (1982, 1991), cognitive appraisal of the situation can be subdivided into three more specific forms of appraisal: primary and secondary appraisal, and re-appraisal, as described in the diagram above.

Research evidence

Some of the earliest evidence indicating the importance of cognitive appraisal was reported by Speisman et al. (1964). The participants were shown a film of a Stone Age ritual in which adolescent boys had their penises deeply incised. Cognitive appraisal was manipulated by varying the soundtrack of the film. Denial was produced by indicating that the film did not show a painful operation, and intellectualisation was produced by considering matters from the perspective of an anthropologist viewing strange native customs. There was also a control condition in which there was no soundtrack. The participants in the denial and intellectualisation conditions were less anxious than those in the control condition in terms of physiological measures (e.g., heart rate).

Lazarus et al. (1965) also demonstrated how one's way of appraising a situation affects the emotion attached to the experience. They showed participants a film entitled "Woodshop" that contained stressful scenes of gruesome accidents in a sawmill. There were three experimental conditions. In group 1 participants were told the people were actors, the events were staged, and no one was actually injured. This was the denial condition. In group 2 (intellectualisation) participants were asked to consider the film in terms of its value for promoting safety at work. A third control group were given no instructions. Stress was assessed by measuring participants' galvanic skin response and they were also asked at the end to evaluate how stressful they thought the film was. Groups 1 and 2 showed lower physiological stress while watching the film and reported less after the film. This demonstrates that the same event can be emotionally stressful or not depending on how its contents are appraised.

Evaluation

Studies such as those by Speisman et al. (1964) and Lazarus et al. (1965) have shown that emotional reactions to situations can be changed if cognitive appraisals are changed. However, there are various problems with cognitive appraisal theory. First, it is not entirely possible to assess the theory because an individual's cognitive appraisals of a situation may occur below the level of conscious awareness (Lazarus, 1991). Second, the studies carried out by Lazarus and others are rather artificial. The participants typically sit passively in an initially unemotional state while they are exposed to emotionally threatening stimuli. In such situations, it is clear that cognitive appraisals can affect emotional responses. In the real world, however, it is likely that the causality can go in the opposite direction, with emotional states influencing the process of cognitive appraisal. Third, it is unlikely that emotional experience depends only on cognitive appraisal. It is probable that other factors (e.g., bodily reactions) also play a part in determining emotional experience.

Finally, we might consider Zajonc's (1984, p.117) contrasting view: "Affect and cognition are separate and partially independent systems and ... although they ordinarily function conjointly, affect could be generated without a prior cognitive process." Zajonc (1980) suggested that there is evidence from the "mere exposure effect" to support this view. Various studies have presented stimuli (such as a melody)

How does Speisman's study demonstrate the effects of cognitive appraisal?

How could you apply these findings to reducing your own levels of arousal in a stressful situation?

Do you think that Zajonc was correct in stating that emotion could be generated without prior cognition?

to participants so that it was below the level of cognitive awareness. In later tests participants could not recognise the stimuli but they still tended to choose previously presented stimuli rather than similar new ones when asked to select the ones they preferred. This indicates that you can have an emotional experience (preference for something) in the absence of cognitive processing—if the information could not be recognised this suggests that it had received no cognitive processing, and it received no cognitive processing because it was perceived below the level of conscious awareness. There are two criticisms of this view. First, it assumes the "preference" is an emotional experience and, second, it assumes that the information received no cognitive processing, whereas many cognitive psychologists acknowledge that cognitive processing can take place without conscious awareness.

> ### Emotion: Is it a physiological or a cognitive experience?
>
> Some kinds of emotional experience are more physiological, others are more cognitive.
>
> - *A physiological experience.* A jet screams over your head, you duck and experience a tightness in your chest. Past experience and individual differences will determine the emotion you might report feeling—fear, surprise, elation. For each of us it will be different, but the basis will be arousal. Such responses are more related to emotion as an adaptive response.
>
> - *A cognitive experience.* You hear that you have passed A level psychology and feel ecstatic, which may lead to physiological sensations.
>
> This might explain why emotion can sometimes occur with arousal and sometimes without it. It also fits in with LeDoux's suggestion that there are two pathways in the brain, one more physiological and the other more related to higher order processing.

Synthesis: Four-factor theory

The major theories of emotion we have considered are generally thought of as being in competition with each other. However, none of them can be regarded as providing complete accounts of emotion. It is increasingly argued that what is needed is a theory combining elements of previous theories. As an example, we can take the four-factor theory of emotion put forward by Parkinson (1994). According to this theory, emotional experience depends on four separate factors:

1. Appraisal of some external stimulus or situation. This is the most important factor, and is the one emphasised by Lazarus (1982, 1991).
2. Reactions of the body (e.g., arousal). This is the factor emphasised in the James–Lange theory.
3. Facial expression. The importance of this factor was shown in a study by Laird (1974, see page 219) in which participants were more amused by cartoons when adopting a facial expression close to a smile than when having an expression resembling a frown.
4. Action tendencies. For example, preparing to advance in a threatening way is associated with anger, whereas preparing to retreat is associated with fear (Frijda, Kuipers, & ter Schure, 1989).

These four factors are not independent of each other. Cognitive appraisal of the situation affects bodily reactions, facial expression, and action tendencies, as well as having a direct effect on emotional experience. It is for this reason that cognitive appraisal is the most important of the four factors.

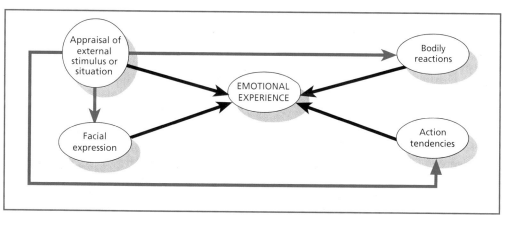

SECTION SUMMARY

Brain Mechanisms of Motivation

❖ Motivational factors help to determine the direction, intensity, and persistence of behaviour. Hunger and thirst are examples of motivated behaviour. Both are controlled by the principle of homeostasis, which is regulated by the hypothalamus.

❖ Early research identified the lateral nucleus of the hypothalamus as a feeding centre, and its ventromedial nucleus as a satiety centre. This hypothalamic theory is oversimplified. An alternative, glucostatic theory, proposes that glucostats are sensitive to blood glucose levels and create a hunger drive when glucose levels are low, a homeostatic system. Lipostatic theory suggests that hunger is initiated when the hypothalamus finds that lipid (fatty acid) levels are low. Theoretical accounts should also explain why people stop eating. Multiple control over the initiation of eating behaviour is likely. Cessation of eating depends in part on a nutrient-monitoring system in the stomach.

❖ There are two main criticisms of homeostatic theory: First, social rather than physiological factors control most of our eating, which can be accounted for by positive–incentive theory. Second, animals that have been "sham fed" do not eat any more than they normally do. Eating disorders include obesity, which may be caused by an insensitivity to leptin which signals high levels of fat; anorexia, which has been linked to malfunctioning of the hypothalamus; and bulimia, which may be related to low levels of serotonin.

❖ Thirst occurs either from extracellular or intracellular water loss. Water moves in and out of cells as a result of osmosis. Osmotic thirst arises when water deprivation leads to changes in osmotic pressure which are detected by osmoreceptors in the hypothalamus leading in turn to thirst and more concentrated urine to conserve water. Volumetric thirst arises when baroreceptors detect low blood volume (e.g., from loss of blood) and this affects the kidneys directly by increasing the release of antidiuretic hormone. Satiety receptors in the mouth and in the intestines cause drinking to stop.

Theories of Motivation

❖ One early attempt to explain motivation was in terms of instincts, a rather circular explanation. Motives can be classified in terms of an intrinsic/extrinsic dimension. Motives can also be classified as cyclic or non-cyclic, and primary or secondary. Finally we can separate theories of motivation into those that are based on physiological systems and those that are psychological.

❖ Drive theories are physiological and based on the notion of homeostasis (maintaining a steady state), e.g., homeostatic drive theory. Drive-reduction theory suggests that physiological needs produce psychological drives. Reduction of needs is rewarding. Behaviour depends on a combination of motivation (drive) and learning (habit). These theories can account for hunger and thirst, but cannot account for those behaviours, such as curiosity, which do not reduce physiological needs. Drive theories ignore cognitive factors, are based on non-human animal studies, and may not apply to all human behaviour. An alternative physiological approach is to explain motivation in terms of optimum levels of arousal (OLA) which describes a return to an optimum state. This can account for curiosity, the effects of sensory overload, thrill seeking, and also extravert personality. However, it is a circular concept.

❖ Psychological theories of motivation focus more on human motives. Murray's need-press theory posits 20 manifest needs which are expressed in the presence of certain environmental factors or "press". Some of these needs have been measured by the Thematic Apperception Test (TAT). The most explored of Murray's needs is the need for achievement (nAch), a concept further developed and researched by McClelland. Despite the empirical support for nAch, the other needs have not been studied extensively, and TAT has been criticised for having low reliability and validity. Maslow presented a humanistic theory of motivation. Physiological or deficiency needs are at the bottom of a hierarchy of needs, moving through to personal growth needs at the top. The inclusion of self-actualisation and esteem needs is a step forward but these may not be universally desirable, and may come from the environment rather than the individual.

❖ Locke's goal-setting theory is relevant to a work setting. The theory recognises that humans are often motivated by long-term goals, whereas other species typically focus on short-term goals. High performance depends on setting hard goals, and being committed to these goals. Locke only focused on conscious intentions, and tended to ignore negative effects of goal setting and commitment (e.g., anxiety if performance does not match up to the goal). The theory also ignores basic needs such as hunger.

❖ Emotion consists of cognitive, physiological, experiential, expressive, and behavioural components. Emotion can be understood in terms of underlying brain mechanisms. The Papez circuit is based on the hippocampus, hypothalamus, and thalamus. This was later modified into the Papez–MacLean limbic model, in which there was more emphasis on the role of the amygdala. More recently, LeDoux argued that there are two brain systems involved in emotion: a rapid response involving the amygdala and autonomic and endocrine changes, and a slower response involving direct transmission of information from the thalamus to the cortex. Limbic theories of emotion are most relevant to fear and anger, and tend to de-emphasise the role of the cortex in emotion. The frontal lobes are also involved in emotion.

Emotion

❖ According to the James–Lange theory, experienced emotion depends on feedback from the bodily changes produced by an emotional stimulus, with each emotion having its own pattern of bodily changes. However, we often experience emotion before or without the relevant bodily changes, and many different emotional states are associated with a broadly similar state of autonomic arousal. It also appears to be possible to experience arousal but no accompanying emotional experience.

❖ The Cannon–Bard theory suggests that an emotional stimulus activates the thalamus and this produces two separate effects: (1) emotional experience, and (2) activation of the hypothalamus and autonomic arousal. This fits in with LeDoux's view that two brain systems are involved with emotion, but the Cannon–Bard theory cannot explain the link between physiological intensity and emotional experience, nor can it explain why a particular emotion is experienced.

❖ Schachter and Singer's cognitive labelling theory proposed that there are two factors that are essential to an emotional experience: (1) the physiological arousal, and (2) a cognitive interpretation or label for the arousal. There has been some research support for the theory, though such studies may lack ecological validity and the effects of arousal on emotional intensity are often much weaker than predicted. The theory can explain why arousal leads to particular states and it led to the development of other cognitive theories.

❖ Lazarus' cognitive appraisal theory. This proposes that emotional experience depends on cognitive appraisal of significant stimuli: primary and secondary appraisal, and re-appraisal. Problems with this theory include the point that in real life emotion may affect cognitive appraisal rather than vice versa. Furthermore, Zajonc suggested that affect and cognition are separate systems, but cognitive appraisal theory assumes that cognitive processing cannot take place without cognitive awareness.

❖ Parkinson's four-factor theory offers a way of combining elements of all the theories, giving greatest emphasis to cognitive appraisal.

FURTHER READING

The topics in this Section are covered in greater depth by P. Gorman (2001) *Motivation and emotion* (London: Routledge), written specifically for the AQA A specification. There are full accounts of motivation (Chapter 10) and emotion (Chapter 17) in J.P.J. Pinel (1997) *Biopsychology (3rd Edn.)* (Boston: Allyn & Bacon). Detailed information about motivation and emotion is provided in Chapters 11–13 of N.R. Carlson (1994) *Physiology of behaviour (5th Edn.)* (Boston: Allyn & Bacon). T. Strongman (1996) *The psychology of emotion (4th Edn.)* (Chichester, UK: Wiley) provides a detailed account of the theories of emotion.

Example Examination Questions

You should spend 30 minutes on each of the questions below, which aim to test the material in this Section.

1. Discuss research studies relating to the role of brain structures in motivational states.   (24 marks)

2. (a) Outline the role of brain structures in motivational states (e.g., hunger and/or thirst).   (12 marks)
    (b) Evaluate explanations of motivational states related to brain structures.   (12 marks)

3. Critically consider **one** physiological approach to explaining motivation.   (24 marks)

4. (a) Describe **one** psychological approach to explaining motivation.   (12 marks)
    (b) Assess the extent to which this approach can account for research evidence.   (12 marks)

5. Describe and evaluate research into the relationship between brain structures and emotional behaviour/experience.   (24 marks)

6. Discuss **one** physiological approach to explaining emotion.   (24 marks)

Examination Tips

Question 1. "Discuss" is an AO1 + AO2 term, therefore you must describe research studies, and then evaluate them. The studies must relate to the role of the brain in, for example, hunger or thirst. If you wish to introduce evidence related to how other physiological mechanisms contribute to motivation then these could be used as a form of evaluation (arguing that motivation is not just controlled by the brain), but such evaluation must be explicit. Evaluation might also concern the methodology of the studies and/or relevance to theoretical accounts of motivation. It could be argued that higher cognitive control is also related to "brain states".

Question 2. In part (a) a summary description only is required ("outline") and therefore marks are awarded for breadth rather than detail. Only material related to brain structures will be creditworthy. Other mechanisms of motivation can be introduced in part (b) as a form of evaluation. This question differs subtly from question 1 because the credit here is for explanations rather than studies. Clearly the same material can be used but not the same structure. In this case you might use studies to support (evaluate) your explanations but the backbone of the essay concerns explanations.

Question 3. You are required to describe and evaluate only one theory and it must be a physiological one. Other theories could be introduced as a means of evaluation but this must be done explicitly—it is not sufficient to merely say "we can evaluate theory x with theory y" and then just describe the second theory. The second theory should be compared and contrasted to help us further understand the strengths and weaknesses of the first theory. Research studies could be used as part of the description, or could be used as evaluation. It is desirable to make this explicit. Other forms of evaluation include implications of the theory and possible practical applications.

Question 4.   Part (a) requires a description (detail as well as breadth are both important) of one approach only. The question requires a psychological approach to motivation, such as Maslow's, but drive-reduction theory (a "combined" theory) would be acceptable and it might also be argued that any physiological theory is essentially psychological because psychology is a broad discipline. In part (b) you are asked to consider whether the approach/theory can account for research evidence. Credit will be given to how effectively you can use the research evidence as support or otherwise for the theory, not for your descriptions of the research evidence as this is the AO2 part of the essay.

Question 5.   The term "research" refers to both theory and studies. Therefore, in this essay you can describe either theories and/or studies, and evaluate them. The danger is that you will have far too much to write and could end up with lots of breadth but insufficient depth for a top mark. Aim to be selective in the argument you propose to present and give sufficient detail. The best approach is likely to be structured around various theories that are evaluated through the use of research evidence. Such evidence can be further evaluated in terms of validity and methodology. The essay refers to "behaviour and experience", so you should ensure that the experiential aspect of emotion is emphasised.

Question 6.   In this essay you must select one physiological theory to describe. Other theories can be presented as a means of evaluation but you should bear the comments for question 3 in mind.

WEB SITES

http://www.uwm.edu/Course/820-101/Kaleta/InS00MotivHunger.htm
Motivation theories and hunger, in "slide" format.

http://www.uwm.edu/Course/820-101/Kaleta/InS00Emotion.htm
Theories of motivation and emotion, in "slide" format.

http://www.vanguard.edu/psychology/webemotion.html
Emotion and motivation links.

http://www.csun.edu/~vcpsy00h/students/hunger.htm
Notes on hunger and eating, with related links.

http://mentalhelp.net/guide/eating.htm
Links to sites related to eating disorders.

http://www.houghton.edu/depts/psychology/intro13/sld001.htm
Motivation and emotion theories, including Maslow's Hierarchy of Needs, presented as "slides".

http://www.gettysburg.edu/~arterber/psy101/emotion1.html
Summary of theories of emotion.

http://www.britannica.com/bcom/eb/article/8/0,5716,115598+10,00.html
Encyclopædia Britannica article on theories of emotion.

http://www.unige.ch/fapse/emotion/welcome.html
Links on the Geneva Emotion Research Group site.

www.a-levelpsychology.co.uk/websites.html
A continually updated list of useful links, including those printed in this book, may be found at the Psychology Press A level psychology site.

PART 3

Cognitive Psychology

The word "cognitive" is derived from a Latin word cognitio meaning "to apprehend" or understand. Cognitive psychologists look at topics such as memory, perception, thought, language, attention, and so on. In other words they are interested in mental processes and seek to explain behaviour in terms of these mental processes.

In your AS studies, you learned about memory and its application to eyewitness testimony. There are many other applications of cognitive psychology, ranging from suggestions about how to improve your memory (useful for examination candidates), to how to improve performance in situations requiring close attention (such as air-traffic control).

7

Attention and Pattern Recognition

This Section considers theories about the ways in which human beings find their way through the mass of stimuli that constantly surround them, avoiding distractions and focusing on the important and relevant inputs. In addition, we will address the ways in which we recognise the complex patterns of signals received by the visual system.

Focused Attention

What is Attention?

The term "attention" has been used in various ways. Sometimes it is used to mean concentration. However, it is most often used to refer to the ability to select part of the information available in the environment for further processing. This latter meaning was emphasised by William James (1890, pp.403–404):

> *Everyone knows what attention is. It is the taking possession of the mind, in clear and vivid form, of one out of what seem several simultaneously possible objects or trains of thought. Focalisation, concentration, of consciousness are of its essence. It implies a withdrawal from some things in order to deal effectively with others.*

There are links among attention, arousal, and alertness. Consider, for example, someone who is drowsily sitting in a comfortable chair. He or she is in a state of low arousal or alertness, and in this state will probably attend little to the environment. Attention is generally "voluntary" in the sense that we decide what to attend to. However, it can be "involuntary" when we are presented with a novel, surprising, or intense stimulus such as a car backfiring.

One or many attentional systems?

Many psychologists (and non-psychologists) assume that all the phenomena of attention depend on a single attentional system. This is most unlikely to be the case, as was pointed out by Allport (1993, pp.203–204):

> *There is no uniform function, or mental operation (in general, no one causal mechanism) to which all so-called attentional phenomena can be attributed ... It seems no more plausible that there should be one unique mechanism, or computational resource, as the*

What do you think Allport might have meant by "folk psychology"?

causal basis of all attentional phenomena than that there should be a unitary causal basis of thought, or perception, or of any other traditional category of folk psychology.

In other words, Allport took the view that attention cannot be seen as one thing. We would regard it as absurd to consider thinking or perception as being caused by one process, and attention is no different. There is not just one source of attention.

Some evidence for Allport's (1993) position comes from studies of brain-damaged patients having problems with attention. Many of them experience difficulties with respect to some attentional abilities, but not to others. Posner and Petersen (1990), for example, used such findings to argue that there are at least three separate visual attentional processes:

- The ability to disengage attention from a given visual stimulus.
- The ability to shift attention from one target stimulus to another.
- The ability to engage attention on a new visual stimulus.

The information-processing approach

The information-processing approach is based on the following major assumptions:

- Information made available by the environment is processed by a series of processing systems (e.g., attention; perception; short-term memory).
- These processing systems transform the information in various systematic ways (e.g., we see 2 x 4 and we think 8).
- The aim of research is to specify the processes and structures (e.g., long-term memory) underlying cognitive performance.
- Information processing in people resembles that in computers.

In your AS level course you studied the information-processing approach in relation to memory. The multi-store model is a clear example of the use of the information-processing metaphor.

If computers process information, does this mean that humans process information in the same way?

Focused auditory and focused visual attention

In the 1950s cognitive psychology took over from behaviourism as the dominant force in psychology. One reason for this was the computer revolution that provided cognitive psychology with a new set of concepts such as input, output, serial processing, and parallel processing. The computer system provided an ideal analogy for what goes on inside a person's head, and might form a good basis for understanding human cognition. The models of attention that we are about to consider are very much information-processing models. Most research has concerned focused auditory attention, so we will start with this.

Focused Auditory Attention

The starting point for these models of focused auditory attention was some research conducted by Cherry (1953) into what he called the "**cocktail party effect**". This describes the experience of being in a room full of people who are talking. You are attending to one person who is speaking to you, and the other conversations are heard just as background noise. How is it possible to tune into one signal and tune all other signals out? Cherry conducted some experiments to find out the answer, as described in the Key Study on the next page.

Methods of investigating focused auditory attention

In the past, most research related to attention has concerned the auditory mode—our focus of effort on things that we hear. This can be investigated using the **dichotic listening task**. What usually happens is that three digits are presented one after the other to one ear, while at the same time three different digits are presented to the other ear. After the digits have been presented, the participants try to recall them in whatever order they prefer. Broadbent (1958) found that participants show a clear preference for recalling the digits ear by ear rather than pair by pair. Thus, for example, if 496 were presented to one ear and 852 to the other ear, recall would be 496852 rather than 489562.

A second method that is used is called a **shadowing task**, where a participant is given two auditory messages, one to each ear. The participant is asked to attend to just one of the messages and repeat it back out loud while ignoring the other message.

Early-selection theories

Cherry's research indicated that listeners are selecting information early on in the process of listening to a message. The participants were unaware of almost everything in the non-attended message except its physical characteristics. Broadbent's theory was the first attempt to explain this.

Broadbent's filter theory

Broadbent's (1958) filter theory used findings from Cherry's shadowing task and Broadbent's dichotic listening task to propose a filter theory of attention. The key assumptions in this theory were as follows:

- Two messages are presented at the same time and gain access in parallel (at the same time) to a **sensory buffer**. This buffer contains information for a very short period of time.
- One of the inputs is then allowed through a filter on the basis of its physical characteristics, in other words the decision about which message to attend to is related to its physical characteristics—such as the message being in a deep female voice. The other input remains in the buffer, possibly for later processing.
- This filter is needed to prevent overloading of the limited-capacity mechanism beyond the filter. Once past the filter the message is processed thoroughly.

Research studies.   This theory handles Cherry's basic findings, with unattended messages being rejected by the filter and thus receiving very little processing. It also accounts for performance on Broadbent's original dichotic listening task (see "Methods of investigating focused auditory attention", opposite), because it is assumed that the filter selects one input on the basis of the most obvious physical characteristics distinguishing the two inputs (i.e., the ear of arrival). However, it does not explain

The cocktail party effect

Colin Cherry, when he was working in an electronics research laboratory at the Massachusetts Institute of Technology, became interested in the "cocktail party effect". The problem is to explain how it is that we can follow just one conversation when several people are talking at once. Cherry (1953) found that our ability to do this involves making use of physical differences between the various auditory messages in order to select the one of interest. These physical differences include differences in the sex of the speaker, in voice intensity, and in the location of the speaker. Cherry demonstrated this by presenting two messages in the same voice to both ears at once (thereby removing these physical differences). When he did this participants found it very hard to separate out the two messages purely on the basis of meaning.

Cherry also carried out studies using a shadowing task, in which one auditory message had to be shadowed (repeated back out loud) while a second auditory message was presented to the other ear. He found that:

- Very little information seemed to be recalled from the unattended message.
- Listeners rarely noticed when the unattended message was spoken in a foreign language or in reversed speech.
- Listeners couldn't say whether the unattended message was continuous prose or isolated words.
- In contrast, physical changes such as the insertion of a pure tone were usually detected.
- Listeners could report the sex of the speaker and the intensity of sound in the unattended message.

The conclusion was that unattended auditory information receives almost no processing except for some recognition of physical characteristics. This finding was supported by other evidence. For example, Moray (1959) arranged for a list of seven words to be played to the unattended ear. The words were repeated five times. Afterwards participants were given a list of words and asked to identify those presented to the unattended ear. They had more or less no recognition of these words.

How do we distinguish and follow one conversation out of many in situations like this?

Discussion points

1. Are you surprised by any of Cherry's findings?
2. Why do you think that Broadbent found Cherry's findings of great interest?

What does the "cocktail party effect" tell us about attention?

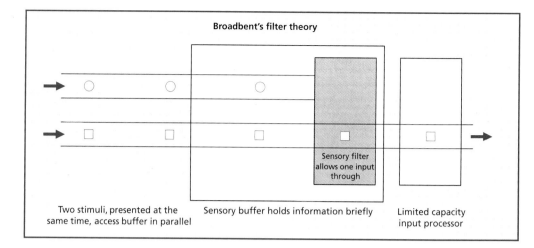

other findings. For example, it is assumed within filter theory that the unattended message is always rejected at an early stage of processing, but this assumption is wrong. The original shadowing studies involved participants with no previous experience of shadowing messages. As a result, they had to devote nearly all of their processing resources to the shadowing task. Underwood (1974) asked participants to detect digits presented in either the shadowed or the non-shadowed message. Participants who had not done the task before detected only 8% of the digits in the non-shadowed message. In contrast, an experienced researcher in the area was able to detect 67% of the non-shadowed digits.

The two messages were very similar (i.e., both auditorily presented verbal messages) in early studies on the shadowing task. Allport, Antonis, and Reynolds (1972) found that the degree of similarity between the two messages had a major impact on memory for the non-shadowed message. When shadowing of auditorily presented passages was combined with auditory presentation of words, memory for the words was very poor. However, when shadowing was combined with picture presentation, memory for the pictures was very good (90% correct). If two inputs differ clearly from each other, then they can both be processed more thoroughly than was allowed for by Broadbent's filter theory.

Broadbent (1958) assumed that there was no processing of the meaning of unattended messages, because the participants had no conscious awareness of their meaning. However, this leaves open the possibility that meaning might be processed without awareness. Von Wright, Anderson, and Stenman (1975) gave their participants two auditorily presented lists of words. They told the participants to shadow one list and to ignore the other one. When a word that had previously been associated with electric shock was presented on the unattended list, there was sometimes a noticeable physiological response. There was the same effect when a word very similar in sound or meaning to the shocked word was presented. These findings suggest that information in the unattended message was processed in terms of both sound and meaning. The most striking finding was that these physiological reactions occurred even though the participants were not consciously aware that the previously shocked word or its associates had been presented. However, as physiological responses were detected on only a fraction of the trials, it seems that thorough processing of unattended information occurred only some of the time.

The electric shocks were relatively mild. Would you consider this to be an example of physical or psychological harm?

Evaluation.   Broadbent's filter theory of attention is of great historical importance. The notion of an information-processing system, with a number of processes linked to each other, first saw the light of day in a systematic fashion in filter theory. That notion has been very influential since then, with information-processing systems being proposed for memory, language processing, and so on, as well as attention. Indeed, it could be argued that cognitive psychology as it is today owes more to Broadbent's filter theory than to any other single contribution.

On the negative side, Broadbent's theory suffered from the fact that it was too inflexible, and some of its limitations have already been discussed in the light of the evidence. The theory predicts that an unattended input will receive minimal processing. In fact, however, there is great variability in the amount of processing devoted to such input. A similar inflexibility of filter theory is shown in its assumption that the filter selects information on the basis of physical features of the input. This assumption is supported by the tendency of participants in the dichotic listening task to recall digits ear by ear. However, a small change in the basic task produces very different results. Gray and Wedderburn (1960) tried a different version of the dichotic listening task where, for example, "who 6 there" was presented to one ear at the same time as "4 goes 1" was presented to the other ear. With this kind of stimulus participants did not report the messages ear by ear, but instead gave them in terms of meaning ("who goes there" followed by "4 6 1"). Thus, selection can occur either *before* or *after* the processing of information from both inputs. The fact that selection can be based on the meaning of presented information is inconsistent with filter theory.

Treisman's attenuation theory

Treisman (1964) proposed an attenuation theory of attention, in which the processing of unattended information is attenuated or reduced. In Broadbent's filter theory, it was proposed that there is a bottleneck early in processing. In Treisman's theory, the location of the bottleneck is more flexible. It is as if people possess a "leaky" filter that makes selective attention less efficient than was assumed by Broadbent (1958).

Let us consider Treisman's theory in a little more detail. Stimulus processing proceeds in a systematic fashion, starting with analyses based on physical cues, and then moving on to analyses based on meaning. If there is not enough processing capacity to allow full stimulus analysis, then some of the later analyses are left out of the processing of unattended stimuli. This theory neatly fits in with Cherry's (1953) finding that it is usually the physical characteristics of unattended inputs (e.g., sex of the speaker) that are noticed rather than their meaning—because usually there is insufficient processing capacity.

According to Treisman's theory, why does it sometimes appear as if information is filtered very early on?

Research studies. Treisman conducted various studies to demonstrate that some processing of the unattended message does take place, thus supporting her model. For example, in one study (Treisman, 1960) she played messages in English and French to participants who were bilingual in these languages. The English message was presented

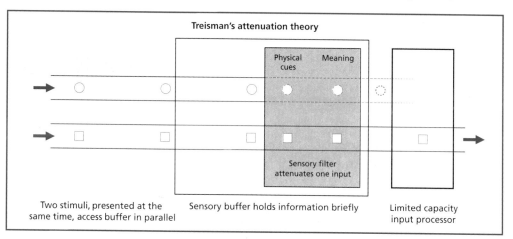

Treisman's attenuation theory

Physical cues   Meaning

Sensory filter attenuates one input

Two stimuli, presented at the same time, access buffer in parallel   Sensory buffer holds information briefly   Limited capacity input processor

to one ear and was to be attended while the French message was to be unattended. The messages had the same meaning and started out with a time delay, but as this delay was reduced the participants recognised that the messages were the same, suggesting that they were doing more than processing the physical characteristics of the unattended message.

Treisman (1964) tested the processing of the unattended message further by playing various messages to the unattended ear: a passage from the same novel as being played to the attended ear, a passage from a biochemical text, a passage in a foreign language, or a set of nonsense syllables. The participants' ability to shadow the attended message was affected by the degree of similarity between the messages played to the attended and unattended ear. The more similar the messages were, the harder it was to shadow the attended message.

Can you think of an everyday example of shadowing an attended message and experiencing interference from an unattended message?

Evaluation.   The extensive processing of unattended sources of information that was embarrassing for filter theory can be accounted for by Treisman's attenuation theory. Treisman's theory is more flexible but is still essentially a single-channel, serial processing theory, ignoring parallel processing. In addition the same findings can also be explained by Deutsch and Deutsch's (1963) late-selection model. We need to consider which theory, Treisman's or Deutsch and Deutsch's, best accounts for the evidence.

Late-selection theories

Deutsch and Deutsch

Deutsch and Deutsch (1963) claimed that all stimuli are analysed fully, with the most important or relevant stimulus determining the response. This theory is like filter theory and attenuation theory in assuming the existence of a bottleneck in processing. However, it places the bottleneck closer to the response end of the processing system, i.e., selection takes place relatively late in the process. This theory is much more a model of parallel processing than of serial processing. At least it is parallel up to the point where a response is selected, but serial thereafter. As selection takes place relatively late, this means that most information is processed in parallel.

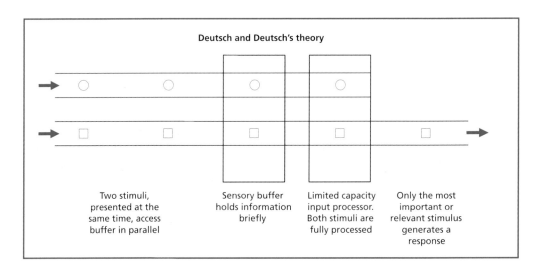

Research studies.   The Deutsch and Deutsch model predicts that a certain amount of unconscious processing is taking place which is why it *appears* that unattended messages are attenuated whereas they are in fact just not accessible. Several studies support this. For example the study by Von Wright et al. (see page 234) indicates that the words in the unattended channel are processed for meaning. In another shadowing experiment, MacKay (1973) played an ambiguous sentence to participants' shadowed side. For example "They threw stones at the bank yesterday". At the same time either the word "river" or the word "money" was played to the unattended ear. Later the participants were given various sentences and asked to identify the one that was closest to what they heard. Was it "They threw stones at the side of the river yesterday" or was it "They threw stones at the savings and loan association yesterday"? Participants selected the interpretation that fitted the word given to the unattended channel. Again, meaning appears to be processed by the unattended side.

Choosing between Treisman and Deutsch and Deutsch. It seems that all these results could potentially be explained in terms of Treisman's attenuation theory, and her theory seems more plausible in some ways. The assumption made by Deutsch and Deutsch that all stimuli are analysed completely, but that most of the analysed information is lost almost at once, seems rather wasteful. In fact, studies by Treisman and Geffen (1967) and by Treisman and Riley (1969) provide support for attenuation theory rather than the theory of Deutsch and Deutsch (1963).

In the study by Treisman and Geffen (1967), the participants shadowed one of two auditory messages, having been told to tap whenever they detected a target word in either message. According to attenuation theory, participants should be less able to analyse data in the non-shadowed message and therefore should be less able to detect targets in the non-shadowed message than in the shadowed one. According to Deutsch and Deutsch, there is complete processing of all stimuli, and so it might be predicted that there would be no difference in detection rates between the two messages. In fact, the detection rate for the shadowed or attended message was 87%, against only 8% for the non-shadowed message.

Deutsch and Deutsch (1967) did not accept that Treisman and Geffen's (1967) findings had disproved their theory. They pointed out that their theory assumes that only *important* inputs lead to responses. As the task used by Treisman and Geffen (1967) required their participants to make two responses (i.e., shadow and tap) to target words in the shadowed message, but only one response (i.e., tap) to targets in the non-shadowed message, the shadowed targets were more important than the non-shadowed ones. Thus, Deutsch and Deutsch's theory could account for the findings.

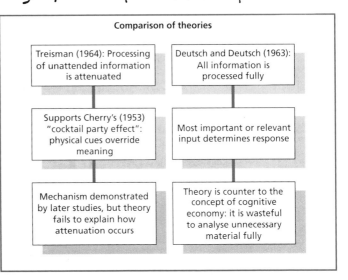

Only important input leads to responses…

Comparison of theories

Treisman (1964): Processing of unattended information is attenuated	Deutsch and Deutsch (1963): All information is processed fully
Supports Cherry's (1953) "cocktail party effect": physical cues override meaning	Most important or relevant input determines response
Mechanism demonstrated by later studies, but theory fails to explain how attenuation occurs	Theory is counter to the concept of cognitive economy: it is wasteful to analyse unnecessary material fully

Treisman and Riley (1969) retaliated by carrying out a study in which exactly the same response was made to targets in either message. Their participants were told to stop shadowing and to tap whenever they detected a target in either message. Many more target words were detected in the shadowed message than in the non-shadowed one, a finding that is hard to explain using the theory of Deutsch and Deutsch.

Johnston and Heinz's theory

A reasonable compromise position was adopted by Johnston and Heinz (1978). They argued that the theories we have considered so far are too inflexible. According to their theory, selection can occur at several different stages of processing. The precise stage at which selection takes place is usually as early in processing as possible in the light of the requirements of the current task. The reason for this is that the demands on processing capacity increase progressively as selection is delayed.

Research studies.   Johnston and Wilson (1980) carried out a study to test this idea. Pairs of words were presented, one to each ear, and the task was to identify target words that

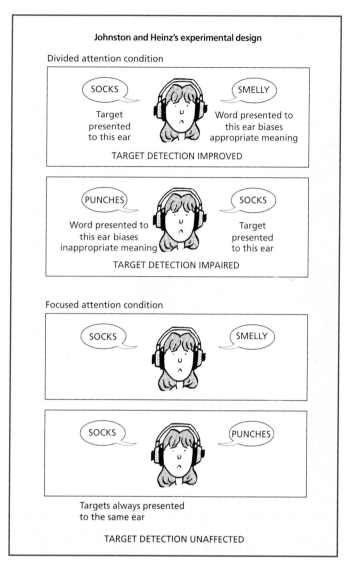

Johnston and Heinz's experimental design

Divided attention condition

SOCKS   SMELLY
Target presented to this ear   Word presented to this ear biases appropriate meaning
TARGET DETECTION IMPROVED

PUNCHES   SOCKS
Word presented to this ear biases inappropriate meaning   Target presented to this ear
TARGET DETECTION IMPAIRED

Focused attention condition

SOCKS   SMELLY

SOCKS   PUNCHES

Targets always presented to the same ear

TARGET DETECTION UNAFFECTED

were members of a given category. The targets were ambiguous words with two different meanings. For example, if the category was "articles of clothing", then "socks" would be a possible target word (meaning either what you wear or to hit something). Each target word was paired with a non-target word that would bias its meaning. For example, "socks" was paired with "smelly" or paired with "punches", or paired with a neutral word such as "Saturday".

When the participants did not know which ear the targets would arrive at (divided attention), target detection was improved by appropriate non-targets and impaired by inappropriate non-targets. Thus, when participants were dividing their attention they were processing both ears for meaning. In contrast, when the participants knew that all the targets would be presented to one ear (focused attention), target detection was unaffected by the appropriateness or otherwise of the non-target word presented at the same time. This suggests that non-targets were not processed for meaning in the focused attention condition. These various findings indicate that the amount of processing received by non-target stimuli is no more than is necessary to perform the main task.

Evaluation.   This model offers a way to interpret all of the evidence considered in this Unit, and offers a bridge to divided attention, the topic to be considered in the next Unit (page 242). However, the model also raises the question of whether it is necessary to have a model of focused attention at all. It may be preferable, as suggested by Johnston and Heinz's study, to have a model that has the capacity to switch attentional focus as required rather than to suppose there is some sort of selection taking place. The models of divided attention offer this possibility.

Furthermore, it may be useful to consider some of the overall limitations of research into focused auditory attention. The failure to shadow the unattended message may be an effect of practice rather than selection. The study by Underwood (1974, see page 234) showed that well-practised participants could shadow much more effectively. In addition we should remember that all studies were conducted in laboratories and may not reflect the complexities of real-life attentional processes. Finally, all of the research has concerned focused auditory attention. Allport et al. (1972) found that if participants had to monitor two messages in different sensory modalities (auditory and visual), their performance improved enormously.

Focused Visual Attention

One of the most common ways of thinking about focused visual attention is by comparing it to a spotlight. When you shine a spotlight on something, everything within a relatively small area can be seen clearly, whereas anything lying outside the spotlight's beam is harder or impossible to see. Various refinements to this basic idea have been suggested. According to Broadbent (1982, p.69), we should

think of selectivity as like a searchlight, with the option of altering the focus. When something seems to be happening ... the beam sharpens and moves to the point of maximum importance.

The zoom-lens model

In similar fashion, Eriksen (1990) developed a **zoom-lens model**. He argued that attention is generally widely distributed, but it can zoom in on certain parts of the visual field if it is necessary to obtain maximum information from them. In other words, the spotlight metaphor implied that the beam of attention is a constant width whereas the zoom lens field can alter depending on circumstances. It is a more flexible process.

This model was investigated by LaBerge (1983, see the Key Study below).

Evaluation of the zoom-lens model

Most of the evidence favours the zoom-lens model over the spotlight metaphor. However, in spite of the attractiveness of the zoom-lens model, it has some limitations. Juola et al. (1991) carried out a study in which a target letter was presented in one of three concentric rings: an inner, a middle, and an outer ring. The participants were given a cue that generally provided accurate information as to the ring in which the target would be presented. If attention is like an adjustable spotlight, then speed and accuracy of target detection would be greatest for targets presented in the inner ring. In fact, performance was best when the target appeared in the ring that had been cued. This suggests that visual attention could be distributed in an O-shaped pattern to include only the outer or middle ring without the inner ring.

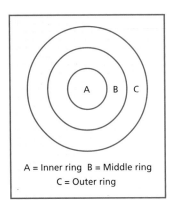

A = Inner ring   B = Middle ring
C = Outer ring

The stimulus for Juola et al.'s (1991) study.

It is proposed within the zoom-lens model that the focus of attention is a given area in visual space. However, there is evidence indicating that we often focus on objects rather than on a particular location. For example, Neisser and Becklen (1975) placed films of two moving scenes on top of each other. They found that the participants could easily attend to one scene while ignoring the other one. This corresponds to everyday life, in which, for example, we seem able to attend to a building while ignoring the trees that partially block our view of it.

Kramer and Hahn (1995) argued that attention does not have to be focused on a single area or on a given object. They found that their participants could attend to two separate areas at the same time, while ignoring distracting stimuli that were presented in between those two areas. They argued that the zoom-lens model was far too inflexible. According to them, attention can be focused on a single area, on objects that are partially obscured by other stimuli, or on two separate areas. Kramer and Hahn (1995, p.385) concluded that their findings "suggest a remarkable degree of attentional

What might be the adaptive significance of being able to focus on objects rather than on a particular location?

The zoom-lens model

The notion of an adjustable attentional beam was investigated by LaBerge (1983). The participants were presented with five-letter words, and they had to perform one of two tasks. One task required them to focus on the entire word, because they had to decide what category the word belonged to. The other task only required the participants to focus on the middle letter, because they were asked to categorise that letter.

In order to decide *where* the participants were attending, LaBerge sometimes presented a probe stimulus requiring a rapid response in the spatial position of one of the five letters of the word, immediately after the word had been presented. He assumed that the probe would be responded to more quickly when it fell within the central attentional beam than when it did not. When the participants had been asked to categorise the middle letter, the reaction time to the probe was significantly faster when it was presented in the spatial position of the middle letter than when it was presented anywhere else. This suggests that the attentional beam was very narrow in that condition. In contrast, the speed of response to the probe was influenced very little by its spatial position when the task involved categorising the word. This suggests that the attentional beam was very broad in that condition. Overall, the findings indicate that the attentional spotlight is of flexible width depending on the precise requirements of the task.

Discussion points

1. Does LaBerge provide convincing evidence that attention is like a zoom lens?

2. What are the limitations of LaBerge's approach?

Is attention focused on the object or the location?

flexibility—that is, the ability to divide attention among non-contiguous [non-adjacent] locations in the visual field".

What happens to unattended visual stimuli? According to both the spotlight and the zoom-lens models, there should be very limited processing of such stimuli. Johnston and Dark (1986, p.56) reviewed the relevant evidence, and came to the following conclusion: "Stimuli outside the spatial focus of attention undergo little or no semantic processing." Francolini and Egeth (1980) were among those reporting findings that are consistent with the conclusion of Johnston and Dark. They gave their participants a circular array of red and black letters or numerals, and told them to count the number of red items while ignoring the black items. Performance speed was reduced when the red items consisted of numerals conflicting with the answer, but there was no interference effect from the black items. These findings suggested that there was little or no processing of the to-be-ignored black items.

Francolini and Egeth made the apparently reasonable assumption that a lack of interference from the to-be-ignored stimuli showed that they were not processed. This assumption is incorrect. Driver and Tipper (1989) carried out a similar study to that of Francolini and Egeth (1980). However, they used more sensitive measures, and found that the meaning of to-be-ignored stimuli was processed.

In sum, the meaning of unattended visual stimuli is processed at least some of the time. There may be less extensive processing of unattended than of attended stimuli, but unattended stimuli do typically receive some processing.

Picking out one unfamiliar face from all these children might take some time, but how quickly would you locate your own face if you were in the picture?

Visual search

Progress in understanding some of the underlying processes involved in focused visual attention has come from studies of **visual search**. In visual search tasks, the participants are presented with a visual display containing several different stimuli, and have to decide as rapidly as possible whether a target stimulus (e.g., the number 4) is present. An example from everyday life might be looking at a school photograph and trying to find yourself. Even if there are dozens of people in the photograph, it usually takes very little time to find your image.

Classic research on visual search was reported by Neisser (1964). He presented his participants with lists of letters, and asked them to detect the letter Z. Performance was faster when the distractor letters contained rounded features (e.g., S, B, P, O, etc.) than when they consisted of straight lines (e.g., E, H, T, L, etc.), presumably because the distractors shared fewer features with the target letter Z in the former condition (see page 256). There was a great increase in speed with practice, suggesting that target detection was becoming automatic.

Feature integration theory

Treisman (1988) put forward a feature integration theory to account for the findings from visual search studies. The theory involves a distinction between objects and features of objects (e.g., colour, size, outlines). Some of the key aspects of this theory are as follows:

* The visual features of objects in the environment are processed rapidly in parallel (i.e., all at the same time) without attention being required; this is the first stage of processing.
* The features are then combined to form objects (e.g., a red chair; a purple flower) by means of a slow, serial process (i.e., one after another); this is the second stage of processing.
* Focused attention on the location of an object provides the "glue" that permits objects to be formed from combined features.
* Features can also be combined on the basis of stored knowledge (e.g., "strawberries are red").
* In the absence of focused attention or relevant stored knowledge, features will be combined in a random fashion; this can produce odd combinations of features known as *illusory conjunctions*.

Research evidence

Treisman and Gelade (1980) reported findings that are relevant to the predictions of feature integration theory. If the target stimulus in a visual search task is defined in terms of a single feature (e.g., something blue), then only the first stage of processing should be needed. As the first stage of processing occurs in parallel, the speed of detection should hardly be affected by the number of items in the display. The findings should be very different, however, if the target is an object defined by a *combination* of features (e.g., a green letter T); these are conjunctive targets. In this case, the second stage of processing and focused attention would be involved. As focused attention operates in a serial fashion, detection speed should be much slower when there are several items in the visual display than when there are few. The findings in positive trials (i.e., when the target was present) were precisely as predicted. The findings in negative trials (i.e., when the target was absent) are of less relevance.

According to feature integration theory, there should be illusory conjunctions or incorrect combinations of features when attention is not focused on the critical part of a visual display. However, illusory conjunctions should not occur when stimuli receive focal attention. Precisely this pattern of results was reported by Treisman and Schmidt (1982).

In spite of the successes of feature integration theory, it does not provide a full account. Treisman and Sato (1990) proposed a modification of the basic theory. They argued that the degree of similarity between the target and the distractors is a factor influencing visual search time. They claimed (with supporting evidence) that visual search for a target defined by more than one feature is usually limited to those distractors having at least one of the features of the target. For example, if you were looking for a blue circle in a display containing blue triangles, black circles, and black triangles, then you would ignore black triangles. This contrasts with the views of Treisman and Gelade (1980), who argued that none of the stimuli would be ignored in such circumstances.

How does this theory of focused visual attention fit with theories of pattern recognition described on pages 254–258?

How and when could you relate feature integration theory to your everyday experience of life?

Divided Attention

How does divided attention
affect work performance?

As was indicated at the beginning of this Section, divided attention or dual-task studies involve the participants trying to perform two tasks at the same time as well as possible. It is of importance in such studies to find out how successfully the two tasks can be performed together. Everyday experience indicates that some tasks can be combined successfully, such as when an experienced motorist drives a car and holds a conversation at the same time. In other cases, however, dual-task performance is often poor. For example, when someone tries to rub their stomach with one hand while patting their head with the other, there can be a complete disruption of performance. These anecdotal examples indicate the need to consider in detail the factors determining how well two tasks can be performed together.

Research into Divided Attention

Task similarity

When we think of pairs of activities that can be performed well together, we tend to think of examples in which the two activities are dissimilar (e.g., driving and talking; reading and listening to music). There is much evidence indicating the importance of task similarity. A relevant study by Allport et al. (1972) was discussed in the last Unit. They found that participants repeating prose passages while learning auditorily presented words had poor long-term memory for the words, but they were able to repeat prose passages and remember pictures that were presented at the same time.

There are various ways in which two tasks can be similar or dissimilar. Wickens (1984) concluded that two tasks interfere with each other if they make use of the same stimulus modality (e.g., visual or auditory), or if they make use of the same stages of processing (e.g., input, internal processing, and output), or if they rely on related memory codes (e.g., verbal or visual).

Response similarity is also important. McLeod (1977) asked his participants to do a tracking task with manual responding at the same time as carrying out a tone-identification task. Some participants had to respond vocally to the tones, whereas others responded with the hand not involved in the tracking task. Performance on the tracking task was worse when there was high response similarity (manual responses on both tasks) than when there was low response similarity (manual responses on one task and vocal ones on the other).

■ Activity: Doing two things at once

The physical task of rubbing your stomach with one hand while patting the top of your head with the other has been used for amusement by children for generations. However, being able to do this well has been suggested as a good indicator of suitability for training as a helicopter pilot, where it is essential to be able to carry out different tasks with each hand! List everyday examples where people are required to do two tasks at the same time. Now consider whether you can actually write an essay while listening to music. Would there be any difference if you listened to a talk radio station? If you feel there would be a difference, can you explain this?

Practice

Common sense indicates that the old saying "Practice makes perfect" is very relevant to dual-task performance. For example, learner drivers find it almost impossible to drive and to hold a conversation at the same time, but expert drivers find it easy. Support for this common-sense position was obtained by Spelke, Hirst, and Neisser (1976) in a study on two students called Diane and John. These students had 2 hours' training a week for 4 months on various tasks. Their first task was to read short stories for comprehension at the same time as they wrote down words to dictation. At first, they found it very hard to do these two tasks together. After 6 weeks of training, however, they were able to read as rapidly and with as much comprehension when taking dictation as when only reading. In addition, the quality of their handwriting had also improved.

Can you think of examples of well-practised tasks where you have learned to do several activities at once?

Spelke et al. found that Diane and John could recall only 35 out of the thousands of words they had written down at dictation. Even when 20 successive dictated words formed a sentence or came from the same semantic category (e.g., four-footed animals), the two students were unaware of it. Spelke et al. gave them further training. As a result, they learned to write down the names of the categories to which the dictated words belonged while maintaining normal reading speed and comprehension.

When two complex tasks are performed well together, it is usually found that the skills involved have been highly practised. For example, expert pianists can play from seen music while repeating or shadowing heard speech (Allport et al., 1972), and an expert typist can type and shadow at the same time (Shaffer, 1975). Such levels of performance are impressive. However, it should be noted that some signs of interference are present in the data from these experts (Broadbent, 1982). In other words they are not able to do the two tasks simultaneously as well as they might do them separately.

The effects of practice: pianist and entertainer Liberace combined chatting to an audience with playing the piano in his stage and television shows.

Task difficulty

It is harder to perform two tasks together when they are difficult or complex than when they are simple. For example, Sullivan (1976) gave her participants the task of shadowing an auditory message and detecting target words on another auditory message at the same time. When the shadowing task was made harder by using a more complex message, fewer targets were detected on the other message.

There are two problems with research on the effects of task difficulty on dual-task performance. One problem is that there are several ways in which one task can be harder than another one. As a result, it is not easy to assess task difficulty with any precision. The other problem is that a task that is hard for one person may be very easy for another. An expert word processor finds typing very easy and undemanding, whereas someone who is just learning to type finds it very hard.

Theoretical Accounts of Divided Attention

We have seen that the extent to which two tasks can be performed successfully together depends on various factors. As a general principle, two dissimilar, highly practised, and simple tasks can typically be performed well together, whereas two similar, novel, and complex tasks cannot. In addition, having to perform two tasks together rather than separately often produces entirely new problems of co-ordination. For example, moving your forefinger in front of you in a circular fashion is very easy. It is also very easy to move both forefingers around in a circular fashion if they both move in the same direction (i.e., both clockwise or anti-clockwise). However, it is harder to move one forefinger clockwise around an imaginary circle while the other forefinger moves anti-clockwise, because the two tasks interfere with each other and resist co-ordination (see Duncan, 1979).

Can you think of examples where you have found that two tasks have interfered with each other, making co-ordination difficult?

Central capacity interference theory

The simplest theoretical explanation of dual-task performance is the central capacity interference theory, which has been favoured by Norman and Bobrow (1975) and by other theorists. There are two crucial assumptions made by this theory:

- There is some central capacity (attention or effort), which has limited resources.
- The ability to perform two tasks together depends on the demands placed on those resources by the two tasks.

It follows that dual-task performance will be poor if the two tasks require more resources than are available. However, the two tasks will be performed successfully if their combined demands for resources are less than the total resources of the central capacity. Some of

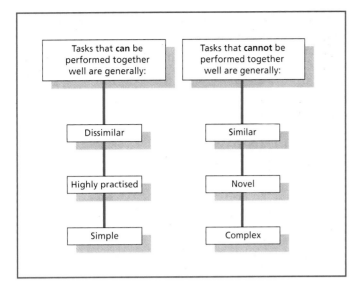

the most convincing evidence comes from a study by Bourke, Duncan, and Nimmo-Smith (1996; see the Key Study below) where participants were given four tasks to perform two at a time. The task that was expected to use a larger amount of resources (generating random numbers) did create greatest interference.

Task difficulty and practice

How does the central capacity interference theory account for the main findings from studies of dual-task performance? The fact that task difficulty is an important factor poses no problem for the theory, because task difficulty is defined simply as the demands placed by the task on the resources of the central capacity. The finding that two demanding tasks (e.g., reading for comprehension and writing at dictation) can sometimes be performed successfully together (e.g., Spelke et al., 1976) seems contrary to the

Support for central capacity

Bourke et al. (1996) provided some of the most convincing evidence for the notion that there is a central capacity that plays a part in determining how well two tasks can be performed together. First of all, they selected four tasks that were designed to be as different as possible from each other.

1. Random generation: the participants were told to try to generate letters at random so they did not form words.
2. Prototype learning: the participants had to work out the features of two patterns or prototypes from seeing various exemplars.
3. Manual task: the participants were told to screw a nut down to the bottom of a bolt and back up to the top, and then down to the bottom of a second bolt and back up, and so on.
4. Tone task: the participants had to detect the occurrence of a given "target" tone.

KEY STUDY EVALUATION — Bourke et al.

As we have seen, the four tasks used by Bourke et al. are very different from each other. If performance depended only on very specific processes, then there would presumably have been little or no interference between tasks. The fact that there was considerable interference is strong evidence for a general central processing capacity. It may have occurred to you that participants with special expertise might have found it easier to combine some of the tasks; for example, a mechanic might be very good at handling nuts and bolts. However, the participants were recent university students, and lacked special expertise for any of the tasks.

With tasks of the nature tested here, does it matter that the sample was biased?

The participants were given two of these tasks to perform at a time, and were told that one task was of more importance than the other. The basic argument was as follows: if there is a central or general capacity, then the task making most demands on this capacity will interfere most with all three of the other tasks. In contrast, the task making fewest demands on this capacity will interfere least with all three of the other tasks.

What did Bourke et al. find? First, they found that these very different tasks did interfere with each other. Second, they discovered that the random generation task interfered the most overall with the performance of the other tasks, and the tone task interfered the least. Third, and of greatest importance, the random generation task consistently interfered most with the prototype, manual, and tone tasks, and it did so whether it was the primary or the secondary task. The tone task consistently interfered least with each of the other three tasks. In other words, the findings were very much in line with the predictions of a general capacity theory.

The main limitation of the study by Bourke et al. is that they did not shed light on the nature of the central capacity. As they admitted (1996, p.544), "The general factor may be a limited pool of processing resource that needs to be invested for a task to be performed. It may be a limited central executive that co-ordinates or monitors other processes and is limited in how much it can deal with at one time ... The method developed here deals only with the existence of a general factor in dual-task decrements, not its nature."

Discussion points

1. Is it surprising that these very different tasks interfered with each other?
2. Why do you think that the random generation task interfered the most with other tasks, whereas the tone task interfered the least?

spirit of the central capacity theory. However, complex tasks can usually only be performed well together after a substantial amount of practice, and the demands on central resources may be reduced through practice. As is discussed later, prolonged practice can lead to some processes becoming automatic and thus not requiring central resources.

Task similarity

The central capacity interference theory can account for the effects of task difficulty and practice. However, it cannot handle some of the effects of task similarity. This can be seen if we consider a study by Segal and Fusella (1970). Their participants had to detect a weak visual or auditory signal while maintaining a visual or an auditory image. As there were two signal-detection tasks and two imagery tasks, there were four possible combinations of tasks: e.g., visual signal plus visual imagery, or visual signal plus auditory imagery.

Performance on the auditory signal task was better when it was combined with the visual imagery task than when it was combined with the auditory imagery task. According to central capacity theorists, this means that the visual imagery task is easier and less demanding of resources than the auditory imagery task. However, inspection of the findings for the visual signal task points to the opposite conclusion. Here performance was better when the visual signal task was combined with the auditory imagery task, suggesting that the auditory imagery task requires fewer resources than the visual imagery task.

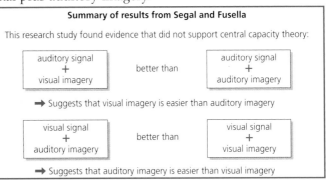

Theory of specific mechanisms

Allport (1989) argued that there are various specific processing mechanisms, each of which has limited capacity. This allows us to make sense of the fact that the degree of similarity between two tasks helps to determine how well they can be performed together. Similar tasks typically compete for the same specific processing mechanisms, and this competition disrupts performance. In contrast, dissimilar tasks tend to use different mechanisms, and so are much less likely to interfere with each other.

Allport's general approach can be illustrated by considering someone who is trying to drive a car and to hold a conversation at the same time. Car driving involves a number of specific skills involving visual perception and motor responses, whereas holding a conversation involves language skills and retrieving information stored in long-term memory about the topic of conversation. It is because such different skills are involved that people are able to drive and to talk at the same time.

According to this view, what tasks might be more difficult to do whilst driving a car?

Combined theory

Eysenck (1984) argued that a theory combining aspects of central capacity interference theory and the theory of specific mechanisms may be more adequate than either theory on its own. According to this view, the effects of task difficulty on dual-task performance are due largely to attention or the central processor, whereas the effects of similarity are due to specific processing resources. The effects of practice occur because tasks that initially require much use of attention or the central processor no longer do so after much practice.

Practical Applications of Divided Attention Research

Predictive testing

We have seen that one of the main reasons why people find it hard to perform two tasks at the same time is because of limited resources. This notion was applied by Ivor Brown in a very practical way in the 1960s. A bus company in England was spending a lot of money in training bus drivers, many of whom failed the driving test for public service vehicles. It was very hard to identify those who were going to fail on the basis of their driving performance during training, because it did not differ noticeably from that of those who passed. Brown came up with an ingenious solution.

Brown argued that unsuccessful trainees were having to put more attentional resources into driving than the successful ones. He tested this idea by using a dual-task set-up (see Eysenck & Eysenck, 1981). A set of eight digits was read every few seconds while the trainees were driving. Each set differed in one digit from the preceding set, and the task was to spot the changed digit. Those trainees who later passed the driving test performed this digit task almost twice as well as those who failed. As a result, much wasted time and money were saved by using the dual performance task for initial selection.

How can you use the concept of limited attentional resources to explain why chatting during a driving lesson is relatively easy whereas a chatty driving examiner on a test could be extremely distracting?

Effects of anxiety

When people are working in a potentially dangerous environment, they become more anxious. What are the effects of anxiety on our ability to carry out two tasks at the same time? You might imagine that anxiety would impair performance on both tasks, but what actually happens is more complex. Weltman, Smith, and Egstrom (1971) made their participants anxious by fooling them into believing that the diving chamber they were in had descended to a depth of 60 feet (18 metres). They were given the main task of detecting small gaps in rings and the subsidiary task of detecting a light when it came on. Anxiety had no effect on performance of the main task, but impaired performance on the subsidiary task. This can best be explained by assuming that the adverse effects of anxiety can be compensated for to some extent by putting most of the available attentional resources into the main task at the expense of the subsidiary one. This may explain why pilots in an emergency situation sometimes ignore vital information that is not normally needed in order to fly safely.

What ethical considerations are involved in studies like the one by Weltman et al. (1971)?

Learning attention management

Gopher (1993) argued that attention management in dual-task situations is a skill that can be learned. He tested this argument using a computer game called *Space Fortress*. This involves controlling the movements of a space ship, firing missiles to destroy a fortress, and avoiding being destroyed. Some Israeli air force cadets were given attentional training on the game, focusing on one task component at a time (e.g., firing missiles). These cadets were twice as likely as other cadets to become qualified pilots within 18 months. This happened in spite of the fact that real flying is much more demanding than *Space Fortress*. What the cadets trained on the game had learned was how to control their attention effectively.

Training in attention management (also known as Nintendo Zelda). Such games may actually contribute to learning to manage attention effectively.

Automatic Processing

As was pointed out earlier, practice often has a dramatic effect on performance. It has often been assumed that this occurs because some processing activities become automatic as a result of prolonged practice. Some of the main criteria for **automatic processes** are as follows:

- They are fast.
- They make no demands on attention.
- They are not available to consciousness.
- They are unavoidable, in the sense that they always occur when an appropriate stimulus is presented.

It has proved hard to find many processes satisfying all of these criteria. For example, the requirement that automatic processes make no demands on attention means that they should have no effect at all on the performance of any attention-demanding task being carried out at the same time. In fact, this is rarely the case (see Hampson, 1989, for a review).

The Stroop effect

Problems with the unavoidability criterion were identified by Kahneman and Henik (1979). They studied the Stroop effect, in which the naming of colours in which words are printed is slowed down by using colour words (e.g., the word BLACK printed in blue). This Stroop effect has often been regarded as involving unavoidable and automatic processing of the colour words. Thus, when you see the word BLACK printed in blue, it is hard to inhibit the tendency to say "black" even though you have been instructed to name the ink colour in which the word is written. However, Kahneman and Henik found that the Stroop effect was much larger when the distracting information (i.e., the colour name) was in the same location as the to-be-named colour rather than in an adjacent location. Thus, the processes producing the Stroop effect are not always totally unavoidable.

> ■ Activity: The Stroop effect
>
> To carry out the Stroop task you will need two sheets of paper, four coloured pens (red, green, yellow, blue) and a stopwatch.
>
> On one sheet of paper, write the colour names red, green, yellow, blue in random order, a total of five times each. However, each colour name must be written in a different colour, e.g. the word "red" written in green ink.
>
> On the other sheet of paper, construct a second list that looks the same as the first one, but where the words are not colour names but other words that occur with the same frequency, e.g. boat, clock, etc.
>
> The experiment will be a repeated measures design, so you need to counterbalance the list presentation (Participant 1 receives List 1 then List 2: Participant 2 receives List 2 then List 1, and so on). The instructions you devise should ask your participants to say the names of the ink colours in each list as rapidly as possible without making any errors. Any errors that are made should be corrected.
>
> Record the times taken and decide how to present your results. Do they concur with those of Kahneman and Henik?

BLACK	**BLUE**	**BLACK**
BLUE	**BLUE**	**BLACK**
BLACK	**BLUE**	**BLUE**
BLUE	**BLACK**	**BLACK**

Skill acquisition

Some of the clearest evidence for automatic processes comes from studies of skill acquisition. Consider, for example, the development of touch-typing skills. As Fitts and Posner (1967) pointed out, there seem to be three stages involved. First, there is the cognitive stage, during which typists rely on rules of which they are consciously aware (e.g., move the index finger of the left hand to the right to type the letter g). Second, there is the associative stage, in which typing errors are gradually detected and eliminated. Third, there is the autonomous stage, in which typing becomes fast, accurate, and automatic.

Can you type fairly automatically? Can you say where the letters on the keyboard are? What would automatic processing predict?

The evidence shows very clearly that typing speed increases greatly with practice, so that a fairly skilled typist can make one keystroke every 60 milliseconds (Fitts & Posner, 1967). However, what is crucial is that the nature as well as the speed of the processes involved changes with training. This is most obvious in the autonomous stage, because most typists in that stage type with very little conscious involvement and can no longer verbalise the rules they used to rely on.

Additional evidence that skilled typing largely relies on automatic processes was reported by Shaffer (1975). He found that skilled typists could shadow or repeat what was said to them with very little effect on their typing performance. He also found that skilled typists could engage in a conversation while typing without it causing much impairment of typing speed or accuracy. This evidence appears to support the criteria of automatic processing.

Skilled touch typists can hold a conversation and attend to other stimuli with very little effect on their typing speed or accuracy.

A theory of controlled and automatic processes

Shiffrin and Schneider (1977) and Schneider and Shiffrin (1977) put forward a theory based on the distinction between controlled and automatic processes. According to their theory, controlled processes are of limited capacity, require attention, and can be used flexibly in changing circumstances. Automatic processes suffer no capacity limitations, do not require attention, and are very hard to modify once they have been learned.

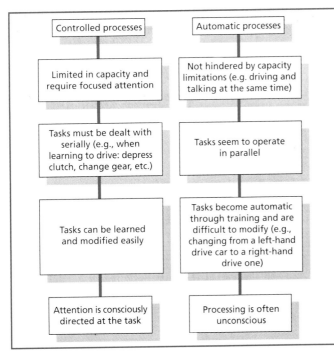

Schneider and Shiffrin (1977) tested these ideas in a series of studies, which are described in the box on the next page. When participants performed a decision task based on automatic routines, the number of items had little effect on their decision times, but when the task involved controlled routines, the number of items progressively slowed them down more. Shiffrin and Schneider (1977) also demonstrated the acquisition of automatic processes in a series of 2100 trials. They then tried to reverse the learning. It took 1000 trials for the learned automatic response to be extinguished, indicating how hard it is to abandon automatic processes.

Advantages and disadvantages of automatic and controlled processes

The greatest advantages of automatic over attentional processes are that they operate much more rapidly, and that many automatic processes can take place at the same time. However, automatic processes are at a disadvantage when there is a change in the environment or in the prevailing conditions, because they lack the adaptability and flexibility of controlled processes. The fact that we possess both automatic and controlled processes allows us to respond rapidly and appropriately to most situations.

Evaluation

The work of Shiffrin and Schneider (1977) and of Schneider and Shiffrin (1977) is important at the theoretical and experimental levels. Theoretically, they drew a clear distinction between automatic and controlled processes, and this distinction has proved very influential. Experimentally, they provided reasonably convincing evidence that the speed of performance can be much affected by whether it is based on automatic or controlled processes.

On the negative side, there is a puzzling discrepancy between theory and data with respect to the identification of automaticity. The theoretical assumption that automatic processes operate in parallel and place no demands on capacity means there should be a slope of zero (i.e., a horizontal line) in the graph relating decision speed to the number of items in the memory set and/or in the visual display when automatic processes are operating. In fact, decision speed was slower in Schneider and Shiffrin's (1977) study when the memory set and the visual display both contained several items.

The greatest weakness of Shiffrin and Schneider's theoretical approach is that it describes rather than explains. The claim that some processes become automatic with practice does not tell us much about what is actually happening. Practice may simply lead to a speeding up of the processes involved in performing a task, or it may lead to a change in the nature of the processes themselves. Cheng (1985) argued that participants in the consistent mapping conditions did not search through the memory set and visual display looking for a match. If, for example, they knew that any consonant in the visual display had to be an item from the memory set, then they simply scanned the visual display looking for a consonant without any regard to which consonants were actually in the memory set. Cheng was probably right, but we cannot tell for sure on the basis of the data provided by Shiffrin and Schneider.

Look at the examples of consistent and varied mapping in the Key Study on the next page. Do you think Cheng's argument is correct?

Instance theory

We have seen that Shiffrin and Schneider (1977) did not really explain how automatic processes develop through practice. Logan (1988) put forward an instance theory that was designed to fill this gap. This theory was based on five main assumptions.

Controlled and automatic processes

Schneider and Shiffrin (1977) tested their theory of controlled versus automatic processes by asking participants to memorise one, two, three, or four items (consonants or numbers); this was called the memory set. They were then shown a visual display containing one, two, three, or four items (consonants or numbers). Finally, they had to decide rapidly whether there was any item that was present in both the memory set and the visual display.

Of crucial importance was the distinction between *consistent mapping* and *varied mapping*. With consistent mapping, only consonants were used as members of the memory set, and only numbers were used as distractors in the visual display (or vice versa). Consider someone who was given only numbers as members of a memory set. If a number was seen in the visual display, it had to be a member of the current memory set. According to Schneider and Shiffrin (1977), the participants' years of practice at distinguishing between letters and numbers allowed them to perform the consistent-mapping task in an automatic fashion. With varied mapping, the memory set consisted of a mixture of consonants and numbers, and so did the visual display. In this condition, it is not possible to use automatic processes.

In order to clarify this key difference between consistent mapping and varied mapping, we will consider a few examples of each:

Consistent mapping

Memory set	Visual display	Response
H B K D	4 3 B 7	Yes
H B K D	9 2 5 3	No
5 2 7 3	J 5 D C	Yes
5 2 7 3	B J G H	No

Varied mapping

Memory set	Visual display	Response
H 4 B 3	5 C G B	Yes
H 4 B 3	2 J 7 C	No
5 8 F 2	G 5 B J	Yes
5 8 F 2	6 D 1 C	No

There was a large difference in performance between the consistent and varied mapping conditions. The number of items in the memory set and visual display had very little effect on decision time with consistent mapping, but had a large effect with varied mapping. According to Schneider and Shiffrin (1977), performance in the consistent-mapping condition reflects the use of automatic processes in parallel. On the other hand, performance in the varied mapping condition reflects the use of attentionally demanding controlled processes operating in a serial fashion. The more items that have to be considered, the slower the decision time.

The notion that automatic processes develop as the result of prolonged practice was studied by Shiffrin and Schneider (1977). They used consistent mapping, with the memory set items always being drawn from the consonants B to L, and the distractors in the visual display always being drawn from the consonants Q to Z, or vice versa. There were 2100 trials, and the dramatic improvement over these trials presumably reflected the development of automatic processes.

After automatic processes had developed, there were a further 2400 trials with the reverse consistent mapping. Thus, for example, if the memory set items were drawn from the first half of the alphabet during the initial 2100 trials, they were taken from the second half of the alphabet during the subsequent 2400 trials. Reversing the consistent mapping greatly impaired performance. The impairment was so great that it took almost 1000 trials for performance to recover to its level at the very start of the experiment. These findings indicate that it is hard to abandon automatic processes that have outlived their usefulness.

Discussion points

1. How useful is this research by Schneider and Shiffrin?

2. Think of some examples of automatic and controlled processes in your everyday life.

1. Separate memory traces are stored away each time a stimulus is presented and processed.
2. Practice with the same stimulus leads to the storage of increased information about the stimulus, and about what to do with it.
3. This increase in the knowledge base with practice permits rapid retrieval of relevant information when the appropriate stimulus is presented.
4. "Automaticity is memory retrieval: performance is automatic when it is based on a single-step direct-access retrieval of past solutions from memory" (Logan, 1988, p.493).
5. In the absence of practice, responding to a stimulus requires thought and the application of rules; after prolonged practice, the appropriate response is stored in memory and can be accessed very rapidly.

What is meant by the phrase "single-step direct-access retrieval of past solutions"?

This theoretical approach provides a useful account of many aspects of automatic processing. Automatic processes are fast because they require only the retrieval of "past solutions" from long-term memory. Such processes have little or no effect on the processing capacity available to perform other tasks, because the retrieval of heavily overlearned information is fairly effortless. Finally, there is no conscious awareness of automatic processes because few processes intervene between the presentation of a stimulus and the retrieval of the appropriate response.

Action Slips

Action slips involve the performance of actions that were not intended. At the most general level, action slips usually result from failures of attention. This is recognised at a common-sense level in the notion of "absent-mindedness". Before discussing theoretical accounts of action slips, however, we will describe some of the main categories. See whether your own action slips seem to fit these categories.

Diary studies

One way of studying action slips is to collect hundreds of examples by means of a diary study. Reason (1979) asked 35 people to keep diaries of their action slips over a 2-week period. Over 400 action slips were reported, most of which belonged to five major categories.

In the study, 40% of the slips involved *storage failures*, in which intentions and actions were either forgotten or recalled incorrectly. Here is one of Reason's examples of a storage failure (1979, p.74): "I started to pour a second kettle of boiling water into a teapot of freshly made tea. I had no recollection of having just made it."

A further 20% of the errors were *test failures*, in which the progress of a planned sequence was not monitored adequately at crucial junctures or choice points. Here is an example (Reason, 1979, p.73): "I meant to get my car out, but as I passed through the back porch on my way to the garage I stopped to put on my Wellington boots and gardening jacket as if to work in the garden."

Subroutine failures accounted for another 18% of the errors; these involved insertions, omissions, or re-orderings of the various stages in an action sequence. Reason (1979, p.73) gave this example: "I sat down to do some work and before starting to write I put my hand up to my face to take my glasses off, but my fingers snapped together rather abruptly because I hadn't been wearing them in the first place."

The remaining two categories occurred only rarely in the diary study. *Discrimination failures* (11%) consisted of failures to discriminate between objects (e.g., mistaking icons on a computer screen). *Programme assembly failures* (5%) involved inappropriate combinations of actions. For example, "I unwrapped a sweet, put the paper in my mouth, and threw the sweet into the waste bucket" (Reason, 1979, p.72).

Evaluation

A diary study such as the one by Reason (1979) provides valuable information about the kinds of action slips that occur in everyday life. However, there are various reasons for not attaching much significance to the reported percentage for each category of action slip. First, the figures are based on those action slips that were detected, and we simply do not know how many cases of each kind of slip were never detected. Second, in order to interpret the percentages, we need to know the number of occasions on which each kind of slip might have occurred but did not. Thus, the small number of discrimination failures may reflect either good discrimination or a relative lack of situations requiring fine discrimination.

What problems may occur if a participant in a diary study is aware of the findings from such studies?

Another problem is that two action slips may be categorised together because they seem superficially similar, even though the underlying mechanisms are actually different. Grudin (1983) carried out videotape analyses of substitution errors in typing, in which the key next to the intended key was struck. Some substitution errors involved the correct finger moving in the wrong direction, but others involved an incorrect key being pressed by the finger that normally strikes it. According to Grudin, the former kind of error is due to faulty execution of an action, whereas the latter is due to faulty assignment of the finger. Thus, we would need more information than is usually available in diary studies in order to identify such subtle differences in underlying processes.

Laboratory studies

In view of the problems with diary studies, it might be argued that laboratory studies offer a way of obtaining more precise data. However, potential disadvantages with the laboratory approach were identified by Sellen and Norman (1992). They pointed out (p.334) that many naturally occurring action slips occur

> *when a person is internally preoccupied or distracted, when both the intended actions and the wrong actions are automatic, and when one is doing familiar tasks in familiar surroundings. Laboratory situations offer completely the opposite conditions. Typically, subjects are given an unfamiliar, highly contrived task to accomplish in a strange environment. Most subjects arrive motivated to perform well and ... are not given to internal preoccupation ... In short, the typical laboratory environment is possibly the least likely place where we are likely to see truly spontaneous, absent-minded errors.*

However, in spite of these problems with laboratory studies, some interesting findings have been obtained, such as the study by Hay and Jacoby (1996), which is reported in the box on the next page.

Theories of action slips

Several theories of action slips have been proposed, including those of Reason (1992) and Sellen and Norman (1992). In spite of differences between these theories, Reason (1992) and Sellen and Norman (1992) agree that there are two modes of control:

- An automatic mode: motor performance is controlled by schemas or organised plans; the schema that determines performance is the strongest one available.
- A conscious control mode: this involves some central processor or attentional system; this mode of control can override the automatic control mode.

Laboratory study of action slips

Hay and Jacoby (1996) argued that action slips are most likely to occur when two conditions are satisfied:

1. The correct response is *not* the strongest or most habitual one.

2. Attention is not fully applied to the task of selecting the correct response.

For example, suppose you are looking for your house key. If it is not in its usual place, you are likely to waste time by looking there first of all. If you are late for an important appointment as well, you may find it hard to focus your attention on thinking about other places in which the key might have been put. As a result, you may spend a lot of time looking in several wrong places.

KEY STUDY EVALUATION — Hay and Jacoby

Hay and Jacoby's research looked at action slips in a laboratory setting. There has been little experimental research in this area. Action slips can be seen to be important in real-life settings. For example, consider a technician on a battleship who has to decide whether an approaching target is hostile or not. Hay and Jacoby found that action slips were most likely to occur when the correct response was not the strongest and had to be made rapidly. This would suggest that for the battleship technician the necessity for speed and previous practice in responding to mainly hostile targets may make an action slip (attacking a non-hostile target) more likely.

Hay and Jacoby tested this theoretical approach in a study in which the participants had to complete paired associates (e.g., knee: b _ n _). Sometimes the correct response on the basis of a previous learning task was also the strongest response (e.g., bend), and sometimes the correct response was *not* the strongest response (e.g., bone). The participants had either 1 second or 3 seconds to respond. Hay and Jacoby argued that action slips would be most likely when the correct response was not the strongest one (i.e., they had learned knee: bone), and when the response had to be made rapidly. As predicted, the error rate in that condition was 45% against a mean of only 30% in the other conditions.

Why is the research by Hay and Jacoby (1996) of major importance? As they themselves pointed out (p.1332), "Very little has been done to examine action ... slips by directly manipulating the likelihood of their occurrence in experimental situations. In the research presented here, we not only manipulated action slips, but also teased apart the roles played by automatic and intentional responding in their production."

Discussion points

1. Does the approach of Hay and Jacoby seem to explain any action slips you have had lately?

2. Are there limitations of the laboratory-based approach used by Hay and Jacoby?

What do we call a tree that grows from acorns? What do you call the white of an egg? If you answered "yolk" then you have demonstrated an action slip.

The advantages of automatic control are that it is fast and that it permits attentional resources to be devoted to other processing activities. Its disadvantages are that it is inflexible, and that action slips occur when there is too much reliance on this mode of control. Conscious control has the advantages that it is less prone to error than automatic control, and that it responds flexibly to environmental changes. However, it operates fairly slowly, and is an effortful process.

According to this theoretical analysis, action slips occur when someone is in the automatic mode of control and the strongest available schema or motor programme is the wrong one. The involvement of the automatic mode of control can be seen in many of Reason's (1979) action slips. One common type of action slip involves repeating an action because the first action has been forgotten (e.g., brushing one's teeth twice in quick succession; trying to start a car engine that has already been started). As we saw earlier in the Section, unattended information is held very briefly and then forgotten. When brushing one's teeth or starting a car occurs in the automatic mode of control, it would be predicted that later memory for what has been done should be very poor. As a result, you would often repeat the action, having forgotten that you did it a few minutes ago!

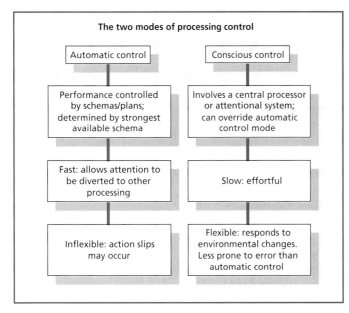

The two modes of processing control

Automatic control
- Performance controlled by schemas/plans; determined by strongest available schema
- Fast: allows attention to be diverted to other processing
- Inflexible: action slips may occur

Conscious control
- Involves a central processor or attentional system; can override automatic control mode
- Slow: effortful
- Flexible: responds to environmental changes. Less prone to error than automatic control

Although these acrobats have practised these actions thousands of times, the consequences of any action slips are too serious for the actions to become purely automatic.

Schema theory

Sellen and Norman (1992) proposed a schema theory, according to which actions are determined by hierarchically arranged **schemas** or organised plans. Note that the term schemas is being used in a different way from that typically found in theories of memory. The highest level schema represents the overall intention or goal (e.g., buying a present), and the lower level schemas correspond to the actions involved in achieving that goal (e.g., taking money out of the bank; taking the train to the shopping centre). Any given schema determines action when its level of activation is high enough, and when the appropriate triggering conditions exist (e.g., getting into the train when it stops at the station). The activation level of the schemas is determined by current intentions and by the immediate situation.

Why do action slips occur according to schema theory? There are a number of possible reasons. First, there may be errors in the formation of an intention. Second, there may be faulty activation of a schema, leading to activation of the wrong schema, or to loss of activation in the right schema. Third, the situation may lead to faulty triggering of active schemas, resulting in action being determined by the wrong schema.

Many of the action slips recorded by Reason (1979) can be related to schema theory. For example, discrimination failures can lead to errors in the formation of an intention, and storage failures for intentions can produce faulty triggering of active schemas.

Evaluation.   It could be argued that action slips are special events produced by their own mechanisms. However, it is probably better to argue (as is done within schema theory) that action slips are "the normal by-products of the design of the human action system" (Sellen & Norman, 1992, p.318). In other words, there is a single action system that normally functions well, but occasionally produces errors in the form of action slips.

Recent theories of action slips emphasise the notion of automatic processing. However, automatic processes are hard to define. More needs to be discovered about the factors leading to automatic processes being used at the wrong time. Recent theories predict correctly that action slips should occur most often with highly practised activities, because automatic processes are most likely to be used with such activities. However, action slips are much more common with actions of minor importance than those regarded as very important. For example, many circus performers carry out well-practised actions, but the element of danger ensures that they do not make use of the automatic mode of control. Recent theories do not seem able to explain such facts.

Pattern Recognition

Pattern recognition is concerned with the identification of two-dimensional and three-dimensional visual stimuli. It is the process of making sense of our visual input. A series of squiggles and shades of colour is recognised as a tree, or a house, or a dog. The process of object recognition is perhaps surprisingly complex, considering we do it all the time and with relatively little difficulty.

Much of pattern recognition research has looked at how letters and numbers are recognised, focusing especially on the issue of how the human perceptual system manages to recognise that A a *a* **A** *A* are all the same letter. We can recognise the letter "A" rapidly and accurately despite considerable variations in typeface, style, and size. How is pattern recognition so successful?

Various theories have been proposed—but they all agree that the basic process involves matching information from the visual stimulus with information stored in memory.

We can recognise words despite the fact that they look considerably different. The complexity of the process is shown by the fact that it is extremely difficult to program machines to do the same task.

Theories of Pattern Recognition

Template theories

The basic idea behind template theories is that there is a miniature copy or template stored in long-term memory corresponding to each of the visual patterns we know. A pattern is recognised on the basis of the template providing the closest match to the stimulus input. Template matching is basically the system used by banks. They have machines using a system of template matching to "read" your bank account number from your cheques. This is a very simple situation, because the digits on cheques are in a standard shape and are in standard locations on the cheque. It is not representative of everyday life, because there are generally enormous variations in the visual stimuli allegedly matching any given template.

One modest improvement in the basic template theory is to assume that the visual stimulus undergoes a *normalisation process* (i.e., producing an internal representation in a standard position, size, and so on) before the search for a matching template begins. Normalisation would help pattern recognition for letters and digits, but it is improbable that it would consistently produce matching with the appropriate template.

Another way of trying to improve template theory would be to assume that there is more than one template for each letter and numeral. This would permit accurate matching of stimulus and template across a wider range of stimuli, but only at the cost of making the theory much more unwieldy.

How effective at pattern recognition are template theories that incorporate the various kinds of improvements just described? Larsen and Bundesen (1992) tried to answer this question by studying machine recognition of digits handwritten by various people. The stimuli were normalised for orientation and size, and several templates were stored for each of the 10 digits. The machine then found the single best match between the presented digit and the stored templates. Pattern recognition occurred on 69% of trials when five templates were stored for each digit, and this improved to 77% when 10 templates were stored, and to 89% when 60 templates were stored. Thus, the number of stored templates did have a significant influence on performance. However, human participants averaged 97% on this task, so machine recognition was well below human recognition.

What features might distinguish the template for a cow from the template for a horse? Or would both of these fit only an "animal" template?

Most template theories are limited, in that pattern recognition depends solely on the one template producing the best match with the visual stimulus. Thus, information concerning the level of match with all the other templates is totally ignored. Larsen and Bundesen (1996) argued that it would be possible to devise an improved template theory by avoiding that limitation. This led them to produce a theory that was a combination of a template theory and a feature theory (see later). The theory is a general one, but they applied it to pattern recognition of digits:

1. There are several stored templates for each digit.
2. Feature analysers or "demons" determine the degree of match between each stored template and the visual stimulus.
3. There are cognitive demons above the feature analysers or demons, one for each digit. Each cognitive demon becomes activated on the basis of degrees of match of its associated feature demons. Thus, information from all templates is taken into account.
4. At the top level of analysis, the decision demon classifies the visual stimulus on the basis of the most activated cognitive demon.

Compare this theory with Treisman's feature integration theory on pages 240–241. Can you see any similarities?

Larsen and Bundesen (1996) found machine recognition for digits based on this theory was 95.3% accurate with an average of 37 templates per type of digit. This level of performance is clearly superior to the levels reported by Larsen and Bundesen (1992), and it is only 2–3% below that of human participants.

Evaluation

Template theories can provide a reasonable account of pattern recognition for simple stimuli, especially if there are normalisation processes and multiple templates for each category of stimuli. In addition, template theories are more effective when they take account of information from all the templates rather than simply the one producing the closest match to the input stimulus.

Template theories have mostly been applied to relatively simple stimuli such as letters and digits. Such theories are less useful when stimuli belong to ill-defined categories for which no single template could possibly suffice (e.g., buildings). Futhermore, template theories do not usually take context effects into account. For example, Palmer (1975) found that briefly presented pictures (e.g., a loaf) could be identified more accurately when they were preceded by a picture of an appropriate context (e.g., a kitchen) than by no context. Template theories also cannot account for the fact that we can recognise many variations of the same letter, as well as the same letters upside down. Jolicoeur and Landau (1984) found that there was only a 15-millisecond delay in recognising a letter upside down, which would require templates of letters in every position in order to recognise them at this speed.

There is no doubt that pattern recognition must involve a match between the stimulus and some internal form, but this matching may take place after further processing.

If the first example is your "template" for the category "buildings", it is easy to see how adaptable humans have to be when recognising other examples of the same group.

Prototype theories

What would be the prototype for the letter "A", or for an apple?

A **prototype** is an idealised abstraction of a pattern, a concept of the basic elements for a category. Like template theory, it is proposed that the incoming stimulus is matched against an internal store of possible patterns. With prototypes, however, we would not need endless examples of the letter "A" but only one prototype. We can then compare all letters to this prototype. If there is a match then the letter is recognised, if there is a mismatch then the pattern would be compared to another prototype.

Evaluation

Clearly prototype theory is a more economical way of explaining a matching process than template theory, in other words it is able to explain the facts in a simpler way and one that requires less complex cognitive processes. Prototype theory can also better explain the speed of the pattern recognition process. It can also explain how we can deal with novel stimuli for which there would be no previous template. The novel stimuli can be compared with various prototypes to find which is the best fit.

However, prototype theory cannot explain the effects of context. For example, if you see the pattern "13" you would recognise this as the number thirteen, but if the same pattern appeared in the context of a group of letters, such as "TA13LE" you might recognise it as the letter "B". The effects of context are further considered on page 260.

We would also have problems distinguishing certain prototypes, for example the prototypes for the letters "B" and "P" are fairly similar yet we rarely make identification mistakes. It may be preferable to use features as the basis for recognition.

Feature theories

According to feature theories, a pattern consists of a set of specific features or attributes. For example, a face could be said to possess various features: a nose, two eyes, a mouth, and so on. These features are then combined, and compared against information stored in memory. In the case of recognising the letter "A", feature theorists would argue that the crucial features are two sloping straight lines and a connecting crossbar.

Research evidence

Strong support for feature detection theory comes from studies of visual search (discussed earlier on pages 240–241), where a target letter has to be found as rapidly as possible in a block of letters. Neisser (1964) compared the time taken to detect the letter "Z" when the distractor letters consisted of straight lines (e.g., W, V) or contained rounded features (e.g., O, G). Performance was faster in the latter condition, presumably because the distractors shared fewer features with the target letter Z.

However, Harvey, Roberts, and Gervais (1983) argued that other factors are also involved. They studied spatial frequency, which is low when alternating light and dark bars are close together, but high when they are further apart. Letters (e.g., "K" and "N") having several features in common were not confused, whereas letters with similar spatial frequencies but few common features were confused. The Pandemonium model is a memorable example of feature detection and is described on the next page.

EXAMPLE OF ARRANGEMENT OF LETTERS	
List 1	List 2
IMVXEW	ODUGQR
WVMEIX	GRODUQ
VXWIEM	DUROQG
MIEWVX	RGOUDQ
IWVXEM	UGQDRO
IXEZVW	GUQZOR
VWEMXI	ODGRUQ
MIVEWX	DRUQGO
WXEIMV	UQGORD

Neisser used stimuli like these to measure the time it took for people to detect the letter Z. He found that they took less time to find it in the block of rounded letters than in the block of "straight line" letters.

Evaluation

Feature theories again ignore the effects of context and of expectations. Weisstein and Harris (1974) asked their participants to detect a line that was embedded in a briefly flashed image. The image was either a three-dimensional form or a less coherent form. According to feature theorists, the target line should always activate the same feature detectors, and the coherence of the form in which it is embedded should have no effect on detection. In fact, target detection was best when the target line was part of the three-dimensional form. Weisstein and Harris called this the "object-superiority effect".

Pattern recognition does not depend solely on listing the features of a stimulus. For example, the letter "A" consists of two oblique uprights and a dash. However, these three

The Pandemonium model of feature detection

Selfridge (1959) described a *Pandemonium model* of feature detection. In this model there are four stages and at each stage "demons" have a specific task.

- An *image demon* records the image that falls on the retina and passes this information to …

- *Feature demons* who analyse the image in terms of its constituent features, such as whether there are angles, curves, sloping lines, and so on. Each feature demon is responsible for one feature; for example, one feature demon "looks for" a right angle whereas another looks for an angle of 30°. As soon as a feature demon recognises its feature, this information is passed to the …

- *Cognitive demons* who are responsible for detecting one pattern. There is one cognitive demon for every capital letter, one for every small letter, one for every digit, and so on. As the cognitive demon recognises more and more of its component features, it shouts louder and louder to the …

- *Decision demon* who has the final task of pattern recognition. The shouting from the various cognitive demons gives the name "Pandemonium" to this model.

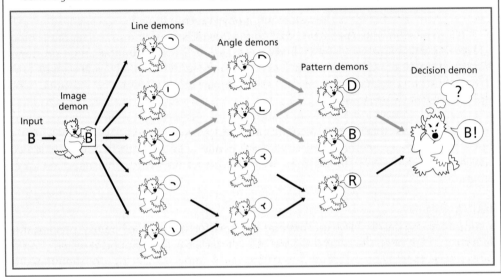

The Pandemonium model, in which information from lines is combined to produce angles, and finally whole letters.

features can be presented in such a way that they are not perceived as an A, like this: \ /—. Thus, we need to consider the *relationships* among features.

Recognition-by-components theory

Biederman (1987) has proposed a more flexible template model that uses the concept of **geons** (geometric ions). Geons are basic three-dimensional shapes such as blocks, cylinders, spheres, arcs, and wedges. Any pattern, shape, or object can be broken down into component geons. For example, a house consists of various sized blocks and rectangles. This theory is also called "recognition-by-components" because the components act as templates. Then these templates permit object recognition (note that strictly speaking this is object rather than pattern recognition).

According to Biederman there are 36 different geons, but when you consider that there are only 44 phonemes in the English language that produce an infinite number of words, then we can see that 36 would be sufficient. In fact it has been calculated that, for example, just three geons arranged in all possible ways could produce 1.4 billion objects (Lund, 2001).

The first step in operating this model is to break the object down into its geon components. Then the individual components can be recognised by a template-matching process. For the complete object to be recognised it is finally necessary to match the components to complete object descriptions, which must include the relationships between the components.

Some examples of Biederman's volumetric primitives called "geons". Note how different objects can be created by combining the same geons in different orientations.

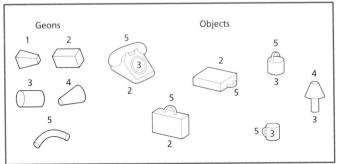

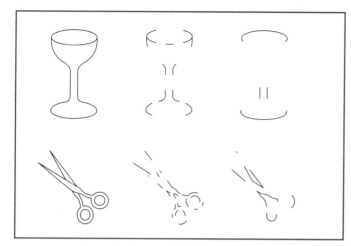

Intact figures (left-hand side), with degraded line drawings either preserving (middle column) or not preserving (far-right column) parts of the contour providing information about concavities.

Biederman's theory has encouraged experimental investigation. Why is this a strength of the theory?

Research evidence

An interesting test of Biederman's theory is the question of how we deal with degraded information, i.e., images that are missing some of their components or geons. Biederman, Ju, and Clapper (1985) showed participants line drawings of objects, some of which contained only three or four of their geons. Even when information was this limited, participants were 90% accurate in their identifications.

In a later study, Biederman (1987) presented degraded images such as those in the illustration on the left. Participants found object recognition harder when information about parts of the contours was missing, specifically those contours related to concavities. This confirms the idea that information about concavities is a key element in object recognition.

Biederman (1987) also proposed that edge information was more crucial than colour. To test this participants were shown line drawings or full-colour photographs of common objects for very brief exposures. Mean identification times were only 11 milliseconds faster when colour was included, even for objects where colour might be expected to be important (such as bananas).

However, some evidence is not supportive. According to Biederman's theory we would expect that object recognition would be impaired if line drawings of objects were divided in such as way that the geons were difficult to detect. However, Cave and Kosslyn (1993) found that dividing objects had very little effect on object recognition.

Evaluation

In sum, there is reasonable experimental support for the kind of theory proposed by Biederman. However, the central theoretical assumptions have not been tested directly. For example, there is no direct evidence that the 36 components or geons postulated by Biederman do actually form the building blocks of object recognition.

The Role of Biological Mechanisms in Pattern Recognition

A different approach to the understanding of pattern recognition is to develop theories that take account of our knowledge of brain functioning. According to Van Kleeck and Kosslyn (1993), this is an era of **cognitive neuroscience**, in which theorists start with the assumption that "the mind is what the brain does".

We will consider two neurobiological explanations of pattern recognition: Hubel and Wiesel's model of feature detection and McClelland and Rumelhart's connectionist approach.

Hubel and Wiesel's model of feature detection

Much of our understanding of basic visual processes stems from the work of David Hubel and Torsten Wiesel (e.g., 1979), who were awarded the Nobel Prize for their studies on cats and monkeys. They recorded the electrical activity of individual cells in the primary visual cortex of the brain (details of the pathways from the eye to the visual cortex are described in Section 8, Perceptual Processes and Development). The animals were shown pictures of lines in different orientations and then the researchers could determine how the brain reacted to these lines.

- *Simple cells* respond most to dark bars in a light field, light bars in a dark field, or to straight edges between areas of light and dark. They respond to stimuli of a

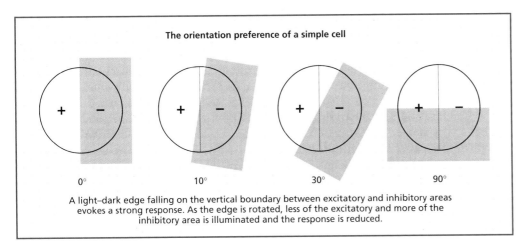

The orientation preference of a simple cell

0°   10°   30°   90°

A light–dark edge falling on the vertical boundary between excitatory and inhibitory areas evokes a strong response. As the edge is rotated, less of the excitatory and more of the inhibitory area is illuminated and the response is reduced.

particular orientation and also each cell responds only to a specific location in the visual field.

- *Complex cells* resemble simple cells in that they respond to straight-line stimuli that are presented in a particular orientation. However, complex cells have larger receptive fields, i.e., they respond to larger areas of vision, and a majority of complex cells respond to stimulation of either eye, whereas nearly all simple cortical cells respond only to stimulation of one eye (left or right). There are many more complex cells than simple cells.
- *Hypercomplex cells* respond to stimuli of a specific length, and also to moving corners and angles. Hypercomplex cells may also respond to complex stimuli such as hands and faces (e.g., Perrett et al., 1994).

Primitive eyes can detect edges. Why is this information important?

Organisation of cells

The primary visual cortex is organised into the three *types* of cell just described. The primary visual cortex is also organised in functional vertical columns that are at right angles to the cortical layers. They are called "functional columns" because each cluster of columns shares the same function, which is analysing the input from the same area of the retina. Within a cluster, half of the cells respond mainly to stimulation from the left eye, whereas the other half respond mostly to stimulation from the same region of the right eye. This enables comparisons to be made between visual inputs to either eye (using binocular disparity for depth perception).

The primary visual cortex appears to act as a kind of gateway to later visual processing. Information passes from here to at least 30 different areas of the brain for higher order processing (Stirling, 2000).

Evaluation

It has been claimed that these cells of the visual cortex are the basis for feature detection. However, it appears that the neurophysiological data are not as straightforward as this early account suggests. More recent research suggests that the functional columns are better described as **blobs** (sensitive to colour) that are surrounded by **inter-blob regions** (sensitive to orientation, some movement, and binocular disparity). This means that the cells are not part of a simple feature detection system. In addition, Bruce, Green, and Georgeson (1996) have questioned the existence of hypercomplex cells. In any case, if we were to need a cell to recognise every face from every angle and cells for every conceivable shape we would run out of cells.

McClelland and Rumelhart's connectionist approach

The traditional approach to understanding brain organisation is to assume that information about each object is stored in a specific location. The connectionist approach suggests that any given object category (e.g., "cat") is represented by a pattern of activity across different processing units spread out in space. McClelland and Rumelhart (1985)

The issue of localised versus distributed processing is discussed in Section 4, Brain and Behaviour.

assumed that there is a network of processing units. Each unit can receive an external input from a visual stimulus and an internal input from other processing units. Connections can either be inhibitory or excitatory. Learning occurs as a result of an altered pattern of activity in the network. After learning has occurred, the network activity corresponding to an entire stimulus pattern can be produced even when only part of the pattern is produced.

What information might be stored in one of these processing units?

McClelland and Rumelhart illustrated this with the following example. Imagine that one has a very small processing network of 24 processing units. This network is exposed to two simple patterns called "Rover" and "Lassie". Eight of the processing units are dedicated to learning to associate the names with their respective patterns, while the remaining 16 units are dedicated to learning the general category "dog". This dog category contains the common characteristics of a dog, constructed from the specific instances and other general but incomplete information. The network would be able to distinguish between "Lassie" and "Rover" patterns and also build up a prototype for "dog" despite only being given incomplete information for this category from the two examples.

Findings with human participants support and clarify this. Participants recognise an object more quickly after seeing it previously. This is called a *priming effect*. With faces, the greatest priming effect is found when the same photograph is presented twice. A smaller priming effect is found when the participant views two different photographs of the same face (as "Lassie" and "Rover" patterns are two different versions of the category "dog"). In other words, our perceptual systems respond to general categorical information but also to the specific information provided by instances of a category.

Why would two different versions of the same face produce less learning than the same photograph seen twice?

Evaluation

One of the major attractions of connectionist networks is that the interconnected networks resemble the network of neurons and synapses found in the brain. More complex models have been developed which take a "layered" approach. Here there are intermediate "hidden" units. Connectionist models can be applied to memory and mental representation generally.

There are grounds for arguing that connectionist models complement rather than challenge previous theories of pattern recognition. For example, Hummel and Biederman (1992) have proposed a connectionist model of Biederman's geon theory. This is a seven-layer network that takes as its input a representation of a line drawing of an object and produces as its output an identification of the object.

Lekhy and Sejnowski (1988) produced a multi-layered network that could recognise the curvature of geometrical shapes. One layer of processing units may correspond to something like the simple and complex cells identified by Hubel and Wiesel.

The Role of Context in Pattern Recognition

We have noted that context is an important issue in pattern recognition. However, most theories of pattern recognition start at the analysis of component parts. For example, according to feature theories a target line should always activate the same feature detectors no matter what context the line appears in. The study by Weisstein and Harris (1974), described on page 256, demonstrated what Weisstein and Harris called the "object-superiority effect" where pattern recognition was found to be improved if a feature was part of a three-dimensional form.

Expectations

Expectations can also affect pattern recognition, acting as a form of context. A simple illustration of the role of expectations is shown in the triangular figure here. Look now before you read on. Unless you are familiar with this trick, you probably read the message in the triangle as "Paris in the spring". Look again, and you will see that the word "the" is repeated. Your expectation that it is a well-known phrase (i.e., **top-down processing**) overrides the information available in the stimulus (i.e., **bottom-up processing**). Tulving

Experimental studies of context effects

Bruner and Minturn (1955) showed how context affects the perception of an identical sensory input. Participants were shown the following stimulus sequences using a tachistoscope to limit exposure times:

L, M, Y, A, 13   16, 17, 10, 12, 13

series 1   series 2

Some participants were given series 1 followed by 2. Others were shown series 2 and then 1, to counterbalance any order effects. The participants were told they were being tested for speed and accuracy. They were asked to draw and to read out each character. Not surprisingly participants tended to close the ambiguous figure (B rather than 13) when shown letters, though the longer the characters were exposed on the tachistoscope the less this effect occurred.

Other studies have demonstrated a similar effect. Siipola (1935) gave participants lists of words that were either animal or nautical words to create a context. At the end of the list was an ambiguous stimulus "sael" or "dack". Participants read "seal", "sail", "duck" or "deck" depending on prior context.

Bugelski and Alampay (1961) showed subjects a series of animal pictures, then the ambiguous ratman shown on the right, followed by a series of human pictures and finally the ratman again (for half of the participants the order was reversed). When participants first saw the ratman, most of them perceived the image in agreement with the first series of pictures. On the second exposure, most of them did not change their perceptions. Therefore "perceptual set" affected their perceptions but subsequent experience didn't significantly alter their initial perceptions.

If participants are shown a series of animal pictures followed by this ambiguous drawing, they tend to see a rat, whereas if the ambiguous drawing is preceded by pictures of people they see a man's face. This illustrates the effect of context on pattern recognition.

and Gold (1963) demonstrated this experimentally. They asked participants to read sentences where certain words were left out. Each sentence ended in a nine-letter word, such as avalanche, raspberry, or collision. The incomplete sentence was shown and then the final word was exposed using a tachistoscope for increasing lengths of time, starting at 10 milliseconds, until the participant recognised the word. For example, a participants might be shown: "More money buys fewer … " and the final target word was "inflation". (The complete sentence was "More money buys fewer products during times of inflation".) The more complete the sentence, the faster participants were able to recognise the final word. As a person reads a sentence, they build up expectations about what will come next. When these are correct, the perceptual process is enhanced in terms of speed of processing. However, the effects of expectations are not as great as suggested here. In essence this was a rather artificial study and people rarely encounter degraded stimuli when reading in everyday life. Expectations are also not always desirable, as the "Iran jet tragedy" indicates (see box).

Bottom-up versus top-down processing

The role of context and expectations can be understood in terms of bottom-up versus top-down processing. Pattern recognition theories start with an analysis of component

CASE STUDY: *Iran Jet Tragedy*

July 3, 1988: Iran Air A300 Airbus shot down by USS *Vincennes* over the Persian Gulf; 290 killed.

How could the USS *Vincennes*, with all its sophisticated gadgetry, mistake a regularly-scheduled passenger plane heading across the Persian Gulf towards Dubai for a military plane poised to attack?

The answer may lie in crew error. There was no malfunction in the radar technology aboard the American warship but it may be that, in the stress of battle, radar operators on the ship convinced themselves that the aircraft they had spotted taking off from an Iranian airport was hostile and intended to attack the *Vincennes*. When they saw this very plane approaching the ship at high speed they mistakenly interpreted this as an attack. This mistake was based on their original misconception.

CASE STUDY: *The Power of Expectations*

The following transcript is of a radio conversation between a US naval ship and the Canadian authorities off the coast of Newfoundland in October 1995:

Canadians: Please divert your course 15 degrees to the south to avoid a collision.

Americans: Recommend you divert your course 15 degrees to the north.

Canadians: Negative. You will have to divert your course 15 degrees to the south to avoid a collision.

Americans: This is the Captain of a US Navy ship. I say again, divert YOUR course.

Canadians: No. I say again, you divert YOUR course.

Americans: THIS IS THE AIRCRAFT CARRIER USS *LINCOLN*. THE SECOND LARGEST SHIP IN THE UNITED STATES ATLANTIC FLEET. WE ARE ACCOMPANIED BY THREE DESTROYERS, THREE CRUISERS AND NUMEROUS SUPPORT VESSELS. I DEMAND THAT YOU CHANGE YOUR COURSE 15 DEGREES NORTH, THAT'S ONE FIVE DEGREES NORTH, OR COUNTERMEASURES WILL BE UNDERTAKEN TO ENSURE THE SAFETY OF THIS SHIP.

Canadians: We are a lighthouse. Your call.

parts, in other words, the first step is to split the whole into smaller bits. This approach to information processing is called **bottom-up processing** where visual analysis depends directly on external stimuli. At the opposite end of the scale there is **top-down processing**, which is influenced by an individual's knowledge and expectations.

Perception often involves a mixture of bottom-up and top-down processing. An especially clear demonstration of this comes from a study by Bruner, Postman, and Rodrigues (1951), in which the participants expected to see ordinary playing cards presented very briefly. When black hearts were presented, some of them claimed to have seen purple or brown hearts. Here we have an almost literal blending of the black colour based on bottom-up processing with the red colour based on top-down processing, due to the expectation that hearts will be red.

In the next Section we will consider theories of perception. As you will see these can be classed as bottom-up theories or top-down theories. There are also theories that combine the two.

Face Recognition

In your AS level studies, the topic of face recognition was considered in the context of eyewitness testimony. A key element of eyewitness testimony is the need to recognise or identify the faces of people involved in a crime. Here we return to the topic of face recognition, in this case as an example of pattern recognition.

The difference between recognising an object and a face

There is evidence that the process of face recognition differs from objection recognition in major ways. Studies of people with brain damage show that the two processes are governed by different areas of the brain. Patients with **prosopagnosia** cannot recognise familiar faces, and this can even extend to their own faces in a mirror. This is not because prosopagnosic patients cannot make the fine discriminations necessary for face recognition, because they generally have few problems in recognising other familiar objects. Farah (1994) obtained evidence that prosopagnosic patients can be good at making precise discriminations for stimuli other than faces. She studied a patient known as LH, who developed prosopagnosia as a result of a car crash. LH and controls were presented with various faces and pairs of spectacles, and were then given a recognition-memory test. LH performed at about the same level as the normal controls in recognising pairs of spectacles, but was at a great disadvantage on face recognition (see figure on the left).

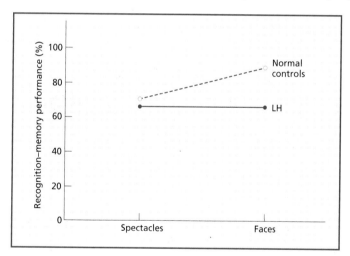

Recognition memory for faces and pairs of spectacles in a prosopagnosic patient (LH) and normal controls.

Bottom-up processing

One possible means of face recognition is via the recognition of individual features, a technique used in Identikit pictures. Bradshaw and Wallace (1971) investigated the value of feature-by-feature recognition by asking participants to make comparisons between pictures of faces (see illustration on facing page). The pictures were assembled using Identikit programmes so that they were composed of the same features. The participants were shown pairs of faces and asked to say whether they were identical or not. The more differences between the faces, the faster participants were at making judgements. This suggests that the participants were analysing each feature separately and in a bottom-up way.

However, this finding may be an artefact of the experiment, because the task participants were asked to do, specifically required making this kind of feature-by-feature comparison. In real life people do use information about individual features

Identikit pictures are motionless. How would this explain why it is often hard to identify a person from an Identikit picture?

(such as eye colour) when recognising faces but they also use information about the overall arrangement of the features. In fact configuration may be more important for recognition of faces. Young et al. (1987) constructed faces by combining the top half of a famous person's face with the bottom half of another famous face. When these combined pictures were aligned as closely as possible, participants found it harder to identify the two contributing people than when they were not as closely aligned. Presumably the close alignment produced a new configuration that interfered with face recognition.

In addition to configuration, motion may be important in face recognition, especially as motion is linked to emotion and there would be good adaptive reasons for people to be sensitive to emotion. The importance of motion was demonstrated in a study by Bruce and Valentine (1988). They arranged it so that participants could only see the motion in faces rather than the features. They did this by attaching lights to a face and filming the face in the dark. Participants could identify the facial expressions (e.g., smiling or frowning) and sometimes could identify the person on the basis of the movements only. This may explain why people appear to perform better in general studies of face recognition than they do in eyewitness identification experiments, because studies of face recognition use the same stimuli (i.e., photographs) at both acquisition and testing. For real identification, eyewitnesses have to match Identikit pictures to the real thing, and there is a less good match.

(a) Starter face

(b) Different nose and chin

(c) Different nose, chin, mouth and hair

(d) Different nose, chin, mouth, eyes, brow and face lines

Examples of faces similar to those used by Bradshaw and Wallace (1971). Face pairs were constructed showing differences in two, four, or seven features.

Innate mechanisms of face recognition

It would make adaptive sense for infants to be born with some ability to distinguish between human faces and other objects. How else could an infant interact with the right class of objects unless it could recognise them in the first place? In a classic experiment, Fantz (1961) demonstrated that neonates (newborns) are able to discriminate between various patterns and most interestingly showed a preference for (or interest in) faces. How could he tell what the infants preferred? He built a special "looking chamber" where infants could lie down on their backs and watch objects hung from the ceiling (see page 300 for an illustration). An observer recorded the attention time given to each object. This is called the visual preference technique. Fantz found that infants as young as 2 days old spent more time looking at complex patterns than plain coloured shapes, and more time looking at a schematic face than any other patterns.

However, it might have been that the face was just a more complex pattern. To test this hypothesis Fantz jumbled up the facial features and still found a distinct preference for the correctly organised facial features. (We should note that the term "preference" may be misleading and "interest" might be more appropriate, as people often look at things not because they like them but because they arouse curiosity, such as looking at a car accident.)

This "facial preference" finding has been replicated in a number of studies, such as Goren et al. (1975) who used slightly different heads. However, it is possible that this apparent innate preference is due to very early operant conditioning. Babies learn to like faces because they are positively reinforced. Babies may initially smile at anything, but only one class of objects smiles back and this is reinforcing. It is also possible that these findings can be explained in terms of infants simply having a preference for symmetrical patterns.

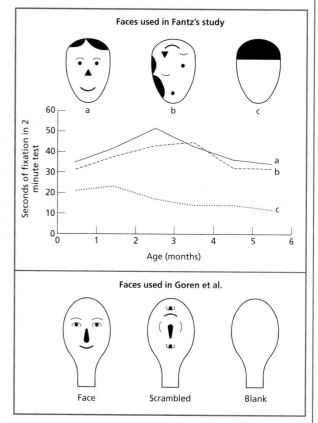

Top-down processing

Much of our day-to-day face recognition involves top-down processing because we are recognising familiar faces. This would explain why you might recognise a shop-assistant in the shop you visit every day to buy your newspaper, but you would take quite a bit longer to recognise the same person if you saw them in the street—if you recognised them at all.

People have excellent memories for familiar faces. Bahrick et al. (1975) demonstrated that people, 35 years later, can still recognise the school photographs of their classmates. They asked 392 ex-high-school students of various ages to free recall the names of any of their classmates, and also showed them a set of appropriate photographs and asked them to identify individuals. Even after 34 years ex-students were still able to name 90% of the photographs of their classmates.

Bruce and Young (1986) have proposed a model for face recognition which suggests that there are two different mechanisms for familiar and unfamiliar face recognition. We have already noted that the recognition of unfamiliar faces involves feature detection (as in Identikit photographs) whereas familiar face recognition involves configural recognition (Yin, 1969).

Bruce and Young's model of face recognition

Bruce and Young (1986) and Burton and Bruce (1993) argued that there are several different types of information that can be obtained from faces, and which correspond to the eight components of their model (see the diagram on the next page). It is worth noting that not every component is involved in recognising every face, and that the model accounts for the differences between recognition of familiar and unfamiliar faces.

- The *recognition of familiar faces* depends mainly on structural encoding, face recognition units, person identity nodes, and name generation.
- The *recognition of unfamiliar faces* involves structural encoding, expression analysis, facial speech analysis, and directed visual processing.

The details of the components are as follows:

- *Structural encoding:* this produces various representations or descriptions of faces.

Would you be able to name your classmates from a photograph after 35 years? Bahrick et al. (1975) found that most people they studied could.

- *Expression analysis:* people's emotional states can be inferred from their facial features.
- *Facial speech analysis:* speech perception can be aided by observation of a speaker's lip movements.
- *Directed visual processing*: specific facial information may be processed selectively.
- *Face recognition units:* they contain structural information about known faces.
- *Person identity nodes:* they provide information about individuals (e.g., their occupation, interests).
- *Name generation:* a person's name is stored separately.
- *Cognitive system:* this contains additional information (e.g., that actors and actresses tend to have attractive faces); this system also influences attentional processes.

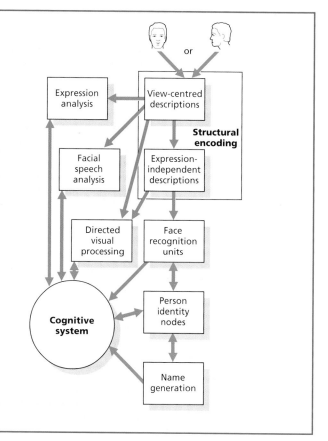

Research evidence

Evidence from patients with brain damage offers support for the distinction between familiar and unfamiliar face recognition. The model would predict that one could find some people who could recognise one but not the other because each involves different systems. Malone et al. (1982) tested one patient who appeared to able to recognise photographs of famous statesmen (14 out of 17 correct) but performed very poorly on a task that involved matching unfamiliar faces.

Another prediction arising from the model would be that one should never be able to put a name to a face without also being able to access other information about the person (such as the person's occupation, or the context in which the person has been encountered in the past). Young, Hay, and Ellis (1985) produced evidence to support this. They asked participants to keep a diary record of the specific problems they experienced in face recognition day by day. There were 1008 incidents altogether, but not once did a participant report putting a name to a face without knowing anything else about the person. In contrast, there were 190 occasions on which a participant could remember a fair amount of information about a person, but was quite unable to think of the person's name.

The Bruce–Young model would predict another problem that should be common. If the appropriate face recognition unit is activated, but the person node is not, then there should be a feeling of familiarity coupled with the inability to think of any relevant information about the person. In the set of incidents collected by Young et al., this was reported on 233 occasions.

It also follows from the model that decisions based on person identity nodes should be made faster than those based on the word generation component. Young et al. (1986) found that participants were much faster at deciding whether a face belonged to a politician than they were at producing the politician's name.

Evaluation

The model of Bruce and Young (1986) provides a coherent account of the various kinds of information we possess about faces, and the ways in which these kinds of information are related to each other. Another significant strength is that differences in the processing of familiar and unfamiliar faces are spelled out.

There are various limitations with the model. First, the cognitive system is vaguely specified. Second, some evidence is inconsistent with the assumption that names can be accessed only via relevant autobiographical information stored at the person identity node. An amnesic patient, ME, could match the faces and names of 88% of famous people for whom she was unable to recall any autobiographical information (de Haan, Young, & Newcombe, 1991).

The model of face recognition proposed by Bruce and Young (1986).

Have you ever recognised a person but been unable to think of that person's name?

The face looks familiar, but can't remember the name!

Third, the theory predicts that some patients should have better recognition for familiar faces than unfamiliar faces, with others showing the opposite pattern. This double dissociation was obtained by Malone et al. (1982), but has proved difficult to replicate. Young et al. (1993) studied 34 brain-damaged men, and assessed their familiar face identification, unfamiliar face matching, and expression analysis. There was only very weak evidence of selective impairment of familiar or unfamiliar face recognition.

Interactive activation and competition model

Burton and Bruce (1993) presented a revised version of the model, as shown in the diagram below. This model takes a connectionist approach. The face recognition units (FRUs) and the name recognition units (NRUs) contain stored information about specific faces and names, respectively. Person identity nodes (PINs) are gateways into semantic information, and can be activated by verbal input about people's names as well as by facial input. Thus they provide information about the familiarity of individuals based on either verbal or facial information. Finally, the semantic information units (SIUs) contain name and other information about individuals (e.g., occupation).

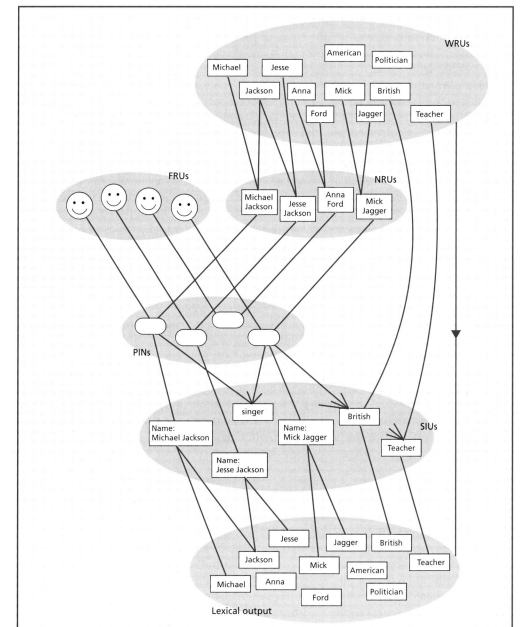

This revised model suggests that it is the person rather than the face that is recognised, and it treats names in the same way as all other information.

Research evidence

The model has been applied to associative priming effects. For example, the time taken to decide whether a face is familiar is reduced when the face of a related person is shown immediately beforehand (e.g., Bruce & Valentine, 1986). According to the model, the first face activates SIUs, which feed back activation to the PIN of that face and related faces. This then speeds up the familiarity decision for the second face. As PINs can be activated by both names and faces, it follows that associative priming for familiarity decisions on faces should be found when the name of a person (e.g., Prince Philip) is followed by the face of a related person (e.g., Queen Elizabeth). Precisely this has been found (e.g., Bruce & Valentine, 1986).

One difference between the interactive activation and competition model and Bruce and Young's (1986) model concerns the storage of name and autobiographical information. These kinds of information are both stored in SIUs in the Burton and Bruce (1993) model, whereas name information can only be accessed after autobiographical information in the Bruce and Young (1986) model. The fact that the amnesic patient, ME (discussed earlier), could match names to faces in spite of being unable to access autobiographical information is more consistent with the Burton and Bruce (1993) model. Cohen (1990) found that faces produced better recall of names than of occupations when the names were meaningful and the occupations were meaningless. This poses problems only for the Bruce and Young (1986) model.

Evaluation

This model can account for the findings from ME, and it can also explain why names are sometimes harder to access than other autobiographical information—because names are less well integrated. Names may be better recalled when they are more meaningful. This revised model is also preferable because it has greater precision.

Burton and Bruce's (1993) interactive activation and competition model also provides an account of prosopagnosia. Burton et al. (1991) simulated prosopagnosia by reducing the weights on the connections from the face recognition units (FRUs) to the person identity nodes (PINs). This reduced the activation of PINs to faces, and meant that faces were often not identified or recognised as familiar. Burton et al. (1991) found that their "lesioned" model used implicit knowledge in a similar way to prosopagnosic patients. Presentation of a face produced some activation of its PIN and the relevant SIUs, and this facilitated performance on tasks requiring the use of implicit knowledge.

SECTION SUMMARY

Focused Attention

❖ Attention is concentration. Focused attention involves the selection of one input from several. Attention is often thought of as consisting of a single, unitary system; in fact, it actually involves a number of different processes. Attention research uses the information-processing metaphor.

❖ Focused auditory attention can be investigated by using the dichotic listening task or asking participants to shadow one message. Cherry's cocktail party effect indicated that only physical characteristics are detected in the non-attended channel. This suggested an early selection model. Broadbent's filter theory proposed that selection takes place on the basis of physical characteristics. A filter is needed to prevent overloading of the limited-capacity mechanism beyond the filter. However, not all evidence is supportive. Detection of the unattended message is improved if participants are practised, and if the two messages are sufficiently different. Detection may also take place unconsciously as evidenced by GSR (galvanic skin response). In some situations messages are not reported ear by ear but rather in terms of meaning. The filter theory was influential but is too inflexible.

❖ Treisman's attenuation theory attempted to cope with the problems by suggesting that the unattended message is not entirely filtered out but just tuned down. The more processing capacity available, the more the unattended message can be processed. Research support includes the processing of bilingual messages for meaning, and difficulty in processing two messages that have similar meaning. This model is more flexible but still involves a filter and serial processing.

❖ Deutsch and Deutsch suggested that selection takes place at a much later stage (late-selection model), all messages are processed in parallel and the one of greatest importance is finally selected for response. The reason we are not aware of this parallel processing is that it is mainly unconscious. Research evidence shows that meaning is unconsciously processed by the unattended side. However this total processing seems rather wasteful of resources and Treisman's theory can account for the same evidence. In addition further studies where participants were able to perform better with the non-shadowed message support Treisman's model in preference to Deutsch and Deutsch's model.

❖ Johnston and Heinz proposed a compromise where selection may take place early or late depending on the requirements of the current task—a theory supported by a task where non-target stimuli were processed no more than was necessary to perform the main task. This is similar to theories of divided attention.

❖ Focused visual attention can be compared to a spotlight with a variable beam. However, this view is an oversimplification, because attention can be used more flexibly than a spotlight. Visual attention can be focused outside a central area and can also focus on objects. Visual stimuli outside the attentional beam receive limited processing, but this can include information about their meaning.

❖ The visual search task can illustrate focused visual attention further. It is easier to locate curved letters in a list of straight-edged characters, a fact that can be explained by feature integration theory.

Divided Attention

❖ Studies on divided attention indicate that we can sometimes perform two tasks at once with no apparent problem, but other pairs of tasks are almost impossible to perform at the same time.

❖ Task similarity makes dual-task performance more difficult. Tasks can be similar in terms of processing modality, stage of processing, related memory codes, or mode of response. Practice can improve dual-task performance considerably, as shown in the study of Diane and John. Task difficulty leads to poorer dual-task performance, though it is not easy to assess task difficulty with any precision.

❖ Many of the findings can be accounted for by the central capacity interference theory. If two tasks require more central capacity resources than are available then performance is affected. Research evidence shows that tasks making greater demands on central capacity (e.g., a random generation task) do interfere with performance of other tasks, whereas this is less true of tasks making fewer demands (e.g., a tone task). Central capacity theory can account for task difficulty and the effects of practice but is not wholly supported by research evidence.

❖ An alternative theory suggests that there are specific processing mechanisms. The two theories can be combined so that the effects of task difficulty on dual-task performance are described as largely due to the central processor, whereas the effects of similarity are due to specific processing resources.

❖ There are useful practical applications of dual-task processing, such as devising screening tests, understanding the effects of anxiety, and perhaps even training individuals to better manage their attentional resources.

❖ Why does practice usually lead to a great improvement in dual-task performance? It can lead to the development of automatic processes, which in theory are rapid, do not rely on attention, are unavailable to consciousness, and are unavoidable. In practice, few processes satisfy all these criteria. Automatic processes tend to place some extra demands as evidenced by research into the Stroop effect. However, practised activities do fit the criteria of automatic processes fairly well.

❖ Shiffrin and Schneider proposed a theory of controlled versus automatic processing where controlled processes are of limited capacity, require attention, and are flexible. Automatic processes have advantages (e.g., speed of operation) and disadvantages (e.g., lack of flexibility), and are relatively difficult to unlearn. The greatest weakness of this approach is that it basically descriptive and not explanatory. The research data also indicate that automatic processes do not happen at zero cost. An alternative, instance theory, is more explanatory—suggesting that automatic processes are faster because they require only the retrieval of "past solutions" from long-term memory.

❖ Action slips are evidence of automatic processes. Diary studies indicate that many action slips depend on storage failures or test failures. However such studies produce unreliable and incomplete data. Laboratory research can overcome these problems, though at a cost of artificiality. Such studies suggest that action slips are most likely when the correct response is not the strongest one, and when attention is not fully applied to the ongoing situation.

❖ One theoretical approach is to distinguish between an automatic control mode and a conscious control mode. Action slips occur during automatic control. Schema theory is an alternative theory, suggesting that actions are determined by hierarchically arranged schemas or organised plans. Action slips occur when, for example, there may be faulty activation of a schema or loss of activation in the right schema. In fact there are very few action slips when people are performing important routines.

Pattern Recognition

❖ Pattern recognition is the process of identifying and attaching meaning to visual input. All theories agree that the basic process involves matching information from the visual stimulus to information stored in memory. Template matching works for machines where there is a finite set of patterns.

❖ Template theory proposes that we have a store of templates and these are matched against an incoming stimulus. This process might be streamlined by "normalisation" but this would still not explain how matches are consistently made. A further possibility would be to have more than one template for each letter and number. Machine simulations of increasing numbers of templates demonstrate increasing accuracy, but still not as good as human pattern recognition. A combination of template theory with feature detection produces machine accuracy equivalent to human accuracy. Template theory on its own cannot account for the effects of context or the speed at which complex and ambiguous stimuli are recognised.

❖ Prototypes are idealised abstractions of a pattern. Each letter needs to be represented by only one prototype. This theory can explain how we would cope with novel stimuli, however it cannot explain context effects, nor how we reliably distinguish between quite similar prototypes.

❖ Patterns consist of features. The Pandemonium model is an example of feature detection. Visual search tasks are used to support feature detection theory, though other evidence suggests that common features do not always slow visual search down. The object-superiority effect indicates that context is important, and relationships among features are also important.

❖ Recognition-by-components theory describes how objects are recognised through the use of 36 constituent geons. Research shows that participants can recognise incomplete objects using geons, though information about concavities is crucial and edge information is more helpful than colour. Some evidence does not fit with the predictions of the theory, such as recognition when geons are difficult to detect. Direct evidence is lacking.

❖ Pattern recognition can be explained and understood at the level of brain organisation. Hubel and Wiesel's model of feature detection is based on the discovery of simple and complex cells in the visual cortex that act as edge, line, and orientation detectors. Each simple cell responds to one retinal area; complex cells have larger receptive fields. Hypercomplex cells respond to combinations of features, such as moving corners and angles. These cells are organised into functional columns so that the inputs for the right and left eye for the same visual field lie next to each other, enabling binocular comparisons. Subsequent research has shown that the simple and complex cells (now called blobs) are not simple feature detectors but have a more complex set of responses.

❖ The connectionist approach assumes that any given object category is represented by a pattern of activity across different processing units. Learning occurs as a result of general categorical information and also the specific information provided by instances of a category. Connectionist models reflect the actual organisation of the brain and complement rather than challenge previous theories of pattern recognition.

❖   Theories of pattern recognition overlook the importance of context. Perceptions are biased by prior context and/or expectations, both of which produce a perceptual set. The set may speed up the process of perception but it may also lead to errors. Expectations are an example of top-down processing whereas pattern recognition theories tend to be bottom-up.

❖   Face recognition is an example of pattern recognition, though evidence from the study of patients with prosopagnosia indicates that different regions of the brain are involved. Bottom-up face recognition can be seen in the use of Identikit pictures. Experimental studies that require feature-by-feature recognition may overemphasise bottom-up processing whereas, in real life, configuration and motion may be more important. Top-down processing explains the ease with which we recognise familiar faces.

❖   Different mechanisms are involved in familiar and unfamiliar face recognition as reflected in Bruce and Young's model. Evidence from studies of brain-damaged patients supports this distinction, as do diary studies that confirm various predictions from the model, such as never knowing a person's name without having access to other information about the person. The model has been influential, though it lacks some important details.

❖   A revised version by Burton and Bruce was produced to account for some anomalous findings. The newer, connectionist model can account for associative priming effects, the differences between the storage of names and autobiographical information, and for prosopagnosia.

FURTHER READING

There is more detailed coverage of the topics discussed here in Part 5 of M.W. Eysenck and M.T. Keane (2000) *Cognitive psychology: A student's handbook (4th Edn.)* (Hove, UK: Psychology Press), and N. Lund (2001) *Attention and pattern recognition* (London: Routledge), written specifically for the AQA A specification. The whole subject of attention research is dealt with in a clear way in E.A. Styles (1997) *The psychology of attention* (Hove, UK: Psychology Press). A useful and more general book on cognitive psychology, which includes useful material on neurocognitive psychology, is D. Groome, H. Dewart, A. Esgale, R. Kemp, N. Towell & K. Gurney (1999) *An introduction to psychology* (London: Routledge).

Example Examination Questions

You should spend 30 minutes on each of the questions below, which aim to test the material in this Section.

1. **(a)** Describe **two** studies of focused (selective) attention.   (12 marks)
    (b) Assess these studies in terms of their implications for explanations of focused attention.   (12 marks)

2. Distinguish between early- and late-selection models of focused attention.   (24 marks)

3. Discuss **two** explanations of divided attention.   (24 marks)

4. Critically consider research into controlled and automatic processing   (24 marks)

5. **(a)** Describe **two** explanations of pattern recognition.   (12 marks)
    (b) Assess these explanations with reference to relevant research studies.   (12 marks)

6. **(a)** Outline findings of research into face recognition.   (12 marks)
    (b) Evaluate this research with reference to theories of face recognition.   (12 marks)

Examination Tips

Question 1.   In part (a) description of two studies is required. It might be helpful to select two studies that have rather different theoretical implications to give yourself more material for part (b). When describing studies you can use the same guidelines as for AS level: write something about the aims, procedures, findings, and conclusions. Do *not* offer any evaluation of the studies, as part (a) is AO1 alone ("describe") and evaluation will receive no credit and cannot be exported to part (b). In part (b) other studies may be used to support your arguments but no credit will be given for descriptions of further studies *per se*, nor will credit be given unless they are used explicitly to enhance your argument.

Question 2.   "Distinguish between" is an AO1 and AO2 injunction that requires a description of the two models for AO1. The AO2 credit is achieved by identifying the differences. There is the obvious point that selection takes place early or later but you might then consider the relative merits or otherwise of each model in terms of research support and cognitive effort required. Ensure that you give a full 15 minutes to the evaluation or you will not access half of the marks.

Question 3.   The question requires a description and evaluation of two explanations/models. Any material on focused attention could be made relevant as a means of evaluation but it is more likely that you would consider research support for each of your models. Practical applications could be used for further evaluation. It is also possible to contrast the two models with each other.

Question 4.   "Critically consider" is an AO1 and AO2 term that requires consideration of both strengths and weaknesses. Criticism can be positive and negative and you are specifically required to do both here. The term "research" refers to both theory and/or studies, providing you with a wealth of possible material. A possible danger would be that you have too much to write about and therefore sacrifice depth for breadth. The top marks are available for an essay that achieves a balance between these two. Therefore it is desirable to be selective and organise your answer to fit the 30 minutes available.

Question 5.   In part (a) you may do best to select two relatively different explanations of pattern recognition. If you describe more than two, only the best two would receive credit. However some explanations have been modified (such as the normalisation process for a template theory) and this could provide extra material under the umbrella of one explanation. In part (b) you can offer any evaluative points you wish but must make some reference to research studies. Other possibilities include contrasts with further explanations or practical applications, as well as considering the success of any explanation in accounting for human behaviour.

Question 6.   Part (a) requires an outline only (a summary description) and focuses on the findings of research rather than descriptions of the studies themselves. Any material on procedures or conclusions will not receive credit. You do not need to refer to lots of studies but it is likely that you will in order to provide sufficient findings. As the term "research" refers to theories or studies you could include the "findings" of certain theories, though this might limit your material for part (b). The requirement for part (b) is to "evaluate these findings". This can be "with reference to theories of face recognition" but can also be in terms of the studies themselves (e.g., methodological flaws) and/or their practical implications. As this is AO2 you must ensure that you are presenting an argument and not just describing studies and/or theories.

WEB SITES

http://www.stir.ac.uk/Departments/ HumanSciences/Psychology/46ac/attention1/
Links to attention-related topics and theories in slide format.

http://www.lehman.cuny.edu/depts/psychology/ sailor/cognition/pattern.html
Summary of theories of pattern recognition.

http://www.cs.rug.nl/~peterkr/FACE/face.html
Face recognition homepage containing lots of links.

8

Perceptual Processes and Development

Seeing the world about us and making sense of it seems very easy. For example, we do not have to think much to know that we are on the pavement, and that there are several cars moving in both directions on the road. In fact, making sense of (or perceiving) the environment is a major achievement. Some of the complexities of vision and perception will be discussed in this Section, together with some of the processes involved in perceptual development.

The Visual System

Structure and Functions of the Visual System

Far more of the brain is devoted to vision than to any other sense modality. Why is that so? There are two main reasons. First, vision is of enormous importance in our lives, and is perhaps even more important than our other senses. Second, the human visual system is engaged in complex processing activities. In the words of Pinel (1997, p.151):

From the tiny, distorted, upside-down, two-dimensional retinal images projected upon the visual receptors lining the backs of our eyes, the visual system creates an accurate, richly detailed, three-dimensional perception.

The eye

Light waves (photons) from objects in the environment pass through the transparent **cornea** at the front of the eye and proceed to the iris, which lies just behind the cornea and gives the eye its distinctive colour. The amount of light that enters the eye is determined by the pupil, which is an opening in the iris. This is achieved by the pupil becoming smaller when the lighting is very bright, and larger when there is relatively little light. The lens focuses light onto the retina at the back of the eye. Each lens adjusts in shape by a process of **accommodation** to bring images into focus on the retina.

Why do we have two eyes? A key reason is because this produces **binocular disparity**, which means that the image of any given object is slightly different on the two retinas. Binocular disparity provides very useful information for the task of constructing a three-dimensional world out of two-dimensional retinal images (see the next Unit for a discussion of perceptual organisation).

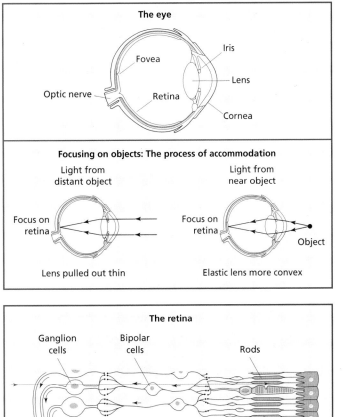

The eye

Fovea

Iris

Lens

Optic nerve

Retina

Cornea

Focusing on objects: The process of accommodation

Light from distant object

Light from near object

Focus on retina

Focus on retina

Object

Lens pulled out thin

Elastic lens more convex

The retina

Ganglion cells

Bipolar cells

Rods

Light

Nerve fibres

Nerve impulses

Cones

Pigment cells

The retina

The retina is fairly complex. It consists of five different layers of cells: photoreceptors, horizontal cells, bipolar cells, amacrine cells, and retinal ganglion cells. The arrangement of these cells is slightly odd. Light from the lens goes through all of the layers until it reaches the receptor cells at the back, after which the neural message goes back through the layers. Impulses from the retina leave the eye via the optic nerve, which is at the front of the retina. This part of the retina is called your "blind spot" because light falling here is not detected. The reason for this inverse arrangement is that the eye is actually an outgrowth from the brain. During evolution, a part of the brain became associated with the eye opening. This part of the brain formed the retina but because the part closest to the eye opening had been the outside of the brain, the cells of the retina continued to face inwards towards the brain!

There are two types of photoreceptors in the retina: **cones** and **rods**. There are about 6 million cones, and they are mostly found in the fovea or central part of the retina. The cones are specialised for colour vision and for sharpness of vision. There are about 125 million rods, and they are concentrated in the outer regions of the retina. Rods are specialised for vision in dim light and for the detection of movement. A retinal ganglion cell receives input from only a few cones but from hundreds of rods. As a result, only rods produce much activity in retinal ganglion cells in poor lighting conditions, but the disadvantage is that under poor lighting conditions the exact location of the stimulus is less clear.

Pathways from eye to cortex

The main pathway between the eye and the visual cortex is the retina-geniculate-striate pathway. This transmits information from the retina to the primary visual cortex or striate cortex via the lateral geniculate nuclei of the thalamus. The entire retina-geniculate-striate system is organised in a similar way to the retinal system. Thus, for example, two stimuli that are adjacent to each other in the retinal image will also be adjacent to each other at higher levels within the system (see Hubel and Wiesel's research on page 258). When the primary visual cortex of blind patients is stimulated by electrodes forming a given shape, they report "seeing" that shape (Dobelle, Mladejovsky, & Girvin, 1974).

Each eye has its own optic nerve, and the two optic nerves meet at the optic chiasm, where the axons from the outer halves of each retina proceed to the hemisphere on the same side, whereas the axons from the inner halves cross over and go to the other hemisphere. Signals then proceed along two optic tracts within the brain. One tract contains signals from the left half of each eye, and the other contains signals from the right half of each eye.

■ Activity: Take a pile of small, differently coloured objects. Pick one up without looking and slowly move it around on the periphery of your vision. You should be able to see it but not make out either the shape or colour. However you can detect the movement. This is because the object is detected by the rods and not the cones of the retina. You can imagine that it is useful to detect movement "out of the corner of your eye" in order to be aware of a predator about to attack!

In another example, draw two small black circles, about 6 inches apart, on a piece of white paper. Cover your left eye and focus on the left circle. Move the paper around until it's about 20cm from your face while staring at one circle. The other circle should disappear, because the image is falling on your blind spot.

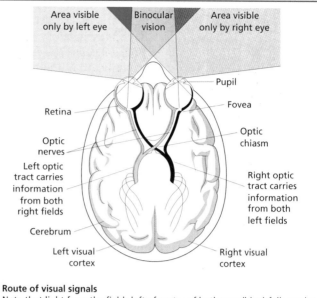

Route of visual signals
Note that light from the fields left of centre of both eyes (blue) falls on the right sides of the two retinas; and information about these fields goes to the right visual cortex. Information about the right fields of vision (grey) goes to the left cortex. Data about binocular vision go to both cortices.

After the optic chiasma, the optic tract proceeds to the lateral geniculate nucleus, which is part of the thalamus. Nerve impulses finally reach the primary visual cortex within the occipital lobe before spreading out to nearby secondary visual cortical areas.

There is one final important feature of the retina-geniculate-striate system. There are two independent channels within this system:

1. The *parvocellular* (or P) *pathway*: this pathway is most sensitive to colour and to fine detail; most of its input comes from cones.
2. The *magnocellular* (or M) *pathway*: this pathway is most sensitive to information about movement; most of its input comes from rods.

The visual cortex is described elsewhere in this book, see pages 149 and 150.

Research into the Nature of Visual Information Processing

Sensations are the raw data of the visual system, the unaltered record of the physical stimulus of light. Perception is the process of summarising and interpreting the raw data in such a way as to give them meaning. This process of perception is considered in the next two Units but elements of the process take place before data even leave the retina.

Processing by the retina

The retina collects 136 million points of light, many of which are repetitive and it would be wasteful to process them all. Therefore it is advantageous for some information to be summarised at the retina. This is the beginning of the process of perception as distinct from sensation.

The bipolar cells begin the process of summation, as each receives impulses from more than one photoreceptor, and each photoreceptor is connected to more than one bipolar cell. In the next layer up, the ganglion cells also receive input from more than one bipolar cell.

Contrast processing

The process of **lateral inhibition** is another means by which retinal information is reduced. When any photosensitive cell is stimulated, it inhibits activity in surrounding cells. The effect of this is to emphasise the borders between light and dark, which enables edge detection or contrast processing.

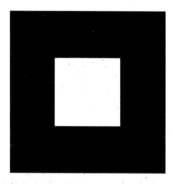

The process of lateral inhibition results in the edges of the square being emphasised. Edge detection is especially important in perception because it helps to define objects.

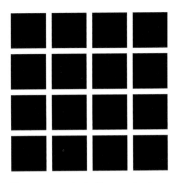

Do you see dark diamonds at the corners of each square? This is an example of lateral inhibition.

The way lateral inhibition takes place is as follows: if you are looking at a white square against a black background, the photons (light energy) emitted from the white square have an excitatory effect on the retina. But at the same time this excitation inhibits adjacent cells. The end result is that the cells responding to the white square are excited, but only at a moderate level because they are also inhibited. At the edge of the square the cells are excited but not inhibited, because these cells are next to cells receiving no light input. Therefore the edges are enhanced.

The visual illusion on the left illustrates lateral inhibition. At the point where the edges of four squares meet, the white areas closest to the square will be least inhibited, whereas the area equidistant between all four corners is again inhibited by surrounding cells. Therefore one appears to see dark diamonds at the "crossroads".

Sensory adaptation

When the lights are turned out in the cinema, you can't see very much. But your eyes quickly adapt to the darkness. This is called **dark–light adaptation**. Eyes also adapt to over-bright conditions, so that if you come indoors on a sunny day it often takes a moment for your vision to return to normal. Usually this light adaptation is faster than dark adaptation.

What factors are responsible for dark–light adaptation? One minor factor relates to changes in the pupil. It dilates in darkness, and this allows more light into the eye. Far more important are changes in the sensitivity of the rods and cones in the retina of the eye. The rods and cones contain photopigments, biochemical substances that react to light photons. When a photopigment such as rhodopsin is exposed to light, it breaks down into its constituent components: vitamin A and a protein molecule, and turns from pinkish-red to a bleached colour. The molecules quickly recombine but if there is a lot of light around, at any one time, a lot of the molecules will be in a bleached state. This means that the eye will be slower to respond to more light stimulation.

When the eye first encounters dark conditions there will only be some rhodopsin molecules that are ready to respond, so there is limited vision. But soon many more of the molecules will have recombined and therefore the reduced photons entering the eye are much more likely to find some intact rhodopsin.

Keeping the image moving

If you stared at an object for a while it would fade because the rhodopsin is bleached out on the retina at those points where the image is. In fact this doesn't happen because there are tiny eye movements which keep the image shifting back and forth—just so as to prevent this problem. Pritchard (1961) demonstrated this by using a device to stabilise the retinal image. A participant looks at a picture which is projected onto a screen using a tiny projector mounted on the participant's cornea. Any movement of the participant's eye is exactly followed by the small slide projector. After a few seconds the participant no longer sees the picture!

The eyes are constantly in motion due to small, rapid jerks called saccades and nystagmus. This means that the image which is thrown on the retina is constantly shifting and thus stimulating different retinal cells. Blinking may be related to this. It is a means of renewing the retinal image as well as sometimes moistening the eye. Otherwise why does blinking increase when extra vigilance is needed?

Colour processing

Why has colour vision developed? After all, if you see an old black-and-white film on television, it is perfectly easy to make sense of the moving images presented to your eyes. There are two main reasons why colour vision is of value to us (Sekuler & Blake, 1994):

- Detection: colour vision helps us to distinguish between an object and its background.
- Discrimination: colour vision makes it easy for us to make fine discriminations among objects (e.g., between ripe and unripe fruit).

What might be the evolutionary benefits of colour vision?

Aside from the question of why we have colour vision, there is also the question of how colour is perceived. We have already noted that the cones in the retina are sensitive to colour, but how does this work? Two theories have been proposed.

Young–Helmholtz theory

Cone receptors contain rhodopsin. This is a light-sensitive photopigment that allows the cone receptors to respond to light. According to the component or *trichromatic* theory put forward by Thomas Young and developed by Hermann von Helmholtz, there are three types of cone receptors differing in the light wavelengths to which they respond most strongly. One type of cone receptor is most sensitive to short-wavelength light, and is most responsive to blue stimuli. A second type of cone receptor is most sensitive to medium-wavelength light, and responds greatly to green stimuli. The third type of cone receptor responds most to long-wavelength light such as that coming from red stimuli. How do we see other colours? According to the theory, many colours activate two or even all three cone types. The perception of yellow is based on the second and third cone types, and white light involves the activation of all three cone types.

Dartnall, Bowmaker, and Mollon (1983) obtained strong support for the Young–Helmholtz theory using a precise technique known as microspectrophotometry. The amount of light absorbed by individual cone receptors at different wavelengths was assessed. All three types of cone receptor assumed by the Young–Helmholtz theory were found. However, this theory cannot account for all aspects of colour perception. For example, most individuals who are colour blind have problems in perceiving red and green, but practically no one has problems with green and blue, and most have a normal ability to perceive red and yellow. These patterns of colour blindness are mysterious from the perspective of the Young–Helmholtz theory. Negative afterimages, which are discussed next, also cannot be explained by the theory.

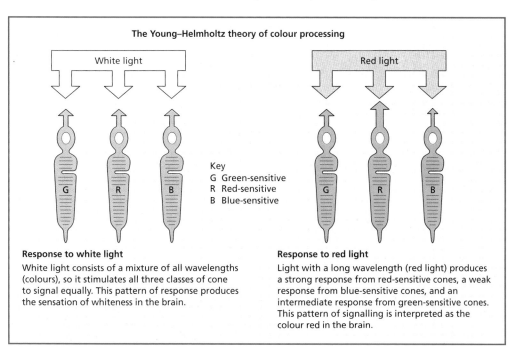

The Young–Helmholtz theory of colour processing

White light

Red light

Key
G Green-sensitive
R Red-sensitive
B Blue-sensitive

Response to white light
White light consists of a mixture of all wavelengths (colours), so it stimulates all three classes of cone to signal equally. This pattern of response produces the sensation of whiteness in the brain.

Response to red light
Light with a long wavelength (red light) produces a strong response from red-sensitive cones, a weak response from blue-sensitive cones, and an intermediate response from green-sensitive cones. This pattern of signalling is interpreted as the colour red in the brain.

Opponent-process theory

Ewald Hering (1878) put forward an opponent-process theory (see diagram on the next page). He assumed there are three types of opponent cells in the visual system. One type of cell produces perception of green when it responds in one way and of red when it responds in a different way. A second type of cell produces perception of blue or yellow in the same way. The third type of cell encodes brightness, and produces white or black.

Some evidence in support of Hering's theory is available from studies of negative afterimages (Pinel, 1997). If you stare at a square of a given colour for several seconds, and then shift your gaze to a white surface, you will see a negative afterimage in the colour predicted from the theory. For example, a green square produces a red afterimage, and a blue square produces a yellow afterimage. In addition, opponent cells have been found in the lateral geniculate nucleus of monkeys (DeValois & DeValois, 1975).

One of the greatest strengths of the opponent-process theory is that it provides an account of colour blindness. According to the theory, colour blindness typically occurs when there is damage to the cells responsible for the perception of red and green, or to those responsible for the perception of yellow and blue. As a result, colour blindness applies to red and green or to yellow and blue, but not to green and blue together.

If you stare at this and then shift your gaze to a white surface, you will see a negative afterimage in yellow, as predicted by the opponent process theory.

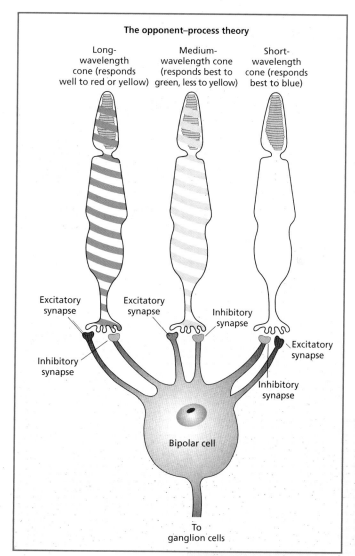

The opponent–process theory

Long-wavelength cone (responds well to red or yellow)

Medium-wavelength cone (responds best to green, less to yellow)

Short-wavelength cone (responds best to blue)

Excitatory synapse

Excitatory synapse

Inhibitory synapse

Excitatory synapse

Inhibitory synapse

Inhibitory synapse

Bipolar cell

To ganglion cells

Possible wiring for a bipolar cell that responds best to yellow light. Yellow light excites both the long- and medium-wave cones. Blue light inhibits the bipolar cell to less than its usual level of firing.

Which theory of colour vision can best explain colour blindness?

Can you think of examples from your own experience that illustrate the phenomenon of colour constancy?

Synthesis

The Young–Helmholtz and Hering theories can be combined, in fact nowadays they are always combined as they describe different aspects of the same process. The three cone types of the Young–Helmholtz theory send signals to the opponent cells of the Hering theory, and this produces the perception of colour. The short-wavelength (blue) cones send excitatory signals to the blue–yellow opponent cells, and long-wavelength (red/yellow) cones send inhibitory signals. If the strength of the excitatory signals is greater than that of the inhibitory signals, blue is seen. If the strength of the inhibitory signals is greater, then yellow is seen. The green–red opponent cells receive excitatory signals from the medium-wavelength (green/yellow) cones, and inhibitory ones from the long-wavelength (red/yellow) cones. Green is seen if the strength of the excitatory signals exceeds that of the inhibitory ones, whereas red is seen if the relative strengths are reversed.

This combined theory is supported by work on colour blindness. As was mentioned earlier, the most common form of colour blindness affects the perception of red and green, which involve the same opponent process. As is predicted by the theory, people with this type of colour blindness typically have a reduced number of medium- or long-wavelength cones (Zeki, 1993).

Colour constancy and the retinex theory

From what has been said so far, you may have the impression that colour vision can be completely explained in neurophysiological terms. That may be true, but various phenomena of colour vision do *not* depend only on the wavelengths of the light reflected from objects. Consider **colour constancy**, which is the tendency for an object to appear to have the same colour under different viewing conditions (see page 296 for more on colour constancy). There are marked differences between natural and artificial light. If our perception of colour were based only on the wavelength of reflected light, then the same object would appear redder in artificial light than in natural light. In fact, we generally show colour constancy in such circumstances.

Why do we show colour constancy? The most obvious reason is because of familiarity. We know that postboxes are bright red, and so they look the same colour whether they are illuminated by the sun or by artificial street lighting. However, that is not the whole story. Land (1977) presented his participants with two displays consisting of rectangular shapes of different colours. He then adjusted the lighting of the displays so that two differently coloured rectangles (one from each display) reflected exactly the same wavelengths of light. However, the two rectangles were seen in their actual colours, showing strong evidence of colour constancy in the absence of familiarity. Finally, Land (1977) found that the two rectangles looked exactly the same (and so colour constancy broke down) when everything else in the two displays was blocked out.

What was happening in Land's study? According to his retinex theory, we decide the colour of a surface by *comparing* its ability to reflect short, medium, and long wavelengths against that of adjacent surfaces. That is why colour constancy breaks down when such comparisons cannot be made. As would be expected from this theory, there are neurons that respond to differences in the wavelengths of light reflected from adjacent surfaces (Zeki, 1993). These neurons are known as dual-opponent colour cells.

Discussion points

1. Why is colour constancy important?

2. How convincing is the evidence for the retinex theory provided by Land (1977)?

Perceptual Organisation

Theories of Visual Perception

Visual perception depends on two types of processing. First, there is **bottom-up processing**, which depends directly on external stimuli. Second, there is **top-down processing**, which is influenced by an individual's knowledge and expectations. Some theorists have emphasised the importance of either bottom-up or top-down processing to visual perception. For example, Gibson (1950, 1966, 1979) focused on bottom-up processes. According to his theory of direct perception, the information provided by the visual environment permits the individual to move around and to interact directly with that environment without internal processes being involved. In contrast, Neisser (1967) and Gregory (1972, 1980) focused on top-down processes. According to their constructivist theory, perception is an active and constructive process that is much influenced by hypotheses and expectations. These theories are considered in some detail next.

Perceptual abilities allow us to interpret our environment.

Gibson's theory of direct perception

Gibson maintained that the environment is sufficiently rich in the data needed for perception that there is no need to infer the involvement of any higher processing. This theory is sometimes called the *ecological theory* because of the claim that perception can be explained solely in terms of the environment. Gibson's interest in perceptual phenomena developed out of being given the assignment of preparing training films for pilots in the Second World War to show the problems pilots experience when landing. This led him to consider the sort of information that was available to pilots. He then spent the next 30 years investigating such environmental data.

Optic array

The starting point for Gibson's theory was the notion that the pattern of light reaching the eye can be thought of as an **optic array** containing all the visual information available at the retina. This optic array provides unambiguous information about the layout of objects in space. This information comes in many forms, including optic flow patterns and texture gradients. Perception involves "picking up" the rich information provided by the optic array in a direct fashion with little or no information processing involved.

Pilots now train on computer simulators, learning how to interpret information from the optic flow about speed, height, and direction, and gaining an understanding of how the plane will react in certain situations.

Optic flow

The first kind of data that Gibson identified were **optic flow patterns**: the point towards which the pilot is moving (called the "pole") seems motionless, with the rest of the visual environment apparently moving away from that point. The farther any part of the landing strip is from the pole, the greater is its apparent speed of movement. According to Gibson, the sensory information available to pilots in optic flow patterns provides them with unambiguous information about their direction, speed, and altitude.

Gibson was so impressed by the wealth of sensory information available to pilots in optic flow patterns that he devoted himself to an analysis of the information available in other situations.

Perception and action

Of particular importance in Gibson's theory was the assumption that there is a close relationship between perception and action. An observer can obtain valuable information about the environment by moving about. For example, optic flow patterns only exist when the individual is in movement. Previous researchers in visual perception had minimised

Why do you thin[?]
researchers mig.
the importance o.

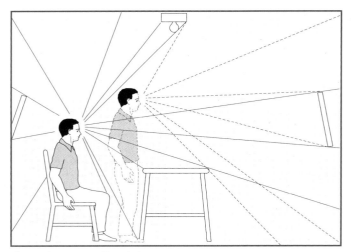

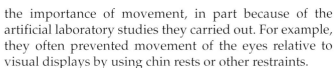

The optic array and how it is transformed by movement.

Horizon ratio relation: the size of an object may get larger as you get closer, but the proportion of that object above and below the horizon remains invariant, i.e., unchanging.

Texture gradients also are perceptual invariants, and communicate distance and depth. The objects seem to become closer together as they recede into the distance.

the importance of movement, in part because of the artificial laboratory studies they carried out. For example, they often prevented movement of the eyes relative to visual displays by using chin rests or other restraints.

Invariants

Gibson argued that important aspects of the optic array remain the same when observers move around their environment; these are known as **invariants**. The pole (the point towards which someone is moving) is an example of an invariant. Another example is the horizon ratio relation: the ratio of an object's height to the distance between its base and the horizon is invariant regardless of its distance from the viewer. According to Gibson, this invariant helps to maintain size constancy.

Texture gradients

Another important invariant in the environment is texture gradient. Gibson argued that texture gradients provide useful information about depth: objects slanting away from you have an increased gradient (rate of change) of texture density as you look from the near edge to the far edge. You may be familiar with the experience of looking for a nice patch of grass on which to have a picnic. You spot one in the distance but as you get closer you find that there are actually a lot of bare patches (Rookes & Willson, 2000). Texture gradients provide us with information about depth and distance because they indicate which things are closer and which are farther away.

Resonance

How do people "pick up" or detect the invariant information provided by the optic array? According to Gibson, there is a process of **resonance**, which he explained by analogy to the workings of a radio. In most houses throughout the Western world, there is almost non-stop electromagnetic radiation from various radio transmitters. When a radio set is switched on, there may be only a hissing sound. If tuned properly, however, speech or music will be clearly heard. In Gibson's terms, the radio is now resonating with the information contained in the electromagnetic radiation.

The analogy suggests we can pick up information from the environment in a fairly automatic and effortless way if we are attuned to that information. The radio operates as

a single unit, in the sense that damage to any part of its circuitry would stop it working. In a similar way, Gibson argued that the nervous system works as a single unit when perceiving.

Affordance

A key part of visual perception involves attaching meaning to the visual information provided to the eyes. It is usually assumed that we perceive the meaning of things in our environment because of top-down processes—relevant knowledge is stored in long-term memory and this tells us what our perceptions mean. Gibson (1979) disagreed with this assumption. He argued that all the potential uses of an object (which he called their **affordances**) are directly perceivable. For example, a ladder "affords" ascent or descent, and a chair "affords" sitting. The notion of affordances was even applied to postboxes by Gibson (1979, p.139):

Affordance is in the eye of the beholder.

> The postbox ... affords letter-mailing to a letter-writing human in a community with a postal system. This fact is perceived when the postbox is identified as such.

Would an orange always "afford" eating?

Most objects give rise to more than one affordance, with the particular affordance that influences behaviour being determined by the perceiver's current state. Thus a hungry person will perceive the affordance of edibility when presented with an orange, and so will eat it. A person who is angry may look at the orange and detect the affordance of a projectile, and so throw the orange at someone.

The notion of affordances is very important to Gibson's theory. It forms part of his attempt to show that all the information needed to make sense of the visual environment is directly present in the visual input. In addition, it conforms to the notion that there is a close relationship between perception and action.

Evaluation of Gibson's theory

Perception and action.   The main strength of Gibson's theory is its emphasis on the notion that the visual environment provides much more information than had previously been thought. He was right in assuming that the moment-by-moment changes in the optic array occurring when we are moving provide very useful information about the layout of the visual environment. Most previous theorists had de-emphasised the importance of movement, and had carried out studies in which the visual environment and the participant were both motionless.

According to Gibson, the meaning that is attached to objects is directly communicated when we look at an object because the potential uses of the object are obvious. One look at a postbox and you can "see" its meaning (a place to put letters).

Accuracy of perception.   Gibson argued that the wealth of information provided in the optic array means that perception is nearly always accurate. What about laboratory studies showing that visual perception can be very inaccurate? According to Gibson, such studies (e.g., of visual illusions) typically involve either very brief stimulus presentations or impoverished stimuli, and so have little relevance to everyday perception. He was right to argue that it can be unwise to assume that the findings from artificial laboratory situations apply to ordinary perception.

Oversimplification.   On the negative side, the processes involved in identifying invariants in the environment, in discovering affordances, and in producing resonance, are much more complex than Gibson indicated. According to Marr (1982, p.30), the major shortcomings of Gibson's analysis result

> from a failure to realise two things. First, the detection of physical invariants ... is exactly and precisely an information-processing problem ...   And second, he vastly under-rated the sheer difficulty of such detection.

Would you class Gibson's theory as a reductionist one?

Internal representation and perception

According to Gibson, a meaningless mark on a piece of paper (e.g., ~) should be enough visual information to permit identification. We could certainly identify it as a squiggle, but if we were to see a note on someone's doorstep that read "A pint of ~ please", we could interpret it correctly using our internal representations from previous experiences of notes on doorsteps. Gibson's theory does not address this issue.

Gibson's theory does not account for visual illusions, e.g., "seeing" water on the road on a hot day.

"Seeing as".   Gibson's theoretical approach applies much better to some aspects of visual perception than to others. This key issue can be approached in terms of the distinction between "seeing" and "seeing as". Fodor and Pylyshyn (1981) clarified this distinction by considering someone called Smith, who is lost at sea. He sees the stars in the night sky, including the Pole Star. However, what may be crucial to his survival is whether he sees the Pole Star as the Pole Star or as just another star. In other words, "seeing as" involves attaching *meaning* to what is being seen. Gibson's notion of affordances was an unsuccessful attempt to explain the meaningfulness of perception. Gibson provided a valuable account of *seeing*, but had little of interest to say about *seeing as*.

The role of memory.   A final weakness of Gibson's approach was his notion that no internal representations (e.g., memories) are needed to explain perception. Bruce, Green, and Georgeson (1996) referred to the work of Menzel (1978) to show the problems flowing from Gibson's position. Chimpanzees were carried around a field, and were shown the locations of 20 pieces of food. When each chimpanzee was then released, it moved around the field picking up the food efficiently. As there could be no relevant information in the light reaching the chimpanzees (because they were now moving independently rather than being carried), they must have made use of stored information in long-term memory to guide their search. This is contrary to the assumptions made by Gibson.

Constructivist theory

Helmholtz (1821–1894) argued that the inadequate information provided by the senses is augmented by *unconscious inferences*, which add meaning to sensory information. He assumed that these inferences were unconscious, because we are usually unaware that we are making inferences while perceiving. Helmholtz's constructivist approach to perception has been developed by theorists such as Gregory (1972, 1980) and Neisser (1967).

The following assumptions are made by most constructivist theorists:

- Perception is an active and constructive process; according to Gordon (1989, p.124), it is "something more than the direct registration of sensations ... other events intervene between stimulation and experience". In other words, perception is more than just sensing physical data; in order to experience seeing something there are other, active processes involved.
- Perception is not directly given by the stimulus input, but rather involves internal hypotheses, expectations, and knowledge, as well as motivational and emotional factors; sensory information is used as the basis for making informed guesses or inferences about the presented stimulus and its meaning.
- Because perception is influenced by hypotheses and expectations that will sometimes be incorrect, perception is prone to error.

What do you see here?

According to Gregory, a perceived object is a hypothesis which is suggested and then tested by sensory data. The stimulus provided to our senses is often incomplete or ambiguous; perception is therefore "driven" by cognitive expectations.

Gregory's theory

The flavour of this theoretical approach was captured by Gregory (1972). He claimed that perceptions are constructions "from the fragmentary scraps of data signalled by the senses and drawn from the brain memory banks, themselves constructions from the snippets of the past". Thus, the inadequate information supplied to the sense organs is used as the basis for making inferences or forming hypotheses about the visual environment.

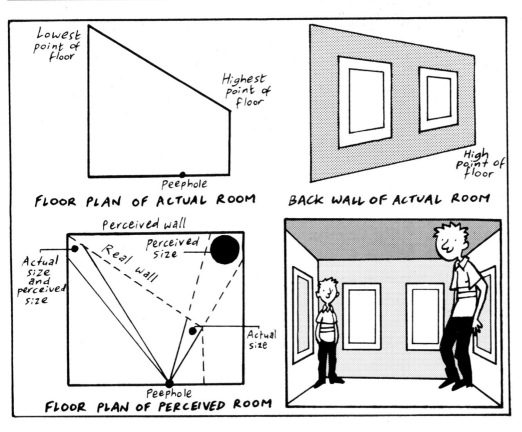

Top: dimensions of the actual Ames room. Bottom: Plan of the perceived room and the room as seen through the peephole.

The influence of expectations

Ittelson (1952) provided an illustration of how expectations can influence perception, based on the Ames distorted room (see the picture above). The room has a very strange shape, but our perception of it is strongly influenced by our expectation that rooms are rectangular. As a result, someone standing in the rear right corner appears to be much taller than someone standing in the rear left corner.

The influence of motivational factors

Constructivist theorists argue that an observer's hypotheses and expectations can be influenced by motivational and emotional factors. Supporting evidence was reported by Schafer and Murphy (1943). They used drawings in which an irregular line had been drawn vertically through a circle so that each half of the circle could be seen as the profile of a different face (see the illustration below). At the start of the study, each face was presented on its own. One face in each pair was associated with winning money, whereas the other face was associated with losing money. When the complete drawings were then shown briefly, the participants were much more likely to report seeing the previously "rewarded" face than the "punished" one. However, it is not clear in this study whether reward affected perceptual experience, or whether it only affected the participants' responses.

Our senses can be deceived by suggestion, such as when hypnosis and relaxation techniques are used as methods of pain relief.

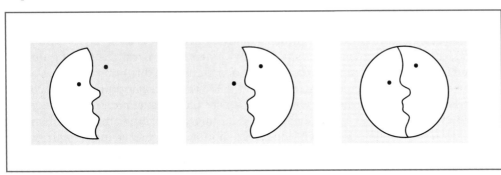

The two stimulus faces and final ambiguous picture used by Schafer and Murphy to demonstrate the effects of motivation on perception.

Other studies: Emotional and motivational factors

Solley and Haigh (1958) examined the role of emotional factors in perception. In two sessions, one before and one after Christmas, they asked children aged between 4 and 8 to draw Santa Claus. As Christmas approached the Santa drawings became larger and more elaborate, but after Christmas the drawings were much smaller. The emotions involved in anticipating Christmas affected how the children depicted Santa and his presents.

Motivational factors were examined by Sandford (1936). Some participants were deprived of food on the day of Sandford's study and then given a word-completion task. Most hungry participants produced BREAD as the word to complete B——D, whereas non-deprived participants tended to produce the word BORED!

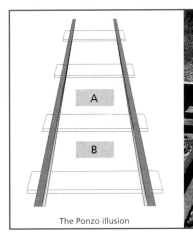

The Ponzo illusion

The Müller–Lyer illusion

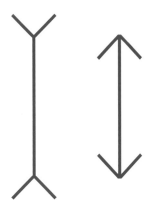

Is it likely that any single theory of the visual illusions will explain all of them?

Explaining visual illusions

Gregory (1970) used the constructivist approach to explain many of the well-known visual illusions. He started with size constancy, in which an object is seen as having the same size whether it is looked at from a short or a long distance away. According to his **misapplied size-constancy theory**, the processes that produce size constancy with three-dimensional objects are sometimes applied inappropriately to the perception of two-dimensional objects. The basic ideas can be understood with reference to the Ponzo illusion shown here. The long lines in the figure look like railway lines or the edges of a road receding into the distance. Thus the top horizontal line can be seen as further away from us than the bottom horizontal line. As rectangles A and B are the same size in the retinal image, it seems the more distant rectangle (A) must actually be larger than the nearer one (B).

Misapplied size-constancy theory can also explain the best-known visual illusion of all, the Müller–Lyer illusion (see below). The vertical lines in the two figures are the same length. However, the vertical line in the figure on the left looks longer than the one in the figure on the right. According to Gregory, the Müller–Lyer figures can be thought of as simple perspective drawings of three-dimensional objects. The left figure looks like the inside corners of a room, whereas the right figure is like the outside corner of a building. Thus, the vertical line in the left figure is in some sense farther away from us than its "fins", whereas the vertical line in the right figure is closer to us than its "fins". As the size of the retinal image is the same for both vertical lines, the principle of size constancy tells us that the line that is farther away (i.e., the one in the left figure) must be longer. This is precisely the Müller–Lyer illusion.

Gregory argued that figures such as the Ponzo and the Müller–Lyer are treated in many ways as three-dimensional objects. Why, then, do they seem flat and two-dimensional? According to Gregory, cues to depth are used automatically whether or not the figures are seen to be lying on a flat surface. Support for this viewpoint comes from the finding that the two-dimensional Müller–Lyer figures do indeed appear three-dimensional when they are presented as luminous models in a dark room. According to Gregory, it is only when these (and other) figures are presented on a flat surface that we do not perceive them as three-dimensional.

It might be thought that the depth cues of two-dimensional drawings would be less effective than those of photographs. Supporting evidence was reported by Leibowitz et al. (1969). They studied the Ponzo illusion, and found that the extent of the illusion was significantly greater with a photograph than with a drawing.

Evaluation of the misapplied size-constancy theory

Gregory's misapplied size-constancy theory is ingenious, and has been regarded as the most adequate theory of the visual illusions. However, Gregory's claim that luminous Müller–Lyer figures are seen three-dimensionally by everyone is incorrect. It is puzzling that the Müller–Lyer illusion can still be seen when the fins on the two figures are replaced by other attachments, such as circles or squares (see diagrams on facing page). Such evidence was interpreted by Matlin and Foley (1997) as supporting the **incorrect comparison theory**, according to which our perception of visual illusions is influenced by parts of the figure that are not being judged. Thus, for example, the vertical lines in the Müller–Lyer illusion may seem longer or shorter than their actual length simply because they form part of a large or small object. (See page 296 for further consideration of theories of visual illusions.)

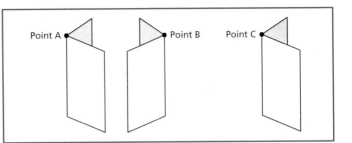

Evidence supporting incorrect comparison theory was reported by Coren and Girgus (1972). The magnitude of the Müller–Lyer illusion was greatly reduced when the fins were in a different colour from the vertical lines. Presumably this made it easier to ignore the fins when deciding on the relative lengths of the two vertical lines.

The strongest evidence that Gregory's theory is incomplete was reported by DeLucia and Hochberg (1991). They used a three-dimensional display consisting of three 2-foot high fins on the floor. Even though it was obvious that all the fins were at the same distance from the viewer (i.e., three-dimensional cues were available), the typical Müller–Lyer effect was obtained. You can check this out for yourself by placing three open books in a line so that the ones on the left and the right are open to the right and the one in the middle is open to the left. The spine of the book in the middle should be the same distance from the spines of the other two books. This finding cannot be explained by Gregory's misapplied size-constancy theory.

On the other hand, cross-cultural evidence (described on pages 307–309) suggests that not all people are susceptible to these illusions. Segall, Campbell, and Herskovits (1963) have argued that some people live in less "carpentered worlds", lacking the straight edges of more urban environments. There is some evidence that, for example, rural Zulus do not respond to the Müller–Lyer illusion—which would support the misapplied size–constancy theory.

In DaLocia and Hochberg's study, three fins that were 2 feet high were positioned on the floor and participants asked to say whether point A was closer to point B than B was to C. The Müller–Lyer illusion persists even though depth is obvious in this three-dimensional situation; a fact that does not fit Gregory's misapplied size-constancy theory.

Evaluation of top-down theory of visual perception

Top-down processes based on expectations, hypotheses, and so on can have a considerable influence on visual perception. Many theorists, such as Gibson, have emphasised the importance of bottom-up processes, and constructivist theorists have performed the valuable service of demonstrating that top-down processes should not be ignored. However, there are some serious problems with the constructivist approach, and the three main ones are discussed here.

The spine of the middle book is closer to the spine of which other book? Now check your answer with a ruler.

Accuracy. Constructivist theorists predict that perception will often be in error, however it is typically accurate. If we always use hypotheses and expectations to interpret sensory data, how is it that these hypotheses and expectations are correct nearly all the time? The obvious answer is that the environment provides much more information than the "fragmentary scraps of data" assumed by constructivist theorists.

Artificial stimuli. Many of the studies carried out by constructivist theorists make use of artificial or unnatural stimuli. As Gordon (1989, p.144) pointed out, such studies involve

the perception of patterns under conditions of brief exposure, drawings which could represent the corners of buildings, glowing objects in darkened corridors ... none of these existed in the African grasslands where human perceptual systems reached their present state of evolutionary development.

Consider, for example, studies involving the very rapid presentation of visual stimuli. Brief presentation reduces the impact of bottom-up processes, thus allowing more scope for top-down processes to operate.

Hypotheses. Constructivist theorists assume that the hypotheses formed by perceivers are the "best guesses" in the light of the available information. However, it is often very hard to persuade observers to change their hypotheses. For example, there is Gregory's (1973) "hollow face" illusion (see picture overleaf). In this illusion, observers looking at a hollow mask of a face from a distance of about 1 metre report seeing a normal face. Even when observers know that it is a hollow face, they still report that it looks normal.

Variants on the Müller–Lyer illusion

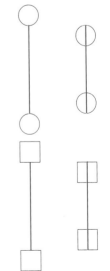

Synthesis: Neisser's cyclic theory

Neisser (1976) provided a synthesis of the direct and constructivist approaches to perception in his cyclic theory. He assumed that there is a perceptual cycle involving schemas, perceptual exploration, and the stimulus environment. Schemas contain collections of knowledge derived from past experience. These serve the function of directing perceptual exploration towards relevant environmental stimuli. Such exploration often leads the perceiver to sample some of the available stimulus information. If the information obtained from the environment fails to match information in the relevant schema, then the information in the schema is modified appropriately.

The perceptual cycle described by Neisser includes elements of bottom-up and top-down processing. Bottom-up processing is represented by the sampling of available environmental information that can modify the current schema. Top-down processing is represented by the notion that schemas influence the course of the information processing involved in perception.

Schemas

The key notion in Neisser's theory is that of schemas or organised knowledge. According to the theory, schemas should reduce the need to analyse all aspects of a visual scene. Evidence for this was reported by Biederman, Glass, and Stacy (1973, see pictures below). Participants were able to recall almost half the objects in photographs of familiar scenes (e.g., a city street) after viewing them for only one-tenth of a second, because the relevant schemas could be used easily. In contrast, when the objects were arranged randomly in the photograph, participants found it much harder to identify and to remember them.

Friedman (1979) reported evidence that visual perception is influenced by schemas. Participants were presented with detailed line drawings of scenes (e.g., a kitchen, an office). The duration of the first look was almost twice as long for unexpected as for

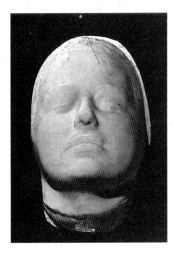

This photograph shows the inside of a hollow mask of a face, but it is very difficult to perceive it as seen "from the back". The viewer tends to perceive it as if they were seeing it from the front.

Testing the Biederman et al. experimental findings

Test the Biederman et al. experimental findings for yourself. Show the scene on the left to someone who has not already seen these pictures, very briefly (Biederman used one-tenth of a second), and see what objects they can recall. Try the random arrangement below on someone else, for the same time period. Again, see how many objects they can remember. Why do you have to show the two pictures to different people? How might this affect your findings?

expected objects, indicating the role of schemas in processing expected objects. It is easier to perceive objects that fit our schemas than objects that do not.

Evaluation

Neisser's (1976) cyclic theory combines some of the best features of the direct and constructivist approaches to perception. Perception often involves top-down processes as well as bottom-up processes, and both types of processes are incorporated into Neisser's perceptual cycle. Another strength of Neisser's theory is its emphasis on schemas. Schema-relevant objects are generally perceived and remembered much better than schema-irrelevant objects.

However, Neisser's cyclic theory is very sketchy, and fails to specify in any detail the processes involved in perception. More specifically, we are not told in detail how relevant schemas direct perceptual exploration, how perceptual exploration determines what is to be sampled in the stimulus environment, or how processing of the stimulus environment then modifies the relevant schemas. Theories, such as Marr's (1982) computational theory (see the box on the next page), indicate that we need much more complex and detailed theories to understand human perception properly.

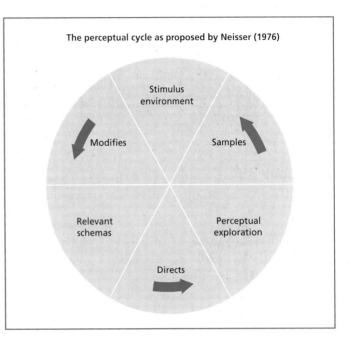

The perceptual cycle as proposed by Neisser (1976)

Features of theory	Direct theories	Constructivist theories	Synthesis
Major concepts			
Top-down or bottom-up?			
Generally learned or innate?			
Stored knowledge needed?			
Weaknesses			

■ Activity: Draw up a table showing comparisons among the different theories of perception.

Perceptual Organisation

Perception involves organising sensory data into meaningful patterns. This organisation happens so naturally and effortlessly that it is hard to believe that organised perception is a substantial achievement. The fact that computers can be programmed to play high-level chess, but still cannot mimic the visual skills of even fairly primitive animals, supports this idea.

The information that arrives at the sense receptors is confusing and disorganised. In the case of vision, there is usually a mosaic of colours, and the retinal sizes and shapes of objects in the environment may correspond very poorly to their actual sizes and shapes. Perceptual organisation requires an ability to detect movement, as well as good depth perception, and an ability to perceive the sizes and colours of objects accurately. These abilities are discussed in what follows.

Marr's computational theory

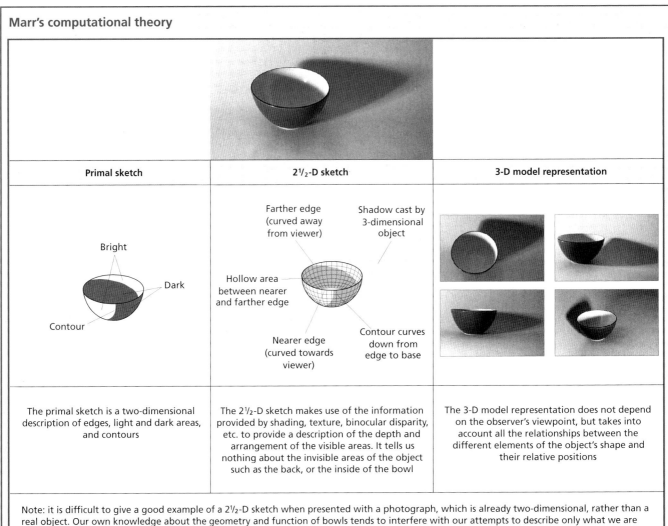

Primal sketch	2¹/₂-D sketch	3-D model representation
The primal sketch is a two-dimensional description of edges, light and dark areas, and contours	The 2¹/₂-D sketch makes use of the information provided by shading, texture, binocular disparity, etc. to provide a description of the depth and arrangement of the visible areas. It tells us nothing about the invisible areas of the object such as the back, or the inside of the bowl	The 3-D model representation does not depend on the observer's viewpoint, but takes into account all the relationships between the different elements of the object's shape and their relative positions

Note: it is difficult to give a good example of a 2¹/₂-D sketch when presented with a photograph, which is already two-dimensional, rather than a real object. Our own knowledge about the geometry and function of bowls tends to interfere with our attempts to describe only what we are actually seeing, rather than what we know is also present!

Marr (1982) proposed a computational theory of visual perception and pattern recognition. According to this theory, visual processing produces a series of representations or descriptions. These representations provide increasingly detailed information about the visual environment. The three main kinds of representation are as follows:

- *Primal sketch*: this provides a two-dimensional description of the main light-intensity changes in the visual input, including information about edges, contours, and indistinct forms, or blobs.
- *2½-D sketch*: this provides a description of the depth and orientation of visible surfaces, making use of information provided by shading, texture, motion, binocular disparity, and so on.
- *3-D model representation*: this provides a three-dimensional description of the shapes of objects and their relative positions; it differs from the 2½-D sketch in that the description does not depend on the observer's viewpoint.

For the purposes of understanding pattern or object recognition, it is most important to consider Marr's 3-D model representation. He assumed that object recognition involves matching information from a 3-D model representation against object information stored in long-term memory. Thus, for example, an object is recognised as a dog if the information in the 3-D model representation matches stored information about the characteristics of dogs more closely than those of any other object.

Marr and Nishihara (1978) argued that the basic units for describing objects should be cylinders having a major axis. These units are organised in a hierarchical way, with high-level units providing information about object shape, and low-level units providing more detailed information.

How does the perceiver identify the major axes of an object? According to Marr and Nishihara, concavities (areas where the contour points into the object) are identified first. Some evidence that concavities are important was reported by Hoffman and Richards (1984). They studied the faces–goblet ambiguous figure. When one of the faces is seen, the concavities make it easy to identify the forehead, nose, lips, and chin. In contrast, when the goblet is seen, the concavities define its base, stem, and bowl.

The work of David Marr is held in high esteem within the field of cognitive psychology. Eysenck (2000, p.287) notes:

"In my opinion, the British psychologist David Marr has contributed more than anyone else in the last 50 years to our understanding of visual perception. His main insight was that visual perception (which seems easy and effortless to us) actually involves a considerable number of complex processes. He then proceeded to identify many of these processes, and was the first person to show how the visual system constructs three-dimensional representations of objects. His achievements were outstanding, even though he died in 1980 at the tragically young age of 35."

Computers may be programmed to surpass human abilities in specific tasks, but they cannot possess the full range of human skills.

The Gestalt approach

The first systematic study of perceptual organisation was carried out by the Gestaltists ("*Gestalt*" is German for "organised whole"). They were a group of German psychologists (including Koffka, Köhler, and Wertheimer) who emigrated to the United States between the two World Wars. They were especially interested in the issue of *perceptual segregation*, i.e., our ability to work out which parts of the visual information presented to us belong together and thus form separate objects. A key aspect of perceptual segregation is the division of the visual field into the figure (central focus of attention) and the ground (everything else).

Principles of perceptual organisation

The Gestaltists proposed several laws of perceptual organisation. However, their most basic principle was the *law of Prägnanz*, which was expressed as follows by Koffka (1935, p.110):

> *Psychological organisation will always be as "good" as the prevailing conditions allow. In this definition the term "good" is undefined.*

In fact, Koffka was unduly vague in his definition. The Gestaltists actually regarded a good form as being the simplest or most uniform of the various possible organisational structures.

The Gestaltist approach can be seen most clearly if we consider some concrete examples shown on the right. Pattern (a) is most naturally seen as three horizontal arrays of dots. This illustrates the Gestalt law of *proximity*, according to which visual elements that are close to each other will tend to be grouped together. In pattern (b), vertical columns rather than horizontal rows are seen. This fits the law of *similarity*, according to which similar visual elements are grouped together. In pattern (c), we see two crossing lines rather than a V-shaped line and an inverted V-shaped line. This fits the law of *good continuation*, which states that those visual elements producing the fewest interruptions to smoothly curving lines are grouped together. Finally, pattern (d) fits the law of *closure*, according to which the missing parts of a figure are "filled in" to complete it. All these laws can be regarded as more specific statements of the fundamental law of Prägnanz.

The faces–goblet ambiguous figure is an example of figure and ground—which is figure and which is ground?

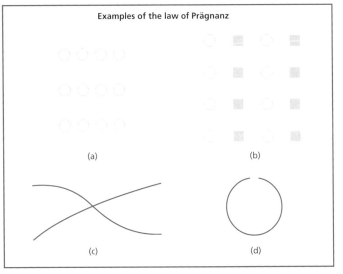

Examples of the law of Prägnanz

(a)

(b)

(c)

(d)

A more difficult figure–ground discrimination.

Evidence for the importance of grouping was reported by Navon (1977, see Key Study below) and Pomerantz and Garner (1973). In the study by Pomerantz and Garner, the participants were presented with stimuli consisting of two brackets arranged in various ways. The task was to sort the stimuli into two piles as quickly as possible depending on whether the left-hand bracket was "(" or ")". In spite of the fact that the participants were instructed to ignore the right-hand bracket, they found it impossible to do this when the two brackets were groupable (e.g., because both brackets were similar in orientation or were close to each other). The evidence for this consisted of slower sorting times for groupable stimuli than for non-groupable ones.

Where do organisational processes come from? The Gestaltists argued that most perceptual organisation reflects the largely innately determined functioning of the perceptual system. However, this is unlikely to be the whole story. Our everyday experiences teach us that those visual elements that are similar and close to each other typically belong to the same visual object, but visual elements that are dissimilar and far apart do not.

What happens when Gestalt laws are in conflict?

The Gestaltists de-emphasised the complexities involved when laws of grouping are in conflict. This issue was addressed recently by Quinlan and Wilton (1998). They used a display such as the one shown in (a) in the figure on the next page, in which there is a conflict between proximity and similarity. About half the participants grouped the stimuli

```
S                 S
S                 S
S                 S
S                 S
S                 S
SSSSSSSSSSSSS
S                 S
S                 S
S                 S
S                 S
S                 S
```

The whole and the parts

One of the key assumptions made by the Gestaltists was that "the whole is more than the sum of its parts". Exactly what they meant by this is a little obscure. However, a testable implication is that the overall Gestalt or whole may be perceived before its parts. This sounds like putting the cart before the horse, because it has usually been assumed that the individual parts or features of a visual stimulus are processed before the overall object is identified. Navon (1977) presented his participants with rather strange stimuli. One was a large letter H formed out of numerous little Ss. In addition, there was a large letter H formed from little Hs, and a large letter S formed from little Ss.

The task on each trial was to identify either the single large letter or the small letters as rapidly as possible. The time taken to identify the large letter was not affected by whether the small letters were the same as the large letter. In contrast, the time taken to identify the small letters was much longer when the large letter differed from them than when it was the same. This happened because information about the whole (i.e., the identity of the large letter) was available before information about the parts (i.e., the identity of the small letters).

Navon's research suggested that early perceptual processing identifies the most important objects. Subsequent perceptual processing then provides a more fine-grained analysis of their detailed structure. However, perceptual processing does not always proceed in this fashion. Kinchla and Wolf (1979) used stimuli constructed in the same way as those of Navon, but they varied the overall size of the stimuli. Their participants heard the name of a letter and were then presented with a visual stimulus. They had to respond "yes" if either the large letter or the small letters matched the letter they had heard. When the overall stimulus was fairly small, the participants were faster at detecting a match with the large letter than with the small letters. This finding resembles those of Navon (1977) in indicating that the large letter is processed first. However, precisely the opposite finding was obtained when the overall stimulus was five times larger. Thus, the parts are processed faster than the whole with large stimuli.

Discussion points

1. What determines whether the whole comes before the parts, or vice versa?
2. What is ingenious about the stimuli used by Navon?

by proximity and half by similarity. Quinlan and Wilton (1998) also used more complex displays like those in (b) and (c) below. Their findings led them to propose the following notions:

Laws of grouping:
(a) display involving a conflict between proximity and similarity; (b) display with a conflict between shape and colour; (c) a different display with a conflict between shape and colour.

- The visual elements in a display are initially grouped or clustered on the basis of proximity.
- Additional processes are used if elements that have provisionally been clustered together differ in one or more features (within-cluster mismatch).

If there is a within-cluster mismatch on features but a between-cluster match, e.g., in (a), then participants choose between grouping based on proximity and on similarity.

If there are within-cluster and between-cluster mismatches, then proximity is ignored, and grouping is often based on colour. In the case of the displays shown in (b) and (c), most participants grouped on the basis of common colour rather than common shape.

Evaluation

The Gestalt laws of organisation seem reasonable. However, they have attracted much criticism. The laws are only descriptive statements that fail to explain why similar visual elements or those close together are grouped. Another limitation is that most of the Gestalt laws relate mainly to the perceived organisation of two-dimensional patterns. Other factors come into play with three-dimensional scenes. For example, it may only be possible to separate out the figure of a chameleon from its background when it moves. Finally, it is hard to apply the Gestalt laws of organisation to certain complex visual stimuli (e.g., stimuli in which similar elements are relatively far apart and dissimilar elements are close together).

Movement perception

The detection of movement is a key part of perceptual organisation. Its importance was shown clearly in the case of a female patient, LM, who had suffered brain damage. She was good at locating stationary objects by sight, and had good colour discrimination, but her movement perception was extremely poor. As a result of this (Zihl et al., 1983, p.315):

> She could not cross the street because of her inability to judge the speed of a car, but she could identify the car itself without difficulty. "When I'm looking at the car first, it seems far away. But then, when I want to cross the road, suddenly the car is very near."

Apparent motion

One of the earliest studies on perception carried out by the Gestaltists was that of Wertheimer (1912). There were two lights in a dark room. When one light was flashed on and off about 50 milliseconds before the other light was flashed on and off, the observers saw a single light appear to move through the dark space separating the two flashed lights. This is known as **apparent motion**, because motion is perceived even though there is no actual motion. Anyone who has ever watched a film has experienced apparent motion. The Gestaltists were interested in apparent motion, because it showed how the whole (perception of motion or movement) could be more than the sum of its parts (two stationary lights).

Would you agree that apparent motion demonstrates that the whole is greater than the sum of its parts?

The law of common fate

The Gestaltists also put forward the law of common fate, according to which visual elements that seem to move together are grouped together. Johansson (1973) attached lights to each of the joints of an actor wearing dark clothes. This actor was then filmed as he moved around in a dark room. Observers saw only a meaningless display of lights

Johansson attached lights to an actor's joints. While the actor stood still in a darkened room, observers could not make sense of the arrangement of the lights. However, as soon as he started to move around, they were able to perceive the lights as defining a human figure. They could even distinguish men from women.

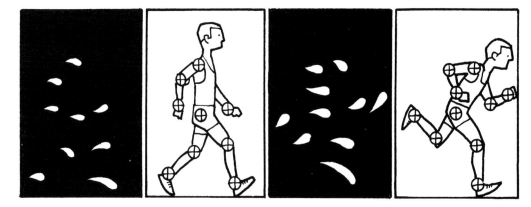

when the actor was at rest, but they perceived a moving human figure when he walked around. This was in spite of the fact that they could not see anything except the lights.

Cutting and Kozlowski (1977) found that observers were good at identifying themselves and others from point-light displays. Kozlowski and Cutting (1978) reported that observers were right about 65% of the time when guessing someone's sex from point-light displays. The observers took account of the fact that men swing their shoulders more than their hips when walking, whereas women show the opposite tendency.

Corollary discharge theory

How can we tell whether changes in the retinal image produced by an object are due to movement of the object or to movement of our eyes? According to corollary discharge theory (e.g., Richards, 1975), the visual system compares the movement registered on the retina with signals about eye movements. When your brain sends a message to your eye muscles, it also sends a copy (known as a corollary or resulting discharge) to the part of the visual system concerned with movement perception. Then whether movement of the retinal image is due to movement in the environment or simply to movement of the eyes can be determined.

Simple evidence supporting corollary discharge theory comes if you press the side of your eyeball gently. There is movement in the retinal image unaccompanied by commands to the eye muscles. As a result, this movement is interpreted by the visual system as being produced by movement in the environment.

However, corollary discharge theory does not provide a complete account of movement perception. As Tresilian (1994, p.336) pointed out, the theory predicts that

> *if the eyes are stationary in the head as the head rotates, the resulting image motion will be interpreted as motion of the environment, yet everyone knows that this does not happen.*

Can you think of occasions when this system fails—when things appear to be moving when neither you nor they are moving?

Thus, we do not rely only on information about eye movements to perceive a stable environment. Movement of the entire retinal image is usually attributed to movement of the head or eye, whereas movement of part of the retinal image is interpreted as movement of an external object.

Depth perception

In visual perception, the two-dimensional retinal image is transformed into perception of a three-dimensional world. In everyday life, cues to depth are often provided by movement either of the observer or of objects in the visual environment. However, the major emphasis here will be on depth cues that are available even if the observer and the objects in the environment are static. These cues can be divided into monocular and binocular cues. **Monocular cues** require the use of only one eye, but can also be used when someone has both eyes open. Such cues clearly exist, because the world still retains a sense of depth with one eye closed. **Binocular cues** are those that involve both eyes being used together.

Monocular cues

There are various monocular cues to depth. They are sometimes known as **pictorial cues**, because they are used by artists trying to create the impression of three-dimensional scenes. One such cue is *linear perspective*. Parallel lines pointing directly away from us seem closer together as they recede into the distance (e.g., railway tracks). This convergence of lines can create a powerful impression of depth in a two-dimensional drawing.

Another aspect of perspective is known as *aerial perspective*. Light is scattered as it travels through the atmosphere, especially if the atmosphere is dusty. As a result, more distant objects lose contrast and seem somewhat hazy.

Another cue related to perspective is texture. Most objects possess *texture*, and textured objects slanting away from us have what Gibson (1979) called a texture gradient. This is an increased gradient (rate of change) of texture density as you look from the front to the back of a slanting object. For example, if you look at a large patterned carpet, the details towards its far end are less clear than those nearer to you.

A further cue is *interposition*, in which a nearer object hides part of a more distant object. Evidence of the power of interposition is provided by Kanizsa's (1976) illusory square (see figure below). There is a strong subjective impression of a white square in front of four black circles. We make sense of the four sectored black discs by perceiving an illusory interposed white square.

Yet another cue to depth is provided by *shading*, or the pattern of light and dark on and around an object. Flat, two-dimensional surfaces do not cause shadows, and so shading provides good evidence for the presence of a three-dimensional object.

Another cue to depth is *familiar size*. If we know an object's actual size, then we can use its retinal image size to provide an estimate of its distance. In one study, when participants looked at playing cards through a peephole, large ones looked farther away than they actually were, whereas undersized playing cards looked closer than was really the case (Ittelson, 1951).

The final monocular cue to be considered is *motion parallax*. This is based on the movement of an object's image over the retina. Consider, for example, two objects moving from left to right across the line of vision at the same speed, but with one object much farther away from the observer than the other. In that case, the image cast by the nearer object would move much faster across the retina.

Binocular and oculomotor cues

All the depth cues discussed so far can be used by a one-eyed person. Depth perception is also achieved using oculomotor cues, the cues from the muscles around the eyes. Two such cues are:

- *Convergence*, which refers to the fact that the eyes turn inwards to focus on an object to a greater extent when the object is very close.
- *Accommodation*, the variation in optical power produced by a thickening of the lens of the eye when focusing on a close object (see diagram on page 274).

Depth perception also depends on binocular cues, which are only available when you have two eyes. *Stereopsis* involves binocular cues, using the disparity in the images projected on the retinas of the two eyes (see diagram on the next page).

Convergence, accommodation, and stereopsis are only effective cues for depth perception over relatively short distances.

There has been controversy about the value of convergence as a cue to distance. The findings have tended to be negative when real objects are used. Accommodation is also of very little use. Its potential value as a depth cue is limited to the region of space immediately in front of you. However, distance judgements based on accommodation are inaccurate, even when the object is at close range (Kunnapas, 1968).

The importance of stereopsis was shown by Wheatstone (1838), who was the inventor of the stereoscope. What happens in a stereoscope is that separate pictures or drawings

This dried-out lake bed is an example of a real-life texture gradient. As the earth slants away from the viewer, the pattern seems to get smaller and less distinct.

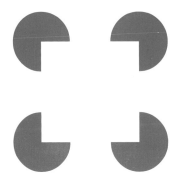

Kanizsa's illusory square— although no square is present, people see the diagram as if it were four blue circles with a white square lying on them.

As the eyes are set a short distance apart, each eye receives a slightly different image from the same scene. The difference in the retinal images, at identical places on each eye, is called binocular disparity. The brain makes use of these slight differences as one way of registering spatial depth. This is the principle of the stereoscope, where photographs taken from slightly different angles, corresponding to the position of each eye, appear to the viewer to fuse as a single three-dimensional image.

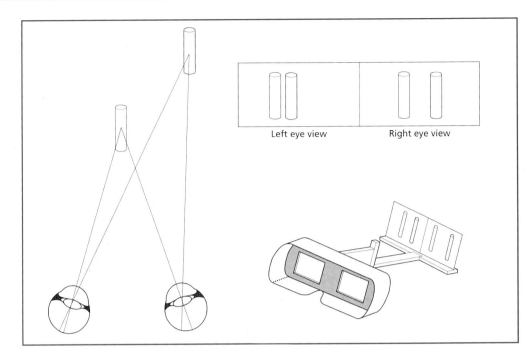

Left eye view   Right eye view

■ Activity: Hold a pen at arm's length; its image will be quite clear. However, as you bring the pen closer to your face, the image will blur because your eyes will no longer be able to converge and focus accurately beyond a certain point.

are presented to the observer so that each eye receives the information it would receive if the objects depicted were actually presented. Stereoscopic vision produces a strong depth effect.

Combining information from cues

So far, we have considered depth cues one at a time. In the real world, however, we generally have access to several depth cues, and so we need to know how information from various cues is combined and integrated. Bruno and Cutting (1988) identified three strategies that might be used by observers who had information available from two or more depth cues:

1. *Additivity*: all the information from different cues is simply added together.
2. *Selection*: information from one cue is used, with information from the other cue or cues being ignored.
3. *Multiplication*: information from different cues interacts in a multiplicative way.

Bruno and Cutting investigated depth perception in a series of studies in which visual displays were observed through one eye only. Their participants had access to four sources of information about depth (e.g., interposition, relative size, and so on) when making decisions about the distance of various objects. The participants used the additivity strategy, because they made equal use of all four sources of information.

It is usually sensible to combine information from depth cues in an additive fashion. Any depth cue provides inaccurate information sometimes, and so relying totally on one cue would often lead to error. In contrast, taking account of all the available information is usually the best way to make sure that depth perception is accurate. However, there are rare cases in which the selection strategy is used. Woodworth and Schlosberg (1954) discussed a study in which two normal playing cards of the same size were attached to stands, with one card being closer to the observer (see diagram on the next page). The observers viewed the two cards monocularly, and the farther card looked more distant. In the next, crucial phase of the study, the corner of the nearer card was clipped, and the two cards were arranged so that the edges of the more distant card seemed to fit exactly the cut-out edges of the nearer card. With monocular vision, the more distant card seemed to be in front of, and partially obscuring, the nearer card. In this case, the cue of interposition overwhelmed the cue of familiar size.

The two stages of the playing-card experiment, as discussed by Woodworth and Schlosberg. When the viewer looks at the first set-up, the card at the back looks farther away (which it is). However, when the front card has been clipped, and the position of the cards rearranged, the back card looks as if it overlaps the front card. The cue of familiar size, telling the viewer that the smaller card must be farther away than the bigger card, is overridden by the cue of interposition, suggesting that the card that appears to obscure part of the other one must be nearer to the viewer, despite its size.

Visual constancies

We are used to objects appearing very similar each time we look at them. For example, the perceived size, shape, and colour of a close friend of yours are likely to change very little over time. The term **visual constancies** is used to refer to the fact that most of the visual characteristics of an object look very similar on different occasions even when there are large changes in the retinal image (e.g., the retinal image of your friend is fairly large when he or she is close to you, but it becomes very small when he or she is a long way away). Psychologists have identified several specific visual constancies, including size constancy, shape constancy, and colour constancy.

Size constancy

Size constancy is the tendency for a given object to appear the same size whether its size in the retinal image is large or small. Why do we show size constancy? A key reason is that we take account of an object's apparent distance when judging its size. For example, an object may be judged to be large even though its retinal image is very small if it is a long way away. The fact that size constancy is often not shown when we look at objects on the ground from the top of a tall building or from a plane may occur because it is hard for us to judge distance accurately.

One of the factors influencing size constancy is familiar size. For example, we know that most adults are between about 1.60 and 1.85 metres tall. We can use this information about familiar size to make accurate assessments of size regardless of whether the retinal image is very large or very small. Evidence of the importance of familiar size was obtained by Schiffman (1967). Observers viewed familiar objects at various distances in the presence or absence of depth cues. Their size estimates were accurate even when depth cues were not available, because they made use of their knowledge of familiar size.

According to the size–distance invariance hypothesis, people work out an object's size by combining information about its retinal size with information about its perceived distance. This theory was supported by Holway and Boring (1941). Participants sat at the intersection of two hallways. A test circle was presented in one hallway, and a comparison circle was presented in the other one. The test circle could be of various sizes and at various distances, and the participants' task was to adjust the comparison circle so that it was the same size as the test circle. Their performance was very good when depth cues were available. However, it became poor when depth cues were removed by placing curtains in the hallway and requiring the participants to look through a peephole.

If size judgements depend on perceived distance, then size constancy should not be found when the perceived distance of an object is very different from its actual distance. The Ames room provides a good example (see page 283). It has a peculiar shape: the floor slopes, and the rear wall is not at right angles to the adjoining walls. In spite of this, the

Have you ever been disappointed when taking a photograph of a distant object (for example, a rock star on stage at a large stadium venue)? When the photograph came back you could hardly see anything. Why does this happen?

Ames room creates the same retinal image as a normal rectangular room when viewed through a peephole. The fact that one end of the rear wall is much farther from the viewer is disguised by making it much higher. The cues suggesting that the rear wall is at right angles to the viewer are so strong that someone walking backwards and forwards in front of it appears to grow and shrink as he or she moves about!

Shape constancy

Shape constancy ensures that we continue to see the shape of a book as a rectangular image despite the fact that the retinal image is rarely rectangular. As we move a book around it takes on numerous forms of a parallelogram or even a trapezoid!

Direct perception theory would claim that we have enough information in the optic array to provide information about such constancy, whereas the constructivists would claim that this ability is learned. The research evidence supports this latter view, that both size and shape constancy are learned early in life (see page 302).

The moon illusion demonstrates the size–distance invariance hypothesis. If you see the moon just as it is rising, you may be staggered by its apparent hugeness. The explanation is that when the moon is overhead, there is nothing else to relate it to except the vastness of the sky. And compared with this vastness, the moon appears small. Near the horizon, there are many familiar objects, such as trees and buildings that provide a sense of scale for judging apparent distance and size.

Colour constancy

Colour constancy is the tendency for an object to appear to have the same colour regardless of the light reflecting from it. For example, the light reflected from objects when they are illuminated by artificial lighting is usually more yellow than when they are illuminated by the sun. However, this generally has very little effect on the objects' perceived colour (Sekuler & Blake, 1994).

Why do we show colour constancy? One reason is that we have learned over the years that most objects tend to have a particular colour. For example, English people know that postboxes are red, and so they tend to always look red even at night under poor lighting conditions.

Land (1977) argued in his retinex theory that we perceive a surface's colour accurately by comparing the light reflected from it against that from adjacent surfaces (see page 278). He obtained evidence for this theory by using two visual displays. The lighting was arranged so that two rectangles having different colours reflected the same wavelengths of light. In spite of this, the two rectangles were seen as different, and their true colours were perceived. It follows from Land's theory that colour constancy would not be found if information about the light reflected from adjacent surfaces were not available. When everything in Land's visual display apart from the two differently coloured rectangles was blocked out, they seemed to have the same colour.

If we see snow on the ground at night, how do we know it is really white when it appears to be much darker?

Colour constancy works best when we are viewing objects in natural light from the sun. It tends to break down when we look at objects in artificial light having a restricted wavelength distribution. As Sekuler and Blake (1994) pointed out, some supermarkets exploit this fact by illuminating their meat products so they look redder than is actually the case.

We continue to see the shape of a book as rectangular despite the fact that the retinal image is rarely rectangular—this is shape constancy.

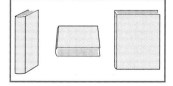

Visual illusions

Visual illusions are not "mistakes" of perception, they illustrate normal functioning in abnormal conditions. We have used visual illusions throughout this Unit to illustrate aspects of perceptual organisation. Gregory (1978) identified four categories of illusion: ambiguous figures, paradoxical figures, fictitious figures, and distortions.

Ambiguous figures

We considered the "ratman" figure earlier (see page 261), an example of a figure that can be interpreted in two different ways. Ambiguous figures rely on contextual cues to resolve their ambiguity. Without contextual cues we may find the image flipping back and forth between the alternatives, as in Necker's cube on the right. The use of contextual cues demonstrates the role of top-down processing in perception because such cues provide expectations.

Paradoxical figures

A paradoxical figure is one that looks realistic at first glance but, on reflection, we realise that it can't work in three dimensions. Two classic examples of this are the Penrose impossible triangle and *Waterfall*, a drawing by M.C. Escher (see below).

Fictitious figures

Fictitious figures are drawings that manage to create an image where there actually is nothing. The Kanizsa square is an example of this (see page 293) where a white square is created by suggestion. This illustrates the strength of the depth cue of interposition.

Distortions

Both the Müller–Lyer illusion and the Ponzo illusion (see page 284 for both of these) create a misperception because they contain cues that normally inform us about

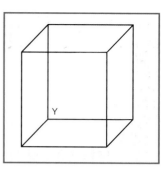

A Necker cube that illustrates the perceptual restructuring in which the corner marked "Y" alternates between being at the back and at the front of the figure.

Putting visual illusions to good use

Someone came up with the innovative idea that you could slow drivers down as they approached a roundabout by giving them the illusion that they were travelling faster than they were. This is done with "optical brakes"—lines drawn across the road that get progressively closer together. The effectiveness of these "brakes" can be explained in terms of **motion parallax**, a cue that is used to perceive relative motion. As an observer moves about, there are systematic movements in the visual field. For example, objects that are closer to the observer move faster in comparison with those in the distance (this contributes to depth perception as well as movement). Another example is that when driving down a road, your sense of speed will be determined by how quickly objects are moving across your eye. Optical brakes provide the illusion that you are moving faster because the lines are moving faster and faster across the observer's eye.

At a road junction or roundabout drivers should be slowing down anyway, but this false feedback from the optical brakes should cause them to slow down even more. The Transport Research Laboratory reports that accidents were reduced by as much as 57% on roads with optical brakes.

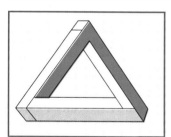

The Penrose triangle (above) and this picture by M.C. Escher, *Waterfall* (right), are both examples of paradoxical figures. The waterfall illusion is achieved by joining several Penrose triangles. As you look at each part of the construction you cannot find any mistakes, but when the print is viewed as a whole you see the problem of water travelling up a flat plane, yet the water is also falling and spinning a miller's wheel. How do the two towers appear relatively the same height yet the left side rises three storeys and the right two? M.C. Escher used many such paradoxical figures in his work.

These creatures are identical in size, although the one in the background appears to be larger than the creature in the foreground due to the depth cues that indicate they are running down a passageway.

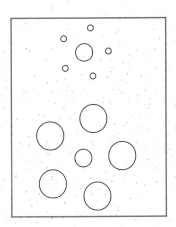

The Ebbinghaus illusion.

> **Auditory illusions**
>
> It is not surprising that there are auditory as well as visual illusions. Auditory illusions are also the consequence of our expectations. Warren and Warren (1970) demonstrated "phonemic restoration". If a sentence is tampered with so that a bleep occurs instead of a particular phoneme, a listener still reports "hearing" the phoneme even when they know it's missing.

depth. These illusions have been used in trying to understand how hypotheses are constructed about our visual world.

Explaining visual illusions

As we have seen earlier, Gregory used the **misapplied size-constancy theory** to explain visual illusions. But this can only explain some illusions and doesn't even appear fully to explain the Müller–Lyer illusion. What other explanations are there?

"Good figure" theory.   The Gestalt psychologists (see page 289) proposed that illusions are the result of our tendency to make best sense out of sensory data. When presented with a row of dots we tend to see them as groups (e.g., ...). Illusions cause one feature to stand out and the visual system makes best sense of the data. Like many explanations, this can explain some illusions, such as the faces–goblet figure on page 289, but not other illusions.

Physiological confusion theories.   Some illusions are the result of physiological processes, such as the dark diamonds effect described on page 276. Carpenter and Blakemore (1973) suggest that other illusions can also be explained in terms of physiology. It is possible that converging or angled lines produce asymmetrical regions of lateral inhibition and this leads to distorted perception. One problem with this explanation is that illusions occur with parallel lines, where lateral inhibition should be symmetrical.

Incorrect comparison theory.   In the earlier discussion of misapplied size-constancy, we also considered the idea that visual illusions occur because our perceptions are influenced by parts of the figure that are not being judged. This theory was supported by research by Coren and Girgus (1972) who found the magnitude of the Müller–Lyer illusion was greatly reduced when the fins were in a different colour from the vertical lines.

The effects of action.   It will be remembered that Gibson emphasised the notion that there is a very close link between perception and action. As he might have predicted, many visual illusions seem to be reduced or eliminated when the participants have to take some form of appropriate action with respect to the figure rather than just observe it (see Milner & Goodale, 1998). For example, consider a study by Aglioti, Goodale, and De Souza (1995) with the Ebbinghaus illusion (see figure on left). In this illusion, the central circle surrounded by smaller circles looks larger than a central circle of the same size surrounded by larger circles. Aglioti et al. (1995) constructed a three-dimensional version of this illusion, and obtained the usual illusion effect. However, when the participants reached to pick up one of the central discs, the maximum grip aperture of their reaching hand was almost entirely determined by the actual size of the disc. Thus, no illusion was apparent in the size of the hand grip.

Evidence supporting the hypothesis that visual illusions can be reduced when action towards the figure is required was reported by Wraga, Creem, and Proffitt (2000). They presented one part of the Müller–Lyer figure on the floor on each trial. The participants either provided a verbal estimate of the length of the line or they walked its length while blindfolded. There was a highly significant visual illusion effect with the verbal estimation task, but there was no illusion effect at all with blind-walking. These findings are especially impressive because the verbal and motor tasks were carefully matched.

Conclusion

The study of illusions is not simply of theoretical interest. A knowledge of illusions can be put to practical use (see the box on page 297) and can help us understand important perceptual errors. The question of whether perception is largely innate or learned is mirrored in the question of whether visual illusions are innate or learned. Some are innate (e.g., those that are the result of lateral inhibition), others are the outcome of experience (e.g., the Ponzo illusion). We will return to the issue of nature or nurture in the next Unit.

Perceptual Development

How much can the newborn baby (or neonate) see and hear? It used to be assumed that the answer was "very little". William James, towards the end of the nineteenth century, described the world of the newborn baby as a "buzzing, blooming confusion, where the infant is seized by eyes, ears, nose and entrails all at once". This suggests that the infant is bombarded by information in all sense modalities, and cannot attach meaning to this information. That view greatly underestimates the capabilities of infants. Many basic perceptual mechanisms are working at a very early age, and infants are not merely helpless observers of their world.

Are there situations where you feel that the world is a "buzzing, blooming confusion"?

Research Methods Used to Study Infants

It is hard to assess perception in infants because they cannot tell us what they can see or hear. However, several methods to assess the perceptual abilities of infants have been developed.

- *Behavioural method*. Various behavioural measures can be taken to discover what infants can perceive. For example, Butterworth and Cicchetti (1978) tested infants in a room in which the walls and the ceiling moved towards and away from them. The infants lost balance, and this loss of balance was always in the expected direction. If the room moved towards them, they swayed forwards, whereas they swayed backwards if the room moved away from them.
- *Preference method*. Two or more stimuli are presented together, and the experimenter simply observes which stimulus attracts the most attention. If infants systematically prefer one stimulus to another, this indicates that they can discriminate between them. This method was used by Fantz (1961) in research discussed later.
- *Habituation method*. A stimulus is presented repeatedly until the infant no longer attends to it; this is known as habituation. When the infant shows habituation to one stimulus, he or she is shown a different stimulus. If the infant responds to the new stimulus, he or she must have discriminated between the two stimuli.

A drawing of the Butterworth and Cicchetti moving room. The walls and ceiling of the room can be moved, although the floor is fixed. The infants experience loss of balance, swaying forwards or backwards, depending on which way the room appears to move.

Why is it an advantage to use newborn babies in research?

- *Eye-movement method.* The eye movements of infants can provide information about their visual perception. For example, if infants are presented with a moving stimulus, the tracking response can be recorded. This indicates whether or not they can distinguish between the moving stimulus and the background against which it is presented. Alternatively, infants can be presented with a visual stimulus, and the pattern of eye movements can be photographed and then examined. Maurer and Salapatek (1976) found that 1-month-old infants looked at the edges and contours of a human face, whereas 2-month-olds focused in a more systematic way on the internal features such as the eyes, nose, and mouth.

- *Physiological method.* Various physiological measures can be used. One way of telling whether infants can discriminate between two stimuli is to measure their visual evoked potentials (brain-wave activity) to each stimulus. Alternatively, if infants show different patterns of heart rate and/or breathing rate to two stimuli, this suggests that the infants perceive the two stimuli to be different. As we will see later, heart rate can also indicate whether infants are frightened or merely interested in a visual stimulus.

- *Visual reinforcement method.* The basic idea is that the infant is given control over the stimulus or stimuli presented to it. For example, Siqueland and DeLucia (1969) gave infants a dummy that was wired up so that their sucking rate could be assessed. A stimulus may be presented only for as long as it continues to produce a high sucking rate, being replaced when it does not. Alternatively, infants can be presented with one stimulus when their sucking rate is high and another stimulus when it is low.

Might newborn babies have had any prior perceptual experience?

Studies of Perceptual Development

Visual preference for faces

It is claimed that visual preference demonstrates the ability to discriminate. Can you offer any other explanation for visual preference?

Fantz (1961) devised the visual preference task, which has proved to be one of the most effective ways of studying infant perception. In essence, two visual stimuli are presented to the infant at the same time, with one being presented to the infant's left and the other to the right. The amount of time spent looking at each stimulus is recorded. If an infant consistently looks at one stimulus more than the other, this selectivity is thought to show the existence of perceptual discrimination.

Fantz showed infants (aged between 4 days and 5 months) head-shaped discs, as shown below. Infants of all ages looked most at the realistic face and least at the blank face. On the basis of such studies, Fantz (1966, pp.171–173) arrived at the following sweeping conclusions:

The experimental apparatus used by Fantz to observe how infants respond to visual stimuli.

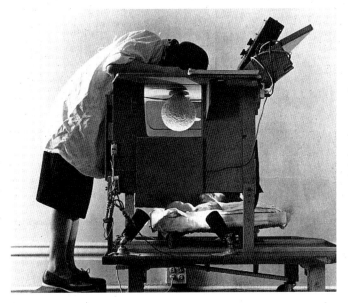

The findings have tended to destroy ... the myth—that the world of the neonate is a big booming confusion, that his visual field is a form of blur, that his mind is a blank slate, that his brain is decorticate, and that his behaviour is limited to reflexes or undirected mass movements. The infant sees a patterned and organised world that he explores discriminatingly within the limited means at his command.

Findings from the visual preference task do not really justify these conclusions. At an experimental level, the difference

in time spent looking at the real and the scrambled faces was fairly small in the study by Fantz (1961). At an interpretive level, it is hard to know whether infants look at the real face because it is a face or because it is a complex, symmetrical visual stimulus. However, Dannemiller and Stephens (1988) made use of computer-generated faces that were constructed so as to control for these factors. Thus, for example, they produced human faces and patterns that had the same level of complexity and symmetry. Three-month-old infants preferred human faces, thus confirming Fantz's findings under well-controlled conditions.

Do you think the Dannemiller and Stephens study had more ecological validity than the Fantz study? Why might the computer-generated faces still be unlike a real human face?

Depth perception

The visual cliff

Gibson and Walk (1960) also argued that infants possess well-developed perceptual skills. They designed a "visual cliff", which was actually a glass-top table. A check pattern was positioned close to the glass under one half of the table (the "shallow" side) and far below the glass under the other half (the "deep" side). Infants between the ages of 6½ months and 12 months were placed on the shallow side of the table, and encouraged to crawl over the edge of the visual cliff on to the deep side by being offered toys or having their mothers call them. Most failed to respond to these incentives, suggesting that they possessed at least some of the elements of depth perception.

Gibson and Walk tested the performance of other species on their visual cliff. Most species (including chicks under 1 day old) avoided the deep side of the visual cliff, suggesting that some aspects of depth perception may be inborn. However, 4-week-old kittens that had been reared in the dark did not avoid the deep side, nor did rats that could detect the glass with their whiskers.

Research on the visual cliff does not necessarily indicate that depth perception is innate. Infants who are several months old might have learned about depth perception from experience. However, there is some intriguing evidence pointing to the importance of learning in the visual cliff situation. Nine-month-old infants had faster heart rates than normal when placed on the deep side, presumably because they were frightened (Campos et al., 1978). However, infants aged between 2 and 5 months actually had slower heart rates than usual when placed on the deep side, suggesting that they were not frightened. This slowing of heart rate probably reflected interest, and it certainly indicates that they detected some difference between the deep and shallow sides of the visual cliff situation.

A drawing of Gibson and Walk's "visual cliff". Babies between 6½ and 12 months of age were reluctant to crawl over the "cliff edge", even when called by their mothers, suggesting that they perceived the drop created by the check pattern.

Retinal image size

Bower et al. (1970) obtained more convincing evidence that infants have some aspects of depth perception. They showed two objects to infants under 2 weeks old. One was large and approached to within 20 centimetres of the infant, whereas the other was small and approached to 8 centimetres. The two objects had the same retinal size (i.e., size at the retina) at their closest point to the infant. In spite of this, the infants were more disturbed by the object that came closer to them, rotating their heads upwards and pulling away from it. Apparently these infants somehow made use of information about depth to identify which object posed the greater threat.

Using evidence from (a) babies and (b) animals in Gibson and Walk's study, would you say that depth perception was more likely to be learned or innate?

Size and shape constancy

Nearly all adults display *size constancy* and *shape constancy*. Size constancy means that a given object is perceived as having the same size regardless of its distance from us, and

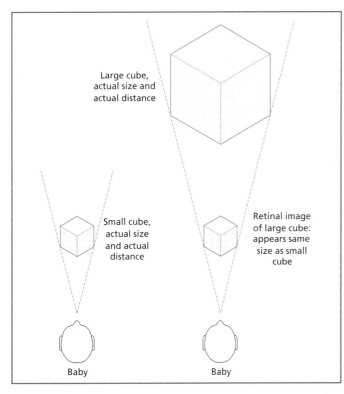

Large cube,
actual size and
actual distance

Small cube,
actual size
and actual
distance

Retinal image
of large cube:
appears same
size as small
cube

Baby

Baby

Two cubes of different sizes may project retinal images of the same size, depending on their distance from the viewer. Bower used this effect to test depth perception and size constancy in infants.

shape constancy means that an object is seen to have the same shape regardless of its orientation. Thus, we see things "as they really are", and are not taken in by variations in the information presented to the retina. This is more of an achievement than might be supposed, because the retinal image of an object is very much smaller when the object is a long way away from us. It is of interest to discover whether infants show evidence of size and shape constancy.

Size constancy

Bower (1966) studied size constancy in infants between 75 and 85 days of age. The first stage of the experiment involved teaching the infants to look at a 30-centimetre cube placed about 1 metre from them. Bower then compared the length of time spent looking at the same cube placed 3 metres from the infant and a 90-centimetre cube placed 3 metres away. The former stimulus had the same size as the original cube, but a much smaller retinal image. In contrast, the latter stimulus had a much greater real size, but the same retinal size as the original cube. Some size constancy was shown, because the infants were almost three times more likely to look at the former than at the latter stimulus object. However, they failed to show complete size constancy, because they were more likely to look at the 30-centimetre cube when it was placed 1 metre away than when it was 3 metres away.

Shape constancy

Evidence for shape constancy in 3-month-old infants has been found using the habituation method (Caron, Caron, & Carlson 1979). Some infants were presented repeatedly with a square forming a trapezoidal shape on the retina until they habituated or lost interest in it. After that, they were presented with a real trapezoid, in which they showed an immediate interest. Thus they had habituated to the real shape rather than to the retinally presented shape.

Innate or learned?

Are the perceptual skills of size and shape constancy innately determined? As Bower was studying infants who were 2 or 3 months of age, they may have learned at least some of the skills involved. However, the exploratory and reaching activities that might lead to the learning of relevant perceptual skills do not usually start in earnest until infants are at least 3 months of age. It makes evolutionary sense for infants to display size and shape constancy at a young age, because this helps them to perceive the world accurately rather than inaccurately. These abilities may be learned through early experience, or they may be biologically driven but only appear after a few months. The same is true of focus (innate effect). Infants are born with a fixed focal length of about 20 centimetres. The eye matures after birth and develops the ability to focus on near and far objects.

If you look at a coin standing on its edge or lying flat on a table, how do you know it is a coin when the image your eye receives differs depending on the coin's position? If you hold same coin at arm's length and bring it slowly towards you, the coin appears to become larger as it gets closer. How do you know it hasn't really changed in size?

Theories of perceptual development

A theory is an attempt to provide a framework for the known facts. What psychological explanations have been proposed for the development of perceptual abilities?

Piaget's enrichment theory

Jean Piaget developed the most influential theory of cognitive development (the development of thinking). This is described in Section 10, Cognitive Development. According to Piaget, the first stage of cognitive development is the **sensori-motor stage** when children under the age of 2 learn to co-ordinate their sensory and motor abilities—

in essence they learn to perceive. Infants acquire their knowledge of the world mainly by acting on it through mouthing, grasping, and manipulating objects. These reflex behaviours are the infant's innate **schemas**. Cognitive development is the growth of these schemas, and they grow as a consequence of experience. The infant is able to **assimilate** certain experiences into existing schemas but other experiences do not fit with what is already known. For example, the infant may put something into his or her mouth and find that it tastes quite bitter in comparison with previous experiences. This requires the development of a new schema for bitter-tasting objects (the process is **accommodation**).

The importance of this, in relation to perceptual development, is that the infant is seen to *enrich* his or her sensory input because schemas provide expectations, and perceptions are influenced by such expectations, as we saw in Gregory's constructivist theory. The infant imposes meaning on sensory data, either making them fit with pre-existing sensory schemas or by generating new ones.

The development of perception depends to a large extent on the infant's growing mobility and ability to act on the environment because in this way schemas are tested. For example, depth perception should be acquired when the infant starts crawling and interacting directly with its surroundings.

However, Piaget probably exaggerated the importance of action in the development of perception. Arterberry, Yonas, and Bensen (1989) showed infants between the ages of 5 and 7 months two identical objects placed on a grid that created the illusion of depth. The two objects were actually the same distance away, but 7-month-old infants reached for the object that looked closer, whereas the 5-month-olds did not. The key finding was that those infants who had had the most experience of crawling showed no more depth perception than the others. This suggests that perceptual development is not dependent on motor abilities.

If depth perception develops around the time an infant starts crawling, does this suggest it is innately driven and due to maturation?

Meadows (1986) discussed other findings that do not seem to fit well with Piaget's theoretical approach. For example, 5-month-olds do not generally reach for objects that are out of reach, even though they have only limited experience of moving around their environment.

Differentiation theory

According to differentiation theory (e.g., Gibson & Spelke, 1983), the stimuli presented to our senses contain all the information needed for accurate perception. Bower (1982) believed that newborns can register all the information that an adult can, but they are simply unable to process it. Differentiation theory sees perceptual development as a question of learning to differentiate between the distinctive features of different classes of objects and the invariant properties that transfer from situation to situation. Perceptual development also involves learning to ignore irrelevant information and learning to pay attention efficiently.

It might be worth noting that the "Gibson" who proposed differentiation theory was not the same "Gibson" who researched the direct perception theory. The former Gibson is Eleanor, wife of the latter Gibson, James!

Evidence that perceptual development does involve learning to identify the crucial features of any stimulus can be seen in a study by Gibson (1969). Children aged between 4 and 8 were asked to select from 13 figures the only one that was identical to a standard stimulus figure (see illustration). The other 12 figures differed slightly from the standard figure in various ways. Some differed in orientation (i.e., the figure was rotated or

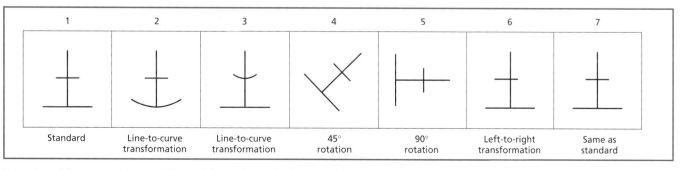

1	2	3	4	5	6	7
Standard	Line-to-curve transformation	Line-to-curve transformation	45° rotation	90° rotation	Left-to-right transformation	Same as standard

Examples of figures used to test children's ability to detect the distinctive features of letter-like forms. Stimulus 1 is the standard. The child's task is to examine each of the comparison stimuli and pick out the one that is the same as the standard.

inverted), and others differed in perspective (i.e., the figure appeared slanted or tilted backwards).

What did Gibson find? The number of errors decreased with age, and the pattern of errors changed. Perspective errors were very common at all ages, but orientation errors showed a sharp decrease between the ages of 4 and 8. These findings may reflect the children's acquisition of the skills involved in reading and writing. Stimulus orientation is not important when a child looks at a toy from different angles, but is crucial in reading and writing for differentiating letters (e.g., the letters b, d, p, and q differ mainly in orientation). In contrast, perspective changes are of little importance whether children are trying to identify objects or letters.

Much evidence indicates that children become progressively better at differentiation. However, perceptual development is likely to involve more than that. Fluent readers perceive the meaning of the sentences they read, and that involves much more than simply differentiating letters from each other.

Does the evidence from Gibson's study suggest that perceptual development is learned or innate?

Evaluation

It appears that children are unexpectedly good at performing a wide range of perceptual tasks. For example, they show good discrimination on the visual preference task, and they exhibit some aspects of depth perception in the visual cliff situation. In addition, they are reasonably good at size and shape constancy.

These abilities improve with experience, as suggested by differentiation theory. However, it is also true that children soon learn to go beyond the actual data presented to their senses and impose their own meaning, as argued by enrichment theory. Research shows that people generate expectations about what they are likely to see and that such expectations are based on past experience.

Slater (1990) summarised the more recent view of an infant's perceptual skills. At birth none of the senses operates at an adult-like level, but they very quickly develop so that an infant is physically capable of adult-like perception. However, the infant's abilities to process the information do not develop as quickly and thus adult-like levels of perceptual ability appear much later. In Slater's (1990, p.262) words:

> *No modality [none of the senses] operates at adult-like levels at birth, but such levels are achieved surprisingly early in infancy, leading to recent conceptualisations of the "competent infant"... early perceptual competence is matched by cognitive incompetence, and much of the reorganisation of perceptual representation is dependent upon the development and construction of cognitive structures that give access to a world of objects, people, language, and events.*

Shaffer (1993) argued that there are three stages of perceptual development during the first year, as shown below.

THREE STAGES OF PERCEPTUAL DEVELOPMENT DURING FIRST YEAR OF LIFE		
Period	**Stage**	**Infants can:**
0–2 months	Stimulus seeking	Discriminate between visual stimuli
2–6 months	Form constructing	Perceive numerous forms and shapes
6–12 months	Form interpretation	Make sense of what they perceive

Most research provides only limited information about the perceptual abilities of infants. The habituation and physiological methods tell us which stimuli can be discriminated by infants, and the preference and visual reinforcement methods also tell us which stimuli are preferred by infants. However, these methods generally do not tell us in detail how the stimuli are perceived and interpreted. The eye-movement and behaviour methods sometimes provide more information about the significance of stimuli for infants, but leave many questions unanswered. For example, infants of 8 months will not crawl over the deep side of the visual cliff, and their heart rate goes up when they are placed on the deep side. These findings indicate clearly that infants find *something* disturbing about the visual cliff, but do not show that they perceive depth like adults.

What is the role of maturation in the development of perceptual processes?

Nature or Nurture?

Studies of human neonates suggest that many perceptual abilities are innate. Gestalt psychologists (see page 289) also believed that the organisation of the perceptual system was innate. If this view is correct, and abilities such as depth perception are inborn, then we should find that all people develop the same abilities regardless of their different personal experiences.

Distortion studies

In the late nineteenth century G.M. Stratton (1896) tested out the effects of wearing a lens on one eye that turned the world upside down (he kept his other eye covered). At first everything looked unreal, but within 5 days he reported that he could walk around with relative ease and write. He took the lens off after 8 days and found that the world he saw "was immediately recognised as the old one of pre-experimental days" yet the fact that everything was now a reversal of what he had grown accustomed to gave it a "bewildering air".

What does this mean in terms of an innate perceptual system? If the system is fixed, it should not be possible for any adaptation to take place. Therefore there is clearly some capacity for learning, but it is possible that all that is being learned is new sensori-motor links. The fact that Stratton found his perception fairly intact after 8 days suggests that it really had not changed. Hess (1956) placed prism lenses on chickens so things appeared 10 degrees to one side of where they actually were. The chickens never learned to adjust their sight so that they could peck in the right place. This suggests that the perceptual systems of other animals may be less flexible than our own.

Is it possible that perceptual systems are different in different animals?

Readjustment studies

Another approach to the study of whether perception is innate or learned has been to consider adults who have regained their sight after a lifetime of blindness. If perception is an innate ability we would expect them to be capable of depth perception and other features of an organised perceptual system. Gregory and Wallace (1963) documented the case history of SB, described in the Case Study below.

CASE STUDY: *SB—Recovery From Blindness*

Some people are born blind because they have cataracts. This means that the lenses of their eyes are not clear but opaque, not letting any light through. In the 1950s it became possible to replace the lens of the eye. This gave a number of people the chance to see for the first time in their lives. SB was a well-known example of this. He was a man of 52 who had longed to see all his life, though his blindness had never especially hindered him and he had always been very active. His progress, and ultimately sad end, were recorded by Gregory and Wallace (1963). When the bandages were first removed he saw a confusion of colours in front of him but knew by the voice that this was his surgeon's face. Within a few days he began to make sense of his visual sensations.

One day he looked out of his fourth-floor hospital window and was curious about the small objects below. He tried to crawl out of the window to touch them, demonstrating a lack of depth perception. He could not see depth in three-dimensional drawings, nor was he disturbed by visual illusions. He continued to touch things to help himself "see", as

he had done when blind. Then he could match his internal concept of the object with his new perceptions. For example, when he was first shown a lathe he shut his eyes and explored it with his hands. Then he opened his eyes and said, "Now that I've felt it I can see it."

This raises questions about what we "see". We assume that our visual images are photographs of the real world. It seems that, in fact, the light patterns recorded by the eye must be organised by the brain before they make sense. It is possible that this is an innate ability that degenerates when not used (consider Blakemore's study of kittens, described later). Or it may be a consequence of experience (learning).

SB's story ends sadly. He never really mastered sight, preferring to use the senses he had become accustomed to and only pretending to "see". He often sat in darkness in the evenings, choosing not to turn on the light. He became very depressed and died 3 years after he gained his sight. "He found disappointment with what he took to be reality" (Gregory & Wallace, 1963, p.114).

Do you feel that ethical issues are involved in the study of "damaged" individuals?

Von Senden (1932) gave a summary of 66 such cases, and reported that initially patients were confused by an array of disordered visual stimuli and found depth judgements particularly difficult. They could distinguish figures against a background and could fixate on the figures and follow them. This suggests that some features of the perceptual system are innate and others are learned. However, there were methodological problems in von Senden's study, including poor motivation on the part of the participants.

Evaluation

Such studies have the advantage of using adults rather than infants. Adults make better research participants because they can provide verbal reports of what they see. The limitation of these data is that it is possible the patients may have undergone physical and psychological trauma when their eyesight was restored. They are also likely to have learned to rely on other senses and may in fact still be using these to aid what appears to be "seeing", for example using touch to assist their perception. Finally, studies of non-human animals who have had no vision from birth (described next) indicate that innate abilities may simply degenerate through lack of use. This could explain why patients with restored vision are unable to regain normal visual perception.

In summary, studies of adults who have regained their sight offer us very little useful evidence.

Deprived environments

What happens if you deliberately restrict an individual's early visual experiences? If perceptual abilities are innate then this early deprivation should not affect subsequent perception. The readjustment studies just described suggest that this may not be true.

Riesen (1950) raised chimpanzees in total darkness until the age of 16 months. When they were allowed to see for the first time, they couldn't distinguish simple patterns. Wiesel (1982) sewed one eye of a kitten shut. If this is done early enough and for long enough the eye becomes blind. These studies suggest that experience is necessary to maintain the innate system, though such total sensory deprivation is likely to have major emotional effects and this might account for the abnormal behaviour later.

Restricted vision

Blakemore and Cooper (1970) conducted a classic study to observe the specific effects that visual experience has on the type of perception that is developed. Kittens were kept in the dark until their eyes opened (they are born with their eyes shut). They were then placed in a drum that had only vertical or only horizontal lines (see illustration on the left). They had a cuff around their neck so that they could see no lines of any other orientation. They did not seem upset by this routine, and sat for long hours inspecting the walls of the tube.

The experimental set-up for Blakemore and Cooper's (1970) studies on visual development in kittens.

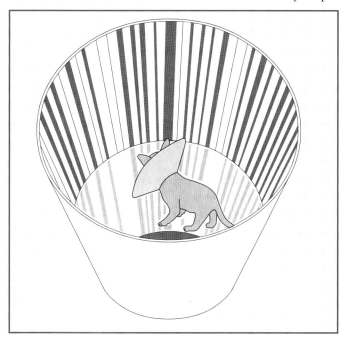

After 5 months the kittens were placed in a normal environment. At first they were clumsy, like any young kitten, but within a short while they were behaving normally except that they were virtually blind for the contours perpendicular to those they had experienced. For example, the vertically experienced kittens only responded to things like table legs (vertical) but tripped over ropes stretched in front of them (horizontal). By anaesthetising the kittens Blakemore and Cooper were able to test the activity of cells in the visual cortex while exposing the eye to horizontal and vertical lines. Blakemore and Cooper found no cells in the deprived kittens' brains that responded to the orientation they had not experienced (research into the visual cortex has demonstrated the existence of cells that are sensitive to lines of particular orientations, see page 258). This suggests that the ability to perceive other line orientations had been lost due to adjustments made in the visual cortex during the critical period. Clearly this could also explain the behaviour of cataract patients.

A study of human response to deprived vision used a naturally-occurring variable—squint eyesight. Banks et al. (1975) studied children born with squint eyesight, a condition where the two eyes do not co-ordinate properly. The effect of this is that the input from the eyes (binocular vision) doesn't match, which limits visual precision. The defect can be corrected with an operation. However Banks et al. found that, if this wasn't done before the age of 4, such children suffered permanently impaired binocular vision. In other words, after a critical age their visual system was no longer capable of change.

Evaluation

Evidence from studies of non-human animals must be treated with caution because it is possible that their perceptual systems are less affected by experience than human perceptual systems, as Hess' study of readjustment in chickens would suggest. However, there is support for the data from naturalistic studies of human behaviour (the cataract patients and children born with squint eyesight). The evidence indicates that it is impossible to separate nature and nurture. The innate components of the perceptual system require experience to maintain them. We are born with a predisposition to adapt to experience.

Cross-cultural or cross-national studies

A final way to consider the nature–nurture question with respect to perception, is to reflect on cultural variation. Given the conclusion from studies of deprivation that experience modifies innate abilities, is this supported by comparisons made between people who have had different visual experiences early in life due to their cultural variations?

Field dependence and field independence

Individuals who are field dependent are more influenced by *external* factors, whereas field-independent people are more influenced by *internal* factors. One way of assessing **field dependence** is by using the tilted room test, in which the room and the chair in which the participant is sitting are moved in different directions. The participant's task is to adjust the chair back into the upright position. Field-dependent people take more account of the tilted room than do field-independent people. Thus their perception is more influenced by background or contextual factors.

Witkin and Berry (1975) extended research on field dependence to include cross-cultural variations in perception. They distinguished between two types of society:

1. Farming/pastoral societies, in which members of the group remain in the same place, tending flocks and/or raising crops.
2. Hunter/gatherer societies, in which small groups move about in search of food.

It could be argued that the clear, undistorted perception of the world associated with field independence is more important in hunter/gatherer societies, whereas those in farming/pastoral societies tend to be field dependent. This would suggest that experience has an effect on the visual system.

There is a tendency, in psychology, to confuse "culture" with "country". A cultural group shares a set of beliefs, values, and practices. Within any one country there are many cultural groups. Many so-called cross-cultural studies in psychology actually involve comparisons between different national groups.

Use of visual illusions

Much of the evidence on cross-cultural variations in perception is based on various visual illusions. We have already referred to the argument by Segall et al. (1963) that the Müller–Lyer illusion would only be perceived by those with experience of a "carpentered environment" containing numerous rectangles, straight lines, and regular corners. People in Western societies live in a carpentered environment, but Zulus living in rural communities do not. Rural Zulus did not show the Müller–Lyer illusion. However, this finding might simply mean that rural Zulus cannot interpret two-dimensional drawings.

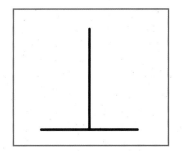

The horizontal–vertical illusion makes it look as if the vertical line is longer than the horizontal line, when in fact they are exactly the same length.

This is unlikely in view of another of Segall et al.'s findings. They studied the horizontal–vertical illusion, which involves overestimating vertical extents relative to horizontal ones in a two-dimensional drawing. Rural Zulus showed the horizontal–vertical illusion to a greater extent than Europeans, presumably because of their greater familiarity with large open spaces.

More evidence of cross-cultural differences was reported by Annis and Frost (1973) in a study on Canadian Cree Indians. Some of them lived in tepees out in the countryside, and some of them lived in cities. Annis and Frost argued that those who lived in cities would be exposed mainly to vertical and horizontal lines in their everyday lives (the "carpentered environment"), whereas those living in tepees would come across lines in all orientations. Both groups were asked to decide whether two lines were parallel. Cree Indians living in tepees were good at this task no matter what angle the lines were presented at. In contrast, those living in cities did much better when the lines were horizontal or vertical than when they were at an angle. These findings suggest the importance of relevant experience to visual perception, and are further supported by a study by Allport and Pettigrew (1957) who made use of an illusion based on a nearly rectangular or trapezoidal "window" fitted with horizontal and vertical bars. When this "window" revolves in a circle, it looks like a rectangular window moving backwards and forwards. People living in cultures without rectangular windows tended not to experience the illusion. Zulus living in rural areas were less likely than Europeans or Zulus living in urban areas to see a rectangle moving backwards and forwards. This study supports the notion that environmental experiences predispose individuals to certain perceptions.

Other researchers have produced different findings. Gregor and McPherson (1965) compared two groups of Australian Aborigines. One group lived in a carpentered environment, but the other group lived in the open air and had very basic housing. The two groups did not differ on either the Müller–Lyer or the horizontal–vertical illusion. Cross-cultural differences in visual illusions may depend more on training and education than on whether or not a given group lives in a carpentered environment.

Interpretation of depth cues

Additional evidence of cross-cultural differences in perception was reported by Turnbull (1961). His subject was a pygmy who lived in dense forests, and so had limited experience of looking at distant objects. This pygmy was taken to an open plain, and shown a herd of buffalo a long way away. He stated that the buffalo were insects, and refused to believe that they really were large animals. Presumably he had never learned to use some of the depth cues described earlier in the way that people in other cultures do. However, this study is limited because only one person was studied, and it is not clear whether he had seen buffalo before.

Use of drawings

Most adults in Western societies are able to interpret two-dimensional drawings and pictures as showing three-dimensional scenes. However, black children and adults in South Africa with little previous experience of such drawings find it very hard to

The eye of the beholder? Are the animals in this picture large animals against a distant background, or small animals close up?

perceive depth in them (Hudson, 1960). There are problems with such cross-cultural research. Deregowski, Muldrow, and Muldrow (1972) found that members of the Me'en in Ethiopia did not respond to drawings of animals on paper, which was an unfamiliar material for them. This might suggest that they had poor ability to make sense of two-dimensional representations. However, when the Me'en were shown animals drawn on cloth (a material familiar to them), they were generally able to recognise them.

Evaluation of cross-cultural research

There are three major limitations with the research in this area. First, it is often hard to interpret the findings. For example, cross-cultural differences in perception could be due to various factors because the experiences of people living in different cultures differ in numerous ways. In future, groups not showing a visual illusion (e.g., the Müller–Lyer) could be studied to find out what kinds of learning experiences they need to show the illusion. The fact that even pigeons show the Müller–Lyer illusion (Malott et al., 1967) suggests we should be careful about assuming that cultural factors are of major importance in determining how the illusion is seen.

Do cultural variations in perception support the view that we process information in a top-down or a bottom-up way?

Second, most studies are limited because they rely on self-report measures. For example, individuals high in trait anxiety may exaggerate how anxious their own behaviour is because of low self-esteem rather than because that is what they actually perceive. Some apparent cross-cultural differences in perception may occur because of cultural differences in the ability to report perceptual experiences in an accurate way. Other cross-cultural differences may depend on differences across languages rather than on actual differences in perception.

Third, much cross-cultural research has focused on two-dimensional visual illusions, and such limited research may tell us little about cultural differences in everyday perception. It is probable that there are large cultural differences in the significance attached to various visual stimuli. For example, members of many African cultures can make much more sense of complex patterns of footprints than can members of Western societies.

Hudson (1960) showed line drawings of three-dimensional scenes to Africans. If they were able to use the three-dimensional depth cues in the picture they would say that the hunter was trying to spear the antelope. However, they tended to say the hunter was trying to spear the elephant. The lack of ability to make sense of Western drawing styles may be due to other things, such as the medium on which the drawing was presented.

Nature and nurture

We have already seen that the question cannot be "nature *or* nurture". Current understanding of the development of the nervous system supports the view that experience is necessary for neurophysiological systems to grow. The brain requires input in order to mature. It is nature *and* nurture. However, given that the two are involved, it is also the case that each individual's particular experiences will influence his or her perceptual tendencies, as illustrated by the research on cultural variation. It would make evolutionary sense for an individual to adapt to the requirements of his or her own environment.

A key reason why the indirect (nurture) and direct (nature) theories differ so much is because the theorists concerned have been pursuing very different goals. Consider the distinction between perception for recognition (in which objects are recognised and identified) and perception for action (in which the precise location of visual stimuli is determined). This distinction, which was proposed by Milner and Goodale (1995, 1998), is supported by evidence from cognitive neuroscience. When visual information is processed in the brain, perception for recognition and perception for action are handled by different "streams", one called the ventral stream and the other called the dorsal stream. Most perception theorists (including Gregory, Marr, and Biederman) have focused on perception for recognition, whereas Gibson emphasised perception for action.

What is ethnocentrism? Why does ethnocentrism lead to limitations in the interpretations of cross-cultural studies?

SECTION SUMMARY

The Visual System

❖ The visual system is of enormous importance in our lives. The lens of the eye focuses light on the retina by the process of accommodation. The retina consists of: photoreceptors, horizontal cells, bipolar cells, amacrine cells, and retinal ganglion cells. There are two kinds of photoreceptors: cones for detailed colour vision and rods for movement and low-level vision. Each bipolar cell receives input from several photoreceptors, and each photoreceptor is connected to more than one bipolar cell.

❖ One optic nerve from each eye carries neurons to the visual cortex. These neurons cross over at the optic chiasma so that the right visual cortex receives input from the right visual field of both eyes and vice versa. The neurons then pass through the lateral geniculate nucleus. There are two independent channels within this system: the parvocellular pathway for colour and fine detail, and the magnocellular pathway for movement.

❖ Perception starts at the retina where data are summarised by bipolar and ganglion cells. Contrast processing is achieved through lateral inhibition. Excitation in one photoreceptor inhibits adjoining cells. This can be seen in the dark diamonds illusion. Sensory (dark–light) adaptation is important in order to maximise perception in light and dark conditions. When dark conditions are first encountered there is less intact rhodopsin available for response to the limited photons, but when this recovers the eye responds more sensitively to fewer photons.

❖ Colour vision offers better detection and discrimination. The Young–Helmholtz theory suggests that there are three types of cones: those that are mainly blue, green, and red sensitive respectively. Different colours activate different combinations of cones. The theory is supported by microspectrophotometry (an analysis of wavelengths) but colour blindness and negative afterimages cannot be explained.

❖ According to opponent-process theory, there are three opponent processes. One process produces green at one extreme and red at the other, the two other opponent processes are blue–yellow, and black–white. Signals from the three types of cone receptors activate these processes. This theory can explain negative afterimages and colour blindness. The most common type of colour blindness affects the perception of red and green, both of which involve the same opponent process.

❖ The Young–Helmholtz and opponent-process theories can be combined: the blue, green, and red cones send signals to the opponent cells. Retinex theory explains that colour vision is achieved by comparing the ability of a surface to reflect short, medium, and long wavelengths against that of adjacent surfaces. This explains why colour constancy breaks down when there are no contrasts.

Perceptual Organisation

❖ Visual processing combines bottom-up with top-down processing.

❖ In his theory of direct perception (bottom-up processing); Gibson emphasised that the visual environment provides much more information than some theorists suggest. There is no need for top-down processing because the optic array is rich in data. Optic flow patterns provide unambiguous information about direction, speed, and altitude. As one moves around the environment, data are produced as some object relationships change while some aspects of the optic array remain the same or invariant, such as the horizon ratio relation and texture gradients. Gibson argued that we detect invariant information from the environment in the same way that a radio receives electromagnetic radiation—this process of resonance is automatic and effortless. He also argued that the potential uses of an object (called affordances) are directly perceivable. Affordance is in the eye of the beholder.

❖ Gibson recognised the importance of movement in perception and that artificial situations create a false picture of real-life perception. However, he underestimated the complexity of the processes underlying visual perception. Gibson's theory explains "seeing" but not "seeing as", and cannot account for the role of memory in perception.

❖ Constructivist theories emphasise (1) the active nature of perception, (2) the use of incomplete sensory information as the basis for making informed guesses, and (3) the likelihood of occasional error. Gregory proposed that perception is the process of forming hypotheses about the visual environment. Research demonstrates how expectations and motivational (top-down) factors can influence our perceptions.

❖ Gregory also suggested that top-down processes and misapplied size-constancy theory can explain visual illusions (e.g., Müller–Lyer). Depth cues make them appear to be three-dimensional. This theory is ingenious but fails to explain why the illusions persist when depth cues are removed. An alternative to this (incorrect comparison theory) proposes that perception is influenced by other features of the display, such as overall length. When three-dimensional cues are provided, the Müller–Lyer illusion persists though it shouldn't. Cross-cultural evidence, on the other hand, may support the possible role of depth cues.

❖ Constructivist theory is correct in identifying a role for expectations in perceptual processes. However, this view overemphasises the incomplete nature of sensory data and the inaccuracy of perception. Research is based on artificial, briefly presented stimuli that reduce the impact of bottom-up processes. If perception is a "best guess", why is it so difficult to change one's hypothesis when given better information?

❖ Neisser's cyclic theory combines bottom-up and top-down processes. Schemas (top-down) direct one's attention, data are sampled (bottom-up), and schemas may be altered. Research evidence supports the role of schemas in facilitating perceptual processes. Marr's theory suggests the complexities involved in processing.

❖ The topic of perceptual organisation is concerned with how we organise sensory data into meaningful patterns. The Gestaltists emphasised perceptual segregation and the law of Prägnanz. Further laws (e.g., those relating to proximity, similarity, good continuation, and closure) all illustrate the law of Prägnanz. The Gestaltists assumed that the whole is more than the sum of its parts, and some evidence supports this assumption. Gestaltists argued that these organisational processes are innate. Recent research has looked at how conflicts are resolved. However, this may not apply to all perceptual organisation. In addition these laws are descriptions rather than explanations, and may only apply to simple, two-dimensional stimuli.

❖ The perception of movement can be explained in terms of the principle of apparent movement (e.g., a moving picture), and the law of common fate (moving dots make sense). A key problem is distinguishing movement of an object from movement of our eyes and/or head—both produce the same retinal image. Data from eye movements (corollary discharge theory) inform the visual system that the eyes have moved and we combine this with analysis of how much of the retinal image has changed. If the whole image is changing, then eye/head movements are involved.

❖ Depth (space) perception depends on various monocular cues such as pictorial cues, linear perspective, aerial perspective, texture, interposition, shading, familiar size, and motion parallax. It also depends on binocular cues: convergence, accommodation, and, most importantly, stereopsis. Information from these depth cues is normally combined in an additive way, but occasionally information from one cue is ignored.

❖ Visual constancy describes the fact that we see things as the same, despite often differing retinal images. Size constancy uses information about depth (distance) and knowledge of familiar size, expressed as the size–distance invariance hypothesis. Shape constancy develops early in life. Colour constancy ensures that we make adjustments for different lighting conditions. Retinex theory proposes that this is done by making colour comparisons between adjacent surfaces.

❖ Visual illusions illustrate normal perceptual organisation by using abnormal conditions. Such illusions can be classified as ambiguous figures (e.g., the "ratman"), paradoxical figures (e.g., the Penrose triangle), fictitious figures (e.g., Kanizsa square) and distortions (e.g., Müller–Lyer illusion). Different illusions can be explained by different theories, such as misapplied size-constancy theory, "good figure" theory, physiological confusion theory, incorrect comparison theory, and the effects of action. An understanding of illusions can be put to practical use, such as in the use of optical brakes on the road.

Perceptual Development

❖ What are the perceptual capabilities of a neonate? There are various methods available for studying perceptual development, including the behavioural, preference, habituation, eye-movement, physiological, and visual reinforcement methods.

❖ Visual preference studies demonstrate that infants show an early preference for the human face over other stimuli, even when features such as complexity and symmetricality are controlled for.

❖ Depth perception in infants was investigated using the visual cliff, which indicated that some animals have depth perception from birth. In humans this may only appear after 6 months, though heart rate measures indicate some awareness of depth even earlier. Ability to perceive depth was demonstrated more convincingly in studies where retinal image size was kept constant. Infants also show some ability to display size and shape constancy. This may be the result of experience or related to innate abilities that mature after birth.

❖ Perceptual development can be explained in terms of enrichment theory, derived from Piaget's theory of sensori-motor development (part of his theory of cognitive development). Piaget argued that schemas generate expectations and these enrich the sensory input. Motor activity is seen as important in the development of schemas, but research studies are not wholly supportive.

❖ The alternative view, differentiation theory, is related to the direct theory of perception. This view suggests that newborns can register all the information that an adult can, but they are simply unable to handle it. Research evidence supports the idea that children do learn to differentiate between visual stimuli (i.e., handle more data with experience).

❖ A synthesis of both theories produces the view that perceptual development is a combination of differentiation and enrichment. The development of perceptual abilities follows a predictable pattern from stimulus seeking to form constructing through to form interpretation. Each of the different methods of conducting research with infants provides us with a different kind of information.

❖ The nature–nurture debate in relation to perception seeks to discover further evidence relating to the extent to which perceptual abilities are innate. Distortion studies indicate that in humans the perceptual system can adapt to changing circumstances, though it may be simply changes in sensori-motor relations that take place. Studies of adults who have regained their sight suggest that some abilities may be innate but even these may degenerate when not used. One difficulty with this evidence is that such adults may have learned alternative perceptual strategies and their behaviour may not be representative. Deprivation studies with non-human animals have found that early sensory deprivation permanently damages perception, though this may equally be due to the psychological effects of sensory deprivation. Studies where cats have experienced a restricted early environment show that related perceptual abilities are lost and that the corresponding areas of the visual cortex do degenerate. A study of children born with squint eyesight confirms that physiological capacity may be affected in the same way in humans. The conclusion is that it is not possible to separate nature and nurture—we are born with a predisposition (nature) to adapt to experience (nurture).

❖ Cultural variation is another way to explore the effects of experience on perceptual development. It may be that the farming way of life promotes field dependence and that the reverse is true of hunter/gatherers. Visual illusions have been used as a way of determining the effects of experience. Some research has found that native Africans are not always able to perceive Western illusions, and in other cases that they are more susceptible to some illusions. Both kinds of evidence generally support the view that perceptual abilities are due to experience, though not all studies concur. The ability to interpret depth cues and two-dimensional pictures may also be related to experience, though equally the findings may be related to problems with cross-cultural research. These problems include difficulties in interpreting cultural differences, and too much reliance on two-dimensional figures and on self-report measures of perception.

❖ It is nature *and* nurture. The brain requires experience in order to develop, but each individual's perceptual abilities are related to experience, which is an adaptive behaviour. There is neuropsychological support for a difference between indirect (nurture) and direct (nature) theories in terms of different processing "streams" that handle recognition and action. Indirect processing concerns recognition and direct processing concerns action.

FURTHER READING

The topics in this Section are covered in greater depth by P. Rookes and J. Willson (2000) *Perception* (London: Routledge), written specifically for the AQA A specification. V. Bruce, P.R. Green, and M.A. Georgeson (1996) *Visual perception: Physiology, psychology, and ecology (3rd Edn.)* (Hove, UK: Psychology Press) covers most of the topics in this Section in detail; in particular they give a very good account of Gibson's approach to perception. R. Sekuler and R. Blake (1994) *Perception (3rd Edn.)* (New York: McGraw-Hill) has good accounts of many topics in visual perception. There is also the classic introduction to the basic phenomena of visual perception by R.L. Gregory (1997) *Eye and brain: The psychology of seeing (5th Edn.)* (Oxford: Oxford University Press).

Example Examination Questions

You should spend 30 minutes on each of the questions below, which aim to test the material in this Section.

1. (a) Describe the structure of the visual system. (12 marks)
   (b) Assess the contribution of the visual system to the process of perception. (12 marks)

2. Discuss the nature of visual information processing (e.g., the processing of contrast, colour, and features). (24 marks)

3. Critically consider **two or more** theories of visual perception. (24 marks)

4. (a) Outline **one** direct theory of visual perception. (12 marks)
   (b) Assess this theory in terms of the extent to which it can explain perceptual organisation. (12 marks)

5. (a) Describe and evaluate **one** study of the development of perceptual abilities. (12 marks)
   (b) Describe and evaluate **one** explanation of perceptual development. (12 marks)

6. Discuss the nature–nurture debate as it applies to perceptual development. (24 marks)

Examination Tips

Question 1.   Part (a) is likely to involve some use of diagrams (a picture is worth a thousand words) but don't just use diagrams—because, on their own, they communicate knowledge but not understanding. In part (b) you should assess the extent to which we can explain perception solely in terms of the visual system. Take care to present an argument rather than simply further description of how perception is achieved. Ideally your argument might be a view of both sides: there are aspects of perception which can be explained in terms of the eye and the visual cortex, but there are other aspects of perception that are top-down, such as the influence of expectations. You can and should refer to research studies to support your arguments.

Question 2.   "Discuss" is an AO1 and AO2 term, therefore you should describe the physiological details of visual information processing—some ideas are provided in the question, such as the processing of contrast (lateral inhibition) and colour processing, but these are examples and not compulsory. The AO2 element of the question is less straightforward. Evaluation can be achieved through the use of alternative explanations, such as retinex theory, or consideration of the adaptive value of such processing systems, or the use of such explanations for understanding visual illusions. You might even consider the value of such knowledge for practical purposes.

Question 3.   "Critically consider" requires that you describe and evaluate theories in terms of their strengths and weaknesses. In order to do this effectively in 30 minutes you will only have time to outline the theories and it is probably best to only consider the two most obvious ones—Gibson's direct perception and Gregory's constructivist theory. As "theories" is in the plural you must include more than one. However, if you choose to describe more than two there is a depth–breadth trade-off (you end up with breadth but are likely to sacrifice depth). You might achieve evaluation by considering the relative strengths and weaknesses of the theories, such as their ability to explain real-life phenomena.

Question 4.   This is a more specific question on the same topic area as question 3. This time you are required to describe only one theory and therefore should give considerably more detail. Note that the type of theory is specified, i.e., direct. This is a legitimate request as types of theory are named in the specification. Other theories may be used in part (b) as a means of assessing the extent to which the first theory can explain perceptual organisation (organisation refers to the perception of depth, movement, constancies and so on) but you will probably have sufficient material for evaluation without this. Remember, in part (b) that description is not required but instead you are presenting an argument about whether your first theory can explain perceptual organisation. The trick here is to use your knowledge effectively in order to construct an argument in answer to the question, rather than just describing evidence.

Question 5.   Both parts of this question are AO1 and AO2. In part (a) there are 6 marks for the description of one study (aims, procedures, findings and conclusions) plus a further 6 marks for evaluation of this study, which might be positive (e.g., confirmation of findings of another study) or negative (e.g., poor methodology or ethical objections). In part (b) you are again required to describe and evaluate, this time an explanation of development. This might be a theory (e.g., differentiation theory) or it might be a more general explanation of how innate factors lead to changes in the perceptual system as it matures. Evaluation could be in terms of contrasting theories/explanations or reference to research studies.

Question 6.   A straightforward question that will require some selectivity to compose a well-structured and well-detailed response in 30 minutes. A balanced answer is desirable, i.e., one that considers both sides of the debate. Commentary should be informed in terms of research (studies and/or theories).

WEB SITES

www.brisray.co.uk/optill/oind.htm
  Many examples of visual illusions.

http://dragon.uml.edu/psych/illusion.html
  Dozens more illusions.

www.skidmore.edu/~hfoley/resources.htm#Visual
  Links about visual perception, illusions, and face recognition.

http://cvs.anu.edu.au/andy/beye/beyehome.html
  See the world as if you were a bee!

http://www.illusionworks.com/
  Comprehensive collection of optical and sensory illusions.

www.a-levelpsychology.co.uk/websites.html
  A continually updated list of useful links, may be found at the Psychology Press
  A level psychology site.

9

Language and Thought

Without language, we would be unable to carry on with our everyday lives. Most of our social interactions with other people rely very heavily on language, and equally much of our knowledge comes from information passed to us in the form of language. According to Sternberg (1995), language can be defined as "an organised means of combining words in order to communicate".

Language and Culture

The word "culture" refers to a set of rules, morals, and methods of interaction shared by one group of people (note that it is the rules etc. and not the group that are the "culture"). These rules and so on are partly learned through language. In this Unit we will explore the relationship between language and the way we behave.

Language and Thought

George Orwell's classic science fiction book *Nineteen Eighty-four* predicted a world where thoughts would be controlled by the state. Orwell wrote, in an appendix to this book, that by the year 2050 the ultimate technology for thought control would be in place—the language he called "Newspeak":

> *The purpose of Newspeak was not only to provide a medium for the expression of the world-view and mental habits proper to the devotees of Ingsoc, but to make other modes of thought impossible. It was intended that when Newspeak had been adopted once and for all and Oldspeak forgotten, a heretical thought—that is one diverging from the principles of Ingsoc—should be literally unthinkable, at least so far as thought is dependent on words.*

Is thought dependent on words?

Watson's approach

One of the earliest attempts to provide a theoretical account of the relationship between language and thought was made by the behaviourists. John Watson, the founder of behaviourism, argued that thinking was nothing more than inner speech. It may be true

John Watson, the American psychologist and founder of behaviourism.

For the interest of Trekkies, Benjamin Whorf was a human and not a Klingon.

that most people sometimes engage in inner speech when thinking about difficult problems, but that is a far cry from Watson's dogmatic position.

The ludicrous nature of Watson's theory was revealed in a witty comment made by the philosopher Herbert Feigl. According to him, Watson "made up his windpipe that he had no mind". Evidence destroying Watson's theory was provided by Smith et al. (1947). Dr Smith showed great bravery by allowing himself to be given a curare derivative (curare was the poison used by American Indians on their arrowheads). This paralysed his entire musculature, so that an artificial respirator had to be used to keep him alive. Because the curare totally prevented any sub-vocal speech, it should also have prevented him from thinking. In fact, he reported that he had been able to think about what was going on around him while paralysed.

The Whorfian hypothesis

An influential theory on the relationship between thought and language was put forward by Benjamin Lee Whorf (1956). He was a fire prevention officer for an insurance company, but spent his spare time working in linguistics. Whorf was much influenced by the obvious differences among the world's languages. For example, Arabic has numerous words describing camels and their disgusting habits, and the Inuit Eskimos have various words to describe snow. In the Thai language, verbs do not have tenses as they do in English. As a result, Thai people often find it hard to use verbs correctly in English to refer to the past or to the future.

Whorf was impressed by these differences among languages. According to his "linguistic relativity hypothesis", language determines (or has a major influence on) thinking. In the words of Whorf (1956, pp.212–213), the linguistic system is

> not merely a reproducing instrument for viewing ideas but rather is itself the shaper of ideas, the program and guide for the individual's mental activity … We dissect nature along lines laid down by our native language.

Whorf also commented on the effect of different languages:

> Formulation of ideas is not an independent process … but is part of a particular grammar [used by an individual] and differs, from slightly to greatly, as between different grammars.

In other words, the language that one person speaks is different to a lesser or greater extent from the language used by others, and these differences can be related to different ways of thinking.

Three hypotheses

It is hard to test the Whorfian hypothesis as it stands. Some clarification of the theoretical issues involved was offered by Miller and McNeill (1969). They argued that there are *three* different hypotheses concerning the effects of language on psychological processes.

- The *strong hypothesis* (the one put forward by Whorf) claims that language determines thinking.
- The *weak hypothesis* states that language affects perception.
- Finally, the *weakest hypothesis* makes the more modest claim that language influences memory, with information that is easily described in a given language being remembered best. Of these three hypotheses, the weakest hypothesis has been tested most often.

Why is it a weaker influence if language affects perception other than thinking? Is perception, or memory, a form of thinking?

The strong hypothesis.　One of the few attempts to test the strong hypothesis was reported by Carroll and Casagrande (1958). They studied Navaho children who spoke only Navaho, Navaho children who spoke Navaho and English, and American children who spoke only English and whose families were of European descent. The importance of form or shape is emphasised more in the Navaho language. For example, Navaho verbs to do with picking up or touching objects differ depending on the shape of the object being handled. According to the strong hypothesis, children who know the Navaho language should show form recognition before those who do not. This is what was found. The children who spoke only Navaho showed form recognition at the earliest age. However, those who spoke Navaho and English were slower to acquire form recognition than those who spoke only English, which is difficult to explain; why would learning English slow their progress down? It is also possible that these differences may be due to experience as much as language. Thus the findings provided mixed support for the strong hypothesis.

How would experience explain these findings?

Weak hypothesis.   The weak hypothesis states that language affects perception. Apparent support for this was obtained by Lenneberg and Roberts (1956). Zuni speakers, who are North American Indian people who come from West New Mexico, made more mistakes in recognising yellows and oranges than did English speakers. As the Zuni language differs from English in having only a single word to describe yellows and oranges, it could be argued that the limited Zuni language caused the difficulties in making perceptual discriminations.

Basic colour words in English

WHITE	**YELLOW**	**PINK**
RED	**BLUE**	**ORANGE**
GREEN	**BROWN**	**GREY**
BLACK	**PURPLE**	

Later research produced findings less favourable to Whorf's hypothesis. Heider (1972) used as her starting point the fact that English and other languages have the same basic 11 colour words, and for each hue there is a best or focal colour. The importance of these focal colours is shown by the finding that English speakers usually find it easier to remember focal colours (such as fire-engine red) than non-focal ones (such as an off-red). If language affects memory, then different results should be obtained with the Dani. They live in New Guinea, and their language has only two basic colour words: *"mili"* for dark, cold colours, and *"mola"* for bright, warm colours. In spite of this, the Dani people showed better recognition memory for focal than for non-focal colours suggesting that language does affect perception (and memory).

Heider's findings are suspect, because the focal colours she used were more perceptually distinct than the non-focal colours. Lucy and Schweder (1979) eliminated this problem, and found that focal colours were *not* remembered any better than non-focal ones.

Other research suggests that language can affect memory for colours. In a study by Schooler and Engstler-Schooler (1990), participants were shown colour chips that were not focal colours, and were or were not asked to label them. Those asked to label the colours did worse than the non-labellers on recognition memory, suggesting that colour memory was distorted by language in the form of labelling.

Language can also affect perceptual processes. Miyawaki et al. (1975) compared English and Japanese speakers with respect to their perception of sounds varying between a pure /l/ and a pure /r/. English speakers made a sharp perceptual distinction between similar sounds on either side of the categorical boundary between "l" and "r"; this is known as categorical speech perception. No such perceptual distinction was made by Japanese speakers, presumably because there is no distinction between /l/ and /r/ in the Japanese language.

Similar findings were reported by Davies (1998). Speakers of English, Setswana, and Russian sorted 65 colours into between 2 and 12 groups on the basis of perceptual similarity. English has 11 basic colour terms, Setswana has 5, and Russian has 12, and it was thought that these differences might influence performance. However, "The most striking feature of the results was the marked similarity of the groups chosen across the three language samples" (Davies, 1998, p.433). In addition, there were minor influences of language. For example, Setswana has only one word to describe green and blue, and Setswana speakers were more likely than English and Russian speakers to group blue and green colours together.

The weakest hypothesis.   Additional evidence that language can influence perception and memory was obtained by Carmichael, Hogan, and Walters (1932). They showed their participants a series of drawings, and told them that each one resembled some well-known object. For example, the same drawing could be labelled as a crescent moon or the letter "C". The participants' subsequent reproductions from memory were influenced by the verbal labels provided for each object as shown in the box below. This demonstrates that language does affect memory.

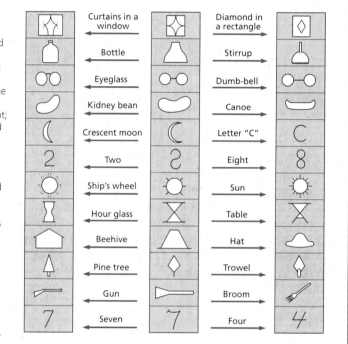

■ Carmichael, Hogan, and Walters (1932)

Carmichael et al.'s study involved two groups of participants who were shown the drawings in the central column here. One group were given the description on the left, and the other group were given the description on the right; for example, one group was told an object was a gun and the other that it was a broom. Later the participants were asked to reproduce the drawings from memory. Their sketches matched the description they were given, not the original drawing, demonstrating that perception is not influenced solely by the stimulus, but is also affected by expectations and knowledge.

Curtains in a window		Diamond in a rectangle
Bottle		Stirrup
Eyeglass		Dumb-bell
Kidney bean		Canoe
Crescent moon		Letter "C"
Two		Eight
Ship's wheel		Sun
Hour glass		Table
Beehive		Hat
Pine tree		Trowel
Gun		Broom
Seven		Four

Evaluation of the Whorfian hypothesis

Whorf's original arguments cannot be accepted. There are various reasons for this. First, he tended to exaggerate the differences among the world's languages. For example, Inuit Eskimos may indeed have various words for snow, but there are several in English as well. Pinker (1994) calls this the "Great Eskimo Vocabulary Hoax", listing the English words: snow, sleet, slush, blizzard, avalanche, hail, hardpack, powder, flurry, dusting, and even snizzling.

Second, there is little evidence that differences between languages have much influence on thought. What is more likely is that the different environmental conditions experienced by different cultures influence what they think about, and this affects the ways in which their language develops. This can be seen in the fact that people who work with horses have a large vocabulary for the different parts of a horse's body and for equipment such as bridles, martingales, and bits. Even if we were taught these words they would do little to affect our thinking. Our thinking would be more affected by working closely with horses, and then experience would dictate the need for different words to reflect the new concepts we had learned.

Third, as Greene (1975) pointed out, it is easy to attach too much significance to the expressions in a given language. For example, users of English talk about the foot of a mountain, but they are well aware that it is very different from a person's foot.

Modified Whorfian hypothesis

Hunt and Agnoli (1991) put forward a modified version of the Whorfian hypothesis. According to Hunt and Agnoli (1991, p.379), "Different languages lend themselves to the transmission of different types of messages." In some languages there may be terms or concepts that make certain logical arguments easier than in another language. This would make it easier to think in that way, but would not preclude a speaker of another language from having the same thought. Thus any given language makes it easy to think in certain ways, but hard to think in other ways. In this sense, language does influence cognition.

Some of the findings we have already discussed are consistent with this modified Whorfian hypothesis. For example, consider Carmichael et al.'s (1932) finding that verbal labels influenced memory. This probably happened because the participants found it easier to rely on those labels when remembering. If it had been essential to remember the drawings accurately, then they might have used more demanding processing strategies.

An example of how language can influence thinking was provided by Hoffman, Lau, and Johnson (1986). Bilingual English-Chinese speakers read descriptions of individuals. These descriptions were deliberately prepared to conform to either Chinese or English stereotypes of personality. For example, there is a stereotype of the artistic type in English, consisting of a mixture of artistic skills, moody and intense temperament, and bohemian lifestyle, but this stereotype does not exist in Chinese. After they had read the descriptions, the participants were asked to provide free impressions of the individuals described. Bilinguals thinking in Chinese made use of Chinese stereotypes in their free impressions, whereas bilinguals thinking in English used English stereotypes. Thus, the inferences we draw can be much influenced by the language in which we are thinking.

Additional evidence that language can influence habits of thought was reported by Ervin-Tripp (1964) in a study on Japanese-American bilinguals. When they were given sentence-completion or word-association tests, their performance resembled that of Japanese-only speakers when they responded in Japanese. However, their answers were like those of English-only speakers when they responded in English.

Evaluation

Hunt and Agnoli (1991) have provided a plausible cognitive account of the Whorfian hypothesis, and there is a fair amount of evidence consistent with it. However, what is lacking is a systematic programme of research to show clearly that language influences thought in the ways specified by Hunt and Agnoli.

In children's education we tend to base our assessment of their understanding of concepts like reversibility on the language the children use, either verbal or written. Can you think of any arguments for and against this that might demonstrate uncertainty about the relationship between language and thought?

The developmental view

Piaget and Vygotsky have contributed the two most influential theories of cognitive development (see Section 10, Cognitive Development). Such theories are concerned with how language and thought develop, as well as all other mental abilities such as memory and perception. We will consider how Piaget and Vygotsky account for the development of language, and the relationship between language and thought in development.

Piaget's view: Thought produces language

According to Piaget, children can only think effectively when they have developed certain cognitive operations and structures. Language is the outcome of a generalised ability to think. For example, suppose that a young child is shown two glasses of the same size and shape containing the same amount of liquid. All the liquid from one of the glasses is then poured into a different glass that is taller and thinner. The child is then asked if the two glasses contain the same amount to drink (this is known as a **conservation task**, see page 366). Children below the age of 7 will often mistakenly argue that there is more liquid in the new, tall glass ("because it's higher") or in the original glass ("because it's wider"). Solving the problem requires the cognitive operation of reversibility, which involves the ability to undo (or reverse) mentally some operation that has been carried out. Older children realise that the liquid in the new glass could be poured back into the original glass, and thus that the two glasses contain the same amount of liquid.

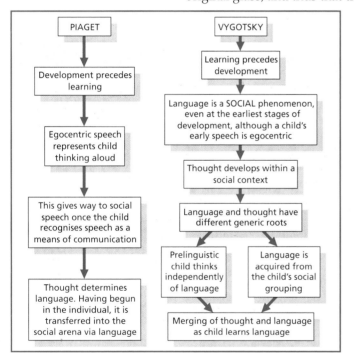

Piaget argued that older children acquire this new mental ability in the course of maturation. This cognitive development, or development of thinking, does not occur as a consequence of language. According to Piaget, thinking influences language development much more than language development influences thinking. Some evidence for this was reported by Sinclair-de-Zwart (1969). She used the two-glass conservation task with children, and asked them to describe the glasses. Sinclair-de-Zwart found that children who could not conserve tended to use absolute rather than comparative terms such as "big" rather than "larger", and used a single term for different dimensions such as "small" to mean "short", "thin", or "few". This suggests important links between language and thought, but which is influenced by which? Sinclair-de-Zwart then tried to teach the nonconservers the verbal skills they were lacking. Only about 10% of those children who were taught the conservation-relevant language showed evidence of conservation thereafter. Thus, language does not benefit thinking very much, and a full understanding of language can only be achieved after the relevant cognitive operations and structures are in place.

Vygotsky's view: Language and thought are separate

According to the Russian Lev Vygotsky, thought and language in the very young child are separate and independent activities. Infants can think before they acquire language, and their early attempts at language often involve repeating what an adult has said without any understanding. Things change when the child reaches the age of 2, when "thought becomes verbal and speech rational" (Vygotsky, 1962).

There are further developments between the ages of 2 and 7. During that time, language develops two rather different uses: (1) it has the *internal* function of being used to monitor and direct internal thoughts; and (2) it has the *external* function of being used to communicate to others what has been thought about internally. Children up to the age of 7 cannot distinguish clearly between these two functions of language. As a result, they produce what is known as **egocentric speech**. According to Vygotsky, egocentric speech serves "mental orientation, conscious understanding; it helps in overcoming difficulties, it is speech for oneself, intimately and usefully connected with the child's thinking. In the end it becomes inner speech".

Crucially, according to Vygotsky, language has the role of embodying culture. When Vygotsky used the concept of "culture" he was referring to the body of knowledge that is held by, for example books and "experts" (persons with greater knowledge), and that is largely transmitted through language. Language and culture are what transform elementary mental functions into higher-order processes. However, Vygotsky did not support the view that language changes the way we think. He suggested that the acquisition of a new word was the *beginning* of the development of a concept rather than the end. In Vygotsky's view, words such as "bigger" do promote changes in conceptual thinking (see the work of Sinclair-de-Zwart, on page 322).

It is less easy to evaluate the significance of Vygotsky's theory than some of the earlier evidence because the predictions are rather vague, though the earlier evidence on linguistic relativity is in accord with Vygotsky's views that language shapes thought. His theory as a whole is assessed in Section 10, Cognitive Development.

Social and Cultural Aspects of Language Use

Sociolinguists claim that language normally functions in a social context, and thus it is important to study it in this context. The concept of linguistic relativity, even in its weakest form, suggests that the language used by any group of people is related to their way of thinking.

One thing to note in this discussion is the interchangeable use of the words "social" and "cultural". In practice it is difficult to distinguish between them. The word "culture" refers to a group of people who share a set of rules, morals, and methods of interaction. "Social" is any behaviour between two or more members of the same species. The rules, morals, and so on of a culture are the products of *socialisation*, that is, we learn them through our social interactions with other members of our culture. Thus "social" and "culture" are interrelated ideas.

Social aspects of language use

When two people speak with one another, there is always more going on than just conveying a message. This is referred to as **paralinguistics**, the study of the subtext in a message. When someone is speaking or even writing, it is not just what they say but how they say it, that provides equally important information. Paralanguage includes all those nonverbal elements such as pauses, pitch, sighs and so on. It also includes "social markers". These are features of a person's speech that permit the listener to classify the speaker in terms of status and group membership. As soon as a person starts to speak most of us can identify their country of origin and perhaps even the region they come from and/or their social class. For example, you can distinguish a Geordie from a Londoner; a country gent from a farmer.

Social markers
The effect of social markers has been examined in studies using the matched-guise technique. Participants are asked to listen to passages that are spoken in different speech

---

Fodor: Specialised language processor

If language processing is separate from thought then we would expect to find a separate cognitive system dedicated to language. This is what Fodor (1983) argued.

If this was true then we would expect that the process of language comprehension would not be influenced by non-linguistic information (e.g., thoughts). As a result, it would be expected that language comprehension should proceed in an entirely bottom-up or stimulus-driven way. In fact, however, top-down processes can affect the processes involved in speech comprehension. For example, Warren and Warren (1970) presented their participants with a recording in which part of a word had been deleted. The participants heard one of the following sentences (the asterisk indicates the deleted portion):

It was found that the *eel was on the axle.
It was found that the *eel was on the shoe.
It was found that the *eel was on the table.
It was found that the *eel was on the orange.

All the participants heard the same speech sound (i.e., "*eel"), but their top-down processes based on the sentence context led them to perceive it differently. Those listening to the first sentence heard "wheel", those listening to the second sentence heard "heel", whereas those exposed to the third and fourth sentences heard "meal" and "peel", respectively.

This appears to show that language and thought are interrelated. However, the fact that brain damage often affects only language processes rather than cognition generally suggests that there are separate processing systems dedicated exclusively to language. Furthermore, as Harris (1990, p.203) pointed out,

Language processing has to be largely independent of other cognitive activities. For, if it were not, we would hear only what we expected to hear and read only what we expected to read.

In what other ways can language be related to social groups?

In the film *My Fair Lady* Professor Henry Higgins aims to teach the cockney flower seller, Eliza Doolittle, to speak "properly" and thus make her into an acceptable member of high society. The speech we use communicates a wealth of information about our social standing.

styles (e.g., accent and dialect altered); the actual content and other paralinguistic cues are kept constant. The listener is asked to rate the speaker in terms of "status variables" (e.g., how able or intelligent the person is) and "solidarity variables" (how likeable the person is). Using this technique Giles and Powesland (1975) found that individuals using **received pronunciation** (RP) English were more favourably evaluated in terms of status and competence than speakers using non-standard English. Examples of non-standard English include urban varieties, such as the accent and dialect used by a person from Newcastle, or minority ethnic groups, such as Hindis in Britain. The reverse is true when looking at the solidarity dimension, For example Hogg et al. (1984) found that Swiss Germans rated speakers of non-standard Swiss German more highly in terms of solidarity than speakers of High German.

What effect does accent have on your perceptions of status and solidarity?

Speech accommodation theory

Speech accommodation theory (Giles, 1984) describes how people modify their speech to suit the context. Two speakers may show convergence in their speech markers when in conversation. High status speakers tend to shift their accent or speech style downwards when speaking to lower status speakers, and low status speakers in turn shift their speech style upwards. Bourhis et al. (1975) suggested that this is a way of communicating interpersonal liking or approval. This bilateral speech convergence may not always occur. In situations where, for example, the low status speaker has a desire for social mobility, there may be unilateral convergence—only the low status speaker adjusts his or her speech style. At the same time there may be unilateral divergence on the part of the high status speaker. This divergence marks the distinctiveness between the two groups, suggesting that it is not likely that the low status speaker will be able to pass into the high status group. Bilateral divergence may also be used to mark disagreement or dislike between two speakers.

When two people are talking they may signal their agreement through convergence of speech styles, whereas they may signal disagreement by divergence. This may be entirely unintentional or, in the case of people who deliberately manage their image, it may be quite intentional.

Research support was obtained by Bourhis and Giles (1977) who observed that Welsh adults accentuated their Welsh accent when speaking with RP English speakers, and Hogg (1985) found that female students shifted their speech style upwards towards that of their male partners.

Diglossia

The term diglossia refers to the existence of two or more varieties or codes that are used within one linguistic culture. Speech accommodation theory describes how we all accommodate our speech markers to suit certain occasions, either consciously or unconsciously. We also change the language we use to suit different occasions. For example, we are all aware that we use one form of speech when speaking with our friends and another form of speech for formal occasions. In some cultures there are quite formal distinctions between a "low" and a "high" style such as in Arabic or Modern Greek. Ferguson (1959) suggested that diglossia was not the same as the distinction made between a standard language and regional dialects. In diglossia the high style (H) is related to the language as used in literature and thus is a more formal version of the language. Diglossia is likely when only a small, elite group in the community are literate.

Differences in the way men and women use language are an interesting form of diglossia, as described in the box on the next page.

Diglossia in Arabic and Modern Greek

In some languages there are two forms of the native language that are used, a high and a low variety. Some examples are given here.

Arabic

High		Low
hiða'un	shoe	*gazma*
'anfun	nose	*manaxir*
ðahaba	went	*rah*
'al'ana	now	*dilwa'ti*

Greek

High		Low
ikos	house	*spiti*
idhor	water	*neró*
éteke	gave birth	*eyénise*
alá	but	*má*

It has been suggested that the use of two different forms may be related to the existence of a literate elite within the society who use the high form.

People adjust what they say to fit the circumstances.

Ethnolinguistic identity theory

Diglossia can be seen on a larger scale, where multilingual nations include a variety of accents, language styles, dialects, and languages. Why do different social groups develop different dialects? Why do people in different countries speak different languages? Why are people so resistant to Esperanto?

You may be able to answer these questions yourself. Have you noticed that you and your friends have some "special" words that have a meaning known only to yourselves? Language is a means of social identity. It is a way of distinguishing "them" and "us".

Giles and Johnson (1981) proposed ethnolinguistic identity theory as a means of explaining this use of language for group identity. We categorise the social world and therefore perceive ourselves as members of various social groups. This is our **social identity**, which may be positive or negative depending on how our ingroup compares with relevant outgroups. Social identity theory suggests that we strive to achieve a positive social identity as a means of increasing personal identity and self-esteem. One of the ways to achieve a positive social identity is through the development of psychological distinctiveness for the group, i.e., a clear demarcation between the

---

Men are from Mars, women are from Venus

A recent, wildly popular book was called *Men are from Mars, women are from Venus*. The author, John Gray, argued that men and women could get along better if they accepted the ways in which they were fundamentally different. In another popular book, *You just don't understand*, Dr Deborah Tannen argued that these male/female differences are related to how men and women use language in a fundamentally different way (Tannen, 1991). She has claimed that men use language to protect their independence and negotiate status, while women use language to seek confirmation and reinforce intimacy. Tannen (1990) notes:

> For women, as for girls, intimacy is the fabric of relationships, and talk is the thread from which it is woven. Little girls create and maintain friendships by exchanging secrets; similarly, women regard conversation as the cornerstone of friendship. So a woman expects her husband to be a new and improved version of a best friend. What is important is not the individual subjects that are discussed but the sense of closeness, of a life shared, that emerges when people tell their thoughts, feelings, and impressions.

> Bonds between boys can be as intense as girls', but they are based less on talking, more on doing things together. Since they don't assume talk is the cement that binds a relationship, men don't know what kind of talk women want, and they don't miss it when it isn't there.

These differences result in inter-sex misunderstanding and communication breakdown. Tannen argues that the differences between masculine and feminine styles of discourse are as great as two different dialects. In fact in some cultures this is true. Bonvillain (1999) gave the following examples from Japanese:

Words used by men		Words used by women
mizu	water	*ohiya*
hara	stomach	*onaka*
umai	delicious	*oisii*
kuu	eat	*taberu*

To what extent do you feel that your accent is important to your sense of social identity? Does your accent or dialect increase the status of your ingroup?

ingroup and outgroups. This where language comes into the picture. If an ingroup regards their language or dialect as a valued dimension of comparison then the group can achieve "psycholinguistic" distinctiveness. Language is an important dimension of group and ethnic (cultural) identity. (The whole topic of social identity theory, and ingroup/outgroup behaviour is discussed at greater length in Section 1, Social Cognition.)

In the case where a social group experiences a negative identity, one strategy may be to redefine the group in various ways such as upgrading their apparently non-standard language or exhuming "dead" languages. We can see this in the way that minority groups take pride in the way they speak, and also in the revitalisation of some languages that were on the verge of disappearance, such as Gaelic and Welsh.

Learning a second language

Some of the issues raised by ethnolinguistic identity theory can be related to the study of learning a second language. Gardner (1979) argues:

> *In the acquisition of a second language, the student is faced with a task of not simply learning new information (vocabulary, grammar, pronunciation, etc) that is part of his own culture but rather acquiring symbolic elements of a different ethnolinguistic community. The new words aren't simply new words for old concepts, the new grammar is not simply a new way of ordering words, and the pronunciations are not simply "different" ways of saying things. These are characteristics of another ethnolinguistic community. Furthermore the student is not being asked to learn about them: he is being asked to acquire them, to make them part of his own language reservoir. This involves imposing elements of another culture into one's own life space.*

Learning a second language is a social process as much as a linguistic one. This is an issue of key importance in multicultural settings. Ball, Giles, and Hewstone (1984) suggest that it is important for members of dominant majority cultures to understand the failures of immigrants to acquire a second language in terms of the complex processes that are involved.

Verbal deprivation theory

Finally we will consider another social aspect of language: the question about whether certain dialects restrict intellectual development. Bernstein (1961) introduced the concept of two different forms of language: an **elaborated** and a **restricted code** (see the Key Study below). The former kind of language allows a user to articulate abstract concepts more easily and, Bernstein suggested, is more likely to be used by middle-class parents and their children, whereas lower-class families are more likely to use a restricted code. Bernstein's **verbal deprivation theory** (a term used by Labov, 1969) was that this language

Elaborated and restricted code

Bernstein (1973) argued that children's use of language is determined in part by the social environment in which they grow up. He distinguished between two language codes or patterns of speech: the restricted code and the elaborated code. The *restricted code* is relatively concrete and descriptive. It is also rather context-dependent, in the sense that it is hard to understand unless one knows the context in which it is being used. In contrast, the *elaborated code* is more complex and abstract, and can easily be understood in the absence of contextual information.

Bernstein (1973, p.203) gave the following examples of the two codes based on descriptions of four pictures showing (1) boys playing football; (2) the ball going through the window of a house; (3) a woman looking out of the window; and (4) the children retreating:

- *Restricted code*: "They're playing football and he kicks it, and it goes through there. It breaks the window and they're looking at it and he comes out and shouts at them because they've broken it. So they run away and then she looks out and she tells them off."
- *Elaborated code*: "Two boys are playing football and one boy kicks the ball and it goes through the window. The ball breaks the window and the boys are looking at it, and a man comes out and shouts at them because they've broken the window. So they run away and then that lady looks out of her window, and she tells the boys off."

Bernstein argued that middle-class children generally use the elaborated code, whereas working-class children use the restricted code. However, many middle-class children can use both codes, whereas many working-class children are limited to the restricted code. The lack of an elaborated code may limit the thinking of working-class children. Teachers in school typically use the elaborated code, and this may disadvantage working-class children.

Evidence that working-class children may have restricted language development was reported by Bernstein (1961). Middle-class and working-class boys who obtained high scores for nonverbal intelligence (e.g., spatial and mathematical ability) were compared on verbal intelligence based on the use of language. The middle-class boys performed equally well on both kinds of intelligence test, whereas the working-class boys obtained lower scores for verbal intelligence. Bernstein argued that the discrepancy between verbal and nonverbal intelligence shown by the working-class boys was due to their reliance on the restricted language code.

Hess and Shipman (1965) studied American mothers and their 4-year-old children. Middle-class mothers used language interactively to discuss issues with their children via questions and answers. In contrast, working-class mothers used language to give orders to their children, and there was less exchange of ideas.

Discussion points

1. How adequate is it to divide language into a restricted code and an elaborated code?
2. What seem to be the main differences between the restricted and elaborated codes?

difference can be used to explain why lower-class children may have limited cognitive development, specifically that their use of a restricted linguistic code limits cognitive development.

If this verbal deprivation theory is correct then it follows that enriched language experience should increase cognitive development in lower-class children. To test this Schwartz et al. (1967) studied two groups of socially disadvantaged primary school children over a period of 2 years. One group received enriched schooling, including work involving their language. The researchers found significant differences on a test of psycholinguistic abilities, supporting the hypothesis that early enrichment helps to offset language disability caused by social disadvantage.

Hart and Risley (1995) also assessed the differences in the language used in different families. They observed 3-year-old children in families categorised as either professional, working class, or on welfare, counting the number of words that were directed towards each child in a week. The difference was enormous—children in professional families had up to 15,000 more words directed towards them in a week than did the children from families on welfare. On the basis of these data, Hart and Risley estimated that the 3-year-olds from professional homes had had 30 million words spoken to them, as opposed to 20 million in the working-class homes and 10 million in the welfare families!

Further support comes from a study by Fowler (1990), which assessed a linguistic enrichment programme designed for parents to use with their very young children. The programme involved language-related games and play. Fowler found that there were significant gains, for example the children used pronouns such as "him" at 18 months, which was 5 months earlier than usual. Of course the question remains about how long these gains might last.

In contrast, the study by Sinclair-de-Zwart (1969), described earlier, suggested that linguistic enrichment may not affect cognitive development (see page 322). Tizard and Hughes (1984) addressed the issue of the explicitness–implicitness of language used by mothers when talking to their daughters. Tizard and Hughes did not find the differences across social classes that would have been expected from Bernstein's theory. Instead, they found that mothers of all social classes were often implicit in talking to their daughters, but became explicit when they felt that it was important to communicate a precise message.

Coul this research be considered to be "socially sensitive"? How might the findings be used?

Evaluation of verbal deprivation theory

There is evidence for the distinction between the elaborated and restricted codes. However, Bernstein's views are oversimplified. There are probably several codes, with the elaborated and restricted codes representing the extremes. At the very least, it is likely that many people use a mixture of the two codes in their everyday speech. Bernstein seems to assume that the elaborated code is superior to the restricted code. In fact, as Harley (1995, p.348) pointed out, "[It] is far from obvious that the working class dialect is impoverished compared to the middle class dialect: it is just different."

Labov's criticisms. Labov (1969) suggested that Bernstein failed to understand the subtleties of non-standard English and therefore his view that lower-class language was restricted was mistaken. In fact, Labov argued, non-standard English is equally capable of representing abstract thought and Bernstein may have simply confused linguistic and social deprivation. Labov (1972) carried out a series of studies into the use of Black English vernacular or dialect by young black people living in the ghetto areas of Harlem, New York. At that time, it was generally argued that the relatively poor school performance of many black children was attributable to their limited command of language. According to Labov, most of the differences between Black English vernacular and standard English are relatively trivial. For example, consider the distinction between the standard English sentence, "He doesn't know anything", and the Black English, "He don't know nothing." The two sentences express the same meaning, and the grammatical complexity of the two sentences is equivalent.

Labov (1972, p.113) pointed out that it can be hard to assess someone's language abilities because of the observer paradox: "To obtain the data most important for linguistic theory, we have to observe how people speak when they are not being observed." What had generally happened in previous research was that the language competence of Black American participants had been assessed by white interviewers. When Labov (1972) used black interviewers, he found a considerable increase in the linguistic fluency of his participants. Speakers of Black English also appeared much more fluent when they were talking in an informal setting about topics that greatly interested them than when they were talking in the school environment about uninteresting matters.

Labov (1972) concluded that Black English was of comparable complexity and sophistication to standard English, a view that is increasingly accepted. However, his conclusion was regarded as controversial in the early 1970s. As Labov (1972, p. 240) noted, "Teachers … are being taught to hear every natural utterance of the [black] child as evidence of his mental inferiority. As linguists, we are unanimous in condemning this view as bad observation, bad theory, and bad practice."

Bernstein's defence.   Finally, we should recall that the evidence for the relationship between language and thought suggested that, at best, language may facilitate thinking but it doesn't determine it. How then could a restricted code restrict cognitive development? Bernstein (1970) attempted to elaborate his original view to suggest a more Vygotskian basis. He argued that the "class system acts upon the deep structure of communication in the process of socialisation". The class structure results in a working class whose knowledge tends to be at the level of context-tied operations (a restricted code) and an elite group who have been taught to use metalanguages for control and innovation. The language of the masses is one that restricts their choice. The elaborated code gives access to "alternative realities", but also may result in an alienation of thought from feeling. Bernstein claims that linguistic codes will only change when the division of labour changes.

Language Acquisition

Perhaps the most remarkable achievement of young children is the breathtaking speed with which they acquire language. By the age of 2, most children use language to communicate hundreds of messages. By the age of 5, children who may not even have started to go to school have mastered most of the grammatical rules of their native language. However, very few parents are consciously aware of the rules of grammar. Thus, young children simply "pick up" the complex rules of grammar without the benefit of much formal teaching.

Stages of Language Development

Language development can be divided into *receptive language* (language comprehension) and *productive language* (language expression or speaking). One-year-old children (and adults as well) have better receptive language than productive language. We underestimate the language skills of children if we assume that their speech reflects all the knowledge of language they have learned.

Children need to learn at least four kinds of knowledge about language (Shaffer, 1993):

- *Phonology*: the sound system of a language.
- *Semantics*: the meaning conveyed by words and sentences.
- *Syntax*: the set of grammatical rules indicating how words may and may not be combined to make sentences.
- *Pragmatics*: the principles determining how language should be modified to fit the context (e.g., we speak in a simpler way to a child than to an adult).

Children usually learn about language in the order listed. They first of all learn to make sounds, followed by developing an understanding of what those sounds mean. After that, they learn grammatical rules and how to change what they say to fit the situation. An interesting feature of this, and one that is important for the theoretical considerations that will shortly follow, is that the sequence of language acquisition is universal.

Early vocalisations

Newborn babies cry when they are distressed. When they are about 3 weeks of age, they produce "fake cries", which seem to occur in the absence of any distress. It is not known for sure why these fake cries are produced, but the reason may be because infants enjoy listening to their own voices. Infants between the ages of about 3 and 5 weeks start to coo. This involves producing vowel-like sounds (e.g., "ooooh") over and over again. Between 4 and 6 months of age, infants start to babble. Babbling consists of combinations of vowels and consonants that do not seem to have any meaning for the infants. *Echolalia* is a form of babbling where infants repeat the same phonemes, such as "mamama". Infants also exhibit some ability to take turns (the pragmatics of conversation) and use gestures (nonverbal communication).

The babbling of infants up to about 6 months of age is rather similar in all parts of the world and in deaf infants as well as hearing ones. However, by about 8 months of age, infants start to show some differences in their babbling which reflect the language they have heard. Indeed, adults can sometimes guess accurately from their babbling whether infants have been exposed to French, Chinese, Arabic, or English (De Boysson-Bardies, Sagart, & Durand, 1984).

One-word stage

Categories

Until the age of about 18 months, young children are limited to single-word utterances. Nelson (1973) studied the first 50 words used by infants, and put those words into categories. The largest category was classes of objects (e.g., cat, car). The next largest category was specific objects (e.g., Mummy, Daddy). The other four categories used by young children were (in descending order of frequency): action words such as "go" and "come"; modifiers (e.g., "mine", "small"); social words (e.g., "please", "no"); and function words (e.g., "for"; "where").

Almost two-thirds of the words used by young children refer to objects or to people. Why is this so? Children refer to things of interest to them, which are mainly the people and objects that surround them.

Mistakes with meanings

Young children often make mistakes with word meanings. Some words are initially used to cover more objects than they should. This is known as **over-extension**. It can be embarrassing, as when a child refers to every man as "Daddy". The opposite mistake, in which the meaning given to a word covers too few objects, is known as **under-extension**. For example, a child may think that the word "cereal" refers only to the brand of cereal the family eats for breakfast.

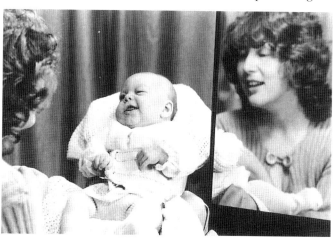

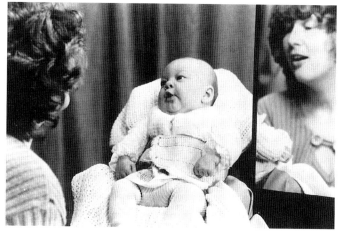

A 6-week-old girl smiles at her mother's face, then responds to gentle baby-talk with cooing vocalisation and a conspicuous hand movement. In the third picture the mother is imitating the preceding vocalisation of her baby.

More meaning in one word

McNeill (1970) referred to the one-word stage as the **holophrastic period**. In this period, young children try to convey much more meaning than their utterances would suggest. For example, an infant who says "ball" while pointing to a ball may mean that he or she would like to play with the ball. McNeill claimed that infants produce one-word utterances because they have a limited attention span and a small vocabulary.

It is hard to test McNeill's notion of a holophrastic period. In its favour is the fact that young children often suggest by their actions or by their tone of voice that they are trying to communicate more than just one word. On the other hand, young children have very limited cognitive development. This must restrict their ability to have complex ideas.

Telegraphic period

The second stage of language development is the **telegraphic period**. It begins at, or shortly after, 18 months of age. Its name arises because the speech of children in this stage is rather like a telegram. Telegrams used to cost so much per word, and so senders of telegrams made them short. Content words such as nouns and verbs were included, but function words such as "a", "the", "and", pronouns, and prepositions were left out. The same is true of the speech of young children. However, they leave out even more than was left out of a telegram. For example, they generally omit plurals and tenses.

Even though young children are largely limited to two-word utterances, they can still communicate a wide range of meanings. One reason for this is that a given two-word utterance can mean different things in different situations. For example, "Daddy chair" may mean "I want to sit in Daddy's chair", "Daddy is sitting in his chair", or "Daddy, sit in your chair!"

Pivot words and open words

Braine (1963) found that early speech consists of two main classes of words: *pivot words* and *open words*. Pivot words always occur in the same place within an utterance, they are few in number, and they are used very often. In contrast, open words appear in different places in different utterances, they are numerous, and each open word is used rarely. Most telegraphic utterances consist of a pivot word plus an open word, and this seems to be a rule that children use. Braine recorded these examples of a pivot word followed by an open word from one child: all clean, all done, all dressed, all messy.

Basic order rule

Another way in which telegraphic speech is based on rules was identified by Roger Brown (1973). He argued that young children possess a basic order rule: a sentence consists of agent + action + object + location (e.g., "Daddy eats lunch at home"). Their two-word utterances follow the basic order rule. For example, an utterance containing an agent will be in the order agent–action (e.g., "Daddy walk") rather than the reverse ("walk Daddy").

How do you think parents learn to decipher the meaning of early vocalisations?

Children should have mastered around 27–45 phonemes (speech sounds) by about 18 months. What might impair this rate of development?

Brown's basic order rule illustrates the child's early use of syntax (sentence construction). Its universal quality suggests that language development at this stage may have strong innate features.

EARLY LANGUAGE ACQUISITION				
Age	0–6 months	6 months–1 year	1–2½ years	2–5 years
Babbling	✓			
Some phonemes learned	✓	✓		
First spoken word		✓		
Beginning of grammatical rules			✓	
Basic rules of grammar acquired				✓

Similarly, action and object will be spoken in the order action–object (e.g., "drink Coke"). Children all over the world construct two-word utterances obeying the basic order rule.

Subsequent developments

Children's language develops considerably between 2½ years and 5 years of age. The most obvious change is in the mean length of utterance, which is usually measured in terms of the number of morphemes (meaningful units) produced. Another important change is based on the learning of what are known as grammatical morphemes. These include prepositions, prefixes, and suffixes (e.g., "in", "on", plural -s, "a", "the"). All children learn the various grammatical morphemes in the same order (de Villiers & de Villiers, 1973). They start with simple ones (e.g., including "in" and "on" in sentences) followed by more complex ones (e.g., reducing "they are" to "they're"). The grammatical morphemes are basically rules that can be applied to several situations.

Over-regularisation

Are children simply imitating the speech of adults rather than actually learning rules? Evidence that they are not comes from children's grammatical errors. A child will say, "The dog runned away", which is a sentence that parents and other adults are unlikely to produce. Presumably the child makes that mistake because he or she is applying the rule that the past tense of a verb is usually formed by adding -ed to the present tense. Using a rule in situations in which it does not apply is known as **over-regularisation** (or over-generalisation).

It could be argued that over-regularisation occurs because children imitate what other children say. However, this cannot explain the findings of Berko (1958) see the Key Study on the next page. This study clearly shows that children apply grammatical rules in a consistent way and the words they produce could not be imitated.

Increasing sophistication

Between the ages of 2½ and 5, children start to use more complex sentences containing a number of ideas. When one of the authors' children, Fleur, was 2 years old, the family were crossing the Channel when her father pointed out to her what he thought was a boat. Her (entirely accurate) reply was "Daddy, that's not a boat, it's a yacht."

Pragmatics

Finally, children at this stage develop a good grasp of pragmatics, in which what they say fits the situation. Shatz and Gelman (1973) analysed the speech of 4-year-old children when talking about a new toy to a 2-year-old or to an adult. The 4-year-olds used complex sentences when talking to the adult. However, they used short sentences when talking to the young child, and focused on holding its attention (e.g., "Look at this!").

Explanations of Language Development

How do young children learn the complexities of language so rapidly and easily? Nativist theorists argue that infants are born with knowledge of the structure of human languages, whereas environmental theorists take the view that language is learned like any other behaviour—as a consequence of imitation and reinforcement.

Nativist theories of child language

Chomsky (1965) presented an enormously influential theory of innate language acquisition, arguing that the human mind is "hard-wired" to acquire language in the same way that we are innately driven to walk on two feet. The "hard-wiring" is a **language acquisition device** (LAD), which enables a child to *innately* acquire language. The device produces universal linguistic rules (*grammar*) when exposed to a native vocabulary, and then transforms this native linguistic input into language.

The language acquisition device is an innate precursor to language acquisition—rather like a chess board without pieces. The chess pieces represent words and the squares are the basis for grammatical constructs. By combining words from different squares in certain orders we create meaning.

Demonstrating over-regularisation

Berko (1958) demonstrated that children do not simply imitate what they hear, as had been suggested by the behaviourists, but that they learn grammatical rules and use them to generate novel, grammatically correct expressions. Berko focused on the rules of morphology. A morpheme is the smallest linguistic unit of meaning. For example, "toes" consists of two morphemes: "toe" and "s". The second morpheme denotes a plural.

Berko tested children's ability to use morphological rules by showing children under the age of 7 a series of cards with either new or known words and asking them to complete a sentence for each. An example is shown on the right. This one tests knowledge of the morphological rule for forming plurals.

The other morphological rules tested were:

- Plurals. Words tested with a picture, as in the illustration on the right: glass, wug, lun, tor, heaf, cra, tass, gutch, kazh, nizz.
- Progressive. A picture showed a man balancing a ball on his nose. "This is a man who knows how to zib. What is he doing? He is _____."
- Past tense. A picture shows a man swinging an object. "This is a man who knows how to rick. He is ricking. He did the same thing yesterday. What did he do yesterday? Yesterday he _____." Other words tested: bing, gling, melt, spow, mot, bod, rang.
- Third person singular. A picture shows a man shaking an object. "This is a man who knows how to naz. He is nazzing. He does it every day. Every day he _____." Also tested: lodge.
- Singular and plural possessive. One animal wearing a hat, then two animals. "This is a niz who owns a hat. Whose hat is it? It is the _____ hat. Now there are two nizzes. They both own hats. Whose hats are they? They are the _____ hats." Other words tested: wug and bik.
- Compound forms. A picture with a man with ball balanced on his nose. "This is a man who knows how to zib. What would you call a man whose job it is to zib? _____."

Altogether participants were shown 27 cards, in a "jumbled order". They were also asked about compound words, such as football, and asked why they thought football was called football. Other compound words used were: afternoon, airplane, birthday, breakfast, blackboard, fireplace, handkerchief, holiday, merry-go-round, newspaper, sunshine, Thanksgiving, Friday.

Berko determined "correct" answers by asking some adults to provide baseline answers. The younger children were generally about 70% correct in their answers and the older children scored better than this, reflecting their progressive understanding of grammatical rules.

Discussion points

1. How does the study of compound words illustrate the acquisition of morphological rules?
2. Berko suggests that these results demonstrate that children gradually acquire and apply grammatical rules. How else could you explain the results?

> ■ Activity: Use Berko's research as the basis for conducting your own research. Use selected sentences and test children of different ages. Make sure you give the test cards to participants in a jumbled order to prevent systematic bias. In using children as participants you should be especially aware of ethical issues.

This is a wug

Now there is another one.
There are two of them.
There are two _____.

Surface structure and deep structure

In developing his theory of a language acquisition device, Chomsky distinguished between the surface structure and the deep structure of a sentence. The surface structure is based on the actual phrases used in a sentence, whereas the deep structure reflects its meaning. For example, the sentence, "Visiting relatives can be boring", has only one surface structure. However, it can mean either that it is sometimes tedious to visit relatives, or that relatives who come on a visit can be boring. The two meanings of this and other sentences are distinguished in the deep structure.

The distinction between surface and deep structure is also important in sentences such as "The man wrote the book", and "The book was written by the man". The meaning of these two sentences is very similar, but this similarity is clear only in the deep structure. The surface structure of the two sentences is different.

Chomsky (1965) introduced the notion of a **transformational grammar**. This allows us to transform the meaning, or deep structure, of a sentence into the actual words in the

Some sentences use different words but have the same meaning, e.g., "The house I live in" and "The house in which I live". Can you list some other sentences that have different surface structure but the same deep structure?

sentence (the surface structure). According to Chomsky, this transformational grammar is innate, and forms a key part of the language acquisition device.

Evaluation.   Chomsky's concern with linguistic structures tends to emphasise correct linguistic acquisition rather than everyday speech, which often includes non-grammatical sentences. The syntax of a sentence may transform the meaning of a collection of words, but it is the meaning itself that most concerns psychologists. Language is a socially constructed as well as a psychologically constructed medium of communication. So it carries with it important signals that extend beyond one-to-one communication. For example, advertisers use the word "natural" to describe a cosmetic, but this is loaded with social meaning rather than just an accurate description of the contents of a bottle. Here the structure of the utterance is of less importance than the meaning that is conveyed by the word "natural".

Universal grammar

Chomsky (1986) later replaced the notion of a language acquisition device with the idea of a universal grammar. According to Chomsky, there are "linguistic universals", which are features found in nearly every language. There are substantive universals and formal universals. Substantive universals concern categories that are common to all languages; noun and verb categories are examples of substantive universals. Formal universals are concerned with the general form of syntactic or grammatical rules.

Word order is a good example of a linguistic universal. Consider the preferred word order for expressing the subject, verb, and object within sentences. There are six possible orderings, two of which (object-verb-subject; object-subject-verb) are very rarely found among the world's languages (Greenberg, 1963). The most popular word order is subject-object-verb (44% of languages), followed by the subject-verb-object word order found in English (35% of languages). Greenberg found that the subject precedes the object in 98% of languages.

Why would the existence of linguistic universals be evidence for the nativist theory?

Where do linguistic universals come from? Chomsky (1986) argued they are innate, but there are other possibilities. Consider the linguistic universals of nouns and verbs, with nouns referring to objects and verbs to actions. Perhaps objects and actions are distinguished in all languages simply because the distinction is such an obvious feature of the environment.

Critical period hypothesis

Did you find it easier to learn your native language as a young child than other languages that you learned later? It probably seems that it was much easier to learn your own language. According to Lenneberg (1967) and other nativists, this common experience supports the "critical period hypothesis". According to this hypothesis, language learning depends on biological maturation—before puberty it is easier to learn a language whereas after that time the biological mechanism has lost some of its flexibility and language learning is harder. This would support the nativist view of language acquisition because acquisition is seen as biologically driven.

According to Lenneberg (1967), the two hemispheres of the brain have the same potential at birth. However, their functions become more specialised and rigid over the years, with language functions typically being located mainly in the left hemisphere. It follows that damage to the left hemisphere at an early age can be overcome by language functions moving to the right hemisphere. This would be harder if the brain damage occurred during adolescence, by which time language is well established in the left hemisphere.

Research studies

Aphasia.   Lenneberg (1967) claimed support for the critical period hypothesis from studies on aphasia, which involves some loss of language due to brain injury. Some children who become aphasic before puberty recover most or all of their lost language functions. Recovery is especially likely if the brain damage occurs before the age of 5. In contrast, brain damage after puberty is often followed by only slow and partial recovery of language. However, other aphasic children fail to support the critical period hypothesis, with the recovery of language functioning being comparable at all ages from early childhood to early adulthood (Harley, 1995).

Second language learning.   The critical period hypothesis has been used to explain why second language learning seems to be harder for older children and adults than for younger children. Newport (1994) looked at second language learning over a long period of time in Asian immigrants to the United States. The younger the children were when they entered the country, the better was their ability to learn complex rules of grammar and other aspects of English. This supports the critical period hypothesis because, as children get older, they are less able to acquire a new grammar.

What other factors might influence the speed at which children learn a second language when they move to another country?

Deprived children

In principle, the best way to test the critical period hypothesis is to consider children who have little chance to learn language during their early years. There have been various reports on "wild" or feral children who were abandoned at birth. For example, there was the "Wild Boy of Aveyron", who was found in an isolated place in the south of France. A French educationalist, Dr Itard, tried to teach the child language, but he only managed to learn two words. Language development in another deprived child is described in the Case Study of "Genie", below.

The evidence suggests there is a critical period for the learning of syntax, and the same is true of phonological learning, for example how to pronounce the words of a language. However, there is less evidence of a critical period for the learning of vocabulary, and many language skills can be acquired after the critical period.

Deaf children

Perhaps the most convincing evidence comes from two studies of language acquisition in deaf children. In one case study, Singleton and Newport (1993) studied a 9-year-old profoundly deaf boy whose parents are also deaf. The parents only learned American Sign Language (ASL) after the age of 15 and were never able to use it grammatically. The boy, however, was observed to be a grammatical user of ASL. How did he learn this when he only had a defective version as a basis for imitation? The explanation is that the parents were beyond the critical age for the acquisition of grammatical language when they learned ASL. They could acquire the vocabulary but not the grammar. Their son, however, was able to apply his "LAD" to the vocabulary and generate a grammatical use of language.

What would "non-grammatical" language be like?

This is even more impressively demonstrated in an observational study of deaf children in Nicaragua. When the Sandinista government reformed education in Nicaragua in 1979 they created the first schools for the deaf, who until then had been isolated from each other. During their play times, the children invented their own sign system that very quickly spread and became known as the Lenguaje de Signos Nicaragüense (LSN). It had no grammar but was an efficient communication system. The most interesting thing about it was that when deaf children around the age of 4 were exposed to LSN they developed something much more fluid and stylised. In fact their version was sufficiently different that it was given a different name, Idioma de Signos Nicaragüense (ISN). The most notable

CASE STUDY: *Genie*

Genie spent most of her time up to the age of 13 in an isolated room (Curtiss, 1977). She had practically no contact with other people, and was punished if she made any sounds. After Genie was rescued in 1970, she learned some aspects of language, especially vocabulary. However, she showed very poor learning of grammatical rules. There are problems in interpreting the evidence from Genie. She was exposed to great social as well as linguistic deprivation, and her father's "justification" for keeping her in isolation was that he thought she was very retarded. Thus, there are various possible reasons for Genie's limited ability to learn language.

Ethical issues: Deprivation studies are useful examples from which we can draw some inferences, but they rarely provide data that can be regarded as scientific. What are some of the ethical issues that arise from looking at the effects of deprivation? Should the psychologist be concerned with compensation for deprivation experienced, e.g. linguistic support for individuals like Genie?

Do the ethical problems concerning work like this outweigh any practical advancement of our understanding as psychologists?

difference was that ISN was grammatical. The older children were presumably beyond the age of acquiring grammar, but the younger children were taking a communication system (LSN) and turning it into a language (ISN). Presumably, they were applying their innate linguistic acquisition device to a linguistic input, something that had been unavailable to the older children at the appropriate age (Pinker, 1994).

Teaching language to non-human animals

In Section 14, Animal Cognition, various attempts to teach human language to non-human animals are described. The general conclusion is that other animals cannot acquire language. They can learn the vocabulary but there is little evidence that they can acquire the grammar. And even if there may be some evidence of grammatical use, it has been acquired with considerable effort. Unlike human children, other animals do not acquire language effortlessly when provided with a native vocabulary.

Conclusion

Harley (1995) concluded that it is reasonable to argue for a weakened version of the critical period hypothesis, according to which some aspects of language are harder to acquire outside the critical period. People of any age and other animals can acquire vocabulary. Grammar appears to be unique to human language. It is grammar that enables language to generate infinite meaning from a limited set of sounds. It is the ability to acquire grammar that may be innately driven, as Chomsky proposed.

Environmental theories

Skinner (1957) claimed that language is acquired by means of **operant conditioning**, in which learning is controlled by reward or reinforcement (see Section 13, Determinants of Animal Behaviour, for a full discussion of operant conditioning). According to this approach, only those utterances of the child that are rewarded or reinforced become stronger. Language develops through a process of **shaping**, in which responses need to become progressively closer to the correct response to be rewarded.

> ■ Activity: In groups of 4–5 people, choose one person and a topic about which they feel confident enough to talk for a while. Observe how their speech changes in response to rewards (smiles, nodding, eye contact, body language, oral responses).
>
> 1. Do they respond to the rewards?
>
> 2. How do they respond in terms of their use of language (less formal, more precise)?
>
> A high degree of change may indicate a response to learning, or may be a consequence of their high level of sociability. Which do you think is more likely?

Imitation is often involved, with the child trying to repeat what his or her parent has just said. This is known as an **echoic response**. Children imitate particular words spoken by their parents and by others, and they also imitate grammatical structures that they hear. Skinner also focused on tacts and mands. A **tact** is involved when the child is rewarded for producing a sound that resembles the correct pronunciation of a word. A **mand** is involved when the child learns a word whose meaning has significance for him or her.

Children do sometimes learn words by imitation or because they are rewarded for saying certain words or sentences. However, detailed analysis of the language behaviour of young children provides evidence against Skinner's theory. Brown, Cazden, and Bellugi (1969) observed the interactions between middle-class American parents and their young children. Parents rewarded or reinforced the speech of their children on the basis of its accuracy or truth rather than the grammar used. According to Skinner's theory this should produce adults whose speech is very truthful but ungrammatical. In fact, of course, the speech of most adults is grammatical but not always very truthful.

Most children develop an excellent command of language very rapidly. Many experts (e.g., Chomsky, 1959) doubt whether such rapid language acquisition would be possible on the basis of imitation and reinforcement alone. It can take some time to learn a single word via reinforcement, and yet children learn thousands of words and a good understanding of grammar.

It seems to follow from Skinner's approach that children should tend to imitate or copy what they have heard other people say. In fact, the telegraphic speech of children under the age of 2 does not usually closely resemble the utterances of other people. As children's language develops, it tends to become more and more creative. Children will often produce sentences that they have never heard before.

Finally, and most importantly, Skinner focused mainly on the learning of specific responses (e.g., pressing a lever; saying a word) by reinforcement. However, much of the knowledge of language possessed by children is not in the form of specific responses at all. They know a lot about grammatical rules, but it does not make much sense to argue that a grammatical rule is a response that can be rewarded. We saw evidence of the learning of rules in the phenomenon of over-regularisation.

How can we study the effects of poor parent–child communication without causing harm?

Motherese

The most important environmental factor in language acquisition is the nature of the social interaction between the mother, or primary carer, and her child. Most mothers adopt a style of speaking to their children known as **motherese** (or parentese). This involves using very short, simple sentences, which gradually become longer and more complex as the child's own use of language develops (Shatz & Gelman, 1973). In order to help their children, mothers typically use sentences that are slightly longer and more complicated than the sentences produced by their children (Bohannon & Warren-Leubecker, 1989).

What factors might determine whether mothers converse with their child about the object of the child's attention?

Mothers, fathers, and other adults also help children's language development by means of expansions. These consist of fuller and more grammatical versions of what the child has just said. For example, a child might say "Cat out", with its mother responding "The cat wants to go out".

Evidence that the way in which the mother talks to her child has an impact on the child's language development was reported by Harris et al. (1986). They found that 78% of what mothers said to their 16-month-old children related to the objects to which the children were attending. However, the situation was different in a group of children whose language development at the age of 2 years was poor. Among these children, only 49% of what mothers said to their children at the age of 16 months related to the object of the child's attention.

What does Harris et al.'s research tell us about the role of language in young children's social development?

Evaluation

The language development of children is greatly helped by conversations with adults involving motherese, expansions, and so on. However, it is not certain that this kind of help is needed for normal language development. As Shaffer (1993) pointed out, there are several cultures (e.g., the Kaluli of New Guinea) in which adults talk to children as if they were adults. In spite of this, children in these cultures seem to develop language at about the normal rate.

The interactionist approach

The evidence in support of some innate capacity for language acquisition seems irrefutable. However, it is also clear that aspects of language acquisition can be explained in terms of reinforcement. These are both necessary conditions for language acquisition, but evidence suggests that they are not sufficient on their own.

There is a third group of theories, described as "interactionist". Social interactionists suggest that language acquisition depends on social stimulation. Consider the following research evidence. Sachs et al. (1981) studied a young boy whose parents were both deaf and did not speak. Although the boy heard language from TV and briefly at nursery school, by the time he was 4 his speech was below age level and structurally idiosyncratic. As speech therapy led to quick improvements this suggests that language will develop only when it is placed in a social context. A similar conclusion might be drawn from the Nicaraguan deaf children described earlier. The schools tried to teach the children lip-reading and speech but were unsuccessful. However, where social forces dictated the necessity for language (in the playground) the children developed their own sign language. Thus the social function of language must also be considered a key factor in acquisition.

The social function of language is a key factor in acquisition.

Bruner (1983) proposed that instead of LAD, children have LASS (a language acquisition support system). According to this system language is the outcome of the interaction between adults (mainly a parent) and the child. The adults play an active role in supporting the child's language acquisition because they provide the vocabulary and the social interaction that necessitates language use.

In the end, all three approaches provide us with a comprehensive account of language acquisition in children.

Problem Solving and Decision Making

Thinking is often considered to be one of the highest expressions of our mental development. If you were asked to add 457 and 638 in your head, you might think "eight and seven is fifteen, then you carry one, so one and five and three is nine, and six and four is ten, so the final answer is … one thousand and ninety-five".

This illustrates several general aspects of thinking. First that individuals are *conscious* of their thoughts, however we tend not be conscious of the processes involved. Second, thinking varies according to how directed it is. Some thinking can be highly *focused*, as in the adding example where there is a clear goal and the steps to reach that goal are known. Other kinds of thinking are much more open-ended—and also less easy to research. Finally, the amount of *knowledge* required for any thinking task varies considerably. In the adding example only a limited amount of knowledge is necessary, whereas the kind of thinking involved in relation to your A2 level studies requires a considerable amount of knowledge (at least it should).

In this Unit we will consider two particular kinds of thinking: problem solving and decision making.

Research into Problem Solving

We will review problem-solving research by broadly following its historical development. So we will begin with a review of early problem-solving research (the Gestalt school), before turning to a treatment of the information-processing theories of problem solving that emerged in the 1950s and 1960s, and finally more recent studies such as the use of analogy.

Early research: The Gestalt school

At the beginning of the twentieth century, adherents of the Gestalt school of psychology extended their theories of perception to problem solving. (See Section 8, Perceptual Processes and Development, for a description of the Gestalt movement in relation to perception.) Before this, problem solving was explained by behaviourists in terms of trial and error learning. Their experiments involved non-human animals. For example, Thorndike placed hungry cats inside a cage within sight of a dish of food. If the cat pushed a pole, the cage door would open. Thorndike observed that at first the cats would thrash about the cage and inevitably at some point would accidentally hit the pole. As a result the door would swing open and the cat would be rewarded with food. Each time the cat was placed back in the cage the same sequence was repeated, however the cats got faster at opening the door with the pole. Thorndike called this trial and error learning. In terms of operant conditioning, the cats had learned to solve the problem by operating on the environment and, as a consequence of their behaviour, receiving rewards. Such rewards are reinforcing and result in the "stamping in" of behaviour.

One of the founders of the Gestalt school, Wolfgang Kohler, disagreed with this formulation and believed that there was more to animal problem solving than trial and error learning. The Gestalt school had been fairly successful in showing that perception was more than conditioning and felt that the same ideas could be applied to problem solving. In terms of perception, Gestaltists had argued, it was possible to *restructure* a stimulus and thus alter one's perception. For example, the Necker cube (see page 297)

Is it reasonable to generalise from non-human animal behaviour to human problem solving?

can be viewed in one of two ways. The change from one view to another is termed "restructuring". Perhaps the same principle could be applied to problem solving—a problem could be restructured in order to solve it.

Gestalt theory can be summarised by the following points:

- Problem-solving behaviour is both *reproductive* and *productive*.
- Reproductive problem solving involves the re-use of previous experience. This can hinder successful problem solving, as seen in, for example, functional fixedness and problem-solving set.
- Productive problem solving is characterised by *insight* into the structure of the problem and by productive *restructurings* of the problem. Insight occurs suddenly and is accompanied by an "ah-ha experience".

Productive problem solving

The classic example of Gestalt research was Kohler's (1925) study on problem solving in apes. The apes had to reach bananas outside their cages, when sticks were the only objects available. On one occasion he observed an ape take two sticks and join them together to reach the bananas, and heralded this as an example of insight. The ape may have used the sticks initially in a trial and error manner but it was only after sitting quietly for a while that the animal produced an insightful solution.

However, there are some question marks about the certainty of this evidence. The previous experiences of this once-wild ape were not known. He may have had previous analogous experiences in the wild and learned to respond in this manner as a result of earlier reinforcement. Birch (1945) found little evidence of this kind of "insightful" problem solving in apes that were raised in captivity.

There are also studies that have involved humans and insight, such as Maier's (1931) "two-string" or "pendulum problem". In the original version of the problem, human participants were brought into a room that had two strings hanging from the ceiling and a number of other objects, such as poles, pliers, and extension cords lying about. The participants were asked to tie together the two strings that were hanging from the ceiling. However, they soon found that when they took hold of one string and went to grab hold of the other, it was too far away for them to reach (see the illustration below). Participants produced a variety of solutions to this problem but the most insightful was the pendulum solution. This involved tying pliers to the ends of the strings and swinging both of them in order to stand in the middle and catch both.

Restructuring

Maier demonstrated a striking example of "problem restructuring" by first allowing participants to get to the point where they were stuck with the two-string problem, and then (apparently accidentally) brushing against the string to set it swinging. Soon after

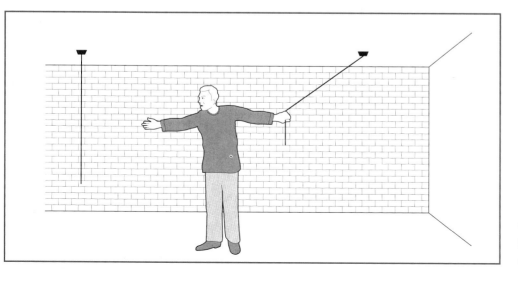

The two-string problem in which it is not possible to reach one string while holding the other.

this was done, participants tended to produce the pendulum solution, even though few of them reported noticing that the experimenter had brushed against the string. According to Maier, this subtle hint resulted in a reorganisation or restructuring of the problem so that a solution emerged.

Functional fixedness

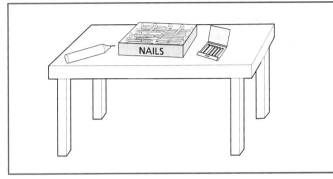

The objects presented to participants in the candle problem.

One of the difficulties with using a reproductive problem-solving strategy is that one re-uses the same strategies in all situations, which restricts one's ability to think creatively when the situation demands. **Functional fixedness** (or mental set) describes the readiness (or lack of it) to solve problems or think in a particular creative manner.

Duncker (1926, 1945) demonstrated functional fixedness in an experiment where participants were given a candle, a box of nails, and several other objects, and asked to attach the candle to the wall so that it did not drip onto the table below (see the illustration on the left). Duncker found that participants tried to nail the candle directly to the wall or to glue it to the wall by melting it. Very few of them thought of using the inside of the nail box as a candle-holder and nailing this to the wall. In Duncker's terms the participants were "fixated" on the box's normal function of holding nails and could not re-conceptualise it in a manner that allowed them to solve the problem. Their problem-solving success was hampered by reproductive behaviour. Similarly, the participants' failure to produce the pendulum solution in the two-string problem can be seen as a case of functional fixedness because they are unable to conceive of the pliers as a pendulum weight.

Problem-solving set

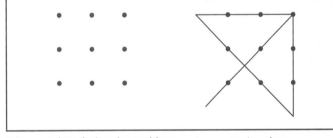

Scheerer's (1963) nine-dot problem requires you to draw four continuous straight lines, connecting all dots without lifting your pen off the paper. Most people find it difficult to solve this because they assume all lines have to stay within the square formed by the dots. In Gestalt terms, participants have "fixated" on the shape, which results in a state of functional fixedness.

Another set of experiments produced by the Gestalt school demonstrated problem-solving set using the water-jug problem (Luchins & Luchins, 1959). In a typical problem you have to imagine that you are given an 8-pint jug full of water, and a 5-pint and a 3-pint jug that are empty (represented as 8-8, 5-0, 3-0, where the first figure represents the size of the jug and the second figure is the amount of water in the jug). Your task is to pour the water from one jug to another until you end up with 4 pints in the 8-pint jug and 4 pints in the 5-pint jug (i.e., 8-4, 5-4, 3-0). Even though this problem seems fairly straightforward the solution takes some time (see the table below for the solution).

In order to demonstrate problem-solving set, Luchins and Luchins had two groups in the experiment: a set and a control condition. The set condition were given a series of problems that could be solved using the same method each time, whereas the control condition received a group of problems that had to be solved using different methods. At the end both groups were tested on a problem that could be solved either using a very simple method or the more complex method that the set condition had been using all along. The control group tended to immediately see the simple solution, whereas the set group opted for their more complex method. In fact they could not "see" the simple method until it was pointed out to them. The set group had, in Gestalt terms, been fixated on the more complex method.

Evaluation of Gestalt theory

The Gestalt approach very usefully showed that problem solving was more than just reproduction of past solutions, as had been suggested by the behaviourists in their idea of trial and error learning, and reinforcement. Gestalt psychologists also demonstrated

Shortest set of moves for Luchins' water-jug problem			
States			
Initial	8-8	5-0	3-0
Intermediate	8-3	5-5	3-0
	8-3	5-2	3-3
	8-6	5-2	3-0
	8-6	5-0	3-2
	8-1	5-5	3-2
	8-1	5-4	3-3
Goal	8-4	5-4	3-0

that when problem solving does rely on past experience this may lead to failure due to functional fixedness or problem-solving set.

The concepts ("insight" and "restructuring") used by the Gestaltist theorists are very attractive and easily understood but they are not sufficiently specific. In order for research to progress it was necessary to find concepts that were more testable.

Post-Gestalt approach

There have been various recent attempts to incorporate key aspects of the Gestalt approach into an information-processing theory of problem solving. We will consider the theory proposed by Ohlsson (1992). According to Ohlsson (1992, p.4), "insight occurs in the context of an impasse [block], which is unmerited in the sense that the thinker is, in fact, competent to solve the problem". The key assumptions of Ohlsson's theory are as follows:

- The way in which a problem is currently represented or structured in the problem solver's mind serves as a memory probe to retrieve related knowledge from long-term memory in the form of operators or possible actions.
- The retrieval process is based on spreading activation among concepts or items of knowledge in long-term memory.
- An impasse or block occurs when the way in which the problem is represented does not permit retrieval of the operators needed to solve the problem.
- The impasse is broken when the problem representation is changed, thus permitting the problem solver to access the necessary knowledge in long-term memory.
- Changing the representation of a problem can occur in various ways: (1) elaboration or addition of new information about the problem; (2) constraint relaxation, in which inhibitions on what is regarded as permissible are removed; (3) re-encoding, in which some aspect of the problem representation is re-interpreted (e.g., a pair of pliers is re-interpreted as a weight in the pendulum problem).
- Insight occurs when an impasse is broken, and the retrieved knowledge operators are sufficient to solve the problem. Insight is complete when the operators lead to a solution in one step; otherwise, it is partial and more time consuming.

There is a reasonable amount of support for the general approach adopted by Ohlsson (1992). For example, Yaniv and Meyer (1987) found that the initial efforts of their participants to access relevant stored information were often unsuccessful. However, these unsuccessful efforts produced spreading activation to other concepts stored in long-term memory. As a result, the participants were more likely to recognise relevant information when it was presented to them.

Knoblich et al. (1999) showed the importance of constraints in reducing the likelihood of insight. They presented their participants with problems such as those shown in the diagram below. As you can see, you would need to know all about Roman numerals in order to solve the problems! The task was always to move a single stick to produce a true

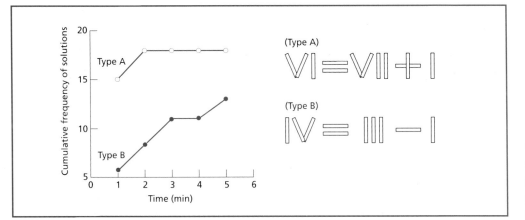

Two of the matchstick problems used by Knoblich et al. (1999), and the cumulative solution rates produced for these types of problems in their study.

statement in place of the initial false one. Some problems (Type A) only require changing two of the values in the equation (e.g., VI = VII + I becomes VII = VI + I). In contrast, other problems (Type B problems) involve a more fundamental change in the representation of the equation (e.g., IV = III – I becomes IV – III = I). Knoblich et al. (1999) argued that it would be much harder for participants to relax the normal constraints of arithmetic (and thus to show insight) for Type B problems than for Type A ones. That was precisely what they found.

Evaluation

Ohlsson's view that insight occurs when there is restructuring of a problem leading to a rapid solution is a useful one. In general terms, as Gilhooly (1996, p.56) pointed out, "Ohlsson's approach is a very promising marriage of Gestalt concerns and information-processing approaches to problem solving." One limitation of Ohlsson's approach is that individual differences have been relatively neglected. It is highly probable that individuals of high intelligence and/or relevant expertise would find it easier to change the representation of a problem.

Information-processing theories

The problem-solving research of Newell and Simon (1972) is the bedrock of the **information-processing framework** and also of all subsequent work in problem solving. (See page 377 for a description of the characteristics of the information-processing approach.)

Problem-space theory

Problem solving can be characterised as being like finding your way through a maze. You start at the entrance to the maze. As you make your way to the centre, there are junctions where you have to make choices. In total there are hundreds of alternative paths through the maze and only some of them will enable you to reach the centre.

Newell and Simon used this analogy as the basis for their problem-solving theory. They suggested that the structure of a problem can be characterised as a set of states, beginning from an initial state (e.g., standing outside the maze), and ending with a goal state (e.g., being in the centre of the maze). During the process of problem solving, actions are performed or "operators applied" (e.g., turn left or right at a junction). The application of these operators results in a move from one state to another—some will lead to dead ends whereas others will facilitate movement towards the goal state. In order to solve a problem there is a whole space of possible states and paths. This **problem space** describes the abstract structure of a problem.

Problem-space theory and the Tower of Hanoi

You may be familiar with the "Tower of Hanoi" problem. There are three vertical pegs and on one peg there are a number of discs piled in order of size so that the largest is at the bottom. The ultimate goal is to move all the discs so they end up in the same order on the last peg. However, only one disc can be moved at a time and you can never have a larger disc on top of a smaller disc. The standard version of the problem uses three discs.

The starting point of the problem is called the *initial knowledge state* (all discs on peg 1). The ultimate goal is all discs, in the same order, on peg 3. This is called the *goal knowledge state*. Movements between pegs are called *mental operators*, which must follow the rule that only one disc can be moved at a time and you can never have a larger disc on top of a smaller disc.

There are many alternative paths between the initial knowledge state and the goal knowledge state, i.e., through the problem space. The strategies that a person uses when trying to solve the problem are called **heuristics**. Heuristics are rules of general principle that are different from **algorithms** in that the latter are procedures that will definitely solve a problem (like a knitting pattern) whereas a heuristic is a strategy that might solve the problem and will save a lot of time and effort in the process.

The initial state and goal state in the Tower of Hanoi problem.

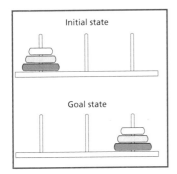

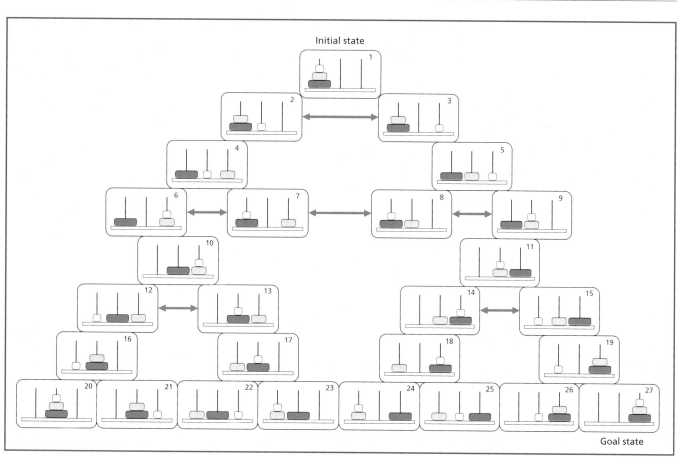

Initial state

Goal state

Means–ends analysis

The **means–ends analysis** is one of the most important heuristic methods proposed by Newell and Simon. It consists of the following steps:

- Note the difference between the current state and the goal state.
- Create a subgoal to reduce this difference.
- Select an operator that will solve this subgoal.

To illustrate means–ends analysis, let us assume that a person solving the Tower of Hanoi problem is two steps away from the solution, for example they are in state 15 in the diagram above. At this point three possible moves can be made (i.e., states 11, 14 and 19), but only one of these will bring you closer to solving the problem. Means–ends analysis proposes that you first note the difference between the current state and the goal state—here an important thing to notice is that the medium disc is on the second peg instead of the third peg. Second, establish a subgoal that reduces this difference—which would be to create a subgoal of moving the medium disc to the third peg. And finally, select an operator that solves this subgoal and apply it—the medium disc will be moved to the third peg and you will be one step closer to the solution.

It is important to remember that this heuristic will not always work but it will often work and will generally save time and effort—all the characteristics of a heuristic.

Research evidence

In order to test problem-space theory it is necessary to create predictions. One such prediction would be that if you can structure a problem into appropriate subgoals, such as "attempt to get the largest disc onto the third peg", then problem-solving performance should improve. One source of such subgoals should be prior experience.

Egan and Greeno (1974) tested this. They gave participants complex five- and six-disc versions of the Tower of Hanoi problem. Some participants received prior experience

Using means–end analysis, the diagram above shows the problem space of legal moves in the Tower of Hanoi problem. If boxes touch each other, or are joined by arrows, this indicates that one can move from one state to the other using a legal operator.

with three- and four-disc problems, whereas the controls did not. The easier versions should have assisted participants because they would have enabled them to develop appropriate subgoals before trying the more complex problems. Egan and Greeno did find that the experimental group deviated less from the shortest solution, though they also had more difficulties in the early stages than the control group. So the strategies that they had learned were helpful nearer to the goal state but not when they were farther away.

The General Problem Solver

Newell and Simon developed a computer program, the **General Problem Solver** (GPS), to mimic the processes used by humans in solving problems. For example, the program used the means–ends analysis. It is possible to compare the steps taken by the computer program in solving a problem with the **protocol** used by a human participant. If the human participant is using the same rules as the GPS then the protocol should match the computer program. However, in the end the GPS was abandoned because it couldn't be applied to human problem solving as had at first been hoped.

The missionaries and cannibals problem

Problem-space theory has also been applied to the hypothetical conundrum where three missionaries and three cannibals need to get across a river in a boat that can only hold a maximum of two. The stumbling block is that there must never be more cannibals than missionaries on either bank or the missionaries will be eaten. There must also always be one person in the boat to row it.

It might help if you try to solve the five missionaries and five cannibals problem now, before reading on.

Simon and Reed (1976) explored a five missionaries and five cannibals version, which can in fact be solved in just 11 moves. However, on average, it takes participants 30 moves to solve the problem.

Simon and Reed analysed the solutions given and identified three strategies or heuristics:

- *Balancing strategy*, where participants simply try to ensure that there is an equal number of missionaries and cannibals on either side.
- *Means–ends strategy* is adopted after a while to try to move nearer to the goal state. This strategy is manifested by people trying to move more people to the goal side of the river.
- An *anti-looping strategy* is important to prevent moves that reverse the immediately preceding move.

Does this description fit the strategies that you used when trying to solve the problem?

Simon and Reed recognised that the key to efficient solving of this problem lay in the moment of strategy shift from the balancing strategy to the means–ends strategy because, if this move is not made at an appropriate moment, one ends up in a blind alley. This would lead to the prediction that any manipulation that would increase the probability of making this strategy shift should result in improved performance. To test this, Simon and Reed worked with two groups of participants. The experimental group were given a hint that they should work to a state where three cannibals were on the goal side of the river on their own without a boat. Because this subgoal involves a state where there are unequal numbers of missionaries and cannibals on either side of the river, it was expected that it should discourage the use of a balancing strategy early on. This prediction was confirmed and experimental participants tended to shift strategies after about four moves whereas those in the control group only shifted after about 15 moves.

Reinterpreting the Gestalt findings

It is possible to use problem-space theory to analyse Luchins' water-jug problem. In the 8-8, 5-0, and 3-0 problem we encountered earlier, the initial state is 8-8, 5-0, and 3-0, and the goal state is 8-8, 5-4, 3-0. The operators

---

■ Activity: Missionaries and cannibals

You can replicate the study by Simon and Reed yourself. Some participants will be in the experimental group and others in the control group. In the control group, explain the missionaries and cannibals problem and ask them to write down the steps they take to solve the problem with five missionaries and five cannibals. With the experimental group give them the hint that they should work to a state where three cannibals are on the goal side of the river on their own without a boat. Again these participants should record their moves.
Which group took fewer moves?

consist of pouring various amounts of water from one jug to another, and the operator restrictions are that the water cannot be added to or flung away.

Attwood and Polson (1976) produced a problem-space analysis of the various heuristics that people would use in solving the water-jug problem, and included assumptions about the limitations on human information processing. The model had the following main points:

- When planning moves, participants only look ahead one move.
- Moves are evaluated using means–ends analysis (participants compare the difference between current state and goal state for two jugs and then decide what next move would bring them closer to the goal state).
- Participants will tend to avoid moves that return them to an immediately preceding state (this is the anti-looping heuristic).
- There are limitations on the number of moves that can be stored in working memory. This is alleviated by transferring information to long-term memory.

As before, the value of making such predictions is testing them in real time. In an experiment, Attwood and Polson (1976) gave participants two problems: 8-8, 5-0, and 3-0, and 24-24, 21-0 and 3-0. In both cases the goal was to distribute the largest jug's water between the two largest jugs (i.e., 8-4, 5-4, 3-0 and 24-12, 21-12, 3-0). The model would predict that the former problem should be more difficult because the latter one can be solved by the means–ends heuristic whereas the former one requires a violation of this heuristic. Attwood and Polson's results confirmed this prediction in terms of the mean number of moves required to solve the problems.

There have also been attempts to explain insight in terms of problem-space theory, as outlined in the box above.

> **Using problem-space theory to explain insight: Ohlsson's (1992) insight theory**
>
> - The representation of insight problems is a matter of interpretation, so there may be many different mental representations of the same problem (i.e., the problems are ill-defined).
> - People have many knowledge operators for solving problems, and therefore operators may have to be retrieved from memory; the retrieval mechanism is spreading activation.
> - The current representation of the problem acts as a memory probe for relevant operators in memory.
> - Impasses occur because the initial representation of the problem is a bad memory probe for retrieving the operators needed to solve the problem.
> - Impasses are broken when the representation of the problem is changed (is reinterpreted, re-presented, or restructured) thus forming a new memory probe that allows the retrieval of the relevant operators.
> - This re-presentation can occur through (1) elaboration, adding new information about the problem from inference of the environment (e.g., hints), (2) constraint relaxation, changing some of the constraints on the goal, (3) re-encoding, changing aspects of the problem representation through recategorisation or deleting some information (e.g., recategorising the pliers in the two-string problems as a *building material* rather than a *tool*).
> - After an impasse is broken a full or partial insight may occur; a full insight occurs if the retrieved operators bridge the gap between the impasse state and the goal state.

Evaluation of problem-space theory

Problem-space theory supports the Gestalt approach to productive problem solving. It shows that people have general heuristics that they can apply to situations about which they have little prior knowledge. Hence they are not merely recollecting solutions to problems, as the behaviourist model would suggest, but are actively and dynamically constructing solutions by applying different heuristics.

Problem-space theory has not been bettered though it has been extended, partly as a result of some of the limitations of the original theory. One major issue is the fact that problem-space theory concentrates on well-defined problems rather than ill-defined ones, and also on problems that lack ecological validity. Subsequent formulations have tried to address the issue of ill-defined problems.

Creativity, analogy, and difficult problems

People often solve problems that involve having to go beyond their knowledge—problems that are novel, unfamiliar, and ill-defined. In such situations we can act creatively.

Traditional approaches to creativity

Wallas (1926) proposed that the process of creatively solving a problem involves four stages:

- *Preparation*, where the problem under consideration is formulated and preliminary attempts are made to solve it.

The mind of a scientist

The following is description of creative problem solving by the French mathematician Henri Poincaré (1913), recounting his work on Fuchsian functions:

> I wanted to represent these functions by the quotient of two series; this idea was perfectly conscious and deliberate; this analogy with elliptic functions guided me. I asked myself what properties these series must have if they existed, and succeeded without difficulty in forming the series I have called theta-Fuchsian.

> Just at that time I left Caen, where I was living, to go on a geologic excursion under the auspices of the school of mines. The changes in travel made me forget my mathematical work. Having reached Coutances, we entered an omnibus to go to some place or other. At the moment when I put my foot on the step an idea came to me, without anything in my former thoughts seeming to have paved the way for it, that the transformations I had used to define Fuchsian functions were identical to those of non-Euclidean geometry. I did not verify the idea; I should not have had time, as, upon taking my seat in the omnibus, I went on with a conversation already commenced, but I felt a perfect certainty.

Poincaré's report fits in perfectly with Wallas' framework for creative problem solving.

- *Incubation*, where the problem is left aside to work on other tasks.
- *Illumination*, where the solution comes to the problem solver as a sudden insight.
- *Verification*, in which the problem solver makes sure the solution actually works.

Support for this stage model has been largely anecdotal, using descriptions of how scientists have solved problems. For example, read the report of the French mathematician Henri Poincaré in the box on the left.

Analogical thinking

Poincaré's account also mentions "analogy". Various creative individuals report solutions to unfamiliar problems based on deep analogies. For example, Rutherford used a solar system analogy to understand the structure of the atom; viewing electrons as revolving around the nucleus in the same way as the planets revolve around the sun. Many problems can be solved by making use of analogical reasoning, in which the solver notices some important similarities between the current problem and some problem solved in the past. Historically, analogical reasoning or thinking was often studied by presenting problems having the form "A is to B as C is to D" (e.g., "North is to south as top is to bottom").

Analogical thinking involves a mapping of the conceptual structure of one set of ideas (called a *base domain*) into another set of ideas (called the *target domain*). Technically this is called analogical mapping, which can be characterised by the following:

- Certain aspects of the base and target domains are *matched*. For example, you notice that objects in the solar system attract each other and that the same is true of objects in an atom.
- Aspects of the base domain that are not present in the target domain are transferred into the latter. For instance, relations about the planets "revolving around" the sun are *transferred* into the atom domain to create some new conceptual structure there (i.e., the electrons revolve around the nucleus).

Rutherford used the solar system analogy to understand the structure of the atom; viewing electrons as revolving around the nucleus in the same way as the planets revolve around the sun. Other relations among the planets may be transferred to the new conceptual structure.

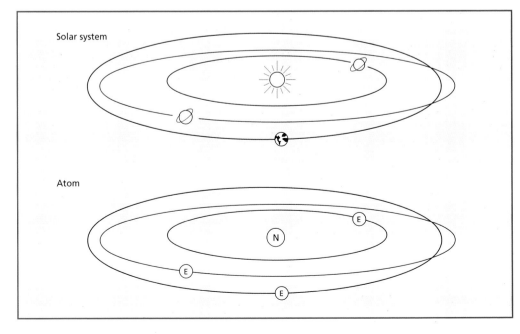

- When the knowledge is transferred from one domain to another, there is a tendency for coherent, integrated pieces of knowledge rather than fragmentary pieces to be transferred. Thus, the integrated knowledge that attraction and weight *cause* the planets to revolve around the sun is transferred before non-integrated information about the earth having life on it.
- Some knowledge is transferred because it is seen as being pragmatically important or goal-relevant in some respects.

Gick and Holyoak (1980) showed how analogies can help in the process of reconceptualising a problem. They used one of Duncker's (1945) problems, the "radiation problem" which involves a doctor's attempt to destroy a malignant tumour using X-rays. The doctor needs to use high-intensity rays to destroy the tumour but these high-intensity rays will also destroy the healthy tissue surrounding the tumour. If the doctor uses low-intensity rays then the healthy tissue will be saved but the tumour will remain unaffected too. This dilemma can be solved by the "convergence solution" which proposes that the doctor send low-intensity rays from a number of different directions so that they converge on the tumour, summing to a high intensity in order to destroy it.

If participants are given this problem, about 10% are able to solve it. However, if they are told a story beforehand that aims to help them reconceptualise the problem, then their ability to solve it improves. The story is about a general attacking a fortress. He cannot use his whole army to attack because the roads leading to the fortress are mined to explode if a large number of troops pass over them. He therefore divides his army into small groups and sends them along different roads so that they converge on the fortress. Participants were asked to memorise this story and, if it was suggested to them that they might use it to solve the radiation problem, then their success rate rose to about 80%. Without the hint, participants did not tend to notice the analogy.

Can you think of your own example of solving problems by analogy?

As with Newell and Simon's attempt to mirror human thought in computer models, computational models have been developed for analogical mapping with somewhat more success. For example, the Incremental Analogy Machine (IAM) (Keane, Ledgeway, & Duff, 1994) predicts that the order in which information is presented will affect speed of solution, a prediction that is confirmed by experiments with humans. However, the question remains as to whether, even when machines parallel human thinking, the underlying processes are the same in human minds and machines.

If a machine produces the same solution as a human, does this mean that it used the same method?

Some recent research has been designed to identify those parts of the brain most involved in analogical thinking. For example, Wharton et al. (1998) obtained PET scans from participants while they solved proportional analogy problems with geometrical shapes. Their findings indicated that analogical mapping is localised in the left prefrontal cortex and left inferior parietal cortex. Some of the functions of working memory also seem to occur in the prefrontal cortex. It is probable that the working memory system is involved in analogical thinking, a notion that forms part of the theory put forward by Hummel and Holyoak (1997). They proposed a connectionist model embodied in a computer simulation called LISA (Learning and Inference with Schemas and Analogies). A key assumption incorporated into LISA is that there are fundamental differences between analogical access and mapping. Mapping takes place initially in a relatively automatic way, and involves comparing features of only a single stored analogue against those of the current problem. This is followed by access that involves retrieval competition among several stored analogues in long-term memory, because only a small number can become accessible to consciousness after any given retrieval attempt. Thus, people's ability to engage in analogical thinking is constrained by the limited capacity of working memory.

Difficult problems

Why are some problems difficult? It is possible to explain problem difficulty in terms of two main limitations: resource limitations (such as on memory) and knowledge limitations. Individuals who are "experts" are characterised by their superior knowledge. For example, deGroot (1965) compared expert chess players with grand masters. He concluded that the essential difference was that grand masters had more knowledge of board positions. Chess players are able to remember previous games and such knowledge increases their ability to evaluate alternative moves.

This expert knowledge may be in terms of facts but it is more likely to be schematic in order to reduce the demand on memory. This again was demonstrated by deGroot, who showed chess players brief presentations of board positions from actual games. The chess masters were able to recall the positions very accurately (91% correct) whereas less expert players were on average 41% correct. This could not be due to memory advantages because when they were tested with randomly arranged configurations the two groups did equally badly. Therefore, it appears that part of expertise is the development of schemas for recognising and encoding various configurations.

Decision Making

We will now turn to a second kind of thinking. In everyday life, we have to make numerous decisions and judgements. How do we do it? In order to answer this question, we will consider some examples.

Risk-taking behaviour in decision making

Many decisions involve some element of risk, where it is necessary to compare possible benefits with potential costs and then decide on the best course of action. One way to explain human risk-taking behaviour is in terms of utility theory.

Utility theory

Suppose that a rare disease found mainly in Asia is expected to kill 600 people in the United States. There are two possible programmes of action to fight the disease. It is estimated that Programme A will save 200 lives, whereas Programme B offers a 1/3 probability that all 600 people will be saved, and a 2/3 probability that no one will be saved.

What psychological theories assume that people behave rationally?

Which of the two programmes is preferable? If we think rationally, then we should take account of the **expected utility** or expected value of each option. This can be worked out by using the following equation:

Expected utility = (probability of a given outcome) x (utility of that outcome)

In this example, the expected utility of Programme A is 1 x 200 = 200 people saved, and the expected utility of Programme B is 0.33 x 600 = 200. Thus, the two programmes are equally useful. In fact, Tversky and Kahneman (1987) found that 72% of their participants chose Programme A. This suggests that their decisions were not made on purely rational grounds. This was further supported when Tversky and Kahneman gave other participants exactly the same problem expressed slightly differently: if Programme A is used, then 400 people will die: if Programme B is used, then there is a 1/3 probability that nobody will die, and a 2/3 probability that 600 people will die. Even though this is the same problem, only 22% of the participants chose Programme A.

Framing the problem

Full-fat milk?
Using the framing effect we can offer an explanation as to why food retailers might advertise or label full-fat milk as "94% fat free" in order to draw customer attention away from its high fat content when compared with skimmed milk. Retailers may have decided to reverse the tendency for customers to associate higher fat content in milk with bad dietary habits by stating the high-percentage fat-free quality of milk.

In the problem we have what is known as a **framing effect**, meaning that the decision is influenced by the phrasing or frame in which the problem is presented. Why did the participants show a framing effect? In the first version of the problem, Programme A is framed in a positive way, with an emphasis on the number of lives that will be saved. In the second version, in contrast, the emphasis is on the number of people who will die.

Loss aversion

The study by Tversky and Kahneman shows that we do not always behave in line with expected utility. There are many other situations in which people do not make use of expected utility. For example, most people show evidence of **loss aversion**, which is the tendency to be much more sensitive to losses than to gains. Kahneman and Tversky (1984) asked participants whether they would accept a bet that involved them winning $20 if a coin came up heads, but paying $10 if it came up tails. The bet should be accepted according to utility theory, but most of the participants rejected it. Thus, they showed loss aversion.

You'll have to drop her to catch me, so are you feeling lucky, punk?

Alternatives to utility theory

Elimination by aspects

Tversky (1972) put forward an elimination-by-aspects theory, according to which the decision maker eliminates options by considering one relevant attribute after another. Someone buying a house may first of all consider the attribute of geographical location, eliminating from further consideration all those houses not lying within a given area. He or she may then consider the attribute of price, eliminating all those properties costing above a given figure. This process continues attribute by attribute until there is only one option left. This strategy has the advantage that it does not involve difficult or complex thinking. However, it suffers from the disadvantage that the final option that is selected depends on the order in which the attributes are considered.

> ■ Activity: Consider the plans you may have for a future career. In deciding on that career, apply Tversky's elimination-by-aspects theory, then compare it to the application of satisficing theory. Which approach do you feel is more convincing? Are there any non-rational factors that might override a decision such as this?

Satisficing

Simon (1978) argued for a different approach known as satisficing theory. This theory is of most use when the various options become available at different points in time. An example is trying to decide who to marry. According to the theory, decision makers set a minimum acceptable level. The first option (e.g., boyfriend or girlfriend) to reach that level is selected. If the initial level of acceptability is set too high or too low, it can be adjusted upwards or downwards to make it more realistic.

Payne (1976) studied the ways in which people chose a flat or apartment from information presented on cards. Most of them started off by using techniques such as elimination by aspects and satisficing to reduce the number of possibilities being considered. After that, they focused on considering the remaining options in a more thorough way.

Reasonableness

Other theorists have argued that people make decisions that are reasonable or justified. Tversky and Shafir (1992) gave their participants the task of deciding whether to buy an attractive package holiday in Hawaii. All the participants were told to imagine that they had just taken a difficult examination. Some were told to imagine that they had passed the examination, some that they had failed the examination, and the rest that it was not known whether they had passed or failed.

Of those participants who had passed the examination, 54% decided to buy the holiday. They had the justification that they deserved to celebrate their success. Of those who had failed, 57% bought the holiday, presumably as a consolation for their disappointment. Of those who did not know what had happened, only 32% decided to buy the holiday. It was hard for the participants in this condition to think of a good justification for taking the holiday when they were in a state of uncertainty.

Summary

We do not generally make decisions in the rational or logical way proposed by utility theory. We are influenced by non-rational factors such as the phrasing or framing of a problem, loss aversion, the desire to be able to justify our decisions, and so on. The precise strategies that we use vary from problem to problem. However, our decision making often makes use of elimination by aspects and/or satisficing. These strategies are not ideal, but usually work fairly well in practice.

Making decisions based on probabilities

Kahneman and Tversky (1973) argued that people often make poor decisions or judgements because they ignore relevant information. Suppose you read in an encyclopaedia that a physical complaint from which you are suffering is one of the symptoms of a rare and unpleasant disease. Suppose further that one person in 5000 has the disease, that the probability of having the physical symptom if you are suffering from the disease is 0.7, and that the probability of having the symptom without also having the disease is 0.01. What is the probability that you have the disease? Most people would argue that there was a high probability that they were suffering from the disease. In actual fact, however, the correct probability is only about 0.014.

Representativeness

> **CASE STUDY:** *Picking Lottery Numbers*
>
> In general, people have a very poor understanding of randomness and probability, as evidenced by the types of numbers commonly selected in the UK National Lottery. Even people who claim to understand that any given number is as likely to come up as any other will be heard to despair: "Oh, I'll never win with that—four numbers in a row!", or "All my numbers are bunched up under 20—I'd better spread them out a bit to get a better pattern." In fact, statistics suggest that you're actually better off picking numbers with a skewed or bunched appearance: you're no more likely to win, but in the unlikely event that you do, you'll be less likely to have to share your prize with anyone else!

How might the representativeness heuristic apply to: (1) the popularity of the National Lottery; (2) travel by plane in preference to car/boat/train?

Why are the probability judgements so inaccurate in the situation of judging whether you have a disease or not? According to Kahneman and Tversky, people decide between various possibilities by considering which one seems to be most representative of, or consistent with, the evidence. In other words, they use a rule of general principle known as the "representativeness heuristic", according to which representative or typical instances of a category are judged to be more probable than unrepresentative ones. What is left out of account is the base-rate information. In the example, this refers to the relative numbers of people suffering from, and not suffering from, the disease. As the number of non-sufferers from the disease is vastly greater than the number of sufferers (4999 out of 5000 people versus 1 out of 5000), this greatly reduces the probability that a person with the physical symptom will actually be suffering from the disease.

Kahneman and Tversky (1972) tested use of the representativeness heuristic, using the following problem:

> *All the families having exactly six children in a particular city were surveyed. In 72 of the families, the exact order of births of boys (B) and girls (G) was G B G B B G. What is your estimate of the number of families surveyed in which the exact order of births was B G B B B B?*

The best estimate is 72, because the probability of having a boy or a girl is the same at 0.5. Thus, any sequence of six children is as likely as any other sequence. However, most of the answers were much lower than 72. According to Kahneman and Tversky, the participants used the representativeness heuristic: the birth order G B G B B G seems more likely than the birth order B G B B B B because it is more representative of the numbers of males and females in the population, and because it appears to be more random.

Tversky and Kahneman (1983) produced even more striking evidence of the kinds of error that can result from using the representativeness heuristic. They found what they called the "conjunction fallacy". The participants were told that an imaginary person called Linda is a former student activist, single, very intelligent, and a philosophy graduate. They were then asked to estimate the probability of her being a bank teller, a feminist, or a feminist bank teller. Most said it was more likely that Linda was a feminist bank teller than a bank teller. This cannot be correct, because the category of bank tellers includes all feminist bank tellers.

Relevance

Do people always rely on the representativeness heuristic and ignore base-rate information? According to Tversky and Kahneman (1980), base-rate information is often used when its causal relevance is made clear. They told their participants that there were two taxi companies in a town, the Blue Company and the Green Company. There was an accident involving a taxi, and the participants' task was to decide the probability that the taxi had been blue. Some participants were told that 50% of the taxis in the town were blue and the other 50% were green, but that 85% of the taxi-related accidents involved green taxis. They were also told that a witness claimed that a blue taxi was involved, but there was a 20% chance that he was mistaken. When the causal relevance of the base-rate information (i.e., the percentage of accidents caused by blue taxis) was made obvious, the participants used that information. Most of them were fairly close to the correct figure of a 59% chance that a blue taxi was involved. When the causal relevance of the base-rate information was not made clear, most participants claimed mistakenly that there was an 80% probability that the taxi was blue.

Availability heuristic

Tversky and Kahneman (1973) studied another heuristic or rule of general principle known as the "availability heuristic". According to this heuristic, probability judgements are sometimes made on the basis of how available relevant examples are in long-term memory. They asked their participants whether each of five letters of the alphabet (K, L, N, R, and V) occurs more often in the first or the third position in English words. All five letters appear in the third position in more words, but the participants mostly argued that each letter appears more often in the first position. This finding depends on the availability heuristic: it is much easier to generate words starting with a given letter than those having the same letter in the third position.

How might you go about testing the strength of the availability heuristic in determining how people make judgements?

Media coverage

Lichtenstein et al. (1978) found that the availability heuristic is used in everyday life. They argued that our judgements about the probabilities of different kinds of lethal events are influenced by the amount of media coverage given to them. Causes of death that receive considerable media coverage (e.g., murder) are judged to be more common than causes of death that receive little publicity (e.g., suicide), even when the less frequently reported lethal events are actually more common. The reason is that we can more readily think of examples of the lethal events that are discussed at length in the media.

Evaluation

The greatest strength of the approach adopted by Kahneman and Tversky is that it captures some of the processes involved in making judgements. We often use rules of general principle or heuristics in our thinking, with important information (e.g., base-rate information) being ignored. In other words, our judgemental thinking is often less precise and rational than we imagine.

How problems are expressed. One weakness in the approach of Kahneman and Tversky is that we are sometimes more capable of making accurate judgements than is predicted by their approach. For example, Fiedler (1988) repeated the conjunction fallacy finding of Tversky and Kahneman (1983; see earlier). About 75% of the participants argued that it was more likely that Linda was a feminist bank teller than that she was a bank teller. However, when other participants were asked to estimate how many out of a hundred people like Linda would be feminist bank tellers and how many would be bank tellers, about 75% argued correctly that more would be bank tellers! If small changes in the wording of a problem can produce major changes in judgemental accuracy, then we must be cautious in interpreting the available findings.

What practical applications might Tversky and Kahneman's research have?

Laboratory studies.   A second weakness of the approach is that it is based too much on artificial laboratory studies. According to Koehler (1996), we are more likely to make use of base-rate information if we have obtained this information through direct experience rather than simply being provided with it in the laboratory. Christensen-Szalanski and Bushyhead (1981) looked at the use of base-rate information by doctors who had found from experience that pneumonia has a low base-rate. These doctors made considerable use of this base-rate information when deciding on a diagnosis.

Tetlock (1991, p.453), makes the point that "Subjects in laboratory studies of cognitive processes rarely feel accountable to others for the positions they take. They function in a social vacuum (or as close an approximation as can be achieved) in which they do not need to worry about the interpersonal consequences of their conduct."

Individual differences.   Some people are much more willing than others to engage in risky decision making, but these individual differences have rarely been studied. An exception was a study by Lopes (1987), who used a short questionnaire to identify risk-averse and risk-seeking participants. According to Lopes (1987, pp.274–275), "Risk-averse people appear to be motivated by a desire for security, whereas risk-seeking people appear to be motivated by a desire for potential ... Risk-averse people look more at the downside and risk seekers more at the upside." The participants had to choose between various lotteries having 100 tickets, all of which had an expected value of about $100. The lotteries varied in terms of risk: at one extreme, all 100 tickets were guaranteed to produce $100; at the other extreme, 31 of the tickets produced nothing and 6 tickets produced over $300. As predicted, the risk-averse participants tended to avoid the riskier lotteries, but that was not the case for the risk-seeking ones.

Lack of a theory.   A final weakness of the approach is that there is no proper theory of what is involved. For example, it seems that use of the availability heuristic involves information retrieved from long-term memory. However, little is known of the processes involved in such retrieval or of the ways in which the retrieved information influences probability judgements.

SECTION SUMMARY

Language and Culture

❖ Language is important in our social relationships (culture) and in our thinking.

❖ Watson, the founder of behaviourism, argued that thinking was nothing more than inner speech but this can't explain how a man who was totally paralysed could still think.

❖ According to Whorf's linguistic relativity hypothesis, language determines (or has a major influence on) thinking. There are three versions of this hypothesis. The strong form proposes that language determines thinking. Research with Navaho children provided some mixed support. The weak form of the hypothesis states that language affects perception. Research studies have compared colour recognition in individuals whose language lacks certain colour words (the Dani and speakers of Zuni) and they appear less able to distinguish certain colours than English speakers. However, the results again are mixed. The weakest form of the hypothesis states that language influences memory, an argument that is hard to refute. This means that Whorf's original arguments cannot be accepted, because he overstated linguistic differences; there is little evidence that language does affect thought, although it does affect aspects of our thinking (e.g., memory); and it is easy to exaggerate the significance of linguistic expressions. A modified version of the linguistic relativity hypothesis (Hunt and Agnoli) suggests that any given language makes it easier to think in certain ways. Support for this has come from the study of bilingual speakers.

❖ Theories of cognitive development offer explanations about how language is related to thought. Piaget argued that language is the outcome of a generalised ability to think; thought produces language. Research does suggest that being taught an appropriate vocabulary does not lead to cognitive development. In contrast, Vygotsky's view was that language plays a central role in cognitive development. Egocentric speech serves the function of directing the child's thinking and also transforms elementary thinking into higher-order processes. However, Vygotsky did not consider that language determines thought—learning a new word is the beginning of a concept rather than the end. Fodor's notion of a separate language processor supports the idea that language and thought can be independent.

❖ The social and cultural aspects of language use allow us to further consider the relationship between language and thought. It is not only what you say but how you say it. Social markers, such as accent and dialogue, provide social information about the speaker. Studies using the matched-guise technique have shown that high status is assigned to speakers using standard language forms whereas high solidarity is assigned to non-standard speakers. Speech accommodation theory explains how speakers use unilateral or bilateral convergence and divergence to indicate interpersonal liking and disagreement, as well as a desire to be upwardly mobile or to resist such changes. Diglossia refers to the existence of two or more varieties or codes that are used within one linguistic culture. In some countries there are high and low forms of the language. Difference in the way men and women use language is an interesting form of diglossia.

❖ Ethnolinguistic identity theory suggests that one's language and dialect are an integral part of social and personal identity. Language and dialect are used as a means of distinguishing the ingroup from outgroups. Negative ingroup identity can be improved through revitalising "dead" languages. Ethnolinguistic group identity has implications for learning a second language, an important issue in multicultural settings.

❖ Verbal deprivation theory proposes that some non-standard forms of English may restrict intellectual development. Bernstein suggested that restricted linguistic code limits cognitive development, whereas elaborated code permits the use of abstract concepts and facilitates cognitive development. Research studies appear to support the notion that working-class children and their parents tend to use restricted codes and that this is related to poorer mental development. In addition enriched language experience has been found to increase cognitive development in working-class children. However the concept of two distinctly different codes is probably an oversimplification and, in any case, the judgement of working-class language as "restricted" may be due to a failure to understand what is being said. Labov's research showed that Black English was equal in complexity. It may be that verbal deprivation theory confuses linguistic and social deprivation.

Language Acquisition

❖ Parents are not consciously aware of teaching their children grammar, yet children master it effortlessly. There are several important features of language acquisition: speech comprehension precedes production; children also learn the following elements of speech in a fixed order: phonology, semantics, syntax, and pragmatics; and finally all children follow the stage sequence when acquiring language. An early stage of language acquisition includes babbling, echolalia, turn-taking, and nonverbal communication. Just before the age of 1 the first words appear. This one-word stage is characterised by over-extension and under-extension as well as the holophrastic use of words. The telegraphic period starts at around 18 months of age, two-word utterances use pivot and open words and follow the basic word order. Subsequent developments include the learning of morphemes and grammar. This can be seen in the classic tendency to over-regularise morpheme rules. Children also learn complex rules of pragmatics.

❖ Chomsky argued that humans possess a language acquisition device (LAD) that enables children to transform a native vocabulary into a grammatical language. Transformational grammar converts surface to deep structure, and vice versa. It may be preferable to express LAD as a universal grammar. Word order is an example of a linguistic universal: subject precedes the object in almost all languages. This may be innate but could also occur because it is an obvious feature of the environment. According to the critical period hypothesis, language learning depends on biological maturation. This view is supported by studies of children with brain damage (aphasia), second language learning, deprived children, deaf children, and trying to teach language to non-human animals. The conclusion is that some aspects of language are not driven by the innate mechanism but it appears that the unique feature of human language—its grammar—is biologically driven and disappears outside a critical period.

❖ The behaviourist approach outlined by Skinner proposes that language develops as a consequence of reinforcement, shaping, and imitation. Further concepts explain the acquisition of language: echoic responses, tacts and mands, and motherese. Children do learn by reward but this imitation cannot explain telegraphic speech nor how grammar would be learned. In some cultures adults talk very little with children yet they learn language.

❖ Nativist theory explains a child's drive to acquire and produce grammatical language, and learning theory explains the vocabulary that is acquired. Nature and nurture are necessary components of language acquisition but nurture includes social influences, as is shown by the social interactionist approach. LASS is an alternative to LAD, whereby language is acquired as the result of social support.

Problem Solving and Decision Making

❖ Thinking is perhaps the highest expression of human mental ability. It is conscious, sometimes highly focused, and involves knowledge.

❖ The Gestalt school investigated problem solving as an extension of their work on perception. Prior to this behaviourists, drawing on research with non-human animals, explained problem solving in terms of trial and error learning and operant conditioning. Gestaltists argued that there was more to problem solving than reproducing past solutions. Productive problem solving results from insight (e.g., Kohler's apes and the two-string problem) and restructuring (e.g., the pendulum solution). Reproductive problem solving results in functional fixedness (e.g., Duncker's candle problem, nine-dot problem) and problem-solving set (e.g., Luchins' water-jug problem). The Gestalt approach demonstrated that there was more to problem solving than reproduction but the concepts of "insight" and "restructuring" were not sufficiently precise. The post-Gestalt approach offers a promising combination of Gestalt concerns and information-processing approaches to problem solving

❖ The information-processing approach of Newell and Simon introduced problem-space theory, which is likened to finding your way through a maze. There is a starting point (initial knowledge state) and an ultimate goal (goal knowledge state). Movements in between (in the problem space) are mental operators that are guided by heuristics. These are efficient strategies that might solve a problem. The most important heuristic is the means–ends analysis, using the following steps: note the difference between the current state and the goal state, create a subgoal to reduce this difference, select an operator that will solve this subgoal.

❖ The predictions from this model have been tested using the Tower of Hanoi problem with some success. The General Problem Solver (GPS) computer programme was based on means–ends analysis but in the end did not mimic human problem-solving behaviour successfully. Performance on the missionaries and cannibals problem was shown to be improved by a hint that resulted in an early strategy shift, as predicted by means–ends analysis. Means–ends analysis can also be applied to the water-jug problem and can explain insight.

❖ Problem-space theory supports the reproductive nature of problem solving. The major limitations are an inability to cope with ill-defined problems and a lack of ecological validity.

❖ Some problems are novel and require creative solutions. Wallas outlined four stages in creative problem solving: preparation, incubation, illumination, and verification. This model fits self-descriptions provided by scientists. Another approach to solving novel problems is the use of analogy, as in Rutherford's use of a solar system analogy to understand the structure of the atom. Analogical mapping involves mapping a base domain (one set of ideas) into the target domain (the ideas that one is trying to explain). This produces new insights into the problem. Research support has used analogy to reconceptualise Duncker's radiation problem and promote faster solution, though this only worked if participants were given a hint. Computer models of analogical mapping, such as the Incremental Analogy Machine (IAM) have been more successful than the GPS. However the underlying processes may not be the same in machines and human minds. Recent research has linked certain areas of the brain (e.g., prefrontal cortex) to analogical thinking. The computer simulation model LISA incorporates this and ideas about access and mapping.

❖ Some problems are difficult because they impose resource limitations and/or knowledge limitations. Experts have greater knowledge but they also have schematic representations of knowledge that reduce demands on memory (resources).

❖ Decision making is part of everyday life. One approach to explaining how people make decisions that involve taking risks is utility theory. This expresses the view that we make rational decisions about the expected utility of a decision by looking at the probability of a given outcome and the utility of that outcome. Research studies show that decisions are not made on such rational grounds. This can be explained in terms of the framing effect—decisions are related to the way the problem was phrased. Further lack of rationality is shown in loss aversion—people resist decisions that have some potential loss involved even though, rationally, the likelihood of winning is greater.

❖ There are various alternatives to utility theory. Elimination-by-aspects theory suggests that decisions are made by eliminating choices on the basis of key attributes, one at a time. This makes decision making simple but may be somewhat arbitrary. Satisficing theory presents the view that we set levels of expected satisfaction that may be adjusted if they are too high or low. Satisficing may help to reduce choices. Finally, reasonableness explains that people make decisions because they feel justified in taking the most desirable option.

❖ When choices are uncertain we have to make judgements in terms of probabilities. One rule of general principle to use is the representativeness heuristic, where people use information about most typical instances and ignore base-rate information. The conjunction fallacy is an example of this and has been demonstrated in research studies. However base-rate information may be used when it is made relevant. A second heuristic, the availability heuristic, is used for probabilistic decisions. Here a decision is made on the basis of how available relevant examples are in long-term memory. An example can be seen in our overestimation of numbers of dangerous crimes because they are more widely covered in the media.

❖ This heuristic approach again emphasises the lack of rationality in decision making. However, people can in fact be quite accurate in decision making. The research findings may be due to the way participants were questioned and also the artificial nature of the tasks, so making people appear less rational than they are. It is important to take social factors and individual differences into account.

FURTHER READING

An interesting discussion of Chomsky's theory and of linguistic relativity can be found in S. Pinker (1994) *The language instinct* (New York: William Morrow & Co., Inc.). K.J. Gilhooly (1995) *Thinking: Directed, undirected and creative (3rd Edn.)* (London: Academic Press); there are thorough discussions of the major types of thinking in this book. T.A. Harley (2001) *The psychology of language: From data to theory (2nd Edn.)* (Hove, UK: Psychology Press); most aspects of language are dealt with very thoroughly in this book, and it is written in a clear fashion, but is rather complicated in parts. R.A. Hudson (1996) *Sociolinguistics (2nd Edn.)* (Cambridge: Cambridge University Press) deals with social aspects of language.

Example Examination Questions

You should spend 30 minutes on each of the questions below, which aim to test the material in this Section.

1. "We dissect nature along the lines laid down by our native languages" (Whorf, 1956).
    Critically consider research related to the linguistic relativity hypothesis.   (24 marks)

2. Discuss investigations into social and cultural aspects of language use.   (24 marks)

3. Describe and evaluate research into the process of language acquisition in humans.   (24 marks)

4. Critically consider the extent to which nativist theories of language acquisition
    can account for research evidence.   (24 marks)

5. (a) Describe **two** studies of problem solving.   (12 marks)
    (b) Assess the extent to which these and/or other studies contribute to our theoretical
         understanding of the nature of problem solving.   (12 marks)

6. Discuss research into risk-taking behaviour.   (24 marks)

Examination Tips

Question 1.   In this question you are not required to specifically address the quotation, though it may help in directing your response. You are required to "critically consider" research, i.e., both the strengths and weaknesses. "Research" refers to theories and studies so you may include both. An important issue will be selectivity in order to compose a well-structured and well-detailed response in 30 minutes. Marks will be lost if you try to cover too much evidence and end up with an essay lacking in detail.

Question 2.   "Discuss" is an AO1/AO2 term requiring a description of relevant investigations. When describing investigations you can use the same guidelines as for AS level: write something about the aims, procedures, findings, and conclusions. There is a vast range of material that could be made relevant in this essay, but ensure that you have some kind of structure to your essay rather than just a "shopping-list" of ideas. Evaluation is likely to be related to methodology and/or theoretical relevance of such investigations.

Question 3.   Studies and/or theories will be creditworthy here in the descriptive part of the answer. If you describe studies then you may evaluate them with reference to theories (stage explanations or nativist/learning theory), and vice versa. Selectivity may well be a problem, as for question 1, and therefore you might focus on certain aspects of language acquisition in humans rather than trying to provide a comprehensive account. Make sure you give a full 15 minutes to the evaluation as otherwise you limit the marks you can access.

Question 4.   This question restricts your answer to a consideration of nativist theory and the question of whether this can account for the research evidence. The descriptive element of the essay is likely to include your knowledge and understanding of nativist theory plus a description of research evidence. These two elements: theory and research evidence should be juxtaposed to decide whether the theory can or cannot account for the evidence. A balanced answer will cover both views (for and against).

Question 5.   In part (a) you should select two relevant studies and describe each in terms of aims, procedures, findings, and conclusions. Evaluation of these studies will not attract credit except in so far as it contributes to part (b) of this question. Here you can use any research evidence and consider the extent that such evidence supports any theoretical positions. As this is the AO2 component of the question you should take care not to describe any theories but instead you should present an argument and use your material to illustrate your argument. The trick here is to use your knowledge effectively in order to construct an argument in answer to the question, rather than just describing evidence. You might employ useful phrases such as "This suggests that …" or "The point this illustrates is …".

Question 6. Research can refer to theories and/or studies and, as suggested for question 3, you may describe one and then use the other as evaluation. Evaluation/commentary may also be achieved through a consideration of logical flaws in a theory, methodological flaws in research studies, practical applications, and so on. It may be possible to go beyond research that is explicitly on risk-taking, and consider other aspects of decision-making as long as this is made relevant as a form of evaluation commentary.

WEB SITES

http://www.mtsu.edu/~dlavery/Whorf/blwquotes.html
Key quotations from Benjamin Whorf's work.

http://www.cc.gatech.edu/~jimmyd/summaries/hunt1991.html
Summary of an important paper by Hunt and Agnoli.

http://www.massey.ac.nz/~i75202/ass200/kmch/contpg.html
Summary of Vygotsky's life and work.

http://members.nbci.com/jbmartins/vygotsky.htm
Vygotsky links.

http://www.piaget.org/
The Jean Piaget Society.

http://www-personal.umich.edu/~andyf/digl_96.htm
Perspectives on Arabic diglossia.

http://www.britannica.com/bcom/eb/article/6/0,5716,118106+2+109772,00.html
Encyclopædia Britannica feature on Modern Greek and its development.

http://www.zhongwen.com/
Huge site that tackles the practical and cultural obstacles facing English speakers wanting to learn Mandarin Chinese.

http://carla.acad.umn.edu/
Center for Advanced Research on Language Acquisition, University of Minnesota, USA.

http://www.june29.com/HLP/
The Human-Languages Page that contains a list of over 2000 language-related links.

http://www.clal.cornell.edu
The Cornell Language Acquisition Lab (CLAL), an American centre for study of first language acquisition.

http://www.theatlantic.com/issues/95sep/ets/labo.htm
Article by Labov on "Academic Ignorance and Black Intelligence" (1972).

http://www.cs.ucd.ie/staff/fcummins/home/CogModels/problemsolving.html#transform
Problem-solving discussion.

http://www.bus.utexas.edu/~dyerj/DA_syllabi/
Decision analysis links.

PART 4

Developmental Psychology

Developmental psychologists study the changes and constancies that occur over a person's lifetime, starting from conception and infancy through to adolescence, adulthood, and finally old age. This approach has also been called lifespan psychology. Developmental psychologists focus on how particular behaviours change as individuals grow older. Changes can be related to maturing and ageing. In children, they look at the changes in the way children think, and how they acquire language. They also look at moral, social, and gender development. Developmental psychologists might also consider changes in adolescence, such as the formation of adult identity; the changes in early and middle adulthood, such as marriage or parenthood; and the changes in late adulthood, such as coping with loss of memory.

10

Cognitive Development

Cognitive development concerns the mental changes that occur during an individual's lifetime. In this Section our focus is on the changes in children's thinking as they get older.

Development of Thinking

Children change and develop in almost every way in the years between infancy and adolescence. However, some of the most dramatic changes take place in terms of cognitive development. The first systematic theory of cognitive development was proposed by a Swiss Psychologist, Jean Piaget (1896–1980). There are several other major theoretical approaches to cognitive development, including those of Vygotsky and the information-processing theorists.

Piaget's Theory

Jean Piaget put forward the most thorough account ever offered of cognitive development. Indeed, such is the richness of his contribution that only the bare outline of his account can be provided here.

Adaptation to the environment

Piaget was interested in how children learn and adapt to the world. In order for adaptation or adjustment to occur, there must be constant interactions between the child and the outside world. According to Piaget, two processes are of key importance:

Jean Piaget, 1896–1980.

When Piaget used the term "adapt" what did he mean?

- **Accommodation**: the individual's cognitive organisation is altered by the need to deal with the environment; in other words, the individual adjusts to the outside world.
- **Assimilation**: the individual deals with new environmental situations on the basis of his or her existing cognitive organisation; in other words, the interpretation of the outside world is adjusted to fit the individual.

Consider the example of an infant playing with different objects. The infant has acquired the concept of a rattle—if you shake a certain object it makes a particular noise. When the infant picks up a new object and this makes the same noise, the infant can *assimilate* this into his or her existing cognitive organisation. The new object fits in with previous

An example of the dominance of assimilation over accommodation —pretending that cardboard boxes are vehicles.

knowledge. However, if the infant picks up another rattle-like object and discovers that makes a mewing sound, the infant must *accommodate* to this new class of objects and form a new concept.

The clearest example of the dominance of assimilation over accommodation is play, in which reality is interpreted according to the individual's whim (e.g., a stick becomes a gun). In contrast, dominance of accommodation over assimilation is seen in imitation, in which the actions of someone else are simply copied.

Schemas and equilibration

There are two other key Piagetian concepts: schemas and equilibration. **Schema** refers to organised knowledge used to guide action. It is a term that is now used throughout psychology but Piaget was one of the first psychologists to use it. Infants are born with innate schemas, such as a sucking schema. Through assimilation and accommodation these innate schemas develop into progressively more complex packets of knowledge about the world. The first schema infants develop is the body schema, when they realise there is an important distinction between "me" and "not me". This body schema helps the infant in its attempts to explore and make sense of the world.

Equilibration is based on the notion that the individual needs to keep a stable internal state (equilibrium) in a changing environment. The child tries to understand its experiences in terms of existing cognitive structures (i.e., schemas). If there is a new experience or a mismatch between the new experience and existing schemas this creates an unpleasant state of *disequilibrium* or lack of balance. The child then uses assimilation and accommodation to restore a state of equilibrium or balance. Thus, disequilibrium motivates the child to learn new skills and knowledge to return to the desired state of equilibrium.

Quantitative versus qualitative change

We can distinguish between two kinds of theorists in the area of child development. One group (e.g., behaviourists) argues that cognitive development only involves changes in the amount of knowledge available to the child, and the efficiency with which that knowledge is used in thinking. According to such theorists, there are no fundamental differences in cognition during development. As a child gets older it is a question of acquiring more knowledge. This is a **quantitative change**, a change in the amount of knowledge rather than the *kind* of knowledge or thinking (a qualitative difference).

The second group of theorists (e.g., Piaget) claim that the ways of thinking found in adolescence are very different from those of early childhood. There is a **qualitative change** in the kind of logic that the child uses. Most importantly, these qualitative changes are the result of innate maturational processes. One can use the analogy of a child learning to walk. No amount of practice will enable a child to walk before he or she is ready. This occurs when the child has matured sufficiently to have the requisite physical skills and co-ordination to do it. Piaget argued that the same was true of cognitive development and, just as learning to walk is a stage in a child's physical development, there are recognisable stages in a child's cognitive development.

Stage theory

Piaget argued that all children pass through various stages. The main assumptions of a stage theory are as follows. First, the stages are determined by innate, maturational changes. Second, although the ages at which different children attain any given stage can vary, the *sequence* of stages should remain the same for all. Third, the cognitive operations and structures defining a stage should form an integrated whole. Despite the notion of a coherence to each stage, Piaget accepted that children in a given stage do not always adopt the mode of thought typical of that stage, and he coined the term **horizontal décalage** to refer to this. The word "décalage" means to move forwards or backwards in French, or simply "a difference". So the concept is Piaget's way of expressing the fact that development is not an even process, some changes progress more rapidly than other changes.

Piaget identified four major stages of cognitive development. The first is the **sensori-motor stage**, which lasts from birth to about 2 years of age. The second is the **pre-operational stage**, spanning the years between 2 and 7. The third is the **concrete operations stage**, which usually occurs between the ages of 7 and 11 or 12. The fourth stage is the **formal operations stage**, which follows on from the stage of concrete operations.

According to Piaget, at each stage there are changes in the way children think. These are qualitative changes. It might help to have an overview of these changes before looking at the specific features of each stage. In the first stage of cognitive development very young children deal with the environment by manipulating objects. This means that sensori-motor development (learning to co-ordinate one's senses with one's motor responses) is basically *intelligence through action*.

In the next stage, which is the stage of pre-operational thought, thinking becomes dominated by *perception*. This contrasts with the third stage, from 7 years onwards, where thinking is more and more influenced by logical considerations, in other words by the ability to engage in logical thinking that is internally consistent. In the pre-operational stage, a child might call all red cars "Daddy's car" because Daddy has a red car. There is a certain logic but it is flawed and not internally consistent—it would not hold up under questioning.

In the third stage of concrete operations, the child's thinking becomes truly logical reasoning; however it can only be applied to objects that are real or can be seen. During the final stage of formal operations, the older child or adult can think logically about potential events or abstract ideas. Examples of such abstract logical thinking include mathematics and thinking about hypothetical ethical issues.

The term "operations" is used to described the internally consistent mental rules that are used in thinking. Thus "pre-operational" refers to the inability to use logical rules; "concrete operations" is the stage when operations depend on concrete examples; and "formal operations" is the ability to conduct abstract logical reasoning.

As you read through the descriptions of all four stages, remember the essence of these stages: knowledge through action, knowledge dominated by perception (what can be seen rather than logical deduction), knowledge through concrete logic, and finally knowledge through abstract reasoning.

Just as children must learn the alphabet before they can read, Piaget defined a set of stages that all children must pass through as they develop.

You have become very adept at sensori-motor co-ordination. Can you think of some examples?

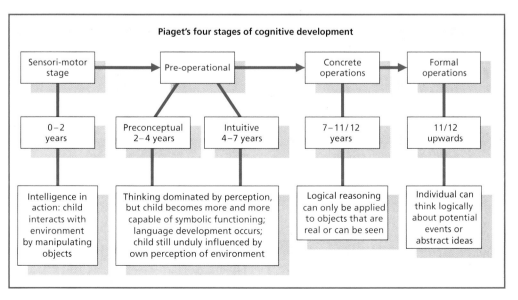

Piaget's four stages of cognitive development

Sensori-motor stage	Pre-operational		Concrete operations	Formal operations
0–2 years	Preconceptual 2–4 years	Intuitive 4–7 years	7–11/12 years	11/12 upwards
Intelligence in action: child interacts with environment by manipulating objects	Thinking dominated by perception, but child becomes more and more capable of symbolic functioning; language development occurs; child still unduly influenced by own perception of environment		Logical reasoning can only be applied to objects that are real or can be seen	Individual can think logically about potential events or abstract ideas

Sensori-motor stage (0–2 years)

What reflexes are babies born with, and how might these develop into conscious activity?

This stage of cognitive development lasts from birth to about 2 years of age, with the infant learning a great deal by moving around. Initially, the baby's schemas consist largely of inborn **reflexes** such as sucking. However, these reflexes change somewhat with experience. For example, babies learn at a very early age to alter the shape of their lips so that they can suck more efficiently.

The key achievement of this stage is **object permanence**. This involves being aware that objects continue to exist when they are no longer in view. In the early part of the sensori-motor stage, the infant has no awareness at all of object permanence: it is literally a case of "out of sight, out of mind". Object permanence develops as the child actively explores his or her environment. Towards the end of its first year, the infant starts to display what is known as **perseverative search**. This involves the infant searching for a concealed object in the place in which it was found some time earlier, rather than in the place in which it was last seen. According to Piaget, this happens because the infant does not regard the object as existing independently of the infant's own behaviour. Perseverative search shows some features of object permanence. However, full object permanence is only achieved towards the end of the sensori-motor stage.

How could the development of a baby's first words be explained in terms of imitation?

The development of imitation is a major achievement of the sensori-motor stage. Imitation allows the infant to add considerably to the range of actions of which it is capable. It develops slowly, becoming more precise over time. Towards the end of the sensori-motor stage, the infant shows evidence of **deferred imitation**, which is the ability to imitate behaviour that was seen before.

Evaluation of the sensori-motor stage.   Piaget identified many of the main kinds of learning shown by infants during the first 2 years. However, he underestimated the abilities of infants in a number of ways. For example, Bower (1982) hid a toy behind a screen. When the screen was lifted a few seconds later, the toy was no longer there. Infants who were 3 or 4 months old showed surprise. This suggests that some aspects of object permanence are present much earlier than was claimed by Piaget. This was also found by Bower and Wishart (1972). They made an object disappear from sight by removing all light from it. However, infra-red television cameras revealed that very young children reached out for the object in the correct direction, suggesting that they had at least some aspects of object permanence.

According to Piaget, deferred imitation only develops towards the end of the second year of life. However, Meltzoff (1988) found that it could occur several months earlier than Piaget believed. Many 9-month-old infants were able to imitate simple actions 24 hours after they had observed them.

Some of Piaget's explanations have not been supported. Piaget assumed that infants showing perseverative search did not remember where the toy had been hidden. However, Baillargeon and Graber (1988) carried out a study in which 8-month-old infants saw a toy being hidden behind one of two screens. Fifteen seconds later they

In the left-hand picture, the baby is reaching for a toy he can see. In the right-hand one, he searches in the same place for it, although in fact it is hidden under the paper on his right.

saw a hand lift the toy out, either from the place in which it had been hidden or from behind the other screen. The infants were only surprised when the toy was lifted from behind the "wrong" screen, indicating that they did remember where it had been put. Thus, perseverative search does *not* occur simply because of faulty memory.

There is another problem with Piaget's explanation of perseverative search. He argued that perseverative search occurs because young children believe that an object's existence depends on their own actions. It follows from this explanation that children who only passively observed the object in its first location should *not* show perseverative search. In fact, infants show as much perseverative search under those conditions as when they have been allowed to find the object in its first location.

Baillargeon and Graber found that 8-month-old infants were surprised when a cup they had seen being put behind the left-hand screen was then retrieved from behind the right-hand screen.

Pre-operational stage (2–7 years)

The child who completes the sensori-motor stage of cognitive development is still not capable of "true" thought. This child operates largely at the level of direct action, whereas the pre-operational child becomes more and more capable of symbolic functioning. The development of language is associated with the cognitive advances of pre-operational children. However, Piaget regarded language development as largely a consequence of more fundamental cognitive changes, rather than as itself a cause of cognitive advance. This is a fundamental feature of Piaget's theory, which was discussed in Section 9, Language and Thought.

Children show considerable cognitive development during the 5 years covered by the pre-operational stage. Accordingly, Piaget divided the pre-operational stage into two sub-stages: the preconceptual (2–4 years) and the intuitive (4–7 years). Two of the cognitive differences between children at the *preconceptual* and *intuitive* stages involve **seriation** and **syncretic thought**.

Seriation.   Seriation tasks require children to arrange objects in order on the basis of a single feature (e.g., height). Piaget and Szeminska (1952) demonstrated that preconceptual children found this very hard to do, and even intuitive children often used a trial-and-error approach.

Syncretic thought.   Syncretic thought can be revealed on tasks where children are asked to select various objects that are all alike. Intuitive children tend to perform this task accurately, for example selecting several yellow objects or square objects. Preconceptual children show limited syncretic thought. The second object they select is the same as the first on one dimension (e.g., size), but then the third object is the same as the second on another dimension (e.g., colour). Thus, syncretic thought occurs because young children focus on two objects at a time, and find it hard to consider the characteristics of several objects at the same time. The most common example of this is lack of the ability to **conserve**, i.e., to recognise that quantity stays the same (is conserved) even when objective appearance changes. Piaget's conservation experiments are described in the Key Study on the next page.

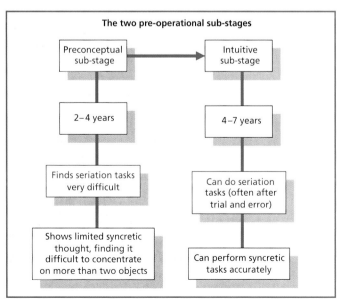

Egocentrism.   Piaget argued that the thinking of pre-operational children is characterised by egocentrism. **Egocentrism** is the tendency to assume that one's way of thinking about things is the only possible way. Piaget studied egocentric thinking in pre-operational children by

Seriation tasks require children to arrange objects in order on the basis of a single feature, such as height.

Conservation tasks

Pre-operational children are unduly influenced by their own perception of the environment. They tend to pay attention to only one aspect of the total situation (this is called **centration** by Piaget). The way in which centration produces errors is shown in studies of **conservation**. Conservation refers to understanding that certain aspects of a visual display do not vary in spite of changes in perceptual aspects. In his classic studies on conservation of quantity, Piaget presented children with two glasses of the same size and shape containing the same quantity of liquid. Once the child has agreed that there is the same quantity of liquid in both glasses, the liquid from one of the glasses is poured into a different glass that is taller and thinner. The child is then asked if the two glasses (the original one and the new one) contain the same amount to drink, or if one contains more. Pre-operational children fail to show conservation. They argue either that there is more liquid in the new container ("because it's higher") or that there is more liquid in the original glass ("because it's wider"). In either case, the child centres or focuses on only one dimension (height or width).

The pre-operational child fails on conservation tasks partly because of centration. However, the child also lacks crucial internalised cognitive operations, according to Piaget. Two cognitive operations are of special relevance to conservation tasks: reversibility and syncretic thought. Reversibility involves the ability to undo, or reverse mentally, some operation that has been carried out. Reversibility allows the realisation that the effect of pouring liquid from one container into another could be negated by simply pouring the liquid back into its original container. Syncretic thought involves the ability to take account of two or more aspects of a situation at the same time. In the case of conservation of quantity, it involves considering height and width together.

KEY STUDY EVALUATION — Conservation

Piaget used the conservation of liquid task to show that pre-operational children lack the internalised cognitive operations of reversibility and syncretic thought. However, it might be interesting to try the same experiment with children from a non-Western environment, such as the bush people of the African Kalahari desert, who are not likely to be familiar with glass beakers filled with water. Would they show conservation or not? Would a lack of conservation necessarily mean that these children could not decentre?

Discussion points

1. In what real-life situations might the ability to conserve be important?

2. What are the limitations of Piaget's research (see General Evaluation on page 371)?

using the three mountains task. Children looked at a model of mountains, and then decided which picture showed the view that would be seen by someone looking at the display from a different angle. Children younger than 8 nearly always selected the photograph of the scene as they themselves saw it. According to Piaget, this error occurred because of their inability to escape from an egocentric perspective.

Egocentrism also involves a lack of differentiation between the self and the world, which makes the child unable to distinguish clearly between psychological and physical events. This produces:

A drawing of the model used in Piaget's three mountains task. Children were shown the model from one angle, then shown photographs of the model from other viewpoints, and asked to choose which view someone standing at one of the other labelled points would see. Pre-operational children usually selected the view from the point at which they themselves had seen the model.

- *Realism*: the tendency to regard psychological events as having a physical existence. Piaget (1967, p.95) provided the following example of realism in a conversation with a child called Engl: "Where is the dream whilst you are dreaming?" "Beside me." "Are your eyes shut when you dream? Where is the dream?" "Over there."
- *Animism*: the tendency to endow physical objects and events with psychological qualities. Young children often attribute consciousness to all things. For example saying "Don't do that or the book will cry."
- *Artificialism*: the tendency to consider that physical objects and events were created by people. For example, I (Michael Eysenck) was walking across Wimbledon Common with my daughter Fleur, aged 3, and told her that the sun would come out when I had counted to 10. When it did so, she was very confident that Daddy could control the sun, and often begged me to make the sun appear on gloomy days!

Piaget's three mountains task required children to reverse a complicated image in their heads. Do you think a failure to do this necessarily shows egocentricity, or is there another explanation?

Evaluation of the pre-operational stage. Piaget identified several limitations in the thinking of pre-operational children. He also provided a theoretical account, arguing that children at this stage lack important cognitive operations (e.g., reversibility). However, Piaget greatly underestimated the cognitive abilities of pre-operational children. For example, Wheldall and Poborca (1980) claimed that children often fail on conservation tasks because they do not understand the question. Accordingly, they devised a nonverbal version of the liquid conservation task. This version was based on operant discrimination learning: the child was rewarded for making the correct choice, and language was not involved. Only 28% of their 6- and 7-year-old participants showed conservation with the standard verbal version, but 50% did so when tested on the nonverbal version. These findings suggest that misunderstanding of language is one factor involved in non-conservation. However, the fact that half of the participants were non-conservers with the nonverbal version indicates that other factors must also be involved.

Other researchers have focused on the issue of whether posing two questions in the conservation task confuses younger children. They might think that, if there are two questions, then there must be two different answers. This research is discussed in the Key Study on the next page.

Bruner, Olver, and Greenfield (1966) argued that pre-operational children may fail to show conservation because they are influenced too much by the altered appearance of the visual display. First, they used the standard version of the liquid conservation task. Then they placed two beakers of different shapes behind a screen with only the tops of the beakers visible. Next water was poured from one beaker into the other behind the screen. When asked whether there was the same amount of water in the second beaker as there had been in the first, children of all ages between 4 and 7 showed much more evidence of conservation than they had in the standard version of the task. Finally, the children were given the standard conservation task for the second time. The percentage of 5-year-olds showing conservation more than trebled from 20% on the first test under

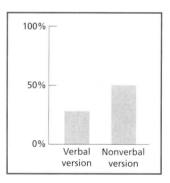

Percentages of children aged 6–7 years who showed conservation on the two versions of Piaget's conservation task (Wheldall & Poborca, 1980).

Give a definition of operant discrimination learning and how it might be demonstrated in Wheldall and Poborca's study.

Asking one question in the conservation experiment

Piaget suggested that younger children cannot cope with conservation tasks because their thinking is not sufficiently mature. Rose and Blank (1974) and Samuel and Bryant (1984) proposed that younger children fail because they find being asked two questions is confusing. The child may well think that the reason the experimenter asks the same question again is because he wants a different answer. This would be especially true because younger children are most susceptible to demand characteristics.

In Samuel and Bryant's study over 200 children aged between 5 and 8½ years were given standard conservation tasks. Some children were given this in the "traditional form" where they were asked two questions: The child is shown the original display with two beakers of liquid or two rows of counters, and asked if the displays are the same. This is followed by the transformation where the water is poured into a taller, thinner glass or one row of counters is spread out. The child is then asked the question a second time.

Another group of children were only asked the question on the second occasion. This is the "one judgement condition". The children were tested on mass (two plasticine cylinders) as well as volume and number.

Younger children did cope better with the task in the one judgement condition than the standard condition; however, there continued to be age differences. In other words the older children always did better. It is, of course, possible that the younger children may still have felt intimidated by the experimental situation and been less able to cope.

Discussion points

1. What conclusions can be drawn from this study in terms of Piaget's theory?
2. What kinds of difficulties are encountered in research with children?

A drawing of the two policemen version of Hughes' (1975) experimental set-up, in which the child is asked to hide a boy doll where neither of the policemen can see him. According to Piaget's egocentrism theory, children should hide the doll in sections A or B, where they themselves can't see him, but in fact Hughes found that 90% of children put the doll in section C—the only one the policemen cannot see.

standard conditions to about 70% on the second test. This shows that the pre-operational children were much more able to conserve when they recognised that appearances were misleading and that their learning could not be explained just by their readiness.

In addition, if Bruner asked the question "Is it still the same water?" this led to a marked increase in the number of children showing conservation. It was argued that such visual manipulation and questions increased the children's *sense of identity*. Identity involves realising that an object remains the same after it has been transformed.

Hughes (1975) argued that poor performance on the three mountains task occurred because the task did not relate to children's experience. He tested this argument by using a piece of apparatus in which two walls intersected at right angles to form what looked like a plus sign. A boy doll and a policeman doll were put into the apparatus, and the child was asked whether the policeman doll could see the boy doll. After that, the child was told to hide the boy so that the policeman could not see him. Nearly all the children could do this. Finally, a second policeman was used, and the children were told to hide the boy doll so that neither of the policemen could see him. According to Piaget, the children should have hidden the boy doll so that they themselves could not see him, and so should have failed the task. In fact, Hughes found that 90% of children between the ages of 3½ and 5 performed the task successfully. Hughes concluded that the main reason why performance was much higher on his task than on the three mountains task used by Piaget was because his task was much more meaningful and interesting for young children.

It is worth re-emphasising the fact that, in all these studies, research showed that more children were capable of the tasks than Piaget had suggested but that differences between the age groups remained.

Concrete operations stage (7–11 years)

Piaget argued that the shift from pre-operational to concrete operational thinking involves an increasing independence of thought from perception (the evidence of your senses). Underlying this shift is the development of various cognitive operations of a logical or mathematical nature, including the actions implied by mathematical symbols (e.g., +, −, ÷, X, >, <, =). The most important cognitive operation is reversibility, which involves the ability to cancel out the effects of a perceptual change by imagining the opposite change. During the concrete operations stage, children can use the various cognitive operations only with respect to specific concrete situations. In the subsequent stage of formal operations, thinking is freed from the immediate situation.

Piaget argued that cognitive operations are usually combined or organised into a system or structure. For example, the operation "greater than" cannot really be considered independently of the operation "less than". Someone will fail to grasp the full meaning of "A is greater than B" unless he or she realises that this statement means that "B is less than A". Piaget coined the term *grouping* to refer to such sets of logically related operations.

One of the tasks used to test conservation of number. Children are asked if there are the same number of beads in the two rows before and after they are rearranged.

What kinds of tasks can children perform in the concrete operations stage that they could not perform previously? One example is based on the notion of **transitivity**, which allows three elements to be placed in the correct order. For example, if Mark is taller than Peter, and Peter is taller than Robert, then it follows from the notion of transitivity that Mark is taller than Robert. Concrete operational children can solve problems such as this one, but they cannot apply the notion of transitivity to abstract problems, such as "if A > B > C, then is A greater than or smaller than C?"

Piaget argued that children should find it easier to achieve conservation on some tasks than on others. Conservation of number (e.g., realising that two rows of objects contain the same number of objects even when they are closer together in one row than in the other) involves fairly simple operations. All the child has to do is to pair each object in one row with an object in the other row. In contrast, consider conservation of volume. This can be tested by placing two identical balls of clay into two identical transparent containers filled to the same level with water. One ball of clay is then moulded into a new shape, and conservation is shown if the child realises that this will not change the amount of water it displaces. Conservation of volume is said to be harder to achieve than conservation of number because it involves taking account of the operations involved in the conservation of liquids and of mass. As predicted, conservation of volume is generally attained some years after conservation of number (e.g., Tomlinson-Keasey et al., 1979).

According to Piaget, most children acquire the various forms of conservation in the same order. First comes conservation of number and liquid at the age of about 6 or 7. Then comes conservation of substance or quantity and of length at about 7 or 8, followed by conservation of weight between the ages of 8 and 10. Finally, there is conservation of volume at about the age of 11 or 12.

Evaluation of the concrete operations stage.   Children between the ages of 7 and 11 typically learn a range of cognitive operations related to mathematics and to logic. However, Piaget's approach is limited. Children during the concrete operations stage acquire an enormous amount of new knowledge, which contributes to their cognitive development. Much of this knowledge owes little to either mathematics or logic. Thus Piaget overlooked vast areas of cognitive development.

This apparatus tests conservation of volume. Children are asked if the liquids will be at the same level again when the new shape of clay is put back into the glass. Conservation of volume is not usually attained until about the age of 11 or 12.

Piaget underestimated the importance of specific experiences in determining performance on conservation tasks. For example, children often show conservation of volume for substances with which they are familiar some time before they show conservation of volume for less familiar ones (Durkin, 1995). This is inconsistent with Piaget's stage-based account of cognitive development.

Formal operations stage (11 upwards)

Formal operational thought involves the ability to think in terms of many possible states of the world. This means

What can you do now, in terms of mental activities, that you were not able to do before you were 11?

In this game, the second player has to work out the four coloured pegs selected by the first player. The second player puts four pegs in the board and the first player provides two pieces of feedback: how many colours are correct, and how many in the correct position. The second player continues to try out various possibilities until the correct combination is found. A formal operational thinker would test possibilities in order to exclude certain combinations. For example, four red pegs could be tried to see if there are any red pegs. A concrete operational thinker would not be able to link successive guesses to eliminate factors.

one's thinking can go beyond the limitations of immediate reality, so one is not tied to perceptions and/or concrete reality. Thus adolescents and adults in the formal operations stage can think in an abstract way, as well as in the concrete way found in the previous stage of cognitive development.

Inhelder and Piaget (1958) suggested the following as a way to decide whether someone is using formal operations when solving a logical problem (such as the pendulum problem described below). If you ask a person to explain how they arrived at an answer to a logical problem, the formal operational thinker will report that they thought of a range of possibilities to account for the problem and used this range to generate hypotheses which could then be tested. The concrete thinker will have thought of a few alternatives and tried each one out in no particular order; when one possibility doesn't work another one is tried with no attempt to logically exclude certain possibilities.

The mathematical game *Mastermind*™ involves abstract logical thinking that occurs at the formal operations stage.

The pendulum problem.   What kinds of problems have been used to study formal operational thought? One task used by Piaget involved presenting the participants with a set of weights and a string that could be lengthened or shortened. The goal was to work out what determines the frequency of the swings of a pendulum formed by suspending a weight on a string from a pole. The factors that are likely to be considered include the length of the string, the weight of the suspended object, the force of the participant's push, and the position from which the pendulum is pushed. In fact, only the length of the string is relevant.

When pre-operational children are presented with this problem, they typically argue mistakenly that the strength of the push they give to the pendulum is the main factor. Concrete operational children often argue that the frequency of swinging of the pendulum is affected by the length of the string, but they cannot isolate that factor from all the others. In contrast, many formal operational children manage to solve the problem. According to Piaget, the ability to solve the pendulum problem requires an understanding of a complicated combinatorial system.

Evaluation of the formal operations stage.   It is probable that Piaget greatly exaggerated the role played by logical reasoning in adolescent and adult thought. Adults in their everyday lives typically deal with problems that have no single perfect solution, and that cannot be solved simply by the rigorous use of logic. Thus, a detailed understanding of mathematics and of logic is of limited value in most adult thinking.

It is also not clear to what extent all adults actually ever do reach this stage of formal operational thinking. For example, Wason and Shapiro (1971) devised a card selection task that requires abstract logical reasoning (see the Key Study on the next page). If this task is given in a concrete form more individuals can solve it, suggesting that not all adults can cope with abstract reasoning.

General evaluation of Piaget's theory

Piaget's theory was an ambitious attempt to explain how children move from being irrational and illogical to being rational and logical. The notion that children learn certain basic operations (e.g., reversibility), and that these operations then allow them to solve a wide range of problems, is a valuable one. No one before Piaget had provided a detailed account of the ways in which children's thinking changes.

We have seen that much of the evidence that Piaget obtained about children's cognitive development is

Children were asked to work out what would affect the frequency of the swings of the pendulum (how many times it would go back and forth in a given period). They were asked to consider changing the weights on the pendulum, the length of the string, how hard they pushed it, and which direction it was pushed in.

Wason and Shapiro

Peter Wason devised the Wason selection task to study deductive reasoning. In the original version, there are four cards lying on a table. Each card has a letter on one side, and a number on the other side. Each participant is told that there is a rule that applies to the four cards. The participant's task is to select only those cards that need to be turned over in order to decide whether or not the rule is correct.

In one of the most used versions of this selection task, the four cards have the following symbols visible: R, G, 2, and 7, and the rule is as follows: "If there is an R on one side of the card, then there is a 2 on the other side of the card". What answer would you give? Most people select either the R card or the R and 2 cards. If you did the same, then you got the answer wrong. The starting point for solving the problem is to recognise that what needs to be done is to see whether any of the cards *fail* to obey the rule. From this point of view, the 2 card is irrelevant. If there is an R on the other side of it, then all that this tells us is that the rule *might* be true. If there is any other letter, then we have found out nothing about the validity of the rule.

The correct answer is to select the cards with R and 7 on them. This answer is produced by only about 5–10% of university students. The reason why the 7 card is necessary is that it would definitely disprove the rule if it had an R on the other side.

Rule: If there is an R on one side of the card, then there is a 2 on the other.

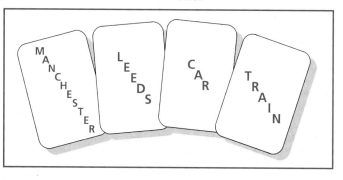

A more concrete version of the Wason selection task.

Wason and Shapiro (1971) argued that the abstract nature of the Wason task makes it hard to solve. They used four cards (Manchester, Leeds, car, and train), and the rule was, "Every time I go to Manchester I travel by car". The task was to select only those cards that needed to be turned over to prove or disprove the rule. The correct answer that the Manchester and train cards need to be turned over was given by 62% of the participants, against only 12% when the task was presented in its abstract form.

Discussion points

1. Why do you think most people find the original version of the Wason selection task so difficult?
2. How can the Wason selection task be made easier?

flawed. He used the **clinical method**, which involves the experimenter discussing the task with the child in an unstandardised and rather unscientific way. A major problem with the clinical method is that it makes considerable demands on the language ability of the child. As a result, Piaget often underestimated the cognitive abilities of children.

Some of the major assumptions on which Piaget's theory is based are inadequate:

What problems does the clinical method pose for anyone attempting to carry out a longitudinal study of a child's development?

1. Stage development

Piaget assumed that all children go through the same sequence of four major cognitive stages. One of the great dangers with stage theories is that the differences between stages will be *overestimated*, whereas those within stages will be *underestimated*. For example, Piaget assumed that children who show conservation of quantity for one material possess the operation of reversibility. As a result, they should show conservation with other materials. In fact, children generally show conservation of quantity for familiar materials some time before they show it for unfamiliar materials. Thus, successful performance depends on *specific* learning experiences as well as on the *general* cognitive operations emphasised by Piaget. In essence, cognitive development proceeds in a much more unsystematic way than Piaget assumed.

2. Performance and competence

Piaget argued that children who fail to solve a problem lack the necessary cognitive structures or competencies. There is an important distinction between performance (which is what the individual actually does) and competence (which is the underlying knowledge). As Shaffer (1993, p.268) pointed out, Piaget had a tendency "to equate *performance* with *competence* (and to ignore other factors that influence children's responses)". Donaldson (1978) drew a distinction between embedded and disembedded language. Embedded language is very much bound up in ongoing events, whereas disembedded language is not. Donaldson argued that children find it much harder to show the abilities they possess when problems are presented in disembedded language. In other words, the gap between competence and performance is greater when disembedded language is used. In similar fashion, students often find mathematics and statistics difficult, because they tend to be disembedded from the immediate experience of students. Donaldson's argument is illustrated by a study with McGarrigle (1974), which is described in the Key Study below.

McGarrigle and Donaldson

McGarrigle and Donaldson (1974) showed that there can be a large discrepancy between competence and performance. They presented 6-year-old children with two rows of counters, following a similar procedure to Piaget's classic conservation experiments. All the children agreed that there were equal numbers of counters in each row. In one condition, the experimenter deliberately messed up one of the rows. Only 16% of the children showed number conservation (i.e., argued that there were the same number of counters in each row). This finding suggests that very few of the children had the underlying competence necessary to show number conservation. However, the findings were very different in a second condition, in which a "naughty teddy bear" messed up one of the rows in what looked like an accidental way. In this condition, 62% of the children showed conservation, saying that there was no change in the number of counters.

Why did McGarrigle and Donaldson find such a large difference between the two conditions? The high level of performance in the "naughty teddy" condition must have occurred because most of the children in fact had a general understanding of number conservation. In the other condition, the fact that the experimenter deliberately altered the situation may have led the children to assume that the experimenter *intended* to change the number of counters in one of the rows. Whether or not that is correct, the fact remains that performance in the "Piaget" condition failed to reflect the underlying level of competence.

KEY STUDY EVALUATION — McGarrigle and Donaldson

Recent research suggests that McGarrigle and Donaldson may also have been mistaken. It is possible that the children were so absorbed in the "naughty teddy" routine that they didn't actually notice the transformation and that is why, with naughty teddy, they said the display hadn't changed. To test this possibility, Moore and Frye (1986) arranged for naughty teddy to actually add a counter (or take one away). Children said no change had taken place, which suggests that they were simply not attending to the display at all.

However, the notion that children may fail to show number conservation because they think the experimenter intended to change the number was further supported by Light et al. (1979). They tested 5- and 6-year-olds in pairs, with both members of each pair being given glass beakers of the same size and containing the same number of pasta shells. They were told the shells would be used to play a competitive game, and so it was essential they had the same number. Then the experimenter pretended to notice that one of the beakers had a badly chipped rim and so might be dangerous to handle. The shells were then transferred to another beaker of a different shape, and the children were asked whether the number of shells in each beaker was the same. Conservation was shown by 70% of the children in this incidental transformation condition, against only 5% in a standard intentional transformation condition. Presumably the change seemed less important when it was seen as merely incidental.

Discussion points

1. Why do you think that McGarrigle and Donaldson found such a large difference between their two conditions?

2. What problems for Piaget's theory arose from his failure to distinguish carefully between performance and competence?

McGarrigle and Donaldson found that when an experimenter rearranged one of a pair of rows of counters, relatively few 6-year-old children thought that the two rows still contained the same number of counters. However, when a teddy bear appeared to mess up the counters accidentally, most children said that the numbers in the rows were still the same.

3. Maturational processes

Piaget (1970) assumed that maturation of the brain and of the nervous system plays an important role in allowing children to move through the successive stages of cognitive development. He also assumed that new cognitive structures can develop when there is a *conflict* between what the child expects to happen and what actually happens. These assumptions are too vague to be of much value in understanding the forces producing cognitive development. Piaget provided a detailed *description* of the major changes in cognitive development, but he did not offer an adequate explanation. He told us *what* cognitive development involves, but not *why* or *how* this development occurs. However, Piaget's approach has given rise to much research, and he remains the most significant theorist on cognitive development.

Vygotsky's Theory

Lev Vygotsky (1896–1934) was a Russian psychologist who emphasised the notion that cognitive development depends very largely on social factors. According to Vygotsky (1981, p.163):

> *Any function in the child's cultural development appears twice, or on two planes. First, it appears on the social plane, and then on the psychological plane.*

As Durkin (1995) pointed out, the child can be thought of as an apprentice who learns directly from social interaction and communication with older children and adults who have the knowledge and skills that the child lacks. This approach is very different from Piaget's, where the emphasis is on the individual acquiring knowledge through a process of self-discovery.

Lev Semeonovich Vygotsky, 1896–1934.

The role of culture

Social factors, or more generally "**culture**", play a key role in cognitive development because, according to Vygotsky, they enable **elementary mental functions** to be transformed into **higher mental functions**. Elementary functions are innate capacities such as attention and sensation. Such functions are possessed by all animals and these will develop to a limited extent through experience. However cultural influences are required to transform them into higher mental functions, such as problem solving and thinking. When Vygotsky used the concept of "culture" he was referring to the body of knowledge that is held by, for example, books and "**experts**" (persons with greater knowledge), and that is largely transmitted through language. Therefore cultural knowledge and language are the means by which cognitive development takes place.

If higher mental functions depend on cultural influences then we would expect to find different higher mental functions in different cultures. Gredler (1992) recorded an example of this. Children in Papua New Guinea are taught a counting system that begins on the thumb of one hand and proceeds up the arm and down to the other fingers, ending at 29. This means that it is very difficult to add and subtract large numbers and this limits mathematical calculations in that culture. We can see another example in the advent of the internet in our cultures. This has the potential of vastly changing the speed of cognitive development in children who can now access huge stores of knowledge.

Has use of the internet affected your own cognitive development?

Vygotsky's four stages

Vygotsky argued that there are four stages in the formation of concepts. He identified these four stages on the basis of a study in which children were presented with wooden blocks provided with labels consisting of nonsense symbols. Each nonsense syllable was used in a consistent way to refer to blocks having certain characteristics, such as circular and thin. The children were given the concept-formation task of deciding on the meaning of each nonsense syllable. Vygotsky's four stages were as follows:

Can you relate any, or all, of these stages to some of the Piagetian concepts you read about earlier?

1. *Vague syncretic stage*: the children failed to use systematic strategies and showed little or no understanding of the concepts.
2. *Complex stage*: non-random strategies were used, but these strategies were not successful in finding the main features of each concept.
3. *Potential concept stage*: systematic strategies were used, but they were limited to focusing on one feature at a time (e.g., shape).
4. *Mature concept stage*: systematic strategies relating to more than one feature at a time were used, and led to successful concept formation.

Zone of proximal development

One of the key notions in Vygotsky's approach to cognitive development is the **zone of proximal development**. This was defined by Vygotsky (1978, p.86) as

> *the distance between the actual developmental level as determined by independent problem solving and the level of potential development as determined through problem solving under adult guidance or in collaboration with more capable peers.*

In other words, children who seem to lack certain skills when tested on their own may perform more effectively in the social context provided by someone with the necessary knowledge. Skills shown in the social situation but not the isolated one fall within the zone of proximal development.

Scaffolding

Wood, Bruner, and Ross (1976) developed Vygotsky's notion of a zone of proximal development. They introduced the concept of **scaffolding**, which refers to the context provided by knowledgeable people such as adults to help children to develop their cognitive skills. An important aspect of scaffolding is that there is a gradual withdrawal of support as the child's knowledge and confidence increase.

Moss (1992) reviewed a number of studies concerned with the scaffolding provided by mothers during the preschool period. There were three main aspects to the mothers' scaffolding strategies. First, the mother instructed her child in new skills that the child could not use on its own. Second, the mother encouraged her child to maintain useful problem solving tactics that it had shown spontaneously. Third, the mother tried to persuade the child to discard immature and inappropriate forms of behaviour.

Left to his own devices, could this boy make his sister a birthday cake? His mother uses scaffolding to create a situation in which he can begin to move into a zone of proximal development.

Language development

Vygotsky attached great importance to the development of language. He argued that language and thought are essentially unrelated during the first stage of development. As a result, young children have "pre-intellectual speech" and "pre-verbal thought". During the second stage, language and thought develop in parallel, and continue to have very little impact on each other. During the third stage, children begin to make use of the speech of others and talking to themselves (private speech) to assist in their thinking and problem solving. An important notion here is that of **intersubjectivity**. This refers to the process by which two individuals whose initial views about a task are different move towards an agreed understanding of what is involved.

Finally, private speech is used routinely in problem solving, and language plays a part in the development of thinking. In other words, language becomes more and more central to cognitive development over the years. Private speech is initially spoken out loud, but then becomes more and more internal. Language generally plays a crucial role when children learn from social interactions with others. Some of the processes involved were described by Berk (1994, p.62):

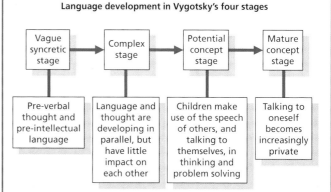

When a child discusses a challenging task with a mentor [someone providing guidance], that individual offers spoken directions and strategies. The child incorporates the language of those dialogues into his or her private speech and then uses it to guide independent efforts.

Research evidence for Vygotsky's approach

Scaffolding

There is considerable experimental evidence that approaches to teaching based on the zone of proximal development and on scaffolding can be very effective. For example, Conner, Knight, and Cross (1997) studied the effects of scaffolding on 2-year-olds, who were asked to perform various problem-solving and literary tasks. Most previous studies had focused only on mothers' scaffolding, but Conner et al. also considered fathers' scaffolding. Mothers and fathers were equally good at scaffolding, and the quality of scaffolding predicted the children's performance on the various tasks during the teaching session.

If scaffolding is to be of real value in education, then clearly its beneficial effects need to last well beyond the original teaching session. Accordingly, Conner et al. conducted a follow-up session. They found that the children who had originally received better scaffolding continued to perform better than those who had received poor scaffolding.

Social context

Wertsch et al. (1980) obtained evidence supporting Vygotsky's view that learning initially emerges in a social context. Mothers and their children between the ages of 2 and 4 were given the task of building a truck so that it looked like a model they could refer to. When the mothers of the younger children looked at the model, this was followed by their children looking at the model on about 90% of occasions. However, the older children's looking behaviour was much less influenced by what their mothers were doing. Thus, social factors in the form of the mother's looking behaviour had much more impact on younger than on older children, as would be expected according to Vygotsky's theory.

Inner speech

Vygotsky's notion that inner speech can be of value in thinking has received support, for example the study by Berk (1994), which is described in the Key Study on the next page. In another study (Hardyck & Petrinovich, 1970), participants read an easy or difficult text. Half of them were told not to use inner speech, whereas the remainder were free to do so. Comprehension of the difficult text was significantly higher when the participants were allowed to use inner speech, but the use of inner speech did not affect comprehension of the easy text. This is consistent with other evidence indicating that inner speech is of most

Children who make use of inner speech tend to perform better on difficult or novel tasks than children who do not use much inner speech.

Berk

Convincing evidence of the important role played by inner speech was reported by Berk (1994). She found that 6-year-olds spent an average of 60% of the time talking to themselves while solving problems in mathematics. Those whose speech contained numerous comments about what needed to be done on the current problem did better at mathematics over the following year. This confirmed Vygotsky's view that self-guiding speech can make it easier for children to direct their actions. Presumably this self-guiding speech made it easier for the children to focus their attention on the task in hand.

Vygotsky argued that private speech diminishes and becomes more internal as children's level of performance improves. Berk (1994) discussed a study in which 4- and 5-year-old children made Lego™ models in each of three sessions. As predicted by Vygotsky, the children's speech became increasingly internalised from session to session as their model-making performance improved. Thus, as Vygotsky assumed, private speech is of most value to children when they are confronted by novel tasks that they do not fully understand.

KEY STUDY EVALUATION — Berk

The usefulness of Vygotsky's theory of diminishing speech depends on what is meant by "speech". For example, some children with learning difficulties are unable to speak but can perform quite well on many types of tasks. Children who are born profoundly deaf and whose families are hearing often find speech difficult or impossible to acquire, but their intelligence is sometimes unimpaired. It is interesting to speculate whether deaf children of deaf parents who grow up using sign language can use signs as their own private "speech" in the way described by Vygotsky.

Discussion points

1. How important do you think that private speech is in children's thinking?

2. Why does private speech become less frequent when children begin to master a task?

---

value when tasks are difficult (Eysenck & Keane, 1995). Behrend et al. (1992) used whispering and observable lip movements as measures of inner speech. Children who used the most inner speech tended to perform difficult tasks better than children who made little use of inner speech.

Evaluation of Vygotsky's approach

There are several significant strengths of Vygotsky's theoretical approach. As he argued, children's cognitive development does depend importantly on the social context and on guidance provided by adults and other children. Piaget underestimated the importance of the social environment, and Vygotsky deserves credit for acknowledging the key role it plays in cognitive development. It follows from Vygotsky's approach that there should be major differences in cognitive development from culture to culture, whereas Piaget argued that children everywhere go through the same sequence of cognitive stages in the same order. There is some evidence for the universal stages emphasised by Piaget (see Eysenck, 1984), but there are also important cultural differences in cognitive development.

There are several limitations with Vygotsky's theoretical approach. First, he has been criticised for exaggerating the importance of the social environment. Children's rate of cognitive development is determined by their level of motivation and interest in learning, as well as by the social support they receive.

Second, the account he offered is rather sketchy. He did not make it clear precisely what kinds of social interaction were most beneficial for learning (e.g., general encouragement versus specific instructions). According to Durkin (1995, p.380), the followers of Vygotsky "offer only superficial accounts of how language is actually used in the course of social interactions".

Third, social interactions between, for example, parent and child do not always have beneficial effects. Indeed, social interactions can make matters worse rather than

Parents can provide their children with an excellent start in acquiring skills if they support and encourage attempts to learn through play.

better. As Durkin (1995, p.375) pointed out, "People confronted with an opposing point of view … dig their heels in, get hot under the collar, refuse to budge, exploit their knowledge as a source of power and control, and so on."

Fourth, Vygotsky assumed that social interactions enhanced cognitive development because of the instruction that was provided. However, there are other reasons why children benefit from social interactions. Light et al. (1994) found on a computer-based task that children learned better in pairs than on their own, even when the other child was merely present and did not say anything. This is known as **social facilitation**, and occurs because the presence of others can have a motivational effect.

Fifth, it would seem from Vygotsky's account that nearly all learning should be fairly easy if children receive the appropriate help from adults and other children. In fact, young children often take months or years to master complex skills even when they are well supported in their schools and homes. This suggests that there are genuine constraints on children's learning that were ignored by Vygotsky.

Vygotsky developed his theory during the last 10 years of his life, before he died of tuberculosis at the tragically early age of 38. At least some of the weaknesses of his approach might have been resolved had he lived longer.

Does social facilitation only apply to young children? Are there times when it might apply to older individuals?

When children are in company they tend to be more motivated to learn—even a boring garden hose needs to be investigated.

Information-processing Approach

Most cognitive psychologists have made use of the information-processing approach in their attempts to understand cognition in adults. According to this approach, the human mind is like is an information-processing system that consists of a small number of *processes* (e.g., attention) and of *structures* (e.g., long-term memory). This system is used in flexible ways to handle all kinds of cognitive tasks ranging from simple mathematics to reading a novel, and from studying French to playing chess. More specifically, it is assumed by information-processing theorists that external stimuli are attended to, then perceived, and then various thought processes (e.g., problem solving) are applied to them. Finally, a decision is made as to what to do with the stimuli, and some kind of response is produced.

What are the implications of the information-processing approach for understanding cognitive development? As Meadows (1994) pointed out, there are various possible ways in which cognitive development might occur within this approach. It might involve a development of each of the basic processes, and/or the ability to use these basic processes efficiently, and/or the overall control and sequencing of these basic processes. Thus, for example, children may develop attentional or perceptual skills as they grow up, the capacity of short-term memory may increase, their problem-solving skills may improve, and so on. Each of these basic processes can combine with the other processes to multiply the kind of thinking the child can use. It is also important to develop executive control to co-ordinate this thinking.

One of the most obvious differences between children and adults is in the size of the knowledge base: on most tasks, adults possess much more relevant knowledge than children. Does this make a difference? Evidence that it can was reported by Chi (1978), who carried out a study on 10-year-old children who were skilled chess players and on adults who knew little about chess. The adults had much better digit recall than the children, but the children's ability to recall chess positions was more than 50% better than that of the adults. The finding that the children recalled chess positions better than the adults indicates the

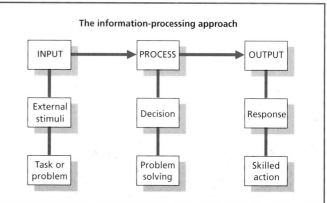

The information-processing approach

INPUT → PROCESS → OUTPUT

External stimuli — Decision — Response

Task or problem — Problem solving — Skilled action

importance of relevant knowledge. Adults generally have superior cognitive processes and ability to perform tasks, and the only obvious advantage possessed by the children was their greater knowledge of chess.

One of the key features of cognitive development from the information-processing perspective is a great increase in **automatic processes**, that is, processes that occur rapidly and with minimal use of processing capacity. Good examples can be found in reading and arithmetic. For most older children and adults, the processes involved in identifying words or simple multiplication (e.g., 5 × 6) are essentially automatic and effortless. For children who are just starting school, these cognitive activities can be very demanding. The basic processes underlying reading and arithmetic become automatic as a result of prolonged practice. (Automatic processing was discussed in Section 7, Attention and Pattern Recognition.)

Approach of Case and Pascual-Leone

Can you recall trying to master a skill, such as multiplication or telling the time, which seemed impossible to grasp but is now automatic?

Case (1974) and Pascual-Leone (1984) were both strongly influenced by Piaget's theoretical approach. They agreed with Piaget that children actively structure their understanding, and that children move from pre-concrete to concrete thinking, and then on to abstract thinking. However, their views differed from those of Piaget in some important ways.

Neo-Piagetian theory

First, they argued that it was desirable to consider cognitive development within an **information-processing framework**. Second, they claimed that it was preferable to focus on specific components of cognitive processing rather than the more general schemas emphasised by Piaget. Third, they argued that much of cognitive development depends on an increase in mental capacity or mental power. These areas of agreement and disagreement with Piaget led them to develop a neo-Piagetian theory of cognitive development.

According to Pascual-Leone (1984), a key aspect of mental capacity is "M". This refers to the number of schemes or units of cognition that a child can attend to or work with at any given time. M increases as children grow up, and this is one of the main reasons for cognitive development. Pascual-Leone assumed that increased M or processing capacity resulted from neurological development.

The information-processing approaches of Pascual-Leone and Case revolve around the notion of schemes or basic units of cognition, which resemble Piaget's schemas. Case (1974) identified three kinds of schemes:

Figurative schemes	Operative schemes	Executive schemes
Internal representations of items of information with which a subject is familiar or of perceptual configurations he or she can recognise	Internal representations of function (rules), which can be applied to one set of figurative schemes in order to generate a new set	Internal representations of procedures, which can be applied in the face of particular problem situations, in an attempt to reach particular objectives
For example: recognising one's own school from a photograph	For example: deciding that two photographs depict the same school	For example: looking at a work colleague and deciding whether to use an operative scheme related to work goals or an operative scheme related to social goals

According to this theory, a child's ability to solve a problem depends on four basic factors. First, there is the range of schemes that the child has available. Second, there is the child's M-power or mental capacity, which increases with age. Third, there is the extent to which the child uses all of its available M-power. Fourth, there is the relative importance that the child gives to perceptual cues on the one hand and to all other cues on the other.

How do children acquire new schemes? Case (1974) suggested that they can be formed by modifying existing schemes. Alternatively, new schemes can be acquired by the combination or consolidation of several existing schemes.

Research evidence

This theory can be applied to many of Piaget's findings. For example, Piaget found that children below the age of 7 generally did not realise that the amount of water remains the same when it is poured from one container into another that is taller and thinner. According to Piaget, this is because these children do not understand the logic of conservation. According to Pascual-Leone (1984), this is often because the children do not have enough mental capacity to hold all the relevant schemes in mind. Suppose that the conservation task were made easier by filling the containers with beads and allowing children to count the number of beads. Piaget would still expect the children to fail, because they have not learned the underlying logic, whereas Case and Pascual-Leone would predict more success, because the demands on mental capacity have been reduced. When this study was carried out, the findings supported the neo-Piagetians rather than Piaget (Bower, 1979).

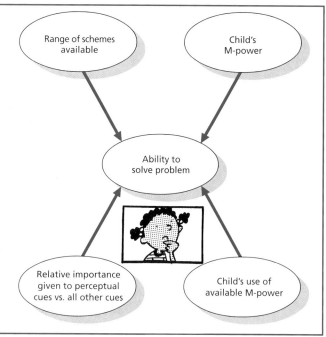

The value of this approach can also be seen in a study discussed by Case (1992). Children and adolescents aged between 10 and 18 were asked to draw a picture of a mother who was looking out of the window of her home and could see her son playing peekaboo with her in the park on the other side of the road. The younger participants found it very hard to do this. They could draw the mother in the house and the boy in the park, but they did not seem to have enough mental capacity to integrate the two parts of the drawing. In contrast, the older participants did produce an integrated drawing, because they had greater M-power.

Evaluation

There are some clear advantages to this theory compared with Piaget's approach. First, the information-processing approach has been applied with great success to the study of adult cognition, and it is reasonable to extend that approach to children's cognition. Second, Piaget argued that children fail to solve problems because they lack the necessary logical or other structures, rather than because of processing limitations. It is argued correctly within the theories of Case and Pascual-Leone that many problem-solving failures in children depend on processing limitations or insufficient M-power. Third, the concepts (e.g., different types of schemes) used by theorists such as Case and Pascual-Leone tend to be easier to measure than the schemas included in Piaget's theory.

On the negative side, there are problems in testing the theory. First, it is often hard to work out how many schemes are required to solve a task, or to decide how many schemes are actually being used by a given child.

Second, it is not at all easy to calculate someone's mental capacity. There is a danger of assuming that success results from sufficient mental capacity and failure results from insufficient mental capacity, without actually measuring mental capacity at all. When that happens, the findings are simply re-described rather than explained.

Third, it is very hard to distinguish between changes in strategies and changes in M-space or mental capacity. As Meadows (1986, p.41) pointed out, "Attempts to measure the size of M-space have to hold strategy and strategy demands constant if they are to distinguish between changes in the size of M-space and changes in the way a stably-sized

If schemas or schemes are hypothetical structures, why might this be a limitation of theories that include them?

COMPARISON OF THE THREE MAIN APPROACHES		
Information-processing	**Vygotsky**	**Piaget**
Children's intellectual development is explained in terms of automatic processes	Children are participating in an interactive process whereby knowledge becomes individualised through socially and culturally determined knowledge	Children's intellectual development can be seen in terms of the individual's adaptation to the environment

space is used." In fact, Case (1985) admitted that children's cognitive development may depend more on changing strategies than on basic mental capacity.

Practical Applications to Education

The theories of cognitive development put forward by Piaget, by Vygotsky, and by information-processing theorists have been very influential in the field of education. Here, we will focus on some of the ways in which their ideas have had an impact on education in schools. However, it is worth noting that many of the educational methods discussed are also used very successfully by parents and others outside the school context.

Piaget's approach

Do you think that children receive more "education" in school or at home?

Piaget himself did not focus very much on the usefulness of his theory for educational practice. However, many people working in education have done precisely that. The Plowden Report in 1967 suggested that some of Piaget's ideas should be used in schools. Years later, the Nuffield Science approach to education was based on the Piagetian notions that children should be actively involved in learning, and that concrete practical work should precede the more abstract aspects of science. Next we consider three of the main ways in which Piagetian theory has been applied in education.

What can children learn?

According to Piaget, what children can learn is determined by their current stage of cognitive development. In other words, it is very much limited to what they are "ready" to learn. More specifically, children can only deal successfully with tasks that make use of the various cognitive structures and operations they have already mastered.

This prediction has received little support. Several attempts have been made to teach concrete operations to preschool children. The ability to perform concrete operational tasks is normally learned at about the age of 7. Thus, it should not be possible on Piagetian theory for much younger children to perform them successfully. However, provision of suitable training to 4-year-olds usually leads to reasonably good performance on such tasks (Brainerd, 1983). In other words, Piaget seems to have underestimated the ability of children to cope with new kinds of intellectual challenge.

How should children be taught?

According to Piaget, children learn best when they engage in a process of active **self-discovery**. Children apply the processes of assimilation and accommodation to their active involvement with the world around them. Teachers can encourage this by creating a state of disequilibrium, in which the child's existing schemas or cognitive structures are shown to be inadequate. Disequilibrium can be created by asking children difficult questions, and by encouraging them to ask questions.

Some of these ideas can be applied to playgroup practices and to children playing with toys. According to Piaget, children will obtain the most benefit from playgroups and from toys when they are actively involved in a process of self-discovery. In what Piaget called mastery play, the child uses new motor schemas in several different situations. This helps to strengthen the child's learning.

Piaget recommended that disequilibrium be created by asking children difficult questions.

Piaget's preferred educational approach can be contrasted with the more traditional approach, in which the teacher provides relatively passive children with knowledge. Piaget argued that this approach (sometimes called **tutorial training**) is much less effective than self-discovery. In his own words, "Every time we teach a child something, we prevent him from discovering it on his own."

Brainerd (1983) reviewed the relevant studies. He concluded that, "although self-discovery training can produce learning, it is generally less effective than tutorial learning". Meadows (1994) arrived at a similar, but broader conclusion: "Piagetian theory emphasises the individual child as the virtually independent constructor of his own development, an emphasis that under-values the contribution of other people to cognitive development and excludes teaching and cultural influences."

Socio-cognitive conflict.   The notion of disequilibrium was developed by neo-Piagetians such as Doise and Mugny (1984). They argued that cognitive development involves the resolution of **socio-cognitive conflict**, which is produced by exposure to the differing views of others. In other words, they emphasised social factors in learning more than Piaget did.

Evidence indicating the importance of socio-cognitive conflict was reported by Ames and Murray (1982), in a study on children aged 6 and 7 who had failed on conservation tasks. Some of the children were given corrective feedback, and others were exposed to children who already knew about conservation. Still others were paired with children who had also failed to conserve, but who had provided a different wrong answer from the one they had produced. Children in the last condition showed the greatest improvement in ability to conserve. Presumably this happened because socio-cognitive conflict and the need to consider the task in detail were greatest in this condition.

The neo-Piagetians also emphasised the importance of **social marking**, which involves conflict between an individual's cognitive understanding and some social rule. Doise et al. (1981) studied conservation of liquid in children between the ages of 4 and 6 who did not initially show conservation. Social marking was induced in some pairs of children by reminding them of the social rule that both children deserved the same reward. Other pairs of children were not reminded of this rule. The children in the social marking condition saw a conflict between the social rule and the apparently different amounts of liquid in the two containers, and this helped them to show conservation. This approach offers useful guidance to educators in suggesting what particular interventions are helpful.

What should children be taught?

Piaget claimed that cognitive development depends very much on children learning a range of schemas or cognitive structures (e.g., operations). Many of these schemas are based on mathematical or logical principles. It follows that it should be useful for children to study mathematics and logic, as well as science subjects that provide illustrations of these principles at work. Of crucial importance is the notion that the learning material must not be too complex and far removed from the child's existing schemas. According to Piaget, children can only learn effectively when they possess the relevant underlying schemas that can be accommodated to new experiences.

The major weakness of Piaget's position is that the cognitive structures he emphasised are of rather limited value for many kinds of learning. It is not clear that concrete and formal operations are of much relevance to the learning of foreign languages or of history. Thus his approach applies only to a small number of subjects taught at school.

Evaluation

In sum, Piaget's ideas have influenced educational practice in several countries. However, the available evidence indicates that this influence has been of limited value. In some cases (e.g., tutorial training), the more traditional approach seems to be superior to Piaget's alternative approach.

Vygotsky's approach

Vygotsky's key contribution to educational practice was the notion that children typically learn best in a social context in which someone who is more knowledgeable carefully guides and encourages their learning efforts. Thus, children can be regarded as apprentices who are taught the necessary skills by those who already possess them, by means of scaffolding. Effective teachers or tutors will generally reduce their control over the learning process when children are performing successfully, but will increase their control when children start making errors.

Most children in Western societies spend many years in school. What implication might this have for trying to apply such a universal theory to all children?

Which group would be predicted to do best according to Vygotsky's theory?

What school subjects are difficult to link with Piaget's theory? Which subjects fit well with the theory?

To be an effective tutor, this father needs to avoid interfering while his son is managing alone, but be prepared to help when the boy gets stuck.

Vygotsky's ideas are relevant at home as well as in the school environment. Some parents do not make use of scaffolding, and do not discuss issues with their children in a way appropriate to their level of understanding. As a result, the children tend to have poor concentration, and find it hard to develop activities (Meadows, 1994).

Peer tutoring

According to Vygotsky, it is important for those involved in educating children to focus on the children's zone of proximal development. It could be argued that the ideal tutors are children who are slightly older and more advanced than the children being taught. Such tutors have useful knowledge to communicate to the children being taught. They should also remember the limitations in their own knowledge and understanding when they were 1 or 2 years younger. The approach we have just described is known as **peer tutoring**, and it has become increasingly popular in schools.

Peer tutoring is generally effective. Barnier (1989) looked at the performance of 6- and 7-year-olds on various spatial and perspective-taking tasks. Those who were exposed to brief sessions of peer tutoring with 7- and 8-year-old tutors performed better than those who were not. The benefits of peer tutoring have been found in various cultures. Ellis and Gauvain (1992) compared 7-year-old Navaho children and Euro-American children who performed a maze game. They were tutored by either one or two 9-year-old tutors working together. The children from both cultures benefited more from the paired tutors than from the individual ones, and the benefit was the same in both cultures. There were some cultural differences in the teaching style of the tutors: the Euro-American tutors gave many more verbal instructions, and were generally less patient.

Collaboration and conflict

Forman and Cazden (1985) found that collaboration as recommended by Vygotsky and conflict as recommended by the neo-Piagetians both have a role to play. They studied 9-year-olds who had to carry out an experiment on chemical reactions. Collaboration among the children was very useful early on when the apparatus had to be set up. Later on, however, when they had to make decisions about how to carry out the experiment (e.g., which combinations of elements would produce which effects), conflict seemed to be more useful than collaboration. An important implication of this study is that any given teaching method is likely to work better in some situations than in others.

Learning through play

Vygotsky also argued that children can learn much through play. According to Vygotsky (1976, p.552):

Peer tutoring: a girl teaches her younger sister to count.

> *In play, the child functions above his average age, above his usual everyday behaviour, in play he is head high above himself.*

Why is this? A key reason is because children at play generally make use of some aspects of their own culture. For example, they may pretend to be a firefighter or a doctor, or they may play with toys that are specific to their culture. This relationship to their own culture enhances learning.

Evaluation

There is convincing evidence that the scaffolding provided by peers or by teachers can be very effective in promoting effective learning at school. However, the Vygotskyan approach has various limitations. First, as Durkin (1995, p.375) pointed out, the whole approach is based on the dubious assumption that, "helpful tutors team up with eager tutees to yield maximum learning outcomes". In fact, as Salomon and Globerson (1989) pointed out, there are several reasons why this assumption is often incorrect. For example, if there is too much status difference between the tutor and the learner, the learner may become uninvolved in the learning process. Another possibility is what Salomon and Globerson called "ganging up on the task", in which the tutor and learner agree that the task is not worth doing properly.

Second, Durkin (1995) argued that the Vygotskyan approach may be better suited to some kinds of tasks than to others. Many of the successful uses of scaffolding have been on construction tasks of various kinds. In contrast, Howe, Tolmie, and Rodgers (1992) studied peer tutoring on a task concerned with understanding motion down an incline. Peer tutoring was of very little benefit, whereas thinking about the underlying ideas proved useful.

Third, the main focus of the Vygotskyan approach to education is on the contribution made by the tutor or expert to the understanding of the child or apprentice. In fact, it is probable that the success or otherwise of scaffolding depends crucially on the responsiveness of the tutor to the thoughts and actions of the child. In other words, those who favour Vygotsky's approach sometimes emphasise *external* factors in learning (e.g., the instructions given by the tutor) while minimising *internal factors* (e.g., the child's knowledge and activities).

Think back to your own experiences at school: which method helped you to learn most successfully?

Does thinking about the ideas underlying a task link more closely with the Piagetian or the information-processing approach?

Information-processing approach

Task analysis and error analysis

There are several implications of the information-processing approach for education. The most important one is that teachers should engage in a careful task analysis of the information they want to communicate to the children in their class. A task analysis involves breaking down the target activity (the information) into constituent elements. This is necessary to ensure that the material is presented in the most effective way so that the child understands the task. It is also of value in identifying the reasons why some children perform a task inaccurately. If teachers have a clear idea of the information and processes needed to perform the task, they can analyse children's errors to see which rules or processes are being used wrongly. We will consider concrete examples of these implications.

Reading.   Information-processing researchers have shown that there are two different ways in which people can read individual words:

1. use is made of rules to translate the written letters and syllables of the word into sound patterns;
2. the word and its pronunciation are found in long-term memory; this approach works best with fairly familiar words.

How was reading taught in your school? What rules of spelling do you remember?

These two ways correspond to two methods of teaching reading: the phonic method, in which the word is broken down into parts (e.g., c-a-t), and the look-and-say or whole-word method. Many teachers used to favour one method or the other, but it is increasingly recognised that the process of learning to read can be speeded up by using a combination of the two methods.

The two approaches to reading (phonic and whole-word) are used separately or together in the wide variety of materials available for teaching and developing reading skills.

Mathematics.   Brown and Burton (1978) used errors to identify children's problems in mathematics. They used the term "bug" to refer to the systematic errors in the arithmetic rules used by children. For example, a child might claim that $736 - 464 = 372$ and that $871 - 663 = 218$ because he or she is using the mistaken rule that subtractions in the hundreds, tens, and units columns are never affected by what has happened in the column to the right. Brown and Burton devised computerised games that provided teachers with training in identifying bugs. As a

result, teachers detected bugs more quickly than before, and they appreciated that some errors in mathematics are due to faulty rules rather than simply to lack of attention.

Other implications
Other implications are as follows:

Implication 1.   Parts of the information-processing system, especially those concerned with attention and short-term memory, have very limited capacity. As a result, it is important that teachers present tasks in such a way that these limited capacities are not overloaded. The development of automatic processes is very useful in this connection. As an example of this, Beck and Carpenter (1986) argued that children often find it hard to understand what they read because their processing capacity is focused on identifying individual words and parts of words. Accordingly, they gave children huge amounts of practice in identifying and making use of sub-word units such as syllables. This led to substantial increases in the speed and accuracy of word recognition, and also produced enhanced comprehension of reading material.

What metacognitive knowledge do you have in relation to taking exams?

Implication 2.   Children benefit from gaining **metacognitive knowledge** about cognitive processes; such knowledge involves understanding the value of various cognitive processes (e.g., knowing that processing of meaning will enhance long-term memory). Children and even adults often lack important metacognitive knowledge. For example, in order to understand a text fully, readers need to focus on the structure of the text, including identifying its main theme. However, children typically lack this metacognitive knowledge, and focus on individual words and sentences rather than the overall structure. Palincsar and Brown (1984) gave children specific training in thinking about the structure of the texts they were reading. This led to a significant increase in their comprehension ability.

Implication 3.   Tasks that involve **implicit learning** need to be taught in a different way from other tasks. Implicit learning was defined by Seger (1994, p.163) as "learning complex information without complete verbalisable knowledge of what is learned". There is often little value in giving people explicit instructions on implicit learning tasks, as is illustrated by the following study.

Berry and Broadbent (1984) used a complex implicit learning task in which a sugar-production factory had to be "managed" to maintain a specific level of sugar output. This task involved implicit learning, because most of those who learned to perform the task effectively were unable to explain the principles underlying their performance. Of key importance, Berry and Broadbent found that giving their participants very explicit instructions about how to control sugar production did not improve performance. Children improve their performance on implicit learning tasks by performing them repeatedly with feedback, rather than by being told what to do.

Evaluation
The information-processing approach has proved of use in education. Its greatest value is that it provides techniques for identifying the processes and strategies required to complete tasks successfully. However, the approach is limited in several ways. First, there are many tasks where it is hard to identify the underlying processes. Second, it is often hard to assess accurately the capacity limitations of any given child, and so the point at which overload will occur is not easy to predict. Third, the information-processing approach often indicates *what* processes are involved in performing a task without specifying *how* children can learn to acquire those processes.

SUMMARY OF THE DIFFERENT APPROACHES TO EDUCATION		
Piaget	**Vygotsky**	**Information-processing**
Child-centred ("discovery learning")	Teacher–child interaction ("social learning")	Development of skills, strategies, and rules

Development of Measured Intelligence

What is Intelligence?

In this Unit we are concerned with the factors involved in the development of children's intelligence test performance (measured intelligence). An obvious starting point is to consider the meaning of intelligence. According to Sternberg (1985, p.45), intelligence is

> *mental activity directed towards purposive adaptation to, and selection and shaping of, real-world environments relevant to one's life.*

There tends to be a gap between such definitions of intelligence and tests of intelligence. Sternberg offered a broad definition of intelligence, which includes the ability to cope successfully with life. In contrast, most intelligence tests measure basic cognitive abilities such as thinking, problem solving, and reasoning. These cognitive abilities are of value when coping with life, but successful individuals tend also to possess various "streetwise" skills not assessed by most intelligence tests. (There is a further discussion of intelligence, and the evolution of this ability, in Section 15, Evolutionary Explanations of Human Behaviour.)

Measured intelligence

The most common measure of intelligence is the intelligence quotient or IQ, obtained from intelligence tests (see box below). This is a measure of general intelligence that does not

---

Intelligence tests

In 1905, Binet and his associate Simon produced a wide range of tests measuring comprehension, memory, and other cognitive processes. This led to numerous later tests. Among the best known of such tests are the Stanford–Binet test produced at Stanford University in 1916, the Wechsler Intelligence Scale for Children, and, in the 1970s, the British Ability Scales.

These and other tests measure several aspects of intelligence. Many contain vocabulary tests in which individuals are asked to define the meanings of words. Tests often also include problems based on analogies (e.g., "Hat is to head as shoe is to ___"), and tests of spatial ability (e.g., "If I start walking northwards, then turn left, and then turn left again, what direction will I be facing?"). They also include vocabulary tests to assess an individual's level of verbal ability.

All the major intelligence tests share key similarities. They have manuals that spell out how the test should be administered. This is important, because the wording of the instructions often affects the tested person's score. The major tests are also alike in that they are **standardised tests**. Standardisation of a test involves giving it to large, representative samples of the age groups for which the test is intended. The meaning of an individual's score can then be evaluated by comparing it against the scores of other people.

It is possible with most standardised tests to obtain several measures of an individual's performance. These measures are mostly of a fairly specific nature (e.g., arithmetic ability or spatial ability). However, the best-known measure is the very general IQ or **intelligence quotient**. This reflects performance on all of the sub-tests contained in an intelligence test, and is thus regarded as an overall measure of intellectual ability.

How is the IQ calculated? An individual's test performance is compared against the scores obtained by other children of his or her age or by other adults in the standardisation sample. Most intelligence tests are devised so that the overall scores are normally distributed: we do not know what the "real" distribution of intelligence looks like. The normal

distribution is a bell-shaped curve in which there are as many scores above the mean as below it. Most scores cluster fairly close to the mean (see graph below), and there are fewer and fewer scores as you move away from it. The spread of scores in a normal distribution is usually indicated by a statistic known as the standard deviation. In a normal distribution, 68% of the scores fall within one standard deviation of the mean or average, and 95% fall within two standard deviations.

Intelligence tests have a mean of 100 and a standard deviation of about 16. Thus, an IQ of 116 is one standard deviation above the mean, and indicates that the individual is more intelligent than 84% of the population. That is because 50% fall below the mean, and a further 34% between the mean and one standard deviation above it.

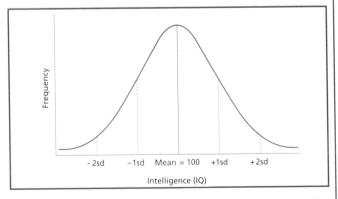

Those with high IQs do not usually perform well on all of the tests within an intelligence test battery, nor do those with low IQs perform poorly on every test. As a result, tests are usually constructed to obtain measures of various abilities (e.g., numerical; spatial; reasoning; perceptual speed). We can obtain a more accurate assessment of an individual's intelligence by considering the profile of his or her performance across these abilities than by focusing only on IQ.

Reliability and validity

Good intelligence tests have high reliability and validity. **Reliability** refers to the extent to which a test provides consistent findings, and **validity** refers to the extent to which a test measures what it is supposed to be measuring. The question of validity is important when considering the use of IQ tests in different cultural settings. In such situations we might ask whether it is valid to test one cultural group using a test derived from another cultural definition of intelligence.

Streetwise skills such as the commercial, bargaining, and economic abilities these children possess are not measured by conventional intelligence tests.

Why do you think drawing might be less valued than a practical skill like wire-shaping in some cultures?

We can see a person's phenotype, but their genotype lies hidden.

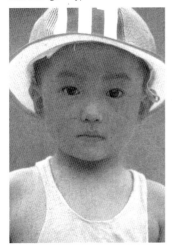

take account of the fact that some people are much more intelligent in some ways than others. For example, consider the case of a boy called Christopher. His tested IQ was 75 or less, which is substantially below the population average of 100. In spite of that, he could speak 17 languages, and many of them fluently (Smith & Tsimpli, 1991).

Class and cultural differences

Another limitation of intelligence tests is that there are various reasons why they may underestimate children's intelligence. First, children may not be well motivated to do their best. Zigler et al. (1973) studied the intelligence test performance of preschool children from poor and middle-class backgrounds. Those from poor backgrounds showed gains of almost 10 points of IQ after a play session or when tested a second time, indicating that their IQ assessed in the normal way was an underestimate. In contrast, middle-class children showed a much smaller increase of about 3 IQ points when given a play session or tested a second time.

Second, most intelligence tests are devised by white, middle-class psychologists from Western societies. As a result, the tests they produce may underestimate the intelligence of those from other cultures or social backgrounds. Some support for this point of view was reported by Williams (1972), who devised the Black Intelligence Test of Cultural Homogeneity (BITCH). This test was aimed at black American children, and white American children did less well on this test than most standard ones.

Third, intelligence tests do not take account of the fact that cultures vary in the skills that are valued. For example, Serpell (1979) compared the performance of English and Zambian children on two tasks. The English children did better at a drawing task, whereas the Zambian children did better on a wire-shaping task. This illustrates the fact that differences between cultures are qualitative rather than quantitative, i.e., no one culture is better than any other culture (a quantitative difference), there simply are variations (a qualitative difference).

Heredity and environment

Why are some children more intelligent than others? At the most general level, there are only two factors that could be responsible: heredity and environment. Heredity consists of each person's genetic endowment, the instructions that tell your body to produce hair of a particular colour, or blood of a particular blood group, or an easy or difficult temperament. Environment consists of the situations and experiences encountered by people in the course of their lives. It is generally assumed that individual differences in intelligence depend on both heredity and environment. As we will see, many psychologists have tried to determine the relative importance of heredity and environment in determining intelligence. However, the Canadian psychologist Donald Hebb argued that this is an essentially meaningless issue. He claimed that it is like asking whether a field's area is determined more by its length or by its width. Of course, its area depends equally on both length and width. In similar fashion, Hebb argued, intelligence depends equally on both heredity and environment.

Hebb's argument is perhaps not as convincing as it sounds. Even though it is clear that the area of a field depends equally on its length and width, we can still reasonably ask whether the areas of different fields vary more because of differences in their lengths or in terms of their widths. In the same way, we can ask whether individual differences in intelligence depend more on differences in genetic endowment or on environmental differences.

Those who believe in the importance of heredity draw a distinction between the **genotype** and the **phenotype**. The genotype is the genetic instructions that each individual is given at conception. These instructions offer a blueprint for characteristics and behaviour but are meaningless until they can be expressed through the environment. The phenotype consists of an individual's observable characteristics. So far as intelligence is concerned, we cannot access the genotype. All that can be done is to assess the phenotype by means of administering an intelligence test.

Why isn't it possible to test an indiviual's genotype directly with an IQ test? How might one assess a person's genotype?

The Role of Genetics

Twin studies

The most popular method of assessing the relative importance of heredity and environment in determining individual differences in intelligence is to conduct a twin study. There are two kinds of twins: **monozygotic twins** and **dizygotic twins**. Monozygotic (MZ) twins derive from the same fertilised ovum, and have essentially identical genotypes. It is for this reason that they are often called identical twins. Dizygotic (DZ) twins derive from two different fertilised ova. As a result, their genotypes are no more similar than those of ordinary siblings. Dizygotic twins are sometimes called fraternal twins.

What would we expect to find in a twin study? If heredity is very important, then monozygotic twins should be considerably more similar in intelligence than dizygotic twins. On the other hand, if environmental factors are all-important, then monozygotic twins should be no more alike than dizygotic twins.

What does the evidence suggest? A review based on 111 studies was published by Bouchard and McGue (1981; see the Key Study overleaf). They left out the findings from Burt's (1955) study, because there is clear evidence that he made up some or all of his data. The mean correlation coefficient for monozygotic twins was +0.86, indicating that monozygotic twins are generally very similar to each other in intelligence. The mean correlation coefficient for dizygotic twins was +0.60, indicating only a moderate degree of similarity in intelligence.

The fact that monozygotic twins were much more similar in intelligence than dizygotic twins suggests that heredity is of major significance in determining intelligence. However, that is on the assumption that the degree of environmental similarity experienced by monozygotic twins is the same as that experienced by dizygotic twins. However, monozygotic twins are treated in a more similar fashion than dizygotic twins in the following ways: parental treatment; playing together; spending time together; dressing in a similar style; and being taught by the same teachers (Loehlin & Nichols, 1976). When these data were considered in detail by Kamin (1981), it emerged that there was an effect of similarity of treatment on similarity of intelligence in the form of IQ.

Intelligence correlation between twins

(Bar chart: Correlation on the y-axis from 0 to 1.00; Type of twins on the x-axis. Identical twins ≈ 0.86; Fraternal twins ≈ 0.60.)

Twins who live apart

In a few twin studies, use has been made of monozygotic twins brought up apart in different families. Such twin pairs would seem to be of particular value in deciding on the relative importance of genetic factors and of environment in determining intelligence. Those arguing that genetic factors are of most importance would expect such twins to resemble each other closely in intelligence. In contrast, those favouring an environmentalist position would argue that placing twins in different environments should ensure that they are not similar in intelligence. According to Bouchard and McGue's (1981) review, the mean correlation coefficient for monozygotic twins brought up apart is +0.72.

The findings from monozygotic twins brought up apart seem on the face of it to provide convincing evidence for the importance of genetic factors. However, there are

The Collister twins: identical twin brothers, married to identical twin sisters.

Bouchard and McGue

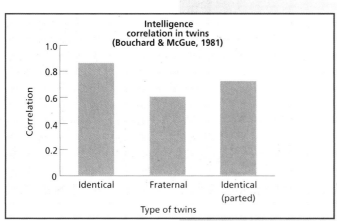

Intelligence correlation in twins (Bouchard & McGue, 1981)

In spite of the problems, much useful information has been obtained from studying twins. Identical or monozygotic twins derive from the same fertilised ovum, and so have essentially identical genotypes. In contrast, fraternal or dizygotic twins derive from two different fertilised ova, and so their genotypes are no more similar than those of two ordinary siblings. If heredity influences intelligence, then we would expect to find that identical twins are more alike in intelligence than are fraternal twins.

In their review of 111 studies, Bouchard and McGue (1981) reported that the mean correlation for identical twins was +0.86, and it was +0.60 for fraternal twins. Thus identical twins are more similar in intelligence than are fraternal twins, and this suggests that heredity plays a part in determining individual differences in intelligence. However, the environment is generally more similar for identical twins than for fraternal twins (Loehlin & Nichols, 1976).

Below are the correlations indicating the similarity of IQ between different groups of relatives. In general terms, relatives who have greater genetic similarity tend to be more similar in IQ. However, relatives having greater genetic similarity tend to live in more similar environments than those with less genetic similarity, which makes it hard to interpret the findings. As Bouchard and McGue (1981) concluded, "Most of the results of studies of family resemblance ... can be interpreted as either supporting the genetic or the environmentalist theory."

Relationship	Mean correlation
Siblings reared apart	+0.24
Siblings reared together	+0.47
Single parent—offspring reared apart	+0.22
Single parent—offspring reared together	+0.42
Half-siblings	+0.31
Cousins	+0.15
Adopted parent—offspring	+0.19

Discussion points

1. How convincing is the evidence reviewed by Bouchard and McGue for the notion that heredity plays an important role in determining individual differences in intelligence?

2. Most of the correlations reported by Bouchard and McGue were based on studies in a small number of Western cultures. Would the same findings be obtained in other cultures?

problems with the evidence. Many of the monozygotic twins brought up apart were, in fact, brought up in different branches of the same family. Other monozygotic twins were actually brought up together for several years before being separated. Thus, many pairs of monozygotic twins actually experience rather similar environments. As a result, at least some of the similarity in IQ of monozygotic twins brought up apart is due to environmental rather than genetic factors. However, the monozygotic twins in the Minnesota Study of Twins Reared Apart were separated in infancy and reared in different environments. In spite of this, their IQs correlated about +0.75 (Bouchard et al. 1990).

Evaluation

The evidence from twin studies suggests that individual differences in intelligence are about 50% due to genetic factors and 50% due to environmental factors. You might have expected this figure to be 75% for genetic factors because of the correlations reported above, but when this correlation is translated into a **heritability estimate** then account is taken of total variability in the population. The details need not concern you but this is an important feature of understanding the relationship between heredity and environment.

In any group of individuals, the more similar the environmental factors shared by the group, the greater will be the effect of genetic factors in determining individual differences in intelligence. Consider the example of a set of seeds. If these seeds are planted in the same pot (identical environment) then any differences must be due to genetic variation, whereas if the seeds are planted in different soils then the environment factors become part of the equation. In terms of humans, this means that if everyone in a society were exposed to precisely the same environmental conditions, then all individual differences in intelligence would be due to genetic factors! On the other hand, in societies in which there are enormous environmental differences between various sections of the community, the role of genetic factors in producing individual differences in intelligence would be rather small.

Dunn and Plomin (1990) found that children reared in the same environment actually had very different experiences.

When considering children raised in the *same* environment, a different argument needs to be considered. The general concept of a shared environment assumes that all children (or seeds) will have the same experiences in that environment. When we consider different environments it is obvious that individuals will have different experiences, but recently researchers have recognised that the same environment does not mean the same *experiences*. Dunn and Plomin (1990) found that children reared in the same environment actually had very different experiences. Differences in their abilities and behaviours could not be not due to the shared environment. They were due (a) to genetic differences and (b) to differences in experience. The latter is referred to as the *non-shared environment*.

In terms of our twin studies, the figure of 50% of individual differences in intelligence being due to heredity applies only to the small number of cultures that have been studied so far. In some cultures this figure may be smaller or larger depending on how similar the environment is.

There are other reasons to be cautious about accepting the apparently obvious conclusion from twin studies that intelligence is 50% genetic. First, there are problems with many of the studies, and it is often unclear whether environmental similarity has been properly controlled.

Can you give examples of large differences in environment between communities living in the same society?

Second, intelligence is assessed by means of IQ obtained from standard intelligence tests. It is debatable whether IQ is an adequate measure of intelligence.

Third, the role of heredity in determining individual differences in intelligence tends to increase with age. According to Plomin (1990), about 30% of individual differences in intelligence among children are due to heredity, and this figure increases to 50% in adolescence, and to more than 50% in adult life. This puzzling change may occur because environmental differences are *smaller* among adults than among children and this is what makes heredity *appear* to contribute more as children grow into adults.

Adoption studies

Another method of assessing the role of genetic and environmental factors in intelligence is by means of adoption studies. The measured intelligence of adopted children might depend more on genetic factors (the intelligence inherited from the biological parents) or it might depend more on environmental factors (related to the intelligence of the adoptive parents).

Horn (1983) discussed the findings from the Texas Adoption Project, which involved almost 500 adopted children. The correlation between the adopted children and their biological mothers for intelligence was +0.28, indicating that there was only a moderate degree of similarity in intelligence. The correlation between the adopted children and their adoptive mothers was even lower at +0.15. Both of these correlations are so low that it is hard to make any definite statements about the roles played by heredity and environment, though it does suggest a greater role for heredity.

The correlations between adopted children and their adoptive mothers, and between adopted children and their biological mothers are so low that they do not allow us to make any definite statements about the roles played by heredity and environment in intelligence.

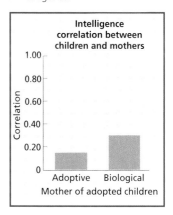

Change over time

Loehlin, Horn, and Willerman (1989) found that there were some differences in the findings when the adopted children were tested again 10 years later. Now the children had an increased correlation with their biological mothers but less with their adoptive mothers. Shared family environment between the adopted children and their adoptive mothers was reduced in importance, whereas genetic factors had a greater influence on the adopted children's intelligence than had been the case 10 years earlier.

The notion that shared family environment has less influence on intelligence as children become older received additional support in a review by Plomin (1988). He reported that the correlation between genetically unrelated children growing up together in adoptive families was about +0.30 for intelligence when they were still children. However, the correlation dropped to zero in adolescence and adulthood. The major reason for this change is presumably because environmental factors outside the home become increasingly important from adolescence onwards. The zero correlation indicates that the influence of any environmental factors within the home does not seem to be long-lasting.

What environmental factors might be expected to influence the development of IQ?

Evaluation

The findings of the study by Capron and Duyne (1989, see the Key Study below) are consistent with those from twin studies in suggesting that about 50% of the variance in intelligence scores is due to genetic factors. However, less clear findings have emerged from other adoption studies (e.g., Horn, 1983), in part because of the problems of interpretation posed by selective placement (children placed in homes similar to those of their biological parents). In many studies, some of the correlation between adopted children and their biological parents is due to selective placement rather than to genetic factors.

Capron and Duyne

High SES biological parent	Low SES biological parent
+	+
High SES adoptive parent	High SES adoptive parent
High SES biological parent	Low SES biological parent
+	+
Low SES adoptive parent	Low SES adoptive parent

The adopted children in this study belonged to one of the four groups shown above.

Capron and Duyne (1989) reported a very impressive adoption study. They made use of four very different groups of adopted children. These groups involved all four possible combinations of biological parents of high or low socio-economic status and adoptive parents of high or low socio-economic status. The predictions are fairly straightforward. The measured intelligence of the adopted children should be related mainly to the socio-economic status of the biological parents if genetic factors are of more importance (because high SES parents are more intelligent and have high IQ children), but should be related mostly to the socio-economic status of the adoptive parents if environmental factors are more important. In fact, the effects of the socio-economic status of the biological and of the adoptive parents were much the same. These findings suggest that genetic and environmental factors were of about equal importance in determining the intelligence of the adopted children.

This study is important for various reasons. First, it is hard to interpret the findings from most adoption studies because of selective placement, which involves adoption agencies placing adopted children into families resembling those of their biological parents in terms of educational and social backgrounds. When there is selective placement, it is hard to disentangle the effects of heredity and environment. The design of the study by Capron and Duyne largely eliminated the issue of selective placement. Second, the use of groups in which there was a large difference between the socio-economic status of the biological parents and that of the adoptive parents is unusual, but has the advantage of making it easier to assess the relative impacts of heredity and environment.

Discussion points

1. Why is the study by Capron and Duyne of importance?

2. Are adoption studies more or less useful than twin studies in trying to decide on the relative importance of heredity and environment in determining individual differences in intelligence?

GENERAL CRITICISMS OF IQ TESTS, ADOPTION STUDIES, AND TWIN STUDIES		
IQ tests	**Adoption studies**	**Twin studies**
Debatable whether IQ is an adequate measurement of intelligence	Selective placement makes it hard to determine the effects of heredity and environment	Environmental similarity often occurs
Cultural differences not always considered	Heredity is less well controlled than in twin studies	Twins raised separately were actually raised by different branches of the same family
		Twins had spent some years together before being separated

Social and Cultural Influences

Environmental factors

We have seen from the findings of twin and adoption studies that environmental factors are of major importance in producing individual differences in measured intelligence. Somewhat more direct evidence for the role of the environment comes from studies in which entire communities have gone through large-scale environmental changes. Wheeler (1932, 1942) studied the members of an isolated community in Tennessee in the United States. This community gradually became more integrated into society as schools and roads were built, and communications with the outside world developed. The children in this community originally had a mean IQ of 82. Ten years later, the children's mean IQ was 93. It seems likely that the environmental changes, in some way, boosted the children's IQ.

How else might one explain this increase in IQ?

The limitation of Wheeler's study is that we do not know which of the many environmental changes within the Tennessee community studied were of most importance in affecting intelligence. As might be expected, there is good evidence that the amount of schooling is important. For example, Ceci (1991) reviewed studies showing that children who start school after the age of 6 have lower IQs than other children. In addition, children's IQs are lower if they miss long periods of schooling through illness or some other reason, and there is a small decline in IQs over the summer holiday.

The HOME inventory

What is needed is to compare several different aspects of the environment in terms of the effects they have on children's level of intelligence. One suitable measure is the Home Observation for Measurement of the Environment (or HOME) inventory. This inventory provides measures in the following six environmental categories:

- Emotional and verbal responsivity of parent.
- Avoidance of restriction and punishment.
- Organisation of physical and temporal environment.
- Provision of appropriate play materials.
- Parental involvement with child.
- Opportunities for variety in daily stimulation.

Gottfried (1984) has addressed the issue of which of these aspects of the home environment have the greatest impact on children's IQs. The evidence from a number of studies indicated that provision of appropriate play materials, parental involvement with the child, and opportunities for variety in daily stimulation predicted children's subsequent IQs better than did any of the other three aspects.

There is a potential problem with this approach. The findings discussed by Gottfried are correlational in nature, and so they cannot be used to show that a stimulating home environment actually increases children's IQs. It is possible that more intelligent parents are more likely than less intelligent ones to provide a stimulating home environment for their children, and that it is the parental intelligence rather than the home environment they provide that is of importance.

A stimulating environment has been said to encourage a child's development. What might this environment include?

Yeates et al. (1983) addressed the causality issue in a longitudinal study of young children. The mother's IQ predicted children's IQs at the age of 2 better than did scores on the HOME inventory. However, the HOME inventory predicted the IQs of the same children at the age of 4 better than did the mother's IQ. These findings suggest that a stimulating home environment is beneficial for children's intellectual development, and that this beneficial effect becomes stronger as children develop.

The Rochester study

Sameroff et al. (1993) reported the findings of the Rochester Longitudinal Study, in which hundreds of children were followed from birth to adolescence. The researchers identified 10 environmental factors that jointly accounted for 49% of individual differences in IQ. This study is reported in detail in the Key Study on the next page.

Operation Headstart

Another way to study the effects of environmental factors on the development of (measured) intelligence is to consider enrichment programmes such as Operation Headstart. In the 1960s there was a political move in the United States to set up an intervention programme that would help disadvantaged children. It was argued that such children lacked some of the early benefits enjoyed by more middle-class children in terms of, for example, health and intellectual stimulation, and that therefore they were disadvantaged even before they started school. Such disadvantages inevitably only got worse and perpetuated a cycle of failure.

In 1965 the first Headstart programmes were run involving half a million children. When the children were compared with a control group after the first year there were small IQ gains; however these were short lived and the financial costs of the programme were over 150 million dollars (Zigler & Muenchow, 1992). Follow-up studies presented a more encouraging picture. Lazar and Darlington (1982) reported that the Headstart children were less likely to be placed in special classes, were more likely to go to college and, in terms of social benefits, were less likely to need welfare assistance or become delinquent. Seitz (1990) also found higher IQs in the Headstart children when they were tested in adolescence, suggesting a delayed effect. This indicates that IQ can be affected by environmental factors.

Evaluation.   Other programmes have found evidence to support this. For example, the Carolina Abecedarian Project (Ramey, 1993) focused on low intelligence mothers and their infants, running a special day-care programme from infancy and giving extra medical attention. By school age the children had higher IQs than a control group but this declined soon thereafter.

Other studies have also tended to find rather minimal effects but this may be because other environmental factors overwhelm the comparatively small influence of the school.

One criticism that has been raised, in terms of methodology, is that the control groups used in the Operation Headstart evaluation may not have actually been comparable because allocation to such groups was not strictly random. However this was not true of the Abecedarian Project and Ramey et al. (1999) reviewed 10 studies that randomly allocated children to the two conditions and concluded that there was firm evidence that Headstart did boost IQ, and that the greater the deprivation suffered by the children the greater the gains achieved by Headstart.

The Rochester Longitudinal Study

Sameroff et al. (1987, 1993) conducted a longitudinal study in New York State to investigate the factors that might be linked to intellectual delay in young children. They selected pregnant women to be part of their study and followed their 215 children, testing the children's IQs at age 4 and 13 (at this point 152 families remained in the sample). The families represented a range of socio-economic backgrounds, maternal age groups, and number of other siblings.

Sameroff et al. identified 10 family risk factors that were related to lower IQ:

- Mother has a history of mental illness.
- Mother did not go to high school.
- Mother has severe anxiety.
- Mother has rigid attitudes and values about her child's development.
- Few positive interactions between mother and child during infancy.
- Head of household has a semi-skilled job.
- Four or more children in the family.
- Father does not live with the family.
- Child belongs to a minority group.
- Family suffered 20 or more stressful events during the child's first 4 years of life.

There was a clear negative association between the number of risk factors associated with a child and the child's IQ, as illustrated in the graph on the right. At age 4 this correlation was –0.58. At age 13 it was –0.61. At the age of 4, high-risk children were 24 times as likely to have IQs below 85 than low-risk children. It was calculated that, on average, each risk factor reduced the child's IQ score by 4 points.

This study shows that environmental factors can be of great importance, and indicates what factors may be especially important. Sameroff et al. (1998) point out that the results have important implications for intervention, suggesting that changing environments should be more effective than relying on individual children's resilience under conditions of accumulated risk.

Discussion points

1. Select one of the risk factors and suggest how it might affect intellectual development.
2. What are the political implications of this study?

KEY STUDY EVALUATION — Sameroff et al.

However, where there are so many interrelated factors, it is not clear whether social class or specific parental behaviours are more important. It is also possible to explain the findings in terms of genetic factors. It is possible that low socio-economic level parents are biologically less intelligent, whereas those with more intelligence become better educated and are able to have higher living standards.

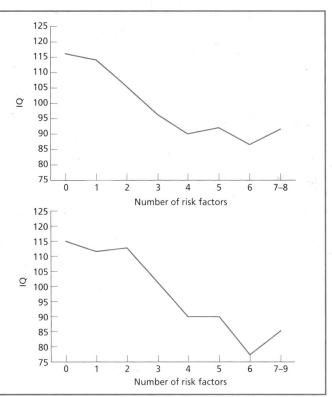

These graphs show the negative association between IQ and number of environmental risk factors. The top graph presents data for mean 4-year old IQ scores, and the bottom graph presents data for mean 13-year old IQ scores.

Intelligence and Race

There has been great political controversy about the fact that the mean difference in IQ between white people and black people in the United States is about 15 points, favouring white people. This is an average figure, and it should be noted that in fact about 20% of black people have a higher IQ than that of the average white person. Most psychologists have assumed that the difference between white people and black people is due to the environmental deprivation suffered by black people. However, Jensen (1969) and H.J. Eysenck (1981) argued that genetic differences might be involved.

This debate has rumbled on. In 1988 Rushton published research that also claimed to demonstrate significant differences in the IQs between white and black children. Quite incredibly the data were based on IQ tests that, although they purported to be "culture-free" (see later), actually rewarded those children who were taught basic arithmetic in school. The white children assessed were US schoolchildren. The black children were from Africa and did not have the same access to school concepts. It is not surprising that they did less well.

More recently, Herrnstein and Murray (1994) published the controversial book *The Bell Curve*, in which they argued that there are genetic differences in IQ. Since these differences are inevitable, why are we wasting money in trying to educate individuals who will never progress beyond a fixed potential? This illustrates the extremely political nature of this debate.

What is "race"?

The first point to make about this controversial issue is that it is of very little scientific interest, in that it is unlikely to tell us anything about the processes involved in human intelligence. This makes it strange that so much time and money have been spent in studying this issue.

The second point is that the issue is meaningless in some ways, because it is based on the incorrect assumption that white people and black people form separate biological groups. There is more genetic variation *within* any so-called racial group than *between* racial groups. Indeed, the whole notion of "race" has been questioned, and seems to have no precise scientific definition. Altogether this suggests that there is little scientific validity in using the term "race".

When groups of white and West Indian children were matched for levels of environmental deprivation, only very small differences in intelligence were found.

The third point is that we cannot carry out definitive research on this issue. We cannot measure accurately the levels of deprivation experienced by black people, nor can we compare the genetic endowment of white people and black people. Even H.J. Eysenck (1981, p.79) admitted that the issue cannot be resolved by experimental evidence: "Can we … argue that genetic studies … give direct support to the hereditarian position? The answer must, I think, be in the negative. The two populations (black and white) are separate populations, and none of the studies carried out on white people alone, such as twin studies, are feasible."

In addition, such research poses major ethical issues. Extreme groups, such as the National Front, have used the findings to promote racial disharmony, which is totally unacceptable. Many working in this area have been insensitive to the dangerous political uses to which their research was likely to be put, and it is an issue that would have been better left unexplored.

Differences in black and white performance on IQ tests

A major reason why black people perform less well than white people on intelligence tests is because of environmental deprivation. Mackintosh (1986) compared white and West Indian children in England. Some of the children were matched for father's job, number of brothers and sisters, family income, and other measures relevant to deprivation, whereas the others were unmatched. In one study, there was a 9-point difference between unmatched groups, but only a 2.6-point difference in the matched groups. Thus, there were very small differences in intelligence between the two groups when they were equated for the level of deprivation.

The fact that IQ tests generally do record differences between black and white individuals might be explained in terms of physical and/or social deprivation associated with lower incomes, poorer housing conditions, lower education, and so on. Alternatively these differences can be explained in terms of cultural variation. According to Vygotksy (earlier in this Section), cognitive development is very much linked to cultural inputs and therefore we would expect to find differences between cultural groups. Such variations were mentioned earlier (see page 386). In order to assess cognitive abilities such as intelligence more fairly one needs to develop culture-fair tests.

Culture-fair tests

Nearly all intelligence tests have been devised by white, middle-class psychologists. It is likely that Australian aboriginals or black people brought up in a very different culture would be disadvantaged by this cultural divide when taking an intelligence test. In similar fashion, members of minority groups might also be disadvantaged when confronted by standard intelligence tests. This issue is important. Legislation designed to ensure equal opportunities for everyone has been passed in Britain, the United States, and numerous other countries. If intelligence tests are biased against certain groups, then there is a real danger that people's rights to have equal opportunities are being infringed.

How should we proceed? According to Sternberg (1994, p.595):

We need to take into account culture in considering both the nature and the assessment of intelligence. Simply translating a test from one language to another scarcely constitutes doing so. Rather, we need to be sensitive to cultural differences that may artificially inflate the scores of one group over another due to the kinds of materials or tasks used to measure intelligence.

One way to do this is to construct what are known as "culture-fair" tests, which consist mainly of abstract and nonverbal items that should not be more familiar to members of one group than another. However, strangely such culture-fair tests tend to produce larger differences in intelligence across cultural groups than are found when conventional verbal tests of intelligence are used (Sternberg, 1994)! In addition, attempts to "translate" American standard tests into Black dialect show no differences. For example when the Stanford–Binet intelligence test was translated into what is known as "Black English" (the English dialect spoken by many Black Americans) and given to black children by black testers, the black children's IQ scores were about the same as when the test was given in its standard form (Quay, 1971).

Why do you think that some "culture-fair" tests produce larger differences in intelligence across cultural groups than standard intelligence tests?

However, rather different findings were obtained with the Black Intelligence Test of Cultural Homogeneity (BITCH), which was designed for Black Americans. White American children did no better than black American children on this test, and sometimes performed worse (Williams, 1972). This suggests that there are cultural differences embedded in tests. The reason why the black children's performance did not improve on the translated test may be because this is based on the assumption that cultural differences are purely linguistic. In reality it is unlikely to be simply a matter of translating a test.

Evaluation of the Heredity/Environment Debate

The studies discussed in this Unit indicate that major environmental changes can produce significant changes in IQ. Thus, they strengthen the notion that intelligence depends to a major extent on environmental factors. However, it has not proved possible to determine precisely which aspects of the environment are most effective in influencing intellectual development. For example, consider the findings of Sameroff et al. (1993; see the Key Study on page 393). They found that environmental factors such as the mother not going to high school and the head of household having a semi-skilled job were associated with low IQ in the children. This does not prove a causal relationship. It is possible that genetic factors play a part in producing these environmental factors *and* in producing low IQ in the children.

Development of Moral Understanding

What are Morals?

What is meant by the term "morality"? According to Shaffer (1993), **morality** implies "a set of principles or ideals that help the individual to distinguish right from wrong and to act on this distinction".

Why is morality important? Society cannot function effectively unless there is some agreement on what is right and wrong. Of course, there are moral and ethical issues (e.g., animal experiments) on which individual members of a given society have very different views. However, if there were controversy on all major moral issues, society would become chaotic.

Shaffer argued that human morality has three components. First, there is the *emotional component*. This is concerned with the feelings (e.g., guilt) associated with moral thoughts and behaviour. Second, there is the *cognitive component*. This is concerned with how we think about moral issues, and make decisions about what is right and wrong. Third, there is the *behavioural component*, which is concerned with how we behave. It includes the extent to which we lie, steal, cheat, or behave honourably.

Why should we distinguish among these components? There is often a significant difference between the components. We may know at the cognitive level that it is wrong to cheat, but we may still cheat at the behavioural level. Some people lead blameless lives (behavioural component), but still feel guilty (emotional component). The title of this Unit is the "development of moral *understanding*". Emotional and cognitive components are part of moral understanding. The behavioural component is a means of assessing the value of theories of moral understanding—what point is there in knowing about moral understanding unless it informs us about behaviour?

The distinction among different moral components is also useful in comparing theories of moral development. Freud and Eisenberg emphasised the emotional component, Piaget and Kohlberg focused on the cognitive component, and social learning theorists concentrated on the behavioural component.

How is moral understanding different to moral behaviour?

Theories of the Development of Moral Thinking

Psychodynamic theory

Sigmund Freud (1856–1939) argued that the human mind consists of three parts: the **id**, **ego**, and **superego**. The id deals with motivational forces (e.g., the sexual instinct); the ego is concerned with conscious thinking; and the superego is concerned with moral issues. The superego is divided into the conscience and the ego-ideal. Our conscience makes us feel guilty or ashamed when we have behaved badly, whereas our ego-ideal

SHAFFER'S COMPONENTS OF HUMAN MORALITY		
Emotional	**Cognitive**	**Behavioural**
Feelings associated with moral behaviour	How we think about moral issues, and decide between right and wrong	How we behave
Theorists: Freud Eisenberg	Theorists: Piaget Kohlberg	Theorists: Bandura Mischel
Approach: Psychodynamic/social cognition	Approach: Cognitive-developmental	Approach: Social learning

makes us feel proud of ourselves when we have behaved well in the face of temptation. (See pages 418–422 for a more detailed description of Freud's theory of personality.)

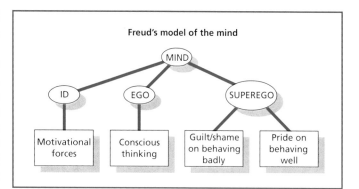

Freud suggested that the superego develops at the age of 5 or 6. Boys develop sexual desires for their mother, leading to an intense rivalry with their father and a desire to get rid of this rival. This state of affairs is known as the **Oedipus complex**. It makes boys feel very fearful, because they are afraid that their father will discover their true feelings. This situation is resolved through the process of **identification**, in which boys come to identify with their father and no longer see him as a rival. Identification leads them to imitate or copy the beliefs and behaviour of their father. As part of the identification process, boys adopt their father's moral standards, and this leads to the formation of the superego. According to Freud, the superego is "the heir of the Oedipus complex".

According to Freud, a similar process occurs in girls at about the same age. Freud (1933) argued that girls are "mortified by the comparison with boys' far superior equipment", for which they blame their mother. A little girl's attention is then directed towards her father, who becomes her love-object and she substitutes her "penis envy" with a wish to have a child. This leads to a kind of resolution similar to the Oedipus conflict and ultimate identification with her same-sex parent. However, Freud concluded that girls never develop quite as strong a sense of justice as boys because they do not experience quite as strong a resolution of their genital conflicts. This is an example of gender bias, an issue that is discussed in more detail in the Unit "Gender Development" in Section 11. However, Freud admitted that, "the majority of men are far behind the masculine ideal [in terms of superego strength]". Jung, a follower of Freud, proposed that a slightly different sequence of events happens in girls. He called this the "**Electra complex**". Electra was another Greek figure. Her mother and her mother's lover killed her father. Electra encouraged her brother to kill her mother. In Jung's analysis, a young girl feels desire for her father and rejects her mother.

Freud developed his ideas about the Oedipus complex at a time when lone-parent families were very rare. What bearing do you think this may have had on his theorising?

Research evidence

The main evidence available to Freud consisted of the accounts of his patients as they tried to remember their childhood, for example Little Hans' (see page 651) experiences of desire for his mother and guilt about his father. Such evidence is weak because it is based on subjective interpretation of events and, in the case of older patients' recollections, a reliance on their fallible memories. Another problem was identified by Meadows (1986, p.162):

there could be no refuting evidence since a demonstration that a person did not experience an Oedipus complex, feel penis-envy, etc., might be taken as evidence for the perfect repression [motivated forgetting] of the person's Oedipus complex, penis-envy, etc.

Freud argued that fear of the same-sex parent was of crucial importance in the development of the superego. Thus parents who are aggressive and administer a lot of punishment might be expected to have children with strong superegos. In fact, the opposite seems to be the case. Parents who make the most use of spanking and other forms of punishment tend to have children who behave badly and who experience little guilt or shame (Hoffman, 1988; see also the Key Study on the next page). However, the evidence is only damaging to Freud if we assume that fear of the same-sex parent depends entirely on the *actual* levels of punishment used by parents. According to Freud, children who *believe* mistakenly that they are punished a lot would be expected to develop a strong superego, but this was not taken into account by Hoffman (1988).

Freud's hypothesis that girls have weaker superegos than boys has been disproved. Hoffman (1975) discussed a number of studies in which the behaviour of children on their own was assessed in order to see whether they did the things they had been told not to

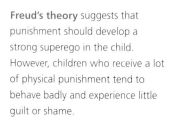

Freud's theory suggests that punishment should develop a strong superego in the child. However, children who receive a lot of physical punishment tend to behave badly and experience little guilt or shame.

Parental role in moral development

The child's early stages of moral development depend very much on its parents. Hoffman (1970) identified three major styles used by parents in the moral development of their children:

1. *Induction*: explaining why a given action is wrong, with special emphasis on its effects on other people.
2. *Power assertion*: using spankings, removal of privileges, and harsh words to exert power over a child.
3. *Love withdrawal*: withholding attention or love when a child behaves badly.

Brody and Shaffer (1982) reviewed studies in which parental style influenced moral development. Induction improved moral development in 86% of those studies. In contrast, power assertion improved moral development in only 18%, and love withdrawal in 42%. As power assertion had a negative effect on moral development in 82% of the studies, it is a very ineffective parenting style. Power assertion produces children who are aggressive and who do not care about others (Zahn-Waxler et al., 1979).

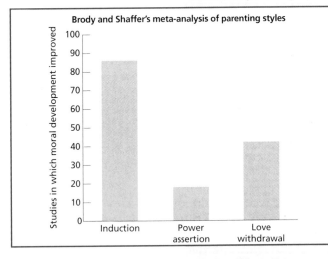

Induction is effective because it provides the child with useful information that helps the development of moral reasoning. Another reason is that induction encourages children to think about other people. Considering the needs and emotions of others is of vital importance if moral development is to occur.

The findings tell us there is an association between parental use of induction and good moral development. The main reason for this association is probably that inductive parenting benefits children's moral development, but that may not be the whole story. Children who are well behaved are more likely to be treated in a reasonable, inductive way by their parents. In contrast, children who are badly behaved and aggressive may cause their parents to use power assertion. Thus, parenting style affects children's behaviour, but children's behaviour may also affect parenting style.

Discussion points

1. Explain how each style might be related to moral behaviour.
2. What components of morality are left out of this account?

---

do. There was no difference between boys and girls in most of the studies. When there was a sex difference, it was the girls (rather than the boys) who were better at resisting temptation. However, it could be argued that ability to resist temptation is not a good measure of superego strength.

Cross-cultural studies have confirmed the findings of Hoffman (1975). Snarey (1985) reviewed 17 studies from 15 different countries around the world. Sex differences in moral development were found in only three of those studies. However, as we shall see, Kohlberg concluded that men *were* more advanced in their moral development—though this evidence has also been criticised by Gilligan, who like Freud suggested that girls were at least different in their moral orientation. It is perhaps worth emphasising the fact that Freud did not say that girls were less morally developed—only that their superegos were less developed because of the weaker identification with the same-sex parent.

If the ability to resist temptation is not a good measure of superego strength, how else might you assess it?

Evaluation

Freud put forward the first detailed theory of moral development. His basic assumptions that parents have a major influence on the moral development of their children, and that many moral values are acquired in the early years of life, are correct. However, most of his specific hypotheses are wrong.

There are several inadequacies with Freud's theory. First, he exaggerated the role of the same-sex parent in the development of children's morality. The evidence indicates that the opposite-sex parent and other children also generally play an important role (Shaffer, 1993).

Freud attached too much weight to emotional factors in morality and not enough to the cognitive processes that help to determine moral behaviour. Theorists such as Piaget and Kohlberg argued that such cognitive processes are the key to moral development. It could also be argued that Freud neglected the behavioural component of morality, which was studied in depth by the social learning theorists.

Freud claimed that children make more dramatic progress in moral development at about the age of 5 or 6 than they do in later childhood or adolescence. In fact, there are large changes in moral reasoning between the ages of 10 and 16 (e.g., Colby et al., 1983; see also Kohlberg's theory on page 402).

Cognitive-developmental theory: Piaget

According to Jean Piaget (e.g., 1932), children's thinking goes through a series of stages (see the first Unit of this Section). The early stages focus on what the child can see and hear, whereas the later stages involve the ability to think in an abstract way about possible events that may never happen. Piaget argued that children's moral reasoning also proceeds through a number of different stages.

Stages in moral development

Piaget began to develop his ideas about moral reasoning by playing marbles with children of different ages. He was interested in seeing how well they understood the rules of the game, how important they thought it was to obey those rules, and so on. His observations led him to propose the following stages of moral development:

In what way is moral reasoning related to moral understanding?

1. *Premoral period* (0–5 years): children in this stage have very little understanding of rules or other aspects of morality.
2. *Stage of moral realism or* **heteronomous morality** (heteronomous means "subject to externally imposed rules") (5–10 years): children at this stage are rather rigid in their thinking—they believe that rules must be obeyed no matter what the circumstances (e.g., it's wrong to tell a lie even if it will spare someone's feelings). Children at this stage think that rules are made by important other people (e.g., parents), and that how bad an action is stems from its consequences, rather than from the actor's intentions. There are two other key features of the moral reasoning of children at this stage. First, they believe in **expiatory punishment**: the naughtier the behaviour, the greater should be the punishment. However, there is no idea that the punishment should fit the crime. For example, a child who drops a freshly

---

Freud's methods

The main source of evidence used by Freud was adults' memories of their childhood. However, not only is this evidence prone to distortion by the person who is remembering, it also cannot be proved or disproved. Freud did not see child patients, but dealt with parents, sometimes only through letters, which has led to speculation about his interpretations of particular behaviours. Freud claimed that the Oedipus and Electra complexes were unconscious phases that a child passed through on his or her way to identifying with the same-sex parent. However, if these phases are unconscious we have no way of proving that they did in fact happen, except indirectly through interpretations of children's behaviour.

A more general criticism of the psychodynamic approach stems from the way in which the theories are formulated. Freud's theory tends to "work backwards", for example, the result leads to the formation of a hypothesis. Freud did not so much predict behaviour as analyse it once it had happened. Finally, the period in which Freud was working must be considered. His patients mostly came from middle-class families, which at the time were ruled by strict disciplinarian regimes. At this point in history, the family would have had the most influence on the developing child. However, today outside pressures such as peer groups, school, and even television and the internet may prove as influential as the family in a child's development.

PIAGET'S STAGES OF MORAL DEVELOPMENT

Premoral	Moral realism (Heteronomous morality)	Moral relativism (Autonomous morality)
0–5 years old	5–10 years old	10 years upwards
Little understanding of rules and other aspects	Rigid thinking: rules must be obeyed Actions are judged by their consequences	Development of flexibility in moral issues Understanding that people differ in moral standards. Rules can be broken and wrong behaviour is not always punished
	Belief in: • Expiatory punishment • Immanent justice	Belief in: • Reciprocal punishment

baked cake on the floor should be spanked rather than having to help to bake another cake. Second, children between the ages of 5 and 10 strongly favour the notion of fairness. This leads them to believe in **immanent justice**, which is the idea that naughty behaviour will always be punished in some way.

3. *Stage of moral relativism or* **autonomous morality** (10 years upwards): children at this stage think in a more flexible way about moral issues. They understand that

moral rules evolve from human relationships, and that people differ in their standards of morality. They also understand that most rules of morality can be broken sometimes. If a violent man with a gun demands to be told where your mother is, it is perfectly acceptable to tell a lie and say that you do not know. There are other major differences from the previous stage. First, the child now thinks that the wrongness of an action depends far more on the individual's intentions than on the consequences of his or her behaviour. Second, children in this stage believe in **reciprocal punishment** rather than expiatory punishment. Thus, the punishment should fit the crime. Third, children in this stage have learned that people often behave wrongly but manage to avoid punishment. Thus, they no longer believe in immanent justice.

What causes development?

Why does moral reasoning change during childhood? According to Piaget, there are two main factors involved. First, young children are egocentric in their thinking, seeing the world only from their own point of view. At about the age of 7, they become less egocentric. Their growing awareness of the fact that other people have a different point of view allows them to develop more mature moral reasoning. This change in the way the child thinks is due to brain maturation that allows the child to comprehend new ideas. Moral development lags behind cognitive development because it depends on the cognitive changes occurring first.

Second, older children develop flexible ideas of morality because they are exposed to the different views of other children of the same age. This leads them to question their own values. In contrast, most younger children have rather rigid ideas of morality. What counts as good or bad behaviour is determined very much by the reactions of their parents.

Can you think of any situations in which adults might also disregard someone's intentions if the consequences of the other person's actions were negative?

Evidence

Children in most Western societies go through Piaget's stages of moral development in the order specified by Piaget (Shaffer, 1993). There is also evidence to support many of the details of the theory. For example, Piaget argued that children in the stage of moral realism judge actions by their consequences rather than by the actor's intentions.

Piaget (1932) obtained evidence for this. Children in this stage were told about a boy called John who opened a door, and by so doing broke 15 cups on the other side of the door. They were also told about Henry, who broke one cup while trying to reach some jam. Even though John had no idea there were any cups there, he was still regarded as being naughtier than Henry because he broke more cups. A further example is given on the next page.

Other evidence indicates that Piaget underestimated the ability of children in the stage of moral realism to take account of the actor's intentions. Costanzo et al. (1973) used stories in which the characters had good or bad intentions, and in which the outcomes were positive or negative. As Piaget had found, young children almost

always ignored the actor's intentions when the consequences were negative. However, they were as likely as older children to take account of the actor's intentions when the consequences were positive.

Evaluation

Piaget was right that there are close links between cognitive development in general and moral development in particular. Another strength of his theoretical approach is that most children in Western societies show the shift from moral realism to moral relativism predicted by Piaget.

On the negative side, young children have more complex ideas about morality than was assumed by Piaget, and some of their moral thinking is more advanced than he claimed. Piaget's assumption that 10- and 11-year-old children have reached an adult level of moral reasoning is incorrect. This was shown in a study by Colby et al. (1983) (described on page 402), who found large changes in moral thinking between the ages of 10 and 16.

Piaget argued that children at the stage of moral realism follow the rules of parents and other authority figures in an uncritical way. However, this only applies to certain parental rules, such as those about honesty and stealing. They are much less willing to allow their parents to make and enforce rules about who they may have as their friends or what they should do in their free time (Shaffer, 1993). This problem may arise because Piaget used the game of marbles and rather simplistic stories as a means of investigating moral behaviour.

Finally, Piaget focused on children's views concerning moral issues, and so he dealt with their knowledge of how they ought to behave. However, their thinking may be rather different from their actual behaviour when faced with a moral dilemma. More generally, Piaget tended to neglect the behavioural component of morality (which was studied by social learning theorists). He also paid little attention to the emotional component of morality (which was emphasised by Freud).

> ### Piaget's moral stories
>
> Piaget used moral stories to investigate what moral decisions children reached. An example is given below with a sample interview with a child.
>
> **STORY 1**: A little boy who is called John is in his room. He is called to dinner. He goes into the dining room. But behind the door there was a chair, and on the chair there was a tray with 15 cups on it. John couldn't have known that there was all this behind the door. He goes in, the door knocks against the tray, "bang" to the 15 cups and they all get broken!
>
> **STORY 2**: Once there was a little boy whose name was Henry. One day when his mother was out he tried to get some jam out of the cupboard. He climbed up on a chair and stretched out his arm. But the jam was too high up and he couldn't reach it and have any. But while he was trying to get it, he knocked over a cup. The cup fell down and broke.
>
> Below is a characteristic response for a child in the stage of moral realism:
>
> *Questioner:* "What did the first boy do?"
> *Child:*   "He broke 15 cups."
> *Questioner:* "And the second one?"
> *Child:*   "He broke a cup by moving roughly."
> *Questioner:* "Is one of the boys naughtier than the other?"
> *Child:*   "The first one is because he knocked over 15 cups."
> *Questioner:* "If you were the daddy, which one would you punish most?"
> *Child:*   "The one who broke 15 cups."
> *Questioner:* "Why did he break them?"
> *Child:*   "The door shut too hard and knocked them over. He didn't do it on purpose."
> *Questioner:* "And why did the other boy break a cup?"
> *Child:*   "Because he was clumsy. When he was getting the jam the cup fell down."
> *Questioner:* "Why did he want to get the jam?"
> *Child:*   "Because he was alone. Because the mother wasn't there."
>
> Piaget (1932), pp.122 and 129

Cognitive-developmental theory: Kohlberg

Lawrence Kohlberg (1927–1987) agreed with Piaget that we need to focus on children's cognitive structures to understand how they think about moral issues. However, Kohlberg's theory differs in several ways from that of Piaget. For example, Kohlberg believed that moral reasoning often continues to develop through adolescence and early adulthood.

Moral dilemmas

The main experimental approach used by Kohlberg involved presenting his participants with a series of moral dilemmas, and then asking them a series of predetermined questions of what they would have done and why. These questions are of key importance because Kohlberg was endeavouring to investigate moral reasoning—how individuals think about moral decisions, rather than moral behaviour.

Each dilemma required them to decide whether it is preferable to uphold some law or other moral principle, or to reject the moral principle in favour of some basic human need. To make clear what Kohlberg (e.g., 1963) did, we will consider one of the moral dilemmas he used.

Do you think that you sometimes behave differently to your moral principles?

In Europe, a woman was dying from cancer. One drug might save her, a form of radium that a druggist in the same town had recently discovered. The druggist was charging 2000 dollars, ten times what the drug cost him to make. The sick woman's husband, Heinz, went to everyone he knew to borrow the money, but he could only get together about half of what the drug cost. He told the druggist that his wife was dying and asked him to sell it cheaper or let him pay later. But the druggist said "No". The husband got desperate and broke into the man's store to steal the drug for his wife.

In what way are Kohlberg's moral dilemmas different from Piaget's moral stories?

The moral principle in this dilemma is that stealing is wrong. However, it was the good motive of wanting to help his sick wife that led Heinz to steal the drug. It is precisely because there are powerful arguments for and against stealing the drug that there is a moral dilemma. (See page 404 for another example of Kohlberg's dilemmas.)

Kohlberg's theory

Kohlberg (1976) developed his stage theory of moral development on the basis of a cross-sectional study, where 72 boys aged between 10 and 16 were interviewed about moral dilemmas, such as the "Heinz dilemma", above. Further details of this research are given in the Key Study on page 404. By analysing the answers participants gave in the interviews, Kohlberg identified different stages and levels of moral reasoning.

Kohlberg followed Piaget in assuming that all children follow the same sequence of stages in their moral development. However, Kohlberg's three levels of moral development (with two stages at each level) do not correspond closely to Piaget's:

Think of an example to illustrate each of Kohlberg's six stages.

Level 1: Pre-conventional morality.   At this level, what is regarded as right and wrong is determined by the rewards or punishments that are likely to follow, rather than by thinking about moral issues. Stage 1 of this level is based on a *punishment-and-obedience orientation*. Stealing is wrong because it involves disobeying authority, and leads to punishment. Stage 2 of this level is based on the notion that the right way to behave is the way that is rewarded. There is more attention to the needs of other people than in stage 1, but mainly on the basis that if you help other people, then they will help you.

Level 2: Conventional morality.   The greatest difference between level 1 and level 2 is that the views and needs of other people are much more important at level 2 than at level 1. At this level, people are very concerned to have the approval of others for their actions, and to avoid being blamed by them for behaving wrongly. At stage 3, the emphasis is on having good intentions, and on behaving in ways that conform to most people's views of good behaviour. At stage 4, children believe that it is important to do one's duty, and to obey the laws or rules of those in authority.

Level 3: Post-conventional or principled morality.   Those at the highest level of post-conventional or principled morality recognise that the laws or rules of authority figures should sometimes be broken. Abstract notions about justice and the need to treat other people with respect can override the need to obey laws and rules. At stage 5, there is a growing recognition that what is morally right may differ from what is legally right. Finally, at stage 6, the individual has developed his or her own principles of conscience. The individual takes into account the likely views of everyone who will be affected by a moral decision. Kohlberg (1981) described this as a kind of "moral musical chairs". In practice, it is very rare for anyone to operate most of the time at stage 6.

Research evidence

Kohlberg assumed that all children follow the same sequence of moral stages. The best way of testing this assumption is to carry out a longitudinal (long-term) study to see how children's moral reasoning changes over time. Colby et al. (1983) conducted a 20-year study of 58 American males (see the graph on page 404). There was a substantial drop in stage 1 and stage 2 moral reasoning between the ages of 10 and 16, with a compensatory increase in stage 3 and stage 4 moral reasoning occurring during the same time period.

NO MORE THAN 4 SCHOOL CHILDREN IN THE SHOP AT ANY TIME

Group pressure can sometimes lead children to behave in unacceptable ways, for example stealing sweets.

Most impressively for Kohlberg's theory, all of the participants progressed through the moral stages in exactly the predicted sequence.

In order to demonstrate that his moral stages were universal, Kohlberg (1969) studied the moral reasoning of children in other countries: Britain, Mexico, Taiwan, Turkey, USA, and Yucatan, finding the same pattern of development. He did find that development tended to be slower in non-industrialised countries. Colby and Kohlberg (1987) reported longitudinal studies in Turkey and Israel that produced similar results. Snarey (1985) reviewed 44 studies from 26 cultures. People in nearly all cultures went through the stages of moral development identified by Kohlberg in the same order. There was little evidence for any stage-skipping or for people returning to an earlier stage of moral development.

However, Kohlberg's claim that the moral thinking of any given individual will be consistently at the same stage has not been supported. Rubin and Trotter (1977) gave their participants several moral dilemmas, and found that many of them responded very differently from one dilemma to the next.

Kohlberg assumed that certain kinds of general cognitive development must occur before an individual can advance a stage in his or her moral reasoning. For example, those whose moral reasoning is at stage 5 make use of abstract principles (e.g., of justice), which presumably requires them to be good at abstract thinking. Tomlinson-Keasey and Keasey (1974) found that those girls of 11 and 12 who showed stage 5 moral reasoning were good at abstract thinking on general tests of cognitive development. However, some of the girls could think abstractly, but failed to show stage 5 moral reasoning. Thus the ability to think abstractly is a necessary (but not sufficient) requirement for someone to attain stage 5 or post-conventional morality.

Evaluation

Kohlberg's theory has the advantage over Piaget's theory in that it provides a more detailed and accurate account of moral development. It appears that children in many cultures work through the various stages of moral reasoning in the order specified by Kohlberg, which would suggest that the theory seems to be on the right lines; however, research in the last decade has questioned this. For example, Miller, Bershoff, and Harwood (1990), in research in India, found that the moral code used tended to give priority to social duties as contrasting with Americans' priority for individual rights. Though later studies have found that, where serious moral issues are concerned, Indian and American views in relation to social responsibilities were more similar (Berry et al.,

Can you think of an example of how Kohlberg's levels of moral development emphasise individual rights?

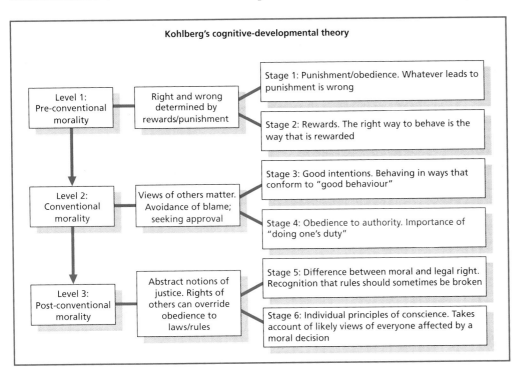

Kohlberg's cognitive-developmental theory

Level 1: Pre-conventional morality	Right and wrong determined by rewards/punishment	Stage 1: Punishment/obedience. Whatever leads to punishment is wrong
		Stage 2: Rewards. The right way to behave is the way that is rewarded
Level 2: Conventional morality	Views of others matter. Avoidance of blame; seeking approval	Stage 3: Good intentions. Behaving in ways that conform to "good behaviour"
		Stage 4: Obedience to authority. Importance of "doing one's duty"
Level 3: Post-conventional morality	Abstract notions of justice. Rights of others can override obedience to laws/rules	Stage 5: Difference between moral and legal right. Recognition that rules should sometimes be broken
		Stage 6: Individual principles of conscience. Takes account of likely views of everyone affected by a moral decision

KEY STUDY EVALUATION — Kohlberg

Kohlberg's theory addresses some of the problems of Piaget's approach, in that it is more flexible and less tied to specific age-based stages of development. Meta-analyses have shown that the six stages of Kohlberg's theoretical framework apply across most cultures, and it is almost universally the case that individuals work through the various stages in the same order. However, individual differences in experience or cultural differences may affect the speed with which a person moves through the stages. For example, in some cultures children can work, be married, or be regarded as full members of adult society at much younger ages than Western children. It is possible that these individuals move through Kohlberg's stages much earlier than Western children do. In addition, some children's lives do not conform to the stereotypical well-balanced family background with a strong moral sense of right and wrong that seems to lie behind some of Kohlberg's stages. This may also have a profound effect on a child's moral development.

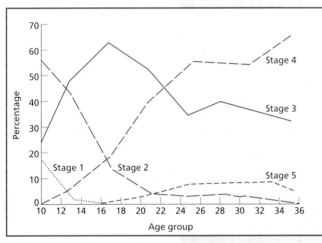

Kohlberg's moral stages studied longitudinally over a 20-year period encompassing ages 10 to 36.

Kohlberg

Kohlberg (1976) developed his stage theory of moral development on the basis of a cross-sectional study, where 72 boys aged between 10 and 16 were interviewed about moral dilemmas, such as the "Heinz dilemma" on page 402 or the one described below.

> In a country in Europe, a poor man named Valjean could find no work, nor could his sister and brother. Without money, he stole food and medicine that they needed. He was captured and sentenced to prison for six years. After a couple of years, he escaped from the prison and went to live in another part of the country under a new name. He saved money and slowly built up a big factory. He gave his workers the highest wages and used most of his profits to build a hospital for people who couldn't afford good medical care. Twenty years had passed when a tailor recognised the factory owner as being Valjean, the escaped convict whom the police had been looking for back in his hometown.

The interviews consisted of a predetermined set of questions, such as "Should the tailor report Valjean to the police?", "Why or why not?", "Does a citizen have a duty or an obligation to report an escaped convict?", "Suppose Valjean were a close friend of the tailor. Should he then report Valjean?".

Each interview lasted 2 hours and the results enabled Kohlberg to classify each boy in terms of his level of moral reasoning. The original sample was followed for a further 20 years (Colby, Kohlberg et al., 1983). The boys and men were tested six times in all, at 3-yearly intervals. The graph on the left shows how moral reasoning developed. At age 10 the children displayed mainly stage 2 reasoning but there were examples of stages 1 and 3. By the age of 22 no one used stage 1 reasoning, and stages 3 and 4 were predominant. By the age of 36, and the end of the study, there was still very little evidence of stage 5 reasoning (about 5%).

Kohlberg's findings were confirmed in a study by Walker et al. (1987) who developed a modified set of nine stages to allow for the fact that reasoning often falls between two of Kohlberg's stages. They still found general agreement with Kohlberg, for example that the equivalent of stage 2 type reasoning dominates at age 10 and stage 3 at age 16.

Discussion points

1. How adequate do you find Kohlberg's use of moral dilemmas to study moral development?

2. What do you think of Kohlberg's stage-based approach to moral development?

1992). Ma (1988) conducted work in China and produced an adaptation of Kohlberg's original theory that included Chinese perspectives such as the "Golden Mean" (behaving as most people in society behave) and "Good Will" (acting in a way that complies with nature). It may be that there are significant cultural differences, especially at the highest level of post-conventional morality, but also some similarities.

Shweder, Mahapatra, and Miller (1990) proposed an alternative post-conventional morality that functions in India. This is based on conceptions of natural law and justice, rather than individualism and social equality.

A further critical issue is the question of whether most people develop beyond stage 4 at all (Shaver & Strong, 1976). In addition, it has proved difficult to make a clear distinction between stage 5 and stage 6 moral reasoning (Colby et al., 1983).

Kohlberg focused on the verbal responses when his participants were given artificial moral dilemmas, rather than on actual moral behaviour. People's responses to those dilemmas may not predict how they would behave in real-life situations. The evidence

Why might there be more cross-cultural similarities over serious moral issues?

is somewhat inconsistent. Santrock (1975) found that children's level of moral reasoning did not predict whether they would cheat when given the chance. However, there is more evidence among adults that the stage of moral reasoning can predict behaviour. Kohlberg (1975) compared cheating behaviour among students at different levels of moral reasoning. About 70% of the students at the pre-conventional level were found to cheat, compared with only 15% of those at the post-conventional level. Students at the conventional level were intermediate (55%). This does appear to support a link between reasoning and behaviour.

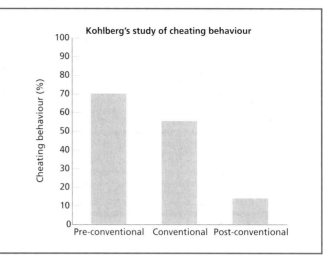

A major criticism of Kohlberg's theory has been its reliance and focus on male morality, an **androcentric** theory. The participants in the baseline study were all males and Gilligan (1977) claimed that essentially Kohlberg had produced a theory that was centred on the way that men approach moral decisions—making decisions in terms of justice rather than in terms of care. Gilligan supported this with her own research (see the Key Study on the next page). Kohlberg's male focus may explain why he found that men were more morally developed than women; he reported that most women were at stage 3 of moral development, whereas men were at stage 4.

Finally, Kohlberg did not consider the emotional component of morality in any detail. For example, the development of emotions such as shame and guilt is important within moral development. This is addressed by theories of pro-social development.

Which is of greater usefulness: a theory of moral reasoning or moral behaviour?

The Development of Moral Behaviour

Social learning theorists such as Albert Bandura (1977) and Walter Mischel (1970) proposed a social learning theory approach that differs from any of the theories considered so far. Thus it can be used as a means of evaluating the other approaches.

Social learning theory

Bandura and Mischel argued that learning experiences of two types are of special importance in influencing moral behaviour:

- Direct tuition: this is based on being rewarded or reinforced for behaving in certain ways, and being punished for behaving in other ways.
- **Observational learning**: moral behaviour can be learned by observing other people being rewarded or punished for behaving in certain ways, and then imitating rewarded behaviour.

According to the theories of Freud, Piaget, and Kohlberg, any given individual is at a certain stage of moral development at a particular time, and this determines the way he or she thinks about most moral issues. As a result, there is a high level of consistency about their moral decisions in different situations. In contrast, it is assumed by social learning theorists that an individual's behaviour in any situation is determined by the rewards and

People may show great inconsistency of behaviour in different situations.

Gilligan and Attanucci

Carol Gilligan (1977, 1982) proposed a theory in response to what she regarded as the Kohlberg's androcentric bias. Kohlberg initially based his theory on interviews with male participants, which suggests that bias may have been introduced. Gilligan argued that a less biased theory should take female views into account and should also consider moral decisions in real-life rather than simply asking participants about hypothetical decisions.

Gilligan (1982) conducted her own research, interviewing women who were facing a real-life dilemma. She interviewed 29 women who were deciding whether or not to have an abortion. She analysed the interviews and concluded that people rely on two different moral injunctions: not to treat others unfairly and not to turn away from someone in need (a "justice" or a "care" orientation). Gilligan suggested that Kohlberg's research was constrained by the assumption that there is only one moral perspective, that of justice. The alternative, care, is observed mainly by women, who tend to be concerned more about people's feelings than about what is "fair". According to Gilligan, Kohlberg showed sexist bias by regarding the morality of justice as superior to the morality of care.

Gilligan developed her own stage theory from her interview analyses and Gilligan and Attanucci (1988) used this for a further analysis of male and female behaviour.

Stage	Justice		Care	
1	1J	Uphold moral standards and withstand pressure to deviate	1C	Concern with what others say and how choices might affect relationships
2	2J	Justice should be tempered with mercy. One should consider the feelings of others, but principles are most important	2C	Sacrificing one's own concerns to the welfare of others. Relationships are more important than conventional rules
3	3J	Although there are "exceptions to the rule", everyone is best served by obedience to universal laws.	3C	Attempting to apply moral rules while valuing the individual and trying not to hurt anyone

Gilligan and Attanucci expected that female participants would favour a care orientation and males would favour a justice orientation. A key feature of this study was that moral reasoning was to be tested in the context of real-life dilemmas, providing greater ecological validity. Eighty men and women aged between 14 and 77 from various walks of life were asked a set of questions about moral conflict and choice, such as "Have you ever been in a situation of moral conflict where you had to make a decision but weren't sure what was the right thing to do?", "Could you describe the situation?", "What were the conflicts for you in that situation?", "What did you do?", "Do you think it was the right thing to do?", "How do you know?". Each participant was interviewed individually for approximately 2 hours, and their answers analysed and classified as care only, care focus (more than 75% care considerations), care justice (less than 75% of either), justice focus, or justice only.

	Care focus and care only	Care justice	Justice focus and justice only
Women	12	12	10
Men	1	15	30

Discussion points

1. Do you think that other ethnic groups (non-American) would respond in the same way?

2. What ethical concerns are raised by Gilligan's research?

punishments he or she has received in similar situations. Thus, people may show great inconsistency of behaviour in different situations.

According to Bandura (1977, 1986), children's moral behaviour changes through development as a result of their experiences. It also changes because there is a shift from *external* to *internal* control. Young children are greatly influenced by the rewards and punishments they receive or see others receive. Older children move in the direction of **self-regulation**, in which they reward themselves for meeting internal standards of behaviour and experience a sense of failure if they do not meet those standards.

How does this theory shed light on the development of moral understanding?

Research evidence

Evidence that moral reasoning can be influenced by observational learning was reported by Bandura and McDonald (1963). Children between the ages of 5 and 11 were exposed to a model who made opposite moral judgements to them, and who was praised by the experimenter for his or her views. After that, the children were tested on their own. Most of them adopted the model's moral standards, and these effects lasted for at least 1 month.

According to social learning theory, there should be inconsistency of moral behaviour across situations. Hartshorne and May (1928) looked at stealing, cheating, and lying in 12,000 children between the ages of 8 and 16. They claimed that there was great inconsistency of behaviour. For example, children who lied in one situation were not particularly likely to lie in another situation. However, a re-analysis of Hartshorne and May's data indicated that the children showed *some* behavioural consistency (Burton, 1976). For example, children who lied in one situation tended to lie in other, related situations, and the same was true for cheating and stealing. In addition, Hartshorne and May (1928) studied children, and there is evidence (Blasi, 1980) that consistency of moral behaviour increases between childhood and adulthood.

*Parke (1977) found that if **children** heard an unpleasant loud noise when they tried to touch a toy, eventually the temptation to play with it was reduced.*

Parke (1977) carried out a study on the effects of punishment on moral behaviour. Children received punishment (a soft or unpleasantly loud buzzer) every time they touched an attractive toy. After that, the experimenter left the room. Children were more likely to resist the temptation to play with the attractive toys when the noise was loud than when it was soft. Parke also found that providing children with good reasons why they should resist temptation was effective, perhaps because it made it easier for them to use self-regulatory processes of self-reinforcement for avoiding temptation.

Evaluation

Social learning theory differs from cognitive-developmental theories in its emphasis on the social factors influencing moral development, and in its focus on moral behaviour rather than moral reasoning. Social learning theorists have shown that moral behaviour is influenced by reward, punishment, and observational learning. As predicted, moral behaviour (especially that of children) has sometimes been found to show inconsistency from one situation to another.

Social learning theory has various limitations. First, it is hard within the theory to understand how general moral principles (e.g., justice, fairness) are learned. Social learning theory does not make it clear how moral development occurs, or why it is that most people go through the same stages of moral development.

Second, most research on moral behaviour carried out by social learning theorists consists of short-term laboratory studies. As a result, according to Miller (1993, p.228):

We know much more about the variables that can affect the learning of social behaviours [e.g., moral behaviour] than about what variables actually operate in the lives of children or what behaviours actually occur at various ages.

Third, the social learning approach focuses very much on the behavioural component of morality at the expense of the cognitive component studied in depth by Piaget and by Kohlberg. It also neglects the emotional component that was emphasised by Freud. As a

Would you consider that any human behaviour is consistent from one situation to another?

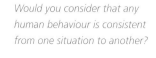

THEORIES OF MORAL DEVELOPMENT		
Theory	**Methods**	**Criticisms**
Psychodynamic	Personal accounts from adults about their childhood experiences.	Relies on accuracy of person's memory. Many of Freud's hypotheses have been proved wrong.
Piaget's cognitive-developmental theory	Telling short stories to illustrate moral points revealed a shift from moral realism to moral relativism.	Piaget may have underestimated the young child's ability to take account of people's intentions. Piaget ignored the behavioural and emotional components of morality.
Kohlberg's cognitive-developmental theory	Through the use of artificial dilemmas, Kohlberg described six stages of moral development that seem to be stable across most cultures.	Most people do not seem to develop beyond stage 4. The distinction between stages 5 and 6 is not clear. Kohlberg also placed little emphasis on the behavioural and emotional components of morality.
Social learning theory	Observational studies and laboratory-based work examined children's moral behaviour rather than moral reasoning.	Theory does not show how general moral principles, e.g., fairness, are learned. Laboratory studies often do not reflect real life. The approach ignores the cognitive and emotional components of moral development.

result, social learning theorists provide us with a rather narrow view of moral development.

Theories of Pro-social Reasoning

Nancy Eisenberg felt that Kohlberg's emphasis on justice and fairness overlooked a key aspect of morality, that of "pro-social" moral reasoning. In Section 3, Pro- and Anti-social Behaviour, we discussed pro-social behaviour in adults, behaviours that aim to benefit others. One particular kind of pro-social behaviour—altruism—aims to help others at a possible cost or risk to the altruist. Why do people behave altruistically? The "empathy-altruism model" (Batson, 1987) suggested that when we see someone else in distress we feel empathy for their distress and are motivated to reduce their and our distress. Empathy describes the ability to comprehend what someone else is feeling.

Eisenberg argued that empathy was a fundamental part of moral development. In order to behave in a just or caring way towards others, one must feel empathy.

Eisenberg's theory

Eisenberg believed, like Piaget and Kohlberg, that changes take place in moral reasoning in parallel with the maturation of general cognitive abilities. Eisenberg particularly emphasised the growth of role-taking skills—the ability to assume the perspective and take the part of another person. These skills in turn assist in the growth of empathy and thus pro-social moral reasoning.

According to Eisenberg, Lennon, and Roth (1983) there are five levels or stages in the development of pro-social reasoning, as shown in the box on the next page.

Research evidence

This theory has been tested by asking children of different ages to decide what they would do if faced by various dilemmas. One of the dilemmas was as follows:

One day a girl named Mary was going to a friend's birthday party. On her way she saw a girl who had fallen down and hurt her leg. The girl asked Mary to go to her house and get her parents so that they could come and take her to a doctor. But if Mary did … she would be late for the party and miss the ice cream, cake, and all the games. What should Mary do?

Children as young as 18 months may show concern when they see other children in distress.

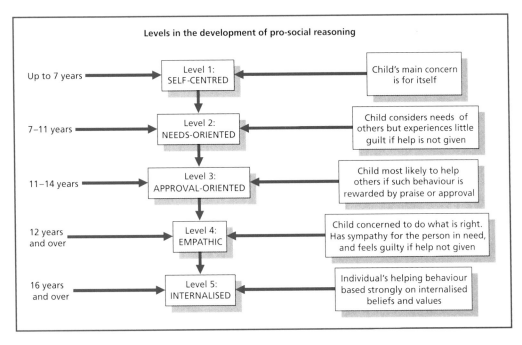

Levels in the development of pro-social reasoning

Age	Level	Description
Up to 7 years	Level 1: SELF-CENTRED	Child's main concern is for itself
7–11 years	Level 2: NEEDS-ORIENTED	Child considers needs of others but experiences little guilt if help is not given
11–14 years	Level 3: APPROVAL-ORIENTED	Child most likely to help others if such behaviour is rewarded by praise or approval
12 years and over	Level 4: EMPATHIC	Child concerned to do what is right. Has sympathy for the person in need, and feels guilty if help not given
16 years and over	Level 5: INTERNALISED	Individual's helping behaviour based strongly on internalised beliefs and values

Eisenberg-Berg and Hand (1979) found that young children tended to be self-centred. Most of them decided that Mary should go to the party and leave the injured girl on her own. In contrast, older children generally decided that it was more important to help the injured girl than to go to the party. Of course, the opinions expressed by children when given such dilemmas may not correspond to their behaviour in everyday life. However, Eisenberg-Berg and Hand obtained some evidence that the level of pro-social reasoning revealed by the dilemmas does predict actual behaviour. Sharing behaviour was more common among children at level 2 of pro-social reasoning than among those at level 1.

Eisenberg et al. (1991) found that empathy (which develops during level 4) plays an important role in producing pro-social thinking. Adolescents given the dilemma about Mary and the injured girl were more likely to decide that Mary should help if they thought about her feelings of pain and anxiety.

According to the theory of Eisenberg et al. (1983), empathy only develops from about the age of 12. However, evidence that empathy may influence pro-social behaviour several years earlier was reported by Zahn-Waxler et al. (1979). Many children between the ages of 18 and 30 months showed obvious concern when they saw other children in distress. The infants may have experienced empathy because their mothers had a particular way of dealing with them when they harmed another child. Their mothers emphasised the distress that their behaviour had caused to the other child. The mothers said things such as, "Don't hit Mary—you've made her cry" or "Put that bat down—you've hurt John."

If the mother of an aggressive child emphasises how much the other child is being hurt, the aggressive child is more likely to feel empathy and stop the undesirable behaviour.

Evaluation

Eisenberg's theory offers a different perspective on the development of moral understanding. It emphasises the importance of emotional factors and focuses on pro-social reasoning rather than issues of wrong-doing. Nevertheless there are strong parallels between this theory and Kohlberg's stage account, and therefore it can be seen as a broadening of Kohlberg's original approach (Bee, 1995).

Eisenberg's approach can be adapted to give useful advice to parents, and others involved with children, about how to raise helpful and altruistic children. For example, emphasising that the consequences of an action matter, and acting as pro-social models for children's behaviour.

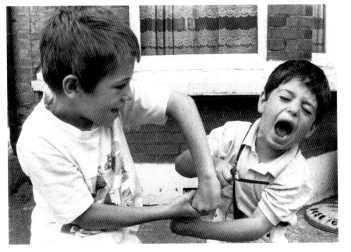

Sociobiological theory

A different approach to understanding the development of pro-social behaviour can be found in sociobiological theory, based on evolutionary principles. According to the theory of evolution, any behaviour that promotes survival and reproduction will be naturally selected and remain in a species' repertoire. Individuals who possess **adaptive** characteristics have a competitive advantage over individuals without such characteristics. This theory can explain many animal behaviours, but it cannot explain altruism because an individual who dies or is injured saving another has reduced their chances of reproduction. Therefore we should not observe altruistic behaviour in the animal world—yet we do.

Sociobiologists offered an explanation for this. It is not the survival of the individual that matters but the survival of the genes. Thus, if an individual dies in order to ensure the survival of other genetically related individuals then this altruistic behaviour is adaptive. This is called **kin selection**.

Sociobiologists further suggest that, if an individual behaves in a pro-social manner towards another, this behaviour may be returned at a later date, thus enhancing the survival of both individuals. This is called **reciprocal altruism** (Trivers, 1971).

Sociobiological theory suggests that we behave pro-socially because we inherit this characteristic. We inherit it because it is adaptive. This is a biological account of the development of pro-social behaviour and is further discussed in Section 3, Pro- and Anti-Social Behaviour (pages 98–133) and Section 13, Determinants of Animal Behaviour (pages 490-529).

SECTION SUMMARY

Development of Thinking

❖ Theories of cognitive development aim to describe and explain the way that children's thinking changes as they get older.

❖ According to Piaget, the child acquires knowledge (adapts to his/her environment) through the twin processes of accommodation (adjustment) and assimilation (taking in). The infant is born with innate schemas that change through interactions with the environment. The driving force is equilibration. Stages are directed by innate, maturational change. All children pass through the same sequence but not necessarily at the same age.

❖ There are four stages of cognitive development: sensori-motor (intelligence develops through action), pre-operational (thinking dominated by perception and lacking internally consistent logic), concrete operations (logical thinking applied to concrete objects), and formal operations (logical thinking can be applied to potential events or abstract ideas).

❖ The sensori-motor stage is characterised by innate schemas (reflexes), object permanence, perseverative search, imitation, and deferred imitation. Critics have demonstrated that Piaget underestimated the abilities of infants at this stage. In addition it appears the perseverative search does not involve the child's active participation.

❖ The pre-operational stage is subdivided into preconceptual and intuitive stages. It is characterised by an inability to demonstrate seriation, syncretic thought (e.g., conservation), centration, egocentric thought (e.g., three mountains experiment), realism, animism, and artificialism. Critics again suggest that Piaget underestimated the cognitive abilities of children at this stage but age differences remain. Children may fail the conservation task because they don't understand the question, or because they are confused by two questions. Certain visual tasks or questions can increase sense of identity and conservation ability. Making the task more meaningful reduces egocentric reasoning.

❖ In the concrete operations stage, children's thinking is no longer dominated by perception and logical reasoning develops, though it is restricted to concrete situations only. Children learn mathematical operations, reversibility, and transitivity. Conservation of volume is harder to achieve than conservation of number; children can conserve in familiar situations. This account may focus too exclusively on logical thinking.

❖ The final stage of formal operations is illustrated by the pendulum problem, solving problems through hypothesis testing. However, adult thought also involves problem solving in situations where there aren't logical solutions. Not all adults may reach this stage.

❖ In general, Piaget's underestimation of children's abilities may be due to his use of the clinical method. Other general criticisms are related to the notion of stages (cognitive development may not be as systematic as the concept of stages suggests), the distinction between performance and competence, and the vagueness of maturation and conflict as concepts to explain why development takes place. Piaget's account may be descriptive rather than explanatory.

❖ Vygotsky emphasised the notion that cognitive development depends very largely on social factors. What children can achieve with the assistance of others is generally more than they can achieve on their own. Culture and "experts" transform elementary into higher mental functions and act in the zone of proximal development.

❖ Vygotsky identified four stages in the formation of concepts: vague syncretic, complex, potential concept, and mature concept stages. Movement through the zone of proximal development leads to cognitive development, and is assisted by scaffolding and language (including intersubjectivity). Research supports the value of scaffolding, the social context, and inner speech in cognitive development.

❖ Vygotsky's approach can explain cultural differences because it is based on the social context; however, the importance of social factors may have been overestimated. In addition, social interactions may result in opposing reactions rather than learning or may simply motivate behaviour (e.g., social facilitation). One might expect learning to be much faster than it is if all that was required was the guidance of experts.

❖ The information-processing approach uses the computer metaphor. Adults tend to have a greater knowledge base and increased automatic processing, which speeds up cognitive processing. The theories of Case and Pascual-Leone adapted Piaget's theory to focus on specific components of cognitive processing rather than more general schemas, and argued for the role of increases in mental capacity or mental power. M (processing capacity) increases with neurological development.

❖ Case suggested that there are three kinds of schemes or basic units of cognition: figurative, operative, and executive. Over time children increase their range of schemes by modifying or combining existing schemes. Cognitive development is the result of increased M-power, and the ability to use it. This can explain Piagetian research findings by arguing that young children have insufficient mental capacity to hold all the relevant schemes in mind. This approach fits well with cognitive research generally, it explains task failure in terms of processing limitations instead of logical reasoning, and it is easy to conduct research into measurable processes. However, it is hard to assess which schemes are being used and to measure M-power.

❖ All theories of cognitive development can be applied to education. According to Piaget, what children can learn is determined by their current stage of cognitive development. Research has not supported this. Piaget's work also suggests that children learn best when engaged in a process of active self-discovery. However, research has shown that the tutorial method is more effective. The neo-Piagetians attach much importance to conflict, and especially socio-cognitive conflict, as a way to promote effective learning at school; social marking is also valuable. Piaget, finally, argued that the study of subjects such as mathematics, logic, and science is valuable for the development of cognitive schemas.

❖ According to Vygotsky, the social context enhances learning. Teachers scaffold the learner by increasing or decreasing support as required. Peer tutoring can be especially effective. The evidence suggests that conflict works well with some learning tasks, whereas collaboration is more effective with others. Play is especially useful in learning because it is often involves cultural activities. However, tutors are not always helpful, especially when the tutor is insensitive to the pupil's needs. The Vygotskian approach isn't useful in all situations, such as conceptual understanding.

❖ The information-processing approach suggests that teaching should be based on a sound understanding of the knowledge and processes required to perform different tasks (task analysis and error analysis). Examples can be found in teaching reading and mathematics. Teaching should also focus on preventing overload of short-term memory, on developing children's metacognitive knowledge, and on avoidance of explicit instructions for implicit learning tasks. This is a useful approach that enables us to identify strategies required to complete tasks successfully. However, it is not possible to identify all underlying processes, capacity limitations are difficult to assess accurately, and having identified a process does not then enable one to know how it can be acquired.

Development of Measured Intelligence

❖ Intelligence enables one to deal effectively with one's environment. Most intelligence tests measure basic cognitive abilities, but not "streetwise" skills. IQ is the numerical estimate produced by such tests. IQ is not always accurate because of social and cultural biases in tests. The key question is whether IQ is related more to heredity or environment. This may be seen as an interaction (two sides of a rectangle) but we still might investigate which contributes more.

❖ Twin studies are one method of research. MZ twins reared together are much more similar than DZ twins in terms of IQ but this may be because MZ twins are treated more similarly. Studies of twins reared apart also support the genetic position, though in some cases the twins were reared in very similar environments. The findings indicate 50% variability due to genetic factors; however, this may arise because of the cultures in which the studies have taken place. In addition we should remember that IQ is an imperfect measure of intelligence and that IQ similarity decreases with age. Adoption studies generally confirm the findings of twin studies, but may be biased by selective placement.

❖ Twin and adoption studies indicate that genetic factors are important but also that environmental factors are influential. Further evidence indicates that improved environmental conditions and schooling are associated with increased IQ. Research with the HOME inventory indicates that provision of appropriate play materials, parental involvement with the child, and variety in daily stimulation are all associated with increased IQ, but it is hard to prove that there is a causal link. The Rochester study identified environmental factors, such as the mother not going to high school or having severe anxiety, that were associated with lower IQ. Operation Headstart demonstrated some positive effects from environmental enrichment.

❖ If IQ is genetically based this might explain the average differences found between American white and black people (about 15 IQ points). This is a highly political argument. Criticisms of such arguments are that investigations of race differences tell us little about the nature of intelligence; that they assume that we can identify distinct racial groups; and that controlled research is possible, whereas we cannot truly isolate genetic and environmental factors. There are also important ethical issues. Environmental deprivation, not genetic factors, may be responsible for most supposed racial differences, and we can also think in terms of qualitative differences associated with culture. IQ tests are potentially socially and culturally biased. Some research suggests that the effects are not as great as has been claimed, though this may be due to the fact that some tests are just translated to make them suitable for another culture. Truly culture-fair tests do show differences.

❖ Morals are concerned with right and wrong, and are vital for society to function. There are emotional, cognitive, and behavioural components associated with morality.

❖ Freud emphasised the notion that moral development depends on children's identification with the same-sex parent at about the age of 5 or 6. In boys the process is described by the Oedipus complex, and in girls as penis-envy or, as Jung suggested, the Electra complex. Moral strength is predicted to be weaker in girls because the resolution is less complete. Research evidence doesn't support a link between harsher parents and greater morality, though it may be important to consider the parents' intentions rather than their behaviour. Research also shows that women do not have weaker moralities. Freud's basic assumptions about age and parental influence are correct. However, he exaggerated the role of the same-sex parent, ignored cognitive and behavioural elements, and suggested that moral development ceased after the age of 6.

❖ According to Piaget, children's thinking develops in stages and this can also be applied to moral reasoning. Piaget observed children's behaviour in games with marbles and identified three major stages: the premoral period, stage of moral realism, and stage of moral relativism. Moral realism is associated with heteronomous morality, expiatory punishment, and immanent justice. Moral relativism is associated with autonomous morality and reciprocal punishment. Moral realism concerns consequences rather than intentions, whereas moral relativism is the reverse. Piaget suggested that development occurs because of decreasing egocentricity and increasing negotiations with others that lead children to question their own values. Piaget used moral stories to demonstrate that younger children do focus on consequences. However this may be oversimplistic— when the consequences are positive they do use intentions. Other problems include an oversimplification of moral thinking and an overestimation of moral reasoning. Piaget assumed that heteronomous children follow their parents in all things, but they may treat some decisions differently. Piaget focused on moral reasoning rather than on either moral behaviour or emotional factors.

❖ Kohlberg expanded Piaget's theory in his six-stage theory. He used moral dilemmas to research the ways that males thought about moral decisions, producing a stage theory of moral reasoning. The three levels are: pre-conventional morality, conventional morality, and post-conventional or principled morality. Kohlberg's original cross-sectional study and subsequent longitudinal study supported this stage theory, as has cross-cultural research. However, other evidence suggests that individuals operate at several levels at one time rather than being consistent, and that being able to think abstractly does not guarantee level 3 of moral reasoning. This account is more detailed than Piaget's; however, there is some doubt if people generally develop beyond stage 4, and whether the stages can predict moral behaviour. Kohlberg overlooked the emotional component of morality and produced a strongly androcentric theory. Gilligan proposed a distinction between a male morality of justice and a female morality of care.

❖ According to social learning theory, moral behaviour in any situation is determined by the rewards and punishments an individual has received in similar situations. This would predict great inconsistency of behaviour in different situations, which is supported by research. There is also research support for the influence of parents, of modelling, and of self-regulation. Social learning theory is useful in its focus on behaviour. However, it is not really a developmental theory, and it does not account for the learning of general moral principles. The evidence is largely experimental and artificial.

❖ Theories of pro-social behaviour have a wider focus. Eisenberg suggested that empathy is a key element of moral and pro-social behaviour. Her theory of the development of pro-social reasoning, like Piaget and Kohlberg's theories, is also a stage theory linked to cognitive maturation. In the five stages she emphasises the growth of role-taking skills. Research again used dilemmas and found support for the theory, though empathy may appear earlier than was predicted. The theory emphasises emotional factors and focuses on pro-social reasoning rather than on issues of wrong-doing. It can be seen as a broadening of Kohlberg's original approach.

❖ Sociobiological theory explains pro-social behaviour as an adaptive means of ensuring the survival of kin and/or those who can return favours. We behave pro-socially because it is an adaptive behaviour that is inherited.

FURTHER READING

The topics in this Section are covered in greater depth by J. Henderson (2001) *Development of thinking* (London: Routledge), written specifically for the AQA A specification. There is good coverage of most aspects of cognitive development in K. Durkin (1995) *Developmental social psychology: From infancy to old age* (Oxford: Blackwell). A very readable account of Piaget's work can be found in the chapter on "Jean Piaget" by Peter Bryant in *Seven pioneers of psychology* (1995) edited by R. Fuller (London: Routledge). The information-processing approach is discussed fully by D.R. Shaffer (1998), *Developmental psychology: Childhood and adolescence (5th Edn.)* (Pacific Grove, CA: Brooks/Cole). Factors associated with the development of intelligence test performance are discussed by M.W. Eysenck (1994a) *Individual differences: Normal and abnormal* (Hove, UK: Psychology Press). Another very up-to-date book written for A level students is by M. Jarvis (2001) *Angles on child psychology* (Cheltenham, UK: Stanley Thornes).

Example Examination Questions

You should spend 30 minutes on each of the questions below, which aim to test the material in this Section.

1. Discuss the applications of **one or more** theories of cognitive development. (24 marks)

2. (a) Describe Vygotsky's theory of cognitive development. (12 marks)
   (b) Evaluate this theory with reference to research evidence and/or other theories of cognitive development. (12 marks)

3. (a) Describe **two** studies that illustrate the role of genetic factors in the development of measured intelligence. (12 marks)
   (b) Evaluate the extent to which these, and/or other studies, provide insight into the role of genetics in the development of intelligence. (12 marks)

4. Discuss the role of genetics **and** cultural differences in the development of measured intelligence. (24 marks)

5. Discuss **one or more** theories of the development of moral understanding. (24 marks)

6. Critically consider the influence of gender and cultural variation on moral development. (24 marks)

Examination Tips

Question 1. "Discuss" is an AO1 and AO2 term. The words "applications" and "theories" are both plural and therefore you must cover more than one application (though the applications may just concern education) and more than one theory. Evaluation may be achieved through reference to research studies but may also involve comparisons between the differing theoretical perspectives.

Question 2. Vygotsky's theory of cognitive development is explicitly named in the specification (as is Piaget's theory and the information-processing approach), thus it is legitimate to specifically ask for a description of one of these theories/approaches. In part

(a) you should aim for a balance between depth and breadth (i.e., cover a number of aspects of the theory, but not as a "shopping list"; detail is required). In part (b) you are given some guidance about evaluation but can include other considerations, such as practical applications and methodological/logical flaws.

Question 3.   When describing studies you can use the same guidelines as for AS level: write something about the aims, procedures, findings, and conclusions. Criticisms of such studies will not be creditworthy here as part (a) is AO1 marks only. The studies selected must illustrate the role of genetic factors but you do not need to explain this link as that is the topic for part (b). Since the second part is AO2 you must ensure that you are presenting an argument about the role of genetic factors and using research studies to support this argument. You should not offer any further *descriptions* of research studies.

Question 4.   This essay requires consideration of both nature and nurture. It is not explicitly required that you use research studies and, given the potential breadth of the material, you may do better to limit your descriptions of such studies and emphasise the arguments for each position. The essay asks about the role of genetics/cultural differences not the evidence to support this, though such evidence may form part of your *critical* consideration. You will need to be selective in order to compose a well-structured and well-detailed response in 30 minutes. Marks will be lost if you try to cover too much evidence and end up with an essay lacking in detail.

Question 5.   In the specification there are no named theories for moral understanding, unlike the theories of cognitive development; Piaget and Kohlberg are given as "e.g.'s". Therefore no question can be asked about a named theory. This essay offers you the opportunity to take the depth or breadth route—either lots of theories in minimal detail or few theories in more detail. For top marks you need to achieve a balance between depth and breadth. Evaluation can be achieved through contrasting different theories, a consideration of whether moral understanding is related to moral behaviour, reference to research studies and their methodological problems, gender bias in theories of moral understanding, and so on.

Question 6.   "Critically consider" is an AO1 and AO2 term. You should consider/describe gender *and* cultural variation, and then evaluate the extent that such variations affect moral development. Support for your argument can be achieved through the use of research (theories and/or studies). It is possible to conclude that such variation actually has no effect (i.e., morals are universal), and this position should be explored as part of a balanced answer (the injunction "critically" requires a consideration of both the strengths and limitations of the argument).

WEB SITES

http://www.piaget.org
   The Jean Piaget Society.

http://members.nbci.com/jbmartins/vygotsky.htm
   Vygotsky links.

http://www.mugu.com/cgi-bin/Upstream/Issues/psychology/IQ/index.html
   Site with various articles related to intelligence and nature/nurture.

http://www.allthetests.com/intelligence.php3
   Selection of intelligence tests.

http://www.ccp.uchicago.edu/grad/Joseph Craig/kohlberg.htm
   Notes on Kohlberg's six stages of moral judgement.

11

Social and Personality Development

In this Section we continue to look at the development of behaviours through childhood and into adolescence. A "big" question in psychology is how personality develops.

Personality Development

What is Personality?

A definition that captures much of what psychologists mean by personality was provided by Child (1968, p.83). He described it as *"more or less stable, internal factors that make one person's behaviour consistent from one time to another, and different from the behaviour other people would manifest in comparable situations"*.

As Hampson (1988) pointed out, the four key words in Child's definition are "stable", "internal", "consistent", and "different". According to Child's perspective, personality is relatively stable or unchanging over time; moods or emotional states may change dramatically over shortish periods of time, but personality does not; personality is internal, and must not be equated with external behaviour; behaviour (e.g., restlessness; lack of eye contact) is relevant, but only because it allows us to draw inferences about someone's underlying personality. If personality is moderately stable over time, and if personality determines behaviour, then it should follow that individuals will behave in a reasonably consistent fashion on different occasions. Finally, there are individual differences in personality, and these differences are revealed by different ways of behaving in a given situation. For example, extraverted people will talk more than introverted ones in a social group.

Freud's account of personality development remains highly influential, so we will start by examining this.

The Psychodynamic Approach

"Psychodynamic" refers to any approach that emphasises the processes of change and development, and moreover any theory that deals with the dynamics of behaviour (the things that drive us to behave in particular ways). Glassman (1995) points out that the psychodynamic approach is distinguished from the cognitive approach chiefly because of this element of motivation. The psychodynamic approach focuses on the role of internal processes (such as motivation) and of past experience shaping personality.

Freud's psychoanalytic theory is the best-known psychodynamic theory. We will also consider Erikson's psychosocial theory.

Sigmund Freud, 1856–1939.

Think of a time when you might have called someone by the wrong name. Was this a "Freudian slip" (an error made as a result of unconscious "intrusions" into conscious behaviour which reveal a person's true feelings)?

Freud's psychoanalytic theory

The term psychoanalysis refers both to Freud's theory of personality and his method of treatment for mental disorder (discussed in Section 18, Treating Mental Disorders). Sigmund Freud practised as a psychiatrist in Vienna in the late nineteenth century and first half of the twentieth century, treating mainly neurotic women. Neurotic illnesses are diseases that appear to be physical, such as hysterical paralysis, but where no physical cause can be found. It was thought at the time that such disturbances did have a physical cause, but Freud proposed that the cause was actually psychological. His understanding of these psychological causes is revealed in his case studies, such as that of Anna O (see the Case Study below).

These case studies of pathological (diseased) behaviour led Freud to propose a theory of normal personality development. In particular, he suggested that adult personality is the result of an interaction between innate drives (such as the desire for pleasure) and early experience (the extent to which early desires were gratified). Freud proposed that individual personality differences can be traced back to the way the early conflicts between desire and experience were handled (in the case of Anna O her conflicts arose when caring for her dying father). These conflicts remain with the adult and exert pressure through unconsciously motivated behaviour. In order to understand how these conflicts arise we first have to look at the structure of the personality.

The structure of the personality

Freud assumed that the mind is metaphorically divided into three parts. First, there is the **id**. This contains innate sexual and aggressive instincts, and is located in the unconscious mind. The sexual instinct is known as libido. The id works in accord with

---

CASE STUDY: *Anna O*

Freud's theory was largely based on the observations he made during consultations with patients. He suggested that his work was similar to that of an archaeologist, who dug away layers of earth before uncovering what he was seeking. In a similar way, the psychiatrist seeks to dig down to the unconscious and discover the key to the individual's personality dynamic.

One of his patients was Anna O, a girl of 21 who had a high degree of intelligence. Her illness first appeared while she was caring for her father, whom she tenderly loved, during a severe illness that led to his death. Anna O developed a severe paralysis of both right extremities, disturbance of eye movements, an intense nausea when she attempted to take nourishment, and at one time for several weeks a loss of the power to drink, in spite of tormenting thirst. Freud's report explains how she occasionally became confused or delirious and mumbled several words to herself. If these same words were later repeated to her when she was in a hypnotic state, she would engage in deeply sad, often poetically beautiful, day dreams. These day dreams commonly took the situation of a girl beside the sick-bed of her father as their starting point. Anna O jokingly called this treatment "chimney sweeping". Freud's colleague Dr Breuer soon hit upon the fact that through such cleansing of the soul more could be accomplished than a temporary removal of the constantly recurring mental "clouds".

During one session, the patient recalled an occasion when she was with her governess, and how that lady's dog, that she abhorred, had drunk out of a glass. Out of respect for the conventions the patient had remained silent at the time of the incident, but now under hypnosis she gave energetic expression to her restrained anger, and then drank a large quantity of water without trouble, and woke from hypnosis with the glass at her lips. The symptom of being unable to drink thereupon vanished permanently.

Freud comments, "Permit me to dwell for a moment on this experience. No one had ever cured an hysterical symptom by such means before, or had come so near understanding its cause. This would be a pregnant discovery if the expectation could be confirmed that still other, perhaps the majority of symptoms, originated in this way and could be removed by the same method.

"Such was indeed the case, almost all the symptoms originated in exactly this way, as we were to discover. The patient's illness originated at the time when she was caring for her sick father, and her symptoms could only be regarded as memory symbols of his sickness and death. While she was seated by her father's sick-bed, she was careful to betray nothing of her anxiety and her painful depression to the patient. When, later, she reproduced the same scene before the physician, the emotion that she had suppressed on the occurrence of the scene burst out with especial strength, as though it had been pent up all along.

"In her normal state she was entirely ignorant of the pathogenic scenes and of their connection with her symptoms. She had forgotten those scenes. When the patient was hypnotized, it was possible, after considerable difficulty, to recall those scenes to her memory, and by this means of recall the symptoms were removed."

Postscript: Anna O was actually Bertha Pappenheim. Jones (1953) claims that her recovery was not as successful as Brewer suggested. She had many relapses and was institutionalised for a while. In later life Bertha remained cool about psychoanalysis, refusing to allow the orphans she cared for to be treated by this method.

Adapted from Sigmund Freud (1910) The origin and development of psychoanalysis. *American Journal of Psychology, 21*, 181–218.

the **pleasure principle**, with the emphasis being on immediate satisfaction. Second, there is the **ego**. This is the conscious, rational mind, and it develops during the first 2 years of life. It works on the **reality principle**, taking account of what is going on in the environment, i.e., in reality. Third, there is the **superego**. This develops at about the age of 5 and embodies the child's conscience and sense of right and wrong. It is formed when the child adopts many of the values of the same-sex parent (the process of identification).

Freud also assumed that there were three levels of the mind: the conscious, the preconscious, and the unconscious. The conscious consists of those thoughts that are currently the focus of attention. The preconscious consists of information and ideas that could be retrieved easily from memory and brought into consciousness. The unconscious consists of information that is either very hard or almost impossible to bring into conscious awareness.

To what extent do you think it is useful to create metaphorical concepts such as these? Are there associated dangers?

Defence mechanisms

An important part of Freud's theory was the notion that there are frequent *conflicts* among the id, ego, and superego. Conflicts cause the individual to experience anxiety, and this leads the ego to devote much time to trying to resolve these conflicts. The ego protects itself by using a number of **defence mechanisms**, which are strategies designed to reduce anxiety.

Anna Freud (1936) used this concept of ego defences to explain the development of the personality, for example "defences against instincts" are the result of developmental conflicts where a child learns defensive behaviours in order to control undesirable instinctive behaviours. Some of the other defences that contribute to the formation of adult personality include:

1. *Repression*. Keeping threatening thoughts out of consciousness. For example, a person may not remember a dental appointment because it is going to be painful.
2. *Displacement*. Unconsciously moving impulses away from a threatening object and towards a less threatening object. For example, someone who has been made angry by their boss may go home and kick the cat.
3. *Projection*. An individual may attribute their undesirable characteristics to others. For example, someone who is very unfriendly may accuse other people of being unfriendly.
4. *Denial*. Refusing to accept the existence or reality of a threatening event. For example, patients suffering from life-threatening diseases often deny that these diseases are affecting their lives.
5. *Intellectualisation*. Thinking about threatening events in ways that remove the emotion from them. An example would be responding to the sinking of a car ferry with considerable loss of life by thinking about ways of improving the design of ferries.

What kinds of experience might be so upsetting that they are kept out of conscious awareness?

Psychosexual development

Freud described early personality development in terms of a series of stages, where in each stage the child's energy or **libido** is focused on a body region. The term "libido" was Freud's word for the psychological and sexual energy produced by the id. When Freud used the word "sexual" he was not referring to sexuality as in sexual intercourse but rather to a more general physical and sensual arousal, perhaps simply a state of pleasure.

These five stages are psychosexual because of this psychological and sexual energy.

1. *Oral stage*: this occurs during the first 18 months of life. During this stage, the infant obtains satisfaction from eating, sucking, and other activities using the mouth.

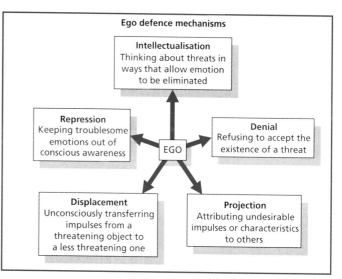

2. *Anal stage*: this occurs between about 18 and 36 months of age. Toilet training occurs during this stage, which may cause conflict.

3. *Phallic stage*: this occurs between 3 and 6 years of age. The genitals become a key source of satisfaction during this stage. At about the age of 5, boys acquire the **Oedipus complex**, in which they have sexual desires for their mother and therefore want to get rid of their father who is a rival. They then also fear their father who might realise what they are thinking. This complex is resolved by identification with their father, involving adopting many of their father's attitudes and developing a superego. Jung (a follower of Freud) suggested that a similar process operates in girls called the **Electra complex**, in which they desire their fathers. Freud's own view was that, during the genital stage, girls come to recognise that they don't have a penis and blame their mother for this. The girl's father now becomes her love-object and she substitutes her "penis-envy" with a wish to have a child. This leads to a kind of resolution and ultimate identification with her same-sex parent.

4. *Latency stage*: this lasts from 6 years of age until the onset of puberty. During this stage, boys and girls spend very little time together.

5. *Genital stage*: this starts from the onset of puberty and continues throughout adult life. During this stage, the main source of sexual pleasure is in the genitals.

Note that the term '"sexual" is roughly equivalent to "physical pleasure".

Personality development

In a sense there are three strands to Freud's theory of personality development: the structure of the personality (id, ego, and superego), defence mechanisms, and stages of psychosexual development. Personality itself develops as an outcome of these three strands. If a child experiences severe problems or excessive pleasure at any stage of development, this leads to **fixation**, in which basic energy or libido becomes attached to that stage for many years. Later in life, adults who experience very stressful conditions are likely to show **regression**, in which their behaviour becomes less mature and like that displayed during a psychosexual stage at which they fixated as children. According to Freud, these processes of fixation and regression play important roles

Useful mnemonic

To help you remember Freud's stages of psychosexual development, the following mnemonic is made from the initial letter of each stage: Old Age Pensioners Love Greens!

FREUD'S STAGES OF PSYCHOSEXUAL DEVELOPMENT

Stage	Approximate age	Summary
Oral	0–18 months	Satisfaction from eating, sucking, etc.
Anal	18–36 months	Interest in and satisfaction from anal region
Phallic	3–6 years	Genitals become source of satisfaction
Latency	6 years old to puberty	Boys and girls spend little time together
Genital	From onset of puberty	Genitals are main source of sexual pleasure

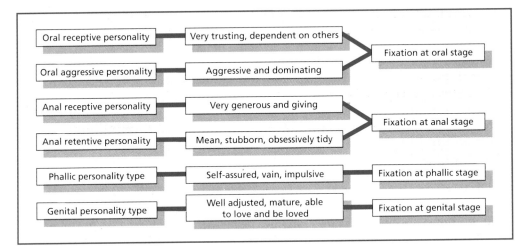

Freud's personality types.

in determining adult personality. Some personality types are shown in the box on the previous page, along with descriptions and a link to the stage of psychosexual development at which fixation may have occurred.

Case studies

Freud's theory was based on the data he collected in his interactions with patients. He never made any notes during a therapeutic session, feeling that any lack of attention during therapy would interfere with its progress and believing that he would be able to record all the important details afterwards. It is likely that these notes were biased by his own expectations and selective recall. In fact, Freud recorded only a very few case histories such as those of Anna O, described earlier, and Little Hans (see page 651).

Little Hans was an unusual case study because it was the only one involving a child, which highlights the fact that Freud's account of child development was almost entirely based on retrospective accounts. It was also, as we have noted, a theory of normal development based on observations of pathological behaviour.

What problems might arise in using retrospective data?

Freud also used self-analysis as an important form of empirical data. He reserved a half-hour at the end of each day for searching self-analysis and was reluctant to accept the validity of any hypothesis unless he had tested it in the context of his own behaviour. Some psychologists might criticise this as a highly subjective form of evidence yet it is probably no more than any scientist does—to ask whether a theory accounts for the facts as you know them. Freud used his own experience as a form of "fact".

Other research evidence

There is other psychological research evidence that can be used to support Freud's theory. The topic of repression in relation to memory has been investigated (and was part of your AS level studies). For example, Myers and Brewin (1994) asked participants to recall childhood memories and found that those who had experienced hostility from their fathers were most likely to repress such memories. In another study, young women who had received hospital treatment for incidents involving sexual abuse were tracked down 17 years later, 38% said they had no conscious recollection of the events for which they were treated (Williams, 1994). Both studies indicate that some people do deal with anxiety by repressing the events that create anxiety.

Another area of cognitive psychology that has drawn on Freud's ideas is that of perceptual defence—the concept that things are likely to be ignored if they are unpleasant or emotionally threatening. This was classically demonstrated in a study by McGinnies (1949) where participants were shown lists of words. The exposure time for each word was increased until the participant was able to correctly identify the word. McGinnies found that emotionally threatening words, such as "raped" and "penis" required longer exposure time than words such as "apple" and "dance". Levinger and Clark (1961) provided similar evidence of the effects of anxiety-provoking words. They gave participants lists of words and asked them to think of an associated word. Later, when participants were asked to recall words, they recalled those that had neutral associations better than those that had an emotional association. This supports the view that emotional thoughts are repressed, presumably because they provoke anxiety.

Do you think there might be ethical objections to this research?

Evaluation of psychoanalytic theory

Freud and his psychoanalytic theory have had an enormous impact on psychology. Williams (1987) commented that:

psychoanalysis has been society's most influential theory of human behaviour ... it profoundly altered Western ideas about human nature and changed the way we viewed ourselves and our experience.

On the other hand, some psychologists object outright to Freud's theory. Freud's method of investigation was to focus on the individual, observing particular "cases" in fine detail. In some ways this is to his credit—a detailed understanding of the way people think and feel (an ideographic approach). However, many people see this approach as a

What disadvantages are there in this idiographic approach?

drawback mainly because Freud's observations were largely based on a rather narrow sample of people: white, middle-class Viennese Victorian women. The theory may not be universally applicable yet certain key concepts have endured. Namely, the emphasis on childhood and on the influence of the unconscious.

Considering that Freud was working in a strict Victorian society, why was sexual behaviour so strongly emphasised in his theory of development?

It has been suggested that Freud may have overemphasised sex because he developed his theory at an historical time of great sexual repression. Understandably this may have caused sex to be something that was repressed in many minds (Banyard & Hayes, 1994). A number of neo-Freudians have adapted Freud's explanation and incorporated more social rather than sexual influences, such as Erik Erikson.

Freud's work was largely with middle-class women in Vienna in the 1890s and 1900s. How relevant do you think his ideas are to other cultures, particularly given the social changes during the twentieth century?

Erikson's psychosocial theory

Erikson's (1959) starting point was the notion that conflicts between the natural processes of maturation and the expectations of society create various crises that the child must try to resolve. Erikson's theory of psychosocial development resembled Freud's theory of psychosexual development in some ways, but its emphasis was much more on the role of social factors and on the development of the ego. There are eight stages of psychosocial development. Everyone goes through these stages in the same order, but people vary enormously in terms of how successfully they cope with each stage. Each stage has possible positive and negative outcomes associated with it; children who have negative outcomes have to deal with their unresolved crises later in life.

The eight stages are outlined in the box on the next page, and the first four are described in detail (the remainder are discussed in Section 12, Adulthood).

Erikson's psychosocial theory emphasised the role of social factors in the development of the ego.

- *Stage 1.* Infancy (0–1 year): the infant develops either trust *or* mistrust in itself and others; the mother or mother figure is the central person in the child's life.
- *Stage 2.* Toddler (2–3 years): the child either becomes more independent *or* has a sense of shame and doubt. Erikson (1959, p.102) described "the sinister forces which are leashed and unleashed, especially in the guerilla warfare of unequal wills; for the child is often unequal to his own violent drives, and parent and child unequal to each other". The parents are the central figures.
- *Stage 3.* Preschool (4–5 years): the child shows initiative *or* experiences guilt. According to Erikson (1959, p.74), "Being firmly convinced that he *is* a person, the child must now find out *what kind* of a person he is going to be ... he wants to be like his parents, who to him appear very powerful and beautiful, although quite unreasonably dangerous". The family is of central importance.
- *Stage 4.* Childhood (6–12 years): the child shows industry and works hard *or* develops a sense of inferiority. According to Erikson (1959, p.82), the child's approach during

PSYCHOSOCIAL DEVELOPMENT—ERIKSON'S STAGES 1–8

Stage	Age	Name	Life crisis	Positive characteristics	Negative characteristics	Social focus
1	0–1	Infancy	Trust vs. mistrust	Trust in self and others	Mistrust in self and others	Mother
2	2–3	Toddler	Autonomy vs. shame	Becoming independent	Sense of shame and doubt	Parents
3	4–5	Preschool	Initiative vs. guilt	Shows initiative	Experiences guilt	Family
4	6–12	Childhood	Industry vs. inferiority	Shows industry	Sense of inferiority	School, friends, home
5	13–19	Adolescence	Identity vs. role confusion	Identity	Role confusion	Peer group
6	20–30	Early adulthood	Intimacy vs. isolation	Intimacy	Isolation	Friends
7	30–60	Middle adulthood	Generativity vs. stagnation	Generativity	Stagnation	Household
8	60+	Old age	Integrity vs. despair	Wisdom	Despair	Humankind

this stage is, "I am what I learn." This learning takes place at school and in friends' houses as well as at home, because the child's social world is expanding.

Children generally show a mixture of the positive and negative outcomes identified here. For example, most infants in stage 1 develop some trust as well as some mistrust. Children for whom the outcomes of each stage are mainly positive develop a stronger and more positive sense of self than children for whom most of the outcomes are negative.

Research evidence

Erikson relied heavily on clinical evidence to provide support for his theory, gathered in his work as a practising therapist. Although such evidence can indicate that a theory is on the right lines, it is generally too anecdotal and imprecise to confirm the theory's details. However, there is some experimental evidence providing indirect support for aspects of Erikson's theory. For example, Erikson argued that trust was a positive outcome of stage 1, whereas mistrust was a negative outcome. The work of Ainsworth on attachment behaviour is relevant (examined in your AS level studies). Ainsworth and Bell (1970) identified three forms of attachment of an infant to its mother. Secure attachment, which is most useful for the infant's psychological development, involves a high level of trust. In contrast, the less desirable resistant attachment and avoidant attachment both involve mistrust and anxiety.

Erikson's general notion that the development of the self during stage 4 (ages 6–12) is increasingly influenced by friends and by schoolmates has received support in the work of Damon and Hart (1988). They asked children of different ages to describe themselves and found that children between the ages of 8 and 11 are much more likely than those between 4 and 7 to describe themselves in comparison with other children. The older children also tended to use more internal, psychological terms to describe themselves, whereas younger children focused on visible and tangible properties and possessions to define themselves, such as "I've got black hair" rather than "I'm a kind person".

What are the major drawbacks of using mainly clinical evidence to formulate a theory, as Erikson did?

Evaluation

Erikson's psychosocial theory possesses various significant strengths. First, its focus on social processes and the development of the ego greatly enlarged the scope of psychodynamic theory. Second, the notion that children face a series of conflicts or crises, with the consequences for their sense of self depending on how well these conflicts are resolved, is a valuable one. Third, Erikson would seem to be correct in arguing that most of the conflicts experienced by infants lie within the family, whereas later conflicts (e.g., in stage 4) spread out to include school and peers.

There are several limitations of the theory. As Miller (1993, p.172) pointed out:

Erikson's theory does not explain in any detail how a child moves from stage to stage or even how he resolves the crisis within a stage. It states what influences the movement (for example, physical maturation, parents, cultural beliefs, to what extent earlier crises were resolved), but not specifically how the movement comes about.

Second, there is little convincing evidence for Erikson's theory. As Dworetzky (1996, p.369) pointed out *hard scientific proof for Erikson's theory is not easy to come by because of the difficulty of examining each of Erikson's stages under controlled laboratory conditions or by other scientific methods.*

According to Erikson, what is the main "cause" of personality development?

The point is that some theories simply do not lend themselves to the kind of research where cause and effect relationships can be indicated. Erikson's emphasis on individual experience rather than observable behaviour means that it has proved quite difficult to test in a scientific manner.

Third, one reason why it is hard to test Erikson's theory is because most of the evidence is correlational. For example, suppose we find that children who show signs of independence at stage 2 develop a stronger sense of self in later childhood than those who do not. This does not prove that independence at stage 2 *caused* a strong sense of self.

Fourth, there is a danger with any stage theory that it presents far too tidy an account of what happens. For example, a conflict between trust and mistrust is said to be central only to the first stage of development, but it could well be argued that this conflict keeps recurring through most people's lives.

Social Learning Approaches

A contrasting approach to the explanation of personality is to consider development purely from the point of view of social interactions. Both Freud and Erikson involved social factors in their account; however, the key to the psychodynamic approach was the explanation of how these external factors interact with internal development. The social learning approach is almost entirely lodged in external social experiences.

Social learning theory

Even 6-month-old children show social interaction.

Social learning theory proposes that all behaviour is the consequence of conditioning: direct or indirect. Classical and operant conditioning theories (described in detail in Section 13, Determinants of Animal Behaviour) explain learning as the consequence of association or reinforcement respectively. Social learning theory extended this to included indirect, or vicarious reinforcement. Personality is learned in the same way as everything else is learned.

Consider the following example. One aspect of personality is humour. A child may tell a joke to a circle of friends and find that they all laugh along with him. This is rewarding and thus increases the likelihood that the child will tell the joke again. If, however, the joke raises no laughter but instead the other children tease him for being little use at telling jokes, then the child is less likely to repeat this behaviour. Thus we have the elements of direct reinforcement (reward) and punishment (decreases the likelihood of a behaviour being repeated).

To continue the example, the same child may watch someone else telling a joke—successfully getting laughs from everyone. This may lead the child to imitate the behaviour of the successful joke teller. This is called vicarious reinforcement. The child observed someone else's behaviour being rewarded and this encouraged him to model his own behaviour on the successful behaviour.

The key elements of social learning are observation, vicarious reinforcement, and modelling or imitation. The essential difference between social learning and learning theory is that the former includes indirect learning which means that cognitive factors must be involved. In order to recall a behaviour to be modelled there must be some internal representation of this model. Traditional learning theory specifically rejected the use of cognitive factors in explanations of behaviour. The origins of social learning theory lie in the work of Albert Bandura (b.1925). In the 1950s he was conducting research into adolescent aggression and felt that learning theory was too simplistic as an explanation for the phenomena that he was observing. Consider the description of his early experiments on aggression that is given in the box on the next page.

Steps in the modelling process

Bandura suggested that there are four steps in the modelling process:

1. *Attention.* If you are going to learn anything, you have to be paying attention. Certain characteristics of the model influence attention. If the model is attractive, or prestigious, or appears to be particularly competent, you will pay more attention. And if the model seems more like yourself, you pay more attention. Parents, peers, and the media are obvious models that command attention.

2. *Retention.* It is obvious that the model must be remembered and recalled. This stage requires reference to cognitive processes.

3. *Reproduction.* You may observe someone telling a joke well but that doesn't mean you can imitate it. Imitation requires personal skills. An interesting feature of imitation is that just imagining oneself doing the activity can improve performance. Athletes, for example, improve their own performance through imagination as well as direct practice.

4. *Motivation.* Finally you need to be motivated to perform the action, which depends on direct and indirect reinforcements and punishments. The first part of the equation is that you observe a behaviour (observational learning) but, after that the likelihood you will repeat it is related to vicarious reinforcement or punishment.

Observational learning

Of the hundreds of studies Bandura was responsible for, one group stands out above the others—the Bobo doll studies. He made a film of one of his students, a young woman, essentially beating up a Bobo doll. In case you don't know, a Bobo doll is an inflatable, egg-shape balloon creature with a weight in the bottom that makes it bob back up when you knock it down. Nowadays, it might have Darth Vader painted on it, but back then it was simply "Bobo" the clown.

The woman punched the clown, shouting "sockeroo!" She kicked it, sat on it, hit it with a little hammer, and so on, shouting various aggressive phrases. Bandura showed his film to groups of kindergartners who, as you might predict, liked it a lot. They then were let out to play. In the playroom, of course, were several observers with pens and clipboards in hand, a brand new Bobo doll, and a few little hammers.

And you might predict as well what the observers recorded: a lot of little kids beating the daylights out of the Bobo doll. They punched it and shouted "sockeroo", kicked it, sat on it, hit it with the little hammers, and so on. In other words, they imitated the young lady in the film, and quite precisely at that.

This might seem like a real nothing of an experiment at first, but consider: these children changed their behaviour without first being rewarded for approximations to that behaviour! And while that may not seem extraordinary to the average parent, teacher, or casual observer of children, it didn't fit so well with standard behaviouristic learning theory. Bandura called the phenomenon observational learning or modelling, and his theory is usually called social learning theory.

From http://www.ship.edu/~cgboeree/bandura.html

There are two specific aspects of social learning theory that were developed by Bandura (1977, 1986) that help explain personality development, which we will consider here. These are the concepts of reciprocal determination and self-efficacy. Learning is influenced by self-regulation (reciprocal determinism) insofar as the learner very much contributes to the learning process. Learning is also affected by the way you feel about yourself (your self-concept or self-efficacy).

Reciprocal determination

One might think that social learning theory, like traditional learning theory, is a determinist account of behaviour. Learning theory suggests that we are shaped by external factors and this leads us to behave in predictable ways. However, Bandura stressed that social learning theory does not represent the individual as a helpless victim of circumstance. Nor did Bandura subscribe to the idea that one can somehow add up internal and external factors and thus explain personality. Bandura felt this was an oversimplification and that it was the *interaction* that was all important (1973, p.43):

> *The environment is only a potentiality, not a fixed property that inevitably impinges on individuals and to which their behaviour eventually adapts. Behaviour partly creates the environment and the resultant environment, in turn influences the behaviour.*

Bandura (1977, 1986) called this interaction **reciprocal determinism**. The personal characteristics of an individual

Bandura emphasised the role of interaction in the learning process.

influence what they select to do in the social environment. These characteristics include personality, beliefs, and cognitive abilities, and these will then determine who a person chooses to spend time with, what kind of activities they take part in, and what they avoid. These selections then, in turn, affect what skills and behaviours are reinforced and what ultimately is learned. An aggressive child, for example, may find that this behaviour is rewarding because the child gets to play with a certain toy. Increased aggressiveness will further shape the child's environment because it may discourage certain other children from playing with the aggressive child. It may just be other aggressive children who maintain the friendship and this will shape the original child's continuing behaviour. People are both products of and producers of their environment.

Self-efficacy

Bandura also stressed the effect of an individual's perceived abilities on his or her learning. This sense of perceived effectiveness is called **self-efficacy**. It is the individual's perception or assessment of his or her ability to cope satisfactorily with given situations. According to Bandura (1977, p.391), self-efficacy judgements are concerned "not with the skills one has but with judgements of what one can do with the skills one possesses".

An individual's sense of self-efficacy in any given situation depends on four factors:

What other effects might high levels of emotional arousal have, for example, in a competitive sports situation?

1. That individual's previous experiences of success and/or failure in that situation.
2. Relevant vicarious experiences, based on observing someone else cope successfully or unsuccessfully with the situation; this is observational learning.
3. Verbal (or social) persuasion: your feelings of self-efficacy may increase if someone argues persuasively that you have the skills needed to succeed in that situation.
4. Emotional arousal: high levels of arousal are often associated with anxiety and failure, and can serve to reduce feelings of self-efficacy.

Research evidence

There is much evidence from studies of children to show the importance of observational learning. Children who see someone else (the model) behave aggressively and being rewarded for this showed observational learning, in that they then behave aggressively themselves (Rosekrans & Hartup, 1967). Those children who

A child who has previously been successful in a situation is more likely to expect to succeed again, whereas one who has previously done poorly may be reluctant to put in much effort or show much interest.

see the aggressive model punished do not behave aggressively because of the potential threat of punishment.

In a general sense, Bandura's approach leads to the prediction that children should develop more "selves" as they develop friendships with more people. Relevant evidence was reported by Harter and Monsour (1992). They asked children of 12, 14, and 16 to describe themselves with their parents, with their friends, and at school. Among the 12-year-olds, about one-third of the attributes they used to describe themselves in their relationship with their parents were also used to describe themselves with friends and at school. In contrast, 16-year-olds tended to describe themselves very differently in the three situations, suggesting that they had developed a number of selves. These findings are consistent with the claim of William James (1890, p.294) that people have many selves: "he [an individual] has as many different selves as there are distinct groups of persons about whose opinion he cares".

The importance of self-efficacy was shown by Bandura and Cervone (1983). Their participants performed a task, and then indicated how satisfied or dissatisfied they would be with the same level of performance during a subsequent session. Those high in self-efficacy exerted much more effort than those low in self-efficacy in the second session, and this was especially the case among participants who were dissatisfied with their initial level of performance.

Evaluation

The most important difference between Bandura's social learning theory and other theories is the notion that people possess more and more different "selves" as they experience an increasing number of situations and activities. This does not seem consistent with the fairly simple views of the self held by most children and adults. This discrepancy may well be due to the limitations of conscious awareness, as was claimed by Baars (1997). He referred to "the extraordinary oversimplification that seems to characterise our self-concept". There is no strong evidence, but Bandura (1986) may well be right that our sense of a single, integrated self is an illusion.

The greatest limitation of the social learning theory approach is that it is not specifically a *developmental* theory. In other words, Bandura does not spell out in detail how children's personality changes in the course of development. The *amount* of information about the self undoubtedly increases during childhood, as Bandura suggests. However, theorists other than Bandura (e.g., Erikson) argue convincingly that the *kinds* of information children possess about the self also change during development, and this is an important omission from social learning theory.

Situationalism

Bandura suggested that personality is not a stable trait of an individual. Mischel and Peake's theory (1982) takes this even further. They referred to the "consistency paradox", the intuitive belief that people are consistent across situations; a belief that stems from our tendency to categorise everything. However, research has failed to show this consistency. Mischel and Peake (1982) confirmed this inconsistency in a study where different individuals were asked to rate the behaviour of 63 students in various situations. The observers were asked to focus on their conscientiousness, and included family and friends of the students plus unknown observers. Mischel and Peake found almost zero correlation in behaviour ratings (i.e., personality) between the different situations.

Mischel (1968) argued instead that individuals exhibit *behavioural specificity*, that is their behaviour is specific to certain situations. In fact their behaviour is determined by the situation because it is reinforced for that situation. An individual will behave aggressively in one situation and meekly in another depending on the reinforcements received. This is *selective reinforcement*.

Mischel (1968) pointed out that the reason we may think that personality is consistent is because we tend to see people in similar situations and therefore they appear to be consistent. People offer excuses for why they are sometimes inconsistent,

If you have studied multiple personality disorder (in Section 16, page 603), then you might consider how this notion of different selves relates to the pathological condition.

Mischel suggested that our different selves are related to different situations. Bandura also suggested that each individual has different selves, but suggested an alternative source. What is it?

such as saying "I'm usually very punctual but when it's raining it throws me off". One advantage of Mischel's theory, therefore, is that he can explain personality inconsistency.

Person variables

Mischel (1993) suggests that there are important individual differences in the way we think and therefore learn, and this inevitably leads to differences in personality development. For example, if you put two people in the same situation they actually behave differently. It is not simply the situation that affects behaviour but the individual's prior learning experience. Mischel calls these differences **person variables**, the product of the individual's total history that in turn mediates the manner in which new experiences affect him/her.

1. *Cognitive and behavioural construction competencies.* What can you do? This refers to an individual's ability to construct particular cognitions and behaviour. These competencies are related to an individual's past experiences. For example, if one individual has learned that shouting is an effective way to resolve an argument while another individual has successfully resolved conflict through quiet reasoning, each individual is likely to behave differently when in a conflict situation.
2. *Encoding strategies and personal constructs.* How do you see it? The selective attention, interpretation, and categorisation of events substantially alters the impact of any stimulus on behaviour. This helps to explain why two people having the same experience see it differently. For example, some parents feel that violence in cartoons is unacceptable. Such a parent might switch off a programme with such content whereas another parent, who interprets punching and shouting as relatively inoffensive behaviour, would not object to the television programme.
3. *Expectancies.* What will happen? Specific expectancies about the consequences of different behaviours in a specific situation are developed on the basis of direct experience, instructions, and observational learning. For example, a child who has had lots of fun in swimming lessons will have a positive view of swimming as a leisure activity whereas a child who perhaps didn't get on very well in swimming lessons because his teacher shouted a lot is likely to see swimming as a less pleasurable activity.
4. *Subjective stimulus values.* What is it worth? What are your goals? Individuals decide whether or not to perform a specific behaviour based on the given value of the outcome. This value system develops on the basis of direct experience, instructions, and observational learning. For example, a person who values peace and solitude will be more attracted by someone who likes walks in the country than someone who likes shopping.
5. *Self-regulatory systems and plans.* How can you achieve it? A person regulates his/her own behaviour by self-imposed goals or standards and self-produced consequences. For example, a girl working in a shop who hopes to become a manageress might report that other employees are pilfering, whereas another shop girl who hates the store and intends to quit soon might keep quiet.

Evaluation

This view of personality gains support from studies of context-dependent learning as examined in your AS level studies (e.g., Abernethy, 1940). There is no doubt that people do learn things in relation to contexts. However, people also generalise learning from one situation to another, which suggests that not all aspects of our personality are situation-specific. If this were the case we would have a sense of fragmentation whereas most individuals feel a unity about themselves. This is in contrast to multiple personality disorder (see Section 16, Issues in Classification and Diagnosis of Psychological Abnormality), a mental disorder where individuals do experience fragmentation. It appears that a sense of unified self is important to mental health.

Gender Development

What is Gender?

When a baby is born, the key question everyone asks is, "Is it a boy or a girl?" As the baby develops, the ways in which it is treated by its parents and other people are influenced by its sex. In the fullness of time, the growing child's thoughts about itself and its place in the world are likely to depend in part on whether it is male or female. Here we are concerned with some of these issues.

Observed Gender Differences

Fixed gender stereotypes are in decline. Few people accept any more that men should go out to work and have little to do with looking after the home and the children, whereas women should stay at home and concern themselves only with the cleaning and children. However, many stereotypes still exist. It is important to consider the actual behaviour of boys and girls. Do the sexes really differ in their behaviour?

One of the most comprehensive studies of sex differences (and quite an old one) was conducted by Eleanor Maccoby and Carol Jacklin (1974). They reviewed over 1500 studies of sex differences and concluded that there were only four significant differences between boys and girls for which there was convincing evidence:

- Girls have greater verbal ability than boys; this difference has been found at most ages during childhood.
- Boys have greater visual and spatial abilities than girls.
- Boys have greater arithmetical ability than girls, but this difference only appears during adolescence.
- Boys are more aggressive than girls physically and verbally.

As Shaffer (1998) pointed out, later research has indicated that there are some other gender differences in behaviour. Girls show more emotional sensitivity than boys. For example, girls from the age of about 5 are more interested than boys in babies, and respond more attentively to them. Girls have less developmental vulnerability than boys, with more boys showing mental retardation, language disorders, and hyperactivity.

Most observed gender differences in behaviour are fairly modest. However, there is increasing evidence in Britain that girls are outperforming boys in nearly all subjects. In 2000 girls outperformed boys at A level for the first time in the 49-year history of the exam. Girls also outperformed boys in every national curriculum subject at GCSE. Across all subjects, 61.1% of the GCSEs taken by girls were graded A* to C compared with 51.9% of the GCSEs taken by boys. Girls traditionally do better than boys in English and in other language skills, while boys still gravitate to science subjects such as maths and physics. Among the top 10 GCSE subjects, the girls' smallest lead was in maths, where they outperformed

KEY TERMS

Sex: the biological fact of being male or female as determined by a pair of chromosomes—females have a pair described as XX while males have a pair described as XY.

Gender: the psychological characteristics associated with being male or female, i.e., masculinity and femininity.

Sexual identity: this is determined by the biological factors that have made us male or female; it can usually be assessed from the genitals.

Gender identity: this is a child's or an adult's awareness of being male or female; it is socially rather than biologically determined, and emerges during the early years of childhood.

Gender (or sex) **role**: a set of expectations that prescribe how males and females should think, act, and feel.

Gender stereotypes: beliefs about the differences between males and females, based on gender roles.

■ Activity: Gender stereotypes

Make a list of stereotypes that are often used to describe males and females. Now categorise these in terms of gender or biology. Are there any that could be supported by evidence, and what evidence could be considered valid?

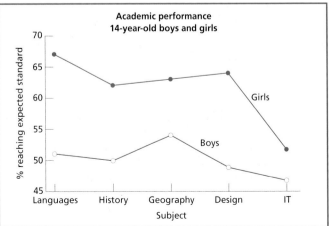

Boys playing with guns—is this nature or nurture?

the boys by 49.7% to 48.8%. Their biggest lead was in art—a gap of 20 percentage points—followed by design and technology, English, and French, a gap in each case of more than 15 points.

In general, there are fewer and smaller differences between the genders than is generally assumed. Why is there this gap between appearance and reality? We tend to misinterpret the evidence of our senses to fit our stereotypes. Condry and Condry (1976) asked college students to watch a videotape of an infant. The ways in which the infant's behaviour was interpreted depended on whether it was referred to as David or Dana. The infant was said to be "angry" in its reaction to a jack-in-the-box if it had been called David, but "anxious" if it had been called Dana.

Psychological Theories of Gender Development

In the following accounts our interest is, in particular, on the development of gender identity (your own sense of your gender) and on gender roles (what you learn about appropriate behaviour for males and females).

Psychoanalytic theory

What does psychoanalytic theory tell us about the development of gender identity?

Part of Freud's psychoanalytic theory was designed to account for gender development (see pages 419–420 for a fuller account). Most theories of gender development are based on the assumption that environmental and cultural influences are of crucial importance. In contrast, Freud de-emphasised such influences, arguing that "anatomy is destiny".

As we saw earlier, Freud argued that boys develop an Oedipus complex, in which they have sexual desires for their mother combined with intense fear of their father. Part of this fear arises because boys think that their fathers may castrate them. The Oedipus complex is resolved by a process of identification with the father. Girls resolve a different crises at the same age ("penis-envy" or the Electra complex) and come to identify, somewhat less strongly with their mother. According to Freud, identification plays a major role in the development of gender stereotypes.

Chodorow (1978) developed an alternative psychoanalytic theory, according to which most young children develop a close relationship with their mother. This relationship then sets the pattern for future relationships. Girls can develop a sense of gender identity based on their close relationship with another female (their mother). By so doing, they associate femininity with feelings of closeness. In contrast, boys have to move away from their close relationship with their mother in order to develop gender identity, and this can make them regard masculinity and closeness as not being associated.

Research evidence

There is some evidence that the father plays a major role in the development of gender stereotypes in boys. Boys whose fathers are missing during the time at which the Oedipus complex develops (around the age of 5) showed fewer gender stereotypes than boys whose fathers were present throughout (Stevenson & Black, 1988). There is also evidence (discussed later) that there are major changes in gender development at around the age of 5.

Fathers may play a major role in the development of sex-typed behaviour in their sons.

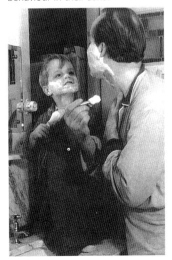

Evaluation

Freud's psychoanalytic theory of the development of gender identity is incorrect in nearly all other respects. His account tells us more about his powers of imagination than about what actually happens. There is no real evidence that boys fear castration or that girls regret not having a penis. Freud argued that the identification process depends on fear, so it might be expected that a boy's identification with his father would be greatest if his father was a threatening figure. In fact, however, boys tend to identify much more with a warm and supportive father than with an overbearing and threatening one (Mussen & Rutherford, 1963).

The psychoanalytic theory of gender development should be regarded largely as a historical curiosity rather than a useful theoretical contribution. However, it was the first systematic attempt to identify a series of developmental stages within which gender development can be understood. Freud focused on the influence of the same-sex parent in influencing gender development in children. By so doing, he ignored the impact of the opposite-sex parent, other members of the family, and other children.

Freud's general approach was limited in various ways, as can be seen if we relate it to other theoretical approaches. The emphasis in Kohlberg's cognitive-developmental theory (see also below) and in gender-schema theory (discussed later) is more on the cognitive factors involved in gender development. The emphasis in social learning theory (also discussed later) is more on the behavioural aspects of gender development.

How might Freud have used his focus on the influence of the same-sex parent to explain homosexuality?

Cognitive-developmental theory: Kohlberg

Lawrence Kohlberg (1966) put forward a cognitive-developmental theory of gender role development. The essence of his approach can be seen by contrasting it with social learning theory, which is discussed later on. According to Kohlberg (1966, p.85), "the child's sex-role concepts are the result of the child's active structuring of his own experience; they are not passive products of social training".

What is meant by a "cognitive-developmental theory", as distinct from a cognitive theory?

There are other important differences between social learning theory and Kohlberg's theory. According to social learning theory, children develop a gender identity as a result of attending to same-sex models. According to Kohlberg, the causality goes in the other direction: children attend to same-sex models because they have already developed a consistent gender identity. It follows from this theory that children find it rewarding to behave in line with their consistent gender identity. In the words of Kohlberg (1966, p.89), "I am a boy; therefore I want to do boy things; therefore the opportunity to do boy things … is rewarding."

The notion of gender identity is of great importance within Kohlberg's cognitive-developmental theory. Children go through three stages in the development of gender identity:

1. *Basic gender identity* (age 2 to 3½ years): boys know they are boys, and girls know they are girls. However, they believe it would be possible to change sex.
2. *Gender stability* (3½ to 4½ years): there is an awareness that sex is stable over time (e.g., boys will become men), but less awareness that sex remains stable across different situations, such as wearing clothes normally worn by members of the opposite sex. When a doll was dressed in transparent clothes so there was a discrepancy between its clothing and its genitals, children in this stage decided on its sex on the basis of clothing (McConaghy, 1979).
3. *Gender consistency* (4½ to 7 years upwards): children at this stage realise that sex remains the same over time and over situations. This is like Piaget's notion of conservation (see Section 10, Cognitive Development).

Research evidence

There is evidence that children do, indeed, progress through the three stages proposed by Kohlberg. In a cross-cultural study, Munroe, Shimmin, and Munroe (1984) found that

KOHLBERG'S STAGES IN THE DEVELOPMENT OF GENDER IDENTITY		
Basic gender identity	**Gender stability**	**Gender consistency**
2–3½ years	3½–4½ years	4½–7 upwards
Aware of sex, but believes it can change	Aware that sex is stable over time, but not over situations	Realises sex remains the same, regardless of time or situation

Do behaviours that are considered "boy things" and "girl things" remain constant over time? Are there illustrative examples from your childhood that are different from your parents' childhood?

Research with preschoolers has helped to determine the development of gender identity.

children in several cultures had the same sequences of stages on the way to full gender identity.

One of the predictions of Kohlberg's theory is that children who have reached the stage of gender consistency will pay more attention to the behaviour of same-sex models than children at earlier stages of gender development. Slaby and Frey (1975) tested this prediction. Children between the ages of 2 and 5 were assessed for gender consistency, assigned to a high or a low gender consistency group, and shown a film of a male and a female performing various activities. Those who were high in gender consistency showed a greater tendency to attend to the same-sex model than those low in gender consistency.

More evidence of the importance of gender consistency was reported by Ruble, Balaban, and Cooper (1981). Preschoolers high and low in gender consistency watched television commercials in which toys were represented as being suitable for boys or for girls. These advertisements had more effect on the attitudes and behaviour of boys and girls high in gender consistency. This offers a more complex perspective on the role of the media in gender behaviours than social learning theory because it suggests that it is not simply a case of exposure to stereotypes in the media but what children bring with them to their media use.

Evaluation

Gender identity does seem to develop through the three stages proposed by Kohlberg. As predicted by the theory, the achievement of full gender identity increases gender role behaviour. In more general terms, the notion that gender development involves children actively interacting with the world around them is valuable, as is the notion that how they interact with the world depends on the extent to which they have developed a consistent gender identity.

There are various problems with Kohlberg's theory. First, gender role behaviour is shown by most boys and girls by the time of their second birthday. This is several years before they have reached gender consistency, and so it cannot be argued that *all* gender role behaviour depends on gender consistency.

Second, Kohlberg (1966, p.98) argued that, "the process of forming a constant [gender] identity is … a part of the general process of conceptual growth". This approach tends to ignore the external factors (e.g., reward and punishment from parents) that determine much early gender role behaviour. More generally, Kohlberg's focus was too much on the individual child, and not enough on the social context that largely determines gender development.

Third, Kohlberg probably exaggerated the importance of cognitive factors in producing gender role behaviour. Huston (1985) pointed out that Kohlberg's theory leads to the prediction that there should be a close relationship between cognitions about gender and gender-typed attitudes and behaviour. In fact, the relationship is not very strong, and is weaker in girls than in boys. It is not clear how these findings can be explained by Kohlberg's theory.

Cognitive-developmental theory: Gender-schema theory

Martin and Halverson (1987) put forward a rather different cognitive-developmental theory known as gender-schema theory. They argued that children as young as 2 or 3 years who have acquired basic gender identity start to form **gender schemas**, which consist of organised sets of beliefs about the sexes. The first schema that is formed is an ingroup/outgroup schema, consisting of organised information about which toys and activities are suitable for boys and which are suitable for girls. Another early schema is an own-gender schema containing information about how to behave in gender-stereotyped ways (e.g., how to dress dolls for a girl). Some of the processes involved in the initial development of gender schemas may include those emphasised by social learning theorists.

A key aspect of gender-schema theory is the notion that children do not simply respond passively to the world. What happens instead is that the gender schemas possessed by children help to determine what they attend to, how they interpret the world, and what they remember of their experiences. In other words, as Shaffer (1993, p.513) argued, "Gender schemas 'structure' experience by providing an organisation for processing social information."

In what other contexts have you come across "schema"? How would you define it?

Research evidence

According to the theory, gender schemas are used by children to organise and make sense of their experiences. If they are exposed to information that does not fit one of their schemas (e.g., a boy combing the hair of his doll), then the information should be distorted to make it fit the schema. Martin and Halverson (1983) tested this prediction. They showed 5- and 6-year-old children pictures of schema-consistent activities (e.g., a girl playing with a doll) and schema-inconsistent activities (e.g., a girl playing with a toy gun). Schema-inconsistent activities were often misremembered 1 week later as schema-consistent (e.g., it had been a boy playing with a toy gun).

Another study that supports gender-schema theory was reported by Bradbard et al. (1986). Boys and girls between the ages of 4 and 9 were presented with gender-neutral objects such as burglar alarms and pizza cutters. They were told that some of the objects were "boy" objects, whereas others were described as "girl" objects. There were two key findings. First, children spent much more time playing with objects that they had been told

Schema-consistent activities

Schema-inconsistent activities

were appropriate to their gender. Second, even a week later the children remembered whether any given object was a "boy" or a "girl" object.

A study by Masters et al. (1979) also supports gender-schema theory. Young children of 4 and 5 were influenced in their choice of toy more by the gender label attached to the toy (e.g., "It's a girl's toy") than by the gender of the model seen playing with the toy. As Durkin (1995) pointed out, children's behaviour seems to be influenced more by the schema, "This is a boy's toy" or "This is a girl's toy" than by a desire to imitate a same-sex model.

Evaluation

One of the main strengths of gender-schema theory is that it helps to explain why children's gender-role beliefs and attitudes often change rather little after middle childhood. The gender schemas that have been established tend to be maintained because schema-consistent information is attended to and remembered. Another strength of the theory is its focus on the child as being actively involved in making sense of the world in the light of its present knowledge.

The limitations of gender-schema theory resemble those of Kohlberg's theory. The theory emphasises too much the role of the individual child in gender development, and de-emphasises the importance of social factors. In addition, it is likely that the importance of schemas and other cognitive factors in determining behaviour is exaggerated within the theory. Another problem is that the theory does not really explain *why* gender schemas develop and take the form they do.

Finally, it is assumed within the theory that it should be possible to change children's behaviour by changing their schemas or stereotypes. In fact, as Durkin (1995, p.185) pointed out, "greater success has been reported in attempts to change concepts than attempts to change behaviour or behavioural intentions". In a similar way, many married couples have *schemas* relating to equality of the sexes and equal division of household chores, but this rarely has much effect on their *behaviour*.

Social learning theory

According to social learning theory (e.g., Bandura, 1977, 1986), the development of gender occurs as a result of the child's social experiences. Generally, children learn to behave in ways that are rewarded by others and to avoid behaving in ways that are punished by others. This is known as direct tuition. As society has expectations about the ways in which boys and girls should behave, the operation of socially delivered rewards and punishments will tend to produce gender stereotypes and gender-appropriate behaviours.

Bandura also argued that children can learn gender stereotypes by observing the actions of various models of the same gender, including other children, parents, and teachers. This is known as observational learning, and was discussed earlier in the Section. It has often been argued that much observational learning of gender stereotypes in children depends on the media, and especially television.

Social learning theory contrasts with cognitive-developmental theory in arguing that rewarding behaviour is behaviour that *others* regard as appropriate. Cognitive-developmental theorists suggest that rewards are gained from doing things that fit one's own concept of gender identity, i.e., gender-appropriate behaviour is self-rewarding.

Research evidence

Gender stereotypes are learned in part through direct tuition. Fagot and Leinbach (1989) carried out a long-term study on children. Parents encouraged gender-appropriate behaviour and discouraged gender-inappropriate behaviour in their children even before the age of 2. For example, girls were rewarded for playing with dolls, and discouraged from climbing trees. Those parents who made the most use of direct tuition tended to have children who behaved in the most gender-stereotyped way. However, these findings are not altogether typical. Lytton and Romney (1991) reviewed numerous studies on the parental treatment of boys and girls. There was a modest tendency for parents to

Think about your own family. Are there specific domestic chores that are done by particular members of the family? Can they be categorised by gender?

Parents may try to discourage what they see as sex-inappropriate behaviour in a variety of ways. Climbing trees while wearing a skirt is more difficult than in trousers or shorts.

encourage gender-stereotyped activities, but boys and girls received equal parental warmth, encouragement of achievement, discipline, and amount of interaction.

Direct tuition is also used by other children. Fagot (1985) studied the behaviour of children aged between 21 and 25 months. Boys made fun of other boys who played with dolls or with a girl, and girls did not like it when one of them started playing with a boy. There are similar pressures from their peers among older children in the years before adolescence. Those who fail to behave in a gender-stereotyped way are the least popular (Sroufe et al., 1993).

Observational learning was studied by Perry and Bussey (1979). Children aged 8 or 9 watched male and female adult models choose between gender-neutral activities (e.g., selecting an apple or a pear). Afterwards, they tended to make the same choices as the same-sex models. These findings suggest that observational learning plays an important role in gender development. However, Barkley et al. (1977) reviewed the literature, and found that children showed a bias in favour of the same-sex model in only 18 out of 81 studies.

Children between the ages of 4 and 11 watch about 3 hours of television a day, which adds up to 1000 hours a year. It would be surprising if this exposure had no impact on children's views of themselves and on gender stereotypes via observational learning. Most of the research indicates there is a modest link between television watching and gender stereotypes. Frueh and McGhee (1975) studied the television viewing habits of children aged between 4 and 12. Those children who watched the most television tended to show more gender-stereotyped behaviour in terms of preferring gender-stereotyped toys. However, this is only correlational evidence, and so we do not know that watching television led to gender-stereotyped behaviour.

Williams (1986) examined gender-role stereotypes in three towns in Canada nicknamed: "Notel" (no television channels); "Unitel" (one channel); and "Multitel" (four channels). Gender-role stereotyping was much greater in the towns with television than in the one without. During the course of the study, Notel gained access to one television channel. This led to increased gender-role stereotyping among children.

Some of the strongest evidence that television can influence gender development was reported by Johnston and

> ■ Activity: Content analysis
>
> In small groups, choose one or two children's television programmes that are currently being shown. Analyse the content of the programmes for sex-role stereotyping and sex-typed behaviour using observational techniques. Your results can then be pooled for general analysis.
>
> If possible, carry out the same study on children's television programmes from the past, many of which are now available on videotape. What differences, if any, do you find between the two?

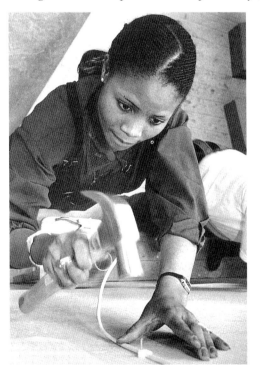

Television programmes that showed men and women taking part in non-traditional sex-typed activities have been found to produce some attitude changes among viewers, but the effects on behaviour were small.

Do you think the Canadian study by Williams (1986) would be able to demonstrate a causal relationship between television and gender-role stereotyping? What other factors in children's lives might have played a part?

Ettema (1982). In the *Freestyle* project, there were a series of television programmes in which non-traditional opportunities and activities were modelled. These programmes produced significant attitude changes away from gender-role stereotypes, and these changes were still present 9 months later. However, the effects on behaviour were rather small.

Evaluation

One of the strengths of the social learning approach is that it takes full account of the social context in which the development of gender occurs. As social learning theorists have claimed, some gender-stereotyped behaviour occurs because it has been rewarded, and gender-inappropriate behaviour is avoided because it has been discouraged or punished. There is also evidence that observational learning is important, but perhaps more with older than with young children.

There are several limitations of social learning theory. First, as Durkin (1995, p.179) pointed out:

> *Research into the effects of the principal mechanisms emphasised by the theory (parental reinforcement, modelling) has not led consistently to the conclusion that they have a major influence.*

Second, some aspects of social learning theory suggest that gender is *passively* acquired through reward and punishment. In reality, children make an active contribution to their own development and this factor is recognised in later versions of social learning theory, such as Bandura's (1986) social cognitive theory, in which the emphasis is on the self and the role it plays in influencing behaviour (see page 425 for a description of reciprocal determinism).

Third, social learning theorists mistakenly assume that learning processes are very similar at any age. For example, consider young children and adolescents watching a film in which a man and a woman are eating a meal together. The observational learning of the young children might focus on the eating behaviour of the same-sex person, whereas the adolescents might focus on his or her social behaviour. Approaches such as Kohlberg's cognitive-developmental theory and gender-schema theory are better equipped to explain developmental changes in learning and cognition.

Fourth, social learning theory focuses on the learning of *specific* ways of behaving. This ignores the fact that there is also a considerable amount of *general* learning. For example, children seem to acquire gender schemas (organised beliefs about the sexes; Martin & Halverson, 1987), and it is hard to explain how this happens in terms of social learning theory.

Biological Theories of Gender Development

Biological theories differ, and contrast with, psychological theories because they are largely focused on the influence of our biological sex on gender behaviour.

Biosocial theory

There are various obvious biological differences between boys and girls. These biological differences produce hormonal differences between the sexes at a very early stage of development. For example, the male sex hormone testosterone is present in greater amounts in male than female foetuses from about the age of 6 weeks, whereas the opposite is the case for the female sex hormone oestrogen (see Durkin, 1995). It has been argued that basic biological and hormonal factors are important in gender identity, and in the development of greater aggressiveness in boys than in girls. However, as Willerman (1979) pointed out:

> *One should not expect too much of the genetic differences between males and females. The two sexes have forty-five/forty-six of their chromosomes in common, and the one that differs (the Y) contains the smallest proportion of genetic material.*

The "Y" chromosome is denoted in this way because it is missing some of the information that is on the "X" chromosome, which is why males are more susceptible to recessive disorders—they only need one gene on that pair because there is no partner on the Y chromosome.

The ideal way of testing biological theories of gender development would be to study individuals in which there is a clear distinction between sexual identity (based on biological factors) and the way in which they are treated socially. Thus, for example, if an individual was born a boy but was treated as a girl, would biological or social factors be more important in their gender development? The ideal study has not been carried out, but approximations to it are discussed next.

Research evidence

Suggestive evidence in support of the biological approach to gender development has been obtained in animal studies. For example, Young, Goy, and Phoenix (1964) gave doses of testosterone to pregnant monkeys. This male sex hormone produced greater aggressiveness and higher frequency of rough-and-tumble play in the mothers' female offspring.

However, gender is not necessarily a matter of biological sex. Early research evidence appeared to suggest that individuals would accept their sex of rearing and learn appropriate gender role behaviours in association with the gender assigned at birth. For example, about 500 people in Britain have what is known as testicular feminising syndrome. They are male in the sense that they have male chromosomes and testicles. However, their bodies do not respond to the male sex hormone testosterone. As a result, they develop a female body shape and their breasts develop. Mrs DW has testicular feminising syndrome. She had always thought of herself as a woman but when she found it impossible to become pregnant she consulted a doctor and found that she was biologically male and had no internal female organs. Nevertheless, she felt that she was a woman and elected to stay in that role, adopting two children (Goldwyn, 1979). This, of course, is a case study of one, which makes it hard to draw firm conclusions. It also isn't entirely clear whether we can say that Mrs DW was influenced by social factors (reared as a girl) or biological ones (exposure to male hormones).

In the case of Mrs DW, what factor or factors do you think were responsible for her gender identity?

Other case studies recorded by Money and Ehrhardt (see the Key Study on the next page) at first appeared to support Goldwyn's conclusion. However, the evidence now appears to suggest that biological sex may have a greater influence than was once thought.

Further support for this latter view comes from a study by Imperato-McGinley et al. (1974) of a family in the Dominican Republic. Four of the sons in the family appeared biologically to be female at birth, and were reared as girls. However, at the age of about 12, they developed male genitals and started to look like ordinary adolescent males. In spite of the fact that all four of them had been reared as girls, and had thought of themselves as females, they seemed to adjust well to the male role. According to Gross' account (1996, p.584), "They have all taken on male roles, do men's jobs, have married women and are accepted as men." These findings suggest that biological factors can be more important than social ones in the formation of gender identity.

Evaluation

Most of the evidence we have considered suggests that biological factors play some role in gender development. Of particular interest are those studies in which there is a fairly direct conflict between biological and social factors, as was the case with the four children in the family from the Dominican Republic. It seemed as if biological factors outweighed social factors. However, it needs to be remembered that the relevant evidence has been obtained from very unusual cases, and it is hard to know whether the findings obtained can be generalised to the ordinary population.

It is important to note that biological theories cannot provide more than a partial explanation. Such theories do not explain the impact of social factors on gender development, and they do not account for the substantial changes in gender roles that have occurred in Western societies in recent decades. As Durkin (1995, p.173) pointed out:

What might be some of the ethical problems encountered by researchers conducting studies into the links between sexual identity and biology?

Money and Ehrhardt

Money and Ehrhardt (1972) discussed cases of females who were exposed to male sex hormones prior to birth. The reason for this was as a treatment to prevent miscarriage in mothers who had a previous history of such difficulties. The effect of the hormones on the foetus was not considered.

Even though their parents treated them as girls, they tended to be tomboys. They played and fought with boys, and avoided more traditional female activities. In addition, they preferred to play with blocks and cars rather than with dolls. However, many of these girls were given the hormone cortisone to prevent them from becoming too masculine anatomically. One of the effects of cortisone is to increase activity level, and this may have made their behaviour more like that expected of boys.

A further consideration is that male hormones during prenatal development have the effect of masculinising the brain (Geschwind & Galaburdam, 1985). This is what makes men behave in a male fashion, such as having a more dominant right hemisphere of the brain, and thus would have the same effect on biological females. Therefore, in such cases the individual is, at least in some sense, biologically male.

However, evidence that social factors can override biology was also reported by Money and Ehrhardt. They studied male identical twins, one of whom had had his penis very severely damaged during a circumcision operation. Money advised the parents that the best solution would be to reassign the boy's gender and rear him as a girl, giving him female hormones at puberty. The parents endeavoured to raise the boy as a girl, calling her Brenda and rewarded gender-appropriate behaviour. Money reported that Brenda played with girls' toys such as dolls and a doll's house, whereas his brother asked for a garage. He was neater and more delicate in his behaviour than his identical twin.

A recent book by Colapinto (2000) describes quite a different reality, of a child who was totally confused and more boyish than his/her brother. Eventually, in adolescence, Brenda chose to return to being a man and later married.

Money had used the case to argue that social factors can overrule biology and many feminists embraced this view because it suggested that many gender prejudices and gender differences are social creations. The reality of this one natural experiment suggests that biology may be more important than some people wish to recognise.

Discussion points

1. How much can studies of such unusual cases tell us about ordinary gender development?

2. Do these cases persuade you that biological factors play a part in gender development?

Biological theories stress the demands of parenting and the possible implications of possible differences in abilities, but have little to say about the other distinguishing characteristic that has evolved in this [human] species: its ability to articulate, share, reflect upon, and change its social practices. Biosocial theory, on the other hand, is an attempt to combine elements of both approaches [i.e., biological and social approaches].

Sociobiological theory

Many aspects of gender behaviour have been explained through sociobiological theory and this is discussed at length in Section 15, Evolutionary Explanations of Human Behaviour.

Briefly, the argument is that males and females look and behave differently because such behaviours are adaptive. All animals are driven to behave in ways that maximise reproduction because this ensures the survival of the individual's **genes**. Thus adaptive behaviours remain in the gene pool and other behaviours tend to disappear.

Males produce thousands of sperm at almost no physical cost. Females produce eggs in limited quantities and at a greater physical cost. Therefore females, especially humans, must ensure that each reproduction is as successful as possible. This would lead us to predict that women seek men with good genes and who can provide resources to help look after a growing child. "Good genes" may be in terms of physical strength or intelligence or, in fact, any characteristic that might be passed on to sons in the next generation because this would ensure that these sons are selected by other females, and the original mother's genes are thus further perpetuated. This is called the **sexy sons hypothesis** (see page 565). Alternatively, "good genes" may be in terms of robustness, as proposed by the **handicapping theory**. Women seek men who can provide robust genes for their offspring and this is indicated by the males' ability to sustain characteristics that incur a physiological cost, such as a peacock's elaborate tail.

Females also look for resources, which may be in terms of money, land, or power. Davis (1990) found that when men advertised for a mate they tended to emphasise their wealth or other resources, and women indicated that they were looking for a high-status, wealthy man, and mentioned their own physical attractiveness.

What does this sociobiological view tell us about gender identity and gender roles?

Research evidence

Cross-cultural studies have supplied evidence that there are universal similarities in gender behaviour, which supports sociobiological theory. For instance, Mead's (1935) classic studies of three cultural groups in New Guinea indicated some gender differences but also gender similarities. In the Mundugumor, both men and women adopted the aggressive, instrumental style of behaviour that is supposed to be more characteristic of males. In the Arapesh, both sexes adopted the caring, expressive style commonly associated with females. Most dramatically, the females in the Tchambuli behaved in an assertive and independent fashion, whereas the males were nurturant and dependent.

At first sight this evidence would seem to suggest that there *are* gender differences and this could be explained in term of social rather than biological, inherited factors. However, within each cultural group the males were *more* aggressive than the women. Even in the Tchambuli it was the men who did most of the fighting in time of war. This supports the idea of inherited gender role behaviours.

Other research has supported these findings. See, for example, the study by Buss (1989) on pages 537–538. Also, Williams and Best (1982) explored gender stereotypes in 30 different national cultures. In each country 100 male and female students were asked to look at a list of adjectives and state whether they were associated with men or women, or both, in their culture. Williams and Best found that there were many similarities across the various cultures. Men were seen as more dominant, aggressive, autonomous, and taking a more *instrumental role*, whereas women were more nurturant, deferent and interested in affiliation, being encouraged to develop an *expressive role*. This finding was also supported by Barry, Bacon, and Child (1957) (see the Key Study on the next page).

Cultural change also applies to historical differences. There have been great changes in most Western societies in recent years. In the mid-twentieth century, many fewer women than men went to university. Nowadays the number of female university students exceeds that of male students in several countries. There is a similar pattern in employment. In spite of these changes, many of the old stereotypes have changed very little. Bergen and Williams (1991) found in the United States that stereotypical views of the sexes in 1988 were remarkably similar to those expressed in 1972. This might be taken as an indication that gender roles are biologically driven.

In most Western societies, there are now more female than male university students.

Evaluation

Most cross-cultural studies have indicated that the cultural expectations and stereotypes for boys and girls are surprisingly similar in otherwise very different cultures. However, Williams and Best (1992) found that such consensus was strongest in **collectivist** societies and weaker in **individualist** societies where gender equality is more influential. This again suggests a cultural difference—the effect of different socialisation practices.

Barry, Bacon, and Child

Socialisation pressures in 110 non-industrialised countries were explored by Barry, Bacon, and Child (1957). They considered five characteristics:

- Nurturance (being supportive).
- Responsibility.
- Obedience.
- Achievement.
- Self-reliance.

There was more pressure on girls than on boys to be nurturant in 75% of the non-industrialised societies, with none showing the opposite pattern. Responsibility was regarded as more important in girls than in boys in 55% of the societies, with 10% showing the opposite. Obedience was stressed for girls more than for boys in 32% of societies, with 3% showing the opposite. There was more pressure on boys than on girls to acquire the other two characteristics. Achievement was emphasised more for boys in 79% of societies (3% showed the opposite), and self-reliance was regarded as more important in boys in 77% of societies, with no societies regarding it as more important in girls.

These findings indicate that the gender-role stereotypes of females being expressive and males being instrumental are very widespread. Related findings were obtained by Williams and Best (1990). Similar gender stereotypes to those found in the United States were present in 24 other countries in Asia, Europe, Oceania, Africa, and the Americas.

Discussion points

1. Are you surprised at the cross-cultural similarities in expectations of males and females?

2. Why do you think there are such consistent gender-specific expectations?

Gender identity and gender roles		
	Gender identity	Gender roles
Psychodynamic theory	Learned through identification with same-sex parent during the phallic stage (aged 3–6 years)	Learned after identification
Cognitive-developmental theory	Consistent gender identity appears around age 4	Gender identity leads child to acquire gender stereotypes
Gender-schema theory	Basic gender identity appears around 2½ and child begins to develop gender schemas	Gender schemas organise knowledge about gender stereotypes and role
Social learning	Learned by attending to same-sex models	Learned through vicarious reinforcement and modelling
Biosocial	Determined largely by biological sex	A combination of biological and social influences
Sociobiological	Biological	Adaptive and biological

Adolescence

Is it possible that adolescence is less stressful today than it was 30 years ago?

It is often assumed that adolescence is a very "difficult" period of life, with adolescents being highly stressed and moody. It is further assumed that adolescents are stressed because they have to cope with enormous changes in their lives. Some of these changes are in sexual behaviour following puberty. There are also large social changes, with adolescents spending much more time with others of the same age and much less time with their parents than they did when they were younger. Adolescence is also a time at which decisions need to be made about the future. Adolescents need to decide which examinations to take, whether or not to apply to university, what to study at university, and so on.

Adolescence is certainly a period of change, and adolescents do have various pressures on them. However, as we will see, it is *not* true that all adolescents become stressed at this time, and some research suggests that adolescents are at no greater risk of being in crisis than adults of all ages. However, rates of mental disorder do peak in adolescence, and moods become more extreme and unstable (Rutter et al., 1976; see the Key Study below).

When does adolescence begin and end? It is convenient to assume that it covers the teenage years from 13 to 19. However, some girls enter puberty at the age of 10 or 11, and so become adolescent before they become teenagers. There are also numerous 20- and 21-year-olds who continue to exhibit many of the signs of adolescence. Adolescence cannot only be defined in terms of age, because some people enter and leave adolescence years earlier than others. In spite of these considerations, we will assume that the stage of development known as adolescence largely centres on the teenage years.

Theories of Social Development in Adolescence: The Psychoanalytic Approach

At the beginning of this Section we considered psychoanalytic theories of personality. Such theories, all derived from Freud's approach, are characterised by the view that the child goes through innate stages during development and each stage is associated with a focus on some aspect of development. Life experiences interact with innate urges to produce adult personality. Freud proposed that, during adolescence, the focus is on adult sexuality (the genital stage) and on independence. These ideas were further developed in Erikson's more psychosocial theory.

The Isle of Wight Study

Rutter et al. (1976) conducted a very large-scale study of adolescents living on the Isle of Wight. The aim of the investigation was to find out more about adolescent turmoil and to further explore Bowlby's hypothesis that early separation was associated with later maladjustment and delinquency. Rutter et al. interviewed 2300 9- to 12-year-olds and their families. The sample was divided into good, fair, and poor families. A good family was defined as one with warm, loving, and secure relationships.

In terms of psychiatric disturbance, Rutter et al. found a small peak in adolescence. Even though there was more psychiatric illness in adolescence than childhood, such disturbance was rare but a reasonable number reported feelings of inner turmoil. Where there were psychiatric problems these had mostly been ongoing since childhood, but in cases where problems did first appear in adolescence there were often family problems which may have acted as a stressor.

In terms of early separation, the study found that, in good and fair homes, separation did not lead to delinquency. When early separation had been due to illness, it was not related to delinquency, but when separations were due to stress in the home the children were four times more likely to become delinquent. This led Rutter et al. to conclude that it is not separation *per se* that causes delinquency, but the stress which often surrounds separation.

Discussion points

1. What conclusions can be reached about the factors that may cause disturbance in adolescence?

2. Data about early childhood was collected retrospectively. How may this have affected the reliability of the data?

Erikson's theory

Erik Erikson (1902–1994), like Freud, used the idea of crises during stages of an individual's life that needed to be resolved before moving on to the next stage. If these crises were not resolved development could not proceed normally. There are two key differences between Erikson and Freud. First, Erikson's crises were not psychosexual but were psychosocial, resolving social rather than physical conflicts. Second, Erikson mapped eight different stages (and crises) across the entire lifespan in contrast with Freud's stages that stop after adolescence. These stages are outlined on pages 422–423 and 459–460. In adolescence the crisis is one of identity.

Erikson's ideas about adolescence stemmed from his observations of emotionally disturbed adolescents during therapy. His views have been influential, and have helped to create the general impression that most adolescents are stressed and uncertain about themselves and about the future. Erikson (1950, 1968, 1969) also argued that adolescents typically experience **identity diffusion**, which involves a strong sense of uncertainty. They need to achieve a sense of identity, which can be defined as "a feeling of being at home in one's body, a sense of 'knowing where one is going', and an inner assuredness of anticipated recognition from those who count" (Erikson, 1950, p.165). Adolescents find it hard to do this, because they are undergoing rapid biological and social changes, and they need to take major decisions in almost all areas of life (e.g., future career). In other words, adolescents typically face an **identity crisis**, because they do not know who they are, or where they are going. Erikson (1950, p.139) argued that the typical adolescent thinks about himself or herself in the following way: "I ain't what I ought to be, I ain't what I'm gonna be, but I ain't what I was."

What do psychologists mean by identity? What is an "identity crisis"? Is an identity crisis healthy or maladaptive?

Erikson (1969, p.22) spelled out in more detail what is involved in this identity crisis:

Adolescence is not an affliction but a normative crisis, i.e., a normal phase of increased conflict … What under prejudiced scrutiny may appear to be the onset of a neurosis is often but an aggravated crisis which might prove to be self-liquidating and, in fact, contributive to the process of identity formation.

■ Activity: Erikson's theory

Consider Erikson's theory in the context of other variables in an adolescent's life:

1. Ingroups: what major stresses, influences, and decisions are part of an adolescent's life?
2. Do you think that most adolescents accomplish identity formation adequately? If not, why not?
3. Erikson's theory is a stage theory. Can one scheme fit all individuals?

A scornful and snobbish hostility towards the role offered in one's family.

Thus, Erikson seemed to think that it was almost essential for adolescents to go through an identity crisis in order to resolve the identity issue and move on to the formation of a stable adult identity.

According to Erikson (1968) adolescents experienced uncertainty about their identity—called identity diffusion. This uncertainty has four major components:

1. *Intimacy*: adolescents fear commitment to others because it may involve a loss of identity.
2. *Diffusion of time*: this "consists of a decided disbelief in the possibility that time may bring change and yet also of a violent fear that it might" (Erikson, 1968, p.169).
3. *Diffusion of industry*: this involves either an inability to concentrate or enormous efforts directed towards a single activity.
4. *Negative identity*: this involves "a scornful and snobbish hostility towards the role offered as proper and desirable in one's family or immediate community" (Erikson, 1968, p.173).

Erikson (1969) assumed that there are some important differences between males and females in identity development: females develop a sense of identity later than males, allegedly because they realise that their identity and social status will depend very much on the type of man they choose to marry. It is unlikely that a theorist would make such assumptions in the greatly changed society in which we now live.

One final point needs to be made about Erikson's theoretical approach. Adolescence typically lasts for several years, and an identity crisis could possibly develop at any point within the teenage years. According to Erikson (1968), however, an identity crisis is more likely to occur in late adolescence than at any earlier time.

Research evidence

Some of the evidence is consistent with the notion that adolescents experience high levels of stress. Smith and Crawford (1986) found that more than 60% of students in secondary school reported at least one instance of suicidal thinking, and 10% had attempted suicide. In fact, suicide is the third-highest cause of death among Americans aged between 15 and 24. However, there are fewer suicides among young adults than among middle-aged adults.

Adolescents in different cultures have quite different educational experiences, and life experiences generally. How might these experiences affect adolescent development?

One of the implications of Erikson's theory is that adolescents should have low self-esteem because of the uncertainties they face. However, the evidence does not support this. If there are changes in self-image during adolescence, those changes are more likely to be positive than negative (Marsh, 1989). Of course, some adolescents do show reduced self-esteem, but this is only common among those who experience several life changes (e.g., change of school; divorcing parents) in a fairly short period of time (Simmons et al., 1987).

Why should a number of critical life changes reduce an adolescent's self-esteem?

There is also some evidence that adolescents are not always highly emotional. For example, Larson and Lampman-Petraitis (1989) assessed the emotional states of American children between the ages of 9 and 15 on an hour-by-hour basis, finding that the onset of adolescence was not associated with increased emotionality. On the other hand, a study by Csikszentmihalyi and Larson (1984) found that adolescent Americans displayed extreme mood swings in the space of 1 hour whereas adults typically take several hours to change from one mood to another.

The evidence generally indicates that problems are more likely to occur early rather than late in adolescence. For example, Larson et al. (1996) found that boys experienced less positive emotion in their family interactions at the ages of 12 and 13, and girls did the same at the ages of 14 and 15. After that, however, the level of positive emotion increased in late adolescence, returning to the level of childhood.

Some studies have addressed the issue of sex differences in identity formation. Douvan and Adelson (1966) obtained support for Erikson's position. Adolescent girls had greater problems than adolescent boys with identity development, and this seemed to be because they focused on the changes in their lives that would result from marriage. In contrast, Waterman (1985) reviewed several studies, and concluded that there was only "weak and inconsistent evidence" that boys and girls follow different routes to identity achievement.

Evaluation

Erikson was correct in his argument that adolescents and young adults typically experience major changes in identity, and that these changes can cause uncertainty and doubt. However, Erikson overstated the case when he focused on the notion of an identity crisis that all adolescents go through. Offer et al. (1988, pp.83–84) reviewed the literature, and came to the following measured conclusion:

> *The most dramatic … findings are those that permit us to characterise the model American teenager as feeling confident, happy, and self-satisfied—a portrait of the American adolescent that contrasts sharply with that drawn by many theorists of adolescent development, who contend that adolescence is pervaded with turmoil, dramatic mood swings, and rebellion.*

On the negative side, most of Erikson's theorising was about male adolescents, and he had relatively little to say about female adolescents. This led Archer (1992, p.29) to argue as follows:

> *A major feminist criticism of Erikson's work is that it portrays a primarily Eurocentric male model of normality.*

Erikson initially argued that identity in males and females differed for biological and anatomical reasons, for example, he referred to the "inner space" or womb as the basis for female identity. However, he changed his mind somewhat thereafter. Erikson (1968, p.273) argued that

> nothing in our interpretation ... is meant to claim that either sex is doomed to one ... mode or another; rather ... these modes "come more naturally".

Erikson did not carry out any experimental studies to test his theoretical ideas. The ideal approach would have been to conduct a longitudinal or long-term study in which people were observed over a period of years starting before adolescence and continuing until after adolescence. In fact, as was mentioned earlier, Erikson relied mainly on his observations of adolescents undergoing therapy. He obtained evidence of an identity crisis in this biased sample, but this does not mean that all adolescents are the same.

Finally, Erikson's views merely *describe* what he regarded as typical of adolescent thinking and behaviour. He did not provide a detailed *explanation* of the processes responsible for creating an identity crisis, nor did he indicate in detail the processes responsible for resolving it.

While searching for an identity, adolescents are already having to cope with physiological changes, changing roles, relationships, the prospect of future work and/or education, and other pressures. All this as they try to discover who they really are, and how they are seen by others.

Erikson uses all these areas of uncertainty, and more, to suggest an identity crisis that adolescents are bound to go through. He has been criticised for his concept of a single identity, and for his research sampling, which has been seen as too small in number and too male-biased. Erikson's ideas about identity have been termed oversimplified, and more elaborate accounts have been given by Marcia and others. Marcia recognised that multiple identities are possible. Others have criticised the fact that Erikson only offers the option that adolescents must go through a crisis.

Erikson was one of the first to develop a stage account of human development, but his stage theories fail to take individual differences fully into account. One stage or plan cannot apply to all people, and much evidence suggests that no two people with basically the same environment will behave in the same way.

Marcia's theory

James Marcia (1966, 1980) was much influenced by Erikson's (1963) notion that adolescents are likely to experience an identity crisis. However, he argued that better methods of assessing adolescents' state of identity diffusion or identity formation were needed. He also argued that Erikson's ideas were oversimplified, and that there are actually various different ways in which adolescents can fail to achieve a stable sense of identity.

CASE STUDY: *Anne Frank*

Anne Frank was a Jewish teenager in the Netherlands during the Second World War. She and members of her family spent 2 years hiding from the occupying Nazis in a secret annexe at the back of a warehouse in Amsterdam, during which time Anne kept a diary of day-to-day events and her thoughts and feelings. Anne was 13 years old when the family went into hiding, and she experienced the difficulties faced by all adolescents as well as the almost unbearable situation of being confined with seven other people, facing hunger, boredom, and the constant fear of discovery. After a year and a half in the secret annexe, Anne wrote:

Everyone thinks I'm showing off when I talk, ridiculous when I'm silent, insolent when I answer, cunning when I have a good idea, lazy when I'm tired, selfish when I eat one bite more than I should, stupid, cowardly, calculating, etc., etc. All day long I hear nothing but what an exasperating child I am, and although I laugh it off and pretend not to mind, I wish I could ask God to give me another personality, one that doesn't antagonize everyone.

After the war, only one member of Anne Frank's family had survived; her father Otto, who edited and published his daughter's diaries. Because of the social climate of the time (1947) Otto Frank edited out many references Anne had made to her sexual feelings and some passages in which she wrote with anger and sometimes hatred about her mother and other family members. A new edition of the diaries, published in 1997, gives a fuller picture of Anne Frank as a normal adolescent, struggling to come to terms with all the changes in her extraordinary and tragically short life.

Marcia's first assumption was that, at any point in time, each adolescent has an identity status. Marcia investigated the possible different kinds of identity status by using a semi-structured interview technique to explore what adolescents thought about occupational choice, religion, and political ideology. In each of these three areas an individual was classified on two dimensions: (1) Have various alternatives been considered seriously in each of the three areas? (crisis); and (2) Have firm commitments been made in those areas? (commitment). Marcia (1967, p.119) defined the key terms here as follows:

> Crisis refers to times during adolescence when the individual seems to be actively involved in choosing among alternative occupations and beliefs. Commitment refers to the degree of personal investment the individual expresses in an occupation or belief.

Marcia concluded from these interviews that there are four possible identity statuses that may be experienced during adolescence:

1. **Identity diffusion**: identity issues have not been considered in detail and no firm commitments have been made for the future.
2. **Foreclosure**: identity issues have not been considered seriously, but future commitments have been made in spite of this.
3. **Moratorium**: there has been an active exploration and consideration of alternatives, but no definite future commitments have been made; this corresponds to Erikson's identity crisis.
4. **Identity achievement**: various alternatives have been carefully considered, and firm future commitments have been made.

Marcia (1966) assumed that adolescents would tend to move from one of the low-identity statuses (foreclosure and diffusion) to one of the high-identity statuses (moratorium and achievement). Adolescents would change their identity status because of the growing external and internal pressures on them to enter the adult world. Not all adolescents would pass through each stage.

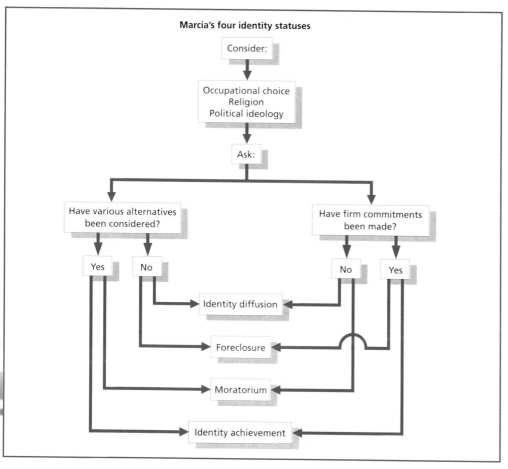

Marcia's four identity statuses

Consider:

Occupational choice
Religion
Political ideology

Ask:

Have various alternatives been considered?

Have firm commitments been made?

Yes   No

No   Yes

Identity diffusion

Foreclosure

Moratorium

Identity achievement

In order to assess the degree of crisis an adolescent was in, what question(s) did Marcia ask?

Research evidence

Marcia's development of Erikson's ideas was largely intended to facilitate empirical research. The stages identified on the previous page are the outcome of Marcia's own research and have received general support from other studies, such as Meilman's (1979) research, described in the Key Study below. Meilman did find evidence of all four identity statuses but also found that many of the characteristics typically associated with adolescence were in fact not typical at all. It appears that some individuals never experienced an identity crisis and that many individuals had still failed to achieve a stable identity by their mid-20s.

Meilman

Some support for Marcia's general approach was reported by Meilman (1979). He assessed the identity statuses of young males ranging in age between 12 and 24 using Marcia's semi-structured interview technique. All of the 12- and nearly all of the 15-year-olds had one of the low-identity statuses. Among the 15-year-olds, 64% had identity diffusion and 32% had foreclosure. Among the 18-year-olds, 48% had identity diffusion and 24% had foreclosure, with 20% having identity achievement. The proportion of identity achievers increased to 40% among the 21-year-olds, and to 56% among the 24-year-olds.

There are two surprising features of Meilman's findings. First, large numbers of people in their early 20s had still failed to achieve a stable identity, indicating that problems over identity are often by no means confined to the years of adolescence. Second, it appears that only a small minority of individuals at any age are in the moratorium period, suggesting that an identity crisis is fairly infrequent during or after adolescence.

Discussion points

1. Does it make sense to put adolescents and young adults into one of only four categories?
2. What confidence can we have in the opinions expressed by the participants in semi-structured interviews?

Marcia (1966) assumed, as did Erikson, that any given adolescent either has or has not forged an identity for himself or herself. In other words, identity formation is all or none. That assumption is an oversimplification, as was shown by Archer (1982). The identity statuses of adolescents who varied in age between 12 and 18 were assessed in the areas of occupational choice, gender roles, religious values, and political ideologies. Only 5% of these adolescents had the same identity status in all four areas, indicating that the great majority of adolescents are at different stages of development towards identity formation in different areas of life.

Erikson (1968) and Marcia (1966) both seem to have assumed that adolescents who have achieved a stable sense of identity are unlikely to go back to an earlier, pre-identity stage. However, Marcia (1976) carried out a follow-up after his initial study, and found that some of the adolescents who had achieved a sense of identity had returned to the foreclosure or diffusion identity status 6 years later.

What experiences might cause an adolescent to go back to an earlier identity status?

Identity status depends more on social and cultural factors than Marcia (1966) assumed. For example, Munro and Adams (1977) found that college students were more likely than those of the same age in full-time work to be in the moratorium period with respect to religious and political identity. This difference may have occurred because time spent at university provides more opportunity for exploration and questioning than is available in the workplace.

One of the key differences between Marcia's theory and that of Erikson is that Marcia argued that there are different ways in which an adolescent can fail to have achieved a sense of identity. Evidence that it is important to distinguish among the moratorium, foreclosure, and diffusion categories was reported by Marcia (1980). Those in the moratorium status felt much more positive about themselves and about the future than did those in the diffusion and foreclosure statuses. These findings are hard to explain from Erikson's theory, because the moratorium status comes closest to his notion of identity crisis.

Evaluation

Marcia's theory is more realistic than that of Erikson, in that it recognises that there are several possible identity statuses. However, it is open to most of the same criticisms. Semi-structured interviews conducted at one point in time cannot provide much evidence about the ways in which adolescents change and develop during the teenage years. It is also not clear whether the answers given by adolescents in these interviews are accurate, or whether they are simply telling the interviewer what they think he or she expects to hear. Furthermore, there is a large difference between describing four identity statuses found among adolescents and explaining in detail how these statuses arise and are replaced by other statuses.

Marcia's whole approach is rather limited. This was shown by Archer (1992, p.33), who asked the following awkward question:

> *Why do we expend all this energy conducting these interviews, listen to these people share life stories, and then walk away with only these four little letters—"A" for identity achievement, "M" for moratorium, "F" for foreclosure, and "D" for identity diffusion?*

Some studies have focused on the factors within the family that may lead adolescents to have different identity statuses. Adolescents in either the identity achievement or moratorium statuses tend to have affectionate parents and the freedom to be individuals in their own right (Waterman, 1982). Adolescents in the identity foreclosure status tend to have close relationships with domineering parents, and those in the identity diffusion status tend to have distant relationships with aloof or uninvolved parents (Waterman, 1982). This suggests that crises are not resolved by individuals.

Theories of Social Development in Adolescence: The Sociological Approach

Erikson and Marcia focused on crises in adolescence, and how healthy psychological development was related to the resolution of crises. The sociological approach takes the view that adolescence is indeed a transitional process *but* the reason for this is not because there are personal crises to be overcome but rather that external factors steer the adolescent in the direction of transition. These external factors include culturally determined pressures from the family, from peers, the school, and other social influences such as the mass media. The net result is that the adolescent is placed under pressure at a time when he or she may be feeling most vulnerable. Vulnerability is due to those physical and psychological changes associated with puberty.

Coleman's focal theory

G. Stanley Hall (1904) suggested that adolescence is a time of "storm and stress" during which the child must experience the turbulent history of the human race in order to reach maturity, referred to as "recapitulation theory".

This view of crisis in adolescence was disputed by Coleman (1974) who argued that, in reality, most adolescents do not experience severe difficulties because they are usually able to "focus on" (thus focal theory) individual problems as they occur. Coleman agreed with the psychoanalytic view that adolescence was a time of role change and thus a time when social adjustments need to be made, but he did not agree that crisis was either inevitable or healthy. Instead, it may well be that those adolescents who experience crisis have other ongoing, externally caused problems which make the adjustment more difficult.

Research evidence

Evidence to support Coleman's views comes from a large scale study, involving 800 boys and girls aged from 11 to 17. Coleman and Hendry (1990) interviewed the young people asking them to discuss topics that were anxiety-provoking, such as self-image, being alone,

Marcia used semi-structured interviews to assess adolescents' identity status. What might be a better method to choose?

From your own experience, do you think Erikson was right, or do you prefer Marcia's more elaborate ideas?

occupational choice, and peer, sexual, and parental relationships. The results showed that each issue seemed to have a different distribution curve, peaking in importance over a particular age. Concerns about peer relations, for example, peaked earlier than occupational choice. In addition, some adolescents came to these issues earlier than normal, and others experienced them later. Adolescent life, therefore, can be seen as a mixture of stability and adjustment in different areas of life at different times. The coincidence of a number of important issues all peaking at once could cause problems but, generally, adolescents navigate carefully through this stage of life, choosing whether to engage with particular issues immediately or later. In this way, they manage their own life stage and are generally successful in coming through unscathed.

Evaluation

There appears to be no reason to suppose that adolescence is necessarily a time of storm and stress, or that such crises need to be weathered for healthy personality development. At the same time it is clear that adolescents do have adjustments to make to their physical and psychological identities.

It may be that Erikson and Marcia, on the one hand, and Coleman on the other, were using the word "crisis" in a rather different sense. Erikson's understanding of a crisis was that it was a fairly normal developmental event, whereas Coleman may well be referring to a more serious disturbance caused by a number of conflicts all occurring at the same time.

Relationships in adolescence

A key part of the sociological approach is to emphasise the role of socialisation in adolescent development, especially the role of family and peers in socialising the adolescent. "Sociological" means that it is concerned with the effects that social groups have on the individual. A classic picture is of the adolescent breaking his or her ties with the family and substituting the influence of the family with peer group culture.

Relationships with parents

Adolescence is traditionally seen as a time of conflict between parents and their children. There are various ways of explaining why this may be. The cognitive-developmental view (e.g., Piaget) might suggest that the young people's newly achieved abilities of hypothetical and abstract thought might lead them to start considering their own opinions leading them into philosophical arguments with parents. Peterson et al. (1986) found that children in the stage of formal operations (aged 11 upwards) were more likely to have heated arguments with their parents, though we cannot be certain whether this is *because* of the stage of formal operations.

A second explanation, from the sociobiological perspective, is that adolescent strivings for independence are adaptive because this enables the adolescent to become directed towards the peer group and ready for entry into adulthood. The psychoanalytic view was also one that regarded independence as a crucial aim of this stage and a necessity for future healthy psychological development.

Some studies have found conflict but many have found that most adolescents are actually quite happy with the situation at home. For example, Offer et al. (1988) surveyed adolescents in various countries (Australia, Bangladesh, Hungary, Israel, Italy, Taiwan, Turkey, United States, and West Germany) and found that 91% denied holding a grudge against their parents and a similar number said their parents were not ashamed of them. Youniss (1989) found that many adolescents reported being very close to their parents. Smetana (1988) identified two different kinds of dispute. One concerns domains under the control of the adolescent, such as sleeping late at the weekend, and the other concerns parental domains, such as not cleaning up after a party, or thieving. The latter were regarded as legitimate areas for parents to continue to exert control whereas the former could lead to parent–child disputes.

Durkin (1997) points out that it is important to bear in mind the fact that conflicts occur between any individuals sharing a house; conflict is part of social life. Discord relates to negotiations over rights and may not result in a rejection of the relationship itself.

In relation to the issue of independence, one might think that adolescents who become emotionally dependent on their peers are compensating for lack of support from home. However, Ryan and Lynch (1989) make an important point that, just in the same way as a securely attached infant is better equipped to form relationships away from primary caregivers, the same is true of adolescents. Therefore, adolescent independence is likely to be the result of good family relationships rather than the outcome of conflict.

Older children can be surprisingly confident about debating.

Are independent adolescents more or less likely to have good relations with their parents?

Relationships with peers

There is no doubt that peers do become increasingly important during adolescence. Palmonari et al. (1989) surveyed Italian 16- to 18-year-olds and found that 90% identified themselves as belonging to a peer group. The roles of such peer groups are various. One important effect may be for emotional support. Buhrmester (1992) found that adolescents who had close peer group relationships were also less prone to anxiety and depression (though, it could be argued that depressed adolescents would find it difficult to form close relationships).

Another important role of the peer group is social conformity. Constanzo and Shaw (1966) conducted conformity experiments along the lines of those of Asch, using participants aged between 7 and 21. They found that conformity peaked at around 11–13 years. Brendt (1979a) investigated conformity using hypothetical situations where the participant was encouraged by another (a peer or an adult) to behave in an anti-social or pro-social way (e.g., stealing a sweet or helping someone with homework). Brendt found that conformity to adults' suggestions decreased with age, whereas the reverse was true of peer conformity. Pro-social conformity peaked around the age of 11–12 whereas antisocial conformity occurred slightly later, at 14–15 years.

Harris (1997) argues that this tendency towards conformity is vital in adolescent development. According to **group socialisation theory**, children and adolescents are shaped far more by their peers than they are by their parents. Only this can explain why siblings are often so very different from each other. Siblings have genetic similarities and they share the same home influences yet they are so different. This must be because they are largely socialised by peers. This makes sense when you consider that, ultimately, we all have to function in the world outside our own home and thus it is important to orient ourselves towards peers rather than families as we get older.

There may be some individual differences. For example, Fuligni and Eccles (1993) questioned nearly 2000 11-year-olds, and found that peer orientation was higher in

One feature of adolescent behaviour is the image of being different while at the same time adolescents are actually highly conformist within their own social group.

adolescents who rated their parents as more authoritarian and where adolescents felt they had few opportunities to be involved in decision making. Adolescents who experience a democratic parenting style may rely less on their peers.

Cultural differences

The account of adolescence that has been presented so far is largely related to European or so-called "Western" culture. In fact, however, there are enormous individual and cultural differences in the adolescent experience (Durkin, 1995).

The individualist and collectivist dimension

Adolescents in the United States and other Western societies generally take several years to achieve a clear sense of adult identity. However, that does not necessarily mean that similar processes are at work in other cultures. Markus and Kitayama (1991) drew a distinction between societies in which there is an *independent* construal of the self and those in which there is an *interdependent* construal of the self. Societies (such as the United States or western Europe) with an independent construal of the self tend to be described as individualistic, egocentric, and self-contained. Societies (such as those in the Far East) with an interdependent construal of the self are described as **collectivist**, connected, or relational. In the latter societies, many of the key decisions of early adulthood are not taken directly by the individual concerned. For example, there may be an arranged marriage, and the individual may be expected to do the same job as his or her father or mother. In such societies, the whole nature of adolescence is different from that in **individualist** societies.

What are the distinctive features of a collectivist society?

No adolescence

Historically, the concept of adolescence is also not universal. Shaffer (1993) claimed that adolescence is an "invention" of the twentieth century. He argued that, when it became illegal to employ children, this created a new section of the population, an "adolescent peer culture", which was isolated from those who were younger and older. They were not able to identify with younger children and were now kept separate from the adult working population. Up until this time there was no "adolescent" phase. It was G. Stanley Hall, writing at the beginning of the nineteenth century, who first identified this period of development. According to Gross (1996), the concept of a "teenager" is even more recent, being coined in the 1950s. Adolescence is therefore historically a new concept and it is also culturally specific.

Evidence that adolescence in the Western sense is not universal was discussed by Condon (1987) in his analysis of the Inuit of the Canadian arctic at the start of the twentieth century. In that society, young women were regarded as adult at puberty. By the time of puberty, they were usually married, and soon thereafter started to have children. Young men were treated as adult when they could build an igloo, hunt large animals on their own, and support themselves and their families. The difficult living conditions in the arctic meant that there was no time for teenagers to spend several years thinking about what they were going to do with their lives.

Difficult living conditions may force adolescents to move straight from childhood to adulthood in order to survive.

Sub-cultural differences

Within Britain there are many cultural groups, and for adolescent members of minority groups there may be particular problems related to identity formation in adolescence because their path to adulthood is not clear cut. Weinreich (1979) reported findings on different groups of adolescent girls in the United Kingdom. Immigrant girls (especially those from Pakistani families) had higher levels of identity diffusion than did girls from the dominant culture. It is fairly common to find that adolescents from ethnic minorities take longer to achieve identity status, perhaps because their lives are more complex and confusing than those of the majority group (Durkin, 1995).

Delinquency

A different kind of sub-culture from ethnic minorities, is the delinquent sub-culture. Much of this Unit has presented the view that young people generally negotiate adolescence with relatively little stress and conflict. But there are a minority for whom this is not true. Hargreaves (1967) studied the different sub-cultures within a school population of 14- to 15-year-old boys in the north of England. The study identified two opposed sub-cultures: a group of academically successful boys, who were also the ones most liked by the teachers and were often prefects, and the "delinquescent" low achievers. Popularity in this group was related to anti-social behaviour. These data suggest that children who are not achieving at school turn to other sources to define success or acceptance, thus forming delinquent sub-cultures.

It is difficult to assess the intellectual ability of such delinquents because they also usually lack the motivation to do well on IQ tests, therefore their poor performance may be due to low motivation rather than low IQ.

One of the possible explanations for delinquency is reputation management theory (Emler, 1984). This follows on from the research of Hargreaves and proposes that for all adolescents the main task is identity formation. For those who can define their reputation in terms of academic success, identity is not a problem. But other adolescents reject socially sanctioned values either because they are academically unsuccessful or because they may distrust the rewards offered by conventional social systems. This view is supported by the social nature of delinquency. Emler et al. (1987) found that most adolescent crime was committed in the company of others. Reicher and Emler (1986) argue that the peer context is critical in constructing social and personal identity and, for some adolescents, delinquency is their main route to doing this. In addition, this can explain why boys are more likely to be delinquent than girls—because there is greater pressure on them to do well at school and therefore failure is more deeply felt (Emler & Reicher, 1995).

SECTION SUMMARY

❖ Personality consists of stable, internal, and consistent characteristics that make each of us different. Psychodynamic theories focus on how internal processes (such as motivation) and past experience shape personality.

Personality Development

❖ Freud developed a theory of personality (psychoanalytic theory) as a way to explain the dynamics that may create pathological behaviours. Innate drives interact with early experiences and may produce conflicts that lead to unhealthy behaviours. The personality consists of the id, ego, and superego. The id and ego are often in conflict because they are driven by the opposing pleasure and reality principles. Conflicts cause the individual to experience anxiety. The ego protects itself against anxiety using defence mechanisms such as repression, displacement, projection, denial, and intellectualisation.

❖ Psychosexual development involves the attachment of the libido to various body regions at different stages of development: oral, anal, and phallic stages are followed by a latent period and finally a genital stage. The phallic stage is important in moral development and includes the Oedipus (Electra) complex, which leads to identification. Personality development is the consequence of over- or undergratification at any stage, leading to a fixation (libido attached to that stage). Anxiety later in life leads to regression to a previously fixated stage.

❖ The theory is derived from and supported by Freud's case studies largely of adults, and women and disturbed individuals. He also used extensive self-analysis to validate his theories. Other research support can be gleaned from studies of repression (motivated forgetting) and perceptual defence. The rather weak research support is a drawback to the theory, as well as the fact that it was based on a unique group of individuals. Case histories produce rich data but can be biased. Nevertheless, Freud's emphasis on childhood and on the unconscious has endured. His overemphasis on sexual forces may be a reflection of his historical period.

❖ Erikson focused on psychosocial rather than psychosexual influences. He outlined eight stages of development, where there are conflicts to be resolved at each stage for healthy development: trust vs. mistrust, autonomy vs. shame, initiative vs. guilt, industry vs. inferiority, identity vs. role confusion, intimacy vs. isolation, generativity vs. stagnation, and integrity vs. despair. Resolution does not mean that one or the other extreme is developed; individuals generally experience a mixture of each outcome. Research support comes from Erikson's clinical studies, from attachment research which indicates the importance of trust, and from studies that show how peers influence self-development. The focus on social processes enlarged the scope of psychodynamic theory, and the notion of crises has been useful. However, the theory does not explain how crises are resolved nor is the research evidence very convincing. It is rather too tidy an account to be realistic.

❖ The social learning approach contrasts with the psychodynamic approach in placing a far greater emphasis on external social influences. Social learning theory explains learning in terms of direct and indirect reinforcement. Personality is learned like everything else. Social learning incorporated cognitive explanations by suggesting that we model our behaviour on others and therefore need an internal representation of that behaviour. Bandura suggested that there are four steps in the modelling process: attention, retention, reproduction, and motivation. He also argued that personality develops as an interaction: people are both products of and producers of their environment (reciprocal determination). An individual's sense of perceived effectiveness (self-efficacy) also influences personality development: previous experiences, relevant vicarious experiences, persuasion, and emotional arousal all create self-efficacy. The principles of social learning theory are well supported by research evidence, except that the theory would predict that individuals should develop multiple selves—which is not congruent with personal experience. However, it may be that our sense of a single, integrated self is an illusion. Social learning theory is not truly a developmental theory.

❖ Mischel's theory of situationalism expanded on the notion that there is no consistency in self or personality. He called this the consistency paradox and proposed instead that individuals exhibit behavioural specificity. We learn to behave differently in different situations because of selective reinforcement. We think people are consistent because we often see them in similar situations. Mischel proposed five person variables that are influenced by experience and influence learning: construction competencies, encoding strategies, expectancies, subjective stimulus values, and self-regulatory systems and plans. These jointly explain how personality develops. This theory is supported by research into context-dependent learning. However the notion of a fragmented self is allied to mental disorder; we need to have a sense of unity in our personality to function effectively.

Gender Development

❖ Gender is a fundamental part of our self-concept. Key terms include: sex, gender, sexual identity, gender identity, gender (or sex) role, and gender stereotypes. Some gender stereotypes are outdated but others are real, such as differences in verbal ability, interest in babies, and performance at school. The differences are exaggerated by our expectations.

❖ According to psychoanalytic theory, anatomy is destiny, meaning that gender development is largely determined by biological factors. Freud argued that identification with the same-sex parent plays a major role in the development of sex-typed behaviour. Chodorow offered an alternative that both sexes identify with their mother; boys ultimately have to move away from this close relationship in order to establish their gender identity. There is some evidence to support this view, boys without fathers when under the age of 5 show fewer gender stereotypes but in general the support is thin. Boys should identify more with a threatening father but they don't.

❖ Kohlberg's cognitive-developmental theory suggests that gender identity is a prerequisite to acquiring gender roles. According to this theory children develop gender identity in three stages: basic gender identity, gender stability, and gender consistency. Research supports the existence of these three stages, as well as other predictions from the theory such as the fact that achievement of gender consistency leads to the predicted increase in sex-typed behaviour. However, it appears that children begin to acquire gender concepts before gender consistency. The exaggeration of internal, cognitive factors and lack of emphasis on social context is a further limitation of the theory.

❖ According to gender-schema theory young children who have acquired basic gender identity start to form gender schemas. Gender schemas actively organise new experiences. Information that is inconsistent with gender schemas tends to be misremembered. This theory can explain why gender-role beliefs often change rather little after middle childhood. Many of the same criticisms apply as for cognitive-developmental theory. In addition there is evidence that gender schemas are not always in accord with gender behaviours.

❖ According to social learning theory, gender development occurs through direct learning and observational learning. As predicted, sex-typed behaviour sometimes occurs because it is rewarded, whereas sex-inappropriate behaviour is avoided because it is discouraged. Research studies also demonstrate the importance of peer reinforcement in learning gender stereotypes, and the importance of observational learning in gender development, involving either live models or the media. Social learning theory takes full account of the social context in which the development of gender occurs. However, social learning theorists focus on learning specific forms of behaviour rather than on general types of learning; they tend to regard children as passive rather than active; and they ignore age differences in receptiveness.

❖ Biological theories of gender development contrast with the social approach. Studies of individuals reared in opposition to their biological sex permit us to contrast the effects of social and biological factors. It appears that social factors are influential but, in some cases at least, biological factors are ultimately important. However, these are very unusual cases. Biosocial theory is an amalgam of biological and social factors.

❖ Sociobiological theory explains gender development in terms of evolutionary processes. Women select males in terms of good genes to enhance the perpetuation of their own genetic line. They also select men with resources to help look after their offspring. These are examples of gender role behaviour. Cross-cultural studies show that universal male and female behaviours (females are nurturant and males are instrumental) are very widespread, and strongest in collectivist cultures, suggesting some biological basis.

Adolescence

❖ Adolescence roughly covers the teenage years, but is better defined in psychological terms rather than by age. It is a time of many changes but it is not necessarily experienced as stressful.

❖ The psychoanalytic approach emphasises biologically driven stages in development. Erikson argued that adolescents experience an identity crisis which is necessary in order to resolve the identity issue and to move on to the formation of a stable adult identity. Adolescents experience uncertainty (identity diffusion) revolving around intimacy, diffusion of time, diffusion of industry, and negative identity. He also argued that females have greater problems than males with identity development, and that an identity crisis is more likely towards the end of adolescence. There is some evidence of stress during adolescence but low self-esteem may be explained by other changes not associated with adolescence *per se*. There appears to be little support for sex differences in identity development or for identity crisis later in adolescence. Possibly, Erikson relied too much on limited observations of a biased sample of emotionally disturbed adolescents. The account is more descriptive than explanatory.

❖ Marcia aimed to find more exact ways of assessing identity crisis and a more complex formulation of how adolescents achieve a stable sense of identity. He argued that there are four identity statuses that may be experienced during adolescence: identity diffusion, foreclosure, moratorium, and identity achievement. Crisis and commitment determine the passage through these statuses. A number of Marcia's (and Erikson's) assumptions have not been supported by research: not all individuals ever reach identity achievement; the identity statuses are less all-or-none than Marcia suggested; there may be a return to earlier stages; and social and cultural factors have been shown to be important. The interview method may produce inaccurate data, and the classification scheme is ultimately reductionist. On the plus side, Marcia showed that the identity crisis takes various different forms (diffusion, foreclosure, and moratorium).

❖ The sociological approach takes the view that transition is forced on the adolescent because of external factors (e.g., pressures from the media) rather than internal identity crises. According to Coleman's focal theory the "storm and stress" view is generally wrong because most adolescents are able to focus on areas of development one at a time, and thus remain fairly unstressed. Research evidence supports this.

❖ The sociological approach emphasises the role of parents and peers in development, especially during adolescence. Parent–adolescent conflict may be related to increased ability to think abstractly (cognitive-developmental view), or an adaptive behaviour to promote independence (sociobiological and psychoanalytic view). In fact many adolescents do not experience conflict with their parents, or at least only conflict over certain areas of their lives such as sleeping habits rather than over more fundamental issues such as moral principles. Discord may be related to social living and not to the relationship itself. Adolescent independence is likely to be the result of good family relationships rather than the outcome of conflict.

❖ Peers become increasingly important during adolescence. They offer emotional support and are a source of social conformity (and security). Adolescents are more conformist than younger children, especially with respect to their peers. Group socialisation theory suggests that peer influence is important because it prepares adolescents to cope with the wider adult world.

❖ There are individual and cultural differences, both of which are related to social processes. In collectivist cultures the society rather than the individual constructs identity. In some non-Western cultures there is no adolescent period. This may also apply to our own culture in the past. Sub-cultural variation also exists, which includes delinquent sub-culture. For some adolescents delinquency may be the only route to social identity, which leads to the assumption that delinquency is sometimes a necessary part of adolescence.

FURTHER READING

The topics in this Section are covered in greater depth by T. Abbott (2001) *Social and personality development* (London: Routledge), written specifically for the AQA A specification. A useful reference for theories of personality can be found in C.S. Hall, G. Lindzey, and J.B. Campbell (1997) *Theories of personality* (New York: John Wiley). There are chapters on gender and adolescence in K. Durkin (1995) *Developmental social psychology: From infancy to old age* (Oxford: Blackwell). J. Kroger (1996) *Identity in adolescence* (London: Routledge) is part of a Routledge series on "adolescence and society" edited by John Coleman.

Example Examination Questions

You should spend 30 minutes on each of the questions below, which aim to test the material in this Section.

1.　Discuss **one** explanation of personality development.　　　　　　　　　　　　(24 marks)

2.　Distinguish between psychodynamic and social learning approaches to the explanation
　　of personality development.　　　　　　　　　　　　　　　　　　　　　　　　(24 marks)

3.　**(a)**　Outline **two** explanations of the development of gender identity.　　　　(12 marks)
　　(b)　Evaluate these explanations.　　　　　　　　　　　　　　　　　　　　(12 marks)

4.　"Narrow gender concepts inevitably limit a person's behavioural repertoire and mean that an
　　individual has to behave in a rigid fashion. People who are less gender-stereotyped are freer
　　to behave in ways that are appropriate to the situation and this is psychologically healthier."

　　Discuss the effects of gender roles and gender identity on behaviour.　　　　　(24 marks)

5.　Critically consider research into social development in adolescence.　　　　　　(24 marks)

6.　Discuss the findings of research into cultural differences in adolescence.　　　　(24 marks)

Examination Tips

Question 1.　"Discuss" is an AO1 and AO2 term, therefore you should describe your chosen theory of personality and then evaluate it. For good marks the description needs to be well-detailed. Evaluation/commentary (AO2) is best if it is embedded in the essay rather than "tacked on" at the end. You might make reference to research studies, methodological flaws in such evidence, and/or make comparisons with other theories. Practical applications are a means of positive evaluation.

Question 2.　"Distinguish between" is an AO1 and AO2 term, therefore you should describe both theories but also aim to draw out the similarities and differences in doing so. It is this compare/contrast that will earn you the AO2 marks. There are numerous ways of contrasting theories such as in terms of their potential for research and their actual research support; in terms of their cultural or gender bias, with respect to the extent the theory covers the life span, and so on. You can use lots of different theories as the question requires that you contrast the two approaches not two theories.

Question 3.　In part (a) the injunction "outline" is used to signal that breadth rather than depth is required here. "Outline" requires a summary description only. You need to cover two explanations of how gender identity develops and should provide a summary description of each. In part (b) you are required to offer any kind of evaluation, which might be achieved through reference to research evidence, a consideration of the conclusions of such studies and their methodology, comparisons with other explanations of gender identity, and any practical applications. Make sure you give a full 15 minutes to the second part or you will lose valuable marks.

Question 4.　In this question you are not required to specifically address the quotation, though it may help in directing your response. The essay requires consideration of the relationship between gender identity/roles and actual behaviour. How does our identity influence the way we behave? You should describe the relationship between roles/identity and behaviour, and at the same time assess the value of such understanding. Upon what sort of evidence is this knowledge based? Is this evidence sound?

Question 5.　"Research" can be either theories or studies. If you describe studies then you may evaluate them with reference to theories and vice versa. When describing studies you can use the same guidelines as for AS level: write something about the aims, procedures, findings, and conclusions. The essay is quite open-ended so it will probably be necessary to be selective in the way you structure your response, otherwise you risk providing too much breadth and not enough detail to communicate good understanding.

Question 6.   The essay requires a focus on the findings only of research (theories and/or studies) and therefore no credit will be given for information about procedures or conclusions except where these are relevant to our knowledge of findings and/or used as an evaluation of the findings. For example, it is likely that you will criticise such findings in terms of the validity of the research procedures. Such criticism may be positive or negative. Note that the essay is limited to cultural differences in adolescence but such differences arguably include many things, for example, historical and gender differences (it may be desirable to be explicit about why these count as "cultural").

WEB SITES

http://www.ship.edu/~cgboeree/perscontents.html
Large site covering personality theories.

http://www.personalityresearch.org
Great ideas in personality, lots of material and links on personality theories and research.

http://www.personalityresearch.org/glossary.html
Glossary of personality terms, with links to related glossaries.

http://www.spsp.org
Society for Personality and Social Psychology homepage.

http://www.freud.org.uk/
The homepage of the Freud Museum, London, which includes links to many Freud-related sites on the internet.

http://freud.t0.or.at/freud/index-e.htm
The homepage of the Freud Museum, Vienna, which is also the online service of the Sigmund Freud Society.

http://www.nwmissouri.edu/nwcourses/martin/general/socialization/tsld014.htm
Notes about Freud on personality development, in "slide" format.

http://snycorva.cortland.edu/~ANDERSMD/ERIK/welcome.HTML
A site about Erik Erikson, including critiques and links.

http://www.gwu.edu/~tip/bandura.html
Overview of Bandura's Social Learning Theory.

http://www.ship.edu/~cgboeree/bandura.html
Introduction to Bandura's theories.

http://www.nd.edu/~rbarger/kohlberg.html
Summary of Kohlberg's stages of moral development.

http://www.aston.ac.uk/psychology/courseinfo/dev2/wk1.html
Sex role development theories.

http://www.stanford.edu/group/adolescent.ctr/
Stanford Center on Adolescence.

http://www.clc.cc.il.us/home/soc455/psycweb/develop/identity.htm
Erikson's and Marcia's theories.

www.a-levelpsychology.co.uk/websites.html
A continually updated list of useful links, including those printed in this book, may be found at the Psychology Press A level psychology site.

12

Adulthood

This Section discusses development from early to late adulthood, and the varying paths we all take. The effects of major changes, such as marriage, parenthood, divorce, retirement, and bereavement, as well as physical and mental ageing, in Western and in other cultures, are explored.

Early and Middle Adulthood

Even casual observation indicates that adults vary enormously in terms of the paths their lives take from the end of adolescence to old age. Some of these differences occur because of differences in personality, motivation, and interests, and some occur because of unexpected and unwanted life events (e.g., divorce; unemployment; illness). However, most adults form close relationships with others, most have one or more children, and most have jobs for much of their adult lives, suggesting that there may be some common life themes running through most people's adulthood. Theorists such as Erikson and Levinson have focused on these common themes, and used them as the basis for identifying the major stages of development in the adult years.

Erikson's Eight Ages of Man

As we saw in Section 11, Social and Personality Development. Erikson identified four stages to cover childhood. Erikson (1950, 1968) divided life during adolescence and adulthood into four further stages, each of which has its own developmental crisis. As with the earlier stages, each of the stages of adolescence and adulthood has a positive outcome and a negative outcome. Those who achieve only a negative outcome at one stage find it harder to cope during subsequent stages. The adolescent and adult stages are as follows (the ages for each stage are very approximate):

* *Stage 5.* Adolescence (13–19 years): this is the stage during which individuals strive to avoid role confusion and develop a sense of identity. The social focus is on peer groups.
* *Stage 6.* Early adulthood (20–30 years): this is the stage during which most adults commit themselves to a love relationship and to intimacy; other adults develop a sense of isolation. The social focus in this stage is on friendships.
* *Stage 7.* Middle adulthood (30–60 years): this is the stage during which most adults commit themselves to productive and socially valuable work (including bringing up their own children and being concerned with others within society), or they

become stagnant and self-centred. Erikson described these two extremes as generativity and stagnation. Generativity refers to "the interest in establishing and guiding the next generation" (Erikson, 1959, p.97). The social focus is on the household.

• *Stage 8*   Old age (60 years onwards): adults in this stage try to make sense of their lives. If they are successful in doing so, they gain wisdom; if they cannot do this, then they experience despair. The social focus is on humankind.

Is it possible to explain these conclusions about gender in an historical context?

In general terms, Erikson seems to have assumed that the three stages of adulthood applied universally to both sexes and to all cultures. However, Erikson (1968) did accept that there were often some differences between men and women in the sequence of stages. For example, men typically achieve a sense of identity before they achieve intimacy with a sexual partner during the stage of early adulthood. In contrast, Erikson argued that most women do not fully achieve a sense of identity until they have found a potential husband. According to him, the reason is that women's identity depends in part on the nature of the man she wishes to marry.

PSYCHOSOCIAL DEVELOPMENT—ERIKSON'S STAGES 5–8

Stage	Name	Age	Life crisis	Positive characteristics	Negative characteristics	Social focus
5	Adolescence	13–19	Identity vs. role confusion	Identity	Role confusion	Peer group
6	Early adulthood	20–30	Intimacy vs. isolation	Intimacy	Isolation	Friends
7	Middle adulthood	30–60	Generativity vs. stagnation	Generativity	Stagnation	Household
8	Old age	60+	Integrity vs. despair	Wisdom	Despair	Humankind

Research evidence

There is some evidence to support Erikson's assumption that men are more likely than women to achieve identity before intimacy. In a study on undergraduate students (reported in Bee, 1994), very few men showed intimacy without identity. In contrast, 52% of women who had not achieved identity nevertheless showed intimacy.

Erikson hypothesised that it is harder for parents to provide their children with a sense of purpose to carry them through adult life when the society in which they are living is going through a period of rapid change. Erikson studied the child-rearing practices of Sioux and Yurok Indians, who were experiencing great social change. He found supporting evidence for his hypothesis in these societies. This confirms the notion of psychosocial change which is central to Erikson's theory.

■ Activity: Design a short questionnaire to use with adults, and ask them about issues relating to intimacy and identity. Are there differences between genders? Is intimacy achieved before or after identity?

Evaluation

Neugarten found that working-class men are more likely than middle-class men to marry early and have children.

Erikson was one of the first psychologists to attempt the difficult task of providing a stage account of the whole of human development, and so he helped to open up the psychology of adulthood as an area of study. It is now generally accepted that people do develop and show significant psychological changes throughout their lives rather than simply during childhood.

However, Erikson's account of adult developmental changes is very sketchy. For example, it is doubtful that it makes much sense to argue that a single stage of development (middle adulthood) covers 30 years of an adult's life.

The most serious problem with stage-based accounts of development is that they imply that most people change and develop in the same ways. There is plentiful evidence that this is not correct. Neugarten (1975) discussed clear evidence that key developmental changes tend to occur at an earlier age for working-class men than for middle-class men. Working-class men tend to get married, have children, and have a full-time job during their early 20s, whereas middle-class men often delay settling down and getting married until their 30s.

The other major problem with Erikson's approach is that it was based on rather limited data. Erikson made use of detailed biographical case studies, such as those of Martin Luther and Mahatma Gandhi, and on his clinical experiences. His approach has the disadvantage that information is obtained from only a small and unrepresentative sample of adults. It also has the disadvantage that Erikson had to rely on whatever information happened to be available (e.g., letters and other documents). It was hard for him to compare different individuals, because he did not have information from the same questionnaires or other measuring instruments as a basis for comparison.

Different generations of people are brought up with slightly different values and aspirations, so how would this distort a general stage theory such as Erikson's?

Levinson's Seasons of Man's Life

Daniel Levinson (1978, 1986) argued that there is a **life cycle**, which consists of a sequence of periods spanning adult life. According to Levinson (1986, p.4), the notion of a life cycle "suggests that there is an underlying order in the human life course; although each individual life is unique, everyone goes through the same basic sequence". Many leading authorities such as Freud and Piaget assumed that development is essentially complete at the end of adolescence. In contrast, Levinson proposed that development continues during adulthood and old age.

Levinson (1986, p.6) argued that there is a **life structure**, which he defined as "the underlying pattern or design of a person's life at a given time". In trying to understand an adult's life structure, it is of crucial importance to focus on his or her relationships with other people who matter to them, and on the ways in which these relationships change over time. What are the main components in the life structure? Levinson (1986, p.6) found that

> *only one or two components—rarely as many as three—occupy a central place in the structure. Most often, marriage–family and occupation are the central components of a person's life, although wide variations occur in their relative weight and in the importance of other components.*

How can we decide the extent to which an individual's life structure has been satisfactory? There are two factors that need to be considered. First, there is the level of success or failure that the individual has had in his or her dealings with the external world. Second, there is the impact of the life structure on the inner self; for example, has the individual had to ignore or neglect some of his or her major desires?

The life cycle

According to Levinson's theory, the life cycle consists of a sequence of eras. Each era has its own psychological and social characteristics, and each era "makes its distinctive contribution to the whole." The move from one era to the next does not occur rapidly. Instead, there are cross-era transitions, which last for about 5 years and which span the time period from the end of one era to the start of the next. Finally, there are also important changes within each era.

The detailed structure of the life cycle is illustrated overleaf. The ages that are given for each part of the life cycle are the most common ones, but in practice there is a range of about 2 years above and below each figure. Here is the proposed structure:

1. *Era of pre-adulthood* (0–22 years): this is the era of most rapid development, as it spans infancy, childhood, and adolescence; the years between 17 and 22 form the early adult transition, in which there is the start of early adulthood as the individual begins to behave as an adult in an adult world.
2. *Era of early adulthood* (17–45 years): according to Levinson (1986, p.5), this is "the era of greatest energy and abundance and of greatest contradiction and stress". This era starts with the early adult transition (17–22 years), during which the individual forms a *Dream*, which comprises his or her major life goals. According to Levinson

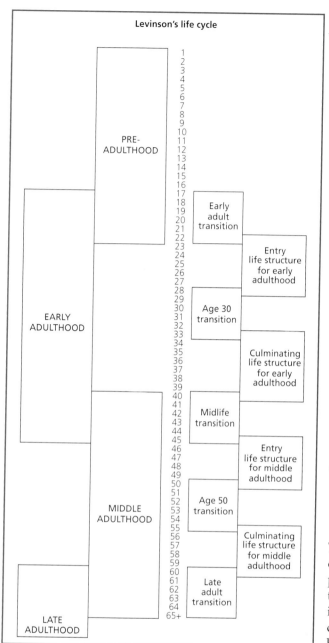

Levinson's life cycle

PRE-ADULTHOOD

EARLY ADULTHOOD

MIDDLE ADULTHOOD

LATE ADULTHOOD

Early adult transition

Entry life structure for early adulthood

Age 30 transition

Culminating life structure for early adulthood

Midlife transition

Entry life structure for middle adulthood

Age 50 transition

Culminating life structure for middle adulthood

Late adult transition

1
2
3
4
5
6
7
8
9
10
11
12
13
14
15
16
17
18
19
20
21
22
23
24
25
26
27
28
29
30
31
32
33
34
35
36
37
38
39
40
41
42
43
44
45
46
47
48
49
50
51
52
53
54
55
56
57
58
59
60
61
62
63
64
65+

(1978, p.92), "If the Dream remains unconnected to his life it may simply die, and with it his sense of aliveness and purpose." The early adult transition is followed by the entry life structure for early adulthood (22–28 years), which is the time during which an initial attempt is made to construct an adult lifestyle. This is followed by the age 30 transition (28–33 years), which is a time for reconsidering and modifying the entry life structure. After that come the culminating life structure for early adulthood (33–40 years), which is the time for trying to realise key aspirations, and the midlife transition (40–45 years), which brings the era of early adulthood to a close and initiates the era of middle adulthood. In this period of transition, people often feel that their lives will never match their dreams. In other words, they have a midlife crisis.

3. *Era of middle adulthood* (40–65 years): this era starts with the midlife transition, followed by the entry life structure for middle adulthood (45–50 years), during which the individual develops a life style for middle age. This is followed by the age 50 transition (50–55 years), during which the life structure from the previous period is reconsidered and modified. The culminating life structure for middle adulthood (55–60 years) is the established life structure towards the end of this era. It is followed by the late adult transition (60–65 years), which spans the end of the era of middle adulthood and the start of the era of late adulthood.

4. *Era of late adulthood* (60+ years): this era begins with the late adult transition, and then moves on to periods concerned with the inevitable adjustments required because of retirement, declining health, and so on.

Two extreme positions are possible with respect to the life cycle. One extreme is to argue that adult development proceeds from one life structure to the next, with a rapid transition between successive structures. The other extreme is to argue that adult development involves almost constant change, with very little stability in the form of life structures being present. Levinson (1986) adopted a compromise

Early adulthood

Middle adulthood

Late adulthood

position, according to which most adults spend about an equal amount of time in fairly stable life structures and in states of transition or change.

Research evidence

Levinson (1978) originally obtained evidence for his theory from interviews with 40 men in their 30s and 40s. There were 10 novelists, 10 biologists, 10 factory workers, and 10 business executives. All of the men were interviewed several times for a total of 10–20 hours over a 3-month period in order to explore in detail the ways in which their life structures had developed during adulthood. He interviewed them again 2 years later, and also interviewed most of their wives. Some years later, Levinson carried out a similar study on 45 women. According to Levinson (1986), both studies indicated a surprisingly great tendency for everyone to proceed through the same periods and eras at about the same ages, though this is not entirely supported by Roberts and Newton (1987) who found gender differences (see the Key Study below).

From your own experience, how would you evaluate Levinson's theory?

Roberts and Newton

Roberts and Newton (1987) investigated adult development in relation to Levinson's theory. They conducted detailed interviews with 39 women. Nearly all of them experienced a transition between the ages of 17 and 22, they had a Dream during that stage, and they went through a transition at about the age of 30. However, there were some important differences between these women and the men studied by Levinson (1978). Men's Dreams tended to revolve around careers, whereas those of women were more complex. Women's Dreams typically included both personal goals (e.g., career) and interpersonal goals (e.g., obligations to others; providing support for a "special man").

How did women resolve this conflict between personal and interpersonal goals? According to Roberts and Newton, many women who have focused mainly on their careers up to the age of 30 start to switch their attention to marriage and family, whereas those who spent their 20s pursuing marriage and family goals begin to think seriously about a career. Thus, the structure of the life cycle is broadly similar in men and women, but there are some important differences in terms of the Dream and major goals.

Discussion points

1. What reasons are there for assuming that young men and young women might have different goals and aspirations?
2. Do you think that there might also be important differences in the structure of the life cycle in individuals from different social classes or from different cultures?

In adolescence there are "developmental universals" such as puberty. Do you think there are developmental universals in adulthood?

Evaluation

The interview method used by Levinson (1986) poses various problems. First, people may not remember clearly what happened to them 20 years earlier. Second, what people say about the past may be deliberately distorted. Third, when the interviewer has a particular theory in mind, this can influence the kinds of questions that are asked and the kinds of answers provided by those being interviewed. Fourth, the fact that Levinson (1978) did not interview anyone who was more than 47 years old in his study on men limits what he can usefully say about men in their 50s and 60s.

Critics of Levinson's theory have often argued that there is no real evidence for a midlife crisis during the early 40s. For example, Vaillant (1977) collected longitudinal data over a period of many years on Harvard graduates. He found that some men did divorce, change jobs, or suffer depression at midlife. However, the frequency of these major changes was about the same throughout adulthood, and there was no real evidence that the early 40s were an unusually difficult or stressful time.

Finally, there is a desperate need for cross-cultural studies in this area, because the structure of the life cycle is likely to be very different in other cultures. For example, there are societies in which life expectancy is only about 40 years. In such societies, it would make little sense to think of the period between 17 and 45 as forming early adulthood!

Could it be that the concept of a midlife crisis, which has been widely popularised, is self-fulfilling?

There are other societies in which women are more or less prohibited from working, and this must influence the Dreams of women in such societies.

Gould's Theory of the Evolution of Adult Consciousness

Gould (1980) extended Freud's theory of personality development (see Section 11, Social and Personality Development) to adulthood, continuing to draw on the ideas of crisis and resolution. The central principle of this theory is that, in order to grow up, you have to progressively give up the fictions of childhood. The "evolution" focus is on how one's consciousness develops in response to life experience.

Research evidence

What comment would you make on the participants that Gould used?

Gould based his stage theory on responses to a questionnaire. The questionnaire was developed through observations of outpatient therapy groups over a period of several months. The patients ranged in age from 16 to over 60. Observers of these "phase of life" groups collected statements that were characteristic of the different age groups. These statements were then placed in a questionnaire and distributed to over 500 white, middle-class people, aged 16–50. There were 160 questions that focused on 10 different areas of life. This enabled Gould to identify statements and concerns that were typical of different age groups. Gould found that the data from his original and later samples indicated close agreement about the kind of statements selected.

Gould calls these statements "false assumptions". They are beliefs that need to be challenged during each phase of development. They are not recipes for successful adulthood but they are developmental issues that "healthy" adults need to address. The four major assumptions are set out in the table below. Gould suggested that false assumptions give us a sense of safety, and protect us from anxiety, which makes it painful to give them up, but they need to be challenged in order for adult consciousness to evolve. Each assumption is typical of particular age groups.

Gould's false assumptions

Age	False assumption	Commentary
18–21	"I will always belong to my parents and believe in their world."	Gould suggested that marriage at this age is an attempt to gain independence but may fail because such marriages are likely to provide greater dependence rather than independence.
22–28	"Doing things my parents' way, with willpower and perseverance, will bring results. But if I become too frustrated, confused, or tired, or am simply unable to cope, they will step in and show me the right way."	Gould referred to this period as "I'm nobody's baby now". The adult must learn that trying is not enough (it would have been enough at a younger age). One's dependence on parents (or a loved one) prevents independence and ultimately leads to feelings of hostility.
28–34	"Life is simple and controllable. There are no significant coexisting contradictory forces within me."	Gould called this phase "opening up what's inside". We may have hidden earlier feelings, goals, interests, and talents, possibly because they caused inner conflict or there wasn't time for such things.
35–45	"There is no evil in me or death in the world. The sinister has been destroyed."	In the midlife transition one must come to terms with mortality. Men have to recognise that success and hard work cannot protect them from dying; women may strike out on their own as a means of challenging man as the protector and coping with their own mortality.

For example, in the phase 22–28 years, the adult may feel, in Gould's (1978, pp.110–111) words:

When our temporary dependence on others to reassure us becomes a fixed requirement—that is, when we expect others to take responsibility for us—we form a conspiracy to avoid confronting our disguised childhood demons. In this conspiracy we don't have to do anything; they, our loved ones, will do all that we can't do for ourselves …

The conspiracy is a no-win situation. Eventually we feel either hostile or dependent and often both. In any case, our simple pact with our loved one becomes a destructive conspiracy that prevents us developing a fuller, more independent adult consciousness.

The gist of these extracts is that dependence on others becomes a "conspiracy", a conspiracy to prevent us taking responsibility for ourselves. But this is a "no-win situation" because you end up wanting support from another and yet also resenting this support. The dependency also prevents independence, which is necessary in order to grow further.

The critical concept here is that the individual has a false assumption (I like being looked after by someone else) and this false assumption prevents healthy development.

To what extent does this struggle between dependence and independence mirror development at earlier ages (e.g., infancy and adolescence)?

Evaluation

The research evidence on which this theory is founded is clearly limited, however the theory provides an interesting approach to understanding adult development. Gould emphasised the misconceptions that individuals need to discard as they progress through adulthood, which has potential use in therapy.

Stage Theories

All three theories discussed in this Unit focus on the idea of discontinuities through life, and of transition points and crises. This may be an unnecessarily negative focus on development, and one that is reflective of our culture as opposed to that of other ethnic groups and also other historical times. In other words, the transitions may be related to the way our society is structured with education up to a certain age, early job and career commitments, end of family involvements, and retirement. This sequence of events is clearly not shared in other cultures where, for example, young people start work at a younger age than in the West and have no thought of "job prospects", and where family commitments do not end.

An alternative approach is to focus more on continuities, such as how personality develops through adulthood, or on life events, the approach taken in the next Unit.

Family and Relationships in Adulthood

A different approach to the study of adulthood is to consider important life events, and the effect of these on an individual's development, rather than expecting to find age-related changes as suggested by the theories of adult development discussed in the previous Unit.

The Life Events Approach

In your AS studies, you considered the Social Readjustment Rating Scale (SRRS) developed by Holmes and Rahe (1967). This is a means of estimating the amount of stress experienced by an individual over a period of time, based on the major life events that the individual has had to cope with. Most adults experience several stressful life events

Do you recall some of the limitations of the SRRS and the life events approach to explaining stress?

Christmas, supposed to be a happy time for joyful family get-togethers, can be a source of considerable stress.

over the years. Close relatives may die, they may get divorced, they may become unemployed, and so on. The Social Readjustment Rating Scale is a list of 43 life events, each of which is assigned a value (out of 100) in terms of its likely impact. You may or may not have been surprised that holidays and Christmas are regarded as sources of stress. However, Holmes and Rahe argued that any change (whether desirable or undesirable) can be stressful. Thus, for example, Holmes and Rahe included marital reconciliation (45 life-change units), gain of a new family member (39), and outstanding personal achievement (28) among the 43 life events.

There have been numerous studies using the Social Readjustment Rating Scale. Those individuals experiencing events totalling more than 300 life-change units (LCUs) over a period of 1 year or so are more at risk for a wide range of physical and mental illnesses. These illnesses include heart attacks, diabetes, TB, asthma, anxiety, and depression. The correlations between life-change units and susceptibility to any particular illness tend to be rather low, rarely exceeding about +0.30. The implication of this is life events have a significant bearing on lifelong development and adjustment.

The Social Readjustment Rating Scale

Rank	Life event	LCU	Rank	Life event	LCU
1	Death of a spouse	100	22	Change in responsibilities at work	29
2	Divorce	73	23	Son/daughter leaves home	29
3	Marital separation	65	24	Trouble with in-laws	29
4	Jail term	63	25	Outstanding personal achievement	28
5	Death of a close family member	63	26	Spouse begins/stops work	26
6	Personal injury or illness	53	27	Begin/end of school	26
7	Marriage	50	28	Change in living conditions	25
8	Fired at work	47	29	Revision of personal habits	24
9	Marital reconciliation	45	30	Trouble with boss	23
10	Retirement	45	31	Change in work hours/conditions	20
11	Change of health of family member	44	32	Change in residence	20
12	Pregnancy	40	33	Change in schools	20
13	Sex difficulties	39	34	Change in recreation	19
14	Gain of new family member	39	35	Change in church activities	19
15	Business readjustment	39	36	Change in social activities	18
16	Change in financial status	38	37	Moderate mortgage or loan	17
17	Death of close friend	37	38	Change in sleeping habits	16
18	Change to different line of work	36	39	Change in number of family get-togethers	15
19	Change in number of arguments with spouse	35	40	Change in eating habits	15
20	Heavy mortgage repayments	31	41	Holiday	13
21	Foreclosure of mortgage or loan	30	42	Christmas	12
			43	Minor violation of the law	11

Adapted from T. Holmes & R. Rahe (1967) The social readjustment rating scale. *Journal of Psychosomatic Research, 11*, 213–218.

Do you think life events tend to occur in clusters?

Evaluation of the life events approach

The approach adopted by Holmes and Rahe (1967) has been very influential, and numerous questionnaire measures of life events have been developed. Their basic assumption that severe life events will increase the probability of being affected by a stress-related illness is a reasonable one that is supported by most of the evidence. On the negative side, there are four key problems with use and interpretation of the Social Readjustment Rating Scale.

Direction of causality

First, it is often not clear whether life events have caused some stress-related illness, or whether stress caused the life events. For example, stress may play an important part in producing life events such as marital separation, change in sleeping habits, or change in eating habits. Schroeder and Costa (1984, pp.859–860) found that

> when health-related, neuroticism-related, and subjective items were included in the life event measure, the customary low-to-moderate correlation with reported illness was obtained. However, ... when these contaminated items were excluded, the remaining items were not correlated with illness, which suggests that illness is essentially independent of the occurrence of life event changes.

Individual variation

The impact of most life events varies from one person to another. For example, marital separation may be less stressful to someone who has already established an intimate relationship with someone else, and who long ago ceased to have any affection for his or her spouse. Brown and Harris (1982) addressed this issue by developing a semi-structured interview approach to life events. This involves detailed questioning about life events in order to understand the background *context*. The likely impact of any given life event on the average person in that context is then assessed. This approach is superior to self-report approaches, but is much more time-consuming.

What are some of the disadvantages of using a semi-structured interview technique?

Memory problems

Memory failures can reduce the usefulness of the Scale. People often cannot remember minor life events from several months ago. Jenkins, Hurst, and Rose (1979) asked their participants to report the life events that had occurred during the same 6-month period, on two occasions 9 months apart. Their total scores were about 40% lower on the second occasion than the first. One way of reducing this problem is to use a structured interview approach in which the interviewer asks several questions about the occurrence and dating of events. Brown and Harris (1982) found that there was much less forgetting when this approach was used.

Desirable vs. undesirable events

Holmes and Rahe (1967) assumed that desirable life events could cause stress-related illnesses. However, most of the evidence does not support that assumption (Paykel, 1974). According to Martin (1989, p.198):

> Desirable events have generally been found to be nonsignificantly related to a variety of dependent measures, and the general consensus at present is that life event measures should include only undesirable events.

Common and Important Life Events in Adulthood

We will now consider three of the life events that are related to high levels of stress: marriage (or partnering), divorce, and parenthood. The problems identified in general for the life events approach, apply equally to each of these individual events.

In addition, many of the issues discussed in Section 2, Relationships, are relevant to the life events discussed here. The formation, maintenance, and dissolution of relationships underlies marriage, divorce, and parenting. In Section 2 we also considered the effects of variations in Western and non-Western cultures on relationships.

Marriage

The high divorce rate and extensive media coverage of marital problems have probably led many people to assume that marriage is a recipe for unhappiness and misery. In fact, most of the evidence suggests exactly the opposite, for example consider the Key Study by Bradburn (1969), below.

Information about some of the reasons why married people tend to be relatively happy was reported by Argyle and Furnham (1983). They found three main factors that determine people's level of satisfaction with different kinds of relationships: material and instrumental help; social and emotional support; and common interests. Spouses were rated higher than those in any kind of non-sexual relationship on all three factors, but especially on material and instrumental help.

Bradburn

What effect do you think the social climate in 1969 might have had on the responses people gave in Bradburn's study? Do people always tell the truth in situations like this?

Bradburn (1969), in a study carried out in the United States, found that 35% of married men and 38% of married women said that they were "very happy". These figures were much higher than those for never-married men and women (18% for each sex). Of those who had been married, but were currently separated, divorced, or widowed, an even smaller percentage were "very happy". For example, only 7% of separated or widowed men said that they were "very happy".

The conclusion that marriage is good for you was strengthened by Bradburn's findings of the percentages of people who admitted that they were "not too happy". Fewer than 10% of married people said that they were "not too happy". This compares with a massive 40% of separated people, as well as over 30% of divorced people. Those who have never been married are less happy than married people. However, they are happier than those who have been married but are no longer in that state, with about 17% of them being "not too happy".

These findings need to be interpreted with care. Divorced people may be less happy than married people mainly because of the fact that they are divorced. However, it is also possible that those who are naturally unhappy and depressed are more likely to become divorced than those who are naturally happy and easy-going.

KEY STUDY EVALUATION — Bradburn

Bradburn's study found that more married people claimed to be very happy compared with single people, 40% of whom said they were "not too happy". However, the study was carried out in 1969 in the United States, at a time when marriage was the norm, and couples who lived together outside marriage were still regarded as slightly outrageous. The demand characteristics of being asked by a stranger about one's happiness at home may have affected married people's responses, as well as those of single people, who in 1969 were expected to aspire to being married.

Discussion points

1. Why might it be that married people are generally happier than those who are not?
2. What are the limitations of self-report measures of happiness?

Graphs showing results from Bradburn's study.

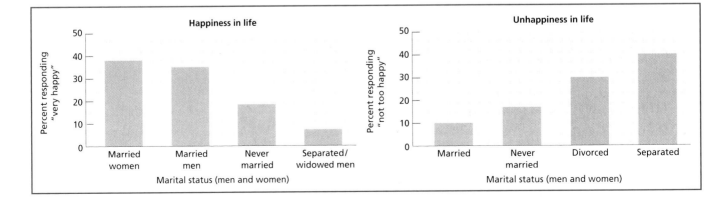

There are two additional points that need to be made. First, many of the studies indicating that marriage is associated with high levels of happiness were carried out many years ago. It is possible that marriage has fewer beneficial effects now than it used to have. Second, there has been a dramatic increase in the number of people cohabiting rather than marrying, and a major reason for this is because cohabitors perceive significant disadvantages in the state of marriage. Therefore marriage itself may no longer be as clearly associated with happiness. According to Cunningham and Antill (1995):

What do you think are the disadvantages and advantages of marriage? Could these explain why more people are cohabiting now?

> *Uneasiness about a lifetime commitment to the present partner or to the institution of marriage continually arises in surveys of cohabitors. Women's uneasiness about the institution of marriage now often stems from their awareness that it is still one of the major sites of gender inequality.*

Changes during marriage

Marital satisfaction tends to change over the years. It has been reported several times (e.g., Glenn & McLanahan, 1982) that there is a U-shaped relationship between marital satisfaction and the length of the marriage. Marital satisfaction declines sharply with the birth of the first child, and only rises again when the last-born child leaves home. One limitation of most of these studies is that married people were usually asked to recall their level of marital satisfaction at different points in the marriage, some of which might have occurred 20 years or more earlier. Obviously, what is recalled over such long periods of time might be inaccurate.

Vaillant and Vaillant (1993) reported a longitudinal study in which married people indicated their level of marital satisfaction at several points over a 40-year period. They found that the husbands' level of marital satisfaction remained about the same over the course of the marriage, and that the wives' level of satisfaction showed a modest decline. The difference between their findings and those of most other researchers could be due to the fact that they did not ask their participants to recall feelings from the distant past. However, there was another important difference between their study and those of other researchers. Their male participants were all graduates from Harvard University, and so on average they were very well off. Their affluence may have prevented them from suffering some of the stresses of child rearing.

A **50th wedding anniversary** celebration.

Mental health

Interpersonal relationships (especially intimate ones) can be very valuable in promoting mental health. For example, married people have much lower rates of mental disorder than single people of the same age (Gove, 1979). Detailed information on this point was provided by Cochrane (1988). He found that the rate of admission to mental hospital was only 0.26% for married people. This was much lower than the rates for those who were not married: 0.77% for single individuals; 0.98% for widowed individuals; and 1.4% for the divorced. There are problems with interpreting these findings. However, the very high figure for divorced people may well occur in part because people who are developing the symptoms of mental disease are more likely to get divorced in the first place.

Social support.   Why do marriage and relationships generally have beneficial effects on mental health? An important reason is the social support that is provided by friends, lovers, and spouses. Much of the relevant evidence was considered in a meta-analysis of 70 studies by Schwarzer and Leppin (1992). They found that there was an overall correlation of −0.22 between social support and depression, indicating that individuals with the most support are least likely to be depressed. However, some of this effect may occur because depressed people are less likely to receive social support.

According to the buffering hypothesis, social support is most effective in improving mental health in stressful conditions. There is some support for this hypothesis. For

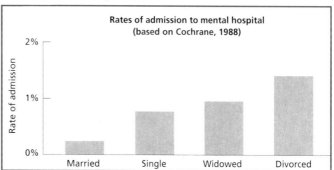

What factors could be the cause of higher rates of mental disorder in divorced people?

example, Cohen and Hoberman (1983) found in high-stress conditions that individuals high in social support reported only two-thirds as many physical symptoms (e.g., headaches, insomnia) as those low in social support. In contrast, social support had no effect on physical symptoms in low-stress conditions.

Thoits (1982) discussed some of the evidence indicating the effectiveness of social support. However, he also pointed out that social support has a number of different dimensions:

- Amount of support.
- Type of support (e.g., emotional versus instrumental).
- Source of support (e.g., spouse, friends, relatives).
- Structure of support networks (e.g., size, accessibility, stability).

Physical health

Evidence that marriage can serve to preserve physical health was obtained by Lynch (1977). Married people were much less likely than single, divorced, or widowed individuals of the same age to die from several kinds of physical conditions. The illnesses of which this was true included diabetes, stroke, various cancers, cirrhosis of the liver, pneumonia, and tuberculosis. The beneficial effects of marriage on physical health were rather stronger in men than in women.

Cultural comparisons

There are significant and important differences in marriage as experienced in different countries. These cultural variations are considered in detail on pages 82–84.

Divorce and separation

Divorce is becoming increasingly common in Western societies. Almost 40% of marriages in Britain end in divorce, and the figure is even higher in the United States. Divorce is especially likely during the first 5 years of marriage, and other "danger periods" are after 15 and 25 years of marriage (Gross, 1996).

Divorce is the second most stressful life event after death of one's spouse according to the Social Readjustment Rating Scale (Holmes & Rahe, 1967). Divorced people tend to have worse mental and physical health than married people (Buunk, 1996). Indeed, their general health is even worse than that of people who are widowed or who have never married.

The stressfulness of divorce depends on a variety of factors. Buunk (1996, p.371) concluded that:

> *Individuals who had a less close relationship with their former partner, who took the initiative to break up or divorce, who are embedded in social networks, and who at present have a satisfying, intimate relationship, are relatively better off. In addition, certain personality characteristics, including high self-esteem, independence, tolerance for change, and egalitarian [favouring equality] sex-role attitudes, facilitate coping with the situation of being divorced.*

The impact of divorce often differs for men and women. Women are likely to suffer more in some ways, because they often lose more financially and have to accept greater parental responsibilities (Rutter & Rutter, 1992). On the other hand, men are less likely than women to initiate divorce proceedings, and they tend to have weaker support networks (Gross, 1996).

Stages

It has been argued that those getting divorced tend to go through a series of stages during the divorce process. For example, Bohannon (1970) proposed the following six stages:

1. *Emotional divorce*: the marriage disintegrates psychologically amid conflict and recrimination.

When divorce was rare and carried a social stigma, cards such as these were unheard of. However, 40% of marriages in Britain now end in divorce.

2. *Legal divorce*: the marriage ends officially and legally.
3. *Economic divorce*: the assets of the divorced couple are divided up.
4. *Co-parental divorce*: issues relating to custody of any children of the marriage and access rights to them are decided.
5. *Community divorce*: the necessary changes are made to relationships with family and friends.
6. *Psychic divorce*: the two divorced people adjust separately to the new state of affairs.

As with most stage theories, it may be doubted whether everyone who gets divorced works their way neatly through these six stages in the specified order.

Research evidence

Studies of the effects of marriage also have looked at the effects of divorce, indicating that it is or will be associated with poorer psychological and physical health. For example, in Cochrane's (1988) study described earlier, the proportion of the population admitted to mental hospitals was 1.4% for divorced individuals, 0.77% for single individuals, and only 0.26% for married people.

Many studies that look at divorce consider especially the effects on the children. Amato et al. (1995) conducted a 12-year study of 2033 married people, some of whom divorced over the course of the study. The researchers were able to interview nearly 500 adult offspring who had lived in the same household as the parents at the time of the initial interviews. They found that:

- In high-conflict families, the young adults were coping better if their parents divorced than if they stayed together.
- In low-conflict families, the young adults coped better if their parents stayed together than if they divorced.

This appears to suggest that conflict is worse than divorce, but where there is low conflict it is better for parents to remain together.

Evaluation

The effects of divorce vary greatly depending on the personalities of those involved, on the nature of the previous relationship between them, and on the existence (or otherwise) of another intimate relationship and a strong social network. The available evidence is limited. Divorced people are less happy and more stressed than non-divorced people, and this could occur because divorce makes people stressed, or because stressed and unhappy people seek divorce. We don't know exactly what is going on, but there is evidence that certain kinds of people tend to divorce. For example, identical twins whose co-twin has divorced are rather more likely to become divorced than identical twins whose co-twin has not divorced (Plomin, 1997). The genetic factors that play a part in determining who becomes divorced may also tend to produce negative emotional states.

Do you think that stress is always a negative factor in people's lives?

Parenting

Gaining a new member of the family is one of the more stressful life events in the Social Readjustment Rating Scale (Holmes & Rahe, 1967). This may seem surprising. However, becoming a parent involves numerous changes in life style, a marked reduction in free time, and a considerable increase in responsibility. It also produces a change of role, with parents defining themselves and being defined by others as occupying the roles of father and mother. As Bee (1994) pointed out, parents with young children have much less time for each other. As a result, they have fewer conversations with each other, less sex, and spend less time doing routine chores together.

These factors help to explain why studies carried out in Western societies consistently indicate that the arrival of the first child reduces marital satisfaction (e.g., Reibstein & Richards, 1992). This adverse effect is found in all religious groups, races, and at all educational levels (Eysenck, 1990). It is stronger in women than in men, in

Could parenting be a factor in the reduction in time parents spend together when a baby is born?

What effect do you think extended families in non-Western cultures might have on the early experiences of parenting.

The life event called "parenthood" loves a vast range of different experiences. Is it possible to offer any kind of global view of its effects on adult development?

Coping with sudden infant death

Some of the stresses of parenthood are rare, but occasionally parents do have to cope with a very sick or dying child. Palmer (1997) conducted interviews with 12 African-American mothers whose infants had died suddenly (SIDS). The aim of the study was to document the social and emotional impact of such deaths. The study considered the mother's reaction to her child's death, avenues of support, coping strategies, multiple stressors, the role of family and religion in dealing with the death, the mother's relationship with the child's father, and the mother's treatment by healthcare workers and the police.

The mother's grief reactions were characterised by intense physical and emotional distress, and self-blame. On average it took the mothers about 2 years to recover such that they felt they could resume normal activities. There was a tendency of many of the fathers to attribute the child's death to the mother. Among the characteristics unique to this group of mothers were the attribution of the death to "God's Will", a need to be "strong" in coping with the infant's death, a tendency in many mothers to isolate themselves from family members despite the family's willingness to lend support, and the prevalence of death in the family, either due to natural or violent causes.

One important point to consider, which is relevant to any bereavement research, is that the sample is biased by the fact that only those willing to be interviewed are participants. It is possible that those who are most especially distressed during bereavement, or those least distressed, may not wish to be interviewed.

Discussion points

1. What ethical considerations might be especially important in research of this kind?

2. What practical value might stem from such research?

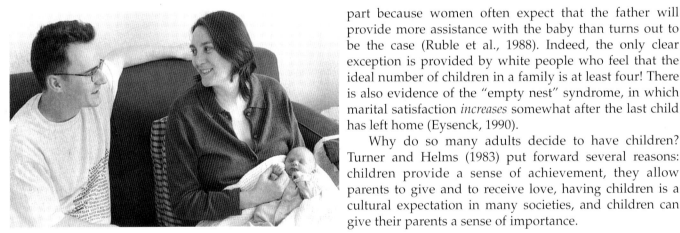

The arrival of a new baby is stressful for both parents.

part because women often expect that the father will provide more assistance with the baby than turns out to be the case (Ruble et al., 1988). Indeed, the only clear exception is provided by white people who feel that the ideal number of children in a family is at least four! There is also evidence of the "empty nest" syndrome, in which marital satisfaction *increases* somewhat after the last child has left home (Eysenck, 1990).

Why do so many adults decide to have children? Turner and Helms (1983) put forward several reasons: children provide a sense of achievement, they allow parents to give and to receive love, having children is a cultural expectation in many societies, and children can give their parents a sense of importance.

Relevant factors

The extent to which parents adjust successfully or unsuccessfully to the arrival of a baby depends on several factors. For example, working-class parents show less dissatisfaction with parenthood than do middle-class parents (Russell, 1974). A possible reason for this is that becoming a parent is more likely to have a serious disruptive effect on the career plans of middle-class women. Having said this, the financial implications may be greater for working-class parents.

In addition, couples differ in how well they adjust to the demands of parenting. Couples who are psychologically close before the birth of their first child are most likely to adjust well to the baby's arrival. For example, couples whose interactions were most positive during the months of pregnancy, and who showed respect to each other when conflicts arose, dealt most successfully with their roles as parents (Heinicke & Guthrie, 1992). Fathers feel more positive about their role and mothers behave more warmly towards their children in couples who confide in each other (Cox et al., 1989).

The age and financial circumstances of parents are also important in determining how well they adjust to having a baby. Couples who are young and who have adequate amounts of money tend to be happier parents than couples who are older and poorer (Bee & Mitchell, 1984).

Is it more likely, today, that older parents would be better off?

As might be expected, the extent to which mothers are satisfied with the role of mother influences their reactions to their children. Lerner and Galambos (1985) carried out a study in the United States, and found that children are more likely to be rejected if their mother is dissatisfied with her role. In addition, the children are more likely to become difficult to handle.

Evaluation

It is very hard to draw general conclusions from research on parenting. There are two main reasons. First, the impact of a baby on its parents depends on numerous factors. These factors include social class, the attitude of the mother to her new role, the psychological closeness of the parents, the extent to which the parents confide in each other, the age of the parents, and the financial means of the parents. Other factors that are likely to be important are whether the baby was planned and whether or not the parents have other young children.

How would you design a study to look at how couples adjust to being parents? What ethical issues might be involved?

Second, the three people in the basic family (father, mother, child) typically interact in complex ways with each other. As a result, it is usually hard to work out exactly *why* any given couple finds parenting a stressful experience. For example, a married couple may argue that parenting is stressful because their child cries a lot and behaves badly. However, it is possible that the child's mother has not behaved with enough warmth and sensitivity to produce secure attachment of the child to its mother. In other words, it is often hard to establish cause and effect.

Cognitive Changes in Late Adulthood

One of the greatest changes during the course of the twentieth century was the dramatic increase in the number of older people in most Western societies. In the United States, for example, the average life span increased by 26 years, and the proportion of people over 65 increased from 1 in 30 to about 1 in 6. As a result of this enormous increase in the number of old people, there has been a growth of interest in trying to understand the ways in which they adjust to the ageing process.

We will also consider two life events that are common to old age, retirement and bereavement, and finally some theoretical accounts of healthy adjustment in old age. In a sense all of this is *cognitive* insofar as the term "cognitive" refers to the way individuals think about their behaviour.

Ageing is not necessarily synonymous with withdrawal from society.

Cognitive Changes in Old Age

There are two opposing views of cognitive abilities in old age. One is the view that our mental abilities decline with age, the other is the picture of the wise older person who may have lost some of their marbles but retains the key elements of knowledge and the ability to use it. Which is true?

Intelligence

Wechsler (1955) compiled the normative data for WAIS, the Wechsler Adult Intelligence Scale. He found that intelligence reaches a peak around the age of 30. However, the sample was cross-sectional, which means that people of different ages were tested at the same point in time. It is probable that people of 60 in 1955 were not as intelligent as the 20-year-olds because when they were younger they had experienced poorer diets and also less sophisticated education. Schaie (1983) found, from a longitudinal study in Seattle, that **cohort effects** equal or exceed age differences. Burns (1966) reported a longitudinal study where a set of people were tested at age 22 and again when they were 56; on average their

Do you think that intellectual decline is an inevitable feature of old age?

IQs were higher when they were older. This supports the view that cross-sectional data may give an inaccurate picture.

There is also the issue of defining intelligence in general. One distinction has been made between "crystallised" and "fluid" intelligence. Cattell (1963) suggested that the latter is a general intellectual capacity, whereas the former encompasses problem solving and knowledge, which comes from experience. Schultz et al. (1980) found declines in fluid intelligence and spontaneous flexibility with age, but they found that some older participants were the best of all. Baltes and Baltes (1990) claim that fluid intelligence actually declines with age but that crystallised intelligence may increase with age.

However, longitudinal studies suffer from their own problems because of selective dropout. When people are tested 30 years later, after the beginning of a study, some participants are no longer willing or available for testing. It is possible that the more intelligent participants are the ones who remain in a study. This can be seen in a study by Larsen (1997). At the start there were over 1000 participants, aged between 30 and 60. Eleven years later, 300 participants were no longer available. Many of these were the ones who had only received primary schooling and had the lowest social status.

There is a further problem with studies of intelligence in old age. Some older people are suffering from illnesses which may affect intellectual capacity, such as Alzheimer's disease. This would affect average statistics and might make it appear that older people are less intelligent.

Memory

There is evidence that memory does decline. For example, Talland (1968) found that participants aged 77 to 89 remembered less than half the number of items that a 20- to 25-year-old age group could recall on a short-term memory task, and also forgot more in the initial 90 seconds after presentation of a three-letter word. Kimmel (1990) suggested that there may be dramatic declines shown in laboratory memory experiments and some everyday memory skills, but older people show highly competent memory skills in other areas, such as long-term recall or expert memory skills (e.g., playing chess).

It is also possible that motivation can account for age differences. In a study on memory performance (Levy & Langer, 1994) it was found that Chinese elderly and those who were profoundly deaf outperformed normal hearing Americans on memory tasks. The explanation offered was that the former two groups had not acquired negative stereotypes of the elderly and thus they had higher expectations of their abilities in old age. The hearing Americans had reduced expectations, which depressed their performance.

One reason for apparent improvement with age, or at least a lack of decline, may be because elderly individuals have sometimes developed strategies for coping with deficits. Warren and Warren (1970) reported that older participants used different strategies for compensating for poorer short-term memories.

Other cognitive tasks

There are many other aspects of cognitive performance. Crossman and Szafran (1956) established that older participants took longer on tasks involving discrimination when the number of alternatives increased. McDonald (1995) found that some older people could not cope with Piaget's three mountains task (see page 367), which requires **decentration**. It may be that they could do the task but, when faced with a difficult situation they reverted to a pre-concrete level of thought.

Problems in assessing ability

Piaget's description of cognitive development is in Section 10. What age group of children cannot decentre?

As we have already noted, it is difficult to truly assess cognitive abilities in old age in *normal* individuals because some elderly have decreased abilities due to the effects of strokes and other progressive illnesses. Birren et al. (1963) examined a group of men aged

65–91; some had no obvious symptoms of disease but, on close medical examination, they in fact had certain mild diseases, which would subtly affect performance.

A further reason for decline is that some elderly lack of stimulation and this may explain their reduced abilities rather than old age *per se*. Institutionalised elderly people may suffer similar ill-effects to children in orphanages. Rubin (1973) found that elderly people living in their own homes performed better on Piagetian tasks than those living in institutions.

Common Life Events in Old Age

Retirement

For many people, retirement is very much looked forward to. It is a time when they can engage in leisure activities, spend time with family and friends, and be relieved of the pressures of work. However, this is not true for everyone. Some people enjoy their working lives for the sense of identity it provides and the social contacts. For both groups, retirement can be like becoming unemployed.

Phases of adjustment
Atchley (1982) describes six phases of adjustment, as outlined in the box on the right. The intention was to outline possible phases that are not necessarily experienced by everyone but suggest a typical experience of retirement. The duration of each phase is also variable. One recommendation arising from this outline is that pre-retirement education can be helpful in preventing the honeymoon phase and the rather inevitable dis-enchantment phase that follows it.

Factors that affect the experience of retirement
There are a several factors that help or hinder the retirement experience. It clearly depends to what extent work was a fundamental part of the individual's life. Some people maintain contact with work colleagues, who may also have retired. For most retired people their circle of social contacts inevitably decreases. In couples, where the wife may have been at home throughout the man's working life, there are major adjustments to be made in having to spend a great deal more time together. This is difficult for both partners.

Work also offers a daily routine, so the individual has to develop a whole new set of routines. This is reflected in Atchley's scheme where the stability phase recognises the need to finally re-establish order. The lack of routine and direction gives the individual a sense of insecurity and possibly uselessness. Some individuals may have had hobbies throughout their working life and thus continue to have a purpose.

Work also provides money and status. Many individuals may not have the money to do the things they would like to do, or failing health may prevent this. Work also gives identity. Some individuals may avoid the loss of identity by continuing with their jobs in an altered capacity, for example acting as an adviser or helping out occasionally. This is more likely for professional jobs, though a loss of identity is also most likely with such jobs. Where an individual has worked in a physically demanding job there may be little loss of identity and there may also be improved health after retirement!

If retirement is voluntary and looked forward to with anticipation and relief then it will be a more pleasant experience than when it is involuntary or possibly earlier than anticipated. We may gain insights into involuntary retirement by looking at research into unemployment (see box overleaf).

Atchley's phases of adjustment to retirement

The pre-retirement phase. Prior to retirement the individual begins to think of some of the consequences such as financial changes and lifestyle changes. This phase is subdivided into "remote" and "near" to express the fact that people start to think about retirement quite a while before it actually happens.

Honeymoon phase. Just after retirement there is a period of relative enjoyment and euphoria. It feels as if one is on holiday and it is usually a very busy time. This is especially so for an individual who has taken voluntary retirement.

Disenchantment phase. Following the elation of the honeymoon phase, the individual may feel disappointment and even depression when much looked-forward-to activities fail to measure up to expectations. Some of the problems may arise because failing health means that it is not possible to do as much as one would have liked, or it is possible that one's partner becomes ill or dies.

Reorientation phase. A time to develop a more realistic approach to retirement and to consider new, previously unplanned activities. The individual may seek new roles such as engaging in voluntary work.

Stability phase. Life has taken on an orderly routine again, where the individual can cope with new opportunities as before retirement.

Termination phase. Ultimately poor health may make self-care impossible and significant lifestyle changes are required.

Involuntary retirement—unemployment

When an older person is forced to retire unexpectedly the experience is similar to becoming unemployed. Conversely, when an individual becomes unemployed at a late stage in life, this effectively becomes retirement. Unemployment differs from most people's experience of retirement because it is sudden and unexpected. But there are overlaps and parallels.

Not surprisingly, the psychological effects of unemployment tend to be negative. For example, Hepworth (1980) compared employed and unemployed British men on a measure of general distress containing items about feelings of anxiety, depression, worthlessness, hopelessness, and so on. The distress scores were six times higher for the unemployed men than for those in employment.

Unemployment also has negative physical effects. Moser et al. (1984) carried out a 10-year longitudinal study on males who were aged between 15 and 64 at the start of the study. Men who were unemployed initially were significantly more likely than employed men to die during the course of the study, and this was especially so for death by suicide or lung cancer.

In spite of the fact that unemployment generally has negative effects, the size of these effects depends on the circumstances in which unemployed people find themselves. For example, unemployment is likely to be especially damaging to a relatively poor middle-aged person who is supporting a large family and who has little chance of finding another job. In contrast, unemployment will have less impact on someone who is wealthy and due to retire anyway. Warr (1987) pointed out that about 10% of unemployed men actually report an improvement in their health since losing their jobs. This mostly happens because their jobs damaged their physical health, but some unemployed men reported improved psychological health as well.

Why does unemployment typically impair psychological and/or physical health? Warr (1987) argued that there are nine environmental factors that influence psychological well-being, with unemployment tending to change all of these factors for the worse:

1. *Availability of money*: unemployed people typically have less money at their disposal.
2. *Opportunity for control*: unemployed people are less able to behave as they choose.
3. *Opportunity for skill use*: this generally decreases as a result of unemployment.
4. *Goals and task demands*: unemployment reduces the demands on people, and can make their behaviour less purposeful and goal-directed.
5. *Variety*: unemployed people tend to have less variety and change in their everyday lives than those in employment.
6. *Physical security*: unemployed people may worry about the loss of adequate housing or may be unable to pay for fuel for heating and lighting.
7. *Opportunity for interpersonal contact*: unemployed people typically have social contact with fewer people than do employed people.
8. *Environmental clarity*: unemployed people tend to be more uncertain about the future than those in employment.
9. *Valued social position*: unemployed people lose the socially approved role they filled when they were employed, and this can cause reduced self-esteem.

You can see that these factors are equally applicable to retirement as well as to unemployment.

Bereavement

According to the Social Readjustment Rating Scale (Holmes & Rahe, 1967), bereavement in the form of death of one's spouse is the most stressful life event that people experience. There are several reasons for this. For most married people, death of their spouse causes considerable emotional trauma, because they have lost the central relationship in their lives. In addition, it typically also requires great changes in the life structure of the bereaved person. Finally, bereavement also has a major impact on the bereaved person's social identity. They lose their role as partner in a marriage, and adopt the lesser role of widow or widower. This can pose particular problems in those societies in which social life is organised mainly around married couples.

Stroebe et al. (1982) argued that the loss of one's spouse affects the survivor's social functioning in four main ways:

1. Loss of social and emotional support: this is the key loss.
2. Loss of social validation of personal judgements: an individual's spouse can help to make them confident about the correctness of their views.
3. Loss of material and task supports: in most marriages, there is some role differentiation, with the husband and wife focusing on different tasks and activities; after bereavement, the survivor has to take on the tasks done hitherto by the spouse.
4. Loss of social protection: the spouse can no longer defend the survivor from unfair treatment by other people.

Stages

Parkes (1986) argued that bereaved people go through a series of stages following the death of their spouse. First, there is a period of shock and numbness. Second, there is a period of intense longing for the dead spouse. Third, there is a prolonged period of depression and general hopelessness. Fourth, the bereaved person does what is possible to construct a new life for himself or herself.

Ramsay and de Groot (1977) argued that the processes involved in coming to terms with bereavement do not occur in the predictable ways assumed by stage theorists. According to them, there are nine components of grief, which may occur in various different orders: (1) shock or numbness; (2) disorganisation or an inability to plan sensibly; (3) denial (e.g., expecting the dead spouse to arrive home); (4) depression; (5) guilt at having neglected the dead spouse or having treated him or her badly; (6) anxiety about the future; (7) aggression (e.g., towards the doctors or members of one's family); (8) resolution or acceptance of what has happened; (9) reintegration or reorganisation of one's life.

It has often been suggested that the final stage of grief involves recovery from bereavement. However, Stroebe et al. (1993) argued that total recovery is often not possible: "if there has been a strong attachment to a lost loved one, emotional involvement is likely to continue, even for a lifetime".

One might also consider the bereavement one feels about one's own death, anticipatory bereavement. Kübler-Ross (1969) outlined "stages of dying", basing this on accounts of bereavement and on interviews with over 200 dying patients. This stage account has been very influential in counselling both dying and bereaved individuals (see box on this page).

Do you think that we deal with death the same way as people did 100 years ago? What differences are there and what psychological consequences could there be?

Evidence

Nearly everyone who is bereaved experiences a range of grief reactions. Indeed, there are still signs of grief and other negative emotions 2½ years after bereavement (Thompson et al., 1991). However, bereavement is somewhat less stressful if the person who dies has been ill for some time beforehand (Eisdorfer & Wilkie, 1977). Bereavement is also less stressful on average when the bereaved person is old rather than young (Stroebe & Stroebe, 1987). An important part of the reason for this is probably that the loss is more likely to be unexpected when the person who dies is young.

Stroebe et al. (1982) reported evidence that those who have been bereaved are at increased risk of death from cirrhosis of the liver, accidents, strokes, coronary heart disease, and violence. Widowers are more at risk than widows so far as deaths from cirrhosis of the liver and violence are concerned. Gallagher-Thompson et al. (1993) carried out a longitudinal study, in which they confirmed that bereaved men and women are at increased risk of premature death. They also found that the bereaved who died were less integrated socially than those who did not: their spouse had been the main person in whom they confided; they had small social networks; and they were generally less involved in social activities.

Gender differences

It is much more common for the wife to be bereaved than for the husband. About 85% of married people who are bereaved are widows, against only 15% who are widowers. It is often argued that men find it harder to adjust to loss of their spouse than do women (Cavenaugh, 1994). One reason is that, for many men, their wife is their only close friend, whereas women tend to have a wider circle of friends. Another reason is that many men lack the housekeeping and cooking skills needed to look after themselves properly. Men tend to be older than women when they are widowed, and this makes it harder for them to cope. In view of this evidence, it is only to be expected that bereaved men are more

> ### Kübler-Ross' stages of dying
>
> The following stages of dying were identified by Kübler-Ross:
>
> 1. *Denial and isolation.* Patient's first response tends to be "No, not me, it cannot be true". This is seen as a healthy manner of coping with shocking, unpleasant news. In the short term it acts as a buffer. In Kübler-Ross' study only three patients remained in denial to the very end. The "isolation" aspect refers to the reaction of others, which is often to avoid a dying (or bereaved) person.
> 2. *Anger.* The beginning of acceptance is to feel anger, "Why me?" The patient may also feel "I am not dead yet!" Kübler-Ross advises carers to deal with the anger by giving comfort and respect.
> 3. *Bargaining.* Once the reality sets in, the anger is not going to be effective, the individual may try to "bargain" by, for example, praying to God or asking just to remain alive until, for example, an expected grandchild is born. Not everyone tries to bargain but it is an attempt to find a little extra time or to find some way out.
> 4. *Depression.* After anger and attempts at appeasement, another characteristic response is depression. Kübler-Ross suggested that there may be "reactive depression", that is feeling depressed about things associated with the illness such as physical disfigurement. There is also "preparatory depression", which is sadness and grief about giving up the things in this world. Kübler-Ross recommended that it is important to allow individuals to express their sorrow in order to reach a final acceptance.
> 5. *Acceptance.* If a patient has been able to work through the preceding phases, he or she may face death with a sense of acceptance. Kübler-Ross commented that the patient may "contemplate his end with a certain degree of quiet expectation". At this time visits with the patient may be quite meaningful for others too.
>
> These stages may not follow in a sequence, but may come and go. They may also be accompanied by *hope* of some last-minute recovery.

Do you think that Gallagher-Thompson et al.'s findings would apply equally to non-Western cultures? What cross-cultural differences might you find?

likely than bereaved women to suffer from ill health and rapid death (Bury & Holme, 1991).

The effects of widowhood on women depend to a large extent on the nature of the relationship they had with their husband. Women who have defined themselves in terms of their husband experience a loss of identity, and generally find it very hard to adjust to widowhood (Lopata, 1979). In contrast, those whose lives have had a broader focus cope better and do not suffer much loss of identity. There is also evidence that widows who have strong relationships with other people (especially their own children) manage to adjust more successfully than those who do not (Field & Minkler, 1988).

Another difference between the sexes is that women who are bereaved are less likely than men to remarry. Lopata (1979) reported that widows are often reluctant to surrender their independence, and they are also concerned about the possibility of being widowed for a second time. In contrast, men often favour remarriage because they find it harder than women to achieve psychological closeness with people outside the home.

It is possible that sex differences in reactions to bereavement are in decline. As Stuart-Hamilton (1994, p.121) suggested, "the current societal re-evaluation of gender roles may eradicate whatever differences there are".

Ways of coping

What other formalised rites may assist the grieving process?

All societies have formalised rites to help cope with the bereavement process. The funeral itself is a key part of this, though even before this people are encouraged to make contact with the dead person to begin the grieving process. In our culture people used to sit with the body in the time before burial, and in some cultures it is still the practice to groom the dead person. There is research that supports the importance of close physical contact as a means of assisting the bereavement process. For example, Dorner and Atwell (1985) found that parents welcomed the hospital's policy of encouraging frequent contact with babies born with spina bifida, and it facilitated the grieving process.

Bereavement is like the ending of all relationships. Duck (1982) described the last phase of relationship breakdown as the "grave-dressing phase" (see page 74). The analogy is not accidental since recovery from bereavement also involves finding some way to interpret the ending and move on.

Explanations of Adjustment to Old Age

Do you think that society's stereotypes of older people lead to a self-fulfilling prophecy effect?

Adjustment to old age is hard for many reasons. Older people have typically retired from paid employment, their friends and close relatives may die, their physical health is declining, and they have reduced opportunities to be involved in society. In addition, they have to cope with negative stereotypes of old age. Goldman and Goldman (1981) asked more than 800 children in various Western countries their views on old age and concluded (1981, p.408) that the mere figures

> *do not convey the revulsion and often disgust expressed about old age by many children of all ages. Descriptions of wrinkled skin, sickness, feebleness and increasing fragility were often accompanied by grimaces and emotional negativisms.*

Older people recognise the negative view of them held by society. Graham and Baker (1989) asked students and people in their 60s to indicate the status level of people of different ages. Both groups agreed that status level is low in young children, rises among those in their teens, 20s, and 30s, and declines in older people. The status level of 80-year-olds was as low as that of 5-year-olds.

What do old people regard as of most importance to allow them to enjoy a good quality of life? Ferris and Branston (1994) found that relationships, social networks, and good health were the three most important factors. The importance of social support was also found by Russell and Catrona (1991). Elderly people with little social support were more likely to develop depressive symptoms over a 1-year period. Many old people have very little money, and so financial security is another important factor. Krause et al. (1991) found in America and in Japan that elderly people with financial problems experienced depression and a sense of worthlessness.

Social disengagement theory

Cumming and Henry (1961) put forward the social disengagement theory. According to the theory, there are various reasons why older people become less and less actively involved in society. Some of the reasons are due to factors beyond the control of the individual, such as compulsory retirement, deaths of relatives and friends, and children moving away from home. In addition, many older people choose to reduce the scope of their social lives, spending more and more of their time on their own. According to Cumming and Henry, progressive disengagement is the best way of adjusting to old age.

These theoretical ideas were developed by Cumming (1975). He argued that there is a gradual shrinkage of the life space in older people. This happens as they come to occupy fewer roles and have social interactions with fewer people. In addition, society has fewer expectations of older people with respect to those roles that they do continue to occupy. Finally, older people actively disengage from most of society, and this is the appropriate way of coping with external and internal pressures. The external pressures include a reduced need by others for the skills and abilities the older person possesses, and the internal pressures include deteriorating physical health and a decreasing level of concern about other people.

Research evidence

Cumming and Henry (1961) provided some support for their disengagement theory. They carried out a 5-year study on people between the ages of 50 and 90 living in Kansas City in the United States. They found substantial evidence that older people do progressively disengage from society. Somewhat different conclusions emerged from a follow-up study of over half of the original sample by Havighurst et al. (1968). They found that older people showed increasing disengagement as they aged. However, those who remained most socially active and involved tended to be the most contented, which is inconsistent with disengagement theory. Studies in the United Kingdom and Australia have found that the majority of elderly people do not show the social disengagement predicted by Cumming and Henry (1961). For example, many of them remain very active socially through the church or through community organisations (see Durkin, 1995).

On the other hand, two findings of Havighurst et al. were more supportive of disengagement theory. First, they found that some of those studied were *disengagers*, meaning that they had chosen to disengage themselves from social activities, but were nevertheless happy. For example, individuals who have always been rather reclusive tend to disengage in their later years (Maddox, 1970).

Second, in spite of their declining levels of social engagement, older adults were less likely than younger ones to experience loneliness. This suggests that disengagement may become progressively more appropriate for people as they age. Lieberman and Coplan (1970) found evidence for disengagement during the last 2 years of life. However, in many cases this disengagement was forced on the individual by ill-health and was not a voluntary choice.

Evidence that older people cope with stressful situations in a more passive and disengaged way than younger people was reported by Folkman et al. (1987). Elderly people reported using passive and emotion-focused coping strategies in stressful

■ Activity: Form groups to address the following questions and report your findings:

1. Is growing old a one-way ticket to decline?
2. If you were designing a study of older people, what design features would you include and why?
3. Do psychologists feel the same now as they have in the past about such issues as intelligence and memory capacities in the older person?
4. Has the way society deals with the older person changed in recent years?

Illness, loneliness, and an unwillingness or inability to cope with day-to-day problems may lead older people to move to sheltered housing or a retirement home.

Do you think that progressive disengagement occurs naturally, due to the factors mentioned in the text, or do people choose to disengage?

Recent studies suggest that the majority of elderly people do not show social disengagement, but instead remain socially active.

Do developmental theories tend to ignore individual differences?

situations, whereas younger people tended to prefer active, problem-focused coping strategies.

Cultural differences

There are important cultural differences in the extent to which older people disengage from society. In many non-Western cultures, elderly people tend to be actively involved in society, and they are given respect and authority because of their age (Tout, 1989). For example, elderly women in India generally maintain an active role in the lives of their community (Merriman, 1984). However, this is not the case with all non-Western cultures. Nomadic peoples who are frequently moving on from one place to the next often show little respect towards the elderly, because they reduce the mobility of the entire group (Tout, 1989).

As the years go by, so Western influences are spreading throughout much of the world. This has led to a marked reduction in the extended family with the grandparents at its head in numerous cultures in Africa and Asia. The growing tendency towards social exclusion of elderly people in some of these cultures was observed by Turnbull (1989) among the Ik people of Uganda. They have experienced a number of stressful social and economic circumstances, which are responsible in part for growing hostility towards the elderly. When outsiders offered help (e.g., medication) to elderly members of the Ik people, considerable resentment was shown towards them for providing assistance to the "dead".

Evaluation

Older people generally show some signs of disengagement from society, although the extent of this disengagement is often less than was suggested by Cumming (1975). In addition, there are more signs of disengagement among older people shortly before death. However, it seems likely that disengagement occurs more because of external factors (e.g., retirement) than because older people *want* to disengage themselves from society.

One of the greatest limitations of disengagement theory is that it is based on the implicit assumption that all older adults are basically similar. This assumption is incorrect, because there are important personality and cultural factors that determine whether or not older people will disengage, as we have seen. It is known that adult personalities change only modestly during the adult years (Conley, 1984), and so those who are sociable and extraverted during the years of early adulthood and middle age are likely to remain sociable and socially engaged into old age. In contrast, there are many middle-aged people who are unsociable, and so are likely to become disengaged years before they reach old age (Bee, 1994). In other words, individual differences in personality allow us to predict fairly well whether any given person will or will not disengage in later life.

Images of old people change with the times. In the 1880s far fewer people survived into their 70s. How would theories such as disengagement theory have applied to people who had no welfare system to help them in their old age? In the 1940s life expectancy had improved for many reasons, and nowadays staying young in outlook and being active are the goals for many aged 70 and over.

CASE STUDY: *Wisdom in Old Age—Laurens van der Post*

Laurens van der Post was born in South Africa in 1906 and died in 1996 at the age of 90. He spent his childhood in Africa, where he developed a closeness with and a fascination for the culture and beliefs of the native people of the Kalahari desert. Later he sailed on a whaling ship and then undertook a long voyage to Japan, which in the 1930s was closed to many Westerners. During the Second World War he fought in the South-East Asian jungle and was taken prisoner by the Japanese. After the war he travelled the world and wrote many books, both fiction and non-fiction, about the cultures and countries he came to know. He was a friend and admirer of the psychiatrist and psychologist Carl Jung.

All this varied experience led van der Post to become a writer and thinker who was deeply concerned with human spirituality, and in his later years he was regarded as a mentor by many people, including the Prince of Wales. In his old age he was valued for his wisdom and insight in a way that is rare in Western society, although it is interesting to note that much of his early life was spent in close contact with non-Western cultures. In a collection of conversations with a friend published in 1986 (Pottiez, 1986, p.146) van der Post is described as " ... like a white Bushman and the earth is your hunting ground". Van der Post himself responds:

> *I do not know ... but I think one's whole life is a search ... the whole of life consists of making your way back to where you came from and becoming reunited with it in greater awareness than when you left it; by then adding to it your own awareness, you become part of the cosmic awareness.*

Disengagement theory also fails to take cultural factors into account. We have seen that there are significant cultural differences in the ways in which older people are regarded. Of particular importance here is the distinction between individualism and collectivism (Triandis, 1994). In Western societies, with their **individualist** emphasis on personal achievement, older people with their declining powers are likely to be at least partially rejected by society. In the **collectivist** societies of Asia and Africa, on the other hand, the greater emphasis on co-operation and supportive groups leads to older people remaining more integrated and engaged with society (Triandis, 1994).

There may, of course, be cohort or generational effects. Those who are elderly now grew up in a society that was much less affluent, in which medical treatment was less developed, and in which life expectancy was less. In contrast, those who are currently young or middle aged are likely on average to be more secure financially and healthier when they become elderly. It is thus possible that any tendency towards disengagement among the current elderly may be greatly reduced in following generations.

Do you think that self-perception could affect the way some people cope with ageing?

Activity theory

Havighurst (1964) and other theorists have put forward a different approach to ageing, known as activity theory. According to this theory, older people become somewhat disengaged from society, not because they choose to, but because that is the way that they are treated by society. For example, many workers are forced to retire against their wishes because they have reached the age of 60 or 65, or for some other reason. It is assumed within activity theory that the best strategy for older people to adopt is to remain as active as they can. This involves hanging on to as many of the activities they were involved in during middle age for as long as possible.

Of particular importance is the need to keep involved in numerous different roles within society, trying to replace any roles that have disappeared with new ones. In other words, they need to maintain their "role count". This can be done by starting new hobbies, joining clubs (e.g., a theatre club), or babysitting their grandchildren.

How would you evaluate activity theory? Perhaps you can think of individuals who fit this profile, but does it apply to everyone?

Research evidence

Evidence that activity theory describes older people better than does disengagement theory was reported by Atchley (1977), who argued that "most people continue to do in retirement the same kinds of things they did when they were working". Atchley reported on the percentages of men and women continuing to fulfil various social roles in their 70s and beyond. Among men aged between 70 and 74 (the figures for men aged 75 and over are in brackets),

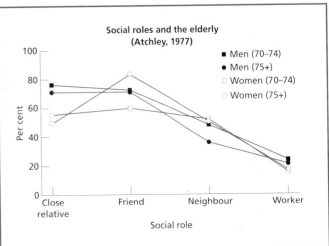

Which data from Atchley's study do you think are most significant?

76% (71%) had contact with close relatives, 72% (71%) had the role of friend, 48% (36%) that of neighbour, and 24% (21%) that of worker. Among women aged between 70 and 74 (the figures for older women are in brackets), 56% (50%) had contact with close relatives, 60% (83%) had the role of friend, 52% (50%) that of neighbour, and 16% (17%) that of worker. Thus, most elderly people in the United States have a variety of active social roles.

Heckhausen (1997) presented evidence that older people remain active and motivated in their lives. He studied three groups of people (20- to 35-year-olds; 40- to 55-year-olds; and those 60 plus) in terms of primary control, which consists of active attempts to change the external world in line with the individual's desires. His key finding was as follows: "primary control striving remains stable across the life span, even though the opportunities for primary control decrease in old age" (p.183). However, there were some age differences in terms of the areas in which the participants tried to exercise primary control. Older people focused more than younger ones on the areas of health, leisure, and community, but they focused less on family, financial, and work goals.

In what ways can living in an institution affect a person psychologically?

Langer and Rodin (1976) studied elderly people living in nursing homes. Those who were encouraged to be active and to look after themselves as much as possible had greater psychological well-being and lived longer than those who were less active. In similar fashion, Yaguchi et al. (1987) found that old people in Japan who remained physically active had higher levels of morale and more life satisfaction than those who were not physically active.

Evaluation

Perhaps the greatest strength of activity theory is that it is based on the recognition that there are important continuities between middle age and old age. In other words, most of the needs and motivational forces that lead middle-aged people to be actively involved in society still apply when they move into old age. Further support for activity theory comes from the frequent finding that the most contented older adults tend to be those who are the most active (e.g., Havighurst et al., 1968; Langer & Rodin, 1976).

The main weakness of activity theory is that it is greatly oversimplified. It takes little or no account of individual differences in personality. Some older adults (such as the disengagers in the Havighurst et al. study) deliberately reduce their activity level and disengage from society, because they find that this approach suits them. Activity theory also pays little attention to factors other than activity level that contribute towards the adjustment made to old age. These factors include physical health, financial security, close relationships, and a strong social network.

Surprising numbers of active elderly people take up as a retirement hobby something related to their working life, for example ex-railway men volunteering to drive steam trains.

Most elderly people are less active than middle-aged people, and so it might be expected that they would be less content as a result. In fact, however, the level of contentment in elderly people is similar to that in the middle aged (see Durkin, 1995).

Synthesis

A central weakness with both disengagement theory and activity theory is that they are based on the oversimplified assumptions that all older people are essentially alike and are exposed to similar circumstances. Stuart-Hamilton (1994, p.127) put forward a more realistic hypothesis

> *disengagement and activity theory describe the optimal strategy for some but not all elderly individuals, and which is the better depends upon a variety of factors, such as: financial circumstances (e.g., can one afford an active lifestyle?); health (e.g., does one still have the vigour for some hobbies?); and personality types (e.g., a lifelong introvert may hate an active lifestyle).*

The notion that there are different ways of coping successfully with old age was supported by Reichard et al. (1962), see the Key Study on the next page.

The disengagement and activity theories both assume that adjustment to old age depends more on *what* you do than on *who* you are. However, there is strong evidence

Reichard et al.

The notion that there are different ways of coping successfully with old age was supported by Reichard et al. (1962). They interviewed 87 Americans aged between 55 and 84, and identified five personality types. Two of these (*hostility*, in which others are blamed for one's misfortune; and *self-hatred*, in which the hostility is turned on oneself) were associated with poor adjustment to old age. In contrast, the other three personality types were associated with fairly successful adjustment to old age.

- *Constructiveness*: this involves coming to terms with the losses of old age, and continuing to interact positively with others.
- *Dependent* or "rocking chair": this involves regarding old age as a time of leisure, and being reliant on others to provide assistance.
- *Defensiveness*: this involves remaining very active, as if pretending that old age has not arrived.

As if pretending that old age has not arrived...

The findings of Reichard et al. are relevant to the disengagement and activity theories. The dependent personality style clearly possesses elements of disengagement, whereas the defensive personality style is primarily based on activity. Thus, we have evidence here that both theories apply reasonably well to certain individuals.

Discussion points

1. Is it possible that personality is more important than age in determining an individual's outlook on life?
2. Does it make sense to assign all old people to one or other out of five categories?

that who you are in terms of personality has a substantial effect on psychological well-being. Costa and McCrae (1980) argued that happy people are those who experience many pleasant emotions and few negative ones. They also argued that those high on extraversion or sociability experience more pleasant emotions than introverts, and that those high on neuroticism (a personality dimension involving being anxious and depressed) experience many negative emotions. As predicted, they found that the happiest people were those who were high on extraversion and low on neuroticism, and the least happy were those low on extraversion and high on neuroticism. McCrae and Costa (1982) later found that precisely the same was the case in a sample of old men.

S E C T I O N   S U M M A R Y

❖ Common life events in adulthood may lead to identifiable themes, which are recognised in theories of adulthood.

❖ According to Erikson's theory, there are three major stages after adolescence: early adulthood, middle adulthood, and old age. The first stage revolves around intimacy vs. isolation, the second stage around generativity vs. stagnation, and the third stage around wisdom vs. despair. Erikson claimed that women do not fully achieve a sense of identity until they marry, whereas men may achieve intimacy before identity. This is supported by research. Studies of groups undergoing social change also support the theory. However, it is a very sketchy account, and it mistakenly implies that most people change and develop in the same ways. It is largely based on limited data from biographical case studies.

❖ Levinson suggested that each individual has a life structure that is based on important components such as relationships and occupation. Satisfaction derived from the life structure is related to success and failure, and impact on the inner self.

Early and Middle Adulthood

The life cycle consists of a series of eras, with lengthy cross-era transitions. The main eras are those of pre-adulthood, early adulthood, middle adulthood, and late adulthood. Adults spend an equal amount of time in fairly stable life structures and in states of transition or change. The evidence for this theory comes mainly from interview data, which are retrospective and may be biased. Levinson's assumption that virtually everyone experiences a midlife crisis has received little support. Such Western theories are unlikely to receive cross-cultural support.

❖ Gould's theory of the evolution of adult consciousness extended Freud's theory of personality development. Gould observed outpatient therapy groups and collated typical statements in age group categories, which were further confirmed by a larger, though still biased sample. These statements illustrate false assumptions, the beliefs that need to be challenged during each phase of development. False assumptions make us feel safe but need to be overcome in order to develop. The theory is founded on limited research but has useful applications in therapy.

❖ Stage theories identify culturally specific transitions and discontinuities. An alternative is to focus on continuities that are not age related, such as life events.

Family and Relationships in Adulthood

❖ Holmes and Rahe proposed that life events can be used to measure the amount of stress experienced by adults. Positive and negative events can be equally stressful. Research indicates a moderate positive correlation between life events and ill health. The life events approach has been criticised because the direction of causality is not clear; it doesn't acknowledge individual variation; the interviews may produce unreliable data because people cannot remember what things have happened; and undesirable events may actually create more stress than desirable ones.

❖ Against this background we should consider particular life events and the effect they have on individuals' development; in particular marriage, divorce, and parenting.

❖ Marriage is associated with happiness, which can be explained because marriage provides help, support, and common interests. Marriage may have a lower association with happiness nowadays as people choose cohabitation instead. Marital satisfaction is represented by a U-shaped curve, though studies rely on recall of past happiness. Married people are less likely to become mentally ill. Marriage provides social support; social support is most effective in improving mental health in stressful conditions (buffering hypothesis). Married individuals enjoy better physical health too. Cultural variations should be considered.

❖ The stress of divorce varies between individuals, and between men and women. The typical stages of divorce are: emotional, legal, economic, co-parental, community, and psychic. The stress associated with divorce may be a cause or an effect. Studies that look at the effect on children suggest that conflict is worse than divorce, but where there is low conflict it is better for parents to remain together. Individual differences may arise because certain kinds of people tend to divorce.

❖ Parenting tends to reduce marital satisfaction, because it reduces the parents' free time and increases their responsibilities. Marital satisfaction may increase after the last child has left home (empty nest syndrome). Adults decide to have children for a sense of achievement, to give and to receive love, due to cultural expectations and/or for a sense of importance. Relevant factors in parental satisfaction include: social class (which may be related to job disruption), closeness of parents prior to birth, and the age and financial circumstances of the couple. Satisfied mothers find relationships with children easier. Complex family interrelationships make it hard to study the effects of parenting because it is unclear whether specific factors are causal or not.

Cognitive Changes in Late Adulthood

❖ Adjustment to old age is affected by physical decline, changes in lifestyle (e.g., retirement, death of friends) and ageist stereotypes that create negative expectations. Reduced social support may lead to depression in the elderly.

❖ Research into cognitive changes has indicated declines in IQ, but this may be due to cohort effects. It also may be that crystallised intelligence is unaffected. On the other hand, longitudinal studies also suffer from selective dropout, which may create apparent increases in IQ in some studies. However, degenerative illness may make it appear that IQ is declining. Memory in experimental studies does decline but the elderly retain many other aspects of good memory function. Motivation and lowered expectations may account for age differences. Further masking effects include the fact that the elderly learn coping strategies and/or cognitive decline is due to a lack of stimulation.

❖ Retirement is a feature of most people's old age, though not everyone looks forward to it. Atchley outlined six phases of adjustment: pre-retirement, honeymoon, disenchantment, reorientation, stability, and termination phases. Not everyone experiences each phase and the duration of each phase is variable. The recognition of such phases may help in providing pre-retirement education. A number of factors that help or hinder the retirement experience are: past enjoyment of work, reliance on work for social contacts, hobbies, money, sense of identity, and whether retirement was voluntary or not. For some individuals retirement is similar to unemployment, which has negative psychological and physical effects. The size of these effects depends on environmental factors such as availability of money, opportunity for control, variety, physical security, opportunity for interpersonal contact, and valued social position. The more opportunities one constructs, the less negative the effects of unemployment—which may be true for retirement as well.

❖ Bereavement in the form of death of one's spouse is the most stressful life event, involving the loss of many things: emotional support, validation of personal judgements, supports, and social protection. Bereavement causes a period of shock and numbness, then intense longing for the dead spouse, then a long period of depression, and finally the construction of a new life. Kübler-Ross interviewed dying patients about their sense of anticipatory bereavement for their own death, and outlined the stages leading to acceptance of this: denial and isolation, anger, bargaining, depression, and finally acceptance. The effects of bereavement are lessened where the death is expected and the person is old. Bereaved individuals are more likely to die themselves than non-bereaved. There are a number of gender differences. Men find bereavement more difficult because, for example, they may not be used to looking after themselves. Some women experience a loss of identity. Men are more likely to remarry. Coping with bereavement may be assisted by cultural rites of passage, such as funeral services, close physical contact with the dead body, and other forms of "grave-dressing".

❖ According to social disengagement theory, reduced active involvement in society is the best way of adjusting to old age because it is an appropriate response to the decreasing roles available and to decreasing abilities. Some research supports this, but other research found that the older people who remained the most active tended to be the most contented, and that active involvement is more the norm in Western cultures studied. It may be that some individuals are "disengagers". Other evidence shows that older people do progressively disengage, though this may be forced on them by ill-health. Older people appear to be more passive than younger ones. There is less disengagement in many non-Western cultures, though not in nomadic societies. Social disengagement theory de-emphasises individual differences.

❖ According to activity theory, older people become disengaged because this is forced on them by society. Adjustment is best served by remaining as active as possible. Older people should maintain their role count. Research suggests that most older people do have a variety of active social roles, and that activity is related to better health and contentment. This theory recognises that there are important similarities between middle age and old age. However, activity theory is oversimplified. It takes little or no account of individual differences in personality, and does not recognise that some individuals cannot choose this option.

❖   A combination of disengagement and activity may be the best solution. The dependent personality style clearly possesses elements of disengagement, whereas the defensive personality style is primarily based on activity. Happy people may also adjust better to old age; happiness is associated with extraversion and a lack of neuroticism.

FURTHER READING

There is clear coverage of adulthood and old age in K. Durkin (1995), *Developmental social psychology: From infancy to old age* (Oxford: Blackwell). The changes that occur in old age are discussed fully by I. Stuart-Hamilton (1994), *The psychology of ageing: An introduction (2nd Edn.)* (London: Jessica Kingsley). The strengths and weaknesses of methods for studying life events are explored by R.A. Martin (1989), "Techniques for data acquisition and analysis in field investigations of stress", in R.W.J. Neufeld (Ed.) (1979), *Advances in the investigation of psychological stress* (New York: Wiley).

Example Examination Questions

You should spend 30 minutes on each of the questions below, which aim to test the material in this Section.

1. (a) Describe **one** theory of early and/or middle adulthood.   (12 marks)
    (b) Assess this theory with reference to research studies.   (12 marks)

2. Critically consider research related to the existence of crises and transitions in early and middle adulthood.   (24 marks)

3. Discuss research into factors associated with divorce, including a consideration of gender differences.   (24 marks)

4. Describe and evaluate the effects of marriage (partnering) on the individual.   (24 marks)

5. Discuss issues surrounding how individuals cope with bereavement.   (24 marks)

6. Discuss research into **two or more** cognitive changes that take place in late adulthood. (24 marks)

Examination Tips

Question 1.   In part (a) you should select one theory and describe it, providing sufficient depth and breadth. The latter is achieved through a consideration of different aspects of the theory. Evaluation (part b) must include some reference to research studies. However, the studies should not be *described*, but used as part of an argument to assess the value of the theory. You may also evaluate the theory through comparisons with other approaches, criticisms of the methodology used in the research studies, practical applications and implications, and so on.

Question 2.   The question requires a description of crises and transitions during early and middle adulthood, with reference to any theories. The AO2 element of the essay should assess the strengths and limitations of this approach, for example, to what extent does the approach reflect reality? To what extent is it supported by research evidence? Are there gender and/or cultural differences?

Question 3.   "Research" can refer to theories and/or studies. Such research should be described and then evaluated. The question provides one suggestion for how you might consider the value of research—gender differences. There are also potential cultural differences and individual differences, both of which offer useful means of evaluating research. Studies related to marriage rather than divorce may be used effectively if they are made explicitly relevant. Note that the question does say "factors associated with divorce" so this points also to issues such as stress and the effects on any children's lives.

Question 4. You are required to describe what effects marriage (partnering) may have on the individual, e.g., in terms of happiness, mental and physical health, and so on. Evaluation may be in terms of research studies (though these may have been used as part of the description), individual and cultural differences, and practical applications. It is also appropriate to offer commentary on the methodology of any research studies insofar as this may bring the findings into question.

Question 5. Again "describe and evaluate" is required ("discuss" = "describe" + "evaluate"), this time looking at issues related to the experience of bereavement. This might involve looking at stages of the bereavement process, factors that make bereavement easier or harder, individual and cultural differences, and so on. Research evidence will be useful in providing more than a commonsense approach. Ensure that you give a full 15 minutes to the AO2 part of the question, otherwise you are throwing away valuable marks.

Question 6. You have a choice of taking the depth route (a few cognitive changes but lots of detail) or the breadth route (a number of cognitive changes identified but therefore less detail for each). Either way a reasonable balance must be achieved for high marks. "Research" is asked for in the question, which can be either theory and/or studies. If research studies are described then theories can be used as a means to evaluate or comment on the studies (and vice versa). Research can also be evaluated in terms of methodological/logical flaws, and practical applications.

WEB SITES

http://www.hope.edu/academic/psychology/335/webrep2/crisis.html
Recent research into the midlife crisis.

http://www.mhhe.com/socscience/devel/common/middleadulthood.htm
Middle adulthood links.

http://www.psychology.org/links/Environment_Behavior_Relationships/Marriage/
Links related to marriage and divorce.

http://www.cygni.org/scales/social_readjustment_rating_scale.htm
The Holmes and Rahe Social Readjustment Rating Scale.

http://www.nlm.nih.gov/medlineplus/bereavement.html
Interesting links about bereavement with children, siblings, and adults.

http://www.soton.ac.uk/~aoh/indexold.htm
Attitudes to Ageing interactive study.

http://epunix.biols.sussex.ac.uk/Home/Julian_Staddon/age.html
Links to useful sites on ageing.

www.a-levelpsychology.co.uk/websites.html
A continually updated list of useful links, including those printed in this book, may be found at the Psychology Press A level psychology site.

PART 5

Comparative Psychology

This area of psychology is called "comparative psychology" because it seeks to make comparisons between the behaviours of different species, with the intention of gaining insights into human behaviour. The study of animal behaviour is a field in its own right, and does not belong wholly to psychology.

In this Part we will be considering explanations of human behaviour that are derived from insights gained in the study of non-human animals. It is a fascinating and increasingly popular area of psychology, and one that is changing very rapidly.

Section 13: Determinants of Animal Behaviour

❖ Why are some behaviours naturally selected?

❖ Why is conditioning such an important explanation for behaviour?

❖ How does social learning differ from learning?

❖ How intelligent are non-human animals?

Section 14: Animal Cognition

❖ How does a homing pigeon find its way home?

❖ Is it possible to teach a monkey to use human language?

❖ What is a bee trying to say with its waggle dance?

❖ Is non-human animal memory the same as human memory?

Section 15: Evolutionary Explanations of Human Behaviour

❖ Why do women choose one man in preference to another?

❖ How does parental investment differ between the sexes?

❖ Do mental illnesses have some evolutionary advantage?

❖ How has intelligence evolved?

13

Determinants of Animal Behaviour

Probably the most important question in comparative psychology is "Why do the members of a given species behave in a certain way?" This Section looks at a variety of answers to this question. It may be an inherited behaviour, or it may be acquired through learning and imitation.

Evolutionary Explanations of Animal Behaviour

In this Unit we will consider explanations in terms of heredity for the behaviour of animals. This is the view that some behaviours are innate or "hard-wired" into the genetic code of the animal in order to promote the survival of the individual, or more specifically the survival of the individual's **genes**. We will see how this argument has been developed.

It is important to separate the concept of "evolution" from the "theory of evolution". Evolution means change. The theory of evolution is an explanation offered for why change occurs in living species. The best-known theory of evolution was developed by Charles Darwin in 1859, but he was not able to explain all behaviours with this theory. Most notable of the behaviours he could not explain is the "paradox of altruism". Our starting point in this Unit will be to discuss the evidence showing that species do evolve. Then we will discuss evolutionary theory and, finally, the paradox of altruism.

The Facts of Evolution

Species: Fixed or changing?

It used to be argued that every species is separate from every other species, and that these differences remain fixed over time. This argument seems to be supported by the evidence of our own eyes. During the course of our lifetime, there are no obvious changes in the cats, dogs, and other species of animals we encounter. However, there is overwhelming evidence that species do change substantially over much longer periods of time than a human lifetime. There are at least three main kinds of evidence supporting the notion that species evolve over time: the fossil record, geographical variation, and selective breeding.

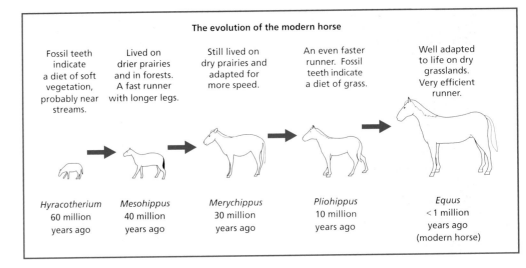

Fossil teeth indicate a diet of soft vegetation, probably near streams.

Hyracotherium
60 million years ago

Lived on drier prairies and in forests. A fast runner with longer legs.

Mesohippus
40 million years ago

Still lived on dry prairies and adapted for more speed.

Merychippus
30 million years ago

An even faster runner. Fossil teeth indicate a diet of grass.

Pliohippus
10 million years ago

Well adapted to life on dry grasslands. Very efficient runner.

Equus
< 1 million years ago (modern horse)

The evolution of the modern horse

Fossil record

Examination of the fossil record reveals that there have been progressive changes over time in the size and shape of many species. However, the fossil record is limited in a number of ways. First, the record is usually very incomplete. Often only some of the bones have been preserved, and there may be gaps in the record extending over thousands or tens of thousands of years. Second, the fossil record at best provides evidence only about the hard parts of an animal, and so it is often not easy to work out in detail what the animal looked like. Third, the fossil record cannot tell us about the behaviour of the members of a species. It is sometimes possible to make well-informed guesses about their behaviour, but that is all.

Ichthyosaurus: a marine reptile from the Jurassic era. Fossil records give us clues to what an animal looked like, but not how it behaved.

Geographical variation

A most important source of evidence about change in living species comes from the study of animals in different geographical locations. In fact geographical variation was the source of inspiration for Darwin's theory of evolution. During his voyages on board HMS *Beagle* Darwin visited the Galapagos Islands where he observed varieties of finch, a type of songbird. He noticed that on some islands finches had thick, heavy beaks, whereas on other islands their beaks were elongated. This difference could be related to differences in diet. On the first set of islands the finches ate hard-shelled seeds, on other islands they fed off insects hiding under rocks. The differences in physical characteristics could be related to the variation in environmental (geographical) conditions. Each species adapts to features of its environment, thus developing unique characteristics that are related to that environment. As Ridley (1995, p.21) pointed out:

At any one place, species do appear as discrete groups of organisms, but if a species is traced across the world its appearance can usually be seen to change from place to place. House sparrows, for example, vary in size, bodily proportions, and colouration across

On his travels to the Galapagos islands in the 1830s, Darwin noticed that on some islands the finches had thick, heavy beaks, whereas on other islands their beaks were elongated. These differences can be related to variation in environmental conditions.

The fact that kangaroos and some other marsupials are only found in Australia tells us that this continent became separated from other continents before these species evolved.

the United States, and the house sparrows of North America visibly differ from those of Europe.

n an interesting twist, evolution has been used to explain geographical change (continental drift). The fact that kangaroos and some other marsupials are only found n Australia tells us that this continent became separated from other continents before hese species evolved. The same principle could explain why there are no snakes in reland.

elective breeding

elective breeding also supports the view that species can change over time. Darwin 1859) was impressed by the way in which breeding programmes can produce, for xample, either racehorses that are light and lean or farm horses that are large and trong. Darwin himself bred pigeons, and observed changes in them from one eneration to the next. He argued that the changes produced artificially by selective reeding are like those that occur under more natural conditions. In other words, f a farmer decides that multiple pregnancy is a desirable characteristic in sheep, hen he or she selects ewes who have given birth to twins and triplets for breeding tock. In nature, there are also "desirable characteristics", such as the ability to run ast or to remember where you left your food, and these are selected—but they re not selected by any person (artificial selection). They are naturally selected, as we ill see.

What behaviours might be desirable in farm stock? How could a farmer try to produce animals with these traits?

Darwin's Theory of Evolution
Natural selection and adaptation

We have seen that there is convincing evidence that species can and do change considerably over long periods of time. What is needed is an explanation of the *processes* involved in producing these changes. Darwin (1859) provided such an explanation in his theory of natural selection. This theory was based on five major assumptions:

All dogs have the same distant ancestors, but selective breeding has resulted in major variations.

1. *Variation*: individuals within a species differ from each other in their physical characteristics (e.g., height) and in their behaviour (e.g., aggressiveness).
2. *Heritability*: some of the variation among members of a species is inherited. As a result, offspring tend to resemble their parents more than they resemble other members of the species.
3. *Competition*: the members of most species produce far more offspring than can survive. Darwin worked out that a pair of elephants could have about 19 million descendants alive 750 years after their birth if there were no problems of survival. However, animals compete for things like mates, food, and places to live. Those individuals who lose the competitions are less likely to reproduce.
4. *Natural selection*: the individuals who survive the process of competition and go on to breed will tend to have characteristics that are better suited to the environment than those who do not. Thus, there is natural selection or "survival of the fittest" (in the sense of survival or reproductive success rather than physical fitness).
5. *Adaptation*: as a result of the process of natural selection, successive generations will tend to be more and more adapted to their environment. They will possess characteristics that increase their abilities to obtain food, survive, and most importantly, to reproduce. Suppose, for example, that a speedy predator eats mainly the members of a given species. If only the fast-moving members of the prey species survive, then that species should evolve over the generations in the direction of becoming on average faster moving.

Darwin was greatly influenced by the work of Malthus (1798). Malthus emphasised the notion that the human population tends to increase considerably over time, whereas the earth's resources (e.g., land, food) either cannot increase or do so only slowly. Malthus worked out what would happen if a couple had three children, all of their children had three children, and so on. After 1? generations, the original couple would have more than one and a half million offspring (see the diagram on page 495), a figure that makes both of the present authors feel guilty at having three children each of our own! Malthus and Darwin were both pessimistic about the chances of any species showing reproductive restraint. As a result, Darwin reasoned, what must happen is that there will be ever-increasing competition for finite resources. Competition exerts **selective pressure** because those who lose, when resources are limited, fail to reproduce.

Cheetahs are the fastest land animals and catch their prey using amazing bursts of speed. They can reach 70mph (110kph) but tire after about 400 metres.

Changes within a species

Darwin (1859) assumed that evolutionary change would generally happen relatively slowly over periods of hundreds or thousands of years. However, the fossil record suggests that changes can occur fairly rapidly. As a result, Gould (1981) argued that a species will sometimes have fairly brief periods of rapid development in between long periods of relative stability. He described this notion as **punctuated equilibrium**.

Rapid development

Grier and Burk (1992) addressed the issue of why it is that some aspects of behaviour seem to have changed much more than others during the course of evolution. They identified four main reasons why evolutionary change might be rapid for some categories of behaviour:

Numbers of descendants after many generations		
Year	Generation	Number of descendants
2000	1st	3
2025	2nd	9
2050	3rd	27
2075	4th	81
2100	5th	243
2125	6th	729
2150	7th	2187
2175	8th	6561
2200	9th	19,683
2225	10th	59,049
2250	11th	177,147
2275	12th	531,441
2300	13th	1,594,323

Based on a new generation every 25 years, where each descendant has three surviving children. This situation is hypothetical as some people do not have three children due to early death, sterility, or choice.

1. Any behaviour that permits a more efficient use of the available resources (e.g., bigger jaws for eating whole animals, or better display tactics for winning territory) will quickly give an advantage to an individual with that characteristic. This will increase their reproductive success.
2. Any behaviour that gives an individual a competitive edge is likely to lead to more rapid evolution, such as a male who is stronger and therefore will win competitions when fighting over the right to impregnate a female. The offspring will be his, and his genes will be perpetuated.
3. Any behaviour used with respect to other members of the same species (e.g., courtship or communication) may be especially likely to show evolutionary change because of the advantage conferred on the possessor. In other words, any behaviour that impresses prospective mates or deters rivals of the same sex is likely to be selected quickly because of the large benefits the successful behaviour brings.
4. Forms of behaviour between the members of two species (e.g., predator–prey interactions, host–parasite interactions) may be subject to rapid change by both species. For example, if a predator has to run fast to catch his/her dinner then this selects for speed of movement in both the predator and prey, as predators become faster so the prey must evolve faster speeds to escape—or a least any prey that survive must have evolved faster speeds (faster prey are naturally selected). This evolution leads to the selection of yet faster speed on the part of the predator and so on. This process is called **co-evolution**.

Stable periods

In contrast, there are other forms of behaviour that tend to remain stable over generations either when there would be no advantage in changing them (see "Evolutionarily stable strategies", described overleaf), or because a superior form of behaviour has simply not appeared in the species in question.

Adaptation is imperfect

It might be thought that the processes of natural selection and adaptation would tend to make the members of a species almost perfectly suited to their environment. This is not what Darwin actually believed. According to Darwin (1872, p.163):

Natural selection tends only to make each organic being as perfect as, or slightly more perfect than, the other

Deep sea octopus

In a study of deep sea life, Wider, Johnsen, and Balser (1999) described one octopus species that lives at depths of 900 metres and feeds on prey too small to grasp with tentacles. The usual suckers on octopus tentacles are therefore redundant and this species does not have the muscles that are normal in shallow-water octopuses. Instead, the sucker-like pads have developed light-emitting cells, which produce the bluish light typical of bioluminescence and attract prey.

How can the principles of natural selection and survival of the fittest be used to explain the physical characteristics of the deep sea octopus?

One theory about the disappearance of the dinosaurs is that they failed to adapt to changes in world climate brought about when a massive meteor hit the earth.

inhabitants of the same country with which it comes into competition … Natural selection will not produce absolute perfection.

Environmental change

One reason why a species' behaviour is not well adapted to the environment is because the environment has changed recently and this creates a mismatch, which will need correcting. Some individuals may have characteristics better suited to the new environment, and these characteristics will now be selected.

If the environment has changed profoundly it is unlikely that the species will be able to adapt. For example, it is speculated that the reason dinosaurs became extinct was due to massive environmental changes after a large meteor hit the earth 65 million years ago. The dinosaurs had little chance of surviving in these new conditions, and there would not have been sufficient time for the slow process of evolution to enable them to adapt.

Evolutionarily stable strategies

Do you think the behaviour of the milk thieves can be better explained by cultural rather than genetic evolution?

Another important reason why species are imperfectly adapted to their environment was identified by Maynard Smith (1976). He argued that natural selection typically produces *stable* behavioural strategies, even when these strategies are not ideal. When an individual animal interacts with other animals, its most adaptive behaviour depends very much on how the other animals behave. For example, it might be adaptive for animals to be very

CASE STUDY: *The Milk Thief*

In 1949 doorstep delivery of bottled milk was becoming increasingly popular. Previously, milk had been decanted into the householder's own jugs and containers, but the new method involved a glass bottle with a foil cap. Housewives began to complain that someone or something was piercing and peeling back the foil cap, and stealing the cream from the top of the milk. As this epidemic of thefts spread, it was discovered that the culprits were several species of tits, the main offenders being blue tits who had discovered a new food source. The behaviour was widespread for 10 years or so, during which time householders learned that a solution was to leave a cup on the doorstep for the milkman to put over the top of the milk bottle. Gradually the milk thefts ceased to be a problem.

However, at about the same time, blue tits began another unusual behaviour. Entering houses and factories, they would embark on an orgy of paper-tearing, ripping up strips of any paper they found: wallpaper, toilet rolls, parcel wrappings, newspapers, and so on. There seemed to be no obvious reward for this behaviour, and scientists were baffled. One explanation put forward by the British Trust for Ornithology was that, because the birds could find so much food so easily, their hunger was satisfied before their hunting drive, so they were imitating tearing bark from trees in search of prey. Before anyone could agree on the true explanation for this odd behaviour, it too died out, and milk-stealing and paper-tearing by blue tits is now almost unknown.

aggressive and inclined to fight (hawks) or it might be adaptive for animals to avoid conflict and fighting (doves). Which is the better strategy? Probably to be a dove and avoid injury from fighting. However, in the real world, that is a risky strategy because of the danger of invasion by hawks. In fact, the most adaptive strategy for a species is for there to be a mixture of hawks and doves, and this is what is found in many species. Maynard Smith referred to this as an **evolutionarily stable strategy (ESS)**. This is "a strategy which when adopted by most members of the population cannot be beaten by any other strategy" (Krebs & Davies, 1993, p.149).

> ■ Activity: Consider the game "scissors, paper, rock"—where scissors cut paper, paper covers rock, and rock smashes scissors. Play this game and speculate on what might be an evolutionarily stable strategy to pursue to win the game.
>
> Answer: All three moves should be equally played but in a random order.

Do you think the adaptive strategy of a mixture of hawks and doves can be applied to humans?

Evidence for the Theory of Natural Selection

Uniformitarianism

Most of the evidence for natural selection is rather indirect. The reason for this is because the processes involved occur over such long periods of time that they cannot be observed directly. Those who use the fossil record or other historical evidence endorse the assumption of **uniformitarianism**. This is the notion that biological and physical processes operate in the same uniform way over time. If we accept the idea of uniformitarianism, then our observations in the present allow us to make inferences about the past. For example if we observe from the fossil record that some dinosaurs had head ornaments then we might conclude that these served the same purpose as the head ornaments on animals today, such as deer. We might also argue that the reason giraffes have long necks is because this enabled them to reach food supplies not being exploited by other animals.

However, there is a constant danger of observing what a given species is like now and working backwards to make up an "explanation" that sounds plausible but lacks direct evidence. For example, we might guess that giraffes have long necks because in the distant past only those giraffes with long necks were able to reach up high enough to obtain food. But we are making an assumption that their food source was high up in trees—this of course may have developed *after* they got the long necks. Hailman (1992, p.127) was very critical of this approach:

How might the principle of uniformitarianism be applied to the case of finches on the Galapagos Islands (see pages 492–493)?

> *The colouration, anatomy, physiology, and behaviour of animals seem so well suited to the environments in which they live that natural selection "must" have adapted the animals to their environments. Come on, can't we do better than that?*

There are examples of somewhat more direct evidence, as we shall see.

Moths, kittiwakes, and empid flies

What has often been regarded as fairly direct support for some of the assumptions of Darwin's theory was obtained by Kettlewell (1955) in a study of moths, described on the next page. Other good evidence for the theory of evolution comes from observations of gulls. There are about 35 species of gulls, and most of them show great similarities in their behaviour. Nearly all these species nest on the ground, but kittiwakes nest on narrow ledges, which are a long way above ground level. Cullen (1957) found that the chicks of most gull species start to roam about away from the nest within about 1 day of hatching. In contrast, the chicks of kittiwakes remain in their nests. The evolutionary significance of this difference is fairly clear. The chicks of kittiwakes might kill themselves if they moved around on narrow ledges, whereas the chicks of other gull species can often avoid danger by running away from it. This nesting behaviour is **adaptive**.

Another example of an evolutionary explanation of a behaviour comes from the courtship behaviour of various species of empid flies. In some species, male flies give

Roaming behaviour in kittiwake chicks would seriously damage the survival of the species.

CASE STUDY: *The Peppered Moth*

What has often been regarded as fairly direct support for some of the assumptions of Darwin's theory was obtained by Kettlewell (1955). He studied two variants of the peppered moth, one of which was darker than the other. The difference in colour is inherited, with the offspring of the darker type being on average darker than those of the lighter type. Both types of peppered moth are eaten by birds such as robins and red-starts that rely on sight to detect them. Kettlewell observed the moths when they were on relatively light lichen-covered trees and when they were on dark, lichenless trees in industrially polluted areas. The lighter coloured moths survived better on the lighter trees and the darker coloured moths survived better on the darker trees.

According to Darwin's theory, the number of darker moths should increase if there is an increase in the proportion of dark trees. Precisely this happened in England due to the industrial revolution, when pollution killed the lichen and coated the trees with sooty deposits. The proportion of peppered moths that were dark apparently went from being almost nil to over half the resident population in a period of about 50 years. However, the evidence that there were few dark peppered moths in the late nineteenth century comes from moth collections. As Hailman (1992, p.126) pointed out, "Those collections were not scientific samples but were made by amateurs ... Perhaps they did not like ugly black moths."

Colour variants of the peppered moth.

prey wrapped in silk to the female during courtship. This is effective, but has the disadvantage that the male has to exert energy to obtain the prey. In other species, the male gives the female nothing. This has the disadvantage that the male is sometimes eaten by the female, probably because the female is not distracted by the presence of the prey wrapped in silk. In evolutionary terms, the optimal behaviour for the male would be to distract the female without the need to catch any prey. Precisely this happens in other species of empid flies, in which the male gives the female an empty silk balloon (Kessel, 1955).

Links between environment and behaviour

One of the best ways of testing evolutionary notions is to study numerous species that differ in their behaviour. The researcher tries to work out which environmental differences have produced the behavioural differences among species. According to Grier and Burk (1992, p.143):

> *This approach is considered as strong or nearly as strong as the genuinely experimental method. In essence, one is merely taking advantage of experiments that have already taken place in nature where there is a sufficiently large sample size to reduce the impact of spurious correlations.*

Ridley (1983) described one such natural experiment. There are numerous species in which the male hangs on to the female for periods of time ranging between days and weeks before fertilisation occurs. This is known as precopulatory guarding, and it is found in arthropods (e.g., spiders and crustaceans), frogs, and toads. Ridley argued that precopulatory guarding might develop through natural selection in species in which the females are receptive for mating for fairly brief but predictable periods of time. On the other hand, precopulatory guarding would not be found in species where the females are continuously receptive for mating or where their receptivity occurs at unpredictable times. His key finding was that these predictions were confirmed in 399 out of 401 species.

Male frogs use precopulatory guarding to ensure that mating is successful.

Evaluation and Development of the Theory of Evolution

Mechanisms of heredity

It is generally accepted that Darwin's (1859) theory of natural selection is essentially correct as far as it goes. However, he did not provide an account of the *mechanisms* involved in heredity. Darwin thought that there might be some blending of characteristics from parents, but the actual mechanism was demonstrated by the experiments of Gregor Mendel (1822–1884), a monk whose work was never known to Darwin. **Mendelian genetics** explains how the units of inheritance combine and produce variation. The discovery of **genes** enables Darwin's theory to be re-expressed in terms of the involvement of genes. In the words of Krebs and Davies (1993, pp.9–10):

> *The individual can be regarded as a temporary vehicle or survival machine by which genes survive and are replicated ... the most successful genes will be those which promote most effectively an individual's survival and reproductive success ... As a result, we would therefore expect individuals to behave so as to promote gene survival.*

Evidence that genetic factors can have powerful influences on behaviour comes from artificial selection experiments. In such experiments, animals are bred so as to produce separate strains that behave very differently from each other. For example, Berthold et al. (1990) carried out a selection study on blackcaps, of which 75% were migratory and 25% were resident. They mated migratory birds with other migratory birds, and they

If the migratory behaviour of the blackcaps was an ESS, what comment might you make about the ethics of the study by Berthold et al.?

Mendelian genetics

Darwin was unable to explain how inherited variation occurred. He thought that there might be some blending of characteristics from parents, but the actual mechanism was demonstrated by the experiments of Gregor Mendel, a monk whose work was only rediscovered after Darwin's death. Mendelian genetics explains how the units of inheritance combine and produce variation.

In a typical experiment Mendel bred red-flowered pea plants with white-flowered ones. He observed that in the first generation there were no white flowers but in the next generation they reappeared in a ratio of 1:3. This could only be explained using the concept of "particulate factors" (later called *genes*). Each plant has a pair of genes for flower colour. To produce a red flower these are RR and to produce white they are ww. Red is *dominant* to white, so a plant that is Rw has a red flower. In the first generation all offspring are Rw. When two Rw individuals breed, their offspring may be RR, Rw, Rw, ww (3 are likely to be red and 1 white).

The plant's **phenotype** is its external appearance (red or white), its **genotype** is the genes. For all sexually reproducing organisms there are often two forms of each gene (called alleles).

Parents:	RR (Red)		ww (White)	
First generation of pea plants:				
	Rw (Red)	Rw (Red)	Rw (Red)	Rw (Red)
Second generation:				
	RR (Red)	Rw (Red)	Rw (Red)	ww (White)

Some characteristics are inherited in this Mendelian way. For example yellow and black Labrador dogs inherit their colour like this, which explains why a black bitch who is genetically black/yellow can have a yellow puppy if she mates with a yellow dog (who must be yellow/yellow because yellow is the recessive gene).

However, **polygenetic inheritance** as opposed to single gene determination is the way most characteristics are inherited. This characteristic is caused by a number of genes, rather than straightforward Mendelian single gene combinations, as in the pea plant example.

The peacock's long tail, apparently an evolutionary error, has an important role to play in attracting a mate.

mated resident birds with other resident birds. After six generations, they produced two separate strains that were either 100% migratory or 100% resident. It is claimed that selection experiments show in an exaggerated form the workings of evolution.

Adaptation

Darwin's theory of evolution states that all characteristics possessed by individual animals should serve the function of making them well adapted to their environment. However, some species possess characteristics that do not seem to serve any useful purpose. For example, the long tail or train of peacocks makes them vulnerable to attack by predators because it reduces their mobility. Darwin (1871) recognised that peacocks' long tails or trains must be functional in some way. He proposed **sexual selection** as a variation of natural selection: peahens find the peacock's long train attractive, and so peacocks with long trains have greater reproductive success than those with short trains, making this an advantageous and adaptive trait Sexual selection is discussed further in Section 15, Evolutionary Explanations of Human Behaviour.

The paradox of altruism

According to Darwin's theory, individual animals should behave in a selfish fashion to compete successfully against other individuals, and so ensure the survival of their genes in the future. However, animals often seem to show altruistic behaviour, which is behaviour that benefits other animals but at some cost to the animal itself or cost to its reproductive potential. Reproductive success is of central importance to the theory of natural selection. It would seem to follow that the processes of natural selection would lead to the gradual disappearance of altruism. Why hasn't this happened? This is called the "paradox of altruism", which we will consider next.

Biological Explanations of Apparent Altruism

Many species show evidence of **altruism** or apparent altruism in their behaviour. Altruistic behaviour has two elements. One is behaving in a way that benefits another animal, and the second is that this is at some potential risk or cost to the altruist. This cost may be in terms of the altruist's own survival and reproduction.

Examples of altruistic behaviour include the suicidal sting of the honeybee and birds' alarm calls, which serve to warn others that a predator is nearby, but which also tell the predator where the altruist is. As we have noted, the existence of altruism or apparent altruism is a paradox that cannot be explained in terms of Darwin's (1859) theory of natural selection.

One possible explanation for altruism is **group selection theory**, as outlined by Wynne-Edwards (1962). A group of animals that possess more favourable characteristics would be more likely to survive to reproduce. For example, birds' warning calls help to ensure the survival of the flock of birds even if they reduce the chances of survival of the individual making the calls. This line of reasoning may sound convincing, but there are problems with it. Selfish individuals in a group composed mainly of altruists would have greater reproductive success than would the altruists. Thus, selfishness would be favoured by natural selection, and would probably eliminate altruism. In addition, natural selection takes place at the level of the individual genes and cannot select a group. It is the individual within the group who possesses advantageous genes and, as that individual is more likely to survive to reproduce, this will facilitate the perpetuation of only that individual's genetic line not the genetic line of the whole group.

Attached to the honeybee's sting is a sac of venom. When the bee attacks, it leaves its sting in its victim, along with the venom sac. Once the bee has lost its sting, it dies, so defending the hive in this way could be seen as altruistic.

Krebs and Davies (1993) suggest that there are four main evolutionary explanations for why animals sometimes exhibit altruistic behaviour. These are as follows:

1. *Kin selection*: an individual can increase its genetic representation in future generations by providing help to its close relatives (kin).
2. *Reciprocity*: one individual behaves altruistically towards a second individual, with the expectation that the second individual will return the favour in the future.
3. *Mutualism*: two individuals may both behave in an altruistic fashion at the same time because they both gain from co-operation.
4. *Manipulation*: an individual is misled or manipulated by another individual into behaving in an apparently altruistic way.

We will consider these four reasons in turn.

Kin selection

Darwin (1859) focused on the individual as the unit of natural selection, and it is difficult from that perspective to account for altruistic behaviour. However, if one regards the gene as the unit of selection then it is possible to explain altruistic behaviour. Animals who are related to each other share genes, especially if we are considering parents and offspring. If an offspring dies then the parent would have to reproduce again, otherwise that is the end of the genetic line. Any parent who is willing to die to save its offspring is more likely to create an enduring genetic line. Thus the gene for altruism is essentially a selfish one that ensures its survival, regardless of the individual carrying the gene.

> **Parental care and altruism**
>
> "Bringing up baby" involves heavy costs to many animal parents: in mammals this includes biological investment in egg production, growth and development of the foetus in the womb, milk production after birth, time and effort spent in care and defence, etc. In birds there is a similar amount of investment in nest building, egg production, incubation, feeding, etc. These behaviours could be argued to be of no benefit to the parents directly, and so could come under the heading of altruism. This altruism is even more marked if the parents are assisted by other family members, i.e. others who share the same genes. Mumme (1992) observed a type of Florida jay whose older broods acted as helpers with younger offspring, with the result that the younger brood had a greatly increased survival rate.

Maynard Smith (1964) introduced the term **kin selection** to describe this new form of selection. Kin selection refers to "the process by which characteristics are favoured due to their beneficial effects on the survival of close relatives, including offspring and non-descendant kin" (Krebs & Davies, 1993, p.266). The term "kin" covers all of an individual's relatives. As we will see, kin selection may well be the most important reason for the evolution of altruism.

*Kin selection is a concept favoured by **sociobiologists** who use it to explain social behaviour in terms of evolutionary processes. The key difference between sociobiology and the theory of evolution is that the former uses the gene rather than the individual as the basic unit of evolution. This explanation was popularised by Richard Dawkins (1976) in his book "The selfish gene". In what way is the gene "selfish"?*

Genetic closeness

A key implication in kin selection is that altruistic behaviour is more likely to be shown towards genetically close relatives than towards other individuals. This idea was summed up by the geneticist J.B.S. Haldane. He argued that he would be willing to sacrifice his own life for the sake of two of his brothers or eight of his cousins—the sum of "relatedness" is equivalent for the two brothers or the eight cousins.

We can understand more clearly what is involved in kin selection by considering the notions of direct and indirect fitness. **Direct fitness** is fitness in terms of gene survival gained through production of offspring, whereas **indirect fitness** is fitness in terms of gene survival gained through helping the survival of non-descendant kin such as siblings, cousins, nephews, and nieces. According to Hamilton (1964), the main reason why animal altruism exists is because of the addition of indirect fitness to direct fitness. The combination of these two forms of fitness is known as inclusive fitness. According to Grier and Burk (1992, p.457), **inclusive fitness** is

> *(1) an individual's reproductive success, plus (2) the extra reproductive success its relatives had because of its behaviour, devalued in each case by the coefficient of relatedness of the relative to the individual, minus (3) the extra offspring the individual had (if any) because of the help it received from its relatives.*

> **Relatedness**
>
> The extent to which any two individuals are genetically related can be expressed using the concept of the **coefficient of relatedness (r)**. This is defined as the probability that an **allele** (a portion of the gene) chosen at random from one individual will also be present in another individual. It can also be thought of as the proportion of the total **genome** present in one individual that is present in another as a result of common ancestry. The r-value between two brothers or sisters is 0.5 as there is a 50% chance that they share any one gene.

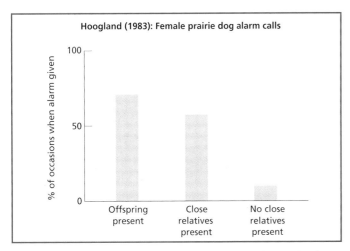

Hoogland (1983): Female prairie dog alarm calls

% of occasions when alarm given

Offspring present / Close relatives present / No close relatives present

Each offspring shares half its genes with its mother and half with its father. Siblings share half of their genes, so offspring:parents and sibling:sibling are just as closely related.

Evidence for kin selection

Alarm calls.   It follows from the idea of kin selection that an individual will be more likely to help a closer relative than a more distant one. This has been supported by research, for example Hoogland (1983) looked at alarm calls in black-tailed prairie dogs, which live in groups known as coteries. Within each coterie there is usually one adult male, three or four adult females, and their offspring. In order to persuade the prairie dogs to give alarm calls, Hoogland presented a stuffed badger, which is a predator of prairie dogs. Female dogs gave the alarm call on 71% of occasions when their offspring were in the coterie, on 58% of occasions when there were only non-descendant close relatives (e.g., siblings) in the coterie, and on only 10% of occasions when no close relatives were present. The figures were similar for male dogs: 51%, 49%, and 25%, respectively. The key finding was that alarm calling was almost as frequent when only non-descendant relatives would benefit as it was when descendant ones were in the coterie. This indicates that altruistic behaviour is shown not just towards offspring but also to other, equally related individuals. Similar evidence comes from a study of Belding's ground squirrels by Sherman (1977) discussed in the Key Study below.

Eusocial insects.   Perhaps the most striking evidence of altruistic behaviour is found among the eusocial or highly social insects, which include all of the ants and termites and several species of wasps and bees. These insects co-operate in nest building, they engage in group foraging to obtain food for the group, there is co-operative care of the young, and the nest is aggressively defended against invaders. A well-known example of such defence is the altruistic suicide of honeybees. When a honeybee stings an invader, its entire sting apparatus is ripped out, causing the bee to die.

Why do eusocial insects behave in such altruistic ways? The single most important reason stems from the fact that most species of eusocial insects have a system of sex determination known as haplodiploidy. **Haplodiploidy** involves males developing from unfertilised eggs, whereas females develop from fertilised eggs. Under haplodiploidy, the

Giving an alarm call alerts other ground squirrels to the presence of a predator, but alerts the predator to the caller's presence and position at the same time.

Belding's ground squirrels

Evidence supporting the notion of kin selection was reported by Sherman (1977) in a study of Belding's ground squirrels in the United States. When the squirrels are only a few weeks old, the young males go off in different directions, whereas the young females typically stay near the area in which they were born. Females who are closely related rarely fight each other, and co-operate to defend each other's young from attackers. However, unrelated ground squirrels drag approximately 80% of the young squirrels from their burrows, and then kill them. This illustrates how kin behave more altruistically than non-kin.

Sherman also studied alarm calls in squirrels when a predator (e.g., weasel, coyote) was approaching. These alarm calls represent altruistic behaviour, because squirrels giving an alarm call increased their chances of being attacked by the predator. As predicted from the kin selection notion, females were much more likely to give these alarm calls when there were close relatives nearby than when only unrelated squirrels were in the area. Those who benefited from the alarm calls were usually the offspring of the squirrel making the calls. However, alarm calls were also given when only parents or non-descendant relatives (e.g., sisters) were nearby. These findings are exactly in line with the notion that altruistic behaviour is more likely to occur when it serves the interests of close relatives than when it does not.

Discussion points

1. Why do you think close relatives benefited in this way?

2. Can you think of reasons why Sherman's research is regarded as being important?

female offspring of a common father get all of his genes, and they also share half of the genes from their common mother. As a result of this unusual arrangement, a female's relatedness to her sisters is 0.75, but her relatedness to her own offspring is only 0.5. This means that she can maximise the chances of her genes surviving by helping her mother, the queen (so that her mother produces more sisters for her), rather than by reproducing herself.

How do we know that the altruistic behaviour of eusocial insects depends on haplodiploidy? Key evidence is that elaborate altruistic societies have developed in 11 insect species in which there is haplodiploidy, but in only one species (diploid termites) in which there is not. However, haplodiploidy cannot be the only factor involved in producing complex altruistic societies. Haplodiploidy is also found in solitary parasitic wasps, which do *not* form themselves into altruistic societies. What other factors are involved? It is likely that a high level of danger from predators and the need to build complex nests play a part in the development of complex societies (Grier & Burk, 1992).

Ants co-operate to bring large amounts of food back to the main group.

Kin recognition.   We have seen that individuals in many species are more likely to behave in an altruistic way when close relatives or kin will benefit than when only non-relatives will gain. This suggests that they can recognise which members of their species are kin and which are not. How does this kin recognition occur? A clue to the answer can be found in the observation that individuals are by no means always accurate on this issue. For example, there are several species of birds in which the parents will ignore their own offspring if they are put outside their nest. However, if a cuckoo or other bird deposits an egg inside their nest, they will look after the bird when it hatches as if it were their own (called **brood parasitism**). These observations suggest that individuals tend to regard any other animal living in their home or with whom they have grown up as kin even if there is no close physical resemblance.

Holmes and Sherman (1982) tested the notion that animals treat those they have grown up with as kin. The pups of ground squirrels were assigned to four kinds of rearing group: siblings reared by one mother; siblings reared by different mothers; non-siblings reared together by one mother; and non-siblings reared by different mothers. When they had grown up, pairs of squirrels selected in various ways from these groups were put together. Animals that had been reared together rarely behaved aggressively to each other, and it made no difference whether or not they were genetically related. Animals that had been reared apart behaved much more aggressively towards each other than did animals that had been reared together. It did not matter whether the animals in the pair were genetically related, except that two sisters who had been reared apart were less aggressive towards each other than were unrelated females reared apart. Thus, the behaviour of squirrels towards each other is based more on whether they have lived close to each other than on whether or not they are kin.

In sum, it is often hard for individuals to be certain whether another member of their species is or is not kin. However, the simple assumption that anyone living in the same nest or other home is kin is generally correct. If a

"Well, he lives in our home, so I guess he must be one of us."

Young ground squirrels reared together behave as if they were genetically related, and are less aggressive towards each other as adults than are related squirrels who have been brought up apart.

special study is set up in which the young of a species are brought up with non-relatives (e.g., Holmes & Sherman, 1982), then animals will make mistakes. However, these kinds of situations rarely arise in nature.

Evaluation of kin selection

There is strong evidence that much altruistic behaviour in animals depends on kin selection. However, it should be noted that there are some complicating factors. First, animals cannot work out how closely they are related to another individual, and so they make use of "rules of thumb" such as that all those in the same nest are closely related. This explains kin recognition as well as brood parasitism. Second, even when altruistic behaviour is influenced by kin selection, it is often also influenced by environmental factors. For example, the presence of dangerous predators may increase the chances that the members of a species will behave altruistically towards each other.

One thing to remember is that the same principles may not apply to human behaviour, where altruistic behaviour may result from cognitive as much as biological processes—referred to as **psychological altruism**.

Reciprocal altruism

Trivers (1971) argued that an animal will behave altruistically towards other animals when this increases the chances that the other animals will then behave altruistically towards it. He used the term **delayed reciprocal altruism** to refer to this state of affairs. The most obvious problem with delayed reciprocal altruism (or reciprocity as it is also known) is the possibility of cheating. If someone behaves altruistically towards you, but you then refuse to help that person, then you have gained overall but they have lost.

Axelrod and Hamilton (1981) discussed the problem of achieving co-operation or reciprocity in terms of the "prisoner's dilemma" (see the box below). This was originally devised to understand human behaviour, but can easily be applied to other species. The basic idea is that each individual animal will do better if it behaves selfishly rather than co-operatively. The next best option is if they both co-operate and the worst option for both of them is if they both act in a selfish way. As Axelrod and Hamilton pointed out, if two animals meet only once, then their best strategy is to behave in a selfish way. However, if they meet numerous times, then other strategies can become more effective.

Delayed reciprocal altruism

In baboon tribes the most successful males in the group mate most often with the females. However, Packer (1977) observed altruistic co-operation between young males. One of them would distract the dominant male—a risky business, as the dominant male is always larger and stronger. The other young male would seize the opportunity to mate with the partner of the dominant male. It seems the favour would be returned on a later occasion, giving both young males the chance of mating and fathering offspring.

The prisoner's dilemma

This game holds a particular fascination for psychologists, because it tests co-operation between people: the outcome of the game always depends on the choices both people make and the degree of co-operation between them. In its typical format, the players are given the hypothetical situation of being arrested for working together to commit a crime. The two "prisoners" are kept apart, and each is questioned by the "police". The same suggestion is made to each one: if he or she (A) will agree to confess and give evidence against the other prisoner (B), then A will be released and B will be severely punished. Each player has two choices: to keep silent in co-operation with their partner, or to defect and confess all.

Both players gain when they co-operate with each other, as each will receive the same small punishment (there being little or no evidence against either). If both players confess, they both lose, because there is now evidence against them both and the penalties will be more severe. However, if one remains silent and the other confesses, the confessor

gets away without a penalty while the other player receives the severe punishment. The dilemma is, of course, that one person can never be sure of the other person's decision.

Activity

Try to simulate the prisoner's dilemma in groups of three. Two people take the prisoner roles, and the third acts as "judge", allocating points. Each prisoner must be unable to see or hear what the other prisoner decides, but can be told their scores at the end of each trial. A scoring method could be:

Both keep silent (co-operation):   Each scores 5 points
A keeps silent, but B confesses: A loses 10 points. B gains 10 points.
B keeps silent, but A confesses: B loses 10 points. A gains 10 points.
Both confess: Each scores no points.

Try the experiment in two conditions: one with no hints, and one using Axelrod's tit-for-tat strategy.

Axelrod (1984) asked 62 scientists to suggest winning strategies for the prisoner's dilemma. The most effective strategy was tit for tat. It involved the individual co-operating on the first occasion. On the second occasion, the individual behaved as the other individual had on the first occasion. After that, the individual simply copied the behaviour of the other individual on the previous occasion. This tit-for-tat strategy works because it encourages the other animal to be co-operative, while discouraging it from being selfish.

What strategy would you use in the prisoner's dilemma?

The tit-for-tat strategy is very effective, and it is an easy strategy for animals to use. However, it is not very clear how this strategy could become established in a species in the first place. Axelrod and Hamilton (1981) suggested that it might be directly linked to kin selection. Considerations of kin selection indicate that co-operative behaviour or reciprocity would be most likely to evolve between close relatives. It could then be that co-operative or reciprocal behaviour is used to identify relatives from non-relatives.

Could reciprocal altruism work if individuals didn't recognise each other?

Evidence for delayed reciprocal altruism

Krebs and Davies (1993) discussed various examples of delayed reciprocal altruism. Fischer (1980) considered spawning in the black hamlet fish, which possesses both male and female characteristics. The fish form pairs, in which one fish releases some eggs, that are then fertilised by the other fish. The two fish then swap roles, and they continue to alternate roles over a 2-hour period. The value of this rather complicated method of spawning is that cheating can be detected at an early stage. Fischer found that when one fish in the pair refused to co-operate, the other fish would not release any more eggs, and would simply swim away.

Delayed reciprocal altruism was also found in vampire bats in Costa Rica by Wilkinson (1984). He formed one large group of bats from two roosts, both of which consisted of unrelated individuals. A bat was removed and denied access to blood. It was then put back into the group. It was far more likely to be given blood by a familiar bat from its roost than by an unfamiliar bat from the other roost. This is as expected, because reciprocity is more likely between animals that know each other. Of particular importance, the starving bat that was given blood by another bat was more likely to give blood to that bat in future than to other bats.

What effect would cheating have on the evolution of reciprocal altruism?

Mutualism

Mutualism is like reciprocity in that it involves two animals behaving in altruistic or co-operative ways towards each other. The difference is that both animals obtain benefits at the same time with mutualism, but the benefits for one of the animals are delayed in the case of reciprocity.

Packer et al. (1991) studied mutualism in prides of lions in Tanzania. In each pride, there are usually a number of related females and between two and six males. The advantage for males of being in a pride is that it increases their chances of reproducing. When there were only two males in a pride, both of them fathered a number of offspring. This suggests the existence of mutualism, or co-operation between them. Mutualism was less obvious when there were more males in a pride. In such prides, at least one of the males did not father any offspring. This can be explained in terms of kin selection. All the males in a large pride were close relatives. As a result, the genes of the males who did not father any offspring survived through the reproductive success of the other males in the pride.

One of the best-known examples of manipulation can be seen in the behaviour of cuckoos. Once a cuckoo egg has been accepted by the host birds, the chick will try to push all the other chicks out of the nest to ensure its own survival.

Manipulation

Sometimes what looks like altruism actually occurs because the animal behaving in an altruistic way has been tricked by the animal that benefits from the altruistic behaviour. Perhaps the best-known example of such

In what way is "manipulation" not an altruistic behaviour?

Is manipulation "apparent" altruism?

Why is spite unknown in the animal world (apart from humans)?

manipulation is the way in which cuckoos can persuade birds of other species to act as hosts by hatching their eggs and caring for their offspring. The female cuckoo places one egg in the host nest, and removes one of the eggs that was already there. After the cuckoo hatches, it rapidly ejects all of the host eggs from the nest.

This manipulation on the part of cuckoos is carefully designed so that the host bird will be less likely to reject the cuckoo's egg. Davies and Brooke (1988) used model cuckoo eggs. They found that the host birds are more likely to reject eggs if they see a stuffed cuckoo on its nest, if the eggs are not like their own eggs, or if they are laid in the nest before the host birds have laid their own eggs. The behaviour of cuckoos placing their eggs in host nests is such as to maximise the chances that the eggs will be accepted by the host birds.

The difference between altruism and selfishness			
		Recipient	
		Gains	Loses
Actor	Gains	mutualism	selfishness
(donor of the act)	Loses	altruism	spite

Classical and Operant Conditioning

In the last Unit we reviewed one kind of explanation for behaviour—the argument that some behaviours are there because they are adaptive and innate. Another form of explanation is that behaviours are learned. In this Unit we will examine two ways to explain learning: classical and operant conditioning. When we use the term conditioning we are describing learning that takes place without conscious awareness. For example, if you hit your head every time you pass by a certain cupboard you will soon *learn* to duck before you pass it. You won't think about it, but will just do it. Experience has conditioned you. The example given here is of operant conditioning. You should be familiar with both **classical conditioning** and **operant conditioning** from your AS level studies but it may be helpful to remind yourself of key points, as well as to consider more detailed aspects of conditioning theory.

You should also remember that conditioning theory is the basis of the **behaviourist** approach in psychology, an approach that focuses on observable behaviours only and rejects any reference to internal cognitive (mental) activity.

Classical Conditioning

Imagine that you have to go to the dentist. As you lie down on the reclining chair, you may feel frightened. Why are you frightened before the dentist has caused you any pain? The sights and sounds of the dentist's surgery lead you to expect or predict that you are shortly going to be in pain. In other words, you have formed an *association* between the neutral stimuli of the surgery and the painful stimuli involved in drilling. Such associations are of central importance in classical conditioning.

Basic findings

The best-known example of classical conditioning comes from the work of Ivan Pavlov (1849–1936), a Russian physiologist. He was conducting research into the digestive system, which required that his experimental dogs were connected to a machine that collected saliva. When the dogs were offered food, saliva production increased. But Pavlov also noticed something particularly interesting—this salivation started to increase as soon as a researcher opened the door to bring them the food. The dogs had learned

Ivan Pavlov, 1849–1936.

that "opening door" signalled "food coming soon". It was in their nature to salivate when they smelled food. This is a *reflex* response. But the dogs had now *learned* a link between "door" and their reflex response (salivation). This is classical conditioning.

In this example, food is an unconditioned stimulus (UCS) and salivation is an unconditioned response (UCR). No learning is required for this stimulus–response (S–R) link, which is why both stimulus and response are described as "unconditioned".

The sound of the door opening is a neutral stimulus (NS). There is no inborn reflex response to hearing a door open.

If an NS and UCS occur together repeatedly they become associated, until eventually the NS also causes the UCR—now the NS is called a conditioned stimulus (CS) and the UCR becomes a conditioned response (CR) to this. The CS on its own will produce the CR. A new S–R link has been learned.

Pavlov discovered a number of features of classical conditioning. One of these was **generalisation**. In later experiments he presented a tone just before the food was presented. The conditioned response of salivation was greatest when the tone used as the conditioned stimulus was the same as had been used during training, but the dogs also responded to other tones. Generalisation is the ability to apply learning in one specific situation to other similar situations. The more similar the tone was to the original, the stronger the salivation response. This is described as a generalisation gradient.

Pavlov also identified the phenomenon of **discrimination**. Suppose that a given tone is paired several times with the sight of food. The dog will learn to salivate to the tone. Then another tone is presented on its own. It produces a smaller amount of salivation than the first tone through generalisation. Next the first tone is paired with food several more times, but the second tone is never paired with food. Salivation to the first tone increases, whereas that to the second tone decreases. In other words, the dog has learned to discriminate between the two tones.

Another key feature of classical conditioning is **experimental extinction**. When Pavlov presented the tone on its own several times, with no food, he found that there was less and less salivation. In other words, the repeated presentation of the conditioned stimulus in the absence of the unconditioned stimulus removes the conditioned response. This finding is known as experimental extinction.

Extinction does not mean that the dog or other animal has lost the relevant conditioned reflex. Animals brought back into the experimental situation after extinction has occurred produce some salivation in response to the tone. This is known as **spontaneous recovery**. It shows that the salivary response to the tone was inhibited rather than lost during extinction.

Explanations of classical conditioning

Time factors

What is going on in the classical conditioning situation? An association is formed between the conditioned and unconditioned stimuli. In order for that to happen, it is important for the two stimuli to occur close together in time. Conditioning is usually greatest when the conditioned stimulus is presented a short time (about half a second)

Learned associations

Imagine something nice, something delicious, your favourite food. Is it strawberries, chocolate, a barbecue, a curry? Think about it and visualise it, and you will find your mouth is watering! There is no such food nearby, you cannot really see, smell, or taste it, but you have learned that you love this food and this learned association has made you salivate. This will not happen if you are presented with a food you have never seen before, as you have not learned an association to it. If your most disliked sort of food were actually presented to you, your mouth would not water either. A different association would have been learned, and possibly a different response too.

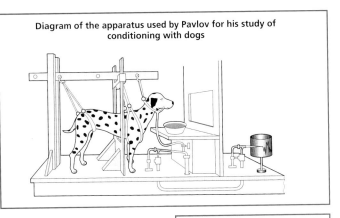

Diagram of the apparatus used by Pavlov for his study of conditioning with dogs

---

Classical conditioning

UCS → UCR

NS + UCS paired

NS (now CS) → UCR (now CR)

Why were the behaviourists such as Watson so interested in Pavlov's findings?

■ Activity: Consider the following situations and, for each, try to identify the UCS, UCR, NS, CS, CR:

A puff of air is directed at your eye. Your reflex response is to blink. At the same time as the air is blown, a bell is sounded. In time, the bell produces a blink response.

As you walk into the examination room you are filled with a sense of dread. There is a smell of roses from outside the window. A few weeks later you smell the same perfume of roses and are filled, inexplicably, with a sense of fear.

■ Activity: It is possible to demonstrate the classical conditioning of the eye-blink reflex. Blow *carefully* (using a drinking straw or similar) a puff of air across a volunteer's eyeball. (You may have to experiment a little to get a strong, reliable blink.) Now pair the puff of air with a gentle tap on the back of the participant's hand. Record the number of pairings required to produce the eye-blink to the tap on the hand alone.

> This means food is coming.

The idea that the dog is actually thinking anything is exactly what behaviourists did *not* suggest. The prediction of what comes next is entirely unconscious and without thought.

Do you think Kamin's study would face difficulties gaining ethical permission today?

before the unconditioned stimulus, and stays on while the unconditioned stimulus is presented. This is called **forward conditioning**. If the unconditioned stimulus is presented shortly before the conditioned stimulus, there is little or no conditioning. This situation is known as **backward conditioning**.

What is important is that the conditioned stimulus (i.e., the tone) allows the dog to unconsciously *predict* that the unconditioned stimulus (i.e., food) is about to be presented. The tone provides a clear indication that food is about to arrive, and so it produces an effect (i.e., salivation) that is similar to that produced by the food itself. Experimental extinction or the disappearance of salivation occurs when the tone no longer predicts the arrival of food. This explains why backward conditioning is so ineffective. If the conditioned stimulus is only presented after the unconditioned stimulus, then it cannot predict its arrival.

Expectation

Kamin (1969) showed that classical conditioning depends on expectation (a mental concept, foreign to behaviourists). The animals in the experimental group received light paired with electric shock, and learned to react with fear and avoidance when the light came on. The animals in the contrast group had no training. Then both groups received a series of trials with a light–tone combination followed by shock. Finally, both groups received only the tone. The contrast group responded with fear to the tone on its own, but the experimental group did not.

What is going on here? The experimental animals learned that light predicted shock, and so they ignored the fact that the tone also predicted shock. The contrast animals learned that the tone predicted shock, because they had not previously learned something different. The term **blocking** is used to refer to what happened with the experimental animals: a conditioned stimulus does not lead to conditioning if another conditioned stimulus is already being used to predict the onset of the unconditioned stimulus.

Rescorla and Wagner (1972) proposed a theory of classical conditioning that accounts for blocking and many other phenomena. According to their theory, conditioning depends on the discrepancy between obtained and expected reinforcement. In the study by Kamin (1969), the shock was fully predicted by the light. Adding the tone did not introduce any discrepancy between obtained and expected reinforcement, and so there was no conditioning to the tone.

Evaluation of classical conditioning

Classical conditioning is an important form of learning and can be used to explain many behaviours in non-human animals and humans, such as phobias (strong fears of certain objects or situations). Classical conditioning was the basis for **behaviourism**. John Watson, the founder of behaviourism, felt that the principles of learning outlined by Pavlov and Thorndike (see later) offered psychology a way to become a more objective science because conditioning involves directly observed behaviours.

One-trial learning

Classical conditioning is more complex than used to be thought. It used to be assumed that classical conditioning occurs only after many training trials, and that the unconditioned stimulus must follow the conditioned stimulus very closely in time. Garcia, Ervin, and Koelling (1966) discovered a dramatic exception to these assumptions. Indeed, it was such an exception to what generally happens that many psychologists at first refused to accept the findings, and Garcia had great difficulty in publishing them.

John Watson, 1878–1958.

Garcia et al. (1966) studied taste aversion. Rats have a strong preference for sweet-tasting foods. Some were given saccharin-flavoured water followed by a drug that caused intestinal illness several hours later. This produced one-trial learning, with the rats only needing to be sick once in order to avoid drinking the water thereafter. Why was conditioning so rapid in this case? Animals are biologically prepared to learn to behave in ways that will ensure their own survival, and it is clearly important for animals to learn to avoid poisoned food.

Preparedness

The early behaviourists assumed that the strong associations needed for classical conditioning could be formed between almost any conditioned stimulus and any unconditioned stimulus. This notion has been disproved, because some associations are much easier to form than others. In one study, rats learned to associate saccharin-flavoured water with illness produced by X-rays, but they did not learn to associate light and sound with illness. It was suggested that rats naturally learn to associate taste with illness, but they are not equipped biologically to associate external stimuli like light and sound with illness. Seligman (1970) called this "**preparedness**"—the tendency for members of a species to be biologically predisposed to acquire certain conditioned responses, which might be encountered in their environment, more easily than others that they might not encounter.

The vapourer moth caterpillar is poisonous, and any animal eating it will be ill or even die. Potential predators must learn to avoid these caterpillars quickly, to minimise illness. If too many are eaten before the predators learn to avoid them, then the brightly coloured signalling strategy is not working.

Language

Classical conditioning is much less important in humans than in other species. A major reason for this is that humans possess language. With other species, extinction usually occurs only slowly and over a fairly long period of time. With humans, simply telling them that the unconditioned stimulus will not be presented again can produce immediate extinction (Davey, 1983). The key point here was expressed by Mackintosh (1994, p.392):

> People have rather more efficient, language- or rule-based forms of learning at their disposal than the laborious formation of associations between a CS [conditioned stimulus] and a US [unconditioned stimulus]. Even behaviour therapy, one of the apparently more successful attempts to apply principles of conditioning to human affairs, has given way to cognitive behaviour therapy or simply cognitive therapy.

However there are instances where this is not true, such as the treatment of phobias that have been acquired through classical conditioning (see Section 18, Treating Mental Disorders).

Does telling a person with a spider phobia that there is nothing to fear bring about the end of their phobia?

Classical conditioning in real life

In laboratory studies of classical conditioning, a *passive* animal is presented with various conditioned and unconditioned stimuli. In real life, however, learning typically involves the animal or human interacting *actively* with the environment. Nevertheless, classical conditioning does explain some natural behaviours. According to Grier and Burk (1992, p.719), "Although usually studied in the laboratory with artificial CSs [conditioned stimuli] such as ringing bells or flashing lights, classical conditioning clearly is a natural phenomenon with real biological value." Taste aversion is one clear example of the biological value of classical conditioning. Grier and Burk also argued that classical conditioning is involved when predators learn to associate certain sounds or smells with potential prey.

Operant Conditioning

In everyday life, people are often persuaded to behave in certain ways by the offer of some reward or reinforcement. For example, students at school deliver the morning papers because they are paid, and amateur athletes take part in competitions because of the praise they receive for performing well. These are two examples of what is known in psychology as operant or instrumental conditioning. Much of operant conditioning is based on the **law of reinforcement**: the probability of a given response occurring increases if that response is followed by a reward or positive reinforcer such as food or praise.

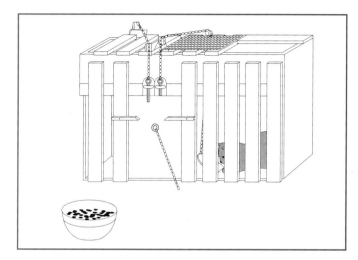

Thorndike demonstrated trial and error learning by placing a cat in a puzzle box. The cat eventually discovered how to get out and on subsequent trials did this immediately, an example of instrumental learning.

Basic findings

Edward Thorndike (1874–1949) extended classical learning theory to include **instrumental learning**. As we noted in Section 9 when looking at problem solving, Thorndike suggested that learning could take place through *trial and error*, rather than just by association as in classical conditioning. He demonstrated this by placing a hungry cat in a "puzzle box" with a fish hanging nearby. The cat struggled to try to get out of the box, and eventually, by accident, tripped the latch of the box and jumped out. The next time the cat was placed in the box, it went through the same sequence of somewhat random behaviours but took less time to escape from the cage. After a few more trials the cat had learned what to do and, each time it was imprisoned, would release the catch immediately. This led Thorndike to state his "Law of Effect": acts that are followed by a positive state of affairs are more likely to recur than acts that are followed by an annoying state of affairs.

- Positive effects (rewards) lead to the *stamping in* of a behaviour.
- Negative effects (punishments) lead to the *stamping out* of behaviour.

This theory of instrumental conditioning was further developed by B.F. Skinner (1904–1990) into **operant conditioning**. Thorndike's and Skinner's approaches were similar in that they concentrated on the *effects* of behaviour rather than Pavlov's focus on the behaviours themselves.

The best-known example of operant conditioning is provided by Skinner (1938). A rat is placed in a cage with a lever (bar) sticking out on one side (see diagram on the facing page). If the lever is pressed, a pellet of food will be delivered. At first the rat presses the lever by accident but soon learns that there is a link between lever pressing and food appearing. Skinner stated that the rat *operated* on the environment. When there was a reward (food) this **reinforced** the likelihood of the behaviour occurring again. When an animal performs a behaviour (or operates on the environment) there are four possible consequences:

Note that reinforcement always makes behaviour more likely.

- *Positive reinforcement* is pleasurable and therefore increases the likelihood of a behaviour occurring again. Examples are receiving food or any reward.
- *Negative reinforcement* refers to the avoidance of an unpleasant stimulus, but the result is that it is also pleasurable (like positive reinforcement) and thus increases the likelihood of a behaviour. For instance, if the floor of a rat's cage was electrified and pressing the lever stopped this, then the rat would be more likely to press the lever. In human terms, an example could be discovering that if you smile sweetly while being told off, the person stops telling you off. This increases the likelihood of the smiling behaviour.
- *Positive punishment* such as receiving an electric shock, decreases the likelihood of a behaviour. For example, if the rat received a shock every time it pressed the lever it would stop doing it. If you get burned when you touch a hot pan, you are not likely to touch it again.
- *Negative punishment* such as removing some food (removing a pleasant stimulus), decreases the likelihood of a behaviour. An example in human terms might be being grounded for staying out late. The removal of a desirable option (going out) reduces the likelihood of staying out late.

B.F. Skinner, 1904–1990.

The probability of a response decreases if it is not followed by a positive reinforcer. This phenomenon, discussed earlier, is known as experimental extinction. As with classical conditioning, there is usually some spontaneous recovery after extinction has occurred.

There are two major types of positive reinforcers or rewards: primary and secondary reinforcers. **Primary reinforcers** are stimuli that are needed to live (e.g., food, water, sleep, air). **Secondary reinforcers** are rewarding because we have learned to associate them with primary reinforcers. Secondary reinforcers include money, praise, and attention. In your AS level studies, one explanation for attachment was couched in terms of secondary reinforcers. Dollard and Miller (1950) suggested that a mother (or person doing the feeding) rewards the infant because she reduces the infant's primary needs for food and water. The rewarding properties of the primary needs then become associated with the mother, who therefore becomes a secondary reinforcer. Her presence alone has become rewarding and the infant shows pleasure whenever he or she hears or sees the mother.

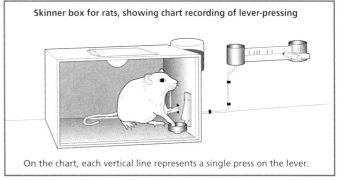

Skinner box for rats, showing chart recording of lever-pressing

On the chart, each vertical line represents a single press on the lever.

A child learns that he can avoid being hit by his father if he smiles. Which kind of reinforcement is this: positive or negative?

Schedules of reinforcement

It seems reasonable that we tend to keep doing things that are rewarded and that we stop doing things that are not rewarded. However, Skinner (1938) found some complexities in operant conditioning. We have looked so far at **continuous reinforcement**, in which the reinforcer or reward is given after every response. However, it is rare in everyday life for our actions to be continuously reinforced. Consider what happens with partial reinforcement, in which only some of the responses are rewarded. Skinner discovered four main schedules of partial reinforcement:

- *Fixed ratio schedule*: every nth (e.g., fifth, tenth) response is rewarded. Workers who receive extra money for achieving certain targets are on this schedule.
- *Variable ratio schedule*: every nth response is rewarded on average, but the gap between two rewarded responses may be very small or fairly large; this schedule is found in fishing and gambling.
- *Fixed interval schedule*: the first response produced after a given interval of time (e.g., 60 seconds) is rewarded. Workers who are paid regularly every week are on this schedule — they receive reward after a given interval of time, but do not need to produce a specific response.
- *Variable interval schedule*: on average, the first response produced after a given interval of time (e.g., 60 seconds) is rewarded. However, the actual interval is sometimes shorter than this and sometimes longer. For example, self-employed workers whose customers make payments at irregular times are rewarded at variable intervals, but they do not need to produce a specific response.

Can you think of some other examples of situations in everyday life involving the various schedules of reinforcement?

Although these gamblers have no idea when or if they will receive a payout, they continue to play. This is an example of the most successful reinforcement schedule —variable ratio reinforcement.

It might be thought that continuous reinforcement (with reward available after every response) would lead to better conditioning than partial reinforcement. In fact, the opposite is the case. Continuous reinforcement leads to the lowest rate of responding, with the variable schedules (especially variable ratio) leading to very fast rates of responding. This helps to explain why gamblers, who receive variable rate reinforcement, often find it hard to stop their addiction.

What about extinction? Those schedules of reinforcement associated with the best conditioning also show the most resistance to extinction. Thus, rats that have been trained on the variable ratio schedule will keep

Circus animals are trained to perform complex routines by using the concept of shaping. The animal trainer gradually works towards the target routine by rewarding behaviours that at first are very simple, but gradually the rewards are given for successively closer approximations to the target.

responding in extinction (in the absence of reward) longer than rats on any other schedule. Rats trained with continuous reinforcement stop responding the soonest. One reason why continuous reinforcement leads to rapid extinction is that there is a very obvious shift from reward being provided on every trial to reward not being provided at all. Animals trained on the variable schedules are used to reward being provided infrequently and irregularly, and so it takes much longer for them to realise that they are no longer going to be rewarded for their responses.

Shaping

One of the features of operant conditioning is that the required response has to be made before it can be reinforced. How can we condition an animal to produce a complex response that it would not produce naturally? Think of some of the routines performed by circus animals. They would never produce such a routine out of the blue so that it could be rewarded. What happens is that the animal trainer gradually works towards the target routine using a process called **shaping**. Learned behaviours are gradually built up through by successive reinforcements for behaviours that are progressively closer and closer to the desired behaviour. Skinner used this technique to teach pigeons to play a basic form of table tennis! He did this by rewarding them every time they made contact with any table-tennis ball (see the picture below). Then he progressively rewarded them for actions that were more and more like the actual game.

Punishment

When a response is followed by an aversive stimulus this is known as **punishment training**. Punishment may not always be effective. For example, if the aversive stimulus occurs shortly after the response, then it has the effect of reducing the likelihood that the response will be produced in future. If there is substantial delay, however, then the effects of the aversive stimulus are much reduced.

If a small child is misbehaving in a supermarket, parents will sometimes offer sweets as a pacifier. Which kind of reinforcement is this? What is the likely outcome for future behaviour?

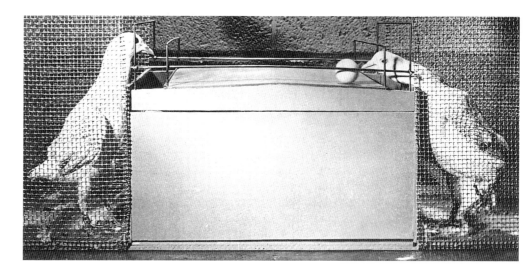

Punishment

Using punishment alone to affect behaviour is regarded by most psychologists today as a technique that is morally and ethically dubious. When this belief is added to research that has shown how punishment on its own has at best only short-lived effects, it is surprising that punishments are still used in so many situations, from family life to warring nations.

Many cultures, such as our own, still use punishment to deal with criminal offenders. Fines or prison sentences are serious punishers in

their own right, but research suggests that they would be more effective if linked to some kind of reward for not re-offending. Figures from the Central Statistical Office (1996) show that punishment alone does not have much success. In England and Wales between 1987 and 1990, three in every five males sent to prison became re-offenders, and in 1991 75% of young male offenders had been reconvicted within 2 years; 12% within 3 months of their release from prison.

In relation to human behaviour, it is clear that sometimes punishment is reinforcing instead of reducing the likelihood that a behaviour is repeated. The attention that is associated with receiving punishment is a reward for some people so that they become more rather than less likely to emit a behaviour.

Skinner claimed that the effects of punishment were short lived. Evidence supporting this view was presented by Estes (1944). Two groups of rats learned to press a lever for food, and were then given a series of extinction trials. One group was given a strong electric shock for every lever press during the early stages of extinction, but the other group was not. The punishment reduced the rate of responding for a while (suppression). However, in the long run the two groups produced the same number of responses. This supports the view that punishment doesn't result in lasting learning or true extinction.

Punishment usually has a more lasting effect when other, desirable behaviours are rewarded at the same time. For example, a child who is punished for putting his or her elbows on the table at mealtime is most likely to stop doing this if he or she is also rewarded for sitting properly.

Behaviours linked to operant conditioning

Avoidance learning

Nearly all drivers stop at red traffic lights because of the possibility of aversive stimuli in the form of an accident or trouble with the police if they do not. This is a situation in which no aversive stimulus is presented if suitable action is taken, and it is an example of **avoidance learning**. Many aversive stimuli strengthen any responses that stop the aversive stimuli being presented, and they are known as *negative reinforcers*.

Avoidance learning can be very effective, as was shown by Solomon and Wynne (1953). Dogs were placed in a two-compartment apparatus. A change in the lighting served as a warning that a strong electric shock was about to be presented. The dogs could avoid being shocked by jumping into the other compartment. Most dogs received a few shocks at the start of the experiment. After that, however, they generally avoided the shock for the remaining 50 or more trials.

Mowrer (1947) put forward a two-process learning theory to account for avoidance learning. According to this theory, the first process involves classical conditioning. The pairing of neutral (e.g., walls of the compartment) and aversive stimuli (electric shock) produces conditioned fear. The second process involves operant conditioning. The avoidance response of jumping into the other compartment is rewarded or reinforced by fear reduction.

Two-process theory provides a plausible account of avoidance learning. However, there are some problems with the notion that the avoidance response occurs to reduce fear. Dogs in the Solomon and Wynne study typically responded to the warning signal in about 1.5 seconds, which is probably too little time for the fear response to have developed. After the avoidance response occurred regularly, the dogs did not behave as if they were anxious. Thus, it is hard to argue that their avoidance behaviour was motivated only by fear reduction.

How could the principles of avoidance learning be used to discourage criminals from re-offending?

Learned helplessness

Seligman (1975) studied another form of learning based on aversive stimuli. Dogs were exposed to electric shocks they could not avoid. After that, they were put in a box with a barrier in the middle. The dogs were given shocks after a warning signal, but they could escape by jumping over the barrier into the other part of the box. In fact, most of the dogs passively accepted the shocks, and did not learn to avoid or escape them. Seligman used the term **learned helplessness** to refer to passive behaviour in situations in which unpleasant stimuli could be escaped or avoided by appropriate action. The animal does not escape because it has learned to be passive.

Dogs who had *not* previously received unavoidable shocks rapidly learned to avoid the shocks by jumping over the barrier as soon as the warning signal was presented. These dogs were simply showing avoidance learning. Dogs who had learned helplessness just remained where they were.

Attribution theory

Seligman (1975) argued that the learned helplessness seen in dogs is very similar to the passive helplessness shown by humans suffering from some kinds of clinical depression (see page 641). A cognitive account of the processes involved in learned helplessness was offered by Abramson, Seligman, and Teasdale (1978). In their attribution theory, they argued that people might attribute failure to an internal cause (themselves) or to an external cause (other people or the situation). For example, your boyfriend finishes your relationship and you are convinced that this is because of your moodiness (an internal cause) or the fact that you have very little money for nice clothes (external cause).

In addition, individuals might attribute failure to a stable cause that was likely to continue in the future or to an unstable cause that might change soon. For example, the moodiness may be a permanent feature of your character (stable) or perhaps it is just because exams are looming ahead (unstable).

Finally, people might attribute failure to a global cause (relevant to many situations) or to a specific cause (relevant only to one situation). For example, you may be moody with everyone (global) or just with your boyfriend because you didn't feel that he really loved you (specific cause).

Abramson et al. argued that people suffering from learned helplessness tend to attribute failure to internal, stable, and global causes. Thus, they feel personally responsible for failure, they think the factors leading to the current failure will continue in the future, and they think those factors will influence other situations.

If you are asked to discuss conditioning in non-human animals, how might you relate the evidence to human behaviour?

Evaluation of operant conditioning

The fact that much of the evidence is based on laboratory studies with non-human animals may reduce the meaningfulness of the concept of operant conditioning for human behaviour, yet it is often very effective. It is possible to control the behaviour of humans and other species by clever use of reinforcement. For example, the training of circus animals and guide-dogs is largely based on the principles of operant conditioning. Operant conditioning has also been used successfully in the treatment of various mental disorders. For example, there is the token economy, in which patients are rewarded for producing desirable behaviour of various kinds. This token economy approach has been used with several kinds of patients including schizophrenics (see Section 18, Treating Mental Disorders).

What examples of operant conditioning can you think of from your own upbringing?

Operant conditioning has been shown in numerous species (see Grier & Burk, 1992). For example, Boycott (1965) trained octopuses to avoid crabs (part of their normal diet). This was done by presenting the octopus with a white square and a crab, and then giving the octopus an electric shock. The octopuses were not shocked when there was no white square, and they learned to take crabs when there was no danger of receiving a shock. Similar operant conditioning procedures were used to train octopuses to take crabs and avoid fish, or vice versa. However, the concept of operant conditioning has some limitations.

Equipotentiality

Skinner seems to have believed that virtually any response could be conditioned in any stimulus situation. This is known as **equipotentiality**. But actually, some forms of operant conditioning are much more difficult to produce than others. Breland and Breland (1961) tried to train a pig to insert a wooden token into a piggy bank for reward. What happened was that the pig picked up the token, but then repeatedly dropped it on the floor. In the words of Breland and Breland, the pig would "root it, drop it again, root it along the way, pick it up, toss it in the air, drop it, root it some more, and so on". They argued that their findings showed evidence of instinctive drift, meaning that what animals learn tends to resemble their instinctive behaviour.

Convincing evidence that instinctive behaviour plays a much larger role in operant conditioning than Skinner believed was provided by Moore (1973). He took films of pigeons pecking at keys for either food or water reward. Students were then asked to decide what the reward was by looking at the films of the pigeons' pecking behaviour. They were correct 87% of the time. Birds pecking for food usually struck the key with an open beak, and made sharp, vigorous pecks. When pecking for water, the pigeons had their bill closed and there was a more sustained contact

with the key. The suggestion is that animal behaviour is governed by innate predispositions as much as, if not more than, reinforcements.

What behaviours would be most easy to condition in rats and mice?

Explanatory deficiencies

According to Skinner, operant conditioning involves forming an association between a given response and a reinforcer. However, as Mackintosh (1994) pointed out, matters are often more complex than that. He gave the example of a rat that is trained to press a lever in a Skinner box in order to obtain sucrose pellets. After that, the rat eats sucrose pellets in a different place. This is followed by an injection of lithium chloride, which conditions an aversion to sucrose pellets. Finally, the rat refrains from pressing the lever in the Skinner box, even though nothing has been done to weaken directly the lever-pressing response.

Mackintosh (1994, p.382) argued that this example illustrates a very important limitation of Skinner's views on operant conditioning:

> *Conditioning is not reducible to the strengthening of new reflexes or stimulus–response connections by the automatic action of a process of reinforcement. It is more profitably viewed as the process by which animals detect and learn about the relationship between events in their environment, be those events stimuli, responses, or reinforcers.*

In similar fashion, Bandura (1977) argued that "Reinforcement serves principally as an informative and motivational operation rather than as a mechanical response strengthener."

Alternative explanations

A further problem is that there are clearly other forms of learning, beyond conditioning, which involve cognitive processes. Skinner's view was that the mind was a "black box"— there was no need to look at what goes on in there in order to understand behaviour. One of the most obvious weaknesses of the conditioning approach is that there are several kinds of learning that do not seem to depend on conditioning principles.

Latent learning.   The principle of operant conditioning is that learning occurs as a consequence of reinforcement or punishment (it is stamped in or stamped out). However, there is evidence that learning can occur in the absence of any reinforcement. This is known as **latent learning**.

Several studies of latent learning have focused on rats running in mazes. Rats who explore a maze but receive no food reward for doing so seem from their behaviour to have learned very little. However, when food is provided in the goal box at the end or centre of the maze, the rats run rapidly to it, thus indicating that latent learning has occurred. In one study, Tolman and Honzik (1930) compared maze running in rats that either were rewarded or were not rewarded. The rewarded group received food at one end of the maze (the goal box) every time they found their way there. The non-rewarded rats spent the same amount of time each day in the maze but there was no food reward. They simply explored the maze. After 10 days, some of the non-rewarded group were given food in the goal box. Very quickly the previously non-rewarded rats were behaving just like the rewarded group, i.e., taking about 4 seconds to travel to the goal box. It had taken the rewarded group the whole 10 days to learn to travel this quickly to the goal box, whereas it took the non-rewarded group a few days to display the same behaviour change. Clearly the non-rewarded rats had been learning during their early days in the maze, though it was in the absence of any reinforcement and also in the absence of any external indication that learning was taking place

Is it reasonable to generalise from the behaviour of rats to other animals, such as monkeys and humans?

("behavioural silence"). Tolman (1948) used the phrase **cognitive map** to describe what it was they had learned.

The main problem with studies of latent learning was raised by Hilgard and Marquis (1961, p.233):

What does Hilgard and Marquis' criticism mean for the unrewarded rats in the maze?

> *It is never possible to state with complete certainty that a given experiment has accomplished its primary objective, that of temporarily eliminating reinforcement for one group of subjects in the experiment.*

Insight learning.   The Gestaltists studied a phenomenon known as **insight learning,** which involves a sudden restructuring or reorganisation of a problem. Insight learning (also called the "aha experience") was studied by Kohler (1925). For example, an ape called Sultan was placed in a cage with some sticks, none of which was long enough to reach a banana he wanted. Suddenly, he joined two sticks together, and was then able to reach the banana.

Birch (1945) studied apes brought up in captivity, and found little evidence of insightful problem solving in them. He pointed out that Kohler's apes had spent part of their lives in the wild, and so might have slowly learned the abilities that looked like sudden insight. In addition, Epstein et al. (1981) have suggested that one could explain apparent insight learning as nothing more than a set of conditioned responses.

Observational learning.   Bandura (1977) argued for the importance of **observational learning**. This is learning that is based on imitating the behaviour of others, especially if their behaviour is seen to be rewarded. Such imitation implies an internal representation of the behaviour, which is stored and used at a later date.

Bandura et al. (1963) showed observational learning in young children who watched a film in which an adult behaved aggressively or non-aggressively towards a large inflated clown known as a Bobo doll. After they had watched the film, the children played with the doll. Those who had seen the adult behave aggressively towards the doll were much more likely to treat it aggressively themselves. (Bandura's work is discussed more fully in Section 3, Pro- and Anti-social Behaviour.)

Bandura argued that the entire operant conditioning approach was very limited. According to him (1977, p.12):

An example of observational learning—attacking a Bobo doll.

> *Psychological theories have traditionally assumed that learning can occur only by performing responses and experiencing their effects. In actuality, virtually all learning phenomena resulting from direct experience occur on a vicarious [second-hand] basis by observing other people's behaviour and its consequences for them.*

Social Learning in Non-human Animals

In our quest to understand the explanations for behaviour in non-human animals we have considered the inheritance of adaptive behaviours and learning through conditioning. In this final Unit, our attention is on different forms of learning—those that involve other animals, i.e., social forms of learning.

Social Learning

Many animals live in groups of two or more **conspecifics**. Group living facilitates social learning for two main reasons. First, it offers the opportunity to learn by observing the behaviour of another and imitating any behaviour that appears to be desirable. The fact that it may appear to be desirable is called **vicarious reinforcement**—one animal receives reinforcement indirectly by observing what happens to another animal. The second reason is that group life presents many situations that require problems to be solved to ensure that individuals survive long enough to reproduce. For example, an individual has to be aware of the interrelationships within the group, needs to co-operate with other group members in foraging, and so on. Such social problems present greater challenges than many environmental problems.

Imitation is more than simply doing the same thing as another conspecific. For example, if one dog starts to bark and a lot of other dogs copy this behaviour we would not call this imitation. This would be social contagion. Imitation involves learning a complex set of behaviours.

There are advantages to social learning. It is much faster and far less costly than trial and error learning because trial and error learning often involves performing behaviours that may be detrimental to survival, or even fatal. A second advantage is that socially learned behaviours are passed from one generation to the next. Cultural transmission has much greater potential than other forms of learning. Cultural transmission (or inheritance) has been compared to genetic inheritance in so far as they both are governed by the principle of natural selection. The basis of natural selection is that any biologically determined behaviour that promotes survival and reproduction is likely to be retained because individuals with these characteristics survive. The same could be said of cultural inheritance. Behaviours that are adaptive will be retained because any individual using this behaviour is more likely to survive and reproduce.

Cultural evolution has the advantage of being much faster than genetic evolution. It is faster because genetic transmission relies on the passing of successive generations and also because it involves small changes, whereas cultural transmission leads to huge changes in a very wide range of behaviours. Brown (1986) argued that rapid cultural evolution will eventually make biological evolution irrelevant. For example, it took 200 million years for the first marine animals to evolve into amphibians, whereas it took 50 years of cultural evolution for man to move from flying to space travel.

Research evidence for imitation

Much of the evidence for the power of imitation as a form of learning comes from naturalistic observations of animals, such as Kawai's (1965) study of Japanese snow monkeys (see the Key Study on the next page) and observations made of blue tits opening the old-fashioned milk bottles with foil tops (see page 496). Fisher and Hinde (1947) argued that this behaviour could not be spread through genetic transmission because it occurred far too quickly. It is most likely that one or a few birds learned through trial and error and reinforcement that they could obtain milk by pecking the bottle tops, and this behaviour was quickly imitated.

This explanation was supported by a laboratory experiment carried out by Sherry and Galef (1984). In the first part of this experiment 16 Canadian black-backed chickadees, a relative of the blue tit, were placed in a cage with a small unopened plastic cream container (the individual portions given out in cafes). Four of the birds did learn that they could open the containers. In the second part of the experiment, the 12 birds that had failed to open the cream containers ("learner" birds) were placed in one of three conditions. Either they were placed in a cage with a "tutor" bird, one that had previously learned to open the cream containers, or they were placed in a cage with an opened container with the intention that this might help them discover the solution for themselves (discovery learning), or they were placed again on their own with an unopened container. Three birds in each of the first two groups learned the trick but the control group remained unenlightened. This experiment demonstrates the importance of imitation in learning.

Imitation and stimulus enhancement

Another conclusion from Sherry and Galef's experiment is that discovery learning is as effective as imitation. This can be explained using the concept of **stimulus enhancement**. An animal may find, by observing the behaviour of another animal, that they become more

Cultural transmission in Japanese snow monkeys

Kawai (1965) conducted a study of Japanese snow monkeys, observing them in their natural environment (a small Japanese island) over a number of years. The dense vegetation on the island made it difficult to observe the animals and therefore the researchers left food on the more open beach. The monkeys quickly learned that the beach was a good source of food and spent more and more time there. On one occasion they watched as one female, whom the researchers called Imo, took a sweet potato to the water and washed it to remove the sand and mud. Could this be an example of insight learning? Possibly, but in any case Imo immediately recognised that this was preferable to eating dirty potatoes and took to washing all her potatoes before eating them. Soon, other monkeys started to do the same thing and eventually 80% of the younger monkeys were washing their potatoes. They apparently saw what Imo did and imitated it. Interestingly this was not true of the older monkeys of whom only 18% took to washing their potatoes. This age difference may be due to the fact that the younger monkeys interact more and therefore had more opportunity to observe the washing behaviour.

The monkeys were also given wheat, which was left on the beach, and they ate this one grain at a time because it was covered in sand. One day, a few years after the potato washing started, Imo was seen to grab a handful of wheat off the beach and throw it into the sea. The dirt sank and the wheat floated, enabling her to collect the now clean wheat. The idea of throwing the wheat into the sea was more remarkable than her first invention because it is quite different from the monkeys' normal behaviour of cleaning food with their hands. This new behaviour was also quickly imitated and both of Imo's innovations became part of the group culture, being transmitted to subsequent generations.

Discussion points

1. The first time that Imo washed the potatoes was described as insight learning. How else could this be explained?

2. In order for other monkeys to imitate Imo's behaviour, what factors must be involved?

aware of certain stimuli in their environment. For example, some of the birds in Sherry and Galef's experiment may simply not have noticed the cream container and therefore not even tried to open it. When they observed the "tutor", this drew their own attention to the container, giving them the opportunity to discover the solution for themselves.

You may be able to solve a problem more quickly if you get a hint. Stimulus enhancement makes you aware of certain stimuli in the environment, things you might have overlooked.

However, stimulus enhancement by a tutor is not always supported by the evidence. Burt and Guilford (1999) trained pigeons to find a box of food under a grid in the floor. Another set of pigeons then watched the original birds while a control group were just given the grid alone. In this study Burt and Guilford found that the control group did better than the birds with a tutor, suggesting that neither imitation nor stimulus enhancement helped the birds in the first group.

Fritz and Kotrschal (1999) concluded, in relation to their own study of social learning and foraging, that it may be impossible to distinguish between social learning and stimulus enhancement.

If it is not possible to distinguish between social learning and stimulus enhancement, are both concepts necessary?

Imitating and tutoring

Sherry and Galef used the term "tutor" to describe the birds who had learned the trick and were acting as teachers to the learner birds, but an important distinction is made between imitation and tutoring. Imitation is a passive process where the individual animal does not deliberately perform an action so that it can be imitated, and the observer may or may not imitate what is seen. Tutoring is an active process where the tutor is modifying its behaviour in some way to accommodate the needs of the learner. Tutoring incurs some costs, perhaps just in terms of time, and therefore in order to remain adaptive there must be some long-term benefit for the tutor. Like altruism, this benefit may be in terms of increased fitness, such as when a parent tutors or teaches its offspring.

Tutoring can be seen in a naturalistic observational study of chimpanzees by Boesch (1991). The chimpanzees had a method for cracking open nuts using a stone for a hammer and a block of wood as an anvil. Mother chimpanzees would leave a hammer near a block to encourage their offspring to discover this tool use. In a few cases Boesch also observed direct teaching where a mother intervened when her offspring was having difficulty. The mother would put the nut in a better position or actually crack the nut for the infant, possibly as a demonstration. In one case, after a mother had watched her daughter trying unsuccessfully to crack some nuts, the mother took the hammer and examined it carefully. Having found a better way to hold the stone, the mother cracked open the nuts. Later, the daughter used the same hammer grip and was now successful. However, the concept of tutoring requires that there is some intention on the part of the tutor, and it is hard to assess the extent to which the mother chimpanzee's behaviour was intentional. In addition our understanding of tutoring includes the notion that the tutor has some idea of what the learner is thinking, which involves a Theory of Mind—a concept we will return to shortly.

Foraging

Virtually all animals engage in **foraging**, which involves a range of different activities many of which involve social learning. It starts with finding a suitable source of food. If the food source is living, then the animal may have to pursue, capture, and kill it. After that, the foraging animal has to handle the prey or prepare it for eating.

Feeding is of vital importance to animals, and so they need to develop effective foraging strategies. More specifically, they need to make various decisions during the course of foraging, such as the following:

- What kind or kinds of food are suitable?
- What is the best search strategy for finding prey?
- How should prey be captured and killed?
- How should killed prey be prepared for eating?
- How much food should be eaten?

Some of these tasks are accomplished as the result of innate behaviour, but many of them are learned either as a consequence of conditioning or social learning. We have already discussed examples of how social learning may influence foraging behaviour in the cases of Japanese snow monkeys and potato washing, and birds opening cream containers. We will now consider some other aspects of foraging, and innate and learned explanations for these.

Recognising suitable foods

In order to identify suitable food an animal needs a **search image**, a template to allow them to identify target food for their species. The ability of toads to recognise their food is innately driven. Toads have a diet mainly restricted to small insects. If you move a small dark piece of paper in front of a toad, it will snap at it. The toad's predisposition to snap at anything small, dark, and moving works well in the natural environment because anything answering this description is invariably an insect. Toads' feeding responses are not much affected by learning but this is not true for many other animals

In what way is innate recognition of suitable food an adaptive behaviour? When might such innate programming be non-adaptive?

Animals need to recognise food and they also need to recognise what food to avoid. Avoidance of poisonous food has already been explained in terms of "preparedness" (see page 509). It is also likely that animals learn through observation to avoid certain foods, otherwise it is difficult to see how poisonous animals would gain any advantage from warning colouration, as in the case of some butterflies or snakes. Other animals must learn to stay away on the basis of second-hand information.

Animals may also learn food preferences from each other. A study by Galef and Wigmore (1983) looked at the effects of one group of rats' food preferences on another group. Rats were paired and placed in cages with normal food. One member of each pair (the demonstrator) was removed and starved for 24 hours and then fed food that was either flavoured with cinnamon or cocoa. The demonstrator was returned to its partner (the observer) for 15 minutes. Following this the observer was given a choice of either cinnamon- or cocoa-flavoured food. The observer rat showed a clear preference for whatever flavour food that had been given to the demonstrator. This finding would explain how animals might exchange information about nearby food sources.

The term "demonstrator" is used in preference to the term "tutor". Can you suggest why?

Best strategies for foraging

Optimal foraging theory (OFT) is an explanation of foraging in terms of achieving a balance between costs and benefits ("optimal" means "best"). This theory was originally proposed by MacArthur and Pianka (1966) and by Emlen (1966). Foraging strategies (the ways that an animal finds food) are designed to maximise the benefits and to minimise the costs. According to the theory, there can be various kinds of benefits and costs. However, the major benefits usually consist of the number of calories consumed. The major costs are generally in the form of expenditure of energy, but can include the risks of being attacked by predators and the use of time.

An excellent example of optimal choice can be seen in one crow species that feeds on whelks. Zach (1979) observed that the crows manage to break open the tough whelk shells by dropping them onto rocks from a great height. The larger whelks provide more food and their shells are easier to break, but they are more costly in terms of carrying the extra weight and having to drop the whelk from a greater height. OFT would predict that gathering larger whelks is a more optimal than gathering smaller whelks at less energy cost—and that is what Zach found.

Zach interpreted this behaviour as being learned and possibly socially learned through imitation. Foragers with well-developed learning strategies will have an advantage over those who are less flexible.

Hunting in groups

One of the reasons for group living is to assist when hunting. Groups can have more effective strategies than individuals, though there is a cost in terms of the food having to go round all the members of the group.

Such communal hunting is found in lions, wolves, killer whales, communal spiders, and other species. Detailed evidence on the effects of group size on hunting success in lions was reported by Schaller (1972). When lions hunted gazelle, wildebeest, zebra, or other prey on their own, their overall success rate was only 15%. This increased to 29% when two lions hunted together, and to 37% when three lions hunted together. The success rate decreased somewhat when there were more than three lions in the hunting group.

Animals that are communal hunters are likely to acquire some of their strategies through social learning. For example, Caro (1980) documented the way mother cats teach their kittens how to capture prey. The mother brings dead prey to the kittens and eats it in front of them. Next time the mother brings dead prey but leaves it for the kittens. Later still, the mother brings an injured but live prey for the kittens to play with. Finally she brings a live prey and releases it for the kitten to try to catch. If the prey escapes the mother recatches it, and offers it again to the kittens. This would appear to be an example of tutoring by the mother.

Kitten tutoring

Intelligence in Non-human Animals

We will now consider the evidence for intelligence in non-human animals. The link between social learning and intelligence is that, in order to imitate the behaviour of another animal, the observing animal must understand that the particular behaviour is linked to the particular outcome. For example, if a learner observes another conspecific lying in wait for a prey, and then pouncing on the prey, the learner must realise that the hunting strategy increased the likelihood of capturing the prey and therefore that it is desirable to imitate the behaviour. This linking requires some form of intelligence. So social learning is evidence for intelligence in non-human animals.

Harré and Lamb (1983) define intelligence as "the all round mental ability (or thinking skills) either of humans or of lower animal species". However the problem with this, and many other definitions of intelligence, is that the terms do not lend themselves to testing. How can we assess whether a non-human animal has intelligence unless we have some objective means of making this assessment? For the purposes of research an operational definition might identify certain behaviours that are regarded as signs of intelligent behaviour. A **Theory of Mind** is one such behaviour. To possess a Theory of Mind is to have an understanding of others' thoughts and emotions, recognising that they are different from one's own. This ability enables one to make predictions of how others will behave.

How would you define intelligence?

Heyes (1998) states that there are six types of behaviour that are representative of an animal that has a Theory of Mind:

1. Imitation
2. Self-recognition
3. Social relationships
4. Role-taking
5. Deception or Machiavellian intelligence
6. Perspective taking.

Imitation

Imitation is regarded as evidence of a Theory of Mind, as we have already pointed out, because it is believed that the imitator has mentally attributed purpose to the behaviour of another, thus imitation is said to involve conscious mental states. The study by Kawai (see page 518) showed an ability to imitate in animals but, as we saw, it was also possible to explain this behaviour in terms of stimulus enhancement, which is a **non-mentalistic behaviour**, i.e., it involves no mental activity. The same could be said of all the other evidence we examined. So it appears that the evidence from research on imitation cannot be taken as clear evidence of intelligence in non-human animals.

Self-recognition

In what way is a mentalistic state evidence of intelligence?

The ability to recognise oneself in a mirror is taken as evidence of self-awareness. Self-awareness refers to consciousness of the self as a separate individual and therefore implies that an animal has developed a self-concept, a mentalistic state.

Gallup (1971) developed the **mirror test** as a means of testing self-recognition. The test involves anaesthetising an animal to enable the researcher to place a red mark (using odourless, non-irritating dye) on the animal's forehead. When the animal regains consciousness, it is observed to see how often it touches its forehead, first in the absence of a mirror and then in the presence of a mirror. An animal with a self-concept should touch this mark when looking in the mirror. Gallup (1977) and others have found that chimpanzees and orang-utans are capable of self-recognition but not other primates or non-primate animals.

This evidence is supported by more naturalistic studies where animals have been shown to adorn their bodies with objects, such as putting bananas on their head, and also using mirrors to inspect areas of their body that would otherwise be inaccessible (Cheney & Seyfarth, 1990).

However, there are some criticisms of the mirror-test approach. First of all another study looked at mirror behaviour in pigeons. Epstein, Lanza, and Skinner (1981) showed that pigeons can learn to use a mirror to help them remove bits of paper that had been stuck to their feathers. Either we have to accept that pigeons do have a Theory of Mind or that the mirror test does not demonstrate the ability to use mental concepts. In view of the fact that autistic children can also use mirrors to inspect their bodies *and* are thought not to have a Theory of Mind, it would seem that the latter explanation is correct, in other words the mirror test is not actually testing Theory of Mind.

Heyes (1998) further suggests that the findings from mirror-test studies are artefacts, that is they arise because of the methods used in the studies. She suggests that the fact that the mirror-present condition always comes quite a long time after the mirror-absent condition means that the primates are much more active and alert in this condition and therefore more able to touch the mark. In addition to this, an examination of the actual data shows that the differences between mirror-absent and mirror-present conditions were not that great.

What is the extraneous variable in these mirror experiments?

In defence of the mirror test we should point out that it is also used to demonstrate self-recognition in infants—except that they are not anaesthetised. Lewis and Brooks-Gunn (1979) used the "rouge test" to argue that infants of a certain age had developed a self-concept. If we accept this evidence, then we must also accept that the mirror test demonstrates self-recognition and a Theory of Mind in some animals (the great ape species) and therefore could be evidence of intelligence.

Social relationships

Chimpanzees can learn to recognise themselves in a mirror and use the mirror to investigate parts of themselves they cannot easily see.

The argument is that, in order for animals to have social relationships, they must have a Theory of Mind. To refer back to the autistic children, autism is a condition where individuals lack the ability to interact with other people, they lack communication skills, and avoid eye contact with others. It is suggested that this can be explained in terms of the Theory of Mind, or rather the lack of it. What autistic children lack is the ability to

understand that other people have separate and different mental states from their own, and this precludes autistic individuals forming a relationship with others, or even communicating with them.

Do social relationships in non-human animals involve a knowledge of their own intentions as well as an understanding of the intentions of other conspecifics? This would be evidence for a Theory of Mind. Stammbach (1988) carried out a field experiment to determine whether or not such mental states were involved in social relationships of long-tailed monkeys. Stammbach trained one monkey in a troop to obtain food by controlling three levers. The other monkeys didn't imitate this behaviour but they did come and sit by the trained monkey, grooming him. It was claimed that this showed that the untrained monkeys recognised the superior knowledge of the trained monkey and groomed him in order to establish a social relationship that might lead to more food. This implies a Theory of Mind because the untrained monkeys demonstrated insight about the mental state of the expert monkey.

However, an alternative, and simpler, explanation is that the untrained monkeys sat near the expert because they were more likely to be rewarded through obtaining food. Thus their behaviour could be explained in terms of non-mentalistic operant conditioning.

Why is conditioning non-mentalistic?

This view is supported by studying similar behaviour in rats (Timberlake & Grant, 1975). One rat was fixed to a food trolley. Other rats soon followed this rat around, but it is presumed that a rat would not have formed a mentalistic concept (because rats are unlikely to be intelligent) and the behaviour was due to associating the trolley-rat with reward.

The conclusion is, once again, that there is not strong evidence to support the idea that non-human social relationships involve mentalistic concepts. There is no doubt that non-human animals do have social relationships but these do not necessitate a knowledge of the other conspecifics' minds. The formation of associations is a much simpler explanation and therefore preferable.

Why is a simpler explanation of a particular behaviour preferable?

Role taking

Role taking concerns the ability to watch the behaviour of another person and understand their intentions. Premack and Woodruff (1978) tested this in a female chimpanzee called Sarah as a means of assessing her ability to understand the human language she was being taught. They showed her videotapes of human actors attempting to solve different problems. For example, in one sequence a person was seen shivering violently next to an unplugged heater or attempting to escape from a locked cage. Just when the actor was about to solve the problem the videotape was stopped and Sarah was shown two pictures of possible solutions, only one of which would be successful. Results showed that Sarah consistently selected the photograph that depicted the actor performing an action that would lead to the correct solution to the problem.

These findings led Premack and Woodruff to be the first to formulate the Theory of Mind hypothesis. They argued that Sarah was able to understand the beliefs and intentions of the actors and only with this knowledge was she able choose the correct picture. However, it is possible that Sarah was able to pick the correct picture because she was using physical cues in the video and photographs to enable her to match them, or she might have been basing her choice on previous familiarity with a given situation.

On the other hand, later studies have supported the view that non-human animals are able to make attributions about the behaviour of another. For example, Povinelli, Nelson, and Boysen (1992) conducted a study with pairs of chimpanzees. One chimpanzee was able to see some food but could not reach it, while the other chimpanzee could not see the food but could touch it. After some training in communication skills, the chimpanzee who could see was able to guide the chimpanzee who could not. However, most importantly, when the roles were reversed the two chimpanzees were immediately able to get the food. This indicates quite a sophisticated level of role taking.

On balance the evidence related to role taking does support the idea that some non-human animals do have a Theory of Mind.

Deception or Machiavellian intelligence

Deception or **Machiavellian intelligence**, is related to the Theory of Mind. In order to intentionally deceive another individual one has to have an understanding of what they know, or rather don't know. Intentional deception involves deliberately manipulating the information that a second animal receives. Premack and Woodruff (1978) provided evidence of this ability in chimpanzees. One chimpanzee saw a trainer place food under one of two containers which were both out of the chimpanzee's reach. Then another trainer entered the room. This trainer was either wearing a green laboratory coat or a white one. The chimpanzee had previously been trained to know that the trainer in the green coat was co-operative—she would help him get the food. The white-coated trainer was competitive—if the trainer chose the right food dish, she would keep it.

What did the chimpanzees do? On most trials they were able to get food with both trainers—they helped the co-operative trainer and deceived the competitive one. The fact that the chimpanzees knew that the competitive trainer would act on their false information is evidence of a Theory of Mind.

However, as before, it is possible to explain the chimpanzees' behaviour in terms of associative learning and not intentional deception. They could have simply learned that they should point to the container with food in it when the trainer has a green laboratory coat on and not when she has a white laboratory coat on as the former is more likely to result in a reward.

Whiten and Byrne (1991) remain convinced that non-human animals are capable of deception, on the basis of their own research and that of other researchers. To convince others they compiled a record of 250 individual observations of such behaviour. Examples include observations of female primates suppressing their usual copulation calls while copulating with a subordinate male to avoid being discovered by the dominant male, or of a vervet monkey making a fake alarm call to get itself out of a tight spot, when cornered by an aggressor (see page 542).

What are your own conclusions about deception, on the basis of this evidence?

Perspective taking

The final behaviour to consider, as evidence for a Theory of Mind in non-human animals, is perspective taking which involves being able to understand that another individual has a different perspective or view from oneself. The best example of this is seen in the Sally–Anne test, conducted with children (see the diagram on the next page). The test involves two dolls, Sally and Anne. Sally puts a marble in her basket and then leaves the room. Anne removes the marble and places it in a box. Sally returns and the observer is asked, "Where will Sally look for her marble?" If the observer answers "in her basket", this is a false belief and demonstrates that the observer has got a Theory of Mind because he or she realises that Sally won't know that the marble has been moved. This test is used to demonstrate a child's ability to take the perspective of another.

Children under the age of 4, and autistic children, have been found to be unable to do this (Baron-Cohen, Leslie & Frith, 1985). Tomasello and Call (1994) tested primates who had been taught human language, and found that none of them passed the Sally–Anne test. However, Hauser (1998) felt that the Sally–Anne test was totally inappropriate for primates and devised his own "ape version". In this version a monkey observes an actor watching an object being hidden. A screen is then placed between the actor and the hiding place, thus preventing the actor seeing that another person has moved the object but the monkey sees this. When the screen is removed the actor either looks in the old location or the correct new location. If the monkey stares longer at the actor when he looks in the new location this is taken as an indication of a Theory of Mind because the monkey knows the actor is looking in the wrong place. In fact this is what both monkeys and very young children did, indicating that they both do have a Theory of Mind after all.

Do you feel that this method is a more suitable means of assessing perspective taking in non-human animals?

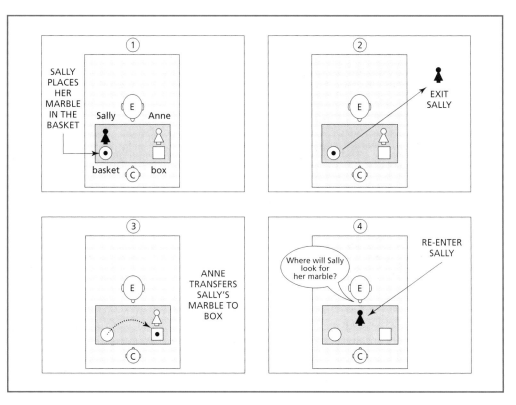

Where do you think Sally will look for her marble? Is this a "false belief"?

Do non-human animals have a Theory of Mind?

On balance the evidence appears to indicate that non-human animals do not have a Theory of Mind (Cartwright, 2001). Any evidence that has looked reasonably promising has also been able to be explained in terms of associative learning. The evidence for deception is probably the strongest but it is still not clear to what extent this is intentional behaviour. The ape version of the Sally–Anne test also provided promising evidence.

However, if non-human animals lack a Theory of Mind (or the ability to be aware of mental concepts) this does not mean they have no intelligence. It is only one possible line of evidence. Intelligence has also been defined as the ability to solve problems and all animals have this capacity in relation to their own environments. Warden (1951) devised a series of intelligence tests for non-human animals. One of them consisted of a cage with three plates on the floor. The animal had to learn to step on one plate which would give it access to food. Once this had been well learned, the task became more complicated. The animal now had to step on two plates to gain access to food. The number of plates that the animal can cope with is taken to be equivalent to its intelligence score. Guinea pigs scored one plate, rats reached two plates, cats got to seven plates, and some monkeys were able to learn a sequence of 22 plates in a given order. Remember that intelligence is equivalent to how you choose to assess it. In this Unit we have considered intelligence in terms of the ability to use a Theory of Mind, but this can be challenged as inappropriate. Other evidence might include the use of language and memory, both discussed in the next Section.

SECTION SUMMARY

❖ We can establish that living species do evolve over long periods of time by looking at three sources of evidence. Fossil records can tell us about physical changes but not about behaviour. Geographical variation demonstrates how similar species develop adaptations in relation to geographical/environmental differences. Artificial breeding shows that it is possible to produce offspring with desirable characteristics by selecting the right breeding stock as parents.

Evolutionary Explanations of Animal Behaviour

❖ Darwin's theory of natural selection offers an explanation of the processes involved in evolution. There are five main assumptions: variation (animals vary), heritability (some variation is inherited), competition (winners will be more likely to reproduce), natural selection (survivors will have characteristics that are better suited to the environment i.e., survival of the fittest), and adaptation (successive generations become better adapted to their environment). Both Malthus and Darwin predicted that there would be ever-increasing competition for finite resources, which acts as a selective pressure.

❖ Punctuated equilibrium describes the alternation between periods of rapid change and relative stability. Rapid change is likely when a behaviour appears that enhances an individual's use of available resources, an individual's competitiveness and ability to compete with members of the same sex for access to reproduction opportunities or to impress members of the opposite sex, and/or interrelationship with members of other species.

❖ Animals are not always perfectly adapted to their environment. This may be because recent environmental change creates a mismatch, or because the current strategy cannot be bettered by any other strategy (an evolutionarily stable strategy, ESS).

❖ The evidence for the theory of natural selection tends to be indirect. The principle of uniformitarianism assumes that the behaviours/characteristics we observe today serve the same function as they would have in the past. This may be incorrect. More direct evidence comes from observations of behaviour in the peppered moth, kittiwake chicks, and male empid flies, all of which exhibit behaviours that have enabled them to be better adapted to their environment. Natural experiments can also be conducted by forming a hypothesis about the relationship between the environment and behaviour and seeing if it is supported by natural evidence.

❖ The theory of evolution has been developed further. The discovery of genes demonstrated the mechanism by which characteristics are inherited. Artificial selection experiments are used to demonstrate this. Sexual selection is used to explain why some animals possess characteristics that might appear to be non-adaptive. The paradox of altruism can only be explained by developing Darwinian theory.

❖ There are four main explanations that can account for biological altruism in terms of evolutionary theory. Group selection theory cannot account for the paradox of altruism because natural selection takes place at the level of the genes. However, kin selection, reciprocity, mutualism, and manipulation can account for this paradox.

❖ Kin selection explains altruism in terms of the selfish gene. Characteristics are favoured due to their beneficial effects on the survival of close relatives. Inclusive fitness involves both direct (one's own) and indirect (one's relatives') fitness. Supporting evidence comes from the studies of warning calls in prairie dogs and Belding's ground squirrels, as well as altruism in eusocial insects which can be explained partly in terms of haplodiploidy. Kin selection relies on kin recognition, largely based on the "rule of thumb" that animals sharing one's home tend to be kin.

❖ Delayed reciprocal altruism is altruism performed with the expectation that the favour will be returned. It is susceptible to cheating and therefore it would be most likely to evolve between close relatives. It has been observed in the black hamlet fish, vampire bats, and olive baboons. Mutualism involves simultaneous reciprocity and has been observed in male lions. Manipulation, as in brood parasitism in cuckoos, is not true altruism because the behaviour is not intentional on the part of the "altruist".

Classical and Operant Conditioning

❖ Learning is a determinant of animal behaviour. Classical conditioning occurs through learned associations between a neutral stimulus (NS) and an unconditioned stimulus (UCS). After conditioning, the NS becomes a conditioned stimulus (CS) that produces the original reflex response (unconditioned response, now a conditioned response, CR). A new S–R link has been formed. Further aspects of classical conditioning include generalisation, discrimination, extinction, and spontaneous recovery. Classical conditioning can be explained in terms of time factors (forward conditioning is most successful) and expectation.

❖ Classical conditioning is more complex than was originally thought. One-trial learning and preparedness suggest the need to incorporate a role for innate factors. Classical conditioning is of less importance in humans because of the input of language. Laboratory studies involve less active involvement in learning than in real life, but classical conditioning can be applied to natural situations, such as taste aversion.

❖ Operant conditioning involves rewards and punishments. It concerns the effects of behaviour. Thorndike proposed that learning can occur through trial and error. Any behaviour that produces a pleasurable state of affairs is stamped in (the Law of Effect). Skinner introduced the concept of reinforcement (both positive and negative) and punishment. Learning takes place when an animal operates on its environment (the *antecedent*). The probability of a *behaviour* being repeated is increased if the behaviour is reinforced (the *consequence*) = the ABC of learning.

❖ Secondary reinforcers develop when a thing with no intrinsic reinforcement value (such as money) is associated with a primary reinforcer, and then becomes reinforcing in itself. Continuous reinforcement is the least effective schedule of reinforcement and variable schedules (especially variable ratio) are the most effective. Complex behaviours can be taught using shaping. Punishment may have only short-lasting effects but can be made more effective if other, desirable behaviours are simultaneously rewarded.

❖ Avoidance learning is the result of classical conditioning (NS paired with aversive stimuli) and operant conditioning (avoidance response is reinforced by fear reduction). When an animal has learned helplessness it will not try to escape from an aversive stimulus. Learned helplessness has been used to explain depression in humans.

❖ Much of the research has low external (ecological) validity which may reduce its meaningfulness, yet operant conditioning has some useful applications, such as in the treatment of mental disorders and in training animals. Animals do not learn all responses with the same ease (equipotentiality), what they learn tends to resemble their instinctive behaviour (instinctive drift). In fact animal behaviour may be governed more by innate predispositions than by reinforcements.

❖ Operant conditioning may be less mechanical than Skinner imagined, it is *one* aspect of the learning process. Cognitive processes are excluded from explanations of conditioning, but they are demonstrated in latent learning and the use of cognitive maps, insight learning, and observational learning and imitation.

Social Learning in Non-human Animals

❖ Social learning is learning that involves other animals. Group living offers the opportunity for vicarious reinforcement and imitation, as well as the need to solve problems arising from group inter-relationships. Social learning is faster and less costly than trial and error learning. It also leads to cultural transmission, a process that is analogous to but faster than genetic transmission.

❖ Research evidence for imitation comes from observational studies of, for example, Japanese snow monkeys and blue tits opening milk bottles, and from experimental studies of, for example, chickadees. Learning may occur through stimulus enhancement rather than imitation, as is demonstrated by discovery learning (where the animal is given just a hint about how to solve the problem). A distinction is made between imitation and tutoring, which incurs a cost to the tutor and involves intentional modification of the tutor's behaviour.

❖ Foraging behaviours include a range of activities related to obtaining food, including food preferences, optimal foraging strategies, and strategies for hunting in groups. Each of these involves both innate and socially learned elements.

❖ Social learning (imitation) is possible evidence for intelligence in non-human animals because the learner must be able to link behaviours with consequences. The ability to use a Theory of Mind is further evidence of intelligence. A Theory of Mind is the ability to have insight into one's own mind and that of others. Heyes suggested that there are six types of behaviour that are representative of an animal that has a Theory of Mind: imitation, self-recognition, social relationships, role-taking, deception or Machiavellian intelligence, and perspective taking.

❖ Imitation can most simply be explained in terms of stimulus enhancement. Self-recognition is assessed using the mirror test which appears to demonstrate a Theory of Mind in the great apes. However, pigeons also appear able to use a mirror, as do autistic children, and neither are thought to possess a Theory of Mind. There are also doubts about the methodology and the magnitude of the results. Research suggests that social relationships in non-human animals involve insight into another animal's mental state, however the research findings can also be explained in terms of the non-mentalistic concept of operant conditioning. Evidence related to role taking does support the idea that some non-human animals do have a Theory of Mind, as in the studies with chimpanzees (Sarah identifying pictures and pairs of chimpanzees taking turns to access food without seeing it). Intentional deception implies a knowledge of what another knows or doesn't know. Experimental evidence can be explained in terms of conditioning but there is much observational support for intentional deception in wild animals. Finally, the ape version of the Sally–Anne test also provided promising evidence of perspective taking.

❖ The overall case for intelligence in non-human animals is not clear in terms of their ability to demonstrate a Theory of Mind. However, this is only one way to define intelligence.

FURTHER READING

The topics in this Section are covered in greater depth by J. Cartwright (2001) *Determinants of animal behaviour* (London: Routledge), written specifically for the AQA A specification. A good general textbook on the topics in this Section, and the next one, is J.M. Pearce (1997) *Animal learning and cognition (2nd Edn.)* (Hove, UK: Psychology Press). R. Dawkins has written various books on the theory of evolution and kin selection such as (1976) *The selfish gene* (Oxford: Oxford University Press) and (1986) *The blind watchmaker* (New York: Norton). A highly readable and up-to-date account of intelligence in non-human animals can be found in E. Linden (1999) *The parrot's lament* (New York: E.P. Dutton).

Example Examination Questions

You should spend 30 minutes on each of the questions below, which aim to test the material in this Section.

1. Discuss evolutionary explanations of behaviour in non-human animals.   (24 marks)

2. Describe and evaluate **two** explanations for biological altruism.   (24 marks)

3. Critically consider the role of classical conditioning in the behaviour of non-human animals.   (24 marks)

4. (a) Outline the nature of operant conditioning.   (12 marks)
   (b) Assess operant conditioning as an explanation of non-human animal behaviour.   (12 marks)

5. Discuss explanations of the role of social learning in the behaviour of non-human animals.   (24 marks)

6. Describe and assess evidence for intelligence in non-human animals.   (24 marks)

Examination Tips

Question 1.   "Discuss" is an AO1 and AO2 term requiring, in this case, a description of evolutionary explanations plus an evaluation of such explanations. Your examples should be restricted to non-human animals though it would be possible to extend your generalisations to human behaviour as a form of commentary (AO2). Evaluation can be achieved by considering the quality of the research evidence and/or contrasting the explanations you present.

Question 2.   The descriptive part of this question is limited to two explanations. You are not restricted to non-human animal behaviour but as the question concerns biological altruism it is likely that you will focus on non-human animal behaviour. Examples of such behaviour are likely to be largely descriptive and thus form part of your explanation rather than the evaluation. It is important to ensure a good balance in description and evaluation in order to access the full 24 marks for the question (12 marks for AO1 and 12 for AO2).

Question 3.   "Critically consider" is an AO1 and AO2 term requiring a description of classical conditioning (in terms of non-human animal behaviours) and an evaluation of this explanation both in terms of its strengths and weaknesses. It would not be appropriate to refer to applications such as the treatment of mental illness as the question is restricted to non-human animals, unless one argued that the value of understanding conditioning in non-human animals is its application to human behaviour.

Question 4.   In part (a) an outline is required because of the breadth of material likely to be included. "Outline" is defined as a "summary description" and marks are available for breadth rather than depth (detail). It is important, nevertheless, to communicate understanding rather than just presenting a list of characteristics. In part (b) you should present both the strengths and weaknesses of operant conditioning as an explanation of behaviour. As for question 3 this might include reference to human behaviour and might also include contrasts with other forms of learning (e.g., classical conditioning, social learning, habituation).

Question 5.   A likely problem in this essay will be lack of selectivity. In order to obtain high marks you need to supply depth and breadth, structure and coherent elaboration. If you try to include everything you know, it is likely to read like a list and lack sufficient detail (AO1 skill) and elaboration (AO2 skill). Evaluation might be achieved by contrasting social learning with other explanations for behaviour in non-human animals (such as innate behaviour or classical and operant conditioning).

Question 6.   This again is a potentially vast topic and therefore you must be selective in the material you use. Note the use of the term "evidence", which means that the backbone of your essay should be research studies that can then be used to present an argument about whether non-human animals are intelligent. "Assess" can be achieved through a critical consideration of the evidence as well as what it tells us about the intelligence of non-human animals.

WEB SITES

http://www.psychologicalscience.net/Psychology_Topics/Comparative/
Comprehensive list of links to comparative psychology sites.

www.talkorigins.org/origins/faqs-evolution.html
Vast collection of articles on evolution, including basic explanations and Darwin's original text.

http://www.almaz.com/nobel/medicine/1904a.html
Links to sites about Ivan Pavlov.

http://elvers.stjoe.udayton.edu/history/people/Watson.html
Links to sites about John Watson.

http://www.cogsci.soton.ac.uk/bbs/Archive/bbs.heyes.html
An edited version of an article by Heyes on animals' theory of mind.

http://www.animalbehavior.org/
Animal Behavior Society homepage.

14

Animal Cognition

The linking theme in this Section is a consideration of the cognitive, or mental, abilities of non-human animals. The ability to navigate, use language (natural and/or human) and to store memories all involve mentalistic activity.

Animal Navigation

To navigate means to find one's way. When travelling over long distances it would be likely that an animal needs some means of direction finding rather than simply recognising known features along the way. "Orientation" means to move in a particular direction without reference to local landmarks, as in using a compass. Animals use this directional sense to get them to the right area (orientation) and then they can use local landmarks (like a map) to find the precise location of their target. This is called true navigation, the combination of compass and map to find an exact location. **Navigation** involves compensating for any displacement and continuing towards an end goal.

Some animals, such as butterflies in migration, navigate to places previously unvisited and use only orientation. Sometimes some adjustment is made for displacement. This can be seen in a study of starling migration by Perdeck (1958). Starlings from northern and eastern Europe tend to migrate in a southwesterly direction during the autumn. Perdeck arranged for young and adult starlings to be transported from the Netherlands to Switzerland, a displacement of their usual starting point. When they were released, the young starlings simply flew in a southwesterly direction. As a result, they arrived in parts of Europe much farther south than is normal for starlings. These birds were clearly using orientation only. In contrast, the adult starlings adjusted their flying direction to take account of the fact that they had been displaced. They flew in a northwesterly direction, and arrived at their normal destination. The adults were able to make adjustments. This shows that animals use both learned and innate techniques when navigating.

Migrant birds also navigate to get home, to their place of origin. This is called **homing behaviour** because instead of finding its way, the animal is actually trying to locate something specific. "Homing" refers to being able to locate a target, such as one's home,

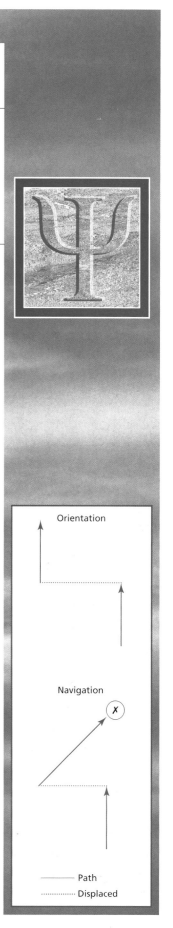

Orientation

Navigation

⊗ x

——— Path
.... Displaced

The difference between directional orientation and navigation can be seen when an animal's intended path (solid line) is experimentally altered (dashed line). When an orienting pathway is changed, the animal continues to orientate in the same direction, but not towards a specific target point. When a navigating pathway is changed, however, the animal compensates for the displacement and travels towards the target point.

Interaction between innate orientation tendencies and experience as shown by displaced migrating starlings in the study by Perdeck (1958).

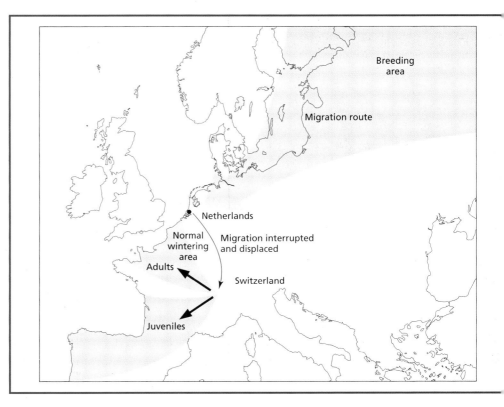

What might be the reason for the difference in behaviour between young and adult starlings in Perdeck's study?

point of origin, or a food store. In essence migration and homing draw on the same capabilities. They may require travel over land, in the air, or in the sea. They may involve journeys of several thousands of miles. Some species are noted for their special abilities such as the homing pigeon, or the salmon who returns to its native river for breeding, or the honeybee in locating its food.

Migration

Migration has been defined as "long-distance travel, usually with a return, to specific locations" (Grier & Burk, 1992, p.243). Migration is found in many species of birds and fish, and generally involves large numbers of animals travelling together. The distances involved can be very impressive. Some examples are given by Grier and Burk (1992). Golden plovers have been known to fly 2400 miles non-stop from Labrador in Canada to South America, and an arctic tern was discovered in the Antarctic 9000 miles away from the place in Russia where it was ringed.

Fish

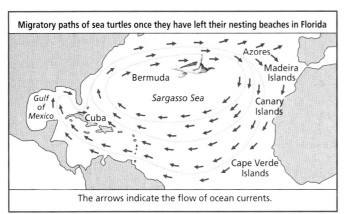

The arrows indicate the flow of ocean currents.

There are several species of fish that migrate over long distances. Two of these species, which have been studied in most detail, are eels and salmon. Atlantic eels live in rivers in western Europe and close to the eastern coast of North America. However, they breed in the Sargasso Sea which is in the western part of the Atlantic ocean. When the young hatch, they drift for at least a year until they reach a river. As you might imagine, it is very hard to track the movements of eels over thousands of miles. As a result it is not surprising that it is not known in detail how the eels find their way to the Sargasso Sea.

More is known about the homing behaviour of salmon. Salmon hatch in streams and rivers, but then spend several years in the ocean hundreds or thousands of miles away. After that, they show an amazing ability to return for breeding purposes to the stream or river in which they were hatched. The possible mechanisms for this homing ability are discussed later.

Birds

Homing pigeons are the best known of the species of homing birds. However, there are several others. For example, pied flycatchers breed in the northern part of Europe and migrate to Africa for the winter. In one study (Berndt & Sternberg, 1969), it was found that a majority of the birds returned very close to where they had been hatched during the breeding season. In another study, a Manx shearwater was flown by plane from England to the east coast of the United States. It managed to find its way back to its nest in 12 days (Matthews, 1953).

Heredity or experience?

Does the migratory and homing behaviour of birds depend on heredity or on experience? The answer varies from one species to another. In the study by Perdeck (1958), described earlier, migration was affected by both innate factors and experience in the older birds. In contrast migration in European storks appears to be largely innate. European storks migrate across the Mediterranean to the same place no matter where in Europe they come from. Young storks in western Europe cross the Mediterranean by the Straits of Gibraltar, so they all start out in a southwesterly direction. Storks from eastern Europe go round the eastern end of the Mediterranean before heading for their migration grounds. How do the storks know which direction to take at the start? Is their directional sense innate? Schuz (1971) took stork eggs from eastern Europe and moved them to nests in western Europe. The young storks flew in a southeasterly direction, rather than the southwesterly direction of storks whose parents were from western Europe. Differences in heredity presumably underlie these differences in direction of flying.

Advantages of migration

There are several costs associated with migration. Migrating long distances can use up a lot of energy, there is the risk of getting lost, and migrating animals may be caught by predators while on their travels. In view of these costs, why does migration occur at all?

The most obvious advantage is to maximise feeding opportunities. When it is cold and there is little food an animal that migrates to more plentiful feeding areas will have an adaptive advantage. Migrating southwards offers the prospect of having better access to food.

There are other advantages to migrating, beyond food. The new environment may offer relief from predation. There may be better breeding territories in the area of migration than in the original area. In addition, competition from another species may be less in the migration area.

Not all birds migrate. The ones who stay have a diet that can be more easily satisfied during winter months, such as feeding on seeds that are available through the winter. In some years migrant species may decide not to migrate, presumably because the environmental cues—such as temperature or reduction in food supplies—have not triggered their migration.

One might ask why the migrants go back. Presumably because they are better adapted to their home environment.

Mechanisms Involved in Navigation

In travel over long distances we are concerned with true navigation, the use of orientation and local landmarks—a compass and a map. Much of this research has focused on homing pigeons, but relevant findings from other species will also be considered.

There are two important general points to be made at the outset. First, it would be wrong to assume that all species of homing birds use the same mechanisms to navigate accurately. Second, some bird species can use various mechanisms in homing, with the one chosen at any given time being determined by the precise circumstances.

It is possible to distinguish between the compass part of navigation (navigation by direction) and the map part (navigation by location). In some cases only the latter would be necessary—as in relatively short journeys.

Navigation by direction

Magnetic information

There is strong evidence that homing pigeons use information from the earth's magnetic field. Lednore and Walcott (1983) devised a way to test this by attaching an electromagnetic coil to the heads of pigeons in order to disrupt their ability to use magnetic information. This did disrupt the pigeons' ability to return home on overcast days, but not on sunny ones. The implication is that pigeons can make use of information from magnetism or from the sun's position to guide their homing behaviour.

What would be the particular advantages of using a sun compass?

Lednore and Walcott used experienced pigeons. Inexperienced pigeons are much less able to navigate accurately on the basis of magnetic information alone, and seem to need information from the sun's position as well (Keeton, 1974). These findings indicate that learning and experience play an important role in the use of magnetic information.

More evidence that pigeons use magnetic information to help them navigate was reported by Walcott and Green (1974). They also fitted electromagnetic coil caps to the heads of homing pigeons. Magnetic fields were then produced by connecting the coils to small batteries. When the pigeons were tested on overcast days, they flew in the correct direction with a certain direction of current flow in the electromagnetic coils. When the direction of the current was reversed, the pigeons flew in the opposite direction.

Other bird species also make use of magnetism. Wiltschko (1972) studied caged European robins that were exposed to changed magnetic fields. Their direction of movement was affected by these changes, indicating that they were making use of magnetic information.

Physiological basis.   If animals are using magnetic cues, then there must be some physiological source of this ability. Beason (1989) conducted research with the bobolink, a bird that migrates from the north to the south of the equator, and found evidence of magnetite in a region of the brain just behind the nose. Magnetite is an iron compound that is magnetic. The responsiveness of this area to magnetic forces was tested by placing microelectrodes in this region of an anaesthetised bobolink. There was electrical activity when electromagnets were used to alter the surrounding magnetic fields.

Human direction finding

Humans are clearly capable of complex and accurate navigation and they have been doing it for at least 6000 years (Waterman, 1989). We use and have used celestial and stellar navigation and local landmarks. Humans have also used magnetic compasses for the last 1000 years, but do humans have an innate means of detecting magnetic information? Some people do claim that they have an excellent sense of direction, which implies an ability to be physiologically sensitive to magnetic cues.

Baker (1987) conducted a series of experiments to test this magnetic ability. Participants were driven around while blindfolded and then asked to indicate the direction towards home, spun round on a chair while blindfolded and wearing earmuffs and then asked to state the compass direction they were facing, or led on a tortuous path through a wood and then asked to indicate the direction home. Baker claims to have demonstrated magnetic abilities, however his findings have not been

replicated. Furthermore, certain aspects of his findings have led to doubts. For example, he claimed that the actual speed that is used to spin a person round is critical. Too much rotation or too little rotation destroys a participant's sense of direction.

Another study, by Murphy (1989), may be more convincing. Participants were spun round in a chair with their eyes shut. After a number of clockwise rotations they were stopped at a randomly selected point and asked to estimate their orientation having originally been shown where north, east, south, and west were. This was repeated in an anticlockwise direction. If they had a brass bar on their head, the same participants were able to report their compass direction, but if they had a magnet attached to their head this ability disappeared. The magnet would have disturbed their magnetic abilities and thus supports the existence of these abilities.

However, Wiltschko and Wiltschko (1988) suggested that it is not possible to detect the earth's magnetic force with magnetite but instead it is more likely to be detected within the visual system. As yet the physiological basis for the detection of magnetic cues is not certain.

The sun's position (celestial navigation)

The sun is clearly a key mechanism in direction finding. Without sun some animals are disoriented. For example, Bellrose (1958) tracked mallards and found that under a clear sky they flew directly towards their target, whereas under an overcast sky they flew in various directions and appeared disoriented. However, for other birds, such as homing pigeons, navigation is still possible without the sun, as Lednore and Walcott (1983) demonstrated. Other animals, such as ants, also use the sun. If they are shielded from direct sunlight and a mirror is used to reflect sunlight from the opposite direction, ants will turn around and walk in the reverse direction until the shade is removed (Santschi, 1911). Salmon also probably use a sun compass to navigate across the ocean but, once they are at their home coast, they distinguish between rivers using smell.

Further evidence about how birds use the sun has been obtained by the use of **clock shifting**. In essence, pigeons or other birds are exposed to artificial light. This light is turned on and off in such a way as to create an artificial day that starts and ends a few hours earlier (or later) than the natural day. After a while, the bird's circadian rhythm or sleep–waking cycle (see Section 5, Biological Rhythms—Sleep and Dreaming) shifts in line with the artificial day. It is assumed that birds exposed to such clock shifting will misinterpret information about the sun's position, because they perceive the time as being several hours earlier or later than is actually the case.

Keeton (1974) used clock shifting to produce a 6-hour shift in the circadian rhythm or sleep–waking cycle of homing pigeons. When the pigeons were released on a sunny day, they set off about 90° away from the homeward direction. In contrast, they showed normal homing behaviour on overcast days. These findings suggest that the pigeons choose to use information from the sun's position when possible, but the shifted circadian rhythm made them misinterpret that information.

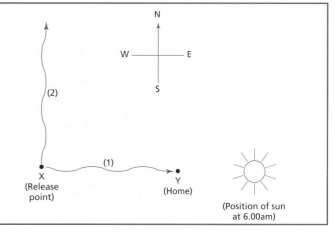

This diagram shows how clock shifting can alter navigation paths in homing pigeons. The correct path is shown in (1), where the pigeon has been kept in natural light. Pigeon 1 "knows" it is 6.00am, and the sun is in the east, so it flies towards the sun. Path (2) is incorrect, as the pigeon has been clock-shifted so it thinks it is midday, with the sun in the south, therefore it flies 90° anticlockwise to the sun. Pigeon 2 believes that it is flying east, but it is actually heading north.

What ethical issues might be involved in this research?

CASE STUDY: *Monarch Butterflies*

Clock shifting has also been used to test monarch butterflies' homing abilities. Colonies fly from the eastern and western USA and Canada to Mexico. Perez, Taylor, and Jander (1977) clock-shifted migrating monarchs by 6 hours and compared them with a laboratory control group. The results showed a statistically significant orientation to the sun in flight direction.

On the other hand, grains of magnetic material have been found in the bodies of adult monarchs (Cocker, 1998), and the area of Mexico to which they migrate is rich in iron ore. Its magnetic reading is 90–100 times greater than normal. This would seem to suggest that monarchs are using their own compass-like ability as well as their sun-map to home in on a natural magnetic beacon as their winter site.

The stars (stellar navigation)

At night animals clearly cannot use the sun. Some bird species make use of information about the stars for navigational purposes. In the study by Bellrose (1958) described earlier, the mallards were also tracked at night by attaching small flashlights to their feet. The mallards all flew in the same direction on clear nights, but were disoriented and flew around aimlessly on overcast nights. Indigo buntings also make much use of information

The sun-arc and map-compass hypothesis

Matthews (1955) proposed that birds learn the path that the sun takes across the sky in their home location. At any location they can then compare the observed path with this home path and, given the time of day, calculate which orientation to take to get home. The flaw in this argument is that the bird would have to spend some time observing the sun's arc before being able to orient itself.

The alternative hypothesis, proposed by Kramer (1953), is called the **map-compass hypothesis**. This suggests that the sun is used for compass information only and something else serves as the map. Grier and Burk (1992) described the following experiment to support this latter hypothesis. If a bird is clock-shifted backwards by 6 hours, moved 100km south to an unfamiliar location and then released at midday, what happens? The bird perceives its home time as 6am. If the sun-arc hypothesis were correct, the bird would look at the sun overhead and think "I am 6 hours east of my home". It would travel west and slightly northwards. The northward adjustment is because the sun would also be too high in the sky because of the southward displacement and therefore the bird needs to travel 100km north. If, however, the map-compass hypothesis were correct, the map system would provide the information that the bird was too far south and needed to travel north. The bird would know that north was 90° to the left of the sun; at 6am the sun should be in the east, whereas in fact our sun is in the south and therefore we would predict that the bird will head east (i.e., 90° to the right).

What actually happens? The birds go east. The remaining problem is that the physical basis of the map system is not known. We should also remember that pigeons can still home on cloudy days, which means they must be using something besides the sun.

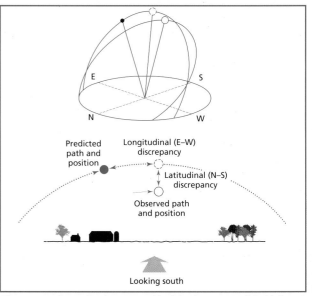

The sun-arc hypothesis proposed by Matthews to explain bird homing. The top diagram shows the view as it would appear to an external viewer. The bottom diagram shows the same thing from the bird's point of view. The hollow circle is the observed sun, and the solid circle is the predicted position. On the path it is taking, the observed sun is too low and too far along in the arc. Therefore, the bird must be north (for the sun to be lower) and east (for the sun to be ahead in its position) of home. To get home the bird must travel south and west.

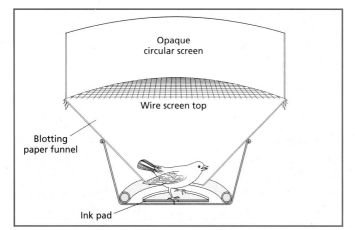

This apparatus is used to record the intended direction of movement of a bird. The bird jumps up the sides of the funnel when it is restless and, because its feet have been inked by the stamp pad, they leave marks showing the intended direction.

from the stars (Emlen, 1975), but many other species (e.g., swans and European robins) do not.

Emlen (1975) tested the ability to use stars by placing naïve indigo buntings in a planetarium, and found that they did respond to the alterations in the night sky. You might wonder how he did this. He used a stamp-pad technique as shown in the diagram on the left. The bird jumps up the sides of the funnel when it is restless and, because its feet have been inked by the stamp pad, they leave marks showing the intended direction of travel.

If an animal is using the stars it must be able to recognise some pattern. It appears that the birds' orientation is based on the position of the north star and the rotation of the stars around this during the night.

Navigation by location

We have already noted that salmon use smell as a navigational device when nearing their home ground. What cues are there to recognise one's home?

Odours

Homing pigeons make use of olfaction, i.e., information about odour. Papi et al. (1972) cut the olfactory nerves of pigeons and found that this affected their ability to orient themselves. The use of local anaesthetics was a somewhat more ethical means of achieving the same thing and also demonstrated disorientation. Other studies have plugged the pigeon's nostril, again finding that homing was disrupted. However, it may well be the discomfort and pain endured by the pigeons that affected their homing behaviour, and this is why they were disoriented, rather than any specific effects on the olfactory system.

Studies of salmon indicate that odour may play a major role in their ability to return to their home stream or river. Hasler (1986) plugged the noses of salmon and found that they homed less accurately than untreated control animals, which suggested that smell is a key element in their homing behaviour. It is likely that each stream has its own distinctive odour or taste. Young salmon learn the odour of their stream, and their memory of this odour directs their homing behaviour.

Instead of blocking smell it is possible to study olfactory influences by altering home odours, or presenting artificial odours to see how this affects homing behaviour. Grier and Burk (1992) reported one study where young salmon were exposed to one of two artificial odours before being released into Lake Michigan. Then two streams running into the lake were scented with one of the artificial odours, and attempts were made to monitor which salmon returned to which stream. More than 90% of the recovered fish went to the stream that had the odour to which they had been exposed when young. These findings show convincingly that homing behaviour in salmon is influenced by smell.

The use of smell has also been documented in homing for honeybees. The smell of each hive is unique and related to the diet of the residents (Ridley, 1986). This is important in ensuring that bees return to their own hive and to prevent outsiders infiltrating the wrong hive. This was demonstrated in a study where two hives were moved to the same location. The researchers observed that inter-hive fighting decreased, possibly because the bees fed on the same flowers and the hive odours were the same. This was confirmed when they divided one hive in half and fed each half different diets. Intra-hive fighting increased, demonstrating the importance of smell in nest identity. This is one means of kin recognition, as discussed in Section 13, Determinants of Animal Behaviour.

Sound

Bats are well known for echolocation. They emit various squeaks and chitters, some of which cannot be detected by the human ear. Spallanzani was the first to demonstrate this ability back in 1793 (Grier & Burk, 1992). He plugged bats' ears and found that they flew about randomly, colliding with everything, demonstrating that bats use their ears for navigation. In the eighteenth century no one believed him, because they didn't know about ultrasound. The sounds are reflected off objects so that bats can detect different shapes and distances. In fact echolocation is used mainly to locate insects for eating. When bats are homing over long distances they may well use magnetic information, and some of them have been known to travel distances of over 1000 kilometres.

Local landmarks

It might be thought that pigeons would make use of visual information to guide their homeward flight, perhaps making use of landmarks identified on the outward trip. However, pigeons released repeatedly from the same site very rarely fly the same route twice. This suggests that they do not carefully follow a series of landmarks. More convincing evidence was reported by Walcott and Schmidt-Koenig (1971). They fitted pigeons with translucent lenses before releasing them 80 miles away from home. The lenses prevented the pigeons from identifying landmarks. However, most of them either found their way home or at least set off in the right direction. Most strikingly of all, pigeons that have been clock-shifted have been known to fly in completely the wrong direction (Keeton, 1974) even when their home loft is visible from the point of release!

Other bird and animal species seem to make more use of visual information. Gannets that were moved to an unfamiliar location tended to fly around over increasingly large areas in a rather random fashion. When they happened to fly over familiar territory, they rapidly found their way back home (Griffin, 1955).

The classic example of the use of local landmarks comes from an experiment with digger wasps by Tinbergen and Kruyt (1938). These wasps dig holes for their nests. When the wasp emerges from its hole, it flies around for a few seconds learning the local landmarks so that it can re-identify the nest site. Tinbergen arranged some pine cones around a nest site (as in the diagram on the next page), acting as artificial landmarks. After the wasp had left, the researchers moved the pine cones to a new location. The returning wasp was then unable to find its home.

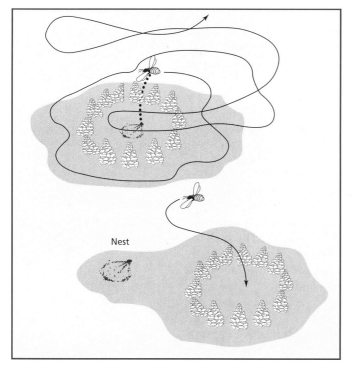

A classic example of the use of landmarks involves digger wasps, who dig a hole for their nest and fly around it for a few seconds learning landmarks. If an artificial landmark is introduced around the nest, such as a ring of pine cones, the wasp will learn this. If the pine cone ring is then moved to another location, the wasp will return with prey to the new location but will be unable to locate the nest entrance.

■ Activity: There are many stories, some of which have been made into films, in which household pets have travelled extremely long distances alone to return to former homes. Assuming that such animals do have some "sense of direction", make a list of the possible explanations for how this sense might function.

The use of local landmarks involves a spatial memory, a topic to be discussed in the Unit on Memory (see page 554).

Evaluation

We have seen that information about the earth's magnetism, the position of the sun, the positions of the stars, olfactory information, and visual landmarks can be used for purposes of navigation. Experienced homing pigeons seem to rely on information from the sun's position if it is available. If it is not available, they use information about the earth's magnetic field. These sources of information are very useful in guiding pigeons in the right general direction. When they have flown fairly close to home, then they probably use visual landmarks to reach their loft.

In spite of the progress that has been made, there is much that remains unclear. For example, *what* is the precise information that birds obtain from the position of the sun, the earth's magnetic field, the positions of the stars, and so on? *How* is that information used to allow birds to arrive at their destination? In general terms, birds need to know the direction in which home lies, as well as at least its approximate distance. In addition, they need to know how to travel in the desired direction. Some of these questions will be explored in the Unit on Memory (see page 553).

Animal Communication and Language

Nearly all species communicate with members of their own species. Many species also communicate with the members of other species (e.g., predators or prey species). The communication signals can take many forms: they may be visual, auditory, chemical, or tactile.

More often than not, human communication is intentional. In other words, the individual who is communicating tries to have a given effect on the person or people to whom the communication is addressed. This is one criterion for "language" as distinct from communication. Another distinction between non-human animal and human communication is that we often communicate about events from the past or what might happen in the future. In contrast, animals typically communicate about the here and now, relating to issues of immediate importance.

We will consider the question of whether human and non-human animal communication is distinct, or whether it would be reasonable to describe some animal communication systems as languages. Studies of non-human animal language include consideration of both natural languages and attempts to teach non-human animals human language

In what ways do humans communicate unintentionally?

First, we will discuss the use of different signalling systems in non-human animals.

Animal Communication

We will consider two definitions of communication here. Burghardt (1970) argued that communication "occurs when one organism emits a stimulus that, when responded to by another organism, confers some advantage … to the signaller or its group". According to Krebs and Davies (1993, p.349), communication is "the process in which actors use specially designed signals or displays to modify the behaviour of reactors".

The key notion that is common to both definitions is that communication requires that the behaviour of the receiver be altered in some way by it. This approach to communication has the advantage that we can observe the receiver's behaviour, and so tell whether communication has occurred.

Why do animals communicate? As Grier and Burk (1992) pointed out, there are many reasons. However, there seem to be four major functions of animal communication:

1. *Survival*: for example, alarm and distress signals are used to warn of predators.
2. *Reproduction*: for example, signals are used during courtship, pair formation, and pair maintenance.
3. *Territory boundaries* and social spacing: for example, aggressive threat, defensive threat, and submissive signals are used between members of a species.
4. *Food*: for example, signals can be given indicating where there is a good food supply.

It might be thought that the number of different signals would be much higher in some classes of species (e.g., mammals) than in others (e.g., birds). However, the evidence does not really support this view. The average number of different signals is slightly higher in mammals than in birds, and in birds than in fish (Moynihan, 1970). There is much more variability between different species of mammals, birds, or fish than between different classes of species.

We will next consider some of the general features of signalling systems in animals. After that, we will discuss specific features of signalling in various species.

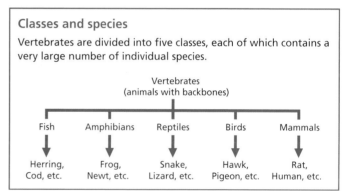

Classes and species

Vertebrates are divided into five classes, each of which contains a very large number of individual species.

Vertebrates
(animals with backbones)

Fish	Amphibians	Reptiles	Birds	Mammals
Herring, Cod, etc.	Frog, Newt, etc.	Snake, Lizard, etc.	Hawk, Pigeon, etc.	Rat, Human, etc.

Channels for communication

As has already been mentioned, the main sensory channels used for animal communication are chemical, visual, auditory, and tactile signals.

Chemical signals

Most chemical signals are called **pheromones**, and were probably developed before signals in other sensory channels. The female silk moth produces bombykol which can be detected by the male over a distance of a mile and obviously helps in mate attraction. Smell is the main method of communication in ants. If an ant finds food, it returns to the nest leaving a trail of pheromones which is then followed by others using their antennae. Ants, like honeybees (see page 537), have colony odours to help recognise colony members and identify intruders. Smell is also used as a means of marking territory, such as a dog urinating or an otter leaving spraints (faeces).

Strengths and limitations.   Chemical signals have various advantages over other signals. Receivers can detect chemical signals even in darkness or when there are numerous objects between sender and receiver. In addition, chemical signals often last for a long time, and are hard for predators to detect and interpret. Both characteristics would apply, for example, to the messages left by dogs.

Pheromones
The function of many pheromones is to attract the opposite sex for mating. Gardeners can now use this mechanism to catch garden pests by buying traps baited with female pheromones from the insect species concerned. The males flock to the traps and are killed before they have the opportunity to reproduce.

On the downside, chemical signals can last too long and so interfere with later chemical signals, and it can take longer to create chemical signals than other kinds of signal. This can be a relatively slow means of communication when compared with, for example, visual or auditory signals.

Visual signals

Many signals produced by animals are visual in nature. Examples include the dance of the honeybee (described on page 543), threat displays where one animal may bare its teeth or sway back and forth, and courtship displays such as the peacock's tail or even the firefly's flashing of its light. Body markings are also much used either as a means of species identification or to indicate potential danger, such as the bold colours on poisonous snakes. Visual signals are related to emotion, such as blushing in humans. The octopus changes colour to express anger or pleasure and cats signal embarrassment when they engage in a displacement activity.

Strengths and limitations.   According to Grier and Burk (1992, p.528), there are several advantages associated with the use of visual communication:

(1) it is transmitted instantaneously; (2) it may carry a large amount of information, assuming the receiver's eyes and brain are capable of processing it all; (3) it is highly directional, permitting the source to be located; and (4) some aspects, such as body colouration, are permanent ... needing to be produced only once.

What are the disadvantages of visual signals? First, they are only effective under reasonable lighting conditions. Second, they are not generally detectable by receivers over long distances. In addition, visual displays are often "expensive" in terms of energy.

Auditory signals

The most obvious example of an auditory signal is bird song, which is described on page 542. Many species use the auditory channel for mating and alarm calls. Aggression may be expressed auditorily as in barking, and some animals have quite a vocabulary as in the vervet monkey, described on page 542. Groups of animals use vocal calls as a means of aiding organisation. Whales also signal group membership by sharing the same song within a group.

Strengths and limitations.   Auditory signals (which are produced by numerous species) possess various advantages. Unlike visual signals, they can be used in the dark. In addition, they can contain much more meaning than chemical signals, and the process of communication is generally fast and efficient. On the negative side, animals often need to use a lot of energy to produce auditory signals. For example, some species of insects lose 2–3% of their body weight during prolonged calling (Dodson et al., 1983). Other problems are that predators can usually detect auditory signals, and auditory signals become very distorted over long distances.

Can you think of an animal that doesn't use auditory signals? Why might this be?

Tactile signals

Tactile signals, which involve touching, are mostly used in combination with other kinds of signals. Tactile signals are used when offspring want to be fed by their parents, during grooming, or to indicate that an individual wants to be carried. For example, young herring gulls peck at the red spot on a parent's beak to elicit feeding. Submissive dogs lick the pack leader's muzzle as a way of communicating recognition of the leader—this may explain why dogs often jump up and try to lick your mouth!

Strengths and limitations.   Tactile communication has the advantage that it does not depend on complex structures such as those involved in sending and receiving auditory signals. It has the disadvantage that it can only be used in situations in which direct contact between two animals is possible.

Other channels

A few species of fish make use of electrical signals, for example various species of electric fish communicate with each other by this means. These signals are used during courtship, and are also used when dominance hierarchies are being set up (Hagedorn & Heiligenberg, 1985).

Overview

Different species of animals vary in terms of the main sensory channel they use for purposes of communication. According to Wilson (1975), most reptiles, fireflies, and fish tend to make more use of the visual channel than of the chemical or auditory channels. Frogs, mosquitoes, and cicadas rely mostly on the auditory channel, and moths and protozoans use mainly the chemical channel. Other species are harder to categorise. Many species of birds rely about equally on the visual and auditory channels, and humans make most use of the auditory channel, followed by the visual channel, with relatively little reliance on the chemical channel.

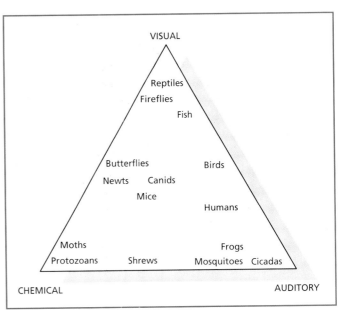

The role of different sensory channels, on a proportional basis, in the communication of different types of animal.

There are often fairly obvious reasons for the channel preferences of a given species. For example, roe deer living in open spaces use mainly visual signals to mark their territories. However, in dense forests their visual signals would not be seen. As a result, in this environment animals make use of loud calls and scents placed in their territory to warn other animals. Under water, it is obvious that auditory signals would be desirable (as in the whale song) though many fish species use colouring for close recognition.

Sometimes, animals send signals in more than one modality at a time. For example, ants use chemical signals in the form of odour trails so that other ants will follow them (Holldobler, 1971). At the same time, they use head movements to indicate whether they are leading to food (side-to-side movements) or to a nest site (backwards-and-forwards movements).

> ### Cockroach trails
>
> Researchers at the University of Florida in Gainesville, USA, found that some cockroaches follow their own dirt trails. As they wander about, they defecate, and other cockroaches also follow this trail, perhaps because it is likely to lead to a food source (Guterman, 1998).

It does not make much sense to ask which sensory channel is the best for communication purposes. Each channel has its own advantages and disadvantages, and effective use of any channel requires that the sender and receiver both possess the appropriate structures (e.g., a larynx; ears; eyes). In general terms, less complex species tend to have more limited sensory abilities than more complex ones, and rely more on chemical and tactile signals.

In what way would an animal's habitat also be an important factor in deciding on what channel is best for communication?

Ritualisation

The signals made by many species tend to be stereotyped, exaggerated, and repetitive. These signals have developed through evolution so that they communicate information more effectively to other animals. The process involved in the progressive development of signals is known as **ritualisation**.

Why does ritualisation occur? There are two reasons: as a consequence of honest signals or because there are also dishonest signals.

Honest signals

It is adaptive for a signal to become less and less ambiguous in order to ensure that the receiver understands the meaning of the communication. One way that ambiguity can be reduced is through the development of increasingly exaggerated forms of communication, i.e., ritualisation. For example, dogs use posture to communicate fear and to appear threatening. It is important that the two different signals are correctly

The way in which a male fiddler crab waves its claw may differentiate one species from another during courtship.

interpreted. Therefore, each signal becomes exaggerated. A fearful dog crouches near the ground, whereas a threatening dog stands erect. Another example of ambiguity reduction is found in the courtship displays of various species of fiddler crabs, in which the male crabs wave their enlarged claw. In some species, there is a rapid series of short claw waves, whereas in others there are only a few, long-lasting claw waves. The patterns of claw waves presumably differ from one species to another in order to make sure that there is no confusion between species.

Dishonest signals

All signals aim to manipulate the behaviour of another into doing things that benefit the signaller. Dawkins and Krebs (1979) have called this the manipulation hypothesis. Such behaviour leads in some cases to dishonest signals. A dishonest signal is one that disadvantages the animal receiving the signal. An example of this is the signalling behaviour of young cuckoos who beg for food from their foster parents. Mantis shrimps provide another example. They have powerful forelimbs which they spread out in a threat display. This is usually an honest signal. However, mantis shrimps shed their hard outer protective covering every two months, and this makes them soft and vulnerable for a few days. They continue to use their threat display during this vulnerable period, even though it is not an honest signal of their ability to fight (Adams & Caldwell, 1990).

If those on the receiving end of the dishonest signal show resistance, then signals may become more exaggerated and stereotyped in order to overcome this resistance. This can be seen in the signals animals use to make themselves look larger. A frightened cat will turn sideways, arch its back, and hiss—a ritualised behaviour. Another example can be seen in the exaggerated behaviour of some ground-nesting birds who drag their wing behind them to look injured with the purpose of leading a predator away from their nest. Such behaviour is not intentional.

Lack of intention is the rule but a possible exception can be seen in the vervet monkey as reported by Cheney and Seyfarth (1990). These monkeys have an alarm call indicating that a leopard is approaching. This causes other monkeys in the group to climb up the nearest tree. A monkey called Kitui was observed giving this call when a male monkey from another group was approaching, but there was no leopard in sight. This caused the strange male to climb a tree, and so stopped him from interfering with the group. On two of these occasions, Kitui walked along the ground giving the leopard call, which he would not have done if he had really thought there was a leopard in the area. (Deception in non-human animals is also discussed in Section 13, Determinants of Animal Behaviour.)

Examples of Animal Communication

Communication in birds

As was mentioned earlier, most species of birds communicate much information through the auditory modality. The precise nature of their songs often depends on the kind of environment in which they live. Hunter and Krebs (1979) made recordings in several countries of the territorial songs of great tits living in dense forest or in open woodland or parkland. Birds in an open environment had songs with

Vervet monkeys respond to each other's "leopard" alarm calls by taking refuge in the nearest tree.

higher maximum frequency, notes that repeated more rapidly, and a wider range of frequencies than did birds living in the forest. This effect was so strong that the songs of great tits in English parkland were more like those of great tits in Iran than those of birds in a dense English forest.

Why does the type of environment or habitat have such large effects on bird song? Wiley and Richards (1978) argued that the songs of birds are designed so that they can be heard by other birds with as little distortion as possible. Distortion can occur in forests because of echoes or reverberations from parts of trees. Such echoes are stronger if there are high-frequency sounds in the song, or if the song contains rapidly repeated notes. In contrast, in an open environment distortion is most likely to occur because gusts of wind cause the song to sound softer or louder from moment to moment.

It follows from the analysis of Wiley and Richards that bird songs in forest conditions should contain low-frequency sounds. They should also consist of pure notes or of trills (quavering sounds) with notes spaced out in time. On the other hand, bird songs in open spaces should consist of high-frequency sounds and should be in the form of rapid trills. The songs of most bird species are in line with these predictions.

Communication in honeybees

Probably the most important kind of information that honeybees need concerns the locations of good sources of food. As a result, they have a well-developed ability to communicate information about where food is to be found. The classic work in this area is by von Frisch (1950). He analysed carefully over 6000 occasions on which a honeybee that had located food returned to its hive and communicated this information to the other bees by moving in specific ways. This was normally done on a vertical surface. When the food was within about 100 metres, the honeybee simply moved around in a circle. When the food was farther away, the bee performed a waggle dance in the form of a figure-of-eight. In this figure-of-eight pattern, the central line indicates the direction of the food source. More specifically, it represents the angle between the hive, the position of the sun, and the food.

How is the distance of the food source communicated in the waggle dance? This distance is indicated by the speed with which the bee dances, with slower speeds being found when the food source is a long way away. The bee dances at the rate of about 25 figures-of-eight per minute when the food source is 500 metres away, compared with about eight per minute when food is 10,000 metres away.

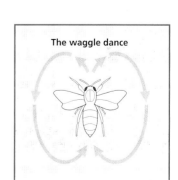

The waggle dance

What problems do you think von Frisch might have had in making his observations?

How well are the other bees able to make use of the information contained in the waggle dance? Von Frisch's findings suggested that the bees made fairly effective use of it. He found that over 60% of the bees went to the food sources that were closest to the hive rather than to ones that were farther away. The speed with which they reached these food sources suggests that the waggle dance had provided the bees with valuable information. However, it is possible that some of the bees found the nearest food sources through smell or vision rather than because of observing a waggle dance.

It used to be assumed that bees responded in an automatic way to the waggle dance. However, it now looks as if matters may not be so simple. Gould (1992) found that bees were very unwilling to use the information in the dance to fly to nectar that had been placed in a boat in the middle of a lake. This may have been because it seemed improbable that food would be found in the middle of a lake, or because bees do not like to fly over water. This suggests that the bees are engaging in some further processing of the information received.

Communication in whales

If you are describing one method of communication in non-human animals you can describe communication in one species or one sensory modality.

Humpback whales communicate with each other by means of elaborate "songs" or combinations of sounds. The notes of the songs are long, and the sounds have an echoing quality about them. Each song lasts for up to 30 minutes, and is then repeated. Typically, whale songs have about six themes, but the number ranges between four and ten. A large group of humpback whales will all sing the same songs. In a long-term study, Payne and Payne (1985) found that the songs changed over time.

The exact meaning of these songs is not known. However, whales sing mainly during their breeding season. It has also been found that whales are most likely to "sing" when they are rounding up fish, coming together as a group, or moving off in different directions.

Some light was shed on the meanings of whale calls by Tyack (1983). When he played tape recordings of whale songs to other whales, they tended to disperse. Whales within a group make calls to each other when they are observing a competition between two males for the attention of a female. When Tyack played a tape recording of such calls to whales, they immediately became very excited.

In sum, most (or all) of the calls made by humpback whales seem to be designed to communicate with other members of their group. Thus, their calls probably serve various social functions.

Communication in dolphins

Impressive evidence of communication between dolphins was reported by Bastion (1967). Two dolphins were kept in separate tanks. They could not see each other, but were within hearing range. One dolphin was taught to press a paddle in order to obtain a reward. When the other dolphin was tested, it was immediately able to perform the task correctly. This suggests that the first dolphin had somehow managed to communicate relevant information about the task to the second dolphin.

"Well, I simply trained them to give me fish by pressing this over and over again."

■ Activity: Before reading the next topic, try to write a working definition of "language". Would you include things like bird calls, or the signalling given by a peacock's tail? What about "body language"? How would sign language or Braille fit into your definition?

Language in Non-human Animals

Language has been defined as being "human communication", a definition that immediately excludes any non-human language. We tend to use the term "language" rather casually, such as in talking about computer "languages" or the language of love. If we want to determine whether or not non-human animals are capable of using a language system, then we need to have some precise criteria. Hockett (1960) put forward a large number of such criteria, some of which are as follows:

- *Semanticity*: the words or other units must have meaning.
- *Arbitrariness*: there must be an arbitrary connection between the form or sound of the word and its meaning.
- *Displacement*: language can be produced in the absence of the object or objects being described.
- *Prevarication*: there is an ability to tell lies and jokes.
- *Productivity*: there is an essentially infinite number of different expressions that can be communicated.

With these criteria in mind we can consider the extent to which non-human animals can use language, both natural forms and attempts to teach non-human animals to use human language.

Can you think of examples of these criteria in the communication systems of non-human animals?

Natural animal languages

The study of evolution (see Section 13, Determinants of Animal Behaviour) indicates that there are many interrelations between animals of different species. Some animals have more highly developed visual abilities, others have a preference for meat rather than vegetarian matter. In all of the characteristics that one could name there is continuity rather than a sharp division. This leads us to ask why language should be any different. Why would this be an ability only found in humans? It may be most fully developed in humans but it would be reasonable to think we would find language systems, as distinct from communication, in other animals as well.

Hockett's list provides us with some criteria, which we will follow in this discussion.

Are most characteristics continuous or discontinuous across species?

Semanticity

In order to determine whether the units of language have meaning we have to look at the effect the units have on the receiver. Cheney and Seyfarth's (1990) study of vervet monkeys provides an example of meaning. The monkeys have three different types of alarm call, each related to a different predator: eagles, leopards, and pythons. A further two calls have been identified as possibilities, those that signal baboons and humans. These different calls are equivalent to a vocabulary.

The other monkeys respond very distinctively to each call. If the call is for an eagle, the other monkeys run into the heavy brush to be safe. The response to the leopard call is to run up a tree and to a python call is to look around to locate the snake. This shows that each call has a specific meaning. Interestingly young vervet monkeys appear able to understand these calls but take time to learn to emit the calls when they spot predators themselves.

Meaning can also be seen in the dance of the honeybee (see page 543).

Arbitrariness

In the case of the vervet monkeys the calls that are used are arbitrary because they do not directly represent the danger. If the alarm was a visual signal where the monkey pointed up or down, then this would not be arbitrary. Dolphins' signals also provide evidence of arbitrariness. Dolphins' main communications consist of sequences of clicks and rattles, whereas sounds made at other times include whistles, squeaks, groans, and chirps. Bright (1984) recorded the sounds made by a male dolphin while it was being captured. When these sounds were played to other dolphins in the same group, they swam away rapidly.

Displacement

Honeybees can provide us with an example of displacement as they describe the location of a honey source that is not present at the time of communication.

Dolphins use an impressive array of vocal signals in communication.

Prevarication, the ability to use language for lying or telling jokes, may exist only in human communication systems.

Prevarication

We considered the ability of non-human animals to tell lies in Section 13, Determinants of Animal Behaviour (page 524). Here we are concerned with the question of whether they naturally use language to do this. Cheney and Seyfarth's (1990) study provides relevant evidence, as described on page 542. One monkey was seen to deliberately signal "leopard approaching" to another male to stop him interfering with the group. This demonstrates the ability to use a call dishonestly.

Productivity

Neither the dance of the honeybee nor vervet monkey calls are capable of producing an infinite number of meaningful expressions using a relatively small set of basic components. Cetaceans, such as dolphins and whales, have one of the most complex communication systems of any animals. Recent research by Janik (2000) documents the richness of dolphin language but there still is nothing to suggest an ability to recombine the signals to produce anything like the expressiveness of human language.

Conclusion

The evidence suggests that there is little basis to argue that non-human animals possess natural language. It is possible that our studies of such systems have not been sophisticated enough but, to date, the major stumbling block is the lack of productivity. One possible explanation for the discontinuity between non-human animal communication and human language is considered in Section 15, Evolutionary Explanations of Human Behaviour. Crow (2000) has argued that language appeared in humans as the result of a single genetic mutation in one individual (see page 583).

Teaching Human Language to Non-human Animals

As we have seen, many animals share a number of the characteristics of a language, though this does not add up

---

Is bird song a language?

Hockett's full list of the criteria for language also included spontaneous acquisition during a critical period of development, as well as cultural transmission. This is true of bird song. Birds that are reared in isolation do not acquire the full repertoire of normal adult birds (Slater, 1981).

Bird song is used for a wide variety of purposes, such as to locate and identify members of the same species (courtship), to identify individuals, to solicit food (begging by chicks), to demarcate territory (aggression), to warn of predators (alarm calls), and simply to sing.

Although these "tunes" could be said to show signs of arbitrariness and displacement, and are quite complex, there is no evidence of productivity. There are too few units to be able to combine them to produce other meanings.

to an ability to use a language spontaneously. However, the fact that other species do not possess language does not necessarily mean that they cannot acquire it. Several attempts have been made to teach apes the basic features of human language, and the findings from such attempts are discussed here.

Why try to teach them?

The issue of whether language can be taught to other species has some theoretical interest. According to Skinner (1957), spoken language is learned in very much the same way as other responses. In other words, utterances that are rewarded or reinforced tend to be strengthened, whereas those that are not rewarded are weakened. As a result, there is nothing special about language, and thus there is no reason why language should not be learned by other species (see Section 9, Language and Thought).

In contrast, Chomsky (1959, 1965) claimed that language is a unique system. It cannot be acquired by other species, because language learning can only occur in species having various innate linguistic mechanisms. According to Chomsky (1959), only the human species has such innate mechanisms, and they form part of the so-called **language acquisition device** (LAD). This device contains the rules of grammar which allow humans to produce an infinite variety of expressions from a fixed vocabulary. The term grammar refers to the existence of a set of rules about how to combine words to produce specific meanings. For example, "The cat chased the dog" and "The dog chased the cat" have different meanings and we know this as a consequence of the rules of combination.

Chomsky believed that children have the ability to generate the rules of grammar when they are exposed to a native vocabulary, and this turns them into language users. Can non-human animals also do this?

Would it be a sufficient demonstration of language abilities for a non-human animal to comprehend human language, or is production essential?

Teaching dolphins to use language

Dolphins have developed a large brain, including a relatively large area of cortex. It has often been argued that these creatures are highly intelligent. As a result, attempts have been made to understand their communication systems and to teach them aspects of language.

Herman, Richards, and Wolz (1984) studied language learning in bottlenosed dolphins. One of them, Akeakamai, was trained in a visual language based on gestures made by a trainer. There was an emphasis on grammar in this language, in the sense that word or symbol order made a difference to the meaning being expressed by the trainer. Akeakamai became very proficient at fetching a given object from among a large number after a training programme in which she was rewarded for responding correctly. She was also able to take one object to another in response to the trainer's gestures. After a lot of training, Akeakamai was presented with new sentences describing combinations of actions that she had not carried out before. She showed her comprehension ability by performing these actions correctly.

Herman et al. (1984) studied another bottlenosed dolphin called Phoenix. He was trained on a language like that used with Akeakamai, except that it was expressed by means of short, computer-generated noises. Phoenix displayed a good ability to respond correctly to instructions in this language, and was good at taking account of word order.

In sum, dolphins show some ability to understand human language and to grasp the basics of grammar. More research is needed to find out whether they can develop their language abilities further than this.

Some of the gestures used to communicate with Akeakamai the dolphin (adapted from Herman et al., 1984)

TAIL-TOUCH

MOUTH

LEFT

WATER

Teaching primates to use language

Hayes and Hayes

Keith and Catharine Hayes brought up a chimpanzee named Viki, and spent six years trying to teach her to speak (Hayes, 1951). At the end of that time, Viki could only say four words: "momma"; "poppa"; "up"; and "cup". Her teachers had to push her lips and mouth into the correct positions at first. However, she finally learned to position her lips and mouth with her own hands to produce the sounds.

Evaluation.   This study was poorly designed. It is not at all natural for chimpanzees to make much use of their vocal cords. Humans can produce about 100 distinct sounds, but chimpanzees can produce only about a dozen. As we will see, later studies abandoned the attempt to make chimpanzees communicate vocally as humans do.

Gardner and Gardner

Washoe spontaneously taught her adopted son Loulis (pictured) the ASL signs she knew.

Attempts to teach language to chimpanzees started in earnest in 1966. Allen and Beatrice Gardner began to teach American Sign Language (ASL) to a 1-year-old female chimpanzee called Washoe. They used operant conditioning techniques. After 4 years of training, Washoe knew 132 signs, and she could arrange them in novel ways. For example, when she saw a swan she signed "water bird" and she used "food drink" for the refrigerator. There was also evidence that she had grasped some of the elements of grammar. She signed "tickle me" much more often than "me tickle", and "baby mine" more often than "mine baby". Washoe also showed the ability to apply the signs she had learned in new situations. For example, she initially learned the sign "open" with reference to a door. After that, she used the sign in the presence of cupboards, drawers, and boxes. In view of what Washoe learned to do, the Gardners concluded that she had learned language.

A key feature of language is that people use it just to pass the time of day, not because they want something. On one occasion, Washoe signed "toothbrush" using the sign for the first time. She didn't do this because she wanted her toothbrush (the toothbrush was just in front of her so she can't have been asking for it). She must have done it simply as a comment.

Fouts (1973) continued work with Washoe to see if she would teach ASL to an adopted son, Loulis. If she did this would be evidence of cultural transmission. The researchers never signed directly to Loulis but by the time he was 5 years old he had learned 51 signs.

Evaluation.   We should be cautious about accepting the conclusions of Gardner and Gardner (1969). Terrace et al. (1979) carried out a detailed analysis of Washoe's behaviour as revealed in a film that was made about her. Most of the grammatical sequences of signs produced by Washoe occurred when she simply imitated the signs that had just been produced by her teacher. The ability to imitate is very different from the ability to grasp grammatical rules. On the other hand, the Gardners have pointed out that Terrace's conclusions were based only on a short film, not the full record of Washoe's behaviour throughout their study.

It is also not clear whether Washoe did actually use consistent word order, which is a requirement of using grammar. The reason Washoe didn't do this may be because this was the limit of chimpanzees' ability to acquire language (in other words they can't). Or it may be because Washoe was never rewarded for the order of words. On the other hand children learning to speak aren't specifically rewarded for word order, yet they do learn it.

In addition, many of the signs that Washoe learned are the same as gestures that occur naturally in apes. These include "tickle" (signed by tickling), "hug" (signed by hugging), and "scratch" (signed by scratching). This would mean she hadn't actually learned anything.

The benefits of being able to communicate with Washoe

When Washoe was 5 years old she left the Gardners' care. Twelve years later they were reunited and Washoe immediately recognised them, and began to play a game she had not been seen playing since she left them. This clearly raises ethical questions concerning the nature of the experience from Washoe's point of view and whether the findings justified the research process.

Another story relates to a time when Washoe had a baby who was born unwell. The trainer removed the infant for treatment and later returned to tell Washoe the infant had died. Washoe thought he was returning with her child and signed "baby" enthusiastically. The trainer signed back, "He is dead, finished". And Washoe dropped her head, moved to a corner and stopped signing. Being able to communicate with humans may have been a good thing for Washoe—or a bad thing, depending on how you view it.

Finally, we should consider the possibility that Washoe was responding to cues from her trainers, rather than spontaneously producing language. There is a well-known case of a horse (Clever Hans) who was taught to be able to add and was able to give his answers by beating his hoof on the ground. It became apparent, in fact, that the horse couldn't add at all but was responding to very subtle cues from his trainer. Perhaps the same thing could explain Washoe's apparent abilities?

Gardner and Gardner (1978) did test Washoe in a situation that would avoid inadvertent cueing. Washoe was asked to name an object that she could see but that could not be seen by the person she was talking to. She was shown 32 items, each on four occasions, and correctly identified them 92 out of 128 times.

Clever Hans, the "counting" horse.

Terrace

One of the most thorough attempts to teach sign language to an ape was made by Herbert Terrace (1979). He and his associates tried to teach American Sign Language to a chimpanzee called Nim Chimpsky (a rather feeble pun on Noam Chomsky). Between 18 and 35 months of age, Nim was observed signing over 19,000 utterances consisting of two or more signs. Analysis of the two-sign combinations consisting of a transitive verb and "me" or "Nim" showed that Nim chose the verb-first order 83% of the time (e.g., "tickle Nim" rather than "Nim tickle").

Most humans sometimes use language to deceive others, and Nim was also able to do this. He noticed that his teachers were very responsive when he signed either "dirty" (meaning he needed to go to the toilet) or "sleep" (meaning that he was tired). He started to use these signs when they were obviously not appropriate, probably because he was bored and wanted more attention.

How might you relate Nim's attention-seeking signing to what you have learned about conditioning?

Evaluation. Nim's achievements looked much less impressive when his performance was compared with that of young children. Children initially produce utterances containing about one-and-a-half words on average. However, this rapidly increases to an average of four or more words per utterance. In contrast, the average length of Nim's utterances remained very steady at about one-and-a-half signs for the whole of the period between 26 and 46 months. In other words, Nim remained at a low level of language achievement, which is greatly exceeded by most young children.

There was another major difference between Nim's language and that of young children. Among children just starting to talk, under 20% of their utterances consist of imitations of their parents' expressions, and about 30% are spontaneous. In contrast, 40% of Nim's signings were merely imitations of what his teacher had just signed, and only 10% were spontaneous. Thus, Nim used language in a much less creative and spontaneous way than even very young children.

There are various possible reasons why Terrace found less evidence of language learning than other researchers (e.g., Gardner & Gardner, 1969) who have made use of American Sign Language. First, Terrace (1979) took more care than previous researchers to distinguish between "true" use of language and mere imitation. Second, a large number of volunteers were used by Terrace in the attempt to teach language to Nim, and some of them may not have been very competent. This could have limited the amount of language acquired by Nim. The Gardners argued that Nim had not received the kind of careful "parenting" that had been given to Washoe and Nim's language was therefore acquired in a less social atmosphere. Nim may have lacked the social impetus for language, which is so important.

Patterson

Patterson (1979) trained a female gorilla called Koko in a modified version of American Sign Language. She had mastered over 400 signs by the age of 10, which is much more than has been achieved by most other apes. She showed some ability to generalise beyond what she had been taught. For example, she was taught the sign for "straw" in the sense of a drinking straw, but then applied it to similar-looking objects such as plastic tubes and cigarettes.

One of Koko's most impressive achievements was her ability to create novel combinations of signs. For example, she signed "white tiger" to indicate a zebra, "false mouth" to mean nose, and "eye-hat" to mean mask. The productivity or creativity involved in these sign combinations is one of the main criteria for genuine language. She also showed some evidence of displacement, or the ability to refer to events that were not currently happening. For example, on one occasion she seemed to be apologising for having bitten someone three days earlier, and on another occasion she used the phrase "dirty toilet" as an insult.

What evidence of prevarication can be found in Koko's language?

Evaluation.   On the negative side, Koko showed little evidence of having mastered syntax or the grammatically correct ordering of words. In addition, most of her communications were rather brief, and were certainly much shorter than is the case even with young children. Thus, Koko only exhibited some of the features of language.

Sometimes Kanzi received spoken instructions through headphones.

Savage-Rumbaugh et al.

The chimpanzees studied by the Gardners and by Terrace were common chimpanzees (*Pan troglodytes*). It has been claimed that bonobo apes (*Pan paniscus*) are more intelligent than common chimpanzees. As a result, Savage-Rumbaugh et al. (1986) decided to study language in a male bonobo ape called Kanzi. In contrast to previous studies based on American Sign Language, Kanzi was taught using a keyboard containing geometric symbols known as lexigrams. Those working with Kanzi sometimes used the keyboard themselves, and sometimes they spoke to him in English.

Most of the earlier work on language learning in great apes had focused on language production rather than on language comprehension. In contrast, Savage-Rumbaugh et al. were as concerned with Kanzi's comprehension skills as with his ability to produce language. One reason for this is that language comprehension develops more quickly and easily in young children than does language production, and the same might be the case with great apes.

In 17 months, Kanzi learned to understand nearly 60 of these symbols, and he was able to produce nearly 50 symbols. After prolonged training, Kanzi mastered the use of 150 different symbols. Savage-Rumbaugh et al. found that Kanzi had developed good comprehension skills. He responded correctly every time to 109 words on a speech comprehension test, and behaved appropriately to 105 action–object utterances (e.g., "Kanzi, go get me a knife").

Kanzi's language learning was greater than that of Washoe, Nim Chimpsky, or Koko. He understood the difference between "Chase Kanzi" and "Kanzi chase". He could even make fairly subtle distinctions, such as that between "Put the pine needles in your ball" and "Can you put the ball on the pine needles?" However, as with Nim Chimpsky, he differed from young children in that the length of his utterances did not increase over time. Indeed, most of his utterances consisted of a single lexigram.

How impressed are you by Kanzi's command of language?

Later, Savage-Rumbaugh (1991) worked with another bonobo ape, Panbanisha, aiming to teach language in the same way that children are taught: they are exposed to it in the course of everyday life, use it to talk about future plans, and they are enculturated by it. Savage-Rumbaugh continued to converse using lexigrams while roaming around the large forest surrounding her home, to ensure that language was being learned in a natural and social setting. The results were a rich use of language: 90% accuracy in being able to identify pictures, novel combinations of words, and introduction of new rules.

Panbanisha also demonstrated prevarication. An experimenter replaced a sweet that was in a box with an insect. When another person was about to open the box, Panbanisha was asked by the first experimenter what the second person was looking for. Panbanisha answered "a sweet". This suggests both prevarication and a **Theory of Mind**, the ability to have insight into the mental state of another (see Section 13, Determinants of Animal Behaviour). Panbanisha also commented that the first researcher had been bad by trying to fool the second person.

Evaluation. Savage-Rumbaugh's research has been the most promising to date and has indicated considerable abilities in non-human animals. However, Terrace (1979) says Kanzi, like the disappointing Nim, is simply "going through a bag of tricks in order to get things". Other critics say there is nothing surprising about chimpanzees associating vocal sounds with objects. On one occasion Kanzi was recorded on videotape being told, "Give the dog a shot." The chimpanzee picked up a hypodermic syringe lying on the ground in front of him, pulled off the cap, and injected a toy dog. But was Kanzi just trained to associate the sound "dog" with the furry thing in front of him and programmed to carry out a stylised routine when he heard "shot"? Does the chimp really understand what he is doing?

Sue Savage-Rumbaugh holds a board displaying lexigrams that Kanzi uses to communicate with her.

Evaluation of attempts to teach language to non-human animals

The issue of whether or not apes can be taught language is important in a number of ways. In principle, it should help to resolve the theoretical controversy between Skinner (1957)

CASE STUDY: *An Interview with Sue Savage-Rumbaugh*

Q. Do your apes speak?

A. They don't speak. They point to printed symbols on a keyboard. Their vocal tract isn't like ours, and they don't make human noises. However, they do make all kinds of ape noises. And I believe they use them to communicate with one another. Now, the apes may not always elect to talk about the same things we do. They might not have a translation for every word in our vocabulary to theirs. But from what I've seen, I believe they are communicating very complex things. Let me give you an example. A few weeks ago, one of our researchers, Mary Chiepelo was out in the yard with Panbanisha. Mary thought she heard a squirrel and so she took the keyboard and said, "There's a squirrel." And Panbanisha said "DOG." Not very much later, three dogs appeared and headed in the direction of the building where Kanzi was. Mary asked Panbanisha, "Does Kanzi see the dogs?" And Panbanisha looked at Mary and said, "A-frame." A-frame is a specific sector of the forest here that has an A-frame hut on it. Mary later went up to "A-frame" and found the fresh footprints of dogs everywhere at the site. Panbanisha knew where they were without seeing them. And that seems to be the kind of information that apes transmit to each other: "There's a dangerous animal around. It's a dog and it's coming towards you."

Q. How do you know when the chimps point to symbols on the keyboard that they are not just pointing to any old thing?

A. We test Kanzi and Panbanisha by either saying English words or showing them pictures. We know that they can find the symbol that corresponds to the word or the picture. If we give similar tests to their siblings who haven't learned language—they fail. Many times, we can verify through actions. For instance, if Kanzi says "Apple chase," which means he wants to play a game of keep away with an apple, we say, 'Yes, let's do." And then, he picks up an apple and runs away and smiles at us.

Q. Some of your critics say that all your apes do is mimic you?

A. If they were mimicking me, they would repeat just what I'm saying, and they don't. They answer my questions. We also have data that shows that only about two percent of their utterances are immediate imitations of ours.

Q. Nonetheless, many in the scientific community accuse you of over-interpreting what your apes do.

A. There are SOME who say that. But none of them have been willing to come spend some time here. Their belief is that there is a thing called human language and that unless Kanzi does everything a human can, he doesn't have it. They refuse to consider what Kanzi does—which is comprehend—as language. And it's not even a matter of disagreeing over what Kanzi does. It's a matter of disagreeing over what to call these facts. They are asking Kanzi to do everything that humans do, which is specious. He'll never do that. It still doesn't negate what he can do.

From Claudia Dreifus (1998) "She talks to apes and, according to her, they talk back". *New York Times*, 14 April.

and Chomsky (1959) that was discussed earlier. In addition, work on this issue may provide some insights into the nature of language.

On the negative side, it is rather artificial to try to teach chimpanzees human language systems to which they are not adapted. It is perhaps unfortunate that so much of the research has made use of a version of American Sign Language that is particularly artificial. The grammatical structure of American Sign Language is different from that of spoken languages, and the version of it used in research is simplified and distorted from the original. As a result, Benderly (1980) concluded as follows: "This rather impoverished form is really not a language, but a manual code for English."

We can only decide whether or not apes have succeeded in acquiring language with reference to Hockett's criteria for language (see earlier). According to Harley (1995, p.14), "If we look at them [attempts to teach apes a human-like language] in terms of Hockett's design features, at first sight all the important ones appear to be present." However, as Harley went on to point out, there is only weak evidence for some of the criteria. For example, apes do not often show displacement, and very rarely refer to objects that have not been seen for a long time. They also show much less evidence of productivity than do most humans.

How else can we evaluate the language performance of chimpanzees? According to Harley (1995, p.18), "A great deal comes down to a comparison of the performance of apes with that of children, and there is considerable disagreement on how well apes come out of this comparison." There are various ways in which the language performance of apes falls short of that of young children. First, apes do not often use language spontaneously, and they very rarely ask questions. Second, the average length of their utterances is much less than that of most young children. Third, there is very little evidence that apes use language to help them think. Fourth, apes use language to refer to the here-and-now, and rarely refer to objects that are not visible or have not been seen for some time.

Chimpanzees have shown only a modest ability to learn language because they have only a limited need or wish to communicate. As Savage-Rumbaugh et al. (1986) concluded:

> *Symbols have merely served to replace or accompany non-verbal gestures the chimpanzee would otherwise employ ... chimpanzees, even with intensive linguistic training, have remained at the level of communication they are endowed with naturally—the ability to indicate ... that they desire you to perform an action upon them or for them.*

"He says the downturn in world trade is adversely affecting banana supply, and warrants a reduction in interest rates".

It is hard to come to any definite conclusions. However, the fact that most human children as young as 2 years old have a much greater command of language than any

■ Activity: Record a summary of the research on primates by completing the table below. Refer to Hockett's criteria for language as much as possible.

	Basic research details	Evidence that language was acquired	Arguments against	Criticisms of methodology
Washoe				
Nim				
Koko				
Kanzi				

trained ape suggests that no ape has developed language in the full sense. Another reason for doubting the language ability of chimpanzees was offered by Chomsky (quoted in Atkinson et al., 1993):

> Looking back at your working definition of language, do you think it is still adequate? How would you change it, if at all, in the light of all these animal studies?

If an animal had a capacity as biologically advantageous as language but somehow hadn't used it until now, it would be an evolutionary miracle, like finding an island of humans who could be taught to fly.

Memory

Non-human animals have memories. Your dog jumps up and down when he sees you; police dogs are given a scent and then can follow it; many animals, as we have just seen, possess or can learn to use a vocabulary. In this Unit we will consider two important behaviours that rely on memory. Navigation by location requires a recall of landmarks or smells. Foraging involves memory in so far as an animal needs to recall where it found food and also may need to recall where it later hid the food.

In your AS level course, you studied human memory. There are clearly going to be some parallels between human and non-human memory as the human brain has evolved from its non-human ancestors.

Memory is the process of retaining information after the original thing is no longer present. There are close links between **learning** and **memory**. Something that is learned is lodged in memory. The two terms are almost synonymous, though learning theorists (**behaviourists**) prefer the concept of "learning" to that of "memory". This is because memory implies internal cognitive processing, whereas the process of learning need only involve observable behaviours. To a great extent the study of memory in non-human animals is and has to be of observable processes, because you can't ask a pigeon to tell you what it remembers. However one can infer internal processes, such as cognitive maps, in order to make sense of the observable data.

What sorts of things can most dogs remember?

Memory in Navigation

Earlier in this Section we discussed the cues that are used by non-human animals when navigating. Magnetic information, the sun, and the stars all provide information on the direction to travel. It is likely that these cues are largely innate although, for example, Perdeck (1958) showed that older starlings use true navigation as distinct from orientation only (see page 531), and Emlen (1975) suggested that indigo buntings do learn the constellation patterns while in the nest. The use of the sun as a directional cue also relies on the biological clock, another innate mechanism.

Navigation involves location as well as direction, and the cues for location finding come from local landmarks and recognising home odours. The ability and predisposition to do this, as in salmon, is again innate but clearly the actual landmark or smell has to be learned. Gould (1987) pointed out that there are two ways that landmarks could be remembered:

1. By recall of a few basic characteristics. This may involve recall of parameters or recall of whole sectors or sequences.
2. By forming a more complete image or pictorial representation. This would be an example of **spatial memory**, the ability to learn environmental layout in order to recall the objects or activities associated with particular places.

Gould (1987) illustrated the distinction between learning a list of parameters and learning a picture with the following example:

To use a human analogy, the information content of an advertisement specifying the important parameters of, say, an automobile (make, model, year, body type, colour, accessories, mileage, etc.) is far lower than the information content of an actual picture of the item for sale; the list of important parameters is clearly an adequate and inexpensive way to store (or communicate) information in certain contexts.

Parameters or pictures?

Earlier we described a study of digger wasps homing using visual landmarks about their nest (Tinbergen & Kruyt, 1938; see page 537). Baerends (1941) also studied digger wasps and found that not only did they use landmarks around the entrance to their nest but they also used more distant landmarks to guide their homeward journey, such as a stone wall or a pond. Baerends suggested that the wasp memorises a sequence of visual cues and uses this stored version to compare with the view on its flight path, to guide it home. The wasps appeared to have several different possible routes but these were not inter-related as in a pictorial representation. This led Baerends to conclude that the wasps were storing visual parameters and not a map.

On the other hand, further variations of Tinbergen and Kruyt's study do support some use of spatial memory (a map) by digger wasps (Tinbergen, 1951). In the original study the circle of pine cones was put in a different place from the nest entrance. In this variation of the original a triangle of pine cones was left over the nest but a circle of stones was placed nearby. The wasps went to the circle of stones. This suggests that the stored parameters related to spatial relationships and were not based on the visual objects.

Gould (1987) came to a similar conclusion with respect to honeybees. He conducted various experiments and concluded that the bees remembered the landmarks pictorially, in essence taking a picture from above and storing this. Gould suggests that there is an adaptive trade-off between remembering a list of features (but not in visual form) and remembering a whole picture. A low-resolution picture would be good enough.

Cognitive maps

A cognitive map is a mental representation of the spatial relationships of an animal's immediate environment. Evidence for the existence of cognitive maps came from a study by Tolman and Honzik (1930). One group of rats spent 10 days in a maze with no reward being given but when a food reward was added on the 11th day these rats learned the route to the food box almost immediately, whereas other rats who had been continually rewarded took nearly 10 days to be able to go directly to the food box. The first group must have been learning something to enable their behaviour to change so comparatively quickly. Tolman used the term **cognitive map** to describe what they had learned. According to behaviourists, learning only takes place as a consequence of reinforcement. In the absence of such reinforcement no learning should have taken place—but it had.

Models of spatial memory

Spatial adaptation model

Sherry et al. (1992) argued that spatial ability will be more developed in some animals than others because some animals have a greater need to use it. If an animal has a life-style that requires spatial ability then those individuals with this ability are better adapted and more likely to survive and reproduce. For example, a squirrel who hides its food needs to be able to relocate it and would rely on spatial memory, whereas a cat is not reliant on food storage. Therefore the argument is that spatial memory evolves because it is adaptive for some animals.

Gaulin and FitzGerald (1989) produced evidence to support this in a study of meadow moles. Male members of the species have a territory that is four times the size of the females' territory. As one would expect, on the basis of the spatial adaptation model, the males showed much superior maze-learning abilities than the females. In contrast, in prairie vole males and females share the same territory, and they also are fairly equal in their ability to learn a path through a maze. Spatial abilities are related to environmental demands for them.

Pliancy model

Day et al. (1999) suggested an alternative model to account for the same facts. They argued that the reason the male meadow moles were better at the maze was not due to a superior spatial ability, but they had just developed more flexible (or pliant) memories. Their memories could cope with forming more complex associations. Evidence to support this was gathered in Day et al.'s own study of two related species of lizard. One of the species lived in an environment where their prey tended to be clumped together—with such a distribution a spatial memory would be adaptive in order to find the prey. The second lizard species had more evenly distributed and mobile prey, and therefore spatial memory would not have offered any particular adaptive advantage.

The lizards were tested on a maze-learning task and no differences between the two species were found, in contrast to the findings with the voles. However, when the lizards were given a non-spatial visual discrimination tasks, the species who had "clumped" prey did better. This suggests that their particular environmental demands were associated with an ability to perform more complex processing than just the spatial memory aspect.

Neurological basis of spatial memory

Spatial memory is linked to the hippocampus. Early memory research thought that the hippocampus was related to memory in general. This was in part due to the study of HM, a patient who had his hippocampus removed (in an attempt to control his epilepsy) and suffered short-term memory loss. Later experiments with rats found that those rats with hippocampal lesions (cuts made to sever the brain connections to the hippocampus) were still able to learn simple discrimination tasks (Kalat, 1998), therefore showing that memory functions were also governed in other areas of the brain.

Later research did find that these brain-damaged rats could not function in situations requiring memory of locations. For example, in the "Morris selection task" (see illustration on the right) Jarrard (1995) found that rats with hippocampal damage were able to find the platform but, unlike normal rats, were unable to remember the location from one trial to another and thus could not escape any faster with each progressive trial. Thus the hippocampus appears to have a specific role in memory—related to locations.

Interestingly, Bingman and Mench (1990) found that pigeons with hippocampal lesions were not disoriented during the initial stages of a homeward flight (using direct rather than location navigation) but when they got close to home they had more difficulties.

Evidence from humans agrees with this. A study of taxi drivers (see page 155) showed that their right hippocampus was active when they were recalling routes around London but not when recalling information about landmarks (Maguire et al., 1997).

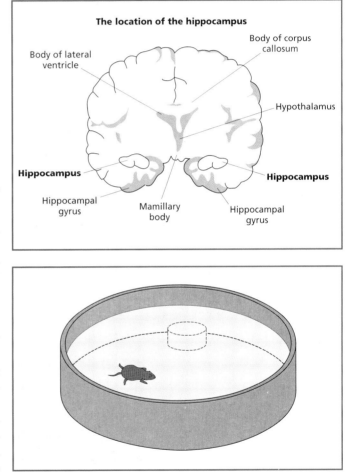

The Morris selection task involves placing a rat in murky water. A platform that would provide support is submerged so the rat cannot see it. Rats with hippocampal damage have trouble remembering the location of the platform.

Memory in Foraging

Foraging behaviours have been examined in detail in Section 13, Determinants of Animal Behaviour. Successful foraging is of major adaptive importance. Most animals spend most of their waking hours searching for food. They aim to expend as little energy as possible in doing this, so it is helpful to know where the best places to search will be. One way to do this is to return to places where food was found before, a strategy that requires a spatial memory. Another strategy is to collect more than one needs at one time and store some of the food in a "food cache" for later use, when there is less food available, such as during the winter months. The role of memory can be seen both in returning to profitable food sites and in relocating places where food has been hidden.

Learning where to find food

Menzel (1971) demonstrated food finding in a group of chimpanzees. The chimpanzees were taken on a winding trail during which food was left in 18 different locations. Later, they were released into the outdoor enclosure. They did not follow the original path taken but went directly to the different food locations. In a later experiment half of the food sites were fruit and the others were vegetables. When the chimpanzees were released they went to the fruit sites first. Both experiments indicate that the chimpanzees were using a spatial representation of the area rather than following a series of visual cues.

Relocating food caches

Some food-storing birds can remember the locations of thousands of stored seeds over a period of several months (Sherry et al., 1981), and MacDonald (1997) documented squirrels retrieving food from food caches after 62 days. One suggestion is that they use smell rather than location to relocate their food cache. This was tested in an experiment by Jacobs and Liman (1991). A number of grey squirrels were released, one at a time, into an enclosed outdoor area. They had 10 nuts to bury and the position of each site they chose was recorded. Later the nuts were replaced by new nuts to remove any possible odour cue. The squirrels were still more likely to recover nuts from their own caches even when they had to travel past other sites, and even 12 days later.

Other animals, such as the black-capped chickadee (Hitchcock & Sherry, 1990) appear to be able to remember food caches for 28 days. There is not always a great advantage in very lengthy recall as, by the time an animal has returned to its cache, some other animal is likely to have found the food.

Food caches and the hippocampus

One interesting finding relates to the hippocampus and food caching. We saw earlier that the hippocampus is involved in spatial memory. Smulders et al. (1995) found that black-capped chickadees had larger hippocampal regions during late autumn, a time when the birds are caching food for winter and therefore would be making large demands on their spatial skills. In general food storing birds have been found to have larger hippocampal regions that non-food-storing animals (Krebs et al. 1989). This suggests that food caching puts a large demand on the hippocampus.

SECTION SUMMARY

Animal Navigation

❖ True navigation involves direction finding (orientation) and location finding (e.g., landmarks). Young starlings use orientation only whereas older starlings can compensate for displacement. Navigation uses both innate and learned abilities. To navigate is to find one's way, homing behaviour is the location of a specific target (e.g., nest, point of origin, or food store). Both navigation and homing employ similar abilities.

❖ Migration relies on navigational abilities. Fish, such as eels and salmon, migrate exceptionally long distances. Eels home in on the Sargasso Sea. Salmon home towards their river of origin. Homing pigeons are well known for their navigational abilities and many other birds also have excellent navigation systems.

❖ Starlings' navigational abilities are both innate and learned, whereas the European stork is mainly influenced by an innate directional sense. The costs of migration include energy expenditure and getting lost, but these are outweighed by advantages. These include better food supplies and mating opportunities, and less predation and competition from other animals. Not all birds migrate and some birds don't migrate every year.

❖ When considering explanations of navigation it is important to remember that animals often use a variety of mechanisms, and that different animals rely on different cues. Navigation by direction may use magnetic information, the sun (celestial), and/or the stars (stellar). Navigation by location may rely on smell (olfactory cues), sound (auditory cues), and/or local landmarks (visual cues).

❖ Studies using electromagnetic coil caps demonstrate that homing pigeons and other birds rely on magnetic information, especially on cloudy days. Young pigeons appear to be less able to use this information. The physiological source for this magnetic ability may lie in a region behind the nose which contains magnetite, though there is some doubt about whether this can detect the earth's magnetic fields.

❖ Many animals, such as homing pigeons, ants, and salmon, use the sun for navigation. Some animals rely exclusively on the sun, such as mallards. Clock-shifting experiments demonstrate how animals use the sun. For example, a bird's circadian rhythm is altered by 6 hours (so it thinks it is 5am instead of 11am). On a sunny day the bird flies at a right angle to the correct path because the sun's position is misinterpreted.

❖ Some birds use the stars, using the position of the north star and the rotation of the stars around this during the night.

❖ The importance of smell has been demonstrated by plugging the noses of homing pigeons and salmon. Both species display disorientation. Experiments have also cut the olfactory nerves of pigeons or used local anaesthetics. It is possible that disorientation is due to the experimental procedures rather than reliance on smell for location finding. Other studies have artificially altered odours and demonstrated more convincingly that animals use odour for location.

❖ Bats use echolocation for navigation, though long-distance travel may involve magnetic information.

❖ Homing pigeons may use visual landmarks, finding homing difficult when wearing translucent lenses. However, they don't rely on visual cues. Other bird and animal species seem to make more use of visual information. Digger wasps memorise the pattern of objects around their nest site.

❖ We know what cues animals use in navigation but not the mechanisms involved or how the information is used.

Animal Communication and Language

❖ Animal communication is both intraspecies and interspecies. Communication requires that the behaviour of the receiver be altered in some way by it. Human language differs from non-human animal communication in various ways, such as being intentional and concerning the past as well as the present. Animal communication relates to survival, reproduction, territory boundaries, and food.

❖ Animals use different sensory channels for communication. Chemical signals are usually pheromones, as used by moths, ants, and even humans. These signals can be used at night, last for a long time, and are hard for predators to detect and interpret. However, they may interfere with later chemical signals, and they are a slow means of communication.

❖ Visual signals, such as the peacock's tail or the markings on a snake, have the advantages of instantaneous transmission, rich information, and being highly directional and permanent. However, they only work under reasonable lighting conditions and over short distances. They are also expensive in terms of energy.

❖ Auditory signals are also "expensive". They may be distorted over long distances and can be heard by predators. On the other hand, they can be used in the dark, and are rich in meaning, fast, and efficient.

❖ Tactile communication is used for social signals and between parents and young. It tends to be simple but can only be used in situations in which direct contact is possible. A few species of fish make use of electrical signals.

❖ The choice of sensory modality is related to environmental conditions. For example, visual signals would not work well in dense vegetation. Choice is also related to possession of the appropriate structures, such as keen eyesight.

❖ Over time communication signals tend to become ritualised: stereotyped, exaggerated, and repetitive. This occurs because (1) it is adaptive for a signal to become less and less ambiguous in order to ensure that the receiver understands the meaning of an honest signal, or (2) the receiver of a dishonest signal shows resistance, so the signal has to become more exaggerated and stereotyped in order to overcome this resistance. All signals manipulate the receiver. A dishonest signal disadvantages the receiver. Most dishonest signals in non-human animals do not involve deliberate deception.

❖ Bird song is adapted to the individual's environment in such a way as to avoid distortion. Each species has a basic repertoire of songs but the specific details are learned through imitation. Honeybees perform a waggle dance to communicate the location of food sources, though other bees may also use cues such as smell. Bees may also interpret the signals rather than just following them automatically. Groups of whales sing to each other. Their songs serve various social functions, such as for foraging, mating, and generally staying in touch with other group members. Dolphins appear able to be quite precise in their communications.

❖ Hockett proposed certain criteria for distinguishing language from communication, such as semanticity, arbitrariness, displacement, prevarication, and productivity. It would be reasonable to expect that there is no discontinuity between animal communication and language. Vervet monkeys demonstrate semanticity, arbitrariness, and prevarication. The dance of the honeybee demonstrates displacement as well as semanticity. Whale communication is also arbitrary and has semanticity. However, no non-human animals appear to be able to produce an infinite variety of signals from a limited repertoire, as is the case with human language. Discontinuity might be explained as the consequence of a single genetic mutation which produced a unique characteristic in humans.

❖ Animals may not naturally produce language but can they be taught to use it? If they can this would provide support for the behaviourist view that language is entirely learned, as opposed to Chomsky's view that humans use language because they are innately hard-wired to do so. The key feature of an innate linguistic device is the ability of children to generate the grammatical rules from exposure to a native vocabulary.

❖ Dolphins show some ability to understand human language and to grasp the basics of grammar.

❖ Early primate research included the Hayes' attempts to teach speech to Viki, without much success. The Gardners used operant conditioning to train Washoe to use sign language (ASL). This female chimpanzee appeared to be able to acquire many key features of language: novel uses of words and word combinations, some grammatical ability, spontaneous production, and cultural transmission. It is possible that Washoe was not genuinely using grammatical rules, though this may be because she was not rewarded for using them. Critics have also suggested that she was responding to inadvertent cues from her trainers, though subsequent research suggests that this was not the case.

❖ Another chimpanzee, Nim, showed some ability to use consistent word order and also used language for deception. However, many of Nim's utterances were imitations and not spontaneous. Nim's comparatively poor performance may be due to Terrace's application of more rigid criteria or because Nim may have lacked the important social impetus for developing language.

❖ Koko, a gorilla, showed some ability to generalise beyond what she had been taught, could create novel combinations of signs, and showed some evidence of displacement. However, there was little evidence of consistent grammar and her utterances were brief.

❖ Kanzi, a male bonobo ape, was taught language using lexigrams. Savage-Rumbaugh et al. focused on comprehension rather than production. Kanzi was able to recognise a large vocabulary and to distinguish between meaning as expressed by different word order. However his utterances again remained much shorter than that of a child. Another bonobo, Panbanisha, has demonstrated further abilities, such as the ability to prevaricate. However, critics still feel unsure whether this is just imitation or true understanding.

❖ It is difficult to interpret the findings from studies of teaching human language to non-human animals. First of all, the experimental version of ASL used, unlike that used by deaf people, may not be a true language. Second, even though many of Hockett's criteria appear to be present, the evidence is rather weak. Third, primates' abilities to acquire language are poor in comparison with the abilities of young humans—in terms of utterance length and ease of acquisition.

❖ The study of memory in non-human animals involves making inferences about non-observable mental processes on the basis of what an animal appears to have learned.

Memory

❖ Navigation relies on a sense of direction (orientation) and location finding. Orientation may be innate but animals need to learn ways of recognising their location. There may be two ways of recalling landmarks: by characteristics or by using a spatial representation. Some research suggests that wasps rely on visual characteristics, though other evidence indicates that both wasps and honeybees use spatial representation for navigation.

❖ How can we account for spatial memories? The spatial adaptation model suggests that animals develop spatial memories if and when it is adaptive to their lifestyle. The pliancy model argues that spatial abilities are the outcome of generally superior and more flexible mental abilities, not just specialised spatial abilities.

❖ Research indicates that spatial memory is controlled by the hippocampus in non-human animals and humans. Pigeons with hippocampal damage are not disoriented (i.e., direction finding is fine) but they have difficulty with location finding.

❖ Spatial memory is also important in foraging. Research shows that animals do not follow a sequence of visual cues to relocate food supplies but that they use spatial representations. The same is true for relocating food caches. Research has also found that food-storing animals tend to have larger hippocampal regions, the area of the brain used by spatial memory.

FURTHER READING

A good general textbook on the topics in this Section, and the last Section, is J.M. Pearce (1997) *Animal learning and cognition (2nd Edn.)* (Hove, UK: Psychology Press). S.J. Shettleworth (1998) *Cognition, evolution and behaviour* (New York: Oxford University Press) is an advanced text but highly informative. E.S. Savage-Rumbaugh et al. (1998) *Apes, language and the human mind* (New York: Oxford University Press) describes Kanzi's day-to-day life and achievements, and discusses the arguments for animal language in primates.

Example Examination Questions

You should spend 30 minutes on each of the questions below, which aim to test the material in this Section.

1. Discuss **two** explanations of animal navigation.   (24 marks)

2. Critically consider research studies into homing and/or migration in non-human animals.   (24 marks)

3. Describe and evaluate the use of **two** different signalling systems in non-human animals.   (24 marks)

4. (a) Describe **two** research studies of animal language.   (12 marks)
    (b) Assess the value of these and/or other research studies of animal language.   (12 marks)

5. (a) Describe **two or more** explanations of memory in non-human animals.   (12 marks)
    (b) Assess the importance of memory in foraging behaviour.   (12 marks)

6. Discuss the importance of memory in navigation (e.g., spatial memory) behaviour in
    non-human animals.   (24 marks)

Examination Tips

Question 1.   "Discuss" is an AO1 and AO2 term. The question is limited to a description of two explanations of animal navigation, such as the sun or magnetic information. A different approach would be to consider navigation in two different animals—each one counting as "one" explanation. Evaluation is likely to refer to research evidence and possible flaws in the methodology. One could also offer contrasting explanations as long as they are explicitly given as evaluation rather than just describing further explanations.

Question 2.   "Critically consider" is also an AO1/AO2 term requiring description of research studies plus evaluation which must include a consideration of the strengths and weaknesses of the studies. When describing studies you can use the same guidelines as for AS level: write something about the aims, procedures, findings, and conclusions. Evaluation may include reference to other research studies that confirm or dispute the original findings, the plausibility of an explanation arising from the study, methodological issues, and even practical applications.

Question 3.   "Two different signalling systems" refers to either two different modalities, such as sight and smell, or two different animals. The question requires that you describe the use of such signals and also evaluate them (i.e., determine the value). This can be done by considering strengths and weaknesses of a particular method, or considering issues of honest/dishonest signals. It would also be possible to make contrasts with signalling systems as long as such material is explicitly presented in this way.

Question 4.   The question refers to "animal language" (as does the specification), which means that human language would be acceptable. In part (a) you must describe two studies, including details such as aims, methods, findings, and conclusions. Any criticisms of such studies would not be creditworthy though such material could be exported to part (b) where a general evaluation is required. If you do introduce further studies into part (b) then further *description* is not required. The second part requires an argument about the value of such research studies, which might include consideration of flawed methodology but also consideration of what such studies tell us—what is the point of such research?

Question 5.   The "two or more" is included to reassure you that two explanations are sufficient but you may want to include more. In such cases there is a depth–breadth trade-off. If you write about a number of explanations (breadth) then the level of detail is necessarily limited. Whereas if only explanations are covered, then there is room for more detail (depth). For top marks a good balance between depth and breadth is required. In part (b) you must assess the importance of memory in foraging behaviour. The trick here is to use your knowledge effectively in order to construct an argument in answer to the question, rather than just offering description. You might employ useful phrases such as "This suggests that …" or "The point this illustrates is …".

Question 6.   For the AO1 element you should describe how memory is involved in navigation. This may include descriptions of navigation behaviour itself but the focus must be on memory. Evaluation will involve a consideration of the extent to which such behaviour does rely on memory. Some animals, such as butterflies, do it with no memory abilities.

WEB SITES

http://www.monarchwatch.org/index2.html
Monarch Watch: a site dedicated to education, conservation, and research on the monarch butterfly, with information on migration and tagging.

http://www.salmoninfo.org/lifecycle.htm
Salmon Information Center, with many links.

http://www.howandwhy.com/General/Pigeon.html
How does a homing pigeon "home"?

http://www.nmnh.si.edu/BIRDNET/index.html
Birdnet: The Ornithological Information Source, including many links.

http://www.dolphin-institute.org/
The Dolphin Institute, based in Hawaii, dedicated to dolphins and whales through education, research, and conservation.

http://www.cwu.edu/~cwuchci/
The Chimpanzee and Human Communication Institute, at the Central Washington University, including a "Friends of Washoe" section.

http://www.koko.org
The Gorilla Language Project (or "Project Koko" after one of the gorillas), the longest continuous inter-species communications project of its kind in the world.

www.animalnews.com/fouts/about.htm
The Washoe project.

http://www.santafe.edu/~johnson/articles.chimp.html
Chimp Talk Debate: Is It Really Language?

http://www.pigeon.psy.tufts.edu/peoplef.htm
Research on animal cognition, with particular reference to pigeons.

http://www.sci.monash.edu.au/psych/research/memory/
Animal Memory Research Team, Monash University, Australia.

http://www.abdn.ac.uk/mammal/
The Mammal Society of Great Britain.

http://www.apa.org/science/anguide.html
American Psychological Association (APA) Guidelines for Ethical Conduct in the Care and Use of Animals.

www.a-levelpsychology.co.uk/websites.html
A continually updated list of useful links, including those printed in this book, may be found at the Psychology Press A level psychology site.

15

Evolutionary Explanations of Human Behaviour

Evolutionary explanations may be less appropriate for human behaviour than for non-human behaviour, because we are influenced by language and consciousness. Nevertheless there has been growing interest in applying the theory of evolution to the behaviour of humans. If you have not covered Section 13, Determinants of Animal Behaviour, in your studies, you will benefit from reading about the theory of evolution there to increase your understanding of the concepts covered here.

Human Reproductive Behaviour

Natural Selection and Sexual Selection

Reproduction is fundamental to the survival of any genetic line. If an individual doesn't reproduce then that's the end of his or her **genes** (unless an individual helps a close relative to reproduce—see the concept of **inclusive fitness** described on page 501). Therefore any characteristic that maximises an individual's ability to reproduce successfully is highly adaptive and likely to be naturally selected. Individuals with these genes go on to form successive generations.

Charles Darwin formulated this theory of evolution by **natural selection** but he was perplexed by several inconsistencies. One of them was the question of why some characteristics endure when they appear to be positively detrimental to the survival of an individual. For example, stags have huge antlers which must be a disadvantage when trying to escape from a predator. One would have thought that stags with small antlers would be naturally selected and therefore we would see no stags with large antlers. To solve this problem, Darwin (1871) outlined the principle of **sexual selection**. He argued that if a characteristic, such as the stag's antlers, increases the individual's chances of reproduction, then this characteristic will be adaptive because that stag will have more offspring. The antlers serve to increase the stag's reproductive fitness. The next question is "Why would stags with larger antlers have increased chances of reproduction?" Because the male stags fight for the right to be the dominant male and to have the right to access the harem of females.

We will start this Unit with a general consideration of sexual selection in non-human animals.

The principle of natural selection would predict that large antlers would reduce a stag's chances of survival. However, this prediction is not supported by our observations—stags do have large antlers. The antlers increase reproductive success and thus are adaptive.

Anisogamy

Males produce sperm and females produce eggs.

- Males produce sperm in thousands at relatively little physiological cost. Therefore their best strategy is to mate with many females, because this should result in the maximum number of offspring to perpetuate their genetic line.
- Females produce eggs, each of which contains a store of food for the growing embryo. This incurs some cost to the female and so eggs are not generally produced in thousands. Selection tends to favour those females who are more discriminating, because females need, for their smaller number of reproductions, to select a mate with good genes. This would ensure the best survival of their genes.

This difference between egg and sperm is termed **anisogamy**, a type of sexual reproduction where the gametes of the two sexes are dissimilar. It is rare to find animals where the two gametes are the same size (isogamy) but it does occur in, for example paramecium, a tiny freshwater organism.

The consequence of anisogamy, and the fact that in many animals (mammals especially) it is the mother who bears the majority of the huge biological cost of producing offspring, is that males tend to compete with other males for the right to fertilise females. This is called **intrasexual selection** ("intra" means "within"). In contrast, females tend to exercise choice and select the best male available. This is called **intersexual selection** ("inter" means "between").

Using words like "selection" and "choice" suggests that these behaviours are intentional—but they aren't. How could this difficulty with description be overcome?

Intrasexual selection

Dimorphism, the difference between males and females, arises because of intrasexual competition. If males have to compete, they need to be able to fight and this tends to result in larger males who have antlers for fighting or colourful tail feathers to attract females. Usually females do not have to compete with other females in order to mate.

There are generally fewer sexually receptive females than males in any population and therefore there is competition between males for the scant resource. This means that dominant males carefully control their hard-won access to impregnate the females. However, non-dominant males have developed other strategies. **Sneak copulation** is an example of this, where a non-dominant male discreetly copulates when the first male is not looking. Some male elephant seals pretend to be females, and are then able to join a harem and sneak copulate when the bull is occupied elsewhere. In order to counteract this males must be very possessive of their females and/or have sex in private. In the Coho salmon there are two male forms. One is much smaller than the other and lurks behind rocks (being small helps with this) to fertilise female eggs surreptitiously. The longer-maturing and larger hooknose male fights for the opportunity to fertilise eggs with other males. The fact that both forms persist shows that both strategies pay off.

Fertilisation of a human egg by a sperm, an example of anisogamy, where the gametes of the two sexes are dissimilar.

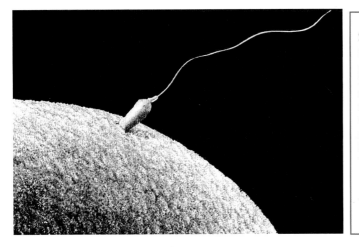

Soay sheep

Research by Brian Preston at University of Stirling (Motluk, 1999) parallels findings on stags. The 3-year study of 100 wild soay sheep on St. Kilda's Isle, Scotland, showed that the larger rams were most successful in mating, seeing off the smaller rams so that they could mate 10 or more times a day. Blood tests on the lambs showed that the majority born from matings that took place early in the 5-week reproductive season in November and December were fathered by the bigger rams. However, lambs born from matings in the last 2 weeks of the season had an equal chance of being fathered by bigger or smaller rams. This shows that at the beginning of the mating season the bigger rams were more successful, and selection was for heaviness. The later fall in success rates could be explained by the larger rams actually running out of sperm: too much success leading to failure!

Another strategy is called sperm competition. Males may compete at the level of their sperm for the right to fertilise an egg. Once a male has inseminated a female, another male's sperm may arrive and there is evidence that the most recently arrived sperm have the advantage.

Intersexual selection

Females tend to do the choosing, but on what basis?

Fisher's hypothesis: The runaway process

Fisher (1930) proposed that, initially, females are attracted to those features of males that have survival value. For example, a bird that has a fairly long tail may be better at flying and so at finding food than one with a short tail. A female will prefer a male with a long tail because her offspring are likely to inherit this characteristic (presuming that the long tail was an inherited characteristic). With progressive generations, males with a more exaggerated form of the long tail are the ones that are selected by females, so the characteristic becomes more and more exaggerated. Fisher called this the **runaway process**.

This hypothesis has also been described as the "sexy sons" hypothesis because females will benefit from mating with a male with desirable characteristics as these will be passed to her sons, and their reproductive chances will be enhanced because they are "sexy". Thus the mother's genes are perpetuated.

As long as the advantages outweigh the disadvantages, the exaggerated characteristic will be perpetuated. It is thought that one reason that the giant deer became extinct was that its antlers had simply become too large through the runaway process. Fossil records show antlers spanning as much as 3 metres. Andersson (1982) supplied experimental evidence to support this hypothesis (see the Key Study on the next page).

The handicap hypothesis

The main alternative to Fisher's hypothesis is Zahavi's (1977) handicap hypothesis. According to this hypothesis, a male adornment such as a long tail is a handicap in terms of survival. Females prefer males with long tails *because* a long tail is a handicap. The argument is that a male bird that is able to survive in spite of having a significant handicap is likely to be genetically superior to other birds. Thus females who prefer handicapped males may be selecting those who tend to possess good genes for survival. Therefore this theory is also called the "good genes" theory, but in this case the good genes are in terms of survival and reproduction, rather than Fisher's view that the good genes would be good in the sense that they will lead to attractive offspring.

The basic notion behind the handicap hypothesis can be seen if we consider a concrete example. Suppose that two men are running around a track at the same speed, but one of them is carrying a heavy load. We would probably assume that the man handicapped by the load is stronger and fitter than the other man. Certain behaviours imply or *indicate* robust genes.

Hamilton and Zuk (1982) put forward a specific version of the handicap hypothesis. They argued that males are only likely to have a long tail or other sexual adornment if they are in good health. An individual who is not in good health could not manage to survive with such an extra drain on energy. Thus, male animals with these adornments are attractive to females because they are likely to be free of diseases.

Møller (1990) tested Hamilton and Zuk's version of the handicap hypothesis. He studied barn swallows in Denmark. First of all, Møller showed that female swallows prefer

> **Mating by proxy**
>
> Researcher Matt Gage of Liverpool University was studying an insect pest, the flour beetle, which destroys stored grain (Walker, 1999). He hoped to find clues to methods of control from the reproductive cycle of the beetles, and he stumbled on a strange strategy of "mating by proxy". This appears to stem from the crowded populations of flour beetles, which are highly promiscuous. The males mate with many females in just a few minutes, and so the females have a succession of matings. Each male uses his spiny genitalia to scrape out the previous male's sperm before replacing it with his own. The ousted sperm stick to the outside of the male's genitalia and survive the journey to the next female where they are deposited. According to Gage, one in eight females was fertilised by a male with which they had not mated. So far, it seems that this strategy is unique in the animal world.

It is a good intersexual strategy, in evolutionary terms, for females to be coy because it permits time to assess a male's fitness (likelihood of reproductive success). Marilyn Monroe knew how to act coyly, as can be seen in this still from the comedy *The Seven Year Itch*.

According to Fisher why will successive generations of birds have longer and longer tails?

The terms "good taste" and "good sense" have sometimes been used to describe these theories. Considering Fisher's and Zahavi's hypotheses, which one do you think is the "good taste" hypothesis and which is the "good sense" one?

Long tails in widow birds

Perhaps the most interesting form of intrasexual selection occurs when some characteristic (e.g., a long tail) evolves over the generations because it is attractive to members of the opposite sex. For example, the males of several species (e.g., peacocks; birds of paradise) are elaborately adorned, and their adornment seems to make them more attractive to females for mating purposes. This form of intrasexual selection may seem straightforward, but it is not really so. For example, the peacock's very long and large tail reduces its chance of escaping from a predator. In addition, it has to eat more because of the weight of its tail.

It seems reasonable to assume that such adornments have developed because females find them attractive. However, it is always useful to have good evidence for any assumption. Andersson (1982) studied long-tailed widow birds in Kenya. The male of the species is fairly small (about the size of a sparrow), but its tail is about 40 centimetres or 16 inches in length. Andersson cut the tails off some males to reduce their length to about 14 centimetres or 6 inches. He lengthened the tails of other males by sticking the detached pieces of tail on to them with superglue, making their tails about 65 centimetres or 26 inches long.

Andersson then measured mating success by counting the number of nests in each male's territory. The males with the artificially lengthened tails had the greatest mating success, indicating that female widow birds are attracted to long tails in male birds. This evidence is convincing, because Andersson experimentally manipulated the length of the tail rather than simply relying on correlational evidence.

Can you explain why Andersson's approach is more convincing than one based on correlational evidence?

Discussion points

1. Why is the research by Andersson of particular value?

2. Do you think that this research provides a good explanation of long tails in male widow birds?

Concar (1995) proposed that the reason we find a symmetrical face attractive is that one needs strong genes to produce symmetricality, and this implies greater fitness (likelihood of reproductive success in terms of fertility and childbearing abilities).

males with long tails. He did this by finding that males with artificially lengthened tails paired up more quickly with female swallows than did normal males. Then he found that baby swallows reared in nests containing numerous blood-sucking mites were more likely to have reduced growth or to die than were those raised in nests with relatively few mites. Finally, he found that male swallows with long tails had offspring with fewer mites on them than did males with short tails. In other words, as predicted by the handicap hypothesis, male barn swallows with longer tails are healthier than those with shorter tails, because they have greater resistance to parasites such as blood-sucking mites.

Non-genetic benefits

Both Fisher's hypothesis and the handicap theory are related to characteristics that are inherited. The female selects a mate because she "thinks" he has characteristics that will be desirable for her offspring. Females may also select mates on the basis of non-inherited characteristics, most especially their possession of resources. In bullfrogs the strongest males are the ones that get the best pond sites, and the females choose the ones with the best site. A good site ensures that there should be plenty of food for the female and her offspring.

In many birds it is usual for the male to stay and help with the rearing of the young, which largely involves helping to provide adequate food supplies. Courtship rituals often involve supplying food, which may be a demonstration of the male's ability to gather resources. In addition a male with a nest site already has a valuable resource.

Human Reproductive Behaviour

The discussion until now has focused on sexual selection in all animals. We will now consider the evidence relating specifically to human reproductive behaviour. In recent years there has been a growing interest in evolutionary explanations of human behaviour and the field has been called **evolutionary psychology**. There are some important limitations when it comes to applying the principles of evolution to human behaviour.

First, the apparent knowledge we have about evolution is largely deduction. We do not know that certain behaviours exist because they are adaptive, it's just that this interpretation makes sense. Second, when applying these explanations to human behaviour we must not overlook the fact that humans are capable of conscious choice and are therefore less driven by innate forces than non-human animals.

Finally, there may be dangers in subscribing to evolutionary explanations of human behaviour because they are determinist. There is nothing intrinsically wrong with a determinist position—after all the intention of scientific research is to uncover causal relationships, a highly determinist aim. However, the danger is being fooled into thinking that an inherited disposition is inescapable, a position that appears to be promoted by some evolutionary explanations. Evolutionary psychologists do not take the position that this is the way humans *must* behave—but sometimes their arguments may sound like this.

Behaviourists also promote a determinist position. Which view is more "dangerous"—behaviourism or evolutionary psychology? (Read the box below.)

It is important to bear these points in mind when reading the following accounts.

Mate choice

Anisogamy, and the fact that women have a lower potential reproductive rate than men, tell us that human males are likely to maximise their reproductive success by having sex with numerous females. They should seek women who are fertile. One way to do this is to seek younger attractive women. Youth and physical attractiveness are good indicators of health.

In contrast, females can bear only a limited number of children, and they invest heavily in each one during the 9 months of pregnancy and for several years thereafter. It follows that women should be more selective than men in their choice of sexual partners. They should prefer men who have good resources, and who are willing to be committed to them over long periods of time.

Various studies have produced support for this view. Buss (1989; see the Key Study on the next page) conducted a cross-cultural study to show that men and women in many different cultures follow the patterns of behaviour predicted by evolutionary theory for the factors that are most valued in a mate. These findings are consistent with those of Davis (1990), who considered the content of personal advertisements in newspapers. Women advertising for a mate tended to emphasise their physical beauty and to indicate that they were looking for a high-status, wealthy man. In contrast, men emphasised their wealth or other resources, and made it clear that they were looking for a physically attractive younger woman. In other words, women regard men as "success objects", whereas men regard women as "sex objects".

Darwinism and the Left

In the years to come, skill will be needed to sift the legitimate from the spurious applications of Darwinism. We already factor knowledge of human nature into our social systems in many ways. Consider the undeniable and biological propensity for humans to fall asleep. This is not something we learn, we are born with this tendency. But modern society relies on the ability and willingness of some individuals to work through the night. A knowledge of biology tells us that there is a price to pay in terms of performance and fatigue, and elementary psychology tells us that we may need inducements to persuade people to work through "unnatural" hours. But it can be done. Biology is not destiny, but it can provide a useful contour map.

This is the approach taken by the Australian philosopher Peter Singer who argues that "it is time to develop a Darwinian Left" (Singer, 1998). For Singer, Darwinism informs us of the price we may have to pay to achieve desirable social goals. Uninformed state attempts to produce socialist societies have failed because they ignored human nature. For Singer, some aspects of human nature show little or no variation across

culture and consequently must be taken into account in any social engineering. Singer's list includes concern for kin, ability to enter into reciprocal relationships with non-kin, hierarchy and rank, and some traditional gender differences. To ignore these is, according to Singer, to risk disaster. The political reformer, like a good craftworker should have a knowledge of the material that he or she works. The trick is to work with the grain rather than against it.

The blank slate approach to human nature that is still unquestioned in some branches of the social sciences would, if it were taken seriously, be a tyrant's licence to manipulate. Liberals would have to stand back powerless and impotent as a tyrannical state moulded its people into instruments of whatever crazy ideology was in fashion. To resurrect culture as the new authority risks all we have gained and threatens to tip us into a state of intellectual bankruptcy and moral free-fall. Fortunately for anyone so inflicted, Darwinism is the best antidote around to the fashionable fallacies of post modernism.

Adapted from Cartwright (2000).

Cross-cultural support for the evolutionary account of mate choice

One way of testing the evolutionary theory of human sexual selection is by carrying out a cross-cultural study of preferred characteristics in mates. If the theory is correct, there should be clear differences in those characteristics preferred by men and by women, and these differences should be consistent across cultures. Some support for these predictions was reported by Buss (1989b), who obtained data from 37 cultures in 33 countries. He found that males in virtually every culture preferred females who were younger than them, and so likely to have good reproductive potential. In contrast, females in all cultures preferred males who were older, and thus more likely to have good resources. As predicted, females rated good financial prospects in a potential mate as more important than did males. It could be argued that males should value physical attractiveness in their mates more highly than females, because of its association with reproductive potential. In 36 out of 37 cultures, males valued physical attractiveness in mates more than did females. Finally, males tended to value chastity in a potential mate more than did females, but the difference between the sexes was not significant in 38% of the cultures sampled.

Discussion points

1. Does this research provide strong support for the evolutionary approach?
2. Why do you think that sex differences in mate preference vary between Western and non-Western cultures?

■ Activity: Westen (1996, p.706) commented on the behaviour of men and women: "Consider the Casanova who professes commitment and then turns out a few months later not to be ready for it; the man who gladly sleeps with a woman on a first date but then does not want to see her again, certainly not for a long-term relationship; or the women who only date men of high status and earning potential."

Westen suggested that all of these behaviours can be explained in evolutionary terms. Try to do this for yourself, by making a list of the different behaviours along with the evolutionary explanations for them. You also might consider why some people might find Westen's comments sexist and offensive.

More evidence supporting the prediction from evolutionary theory that females should be more selective than males in their choice of sexual partners was reported by Clark and Hatfield (1989). Attractive male and female students approached students of the opposite sex, and asked each student if he or she would sleep with them that night. As you have probably guessed, this offer was received much more eagerly by male students than by female ones. None of the female students accepted the invitation, whereas 75% of the male students did. This supports the view that men are easily persuaded to have sex whereas women are more choosy.

Parental investment

Females typically differ from males in having a higher level of **parental investment**. Parental investment was defined by Trivers (1972) as "any investment by the parent in an individual offspring that increases the offspring's chance of surviving (and hence reproductive success) at the cost of the parent's ability to invest in other offspring." Parental investment can take many forms. The nutrients contained in eggs are an important form of parental investment, but such investment also includes retaining eggs in the body, providing embryos with food through a placenta, and building a nest to shelter the eggs and/or the offspring. After the offspring have been born, parental investment can involve feeding them, defending them against predators, and spending time providing them with knowledge relevant to their future survival.

Female and male investment

In mammals, female investment in her offspring is greater than male investment, because of the female's efforts during pregnancy. For example, female elephant seals are pregnant for several months before giving birth to a pup that may weigh as much as 50kg or 8 stone

After the pup is born, the mother loses up to 200kg or 31 stone in weight during the first few weeks of feeding.

What are the implications of the greater parental investment of females than males? As Trivers (1972) pointed out:

> *Where one sex invests considerably more than the other, members of the latter will compete among themselves to mate with members of the former.*

Thus, we would expect in most species that males would compete with each other for the right to mate with females, rather than vice versa. The reason is that females have more to lose from having offspring from an unsuitable mate, and so they are more careful in their choice of mate.

When selecting a mate it is in the female's interests to find one who will provide the greatest parental investment. However, there is a problem here. Most of the parental investment provided by males occurs *after* conception has occurred, by which time it is too late for the female to change her mind! What happens in many species is that the courtship behaviour of males allows females to predict the likely level of parental investment they will provide later on. For example, the amount of feeding provided by male terns during courtship predicts the amount of feeding of the chicks that they will subsequently provide (Wiggins & Morris, 1986).

Sex-role reversal

It is important to note that Trivers (1972) did not argue that females in every species would have greater parental investment than males (see the Case Study below). His key notion was that the sex having more parental investment would tend to be more selective when mating than would the other sex.

CASE STUDY: *The Stickleback*

The three-spined stickleback is found throughout the northern hemisphere in both fresh and salt water. They are 5–10 centimetres long. In spring, each male leaves the school of fish and stakes out his own territory. All intruders (male or female) are chased away.

The male builds a nest, consisting of a shallow pit, about 2 inches square, dug into the sand. The male shapes some weeds into a mound with his snout and finally he bores a tunnel through the mound by wriggling through it. The tunnel is slightly shorter than the male. At this point the male changes colour, from his normal grey to bright red on his underbelly and bluish white on his back. Females have also become "ready"—they have grown shiny and bulky because they are carrying their eggs.

When a female enters the male's territory he swims towards her in a series of zigzags. The female acknowledges this with a special "head-up" posture. He then swims towards the nest and she follows. He makes a few thrusts with his snout into the entrance, turns on his side, raises his spines, and quivers. She enters the nest, with her head and tail sticking out of each end. The male prods her tail end, which causes her to lay her eggs in his nest. She then glides out of the nest and he enters quickly to fertilise them. Finally he chases her away and goes looking for another partner.

The male may escort three, four or even five females into his nest, fertilising each clutch of eggs in turn. After that he grows hostile towards females and his colour returns to the normal grey. Now he looks after his eggs, chasing predators away and fanning water over the eggs with his fins to ensure a good supply of oxygen. For the first few days after the eggs hatch, the male keeps them all together. He chases any stragglers and brings them back to the nest in his mouth. Eventually they go out into the world and join young sticklebacks from other broods.

In this species the male makes a much larger parental investment than the female.

The female stickleback swims into the nest and the male prods the base of her tail, causing her to lay her eggs. The female is then chased away from the nest and the male enters it and fertilises the eggs. The male then fans water over the eggs to enrich their oxygen supply.

Females generally care for offspring as a consequence of needing to protect their larger parental investment.

Shared care

In humans, joint parental investment is necessary because of the long time it takes to pass through childhood. There are many customs we observe that help females ensure that male parental investment will be forthcoming. For example, traditionally when a man asked a woman for her hand in marriage he would have been expected to show that he would be able to provide for a family. Women might also provide material goods in the form of what was called their "bottom drawer" or their dowry. In order to be ready to set up a family it was important to ensure that the necessary resources were there. Marriage itself is a way of ensuring that the female has some rights over her husband and that even if he should depart, she will continue to gain support from him.

In Western society today we are observing some reversal of sex roles. A number of men stay at home to care for their children while their partners go out to work. In general, men are far more willing to take on traditionally female tasks such as nappy changing and childminding duties. This reflects the fact that humans are not necessarily subject to biological forces and can alter genetic directions through conscious choice.

Mating systems

There are a number of different social systems for mating: one male and one female, or one male and several females, and so on.

Monogamy

Monogamy refers to one male pairing with one female ("mono" means "one"). In some animals monogamy is for life, such as in swans. This is called perennial monogamy. In other animals, such as songbirds, monogamy may be for one breeding season only (annual monogamy).

Polygamy

Polygamy is one individual of one sex mating with many individuals of the other sex ("poly" means "many"). **Polygyny** refers to one male and many women ("gyny" means female"). A common example of this is the harem where one man has many wives. There is also serial polygyny, where a male bonds with one female for a while and then moves on to another.

Polygyny has obvious advantages for males as they gain by maximising their reproduction. One might think, from an evolutionary point of view, that females would prefer monogamy because then they have a mate to provide resources solely for them. However, polygyny can provide a high level of resources and has proved a successful way to rear children, such as is the case in many animals (e.g., lions). Females in a harem have a dominant male with presumably "good" genes because that male fought others for the right to mate. The group will share parental care and resources. Songbirds were thought to be monogamous, but more recently it has been recognised that, when resources are plentiful, a male will do better to engage a second or even third mate (Lack, 1968). In this situation the female continues to get the same level of support from the male.

Seals commonly practise polygyny, in which several females are defended and mated by one male.

Polyandry describes a mating system where one female has many males ("andry" means "male"). This is rare in humans but has been documented in Tibet, where a woman may marry two or more brothers. This is necessitated by the harsh living conditions where it takes at least two men to manage a farm. With two brothers, all parents share a genetic interest in all the children (Dickemann, 1985).

Polygynandry

Polygynandry, or promiscuity, is where many males mate with many females. Such promiscuity is rare in the animal kingdom but has been observed in chimpanzees and songbirds such as the dunnock. Halliday and Arnold (1987) identified several advantages for promiscuity, including the following: (1) it may produce greater genetic diversity in the offspring; (2) it may persuade a number of males to guard the brood; and (3) it may reduce the negative effects of males engaging in sexual competition.

Mating systems, parental investment, and parental care

The choice of mating system for any species is related to parental investment (see the box on the next page). In the stickleback it is the male who has made the larger investment, in terms of energy, and polygyny is the rule—one male mates with many females. In species where both partners share care, monogamy is likely because both partners benefit from protecting their investment.

Which comes first, mating system or parental investment? It is parental investment that dictates how much investment is made from the start but, in non-human animals, it appears that if a partner can desert, and his or her reproductive success is enhanced by this, then he or she will desert, and this affects the mating system. For example, in the case of animals where eggs are externally fertilised (like the stickleback) the female can leave first because the male fertilises the eggs after she has laid them. This results, in most cases, in male care and polyandry. It may also result in no care. If there are sufficient eggs then both parents have protected their investment through sheer numbers.

In the case of internal fertilisation, the male can desert and often does. The female, who has made a major

---

Women are promiscuous, naturally

"So many men, so little time!" The actress Mae West jested about it, but scientists—male ones anyway—are convinced they have proved it. Women—far from being naturally monogamous—are, like men, naturally promiscuous. Biologists believe that women are genetically programmed to have sex with several different men in order to increase their chances of healthy children.

This theory helps to explain the high incidence of mistaken paternity. One study suggested that as many as one in seven people may not be the biological child of the man he or she thinks is the father.

Two recent reports have added to a growing body of evidence that females from across the animal kingdom—including birds, bees, fish, scorpions, crabs, reptiles, and mammals—are promiscuous. Promiscuity is suggested by the "good gene" theory, as shown in the great weed warbler. The female warbler may nest with a male with a small song repertoire but she will seek "extra-pair copulation" with males with big song repertoires, which tend to live longer. This way she gets the best offspring (from mate 2) and they are looked after (by mate 1).

"We don't all get the exact partner we want, we make some kind of compromise. That's true of humans as well. A woman might find a man who is good at providing food and looking after children, but she doesn't necessarily want him to be the father of her kids," says Tim Birkhead, professor of evolutionary psychology.

The only comfort that men can take from the animal world is that females have an incentive not to have all their offspring from adulterous liaisons.

"If they are totally unfaithful to their social partner, they might just be abandoned," said Birkhead.

Adapted from A. Brown (2000) "Women are promiscuous, naturally." *The Observer, 3 September.*

Mating systems and parental care

1. **Monogamy**: there is a pair bond between a male and a female, which may last for an entire breeding season or even a lifetime; often both parents protect the eggs or young, and co-operate in rearing the offspring.
2. **Polygyny**: a male mates with several females, whereas a female usually mates with only one male; females are more likely than males to provide the parental care.
3. **Polyandry**: a female mates with several males, whereas a male usually mates with only one female; in this mating system, males generally provide the parental care.
4. **Polygynandry** or **promiscuity**: males and females both mate with several members of the opposite sex; parental care may be provided by members of either sex.

Mating systems and the environment

Crook (1964) studied many species of weaver bird and related mating strategies and social organisation to ecology:

- In the forest, insect food is dispersed and relatively scarce. Therefore parents form monogamous bonds and feed solitarily. They reduce predation risks through light colouration and camouflaged nests.
- In the savannah, seed food is abundant in patches. Efficient foraging is achieved by groups rather than individuals but there are few nesting sites, so what there is must be shared. This favours competition, intraspecies rivalry, and brighter plumage. Polygyny is likely because the males who gain the best nest sites can attract several females.

investment in pregnancy, is likely to stay and care. This will result in polygyny or monogamy. The partner left "holding the baby" generally ends up caring for the offspring. A partner who leaves enhances his or her own reproductive success because he/she can go off and breed again, *unless* in leaving this reduces the chance of their current offspring surviving—then they stay! If the presence of both parents is important to ensure the survival of current offspring then it pays for both parents to stay.

Are humans monogamous by nature?

The answer is probably no. Despite the fact that humans are basically regarded as a monogamous species (Grier & Burk, 1992) there is evidence from studies across different cultures that humans tend towards polygyny (see the pie chart below).

There is other evidence of our natural tendency to polygyny. The fact that humans exhibit dimorphism (males and females are quite different in form) is evidence of competition and polygyny. Males only have to compete when females are a scant resource. Such conditions favour polygyny. Where competition between males is great, males have to develop means of winning any competitions for females. One way of doing this is through fighting, so males tend to be bigger. Another way is through attracting females, so males develop special plumage or other attractive features. However the dimorphism in humans is not as pronounced as in some animals (such as peacocks) which suggests only a low degree of polygyny.

Another means by which males compete is through sperm competition (see page 565). Males who have to compete need to produce more sperm and hence have larger testicles. Short (1991) investigated this "testicular effect". Chimpanzees have huge testicles, relative to body weight, in comparison with gorillas (60g:50kg compared with 10g:250kg). Therefore we would expect great competition among male chimpanzees but little in gorillas. This fits with the fact that chimpanzees have a mainly polygynandrous system whereas gorillas live in harems (polygyny). Human male testicles are intermediate between chimpanzees and gorillas (10g:70kg), which suggests a tendency toward polygyny or even polygynandry.

Evaluation of mating systems

Evolutionary psychologists have realised recently that the concept of mating system doesn't quite work. An approach based on mating systems exaggerates the extent to which sexual behaviour is similar within any given species. More specifically, this approach ignores the considerable individual differences in sexual behaviour within a species.

An alternative approach is based on mating *strategies*. According to this approach the sexual behaviour of individual males and females of a given species depends on the precise circumstances in which they find themselves. We have seen that this is the case with birds, where there is a tendency to switch from one system to another in response to general environmental conditions. The same can be seen in human societies. Under some conditions polygamy may be the best option for both males and females.

Therefore the current view is that the most adaptive strategy is for a species to have a range of options and be flexible about changing to fit varying environmental conditions rather than conforming closely to the mating system that any given species is "supposed to follow. In some bird species all four mating strategies are exhibited at different times such as in dunnocks (Davies & Lundberg, 1984).

In human societies the tendency is towards polygyny, but monogamy will dominate when the benefits of polygyny for the male are outweighed by the benefits of

Human mating systems in traditional cultures prior to Western influence.

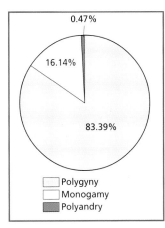

0.47%

16.14%

83.39%

☐ Polygyny
☐ Monogamy
▨ Polyandry

monogamy, for instance when male help is essential to female success. Like all species, humans have a set of alternative strategies which are selected in relation to prevailing conditions.

Explaining other human reproductive behaviours

Adultery

In songbirds, it has been observed that under good environmental conditions males may manage several nest sites to maximise their reproduction. We could translate this into adultery in human terms. Males, given the chance, have nothing to lose and everything to gain by adultery unless they are found out.

Ridley (1993) reported that over 20% of children in the UK are offspring of males other than their presumed father. This suggests that women are at least as adulterous as men. Why are women adulterous? As we have seen, there are advantages for both sexes from promiscuity. Women may stand to gain by improving the quality of their offspring by selecting different mates, whereas males can increase the quantity. If a woman is found out and loses her partner she risks losing protection and resources. Her protection may lie in ensuring emotional ties.

On the other hand, this hypothesis is based on the astonishing figure produced by Ridley. There is reason to doubt that mistaken paternity is as high as 20%. The fault may lie with data based on a small and self-selected sample. A more recent study in Switzerland (Sasse et al., 1994) tested a more representative sample of 1600 children and found that fewer than 1.4% of the children were raised by a presumed father who was actually not their biological one.

Chastity

Wilson (1975) claimed that women and men adopt different sexual strategies because women have to devote a considerable amount of time to their offspring, both during pregnancy and thereafter. In contrast, men can maximise their reproductive potential by having sex with numerous women. Women can be sure that any child they produce is really theirs, whereas men lack this certainty. As a result, men feel a need to control female sexuality so that they can be as sure as possible that any child they protect is carrying their genes. Women have not got this problem because they are fairly certain that any child is theirs. Thus evolutionary psychologists predict that men will place a premium on chastity whereas women are not as concerned.

This is supported in cross-cultural evidence from Buss (1989b) where in 62% of the 37 cultures assessed it was found that males valued chastity more than females, and in the remaining countries (38%) there was no difference. In no culture was chastity more highly valued by females.

Jealousy

Buss et al. (1992) also showed a link with jealousy. Men protect their women by expressing jealousy. Male and female undergraduates were interviewed about their attitudes to the sexual or emotional infidelity of their partners. The men showed greater concern about sexual infidelity, whereas women were less concerned by just sexual infidelity and were more concerned that emotional interest may be aroused.

Rape

Thornhill et al. (2000) have recently presented a controversial case for rape as an example of an evolved mating strategy. Thornhill and Thornhill (1983) argued that men who are unable to mate, for whatever reasons, are driven to select an alternative strategy. In the history of reproductive evolution human males have exercised various options, all with a common aim of reproducing their genetic line. Rape, Thornhill and Thornhill argue, is one of these strategies. It is an evolved alternative that is primarily employed by men who cannot effectively compete for resources and thus do not have the status necessary to attract and reproduce successfully with desirable mates. Such men may incorporate rape into their behaviour repetoire.

Clearly many would see this as an absurd claim and an attempt to vindicate rapists by showing rape to be "natural".

Thornhill (1980) has collected some support for this hypothesis. Apparently similar behaviour has been observed in the male Panorpa scorpion fly, which inseminates unwilling females by securing their wings in an abdominal clamp. Thornhill further argued that males should be most strongly selected to rape in species in which they provide resources important for female reproduction. In such species, the strength of selection on males to rape should exceed the strength of selection on females to prevent rape. However, this is a dangerous idea when applied to human societies.

This is an example of sexually sensitive research. What argument would you offer to challenge the conclusions?

Evaluation

Evolutionary psychology has been used to explain a whole range of human behaviours in terms of the value of these behaviours for reproduction. The aim of any behaviour, or rather its adaptiveness, is directed at maximising the reproductive success for the individual.

A major problem with this approach to human reproductive behaviour is that it de-emphasises the importance of social and cultural influences. There have been enormous changes in human sexual behaviour and in sexual attitudes during the past 50 years, and these changes simply cannot be explained in evolutionary terms.

A further major problem is that fact that such evolutionary arguments are difficult to falsify. For example, it could be claimed that *monogamous* relationships are likely when resources are poor, because then a man would be unlikely to attract more than one female, let alone sustain more than one female and their offspring. On the other hand, it might be argued that *polygyny* is likely in times of scant resources, because women would do better to group together and share the gathering of whatever is available. In lion prides the females do the hunting as well as the child care, so it is not always necessary to have a male as provider.

Nevertheless, evolutionary accounts of reproductive behaviour cannot be said to be boring!

You might contrast these views with those of Singer in the box on page 567.

The ability to wrestle with a mammoth went down well with the ladies.

Evolutionary psychology: A comment

Evolutionary psychology—EP for short—is more than just a product of academia. It is a phenomenon of evolution all by itself. It has existed as a separate discipline for barely 20 years, yet it appears to be taking over the world. Evolutionary psychologists (EPs) conclude that human behaviour can best be understood, not with foreground reference to the contemporary social conditions, but by attributing it to processes that took place in the Stone Age. It is an EP axiom that the most basic human instinct is to reproduce and that men and women go about this in different ways. After all, our distant forebears had distinctly separate needs: women, being the carriers and bearers of children in perilous conditions, had an interest in choosing mates who were hearty, healthy, and liked to stick around to fight off marauding mammoths and maybe barbecue them too; men by contrast had more to gain from promiscuity, partly because they didn't pay for it with pregnancy, partly because for them it was the most effective way of fulfilling their prime directive of perpetuating their genes.

Steven Rose accuses EPs of having a "Flintstones view" of the human past based on "endless speculation". Rose sees EPs as gripped by chronic tunnel vision, "insisting on groping for some adaptionist explanation for everything when all sorts of local or social factors might easily account for the

activity they're trying to study". Some EP findings are extrapolated from studies of other species. Rose has particular scorn for these "dubious animal behaviourists writing scientific pornography".

EP lends a momentum and veneer of intellectual validity to the media's obsession with sex. The press is cluttered with EP pronouncements. We've been informed, for example, that all over the world the key indicator to a man of a woman's fertility is the relationship of her hip measurement to that of her waist. A ratio of 0.7 is deemed ideal. How do we know? Because an EP from the University of Texas did a survey.

One of the most vaunted EPs is David Buss, who used evidence from 37 different cultures to make the case that men and women everywhere played the mating game in different ways, with men being interested in more casual sex and women being more concerned about commitment. And, of course, the explanation for these findings could only be evolutionary, disproving the theories of social scientists who have held that such differences have cultural—and therefore alterable—explanations. "What we have is in fact just the opposite," said Buss. Make way for the new cocks of the walk.

Adapted from an article by D. Hill in The *Observer*, Sunday 27 February 2000.

Evolutionary Explanations of Mental Disorders

The mental disorders anorexia nervosa and bulimia nervosa were considered as part of your AS level studies, and mental disorders are further considered in your A2 studies, in Section 17, Psychopathology. In this Unit we will focus on evolutionary explanations for mental disorders and direct you to read about the symptoms of particular disorders and alternative explanations in Section 17.

Evolutionary Explanations of Human Mental Disorders

In order to understand the principles of evolution, you should read the first Unit in this Part (pages 491–506), and the summary (pages 525–526). In terms of mental disorders the basic argument is that (1) mental disorders can be observed in humans and the historical record shows that this is not a recent development, (2) some mental disorders are inherited, (3) the persistence of such disorders suggests that they may have some adaptive value. This seems hard to accept when one considers the disabling nature of mental disorders such as anorexia nervosa and depression. This would lead us to expect that a person with a mental disorder would have reduced reproductive success and, if such disorders are inherited, this would result in the disappearance of such disorders.

Genome lag

It is argued that most of our inherited behaviours stem from the time of the **environment of evolutionary adaptation** (EEA), the period in human evolution during which our genes were shaped and naturally selected to solve survival problems operating then. This was roughly between 35,000 and 3 million years ago. Some of these behaviours are not especially adaptive today, but they have not been eliminated from our behavioural repertoire by **natural selection**. This is called "genome lag" because the evolution of the genome has lagged behind environmental changes.

    One example of this is our response to stressors. In your AS level studies you learned about the way animals, including humans, respond to stressors. The initial rush of adrenaline, and the "fight or flight" response, is important for survival. In common with other animals the stress response enabled our very distant ancestors to respond appropriately to environmental threats, such as stampeding buffalo, which really did threaten survival. Those individuals who had a rapid and effective stress response were more likely to survive. Now, we have a physiological stress mechanism that is not suited to our lifestyle. Modern stressors are things like noise, overcrowding, and pressure of too much work. They are often things over which we have no control. In such situations a stress response is not very adaptive. First of all running away is unlikely to be desirable—it would probably be more adaptive to respond to a stressor with parasympathetic arousal (relaxation). Second, modern stress situations are often ongoing and therefore we do end up in the state described by Selye's GAS model (described in your AS level course). This was not the original outcome of the stress response. In our evolutionary past we saw the threat (say a buffalo), became aroused (in terms of the **autonomic nervous system**), ran away, and the stressor was gone, so autonomic activity could return to normal. Today our stressors remain with us, and we end up ill. In relation to mental illness we can argue that humans are not adapted to urban life and the stressors of this environment may underlie mental disorder.

Evaluation

On the other hand, it could be argued that today's environment and that of the EEA are not that different. Many aspects of our day-to-day life are probably the same and we have the same concerns—finding resources, forming relationships, raising children, coping with

fight or flight is of little use in the modern world.

death and injury, and so on. Cartwright (2001) wryly comments that "One of the ironies of the modern condition is that we launch high tech satellites into orbit around the planet to beam down soap operas and pornography."

It is also possible that the reason for this genome lag is that the genes continue to offer some benefits, and that is why they remain in our gene pool. Temple Grandin, a high-achieving autistic, has argued this point:

> *Aware adults with autism and their parents are often angry about autism. They may ask why nature or God created such horrible conditions as autism, manic depression, and schizophrenia. However, if the genes that caused these conditions were eliminated there might be a terrible price to pay. It is possible that persons with bits of these traits are more creative, or possibly even geniuses … If science eliminated these genes, maybe the whole world would be taken over by accountants. (Sacks, 1995, p.278).*

Increased fitness

Temple Grandin's argument leads us to a second possibility—that the genes underlying certain mental disorders are also responsible for other, more desirable traits. Evolutionary theory has been used to explain certain disease symptoms and offer advice on suitable forms of treatment. Symptoms such as vomiting, coughing, running a temperature, and avoidance of certain foods may be a necessary part of the body's response to physical illness and thus are desirable and adaptive. For example, when lizards are ill they seek a warm place to lie in the sun. This is part of their normal temperature regulation as they are cold-blooded, but when they are ill they appear to tolerate even hotter conditions. Kluger (1990) found that if lizards who are ill are prevented from obtaining this extra warming, the result is that they die. This suggests that fever may be a way of killing off the pathogens associated with an illness.

It could be argued that similar principles apply to mental illness; that some of the symptoms can be seen as adaptive behaviours. For example anxiety, and the associated responses to it, are adaptive behaviours. Increased fitness also explains sickle cell anaemia (see the box below) and similarly it has been argued that aspects of mania (as part of manic depression) may be traits of the greatest world leaders.

Alternatively the mental disorder gene or set of genes may be linked in some way to increased fertility, and this would explain why it is perpetuated. Either way the characteristic remains naturally selected.

Other possible explanations

Some mental disorders may persist not because they are associated with characteristics that have been naturally selected, but simply because they are not weeded out, as they manifest themselves after breeding. This can be seen in the condition called Huntington's chorea, a genetic condition that only appears in middle life and is inevitably fatal. A child whose parent has developed Huntington's chorea has a 50:50 chance of developing it him or herself.

Another possibility is that the gene for a disorder is recessive and therefore would only be expressed when passed to a child by *both* parents, as in the case of haemophilia, a condition in which one's blood doesn't clot and that may result in bleeding to death. Most people who carry this gene do not exhibit the disorder because they have only one of the gene pair. Thus the gene continues to be passed on silently, only occasionally being expressed when both parents are carriers and they both pass the gene to their offspring. This means that there is little opportunity for natural selection for or against this gene.

Sickle cell anaemia

There are a number of well-established cases of maladaptive genes surviving against apparent odds in the human gene pool. A simple change to the base sequence on our DNA is known to cause the distressing condition of sickle cell anaemia. This condition occurs when an individual inherits a defective gene from both parents, and results in a proliferation of sickle-shaped cells in the blood. These cells are quickly broken down by the body, and the result is that the blood does not flow smoothly and parts of the body are deprived of oxygen. The physical symptoms range from anaemia, physical weakness, pain, damage to major organs, brain damage, and heart failure. There is no cure for the condition, which causes the deaths of about 100,000 people world-wide each year. Sickle cell anaemia is by far the most common inherited disorder among African-Americans and affects one in 500 of all African-American children born in the USA.

The reason that sickle cell anaemia has such high frequency among African-Americans, and the fact that natural selection has not eliminated it (many of those suffering die before they can reproduce), is probably due to the fact that in Africa possession of one copy of the sickle cell gene confers some resistance to malaria. People who inherit only one copy of the sickle cell gene are said to have the sickle cell trait and only some of their red blood cells are oddly shaped. The malarial parasite (*Plasmodium*) cannot complete its life cycle in the mutant cells and therefore those with the sickle cell trait are resistant to malaria. It is the prevalence of malaria in African countries that explains why this apparently maladaptive gene survived in the gene pool and is now found among African-Americans.

Adapted from Allison (1954).

Applying Evolutionary Explanations to Mental Disorders

The three main disorders that will be examined in Section 17, Psychopathology, are schizophrenia, depression, and anxiety disorders. Here we will consider possible evolutionary explanations for each of these.

Schizophrenia

Schizophrenia is a complex disorder with a range of subtypes (see page 629). The research evidence strongly suggests that there is a genetic basis for schizophrenia. This evidence comes from twin and adoption studies, as well as studies of biochemical abnormalities (see pages 629–632). At the same time there is also evidence of some environmental component because identical twins do not always both develop the disorder. The **diathesis–stress** model expresses this relationship: individuals are born with a predisposition for the disorder but it is only expressed when environmental stressors act as a trigger.

Group-splitting hypothesis

Stevens and Price (1996) have developed an evolutionary account of schizophrenia called the **group-splitting hypothesis**. The characteristics of the schizoid personality serve an adaptive function under certain conditions. These characteristics include mood changes, bizarre beliefs, hallucinations, delusions, and strange speech. A "crazy" individual may act as a leader and enable one subgroup to split off from a main group, a valuable function at times when the main group has become too large to be optimum. As group size increases so do risks from predation, difficulties in finding enough food, and intragroup rivalries. Dunbar (1996) estimated that between 100 and 150 was an optimum group size.

There are many examples of schizoid personalities who have become leaders. A recent example was the cult leader David Koresh of the Branch Davidians who died with a group of followers at Waco, Texas in 1995. One member reported that "David was planning to lead the group to Israel to re-take Jerusalem. He taught that there would be a big battle between the forces of the world and his people." In this instance the plans may have been too crazy, but one might imagine that some leaders are possessed by extraordinary ideas that do mean a radical and healthy change for the group.

Origin of language theory

Crow (2000) has suggested that schizophrenia is the price that humans pay for language. This would explain the central paradox of schizophrenia—that despite the fact that the disorder should reduce reproductive capacity, the apparently genetic condition persists. In contrast language has clear adaptive advantages in terms of enabling the users to engage in precise communication. It may also have advantages for reproductive success

Crow's theory is further described in the box at the bottom of page 583.

The ability to use language is usually adaptive. When might this not be true?

because it enables the user to be superior in intersexual selection. Crow proposes that a genetic mutation on the Y-chromosome at some time in our ancestral past led to the development of language but it also predisposed individuals to certain mental illnesses. Crow argues that a disorder like schizophrenia involves a breakdown in the brain's internal linguistic controls. Schizophrenics often believe they are hearing voices and/or may use atypical language. In some individuals language may not be lateralised (located only in the left hemisphere, which is the normal state of affairs) and this disrupts certain mechanisms of language, such as the ability of an individual to distinguish his thoughts from the speech output that he generates and the speech input that he receives and decodes from others. The result is schizophrenia.

Depression

There are two categories of depression: unipolar and bipolar (manic depression).

Unipolar depression

It seems reasonable to suppose that lowered mood (sadness) is an appropriate response to certain situations. It may even be adaptive in the same way that emotional responses in general serve important adaptive functions to motivate behaviour. Nesse and Williams (1995) suggest that in certain situations it may be a better strategy to sit tight and do nothing. For example, our hunter-gatherer ancestors might have increased their survival if they were disinclined to venture out in bad weather but instead experienced low mood and stayed indoors.

When might it be useful to feel depressed?

The rank theory of depression suggests that it is important for survival that an individual who is the loser in a contest (i.e., loses rank) should accept the loss to prevent further injury from re-engaging his (or her) defeater, an act of "damage limitation". The adaptive significance of depression is that it discourages the individual from further efforts.

A further possible evolutionary explanation for unipolar depression is based on the "genome lag" explanation. Nesse and Williams (1995) suggest that rates of depression are increasing and it is possible that depression is a consequence of life in highly developed, urban societies that are very competitive. People, especially young people, are presented with many images of ideal lives and material possessions by the media. Such competition and longing leads individuals to feel dissatisfied, and depressed.

Bipolar depression

There is stronger evidence for the inheritance of bipolar depression than for unipolar depression, again from twin studies and adoption studies. It has been suggested that the manic phase of bipolar disorder is related to creativity and charismatic leadership, and thus would be an adaptive trait.

Winston Churchill, Abraham Lincoln, Vincent Van Gogh, Graham Greene, Ludwig van Beethoven … the list is endless. These have all been said to be sufferers of manic depression. The argument is that creativity is linked in some way to the same genes that underlie manic depression. Without one we would not have the other.

Anxiety disorders

"Anxiety disorders" are a group of mental disorders characterised by levels of fear and apprehension that are disproportionate to any threat posed. Anxiety, like depression, is an emotion. Anxiety, like stress, is adaptive. Anxiety places an animal in a state of arousal (the "fight or flight" response), ready to deal with an environmental threat. Anxiety also ensures that situations of danger are approached cautiously.

Such useful forms of anxiety can become crippling and disabling when the anxiety becomes disproportionate to any problem experienced, such is the case in phobias and obsessive-compulsive disorder. In each of these, natural anxiety reactions have become exaggerated probably through conditioning, as can be seen in the case study of Little Albert, illustrating classical conditioning (see the Key Study on the facing page). Anxiety is also enhanced through operant conditioning, as we can see in obsessive-compulsive disorder.

Little Albert

According to the behaviourists, specific phobias develop through two kinds of conditioning. First, a neutral or conditioned stimulus can come to produce fear if, on several occasions, it is presented at the same time as an unpleasant or unconditioned stimulus. For example, Watson and Rayner (1920) studied an 11-month-old boy called Albert. He was a calm child, but the loud noise produced by striking a steel bar made him cry. He became frightened of a rat when the sight of the rat was paired seven times with a loud noise. This involved classical conditioning.

What happened after that was that the fear produced by the previously neutral stimulus (i.e. the rat) was reduced by avoiding it thereafter. "Albert not only became greatly disturbed at the sight of a rat, but this fear had spread to include a white rabbit, cotton wool, a fur coat and the experimenter's (white) hair" (Jones, 1925). However, it has often proved hard to condition people to fear neutral stimuli by pairing them with unpleasant ones in the laboratory (Davison & Neale, 1996).

The development of phobias can be explained by Mowrer's (1947) two-process theory. The first stage involves classical conditioning (e.g. linking the white rat and the loud noise). Then the second stage involves operant conditioning, because avoidance of the phobic stimulus reduces fear and is thus reinforcing.

Some of the evidence supports the conditioning account. According to Barlow and Durand (1995), about 50% of those with a specific phobia of driving remember a traumatic experience while driving (e.g. a car accident) as having caused the onset of the phobia. Barlow and Durand also noted that nearly everyone they have treated for a choking phobia has had some very unpleasant choking experience in the past.

Discussion points

1. How convincing is the behavioural or conditioning account of specific phobias in the light of the evidence?

2. Can a conditioning account explain the relative frequency of different phobias?

Phobias

A phobia is a strong and irrational fear of something. The emotion of fear may have some adaptive value. Seligman (1970) used the term "**preparedness**" to describe the tendency for members of a species to be biologically predisposed to acquire certain conditioned responses more easily than others. One of these responses would be a fear of things that were probably associated with danger to primitive humans, such as insects, heights, and small animals. Consider poisonous snakes for example—you may only have one chance to escape and so there would be survival value in having an innate predisposition to avoid them.

Bennett-Levy and Marteau (1984) conducted a correlational study that supported the idea that we are born with a readiness to fear certain objects (and we would presume that this readiness has adaptive advantages). Participants were given a list of 29 animals and asked to rate them in terms of their perceived ugliness, perceived harmfulness and their own fear of the animal. Fear was strongly correlated with the animal's appearance. In particular, the more the animal's appearance was different from the human form, the more the animal was feared. Such differences were in terms of having more legs or an unpleasant skin texture.

The suggestion is that this innate fear would be a basis for a phobia. Subsequent avoidance of the phobic stimulus is rewarding because it reduces anxiety levels, and thus a phobia would develop as a result of operant conditioning.

Obsessive-compulsive disorder

This disorder is characterised by a combination of obsessive thoughts and compulsive acts. The compulsive rituals are often concerned with hygiene, such as

■ Activity: Coursework idea

The following idea was described in McIlveen et al. (1992) based on the study by Bennett-Levy and Marteau (see text).

There was a flaw in the original study in that perceived harmfulness was not controlled for, and it might be that this could explain the findings. In your study you could compile a list of feared and not-feared animals and ask participants to rate them on perceived fear, harmfulness, and strangeness using a 3-point scale for each item. In other words rate, for example, perceived harmfulness of a spider on a 1–3 scale, where 3 is very harmful. Then place all the participants' results together, so you have a total score for the fearfulness of spiders, their harmfulness, and their strangeness. Finally correlate fear and harmfulness, fear and strangeness, and harmfulness and strangeness.

washing oneself or cleaning for several hours each day to eradicate any possible contamination.

One explanation offered for the cause of obsessive-compulsive behaviour is that the individual experiences intense anxiety from the obsessive thoughts. The hygiene ritual is found to reduce the anxiety and is thus rewarding, so as a result of operant conditioning the compulsive rituals are repeated. Obsessive-compulsive disorder has been shown to have genetic links. It is possible that the ritualistic behaviours have an evolutionary basis as well. There would be an evolutionary advantage in extra vigilance with tasks involved with cleaning and checking.

Evaluation of Evolutionary Explanations of Human Mental Disorders

This is a fairly new field and therefore the explanations perhaps lack refinement and/or research evidence at present.

A prerequisite to the evolutionary argument is that the behaviour must be inherited, or at least there must be an inherited predisposition to the disorder. Evolutionary explanations can account for the fact that many mental disorders do run in families. It is important to remember that the mental disorders are not adaptive in themselves, but they are linked to behaviours that are adaptive.

There is a potential benefit from the evolutionary approach in its application to the treatment of mental disorders—**evolutionary psychiatry**. Nesse and Williams (1995) argue the strengths of this approach by making an analogy with the way physical diseases are viewed. If a patient has a cough it is more useful to understand the function of the cough, which may then lead you to the root of the problem. Instead what psychiatry currently does, in terms of the cough analogy, is to understand the neural mechanisms underlying the cough and describe when coughing takes place, and perhaps catalogue different kinds of cough. Through this analogy we can see that mental illnesses might be more profitably treated—and/or accepted—if we understand the function of the behaviours. This permits us to understand the adaptive nature of apparently maladaptive behaviours.

Finally we should remember that there are a number of different approaches that can be used as a means of evaluation of evolutionary explanations. These alternatives are presented in Section 17, Psychopathology.

Evolution of Intelligence

What is Intelligence?

In Section 13, Determinants of Animal Behaviour, we considered the evidence for intelligence in non-human animals, giving one definition as "… the all round mental ability (or thinking skills) either of humans or of lower animal species". In this sense intelligence can be taken as equivalent to a collection of mental abilities. These abilities include problem solving, reasoning, memory, language, and so on. Many non-human animals possess some of these abilities, as we have seen, for example, in the Unit on memory in non-human animals.

Intelligence is therefore a cluster of abilities, but it can also be seen as the ability to deal effectively and adaptively with the environment. An animal that can respond more effectively to environmental challenges will be more likely to survive and reproduce. In this Unit we are concerned especially with the evolution of human intelligence, though this is on a continuum with the evolution of the same skills in other species.

Evolutionary Factors in the Development of Human Intelligence

Intelligence must have evolved because it was an adaptive ability for any individual to possess. Could it be that an individual with more intelligence had greater reproductive success? Why might that be the case?

Ecological theory

In Section 13, Determinants of Animal Behaviour, we looked at foraging behaviour and also at the memory requirements needed to forage successfully (remembering where one found a good source of food, remembering where one might have stored it in a food cache). Hunting benefits even more from cognitive abilities such as planning, and co-ordination with other animals. The ecological theory for the development of intelligence suggests it is the demands for successful foraging that make the development of many mental abilities adaptive. The word "ecological" refers to the environmental demands.

This applies very particularly to tool use in humans and those other animals that use tools. Tool use is often associated with food—gathering or eating. For example, the first stone tools were used by human ancestors some 2.5 million years ago. Gradually tool use in humans has become more sophisticated. It is likely that those humans who could use tools would have had an adaptive advantage over those who could not, and this "tool-use" intelligence would have been naturally selected.

Social theory

A second view is that intelligence evolved as a result of the problems presented by group living. Group living confers many advantages on individuals, such as increasing survival and reproductive potential. A group can cope better with predators by having lookouts or using strategies to confuse the predator, groups can often forage more effectively by using co-operative hunting, and group life facilitates mating.

Group life presents situations that require problems to be solved to ensure that individuals survive long enough to reproduce. For example, an individual has to be aware of the inter-relationships within the group, needs to co-operate with other group members in foraging, and so on. An individual who can solve social problems is more likely to survive and reproduce. Therefore this ability is favoured by natural selection.

In addition to the problems posed by group living, social life requires an ability to understand the intentions of others. This is called the **Theory of Mind**. To possess a Theory of Mind is to have an understanding of others' thoughts and emotions, recognising that they are different from one's own. This ability enables one to make predictions of how others will behave. Evidence for the Theory of Mind in non-human animals was considered earlier on pages 521–525. Individuals without a Theory of Mind find social relationships more difficult. There is evidence that autistic individuals lack a Theory of Mind (Baron-Cohen, Leslie, & Frith, 1985) and they are also characterised by their social withdrawal. Theory of Mind is likely to be favoured by natural selection in so far as it promotes social relationships.

An important aspect of sophisticated group living is the ability to detect cheats. The ability to cheat, or **Machiavellian intelligence**, is related to the Theory of Mind. The individual doing the cheating must know how the world appears to another individual. Ultimately cheats would undermine social structure, therefore detection of cheating is an adaptive behaviour. Cosmides (1989) proposed that this is demonstrated in the human ability to be especially good at solving puzzles related to social concerns. An example of this can be seen in Wason's selection task (described on page 371). Participants are given four cards, each with one symbol visible, for example: R, G, 2, and 7. They are then told to prove the rule: "If there is an R on one side of the card, then there is a 2 on the other side of the card". Most people give the wrong answer (the right answer is to select the

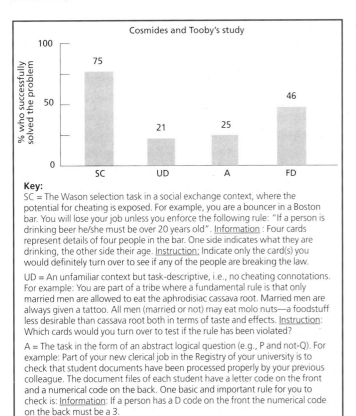

Key:

SC = The Wason selection task in a social exchange context, where the potential for cheating is exposed. For example, you are a bouncer in a Boston bar. You will lose your job unless you enforce the following rule: "If a person is drinking beer he/she must be over 20 years old". Information : Four cards represent details of four people in the bar. One side indicates what they are drinking, the other side their age. Instruction: Indicate only the card(s) you would definitely turn over to see if any of the people are breaking the law.

UD = An unfamiliar context but task-descriptive, i.e., no cheating connotations. For example: You are part of a tribe where a fundamental rule is that only married men are allowed to eat the aphrodisiac cassava root. Married men are always given a tattoo. All men (married or not) may eat molo nuts—a foodstuff less desirable than cassava root both in terms of taste and effects. Instruction: Which cards would you turn over to test if the rule has been violated?

A = The task in the form of an abstract logical question (e.g., P and not-Q). For example: Part of your new clerical job in the Registry of your university is to check that student documents have been processed properly by your previous colleague. The document files of each student have a letter code on the front and a numerical code on the back. One basic and important rule for you to check is: Information: If a person has a D code on the front the numerical code on the back must be a 3.

FD = Familiar context but descriptive without cheating implications. For example, the drinking problem but in a totally alien cultural setting.

cards with R and 7 on them). However, if participants are given the same task but in a less abstract version, more people are successful. For example, four cards (Manchester, Leeds, car, and train), and the rule, "Every time I go to Manchester I travel by car". The correct answer is Manchester and train.

According to Cosmides the reason we find the concrete example easier is that it involves social relations and this is what our intelligence is adapted to cope with. Thus we are able to detect cheats. Cosmides and Tooby (1992) further demonstrated the particular point of cheating in an adaptation of the Wason selection task. There were four conditions in this study, shown under the graph on the left. This clearly supports the view that our intelligence is especially good at dealing with social situations where cheating may be involved.

There is support for this social theory when one considers the fact that most intelligent animals are highly social. Almost all primates are social with the exception of baboons and orangutans; whales, dolphins, elephants, lions, and so on are all highly social. However, it is hard to know which came first. It could be that intelligent animals were thus able to cope with the demands of social living. Or it could be, as argued by social theory, that selective pressures meant that the more intelligent individuals achieved reproductive success through their better social abilities.

Ecological or social?

Do social problems present greater challenges than environmental problems, or vice versa? Which can be held more responsible for the evolution of intelligence? Dunbar (1993) offered a means of testing this. He argued that the neocortex is the area of the brain most responsible for higher-order thinking. This area should correlate most highly with whichever factor—social or environmental—is most responsible for the need for intelligence in humans and other primates. Dunbar found no relationship between the size of the neocortex and environmental complexity in a range of different primates, but he did find a strong correlation between size of neocortex and group size, as an indication of the complexity of social relationships.

This research suggests that social theory better explains the evolution of intelligence.

Sexual selection theory

There is a third possible explanation for why intelligence evolved. It is because intelligence is a trait that was *sexually* selected (as distinct from naturally selected). Intelligence is seen as a sexy trait, in the same way that the peacock's tail feathers are sexy. Intelligence would include behaviours like the ability to be entertaining, or to be successful at hunting. Females prefer men who are intelligent and this means that the trait of intelligence becomes progressively stronger. This would be an example of the runaway hypothesis for intersexual selection (see page 565). Miller (1998) suggests that this sexual selection explains why men have been more creative in the arts than women because in this way they could demonstrate their intelligence and win the sexual favours of a woman.

Do you agree that women have been less creative in the arts than men? What reasons could you give for this belief?

There was selective pressure on females as well because they needed bigger brains to decode the male's new abilities—abilities to entertain, produce art and music, and also to use language (see the box on the facing page). Thus there is selective pressure on both males and females to be intelligent.

Support for the sexiness of intelligence comes from surveys of what characteristics people seek in partners. Miller (1996) reports that intelligence consistently comes at the top of the list despite the fact that it is not related to such obvious indicators of reproductive success as health, fertility, and command of resources. Therefore, according to evolutionary psychologists, there must be some other way that intelligence is related to sexual selection (what people find attractive in a mate). The answer is that intelligence is a runaway trait. In evaluation of this argument, one might consider research on interpersonal relationships (see Section 2, Relationships) which indicates that a host of factors are related to interpersonal attraction, not just intelligence.

Do you think that intelligent members of the opposite sex are more "sexy"?

One argument that favours the view that sexual selection is responsible for intelligence is the fact that the human brain has increased in size tremendously (and the male brain is bigger than the female brain, even when different body weight is taken into account, see later). In the last 3 million years the human brain has trebled in size, a very rapid change in evolutionary terms. Sexual selection exerts the kind of pressure that could explain this rapid change because it directly selects for reproductive success.

Self-feeding co-evolution

It is likely that mental abilities and brain growth have co-evolved. **Co-evolution** describes the process whereby two characteristics evolve in tandem. For example, as a predatory species evolves the ability to run faster then the same must happen in its prey otherwise they will quickly die out. If the prey die out, so may the predator. What remain in nature are those prey–predator relationships where co-evolution has taken place.

Dawkins (1998) has applied the same principle to the evolution of intelligence. There is on the one hand demand for greater mental abilities, especially language, because they are advantageous for survival and reproduction (in computer terms we can call this "software" demands). At the same time, these mental abilities are dependent on hardware evolution—the growth and organisation of the brain to accommodate the new mental abilities. This leads us to consider the size of the human brain.

The Human Brain

In the previous discussion, it has been assumed that there is a positive correlation between brain size and intelligence. Is this a reasonable assumption? Is the size of human brain positively related to intelligence?

Brain growth, language, and schizophrenia

Language may have been a critical development in human intelligence. Crow (1998) has proposed a startling theory that links intelligence to the development of language, brain growth, and also to schizophrenia, as this excerpt suggests:

"Oxford University professor of psychiatry, Tim Crow, believes that an abrupt alteration in our brain's wiring gave us control of the earth. 'Language appeared very quickly and provided us with a unique ability to exchange complex ideas, thus giving us a powerful advantage over other types of human being,' he said. About 100,000 years ago, different species of human had established themselves in different corners of the globe: Neanderthals in Europe and *Homo erectus* in the Far East. Then a new breed of upstart Earthlings appeared on the scene: *Homo sapiens*, who emerged out of Africa and began to spread, with remarkable speed, across the planet. About 30,000 years ago *Homo sapiens* was all that was left. It would appear that this species possessed some key advantage over the others.

"But what was it, and how did we acquire it? Most scientists agree that this advantage must have been a dramatic improvement in the language skills of *Homo sapiens*. Crow has a dramatic solution. He proposes that

a freak mutation occurred in a single, male member of early *Homo sapiens*. This gene, which Crow believes can be traced to the Y-chromosome (possessed only by males), triggered a cascade of biological changes that swept through our species.

"The first man to manifest the gift of the gab would have been favoured strongly for sexual selection. His genes would have spread quickly.

"This capacity for complex speech also brought major disadvantages, in particular it triggered the appearance of schizophrenia in our species. Our sophisticated language controls occasionally go wrong. 'Schizophrenia is a linguistic breakdown in which the sufferer distinguishes his thoughts from his speech output and the speech input that he receives from others,' said Crow.

"It is a startling view of understanding schizophrenia and has sparked considerable scientific interest among other researchers, especially as Crow has a reputation for individualistic brilliance."

Adapted from Robin McKie "Gene glitch made the first man speak" The *Observer*, 26 March 2000.

The cerebral cortex

The outer layer of the human brain is called the **cerebral cortex**. When you look at the brain, it is mostly cortex that you see but it is only 2 millimetres thick. The cerebral cortex has a bumpy, folded appearance and it is these bumps that greatly increase its volume. If you flattened the cortex out it would cover a square measuring 50 x 50cm. It is grey in colour because it largely contains cell bodies rather than the axons that link one area of the brain to another.

The cortex is what distinguishes the brain of mammals from the brain of lower animals. And the human brain has a far larger frontal cortex than other mammals (darker areas in diagram below). The cortex has great importance for our ability to perceive, think, and use language, and is highly related to intelligence.

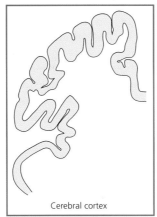

Cerebral cortex

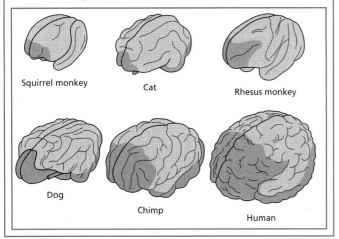

Squirrel monkey

Cat

Rhesus monkey

Dog

Chimp

Human

Brain size and intelligence

The human brain is significantly larger (proportionately) than any other animal brain. Proportion is important because larger animals tend to have bigger brains to manage their bodies but their brain:body ratio is smaller than that for humans.

Is bigger better? One simple line of argument is that bigger brains incur a physiological cost, and also make birth more difficult. Therefore there must be some adaptive advantage to having a bigger brain, otherwise it would not be naturally selected.

Comparative studies

Other evidence that intelligence is related to brain size comes from comparative studies of brain size. For example, Rumbaugh, Savage-Rumbaugh, and Washburn (1996) demonstrated this in a study with 12 different primate species. Each animal was trained to perform a task, such as picking up a square instead of a triangle to find food. Then they were trained to do a second task, such as picking up a circle instead of a hexagon. Rumbaugh et al. found that in the larger-brained primates (e.g., gorilla, chimpanzee) training on task one facilitated performance on task two, whereas in smaller-brained primates (e.g., lemur, talapoin) the learning on task one interfered with learning a similar task. This supports the view that an animal with a larger brain is capable of more intelligent behaviour (transfer of learning).

There is one important danger when conducting comparative studies. One animal may perform less well, not because it has poorer abilities but because it is tested on unnatural tasks. Kalat (1998) gives the following example. One study found that rats appeared unable to pick the "odd one out" when shown three items, two of which were the same. However, later the rats were tested on essentially the same tasks but this time they were given three smells. Now they demonstrated that they did have a grasp of the idea of oddity. Kalat points out that if humans were tested on smells, they might find the "odd one out" task difficult which would lead one to conclude that they lacked this mental ability.

As you can see, higher animals have progressively more forebrain, the area of the brain involved in higher-order thinking. In mammals this forebrain has become highly folded. This development suggests a link between physical characteristics of the brain and intelligence.

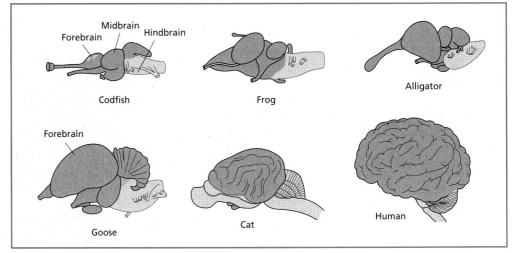

Forebrain   Midbrain   Hindbrain

Codfish

Frog

Alligator

Forebrain

Goose

Cat

Human

Correlating IQ with brain size

Research has looked at the relationship between human brain size and intelligence. Early studies concluded that there was no significant relationship, however this may be due to the fact that there were no accurate ways of measuring brain size (skull size is not a good indicator of brain size). Modern methods, such as MRI scanning (see page 139) provide accurate measurements. Using this method Willerman et al. (1991) studied a selection of college students, chosen to provide a good spread of IQ scores. They found a correlation of 0.51 between IQ and brain:body ratio. In addition they found that the higher-IQ students as a group had larger brains than the low-IQ group.

Why is it necessary to use brain:body ratio in this correlation?

One problem with this study was the unrepresentativeness of the sample. A further issue for any study that uses IQ as the measure of intelligence relates to the criticisms that have been made of IQ tests (see page 385).

Intelligence and inheritance

It might be argued that, if brain size is related to intelligence, and brain size is caused by genes, then intelligence is inherited. Brain size is obviously caused by genes, as we can see when we compare the brain size of humans with, for example, chimpanzees. The size of the human brain is part of our genetic make-up, and humans have brains that are bigger than any other primate in relative terms.

However, when we compare the brain of one human with another, the individual differences in brain size are partly genetic but also partly due to environment. Brain development is related to improved diet, especially a mother's health and nutrition during pregnancy because most brain growth takes place before birth. Some further growth takes place in the period just after birth, but that's it. Babies who have been fed breast milk have higher IQs later in life (e.g., Lucas et al., 1992) which can be explained by the fact that breast milk contains fatty substances that are important to brain growth.

A recent examination of Einstein's brain showed that his inferior parietal region, which is linked to imagery and mathematics, was 15% wider than average. Furthermore, the groove that normally runs from the front of the brain to the back did not extend all the way, suggesting that Einstein's brain cells were packed close together permitting more interconnections.

IQ and sex

Men, on average, have larger brains than women, but men, on average, do not have higher IQs. One obvious explanation would be that men tend to be larger therefore they have a larger brain to manage their slightly bigger bodies. But then we would equally expect short, light people to do less well on IQ tests than tall, heavy people. However this is not the case.

The answer may lie in differences in brain organisation as distinct from overall size. Though women may have smaller brains, they appear to have slightly better organised ones. For example, women have a larger corpus callosum (the nerve fibres that connect the two brain hemispheres) and this means slightly better communication (Johnson et al., 1996).

Brain organisation and intelligence

Perhaps organisation is more important than size, or at least equally important. After the death of the great scientist Albert Einstein his brain was examined to see if there was anything remarkable about it. In fact it was normal in size and structure, but there were some differences in terms of organisation. For example, the neurons in his prefrontal cortex were more tightly packed. This may be the cause or the effect of his intellectual powers, but the fact remains that it was not size but organisation that was related to intelligence.

The human brain in general is more highly organised than the brains of other animals. For example the localisation of particular functions, such as language, can be found to a greater degree in humans. Localisation refers to the fact that different regions of the brain are involved in specific and separate aspects of psychological functioning (see Section 4, Brain and Behaviour).

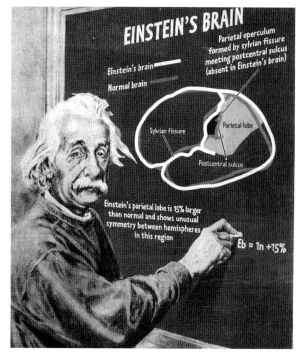

EINSTEIN'S BRAIN

Einstein's brain
Normal brain

Parietal operculum formed by sylvian fissure meeting postcentral sulcus (absent in Einstein's brain)

Sylvian fissure

Parietal lobe

Postcentral sulcus

Einstein's parietal lobe is 15% larger than normal and shows unusual symmetry between hemispheres in this region

Eb = 1n +15%

SECTION   SUMMARY

Human Reproductive Behaviour

❖ The principle of natural selection is that any behaviour that is adaptive, and has some genetic component, is passed on to successive generations because of selective pressure. Some characteristics are selected because they increase the reproductive fitness of the individual in mating contests. This is called sexual selection.

❖ Male reproductive success is enhanced by fertilising as many eggs as possible, which costs relatively little. However males have to compete with other males to mate with females. This is called an intrasexual strategy.

❖ Female reproductive success is enhanced by having few offspring but ensuring that these offspring survive and are healthy, which includes selection of the best mate. This is an intersexual strategy.

❖ Intrasexual selection results in dimorphism because competition between males leads to increased size and adornments to attract females. The fewer females available, the greater the competition between males. Non-dominant males have developed other adaptive strategies to promote their reproductive success, such as sneak copulation and sperm competition.

❖ What is the basis for intersexual selection? Fisher proposed that females choose males with characteristics that promote survival. Over time, these characteristics become exaggerated (the runaway hypothesis). Females continue to choose males with these characteristics because they have "sexy" sons. Zahavi's handicap theory suggests that females choose males with a handicap because this indicates genetic robustness. Coping with a handicap, such as a long tail, may also indicate good health. Females also select males for non-genetic benefits, such as resources.

❖ When applying the principles of evolution to human behaviour we should remember that such explanations may overemphasise the influence of innate factors on human behaviour, and they suggest a determinist view of how we behave.

❖ Anisogamy predicts that males will look for fertile women and women will prefer men who offer resources. Research evidence using cross-cultural studies and newspaper advertisements supports these predictions in humans.

❖ Parental investment is the effort made by either parent that increases the offspring's chance of surviving at the cost of the parent's ability to invest in other offspring. Females tend to make a greater parental investment and this leads to greater choosiness. Females assess male potential during courtship rituals. In some animals, such as sticklebacks, males make a greater parental investment. Humans tend towards shared care, as reflected in many cultural practices. Conscious decisions also affect parental investment in humans.

❖ Each different mating system offers advantages for both sexes. Monogamy is related to shared parental care and ensures help for females in terms of resources. Polygyny maximises reproductive success for males and may offer advantages for females in terms of shared care and good genes. Polyandry is rare in humans but has benefits when males are related. Polygynandry may offer advantages in terms of greater genetic variation for both males and females. The choice of mating strategy for any individual is related to parental investment. The parent left "holding the baby" is often the one who stays and does the caring. If both parents are needed to ensure offspring survival then it pays for them both to stay.

❖ Evidence suggests that human males are polygynous by nature, based on observations of human societies. The testicular effect also suggests a tendency towards polygynandry, in that women too are seeking extra-pair copulations.

❖ It is more appropriate to talk in terms of mating strategies rather than systems, as each species appears to practise different strategies in response to prevailing conditions, rather than having one system.

❖ There is evidence that both men and women are adulterous. Men encourage chastity as a means of preventing this. Jealousy may also have evolved as a strategy to prevent adultery, though men are more concerned with sexual jealousy and women with emotional jealousy. Rape has been explained from an evolutionary perspective as a means of ensuring reproduction for men who cannot effectively compete for resources and thus cannot attract females.

❖ Evolutionary accounts of human reproductive behaviour de-emphasise the importance of social and cultural influences and are difficult to falsify.

❖ We seek evolutionary explanations of mental disorders because the persistence of these disorders, if they are inherited, suggests they must have some adaptive value, or be related to behaviours that have some adaptive value.

❖ Genome lag is one possible explanation, suggesting that modern behaviours evolved at a time when selective pressures were different (the environment of evolutionary adaptation). The pressures of modern life may turn once adaptive behaviours into maladaptive ones. However, it can be argued that there are only small differences between the EEA and life today. Alternatively, the genes responsible for mental disorders may be linked to behaviours that continue to be desirable.

❖ Increased fitness is a second explanation. Certain responses to physical illness are seen as adaptive and the same might be true for symptoms of mental disorders. The same gene for a mental disorder may, for example, increase creativity and/or reproductivity, and thus remains naturally selected.

❖ Some mental disorders may persist not because they are associated with characteristics that have been naturally selected, but simply because they only appear after breeding and are not selected against. Another reason might be that the gene is recessive and thus rarely exposed to selective pressure.

❖ There is strong evidence that a predisposition for schizophrenia is inherited. The group-splitting hypothesis suggests that the schizoid personality can serve an adaptive function when group size has reached a optimum limit, and group division would be adaptive. The origin of language theory suggests that schizophrenia is the price humans pay for language, because schizophrenia involves a breakdown in the brain's internal linguistic controls.

❖ Unipolar depression is related to lowered mood (sadness), which may have adaptive significance because it prevents one being overactive in inappropriate situations. The rank theory of depression proposes that depression is adaptive because it discourages an individual who has lost rank in a fight from further fighting (damage limitation). Genome lag would suggest that urban living creates a sense of competitiveness and thus depression. Bipolar depression appears to be linked to creativity and thus is an example of increased fitness.

❖ Anxiety disorders are characterised by high levels of anxiety, which like stress, can be adaptive. But anxiety can become disabling under certain circumstances. Phobias may be based on innate predispositions to be afraid of potentially harmful animals (preparedness). Operant conditioning then exaggerates natural fears. Obsessive-compulsive disorder involves intense anxiety from the obsessive thoughts. Rituals reduce anxiety and are thus rewarding. Both ritual behaviour and a predisposition to obsessive-compulsive disorder are possibly inherited.

❖ Evolutionary explanations depend on evidence for the inherited predisposition to mental disorders. More research is needed but this approach benefits from taking a functional approach rather than the more descriptive one of traditional psychiatry.

❖ Evolutionary explanations can be evaluated with reference to other explanations for mental disorders, discussed in Section 17, Psychopathology.

Evolutionary Explanations of Mental Disorders

❖ Intelligence is a cluster of mental abilities, and is also the ability to deal effectively with the environment. In what way is it an adaptive trait?

❖ The ecological theory suggests that it is the demands for successful foraging that make the development of many mental abilities adaptive.

❖ Alternatively, social theory proposes that intelligence evolved as a result of the problems presented by group living. Social life also requires a Theory of Mind and may involve the need for Machiavellian intelligence. Humans find it easier to solve social problems, supporting the link between social living and intelligence. Most

Evolution of Intelligence

social animals are intelligent, but there is some question about which comes first: intelligence or social life.

❖ The size of the neocortex correlates with social complexity rather than environmental complexity suggesting that social theory better explains the evolution of intelligence.

❖ Sexual selection is a third explanation for why intelligence evolved. Intelligence is a sexy, "runaway" trait in males. Females also have to be intelligent to appreciate the male's abilities. Thus there is selective pressure on both males and females to be intelligent. Support for this comes from the fact that people consistently select intelligence as the trait they look for in a mate. In addition sexual selection for intelligence can also explain the rapid growth in the human brain because sexual selection selects directly for reproductive success.

❖ A final explanation for the evolution of intelligence is self-feeding co-evolution, where the software (i.e., mental abilities) evolve simultaneously with the hardware (the brain) because they are mutually interdependent. This is called co-evolution.

❖ Is brain size positively related to intelligence? Human brain:body ratio is comparatively large. There must be some advantage to a large brain, because such increased size incurs a cost. One way to answer this question is through comparative studies which support the view that an animal with a larger brain is capable of more intelligent behaviour. Comparative studies do run the risk of underestimating abilities because animals are tested on unnatural tasks. A second approach is to look at the correlation between IQ and brain size. Recent studies using MRI have found a significant positive correlation. However, IQ tests have been questioned in terms of validity.

❖ Brain size is partly inherited, but it is also related to very early environment and diet. Brain size is related to sex—males have larger brains but they do not have higher IQs. This discrepancy may be due to the fact that women's brains are better organised, so compensating for the smaller size. Organisation may be more important than size, and human brains are more highly organised than the brains of other non-human animals.

FURTHER READING

The topics in this Section are covered in greater depth by J. Cartwright (2001) *Evolutionary explanations of human behaviour* (London: Routledge), written specifically for the AQA A specification. Reproductive strategies are intelligently discussed in a lavishly illustrated book by R. Short and M. Potts (1999) *Ever since Adam and Eve: The evolution of human sexuality* (Cambridge: Cambridge University Press). The evolution of mental illness is discussed by A. Stevens and J. Price (1996) *Evolutionary psychiatry* (London: Routledge).

Example Examination Questions

You should spend 30 minutes on each of the questions below, which aim to test the material in this Section.

1. **(a)** Outline evolutionary explanations for human reproductive behaviour.   (12 marks)
    (b) Critically assess these explanations.   (12 marks)

2. **(a)** Describe sex differences in parental investment.   (12 marks)
    (b) Assess the implications of these sex differences in human parental investment.   (12 marks)

3. Discuss **two** evolutionary explanations of human mental disorders.   (24 marks)

4. Critically consider evolutionary explanations of depression.   (24 marks)

5. Discuss evolutionary factors in the development of human intelligence.   (24 marks)

6. Discuss the relationship between brain size and intelligence in humans.   (24 marks)

Examination Tips

Question 1. The injunction "outline" requires a summary description rather than one given in detail. Therefore, in this question, your aim is to provide a number of different explanations rather than focusing on the detail. Your descriptions should nonetheless contain enough information to communicate understanding. In part (b) you are required to present evaluation of the explanations, including a consideration of both their strengths and weaknesses. Such critical assessment may involve reference to research support or to the relevance of such explanations for human behaviour. Note that, if research studies are used, then credit will not be given for a description of the studies but for the effective use of such material.

Question 2. Part (a) involves a description of a number of sex differences in relation to parental investment. There is a depth–breadth trade-off—you may describe many differences and thus have less time for detail, or vice versa. A good mark can only be given where a good balance has been achieved between depth (detail) and breadth. In part (b) you must consider further implications of such sex differences. For example, the issue about which parent stays to care. This same issue may have been included in part (a), in which case you might consider a further implication in terms of subsequent reproduction. This illustrates the fact that AO1 and AO2 are not so much a matter of what you say, but how you use the material.

Question 3. "Discuss" is an AO1 and AO2 term. The question requires that you describe and evaluate two explanations. This can be achieved by explaining two different mental disorders (such as schizophrenia and depression) or by considering two general explanations (such as genome lag and increased fitness). When evaluating these explanations you might offer a contrast with other evolutionary or non-evolutionary explanations. It is important to use such contrasting evidence effectively to be awarded high marks. Research studies would also be useful for evaluation, as would practical applications.

Question 4. "Critically consider" is an AO1/AO2 term that further demands a consideration of both strengths and weaknesses. Thus you need to describe two or more evolutionary explanations of depression (because "explanations" is plural), and evaluate these as suggested in question 3. It is legitimate for the examiner to ask specifically about depression as it is given as an "including" in the specification.

Question 5. The question requires you to consider how we can use the theory of evolution to explain why and how intelligence appeared in humans. You must include at least two factors and should aim to provide sufficient detail for each factor. Evaluation may be through the use of research studies (which may be criticised themselves) as well as an analysis of the logical nature of the arguments presented. The extent to which you use the material effectively rather than just, for example, describing research studies will determine the number of marks awarded.

Question 6. This is a straightforward and rather general question. The risk may be that you know too much and therefore present a rather unstructured account, squeezing everything in. It is advisable to try to be selective and outline a logical flow of ideas about brain size and intelligence, illustrating this outline with examples and research studies, as well as an evaluation of your explanations.

WEB SITES

http://www.literature.org/authors/darwin-charles/the-origin-of-species/
   Text from Darwin's "Origin of Species".

http://www.evolutionary.org/
   Evolutionary theory homepage.

http://www.ocfoundation.org/
   Obsessive–Compulsive Foundation homepage.

http://ethology.zool.su.se/cartoon/
   Article on receiver biases and sexual selection, in cartoon format.

PART 6

Individual Differences

The study of "individual differences" is the study of the ways that individuals differ in terms of their psychological characteristics. Individuals differ physically in terms of height and hair colour. They differ psychologically in terms of intelligence, aggressiveness, willingness to conform, masculinity and femininity, and just about every behaviour you can think of.

An important individual difference can be found in the degree to which a person is mentally healthy. This is specifically referred to as the study of **abnormal** or **atypical psychology**. Psychologists who have an interest in abnormal or atypical behaviour study childhood and adult disorders such as dyslexia, autism, schizophrenia, and depression, seeking to find explanations for such difficulties and to find valid methods of treatment.

This Part is divided into three Sections. In Section A of your examination paper there will be one question for each of these Sections. The questions set on this Part differ from those from the first five Parts because "individual differences" is only part of Unit 5 of the examination, the synoptic

paper, along with "perspectives" (Part 7). There are four important differences in this examination paper: (1) you must answer one question from this Part only, (2) you have 40 minutes to answer this question instead of the 30 minutes for questions on Unit 4 of the examination, (3) your answer will be marked out of 30 instead of 24 marks, and (4) your answer will be marked in terms of an additional criterion: synopticity. "Synopticity" is defined as your "understanding and critical appreciation of the breadth and range of different theoretical perspectives and/or methodological approaches relevant to any question" (AQA specification). Thus it is important, throughout this Part, to be aware of different theoretical perspectives and methodological approaches in relation to the topics under consideration.

Section B of the examination is on issues and debates. There will be four questions, two on "issues" and two on "debates", (see Part 7) and candidates select one from all four. Section C is the "approaches" question (see Part 7). Candidates select one question from the two provided, but these two are not taken from any Section.

591

16

Issues in Classification and Diagnosis of Psychological Abnormality

A mental disorder is "A clinically significant behaviour or psychological syndrome or pattern that occurs in a person and that is associated with present distress (a painful symptom) or disability (impairment of one or more important areas of functioning) or with a significantly increased risk of suffering death, pain, disability, or an important loss of freedom. In addition, this syndrome or pattern must not be merely an expectable response to a particular event, for example, the death of a loved one."

Classificatory Systems

Nearly all psychiatrists and clinical psychologists accept that abnormality or mental disorder exists. They also accept that those individuals who exhibit abnormal symptoms should receive a psychiatric diagnosis or label which specifies the nature of the abnormality. This psychiatric diagnosis is assumed to be of value when it comes to determining the appropriate form of treatment. Diagnosis depends on being able to classify.

Those who advocate the use of classification typically point to its successful use in the treatment of physical illness. Doctors rarely prescribe any treatment to a sick patient until they have satisfied themselves that they have diagnosed correctly the nature of his or her illness. The substantial increase in longevity in most Western societies over the past 100 years is partly due to the success of this approach, referred to as the **medical model**.

Symptoms and Syndromes

The starting point for any attempt to classify mental disorders is identification of the patient's **symptoms**. However, the same (or very similar) symptoms are found in what are otherwise quite different mental disorders. For example, anxiety is a major symptom in generalised anxiety disorder, obsessive-compulsive disorder, and the phobias. As a result, the emphasis in most classificatory systems is not on individual symptoms but on **syndromes** (sets of symptoms that are generally found together).

The **symptom–syndrome approach** to abnormality owes much to the work of Emil Kraepelin (1856–1926). In medicine, it is usual to diagnose physical diseases on the basis of physical symptoms, and Kraepelin felt that the same approach was suitable for mental illness. He emphasised the use of physical or behavioural symptoms (e.g., insomnia, disorganised speech) rather than less precise symptoms such as poor social adjustment or misplaced drives.

Different patients with the same syndromes (e.g., schizophrenia) rarely present the same symptoms. There is a grey area in which the fit between a patient's symptoms and those forming the syndrome of a diagnostic category is relatively poor. In such cases, it is hard to know whether or not the diagnostic category is appropriate.

Why classify?

Given this poor match between symptoms and syndromes, you might wonder why it is necessary to classify disorders at all. There are three main reasons for classification:

1. *For treatment.* In order to decide on a suitable treatment for a disease it is first of all necessary to determine *what* the patient is suffering from. In terms of physical disease, the treatment for a cold is significantly different from that for meningitis. It is critical for a doctor to make a note of the various symptoms exhibited by the patient and decide what these symptoms collectively mean. In other words, the doctor will make a diagnosis of the patient's condition. Diagnosis depends on having a classification scheme. Diagnosis leads to treatment. A psychiatrist or clinical psychology will diagnose, for example, manic depression and prescribe lithium, or will diagnose seasonal affective disorder and prescribe light therapy. One can only decide on a treatment following a diagnosis, which in turn depends on identifying a syndrome on the basis of the existence of certain symptoms.

2. *For research.* In order to identify a *syndrome*, it is first necessary to recognise a group of *symptoms* that co-occur. Having identified a syndrome it is then possible to test various treatments. Syphilis is a classic of example of this. It is a disease that manifests itself as mental illness. An individual exhibits symptoms such as delusion, forgetfulness, and mental deterioration. Eventually paralysis sets in followed by death. These symptoms were recorded by various people over the centuries and little was made of it until one medical student formally described the symptoms of the disorder. He argued that deterioration, paralysis, and death were a distinct syndrome, to be called general paresis (Rosenhan & Seligman, 1989). A link was suspected between general paresis and the syphilis bacterium, a link that was formally established by von Krafft-Ebing late in the nineteenth century. Once the cause was known a cure could be found, which happened in 1909, and general paresis became a condition that was easily treated and no longer necessarily fatal.

3. *For the individual and their family.* In the case of some conditions, psychological or physical, it is reassuring to be given a diagnosis so that one no longer feels one is imagining things. Knowing (or thinking) that there is something genuinely wrong may help recovery. On the other hand, it may be mistakenly seen as a solution, whereas this is not necessarily the case as (a) diagnosis is not necessarily **reliable** or **valid**, and (b) not all illnesses have suitable treatments.

The concepts of reliability and validity should not be new to you. They are fundamentally important issues with relation to classification and diagnosis.

DSM and ICD Definitions of Mental Disorder

At present there are two classification systems in general use: the **Diagnostic and Statistical Manual** (DSM) and the **International Classification of Diseases and Health Related Problems** (ICD). The latter is produced by the World Health Organisation and used in Europe with the main purpose of enabling the collection of health statistics world-wide. It is not primarily a diagnostic tool and for many years did not include mental illnesses at all. DSM is produced by the American Psychological Association.

Such systems are under constant revision and are given numbers. The versions in current use are DSM-IV and ICD-10, reflecting their revision number. In the following pages we will consider the history of these systems as well as their contents. This will be followed by an assessment of the value of these systems.

Other countries have developed their own classification systems. For example, there is also a Chinese Classification of Mental Disorders (CCMD).

Models of abnormality

One point to remember is that this approach to the treatment of mental illness is based on the medical (biological) model. In your AS level studies you considered both medical and psychological models of abnormality. The cognitive and behavioural models (both psychological) place less emphasis on the detection of syndromes and more on identifying symptoms that need to be removed. As such these models have less need for classifications systems, or they may use classification schemes more appropriate to the model. For example, a behavioural classification scheme is considered in the box below.

An alternative approach to classification: The behavioural approach

DSM and ICD are the two main classificatory systems, but they are appropriate only to the medical model of abnormality. Behaviourists recommend behavioural therapies as a means of treating mental disorders. The basis of these therapies is classical and operant conditioning. In order to apply these techniques it is first necessary to identify the deviant or maladaptive behaviours. Goldfried and Davison (1976) have devised a classification scheme that can be used for this purpose.

There are five categories:

I. *Difficulties in stimulus control of behaviour*. It may be that particular stimuli produce inappropriate behaviours or that different stimuli do not produce different behaviours.
II. *Deficient behavioural repertoires*, in other words the individual does not have the appropriate skills for day-to-day living.
III. *Aversive behavioural repertoires*, for example an individual behaves in ways that are unpleasant, irritating, or harmful to others.
IV. *Difficulties with incentive systems*, for example, the individual is experiencing rewards for things that are harmful, such as restricting food intake.
V. *Aversive self-reinforcing systems*, which describes people who have unrealistic expectations and are overcritical of themselves.

The aim of the classification is to permit the therapist to isolate the variables that can become the focus of treatment. There is some evidence that this system has higher reliability and validity than DSM (Bellack & Hersen, 1980).

Diagnostic and Statistical Manual: DSM

The current version of the *Diagnostic and Statistical Manual of Mental Disorders* (DSM-IV), published in 1994, is the most widely used classificatory system. The first version of DSM was published in 1952, and was replaced by DSM-II in 1968. The main problem with DSM-II was its great unreliability, in the sense that two psychiatrists would often produce very different diagnoses of the same patient. Spitzer and Fleiss (1974) reviewed studies on the reliability of DSM-II. They concluded that reliability reached acceptable levels only with the broad categories of mental retardation, alcoholism, and organic brain syndrome.

DSM-II was very unreliable because many of its symptom definitions were vague. Attempts were made with DSM-III (1980) and DSM-III-R (1987) to offer more precise definitions. For example, DSM-II was vague about the length of time involved in a "major depressive episode". In contrast, DSM-III-R specified that five symptoms (including either depressed mood or loss of interest or pleasure) should be present over a 2-week period in order to qualify.

DSM-III and DSM-III-R were also an improvement over earlier versions of DSM in another important way. The two versions of DSM-III focus very much on diagnosing patients on the basis of their observable symptoms. This contrasts with DSM-I and DSM-II, in which there was a strong emphasis on the supposed causes

---

■ Activity: Reliability of DSM

Examine the reasons why previous versions of the DSM (DSM-II, III, and III-R) proved to be unreliable. Compare the most recent version with these earlier ones for reliability, writing your answers in the following format:

	Strengths	Weaknesses
DSM-II	Broad categories of mental disorders, e.g., "mental retardation"	Vague definitions of symptoms

Try to use various other reference sources to help make your answer as full as possible.

What "theories" are used in the construction of a classification scheme?

of mental disorders. Thus, there was a shift from a theoretically based approach to one that is more descriptive. That was desirable, because the theories used in the construction of DSM-I and DSM-II were flawed in various ways.

There was a final important change between DSM-II and DSM-III. In DSM-II, the diagnosis consisted of a single category or label (e.g., schizophrenia). In contrast, DSM-III, DSM-III-R, and DSM-IV are all based on a *multi-axial system*, in which the patient is evaluated on five different axes or scales. The current version, DSM-IV, is described in the Key Study below.

Axes and features of DSM-IV

The first three axes or scales of DSM-IV are always used, whereas the last two are optional. Here are the axes:

Axis 1: Clinical disorders: this axis permits the patient's disorder to be diagnosed.
Axis 2: Personality disorders and mental retardation: this axis is used to identify long-term patterns of impaired functioning stemming from personality disorders or mental retardation.
Axis 3: General medical conditions: this axis concerns any physical illness that might influence the patient's emotional state or ability to function effectively.
Axis 4: Psychosocial and environmental problems: this axis is concerned with any significant stressful events that occurred within 12 months of the onset of the mental disorder.
Axis 5: Global assessment of functioning: this axis provides an overall measure of the patient's functioning at work and at leisure on a 100-point scale.

DSM-IV contains over 200 mental disorders arranged into various categories. Here (with brief descriptions) are some of the main categories used in DSM-IV for axes 1 and 2:

- *Disorders of infancy, childhood, or adolescence*: these cover a wide range of disorders (e.g., emotional, physical, behavioural, intellectual); specific examples are mental retardation, depression, and separation anxiety.
- *Cognitive impairment disorders*: these involve reduced cognitive ability caused by brain damage through disease, injury, or medical condition; examples are dementia (e.g., Alzheimer's disease) and delirium, in which there is a clouding of consciousness.
- *Substance-related disorders*: these disorders involve personal and social impairment caused by the excessive use of drugs or alcohol.
- *Schizophrenia and other psychotic disorders*: these disorders involve a partial or total loss of contact with reality; schizophrenia with its distortions of thought, emotion, and behaviour is the most common disorder in this category.
- *Mood disorders*: these include depressive disorders and bipolar disorders, in which there are periods of mania or great excitement as well as periods of depression.
- *Anxiety disorders*: there are 12 anxiety disorders (e.g., panic disorder, generalised anxiety disorder, post-traumatic stress disorder), each of which involves excessive anxiety for certain situations or stimuli.
- *Somatoform disorders*: these involve preoccupations with the body or with physical illness stemming from psychological causes; examples are somatisation disorder (numerous medical complaints in the absence of actual illness) and conversion disorder (a psychological

problem produces a medical complaint that lacks a medical basis).

- *Dissociative disorders*: dissociative amnesia, dissociative fugue, dissociative identity disorder (multiple personality disorder).
- *Sexual and gender identity disorders*: these include orgasm disorders and sexual sadism, in which sexual pleasure is obtained by hurting another person.
- *Eating disorders*: these involve potentially dangerous abnormal eating patterns; examples are bulimia nervosa (binge eating usually followed by vomiting or purging) and anorexia nervosa (excessive weight loss produced by a preoccupation with thinness).
- *Impulse control disorder*: these are disorders involving difficulties in controlling impulses, which are not featured elsewhere in DSM-IV; an example is kleptomania, which is the psychological compulsion to steal things.
- *Personality disorders*: these are long-term, maladaptive patterns of dealing with life (e.g., anti-social personality disorder, in which the needs of others are ignored).

Some more general features of DSM-IV should be mentioned before providing an overall evaluation of its value. First, as stated before, the disorders identified in DSM-IV are defined by descriptive and observable symptoms rather than by those features that are believed to cause each disorder. Second, each diagnostic category used in DSM-IV is based on prototypes (a set of features characteristic of the category). It is assumed that some symptoms are essential, but that others may or may not be present. For example, the diagnosis of generalised anxiety disorder requires the presence of excessive worry and anxiety. However, it requires only three of the following symptoms: restlessness, being easily fatigued, difficulty concentrating, irritability, muscle tension, and sleep disturbance.

Third, DSM-IV (in common with DSM-III and DSM-III-R) was based in part on the findings of *field trials*, in which diagnostic issues were studied by means of programmes of research. Spitzer, Williams, Kass, and Davies (1989) carried out a field trial to decide whether to introduce "self-defeating personality disorder" into DSM-IV. This proposed personality disorder consisted of symptoms such as behaving in a self-sacrificing way, and choosing situations that are likely to lead to disappointment. The field trial produced clear findings. The symptoms of self-defeating personality disorder were so similar to those of existing personality disorders that there was no need to add it to DSM-IV.

> ### KEY STUDY EVALUATION — DSM-IV axes
>
> The five axes of DSM-IV are designed to incorporate a wide variation in causes, symptoms, and behavioural effects of mental disorders. Axis 1, clinical disorders, includes all recognised disorders apart from "personality disorders" and "mental retardation", which are considered to be qualitatively different in origin and prognosis. These two forms of mental disorder are reserved for axis 2. Axis 3 provides additional evidence of the known connections between physical conditions and psychological disorders, e.g. post-natal depression or long-term alcoholism.
>
> Use of axes 4 and 5 is not compulsory. They refer more to the social functioning of the individual. Axis 4 acknowledges situational factors that may have occurred recently prior to the onset of a particular problem. A person suffering from PTSD (post-traumatic stress disorder) would necessarily have had a distressing experience in recent months, although even 12 months may not be a long enough time for the disorder to manifest itself. Determining the contribution of life events such as bereavement or divorce presents difficulties, because there may be an interdependent relationship between a person's response to life events and their pre-existing psychological condition. Some personality disorders will occur irrespective of situational factors.
>
> Axis 5 also addresses the social functioning of the individual, but unlike axis 4 it assesses the person's ability to adapt to the demands of everyday life. Serious maladaption such as violent behaviour or failure to carry out basic personal hygiene would necessitate some sort of intervention.

Discussion points

1. DSM-IV was based on much research and on experience with earlier versions of DSM. How successful does it seem to be (see the Evaluation section in the main text)?
2. DSM-IV is often regarded as the best classificatory system that we have for mental disorders. Is it worthwhile to develop such classificatory systems?

Evaluation of DSM-IV

The two important issues, with regard to evaluating DSM, are reliability and validity.

Reliability

Reliability is high if different psychiatrists agree on patients' diagnoses using the classification scheme. This is known as **inter-judge reliability**. Fairly detailed evidence on the reliability of DSM-III is available. Inter-judge reliability on some of the major diagnostic categories in DSM-III is as follows (a correlation of about +0.7 or above indicates high reliability):

- Psychosexual disorders: +0.92
- Schizophrenic disorders: +0.81
- Anxiety disorders: +0.63
- Personality disorders: +0.56

CASE STUDY: *An Example of Using DSM-IV*

The client: Mark is a 56-year-old machine operator who was referred for treatment by his supervisor. The supervisor noted that Mark's work had deteriorated in the past 4 months. Mark was frequently absent from work, had difficulty getting along with others, and often had a strong odour of liquor on his breath after his lunch break. The supervisor knew Mark was a heavy drinker and suspected that Mark's performance was affected by heavy alcohol consumption. In truth, Mark could not stay away from drinking. He consumed alcohol every day; during weekends, he averaged about 16 ounces of Scotch per day. Although he had been a heavy drinker for 30 years, his consumption had increased after his wife had divorced him 6 months ago. She claimed she could no longer tolerate his drinking, extreme jealousy, and unwarranted suspicions concerning her marital fidelity. Co-workers avoided Mark because he was a cold, unemotional person who distrusted others.

During interviews with the therapist, Mark revealed very little about himself. He blamed others for his drinking problems: if his wife had been faithful or if others were not out to get him, he would drink less. Mark appeared to overreact to any perceived criticisms of himself. A medical examination revealed that Mark was developing cirrhosis of the liver as a result of his chronic and heavy drinking.

The evaluation: Mark's heavy use of alcohol, which interfered with his functioning, resulted in an alcohol abuse diagnosis on axis I. Mark also exhibited a personality disorder, which was diagnosed as paranoid personality on axis II because of his suspiciousness, hypervigilance, and other behaviours. Cirrhosis of the liver was noted on axis III. The clinician noted Mark's divorce and difficulties in his job on axis IV. Mark was given 54 on the Global Assessment of Functioning scale (GAF), used in axis V to rate his current level of functioning, mainly because he was experiencing difficulty at work and in his social relationships. Mark's diagnosis was as follows:

Axis I—Clinical syndrome: alcohol abuse.

Axis II—Personality disorder: paranoid personality.

Axis III—Physical disorder: cirrhosis.

Axis IV—Psychosocial and environmental problems: (1) problems with primary support group (divorce), (2) occupational problems.

Axis V—Current GAF, 54.

From D. Sue, D.W. Sue, & S. Sue (1994) *Understanding abnormal behaviour (4th Edn.)* (p.124) (Boston: Houghton Mifflin)

How would you explain the tendency for the correlation reliability to be higher for psychosexual disorders than for personality disorders?

As can be seen, the reliability of DSM-III varies considerably from category to category. The reliability of diagnosing personality disorders may be low because there are several different personality disorders and they have overlapping symptoms. The reliability of DSM-IV is almost certainly higher than that of DSM-III.

Validity

Validity is concerned with the extent to which the classificatory system measures what it claims to measure. It is much harder to assess than reliability. There are at least three kinds of validity of relevance to DSM-IV:

- *Aetiological validity*: this is high when the aetiology (cause) of a disorder is the same for most patients suffering from it, in other words we expect a syndrome to have a specific cause. For example, measles is caused by a specific microbe and we would equally expect a syndrome such as schizophrenia to have a specific cause.
- *Descriptive validity*: this concerns the extent to which patients in the various diagnostic categories differ from each other. It is important that each syndrome is distinct from each other syndrome otherwise it may sometimes not be clear what category a patient should be placed in.
- *Predictive validity*: this concerns the extent to which the diagnostic categories allow us to predict the course and the outcome of treatment. A diagnostic category is only useful if it has this predictive ability.

It should be noted that reliability and validity are not entirely independent. A classificatory system that is unreliable cannot be valid.

There is little evidence on validity. The aetiological validity is probably fairly low for most of the categories of mental disorder, because the causes of any given disorder vary considerably from person to person. The descriptive validity of DSM-IV is reduced by **comorbidity**, which is the presence of two or more disorders in the same person at any given time. For example, up to two-thirds of patients with an anxiety disorder have also been diagnosed with one or more additional anxiety disorders (Eysenck, 1997). Such extensive comorbidity blurs the distinctions among categories. The predictive validity of DSM-IV is unknown. However, the facts that the precise form of treatment increasingly depends on the diagnosis, and that treatment is becoming more effective, suggest that its predictive validity may be fairly good.

Which disorders appear to have a greater chance of aetiological validity?

International Classification of Diseases and Health Related Problems (ICD)

Mental disorders were first included by the World Health Organisation in the sixth edition of ICD in 1948. However, this and some of the following editions of ICD had little impact, because of their low reliability and their reliance on unproven theories. The situation was improved in 1993, with the publication of ICD-10. According to ICD-10, there are 11 major categories of mental disorder, shown in the box on the right.

> **Major categories of mental disorder in ICD-10**
> * Organic, including symptomatic, disorders.
> * Schizophrenia, schizotypal, and delusional disorders.
> * Mental and behavioural disorders due to psychoactive substance use.
> * Mood (affective) disorders.
> * Neurotic, stress-related, and somatoform disorders.
> * Behavioural and emotional disorders with onset usually occurring in childhood and adolescence.
> * Disorders of psychological development.
> * Mental retardation.
> * Disorders of adult personality and behaviour.
> * Behavioural syndromes associated with physiological disturbances and physical factors.
> * Unspecified mental disorder.

Evaluation of ICD-10

The situation with respect to the reliability and validity of ICD-10 is similar to that with respect to DSM-IV. That is to say, it has reasonable reliability, but there is little detailed information on its validity. According to Costello, Costello, and Holmes (1995), ICD-10 seems to be more reliable than either ICD-9 or DSM-III-R. However, there must be doubts as to whether it is more reliable than DSM-IV. The categories in DSM-IV tend to be more specific, and the defining symptoms are more precise. In general terms, increased category specificity and symptom precision are associated with higher reliability.

As with DSM-IV, the aetiological validity of ICD-10 is low. Its descriptive validity is also likely to be low, given the prevalence of comorbidity in diagnoses based on ICD-10. Finally, the usefulness of ICD-10 diagnoses as the basis for deciding on the appropriate treatment suggests that its predictive validity may be reasonable.

How would you explain the increased category-specificity of the DSM-IV and its more precise descriptions of symptoms, in comparison with the ICD? Why would this lead to greater reliability?

Comparing ICD and DSM

Early versions of ICD and DSM were very different from each other, but that is no longer the case with ICD-10 and DSM-IV. For example, there are close resemblances between schizophrenia, schizotypal, and delusional disorders in ICD-10 and schizophrenia and other psychotic disorders in DSM-IV; between mental and behavioural disorders due to psychoactive substance use in ICD-10 and substance-related disorders in DSM-IV; and between mood (affective) disorders in ICD-10 and mood disorders in DSM-IV.

In more general terms, ICD-10 and DSM-IV are both based on a set of categories of mental disorder, each of which has its own set of symptoms or **operational diagnostic criteria**. Both systems operate in a similar way using these criteria. In order for a diagnosis to be made, one or two core symptoms should be identified and it is expected that several others will have been present for a reasonable period of time. In some cases the classification system will identify symptoms that should *not* be present in order for a diagnosis to be made.

In spite of the similarities between ICD-10 and DSM-IV, there are some important differences. There are 16 major categories of mental disorder in DSM-IV compared with only 11 in ICD-10, mainly because the categories in ICD-10 tend to be more general. In addition, some of the major categories in DSM-IV (e.g., sexual and gender identity, eating disorders) are not represented directly in ICD-10.

Is it easier to identify syndromes based on the presence or on the absence of key symptoms?

Difficulties in Classifying Psychological Abnormality

The system of classifying and diagnosing mental disorder is based on the medical approach to physical illness. What problems arise when trying to extend this to psychological abnormality?

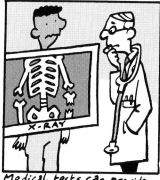

Medical tests can provide an instant diagnosis.

Difficulties with diagnosis

Are there important parallels between physical illness and mental illness or disorder? It is more difficult to diagnose mental disorders than physical illnesses. Many of the symptoms reported by those suffering from mental disorders are subjective (e.g., "I feel very depressed"; "Life does not seem worthwhile"). This is a real problem, because people may differ considerably in what they mean by being "very depressed". In contrast, doctors trying to diagnose a physical illness often have information about the *signs* of disease (the findings from medical or laboratory tests such as X-rays) as well as about the patient's *symptoms* (their account of the ways in which they feel ill). The findings from medical tests often provide much more precise information than is available to psychiatrists and clinical psychologists. For example, an X-ray can prove that a patient has a broken bone in his or her foot, and a blood test can reveal that someone is suffering from malaria.

There is another important difference between physical illness and mental disorder. The **aetiology** (cause of a disease) of most physical diseases is known, whereas that of mental disorders is usually only partially known. For example, malaria is caused by infected mosquitoes, and a diagnosis of malaria can be confirmed by establishing that the patient has recently visited a part of the world in which there are many infected mosquitoes. In contrast, psychiatrists or clinical psychologists diagnosing a mental disorder cannot usually check the accuracy of their diagnosis by establishing the cause.

However, the differences between medical diagnosis and psychiatric diagnosis are often less extreme than has been suggested so far. For example, the only symptom reported by a patient with backache may be a certain amount of pain, and there may be no relevant medical tests that could be carried out. This symptom is as subjective as the symptoms reported by mental patients. Falek and Moser (1975) found that doctors often disagreed among themselves on the diagnoses of physical illness such as angina, tonsillitis, and emphysema. Indeed, disagreement was as great as that for the diagnosis of schizophrenia among psychiatrists. However, the level of agreement among the doctors would undoubtedly have been greater if they had had the results of medical tests available to them before making their diagnosis.

Why might doctors fail to agree when diagnosing tonsillitis?

Reliability and validity

A classic study by Rosenhan (1973) raised serious questions about the reliability and validity of psychiatric diagnoses (see the Key Study on the next page). "Pseudopatients" were diagnosed as schizophrenic and, in a second study, real patients were sometimes identified as pseudopatients. In addition there was not total agreement among psychiatrists about the diagnoses. It may be that psychiatrists are more inclined to call a healthy person sick rather than a sick person healthy because it is potentially dangerous to release a sick person without treatment (whether they are physically or mentally ill). Rosenhan calls this a "type two error", a false judgement made in order to avoid failing to diagnose a real illness. In the case of failing to correctly diagnose a real patient, it may be that psychiatrists were now making more type one errors (calling a sick person healthy) because they were trying to avoid making type two errors!

However, DSM and ICD may not be as lacking in reliability or validity as Rosenhan's study suggests. The evidence considered earlier demonstrated reasonable reliability and validity for both DSM-IV and ICD-10. Nevertheless, it is possible that an emphasis on reliability carries dangers with it. According to Barlow and Durand (1995, p.112), this emphasis "is understandable, since reliability has been so difficult to achieve. But it is not hard to achieve reliability if you are willing to sacrifice validity". You can achieve high reliability by using very precise criteria for each disorder. For example, the key criterion for generalised anxiety disorder in DSM-IV is as follows: "Excessive anxiety and worry (apprehensive expectation), occurring more days than not for at least 6 months, about a number of events or activities." This is fairly precise, but has the obvious disadvantage that the time period of 6 months is arbitrary: someone who suffers from excessive worry for 6 months is unlikely to differ much from someone who only suffers for 5 months.

Rosenhan's study of sane people in insane places

David Rosenhan (1973) argued that psychiatric classification can be very inaccurate. In his controversial study, eight normal people (five men and three women) tried to gain admission to 12 different psychiatric hospitals. They all complained of hearing indistinct voices, which seemed to be saying "empty", "hollow", and "thud". Even though this was the only symptom they claimed to have, seven of them were diagnosed as suffering from schizophrenia, which is a very severe condition involving substantial distortions of thought, emotion, and behaviour.

After these eight normal people were admitted to psychiatric wards, all of them said that they felt fine, and that they no longer had any symptoms. However, it took an average of 19 days before they were discharged. For seven of them, the psychiatric classification at the time of discharge was "schizophrenia in remission". This classification carried with it the implication that they might become schizophrenic again in the future.

Rosenhan was not content with having apparently found that the sane can be classified as insane. He next decided to see whether the insane could be classified as sane. He told the staff at a psychiatric hospital that one or more pseudopatients (normal people pretending to have schizophrenic symptoms) would try to gain admittance to the hospital. No pseudopatients actually appeared, but 41 genuine patients were judged with great confidence to be pseudopatients by at least one member of staff. Nineteen of these genuine patients were suspected of being frauds by one psychiatrist plus another member of staff. Rosenhan (1973) concluded, "It is clear that we cannot distinguish the sane from the insane in psychiatric hospitals."

If we accept Rosenhan's conclusions, then attempts at classification appear doomed. However, there are various limitations in his study. The most powerful argument against Rosenhan's findings was provided by Kety (1974), who offered the following analogy:

> If I were to drink a quart of blood and, concealing what I had done, come to the emergency room of any hospital vomiting blood, the behaviour of the staff would be quite predictable. If they labelled and treated me as having a bleeding peptic ulcer, I doubt that I could argue convincingly that medical science does not know how to diagnose that condition.

Psychiatrists can hardly be blamed for not expecting completely normal people to try to gain admittance to a psychiatric hospital. Errors of diagnosis were made under the very unusual conditions of Rosenhan's (1973) study. However, that does not mean that psychiatrists generally cannot distinguish between the normal and the abnormal.

Rosenhan's findings are actually less dramatic than they seem to be. The diagnosis "schizophrenia in remission" is used very rarely. It suggests that many of the psychiatrists were unconvinced that the patients had really suffered from schizophrenia. This is confirmed by the fact that these normal patients were released within a few days of admission. In the early 1970s, many schizophrenic patients spent years in hospital before being allowed to leave.

This study relied on the use of deception. Do the ends justify the means?

Discussion points

1. What do you think of Rosenhan's research?
2. Did Rosenhan show that psychiatrists cannot tell the difference between the sane and the insane?

Classificatory systems such as DSM-IV and ICD-10 are based on the assumption that we can assign individuals neatly to certain categories. However, many of the symptoms defining their categories are found in much of the population. For example, the key symptom of panic disorder is the existence of recurring panic attacks. However, Norton, Dorward, and Cox (1986) found that 35% of college students had

---

KEY STUDY EVALUATION — Rosenhan

Rosenhan's research in the early 1970s exposed the imprecision of psychiatric diagnosis. Psychiatrists are often unable to verify patients' symptoms, and can only rely on observable behaviour. A number of observations can be made about Rosenhan's research. First, his findings demonstrate the lack of scientific evidence on which medical diagnoses can be made—a crucial issue when an individual's personal liberty may be at stake. Second, the use of somatic treatments such as drugs and ECT (electro-convulsive therapy) was the subject of much discussion in the 1960s and 1970s. Although Rosenhan's fake patients were not subjected to these treatments, the study underlined the need for caution when making decisions about appropriate types of therapy.

The main concerns about Rosenhan's research are ethical ones. In both studies, professionals were deliberately misled about the true status of patients. The deception of professionals whose job it is to treat people with mental disorders is no more ethically justified than deception of patients or participants in a study. However, it is probable that a more open investigation, with the full knowledge and co-operation of the psychiatrists, would have failed to reveal anything of interest.

A further issue concerns the welfare of the genuine patients. During Rosenhan's second study, it would have been possible for a patient who was exhibiting normal behaviour, but in fact was suffering from a spasmodic mental disorder, to be mistakenly discharged from psychiatric care.

experienced one or more DSM-III defined panic attacks over the preceding year. In similar fashion, Rachman and de Silva (1978) found that the obsessions and compulsions found in patients with obsessive-compulsive disorder are also found in over half the "normal" population. Such findings make it hard to justify the notion of neat categories.

Labelling

A powerful argument against classifying mental disorders was provided by Scheff (1966) in his **labelling theory**. He argued that someone who acquires the stigma (mark of social disgrace) of a psychiatric diagnosis or label will be treated as a mentally ill person. As a result, his or her behaviour may change in directions that make the label more appropriate than it was in the first place. Labels create expectations on the part of the patient and others. These expectations may lead to behaviours that confirm the original diagnosis.

Thus, rather than the symptoms leading to the psychiatric label or diagnosis, it may sometimes be the case that the label plays a part in creating the symptoms.

Rosenhan (1973) found that the way in which someone is treated is influenced by the label they have been given. On numerous occasions, Rosenhan's normal patients with a diagnosis of schizophrenia approached a staff member in their psychiatric ward with a polite request for information. These requests were ignored 88% of the time by nurses and attendants, and 71% of the time by psychiatrists. This unresponsiveness by the psychiatric staff suggests that those who are labelled as schizophrenic are regarded as having very low status. Such treatment could clearly increase the severity of the symptoms experienced by real schizophrenics.

In what way might the effects of labelling be applied to other groups, e.g., football fans? What similarities exist between these other groups and people who have been labelled "mentally ill"?

Labels and symptoms

Imagine that you are in a situation where you have been wrongly diagnosed as suffering from a mental disorder such as schizophrenia. How would you react to such a situation? Would you be incredulous? Furious? Tearful? Shocked and withdrawn? How could all those emotions be interpreted by those people whose job it is to assess your mental condition?

Anti-psychiatry

Thomas Szasz (1962, 1974) took a particularly strong view of the meaninglessness of psychiatric labels or classification. His basic argument was that mental illness is a myth. In his own words (Szasz, 1962), "Strictly speaking … disease or illness can affect only the body. Hence, there can be no such thing as mental illness." Why, then, do psychiatrists and clinical psychologists pretend that there is such a thing as mental illness? According to Szasz (1974), society uses stigmatising labels to exclude those whose behaviour fails to conform to society's norms. Such labels include the following: criminal, prostitute, gypsy, foreigner. "Mental illness" is simply a stigmatising label used to exclude non-conformists from society.

The Scottish psychiatrist R.D. Laing agreed with Szasz (1962) that patients are given psychiatric diagnoses because their behaviour is different from that of most other members of society rather than because they have some actual illness. Szasz suggested that mental illness is better represented as a "problem in living" because the symptoms are socially expressed. Laing argued that it is society rather than the patient that is to blame. According to Laing (1967), "By the time the new human being is 15 or so, we are left with a being like ourselves, a half-crazed creature more or less adjusted to a mad world. This is normality in our present age."

Are the norms that society uses to judge people's behaviour stable across different cultures? How might this be relevant to people who settle as immigrants in a different culture from their own?

Commentary on the anti-psychiatry view

Critics of Szasz (e.g., Dammann, 1997) have argued that he used the terms "disease" and "illness" in a very narrow sense, and that it is not reasonable to draw a sharp distinction between physical illness and mental conditions. For example, an outstanding sportswoman who breaks her leg has a physical injury, but is also likely to experience psychological problems as a result.

Critics of Laing have pointed out that his tendency to blame parents in some way for their child's mental condition has been seen elsewhere as a narrow conception of the complexities of mental illness. For example, at one time it was suggested that autism was caused by a "refrigerator mother" (Kanner, 1943).

Social and cultural issues

A major threat to the validity of classification schemes is the question of culture bias, as well as social and gender bias. Classification schemes are devised by Western practitioners and, not surprisingly, the basis of these schemes is related to the experiences and values of these practitioners. The issue of **cultural relativism** was considered in your AS level studies in relation to attempts to define abnormality. It is not possible to make absolute statements about what is normal or abnormal in human behaviour and therefore, inevitably, definitions of abnormality are based on value judgements and these are culturally specific.

Notions of abnormality not only vary from one ethnic group to another, but also within the same culture at different periods in history. For example, the way in which homosexuality is regarded has altered over successive editions of DSM, the system used to classify mental illness in America. In DSM-II, which was published in 1968, homosexuality was classified as a sexual deviation. In DSM-III, published in 1980, homosexuality was no longer categorised as a mental disorder. However, there was a new category of "ego-dystonic homosexuality". This was to be used only for homosexuals who wished to become heterosexual. In DSM-III-R, the category of ego-dystonic homosexuality had disappeared. However, there was a category of "sexual disorder not otherwise specified", with "persistent and marked distress about one's sexual orientation" being included. This remains the case in DSM-IV. On a lay person's level, many people continue to view homosexuality as an aberrant mental state.

Culture, gender, and social bias are considered in greater detail later in this Section.

DSM aims to provide an objective means of assessing mental disorders. To what extent might it apply only to our culture?

Homosexuality ceased to be categorised as a mental disorder in the 1980 edition of DSM.

Alternatives to classification

Earlier we noted that there are alternatives to the medical classification schemes such as behavioural classification (see the box on page 595). All these schemes are essentially **nomothetic** in their approach. That is they involve making generalisations about groups of people on the basis of large scale studies of behaviour. The alternative is the **idiographic approach**, which is concerned with the unique case and aims to analyse each patient on his or her own merit. This approach is taken by a minority of practitioners but has the advantage of avoiding many of the problems identified above. However, the difficulty is that this makes it very hard to develop an understanding of the causes of mental disorder (and of the appropriate form of treatment). Grouping patients according to their diagnoses provides a good basis for an exploration of the factors responsible for any given type of disorder, and for the development of effective forms of treatment.

Classificatory systems (e.g., DSM) increasingly make some allowance for uniqueness, while also focusing on the ways in which different patients are similar. According to Gelder et al. (1989), "The use of classification can certainly be combined with consideration of a patient's unique qualities, indeed it is important to combine the two."

If you were experiencing psychological problems, would you prefer to be analysed by a therapist using an idiographic approach or nomothetic approach?

Multiple Personality Disorder (Dissociative Identity Disorder)

DSM and ICD identify various mental disorders, such as schizophrenia, depression, and anxiety disorders. We will consider the characteristics and causes of these disorders in Section 17, Psychopathology. In this Unit we will focus on one particular syndrome or disorder—**multiple personality disorder** (MPD), now termed **dissociative identity disorder** (DID). The reason that this disorder is placed here is because it highlights some key issues in relation to the classification and diagnosis of psychological abnormality. We will start this account with a definition of the syndrome and a consideration of some case histories to illustrate the common symptoms.

What is Multiple Personality Disorder?

Clinical characteristics

DSM-IV identifies the following characteristics as typical of MPD/DID:

- The presence of two or more distinct identities or personality states, each with its own relatively enduring pattern of perceiving, relating to, and thinking about the environment and self.
- At least two of these identities or personality states recurrently take control of the person's behaviour.
- An inability to recall important personal information, the extent of which is too great to be explained by ordinary forgetfulness.
- The disturbance is not due to the direct physiological effects of a substance (e.g., alcohol abuse) or a general medical condition (e.g., epilepsy). In children, the symptoms are not attributable to imaginary playmates or other fantasy play.

The classic story of Dr Jekyll and Mr Hyde has been explained as a case of multiple personality disorder. An alternative explanation is that it isn't a disorder but rather a convenient way for a deranged mind to explain unacceptable behaviour to the sane part of itself.

It is important to recognise the distinction between this syndrome and schizophrenia. MPD involves the presence of distinct identities, whereas schizophrenia does not result in two or more complete identities. A schizophrenic is one person who is fragmented—the so-called "split personality". Moreover MPD is a personality disorder, meaning that it is a condition that is deeply ingrained and enduring rather than being characterised as *episodes* of disordered thinking.

MPD is classified under the heading of **dissociative disorders** because of the characteristic dissociation between areas of conscious behaviour. Other dissociative disorders include dissociative amnesia where a person's memory becomes detached from the rest of their conscious awareness, and depersonalisation disorder where an individual feels a sense of detachment from their environment as if they were in a dream.

In the most recent version of DSM, MPD has been relabelled as "dissociative identity disorder" to emphasise the dissociative aspect of the disorder. Allison and Schwartz (1980) argue, on the basis of extensive work with MPD patients, that MPD and DID are actually two different groups of dissociators. MPD patients have many identities living in one body, none of which is a central personality. The individual is not one person with various identities but simply multiple identities. DID promotes the view that the disorder is actually a failure to integrate various aspects of identity into a unified personality. If this is the case, then the goal of therapy is to help the patient come to realise that they are one person rather than multiple identities, and this should aid reintegration; in the case of MPD, the task of therapy is to help the alternative personalities (or "alters") arrive at one "agreed" personality.

ICD continues to use the term "multiple personality disorder", and in this discussion we will refer to MPD as representative of both MPD and DID.

Case studies of multiple personality disorder

Most people find the idea of multiple personalities quite fascinating, which explains why several case histories have been given the Hollywood film treatment: *The Three Faces of Eve* and *Sybil* are both films based on actual case histories, which are described on pages 605 and 606.

Case histories illustrate further characteristics of the disorder. It appears that at any time only one personality or identity is evident. Some personalities are aware of the existence of other personalities, or they may experience blackouts when another personality is "out". The personalities differ significantly in their characteristics, such as that of Eve White and Eve Black. Many patients appear to have a lot more than just two or three personalities and each identity may have its own unique memories. The personalities may differ in terms of age and gender, and each personality "sees" him- or herself as this character. Some researchers have found differences between the personalities in terms of personality test scores, interests, learning ability, sexual orientation, smoking habits, blood

The three faces of Eve

Thigpen and Cleckley (1954) recorded the case history of one of their patients, a 25-year-old married woman given the name "Eve White". Until this carefully documented case history was presented, multiple personality had a rather mythical status in psychiatry. The details of the three Eves gave the illness a more respected status, although Thigpen and Cleckley regarded it as a very rare disorder, a status that rapidly changed over the subsequent 40 years.

Eve White had been experiencing "severe and blinding headaches" and unexplained blackouts—periods of time when she couldn't remember what she had done. Her doctor could find no physical cause and therefore referred her to a psychiatrist. During the course of early treatments she appeared to be getting better, then one day a letter arrived, written in a neat script handwriting. Strangely the letter ended with a few lines written in quite a different handwriting and using language quite unlike the usually matter-of-fact Eve White. On her next visit to the psychiatrist, Eve White said she had started a letter but never sent it. During this interview she became agitated and finally asked if hearing voices was a sign of insanity. At this moment she put her hands to her head as if in great pain and, after a tense moment of silence, a newcomer appeared who was a complete contrast to Eve White. She was mischievous and carefree, and introduced herself as Eve Black.

It appeared that Eve Black had been around since Eve's early childhood but Eve White had no knowledge of her existence until after she emerged in the psychiatrists' office. On the other hand, Eve Black was aware of all that Eve White did and was quite scornful of Eve White's emotional problems. She claimed that during childhood she often emerged to play pranks, though she also often lied so it was difficult to know whether what she was saying was real or whether she was just making it up. However, Eve White did confirm many of the episodes by recalling times when she was inexplicably punished. Her parents and husband also confirmed Eve Black's stories.

Eve Black denied any association with the child or the husband. She had never made herself known to them and their first knowledge of her existence was when a meeting was arranged in the psychiatrist's office. Eve Black claimed to have been married to someone else though she said she never had sex with him. This had apparently led him to beat her. However, Eve White didn't recall any of this. Eve Black's explanation was that she was able to selectively erase items from Eve White's memory. This was confirmed by several experiments tried by the psychiatrist.

The psychiatrists used psychological tests to distinguish between the two Eves, and found minor differences in IQ, Eve White had an IQ score of 110 and a high memory function. Eve

The actress Joanne Woodward used different expressions, make-up, and clothes to portray the different "personalities" of Chris Sizemore in the film *The Three Faces of Eve*.

Why is independent corroboration likely to be quite important when considering the spontaneous nature of MPD?

Black scored 104 with a lower memory function. Personality tests revealed that Eve White was found to have a hysterical tendency and to be emotionally repressed. Eve Black displayed rigidity, anxiety, and a tendency to regress to more childlike behaviour. In fact "Black" was Eve White's maiden name. It was therefore suggested that these personalities are the same person at different stages of her life, Eve Black was the younger Eve White. Eve White was the more dominant personality. She was also the only one who could be hypnotised.

Psychological tests revealed further differences between Eve White and Black. Eve White found it hard to express hostility towards her own mother but Eve Black could. Eve Black also expressed intolerance of Eve White's marital predicament. This white and black pattern started early in life. When Eve White's twin sisters were born she felt rejected by her parents; however, she loved them dearly. Eve Black on the other hand hated them. So Eve White showed care and tolerance, whereas Eve Black was intolerant and self-centred. In a sense Eve Black's role was to embody all the angry feelings, thus enabling Eve White to maintain a nice, loving persona.

During the course of therapy Eve White decided to leave her husband and, at that time, her daughter went to live with her grandparents. The headaches and voices disappeared and she managed to do well at her job and achieve some stability. Then, after 8 months, the situation changed for the worse again. The headaches and blackouts returned. She found it hard to work and became very distressed.

During one session of hypnosis she stopped talking, her head dropped and, after a silence of two minutes, she blinked, looked around and said to the therapist "Who are you?" This new person called herself Jane. Jane was more mature and bold than Eve White but not difficult like Eve Black. She could be superficially described as a compromise between the two Eves and was aware of everything the other two did. The psychiatrists hoped that, eventually, Jane would provide the satisfactory reintegration of Eve's personality, and for a while this seemed possible.

However, some time later a fourth personality, Evelyn, appeared at another crisis in Eve's life. She had access to the memories of the others, was again more mature and responsible, and altogether a more complete person than the others. It also emerged that there had been at least nine other personalities before Eve Black and there were others after Evelyn. There may have been 22 altogether. In 1975 the real Eve came forward, Mrs Chris Sizemore. She reported that she had gradually learned to assimilate all her separate selves and to successfully cope with the pressures of life.

Discussion points

1. List examples from this case study to illustrate the four criteria of MPD.

2. What evidence is there that the multiple personalities were not just play-acting?

CASE STUDY: *Sybil*

"Sybil" was Shirley Ardell Mason, born in 1923, in Dodge Center, Minnesota. Like "Eve White", "Sybil's" story was made into a film, but whereas the impact of the Eve White story was to legitimise the concept of MPD, the Sybil story eventually led to questions about whether MPD patients are genuine.

Sybil first visited a psychiatrist, Dr Cornelia Wilbur, in 1954 when Sybil was a graduate student at Columbia University. The story became famous when a book and later a film documented the case history. During treatment more than a dozen distinct personalities emerged, including two males ("Mike" and "Sid"), a baby ("Ruthie"), and other adults.

There has been no reason to question Sybil's story until recently. A psychiatrist, Dr Herbert Spiegel had occasionally stepped in for Dr Wilbur when she had to be away. Spiegel expressed grave doubts about the validity of Sybil's other personalities in an interview in 1997. This triggered a recollection in one of Wilbur's colleagues, Robert Rieber (1999) that he actually had tape recordings of the sessions with Sybil, and he now listened to them. In an analysis of these tapes, Rieber quotes

endless instances of how Wilbur had actually created the other identities rather than it being the case that these identities spontaneously emerged during therapy. For example, Wilbur describes the interview to a colleague, "And I said, well, there's a personality who calls herself Peggy. Ah, uh, I said she is pretty self-assertive ... she can do things you can't, and she [Sybil] was, uh, obviously perturbed by this." In another tape Wilbur says to Sybil "... isn't there some connection between you and these other personalities?" and went on to explain to Sybil that she was a multiple personality and there was a connection. Rieber concludes that Wilbur was planting ideas in Sybil's mind rather than probing her. His main concern is that memories can so easily be created, especially in MPD cases, and this is clearly what Wilbur had done. Furthermore, Wilbur planted other ideas in Sybil's head: "You don't love your mother. You mother is wicked, bad, cruel, painful ... If you don't hate her you ought to."

Rieber concludes that the case was a "conscious misrepresentation of the facts ... Once you start making up a story to suit your own needs it can take on a life of its own."

pressure, and EEG (Lester, 1977). Jens and Evans (1983) even report that women with MPD menstruate most of the time because each personality has a separate cycle!

Incidence

At the time the "three faces of Eve" study was first published in the 1950s, very few MPD cases had ever been recorded. However, since that time there has almost been an epidemic. According to Sue et al. (1994) one clinician alone diagnosed 130 cases. There is reason to be concerned about both overdiagnosis and underdiagnosis.

Underdiagnosis

Some clinicians feel that the condition is underdiagnosed because the symptoms are not recognised. Salley (1988) gave the following description of a misdiagnosis in the case of a man aged 37 who had reported the symptoms associated with MPD since the age of 6. He had experienced blackouts, there were things that he did for which he had no memory, and also behaviour and personality changes had been observed. During his life he had been variously diagnosed as having an organic brain condition, schizoid personality, undifferentiated schizophrenia, and seizure disorder. Individuals with MPD frequently complain of hearing voices and this is taken as a symptom of schizophrenia, whereas, as we have seen in the case of Eve White, this is actually the other personality talking. There is no doubt that it is sometimes difficult to distinguish between various conditions.

Overdiagnosis

At the other extreme there is also overdiagnosis of the condition. In a study in Switzerland Modestin (1992) found very few cases of MPD (less than 1% of psychiatric patients) but half of these were accounted for by three psychiatrists. This suggests that some psychiatrists may be more likely to make this diagnosis. Thigpen and Cleckley, after their landmark case history, received thousands of patient referrals and only diagnosed one further case. So why are there so many cases of MPD in certain quarters?

Genuineness of patients

One possible explanation is that some patients are faking the symptoms in order to get attention, or to save themselves from criminal prosecution. In one well-documented case, Kenneth Bianchi, the "Hillside Strangler", pleaded guilty by reason of insanity to a string

---

The case study approach to research

The case study approach has the advantage of collecting a rich amount of data—one has the opportunity to focus in depth on the details of one particular case (the case could be one school or, as in this unit, one individual). It also is often the only way to study certain behaviours, especially mental disorders where there are not that many individuals who could form the basis of a large-scale study.

The case study approach has the disadvantage of being subjective. Data are invariably collected largely through interviews where the interviewer gets to know his or her participant rather well and is therefore likely to become biased. For example, he or she may develop expectations about what the participant is likely to say in one particular situation and this will affect what they "hear". The case study approach is also likely to rely on retrospective data, which is information recalled from childhood. This again is prone to bias—people find what they are looking for, and childhood memories may be very unreliable. A final drawback to the case study approach is that such studies cannot be replicated because they are based on usually unique circumstances and individuals. Replication is a key way of demonstrating the validity of any research outcome. We believe that, if a finding is true, then it should occur again if the same research procedures are followed.

"Multiple disorder" defence placed on trial

Lawyers defending "vampire cult" members, facing the death penalty for the brutal murder of an elderly Florida couple, may present what they see as the perfect defence—that the accused teenagers were, literally, not themselves. Multiple Personality Disorder—the condition whereby several identities co-exist within the same person—has recently become one of America's most fashionable problems.

But is it anything more than a psychiatric con-trick? Worse, are those "treating" the condition causing it in the first place? Certainly, it is in their interests to foster an epidemic. A growing number of doctors and psychologists are voicing doubts about the validity of MPD and calling for it to be abandoned as a serious diagnosis. In doing so, they are taking on a formidable coalition of interest groups. The American Psychological Association estimates that at least 2500 professionals are

involved with the treatment of MPD. The condition, almost unknown 30 years ago, now affects up to 2 per cent of the American population or 5 million people, almost all women.

Critics say that high-profile examples, such as the television personality Roseanne who claims to have more than 20 personalities, explain the explosion in the number of cases in the past decade. A new book, *Multiple Identities and False Memories*, demolishes the diagnosis and describes it as a "social construction", rather than a medical condition, which suits therapists as much as patients. Its author, Dr Nicholas Spanos, suggests that multiple personalities have been observed in women since the sixteenth century, when they were attributed to "demons" and exorcised by priests.

Adapted from James Langton, *The Telegraph*, 26 January 1997

of murders, arguing that he had MPD, as described in the Case Study below. You might also consider the article " 'Multiple disorder' defence placed on trial" (see previous page).

In another extraordinary court case the tables were turned. In 1990 a Wisconsin man was tried for raping a 26-year-old woman who, it turned out, claimed to suffer from MPD. The woman had consented to sex but her other personalities had not! Another personality—that of a 6-year-old girl—replaced her during the act. At the start of the trial each of the 21 alleged personalities "inside" the victim had to be sworn in separately.

Iatrogenesis

The term **"iatrogenic"** refers to disorders that are produced by a physician or therapist unwittingly through selective attention and expectations. Merskey (1992) believes that the separate personalities that appear in therapy are actually produced by unwitting therapists. The therapist who believes in MPD may convey his or her expectations to the patients through suggestion and social reinforcement. This could explain why certain psychiatrists have a far greater incidence of MPD patients.

Spanos et al. (1985) have argued that hypnosis is the key to this iatrogenic effect. Treatment of MPD patients invariably involves hypnosis. Therapists attempt to enable

---

CASE STUDY: *The Hillside Strangler—A Fake Multiple Personality?*

In the autumn and winter of 1977–1978, the nude bodies of 10 women were found on various hillsides of Los Angeles County. All had been raped and then strangled. This was followed by two similar murders in Washington State, which led to the arrest of Kenneth Bianchi, who claimed to have been driving his car some distance from the crime scene when the victims were killed. When confronted with facts, which made his alibi impossible to believe, he then claimed he had fabricated the story to fill in the gap in his memory for the time span in question.

A forensic psychiatrist interviewed Bianchi and reported that Bianchi gave a history of repeated spells of amnesia since childhood and recommended using hypnosis to further understand Bianchi's state of mind. During a hypnotic interview an alter-personality, "Steve", appeared, claiming responsibility for the two local killings and involvement in nine of the 10 Los Angeles deaths. On 30 March 1979, the defence entered a plea of not guilty by reason of insanity, based on the possibility that Bianchi suffered from the multiple personality syndrome at the time of the offences.

Leading experts on dissociative disorders and hypnosis were brought in to determine the validity of this claim, and they argued that Bianchi was faking for four reasons:

1. The personality called "Steve" was not a stable identity. During the course of a number of interviews his personality changed from polite and passive to aggressive and abusive. This is not typical of multiples or "alters" who usually have a very clearly defined personality.
2. When it was suggested to Bianchi that MPD patients often have a number of different personalities, a new one called "Billy" emerged.
3. Usually people who know the MPD patient well can provide corroborating evidence, such as Eve White's husband reporting strange, inexplicable episodes. No one who knew Bianchi well could offer external corroboration.
4. When apparently hypnotised Bianchi showed the characteristics of a "simulator". This is a person who appears to be hypnotised but is actually just playing the part. This can be demonstrated by asking the hypnotised person to do certain things such as imagine there is a chair in the middle of the room. A truly hypnotised person actually walks round the chair whereas a simulator bumps into it.

Bianchi was eventually diagnosed to be suffering from anti-social (dissocial) personality disorder, not MPD. It turned out that he had committed most of the crimes with his cousin, Angelo Buono. Both men were given sentences of life imprisonment.

Kenneth Bianchi, known as the Hillside Strangler, was determined by experts to be faking multiple personality disorder.

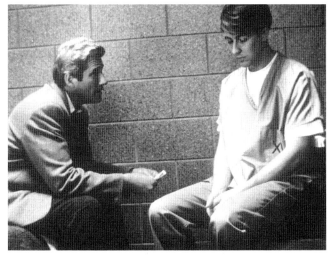

Edward Norton and Richard Gere starred in the film *Primal Fear*, which is based on someone faking MPD to escape a murder charge, and succeeding.

patients to reveal their feelings by implanting possible suggestions about, for example, other personalities or other feelings. Individuals who are peripherally aware of MPD take up such suggestions and display characteristics of MPD. Once a "personality" has been given a name and other features of its identity, it becomes a reality. Spanos et al. presented evidence to support this hypothesis (see the Key Study below). The case of "Sybil" also supports the view that MPD may be iatrogenically rather than spontaneously caused (see page 606).

Explanations of Multiple Personality Disorder

It therefore appears possible that MPD doesn't exist at all as a "real" condition. However, there are alternative viewpoints based on some of the models of abnormality covered in

If MPD is a "spontaneous," i.e., "real" condition, then what is the cause? Eating disorders are explained in terms of various models of abnormality. Which model fits MPD best?

Do therapists create MPD in their patients?

Spanos et al. (1985) have argued that there are a number of factors that may explain the how and why of iatrogenically caused MPD:

1. The syndrome has become well known. Many people are familiar with the disorder and its characteristics through media reports.
2. Certain therapeutic techniques lend themselves to suggestion, especially if hypnosis is used in therapy. Where a patient is placed in a hypnotic trance it becomes relatively easy to "create" multiple personalities. The therapist is not doing this consciously but, in the spirit of therapy, is attempting to enable other characteristics and feelings of the person to be expressed. It is noteworthy that hypnosis has invariably been used in cases of MPD.
3. MPD patients may feel special because it is an unusual and intriguing diagnosis. Therapists become very attentive to such patients.
4. Once it appears that a patient has several personalities these quickly "solidify", being given names and the appearance of reality. It becomes easy to believe in their existence.

Spanos et al. (1985) tested this hypothesis by arranging for male and female students to play the role of an accused murderer (Harry or Betty Hodgins). There were three conditions:

Group A: Full suggestion. Participants were hypnotised and told that "there might be another part of Harry/Betty that feels somewhat differently to the part I've talked to, and I'd like to communicate with that part". If the "part" responded it was asked further questions about its name, identity, and so on.

Group B: Part suggestion. Participants were hypnotised but not given as clear a hint. They were simply told that individuals sometimes block certain feelings and that hypnosis can help to access such thoughts. They were told that, when the hypnotist/psychiatrist put his hand on the participant's shoulder he would be in contact with that other part of the participant.

Group C: Participants were not hypnotised but were given the same suggestions as participants in group B.

More than 80% of the participants in group A indicated that they did have another personality. They also demonstrated amnesia for the other personality when they existed as Harry or Betty. Psychological tests revealed distinct personalities.

About 30% of the participants in group B also revealed a different personality but none of the control group did.

This supports the notion that different personalities emerge as a response to (1) the suggestions that are made and (2) the "patient's" susceptibility to suggestions (i.e., being hypnotised). It is supposed that the participants knew about the behaviour of MPD sufferers and used this as a model for how to respond to the suggestions.

Discussion points

1. It is suggested here that MPD is the result of suggestion from the psychiatrist. Why might a psychiatrist do this?
2. How do these findings explain the fact that some psychiatrists diagnose more MPD cases than others?

your AS level studies. These models were used to explain eating disorders. Here we will use some of them to explain MPD.

Psychodynamic model

According to the psychodynamic or psychoanalytic view, MPD is related to the repression of unpleasant or traumatic events. Repression is a form of ego defence, in other words a means of protecting oneself (the "ego" in psychoanalytic terms) from anxiety. When it is not possible to completely repress such threatening thoughts, possibly because they are so threatening, then separation or dissociation of certain mental processes occurs, ultimately resulting in the formation of separate identities.

In Freudian theory there are three personality structures. Developmentally, there is first of all the id, the primitive part of yourself that is driven by the pleasure principle—"it" gets what it wants. The id is present at birth. Before the age of 2, the second personality structure develops, the ego or sense of self ("I"). The ego is driven by the reality principle, which makes the child accommodate to the demands of the environment. The ego is equivalent to our rational mind and it must modify the demands of the id. Later we develop a superego, which is roughly equivalent to our conscience, our moral self.

The id, ego, and superego are inevitably in conflict, with the ego in the role of mediator. For some people this clash is beyond the resources of the ego. The result is a schism and the formation of separate identities. Anxieties and fragmentation are replaced by a sense of unity and identity—although this exists in several different personalities.

It is thought that this often results from a series of traumatic events in early childhood combined with the inability to escape. Shapiro (1991) suggests that one or more of the personalities takes the "pain" to protect the others. Dissociation is a strategy for survival, for coping with unbearable but inescapable emotions.

Evaluation

Many studies report that MPD patients have suffered early sexual abuse or other trauma. For example, Putnam, Guroff, Silberman, et al. (1986) reported that 97% of MPD patients have experienced child abuse.

For a general consideration of some of the criticisms of psychodynamic theory, see pages 766–767.

The behavioural model

The behavioural model explains mental disorders in terms of reinforcement and learning. MPD patients may be characterised by their inability to handle emotional conflicts. Such individuals experience relief (which is reinforcing) by blocking out disturbing thoughts. They soon learn to use this as a strategy for dealing with highly emotional situations. Clearly this also fits with the data that MPD sufferers have experienced early traumas.

The behavioural explanation of MPD also relates to the situational theory of personality (see the box on the left). In essence this theory proposes that none of us have a consistent personality. We learn to behave appropriately in particular situations because of selective reinforcement. In one situation, certain behaviours are rewarded whereas they are not rewarded elsewhere, and vice versa. Therefore we learn what to do when it is appropriate. MPD patients are adjusting their personality, mannerisms, and even their clothes to fit different situations. They are not displaying different personalities but a therapist may misinterpret these significantly different behaviours and inadvertently create a disorder.

The situational theory of personality and self theory

The situational theory of personality raises the question of the extent to which any of us are truly one identity. Is MPD an exaggeration of what we all experience? Have you ever said "I wasn't behaving like myself?" To what extent are we all able to engage in a mild form of dissociation when we behave in ways that are unacceptable? Carl Rogers (1951), in his self theory of personality, suggests that this sort of dissociation underlies maladjustment. When an individual says "that isn't like me" he or she is excluding that behaviour from their self-concept and therefore cannot control it. Psychological maladjustment exists when the individual denies experiences that therefore cannot be admitted into the self-structure and cannot be controlled. This leads to psychological tension. This is likely to occur especially when an individual maintains a rigid self-structure.

The way to resolve this is for the individual to accept their inconsistencies, thus allowing them to be less rigid and to be able to revise their self-structure. When such threat to self-structure is removed then the person may be capable of perceiving inconsistencies and revising their self-structure to assimilate the inconsistencies.

Evaluation

Behavioural explanations are generally criticised for the fact that they apply more to non-human behaviour. When considering a complex behaviour such as MPD it seems inappropriate to focus on observable behaviour only, as is the case with the behavioural approach. It is likely that cognitive factors are also important and that the principles of reinforcement alone cannot explain the development of MPD.

How can you use these explanations of MPD to support the "spontaneous" argument for MPD?

State-dependent learning

The situational theory of personality is related to state-dependent learning. In your AS level studies on memory you considered research that showed that situational cues can enhance recall. For example, Abernethy's (1940) experiment that demonstrated that students can do better on a test if it takes place in the same classroom as the initial learning took place, and with the same teacher. We also considered **mood-state-dependent memory**.

It may be that this phenomenon can lead to MPD when some individuals have clusters of distinct memories that are recalled in certain contexts. This would fit in with the observations of how different personalities emerge on certain occasions and sometimes a new personality emerges that hadn't appeared before. Presumably this is a memory cluster that had not been triggered for some time but a new emotional context may suddenly access it.

Self-hypnosis

A characteristic of MPD patients is that they appear highly susceptible to hypnosis. In addition to this there are characteristics of hypnosis that resemble MPD. Hilgard (1986) put forward the **neo-dissociation theory** of hypnosis, which suggests that hypnosis is an altered state where consciousness is split into several streams somewhat independent of each other. This explains some of the phenomena that have been demonstrated with hypnosis, such as access to memories not usually available and reduced sensitivity to pain. Hypnotic amnesia may occur because the "forgotten" memories are dissociated or separated from conscious control, and so cannot be retrieved voluntarily. There is also evidence of dissociation with hypnotic analgesia, in which suggestions that pain will not be experienced are often effective when given in the hypnotic state.

Neo-dissociation theory can also explain the **hidden observer phenomenon**. This involves taking a hypnotised person and giving him or her the following instructions: "When I place my hand on your shoulder, I shall be able to talk to a hidden part of you that knows things are going on in your body, things that are unknown to the part of you to which I am now talking ... You will remember that there is a part of you that knows many things that are going on that may be hidden from either your normal consciousness or the hypnotised part of you" (Knox et al., 1974, p.842). A good example of the hidden observer phenomenon was discussed by Hilgard (1986). He used the cold pressor test, in which the participant's arms are kept in ice-cold water for as long as possible. Most people can only tolerate this for about 25 seconds. However, hypnotised individuals who are told that they will not experience any pain keep their arms in the water for about 40 seconds, and report much less pain than non-hypnotised individuals. The hidden observer, who was told to "remain out of consciousness" until summoned up later, then reported a very intense experience of pain. In other words, the consciousness of these hypnotised individuals seemed to divide into two parts.

According to Hilgard (1986), the hidden part is protected from awareness of pain by an amnesic barrier. However, Spanos (1989) takes the view that hypnosis is not an altered state. He argues that hypnotised individuals simply report what they think they should report. He found that "hidden observers" can be led to report high or low levels of pain depending on the expectations they have been given.

If hypnosis is a state of dissociation, as suggested by Hilgard, then it is possible that MPD sufferers are able to place themselves in a trance-like state.

Neo-dissociation theory suggests that hypnosis reveals more than one stream of consciousness.

Social construction

Alternatively, as we have suggested, both hypnosis and MPD are social constructions. In other words they are products of our culture, created inadvertently by therapists and sufferers alike. They are both a consequence of role-playing and/or the influence of a number of social or experimental variables such as demand characteristics and experimenter bias.

This view is supported by research on the iatrogenic nature of hypnosis, discussed earlier. However, it may well be that many MPD patients are the outcome of such iatrogenic factors but at the same time the basis for this influence is a bedrock of some real cases. As Lilienfield et al. (1999) point out "much of the psychological raw material from which [MPD] is sculpted exists prior to professional intervention". It may well be that some individuals, such as Ken Bianchi, can fake MPD and that some patients, such as Sybil, are acting roles in order to gain attention or please their therapist. But other patients may well be genuine, and there is a large catalogue of such case histories. Scroppo et al. (1998) compared 21 MPD patients with 21 non-MPD patients and concluded that there is a genuine and distinct set of symptoms that underlie the disorder, and this supports the notion of a real syndrome.

Biological model

There may even be some biological basis for the behaviour. For example, Pucetti (1977) has proposed a "double brain theory" where it is suggested that we all have two minds, the left and right hemisphere of our brain. Multiple personality would be the result of alternate functioning between the right and left hemispheres. It is true that **split-brain patients**, whose hemispheric connections have been severed, do have two separate streams of consciousness, although it is not clear whether or not this is the equivalent of two separate personalities (see page 156 for a discussion of split-brain patients). Perhaps this separation is more pronounced in MPD patients and this means they are more susceptible to dissociation as in hypnosis. However, this explanation might account for two personalities but not the multiple personalities that are common in MPD.

What do you conclude? Is MPD iatrogenic or spontaneous? And if spontaneous, how would you explain its cause?

Culture-bound Syndromes

The major classificatory systems are based very much on Western conceptions of abnormality and mental disorder. In recent years, however, there has been a growing recognition that it is important to take account of cultural and sub-cultural differences. DSM-IV takes issue with the phenomena known as **culture-bound syndromes** (CBS), defining them as

> *recurrent, locality-specific patterns of aberrant behaviour and troubling experience that may or may not be linked to a particular DSM-IV diagnostic category. Many of these patterns are indigenously considered to be "illnesses", or at least afflictions, and most have local names.*

However, Kleinman and Cohen (1997, p.76) dismissed the appendix to DSM-IV as "little more than a sop thrown to cultural psychiatrists and psychiatric anthropologists". In addition, many Western experts argue that most culture-bound syndromes are simply *variations* on disorders contained within DSM-IV. This may be correct, or it may be that at least some culture-bound disorders are really unique to a specific culture.

In this Unit we will consider the nature and validity of CBSs, as well as wider issues of cultural and sub-cultural differences in the classification and diagnosis of psychological abnormality.

Are There Culture-bound Syndromes?

There is a large range of culturally related disorders that are reported in the literature. Humphreys (1999) has identified at least 36 of them and Berry et al. (1992) described some of the more exotic ones (see the box on the right). In addition to CBSs of an exotic nature, we might also consider examples from our own culture, such as anorexia nervosa. We will start with a consideration of those that may be unfamiliar.

Examples of culture-bound syndromes

Koro

Koro, or "genital retraction syndrome" is a disorder found in south and east Asia. It is characterised by extreme anxiety due to the fear that one's penis or nipples will recede into the body, and possibly cause death. Koro was first reported in the Western medical press in 1895. The syndrome has evolved since that time, shifting towards the concept of disordered body-image perception (Chowdhury, 1998).

There have been cases of koro outside Asia and, though rare, these challenge the view that it is a culture-bound syndrome. Bernstein and Gaw (1990) reported the case of a 25-year-old Cantonese man with koro who was living in the US. Tobin (1996) described a case of koro in a 20-year-old single Irish man with one child. He had recently become impotent and believed that his genitalia were shrinking and that further shrinkage was going to kill him. It was significant that the man had a very marked family history of psychotic and affective illness. Also, prior to the illness the patient had been under considerable stress, due to his perceived lack of manliness in not providing for his child. Thus there is the suggestion that other factors may have predisposed him to the illness and that it is the symptoms that are unique and culturally unfamiliar, not the underlying causes.

Amok

You are no doubt familiar with the phrase "to run amok". "Amok" is a Malay term meaning "to engage in battle furiously". This behaviour has also been likened to the Viking behaviour "berserker" (as in "going berserk"). Both *amok* and *berserker* describe the kind of wild behaviour exhibited just before going into battle.

In south-east Asia the term "amok" has been used to describe a form of mental disorder where the individual behaves in a wild and aggressive manner for a limited period of time. Knecht (1999) reports that the syndrome has been well known for many centuries in the Malay culture. It consists of a characteristic sequence of stages including a first phase of dismal brooding; then an outburst of aggression with furious, often lethal attacks against random victims; followed by terminal sleep and the claim of amnesia. Quasi-amok is a feeble version of the full-blown phenomenon. It features sham attacks against the people within reach, but these individuals never quite overcome their inhibition to kill.

Like koro, amok and quasi-amok are also observed in other parts of the world. For example, Westermeyer (1973) recorded 18 case histories of young men in Laos who ran amok, though only one was eventually diagnosed with a mental disorder. In Britain and the US there have been many of incidents that could be classified as amok, such as Michael Ryan's rampage in Hungerford in 1987, Thomas Hamilton's murderous siege in Dunblane in 1996, Charles Whitman who gunned down 16 people from a tower on the Texas

---

Some "exotic" mental disorders

In the literature of cultural psychiatry there are numerous "exotic" mental disorders that have been described. A sampling of these is provided here:

Brain fag involves problems of academic learning, headache, eye fatigue, and an inability to concentrate. It appears widely in West African students often just prior to school and university examinations, and is virtually unknown outside that culture area. (Though you may wish to dispute this!)

Latah involves imitative behaviour (usually among women) that seems beyond control; movements and speech are copied, and individuals in this state are compliant to commands to do things outside their range of behaviour (for example, to utter obscenities). Its onset is often the result of a sudden or startling stimulus. The term latah means "ticklish" in the Malay language.

Piblogtoq involves an uncontrollable urge to leave one's shelter, tear off one's clothes, and expose oneself to the Arctic weather. It has been identified in Greenland, Alaska, and the Canadian Arctic and has been linked both to isolated environmental conditions and to limited calcium uptake during long sunless winters.

Witiko involves a distaste for ordinary food and feelings of depression and anxiety, leading to possession by the witiko spirit (a giant man-eating monster) and often resulting in homicide and cannibalism. It occurs among Canadian Indians and has been interpreted as an extreme form of starvation anxiety. If a cure is not attained, the witiko sufferer often pleads for death to avoid his cannibalistic desires.

Adapted from Berry et al. (1992) *Cross-cultural psychology* (Cambridge: Cambridge University Press).

university campus in 1966, the Columbine school murders, and so on. However, amok would not be the diagnosis in these cases; had psychiatric diagnosis been attempted it might have been of schizoid personalities. In different cultures, different terms may be used to describe a similar syndrome.

Dhat

Dhat syndrome is a culture-bound sex neurosis of males of the Indian subcontinent. Sufferers have multiple somatic complaints, and blame their physical and mental exhaustion on the presence of semen in their urine. The origins of this lie in the Hindu belief that semen is produced in the blood, and that the loss of semen will result in mental and physical illness. We might even connect this belief to the view in our own culture that masturbation (loss of semen) is sinful and a threat to health.

Chadda and Ahuja (1990) examined a number of patients with dhat and concluded that they were suffering from either neurotic depression or anxiety neurosis. Mumford (1996) also concluded, in a large-scale study of men in India, that the dhat complaint should be primarily regarded not as the focus of a culture-bound syndrome, but as a culturally determined symptom associated with depression. In this case we have an underlying disorder—depression—which is expressed differently in different cultures.

Anorexia nervosa

We might also consider the extent to which illnesses that are identified in DSM are also culture bound insofar as they are "locality-specific patterns of aberrant behaviour". The evidence suggests that eating disorders, such as **anorexia nervosa**, are culture-bound disorders because they primarily occur in Western cultures. It may well be that the predisposition towards a mental disorder exists in certain individuals and the form of this disorder is affected by culturally familiar behaviours. For example, Holland et al. (1988) found that in cases where one twin had anorexia many of the twin partners also suffered from an eating disorder but, where this wasn't the case, a number of them suffered from another psychiatric disorder.

Schizophrenia

We shouldn't forget that the notion of culture extends to different historical periods as well as different ethnic settings. We can see historical variations in the way that symptoms of mental disorder are expressed. For example, one of the current symptoms of schizophrenia is thought control by the television or radio. Clearly no schizophrenic in the early nineteenth century could have experienced such symptoms.

A culture-bound syndrome: Sleep paralysis

Have you ever found yourself lying fully conscious or in a dream-like state, unable to move or cry out, but able to see and hear ... or somehow sense the presence of unknown beings?

On the Web there are many reports from individuals who suffer from this disorder. They describe being unable to move at all for sometimes up to 10 minutes, feeling neither asleep nor awake, and sometimes hearing voices. Such episodes do not occur nightly. It has been suggested that sleep paralysis may underlie alien abduction experiences, where individuals very often report paralysis, out-of-body experiences, and fear before the aliens appear. Usually the person awakens in the night unable to move or cry out, alien beings approach the bed and float the helpless, paralysed abductee up to a spaceship for a frightening medical examination.

The Japanese call this condition "Kanashibari" and accept it as quite usual. The Chinese label it as a mental disorder, qi-gong psychotic reaction, and include it in their classification scheme. Qi-gong psychotic reaction is described in DSM-IV as "an acute, time-limited episode characterized by dissociative, paranoid, or other psychotic or non-

psychotic symptoms", and that "especially vulnerable are individuals who become overly involved" in qi-gong. The Chinese explain the aetiology of the disorder as having its roots in qi-gong, a form of martial art and exercise regime where participants aim to project their qi into the bodies of participants at qi-gong meetings, and to enhance the vital force of participants by so doing. Many participants claim to benefit from these practices, and even to find relief from longstanding physical or psychiatric ailments. Some, however, may develop a syndrome known as qi-gong psychotic reaction.

Lim and Keh-Ming (1996) describe a 57-year-old Chinese-American man who presented with a 3-week history of auditory and visual hallucinations. The patient had begun qi-gong practices as therapy for chronic problems with kidney stones. After several days of intensive qi-gong, he began hearing voices telling him how to practise qi-gong, and to believe that he had contacted beings from another dimension. He sought help from the qi-gong masters, but to no avail. His wife took him to see a psychiatrist, who diagnosed him with schizophrenia form disorder and treated him with anti-psychotic medications.

Culture-bound or culturally relative?

Berry et al. (1992) comment that the sheer intrigue of these exotic-sounding disorders attracts the view that there are some unique cultural differences (i.e., culture-bound). However, it may be that apparently culturally relative symptoms are simply local expressions of universal disorders (**cultural universality**). We have noted that this may be true for dhat. In addition, Yap (1969) notes that latah (from Malaya) and susto (from Peru) are both brought on by a sudden or frightening stimulus, and are simply different cultural expressions of a "primary fear reaction". Susto is expressed as apathy, depression, and anxiety, whereas latah sufferers exhibit uncontrollable movements and imitative behaviour. Yap also regards amok as a "rage reaction", and witiko as a "possession state". All of these conditions are recognised by Western psychiatry and included in their classification schemes. In a true CBS the cultural symptoms would be primary rather than being a cultural overlay of a universal mental disorder.

An illness that is universal is then *expressed* differently in different cultures (i.e., **cultural relativism**). The symptoms are at least partly determined by the values, social norms, and lifestyles found within any culture. We may conclude that apparently culture-bound disorders are actually universal disorders that are labelled and explained differently, as in the case of amok.

Vandereycken and Hoek (1992) define a CBS as "a constellation of signs or symptoms, categorized as a dysfunction or disease, that is restricted to certain cultures primarily by reason of distinctive psychosocial features of those cultures". According to this definition, does the evidence support the existence of CBSs?

Cultural universality

Which mental disorders are found world-wide? According to Kendall and Hammen (1995), schizophrenia, depression, manic depression, some anxiety disorders, and dementia or mental deterioration are found in all cultures. There is probably more cross-cultural evidence about schizophrenia than about any other mental disorder, and so we will now consider that evidence.

Schizophrenia as a universal syndrome

Incidence.   The World Health Organisation carried out a large-scale, cross-cultural study of schizophrenia (Sartorius et al., 1986). In most countries, there was about a 1% risk of developing schizophrenia at some point between the ages of 15 and 54. As might be expected, the figure varied somewhat from country to country. For example, it was almost 2.5% in rural India, compared with only 0.55% in Denmark and Honolulu. These findings suggest that schizophrenia depends only modestly on cultural factors.

Symptoms.   In an earlier study, the World Health Organisation (1981) considered the *symptoms* of schizophrenia in nine countries: England, China, India, Colombia, the United States, Denmark, the Soviet Union, Nigeria, and Czechoslovakia. Several symptoms were commonly found across these countries. Some of the most common symptoms were as follows (the percentage of schizophrenics having each symptom is in brackets): lack of insight (97%); auditory hallucinations (74%); verbal hallucinations (70%); suspiciousness (66%); lack of emotion (66%). It would seem from this evidence that the symptoms that are regarded as central to schizophrenia are also much the same across cultures.

However, there are some cultural differences in the symptoms of schizophrenia. Alaskan Inuit have a concept of "being crazy". It resembles our notion of schizophrenia, in that the symptoms include talking to oneself, screaming at people who do not exist, and making odd facial expressions. However, the Inuit concept also includes thinking one is an animal, drinking urine, killing dogs, and believing that a loved one was murdered by witchcraft.

Types.   In spite of the findings discussed so far, there are some differences in the incidence of types of schizophrenia from one country to another. Three types of schizophrenia are: paranoid schizophrenia (involving delusions of persecution); catatonic schizophrenia (involving immobility); and hebephrenic schizophrenia (involving disorganised speech and behaviour). Catatonic and hebephrenic schizophrenia are much more common in developing countries than in developed ones, whereas the opposite is the case for paranoid schizophrenia (Kleinman & Cohen, 1997).

The way in which schizophrenia is diagnosed varies somewhat from country to country. Sartorius et al. (1986) found that 40% of schizophrenic patients in developed countries (e.g., England, the United States) had the disorder in a severe and long-lasting form, compared with only 24% in developing countries (e.g., Nigeria, India).

Explaining cultural difference

In most of the cross-cultural studies on the frequency of various mental disorders, the emphasis has been on identifying and providing a description of the differences among cultures. What is usually lacking is an explanation of these differences.

The suppression–facilitation model

Weisz et al. (1987) tried to explain the differences in their suppression–facilitation model. According to this model, forms of behaviour that are discouraged within a culture will be suppressed and so observed only rarely. In contrast, forms of behaviour that are rewarded within a culture will be facilitated, and so produced to excess.

Weisz et al. applied their model to Thailand and the United States. In Thailand, parents strongly dislike under-controlled or aggressive behaviour. In the United States, on the other hand, under-controlled behaviour in the form of independence or assertiveness is encouraged. Weisz et al. studied about 400 children in each country who had been referred to a clinic with behaviour problems. As predicted, more of the Thai children than the American children showed over-controlled behaviour, whereas under-controlled behaviour was more common in the American than in the Thai children.

Some of these cultural differences may be more apparent than real. Weisz et al. (1995) observed children's behaviour in schools in the United States and Thailand. The American children were twice as disruptive as the Thai children in terms of talking and being out of their seats. In spite of this, the Thai children were perceived by their teachers as having significantly more behaviour problems than were the American children by theirs.

Why do cultures vary in the types of behaviour they encourage and discourage?

Misdiagnosis

Stevens (1987) argued convincingly that the main reason for the differences cited earlier is misdiagnosis in the developing countries. The fact that 36% of Nigerian patients and 27% of Indian patients recovered in under a month suggests that they had not really been suffering from schizophrenia in the first place.

Differential diagnosis

A third possibility for explaining cultural differences in schizophrenia is the existence of cultural biases in the diagnosis of mental disorders. Cochrane and Sashidharan (1995) report that black African-Caribbean immigrants in the UK are up to seven times more likely than white people to receive a diagnosis of schizophrenia. This difference does not seem to be due to the stresses of being a recent arrival in a new country, because it tends to be slightly larger among second-generation African-Caribbeans. Furthermore, the rate of diagnosis of schizophrenia in the United Kingdom for South Asians is about the same as for the white population (Cochrane, 1983).

Fairly good evidence of cultural bias was reported by Blake (1973). He found that clinicians were more likely to use a diagnosis of schizophrenia if the case study described the patient as African-American rather than as White. In similar fashion, Luepnitz, Randolph, and Gutsch (1982) found that a given set of symptoms was much more likely to produce a diagnosis of alcoholism for a lower-class African-American than for a middle-class white person.

Schizophrenia in Ireland

Murphy (1982) found that Irish Catholics were four times more likely to be hospitalised for schizophrenia than those in England. In Northern Ireland the rates were lower but the Catholics were twice as likely to be hospitalised as non-Catholics. How can we explain these differences? Murphy suggests that one possibility is that the "sometimes savage Irish wit of the Irish culture encourages ambivalence toward individual independence", in other words they are encouraged to use double-think. Second, it is possible that Irish psychiatrists may be reluctant to return poor rural Catholics to isolated homes and this makes it appear that rates of schizophrenia are higher.

Why might the rates of diagnosis vary across cultures? One reason is that the symptoms associated with a disorder may vary from culture to culture in ways discussed earlier (cultural relativism). These variations are not catered for in diagnostic systems such as DSM-IV or ICD-10. For example, people in the United Kingdom or the United States who are suffering from depression typically complain of feelings of worthlessness and hopelessness, and loss of interest in most activities. In contrast, Nigerians who are depressed often complain of burning sensations in the body, crawling sensations in the head or legs, and a feeling that the stomach is bloated with water (Ebigno, 1986).

Reducing cultural bias.   What can be done to reduce cultural bias in diagnosis? Some interesting answers to that question are provided in DSM-IV. One possibility is to take account of language differences between the therapist and the patient. A second possibility is for the therapist to become familiar with the ways in which the members of each cultural group discuss their own distress. A third possibility is to find out the extent to which each patient identifies with different cultural groups, and then to make use of that information before deciding on a diagnosis.

In the UK, a person of African-Caribbean descent is more likely than a white person to be diagnosed with schizophrenia, and this is likely to be due to cultural bias.

Cultural Issues in the Classification and Diagnosis of Psychological Abnormality

This leads us to consider the wider issues with regard to the classification and diagnosis of psychological abnormality. As we have just seen there is evidence of cultural bias in relation to the diagnosis of schizophrenia. We may also consider culture bias in terms of sub-cultures. Both gender and social class are sub-cultures, inasmuch as they can be identified as distinct groups who share attitudes, values, and so on.

Gender differences and gender biases

There are clear gender differences with respect to several mental disorders. Two of the most striking examples are the eating disorders anorexia nervosa and bulimia nervosa, where over 90% of those diagnosed as having either disorder are female. Robins et al. (1984) considered gender differences in the lifetime occurrence of various other disorders across three American cities. Men had a higher rate of alcohol abuse than women (27% vs. 4%, respectively), and they also had more anti-social conduct (5% vs. 1%, respectively). In contrast, women were more likely to have major depression (8% vs. 2%) or a specific phobia (9% vs. 4%).

Explaining gender differences

Why do these gender differences occur? The answer varies across disorders, with some gender differences being genuine, whereas others reflect various **gender biases**. In terms of depression the reasons for higher rates in women may be due to the fact that women often have to cope with sex discrimination and with relative powerlessness, and depression may be one of the results of such stressful circumstances. Alternatively, physiological processes in women (including the menstrual cycle and the menopause) may make them more vulnerable than men to depression.

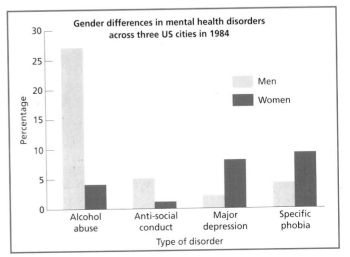

On the other hand, there is evidence that gender bias may be a factor with several other mental disorders. Such bias can occur for various reasons, four of which were identified by Worell and Remer (1992):

- Disregarding environmental context: the focus in most classificatory systems is on the individual's symptoms rather than on his or her circumstances; this may produce gender bias if female patients are having to cope with more difficult circumstances than male patients.
- Differential diagnosis on the basis of gender: this can occur when the patient's symptoms are interpreted in terms of traditional sex-role stereotypes, leading the therapist to exaggerate the numbers of women having so-called "women's disorders" and the numbers of men having "men's disorders".
- Therapist misjudgement: traditional sex-role stereotyping may increase the chances that the therapist will detect symptoms of submissiveness or dependence in female patients and of aggressiveness in male patients.
- Theoretical orientation: the therapist may have various theoretical biases related to gender, and these theoretical biases may distort the process of assessment and diagnosis.

Gender bias

With reference to the reasons given by Worell and Remer for gender bias in the diagnosis of mental disorder:

- What "difficult circumstances" arise more frequently for women than for men?
- Which disorders are doctors (medical or psychological) more likely to identify with being female?
- Which approaches make distinctions between the sexes, e.g., psychodynamic notions of sexuality?

Research evidence

Evidence of the existence of gender biases in diagnosis was reported by Ford and Widiger (1989). They presented therapists with written case studies of one patient with anti-social personality disorder (irresponsible and reckless behaviour) and of another patient with histrionic personality disorder (excessive emotionality and attention seeking). Each patient was sometimes identified as male and sometimes as female, and the therapists had to decide on the appropriate diagnosis. Anti-social personality disorder was correctly diagnosed over 40% of the time when the patient was male, but under 20% of the time when the patient was female. In contrast, histrionic personality disorder was correctly diagnosed much more often when the patient was female: nearly 80% vs. just over 30%.

Why are therapists reluctant to diagnose male patients as suffering from histrionic personality disorder, and female patients as suffering from anti-social personality disorder?

The findings of Ford and Widiger indicate a strong bias from traditional sex-role stereotypes. Evidence on these stereotypes was obtained by Broverman et al. (1981). They asked clinicians to identify the characteristics of the healthy adult, the healthy man, and the healthy woman. The characteristics of the healthy adult and the healthy man were rather similar, including adjectives such as independent, decisive, and assertive. In contrast, the adjectives used to describe the healthy woman included words such as dependent, submissive, and emotional.

Bias in the definitions of abnormality

The findings of Broverman et al. (1981) suggest that there may be other forms of gender bias in the diagnosis of mental disorders. If health and normality are defined with respect to the sex-role stereotype of men, then the symptoms of abnormality in classificatory systems may be based on deviations from this stereotype. If this were to happen, it would discriminate unfairly against women. Kendall and Hammen (1995, p.23) argued that precisely this may already be happening:

Some have argued that the DSM includes, or is being pressed to include, diagnoses that are unfair to women and that it labels as a disorder certain kinds of symptoms that women have but men do not.

As an example, they refer to a severe form of premenstrual distress that was considered for inclusion in DSM-IV. It might be argued, alternatively, that is unfair to not include such symptoms because if no diagnosis is made then no treatment can be given. No one would regard breast examination as being unfair to women yet it clearly involves women and not men.

Suppression–facilitation

The findings of Broverman et al. (1981) suggest a further reason for gender bias in the diagnosis of mental disorders. If we assume that men in Western cultures believe it is important for them to be independent, then they may be less likely than women to seek psychiatric assistance when it is needed. Nolen-Hoeksma (1990) argued that men respond to depression with distracting activities (e.g., watching television, playing sport), whereas women tend to ruminate or ponder on life and to blame themselves. She reported evidence showing that the male coping style is more effective than the female coping style in reducing the level of depression.

> **■ Activity: Sex stereotyping**
>
> List the characteristics thought to be indicative of a healthy male and those for a healthy female. Now reverse the characteristics and make an assessment of their usefulness in determining mental health, e.g., emotionality in a man may be considered a sign of weakness or instability.
>
> Discuss in small groups notions of normality that would avoid the use of sex stereotyping. Devise a new list of sex-neutral characteristics indicating mental health.

Social class bias

There are variations across social classes in the likelihood of receiving various diagnoses, with social class generally being assessed on the basis of occupation. In general terms, what is usually found is that people belonging to the lower classes are more likely than those belonging to the middle class to be diagnosed with severe disorders. However, this is not always the case. Eating disorders, for example, are more prevalent in middle-class individuals.

There are various reasons for apparent social class bias in diagnosing mental illness. Mental health professionals have been found to make less encouraging clinical decisions with patients from the lower classes (Umbenhauer & DeWitte, 1978), such as offering them less effective therapeutic interventions. Another possibility is that those from higher social classes have more coping strategies at their disposal. For example, the fact that they tend to have more money means that they are more likely to be able to afford to go to a health farm or on holiday when feeling highly stressed. Powerful evidence of the impact of wealth was reported by Bruce, Takeuchi, and Leaf (1991). People above and below the poverty line who had no mental illness at first assessment were assessed again 6 months later. Those living below the poverty line were more than twice as likely to have developed alcohol abuse or dependence, bipolar disorder, or major depression during that period, and a staggering 80 times more likely to have developed schizophrenia.

The relationship between social class and mental disorder has been explored more thoroughly with schizophrenia than with any other disorder. As a result, we will focus on schizophrenia.

People living below the poverty line are more likely to develop some mental disorders than those in comfortable financial circumstances.

Schizophrenia

Members of the lower social classes are much more likely than those of the higher social classes to be diagnosed as suffering from schizophrenia (Barlow & Durand, 1995). There are several possible explanations of this finding, three of which are considered next.

First, it is possible that there is a bias, with clinicians being more willing to use the diagnosis of schizophrenia when considering the symptoms of individuals from lower social classes. Johnstone (1989) reviewed several studies which showed that lower-class patients were more likely than middle-class patients to be given serious diagnoses (such as schizophrenia), even when there were few if any differences in symptoms.

Second, there is the social causation hypothesis. According to this hypothesis, members of the lowest classes in society tend to experience more stressful lives, because of poverty, unemployment, poorer physical health, and so on. Stress is also likely through discrimination, because ethnic and racial minorities in many

How does the social causation hypothesis conflict with the medical model argument that severe psychotic illnesses can be approached in the same way as a physical illness?

cultures tend to belong to the lower social classes. The high level of stress makes them more vulnerable than members of the middle class to schizophrenia. This hypothesis is a reasonable one, but there is little evidence providing direct support for it.

Third, there is the social drift hypothesis. According to this hypothesis, individuals who develop schizophrenia are likely to lose their jobs and so their social status is reduced. In other words, schizophrenia causes reduced social status, rather than low social status causing schizophrenia. If that is the case, then schizophrenics should tend to belong to a lower social class than their parents. Turner and Wagonfeld (1967) found this when he compared schizophrenics and their fathers. However, the fathers also tended to belong to the lower social classes themselves, which is in line with the social causation hypothesis.

What conclusions can we come to regarding the explanation of the relationship between schizophrenia and social class? According to Halgin and Whitbourne (1997, p.361), "far too little research has been done ... to resolve the contrasting viewpoints of the social causation and social drift hypotheses". However, there is one key finding that is hard to account for on the social causation hypothesis. As we saw earlier, the rates of schizophrenia are fairly similar across numerous cultures (Sartorius et al., 1986). This happens in spite of the fact that these cultures vary enormously in some of the factors (e.g., poverty, physical health) claimed by the social causation hypothesis to be important determinants of schizophrenia.

Conclusion regarding culture-bound syndromes

In a sense these sub-cultural differences and biases are examples of culture-bound syndromes. If we return to our initial definition that CBSs are "locality-specific patterns of aberrant behaviour and troubling experience that may or may not be linked to a particular DSM-IV diagnostic category" then we can see that mental disorders are highly susceptible to association with sub-cultural and cultural practices.

In order for mental disorders to be adequately treated we need to recognise these cultural and sub-cultural biases.

S E C T I O N   S U M M A R Y

Classificatory Systems

❖ The medical model of physical illness has been adapted as a means of diagnosing and treating mental disorder using reliable and valid classification systems. Most classificatory systems focus on syndromes or sets of symptoms that are generally found together, though the match between symptoms and syndromes is not exact. The classificatory systems that are available to us allow us to do a number of things: (1) administer appropriate treatments once a syndrome has been diagnosed by its symptoms; (2) discover suitable treatments; and (3) reassure the patient and their family.

❖ The most widely used classificatory system is DSM-IV, which employs a descriptive approach based on observable symptoms. The former version DSM-II was vague and unreliable. DSM-III and DSM-IV have the advantage because they focus on observable symptoms rather than theoretical cause. DSM-IV is a multi-axial system in which the patient is evaluated on five axes or scales. There are over 200 mental disorders in 16 main categories in DSM-IV, and most disorders are based on prototypes. Categories are based on field trials.

❖ The current classificatory system of DSM-IV has generally good inter-judge reliability, though this varies from category to category. Aetiological validity is low because of the influence of individual differences. Comorbidity reduces descriptive validity, and predictive validity may be fairly good.

❖ ICD is mainly used for collecting statistics, whereas DSM is used as a diagnostic tool. ICD-6 was the first system to include mental disorders. However, unfortunately it had low reliability. ICD-10 has 11 major categories of mental disorders, some of which resemble categories in DSM-IV. ICD-10 may be less reliable than DSM-IV because the defining symptoms are less precise. Validity is similar to DSM; aetiological validity is low because of the influence of individual differences, comorbidity reduces descriptive validity, and predictive validity may be fairly good.

❖ The latest revisions of DSM and ICD have converged, with many common categories, in addition to the fact that they both use operational diagnostic criteria. Some of these criteria identify symptoms that should not be present as well as those that should be present for a diagnosis to be made. There are differences between the two systems: DSM-IV has more categories and ICD-10 has broader categories.

❖ Most clinicians accept the value of classification symptoms for determining the appropriate form of treatment. However, a central concept to note is that diagnosing mental illness isn't the same as diagnosing "physical illness". Unlike mental illnesses, physical illnesses have signs as well as symptoms, and usually have known causes (aetiology) that enable one to check the accuracy of a diagnosis.

❖ The problems of reliability and validity can be considered at a more general level. Rosenhan's study suggests that psychiatric diagnoses lack reliability and validity. However, the findings of Rosenhan's study can be explained in terms of understandable type one and type two errors as well as the artificiality of the situation. A simple way to summarise this is that high reliability is gained by sacrificing validity. High validity, through the use of "neat" categories, may be an impossible goal.

❖ Labelling is a further difficulty. Labels may be self-fulfilling, affecting a patient's behaviour and that of others. In addition to this, labels may stigmatise individuals and suggest that mental illnesses are real. However, it may be that mental illnesses can be accounted for in different ways. Some psychiatrists feel that mental illnesses are symptoms of society rather than the individuals they treat.

❖ A final problem in classification is the issue of social and cultural biases, including gender and historical differences in the way mental disorders are classified. Such biases are extremely important and must be acknowledged.

Multiple Personality Disorder (Dissociative Identity Disorder)

❖ MPD is characterised by the existence of more than two identities that recurrently take control of an individual and by the occurrence of episodes of lost recall, none of which can be explained by physical causes. MPD differs from schizophrenia (a fragmented personality) and is counted as a type of dissociative disorder. It has been argued by some psychiatrists that MPD and DID are completely different disorders.

❖ The case history of Eve White/Eve Black started an epidemic of MPD. Eve White was repressed and gentle, whereas Eve Black was wicked and more able to express anger. A third identity, Jane, helped resolve the difficulties that arose between Eve White and Eve Black. The case study approach is a valuable tool that produces rich data, but it is subjective and cannot be confirmed through replication.

❖ MPD may be underdiagnosed because of a failure to distinguish between MPD and, for example, schizophrenia, which can have similar symptoms. Alternatively, MPD may be overdiagnosed either because patients aren't genuine (such as in the case of the Hillside Strangler, Kenneth Bianchi) or due to unwitting encouragement by therapists (iatrogenesis, such as in the case of Sybil). Patients who are hypnotised and peripherally aware of MPD may respond to suggestion by "producing" separate identities.

❖ Explanations of MPD include the psychodynamic model, which suggests that an inability to repress anxiety may cause dissociation, and this is an adaptive response to traumatic events.

❖ According to the behavioural model MPD sufferers cope with early traumas by blocking emotional thoughts, which is reinforcing. Alternatively selective reinforcement in different situations leads to distinct behavioural clusters that are misinterpreted by a therapist.

❖ State-dependent learning can also explain situation-specific identities that emerge given contextual cues.

❖ A further possibility is that MPD patients are able to self-hypnotise; the characteristics of MPD fit in with the neo-dissociation theory of hypnosis, and the evidence that hypnotised individuals can access forgotten memories and ignore pain further supports the self-hypnosis explanation.

❖ Concepts such as the hidden observer phenomenon and amnesiac barriers also fit in with MPD.

❖ It may be, on the other hand, that MPD (like hypnosis) is a social construction, or at least this may explain some cases of MPD.

❖ Finally, there may even be a biological basis for MPD, as suggested by double-brain theory.

Culture-bound Syndromes

❖ CBSs are locality-specific patterns of aberrant behaviour. Examples include koro, found mainly but not exclusively in Asia, where individuals experience anxiety related to shrinkage of genitalia; and amok, again found in Asia and concerning episodes of murderous behaviour. The same symptoms may not be described as amok in Western culture. Dhat is a fear of semen in the urine but may be fundamentally a form of depression. The eating disorder anorexia nervosa is primarily restricted to Western culture, and symptoms of schizophrenia are related to historical context.

❖ The evidence suggests that culturally relative symptoms are simply local expressions of universal disorders rather than being locality-specific disorders. There is both cultural universality (underlying *syndromes* are universal) and cultural relativism (the *symptoms* are at least partly determined by cultural norms). Many disorders, including schizophrenia, are found in all cultures. The incidence of schizophrenia is fairly constant world-wide and in many countries there are common symptoms, though there are also some differences in the symptoms expressed and variation in the incidence of different types of schizophrenia. Differences might be explained by the suppression–facilitation model, which suggests that some cultures suppress certain behaviours, whereas other cultures encourage their expression. Differences might also be explained by misdiagnosis or differential diagnosis due to cultural relativism in symptoms that are not recognised by classificatory systems. It may be possible to reduce such cultural bias in diagnosis.

❖ Wider cultural issues in the classification and diagnosis of psychological abnormality include a consideration of sub-cultural differences. Gender bias is suggested by the fact that certain disorders are more common in women (eating disorders and depression) whereas other disorders are more common in men (alcohol abuse and anti-social conduct). Some gender differences are genuine, whereas others reflect various gender biases due to a disregard of the environmental context, differential diagnosis on the basis of gender because of traditional sex-role stereotypes, therapist misjudgement, and theoretical orientation of the therapist. Research evidence suggests a strong bias from traditional sex-role stereotypes that in turn leads to biased diagnoses. It may even be that classification schemes are based on conceptions of health and normality in men and thus discriminate unfairly against women. Finally, suppression–facilitation may explain why fewer men present with symptoms of certain disorders.

❖ Social class bias is evidenced by higher rates of mental disorder in lower occupational groups. This may be due to less effective assistance from clinicians or because higher social class is related to better coping strategies and better financial resources.

❖ Schizophrenia is a disorder that is more prevalent in lower classes. This could be because the diagnosis of schizophrenia is less readily made with middle-class patients, or it could be a consequence of social causation (lower-class living conditions are more stressful), or social drift (schizophrenics lose jobs and become lower class). The fact that schizophrenia occurs at about the same rate across different countries argues against the social causation hypothesis.

FURTHER READING

The topics in this Section are covered in greater depth by S. Cave (2001) *Classification and diagnosis of psychological abnormality* (London: Routledge), written specifically for the AQA A specification. General textbooks on abnormal psychology will provide useful material, such as P.C. Kendall and C. Hammen (1998) *Abnormal psychology (2nd Edn.)* (Boston: Houghton Mifflin), and D.H. Barlow and V.M. Durand (1995) *Abnormal psychology: An integrative approach* (New York: Brooks/Cole). A classic text, now out of print, is R.C. Simons and C.C. Hughes (Eds) (1985) *The culture-bound syndromes: Folk illnesses of psychiatric and anthropological interest* (Dordrecht, The Netherlands: D. Reidel). Further material on culture-bound syndromes can be found in P.M. Yap (1974) *Comparative psychiatry* (Toronto: University of Toronto Press). There are interesting accounts of the cases of Eve and Sybil in C.H. Thigpen, and H. Cleckley (1957) *The three faces of Eve* (New York: McGraw-Hill), in R. Gross (1999) *Key studies in psychology (3rd Edn.)* (London: Hodder & Stoughton), and F.R. Schreiber (1975) *Sybil* (London: Penguin). You can also read about another case of multiple personality disorder in D. Keyes (1995) *The minds of Billy Milligan* (Bantam Books).

Example Examination Questions

You should spend 40 minutes on each of the questions below, which aim to test the material in this Section. Unlike questions from Unit 4 of the examination, covered in Parts 1–5 of this book, the questions in the Individual Differences section of the Unit 5 examination, covered in this Part, are marked out of 30 and an additional criterion is used in assessment: synopticity. "Synopticity" is defined as your "understanding and critical appreciation of the breadth and range of different theoretical perspectives and/or methodological approaches relevant to any questions" (AQA specification).

1. (a) Outline the current version of DSM. (15 marks)
   (b) Critically assess the validity of this classification scheme. (15 marks)

2. Distinguish between current versions of DSM and ICD as alternative approaches to the classification of psychological abnormality. (30 marks)

3. (a) Describe **two or more** case studies of multiple personality disorder (dissociative identity disorder). (15 marks)
   (b) Assess the value of these and/or other case studies in terms of the insights they provide into multiple personality disorder. (15 marks)

4. Discuss the extent to which multiple personality disorder (dissociative identity disorder) is a spontaneous or iatrogenic (manufactured by the therapist) phenomenon. (30 marks)

5. Describe and evaluate arguments for and against the existence of culture-bound syndromes. (30 marks)

6. "DSM-IV identifies the existence of mental disorders that are locality-specific patterns of aberrant behaviour and which may not be linked to other diagnostic categories in DSM-IV."

   Discuss the problems raised by culture-bound syndromes for the classification and diagnosis of psychological abnormality. (30 marks)

Examination Tips

Question 1.   The injunction "outline" is used to signal the fact that less detail is required and more attention to breadth. The key to high marks is attempting to provide more than just a list of the DSM categories, and instead provide more of an overview of how the system works. In part (b) you should present the strengths and weaknesses of the classification scheme in terms of its validity (or "trueness"). An unreliable classification scheme is not valid and therefore reliability can be assessed as well.

Question 2.   "Distinguish between" is an AO1 and AO2 term requiring you to describe the two classification schemes, and then identify those features that are similar and those that are different. Any other form of evaluation will not be creditworthy in this question except if it enables us to see the differences between the two schemes.

Question 3.   In Unit 5 you have more time to write your answers but you also must ensure that you include synoptic material. In order to do this the questions must provide opportunities for making links across the specification. Thus, in the first part of this question, you are given the opportunity to cover as many studies as you wish in order to achieve synopticity in AO1 (for example using case studies that focus on different aspects of the problem or which use rather different approaches to studying the case). In part (b) you are required to assess the value of these studies by considering what they tell us about MPD. You might consider what light they shed on the spontaneous vs. iatrogenic debate, or consider what other insights the case studies have provided. You could further consider their value in methodological terms.

Question 4.   You must both describe and evaluate the extent to which MPD is spontaneous or iatrogenic. This will involve an explanation of both positions, which may be enhanced with examples and case studies. The case studies may additionally be used for evaluation by saying "This shows that …". You must ensure that you cover both description and evaluation in this essay to access the full marks available.

Question 5.   The backbone of this essay will be your arguments for and against the existence of culture-bound syndromes. Research studies can be used to illustrate and/or evaluate the arguments but the question does not ask you describe what you know about culture-bound syndromes or case studies of the same. The focus is on whether or not they exist. As this essay is assessed in terms of synopticity it is important that you try to refer to various perspectives, issues, and debates, and make links across the specification.

Question 6.   You are not required to refer to the quotation in your answer but it is there to suggest ways of answering the question. Culture-bound syndromes are included in this part of the specification precisely because of the issues they raise for classification and diagnosis. This question ties together several parts of this Section. Can we accept the existence of culture-bound syndromes? And then, if we do accept that they exist, what are the implications for diagnosis and treatment?

WEB SITES

http://www.mentalhealth.com/
   Major site with lots of information about disorders, diagnosis, and treatments, as well as numerous links to other sites.

http://mentalhelp.net/disorders/dsmcodes.htm
   A list of DSM-IV codes.

http://www.psych.org/clin_res/q_a.cfm
   Questions and answers about DSM-IV on the American Psychiatric Association website.

WEB SITES *continued*

http://www.who.int/whosis/icd10/
Information on the ICD-10, on the World Health Organisation's official homepage.

http://www.garysturt.free-online.co.uk/rosenhan.htm
Notes on "On being sane in insane places" by Rosenhan.

http://www.antipsychiatry.org/
The anti-psychiatry viewpoint.

http://www.dissociation.com/
All about Multiple Personality Disorder and how it differs from Dissociative Identity Disorder.

http://www.crimelibrary.com/serials/hillside/hillmain.htm
Summary of the case of Kenneth Bianchi, the Hillside Strangler.

http://www.issd.org/
Designed for mental health professionals, this organisation is devoted to research, training, and treatment of dissociative disorders.

http://www.dmoz.org/Health/Mental_Health/Disorders/
Multiple_Personality/
Multiple Personality Disorder links.

http://www.nami.org/
NAMI: "Nation's Voice on Mental Illness".

http://weber.ucsd.edu/~thall/cbs_intro.html
Introduction to culture-bound syndromes.

http://weber.ucsd.edu/~thall/cbs_frame.html
Glossary of culture-bound syndromes.

http://weber.ucsd.edu/~thall/cbs_koro.html
Description of "koro", a culture-bound syndrome of south and east Asia.

http://www.bangladeshinfo.com/doctor/doctor_sexmyth2.php3
Questions and answers about dhat syndrome.

http://www.arts.uwaterloo.ca/~acheyne/S_P.html
Sleep paralysis page, with numerous interesting links.

http://www.sleepdisorders.about.com/health/sleepdisorders/library/weekly/
aa042099.htm
The terror of sleep paralysis, with links.

http://www.schizophrenia.com/
Schizophrenia information and links.

http://peabody.vanderbilt.edu/depts/psych_and_hd/faculty/WeissB/
WeissB.html
Notes on the suppression–facilitation model.

www.a-levelpsychology.co.uk/websites.html
A continually updated list of useful links, including those printed in this book, may be found at the Psychology Press A level psychology site.

17

Psychopathology

What is **psychopathology**? According to Davison and Neale (1996), it is "the field concerned with the nature and development of mental disorders" (p.G–20). Psychopathology is the subject matter of this Section.

Schizophrenia

Causes of Mental Disorder

One of the key issues in abnormal psychology is to understand *why* some people suffer from psychological disorders such as depression or schizophrenia. When considering the causes of a mental disorder, it is helpful to start by distinguishing between two categories of factors:

1. *Biological factors*, as used by the **medical model**, for example:
   * *Genetic factors*: twin studies, family studies, and adoption studies may indicate that some people are genetically more vulnerable than others to developing a disorder.
   * *Brain biochemistry*: individuals with unusually high or low levels of certain brain chemicals may be vulnerable to psychological disorders.
   * *Evolutionary explanations*: a relatively recent approach to the causation of mental disorder has used the principles of evolution as a basis for explanation. Such explanations are considered in detail in Section 15, Evolutionary Explanations of Human Behaviour.

2. *Psychological factors*, as used by **behavioural**, **cognitive**, **humanistic**, and **psychodynamic models**, for example:
   * *Cultural factors*: cultural values and expectations may be important in causing some disorders; for example, most Western cultures emphasise the desirability of thinness in women, and this may help to trigger eating disorders.
   * *Social factors*: individuals who experience severe life events (e.g., divorce, unemployment) may be at risk for various psychological disorders, as may those who lack social support or belong to poorly functioning families.
   * *Experiential factors*: interactions with the environment result in learning or conditioning, which may explain some mental disorders such as phobias.

These factors *interact*. For example, someone may have a very high or a very low level of a given brain chemical because of genetic factors or because he or she has recently experienced a severe life event. Another example concerns the impact of cultural

expectations on eating disorders. This is clearly not the *only* factor causing eating disorders because the overwhelming majority of women in Western societies do not suffer from eating disorders. Eating disorders occur in individuals who are exposed to cultural expectations of thinness *and* who are vulnerable (e.g., because of genetic factors).

The multi-dimensional approach

The description of causal factors raises the questions of whether a disorder is caused by a single factor or many of them. According to one-dimensional models, the origins of a psychological disorder can be traced to a single underlying cause. For example, it might be argued that severe depression is caused by a major loss (e.g., death of a loved one), or that schizophrenia is caused by genetic factors. One-dimensional models are now regarded as greatly oversimplified. They have been replaced by multi-dimensional models, in which it is recognised that abnormal behaviour is typically caused by several different factors.

The multi-dimensional approach to psychopathology is often expressed in the form of the **diathesis–stress model**. According to this model, the occurrence of psychological disorders depends on two factors:

1. *Diathesis*: a genetic vulnerability or predisposition to disease or disorder.
2. *Stress*: some severe or disturbing environmental event. Note that the term "stress" is used in a very broad sense and might include, for example, drug-taking or any event that places an extra burden on the individual psychologically and/or physically.

Can you relate the diathesis–stress model to the dichotomy of nature and nurture?

The key notion in the diathesis–stress model is that both diathesis or genetic vulnerability *and* stress are necessary for a psychological disorder to occur.

Clinical Characteristics of Schizophrenia

Schizophrenia is a very serious condition. The term schizophrenia comes from two Greek words: *schizo* meaning "split" and *phren* meaning "mind". On average, the rates of schizophrenia during the course of a person's life are about 1% of the population (see page 430). The symptoms exhibited vary somewhat, but typically include problems with attention, thinking, social relationships, motivation, and emotion. According to DSM-IV (the *Diagnostic and Statistical Manual, Volume 4*), the criteria for schizophrenia include:

1. Two or more of the following symptoms, each of which must have been present for a significant period of time over a 1-month period: delusions, hallucinations, disorganised speech, grossly disorganised or catatonic (rigid) behaviour; and negative symptoms (lack of emotion, lack of motivation, speaking very little or uninformatively); only one symptom is needed if the delusions are bizarre, or if the hallucinations consist of a voice commenting on the individual's behaviour.
2. Continuous signs of disturbance over a period of at least 6 months.
3. Social and/or occupational dysfunction or poor functioning.

Schizophrenics generally have confused thinking, and often suffer from delusions. Many of these delusions involve what are known as "ideas of reference", in which the schizophrenic patient attaches great personal significance to external objects or events. Thus, for example, a schizophrenic seeing his neighbours talking may be convinced that they are plotting to kill him.

Schizophrenics often suffer from hallucinations. Delusions arise from mistaken interpretations of actual objects and events, but hallucinations occur in the absence of any external stimulus. Most schizophrenic hallucinations consist of voices, usually saying something of personal relevance to the patient. McGuigan (1966) suggested that these auditory hallucinations occur because patients mistake their own inner speech for someone else's voice. He found that the patient's larynx was often active during the time

Schizophrenics often suffer from delusions, misinterpreting ordinary events, such as conversations between other people, as being about themselves.

hat the auditory hallucination was being experienced. More recent studies have confirmed this explanation of hallucinations (Frith, 1992).

Language impairments characterise schizophrenia. Patients may repeat sounds (echolalia) or use invented words (neologisms). Their speech may seem illogical and involve abrupt shifts from one theme to another. This is described as "knight's move thinking" because, in chess, the knight is only permitted to move in an L-shape (for example, two squares forward and one to the right). In some cases the patient's speech can be so jumbled that it is described as "word salad". The impairment of language has led some theorists to suggest that there is a link between the evolution of language in humans and schizophrenia—that schizophrenia is the price we pay for having language (see the box on page 632).

Finally, there are some schizophrenics whose behaviour is even more bizarre. One of the most common behavioural abnormalities is to remain almost motionless for hours at a time. Some patients make strange grimaces or repeat an odd gesture over and over again.

There are positive and negative symptoms. Positive symptoms include delusions, hallucinations, and bizarre forms of behaviour. Negative symptoms include an absence of emotion and motivation, language deficits, general apathy, and an avoidance of social activity.

About one-third of patients have a single episode or a few brief episodes of schizophrenia and then recover fully. A further one-third have occasional episodes of the disorder throughout their lives and, in between these, they are able to function reasonably effectively. The remaining third deteriorate over a series of episodes, each of which becomes progressively more incapacitating. Those patients for whom schizophrenia comes on suddenly tend to have a better prognosis, and the same is true for patients where the positive symptoms predominate.

Types of schizophrenia

According to DSM-IV, there are five main types of schizophrenia:

- *Disorganised schizophrenia*: this type involves great disorganisation, including delusions, hallucinations, incoherent speech, and large mood swings.
- *Catatonic schizophrenia*: the main feature is almost total immobility for hours at a time, with the patient simply staring blankly.
- *Paranoid schizophrenia*: this type involves delusions of various kinds.
- *Undifferentiated schizophrenia*: this is a broad category which includes patients who do not clearly belong within any other category.
- *Residual schizophrenia*: this type consists of patients who are only experiencing mild symptoms.

Biological Explanation: Genetic Factors

Twin studies

Schizophrenia depends in part on genetic factors. Much of the relevant evidence comes from the study of twins, one of whom is known to be schizophrenic. Researchers want to establish the probability that the other twin is also schizophrenic—a state of affairs known as **concordance**. Gottesman (1991) summarised about 40 studies. The concordance rate is about 48% if you have a monozygotic or identical twin with schizophrenia, but only 17% if you have a dizygotic or fraternal twin with schizophrenia.

What clinical characteristics of schizophrenia can be seen in this Case Study of WG?

CASE STUDY: *A Schizophrenic*

A young man of 19 (WG) was admitted to the psychiatric services on the grounds of a dramatic change in character. His parents described him as always being extremely shy with no close friends, but in the last few months he had gone from being an average-performing student to failing his studies and leaving college. Having excelled in non-team sports such as swimming and athletics, he was now taking no exercise at all. WG had seldom mentioned health matters, but now complained of problems with his head and chest. After being admitted, WG spent most of his time staring out of the window, and uncharacteristically not taking care over his appearance. Staff found it difficult to converse with him and he offered no information about himself, making an ordinary diagnostic interview impossible. WG would usually answer direct questions, but in a flat emotionless tone. Sometimes his answers were not even connected to the question, and staff would find themselves wondering what the conversation had been about. There were also occasions when there was a complete mismatch between WG's emotional expression and the words he spoke. For example, he giggled continuously when speaking about a serious illness that had left his mother bedridden. On one occasion, WG became very agitated and spoke of "electrical sensations" in his brain. At other times he spoke of being influenced by a force outside himself, which took the form of a voice urging him to commit acts of violence against his parents. He claimed that the voice repeated the command "You'll have to do it". (Adapted from Hofling, 1974.)

Some of the most striking support for genetic factors was reported by Rosenthal (1963). He studied quadruplets, in which all four girls were identical to each other. Amazingly, all four of them developed schizophrenia, although they did differ somewhat in age of onset and the precise symptoms. They were known as the Genain (dreadful genes) quadruplets. It may be worth noting that they did also have a dreadful and aberrant childhood so, as with most evidence, the conclusion is not clear cut.

Evaluation

There is strong evidence of genetic factors in schizophrenia from the studies of twins. It is worth noting that the concordance rates are not 100% and therefore even this data does not exclude environmental input.

The high concordance rates in monozygotic twins may be explained by the fact that they tend to be treated more similarly than dizygotic twins (Loehlin & Nichols, 1976),

Identical (monozygotic) twins are not only genetically identical; they are also more likely to be treated identically by their family.

and this greater environmental similarity, rather than genetic similarity, may be responsible for the higher level of concordance than in dizygotic twins.

There are two arguments against this view. First, monozygotic twins *elicit* more similar treatment from their parents than do dizygotic twins (Lytton, 1977). This suggests that the greater genetic similarity of identical twins may be a cause, rather than an effect, of their more similar parental treatment. Second, schizophrenia concordance rates for monozygotic twins brought up apart are similar to those for monozygotic twins brought up together (Shields, 1962). The high concordance rate for monozygotic twins brought up apart is presumably not due to a high level of environmental similarity, although critics (e.g., Kamin, 1977) have suggested that some of the reared apart twins in Shields' study had not always spent the whole of their childhood apart and some were raised by relatives and even went to the same school.

Family studies

Gottesman (1991) reviewed other concordance rates. If both your parents have schizophrenia, then you have a 46% chance of developing schizophrenia as well. The concordance rate is 16% if one of your parents has schizophrenia, and it is 8% if a sibling has schizophrenia. These concordance rates should be compared against the 1% probability of someone selected at random suffering from schizophrenia.

Finally, Gottesman and Bertelsen (1989) reported some convincing findings on the importance of genetic factors. One of their findings was that their participants had a 17% chance of being schizophrenic if they had a parent who was an identical twin and who had schizophrenia. This could be due to either heredity or environment. However, they also studied participants with a parent who was an identical twin and did not have schizophrenia, but whose identical twin did. These participants also had a 17% chance

Research by Gottesman (1991) indicates that schizophrenia tends to run in families.

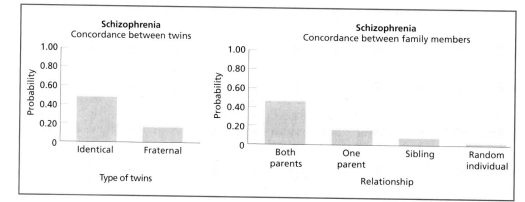

of being schizophrenic. In other words, what is of most importance is the genes that are handed on by the parents.

Evaluation

The evidence reported by Gottesman indicates clearly that schizophrenia runs in families. Furthermore, as predicted by the genetic hypothesis, the concordance rate is much higher between relatives having high genetic similarity. However, the fact that family members who are more similar genetically tend to spend more time together means that environmental factors are also indicated in this evidence.

What are the limitations of twin and family studies of schizophrenia?

Adoption studies

The notion that genetic factors are important in producing schizophrenia is supported by adoption studies. One approach is to look at adopted children, one of whose parents has schizophrenia. Tienari (1991) did this in Finland. He managed to find 155 schizophrenic mothers who had given up their children for adoption, and they were compared against 155 adopted children not having a schizophrenic parent. There was a large difference in the incidence of schizophrenia in these two groups when they were adults: 10.3% of those with schizophrenic mothers had developed schizophrenia compared with only 1.1% of those without schizophrenic mothers.

Kety et al. (1978) considered adults who had been adopted at an early age between 1924 and 1947. Half had been diagnosed as suffering from schizophrenia and the other half had not. The two groups were matched on variables such as sex and age. The rate of schizophrenia was greater among the *biological* relatives of those with schizophrenia than those without, which is as expected if genetic factors are important. The rate of schizophrenia did not differ for *adoptive* families that had adopted a child who became, or did not become, schizophrenic. This suggests that environmental factors had little impact on the development of schizophrenia.

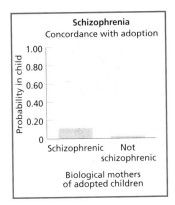

Evaluation

Although Kety et al.'s findings appear to support the importance of genetic factors in schizophrenia, it is worth noting that these statistics were gathered from a time-span of over 70 years. Earlier interpretations of symptoms were different from today, and probably less uniform.

Biological Explanation: Brain Biochemistry

Genetic factors may lead to differences in brain chemistry, so that it is the brain chemistry that is the immediate causal factor. Biochemical abnormalities may be important in the development and maintenance of schizophrenia. For example, schizophrenia may result in part from excess levels of the neurotransmitter dopamine (Seidman, 1983). A slightly different view is that neurons in the brains of schizophrenic patients are oversensitive to dopamine.

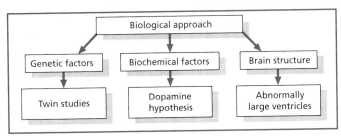

The dopamine hypothesis

Various kinds of evidence suggest that dopamine plays a role in schizophrenia. For example, neuroleptic drugs that block dopamine seem to reduce the symptoms of schizophrenia. The **phenothiazines** are neuroleptic drugs that block dopamine at the synapse (i.e., the juncture between the axon of one neuron and the dendrite of another neuron). The phenothiazines typically reduce many of the symptoms of schizophrenia (Davison & Neale, 1996). However, they have more effect on positive symptoms such as delusions and hallucinations than on negative symptoms such as apathy and immobility.

Other evidence supports the notion that dopamine is involved in schizophrenia. For example, the drug L-dopa, which increases dopamine levels, can produce many of the symptoms of schizophrenia (Davidson et al., 1987). In similar fashion, the symptoms of schizophrenic patients often become worse when they are given amphetamine, which activates dopamine (van Kammen, Docherty, & Bunney, 1982).

Findings from patients suffering from Parkinson's disease are of relevance. Low levels of dopamine are found in Parkinson's patients, and the symptoms of the disease include uncontrolled movements of the limbs. Similar uncontrolled movements are found in schizophrenics given neuroleptic drugs, presumably because these drugs reduce dopamine levels.

Problems with the dopamine hypothesis

As Barlow and Durand (1995) pointed out, there are some problems with the dopamine hypothesis. Neuroleptic drugs block dopamine fairly rapidly, but generally fail to reduce the symptoms of schizophrenia for days or weeks thereafter. This is puzzling if high levels of dopamine are responsible for maintaining the symptoms. What is also puzzling from the perspective of the dopamine hypothesis is that the fairly new drug clozapine is frequently more effective than the neuroleptics in reducing schizophrenic symptoms (Kane et al., 1988). Clozapine blocks dopamine activity less than the neuroleptics, and so it should be less effective according to the dopamine hypothesis.

How can we explain the effectiveness of clozapine? According to Barlow and Durand (1995), there is growing support for the view that two neurotransmitters, dopamine and serotonin, both play a role in producing the symptoms of schizophrenia. Clozapine blocks both of these neurotransmitters, which is not the case with the neuroleptics.

Does the evidence indicate whether schizophrenics might have excess dopamine (or serotonin), or are just more sensitive to it?

The evidence on the relationship between schizophrenia and dopamine levels is mostly correlational in nature. As a result, we do not know whether the changed dopamine activity in schizophrenics occurs *before* or *after* the onset of the disorder. If it occurs after, then clearly dopamine plays no part in causing schizophrenic symptoms.

Biological Explanation: Brain Structure

Could you use this knowledge to diagnose schizophrenia? How reliable would the diagnosis be?

There are several sophisticated techniques for studying the brain (see Section 4, Brain and Behaviour), some of which have been used to study brain structure in schizophrenics. Pahl, Swayze, and Andreasen (1990) reviewed almost 50 studies, the great majority of which found abnormally large lateral ventricles (liquid-filled cavities) in the brains of schizophrenics. Further evidence of the involvement of the ventricles was reported by Suddath et al. (1990). They used magnetic resonance imaging (MRI) to obtain pictures of brain structure from monozygotic or identical twin pairs in which only one twin had schizophrenia. The schizophrenic twin generally had more enlarged ventricles and reduced anterior hypothalamus. Indeed, the differences were so large that the schizophrenic twin could be identified readily from the brain images in 12 out of 15 twin pairs.

Other parts of the brain may also be involved. Buchsbaum et al. (1984) used PET scans with schizophrenics and normals. The schizophrenics had lower metabolic rates than the normals in the prefrontal cortex while performing psychological tests.

Evaluation

The extent to which the brain abnormalities in schizophrenic patients are due to genetic factors is not clear. However, Suddath et al.'s (1990) finding that there were clear differences in brain structure between schizophrenics and their non-schizophrenic identical twins suggests that environmental factors must be of importance.

Biological explanation: The evolutionary approach

Several intriguing evolutionary explanations have been suggested for schizophrenia. These are discussed in greater detail in Section 15, Evolutionary Explanations of Human Behaviour.

In essence the evolutionary view is that schizophrenia is at least in part genetic and the gene for schizophrenia must offer some advantage in order to explain why it has remained in the gene pool.

One possibility is the **group-splitting hypothesis** (Stevens & Price, 1996). The personality characteristics of the schizophrenic include bizarre beliefs, hallucinations, delusions, and strange speech. A "crazy" individual may act as a leader and enable one subgroup to split off from a main group, a valuable function at times when the main group has become too large to be optimum.

A second explanation has been advanced in relation to the origin of language. Crow (2000) has suggested that schizophrenia is the price that humans pay for language. He points out that schizophrenia involves a breakdown in the brain's internal linguistic controls. Schizophrenics often believe they are hearing voices and/or may use atypical language. Thus schizophrenia is an outcome of linguistic ability, when the processor goes wrong.

Psychological Explanation: Psychodynamic Approach

Freud was mainly interested in the neuroses, such as anxiety and depression. He assumed that neuroses occurred as a result of severe conflicts and traumatic experiences. Information about these conflicts and traumas is stored in the unconscious mind, and treatment involves trying to resolve these internal conflicts. See Section 11, Social and Personality Development, for a discussion of Freud's personality theory.

Freud argued that conflicts and traumas are also of importance in schizophrenia. However, an important difference is that schizophrenics have regressed or returned to an earlier stage of psychosexual development whereas this is not true for anxious or depressed patients. More specifically, they have regressed to a state of primary narcissism (or great self-interest), which occurs early in the oral stage. In this state, the ego or rational part of the mind has not separated from the id or sexual instinct. The importance of this is that the ego is involved in reality testing and responding appropriately to the external world. Schizophrenics have a loss of contact with reality because their ego is no longer functioning properly.

Freud argued that schizophrenics were driven by strong sexual impulses. That helps to explain why schizophrenia often develops in late adolescence. Later psychodynamic theorists tended to be unconvinced about the involvement of sexual impulses, preferring to emphasise the role of aggression in schizophrenia.

Is it possible that patients diagnosed as schizophrenic by Freud may have had different characteristics to patients today?

Evaluation

The psychodynamic approach to schizophrenia is limited for several reasons. First, it is very speculative, and is not supported by much evidence. Second, the notion that adult schizophrenics resemble infants in many ways is not very sensible. Third, the psychodynamic approach ignores the role of genetic factors in the development of schizophrenia. The psychodynamic approach is evaluated more generally on pages 766–767.

Psychological Explanation: Behavioural Approach

According to the behavioural approach, learning plays a key role in causing schizophrenia. Early experience of punishment may lead children to retreat into a rewarding inner world. This causes others to label them as "odd" or "peculiar". According to Scheff's (1966) labelling theory, individuals who have been labelled in this way may continue to act in ways that conform to the label. Their bizarre behaviour may be rewarded with attention and sympathy for behaving bizarrely; this is known as secondary gain. This bizarre behaviour becomes more and more exaggerated, and eventually is labelled as schizophrenia.

Evaluation

The fact that schizophrenics often respond to reinforcement when used in therapy provides modest support for the behavioural approach. For example, schizophrenics have learned to make their own beds and to comb their hair when rewarded for doing so (Ayllon & Azrin, 1968). However, the behavioural approach ignores the genetic evidence and it trivialises a very serious disorder, as is shown in the following anecdote. The schizophrenia expert Paul Meehl was giving a lecture, when a member of the audience interrupted and argued in favour of labelling theory. Meehl states: "I was thinking of a patient … who kept his finger up his arse to 'keep his thoughts from running out', while with his other hand he tried to tear out his hair because it really 'belonged to his father'. And here was this man telling me that he was doing these things because someone had called him a schizophrenic" (Kimble et al., 1980, p.453).

The behavioural approach is evaluated more generally on pages 762–763.

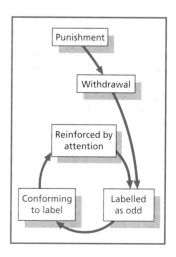

Constant reinforcement for odd or bizarre behaviour may cause a continuous cycle.

Psychological Explanation: Social Factors

To what extent do you think that it is important to relate the different types of schizophrenia to the different explanations?

If schizophrenia was determined entirely by genetic factors, then the concordance rate for monozygotic or identical twins would be close to 100%. As it is actually under 50%, it is probable that several social or environmental factors contribute to the development of schizophrenia.

Interpersonal communication

Some theorists have argued that there are abnormal and inadequate patterns of communication within the families of schizophrenic patients. Bateson et al. (1956) put forward a **double-bind theory**, according to which the members of families of schizophrenics communicate in a destructively ambiguous fashion. For example, the mother will tell her child that she loves him, but in a tone of voice that does not indicate love. The double-bind theory accounts in part for the confused thinking of schizophrenic patients. However, it suffers from the serious problem that there is very little evidence supporting it.

The families of schizophrenics tend to have inadequate interpersonal communication. Mischler and Waxler (1968) found that mothers talking to their schizophrenic daughters were rather aloof and unresponsive. However, the same mothers behaved in a much more normal and responsive way when talking to their normal daughters. Thus, the presence of a schizophrenic patient in the family may cause poor communication patterns rather than the other way around.

Expressed emotion

In spite of the lack of support for double-bind theory, there is evidence that the interactions within families can play a key role in maintaining the symptoms of individuals who are already suffering from schizophrenia. What seems to be important is the extent to which a family engages in **expressed emotion**, which involves criticism, hostility, and emotional over-involvement. Individuals who have suffered from schizophrenia and who live in families with high expressed emotion are nearly four times as likely to relapse compared with those who live in families with low expressed emotion (Kavanagh, 1992).

The direction of causality is not clear in studies of expressed emotion. One possibility is that expressed emotion within the family causes relapse. Another possibility is that individuals who are in poor psychological shape are more likely to provoke expressed emotion from members of their family.

Other social factors

If one of your relatives has suffered from a mental disorder, what reasons are there for you not to worry that you may also develop the same disorder?

Other social factors may be important. Mednick and Schulsinger (1968) studied individuals between the ages of 15 and 25 with a schizophrenic mother. Those individuals were more likely to develop the negative symptoms of schizophrenia if there had been pregnancy and birth complications, and they were more likely to develop the positive symptoms if there was instability within the family.

The social causation hypothesis

Social factors are emphasised by the **social causation hypothesis** (see page 619). This hypothesis was designed to explain why it is that schizophrenics tend to belong to the lower social classes. According to this hypothesis, members of the lower social classes have more stressful lives than middle-class people, and this makes them more vulnerable to schizophrenia. The key issue here is whether belonging to the lower social classes makes individuals likely to develop schizophrenia, or whether developing schizophrenia leads to reduced social status, the **social drift hypothesis** described on page 620. There is some evidence that being in the lower social classes can precede the onset of schizophrenia.

Turner and Wagonfeld (1967) found that the fathers of schizophrenics tended to belong to the lower social classes.

Stress

Finally, stressful life events sometimes help to trigger the onset of schizophrenia. Day et al. (1987) carried out a study in several countries. They found that schizophrenics tended to have experienced a high number of stressful life events in the few weeks before the onset of schizophrenia.

Conclusion

The diathesis–stress model proposes that a complete explanation of any mental disorder is likely to involve both a predisposition to the disorder and a stressor which triggers the appearance of the symptoms. This can be seen to apply to schizophrenia where there is clear evidence of a genetic link, yet we have seen that not everyone who inherits the genetic component (as in identical twins) becomes schizophrenic. We can explain this in terms of the psychological factors that trigger the disorder, such as troubled families or stressful life events.

What are the practical applications of theories of schizophrenia?

The importance of understanding the causes of schizophrenia lies in the decision of what form of treatment is desirable. Biological explanations lead to biological methods of treatment and behavioural explanations to behavioural methods of treatment. The topic of treating mental disorders is examined in the next Section of this Part. In terms of schizophrenia, the most successful therapy has been chemotherapy, a biological approach. This does not offer a cure but provides relief for sufferers and, in the case of schizophrenics who may cause injury to others, protects the general public as long as such individuals continue to take their medication.

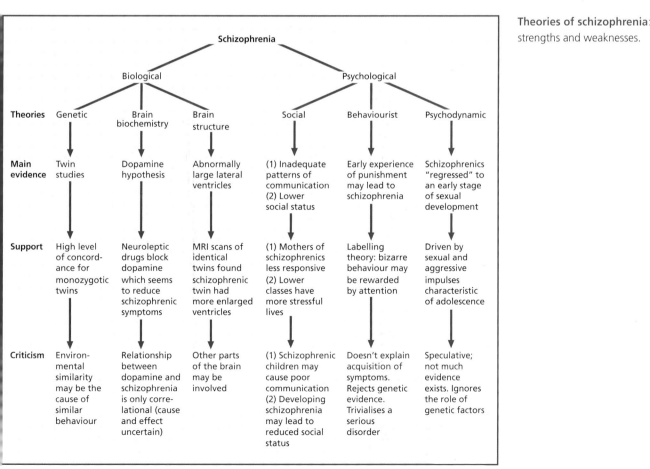

Theories of schizophrenia: strengths and weaknesses.

	Biological			Psychological		
Theories	Genetic	Brain biochemistry	Brain structure	Social	Behaviourist	Psychodynamic
Main evidence	Twin studies	Dopamine hypothesis	Abnormally large lateral ventricles	(1) Inadequate patterns of communication (2) Lower social status	Early experience of punishment may lead to schizophrenia	Schizophrenics "regressed" to an early stage of sexual development
Support	High level of concordance for monozygotic twins	Neuroleptic drugs block dopamine which seems to reduce schizophrenic symptoms	MRI scans of identical twins found schizophrenic twin had more enlarged ventricles	(1) Mothers of schizophrenics less responsive (2) Lower classes have more stressful lives	Labelling theory: bizarre behaviour may be rewarded by attention	Driven by sexual and aggressive impulses characteristic of adolescence
Criticism	Environmental similarity may be the cause of similar behaviour	Relationship between dopamine and schizophrenia is only correlational (cause and effect uncertain)	Other parts of the brain may be involved	(1) Schizophrenic children may cause poor communication (2) Developing schizophrenia may lead to reduced social status	Doesn't explain acquisition of symptoms. Rejects genetic evidence. Trivialises a serious disorder	Speculative; not much evidence exists. Ignores the role of genetic factors

Depression

Clinical Characteristics

Why do you think twice as many reported cases of depression involve women rather than men?

There is a key distinction between *major depression* (sometimes called unipolar depression) and *bipolar disorder* (also known as manic-depressive disorder). According to DSM-IV, the diagnosis of a major depressive episode requires that five symptoms occur nearly every day for a minimum of 2 weeks. These symptoms are as follows:

- *Emotional symptoms*: sad, depressed mood; loss of pleasure in usual activities.
- *Motivational symptoms*: changes in activity level; passivity; loss of interest and energy.
- *Somatic symptoms*: difficulties in sleeping (insomnia) or increased sleeping (hypersomnia); weight loss or gain; tiredness.
- *Cognitive symptoms*: negative self-concept, hopelessness, pessimism, lack of self-esteem, self-blame, and self-reproach; problems with concentration or the ability to think clearly; recurring thoughts of suicide or death.

Marilyn Monroe suffered with unipolar, or major, depression. Famous people who suffered with bipolar depression include Sir Winston Churchill, Abraham Lincoln, and Virginia Woolf.

Patients with bipolar depression experience both depression and mania (a mood state involving elation, talkativeness, and unjustified high self-esteem). About 10% of men and 20% of women become clinically depressed at some time in their lives. Over 90% of them suffer from unipolar rather than bipolar depression.

In addition to the distinction between unipolar and bipolar depression, there is also a distinction in unipolar depression between reactive and endogenous depression. **Reactive depression** is caused by some stressful event(s), such as the death of a close friend. The event triggers an episode of depression. **Endogenous depression** is caused from within the person, for instance it may be due to hormonal imbalances. Neither of these categories are represented in the classification schemes DSM and ICD (discussed in Section 16) but the distinction is an important one for understanding the causes of depression. Endogenous depression is linked to biological factors, whereas with reactive depression an individual may have a genetic predisposition to depression but it is psychological factors that are a primary cause.

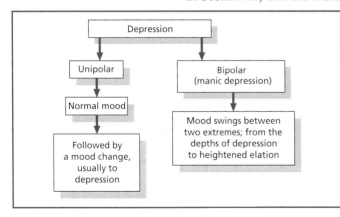

Biological Explanation: Genetic Factors

Family studies

Family studies suggest the involvement of genetic factors. Gershon (1990) presented the findings from numerous

---

CASE STUDY: *Manic Behaviour in Manic Depression*

Robert B had been a successful dentist for 25 years, providing well for his wife and family. One morning he woke up with the idea that he was the best dental surgeon in the world, and that he should try to treat as many people as possible. As a result, he set about enlarging his practice from 2 chairs to 20, planning to treat patients simultaneously. He phoned builders and ordered the necessary equipment. After a day of feeling irritable that there had been delays, he decided to do the work himself and began to knock down the walls. When this proved difficult, he became frustrated and began to smash his X-ray equipment and washbasins. Robert B's family were unaware of his behaviour until patients began to phone his wife after being turned away from the dental surgery. When she mentioned the phone calls to him, Robert B "ranted and raved" at her for 15 minutes. She described her husband as looking "haggard, wild-eyed and run down", and his speech was "over-excited". After several days of this behaviour, Mrs B phoned her daughters and asked them to come over with their husbands to help. On the evening of their visit Robert B began to "brag about his sexual prowess and make aggressive advances towards his daughters". When one of his sons-in-law tried to intervene he was attacked with a chair. Robert B was admitted to hospital, and subsequently it was found that he had had a history of such behaviour.

family studies in which depression was assessed in the first-degree relatives of patients with depression. For both major depression and bipolar disorder, the rates of depression were about two to three times the rates in the general population.

One particular study claimed to identify a gene that might be responsible. Egeland et al. (1987) studied the Amish, a small religious community living in Pennsylvania. The community has a relatively low incidence of major depressive illness, in comparison with the surrounding communities, but one family that was studied had an extremely high level of bipolar disorder. Eleven out of 81 members had manic depression. On examination of their genes it was found that two marker genes on chromosome 11 appeared to be different. Importantly, these genes were "neighbours" of those genes that are involved in the production of monoamines, a biochemical implicated in depression (see later).

The Amish people of Pennsylvania have a relatively high incidence of bipolar disorder. One study found that this predisposition may be carried on chromosome 11, but the finding has not been replicated.

Evaluation

Gene-mapping studies are very attractive but in this case subsequent attempts to support Egeland et al.'s findings have not been successful. For example, Hodgkinson (1987) studied extended families in Iceland and found no evidence of the different genes in relation to manic depression. It is possible that, in family groups, other factors such as patterns of interaction, may account for depressive illness.

Adoption studies

Additional evidence supporting the notion that genetic factors are of importance comes from adoption studies. Wender et al. (1986) found that the biological relatives of adopted sufferers from major depression were about eight times more likely than adoptive relatives to have had major depression themselves. In similar fashion, it has been found with adopted children who later developed depression that their biological parents were eight times as likely as their adoptive parents to have suffered from clinical depression (Wender et al., 1986).

Twin studies

The clearest evidence about the role of genetic factors in the development of major depression and bipolar depression comes from studies on monozygotic and dizygotic twins. Allen (1976) reviewed the relevant studies. For major depression, the mean concordance rate was 40% for monozygotic or identical twins, whereas it was only 11% for dizygotic twins. For bipolar disorder, the mean concordance rate was 72% for monozygotic twins, compared with 14% for dizygotic twins. Similar findings were reported in a large study by Bertelsen, Harvald, and Hauge (1977). They found a concordance rate for major depression of 59% for monozygotic twins and of 30% for dizygotic twins. For bipolar disorder, the concordance rate was 80% for identical twins and 16% for fraternal twins. In the population at large, about 5% have been diagnosed with major depression and 1% with bipolar disorder, and all of the figures for monozygotic and dizygotic twins are much higher.

These findings suggest that genetic factors are involved in both types of depression, and that their involvement is greater for bipolar than for major depression. However, it is not known whether the monozygotic and dizygotic twin pairs experienced equally similar environments. As a result, it is possible that some of the higher concordance rate for monozygotic than for dizygotic twins reflects environmental rather than genetic influences.

The APA A specifications include unipolar (major) depression only. How might you use information about bipolar disorder?

Is the evidence of genetic factors in depression stronger or weaker than in schizophrenia?

Biological Explanation: Brain Biochemistry

What role was suggested for dopamine and serotonin in relation to schizophrenia.

There has been much interest in the possibility that depressed patients might have either elevated or reduced levels of various neurotransmitters. Numerous theories have been put forward in this area, many of them based on the notion that low levels of the neurotransmitters noradrenaline and serotonin may play a role in the development of depression. It has also been suggested that there may be increased levels of these neurotransmitters when bipolar disorder patients are in their manic phase.

The permissive amine theory

Kety (1975) put forward a **permissive amine theory** of mood disorder. According to this theory, the level of noradrenaline is generally controlled by the level of serotonin. When the level of serotonin is low, however, noradrenaline levels are less controlled, and so they may fluctuate wildly. A third neurotransmitter, dopamine, is also involved.

Noradrenaline, serotonin, and dopamine are all neurotransmitters of the monoamine (catecholamine) group, which explains the name "permissive amine" theory. **Neurotransmitters** act at the synapses, or junctions, between neurons in the brain. They may either facilitate or block nervous transmission. Noradrenaline is associated with physiological arousal in general, a fact you may recall from your studies of stress at AS level. Serotonin is also related to arousal and sleep; increases in serotonin generally reduce arousal. Dopamine is normally inhibited by serotonin and has been linked with schizophrenia (see page 631). Under normal conditions all three neurotransmitters play a role in arousal and also are related to mood.

It is suggested that, in depression, serotonin levels are low as a consequence of individual differences that are inherited, and the abnormal serotonin level prevents adequate control of the other two neurotransmitters. Support for this hypothesis comes from studies that establish a link between mood and these monoamines, and from studies of the effects of anti-depressant drugs.

Mood and monoamine transmitters

Teuting, Rosen, and Hirschfeld (1981) compared the substances found in the urine of depressed patients and normals. Compounds that are produced as a by-product of the action of enzymes on noradrenaline and serotonin were present in smaller amounts in the urine of depressed patients. This finding suggests that depressed patients have lower levels of noradrenaline and serotonin. Kety (1975) found very high levels of compounds derived from noradrenaline in the urine of patients suffering from mania.

Evaluation.   It is hard to know whether the high or low levels of noradrenaline and serotonin helped to cause the depression, or whether the depression altered the levels of those neurotransmitters.

Anti-depressants

Anti-depressant drugs such as the monoamine oxidase inhibitors (MAOIs) increase the active levels of noradrenaline and serotonin in depressed patients, and typically reduce the symptoms of depression (see Section 18, Treating Mental Disorders). Lithium carbonate, which is very effective in reducing manic symptoms in bipolar disorder, is thought to decrease the availability of noradrenaline and serotonin. These drug effects suggest the potential importance of altered levels of serotonin and noradrenaline.

Evaluation.   However, the drugs rapidly affect neurotransmitter levels, but take much longer to reduce the symptoms of depression or mania. It is possible that the MAOIs reduce depression by increasing the sensitivity of receiving neurons, and it takes time for this increased sensitivity to occur.

It is important to note that these drug effects do not provide *direct* evidence of what causes depression in the first place. For example, aspirin can cure a headache, but that does not mean that it was an absence of aspirin that produced the headache! MacLeod (1998) called this the **treatment aetiology fallacy**—the mistaken notion that the success of a given form of treatment reveals the cause of the disorder.

Biological Explanation: Endocrine System

The endocrine system produces hormones that have an influence over a huge range of behaviours: growth, menstruation, sleep, sexual activity, and so on. There are a number of conditions that are linked to hormone changes and where depression is a major symptom. Examples include premenstrual syndrome (PMS), postpartum depression (PPD), and seasonal affective disorder (SAD). The latter is discussed on page 175.

Premenstrual syndrome (PMS)

The female menstrual cycle involves changes in the levels of oestrogen and progesterone over the monthly cycle. In the week or two prior to menstruation, some women develop symptoms such as irritability, bloating, breast tenderness, mood swings, decreased ability to concentrate, depression, headache, acne, and constipation. These changes are related to the hormonal fluctuations.

Abramowitz, Baker, and Fleischer (1982) studied the female admissions to one psychiatric hospital and found that 41% entered on the day before or the first day of their menstrual period. Another study, this time looking at women in the normal population, found depressive symptoms during the premenstrual period in about 43% of the women interviewed (Halbreich, Endicott, & Nee, 1983)

Postpartum depression (PPD)

About 20% of women report moderate depression in the period after giving birth and a few of these women become chronically depressed. In extreme cases severe depression has led mothers to commit infanticide. Symptoms include sadness, anxiety, tearfulness, and trouble sleeping. These symptoms usually appear within several days of delivery and go away by 10 to 12 days after the birth.

Women who have recently given birth undergo massive hormonal changes and this is one possible explanation for postpartum depression. A further possibility is that levels of the stress hormone cortisol are very low after birth (see later) and this may make it difficult for women to cope with stress in the period after birth.

Evaluation. In many cases women who suffer postpartum depression have previously had episodes of clinical depression. This suggests that PPD is a combination of hormonal imbalances and a pre-existing predisposition to depression. Lack of emotional support, low self-esteem, and unrealistic ideas about motherhood are also found in cases of PPD, suggesting that psychological factors are important.

Cortisol

The role of cortisol may be important in depression generally. Levels of cortisol tend to be elevated in depressed patients (Barlow & Durand, 1995). The notion that cortisol may be relevant to depression has been examined by using the dexamethasone suppression test. Dexamethasone suppresses cortisol secretion in normals, but about 50% of depressed

Depression and diet

Explanations of depression that are based on biological factors are generally related to endogenous depression, i.e., depression that is caused by internal factors. There is some evidence that what you eat may affect your mood and may, in extreme cases, lead to depression.

Tryptophan is a substance that is found in some foods, such as maize and other starchy foods. Delgado et al. (1990) found that acute tryptophan depletion (ATD) induces a temporary relapse in patients suffering from major depressive disorder. This is supported in a study by Smith et al. (1997) who found that women experienced depression when tryptophan was removed from their diets. In addition it has been suggested that serotonin may be involved in some cases of eating disorder, and that the reason why bulimics often eat a lot of starchy foods is in order to increase their levels of tryptophan and serotonin.

Explanations of depression that focus on the activity of neurotransmitters or fluctuating levels of hormones are concerned with endogenous rather than reactive depression.

Is PPD likely to be due entirely to biological factors?

patients show very little suppression (Carroll et al., 1980). Presumably this happens because the levels of cortisol are so high in these patients that they cannot be easily suppressed.

High levels of cortisol are not specific to depression. Can the same be said for dopamine?

Evaluation.   There are two limitations with the cortisol research. First, reduced suppression on the dexamethasone suppression test is also found in anxiety disorders and other mental disorders, and so high levels of cortisol are not specific to depression. Second, high cortisol levels may be a result of depression rather than forming part of the cause.

Psychological Explanation: Psychodynamic Approach

Freud's psychoanalytic theory is an example of the psychodynamic approach. Freud argued that depression is like grief, in that it often occurs as a reaction to the loss of an important relationship. However, there is an important difference, because depressed people regard themselves as worthless. What happens is that the individual identifies with the lost person, so that repressed anger towards the lost person is directed inwards towards the self. This inner-directed anger reduces the individual's self-esteem, and makes him or her vulnerable to experiencing depression in the future.

Freud distinguished between actual losses (e.g., death of a loved one) and symbolic losses (e.g., loss of a job). Both kinds of losses can produce depression by causing the individual to re-experience childhood episodes when they experienced loss of affection from some significant person (e.g., a parent).

Job loss may cause depression affecting the person's belief in his or her abilities and future prospects.

What about bipolar disorder? According to Freud, the depressive phase occurs when the individual's superego or conscience is dominant. In contrast, the manic phase occurs when the individual's ego or rational mind asserts itself, and he or she feels in control.

In order to avoid loss turning into depression, the individual needs to engage in a period of mourning work, during which he or she recalls memories of the lost one. This allows the individual to separate himself or herself from the lost person, and so reduce the inner-directed anger. However, individuals who are very dependent on others for their sense of self-esteem may be unable to do this, and so remain extremely depressed.

Biological explanation: The evolutionary approach

Several intriguing evolutionary explanations have been suggested for depression. These were discussed in detail in Section 15, Evolutionary Explanations of Human Behaviour.

In essence the evolutionary view is that depression is in part genetic and the gene for schizophrenia must offer some advantage in order to explain why it has remained in the gene pool.

Depression could be an adaptive response to certain situations. Nesse and Williams (1995) suggest that in certain situations it may be a better strategy to sit tight and do nothing. For example, our hunter-gatherer ancestors might have increased their survival if they were disinclined to venture out in bad weather but instead experienced low mood and stayed indoors. However, what was an adaptive response in the past may no longer be so. Nesse and Williams argue that in competitive urban societies depression is increasing because we are not

psychologically equipped to deal with the pressures. We retreat to "sit and wait". This is referred to as "genome lag". Our genetic make-up fits us for the **environment of evolutionary adaptation (EEA)**, not for now.

The *rank theory of depression* suggests that it is important for survival that an individual who is the loser in a contest (i.e., loses rank) should accept the loss to prevent further injury from re-engaging his (or her) defeater, an act of "damage limitation". The adaptive significance of depression is that it discourages the individual from further efforts.

Aspects of bipolar depression have also been explained in evolutionary terms. It has been suggested that the manic phase of bipolar disorder is related to creativity and charismatic leadership, and thus would be an adaptive trait.

Evaluation

There is good evidence that depression is caused in part by loss events. For example, Finlay-Jones and Brown (1981) found that depressed patients experienced more stressful life events than normal controls in the year before onset of the depression, and most of these were loss events. However, the details of the psychodynamic approach are incorrect. Freud would predict that the repressed anger and hostility of depressed people would emerge at least partly in their dreams, but Beck and Ward (1961) found no evidence of this. Freud would also predict that depressed people should express anger and hostility mainly towards themselves. In fact, they express considerable anger and hostility towards those close to them (Weissman, Klerman, & Paykel, 1971).

Finally, it follows from Freud's theory that individuals who experienced some major loss early in their lives should be more vulnerable than others to developing clinical depression in adult life. The evidence is inconsistent, but often suggests that early loss does not predict adult depression (Crook & Eliot, 1980), though the opposite was found by Bifulco et al. (1992, see box above).

> **Separation and loss**
>
> You might also consider **anaclitic depression**, from your AS level studies, which is a state of resigned helplessness and loss of appetite in young children who have been separated from their mothers. Bowlby's (1969) theory of attachment proposed that there might be long-term emotional damage as a consequence of early loss. Bifulco et al. (1992) offered support for this in a study of about 250 women who had lost mothers, through separation or death, before they were 17. They found that loss of their mother through separation or death doubles the risk of depressive and anxiety disorders in adult women. The rate of depression was especially high among those whose mothers had died before the child reached the age of 6.

Psychological Explanation: Behavioural Approach

Reinforcement

Lewinsohn (1974) put forward a behavioural theory based on the notion that depression occurs as a result of a reduction in the level of reinforcement or reward. This relates to the psychodynamic view that depression is caused by the loss of an important relationship, because important relationships are a major source of positive reinforcement. There is also a reduction in reinforcement with other losses, such as being made redundant. People who become depressed because of a major loss may be reinforced in being depressed by the sympathy and understanding shown by other people.

Lewinsohn's behavioural theory clearly presents an oversimplified view of the causes of depression. For example, many people experience major losses without becoming depressed, and the theory does not explain how this happens. The theory also omits any consideration of other causes of depression such as genetic factors.

Learned helplessness

Seligman's (1975) theory and research on learned helplessness have probably been more influential than any other behavioural approach to depression. **Learned helplessness** refers to the passive behaviour shown when animals or humans believe that punishment is unavoidable. In his original studies, Seligman exposed dogs to electric shocks they could not avoid. After that, they were put in a box with a barrier in the middle. The dogs were given shocks after a warning signal, but they could escape by jumping over the barrier into the other part of the box. However, most of the dogs passively accepted the shocks, and did not learn to escape. Seligman described this as learned helplessness, and argued that it was very similar to the behaviour shown by depressed people.

What is wrong with applying the results of a laboratory experiment on dogs to humans in society?

Evaluation of learned helplessness research

Seligman used dogs to illustrate how lack of control over one's experiences might contribute to feeling helpless. In his experiments each dog was "yoked" with another

Why might Seligman's experiments be considered unethical today?

How might the idea of learned helplessness be applied to battered wife syndrome?

dog. The first dog learned to escape from electric shocks, whereas whether the second dog received a shock or not depended on the expertise of its partner. Later in the experiment the dogs were separated and put into a "shuttle box" where they could escape an electrified floor by jumping over a partition. The dogs that had previously learned to avoid shocks soon learned to jump the partition. However, the dogs who had been yoked behaved passively and gave up trying to escape soon after being put in the shuttle box.

From this research it appears that the most important factor in the animals' behaviour was not the electric shocks, but the failure to learn avoidance. The dogs had learned that they were helpless, so they displayed inappropriate behaviour in the shuttle box and didn't try to escape. Seligman went on to propose that depression in humans may be due to learned helplessness. For example, stressful situations may be experienced as unavoidable and not under the control of the individual.

Although symptoms of learned helplessness in Seligman's dogs and symptoms of depression in humans do appear to be similar, there are problems with these conclusions. The experiments were carried out on dogs in controlled conditions, but do the findings apply to humans in society? Later research indicated that what may be important is not so much the learned helplessness that a person feels, but the way in which the individual might perceive and react to the stressful situation.

Psychological Explanation: Cognitive Approach

If drug therapy is a treatment, what does this suggest about the cause of manic depression?

Abramson et al. (1978) developed Seligman's learned helplessness theory by focusing on the thoughts of people experiencing learned helplessness. Abrahamson et al. started by arguing that people respond to failure in various ways:

- Individuals either attribute the failure to an *internal* cause (themselves) or to an *external* cause (other people, circumstances). For example, your boyfriend finishes your relationship and you are convinced it is because of your moodiness (internal cause) or the fact that you have little money for nice clothes (external cause).
- Individuals either attribute the failure to a *stable* cause (likely to continue in future) or to an *unstable* cause (might easily change in future). For example, the moodiness may be a permanent feature of your character (stable) or perhaps it is just because exams are looming ahead (unstable).

Individuals suffering from depression see themselves as failures, and often attribute this to faults within themselves that cannot be changed.

- Individuals either attribute the failure to a *global* cause (applying to a wide range of situations) or to a *specific* cause (applying to only one situation). For example, you may be moody with everyone (global) or just with your boyfriend because you didn't feel that he really loved you (specific cause).

People with learned helplessness attribute failure to internal, stable, and global causes. In other words, they feel personally responsible for failure, they think the factors causing that failure will persist, and they think that those factors will influence most situations in future. In view of these negative and pessimistic thoughts, it is no wonder that sufferers from learned helplessness are depressed.

Depressive schemas

Beck and Clark (1988) also argued that cognitive factors may play an important role in the development of

Measuring depressive symptoms

Beck (1967) developed the most widely used inventory of depressive symptoms. Each question assesses one symptom of depression, and provides a score for severity of that symptom on a scale of 0 to 3. The symptoms are divided into mood, thought, motivation and physical characteristics. The inventory is not intended to be used to diagnose depression, but just to assess the range of symptoms present and the severity.

Research has shown that a "normal" American college student would score above 3 or 4. Mildly depressed students score between 5 and 9, and a score above 10 suggests moderate to severe depression. If an individual scored more than 10 for a period of more than two weeks, he or she should seek help.

Adapted from D.L. Rosenhan and M.E.P. Seligman (1989) *Abnormal psychology* (2nd Edn.). London: Norton.

Beck Depression Inventory (Beck, 1967)

An individual is asked to describe how they are feeling right now.

Mood A (sadness)

0   I do not feel sad.
1   I feel blue or sad.
2a   I am blue or sad all the time and I can't snap out of it.
2b   I am so sad or unhappy that it is quite painful
3   I am so sad or unhappy that I can't stand it.

Mood B (interest in others)

0   I have not lost interest in other people.
1   I am less interested in other people now than I used to be.
2   I have lost most of my interest in other people and have little feeling for them.
3   I have lost all of my interest in other people and don't care about them at all.

Thought C (pessimism)

0   I am not particularly pessimistic or discouraged about the future.
1   I feel discouraged about the future.
2a   I feel I have nothing to look forward to.
2b   I feel that I won't ever get over my troubles.

3   I feel that the future is hopeless and that things cannot improve.

Thought D (failure)

0   I do not feel like a failure.
1   I feel I have failed more than the average person.
2   I feel I have accomplished very little that is worthwhile or that means anything.
3   I feel I am a complete failure as a person (parent, husband, wife).

Motivation E (work initiation)

0   I can work about as well as before.
1a   It takes extra effort to get started at doing something.
1b   I don't work as well as I used to.
2   I have to push myself very hard to do anything.
3   I can't do any work at all.

Motivation F (suicide)

0   I don't have any thoughts of harming myself.
1   I have thoughts of harming myself but I would not carry them out.
2a   I feel I would be better off dead.
2b   I feel my family would be better off if I were dead.
3a   I have definite plans about committing suicide.
3b   I would kill myself if I could.

Physical G (appetite)

0   My appetite is no worse than usual.
1   My appetite is not as good as it used to be.
2   My appetite is much worse now.
3   I have no appetite at all any more.

Physical H (sleep loss)

0   I can sleep as well as usual.
1   I wake up more tired in the morning than I used to.
2   I wake up 1–2 hours earlier than usual and find it hard to get back to sleep.
3   I wake up early every day and can't get more than 5 hours of sleep.

Beck, A.T. (1967). *Depression: Clinical, experimental, and theoretical aspects*. New York: Hoeber.

depression. They referred to depressive schemas, which consist of organised information stored in long-term memory. Beck and Clark's (1988, p.26) cognitive theory is as follows:

> *The schematic organisation of the clinically depressed individual is dominated by an overwhelming negativity. A negative cognitive trait is evident in the depressed person's view of the self, world, and future … As a result of these negative maladaptive schemas, the depressed person views himself as inadequate, deprived and worthless, the world as presenting insurmountable obstacles, and the future as utterly bleak and hopeless.*

The term **cognitive triad** is used to refer to the three elements: the depressed person's negative views of himself or herself, the world, and the future.

The cognitive triad

"I am helpless and inadequate"

"The world is full of insuperable obstacles"

"I am worthless, so there's no chance of the future being better than the present"

Evaluation

Depressed people undoubtedly have the kinds of negative thoughts described by Abramson et al. (1978) and by Beck and Clark (1988). Do these negative thoughts help to cause depression, or do they merely occur as a result of being depressed? Lewinsohn et al. (1981, p.218) carried out a prospective study in which negative attitudes and thoughts were assessed *before* any of the participants became depressed. Here are their conclusions:

> *Future depressives did not subscribe to irrational beliefs, they did not have lower expectancies for positive outcomes or higher expectancies for negative outcomes, they did not attribute success experiences to external causes and failure experiences to internal causes ... People who are vulnerable to depression are not characterised by stable patterns of negative cognitions.*

Most of the evidence suggests that negative thoughts and attitudes are caused by depression rather than the opposite direction of causality. However, Nolen-Hoeksma, Girgus, and Seligman (1992) found that a negative attributional style in older children predicted the development of depressive symptoms in response to stressful life events. Therefore negative thoughts may make people vulnerable to depression.

Therapies based on this cognitive view of depression have proved very successful, as discussed in the next Section of this book. However, one must be careful about suggesting that the success of a treatment reveals the cause of the disorder, a problem called the treatment aetiology fallacy, described earlier.

Identify some of the symptoms of depression that are given in this Case Study.

Suggest two possible factors that may have caused Paul's depression.

CASE STUDY: *Major (Unipolar) Depression*

Paul was a twenty-year-old college senior majoring in chemistry. He first came to the student psychiatric clinic complaining of headaches and a vague assortment of somatic problems. Throughout the interview, Paul seemed severely depressed and unable to work up enough energy to talk with the therapist. Even though he had maintained a B+ average, he felt like a failure.

His parents had always had high expectations for Paul, their eldest son, and had transmitted these feelings to him from his earliest childhood. His father, a successful thoracic surgeon, had his heart set on Paul's becoming a doctor. The parents saw academic success as very important, and Paul did exceptionally well in school. Although his teachers praised him for being an outstanding student, his parents seemed to take his successes for granted. In fact they often made statements such as "You can do better". When he failed at something, his parents would make it obvious to him that they not only were disappointed but felt disgraced as well. This pattern of punishment for failures without recognition of successes, combined with his parents' high expectations, led to the development in Paul of an extremely negative self-concept.

From Sue et al. (1994) *Understanding abnormal behaviour* (p.373) (Boston: Houghton Mifflin)

Psychological Explanation: Social Factors

Patients suffering from major depression typically experience an above average number of stressful **life events** in the period before the onset of depression. For example, Brown and Harris (1978) carried out an interview study on women in London. They found that 61% of the depressed women had experienced at least one very stressful life event in the 8 months before interview, compared with 19% of non-depressed women. However, many women manage to cope with major life events without becoming clinically depressed. Of those women who experienced a serious life event, 37% of those without an intimate friend became depressed, compared with only 10% of those who did have a very close friend. This suggests that social support, another social factor, may moderate the effects of life events on depression.

LIFE EVENTS

Rank	Life event	Stress value
1	Death of a spouse	100
2	Divorce	73
3	Marital separation	65
13	Sex difficulties	39
23	Son or daughter leaving	29
38	Change in sleeping habits	16
41	Vacation	13

Adapted from T. Holmes and R. Rahe (1967), The social readjustment rating scale. *Journal of Psychosomatic Research*, *11*, 213–218.

The findings of Brown and Harris (1978) have been replicated several times. Brown (1989) reviewed the various studies. On average, about 55% of depressed patients had at least one severe life event in the months before onset, compared with only about 17% of controls.

How might the diathesis–stress model be used to explain depression?

Evaluation

There are two main limitations of most life-event studies. First, the information is obtained retrospectively several months afterwards, and so there may be problems in remembering clearly what has happened. Second, the meaning of a life event depends on the context in which it happens. For example, losing your job is very serious if you have a large family to support, but may be much less serious if you are nearing the normal retirement age and have a large pension. This second limitation does not apply to the research of Brown and Harris (1978), because they took full account of the context in which the life events occurred.

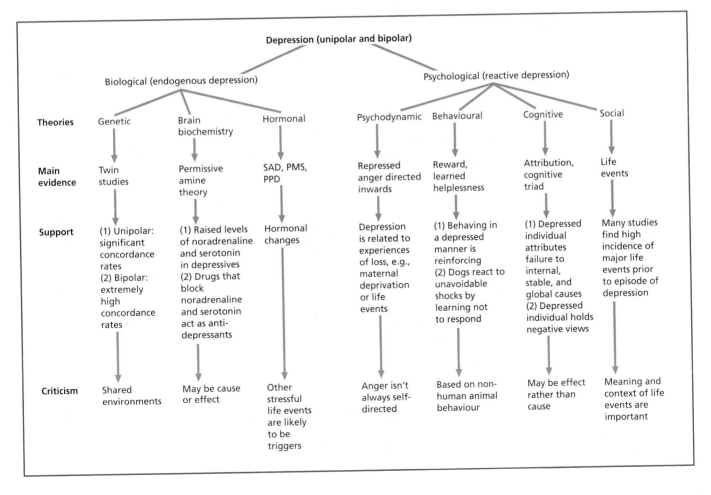

■ Activity: Compile a set of everyday situations or problems (e.g., not doing well in a particular subject, being late for school, not handing in homework). Ask each other about these problems and decide from the participants' answers which factors are involved. Draw up a table of responses like the examples here.

EXAMPLE:

Question 1 Are there any subjects that you are not doing well in, and if so, why do you think this is?

Participant A: I'm hopeless at maths, it's my own fault. (Internal factor)

Participant B: I'm doing badly in maths, because the teacher is awful. (External factor)

	Internal	External	Stable	Unstable	Global	Specific
Q1	✓					
Q2						

	Internal	External	Stable	Unstable	Global	Specific
Q1		✓				
Q2						

Anxiety Disorders

A number of disorders are classified as "anxiety disorders" because they share one clinical characteristic: anxiety. Anxiety is an adaptive response that is important to ensure survival. In certain circumstances it is important for an animal to experience anxiety because it places it in a state of heightened arousal ready to respond to the danger. However, anxiety can become a chronic and disabling response. An individual with an anxiety disorder experiences anxiety that is quite disproportionate to any threat that is posed.

ICD-10 and DSM-IV include the following anxiety disorders: phobias (phobic anxiety disorders), panic disorder, generalised anxiety disorder, obsessive-compulsive disorder, and reaction to severe stress and adjustment disorder (e.g., post-traumatic disorder). In this Unit we will consider one of these: phobias. Some of the other anxiety disorders will be referred to as and when appropriate.

Phobias

Phobias involve a high level of fear of some object or situation, with the level of fear being so strong that the object or situation is avoided whenever possible. There are various different categories of phobia: specific phobia, social phobia, and agoraphobia. We will describe each type of phobia in turn.

Comparisons

About 6% or 7% of the population suffer from phobias. Some phobias are more disruptive of everyday life than others. Agoraphobia and social phobia are usually very disabling, whereas specific phobias such as snake or spider phobias generally have less impact on the phobic's enjoyment of life. About 50% of all phobics seen clinically are suffering from agoraphobia with panic disorder.

Types of phobia

Specific phobia

Specific phobia involves strong and irrational fear of some specific object or situation. Specific phobias include fear of spiders and fear of snakes, but there are hundreds of different specific phobias. DSM-IV identified four major sub-types of specific phobia:

- Animal type.
- Natural environment type: this includes fear of heights, fear of water, and fear of storms.

- Blood-injection-injury type.
- Situational type: this includes fears about being in various situations, such as in a plane, a lift, or an enclosed space (claustrophobia).

In addition, there is a fifth category labelled "other type". This covers all specific phobias that do not fit any of the four major sub-types.

According to DSM-IV, these are the major diagnostic criteria for specific phobia:

- Marked and persistent fear of a specific object or situation.
- Exposure to the phobic stimulus nearly always produces a rapid anxiety response.
- The individual recognises that his or her fear of the phobic object or situation is excessive.
- The phobic stimulus is either avoided or responded to with great anxiety.
- The phobic reactions interfere significantly with the individual's working or social life, or he or she is very distressed about the phobia.
- In individuals under the age of 18, the phobia has lasted for at least 6 months.

Unusual phobias include triskaidekaphobia, *the fear of the number 13;* siderophobia, *a fear of railways; and* monophobia, *a fear of being alone.*

Social phobia

Social phobia involves extreme concern about one's own behaviour and the reactions of others. Social phobia can be either generalised or specific. As the terms imply, individuals with social phobia generalised type are very shy in nearly all situations, whereas those with social phobia specific type mainly become extremely shy in only a few situations (e.g., public speaking). The main diagnostic criteria for social phobia given in DSM-IV include the following:

- Marked and persistent fear of one or more situations in which the individual will be exposed to unfamiliar people or to the scrutiny of others.
- Exposure to the feared social situation nearly always produces a high level of anxiety.
- The individual recognises that the fear experienced is excessive.
- The feared situations are either avoided or responded to with great anxiety.
- The phobic reactions interfere significantly with the individual's working or social life, or there is marked distress about the phobia.

Social phobia is more common in females than in males, with about 70% of sufferers being female. According to Barlow and Durand (1995, p.186), social phobia "tends to be more prevalent in people who are younger (aged 18–29 years), less educated, single, and of lower socioeconomic class".

CASE STUDY: *A Phobia*

A young student in his first year at university was referred to a therapist after seeking help at the student health centre. During initial interviews he spoke of feeling frightened and often panicking when heading for his classes. He claimed he felt comfortable in his room, but was unable to concentrate on his work or to face other people. He admitted to fears of catching syphilis and of going bald. These fears were so intense that at times he would compulsively scrub his hands, head, and genitals so hard that they would bleed. He was reluctant to touch door handles and would never use public toilets. The student admitted that he knew his fears were irrational, but felt that he would be in even more "mental anguish" if he did not take these precautions.

In later sessions with the therapist, the student's history revealed previous concerns about his sexual identity. As a child he harboured feelings of inferiority because he had not been as fast or as strong as his peers. These feelings were reinforced by his mother who had not encouraged him to play rough games in case he got hurt. At puberty the student had also worried that he might be sexually deficient. At a summer camp he had discovered that he was underdeveloped sexually compared with the other boys. He had even wondered if he was developing into a girl. Although he did in fact mature into a young man, he constantly worried about his masculine identity, even fantasising that he was a girl. The student admitted that at times his anxiety was so great that he considered suicide.

Adapted from Kleinmuntz (1974).

Stage-fright: an example of fear when facing the scrutiny of others.

Can you suggest other reasons why more women than men are agoraphobic?

Agoraphobia

Agoraphobia involves great fear of open or public places. Agoraphobia on its own is rather rare, as was pointed out in DSM-IV (APA, 1994). In most cases, the panic disorder starts before the agoraphobia. Individuals who are very frightened of having panic attacks feel less secure when away from familiar surroundings and people, and know that they would be very embarrassed if they had a panic attack in public. These concerns lead them to avoid open or public places, and so agoraphobia is added to the panic disorder (see Case Study below).

Panic disorder with agoraphobia is defined by the following criteria in DSM-IV:

- Recurrent unexpected panic attacks.
- At least one panic attack has been followed by at least 1 month of worry about the attack, concern about having more panic attacks, or changes in behaviour resulting from the attack.
- Agoraphobia, in which there is anxiety about being in situations from which escape might be hard or embarrassing in the event of a panic attack.
- The panic attacks are not due to use of some substance.

What is the definition of a panic attack?

According to DSM-IV, a panic attack involves intense fear or discomfort, with four or more bodily symptoms suddenly appearing. These symptoms include palpitations, shortness of breath, accelerated heart rate, a feeling of choking, nausea, sweating, chest pain, feeling dizzy, and fear of dying.

People between the ages of about 25 and 29 are most likely to develop panic disorder. About 75% of those who suffer from agoraphobia are female. One reason why men show less agoraphobic avoidance than women is because they are more likely to drink heavily so that they can go out in public (Barlow & Durand, 1995).

```
┌─────────────────────────┐
│     Panic disorder      │
└─────────────────────────┘
            │
            ▼
┌─────────────────────────┐
│   Produces anxiety that │
│   an attack might occur │
└─────────────────────────┘
            │
            ▼
┌─────────────────────────┐
│   Embarrassment about   │
│   having an attack out  │
│        in public        │
└─────────────────────────┘
            │
            ▼
┌─────────────────────────┐
│     Agoraphobia +       │
│      panic attack       │
└─────────────────────────┘
```

Biological Explanation: Genetic Factors

The main evidence on genetic factors in the development of the phobias comes from twin studies, although some family studies have also been carried out. Genetic factors are most relevant for agoraphobia and least relevant for specific phobias, with social phobia intermediate.

CASE STUDY: *Sarah—A Case of Agoraphobia*

Sarah, a woman in her mid-30s, was shopping for bargains in a crowded department store during the January sales. Without warning and without knowing why, she suddenly felt anxious and dizzy. She worried that she was about to faint or have a heart attack. She dropped her shopping and rushed straight home. As she neared home, she noticed that her feelings of panic lessened.

A few days later she decided to go shopping again. On entering the store, she felt herself becoming increasingly anxious. After a few minutes, she had become so anxious that a shopkeeper asked her if she was OK and took her to a first-aid room. Once there her feelings of panic became worse and she became particularly embarrassed at all the attention she was attracting.

After this she avoided going to the large store again. She even started to worry when going into smaller shops because she thought she might

have another panic attack, and this worry turned into intense anxiety. Eventually she stopped shopping altogether, asking her husband to do it for her.

Over the next few months, Sarah found that she had panic attacks in more and more places. The typical pattern was that she became progressively more anxious the further away from her house she got. She tried to avoid the places where she might have a panic attack, but as the months passed, she found that this restricted her activities. Some days she found it impossible to leave the house at all. She felt that her marriage was becoming strained and that her husband resented her dependence on him.

Adapted from J.D. Stirling and J.S.E. Hellewell (1999)
Psychopathology (London: Routledge).

Panic disorder with agoraphobia

As far as panic disorder with agoraphobia is concerned, Torgersen (1983) considered pairs of monozygotic or identical twins and dizygotic or fraternal twins, at least one of whom had panic disorder. The concordance rate was 31% for identical twins against 0% for fraternal twins. Harris et al. (1983) found that the close relatives of agoraphobic patients were more likely to be suffering from agoraphobia than were the close relatives of non-anxious individuals. Noyes et al. (1986) found that 12% of the relatives of agoraphobics also had agoraphobia, and 17% suffered from panic disorder. Both of these percentage figures are greater than for controls.

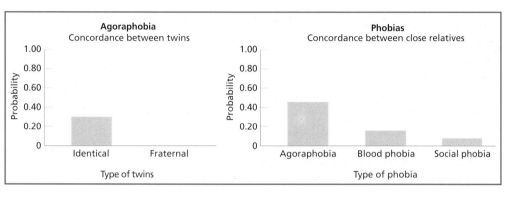

Torgersen (1983) and Noyes et al. (1986) studied twins and families of people suffering from panic disorder with agoraphobia.

Genetics or imitation?

These findings are consistent with the view that genetic factors play a part in the development of agoraphobia. However, there are some problems with interpreting these findings, especially those of Harris et al. (1983). The close relative of an agoraphobic patient may tend to become agoraphobic because he or she imitates the behaviour displayed by the patient, rather than because of genetic inheritance. This would be the explanation offered by **social learning theory**.

Specific phobia

As far as specific phobia is concerned, Fyer et al. (1990) found that 31% of close relatives of individuals with specific phobias also had a phobia. More striking findings were reported by Ost (1989) in a study on blood phobics. In 64% of the cases, these blood phobics had at least one close relative who also suffered from blood phobia. The findings from these two studies are consistent with the notion that genetic factors are involved. However, the experience of having a close relative with a specific phobia may help to trigger a phobia in close relatives.

Social phobia

As far as social phobia is concerned, Fyer et al. (1993) discovered that 16% of the close relatives of social phobics developed the same disorder, against only 5% of the relatives of individuals without social phobia. However, Skre et al. (1993) found that the concordance rate for social phobia was similar in identical and fraternal twin pairs, leading them to conclude that social phobia is caused mainly by environmental influences.

In spite of the findings of Skre et al. (1993), there is indirect evidence that genetic factors may play a part in the development of social phobia. Individual differences in personality depend to some extent on genetic factors (see Thomas, Chess, & Birch, 1970), and there are substantial differences in personality between social phobics and normals. Stemberger, Turner, and Beidel (1995) found that social phobics are extremely introverted. Why might introversion be of relevance to social phobia? Introverted people are sometimes more sensitive about social situations and may have difficulties with social skills, which could lead to the excessive concern about the opinions of others shown by social phobics.

More unusual phobias: anthrophobia, *a fear of men, and* hippophobia, *a fear of horses.*

Biological explanation: The evolution of phobias

If phobias develop because of accidental pairings of a neutral and a fearful or aversive stimulus, then people could become phobic to almost anything. In fact, many more people have phobias about spiders and snakes than about cars, even though we see cars much more often and they are considerably more dangerous. Seligman (1971) argued that the objects and situations forming the basis of most phobias were real sources of danger hundreds or thousands of years ago, and only those individuals who were sensitive to such objects and situations were favoured by evolution. Thus, there is a "preparedness" or biological predisposition to be sensitive to, and to become phobic about, certain stimuli rather than others.

Phobias were discussed in Section 15, Evolutionary Explanations of Human Behaviour.

Biological Explanation: Neurophysiology

It is possible that individuals who generally have a high level of physiological arousal are more vulnerable to the development of phobias. There is some evidence that patients suffering from panic disorder with agoraphobia or with social phobia have high levels of arousal (Lader & Mathews, 1968). However, it is not clear from such evidence whether the high levels of arousal helped to cause the phobia, or whether the phobia led to the increased arousal.

Evaluation

In what way does this data suggest a cognitive rather than a physiological interpretation of panic disorder?

Other evidence suggests that panic disorder with agoraphobia is often *not* associated with increased physiological activity. There have been several studies in which panic patients have been exposed to biological challenges such as inhalation of a mixture of carbon dioxide and oxygen. These biological challenges often produce panic attacks in patients suffering from panic disorder with agoraphobia, but rarely do so in normal controls. In terms of physiological responses, the effects of biological challenge on heart rate, respiratory rate, blood pressure, and so on are comparable in patients and in normal controls (see Eysenck, 1997, for a review). Thus, patients suffering from panic disorder with agoraphobia differ from normal controls in the way they *interpret* their bodily symptoms rather than in terms of their actual physiological responsiveness. In other words, these findings support a *cognitive* rather than a physiological account of panic disorder with agoraphobia.

Psychological Explanation: Psychodynamic Theory

According to Freud, phobias are a defence against the anxiety that is produced when the impulses of the id or sexual instinct are repressed or forced into the unconscious. This theory is illustrated in Freud's case study of Little Hans, who developed a phobia of horses, described in the Case Study on the next page.

Little Hans

Little Hans only showed his fear of horses when he saw them pulling a cart at speed—he was not frightened of horses without carts, or of horses pulling carts at a walking pace.

According to Freud, Little Hans was sexually attracted to his mother, but was very frightened that he would be punished for this by his father. Horses resembled his father in that their black muzzles and blinkers looked like his moustache and glasses, and so Little Hans transferred or displaced his fear of his father on to horses.

Separation anxiety

According to the psychodynamic approach (e.g., Bowlby, 1973), **separation anxiety** in children may make them more likely to develop panic disorder with agoraphobia as a result. Separation anxiety occurs when a child experiences the threat of separation from an important caregiver such as its mother or father. However, there is little evidence that patients suffering from panic disorder with agoraphobia experienced more childhood separation anxiety than other people.

CASE STUDY: *Little Hans*

The case study of Little Hans (the 5-year-old phobic boy) is unusual for several reasons. It is Freud's only analysis of a child rather than an adult. This enabled Freud to test his hypotheses about child sexuality. The case study was also unusual in that Freud's analysis was indirect as almost all of the interviews and observations were made by the boy's father and passed on to Freud. Hans' father was Max Graf, a music critic and early supporter of Freud and member of the psychoanalytic society. Hans' father wrote to Freud when the boy was 5 years old, describing the main problem: "He is afraid a horse will bite him in the street, and this fear seems somehow connected with his having been frightened by a large penis." Freud only met Hans on two occasions. The recording of information and direct interviews were undertaken by Hans' father who then corresponded and discussed the case at length with Freud.

The chief features of the case history (chronologically) are outlined here:

- Hans was fascinated by his "widdler" (his penis). He observed that animals had big ones and it was likely that his parents had big ones too because they were grown up.
- Hans spent a lot of time alone with his mother over the summer holiday and realised he liked having her to himself. He wished his father would stay away. He also felt hostile towards his new baby sister who further separated Hans from his mother. He expressed this indirectly in his fear of baths because he thought his mother would drop him (in fact, he *wished* his mother would drop his little sister, a desire which was projected elsewhere because of the anxiety it aroused).
- There were two strands to his anxiety about horses. First, Hans once heard a man saying to a child "Don't put your finger to the white horse or it'll bite you." Second, Hans asked his mother if she would like to put her finger on his widdler. His mother told him this would not be proper. Therefore, it is suggested that Hans learned that touching a white horse or a widdler was undesirable. Hans' desire (libido) for his mother created a sense of anxiety and fear that she might leave him if he persisted. Unconsciously this anxiety was projected elsewhere: he became afraid of being bitten by a white horse.

- More anxiety was created by the fact that Hans' mother told Hans that, if he played with his widdler it would be cut off. Hans' father told Hans that women have no widdler. Hans reasoned that his mother's must have been cut off—and she might do the same to him.
- There were two pieces of symbolism. First, Hans had a dream about two giraffes, he took away the crumpled one and this made the big one cry out. This might represent Hans' wish to take away his mother (crumpled one) causing his father to cry out (big giraffe—possible symbol of penis). Hans sat on the crumpled one (trying to claim his mother for himself). Second, Freud suggested to Hans that the black around the horses' mouths and the blinkers in front of their eyes were symbols for his father's moustache and glasses. Hans might envy these symbols of adulthood because they could give him the right to have a woman's love.
- Hans developed further anxieties about horses. Hans told his father that he was afraid of horses falling down, and if they were laden (e.g., with furniture) this might lead them to fall down. Hans also remembered seeing a horse fall down and thinking it was dead; since he secretly wished his father would fall down dead this made Hans feel more anxious.
- Hans now became preoccupied with bowel movements ("lumf"). His sister was lumf-like, as was a laden cart. So laden vehicles represented pregnancy and when they overturned it symbolised giving birth. Thus the falling horse was both his dying father and his mother giving birth.
- Finally, Hans became less afraid of horses. He developed two final fantasies which showed that his feelings about his father were resolved: (1) "The plumber came and first he took away my behind with a pair of pincers, and then he gave me another, and then the same with my widdler"; (2) Hans told his father that he was now the daddy and not the mummy of his imaginary children, thus showing that he had moved from wishing his father dead to identifying with him.

Evaluation

It would be predicted from this account that Hans would have shown a phobic reaction every time he saw a horse. In fact, he *only* showed his phobia when he saw a horse pulling a cart at high speed, though this was further explained by the link between the laden cart and Hans' repressed feelings about his sister.

A general criticism of Freudian explanations that applies here is that it is possible to produce an account for anything using these concepts. In addition we can explain Hans' phobia in other, simpler ways. The horse phobia originally developed after Hans had seen a serious accident involving a horse and cart moving at high speed, and this may have produced a conditioned fear response (see the Key Study on the next page).

In general the psychodynamic approach has not received much support, and it ignores many factors associated with phobias (e.g., genetic and social).

How would you suggest that a behaviourist might explain Hans' fear of horses (you might consider the accident that Hans witnessed)?

Psychological Explanation: Behavioural Approach

Classical and operant conditioning

According to the behaviourists, specific phobias develop through two kinds of conditioning. First, a neutral or conditioned stimulus can come to produce fear if, on several occasions, it is presented at the same time as an unpleasant or unconditioned stimulus. For example, Watson and Rayner (1920) studied an 11-month-old boy called Albert (see the Key Study below). He was a calm child, but the loud noise produced by striking a steel bar made him cry. He became frightened of a rat when the sight of the rat was paired seven times with a loud noise. This involved classical conditioning.

The classical conditioning of the fear response

John B. Watson was taken with Pavlov's concept of classical conditioning and believed that it could make psychology a more objective science. With his assistant Rosalie Rayner (Watson & Rayner, 1920), Watson sought to demonstrate that one could explain complex human behaviours using the principles of classical conditioning. They did this by exposing the 11-month-old Albert first to a neutral stimulus (a white rat), and then pairing this with a loud noise. The loud noise was an unconditioned stimulus that produced an unconditioned fear response. Albert quickly learned to show the same fear response to the white rat, thus demonstrating how fear can be learned when a previously neutral stimulus is paired with something that naturally provokes fear.

Mowrer (1947) suggested that phobias are actually the result of a slightly more complex process, involving both classical and operant conditioning. This is called two-process theory. In the first stage, the fear response is learned through classical conditioning (e.g., linking the white rat and the loud noise). The second stage involves operant conditioning, where avoidance of the phobic stimulus serves to reduce fear and acts as a negative reinforcement (stamping the behaviour in).

There is evidence to support this theory. Barlow and Durand (1995) report that about 50% of those with a specific phobia of driving remember a traumatic experience while driving as having caused the onset of the phobia. On the other hand, Menzies and Clarke (1993) found that only 2% of individuals suffering from water phobia reported a direct fearful experience with water. DiNardo et al. (1988) found that many normal people had experienced fearful encounters with dogs but did not develop a phobia of dogs, though 50% of dog phobics had had a fearful encounter with a dog.

Discussion points

1. How might one explain why only some individuals go on to develop a phobia after a fearful experience?
2. How convincing is the behavioural or conditioning account of specific phobias in the light of the evidence?

Albert is shown the rat at the same time as he hears a loud noise.

What happened after that was that the fear produced by the previously neutral stimulus (i.e., the rat) was reduced by avoiding it thereafter. "Albert not only became greatly disturbed at the sight of a rat, but this fear had spread to include a white rabbit, cotton wool, a fur coat and the experimenter's (white) hair" (Jones, 1925). However, it has often proved hard to condition people to fear neutral stimuli by pairing them with unpleasant ones in the laboratory (Davison & Neale, 1996).

The development of phobias can be explained by Mowrer's (1947) two-process theory. The first stage involves classical conditioning (e.g., linking the white rat and the loud noise). Then the second stage involves operant conditioning, because avoidance of the phobic stimulus reduces fear and is thus reinforcing.

Some of the evidence supports the conditioning account. According to Barlow and Durand (1995), about 50% of those with specific phobia of driving remember a traumatic experience while driving (e.g., a car accident) as having caused the onset of the phobia. Barlow and Durand also noted that nearly everyone they have treated for choking phobia has had some very unpleasant choking experience in the past.

Evaluation

In order to obtain support for the conditioning account of specific phobias, we need to show that phobic patients are much more likely than other people to have had a frightening experience with the phobic object. However, the crucial normal control group is often missing. Consider, for example, the study by DiNardo et al. (1988), in which both dog phobics and normal controls without dog phobia had had anxious encounters with dogs!

Keuthen (1980) reported that half of all phobics could not remember any highly unpleasant experiences relating to the phobic object. Those who favour a conditioning account have argued that phobics often forget conditioning experiences that happened many years previously. In order to reduce this problem, Menzies and Clarke (1993) carried out a study on child participants suffering from water phobia. Only 2% of them reported a direct conditioning experience involving water.

However, in defence of the behaviourist view it could be argued that children often have very poor recall for events in early childhood. They may also have repressed the memory of a traumatic event or may not have realised that the event involved water (for example the traumatic event may have taken place beside a stream and thus the sound of water created a phobia). Finally, the behaviourist concept of **stimulus generalisation** suggests that a fear response may be learned about one thing (Albert's fear of a white rat) but then generalised to other apparently quite different things (Albert also reportedly showed a fear reaction to Santa Claus).

Modelling and information transmission

Bandura (1986) developed conditioning theory by showing the importance of modelling or observational learning. Individuals learn to imitate the behaviour of others, especially those whose behaviour is seen to be rewarded or reinforced. Mineka et al. (1984) found that monkeys could develop snake phobia simply by watching another monkey experience fear in the presence of a snake. Another possible way in which phobias could be acquired is through information transmission. What happens is that fear-producing information about the phobic object leads to the development of a phobia. Ost (1985) described the case of a woman who was a severe snake phobic. She had been told repeatedly about the dangers of snakes, and had been strongly encouraged to wear rubber boots to protect herself against snakes. She finally reached the point where she wore rubber boots even when going to the local shops.

Some phobias can be acquired through modelling or information transmission. However, modelling or observational learning seems to be of less importance in producing specific phobias in humans than in other species (Menzies & Clarke, 1994), and there are only a few well-documented cases in which information transmission has led to phobias (see Eysenck, 1997). Merckelbach et al. (1996) argued on the basis of the evidence that claustrophobia or fear of enclosed spaces rarely occurs as a result of modelling

Can a conditioning account explain the relative frequency of different phobias?

How might a fear response in a child be rewarded or reinforced?

or information transmission. In contrast, "In small-animal phobias, but also blood-injection-injury phobia, the predominant pathways to fear are modelling and negative information transmission" (Merckelbach et al., 1996, p.354).

Psychological Explanation: Cognitive Approach

According to cognitive therapists such as Beck and Emery (1985), anxious patients have various **cognitive biases,** which cause them to exaggerate the threats posed by external and internal stimuli. There is good evidence for cognitive biases in phobics. As far as specific phobics are concerned, Tomarken et al. (1989) presented individuals who were high and low in fears of snakes or spiders with a series of fear-relevant and fear-irrelevant slides. Each slide was followed by an electric shock, a tone, or nothing. The phobic participants greatly overestimated the number of times fear-relevant slides were followed by shock. This is known as covariation bias or **illusory correlation**, where individuals perceive relationships where none exist, thus demonstrating a bias (see page 35). This could help to account for the high level of anxiety produced by phobic stimuli.

Social phobia

Social phobics have a cognitive bias, in that they perceive their behaviour in social situations to be more negative than it appears to observers (Stopa & Clark, 1993). This cognitive bias may help to explain social phobics' fears of being evaluated by others.

Panic disorder

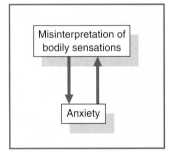

Clark et al. (1988) assessed the ways in which patients suffering from panic disorder or panic disorder with agoraphobia interpret a range of ambiguous events. These patients showed a cognitive bias for their own bodily sensations. For example, they tended to interpret an increase in heart rate as indicating that there was something wrong with their heart. These findings fit in well with Clark's (1986) cognitive theory of panic disorder, according to which panic disorder patients tend to interpret their bodily sensations in a catastrophic or life-threatening way. This makes them more anxious, and this in turn increases the tendency to have catastrophic thoughts about their bodily sensations.

Why do agoraphobics with panic disorder misinterpret their bodily sensations? One possibility is that some previous physical illness has made them more concerned than most people about their bodily well-being. Relevant evidence was reported by Verburg et al. (1995). Of their panic disorder patients, 43% had suffered from at least one respiratory disease, compared with only 16% of patients with other anxiety disorders.

Cause or result?

There is clear evidence that phobic patients have a range of cognitive biases, which lead them to misinterpret their phobic stimuli. However, it has proved very hard to show that these cognitive biases play a part in *causing* phobias rather than simply being a result of having a phobia. The strongest evidence that cognitive biases may be causally involved in phobias was obtained in an unpublished study by Schmidt (discussed in Eysenck, 1997). He assessed the cognitive tendency to respond anxiously to one's own bodily sensations among recruits to the US Air Force Academy who went through stressful basic training. Those with the greatest sensitivity to their own bodily sensations at the start of training were most likely to experience panic attacks thereafter.

Research at the US Air Force Academy showed that those recruits who were aware of, and anxious about, their own bodily sensations, such as increased sweating, raised heart rate, or shortness of breath, were more likely to suffer panic attacks as their training progressed.

Psychological Explanation: Social Factors

Parental rearing styles

It is possible that parental rearing styles have an important impact on the development of phobias. This hypothesis was considered by Gerlsman, Emmelkamp, and Arrindell (1990). They reviewed the literature on parental rearing practices in anxious patients, focusing on the dimension of affection and control or over-protection. They found that phobics (especially social phobics and agoraphobics) were lower than normal controls on parental affection and higher on parental control or over-protection.

Evaluation

Studies on rearing practices have the limitation that they are based on information obtained years after the event. Another limitation is that all we have are correlations between rearing practices and anxiety disorders, and correlations cannot prove causes.

How might the diathesis–stress model be used to explain the development of phobias?

Life events

There is evidence that phobic patients tend to experience more serious life events than normal controls in the year or so before the onset of the phobia. In a study by Kleiner and Marshall (1987), 84% of agoraphobics reported having experienced family problems in the months before they had their first panic attack. In similar fashion, Barrett (1979) found that panic disorder patients reported significantly more undesirable life events in the 6 months prior to onset of their anxiety disorder than did controls over a 6-month period.

What other life events fit into Finlay-Jones and Brown's categories of "threatens the future" and "represents loss"?

Finlay-Jones and Brown (1981) found a difference between anxious and depressed patients in terms of the kinds of life events they had experienced in the 12 months prior to onset of their disorder. Both groups had experienced an above-average number of life events, but those of anxious patients tended to be danger events (involving future threats), whereas those of depressed patients tended to be loss events (involving past losses).

Evaluation

The main problem with most studies is that the information about life events is obtained some time after the events in question. As a result, some events may have been forgotten, or are remembered in a distorted form.

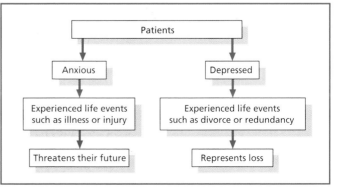

SECTION SUMMARY

Schizophrenia

❖ Causes of a mental disorder can be grouped into biological factors (genetic, brain biochemistry, evolutionary explanations) and psychological factors (cultural, social, experiential). These factors interact so that, for example, genetic factors may be a primary cause or may be the consequence of life experiences. The multi-dimensional approach recognises that abnormal behaviour is typically caused by several different factors. For example, the diathesis–stress model combines genetic vulnerability with stress as joint causes of mental disorder.

❖ Schizophrenia is diagnosed when there are continuous signs of disturbance for at least 6 months. Such signs would include two or more positive symptoms (e.g., delusions, hallucinations, bizarre forms of behaviour) and/or negative symptoms (e.g., lack of emotion). Schizophrenia is classified into different types: disorganised, catatonic, paranoid, undifferentiated, and residual schizophrenia.

❖ The first biological factor considered is genetics. Monozygotic twins have higher concordance rates for schizophrenia than dizygotic twins but this may be because they are treated more similarly. However, they may elicit more similar treatment and monozygotic twins reared apart still show concordance. Family studies support the importance of genetic factors, especially where a schizophrenic has a parent without the disorder but whose identical twin did have the disorder. Family studies also show that the closer the relative genetically the higher the concordance, though this could be due to more similar environments. Adoption studies give strong support to the importance of genetic factors in schizophrenia, though some data were gathered over a prolonged period at a time when diagnoses were less reliable.

❖ Differences in brain chemistry may be due to genetic factors. There is evidence that dopamine overproduction or oversensitivity is linked to schizophrenia. Evidence for the dopamine hypothesis comes from observations that drugs that reduce dopamine levels (neuroleptics) also reduce symptoms of schizophrenia, and drugs that increase dopamine levels (L-dopa) produce schizophrenic-like symptoms. However, neuroleptics take a while to work which wouldn't be predicted by the dopamine hypothesis. Clozapine is more effective than the neuroleptics in reducing schizophrenic symptoms. Clozapine blocks both dopamine and serotonin, implicating serotonin as a further factor in schizophrenia. Dopamine may be a cause or an effect.

❖ In terms of brain differences, schizophrenics have been found to have abnormally large lateral ventricles. This has been found to be true in a twin who has the disorder, whereas the other twin's brain is normal. This again may be a cause or an effect; if it is a cause then it may be related to genetic factors.

❖ The psychodynamic view, as described by Freud, is that schizophrenics have regressed to a state of primary narcissism and have lost contact with reality because their ego is no longer functioning properly. This view is not supported by research studies, nor can it account for the genetic evidence.

❖ According to the behavioural approach, early experience of punishment may lead children to retreat into a rewarding inner world. Once labelled as "odd" they may continue to behave in this way (labelling theory). This view is supported by the successful use of reinforcement to treat schizophrenics. However, it ignores the genetic evidence and it is unlikely that some of the bizarre behaviours associated with schizophrenia would really result from labelling.

❖ Social or environmental factors can be used to account for the fact that concordance rates are never 100%. The double-bind theory proposes that schizophrenics' families communicate in a destructively ambiguous fashion which could explain the confused thinking characteristic of schizophrenia. High levels of expressed emotion within families may help maintain schizophrenia, or this may be a response to a schizophrenic family member. Positive and negative symptoms may be related to certain family events such as birth complications. Social causation hypothesis suggests that the stress of being in the impoverished lower classes leads to schizophrenia, which can explain the higher incidence of schizophrenia in such populations. Equally the social drift hypothesis can explain this link. Other stressors may trigger schizophrenia, a view supported by the fact that individuals have often experienced a high number of stressful life events in the few weeks before the onset of schizophrenia.

❖ The diathesis–stress model combines genetic and social factors, and can explain why concordance rates are not 100%. An understanding of the causes of the disease is important in deciding on suitable treatment. Drug therapies are proving effective though they are not cures.

Depression

❖ Unipolar (major) depression is characterised by the following symptoms having been present daily for more than 2 weeks: emotional symptoms (e.g., lowered mood), motivational symptoms (e.g., loss of interest), somatic symptoms (insomnia or hypersomnia, tiredness), and cognitive symptoms (e.g., negative self-concept, thoughts of suicide). Bipolar depression is much rarer and includes episodes of mania. Endogenous depression is likely to be due to biological factors, whereas reactive depression is primarily psychological.

❖ Evidence for the role of genetic factors comes from family studies with higher than normal incidence among first-degree relatives. Some attempt has been made at gene mapping though the findings have not been replicated. Studies of adopted children show much higher incidence of depression in their biological rather than adoptive parents. Concordance rates are higher in monozygotic twins than for dizygotic twins, and this is stronger for bipolar than unipolar disorder. It is possible that the higher concordance rates are due to greater environmental similarity for monozygotic twins.

❖ Brain biochemistry is the second explanation, exemplified by the permissive amine theory, according to which low levels of serotonin lead to fluctuations in noradrenaline and dopamine. All three are neurotransmitters of the monoamine group. Support comes from studies of monoamine levels in the urine of depressed individuals (levels were low) and the fact that monoamine oxidase inhibitors (MAOIs) reduce depression. However, this evidence is indirect and it is not clear whether the neurotransmitters are a cause or an effect of depression. Evidence based on drug action is subject to the treatment aetiology fallacy.

❖ Changes in endocrine production are also linked to depression, for example in premenstrual syndrome (PMS), postpartum depression (PPD), and seasonal affective disorder (SAD). PMS occurs during a time of hormonal change just before menstruation. PPD may be a combination of hormonal imbalances and a predisposition to depression; psychological factors such as poor emotional support are also implicated. Levels of cortisol appear to be abnormally high in depressed individuals, though cortisol is also linked to anxiety and may be a cause or an effect of depression.

❖ The psychodynamic view of depression is that it is a response to loss where repressed anger towards the object of loss is directed inwards, reducing the individual's self-esteem. Losses in adulthood lead to re-experiencing the emotions felt in childhood relating to loss of affection from some significant person (e.g., a parent). Evidence shows that women who experienced early loss through death of their mother were more prone to depression later. Mourning one's losses helps to prevent depression. However, some predictions from this theory are not borne out, for example repressed anger and hostility do not appear in dreams, depressed people do not just direct anger inwards, and vulnerability to depression following early loss is not always the case.

❖ According to the behavioural view, losses may reduce positive reinforcement, and this would explain depression. Furthermore attention gained from being depressed may itself be rewarding and perpetuate the behaviour. Research has demonstrated that individuals may learn to behave in a helpless manner (learned helplessness), a response similar to depressed behaviour.

❖ Learned helplessness was developed into a cognitive account. Depressed individuals have a unique cognitive style where failure is attributed to internal, stable, and global causes. A different cognitive approach focuses on the role of depressive schemas: the individual has negative views of himself/herself, the world, and the future. This is the cognitive triad. Most of the evidence suggests that negative thoughts are caused by depression rather than vice versa, though one study found that children with a negative attributional style were later more prone to depression.

❖ An important social factor in depression is the effect of major life events. Depression often occurs when a person has to cope with a number of these. The impact of major life events may be lessened by another social factor—support from friends. One limitation to this approach is the fact that life events mean different things to different people.

Anxiety Disorders

❖ Anxiety is an adaptive response but becomes non-adaptive, as in an anxiety disorder, when it is quite disproportionate to any threat that is posed. Examples of anxiety disorders include panic disorder, generalised anxiety disorder, obsessive-compulsive disorder, adjustment disorder (e.g., post-traumatic disorder), and phobias.

❖ Characteristics of specific phobias (e.g., claustrophobia, fear of flying, fear of spiders) include persistent fear, excessive anxiety response to feared object leading to avoidance, awareness that anxiety is excessive, and interference with working or social life. Social phobias (e.g., shyness, fear of public speaking) are distinguished by fear of exposure to unfamiliar people and certain social situations. Agoraphobia (panic disorder with agoraphobia) is usually preceded by panic attacks; a fear of having such an attack in public leads the sufferer to avoid going out. The agoraphobic worries about future panic attacks and is anxious in situations where escape would be difficult. Panic attacks are characterised by palpitations, shortness of breath, accelerated heart rate, a feeling of choking, nausea, sweating, chest pain, feeling dizzy, and fear of dying. Many of these disorders are more common in women, and in younger people.

❖ The role of genetic factors in panic disorder with agoraphobia has been demonstrated in twin and family studies. In one study concordance was nil for dizygotic twins but moderate for monozygotic twins. However, individuals may be imitating each other (social learning theory). The picture is similar for specific phobias but there is some evidence that social phobias are influenced by environmental factors, though introversion may be inherited and this might predispose individuals to develop a social phobia.

❖ Neurophysiology is a second biological explanation. Phobics may have higher levels of arousal, though this could be a cause or an effect of an anxiety disorder. Tests using biological challenges indicate that patients suffering from panic disorder with agoraphobia differ in the way they interpret their bodily symptoms rather than in terms of their actual physiological responsiveness, supporting a cognitive model. Evolutionary explanations should also be considered as an example of biological factors in phobias.

❖ According to Freud, phobias are a means of coping with the anxiety produced from the repression of, for example, sexual desires as illustrated by the case of Little Hans. The boy's fear of horses was explained as a means of dealing with the guilt he felt about having sexual desires for his mother. However, one could explain this fear as a conditioned response. The psychodynamic approach also suggests that early separation anxiety may predispose individuals to develop panic disorder with agoraphobia.

❖ According to the behavioural approach, phobias develop as a result of classical conditioning (the neutral object is paired with something that creates anxiety) and operant conditioning (avoidance of the feared stimulus reduces anxiety and is reinforcing). This is called two-process theory. The experiment with Little Albert demonstrated classical conditioning of a fear response. However, research indicates that phobias do not depend on having previous frightening encounters, and people who do have frightening encounters don't always develop phobias. Modelling and information transmission are behavioural explanations that may apply to some specific phobias.

❖ The cognitive approach proposes that phobics have cognitive biases which cause them to exaggerate the threat posed by certain stimuli. This is supported by the bias produced by illusory correlations. According to the cognitive theory of panic disorder, such patients interpret their bodily sensations in a catastrophic way. This may occur because of past serious illnesses which made them anxious about bodily sensations. There is some evidence that such biases are a cause rather than an effect.

❖ Finally, social factors may be used to explain the development of phobias. Phobics may have experienced low parental affection and high parental control or over-protection. Anxiety disorders may occur when a person experiences an above average number of life events; anxious patients tend to experience danger events, whereas depressed patients experience loss events.

FURTHER READING

The topics in this Section are covered in greater depth by J.D. Stirling and J. Hellewell (2000) *Psychopathology* (London: Routledge), written specifically for the AQA A specification. There is reader-friendly coverage of the mental disorders discussed in this Section in P.C. Kendall and C. Hammen (1998) *Abnormal psychology (2nd Edn.)* (Boston: Houghton Mifflin). The evidence on causal factors in mental disorders is discussed fully in D.H. Barlow and V.M. Durand (1995) *Abnormal psychology: An integrative approach* (New York: Brooks/Cole); Chapter 5 on anxiety disorders is especially good, because David Barlow is one of the world's leading authorities on anxiety. Another textbook with good coverage of most mental disorders is the well-established G.C. Davison and J.M. Neale (1996) *Abnormal psychology (revised 6th Edn.)* (New York: Wiley).

Example Examination Questions

You should spend 40 minutes on each of the questions below, which aim to test the material in this Section. Unlike questions from Unit 4 of the examination, covered in Parts 1–5 of this book, the questions in the Individual Differences section of the Unit 5 examination, covered in this Part, are marked out of 30 and an additional criterion is used in assessment: synopticity. "Synopticity" is defined as your "understanding and critical appreciation of the breadth and range of different theoretical perspectives and/or methodological approaches relevant to any questions" (AQA specification).

1. Describe and evaluate the possible contributions of biological factors to schizophrenia. (30 marks)

2. (a) Outline the clinical characteristics of schizophrenia. (10 marks)
   (b) Outline **one** explanation of schizophrenia, and evaluate this explanation in terms of research studies **and/or** alternative explanations. (20 marks)

3. "There are many different kinds of depression, for example unipolar and bipolar, and endogenous and reactive."

   Discuss the possible explanations for depression, including the evidence on which these explanations are based. (30 marks)

4. (a) Outline the clinical characteristics of depression (unipolar). (5 marks)
   (b) Discuss psychological explanations of depression. (25 marks)

5. Describe and evaluate possible contributions of biological factors to any **one** anxiety disorder. (30 marks)

6. Critically consider the research evidence for psychological explanations of any **one** anxiety disorder. (30 marks)

Examination Tips

Question 1. The descriptive part of this essay concerns biological explanations for schizophrenia, of which there are a large range. Candidates usually present the evidence for such explanations as part of the descriptive material and then evaluate the methodology of such studies or the logic of the explanations. Further evaluation can be given in terms of alternative explanations, such as social and family relationships. It is important to ensure that such alternatives are not just further descriptions but are used explicitly and exclusively as evaluations. Using alternative explanations contributes to the synoptic element of the essay as do any links you are able to make across the specification, such as reference to stress research or evolutionary, behaviourist, and psychodynamic explanations.

Question 2. The division of marks in this question is unusual as some of the AO1 marks are in part (b). In part (a) you are asked for a straightforward list of characteristics. The injunction "outline" is used to indicate that breadth rather than detail is required, though some detail is necessary to demonstrate understanding. You should spend just over 10 minutes on this part of the answer. In part (b) there are 5 marks for another outline, this time of one explanation. If you choose the biological explanation you can include, under this umbrella, a number of different kinds of biological explanation, and leave the research studies to form part of your evaluation. As in question 1, ensure that any alternative explanations used are not just tacked on with a linking sentence "I can evaluate the biological explanations by looking at alternatives", but that you make a genuine effort to use alternative explanations as a point of contrast and evaluation.

Question 3. You are not required to refer to the quotation in your answer but it is there to suggest ways of answering the question. "Discuss" is an AO1 and AO2 term. You are invited to describe any explanations of depression and the evidence on which they are based. The likely problem is that you will have too much to write and therefore, in order to produce a good answer, need to be selective in the way you approach this question, concentrating on the explanations you can give in the greatest detail. You might use other explanations as a form of evaluation, or simply mention them briefly at the end, saying that they have little support. You might also select explanations that are most likely to demonstrate most synopticity.

Question 4. This question, like question 2, has an unusual mark division. Part (a) requires a summary description of the clinical characteristics of *unipolar* depression (this being the only form of depression identified in the specification). You should spend about 5 minutes on this. In part (b) "discuss" is an AO1 and AO2 term. There are 10 marks for a description of psychological explanations and a further 15 marks for an evaluation of these explanations. Thus you should divide your time accordingly. It may be advisable to use evidence as a form of evaluation rather than description, and present a range of explanations in order to attract synoptic credit.

Question 5. The specification requires knowledge of only one anxiety disorder. If you present more than one, they will all be marked but credit only given to the best one. This is not good practice in an examination and it would be better to use further knowledge of this kind as a form of evaluation (e.g., "other anxiety disorders are also explained like this"). The comments written for question 1 apply here.

Question 6. In this essay you are required to focus on research evidence rather than explanations. A critical consideration of such evidence involves reference to both strengths and limitations of, for example, the methodology, practical application and/or ethics of such research. Further evaluation may be in terms of how the evidence may be used to construct explanations. As always bear the synopticity issue in mind.

WEB SITES

http://www.schizophrenia.com/
  Schizophrenia information and links.

http://mentalhelp.net/
  Huge site about mental disorders and treatment.

http://schizophrenia.mentalhelp.net/
  Schizophrenia area of the Mentalhelp site.

http://www.mentalhealth.com/
  Major site with lots of information about disorders, diagnosis, and treatments, as well as numerous links to other sites.

http://mentalhelp.net/guide/schizo.htm
  Many schizophrenia-related links, including articles about its causes and symptoms.

http://www.rcpsych.ac.uk/info/schiz.htm
  Schizophrenia information on the website of the Royal College of Psychiatrists, UK.

http://www.excite.com/health/mental_health/schizophrenia_psych/publications/
  Many links to articles on schizophrenia, some focusing on biological explanations.

http://www.depression.com/
  Major "news" site about depression.

http://www.depressionalliance.org/links/pages/index.html
  Extensive links section on the UK-based Depression Alliance site.

http://www.iop.kcl.ac.uk/main/MHealth/MFS/default.htm
  The Maudsley Family Study (UK) page addressing the issues of whether manic depression runs in families, as well as the role of one's environment.

http://www.blarg.net/~charlatn/Depression.html
  A personal account of major depression by a sufferer; this site also includes many links.

http://www.beckinstitute.org/
  Beck Institute for Cognitive Therapy and Research, under the leadership of its President, the founder of Cognitive Therapy, Aaron T. Beck.

http://phobialist.com/
  Huge list of phobia, which professes to offer no explanations or cures!

http://www.nimh.nih.gov/anxiety/sophri4.cfm
  Information on social phobia.

http://www.nlm.nih.gov/medlineplus/phobias.html
  Phobia links.

http://www.hydra.umn.edu/fobo/hans1.html
  The case of Freud's Little Hans.

www.a-levelpsychology.co.uk/websites.html
  A continually updated list of useful links, including those printed in this book, may be found at the Psychology Press A level psychology site.

18

Treating Mental Disorders

This Section is concerned with the main therapies used to treat mental disorders: biological (somatic), behavioural, cognitive–behavioural, and psychodynamic. There are important issues surrounding the use of these therapies, such as their effectiveness and the ethics of their use.

Biological (Somatic) Therapies

Medical doctors have claimed that mental illness resembles physical illness. According to this medical model, so-called mental illness depends on some underlying organic problem, and the best form of treatment involves direct manipulation of the physiological system within the body. **Somatic therapy** (a major part of which is drug therapy) is the term for this method of treatment.

The four major models of abnormality

There are four major models of abnormality, which were covered in your AS level studies. Each of these models provides explanations of the origins of mental disorders, and each is associated with certain forms of treatment.

The **medical model** proposes that the causes of mental disorders resemble those of physical illnesses. Clusters of symptoms can be identified and a diagnosis made, followed by suitable treatment. There is some evidence that infection, genetics, biochemistry, and/or neuroanatomy may account for mental disorders. If the causes are physical then the treatments should be physical as well, and the medical model recommends direct manipulation of the body processes, such as using drugs, ECT, and psychosurgery. This model is less appropriate for disorders with psychological symptoms, such as phobias.

The **behavioural model** suggests that mental disorders are caused by learning maladaptive behaviour via conditioning or observational learning. Logically, anything that is learned can be unlearned using the same techniques. The approach is best for explaining (and treating) those disorders that emphasise external behaviours, such as phobias. The behavioural model is perhaps oversimplified and

more appropriate to non-human animal behaviour. Ethically, there are advantages such as the lack of blame attached to a person with a mental disorder, but the treatments can be psychologically painful and manipulative.

According to the **psychodynamic model**, the roots of mental disorder are to be found in unresolved conflicts and traumas from childhood. This model may focus too much on the past at the cost of understanding current problems, and too much on sexual problems rather than interpersonal and social issues. Ethical concerns include the problem of false memory syndrome and the sexist nature of the theory. The approach is best for conditions where patients have insight, such as some anxiety disorders, though it has not proved very effective with phobias.

The **cognitive model** takes the view that distorted and irrational beliefs are crucially involved in most mental disorders. Limitations of the cognitive model include the problem of whether distorted thinking is a cause or an effect, and the circularity of the explanations. The model suggests that individuals are to blame for their problems. The cognitive-behavioural model is a recent and popular development, combining both cognitive and behavioural approaches.

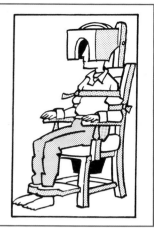

Early somatic therapy

There have been many bizarre treatments for mental illness over the course of history, from blood-letting and purging (use of laxatives) to ice baths. In 1810, Dr Benjamin Rush invented the restraining chair illustrated here. Herman and Green (1991) quote his description of its effectiveness:

> I have contrived a chair and introduced it to our Hospital to assist in curing madness. It binds and confines every part of the body. By keeping the trunk erect, it lessens the impetus of blood toward the brain ... It acts as a sedative to the tongue and temper as well as to the blood vessels.

Rush coined the word *Tranquilliser* as a name for his apparatus and patients were confined in it for up to 24 hours at a time. No one today would be surprised that this would subdue anyone, regardless of their mental state.

The early history of somatic therapy was not very encouraging. As far back as the Middle Ages, those suffering from mental illness had holes cut in their skulls to allow the devils allegedly causing the illness to escape. This practice, which is known as **trepanning**, cannot be recommended. It did not produce any cures, and many of those subjected to trepanning did not survive the operation.

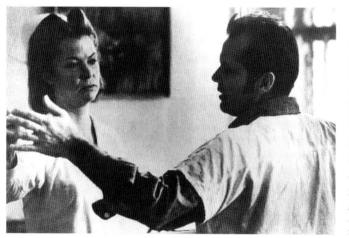

In the film *One Flew Over the Cuckoo's Nest*, Jack Nicholson played Randle Patrick McMurphy, who inspired and awakened his fellow patients, while falling out with the authorities. Eventually, the character is lobotomised, and becomes calmer and easier to handle, but loses all his intellectual spark and energy.

In view of the dangers of lobotomies, it is ironic that Moniz was shot in the spine by one of his own lobotomised patients.

Psychosurgery

Psychosurgery is the use of brain surgery to reduce psychological or behavioural disorders. Pioneering work was carried out by Antonio Egas Moniz in the 1930s (see page 216). He used the surgical method of **prefrontal lobotomy**, in which fibres running from the frontal lobes to other parts of the brain were cut. In the film, *One Flew Over the Cuckoo's Nest*, a lobotomy operation ends Randle Patrick McMurphy's rebellion against the hospital authorities. Moniz and others claimed that this operation made schizophrenic and other patients less violent and agitated, and much easier to manage. This form of psychosurgery caught onto such an extent that about 70,000 lobotomies were carried out between 1935 and 1955.

Lobotomies typically made patients calmer. However, the side-effects were so serious that they are very rarely performed any more. These side-effects include apathy, diminished intellectual powers, impaired judgements, and even coma and death.

More modern methods of psychosurgery

One of the criticisms of lobotomies was their very imprecise nature. Since lobotomies were first performed, a variety of more refined techniques have been introduced. The **prefrontal leukotomy** involves drilling two holes in either side of the skull and inserting needles to sever specific nerve fibres, thus effecting a functional removal of areas of the brain.

Stereotactic neurosurgery is an even more refined method that requires only a small opening to be made in the patient's skull, under local anaesthesia. Then, a thin straight probe is introduced into the brain, and using a remarkably precise system of geometrical coordinates (see page 142), it is targeted onto the internal structure of the brain that the neurosurgeon wants to remove. In this way, quantities of nervous tissue as small as a few cubic millimetres, totally inside the brain, can be lesioned without destroying other parts of the brain.

This method is used in surgeries that target specific regions of the brain. For example **amygdalotomies** and **cingulotomies**. In an amygdalotomy the amygdala, which is the part of the brain involved in anger, is destroyed by directing fine wire electrodes at it through a small hole drilled in the skull. Strong currents are then passed through the electrode, destroying the tissue around its tip. Cosgrove et al. (1996) described their recent work using cingulotomies to relieve emotional distress and reduce abnormal behaviour. The target of their operations, the cingulate gyrus, is a thin ribbon of grey matter believed to play a role in human emotional states.

Effectiveness

Amygdalotomies were carried out on violent criminals, especially in the United States during the 1950s and 1960s. The operations were usually a success, in that those operated on became less aggressive. However, there were very serious side-effects. Patients often became confused, lacking in motivation, and unable to work (Eysenck & Eysenck, 1989). As a result, this form of psychosurgery is almost never carried out any more.

Between 1991 and 1995, Cosgrove et al. performed cingulotomies on 34 patients suffering from depressive or anxiety disorders and claimed that there was improvement in about one-third of the patients, all of whom had severe illnesses that had proved resistant to all other available therapies. It is possible that psychosurgery can be effective if it is performed precisely and on the right patients. However, there are ethical issues surrounding such permanent damage. In the UK, the Mental Health Act requires a patient's consent for psychosurgery, as well as an opinion from a second doctor.

> **Ethical issues: Psychosurgery**
>
> Consider the following moral objections to psychosurgery as a means of alleviating psychotic symptoms:
>
> - Damage to cognitive capacities, e.g., memory, reasoning.
> - Interference in an individual's exercise of his or her own free will.
> - Irreversible alteration of the person's thought processes.

Electroconvulsive Shock Treatment

Electroconvulsive shock treatment (ECT) has its origins in the observation that epileptics rarely suffered from schizophrenia. It was thought that perhaps, in some way, the seizures associated with epilepsy would prevent schizophrenia. In the 1930s a psychiatrist, Sakel, injected insulin into patients, which led to convulsions and coma. The behaviour of some schizophrenic patients did improve. In 1938 two Italian psychiatrists, Cerletti and Bini, first used electric shock to induce seizures.

What used to happen in ECT was that a strong electric current was passed for about half a second between two electrodes attached to each side of the depressed patient's forehead. This current caused almost immediate loss of consciousness and a convulsive seizure. Nowadays, an electric current of between 70 and 130 volts is generally passed through only the non-dominant brain hemisphere, and an anaesthetic and muscle relaxants are given before the treatment itself. As a result, the patient is unconscious during ECT and there are fewer muscular spasms than before. Additional precautions include giving the patient oxygen before and after treatment, and using a mouth gag to prevent the patient biting his or her lips and tongue.

In the past there were cases of broken bones and bruising as a consequence of the restraints that were used, but today the whole treatment is considerably more humane. The convulsion lasts for a maximum of 2 minutes and is only visible as a slight twitching of facial muscles and perhaps the person's toes. Typically a patient will receive between six and nine treatments over a period of a month.

Effectiveness

ECT is now rarely used for schizophrenia; however, it appears to be successful for cases of severe depression. Fink (1985) concluded, from a review of studies on ECT using measures such as suicide rates, that it is effective in over 60% of psychotic-depressive patients. However, Sackheim et al. (1993) found that there was a high relapse rate within a year suggesting that relief was temporary and not a cure.

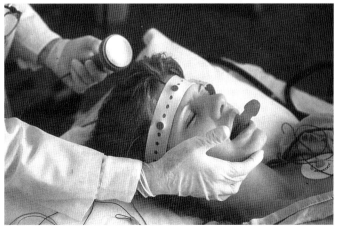

Electroconvulsive shock therapy has been found to be quite effective in cases of severe depression, though the reasons why it might be effective are uncertain.

Assumptions of the medical model
• All mental disorders have a physical cause (micro-organisms, genetics, biochemistry, or neuroanatomy).
• Mental illnesses can be described in terms of clusters of symptoms.
• Symptoms can be identified, leading to the diagnosis of an illness.
• Diagnosis leads to appropriate physical treatments.

Why is ECT sometimes used rather than drugs in the treatment of depression? The main reason is that some severely depressed patients fail to respond to drugs, but do respond to ECT. Janicak et al. (1985) found that 80% of all severely depressed patients respond well to ECT, compared with 64% given drug therapy. It might be suggested that the greater improvement rates for ECT are due to patients' expectations about the successfulness of the therapy rather than the shocks themselves. However, patients undergoing a "sham" ECT procedure in which no shocks are presented show much less improvement than those receiving ECT (Barlow & Durand, 1995). A useful feature of ECT is that it typically reduces depression more rapidly than do anti-depressant drugs. This is of special value when there are concerns that a depressed patient may commit suicide.

Appropriateness

On the negative side, we have little idea of precisely why ECT is so effective and therefore might question how appropriate it is to use as a therapy. One might justify its use by saying that it works, but this is no better than justifying kicking the television as a method of repair for the same reason (assuming that kicking the television does occasionally work—probably because of some third intervening variable).

Current understanding suggests three possible explanations for the effectiveness of ECT. First, ECT may act as a punishment. If maladaptive behaviours have been learned, then punishment will extinguish that S–R link. However, sub-convulsive shocks do not appear to change behaviour but are equally as unpleasant as those shocks that do cause convulsions. As ECT is now done under anaesthetic it also may be less of a punishment in any case.

Second, it has been suggested that the convulsions lead to memory loss and allow some restructuring of disordered thinking. However, unilateral ECT leads to minimal memory disruption yet is still effective.

The third explanation is linked to the permissive amine theory of mood disorders (see page 638). ECT appears to lower the level of noradrenaline and reduce serotonin re-uptake, which will reduce depression. However, for some patients ECT effects a permanent cure, and the alteration of neurotransmitter levels would be temporary.

Ethical considerations

The link between ECT and abuse remains, and it is still seen by many as a form of punishment and a sign of the control wielded by psychiatrists. Any technique that involves direct intervention with brain states is viewed with suspicion.

Given that the full implications of ECT are poorly understood, do you think it is ever right to administer such treatments to vulnerable patients?

Drug Therapy

Drug therapy has been used in the treatment of several disorders. In this discussion, we will focus on drug therapy as applied to depression, anxiety disorders, and schizophrenia.

Depression

Drug therapy has been used in the treatment of patients suffering from major depression and from bipolar disorder (see Section 17, Psychopathology). It has been argued that depression involves a shortage of **monoamines**, which are a type of neurotransmitter including dopamine, serotonin, and noradrenaline. It follows that an effective drug therapy for depression might involve using drugs that increase the supply of these neurotransmitters. Two groups of such drugs are the monoamine oxidase inhibitors (MAOIs) and the tricyclics. The MAOIs work by inhibiting monoamine oxidase, which leads to increased levels of neurotransmitters such as noradrenaline and serotonin. Tricyclics also enhance the action of monamines in a slightly different way (see the diagram on the next page).

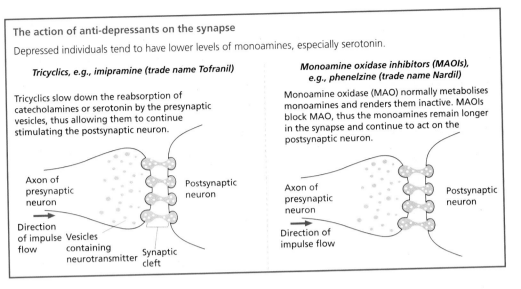

The action of anti-depressants on the synapse

Depressed individuals tend to have lower levels of monoamines, especially serotonin.

Tricyclics, e.g., imipramine (trade name Tofranil)

Tricyclics slow down the reabsorption of catecholamines or serotonin by the presynaptic vesicles, thus allowing them to continue stimulating the postsynaptic neuron.

Axon of presynaptic neuron

Postsynaptic neuron

Direction of impulse flow

Vesicles containing neurotransmitter

Synaptic cleft

Monoamine oxidase inhibitors (MAOIs), e.g., phenelzine (trade name Nardil)

Monoamine oxidase (MAO) normally metabolises monoamines and renders them inactive. MAOIs block MAO, thus the monoamines remain longer in the synapse and continue to act on the postsynaptic neuron.

Axon of presynaptic neuron

Postsynaptic neuron

Direction of impulse flow

A third group of drugs, the selective serotonin re-uptake inhibitors (SSRIs), are specific to serotonin. For example, fluoxetine (trade name Prozac) prevents the re-uptake of serotonin by the presynaptic neuron, so leaving it to have an enhanced effect on the postsynaptic neuron.

The tricyclics are generally more effective than the MAOIs, and produce fewer side-effects. However, the tricyclics can produce dizziness, blurred vision, and dryness of the mouth. It is not very clear why the various drugs are ineffective with some patients. However, the tricyclics tend to be more effective with fairly severe forms of depression (Stern, Rush, & Mendels, 1980), perhaps because abnormalities in the levels of monoamines are most likely to be found in severely depressed patients.

It could be argued that the tricyclics and the MAOIs are simply stimulants producing physiological activation, rather than drugs that correct depressed patients' biochemical deficits. However, most of the evidence is inconsistent with that notion. Neither the tricyclics nor the MAOIs have much effect on the mood of normal individuals who do not have biochemical deficits (Cole & Davis, 1975).

Drug treatment for the manic phase of bipolar disorder has lagged behind that for major depression. However, lithium carbonate produces rapid improvement in most manic patients, and can delay the onset of depression in patients suffering from bipolar disorder. Lithium carbonate reduces the occurrence of manic and depressed episodes in about 80% of patients with bipolar disorder (Gerbino, Oleshansky, & Gershon, 1978). Before lithium carbonate was introduced, the suicide rate of bipolar disorder patients was about 15%, whereas it is now much lower.

Lithium carbonate can have serious side-effects on the central nervous system, on the cardiovascular system, and on the digestive system, and an overdose can be fatal.

It has sometimes been suggested that manic depression is higher among very creative people, and that the manic phase of the disorder can particularly heighten creativity. How might this affect some sufferers' decisions about whether or not to take drug treatment such as lithium carbonate?

CASE STUDY: *Virginia Woolf*

The author Virginia Woolf, who committed suicide in 1941 at the age of 59, was plagued by an intermittent form of depression. This affliction appears to have been bipolar depression, but was accompanied by extreme physical symptoms and psychotic delusions. In her biography of Woolf, Hermione Lee (1997) unravels the series of treatments administered to Woolf between 1895, when she experienced her first breakdown, and the 1930s. Later, Woolf's husband Leonard made detailed notes on her breakdowns (Lee, 1997, pp.178–179):

In the manic stage she was extremely excited; the mind raced; she talked volubly and, at the height of the attack, incoherently; she had delusions and heard voices ... During the depressive stage all her thoughts and emotions were the exact opposite ... she was in the depths of melancholia and despair; she scarcely spoke; refused

to eat; refused to believe that she was ill and insisted that her condition was due to her own guilt.

During the period from 1890 to 1930, Woolf consulted more than 12 different doctors, but the treatments barely altered during this time. They tended to consist of milk and meat diets to redress her weight loss; rest to alleviate her agitation; sleep and fresh air to help her regain her energy. Lithium had not yet been discovered as a treatment for manic depression. Instead, bromide, veronal, and chloral, most of which are sedatives, were prescribed. Lee points out that there is great uncertainty about the neuropsychiatric effects of some of these drugs, and Woolf's manic episodes may well have been the result of taking these chemicals.

Discontinuation of lithium carbonate increases the chances that the symptoms of bipolar disorder will recur, so it tends to be used on a continuous basis.

In sum, various drugs (especially Prozac) are very effective at reducing patients' levels of depression. However, the drugs affect the symptoms rather than the underlying problems causing the depression. Thus, it is desirable for other forms of therapy to be used alongside drug therapy to produce rapid recovery.

Anxiety disorders

In what instances might a GP feel justified in prescribing drugs such as Valium or Librium? What does "tolerance" to drugs mean and what are the problems associated with this and the treatment of anxiety disorders? What other forms of treatment would benefit an anxious patient, together with or instead of drugs?

Patients suffering from anxiety (e.g., those with generalised anxiety disorder) are often given minor tranquillisers to reduce anxiety and permit normal functioning. At one time, **barbiturates** were the most used form of anti-anxiety drug. They are depressants of the central nervous system, and long-acting barbiturates are effective in reducing anxiety. However, they have various side-effects. These include problems of concentration, lack of co-ordination, and slurred speech. In addition, the barbiturates tend to be addictive. Anxious patients who stop taking barbiturates report numerous symptoms such as delirium, irritability, and increased sweating.

The problems with the barbiturates led to their replacement by the benzodiazepines (e.g., Valium, Librium) in the 1960s. The benzodiazepines are more precise than the barbiturates in their functioning, and so typically produce fewer side-effects. However, they often have sedative effects, with patients reporting drowsiness and lethargy. They can also impair long-term memory. There can be unfortunate withdrawal symptoms when patients stop taking them, and there are potential problems of addiction.

Although it is clear that the benzodiazepines are much safer than the barbiturates, the search has continued for other anti-anxiety drugs that will reduce anxiety without producing the side-effects of previous drugs. One such drug is Buspirone, which does not seem to have the potentially dangerous sedative effects of the benzodiazepines. However, more research is needed to establish whether or not it has any unwanted side-effects.

Drug therapy can be useful in providing rapid reduction of anxiety in patients who are very distressed. However, anti-anxiety drugs are only designed to reduce the symptoms of anxiety, and do not address the underlying problems. Anti-anxiety drugs should generally only be used over fairly short periods of time, and should be used in combination with other forms of therapy.

Schizophrenia

To what extent should practical concerns take precedence over ethical issues?

Neuroleptic drugs (drugs that reduce psychotic symptoms but can also produce some of the symptoms of neurological diseases) are often used in the treatment of schizophrenia. Common neuroleptic drugs include the phenothiazines, the butyrophenones, and the thioxanthenes. They reduce the positive symptoms of schizophrenia (e.g., delusions, hallucinations) but have little effect on the negative symptoms (e.g., lack of motivation and emotion, social withdrawal).

Ethical issues: Informed consent

There is a proven link between the use of neuroleptic drugs and the onset of Parkinson's disease, in which the midbrain fails to produce enough dopamine, a chemical that helps to control movement. What ethical issues with regard to informed consent are raised by this fact?

Ethical issues: Compulsory medication

The reduction of the more severe symptoms of schizophrenia has obvious advantages for the carers and families of schizophrenics. Does this mean that patients could or should be given medication without their consent? Are there any differences between the human rights of a schizophrenic person and those of any other patient visiting their doctor? Should the human rights of one person take precedence over those of another person?

Another commonly used drug is clozapine, which is a neuroleptic drug that seems to have fewer side-effects than some others. However, as Kendall and Hammen (1998) have pointed out, it has two important limitations. First, it is much more expensive than most other drugs for schizophrenia, and this restricts its availability. Second, it can produce a potentially fatal blood disease in 1–2% of schizophrenic patients.

In spite of the usefulness of neuroleptic drugs, they have serious limitations. Windgassen (1992) found that about half of schizophrenic patients taking neuroleptics reported grogginess or sedation, 18% reported problems with concentration, 16% had problems with salivation, and 16% had blurred vision. In view of these side-effects, neuroleptic drugs are generally given in the smallest possible doses, and there are *"drug holidays"* during which no drugs are given. Schizophrenic patients are often reluctant to take neuroleptic drugs. As a result, they are sometimes given injections of long-lasting neuroleptics, thus removing the decision whether or not to take a tablet.

The drugs used to treat schizophrenia have the great advantage that schizophrenic patients no longer need to be restrained in straitjackets. However, they have significant disadvantages. First, as we have seen, they have several unfortunate side-effects. Second, the drugs basically reduce symptoms, and cannot be regarded as providing a cure for schizophrenia.

Disorder	Drug/group of drugs	How they work	Drawbacks
Depression (major)	Monoamine oxidase inhibitors (MAOIs)	Inhibit oxidation of monoamines (neurotransmitters, including dopamine, serotonin, and nor-adrenaline), so that levels increase	A range of side-effects
	Tricyclics	As MAOIs	Dizziness, blurred vision, dry mouth
	Tetracyclics (e.g., Prozac)	As MAOIs, but mainly affect levels of serotonin	Preoccupation with suicide and violence
Depression (bipolar)	Lithium carbonate	Anti-mania, but mechanism is imperfectly understood	Side-effects on CNS, cardiovascular, and digestive systems. Overdose can be fatal
Anxiety disorders	Barbiturates	Treat symptoms of anxiety: palpitations, shortness of breath, accelerated heart rate, feeling of choking, nausea, dizziness, etc.	Problems of concentration, lack of co-ordination, slurred speech. Addictive. Withdrawal symptoms include delirium, irritability
	Benzodiazepines (e.g., Valium, Librium)	Have a sedative effect on the CNS	Drowsiness, lethargy, impairments of long-term memory. Withdrawal symptoms and possible addiction
	Buspirone	Stimulates serotonin receptors in the brain	Does not appear to have sedative effect, but other side-effects not yet established
Schizophrenia	Neuroleptic drugs (e.g. phenothiazines butyrophenones, thioxanthenes)	Reduce delusions, hallucinations	Little effect on lack of motivation and emotion, social withdrawal. Some patients report grogginess, sedation, difficulty concentrating, dry mouth, blurred vision
	Clozapine	As neuroleptics, but with fewer side-effects	Expensive. May produce fatal blood disease in 1–2% of patients

Evaluation of chemotherapy

There are various problems with chemotherapy. First, it tends to take responsibility away from the patient and give it directly to the therapist or psychiatrist. Some people feel that drugs are used to keep patients quiet, i.e., for the benefit of the institution and for society, rather than for the patient. Second, there is the problem of compliance with treatment. Patients often dislike taking drugs that have serious side-effects, and it is hard for therapists to make sure that the drugs are being taken as and when they should be. There have been tragic results in some cases where schizophrenic patients have stopped taking their medication. Third, there is the problem that chemotherapy involves treating the symptoms rather than the underlying reasons. As a result, there is a real danger that the symptoms will reappear when chemotherapy comes to an end, or the patient simply has to take the drugs for life. This is a problem in light of the various side-effects there are with drugs. Finally, the fact that drugs are not equally effective with all patients raises questions about their usefulness.

How would you explain the fact that drugs do not always have the same effect on all people? What other factors may interfere?

CASE STUDY: *Chemotherapy Saves Lives*

Novelist blames depression in son's apparent overdose
Danielle Steel says he was manic-depressive

When Nicholas Traina was found dead of an apparent overdose during the weekend, his mother, novelist Danielle Steel, was heartbroken but not entirely surprised. Though her 19-year-old son had a history of drug use, the problem was much deeper: for his entire short life, Traina was tormented by mental illness.

"The only time he messed around with drugs was when his medications failed him and he was desperate," Steel told *The Chronicle* in the first interview she has given since her son's death on Saturday. "This was not some wild kid, this was a very sick kid. The awful thing is I knew for years. He was manic-depressive, and wrestled with mental illness all his life. The biggest agony of my life is that for years, no one would listen to me that he was sick until we found a doctor in LA about 4 years ago who gave him amazing medication. He understood because he was manic-depressive, too."

Adapted from an article in the *San Francisco Chronicle*
17 September 1997

To Dad, girl was Satan and thought he was Messiah when he killed daughter, 6, court told

Paranoid schizophrenic Ron England believed he was the Messiah ridding the world of evil when he murdered his mother and 6-year-old daughter, a psychiatrist says.

Dr Ian Jacques told a coroner's inquest yesterday England still does not believe his daughter, Jenny, and her grandma, Marian Johnston, are dead.

Jacques said England—who'd sworn off medication treating his severe mental illness—was "almost functioning on auto-pilot and getting his instructions (to kill) from television." England called 911 on April 2, 1996, to report he'd killed his mother and daughter at their home in Bowmanville. Marian Johnston, 79, was found slumped on her bed in pyjamas, housecoat and black boots. The former public health nurse, who'd helped England win supervised custody of Jenny over her biological parents, had been stabbed 34 times. On the floor lay Jenny with a knife embedded in her heart. She'd been stabbed 89 times.

Adapted from an article in the *Toronto Sun*

On the other hand, chemotherapy has allowed a great number of people to lead relatively normal lives despite underlying disorders. It may prevent suicide during a deeply depressed episode in a person's life and it may also make the world safer for other people (see the Case Study above).

General Issues for Evaluating Therapies

In the other two Units of this Section we will consider further methods of treatment for mental disorders, but first it is worth considering the basis for evaluating the effectiveness of any therapy, and the main ethical issues that should be considered. These discussions should help you to better understand the issues already touched and to better evaluate these issues as you read on.

How to assess effectiveness

In order to assess the effectiveness of a given form of therapy, it is usual to compare the percentage of clients receiving that therapy who recover with the recovery percentage among clients receiving either no therapy or a different form of therapy. There are various problems associated with this way of assessing the effectiveness of therapy. Some of the main ones are as follows:

What are the possible reasons why it may be unethical to compare effects between a treated group of depressives (using drugs) and an untreated control group (using a placebo)?

- There are numerous different ways of defining and assessing recovery (e.g., in terms of behaviour or in terms of self-report measures); for example, the goal of therapy for psychodynamic therapists is to resolve internal conflicts, whereas for behaviour therapists it is to change overt behaviour. The ideal approach would be to obtain a wide range of self-report, behavioural, and physiological measures.
- Therapy that is effective in producing recovery may or may not be effective in preventing relapse (return of the disorder); thus therapy that seems effective in the short term may or may not be so in the long term.
- It is generally unethical to compare the effects of a given form of therapy with those found in a control group of patients who are denied treatment.
- It is often hard to tell whether any beneficial effects of therapy are due to specific factors (features that are unique to that form of therapy) or to common factors (e.g., patient expectations, personal qualities of the therapist).
- Clients with the same diagnosis often differ considerably in terms of the severity of their symptoms and in the precise pattern of symptoms they exhibit.
- Any given form of therapy tends to be given in a different way by different therapists. As Lazarus and Davison (1971, p.203) pointed out, "The clinician …

approaches his work with … a framework for ordering the complex data that are his domain. But frameworks are insufficient. The clinician … must fill out the theoretical skeleton. Individual cases present problems that always call for knowledge beyond basic psychological principles."

- The effectiveness of therapy depends in part on the skills and personal qualities of the therapist as well as on the content of the therapy itself.

> ### Individual cases
>
> The diagnosis and treatment of a person suffering from, for example, an eating disorder is likely to vary from one individual to another, depending on the person's symptoms, their severity, and the individual case history. The effectiveness of the treatment may therefore hinge on the extent of the therapist's knowledge and understanding of each individual case, rather than on a specific psychological approach to eating disorders.

- It cannot be assumed that patients are allocated *randomly* to different forms of therapy; there is some *self-selection*, with patients often having some say over the therapy they will receive. This complicates the issue of comparing different forms of therapy.
- Some forms of therapy may work much better with some kinds of patients than with others. For example, there is evidence that psychodynamic therapy works best with patients who are young, attractive, verbally skilled, intelligent, and successful (Garfield, 1980). (If you take the first letters of young, attractive, and so on, you arrive at YAVIS, which may assist your memory for this list!)
- The **hello–goodbye effect** describes how patients are likely to exaggerate their symptoms prior to treatment and exaggerate their recovery afterwards, especially in order to please their therapist. The result is that some therapeutic interventions may appear successful.

After reading this list, what would you conclude about the feasibility of evaluating the effectiveness of any therapy?

Strupp (1996) argued that the effectiveness of any given form of therapy should be considered from three different perspectives. First, there is the perspective of society. This includes the individual's ability to function in society and the individual's adherence to social norms. Second, there is the client's own perspective. This includes the client's overall subjective well-being. Third, there is the therapist's perspective. This includes relating the client's thinking and behaviour to the theoretical framework of mental disorder underlying the form of therapy used by the therapist. The extent to which a client has recovered may vary considerably from one perspective to another.

Why might some therapists prefer to use the term "client" instead of "patient"?

Control groups

Suppose we find that clients receiving a given form of therapy are no more likely to recover than those in a control group not receiving any systematic therapy. Does this prove that the therapy is totally ineffective? It does not, because of the **placebo effect**. This effect has been found in drug research, where it refers to the finding that patients who are given a neutral substance (e.g., a salt tablet), but told they have been given a strong drug, will often show signs of medical improvement. Thus, the mistaken belief that one has received an effective form of treatment can produce strong beneficial effects. In similar fashion, according to Mair (1992), control clients who are led to expect that they will show improvement may do so:

Do you think that by seeking help in the form of any kind of therapy, clients are in fact expressing hope for the future? Might this contribute to the placebo effect?

> *As a symbolic communication that combats demoralisation by inspiring the patient's hopes for relief, administration of a placebo is a form of psychotherapy. It is therefore not surprising that placebos can provide marked relief in patients who seek psychotherapy.*

General studies of therapy

Various studies have used the **meta-analysis** technique to compare the effectiveness of different therapies. Once we have had a chance to review the various different kinds of therapy in the rest of this Section, we will consider the findings from these comparative studies (see page 686).

Ethical issues in therapy

There is general agreement that there are important ethical issues concerning therapy. These are associated with the more general topic of issues in psychological research (see pages 706–716). Here we will briefly consider some of the ethical issues that relate to therapy.

Informed consent

It may seem obvious that therapy should only be carried out with the full informed consent of the client. To achieve that, the patient should be fully informed about the various forms of treatment that are available, about the probability of success of each treatment, about any possible dangers or side-effects, about the right to terminate treatment at any time, and about the likely cost of treatment. Evidence of the value of informed consent was reported by Devine and Fernald (1973). Snake phobics were shown four films of different forms of treatment. Those who were given their preferred form of treatment showed more recovery than those who were not.

Why might informed consent increase the effectiveness of a therapy?

There are strong ethical and practical reasons in favour of informed consent. In practice, as is discussed next, there are several reasons why full informed consent is not achieved.

First, the therapist may not have detailed information about the respective benefits and costs of different forms of treatment. In addition, some forms of treatment are very successful with some patients, but cause serious problems with others. These considerations mean that the therapist may be unable to provide the patient with enough information to come to a clear decision.

Second, the client or patient may find it hard to remember the information that he or she has been given by the therapist. Evidence on this issue was obtained by Irwin et al. (1985). They engaged in detailed questioning of patients who had said they understood the benefits and possible side-effects of a form of treatment. In fact, about 75% of them were mistaken, because they had forgotten important information.

Third, many clients are not in a position to provide full informed consent. Examples include young children, those with severe learning difficulties, and schizophrenic patients. As far as schizophrenics are concerned, however, there is evidence (discussed by Davison & Neale, 1996) that they vary considerably in their ability to give informed consent. What typically happens when clients are unable to give informed consent is that a guardian or close relative provides it.

Fourth, clients may agree to a form of treatment because of their exaggerated respect for the expertise of the therapist, rather than because of information about the likely benefits and costs of that treatment. This is perhaps especially likely to occur when the client has little or no prior knowledge of different forms of treatment.

If a relative gives informal consent, might there be a conflict of interest?

Finally, we might consider the difficult problem of informed consent to treatment in cases in which the patient is likely to die without such treatment. The authorities may be in a difficult position with respect to informed consent in such cases. Dwyer (2000, personal communication) reports the case of an adult anorexic who refused to give her consent for treatment and subsequently died. The deceased's family took the health authority to court on the basis that they should have treated the patient even in the absence of her consent.

Confidentiality

Confidentiality is of basic importance in therapy. It is essential if the client is to trust the therapist, and so to feel free to disclose intimate details or his or her life. The law ensures confidentiality in most circumstances. For example, the Police and Criminal Evidence Act (1984) contains within it the requirement that there must be an order signed by a judge before the authorities can consider trying to gain access to a client's confidential records.

MacLeod (1998) pointed out that absolute confidentiality is unusual. For example, cases are discussed with other therapists working in the same place (e.g., a National Health Service Trust). This is done to ensure that clients obtain the best possible treatment, and is not a matter for great concern. However, sensitive information about a patient is sometimes revealed to others *outside* the organisation for which the therapist works. Some examples are considered next.

Suppose that it emerges during therapy that the client is thinking of killing someone against whom he or she has a grudge. If the therapist believes this is a serious threat, then he or she is under an obligation to tell the relevant authorities, to ensure that the threat is not carried out. There are two sets of circumstances in which therapists in the United Kingdom have a legal obligation to disclose information about their clients to the relevant authorities. First, when the information is relevant to acts of terrorism. Second, when the information is of relevance to the welfare of children.

Effectiveness of Somatic Therapy

Finally, let us return to the question of how effective somatic therapies are. Most forms of somatic therapy (with the exception of psychosurgery) have proved fairly effective. There are common themes running through drug therapy for anxiety, depression, and schizophrenia. First, drugs are usually effective in producing a rapid reduction in symptoms. This can be very valuable, because drugs reduce distress, and may stop patients from attempting suicide. Another reason why drugs are useful with schizophrenia is because they may permit schizophrenic patients to benefit from therapy based on the attainment of insight (e.g., psychodynamic therapy).

Second, nearly all somatic therapies used in therapy have side-effects, and these side-effects can be serious and even dangerous. Third, most somatic therapies reduce the symptoms of a disorder, but do not provide a cure. However, they can form part of a combined therapeutic approach designed to produce a cure. Somatic therapies also have the benefit of requiring little effort on the part of the patient and being more suitable for patients who find it difficult to express their thoughts and feelings.

Somatic therapy emphasises changes in the physiological and biochemical systems, and so it seems especially appropriate to the treatment of disorders involving physiological and/or biochemical abnormalities. A clear example is schizophrenia. Drug therapy is also appropriate when patients are in state of great distress (e.g., anxiety disorders, depression). However, it is generally not sufficient on its own. For example, consider panic disorder. As we saw in Section 17, Psychopathology, these patients greatly exaggerate the seriousness of their own physiological symptoms. As a result, cognitive-behavioural therapy designed to reduce these exaggerated cognitions is more effective than drug therapy in producing recovery from panic disorder (Eysenck, 1997).

In general terms, somatic therapy is inappropriate for disorders that are not clearly based on physiological or biochemical abnormalities. For example, cultural values and expectations play an important role in producing eating disorders, and so somatic therapy is unlikely to be of much relevance.

Behavioural Therapies

Behavioural therapy was developed during the late 1950s and 1960s. The underlying notions are that most forms of mental illness occur through maladaptive learning, and that the best treatment consists of appropriate new learning or re-education. Behaviour therapists believe that abnormal behaviour develops through conditioning, and that it is through the use of the principles of conditioning that clients can recover. In other words, behavioural therapy is based on the assumption that classical and operant conditioning can change unwanted behaviour into a more desirable pattern. An important feature of behavioural therapy is its focus on *current* problems and behaviour, and on attempts to remove any symptoms that the patient finds troublesome. This contrasts greatly with psychodynamic therapy, where the focus is much more on trying to uncover unresolved conflicts from childhood.

Classical conditioning

- Unconditioned stimulus (UCS), e.g., food → causes → reflex response, e.g., salivation.
- Neutral stimulus (NS), e.g., bell → causes → no response.
- NS and UCS are paired in time (they occur at the same time).
- NS (e.g., bell) is now a conditioned stimulus (CS) → which produces → a conditioned response (CR) [a new stimulus–response link is learned, the bell causes salivation].

Operant conditioning

- A behaviour that has a positive effect is more likely to be repeated.
- Positive and negative reinforcement (escape from aversive stimulus) are agreeable.
- Punishment is disagreeable.

One of the distinguishing features of behavioural therapy is that more than other forms of therapy it is based on the scientific approach. As MacLeod (1998, p.571) pointed out:

> *The behavioural model of disorders and behaviour was a direct application of behavioural principles from experimental psychology, and was closely related to laboratory-based studies of learning (conditioning) which were often carried out on rats. As such, behavioural therapy has been … closely connected with scientific methodology, both in elaborating the principles of therapy and in evaluating the success of therapy.*

The key ingredients in classical and operant conditioning are discussed in Section 13, Determinants of Animal Behaviour, and will not be repeated here, though a summary is given in the box above. What will be done here is to discuss some of the main forms of treatment used by behaviour therapists. After a brief general evaluation, we will deal with three forms of treatment based mainly on classical conditioning, and then consider treatment based on operant conditioning. It has sometimes been argued that the term "behavioural therapy" should be restricted to forms of therapy based on classical conditioning, with the term "behaviour modification" being used to apply to forms of therapy involving operant conditioning. What is done here is to use the term "Behavioural therapy" in a general way to cover any therapy based on conditioning principles.

How would you use behavioural therapy to address the maladaptive behaviour of compulsive lying?

General evaluation of behavioural therapy

There are three persistent criticisms of behavioural therapy. First, as Kendall and Hammen (1998, p.75) pointed out:

> *Critics have described behavioural therapy as mechanical in its application and as limiting the benefits of treatment to changes in observable behaviour.*

Second, it has been argued that the focus of behaviour therapists on eliminating symptoms is very limited. In particular, it has been claimed by psychodynamic therapists that the failure to consider the underlying causes of mental illness leads to the danger of **symptom substitution**. In other words, one symptom may be eliminated, but the underlying problems lead to its replacement with another symptom.

Third, there is what is known as the problem of generalisation. The application of behavioural therapy may serve to produce the desired behaviour by the patient in the therapist's room. However, it does not necessarily follow that the same behaviour will be produced in other situations.

This 18cm poisonous spider is perhaps more terrifying than the type that would be used in flooding!

Behavioural therapies based on classical conditioning

Flooding or exposure

According to behaviour therapists, phobic fears (e.g., of spiders) are acquired by means of classical conditioning, in which the phobic stimulus is associated with a painful or aversive stimulus that creates fear. This fear can be reduced by avoiding the phobic stimulus.

One way of breaking the link between the conditioned stimulus (e.g., spider) and fear is by experimental extinction. This can be achieved by a technique known as **flooding** or exposure, in which the client is exposed to an extremely fear-provoking situation. In the case of a spider phobic, the client could either be put in a room full of spiders or asked to imagine being surrounded by dozens of spiders. The client is initially flooded or overwhelmed by fear and anxiety. However, the fear typically starts to subside after some time. If the client can be persuaded to remain in the situation for long enough, there is often a marked reduction in fear.

Why is flooding or exposure effective? It teaches the patient that there is no objective basis to his or her fears (e.g., the spiders do not actually cause any bodily harm). In everyday life, the phobic person would avoid those stimuli relevant to the phobia, and so would have no chance to learn this.

The main problem with the flooding technique is that it is deliberately designed to produce very high levels of fear. It can, therefore, have a very disturbing effect on the client. If the client feels compelled to bring the session to a premature end, this may teach him or her that avoidance of the phobic stimulus is rewarding, in the sense that it leads to reduced fear. This can make later treatment of the phobic harder.

You might consider Mowror's two-process theory for phobias, described on page 652.

Systematic desensitisation

Joseph Wolpe (1958) developed an alternative form of behavioural therapy for phobic patients known as **systematic desensitisation**. It is based on **counterconditioning**, and involves the attempt to replace the fear response to phobic stimuli with a new response that is incompatible with fear. This new response is usually muscle relaxation. Clients are initially given special training in deep relaxation until they can rapidly achieve muscle relaxation when instructed to do so.

What happens next is that the client and the therapist together construct what is known as an "anxiety hierarchy", in which the client's feared situations are ordered from the least to the most anxiety-provoking. Thus, for example, a spider phobic might regard one small, stationary spider 5 metres away as only modestly threatening, but a large, rapidly moving spider 1 metre away as highly threatening. The client reaches a state of deep relaxation, and is then asked to imagine (or is confronted by) the least threatening situation in the anxiety hierarchy. The client repeatedly imagines (or is confronted by) this situation until it fails to evoke any anxiety at all, indicating that the counterconditioning has been successful. This process is repeated while working through all of the situations in the anxiety hierarchy until the most anxiety-provoking situation of all is reached.

Do you think the approach of systematic desensitisation relies more on biological factors or on the sense of power and control gained by the clients?

Fear of dogs

If an individual has a fear of dogs, systematic desensitisation could be used to overcome this. The client might have learned their fear in the following way:

- Child is bitten by dog. Unpleasant bite (UCS) ➔ fear (UCR).
- Dog (NS) paired with UCS, becomes CS ➔ fear (now CR).

This can be overcome by associating the dog with a new response—relaxation.

- Dog (CS) ➔ fear (CR).
- Dog paired with new UCS (relaxation) ➔ pleasant feelings (CR).

Aversion therapy

Aversion therapy is used when there are stimulus situations and associated behaviour patterns that are attractive to the client, but which the therapist and the client both regard as undesirable. For example, alcoholics enjoy going to pubs and consuming large amounts of alcohol. **Aversion therapy** involves associating such stimuli and behaviour with a very unpleasant unconditioned stimulus, such as an electric shock. The client thus learns to associate the undesirable behaviour with the electric shock, and a link is formed between the undesirable behaviour and the reflex response to an electric shock.

In the case of alcoholism, what is often done is to require the client to take a sip of alcohol while under the effect of a nausea-inducing drug. Sipping the drink is followed almost at once by vomiting. In future the smell of alcohol produces a memory of vomiting and should stop drinking.

Apart from ethical considerations (discussed on page 671), there are two other issues relating to the use of aversion therapy. First, it is not very clear how the

---

Uses of aversion therapy

Consider the application of aversion therapy to treat:

- Compulsive gambling.
- Sexual perversion (e.g. "flashing").

Assess the probable degree of success in treating either of these forms of maladaptive behaviour. How important is it for the client to want their behaviour to change?

<table>
<tr><td colspan="3">Aversion therapy</td></tr>
</table>

Aversion therapy
- (UCS) Electric shock → (UCR) fear
- (NS) Pornographic pictures → pleasure

Conditioning: Pornographic pictures associated with electric shock
- (CS) Pornographic pictures → (CR) fear
- (UCS) Vomiting → (UCR) displeasure
- (NS) Alcohol → pleasure

Conditioning: Alcohol associated with vomiting
- (CS) Alcohol → (CR) displeasure

shocks or drugs have their effects. It may be that they make the previously attractive *stimulus* (e.g., sight of alcohol) aversive, or it may be that they inhibit the *behaviour* of drinking. Second, there are doubts about the long-term effectiveness of aversion therapy. It can have dramatic effects in the therapist's office. However, it is often much less effective in the outside world, where no nausea-inducing drug has been taken and it is obvious that no shocks will be given (Barlow & Durand, 1995).

People are often sick after drinking too much alcohol. According to aversion therapy this should put them off drinking. Why doesn't this appear to happen?

Behavioural therapies based on operant conditioning

So far we have focused on forms of behavioural therapy based on classical conditioning. However, much behaviour involves the use of operant conditioning. Therapy using operant conditioning is based on a careful analysis of the maladaptive behaviour of the client, and on the reinforcers or rewards which maintain that behaviour. When the therapist has a clear idea of the current patterns of behaviour and their causes, he or she will try to produce environmental changes to increase the rewards for adaptive behaviour and decrease the rewards for maladaptive behaviour.

There are various techniques open to the behaviour therapist using operant conditioning:

- *Extinction*: if a maladaptive behaviour is performed by a patient because it is followed by positive reinforcement, then the incidence of that behaviour can be reduced or extinguished by ensuring that the behaviour is no longer followed by reward. Crooks and Stein (1991) discussed an example of extinction involving a 20-year-old woman who picked away at any small spot or blemish on her face until it started bleeding. This compulsive behaviour seemed to be rewarded by the attention she received from her fiancé and from her family. When this behaviour was ignored, but her desirable forms of behaviour received attention, she rapidly stopped exhibiting her compulsive behaviour.

- *Selective punishment*: a specific maladaptive behaviour is punished by means of an aversive stimulus (e.g., electric shock) whenever it occurs; this is part of what is involved in aversion therapy

- *Selective positive reinforcement*: a specific adaptive behaviour (or "target behaviour") is selected, and positive reinforcement is provided whenever this target behaviour is produced by the patient. This is the approach used by token economies (see text below).

All three of the operant conditioning techniques are limited by ethical considerations. Which of the three presents the most ethical problems? Why do you think this is the case?

Token economies

One important form of therapy based on selective positive reinforcement or reward is the token economy. This is used with institutionalised patients, who are given tokens (e.g., coloured counters) for behaving in appropriate ways. These tokens can later be used to obtain various privileges (e.g., playing snooker; cigarettes). Ayllon and Azrin (1968) carried out a classic study. Female patients who had been hospitalised for an average of 16 years were rewarded with plastic tokens for actions such as making their beds or combing their hair. The tokens were exchanged for pleasant activities such as seeing a film or having an additional visit to the canteen. This token economy was very successful. The number of chores the patients performed each day increased from about five to over 40 when this behaviour was rewarded with tokens.

Paul and Lentz (1977) used a token economy with long-term hospitalised schizophrenic patients. As a result, the patients developed various social and work-related skills, they became better able to look after themselves, and their symptoms were reduced. These findings are all the more impressive in that they were achieved at the same time as there was a substantial reduction in the number of drugs being given to the patients.

Evaluation

The main problem with token economies is that the beneficial effects they produce are often greatly reduced when good behaviour is no longer followed by the rewards that the patients have grown used to receiving. Thus, there is a danger that token economies may produce only token (i.e., minimal) learning. There is no easy answer to this problem. Token economies work because the environment is carefully structured so that good behaviour is consistently rewarded and bad behaviour is not. The outside world is very different, and patients find it hard to *transfer* what they have learned in a token economy to the much less structured environment outside the institution.

What does the word "token" refer to in "token economies"?

One reason for the poor transfer may be that patients have been selectively reinforced in particular situations and therefore would only reproduce the rewarded behaviour in that situation. This is an example of **context-dependent learning**.

What could be done to increase transfer of learning to the outside world?

A second problem is that the use of external rewards may actually destroy intrinsic motivation (see the box on page 207). Rewarding people for the absence of negative behaviour, rather than when positive behaviour actually occurs, may not effect a change in the person, because they are not making a moral decision based on the protection of their own self-esteem, but rather for an external reward.

Third, this form of therapy underestimates the importance of cognitive processes. Although the use of incentives to reward good behaviour may eradicate undesirable behaviour, it may also fail to build a patient's personal autonomy. This will be essential when he or she is faced with choices about how to behave in a given setting.

Fourth, token economies reward patients for socially acceptable behaviour, but they do not allow for variations in patients' capabilities. These may result in fewer tokens being given to the more maladapted individuals because they are more unstable and less able to learn new skills. This might have the undesirable effect of creating a hierarchy in which self-esteem becomes weakened among the more vulnerable people.

Finally, we should consider the ethics of behaviour manipulation. The "desired behaviours" or goals are decided by the institution and may not be acceptable to the patient, given a free choice.

Modelling

Modelling is another form of behavioural therapy, based on the principles of vicarious reinforcement and social learning theory. Modelling can also be used in order to treat phobias. A patient watches the therapist experiencing the phobic situation and then imitates the same behaviour. Bandura, Blanchard, and Ritter (1969) found that the therapy was most effective when working with a live example of the feared object (such as a real snake) rather than a symbolic representation. Modelling has been successfully used to help people cope better in social situations and situations they found fearful, such as going to the dentist. They watch other people coping well in such situations and then imitate their behaviour.

Modelling has been extended to wider use as **social skills training**. This is particularly useful in cases of individuals who lack important social skills, such as bullies or autistic children. Goddard and Cross (1987) described a course developed for disruptive pupils which included skills such as listening, apologising, dealing with teasing and bullying, and gaining feedback from video recordings. In all cases long-term benefits were gained by training the parents so that they could continue the programmes at home. Lovaas et al. (1967) trained autistic children in language skills using shaping and positive reinforcement. "Time out'" is a technique used to train hyperactive children. When they behave uncontrollably they receive attention which, despite being negative, is positively reinforcing. In order to break this cycle, unacceptable behaviour is treated with time in temporary isolation until they calm down. To be effective this should be accompanied by child-centred attention for good behaviour.

Empirical support for the power of social skills training was provided in a study by Cooke and Apolloni (1976). Children who were excessive shy or solitary were exposed

<table>
<tr><td>

Assumptions of the behavioural model

- All behaviour is learned, and maladaptive behaviour is no different.
- This learning can be understood in terms of the principles of conditioning and modelling.
- What was learned can be unlearned, using the same principles.
- The same laws apply to human and non-human animal behaviour.

</td></tr>
</table>

to live models who demonstrated various social skills, such as smiling at others, sharing, initiating positive physical contact, and giving verbal compliments. The study found that the same behaviours did increase in the target children and, in addition, the children showed increases in other positive social behaviours that had not been modelled. Also, the behaviours of untrained children in contact with the target child also showed increases in positive social behaviours.

Modelling works best when the model is similar to the child, for example the model initially acts shy and withdrawn, and when the actions to be imitated are accompanied by some form of commentary that directs the observer's attention to the purposes and benefits of the actions (Asher, Renshaw, & Hymel, 1982).

Effectiveness of Behavioural Therapy

Behavioural therapy is a moderately effective form of therapy. Smith et al. (1980) found that behavioural therapy was as effective as other major forms of therapy. Subsequent reviews of the literature have suggested that behavioural therapy and cognitive behavioural therapy are usually more effective than psychodynamic therapy (see the next Unit).

Behavioural therapy, especially exposure, is often very effective with anxiety disorders. Ost (1989) used one-session exposure on patients with specific phobias and reported that "90% of the patients obtained a clinically significant improvement ... which was maintained after an average of 4 years". One of the few anxiety disorders for which exposure is not very effective is obsessive-compulsive disorder. Van Oppen et al. (1995) found that 17% of patients with obsessive-compulsive disorder recovered after exposure therapy, compared with 39% who received cognitive therapy.

The success of some forms of behavioural therapy does not depend on the factor claimed by behaviour therapists to be responsible. For example, Wolpe (1958) assumed that systematic desensitisation works because clients learn to link a relaxation response to phobic stimuli. Lick (1975) obtained evidence that this is not the whole story. He told his clients that he was presenting them with subliminal phobic stimuli (i.e., below the level of conscious awareness) and that repetition of these stimuli reduced their physiological fear reactions. In fact, he did not present any stimuli, and the feedback about physiological responses was fake! In view of Lick's (1975) total failure to follow the "correct" procedures, it would be expected by behaviour therapists that the therapy should have been ineffective. In fact, Lick's "make-believe" procedure was successful in reducing the clients' fear responses to phobic stimuli. Presumably the "make-believe" procedure made the clients think they could control their fear, even though the counterconditioning emphasised by behaviour therapists did not occur. It also may be that the relationship between client and therapist is important to recovery, even in behavioural therapies.

Behavioural therapy is most appropriate in the treatment of disorders in which behavioural symptoms are central, and is least appropriate when the key symptoms are internal. For example, specific phobics have the behavioural symptom of avoidance of the phobic stimulus, and behavioural therapy works well with that disorder (Ost, 1989). In contrast, many of the key symptoms of obsessive-compulsive disorder are in the form of internal thoughts and obsessions, and behavioural therapy is no more than modestly effective (van Oppen et al., 1995).

Behavioural therapy is also not very appropriate when dealing with serious disorders having a substantial genetic component. The prime example here is schizophrenia. Token economies have been successful in modifying the behaviour of schizophrenics in desirable ways, but no form of behavioural therapy has removed the main symptoms of schizophrenia.

Does the fact that clients in Lick's study experienced a positive outcome override the ethical problems of the deception he used?

In any therapy, how does one know if effectiveness is due to personal characteristics of the therapist rather than the therapy itself?

Alternatives to Biological and Behavioural Therapies

In this Unit we will consider two further approaches to the treatment of mental disorders.

Cognitive Therapy

Behavioural therapy focuses on external stimuli and responses, and ignores the cognitive processes (e.g., thoughts, beliefs) happening between stimulus and response. This omission was dealt with in the early 1960s with the introduction of **cognitive therapy**, based on the assumption that successful treatment can involve changing or restructuring clients' cognitions or thinking.

Ellis' rational-emotive therapy (RET)

Albert Ellis (1962) was one of the first therapists to put forward a version of cognitive therapy. He argued that anxiety and depression occur as the end points in a three-point sequence, as illustrated in the diagram below.

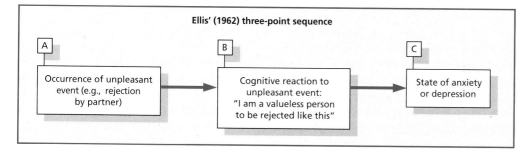

According to this A–B–C model, anxiety and depression do not occur as a direct result of unpleasant events. More precisely, these negative mood states are produced by the irrational thoughts that follow from the occurrence of unpleasant events. The interpretations that are produced at point B depend on the individual's belief system.

Ellis (1962) developed **rational-emotive therapy** as a way of removing irrational and self-defeating thoughts and replacing them with more rational and positive ones. As Ellis (1978) pointed out:

> *If he [the individual] wants to be minimally disturbable and maximally sane, he'd better substitute for all his absolutistic "It's terribles" two other words which he does not parrot or give lip-service to but which he incisively thinks through and accepts—namely, "Too bad!" or "Tough shit!".*

In more technical terms, Ellis argued that individuals who are anxious or depressed should create a point D. This is a dispute belief system that allows them to interpret life's events in ways that do not cause them emotional distress.

Rational-emotive therapy starts with the therapist making patients aware of the self-defeating nature of many of their beliefs. Patients are then encouraged to ask themselves searching questions about these beliefs in order to discover whether these beliefs are rational and logical. For example, patients may be told to ask themselves questions such as the following: "Why do I have to be liked by everybody?"; "Why is it so terrible if I can't have my own way all the time?"; "Does it really matter if I am not competent in every way?" After that, patients are taught to replace their faulty and irrational beliefs with more realistic ones (e.g., "It is impossible to be liked by everybody, but most people like me"; "My life can be happy even if I sometimes can't do what I want"; "I will strive to be fairly competent, and accept that perfection cannot be achieved"). The crucial final step is for patients to have *full acceptance* of these new, rational beliefs.

Do you sometimes deal with problems in the way that Ellis suggests?

■ Activity: Devise a situation like the following example and describe how the thoughts, emotions, and behaviour that result from it could be changed.

It is your birthday and you are given a surprise invitation to meet your friends at lunchtime to celebrate. You are disappointed to find that your best friend does not join you and gives no reason or apology.

	Irrational/negative	Rational/positive
Thoughts	He/she is annoyed with you but won't say why	Maybe he/she was under pressure with work, etc.
Emotions	Hurt and upset. Perhaps you aren't friends after all	Disappointed, but sure you'll get together soon to celebrate
Behaviour	Treat him/her with cool detachment next time you meet	Ring him/her to arrange to meet

Convincing evidence that anxious patients are much more likely than normals to have irrational beliefs was reported by Newmark et al. (1973). They found that 65% of anxious patients (but only 2% of normals) agreed with the statement, "It is essential that one be loved or approved of by virtually everyone in his community." The statement, "One must be perfectly competent, adequate, and achieving to consider oneself worthwhile", was agreed with by 80% of anxious patients compared with 25% of normals.

Evaluation of Ellis' approach

Therapists using rational-emotive therapy tend to be much more argumentative than those using client-centred therapy (see the box on page 686), and they show less concern for the sensitivities of their clients. It may well be that which form of therapy is preferable depends on the individual client. For example, there is evidence that rational-emotive therapy is especially effective with clients who feel guilty because of their own perceived inadequacies and who generally impose high demands on themselves (Brandsma, Maultsby, & Welsh, 1978). Rational-emotive therapy seems more suitable for individuals suffering from anxiety or depression than for those with severe thought disorders (Barlow & Durand, 1995).

Why does rational-emotive therapy appear to be more effective with individuals suffering from anxiety or depression than those who have severe thought disorders?

Beck's cognitive therapy

Probably the most influential cognitive therapist is Aaron Beck. He has developed forms of cognitive therapy for anxiety, but is better known for his work on depression. Beck (1976) argued that therapy for depression should involve uncovering and challenging the negative and unrealistic beliefs of depressed clients. Of great importance is the **cognitive triad**. This consists of negative thoughts which depressed individuals have about themselves, about the world, and about the future (see also page 643). Depressed clients typically regard *themselves* as helpless, worthless, and inadequate. They interpret events in the *world* in an unrealistically negative and defeatist way, and they see the world as posing obstacles that cannot be handled. The final part of the cognitive triad involves depressed individuals seeing the *future* as totally hopeless, because their worthlessness will prevent any improvement occurring in their situation.

Think of an occasion when you felt helpless or worthless. Could you try to reinterpret the situation in a more positive way?

According to Beck et al. (1979), the first stage of cognitive therapy involves the therapist and the client agreeing on the nature of the problem and on the goals for therapy. This stage is called collaborative empiricism. The client's negative thoughts are then tested out by the therapist challenging them or by the client engaging in certain forms of behaviour between therapy sessions. It is hoped that the client will come to accept that many of his or her negative thoughts are irrational and unrealistic. For example, a depressed client who argues that people are always avoiding him or her can be asked to keep a diary of specific

Assumptions of the cognitive model
- Maladaptive behaviour is caused by faulty and irrational cognitions.
- It is the way you think about a problem, rather than the problem itself, which causes mental disorder.
- Individuals can overcome mental disorders by learning to use more appropriate cognitions.
- Aim to be positive and rational.

occasions on which this happens. It is very likely that it happens much less often than the patient imagines.

Cognitive therapy: A summary

Cognitive therapists differ among themselves in terms of the approaches they adopt towards their clients. However, the common features were identified by Beck and Weishaar (1989, p.308):

> Cognitive therapy consists of highly specific learning experiences designed to teach patients (1) to monitor their negative, automatic thoughts (cognitions); (2) to recognise the connections between cognition, affect, and behaviour; (3) to examine the evidence for and against distorted automatic thoughts; (4) to substitute more reality-oriented interpretations for these biased cognitions; and (5) to learn to identify and alter the beliefs that predispose them to distort their experiences.

Cognitive-behavioural Therapy (CBT)

In recent years, there have been increasing efforts to add some of the more successful features of behavioural therapy to cognitive therapy. This combination is referred to as **cognitive-behavioural therapy**. According to Kendall and Hammen (1998), the four basic assumptions underlying cognitive-behavioural therapy are as follows:

In what ways might a person's thoughts about themselves influence the way they react in a particular situation?

1. Patients typically respond on the basis of their *interpretations* of themselves and the world around them rather than on the basis of what is *actually* the case.
2. Thoughts, behaviour, and feelings are all interrelated, and they all influence each other. Thus, it would be wrong to identify one of these factors (e.g., behaviour) as being more important than the others.
3. In order for therapeutic interventions to be successful, they need to clarify, and to change, the ways people think about themselves and about the world around them.
4. It is very desirable to try to change both the client's cognitive processes and his or her behaviour, because the benefits of therapy are likely to be greater than when only cognitive processes or behaviour are changed.

We have already considered some of the ways in which cognitive therapists such as Ellis (1962) and Beck (1976) try to restructure the thoughts and beliefs of their clients. They also try to change the behaviour of their clients in a fairly direct fashion, and so can be regarded as cognitive-behavioural therapists. Beck (1976) instructs his clients to monitor and log their thought processes between therapy sessions. He also emphasises the use of homework assignments that require clients to behave in ways in which they were previously unable to behave. A client suffering from a high level of social anxiety might be told to initiate conversations with everyone in his or her office over the following few days. A crucial ingredient in such homework assignments is *hypothesis testing*. Clients typically predict that carrying out their homework assignments will make them feel anxious or depressed, and so they are told to test these predictions. What generally happens is that the clients' hypotheses are shown to be too pessimistic, and this speeds up the rate of recovery.

Effectiveness of Cognitive and Cognitive-behavioural Therapy

Cognitive therapy and cognitive-behavioural therapy both involve taking full account of the client's own views of the world, no matter how distorted those views might be. If one is trying to produce beneficial change, then it is of value to have clear evidence of the client's present state. There are some advantages of cognitive-behavioural therapy over cognitive therapy, in that many of the symptoms about which clients are concerned are related to their behaviour. As a result, it is reasonable to try to change behaviour *directly*, as well as *indirectly* by changing some of their thoughts and beliefs.

Beck's approach is more developed and sophisticated than that of Ellis. Ellis tends to assume that rather similar irrational beliefs underlie most mental disorders, whereas Beck argues that specific irrational beliefs tend to be associated with each disorder. In spite of the limitations of Ellis's rational-emotive therapy, it is reasonably effective. Engels, Garnefski, and Diekstra (1993) found, across 28 studies, that rational-emotive therapy was as effective as systematic desensitisation and markedly superior to no treatment.

Cognitive-behavioural therapy has proved successful in the treatment of depression and anxiety disorders, and Meichenbaum (1985) has shown its effectiveness in stress reduction (this was discussed in your AS level studies). However, it is of little value in the treatment of disorders that do not involve irrational beliefs. Dobson (1989) reviewed 28 studies of therapy for depression. He concluded that cognitive therapy compared favourably to other forms of psychotherapy in most of the studies. Cognitive-behavioural therapy works well with nearly all anxiety disorders (Eysenck, 1997), but is especially effective with panic disorder. According to Rachman (1993, p.279), "As far as anxiety disorders are concerned, the greatest theoretical and clinical progress has been made in applying cognitive-behavioural therapy (CBT) to the … treatment of panic." It is also more effective than behavioural therapy in the treatment of obsessive-compulsive disorder (van Oppen et al., 1995).

Cognitive-behavioural therapy combines the advantages of cognitive therapy and behavioural therapy, and so provides appropriate forms of treatment for a wide range of disorders. As it is also a very inexpensive and cost-effective form of treatment, it is being used increasingly in Britain and the United States as the preferred form of therapy. Cognitive-behavioural therapy has limited appropriateness for the treatment of schizophrenia. However, schizophrenia is a very serious disorder that has proved extremely hard to treat successfully.

Are there any ethical problems involved in using cost-effectiveness as a criterion for the choice of a preferred form of therapy?

Psychodynamic Therapy

Psychodynamic therapy is based on psychoanalysis, and was introduced by Sigmund Freud at the start of the twentieth century. Some of the principles of psychoanalysis were developed in various ways by Freud's followers such as Carl Jung and Alfred Adler.

Psychoanalysis

According to Freud, neuroses such as the anxiety disorders occur as a result of conflicts among the three parts of the mind: the ego (rational mind); the id (sexual and other instincts); and the superego (conscience). These conflicts, many of which go back to early childhood, cause the ego to use various defence mechanisms to protect itself (see page 419). The key defence mechanism is repression. **Repression** consists of forcing painful, threatening, or unacceptable thoughts and memories out of consciousness into the unconscious mind. The forces of repression then prevent these thoughts and memories from reappearing in consciousness. The repressed ideas concern impulses or memories that the client could not think about without feeling intense anxiety. Repressed memories mostly refer to childhood, and to the conflicts between the instinctive (e.g., sexual) motives of the child and the restraints imposed by his or her parents. Repression serves the function of reducing the level of anxiety experienced by the client.

According to Freud, adults who experience great personal problems tend to show regression (not repression!). Regression involves going backwards through the stages of psychosexual development they went through in childhood (see Section 11, Social and Personality Development, for a detailed description of Freud's theory of personality).

Sigmund Freud, 1856–1939.

Children often fixate or spend an unusually long time at a given stage of psychosexual development if it is associated with conflicts or excessive gratification, and regression typically occurs back to a stage at which the person had previously fixated.

Freud argued that the way to cure neurosis was to allow the client to gain access to his or her repressed ideas and conflicts, and to encourage him or her to face up to whatever emerged from the unconscious. He insisted the client should focus on the feelings associated with the repressed ideas, and should not simply regard them unemotionally. Freud used the term **insight** to refer to these processes. The ultimate goal of psychoanalysis is to provide the client with insight. There are great obstacles in the way, because the emergence of very painful ideas and memories into consciousness produces an extremely high level of anxiety. As a result, the attempt to uncover repressed ideas meets much resistance from the client.

Freud (1917, p.289) described some of the forms that resistance can take:

> The patient attempts to escape by every possible means. First he says nothing comes into his head, then that so much comes into his head that he can't grasp any of it … At last he admits that he really cannot say something, he is ashamed to … So it goes on, with untold variations.

Freud and the other psychoanalysts used various methods to uncover repressed ideas, and to permit the client to gain insight into his or her unresolved problems. The three main methods are as follows: hypnosis, free association, and dream analysis.

Hypnosis

The use of hypnosis came first in the history of psychoanalysis. Freud and Breuer (1895) treated a 21-year-old woman called Anna O, who suffered from several neurotic symptoms such as paralysis and nervous coughs (see page 418). Hypnosis uncovered a repressed memory of Anna hearing the sound of dance music coming from a nearby house as she was nursing her dying father, and her guilty feeling that she would rather be dancing than looking after her father. Her nervous coughing stopped after that repressed memory came to light.

Freud gradually lost interest in hypnosis, partly because many clients were hard or impossible to hypnotise. Another problem is that people under hypnosis become very suggestible. As a result, little reliance can be placed on the accuracy of what they claim to remember when in the hypnotised state.

Free association

The method of free association is very simple. The client is encouraged to say the first thing that comes into his or her mind. It is hoped that fragments of repressed memories will emerge in the course of free association. However, as we have seen, free association may not prove useful if the client shows resistance, and is reluctant to say what he or she is thinking. On the other hand, the presence of resistance (e.g., an excessively long pause) often provides a strong clue that the client is getting close to some important repressed idea in his or her thinking, and that further probing by the therapist is called for.

Dream analysis

According to Freud, the analysis of dreams provides "the via regia [royal road] to the unconscious". He argued that there is a censor in the mind that keeps repressed material out of conscious awareness; this censor is less vigilant during sleep. As a result, repressed ideas from the unconscious are more likely to appear in dreams than in waking thought. These ideas usually emerge in disguised

The client is reluctant to say what he or she is really thinking.

Why do you think someone who seeks psychodynamic and other forms of therapy is often called a client rather than a patient?

Given the suggestibility of people under hypnosis and the possibility that they might then falsely recall things that did not really happen, what are the ethical dangers involved in using hypnosis as a form of therapy?

Dream analysis

There are various schools of thought on the significance of dreams and their possible biological function. Freud and Jung believed that dreams signified the thoughts and feelings of the unconscious mind and are therefore necessary to allow the mind to explore them. Others have suggested that dreams perform no concrete function, but this view has been contested by referring to examples of sleep deprivation. Sleep-deprived participants tend to experience an increase in dreaming sleep when they are finally permitted to sleep.

What is your view on the role of dreams? How might psychologists test your views scientifically?

When evaluating Freud's theory of dreams you might contrast it with other theories of dreams (see Section 5, Biological Rhythms: Sleep and Dreaming). Some other theories just suggest that dreams are the flotsam of brain activity during sleep and that dreams have no meaning.

Freud developed his theory in the early part of the twentieth century when attitudes to sex and sexuality were very different from today. What effect do you think this might have on the development of psychodynamic therapy?

form because of their unacceptable nature. For example, the ideas may be altered by the process of condensation (combining various ideas into a smaller number) or by displacement (shifting emotion from the appropriate object to another one). The best-known examples of displacement involve sexual symbolism, such as someone dreaming about riding a horse rather than having sex.

Freud distinguished between the actual dream (called the **manifest content**) and the underlying repressed ideas (called the **latent content**; see Section 5, Biological Rhythms: Sleep and Dreaming). The unacceptable content of the latent dream is changed into the more acceptable content of the manifest dream. Why do people dream? According to Freud, the main purpose is wish fulfilment: we dream about things that we would like to see happen. Thus, dream analysis can prove useful in making sense of the neurotic client's basic motives.

How plausible is Freud's theory of dreams? A dreamer's major concerns are often expressed in a symbolic fashion rather than directly. For example, patients who are due to have major surgery sometimes dream about standing on an unsteady bridge or falling from a tall ladder, rather than about having an operation (Breger, Hunter, & Lane 1971). The notion that dream symbols are used to disguise unacceptable ideas has been challenged. Hall (1953) suggested that thinking is simpler and more concrete when we are asleep than when we are awake, and that dream symbols are a useful shorthand way of expressing underlying ideas.

Interpretation

Psychoanalysis depends heavily on the therapist's interpretation of what the client says. How, for example, does the therapist know that a girl dreaming about riding a horse is actually thinking about having sex rather than simply about horse-riding? Freud argued that the acid test was the client's reaction to the therapist's proposed interpretation. If the client accepts the accuracy of the interpretation, then it is probably correct. If the client vehemently rejects the therapist's interpretation of a dream, that may simply be resistance by the client's conscious mind to an unacceptable but entirely accurate interpretation.

There is a problem here. The therapist can use either the client's acceptance or denial of the reasonableness of a dream interpretation as supporting evidence that the interpretation is correct! Freud argued that we can regard psychoanalysis as similar to solving a jigsaw puzzle. It may be hard to decide whether a given interpretation is correct, or to decide where to place a particular piece of the puzzle. However, the interpretations of dozens of a client's free associations and dreams should form a coherent picture, just as the pieces of a jigsaw puzzle can only be arranged in one way.

A factor that complicates the interpretation of what clients say and do is what Freud referred to as reaction formation. The basic idea is that the ego may transform unacceptable desires into acceptable ones to protect itself. For example, a person who has homosexual tendencies but feels uncomfortable about this may claim to be strongly opposed to homosexuality.

Transference

Freud emphasised the notion that the client should gain access not only to repressed information but also to the feelings that accompanied it. A major factor in ensuring adequate emotional involvement on the client's part is provided by **transference**, which involves the client transferring onto the therapist powerful emotional reactions that were previously directed at his or her own parents (or other highly significant individuals). As Gleitman (1986, p.696) pointed out, transference provides "a kind of emotional reliving of the unresolved problems of the patient's childhood".

A crucial aspect of transference is that the therapist responds in a neutral way to the client's emotional outpourings. The fact that the therapist will not retaliate in any way allows the client freedom to express long-repressed anger or hostility to his or her parents. The neutrality of the therapist helps to make it clear to the client that his or her emotional outbursts stem from repressed memories rather than from the therapeutic situation itself. Transference may also occur simply because the person becomes very frustrated at the neutral reactions and lack of feedback provided by the therapist!

Ego analysis

Karen Horney, Anna Freud, Erik Erikson, and others modified the traditional psychoanalytic approach to therapy in the 1940s and 1950s. Their approach is known as ego analysis. **Ego analysis** is based on the notion that the ego or rational mind is important, and that therapy should focus on strengthening the ego so that it can achieve more gratification. This contrasts with Freud's emphasis on gratification of the wishes of the id or sexual instinct.

Ego analysis makes use of free association and most of the other techniques associated with psychoanalysis. However, it focuses much more on the patient's current social and interpersonal problems than on their childhood experiences. Another difference is that ego analysts regard society as being a positive force in most people's lives, whereas Freud emphasised the ways in which society inhibits individuals.

Kleinian psychodynamic therapy

Another neo-Freudian approach to therapy is based on Klein's object relations theory. The main focus of this theory is on early relationships and the effects that these relations have on later life. In particular it is how these early relationships, most importantly with one's primary caregiver, affect our ability to relate to others. The emphasis is on significant early figures rather than on the id and ego, and on social rather than biological forces. Adults with emotional problems use the therapy relationship to work through early difficulties, though the emphasis is more on the problems here and now rather than in the past. The therapist seeks to identify consistent relationship problems, and to find ways to improve these.

Kleinian therapy was extended to play therapy. In play therapy children are given the same opportunities as adults to work through their anxieties and repressed feelings. However, as children do not have the verbal skills to do this, play is used as a medium for communication.

How might a therapist help a client strengthen their rational mind by: (a) changing a negative behaviour pattern when relating to others; (b) fulfilling a personal ambition?

Assumptions of the psychodynamic model
- Much of our behaviour is driven by unconscious motives.
- Childhood is a critical period in development.
- Mental disorders arise from unresolved, unconscious conflicts originating in childhood.
- Resolution occurs through accessing and coming to terms with repressed ideas and conflicts.

Effectiveness of Psychodynamic Therapy

The first systematic attempt to evaluate the effectiveness of psychoanalysis was reported by Hans J. Eysenck (1952), who reviewed studies in which clients either received psychoanalysis or did not receive any systematic treatment. The figures were striking: 72% of clients with no proper treatment recovered over a period of 2 years (this is known as **spontaneous remission**), compared with only 44% of those receiving psychoanalysis. These findings imply that psychoanalysis is actually bad for you!

The findings reported by Eysenck cannot be accepted at face value. He counted clients who dropped out of psychoanalysis as clients for whom therapy had failed. If these clients are excluded, then the recovery rate was 66% for patients receiving psychoanalysis. In addition, there are great doubts as to whether the studies on psychoanalysis and on spontaneous remission were comparable in the severity of the initial disorders and the criteria for recovery. Bergin (1971) considered the same information used by Eysenck (1952), but used different criteria for recovery. According to his analyses, psychoanalysis produced an 83% success rate, whereas the spontaneous remission rate was only 30%.

Sloane et al. (1975) carried out a detailed study, mainly on patients with anxiety disorder. Behavioural therapy and ego analysis both produced an 80% improvement rate, which was greater than the 48% found in the waiting-list control group. However, the three groups did not differ at the 8-month follow-up, because the control patients had

Bergin and Eysenck each analysed the same data but reached different conclusions. How can you explain this?

improved considerably. Thus, psychodynamic therapy in the form of ego analysis was as effective as behavioural therapy, and produced more rapid recovery than no treatment.

Psychodynamic therapy is more appropriate for the treatment of some disorders than others. It has proved of value in the treatment of anxiety disorders, depression, and some sexual disorders, but is considerably less effective in the treatment of schizophrenia (Luborsky & Spence, 1978). The central focus of psychodynamic therapy is to permit the client to gain insight into himself or herself. Patients (such as schizophrenics who are not taking drug therapies) who cannot do this are unsuitable for this form of therapy.

Psychodynamic therapies may be best for YAVIS types. Do you remember what this is (see page 671)?

Psychodynamic therapy is most appropriate for some types of individuals. Some of the relevant evidence was discussed by Luborsky and Spence (1978): patients who are better educated benefit more from psychodynamic therapy, perhaps because language skills are so important in therapy. Psychodynamic therapy may not be very appropriate for adults who genuinely had very happy and contented childhoods. If they have very few repressed childhood memories, there is little opportunity for them to gain insight into the meaning of their childhood suffering.

Modern psychodynamic therapies, such as ego analysis and Kleinian therapy, have extended classical approaches in several useful ways such as enabling work to be done with children, and also with groups and over shorter periods of time.

Comparisons Between Therapies: Meta-analysis

Smith, Glass, and Miller (1980) reviewed 475 studies in which the effectiveness of various therapies had been evaluated. In order to be included in the review, each study had to involve a comparison group drawn from the same population, who were treated differently (e.g., untreated). Smith et al. carried out a meta-analysis, which involves combining the data from numerous studies so that an accurate estimate can be made of the effectiveness of each form of treatment. The studies varied considerably. Some involved comparisons between different forms of therapy, whereas others involved

---

Humanistic therapy

The humanistic approach underlies one of the most common approaches to helping people with emotional problems—counselling or **client-centred therapy** (Rogers, 1951, 1959). (This therapy is not mentioned in the A2 specification but we think it is important to outline some of the key points of this approach.)

Humanistic therapy, like the psychoanalytic approach, was designed to change the functioning of the mind. Rogers' starting point for this form of therapy was the concept of self. Individuals often experience problems and seek therapy when there is incongruence (or major discrepancies) between the self-concept and the ideal self. For Rogers (1986) the main assumption lying behind client-centred therapy was:

> The individual has within him or herself, vast resources of self-understanding, for altering his or her self-concept, attitudes and self-directing behaviour, and … these resources can be tapped if only a definable climate of facilitative psychological attitudes can be provided.

According to Rogers (1951), the way in which the therapist or facilitator behaves towards the client is of key importance in determining the success of treatment. Rogers argued that therapists should be:

- Unconditional in positive regard: this involves the therapist accepting and valuing the client, and avoiding being critical or judgemental.
- Genuine, in the sense of allowing their true feelings and thoughts to emerge.

- Empathic (i.e., understanding the other person's feelings).

Client-centred therapy involves the client discussing his or her self-concept and life goals with the facilitator. The facilitator invites the client to interpret or make sense of his or her experience, and enables the client to do this through unconditional positive regard and empathetic understanding. This increases the client's self-esteem and permits him or her to accept those parts of self into the self-structure that were previously excluded from the self-concept (see "self theory" on page 610). This allows the client to reduce the discrepancy between his or her self-concept and ideal self. It also allows the client to develop a greater sense of being in control of his or her destiny because the client controls the therapeutic process. Client-centred therapy differs from psychodynamic therapy in that the focus is very much on current concerns and hopes for the future, whereas the emphasis in Freudian psychodynamic therapy is on childhood experiences.

Rogers originally believed that his client-centred therapy was non-directive, in the sense that the therapist did not provide the client with solutions but expected that the client would find his or her own answers. However, Truax (1966) recorded some therapy sessions between Rogers and his clients. What emerged was that Rogers was much more likely to reward or encourage his clients when they produced positive statements and seemed to be making progress. In other words, Rogers was directing the thoughts of his clients much more than he had intended.

comparisons between therapy and no treatment. Several different **outcome measures** were used in many of the studies, ranging from self-report measures to behavioural and physiological measures of various kinds. Altogether, there were 1776 outcome measures from the 475 studies. These 475 studies considered by Smith et al. were unrepresentative of most clinical outcome studies in that more than 50% of the patients receiving treatment were students.

Smith et al. (1980) concluded: "Different types of psychotherapy (verbal or behavioural, psychodynamic, client-centred, or systematic desensitisation) do not produce different types or degrees of benefit." On average, their analyses indicated that a client receiving any systematic form of psychotherapy was better off than 80% of controls in terms of recovery. They reported that the effectiveness of therapy did not depend on its length. As behavioural therapy typically takes much less time than psychodynamic therapy, that is an argument for preferring behavioural therapy.

The approach adopted by Smith et al. was limited in a number of ways. They failed to include all the existing studies in their review. In addition, they gave equal weight to all studies, regardless of quality. This is serious, because it has been argued (Prioleau, Murdock, & Brody, 1983) that only 32 of the studies considered by Smith et al. were based on sound methods.

Smith et al. found that the beliefs and preferences of therapists were important in determining the effectiveness of therapy. Any form of therapy was more effective when it was provided by therapists who believed strongly in that therapy. However, it is important to note that recovery in most of the studies was assessed by experts who did not know which form of therapy any patient had received.

Would it be possible to offer effective therapy if one did not believe in that particular approach?

Smith et al. also found that some forms of therapy were especially effective with certain disorders. Cognitive therapy and cognitive-behavioural therapy were most effective with specific phobias, fear, and anxiety. Client-centred therapy worked best with clients having low self-esteem.

Rosenhan and Seligman (1995) considered the issue of the most effective forms of therapy for different disorders. Some of their conclusions were as follows:

- *Anxieties, fears, phobias, and panic*: systematic desensitisation, cognitive therapy, and drugs (benzodiazepines) are among the best forms of therapy.
- *Depression*: cognitive therapy, electroconvulsive treatment, and drugs (e.g., Prozac) are all very effective.
- *Schizophrenia*: drugs (neuroleptics such as chlorpromazine) and family intervention (involving communication skills) are effective.

Wampold et al. (1997, p.211) carried out a meta-analysis on studies in which two or more forms of therapy had been compared directly, and in which the same outcome measures had been applied to patients receiving different forms of therapy. Their findings suggested that the beneficial effects of all forms of therapy are essentially the same. They concluded:

> *Why is it that researchers persist in attempts to find treatment differences, when they know that these effects are small in comparison to other effects, such as therapists' effects ... or effects of treatment versus no-treatment comparisons?*

Evaluation of meta-analyses of therapy

We need to be cautious about interpreting the evidence from meta-analyses, because most of them are limited in various ways. According to Matt and Navarro (1997, p.20; see the Key Study overleaf)

> *psychotherapy outcome studies do not adequately represent patient populations, settings, interventions, and outcomes commonly found in clinical practice ... [They] overrepresent anxiety disorders ... younger age groups and student patients ... recruited rather than referred patients ... and difficult to treat patients ... Settings were found to overrepresent outpatient settings, universities, highly controlled environments and to underrepresent*

Matt and Navarro

Matt and Navarro (1997) considered evidence from 63 meta-analyses of the effects of therapy. Across the 28 meta-analyses providing relevant data, the mean effect size was 0.67, meaning that 75% of patients improved more than untreated controls. This is somewhat lower than the figure reported by Smith et al. (1980).

Matt and Navarro also addressed the issue of whether the effects of therapy are due to specific effects or to common effects (e.g., placebo effects). They did this by focusing on 10 meta-analyses in which three types of group were compared:

1. Specific therapy groups, for whom any benefits may depend on specific effects or common effects.

2. Placebo control groups (involving general encouragement but no specific therapy), for whom any benefits are likely to depend on common effects.

3. Waiting-list control groups, for whom no benefits are expected.

The evidence indicated that 57% of placebo control patients did better than the average waiting-list control patient, indicating that common or placebo effects exist. However, 75% of the patients receiving specific therapy did better than the average placebo control patient, indicating that specific effects are almost four times more powerful than common or placebo effects.

KEY STUDY EVALUATION — Matt and Navarro

A major criticism of Matt and Navarro's research concerns its lack of standardisation. The specific conditions of individual cases are vital in determining the effectiveness of therapy. Linked to this is the timescale used. Regression or relapse would indicate failure of therapy, but this is impossible to discover from Matt and Navarro's study. A much lengthier approach, capable of handling disparate sets of data, with a methodology using detailed case notes and follow-up research would be needed to address this problem.

Accuracy is difficult to determine in meta-analyses, and it would be of value to consider making more use of the case-study-centred approach. The inevitable cost and time implications militate against this more focused type of study. However, if psychologists wish to make any real impact on the effectiveness of therapy, it would make sense to involve clients' own testimonies as valid forms of data, rather than relying only on notes based on second-hand observation. This may not give such a tidy result, but might be an improvement in some ways on the sweeping generalisations that often result from meta-analyses.

Do different forms of therapy vary in their general effectiveness? Matt and Navarro (1997, p.22) considered the relevant meta-analyses, and concluded as follows: "Typically, differences favoured behavioural and cognitive therapy approaches over psychodynamic and client-centred approaches." However, they accepted that it was hard to interpret such differences because there was no standardisation of disorder severity, outcome measures, and so on.

Discussion points

1. What are the strengths and weaknesses of meta-analyses as a way of discovering the effectiveness of therapy?

2. How impressed are you by the apparent effectiveness of most forms of therapy revealed by Matt and Navarro?

clinical practice and psychiatric setting. As for types of interventions, meta-analysts note the overrepresentation of cognitive and behavioural interventions, therapists in training or with little experience … and interventions targeting fairly circumscribed [limited] and behavioural problems … With respect to outcomes, several meta-analysts have argued … there is overreliance on self-report measures, therapist ratings, and behavioural measures.

Processes involved in therapy·

The effectiveness of any form of therapy depends on specific factors unique to that therapy, and common factors such as warmth, acceptance, and empathy on the part of the therapist. The fact that different therapies are of roughly equal effectiveness suggests that common factors are important. Indeed, it has been argued that about 85% of the variation in the effectiveness of therapy depends on common rather than specific factors (Strupp, 1996).

Positive common factors

Sloane et al. (1975) conducted a study on patients who had derived benefit from either behavioural therapy or insight-oriented therapy. The two groups were asked to indicate those aspects of therapy that they had found useful. In spite of the large differences in the treatment received, the two groups identified very much the same factors. The helpful factors included the therapist's personality, being able to talk to a sympathetic person, and the therapist's encouragement to handle issues that the patients found hard to deal with. Thus the same common factors are of major importance in both forms of therapy.

Negative outcomes

Mohr (1995) focused on some of the common factors in therapy that seem to produce negative outcomes, in which therapy actually makes the patient's condition worse rather than better. Therapists who show a lack of empathy, who underestimate the severity of the patient's problems, or who disagree with the patient about the process of therapy are most likely to provide unsuccessful treatment. On the other side, patients who are poorly motivated, who expect that therapy will be easy, or who have very poor interpersonal skills are most likely to experience negative outcomes.

...warmth, acceptance and empathy on the part of the therapist.

Specific factors

In spite of the importance of common factors, it is important not to ignore the role of specific factors. Consider, for example, treatment for depression. Drug therapy and cognitive therapy are both equally effective in producing recovery from depression (e.g., Barber & DeRubeis, 1989). However, drug therapy is only designed to reduce the symptoms of depression, whereas cognitive therapy or cognitive-behavioural therapy is intended to equip clients with more realistic and positive beliefs about themselves and their situation. As might be expected, patients who have been treated for depression with drug therapy are more likely to relapse into depression in the year following recovery than are patients who received cognitive-behavioural therapy (Barber & DeRubeis, 1989). Thus, some of the specific factors involved in cognitive-behavioural therapy for depression have greater long-term effectiveness than those involved in drug therapy.

SECTION SUMMARY

Biological (Somatic) Therapies

❖ Early treatments for mental disorders included trepanning which was a highly dangerous and ineffective practice. Moniz pioneered psychosurgery in the 1930s, introducing the prefrontal lobotomy as a method of controlling violent patients. Major side-effects led to abandoning this approach but recent methods have improved precision so that only very specific areas of the brain are destroyed. Prefrontal leukotomy involves inserting fine needles to destroy nerve fibres. Stereotactic neurosurgery is even more refined and can be done under local anaesthesia. Amygdalotomies and cingulotomies have been performed to reduce aggression and curb emotion. In the case of the former there were still serious side-effects but cingulotomies are used with some success. The ethics of causing permanent brain damage remain questionable.

❖ Electroconvulsive shock treatment (ECT) also had its origins in the early twentieth century. Initially it was thought to be a possible treatment for schizophrenia but it has proved successful for depression. Today a weak electric current is usually applied to the non-dominant brain hemisphere along with muscle relaxants and an anaesthetic. The patient shows mild twitching and experiences little discomfort.

❖ ECT is used for cases of severe depression with some degree of effectiveness, though it is not seen as a cure for depression. ECT is preferred to drugs in some cases because some patients respond to ECT but not to drugs, and ECT is also faster acting. Improvements may be due to expectations, but sham treatments showed much less improvement.

❖ When considering the appropriateness of the treatment it is relevant to consider explanations for how the treatment works. First, ECT may act as a punishment though sub-convulsive shocks do not appear to change behaviour but are equally as unpleasant. Second, associated memory loss may allow some restructuring of disordered thinking, though unilateral ECT leads to minimal memory disruption yet is still effective. Third, levels of noradrenaline and serotonin are reduced, which wouldn't explain why some patients do experience a permanent cure. Ethical concerns remain because of the direct nature of brain intervention.

❖ The third form of biological therapy is chemotherapy. Depression is treated with MAOIs and the tricyclics, which increase levels of noradrenaline and serotonin, as well as SSRIs which affect serotonin only. They all reduce the symptoms of depression. Tricyclics tend to be more effective with severe depression and have fewer side-effects, though there are still some associated problems. There are individual differences in effectiveness. None of these drugs have much effect on the mood of normal individuals, supporting the view that they do not simply cause physiological arousal.

❖ Lithium carbonate reduces the occurrence of manic and depressed episodes in bipolar depressives. Anxiety disorders used to be treated by barbiturates until they were replaced by the benzodiazepines, though these often have sedative effects. Buspirone is a new drug with fewer side effects. Schizophrenia is treated with neuroleptics though these have little effect on the negative symptoms. Side-effects can be alleviated by "drug holidays". The drug may be given as an injection to ensure it is taken.

❖ There are various problems with chemotherapy. It tends to take responsibility away from the patient, patients may not comply with treatment, chemotherapy treats symptoms rather than causes, and drugs are not always effective. However, chemotherapy has allowed a great number of people to lead relatively normal lives.

❖ Effectiveness of any therapy can be assessed by comparing recovery rates of individuals who do or do not receive therapy. Problems with this are that the definition of "recovery" varies, patients may still relapse, it is unethical to withhold treatment, effects may be due to common factors, each patient has unique symptoms, each therapist has unique characteristics, patients are self-selected samples, some therapies work better for some patients, and apparent recovery may be due to the hello–goodbye effect. Therapies can be evaluated from the point of view of society, the individual and the therapist. Recovery in control groups may be due to the placebo effect.

❖ Therapy raises a number of ethical issues. Therapy is normally only carried out with the full informed consent of the client, which enhances its effectiveness. However, this is not always possible because appropriate information is not available, patients forget the information or cannot understand it, and choices are based on the therapist rather than the treatment. Confidentiality is also an issue. Somatic therapies are effective for disorders that have a biological basis. They can produce rapid results and require little effort from the patient, but they have side-effects and are not cures.

Behavioural Therapies

❖ Behavioural therapy involves the use of classical and operant conditioning to change unwanted behaviour into something more desirable. Maladaptive behaviours that were learned can be unlearned. Therapy focuses on behaviour and symptom removal. Criticisms are made of its mechanistic nature, and the problems of symptom substitution and lack of generalisation.

❖ The therapies based on classical conditioning include flooding, systematic desensitisation, and aversion therapy.

❖ Flooding aims to break the phobic cycle by demonstrating that there is no basis to the fear, but it may be disturbing and result in increased resistance. Systematic desensitisation involves counterconditioning. An anxiety hierarchy is constructed and at each stage the client practises relaxation to learn a new response that is incompatible with fear.

❖ Aversion therapy involves pairing the undesired behaviour (NS) with a very unpleasant stimulus (UCS) to produce a new response (CR) to the undesired behaviour, and so suppress it. This learning may not transfer to the real world.

- Behavioural therapies based on operant conditioning aim to identify how maladaptive behaviours are being reinforced, and to decrease them while increasing reinforcement for adaptive behaviours. This can be done using extinction, selective punishment, and selective positive reinforcement. Token economies offer rewards for achieving small behavioural goals. They have proved successful but the beneficial effects may disappear when the rewards are no longer given. This may be due to the nature of context-dependent learning, or the fact that rewards destroy intrinsic motivation. The therapy also underestimates the importance of cognitive processes. Variations in patient capabilities and ethics should also be considered.
- Modelling therapy is based on vicarious reinforcement and imitation, and has been extended to social skills training which is effective with, for example, disruptive pupils and autistic children.
- Research indicates reasonable success for behavioural therapies but such success may be due to expectations and/or therapist variables. Behavioural therapies are most suitable for disorders where behavioural symptoms are central.

- Cognitive therapy involves changing or restructuring negative irrational beliefs and thoughts into more positive and rational ones. Its development owes much to the work of Ellis and Beck. Ellis's rational-emotional therapy involves challenging the client's self-defeating beliefs and replacing them with more realistic ones. Anxious patients do appear to hold more irrational beliefs. RET may be suitable for certain individuals and for certain disorders.
- Beck used the concept of the cognitive triad to express the negative beliefs that depressed individuals hold about themselves, the world and the future. Therapy involves collaborative empiricism (joint discussion of the problem and goals) and challenging negative thoughts directly or by setting tasks for the client (e.g., hypothesis testing).
- Recently, cognitive therapy has evolved into cognitive-behavioural therapy, which includes elements of behavioural therapy. The central assumption is that the client's thinking and behaviour both need to change in order to produce the most beneficial effects. CBT has been demonstrated as effective with depression and anxiety disorders, especially panic disorder. It is a cost-effective treatment and increasingly popular.
- Two examples of psychodynamic therapy are considered: psychoanalysis and ego analysis. Psychoanalysis is based on Freud's personality theory. Freud argued that individuals with mental disorders have repressed threatening thoughts and feelings. Adults with personal problems regress to earlier stages of psychosexual development, especially to a stage where earlier fixations occurred. Neurosis can be cured through insight into repressed ideas but this produces high levels of anxiety. Techniques such as hypnosis, free association, and dream analysis are used. Freud abandoned hypnosis because of problems of suggestion. Free association may be threatened by resistance. Dream analysis focuses on the latent content. Dreams are wish fulfilment.
- Psychoanalysis relies very much on the therapist's interpretations of what the client says, and these interpretations may be wrong. A client's acceptance or denial of an interpretation is seen as proof of correctness. Interpretation is further complicated by reaction formation. Therapy often involves transference, with the client transferring strong emotions towards someone of major significance in his/her life onto the therapist and thus dealing with repressed feelings.
- Ego analysis aims to strengthen the rational mind and focuses more on current social problems. Kleinian object relations therapy focuses on early relationships and using the relationship with the therapist to work through early problems. Play therapy is an extension of this work.
- There has been controversy about the effectiveness of psychoanalysis, but it is generally accepted as reasonably effective. It is successful with anxiety disorders, depression and sexual disorders but not with schizophrenia where patients do not have the ability to be insightful. Psychodynamic therapy is suitable for articulate

Alternatives to Biological and Behavioural Therapies

individuals and not for those with happy childhoods where repression would not be a factor in their maladjustment. Modern psychodynamic therapies have extended the approach to children, group work, and to shorter durations.

❖   One large-scale meta-analysis suggested that most forms of therapy are about equally effective, with clients being better off than 80% of controls in terms of recovery. Length of therapy was not important, which suggests that short therapies might as well be used, such as behaviour therapy. Therapies were most effective when provided by a therapist who believed strongly in the therapy being used, and each form of therapy was more effective with some disorders than with others. Meta-analysis is not without problems, such as the lack of comparability. Many of the beneficial effects of therapy are due to common factors rather than specific factors. Common factors are related to both positive and negative outcomes. Specific factors may be important in effecting cures rather than relief.

FURTHER READING

The topics in this Section are covered in greater depth by S. Cave (1999) *Therapeutic approaches in psychology* (London: Routledge), written specifically for the AQA A specification. W. Dryden (1996) *Individual therapy: A handbook* (Milton Keynes, UK: Open University Press) contains chapters on all the therapies. There are several good textbooks in abnormal psychology that cover the main therapeutic approaches. They include P.C. Kendall and C. Hammen (1998) *Abnormal psychology: Understanding human problems (2nd Edn.)* (Boston: Houghton Mifflin), and D.H. Barlow and V.M. Durand (1995) *Abnormal psychology: An integrative approach* (New York: Brooks/Cole).

Example Examination Questions

You should spend 40 minutes on each of the questions below, which aim to test the material in this Section. Unlike questions from Unit 4 of the examination, covered in Parts 1–5 of this book, the questions in the Individual Differences section of the Unit 5 examination, covered in this Part, are marked out of 30 and an additional criterion is used in assessment: synopticity. "Synopticity" is defined as your "understanding and critical appreciation of the breadth and range of different theoretical perspectives and/or methodological approaches relevant to any questions" (AQA specification).

1.   Discuss issues surrounding the use of biological (somatic) therapies.   **(30 marks)**

2.   **(a)** Describe the use and mode of action of any **two** biological (somatic) therapies used
          in the treatment of mental disorders.   **(15 marks)**
     (b) Evaluate these therapies in terms of the issues surrounding their use (e.g.,
          appropriateness and effectiveness).   **(15 marks)**

3.   Distinguish between those behavioural therapies based on classical conditioning and those
     based on operant conditioning.   **(30 marks)**

4.   **(a)** Describe the use and mode of action of **two or more** behavioural therapies based on
          operant conditioning.   **(15 marks)**
     (b) Justify the use of these therapies in the treatment of psychological disorders.   **(15 marks)**

5.   "One of the greatest problems for any patient suffering from mental disorder is the question
     of how to choose the best and most appropriate therapy."

     Distinguish between any **two** types of therapies for mental disorders.   **(30 marks)**

6.   Discuss the use of **two** therapies that are derived from the psychodynamic **or**
     cognitive-behavioural models of abnormality.   **(30 marks)**

Examination Tips

Question 1.   "Discuss" is an AO1 and AO2 term requiring description plus evaluation. In the specification, likely issues are identified as the appropriateness and effectiveness of such therapies but you might consider other issues as well, such as ethical concerns. It is important that you give equal weight to your description as well as the evaluation in order to access full marks, and that you are aware of the synoptic criteria that are also assessed here.

Question 2.   The phrase "use and mode of action" comes from the specification and encourages you to do more than list features of your two chosen therapies. If you consider more than two therapies only the best two will be credited. In part (b) you are specifically required to assess the therapies in terms of issues surrounding their use. It might still be possible to draw comparisons between therapies as long as this was related to an issue such as effectiveness (one therapy is more effective than another in certain situations).

Question 3.   "Distinguish between" is an AO1 and AO2 term that requires you to describe behavioural therapies based on classical and operant conditioning for the AO1 marks and then distinguish between them for AO2. The danger will be that you have a great deal to write for AO1 and little for AO2. It will be important to be selective when describing therapies in order to restrict the time spent on this half of the essay. It is possible to make distinctions in terms of effectiveness, ethics, applicability to different patients, research support, and so on. Credit will also be awarded for any similarities that are identified (e.g., lack of distinctiveness). Behavioural therapies as a whole may be contrasted with other approaches.

Question 4.   This question is restricted to operant conditioning only. Part (a) requires a description of at least two therapies. There is a depth–breadth trade-off here as increasing breadth (more than two therapies) is likely to incur a cost in terms of depth, and both are needed for top marks. In part (b) you must assess the effectiveness and appropriateness of these therapies and thus justify their use. Synopticity can be demonstrated by reference to other approaches, which may be more or less useful, as well as considering other overarching issues such as ethics and determinism.

Question 5. You are not required to refer to the quotation in your answer but it is there to suggest ways of answering the question. The question allows you to select any therapies for discussion—you might contrast behavioural with psychodynamic approaches, or be more particular in comparing aversion therapy with psychoanalysis. The former approach is likely to be most fruitful because of the breadth of material available. As in question 3 you must take care not to write too much description and therefore fail to attract marks for evaluation.

Question 6.   The specification states that you only have to study psychodynamic *or* cognitive-behavioural models of abnormality. Some candidates may find it difficult to achieve a reasonable balance when describing two therapies from one model, knowing one better than the other—as in the case of psychoanalysis and one other example of a psychodynamic therapy. If only one therapy is covered then partial performance penalties will apply for both AO1 and AO2 (maximum of 10 marks each). If only one therapy is evaluated then there are partial performance penalties on AO2.

WEB SITES

http://www.aabt.org/related/related.htm
Links to behaviour therapy sites on the homepage of the Association for the Advancement of Behavior Therapy.

http://www.antipsychiatry.org/ect.htm
Arguments against electroconvulsive shock treatment.

http://neurosurgery.mgh.harvard.edu/psysurg.htm
Article on psychosurgery.

http://www.psychologyinfo.com/depression/cognitive.htm
Using cognitive therapy to tackle depression.

PART 7

Perspectives

This Part is different from all the other Parts in the book because it covers the **synoptic** element of your A level course. Synopticity can be defined as: "the ability to demonstrate an understanding and critical appreciation of the breadth of theoretical and methodological approaches in psychology." In AQA specification A the "synoptic paper" (Unit 5) counts for 20% of your entire A level mark (40% of the A2 examination).

Why is synopticity so important? The essence of studying Advanced level psychology is to gain an appreciation of psychology. This is not the same as learning about why people remember and forget or what factors contribute to an emotional experience. These are all areas of psychology. The intention is that you will develop informed opinions about the breadth of theoretical and methodological approaches in psychology. Therefore, the synoptic paper is the last one you take, in which you can demonstrate your knowledge on these overarching topics.

When answering synoptic questions in the examination it is vital that you draw on your knowledge from other Sections in this book to support your arguments. In the examination you will only be able to answer one question on issues and debates, so you only need to cover one of these thoroughly (i.e., either issues or debates).

You must also answer one question on approaches, but do not need to cover all those in Section 21, Approaches in Psychology. The bare minimum is two. Your choice will depend on the areas of psychology you have studied. For example, if you have not covered Freud's theory of personality in Section 11, Social and Personality Development, then you would be less able to use the psychodynamic approach than a candidate who has studied that Section.

19

Issues

Throughout your studies certain issues have been considered repeatedly: gender, culture, and ethics. In this Section you have the opportunity to reflect on these issues in relation to your studies so far.

Gender Bias

The term "bias" is used to suggest that a person's or society's views are distorted in some systematic way. In psychology, there is evidence that gender is presented in a biased way and this bias leads to a misrepresentation of women. Consider the following example. The performance of participants in psychological research tends to be influenced by the expectations of the investigator. Many people still have lower expectations for women than for men. This would lead us to collect data that show poorer task performance in women (for example, on a memory task). Research data are used to formulate theories and these theories may well be gender biased because of the baseline data.

In this Unit we will explore different areas and aspects of gender bias, and how this affects psychological knowledge.

Gender Stereotypes

There are many popular (and misleading) stereotypes about the differences between the sexes. For example, it has often been claimed that women are more emotional than men. This was expressed poetically by Alfred, Lord Tennyson:

Man for the sword and for the needle she:
Man with the head and woman with the heart.

Stereotypes about gender have been fairly common in psychology as well as in society at large. One of the worst offenders was Sigmund Freud. He argued that anatomy is destiny, meaning that there are great psychological differences between men and women because of their anatomical differences. For example, Freud claimed that young girls suffer from "penis envy" when they find out that boys have a penis but they do not (see page 430 for a discussion of this).

The greatest difficulty lies in distinguishing "real" from culturally created gender differences. There are real differences, or at least that was the conclusion reached by Maccoby and Jacklin (1974) in a review of research on sex differences. They concluded that there were only four differences between boys and girls for which there was strong evidence. This is a much smaller number of gender differences than would have been

Research on sex differences is discussed on page 429.

Maccoby and Jacklin (1974) found strong evidence for only four differences between boys' and girls' behaviour and abilities.

predicted by most psychologists. The four differences identified by Maccoby and Jacklin were as follows:

- Girls have greater verbal ability than boys.
- Boys have greater visual and spatial abilities than girls (e.g., arranging blocks in specified patterns).
- Boys have greater arithmetical ability than girls, but this difference only appears at adolescence.
- Girls are less aggressive than boys: this is found in nearly all cultures, and is usually present from about 2 years of age.

Most of these differences are fairly small, and there is much overlap in behaviour between boys and girls. Sex differences in abilities (verbal, visual, spatial, and mathematical) are even smaller now than they were in the early 1970s (Hyde & Linn, 1988).

However, as Shaffer (1993) pointed out, there are some differences that were not identified by Maccoby and Jacklin (1974). First, girls show more emotional sensitivity (e.g., they respond more attentively to babies). Second, girls are less vulnerable developmentally than boys, and they are less likely to suffer from learning disabilities, various language disorders, or hyperactivity. Third, boys tend to be more physically active than girls. Fourth, girls tend to be more timid than boys when they are in unfamiliar situations.

In a large-scale survey of gender stereotypes in 30 different national cultures, Williams and Best (1982) found that there were many similarities across the various cultures. Men were seen as more dominant, aggressive, and autonomous; a more *instrumental role*. Women were more nurturant, deferent, and interested in affiliation; being encouraged to develop an *expressive role*. This suggests some kind of universal, biological basis for gender stereotypes.

Alpha Bias and Beta Bias

Why is alpha bias more common than beta bias?

If there are real gender differences, how does that affect psychological research? Hare-Mustin and Marecek (1988) considered the issue of gender bias in psychology in detail. Their starting point was that there are two basic forms of gender bias: **alpha bias** and **beta bias**. According to Hare-Mustin and Marecek (1988, p.457), "Alpha bias is the tendency to exaggerate differences; beta bias is the tendency to minimise or ignore differences." They used the term "bias" to refer to an inclination to focus on certain aspects of experience rather than on others.

Within Western cultures, alpha bias has been more common than beta bias. For example, Freud claimed that children's superego or conscience develops when they identify with the same-sex parent. Girls do not identify with their mother as strongly as boys identify with their father. As a result, Freud argued that girls develop weaker superegos than boys (see Section 10, Cognitive Development). However, Freud did admit that "the majority of men are far behind the masculine ideal [in terms of strength of superego]". The evidence does not support Freud. Hoffman (1975) discussed studies in which the tendency of children to do what they had been told not to do was assessed. The behaviour of boys and girls did not differ in most of the studies. When there was a sex difference, it was the girls (rather than the boys) who were better at resisting temptation.

Hare-Mustin and Marecek (1988) argued that beta bias, or the tendency to minimise or ignore sex differences, is less common than alpha bias. They suggested that Bem's (1974) theory of psychological androgyny is an example of beta bias. According to that theory, it is psychologically more healthy to be androgynous (having a mixture of positive masculine and feminine characteristics) than to have only masculine or only feminine characteristics. Individuals who can respond to any situation with either masculine (instrumental) characteristics or feminine (expressive) characteristics are more flexible than an individual who behaves in a more sex-stereotyped way.

Beta bias in research studies

There is evidence of beta bias in experimental research, i.e., a tendency to reduce or minimise gender differences. Male and female participants are used in most studies, but there is typically no attempt to analyse the data to see whether there are significant sex differences. It may be possible that sex differences are found in psychological research because researchers ignore the differential treatment of participants. Male experimenters may treat their female participants differently from their male ones. Rosenthal (1966) reported that they were more pleasant, friendly, honest, and encouraging with female than with male participants. Such findings led Rosenthal (1966) to conclude: "Male and female subjects may, psychologically, simply not be in the same experiment at all."

How might an experimenter control for this differential treatment of men and women?

This means that, because researchers act as if there are no sex differences, they end up providing evidence that there are such differences. In other words beta bias tends to produce sex differences.

Beta bias in psychological theories

The same reasoning can be applied to some psychological theories that show evidence of beta bias. Kohlberg (1963) put forward a theory of moral development based mainly on studies of moral dilemmas with males as the main actors and with males as participants. He claimed that men tended to be at a higher level of moral development than women (see Section 10, Cognitive Development). Kohlberg assumed that there were minimal differences between men and women in terms of moral thinking (a beta bias) and therefore it would not matter if he used only male participants because this would still represent all people. The outcome is a demonstration of gender differences.

How would you measure moral development in a way that is not gender-specific?

Kohlberg's claim that men were morally superior to women was disputed by Gilligan (1977). She argued that Kohlberg had focused too much on the morality of justice and too little on the morality of care. According to her, boys develop the morality of justice, whereas girls develop the morality of care. Gilligan (1982) reported evidence that supported her position (see page 406).

In fact, most of the evidence indicates that there are small or non-existent differences in moral reasoning between males and females. For example, Walker et al. (1987) reported a meta-analysis, in which only eight out of 54 studies revealed significant evidence of sex differences in moral development. That confirms Gilligan's view that Kohlberg had unfairly concluded that female moral development was less advanced than male moral development. However, as Durkin (1995, p.493) pointed out, Gilligan's "critical perspective did serve the purpose of opening up the study of moral development in important ways by broadening conceptions of what morality is and how it should be measured".

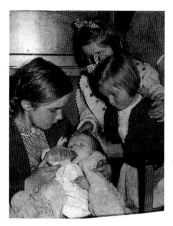

Girls are more likely than boys to respond attentively to babies.

An androcentric view of human nature

The result of beta bias in psychological research is that we end up with a view of human nature that purports to apply to men and women alike, but in fact has a male or **androcentric bias**. This is true of Kohlberg's theory of moral development. It is also true of other areas of research. Asch's (1955) conformity studies involved all male participants. In fact the same is true of many of the other conformity studies (e.g., Perrin & Spencer, 1980). Psychological theories of conformity are thus based largely on male behaviour. Eagly (1978) found that women may be even more conformist, or at least they are more oriented towards interpersonal goals and therefore *appear* to be more conformist in experimental situations. What is clear is that a failure to attend to gender issues has both oversimplified, exaggerated and/or fudged gender differences!

Moscovici's (1969) classic study on minority influence used all female participants. Perhaps if he had used male participants, minority influence would have appeared to be less significant.

Sherif et al.'s (1961) study of boys at a summer camp involved all boys, and Erikson's (1968) research into lifespan development also involved all male interviews. What other studies used all male or all female participants? How may this have affected the theories derived from the data?

Social constructionism is discussed in more detail on page 776.

Facts and Values

The discussion so far has assumed that there are *facts* about gender. A different view is favoured by **social constructionists** such as Gergen (1985). They argue that there are no facts. There are *values* and these determine what are regarded as facts. We construct our reality through shared conversations about the social and physical world. In other words, "scientific knowledge, like all other knowledge, cannot be disinterested or politically neutral" (Hare-Mustin & Marecek, 1988, p.456). Thus we may be "fooled" into believing that our knowledge of gender facts is "real", whereas they are social constructions.

Such facts may have serious repercussions. Burns (1993, p.103) provided an example of how society's values can influence the approach taken to studying women. She pointed out that a major focus of research on women with learning disabilities is on "sexuality and the issues and concerns surrounding women with learning disabilities becoming pregnant, having babies, being sterilised, using contraception, managing periods and being sexually abused." In other words, such women are seen in a negative way in terms of the possible problems they may cause. As Burns (1993, p.103) pointed out, "the consequence of this position is to deny women with learning disabilities a positive identity and role as a woman".

■ Activity: Make a list of value-free factual points about the experience of studying psychology. Now make a second list of value-free factual points about female psychology students. How difficult was it to construct non-judgemental views for either list? To what extent did gender appear to be an issue?

Feminist psychology

Traditional psychology has also sought to explain behaviour in terms of internal causes, such as biological sex differences. This has led to inevitable gender biases in psychological theories. The alternative, social constructionist approach aims to understand behaviour in terms of social processes and thus find a way to greater equality. Feminist psychologists argue that there may be real sex differences but socially determined stereotypes make a far greater contribution to perceived differences.

Feminist psychology takes the view that a prerequisite to any social change with respect to gender roles must be a revision of our "facts" about gender. Whether such facts are true or not, they perpetuate our beliefs about women. Feminist psychology is a branch of psychology that aims to redress the imbalances in psychology.

Pre-menstrual syndrome is described on page 639. In what way is this an example of how female behaviour has been pathologised because it does not fit with male norms for behaviour?

One way to redress the balance is to use evidence that women may be inferior to provide women with greater support. For example, Eagly (1978) acknowledged that women may be less effective leaders than men but this knowledge should be used to develop suitable training programmes.

A further way to redress the balance is to become aware of how androcentric theories inevitably lead to the view that female behaviour is abnormal (see the box "Battered women's syndrome", below). Bem (1994) argued that in a male-centred world, female differences are transformed into female disadvantages. Bem (1993) used the concept of an "enculturated lens" to suggest that the view of gender that we receive from our culture

Battered women's syndrome

Bem (1993) used battered women's syndrome as an example of how society constructs frameworks that pathologise women's behaviour. Bem argued that women who live with highly aggressive partners have now been given a means of legal defence in cases where they have killed their partner, often in circumstances where they were not directly provoked—the battered women's syndrome. The recognition of this syndrome allows women to argue that any attack on their partners, whether it was directly provoked or not, was justified by the general treatment they were receiving from their partners over a prolonged period.

However, at the same time, the idea of a "syndrome" turns the woman's behaviour into something that is pathological, i.e., a behaviour that is somehow "sick" ("pathological" means "diseased"). This "sickness" in

the woman deflects our attention from the sickness inherent in society that allows some men to feel justified in their behaviour.

Furthermore, feminist lawyers point out that the law itself is androcentric because the concept of self-defence is related to male–male encounters (more usual). If one person attacks another, one can plead self-defence as long as the second person was in immediate danger of serious or deadly injury. This cannot be applied to the battered woman, who usually defends herself at a time other than when she is in immediate danger. Alternatively, it could be argued that as she has not been killed in the past, then she has never actually been in such danger. The law does not allow for a form of self-defence that is not within this male–male context because the law is defined by male interactions.

misshapes how we see men and women. Bem (1993, p.2) suggested that we should make those lenses

visible rather than invisible, to enable us to look at the culture's gender lenses rather than through them, for it is only when Americans apprehend the more subtle and systemic ways in which the culture reproduces male power that they will finally comprehend the unfinished business of the feminists' agenda.

In sum, there is evidence of gender bias within psychology. However, most of the clearest examples of such bias occurred a long time ago. This suggests that psychologists have become more concerned to avoid gender bias.

Cultural Bias

Research in psychology has for very many years been dominated by the United States. According to Rosenzweig (1992), 64% of the world's 56,000 researchers in psychology are Americans. Their impact on textbooks in psychology is often even greater. For example, consider Baron and Byrne's (1991) textbook on social psychology. In that book, 94% of the studies referred to were from North America, compared with 2% from Europe, 1% from Australasia, and 3% from the rest of the world.

Facts like those just mentioned are of relevance to **cross-cultural psychology**, in which different cultures are studied and compared. What is a culture? According to Smith and Bond (1993, p.36), a **culture** "is a *relatively organised* system of shared meanings." For example, the word "work" has a rather different meaning in the Japanese culture than in others. In Japan, it typically includes going drinking after normal working hours, and sharing in other recreational activities with one's work colleagues. Most cross-cultural psychology has involved comparisons between different nations or *countries*. This suffers from the problem that a country is generally not the same as a culture. For example, there are several cultures within a single country such as the United States.

The Japanese work culture includes the requirement to socialise outside working hours with colleagues.

> **Cross-cultural psychology**
>
> Cross-cultural psychology is like comparative psychology where different species of animals are studied with the intention of making comparisons with human behaviour, and therefore learning more about the latter. Cultural variation also allows us to observe the effects of different social practices on behaviour.

Cultural Differences

It is often assumed that what is true of our culture or country is also true of most other cultures or countries. Many psychologists who carry out studies in the United States or in the United Kingdom make that assumption. However, the assumption is wrong. For example, an attempt was made to repeat the findings of six American studies on an Israeli population similar to that used in the American studies (Amir & Sharon, 1987). There were 64 significant findings in the American studies, only 24 of which were repeated among the Israeli participants. The other 40 findings were not repeated. In addition, there were six new findings in the Israeli sample that had not been obtained in the American studies.

What are the main differences between cultures? Westen (1996, p.679) expressed some of them in vivid terms:

By twentieth century Western standards, nearly every human who has ever lived outside the contemporary West is lazy, passive, and lacking in industriousness. In contrast, by

What is meant by the term "sub-culture"?

Consider evidence for the view that Westerners shun laziness, passivity, and low productivity. Where do these attitudes come from?

the standards of most cultures in human history, most Westerners are self-centred and frenetic.

Our culture also differs from many others in more fundamental ways, including the ways in which we think of ourselves. As Westen (1996, p.693) pointed out:

> *The prefix "self-", as in "self-esteem" or "self-representation", did not evolve in the English language until around the time of the Industrial Revolution … The contemporary Western view of the person is of a bounded individual, distinct from others, who is defined by more or less idiosyncratic attributes. In contrast, most cultures, particularly the nonliterate tribal societies … view the person in her social and familial context, so that the self-concept is far less distinctly bounded.*

Hofstede

Evidence consistent with Westen's position was reported by Hofstede (1980). He carried out a survey of work-related values among workers in a large multinational company. These workers came from 40 different countries. One of the main dimensions that emerged from the survey was that of individualism–collectivism. Individualism involves an emphasis on individual needs and self-development rather than on group needs, whereas collectivism is based on group needs taking precedence over individual ones. The United States had the highest score for individualism of any country, the United Kingdom was third, and France was tenth. Of special interest was Hofstede's finding that individualism correlated +0.82 with modernity as measured by national wealth. This indicates that there is a strong tendency for wealthier countries to be individualistic and self-centred.

Discussion points

1. Why are the people in wealthier countries more individualist than those in poorer countries?
2. What are the advantages and disadvantages of the individualist and collectivist approaches?

The concept of self and of individual importance is related to societies that are described as **individualist**. Such social groups are contrasted with more **collectivist** cultures where the emphasis is on sharing tasks, belongings, and income. The people in such cultures may live in large family groups and value interdependence. The emphasis is on "we-ness" rather than "I", as illustrated in the text by Nobles (see the Key Study opposite). Examples of such cultures include Israeli *kibbutzim*, many African cultures, and communes.

Effects of individualism versus collectivism

Throughout this book we have provided examples of how individualist and collectivist culture is related to differences in behaviour. For instance, in Section 1, Social Cognition we considered attribution theory—how individuals explain the behaviour of others. Attributions that are made by people from a collectivist culture tend to be contextualised whereas attributions made by people in individualist cultures tend to be more focused on personal choice. It is also the case that the self-serving bias is stronger in individualist cultures than in collectivist ones, and that the fundamental attribution error is less common in collectivist cultures than in individualist cultures. Attribution theories are discussed on pages 18–22.

Psychological theories of relationship formation and maintenance are also related to individualist versus collectivist cultures (see Section 2, Relationships, especially pages 82–84). Altruistic and pro-social behaviour is generally greater in collectivist cultures (see pages 119–120). Humanistic theories of motivation include the need for achievement as a motivating factor, but this may relate to individualist cultures only. Gender equality has

The extended self: Rethinking the so-called Negro self-concept

Nobles (1976) presents a very strong argument regarding the dominance of psychology by white, **Eurocentric** attitudes. He suggests that European psychologists have presented a view of humankind that is based on one particular kind of culture and not representative of all people. The European worldview is oriented along the principles of (1) survival of the fittest and (2) control over nature. These, in turn, affect European values and customs. The emphasis on competition, individual rights, independence, and uniqueness is clearly linked to these guiding principles.

On the other hand, if one examines the African worldview, one can readily see differences from the European one. Rather than the survival of the fittest and control over nature, the African worldview is oriented by the principles of (1) survival of the tribe and (2) oneness with nature. Values that are consistent with these guiding principles are co-operation, interdependence, and collective responsibility.

The African self-concept is, by definition, "we" instead of "I". The African philosophic tradition recognises that it is only in terms of one's people that the "individual" becomes conscious of one's own being. It is only through others that one learns one's duties and responsibilities towards oneself and the collective self.

As a result, Nobles describes the traditional African conception of self, as an "extended self". Self-awareness or self-conception is not, therefore, limited (as in the Euro-American tradition) to just the cognitive awareness of one's uniqueness, individuality, and historical finiteness. It is, in the African tradition, awareness of self as the awareness of one's historical consciousness (collective spirituality) and the subsequent sense of "we" or being One.

The concept "Negro" refers to African individuals who attempt to deny their Africanity because they are caught in a contradiction between two philosophical systems—the African (black) and Euro-American (white). To be a "Negro" therefore, is to be in a state of philosophical confusion. Nobles further argued that the Negro self-concept is an example of scientific colonialism because (1) data are exported from a foreign community and processed into manufactured goods (articles, books, etc.), (2) the centre of gravity for acquiring knowledge about Negroes is located outside of the Negroes themselves, (3) there is an assumption of unlimited right of access to data, (4) it is a profitable enterprise.

Discussion points

1. Can you think of an area of psychology that you have studied where this confusion between the European and African tradition has led to a false understanding of human nature?
2. Explain in what way psychology has forced a kind of scientific colonialism on non-Europeans.

been found to be more common in individualist cultures, whereas collectivist cultures require more separation of roles, which is often along gender lines. Theories of adolescence and old age relate to cultural differences (see for example pages 450 and 480).

Emic and Etic Constructs

Berry (1969) drew a distinction between emic constructs and etic constructs. **Emic constructs** are specific to a given culture, and so vary from one culture to another. In contrast, **etic constructs** refer to universal factors that hold across all cultures. One useful way to remember this is in terms of the distinction between "phonemics" and "phonetics". Both involve the study of the sounds of words (phonemes) but phonemics is the study of sounds as they contribute to meaning *in a particular language*, whereas phonetics is the study of universal sounds independent of meaning. The notion of the "family" is an example of an etic construct whereas the "nuclear family" (just parents and children) is an emic construct. According to Berry, what has happened fairly often in the history of psychology is that what are actually emic constructs are assumed to be etic constructs.

The study of intelligence can be used to illustrate this point. It has often been argued that the same abilities of problem solving, reasoning, memory, and so on define

Try to generate other examples of emic and etic constructs.

intelligence in every culture. Berry (1974) disagreed strongly with that view. He favoured a viewpoint known as cultural relativism. According to this viewpoint, the meaning of intelligence is rather different in each culture. For example, as Sternberg (1985, p.53) pointed out:

> *coordination skills that may be essential to life in a preliterate society (e.g., those motor skills required for shooting a bow and arrow) may be all but irrelevant to intelligent behaviour for most people in a literate and more "developed" society.*

Cole et al. (1971) provided further evidence of the emic nature of the concept of intelligence. They asked adult members of the Kpelle tribe in Africa to sort familiar objects into groups. In most Western societies, people would sort the objects into categories (e.g., foods; tools). What the Kpelle tribespeople did was to sort them into functional groups (e.g., a knife with an orange, because an orange can be cut by a knife). Thus, what is regarded as intelligent behaviour can differ from one culture to another. By the way, the Kpelle tribespeople showed that they could sort the objects into categories when asked to do so—they did not naturally do this, because they thought it was a stupid way of sorting.

Imposed etic

An **imposed etic** is a technique or theory that is rooted in a researcher's own culture, such as an intelligence test, and then used to study other cultures. Psychologists have studied obedience, moral development, and attachment in various cultures using measures designed within our own culture. This includes measures such as Kohlberg's moral dilemmas (see page 404) and the Strange Situation that was included in your AS level studies. The methods used to diagnose and treat mental disorders are also imposed etics (see pages 603 and 616).

Culture bias in IQ tests is discussed on page 386.

The general insensitivity to cultural differences reveals itself clearly in the personality area. Most studies of personality in non-Western cultures have assessed personality by means of translated versions of Western tests rather than by devising new, culture-relevant tests (i.e., they use an imposed etic). Evidence that personality structure may vary from one culture to another was reported by Kuo-shu Yang and Bond (1990). They asked students in Taiwan to describe several people they knew using two sets of adjectives. One set of adjectives was drawn from Cattell's 16PF test, whereas the other set was taken from Chinese newspapers. The factors derived from an analysis of Cattell's adjectives are also known as Big Five personality factors (extraversion, agreeableness, emotional stability, culture, and conscientiousness). Kuo-shu Yang and Bond found that five different factors emerged from an analysis of the adjectives taken from the Chinese newspapers: social orientation, expressiveness, competence, self-control, and optimism. There is some agreement between the two sets of factors. For example, the Big Five factor of agreeableness correlated +0.66 with social orientation, and emotional stability correlated +0.55 with competence. However, the overall similarity between the two sets of personality factors is fairly low, suggesting that personality structure in Taiwanese culture differs from that in Western cultures. Thus it is inappropriate to use a Western personality test to assess personality in another culture.

What social psychological explanations can you give for the results of Kuo-shu Yang and Bond's study?

Derived etics

Berry (1969) proposed that an alternative method of study might be used, one that is similar to the techniques used by anthropologists. He called this a **derived etic**, where a series of emic studies take place in a local setting conducted by local researchers using local techniques. Such studies can build up a picture of human behaviour in a manner similar to the **ethnographic** approach taken by anthropologists. This is the study of different cultures through the use of comparisons. By making comparisons between cultures we can learn more about a target culture, rather like the way that *comparative psychology* can enlighten us about human behaviour.

Biases in cross-cultural research

One final consideration, in relation to cross-cultural research, is the bias involved when an observer conducts research in a foreign culture. A classic example of such research is the studies conducted by Margaret Mead (1935) where she observed three tribes in New Guinea (see pages 102 and 439). Mead concluded that the Mundugumor tribe were all aggressive (masculine quality) regardless of sex. Neither gender gave much attention to child rearing. In contrast the Arapesh were all warm, emotional, and non-aggressive (feminine qualities). Husbands and wives shared everything, including pregnancy: the men took to bed during childbirth! The Tchambuli exhibited a reversal of our own gender roles. Women reared the children but also looked after commerce outside the tribe. The men spent their time in social activities, and were more emotional and artistic.

But how reliable are observations made of individuals in different cultural situations? The greatest problem is the effect that expectations have on what the observer sees. The study of perception tells us this. Perception is a "top-down process": much of what we see (or hear) is incomplete and ambiguous. Therefore we have to impose our own meaning in order to interpret these data. We draw on past experience and expectations. Expectations also influence the categories that are selected and the way that data are recorded (see Section 8, Perceptual Processes and Development).

A further problem for cross-cultural research is that foreign researchers may simply misinterpret the language or cultural practices and draw erroneous inferences. It is also true that they are likely to sample a very small group of individuals within the culture they are studying and this sample may be unrepresentative. Participants who are aware that they are being observed may not behave naturally. For example, concerning another study undertaken by Mead of puberty in Samoa (1928), Freeman (1983) criticised Mead's conclusions, arguing that she may not have established sufficient trust with the Samoan people to expect total honesty from them. One woman in Samoa told Freeman that she had not been honest with Mead about her sexual experiences. Freeman also claimed that Mead was not sufficiently closely involved with the Samoan people and that she saw only what she wanted to see.

Racial Bias

Racial bias is a particularly unpleasant form of cultural bias. Some of the ways in which it manifests itself were discussed by Howitt and Owusu-Bempah (1990). They considered every issue of the *British Journal of Social and Clinical Psychology* between 1962 and 1980. They were dismayed at the way in which Western personality tests such as the 16PF were used inappropriately in non-Western cultures. As they pointed out (p.399), "There were no studies which attempted to explore, for example, the Ghanaian or Chinese personality structures in their own terms rather than through Western eyes."

Racism in relation to intelligence is considered on page 393.

Owusu-Bempah and Howitt (1994) claimed to have found evidence of racism in the well-known textbook by Atkinson, Atkinson, Smith, and Bem (1993). They pointed out that Atkinson et al. tended to categorise Western cultures together, and to do the same for non-Western ones. This included referring to work on African tribes without bothering to specify which tribe or tribes had been studied. Owusu-Bempah and Howitt (1994, p.165) argued as follows: "The *cumulative* effect of this is the 'naturalness' of white people and their ways of life, and the resultant exclusion ... of black people and their cultures."

The central point made by Owusu-Bempah and Howitt (1994) was that Atkinson et al. (1993) evaluated other cultures in relation to the technological and cultural achievements of the United States and Europe. In their own words (1994, p.163):

What do you think is meant by the phrase "in their own terms" when applied to personality structures in different cultures?

Cultures that fall short of this arbitrary Euro-centric standard are frequently described as "primitive", "undeveloped" or, at best, "developing". Religion, morality, community spirit, etc., are ignored in this racist ideological league table.

In sum, many Western psychologists have written in insensitive ways about cross-cultural differences. Sometimes the mistaken impression may have been given that some cultures are "better" than others rather than simply different. There are certainly grounds for concern, but thankfully any explicit or implicit racism is very much in decline.

Ethical Issues

The topic of ethical issues was explored in your AS level studies. It is not our intention to cover the same material again but, instead, to consider some wider ethical issues in relation to what is acceptable in psychological research.

For your reference the British Psychological Society Ethical Guidelines for Research with Human Participants are given on pages 708 and 709. Before looking at the guidelines you should try the research activities on the left and below to review your familiarity with ethical issues.

> ■ Activity 1: Ethical issues
>
> List all the ethical issues that you can recall and for each of them write a further two sentences, explaining how a researcher might deal with such issues.

Ethics in Social Influence Research

To begin, we will outline some of the issues raised by social influence research.

Milgram

Milgram's (1963, 1974) research on obedience to authority was carried out in the days before most institutions had ethical committees responsible for ensuring the ethical acceptability of all research. He asked his participants to administer very strong (and

> ■ Activity 2: Ethical issues
>
> For each of the ethical issues listed below, identify an area in your AS and/or A2 studies which exemplifies the issue, and write a few sentences of commentary (i.e., points that should be considered in relation to the issue). (You can add more examples to the table.)
>
> | | Research study to exemplify the issue | Commentary |
> |---|---|---|
> | Deception in a field experiment | | |
> | Informed consent in a laboratory experiment | | |
> | Confidentiality in a survey | | |
> | Right to withdraw in any kind of research study | | |
> | Privacy in an observational study | | |
> | Protection from harm in a psychology experiment | | |
>
> When you are answering an examination question on ethical issues, ensure that you discuss a good variety of ethical problems as well as a variety of different kinds of research (rather than just using Milgram and Zimbardo as your examples).

To what extent do ethical guidelines protect participants in psychological research?

possibly lethal) electric shocks to someone who was said to suffer from a heart condition. It is very unlikely that an ethical committee would permit an experimenter to carry out the type of research done by Milgram, which explains why very few such studies have been undertaken in recent years. Milgram's research failed to fulfil some criteria that are now regarded as very important. The participants were deceived about key aspects of the study, such as the fact that the other person did not actually receive any shocks. When any of the participants said they wanted to leave the experiment or to stop giving electric shocks, they were told that they had to continue with the experiment. Nowadays it is standard practice to make it clear to participants that they have the right to withdraw from the experiment at any time without providing an explanation. However, Milgram's research did provide us with important insights into obedience to authority.

Zimbardo

Zimbardo's (1973) Stanford prison experiment is another study from many years ago that raises considerable ethical issues. In this study, a mock prison was set up with mock guards and mock prisoners. Some of the mock guards behaved very aggressively, causing four of the mock prisoners to be released because of "extreme depression, disorganised thinking, uncontrollable crying and fits of rage" (Zimbardo, 1973). Savin (1973) compared

CASE STUDY: *Drawing Santa Claus*

Some studies that involve deception of participants can still be regarded as ethically acceptable. One such study was carried out by Solley and Haigh in 1957 (described in Solley & Murphy, 1960). It involved a study on children focusing on a phenomenon resembling "perceptual set". Perceptual set is a bias to perceive a stimulus in a particular way as opposed to any other way, and can arise from external cues (the environment) or internal forces (emotions) which make the individual more sensitive to the stimuli.

In their study, Solley and Haigh asked children aged between 4 and 8 to draw pictures of Santa Claus and his gifts. The children drew their pictures before and after Christmas. Solley and Haigh suggested that emotional set (anticipation of the excitement of

Christmas) would lead to increased sensitivity resulting in larger, more elaborate drawings before Christmas, whereas after Christmas, reduced sensitivity would lead to smaller, less detailed drawings. The study indicated that increased sensitivity had indeed affected perceptual organisation.

The children involved in this study were deceived about the real reason for the research. In order to produce natural and realistic results, the children had to be naive about what might be expected of them. However, in this case deception did not lead to the participants experiencing any form of stress and so could be justified. This study was also ecologically valid, as it generated valuable insights into the effect of perceptual set.

Solley and Haigh's experiment was recently replicated with some Cornish children, with these results. The two larger, more elaborate versions were drawn just before Christmas, but after Christmas they produced the smaller, simple drawings.

Ethical Principles for Conducting Research with Human Participants

Reproduced from *The Psychologist* (January 1993, 6, 33–35)

1 Introduction

1.1 The principles given below are intended to apply to research with human participants. Principles of conduct in professional practice are to be found in the Society's Code of Conduct and in the advisory documents prepared by the Divisions, Sections and Special Groups of the Society.

1.2 Participants in psychological research should have confidence in the investigators. Good psychological research is possible only if there is mutual respect and confidence between investigators and participants. Psychological investigators are potentially interested in all aspects of human behaviour and conscious experience. However, for ethical reasons, some areas of human experience and behaviour may be beyond the reach of experiment, observation or other form of psychological investigation. Ethical guidelines are necessary to clarify the conditions under which psychological research is acceptable.

1.3 The principles given below supplement for researchers with human participants the general ethical principles of members of the Society as stated in the British Psychological Society's Code of Conduct (1985) and any subsequent amendments to this Code. Members of the British Psychological Society are expected to abide by both the Code of Conduct and the fuller principles expressed here. Members should also draw the principles to the attention of research colleagues who are not members of the Society. Members should encourage colleagues to adopt them and ensure that they are followed by all researchers whom they supervise (e.g. research assistants, postgraduate, undergraduate, A-Level and GCSE students).

1.4 In recent years, there has been an increase in legal actions by members of the general public against professionals for alleged misconduct. Researchers must recognise the possibility of such legal action, if they infringe the rights and dignity of participants in their research.

2 General

2.1 In all circumstances, investigators must consider the ethical implications and psychological consequences for the participants in their research. The essential principle is that the investigation should be considered from the standpoint of all participants; foreseeable threats to their psychological well-being, health, values or dignity should be eliminated. Investigators should recognise that, in our multi-cultural and multi-ethnic society and where investigations involve individuals of different ages, gender and social background, the investigators may not have sufficient knowledge of the implications of an investigation for the participants. It should be borne in mind that the best judges of whether an investigation will cause offence may be members of the population from which the participants in the research are to be drawn.

3 Consent

3.1 Whenever possible, the investigator should inform all participants of the objectives of the investigation. The investigator should inform the participants of all aspects of the research or intervention that might reasonably be expected to influence willingness to participate. The investigator should, normally, explain all other aspects of the research or intervention about which the participants enquire. Failure

to make full disclosure prior to obtaining informed consent rec additional safeguards to protect the welfare and dignity c participants (see Section 4).

3.2 Research with children or with participants who impairments that will limit understanding and/or communic such that they are unable to give their real consent requires s safeguarding procedures.

3.3 Where possible, the real consent of children and of adults impairments in understanding or communication should be obt In addition, where research involves any persons under sixteen of age, consent should be obtained from parents or from those *parentis*. If the nature of the research precludes consent being obt from parents or permission being obtained from teachers, k proceeding with the research, the investigator must obtain apr from an Ethics Committee.

3.4 Where real consent cannot be obtained from adults impairments in understanding or communication, wherever po the investigator should consult a person well-placed to apprecia participant's reaction, such as a member of the person's family must obtain the disinterested approval of the research independent advisors.

3.5 When research is being conducted with detained per particular care should be taken over informed consent, p attention to the special circumstances which may affect the per ability to give free informed consent.

3.6 Investigators should realise that they are often in a positi authority or influence over participants who may be their stue employees or clients. This relationship must not be allow pressurise the participants to take part in, or remain i investigation.

3.7 The payment of participants must not be used to induce th risk harm beyond that which they risk without payment in normal lifestyle.

3.8 If harm, unusual discomfort, or other negative consequenc the individual's future life might occur, the investigator must c the disinterested approval of independent advisors, infor participants, and obtain informed, real consent from each of

3.9 In longitudinal research, consent may need to be obtained on than one occasion.

4 Deception

4.1 The withholding of information or the misleading of partic is unacceptable if the participants are typically likely to obj show unease once debriefed. Where this is in any doubt, appro consultation must precede the investigation. Consultation i carried out with individuals who share the social and cu background of the participants in the research, but the advice of committees or experienced and disinterested colleagues m sufficient.

4.2 Intentional deception of the participants over the purpos general nature of the investigation should be avoided whe possible. Participants should never be deliberately misled w extremely strong scientific or medical justification. Even then

be strict controls and the disinterested approval of
dent advisors.

ay be impossible to study some psychological processes
withholding information about the true object of the study
rately misleading the participants. Before conducting such a
e investigator has a special responsibility to (a) determine that
ve procedures avoiding concealment or deception are not
; (b) ensure that the participants are provided with sufficient
ion at the earliest stage; and (c) consult appropriately upon
that the withholding of information or deliberate deception
eceived.

riefing

udies where the participants are aware that they have taken
an investigation, when the data have been collected, the
ator should provide the participants with any necessary
ion to complete their understanding of the nature of the
. The investigator should discuss with the participants their
ce of the research in order to monitor any unforeseen negative
r misconceptions.

iefing does not provide a justification for unethical aspects
estigation.

e effects which may be produced by an experiment will not
ted by a verbal description following the research.
ators have a responsibility to ensure that participants receive
ssary debriefing in the form of active intervention before they
research setting.

hdrawal from the Investigation

e onset of the investigation investigators should make plain
pants their right to withdraw from the research at any time,
ive of whether or not payment or other inducement has been
It is recognised that this may be difficult in certain
ional or organisational settings, but nevertheless the
ator must attempt to ensure that participants (including
) know of their right to withdraw. When testing children,
ce of the testing situation may be taken as evidence of failure
nt to the procedure and should be acknowledged.

e light of experience of the investigation, or as a result of
ng, the participant has the right to withdraw retrospectively
sent given, and to require that their own data, including
gs, be destroyed.

fidentiality

ect to the requirements of legislation, including the Data
n Act, information obtained about a participant during an
ation is confidential unless otherwise agreed in advance.
ators who are put under pressure to disclose confidential
ion should draw this point to the attention of those exerting
ssure. Participants in psychological research have a right to
nat information they provide will be treated confidentially
ublished, will not be identifiable as theirs. In the event that
ntiality and/or anonymity cannot be guaranteed, the
nt must be warned of this in advance of agreeing to
te.

ection of Participants

stigators have a primary responsibility to protect participants
ysical and mental harm during the investigation. Normally,
of harm must be no greater than in ordinary life, i.e.
nts should not be exposed to risks greater than or additional
encountered in their normal lifestyle. Where the risk of harm
r than in ordinary life the provisions of 3.8 should apply.
nts must be asked about any factors in the procedure that

might create a risk, such as pre-existing medical conditions, and must be advised of any special action they should take to avoid risk.

8.2 Participants should be informed of procedures for contacting the investigator within a reasonable time period following participation should stress, potential harm, or related questions or concern arise despite the precautions required by these Principles. Where research procedures might result in undesirable consequences for participants, the investigator has the responsibility to detect and remove or correct these consequences.

8.3 Where research may involve behaviour or experiences that participants may regard as personal and private the participants must be protected from stress by all appropriate measures, including the assurances that answers to personal questions need not be given. There should be no concealment or deception when seeking information that might encroach on privacy.

8.4 In research involving children, great caution should be exercised when discussing the results with parents, teachers or others in *loco parentis*, since evaluative statements may carry unintended weight.

9 Observational Research

9.1 Studies based upon observation must respect the privacy and pyschological well-being of the individuals studied. Unless those observed give their consent to being observed, observational research is only acceptable in situations where those observed would expect to be observed by strangers. Additionally, particular account should be taken of local cultural values and of the possibility of intruding upon the privacy of individuals who, even while in a normal public space, may believe they are unobserved.

10 Giving Advice

10.1 During research, an investigator may obtain evidence of psychological or physical problems of which a participant is, apparently, unaware. In such a case, the investigator has a responsibility to inform the participant if the investigator believes that by not doing so the participant's future well-being may be endangered.

10.2 If, in the normal course of psychological research, or as a result of problems detected as in 10.1, a participant solicits advice concerning educational, personality, behavioural or health issues, caution should be exercised. If the issue is serious and the investigator is not qualified to offer assistance, the appropriate source of professional advice should be recommended. Further details on the giving of advice will be found in the Society's Code of Conduct.

10.3 In some kinds of investigation the giving of advice is appropriate if this forms an intrinsic part of the research and has been agreed in advance.

11 Colleagues

11.1 Investigators share responsibility for the ethical treatment of research participants with their collaborators, assistants, students and employees. A psychologist who believes that another psychologist or investigator may be conducting research that is not in accordance with the principles above should encourage that investigator to re-evaluate the research.

Reference

The British Psychological Society. (1985). A Code of Conduct for Psychologists. *Bulletin of The British Psychological Society, 38,* 41–43.

See also proposed revisions to this code in *The Psychologist, 5,* 562–563.

Copies of this article may be obtained from The British Psychological Society, St. Andrews House, 48 Princess Road East, Leicester LE1 7DR.

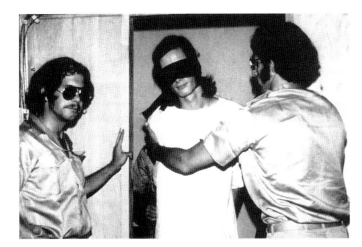

Zimbardo tried to minimise the after-effects of participation in his Stanford prison experiment by asking the participants to sign an informed consent form before the experiment began. Even so, some of the mock guards became very aggressive during the experiment, and four of the mock prisoners had to be released early.

Zimbardo to used-car salesmen and others "whose rol tempt them to be as obnoxious as the law allows". H concluded that:

> *Professors who ... deceive, humiliate, and otherwise mistreat their students, are subverting the atmosphere of mutual trust and intellectual honesty without which, as we are fond of telling outsiders who want to meddle in our affairs, neither education nor free inquiry can flourish.*

Zimbardo pointed out that all of his participants had signe a formal informed consent form, which indicated that the would be an invasion of privacy, loss of some civil righ and harassment. He also noted that day-long debriefin sessions were held with the participants, so that they cou understand the moral conflicts being studied. However, Zimbardo failed to protect h participants from physical and mental harm. It was entirely predictable that the mo guards would attack the mock prisoners, because that is exactly what had happened a pilot study that Zimbardo carried out before the main study.

Asch

A well-known example of research involving deception is the work of Asch (1951, 195 He gave participants the task of deciding which one of three lines was equal in length a standard line. This task was done in groups of between four and 11 people, all but o of whom were "stooge" participants working under instructions from the experiment The participants gave their judgements one at a time, and the seating was arranged that the genuine participant gave his or her opinion last. On key trials, all the stoo participants gave the same wrong answer. The aim of the experiment was to see wheth the genuine participants would conform to group pressure, which happened on abo one-third of the trials. If the participants had been told the experiment was designed study conformity to group pressure, and that all the other participants were stooges the experimenter, then this important study would have been pointless.

Socially Sensitive Research

As we have seen, ethical guidelines focus mainly on the well-being and protection of tho who participate in experiments. However, much research raises issues of relevance society as a whole. As a result, psychologists need to be concerned about broader ethic issues. This is true of nearly all psychological research, but is especially true of social sensitive research. This was defined by Sieber and Stanley (1988, p.49) as:

> *studies in which there are potential social consequences or implications either directly for the participants in research or the class of individuals represented by the research.*

Socially sensitive research can produce risks for many people other than those direct involved as participants. Among the non-participants at risk, according to Sieber an Stanley, are the following:

- Members of the groups (e.g., racial; religious) to which the participants belong.
- People closely associated with the participants (e.g., family; friends).
- The experimenter or experimenters.
- The research institution to which the experimenter or experimenters belong.

Which are more important, the interests of the individual or the interests of society as a whole?

In their thorough discussion of socially sensitive research, Sieber and Stanley argued th important ethical concerns can arise with respect to four major aspects of such researc

- Deciding on the research question or hypothesis to be tested.
- The conduct of research and the treatment of participants.
- The institutional context (e.g., the organisation in which the research is carried out may make unjustified use of the findings).
- Interpretation and application of research findings, especially the application of findings in ways far removed from the intentions of the experimenter.

> **Application of findings**
>
> The research carried out by psychologists such as John Bowlby and Sir Cyril Burt, among others, had a profound effect on social policy. These studies examined the role of the mother in child care, and the development of IQ, and resulted in policies such as encouraging mothers to stay at home rather than going out to work, and the introduction of the 11-plus examination. The studies posed ethical dilemmas for the researchers because their findings could be used to manipulate human behaviour and life choices, as well as adding to the knowledge base of science.

What are the kinds of problems that can occur in each of these aspects of research? We have already discussed at some length issues relating to the conduct of research and the treatment of participants in your AS book. Accordingly, we will focus on the other three aspects here.

The research question

The first part of the research process involves deciding on the question or questions that the research is designed to answer. Simply asking certain questions can pose ethical issues. For example, suppose that a researcher asks the question, "Are there racial differences in intelligence?", and decides to answer it in a study. It is likely (but not certain) that he or she assumes that there are racial differences in intelligence, and that this assumption is motivating the research. In similar fashion, most researchers who carry out twin studies to decide the extent to which criminality is inherited probably assume that genetic factors are important. The very fact that this issue is being investigated may cause concern to the relatives of criminals.

The institutional context

The institutional context can pose ethical issues in at least two ways. First, if the institutional context is perceived to be prestigious or intimidating, it may make the participants feel powerless and thus affect their behaviour. This happened in the work of Milgram (1974), in which he studied obedience to authority in the form of a willingness to administer very strong electric shocks. When the research setting was Yale University, 65% of the participants were fully obedient. This figure dropped to 48% when the setting was a run-down office building. Second, when research is carried out in a company, there can be various ethical problems with respect to the ways in which those running the company use the findings. For example, suppose that a researcher finds that the average stress levels in a company are only moderate. This may lead the company to abandon plans to offer stress counselling to their workers.

Research into sleep deprivation has shown that people are easily confused when under stress from lack of sleep. This apparently innocent finding may have been incorporated into the indoctrination procedures of cults, such as the People's Temple—the followers of Jim Jones who committed mass suicide in Guyana in 1978.

Interpretation and application

No one doubts that researchers should be concerned about the ways in which their findings are interpreted and applied. However, we need to distinguish between those uses of research findings that are predictable and those that are not. For example, it was predictable that the National Front and other organisations of the extreme right would use findings of racial differences in intelligence for their own ends. However, researchers studying the effects of sleep deprivation could not reasonably have expected that their findings would be used in brainwashing and cult indoctrination.

Eyewitness testimony

By now, you may have decided that socially sensitive research should be avoided altogether. However, some socially sensitive research is wholly desirable and of real benefit to society. Consider, for example, research on eyewitness testimony (from your AS studies). This research has shown convincingly that the memories of eyewitnesses for events are fragile and easily distorted. An implication is that defendants should not be found guilty solely on the basis of eyewitness identification. However, in the United States in 1973, there were nearly 350 cases in which eyewitness identification was the only evidence of guilt. In 74% of these cases, the defendant was convicted.

As a result of psychological research, courts and juries are less impressed by eyewitness testimony than they used to be. However, there was a time when such research was ignored. The Devlin Report on Evidence of Identification in Criminal Cases was published in the United Kingdom in 1976. One of its main conclusions was as follows: "The stage seems not yet to have been reached at which the conclusions of psychological research are sufficiently widely accepted or tailored to the needs of the judicial process to become the basis for procedural change."

Evaluation

There is some evidence that socially sensitive research (at least in the United States) is more likely than non-sensitive research to be rejected by institutional ethical committees. Ceci et al. (1985) found that the rejection rate was about twice as great. There are some valid reasons for this. The very fact that certain socially sensitive issues are being studied by psychologists can suggest to society at large that these issues are real and important. For example, the fact that psychologists have compared the intelligence of different races implies that there are racial differences, and that intelligence exists and can be measured.

Socially sensitive research can be used to justify various forms of discrimination against individuals or groups. In the most extreme cases, the findings of psychological studies have even been used to produce discriminatory changes in the laws and regulations within a given society. Thus the findings of socially sensitive research can be used to justify new (and often unwarranted) forms of social control.

Using psychological research for social control

A case in point occurred in the United States when intelligence tests were developed in the early years of the twentieth century. Between 1910 and 1920, several American states passed laws designed to prevent certain categories of people (including those of low intelligence) from having children. Psychologists often exerted pressure to have these laws passed. For example, the prominent Californian psychologist Lewis Terman argued as follows: "If we would preserve our state for a class of people worthy to possess it, we must prevent, as far as possible, the propagation of mental degenerates."

As a result of Terman's views, and those of other psychologists, a Californian law of 1918 required all compulsory sterilisations to be approved by a board including "a clinical psychologist holding the degree of PhD". In similar fashion, pressure by psychologists helped to persuade the state of Iowa to legislate in 1913 for "the prevention of the procreation of criminals, rapists, idiots, feeble-minded, imbeciles, lunatics, drunkards, drug fiends, epileptics, syphilitics, moral and sexual perverts, and diseased and degenerate persons".

No psychologists nowadays would agree with the introduction of such harsh measures. However, some psychologists in the second half of the twentieth century argued that psychological principles should be used for purposes of social control. For example, B.F. Skinner claimed that we can determine and control people's behaviour by providing the appropriate rewards at the appropriate times: "Operant conditioning shapes behaviour as a sculptor shapes a lump of clay." Skinner (1948), in his novel *Walden Two*, described the use of operant conditioning to create an ideal society. He envisaged a high degree of external control in this society, with children being raised

Which different groups of people do you think might face prejudice and discrimination because of findings of socially sensitive research?

mainly by child rearing professionals, and government being by self-perpetuating committees rather than by elected representatives. In a sense, behavioural methods of treatment for abnormal behaviour do exert this kind of control (see Section 18, Treating Mental Disorders).

Defending socially sensitive research

The case in favour of socially sensitive research was made by Scarr (1988, p.56). She argued as follows:

> *Science is in desperate need of good studies that highlight race and gender variables … to inform us of what we need to do to help underrepresented people to succeed in this society. Unlike the ostrich, we cannot afford to hide our heads for fear of socially uncomfortable discoveries.*

Scarr made another important point, arguing that there are very good reasons why most ethical guidelines focus much more on the protection of the participants in experiments than on the protection of the groups to which they belong. In essence, researchers can usually predict fairly accurately the direct effects of their experiment on the participants. However, they are unlikely to be able to predict the indirect effects on the groups to which the participants belong until the outcomes of the experiment are known.

We have considered several advantages and disadvantages of socially sensitive research. It is important to strike a balance. The American Psychological Association tried to do this in its *Ethical principles in the conduct of research with human participants* (1982, p.74):

> *On one side is an obligation to research participants who may not wish to see derogatory information … published about their valued groups. On the other side is an obligation to publish findings one believes relevant to scientific progress, an objective that in the investigator's views will contribute to the eventual understanding and amelioration of social and personal problems.*

Socially Sensitive Research Areas

There are many examples of socially sensitive research areas. Some of the more important ones include race-related research, research on "alternative" sexuality, and research on social and cultural diversity.

Race-related research

The best known (or most notorious) race-related research in psychology has focused on racial differences in intelligence, especially between black and white people in the United States (see Section 10, Cognitive Development). Our concern here is with the ethical issues involved. First we will consider the arguments in favour of carrying out such research, then this will be followed by the arguments against permitting such research to be done.

One of the main arguments in favour of race-related research is that researchers should be free to carry out whatever research seems important to them. If governments start passing laws to prohibit certain kinds of research, then there is a real danger that research will be stopped for political rather than for ethical reasons. What about the ethics of publishing the findings of race-related research that may be used by racists for their own unacceptable purposes? H.J. Eysenck (1981, pp.167–168) argued that

> *it should not be assumed that those who feel that they have a duty to society to make known the results of empirical work are guided by less lofty ethical aspirations than those who hold the opposite view … the obvious social problem produced by the existence of racial and class differences in ability can only be solved, alleviated or attenuated by greater*

Who controls what is acceptable behaviour? Should an individual's behaviour be modified to conform to cultural standards?

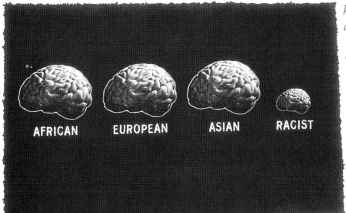

knowledge ... it is ethically indefensible to refrain from acquiring such knowledge and making it available to society.

One of the strongest arguments against race-related research into intelligence is that the findings are often based on faulty research methods and are used in unacceptable ways. For example, Goddard (1913) gave intelligence tests to immigrants arriving in New York. He claimed that his findings demonstrated that 87% of Russians, 83% of Jews, 80% of Hungarians, and 79% of Italians were "feeble-minded". Goddard reached this ludicrous conclusion by ignoring the obvious fact that most of these immigrants had a very limited command of the English language.

Subsequent work on immigrant soldiers in the United States seemed to confirm Goddard's findings, while also showing that immigrants from Great Britain and Scandinavia performed better. These various findings were used by the American government in 1924 to introduce national origin quotas to reduce the level of immigration from southern and eastern Europe.

A second argument against much race-related research is that it is almost meaningless given the fact that black and white people in the United States do not form biological groups. It is also fairly pointless, because it is impossible to discover for certain precisely why there are race differences in intelligence.

Another argument is that such research does not possess any particular scientific interest, in that it offers no prospect of shedding light on the processes and mechanisms involved in intelligence. If it could be shown that all racial differences in intelligence are due to environmental factors, this would tell us nothing about the different problem-solving strategies used by those high and low in intelligence.

Finally, such research has no obvious policy implications. It should be the goal of every society to provide good opportunities for everyone regardless of race, and this is true irrespective of the factors producing racial differences in intelligence.

This poster was produced by the European Youth Campaign Against Racism and the Commission for Racial Equality.

Is knowing how intelligent you are important to having a happy life?

A major focus of race-related research in psychology has been on racial differences in intelligence. One of the arguments against permitting such research is that it moves society no nearer the goal of providing good opportunities for all.

"Alternative" sexuality

According to Kitzinger and Coyle (1995), research on gays and lesbians has gone through three distinct phases:

1. **Heterosexual bias**: the notion that heterosexuality is more natural than, and superior to, homosexuality (see the Key Study on the next page).
2. **Liberal humanism**: this is based on the assumption that homosexual and heterosexual couples have an underlying similarity in their relationships.
3. Liberal humanism plus: what is added to the liberal humanistic view is an increased recognition of the specific characteristics of gay and lesbian relationships.

Liberal humanism

The second phase of research described by Kitzinger and Coyle was based on the liberal humanistic approach. This approach rejected the notion that gays and lesbians are inferior to heterosexuals, and accepted that they should be regarded as individuals rather than as members of a group defined by sexual orientation. It was accepted within this approach that homosexuality is as natural and normal as heterosexuality.

Kurdek and Schmitt (1986) carried out a typical study within the liberal humanistic perspective. They compared gay, lesbian, married heterosexual, and heterosexual cohabiting couples. These couples were assessed for relationship quality based on love for their partner, liking

Morin

Morin (1977) obtained convincing evidence of heterosexual bias in his review of studies on gays and lesbians published between 1967 and 1974. He found that about 70% of these studies addressed issues such as whether homosexuals are mentally ill, ways in which homosexuality can be identified, and the causes of homosexuality. Focusing on such issues suggests that being homosexual was regarded almost like a disease that needed to be "cured".

This biased approach to research, with its clear implication that gays and lesbians are inferior to heterosexuals, poses serious ethical issues relating to discrimination against gays and lesbians. The American Psychological Association in 1975 took steps to prevent such discrimination by adopting the following resolution:

> Homosexuality per se implies no impairment in judgement, stability, reliability, or general social or vocational capabilities. Further, the American Psychological Association urges all mental health professionals to take the lead in removing the stigma of mental illness that has long been associated with homosexual orientations.

Another feature of the research reviewed by Morin (1977) was that 82% of the studies compared gays and/or lesbians against heterosexual individuals. This poses ethical problems, because it misleadingly implies that all gays and lesbians possess the same characteristics that distinguish them from heterosexuals. In fact, of course, gays, lesbians, and heterosexuals are all individuals. Knowing about someone's sexual orientations tells us little or nothing about that person's attitudes, personality, and behaviour.

> ### Homosexuality and the DSM
>
> The decision to remove homosexuality from the DSM (Diagnostic and Statistical Manual) was taken in the 1970s, and it was finally removed from the DSM in 1980. Before that, homosexuality was seen as abnormal behaviour that needed to be "cured" like other forms of illness.

Discussion points

1. How can alternative sexuality be studied in an ethically acceptable way?
2. Can psychological research change some of the unfortunate and misleading stereotypes that prevail in this area?

Does the socially sensitive nature of research related to homosexuals mean that it shouldn't be conducted at all?

their partner, and relationship satisfaction. The gay, lesbian, and married heterosexual couples all had very similar levels of relationship quality, with heterosexual cohabiting couples being significantly lower. These findings support the view of an underlying similarity between homosexuals and heterosexuals.

The liberal humanist approach is limited rather than ethically dubious, but it does raise ethical issues. It has two major limitations. First, there is an assumption that gays and lesbians conform to heterosexual norms in their attitudes and behaviour. As a result, according to Kitzinger and Coyle (1995, p.67), "Researchers … have tended to ignore, distort or pathologise [regard as a disease] those aspects of lesbian and gay relationships which cannot easily be assimilated into heterosexual models." There is an ethical problem here, because it is implicitly assumed that differences between homosexuals and heterosexuals reflect badly on homosexuals.

Second, the approach tends to ignore the difficulties with which gays and lesbians have to contend in terms of the prejudices of society. Some of these difficulties were identified by Kitzinger and Coyle:

> *Lesbian and gay couples are struggling to build and to maintain relationships in the context of a society which often denies their existence, condemns their sexuality, penalises their partnerships and derides their love for each other.*

The Kurdek and Schmitt study assessed relationship quality in gay, lesbian, married heterosexual, and cohabiting heterosexual couples. The findings supported the liberal humanistic view of an underlying similarity between homosexual and heterosexual relationships.

Liberal humanism plus

The third phase of research on gays and lesbians (liberal humanism plus) is gradually becoming more prominent. This approach accepts the equality of homosexuals and heterosexuals. However, it also recognises that there are

some important differences between the relationships of gays and lesbians on the one hand and heterosexuals on the other, based in part on the negative views of gay and lesbian relationships adopted by large sections of society. It is the only approach that manages to avoid most ethical problems.

Social and cultural diversity

By learning to value different cultures and beings, children can develop a positive self-image, and so increase the likelihood of tolerance within the wider society.

We have discussed the importance of ensuring that psychological research is sensitive to ethical issues relating to race and sexuality. Similar issues are raised by research that is concerned with social and/or cultural diversity. Here we will consider research on **ethnic groups**; that is, cultural groups living within a larger society. These ethnic groups can be defined in racial, religious, or other terms. The ethical issues raised by research on ethnic groups will be discussed after their position in society has been covered.

One of the key issues that members of an ethnic group have to address is that of **acculturation strategy**. This has two main aspects:

How might schools encourage integration of different cultures into the curriculum (e.g., by celebrating different cultural festivals)?

1. The extent to which they want to retain their original cultural identity and customs.
2. The extent to which they seek contact with other groups in society.

As Berry (1997) pointed out, the fact that people have two choices to make (each of which can be for or against) means that there are four major acculturation strategies:

- *Integration*: retaining one's own cultural identity while also seeking contact with other groups.
- *Separation*: retaining one's own cultural identity and avoiding contact with other groups.
- *Assimilation*: losing one's own cultural identity and moving into the larger society.
- *Marginalisation*: relatively little contact with one's own culture or with other cultures.

It can be difficult for members of ethnic groups to integrate into a larger society without compromising religious or ethnic beliefs when those beliefs call for them to dress in a way that makes them look different from the majority.

Most of the research has indicated that members of ethnic groups experience stress as they strive to find the most suitable acculturation strategy. However, the typical finding is that acculturative stress is lowest among those adopting the integration option, and is highest among those who are marginalised (Berry, 1997). As might be expected, acculturative stress is lower when there is a high level of tolerance for diverse ethnic attitudes and behaviour within the larger society.

Why are acculturation strategy and acculturative stress relevant to ethical issues? There are three main reasons. First, the fact that many members of ethnic groups experience acculturative stress means that they are on average more vulnerable psychologically than members of the dominant cultural group. Second, research findings that seem to indicate that members of an ethnic group are inferior to the dominant cultural group may make members of the dominant cultural group less willing to have contact with them. This makes it harder for members of an ethnic group to adopt the integration or assimilation strategies.

Third, research findings that cast an unfavourable light on the members of an ethnic group may make them question their own cultural values. In extreme cases, this can lead to marginalisation and to the stress caused by lacking any stable sense of cultural identity.

In sum, it is important for all investigators to have an awareness of the pressures experienced by many ethnic groups. Investigators then need to ensure that their research (and the findings resulting from it) does not increase those pressures.

The Use of Non-human Animals

Animals in Research

Animals and medicines

Animal research has been very useful in the medical field, and has led to the saving of millions of human lives. For example, Alexander Fleming discovered penicillin in 1928. However, it was only in 1940 that research on mice showed that penicillin was a very effective antibiotic. Another example concerns kidney dialysis, which is required by about 200,000 people every year in the United Sates if they are to stay alive. The drug heparin is essential for dialysis, and it has to be extracted from animal tissues, and then tested for safety on anaesthetised animals.

Animals and psychological research

The benefits of animal research are less clear in psychology than in medicine. However, there are several reasons why psychologists use non-human animals in so many of their experiments.

Research involving physical harm

It is possible (although there are major ethical considerations) to carry out surgical procedures on non-human animals that simply would not be permissible with humans. Gray (1985) discussed animal research designed to identify those parts of the brain associated with anxiety. This animal research stemmed from work on humans, in which it was found that anti-anxiety drugs such as the benzodiazepines and alcohol had 19 separate effects. These findings were compared against those of animal studies in which the effects of septo-hippocampal lesions or cuts were observed. The effects of these lesions were very similar to those of anti-anxiety drugs in humans in 18 out of 19 cases. It is probable that the septo-hippocampal system is involved in anxiety, and so lesions or cuts in it produce the same non-anxious behaviour as anti-anxiety drugs.

Social deprivation

It is possible to expose non-human animals to prolonged periods of social or other forms of deprivation. For example, studies have been carried out on monkeys that were not allowed to interact with other monkeys for the first few months of life. When monkeys that had been brought up in isolation were brought together, they reacted very aggressively (Harlow & Mears, 1979). Early isolation also produced a virtual absence of a sex life in adulthood. These findings indicate the potentially severe effects of social isolation.

Monkeys reared in isolation react very aggressively when they are brought together (Harlow & Mears, 1979). This sort of social deprivation would be unacceptable in an experiment on human beings.

Heredity and early experiences

The members of many species develop and reproduce over much shorter time periods than do members of the human species. As a result, it is much more feasible to carry out studies focusing on the effects of either heredity or early experience on behaviour in such species. For example, in one study a breeding programme was used to produce rats that were either reactive or non-reactive to loud noise and bright lights (Eysenck & Broadhurst, 1964). The reactive rats were found to be much more anxious than the non-reactive ones in a wide range of situations. These findings suggest that individual differences in anxiety depend in part on genetic factors.

Simple and complex behaviours

It is generally accepted that the human species is more complex than other species. It may thus be easier to understand the behaviour of other species than that of humans. This makes animal research very useful, provided we assume that other species are

Instead of using poison to deter birds from eating crops, a recent programme of research into animal behaviour has led to the development of more effective scarecrows.

broadly similar to our own. This line of argument was used by the behaviourists to justify the fact that rats (rather than humans) were used in most of their experiments.

Beneficial non-human animal research

Much animal research is acceptable to nearly everyone because it is clear that the ends justify the means. Malim, Birch, and Wadeley (1992) discussed examples of such animal research. One programme of research was designed to provide us with a better understanding of the behaviour of animals that damage crops. This research led to the development of more effective scarecrows, so that more unpleasant methods of preventing crop damage (e.g., poison) were no longer needed. In this case, animal research actually served to produce a large reduction in animal suffering.

Another example of animal research that was almost entirely beneficial in its effects was reported by Simmons (1981). Pigeons were carefully trained by means of operant conditioning to detect life rafts floating on the sea. Pigeons have excellent vision, and so their detection performance was much better than that of helicopter crews: 85% detection compared with only 50%. In this case, animal research has enabled many human lives to be saved.

Psychological examinations of animals can produce benefits for the animals themselves as well as for humans. Examples include wildlife management programmes, efforts to preserve endangered species, and conservation programmes.

Numbers of animals used

How many animals are used in psychological research? Thomas and Blackman (1991) answered that question for psychology departments in the United Kingdom in 1977 and 1989. The figure for the earlier year was 8694 animals, whereas it was only 3708 animals in 1989. This dramatic reduction over a 12-year period has almost certainly continued since 1989. Several species were used in psychological research, but about 95% of the total was accounted for by just three species: the mouse, the rat, and the pigeon.

The total figures for animal research of all kinds are declining year by year, but are still very high. According to Mukerjee (1997), about 1.5 million primates, dogs, cats, guinea pigs, rabbits, hamsters, and other similar species are used in laboratories in the United States each year. In addition, however, about 17 million rats, mice, and birds are used in American research every year.

Society's Views

In the long run, the ethical principles applied to animal research depend on the views of society at large. However, there are enormous differences of opinion among members of the public. Some people are totally opposed to all animal experiments, whereas others are in favour of animal experiments so long as unnecessary suffering is avoided. In order to obtain some factual information, Furnham and Pinder (1990) gave a questionnaire examining attitudes to animal experimentation to 247 young adults. Their average views were not extremely for or against animal research. For example, they agreed on average with the statements that "Research from animal labs produces great benefits in the lives of both animals and people", and "There should be more animal experimentation in areas of medicine where cures are not yet known (AIDS etc.)", and they disagreed with the statement, "I believe in total abolition of animal experiments". On the other hand, they agreed that "All lethal experiments on animals of all sorts should be banned", and "There is no justification for the use of animal experimentation in the testing of cosmetics", and

Between 1977 and 1989 the numbers of animals used in experiments in the UK reduced considerably.

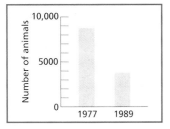

they disagreed with the statement that "Fundamental (for no specific purpose) research using animals is valid".

Furnham and Pinder found that different groups varied in terms of how much they were opposed to animal experimentation. Females were more opposed than males, left-wing people were more opposed than right-wing people, and vegetarians were more opposed than non-vegetarians. Other studies have indicated that people who are older or less educated tend to be more in favour of animal experiments than those who are younger or better educated (Mukerjee, 1997). Thus, no set of ethical principles for animal experimentation could possibly satisfy all of these different groups of people.

Is the rise of vegetarianism, anti-hunting lobbies, and conservation groups responsible for changing attitudes to the use of animals in research?

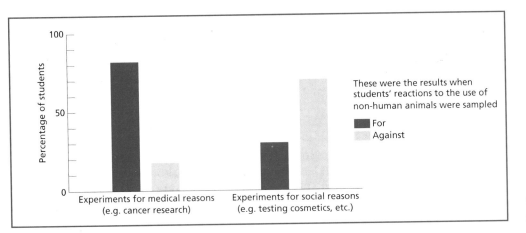

These were the results when students' reactions to the use of non-human animals were sampled
■ For
▢ Against

What factors might account for these results?

Cross-cultural differences

There are also important cultural differences in attitudes towards animal research. Mukerjee pointed out that there is a higher level of public support for animal research in the United States than in Europe. However, even in the United States, there has been a decline in support. In 1985, 63% of Americans agreed with the statement that "scientists should be allowed to do research that causes pain and injury to animals like dogs and chimpanzees *if* it produces new information about human health problems". Ten years later, that figure had dropped to 53%.

Change over time

It is not surprising that the views of society have changed over the years. As Herzog (1988) pointed out, our moral codes depend on what he referred to as "human psychology". In other words, our particular values, emotions, and beliefs determine our position on ethical issues. Herzog argued that an alternative approach would be one based on "pure reason", but ethical issues do not lend themselves to any simple logical resolution.

Speciesism

Human participants in experiments must have their rights and feelings protected by requiring experimenters to follow strict ethical guidelines. However, a key issue is whether non-human participants deserve (as far as possible) to be as fully protected as humans by ethical guidelines. This issue relates to the notion of **speciesism**, which is "discrimination and exploitation based upon a difference in species" (Ryder, 1990). As we will see, some writers (e.g., Gray, 1991) are in favour of speciesism, whereas others (e.g., Ryder, 1990, 1991; Singer, 1991) are strongly opposed to it.

Dogs, dogs, dogs

An American city council held a public meeting to decide whether they should give the animals kept in the city pound (who had been abandoned by their owners) to scientific research. At the meeting one woman spoke of how her baby's life had been saved by an operation that had been pioneered on dogs. She asked whether the audience would rather save children or dogs, to which they replied "Dogs, dogs, dogs" (Flanagan, 1988).

In terms of human evolution, this response does not bode well for our species. On the other hand the laws of natural selection suggest that those humans with genes that favour their own species will be the ones who survive!

Gray accepted that it is ethically wrong to inflict unnecessary pain on the members of any species. However, he also argued that, "we owe a special duty to members of our own species" (1991, p.197). It is thus acceptable to inflict a fairly high level of suffering on animals to avoid a smaller level of suffering by humans, as is often the case in medical research. However, Gray accepted that there comes a point at which the level of suffering inflicted on animals becomes unacceptable. Gray's major reason for believing in speciesism is that, "It is likely … to be better for lions, tigers, mice and men if they each put the interests of their conspecifics [members of their own species] ahead of those of members of other species" (1991, p.198). In his opinion, there are powerful evolutionary and biological reasons for this preference, namely that in order to perpetuate one's genes one should place greater value on individuals who are more closely related (the concept of **kin selection**).

Speciesism and racism

According to Singer (1991), the notion that we should put the interests of our own species above those of other species can lead to the idea that we should give preference to the members of our own race over those of other races. Thus, there are links between speciesism and racism, and both should be avoided. However, while he regarded himself as a non-speciesist, Singer was willing to favour the human species over other species in certain circumstances. For example, if he saw a lion fighting a man, he would shoot the lion rather than let the man die. His reasoning was that it is better to save the life of a being that can plan for the future than a being that cannot.

Ryder (1991, p.201) put forward a powerful argument against speciesism. He proposed that speciesism, racism, and sexism all

> *discriminate unjustly against individuals on irrelevant grounds such as skin colour, physical sexual characteristics and quadrupedality [having four legs]. The infliction of pain or distress upon others without consent is wrong—regardless of their race, sex, or species.*

We are more willing to inflict suffering on species other than our own, and on species for which we feel fear or disgust. Rats are among the most commonly used laboratory animals, but the pet owner in the picture would be as unhappy about inflicting pain on one as he would be about inflicting pain on a puppy or kitten.

Ryder also rejected Gray's argument that speciesism is acceptable because it has biological origins. According to him, what is ethically right should not be based on biology. As Ryder pointed out, "Presumably, Gray would also defend rape, pillage, and murder … where these behaviours have 'biological origins'" (1991, p.201).

Ethical Issues

The position that is taken on the issue of using animals in research depends on how similar to humans other species are seen to be. It is much less reasonable to use animals in a wide range of experiments if they are rather similar to us than if they are very different. Views on the similarity of our species to others have changed very much over the centuries. At one extreme is the seventeenth-century philosopher René Descartes. He argued that animals are very much like machines, and that they lack the soul (with its powers of thinking) that is the supreme human characteristic. It follows from this position that animals are inferior to humans.

The views of Charles Darwin (1859) stand in stark contrast to those of Descartes. According to Darwin, the human species has evolved out of other species. As a result, we are all members of the animal kingdom. It is hard from the evolutionary perspective to cling to the notion that we are radically different from other species. We may be more intelligent, of course, but this is simply a matter of degree. In support of Darwin's argument is the fact that the basic physiology and nervous system of nearly all mammalian species are very similar.

Darwin's (1872) work on emotions is of particular importance to the use of animals in research. He was impressed by the similarities in the expression of emotional states between humans and other species. His findings suggest that it might be unwise to assume that animals experience emotions in very different ways from humans. We cannot be certain, however, because there is no way of knowing the emotional experiences of members of other species.

Many psychologists do not believe that the human species is similar to other species. Humanistic psychologists argued that a key feature of humans is our need for self-actualisation, which involves full realisation of our potential in all ways. Other species lack this need, focusing instead on much more basic needs such as those for food, drink, and sex. Within the context of the humanistic approach, members of the human species are very different and much more complex than the members of any other species. There are ethical problems for animal research regardless of the position one adopts on the issue of the relationship between the human and other species. If other species are very different from us, then studies on them cannot tell us about human behaviour. On the other hand, as Mukerjee (1997, p.77) pointed out:

> If animals are close enough to humans that their bodies, brains, and even psyches [minds] are good models for the human condition, then ethical dilemmas must surely arise in using them.

Washoe the chimpanzee was taught to communicate with humans using American Sign Language signs. She still enjoys the company of humans after being part of a study that began in 1966. Have we as humans a responsibility to care for Washoe for the rest of her life, even though she is over 30 years old and has a life expectancy of 60 years?

Types of morality

It is important to distinguish between **absolute morality** and **relative morality**. Immanuel Kant and other philosophers argued in favour of an absolute morality in which the ends cannot justify the means. In contrast, most people probably agree with the notion of relative morality, according to which the acceptability of actions is judged in terms of the benefits that accrue.

Absolute morality
The notion of an absolute morality may have some appeal, but it tends to be inflexible and unrealistic in practice. For example, the moral principle "Always tell the truth" sounds very reasonable. However, if a madman with a gun demands to know where your mother is, it would make very little sense to adhere to the principle.

Relative morality
The alternative view that the ends can justify the means is favoured by most psychologists. It was expressed in the following terms by the American Psychological Association Committee on Ethical Standards in Psychological Research: "The general ethical question is whether there is a negative effect upon the dignity and welfare of the participants that the importance of the research does not warrant."

Costs and benefits
The notion that decisions about the use of animals in research should be based on an analysis of the benefits and costs involved is sensible. Suppose, for example, a proposed experiment will inflict considerable pain on several animals. This would surely seem less acceptable if the experiment were designed to produce improved cosmetics than if it were intended to lead to the development of treatment for a dreadful disease affecting humans.

When do the ends justify the means? If we cannot ask an animal directly how much pain it is suffering, is it safe to guess how it feels just from observing the animal's behaviour? Do you know for certain when a cat is in distress?

In practice, however, there can be problems. First, it is often impossible to know what the benefits and costs of a piece of research are going to be until after the experiment has been carried out. Second, one person's assessment of the benefits and costs of a piece of research may not agree with someone else's.

Levels of suffering

There is the difficult matter of deciding how much suffering a given experimental procedure inflicts on an animal. As we cannot ask an animal directly what it is experiencing, we have to rely on its behaviour. However, this may be a misleading guide to its feelings. What needs to be done is to find out as much as possible about each species. In spite of the problems involved in assessing animal distress, attempts have been made in several countries such as Australia, Canada, and the Netherlands to develop pain scales. According to this form of assessment, 54% of the animals used in the Netherlands in 1995 suffered minor discomfort, 26% had moderate discomfort, and the remaining 20% suffered severe discomfort.

Is it possible to empathise with the suffering experienced by another species?

Ethical Principles

In general terms, most animal researchers subscribe to what are sometimes known as the "three Rs":

- *Replacement* of animals by other research methods.
- *Reduction* in the number of animals used by means of more advanced statistical techniques.
- *Refinement* of experimental procedures to reduce animal suffering.

Use of the three Rs has proved very fruitful. For example, 5000 monkeys a year were used in the Netherlands in the 1970s to produce polio vaccines. During the 1990s, the number was reduced to only 10 monkeys.

The most obvious problem with the use of animals in research is that many of the ethical principles guiding research on human participants cannot be applied. For example, it is impossible for animals to give voluntary informed consent to take part in an experiment, and they cannot be debriefed at the end. Bateson (1986) argued that there are three main criteria that should be taken into account when deciding whether a study on animals is justifiable (this is often known as Bateson's decision cube):

1. The quality of the research: this can be assessed by the funding agency.
2. The amount of animal suffering: this can be assessed from the animal's behaviour and any signs of stress.
3. Likelihood of benefit: this is important, but can be hard to judge ahead of time.

Field experimenters can disrupt the animal's natural environment. This can continue to be stressful to the animal long after the experiment has finished.

Animal research of high quality, involving minimal suffering, and with a high probability of benefit is the most justifiable. In contrast, animal research of poor quality, involving considerable suffering, and offering a low probability of benefit is hard to justify.

UK guidelines

It is very important for psychologists to develop ethical guidelines to protect animals' rights, and to prevent the animals from suffering or being exploited. Most institutions regard the use of animals in research as being such a sensitive matter that it is normal practice for all proposed animal experiments to be carefully considered by an ethical committee. In the United Kingdom, the Home Office has overall control. Anyone who wants to carry out animal research must have a licence, and inspectors from the Home Office regularly inspect all animal facilities. All research on

Do you think the things that are considered benefits to human society are fixed, or do they vary across cultures and over time? Do the needs of human societies change over time? How might this affect how we decide whether research is ethically acceptable or not?

vertebrates in the United Kingdom is governed by the Animals (Scientific Procedures) Act of 1986. This Act contains numerous safeguards to ensure that vertebrate research is ethically sound.

Investigators in most countries who are planning studies on animals are required to make use of ethical guidelines. Within the United Kingdom, the most important guidelines are those that were issued by the British Psychological Society in 1985. These guidelines state that researchers should "avoid, or at least minimise discomfort to living animals". They represent a systematic attempt to provide a comprehensive set of rules and recommendations to guide the behaviour of any investigators who wish to carry out experiments on non-human participants. The main points of these guidelines are given in the box below.

Consider the normal eating and drinking habits of the animals being studied.

Research with non-human animals

The British Psychological Society, the professional and regulatory body for psychology in the UK, has published detailed guidance and good practice for psychologists carrying out research work with animals. The full version of the guidelines can be obtained from www.bps.org.uk/documents/Code.pdf. To summarise, the guidance covers issues such as legislation, choice of species, number of animals, procedures, procurement of animals, housing and animal care, final disposal of animals, animals in psychology teaching, the use of animals for therapeutic purposes, and obtaining further information about the care and use of animals in research.

The following points provide a general guide to the sorts of issues that a researcher using animals would have to consider:

- Investigators must be aware of all relevant current legislation. They must comply with all of the laws protecting animals.
- Any investigator who intends to harm or stress animals must consider whether the knowledge to be gained justifies the procedure. Thus trivial experiments should not be carried out on animals even if they will suffer only low levels of harm or stress.
- Account needs to be taken of the differences between species in terms of the pain or discomfort they are likely to experience from a given procedure. If there is any choice, then the members of whichever species will suffer the least should be selected.
- Experiments should be carefully designed in order to minimise the number of animals that are required. Statistical tests that allow several factors to be considered together should be used.
- Experiments should not be carried out on the members of any endangered species. The only exception is if the experiment is part of a conservation programme.
- Investigators need to ensure that they obtain animals from reputable suppliers, and that they are provided with detailed information about their history, including any previous laboratory studies in which they have participated. In addition, investigators should confirm that animals are handled appropriately and with minimal stress during transit.
- Care should be taken with respect to caging conditions. There are clear differences among species in reactions to caging in isolation and in the effects of high density or crowding. Information on the recommended requirements for the members of the species being caged should be followed.
- Investigators engaged in fieldwork should disturb the animals being studied as little as possible. Breeding and even survival can be markedly affected by simple observations. Marking animals for identification or attaching radio transmitters may stress them, as may their capture and recapture.
- Animal aggression or predation should be studied in the field rather than by means of staged encounters. If it is necessary to make use of staged encounters, then efforts should be made to use models or animals behind glass.
- Care should be taken with studies in which animals are deprived of food or water. Consider the normal eating and drinking habits of the animals being studied, and also to pay attention to their metabolic requirements.
- Investigators should only use procedures causing pain or distress if there are no other ways in which the experiment can be carried out. In such cases, it is illegal for investigators in the United Kingdom to cause pain or distress unless they hold a Home Office licence together with the relevant certificates.
- No surgical or pharmacological procedures can be carried out on vertebrate animals in the United Kingdom unless the investigators have a Home Office licence plus the relevant certificate. Further safeguards are that only experienced staff should perform these procedures, that the investigators should take steps to prevent post-operative infection, and that they know about the technical aspects of anaesthesia.
- It is essential that animals receive adequate care following an operation; this may involve the use of local anaesthetics and/or nursing. It is also essential that there is frequent monitoring of each animal's condition. If an animal suffers severe and enduring pain, then it must be killed using recommended procedures for euthanasia.
- The investigator should obtain a second opinion if he or she is unsure about the condition of any animals involved in an experiment. This second opinion must come from someone who has no direct involvement in the experiment, and is best provided by a qualified veterinarian.

Types of Animal Research

One final, important point to make is that not all psychological investigations of animals consist of laboratory studies. Cuthill (1991) considered over 900 research papers, and found that 46% of them were field studies carried out in the wild. About one-third of the field studies were field experiments, meaning that they involved some kind of experimental manipulation. The four most common types of manipulation used in these studies were as follows:

1. Dummies: these were mainly stuffed dummy predators; in order to be effective, they need to be realistic, and this means that they cause much distress to animals who encounter them.
2. Non-trivial handling: tagging or marking of animals so they can be identified subsequently is an example of this; as mentioned already, this can be a stressful procedure.
3. Playback of recorded signals: these recorded signals are generally realistic; if they are alarm calls, then this can lead to high levels of distress.
4. Food addition: when the experimenter artificially introduces food into an area, it can cause territorial disputes and fights; it can also lead to undesirable changes in the availability of the animals' normal sources of food supply. Thus food addition can have serious consequences for the animals affected.

Animals are often marked for identification, or have radio transmitters attached to them, to track and observe them in the wild. This may cause significant stress to the animals being observed and might affect their behaviour and possibly even survival.

■ Activity: The use of non-human animals in psychological research
List studies that you are familiar with that involved non-human animals. Use the headings given below. You may add more.

	Researcher's name(s)	Aims, procedures, findings and conclusions	Ethical concerns
Laboratory experiment			
Field experiment			
Naturalistic observation			
Correlational study			

Remember, when commenting on non-human animal research, that there are many different kinds of research methods and each has its own ethical limitations.

SECTION SUMMARY

Gender Bias

❖ A bias is a systematic distortion of one's beliefs. Gender stereotypes create a bias in our understanding of gender behaviours, such as Freud's concept of penis envy in girls. The difficulty lies in distinguishing "real" from culturally created gender differences. Evidence suggests that there are a small number of real differences, confirmed through cross-cultural studies.

❖ One form of gender bias is alpha bias, which is the tendency to exaggerate gender differences. The other form of gender bias is beta bias, which is the tendency to minimise or ignore gender differences. In the Western world, alpha bias has been more common than beta bias. Freud's theory of moral development is an example of alpha bias and Bem's theory of androgyny an example of beta bias. Studies that use male and female participants, and ignore the inevitably differential treatment given to males and females, result in a beta bias and, curiously, a demonstration of gender differences. Theories constructed with data from male participants only (such as Kohlberg's theory of moral development) assume that there are minimal differences (beta bias) and therefore using male participants only should not matter. The outcome is a demonstration of gender differences.

❖ Beta bias tends to produce a view of human nature that is male biased or androcentric. Theories, such as those of conformity, may be restricted to male behaviour but we have been led to believe that they apply to men and women equally. This may oversimplify gender differences and our view of human behaviour.

❖ A key issue with respect to gender bias is the extent to which values determine facts. Social constructionists suggest that facts are socially constructed. Such facts may have serious repercussions, for example in the treatment of women with learning disabilities. Whether such facts are true or not, they perpetuate our beliefs about women. Feminist psychology is a branch of psychology that aims to redress the imbalances in psychology. One way to do this is to use evidence that women may be inferior to provide women with greater support e.g., leadership training. Another approach is to become aware of how androcentric theories turn female differences into female disadvantages, as in the case of battered women's syndrome. Bem suggested that we should make our "enculturated lenses" visible, and thus overcome the bias created by cultural views.

Cultural Bias

❖ Culture can be defined as is a relatively organised system of shared meanings. There is some tendency to confuse the idea of a cultural group with people living in one country.

❖ Many psychologists in the Western world have ignored important cross-cultural differences. A major distinction is made between individualist and collectivist cultures, particularly in terms of the self-concept. This distinction is important in understanding behaviour, as shown, for example, in studies of attribution and of motivation.

❖ It is important to distinguish between emic constructs, which are specific to a given culture, and etic constructs, which are universal. Intelligence is regarded as an etic construct but there is evidence of it being emic. Such misrepresentations have led psychologists to use tools developed in their own culture to measure behaviour in other cultures (imposed etics), such as the Strange Situation and Cattell's personality test. This results in low validity for such studies. Derived etics offer a solution by taking the findings from a variety of emic studies and making comparisons between cultures. Cross-cultural research is further hampered by observer bias, and the use of small samples that are often unrepresentative.

❖ Racial bias is a particular example of cultural bias in psychology. It often involves grouping together quite distinct cultures as in the case of "African tribes". It also leads to evaluations of other cultures in relation to the technological and cultural achievements of the United States and Europe, and the conclusion that other cultures are primitive or undeveloped. Implicit racism is often insensitive and perpetuates erroneous stereotypes.

Ethical Issues

❖ The ethical rights of human participants in psychological research are protected by ethical guidelines, though ultimately these are not always successful. Participants should give their voluntary informed consent before taking part in an experiment. They should also be told that they have the right to withdraw at any time without giving a reason. At the end of the experiment, there should be a debriefing period in which the experiment is discussed fully. Another safeguard is confidentiality, with no information about individual participants being divulged. Privacy and protection from psychological and physical harm are critical. Professional organisations such as the British Psychological Society publish detailed ethical guidelines, and most research institutions have ethical committees. Social influence research provides us with a number of examples where ethical rights were infringed and/or ethical guidelines did not work successfully.

❖ Socially sensitive research is concerned with studies where there are potential social consequences. Ethical guidelines focus mainly on protection of the participants. However, it is important with socially sensitive research to consider the protection of groups to which the participants belong and those closely associated with the participants. These broader social issues need to be considered with respect to the research question selected, the conduct of the research, the institutional context, and the interpretation and application of research findings. The choice of research question reflects the researcher's assumptions and may bias the research process from the outset. The institutional context may make the participants feel powerless, or those running the organisation in which the research takes place may misuse the findings. The findings of socially sensitive research may be applied in dubious ways not anticipated by the researcher, or the research may be used to justify new forms of social control.

❖ On the positive side, socially sensitive research may provide useful information to help minority groups, as in the case of eyewitness testimony. In addition, ethical committees do frequently reject research with potentially sensitive social consequences. Researchers cannot generally be expected to foresee what they will find or how such findings will be used by others. However, the findings of socially sensitive research have been used to justify new (and often unwarranted) forms of social control. In the past, psychologists have advocated sterilisation for undesirable groups of potential parents, and more recently behaviourists have suggested that psychological research can be applied to social control. Such control is exerted through behavioural forms of therapy for mental disorders. However, preventing socially sensitive research may be counterproductive to understanding social inequalities. There is a balance to be struck.

❖ Race-related research has been defended on the grounds that it is ethically indefensible to refrain from acquiring such knowledge and making it available to society. An important counter-argument is the fact that such findings may be based on faulty research methods and are used in unacceptable ways. In addition, race-related research on intelligence in the United States is almost meaningless, because black and white people do not form distinct biological groups. It is not possible to discover for certain why race differences occur, and the research does not have any obvious policy implications.

❖ Early research on "alternative" sexuality suffered from heterosexual bias, tending to regard homosexuality as a disease that needed to be "cured". This was replaced by a liberal humanistic approach. The limitations to this approach are the inherent assumption that homosexuals conform to heterosexual norms, and the fact that it ignores the problems created by the prejudice that homosexuals have to contend with. More recently, an ethically acceptable approach (which may be called liberal humanism plus) has evolved.

❖ Research on social and cultural diversity is socially sensitive. Ethnic groups often experience acculturative stress, which may be resolved through integration, separation, assimilation, or marginalisation. Acculturative stress is lowest among those adopting the integration option, and is highest among those who are marginalised. Acculturative stress makes individuals more vulnerable psychologically. Research that suggests ethnic minorities are inferior may make members of the dominant cultural group less willing to have contact with them, which makes integration more difficult and may make them question their own cultural values, leading sometimes to marginalisation. Investigators need to ensure that their research does not increase pressures on ethnic minorities.

❖ The benefits of animal research are less clear in psychology than in medicine. Animals are used in experiments because some procedures would not be permissible with humans, either those involving physical harm or social deprivation. It is easier to use animals, especially to study the effects of heredity, because they reproduce over much shorter time periods than humans, and because it is easier to understand their behaviour. Objections are not raised about some non-human animal research because it benefits non-human animals and/or humans. The reality is that there has been a great decline in non-human animal research.

❖ Females, left-wing people, and vegetarians are more opposed to animal experimentation than males, right-wing people, and non-vegetarians. No set of ethical principles for animal experimentation could possibly satisfy all of these different groups. There are also cultural and historical differences in attitudes.

❖ Speciesism refers to the discrimination and exploitation of another species based on the fact that it is different from our own. Speciesism can be defended on the grounds that we owe a special duty to our own species, and there are powerful evolutionary reasons for this preference. Speciesism can be opposed on the basis that it resembles racism and sexism, and, like these "isms", discriminates unjustly against individuals on irrelevant grounds. The evolutionary argument could equally be applied to, for example, rape.

❖ Darwin argued that there are important similarities between the human species and other species, for example in terms of emotional expressions. Humanistic psychologists have emphasised the differences, pointing to aspects of human behaviour such as the drive for self-actualisation. If there are differences then such research is acceptable, but at the same it could be argued that such differences make the research irrelevant.

❖ The views of most people on animal experimentation are based on relative morality. However an analysis based on relative costs and benefits presumes that one can anticipate both of these before conducting the research, and that we can assess levels of suffering.

❖ Ethical principles in relation to non-human animals can be represented by the three Rs: replacement with other methods, reduction in numbers, and refinement of procedures. One ethical problem is that animals cannot be given the same rights as human participants, such as informed consent. Bateson's decision cube suggests that researchers should consider the quality of the research, the amount of suffering, and likelihood of benefit. Ethical committees, ethical guidelines and the Home Office try to ensure appropriate conduct in non-human animal research. One should remember that not all studies with non-human animals involve laboratory experimentation.

**The Use of
Non-human Animals**

FURTHER READING

Many of the issues discussed in this Part are also dealt with in M.W. Eysenck (1994a) *Perspectives on psychology* (Hove, UK: Psychology Press). Another textbook in this area is A. Wadeley, A. Birch, and A. Malim (1997) *Perspectives in psychology (2nd Edn.)* (London: Macmillan). There is good coverage of gender issues in R. Unger and M. Crawford (1996) *Women and gender: A feminist psychology (2nd Edn.)* (New York: McGraw-Hill). Cross-cultural research and the issues it raises are discussed in P. Smith and M.H. Bond (1998) *Social psychology across cultures: Analysis and perspectives (2nd Edn.)* (New York: Harvester). A.J. Kimmel (1996) *Ethical issues in behavioural research* (Cambridge, MA: Blackwell), covers ethical issues, whereas J.E. Sieber and B. Stanley (1988) Ethical and professional dimensions of socially sensitive research, *American Psychologist, 43(1)*, 49–55, offers a consideration of socially sensitive research.

Example Examination Questions

You should spend 40 minutes on each of the questions below, which aim to test the material in this Section. Unlike questions from Unit 4 of the examination, covered in Parts 1–5 of this book, the questions on Perspectives (Unit 5 examination) are marked out of 30 and an additional criterion is used in assessment: synopticity. "Synopticity" is defined as your "understanding and critical appreciation of the breadth and range of different theoretical perspectives and/or methodological approaches relevant to any question" (AQA specification).

1. Describe gender biases in psychological research and assess how these biases may have influenced such research.   **(30 marks)**

2. "Some psychological theories are derived from research studies where there were only American male participants but nevertheless the theory is claimed to apply to all human beings."

    Discuss the extent to which psychological theories are biased in terms of gender **and** culture.   **(30 marks)**

3. Discuss the extent to which cultural bias is a problem in psychological research.   **(30 marks)**

4. Describe and evaluate the special ethical problems faced by psychologists when carrying out socially sensitive research.   **(30 marks)**

5. (a) Describe ethical issues that may arise in psychological investigations using humans.   **(15 marks)**
    (b) Assess how effectively psychologists have dealt with such issues.   **(15 marks)**

6. Critically consider the arguments for **and** against the use of non-human animals in psychological research.   **(30 marks)**

7. "Both behaviourists and ethologists rely on studies of non-human animals to formulate their theories."

    Discuss the use of non-human animals in psychological research.   **(30 marks)**

Examination Tips

Question 1.   The AO1 component of this question requires a description of gender biases. These do not have to be set into the context of psychological research but using actual examples is a means of extending your description, and will be helpful for the AO2 component. "Research" is a term that refers to both theories and/or studies. In order to satisfy the synoptic criteria it will be desirable to select examples across a range of different topics and approaches. For the "assess" (AO2) you need to present an argument about whether these biases are critical to the research mentioned. To what extent do the biases bias our views?

Question 2.   The question does not require that you address the quotation but the quotation is intended to be helpful in indicating areas for discussion. It points out that bias in research studies leads to biased theories "Discuss" is an AO1 and AO2 term, therefore you need to describe biases of both gender and culture in psychological theories, and assess the extent to which psychological theories are biased. A balanced answer will look at examples of both biased and unbiased theories. If you only discuss gender or culture then a partial performance penalty would apply (maximum of 10 marks for AO1 and 10 marks for AO2).

Question 3.   This question concerns cultural bias only, though it could be argued that gender groups are a form of cultural group (sharing the same beliefs and so on). "Research" covers theories and studies, thus you can describe instances of cultural bias in research studies only, and/or in theories. The AO2 element requires an evaluation of the extent to which psychological research is biased and, as for question 2, you should present a balanced view. In addition you should consider whether such bias is a problem, for example in the treatment of mental illness or our understanding of intelligence. Synopticity can be achieved by a consideration of research across the specification as well as reference to different approaches and perspectives.

Question 4.   The question requires a focus on those ethical problems that are especially difficult in socially sensitive research—though it could be argued that all ethical issues are a problem in socially sensitive research but just simply more so. Reference to examples of socially sensitive research will be an important means of evaluating the ethical problems and how they might be resolved. It is important to maintain a focus on the issue of socially sensitive research otherwise marks will be lost for not answering the question set and just writing a general ethics answer.

Question 5.   Part (a) requires a description of ethical issues. For top marks this needs to demonstrate a balance between depth and breadth. Therefore a list of points is unlikely to attract high marks because lists lack detail. Furthermore, if the list comprises ethical guidelines this would be rather limited because the question refers to issues not guidelines, which are means of resolving ethical issues. It may help to use examples as part of your description, and this will increase synopticity. For part (b) you are required to assess the effectiveness of psychologists' attempts to deal with such issues. You are likely to refer to guidelines but will get only minimal credit if you describe these. Such material must be used to construct an argument in answer to the question.

Question 6.   You should consider both the strengths limitations of arguments for the use of non-human animals in psychological research, and do the same for the arguments against their use. Considerations should relate to different kinds of methodologies (providing synopticity) as well as different approaches and also you should examine both appropriateness and ethics. You should ensure that there are equal amounts of description and evaluation in your answer to attract the full range of marks.

Question 7.   Again you are not required to address the quotation but it is there to offer some ideas—the notion that non-human animal research comes in many different forms. Reference to different approaches and kinds of research is important for synopticity. The question requires that you both describe the use of non-human animals and assess their use. In a balanced answer this would include consideration of their usefulness as well as the ethical issues such as pain.

WEB SITES

http://www.bps.org.uk/about/rules5.cfm
  British Psychological Association's rules for psychologists, with downloadable Code of Conduct, Ethical Principles and Guidelines.

http://www.apa.org/pi/guide.html
  American Psychological Association (APA) Guidelines for Providers of Psychological Services to Ethnic, Linguistic, and Culturally Diverse Populations.

http://www.stonewall.org.uk/
  British organisation promoting legal equality and social justice for lesbians, gay men, and bisexuals.

http://www.homeoffice.gov.uk/animact/aspag.htm
  Animals (Scientific Procedures) Act 1986, on the United Kingdom Home Office web site.

20

Debates

The synoptic content of this Section focuses on debates that concern psychologists. A debate is discussion of an issue, usually involving the consideration of different sides of a question. As you are already aware, none of these debates is simply "one *or* the other"; there is usually some reasonable middle ground.

Free Will and Determinism

The issue of **free will** versus **determinism** has occupied philosophers and psychologists for centuries. According to those who believe in determinism, people's actions are totally determined by the external and internal forces operating on them. An example of an external force would be the influence of parents when rewarding certain behaviours. An example of an internal force could be hormones.

Those who believe in free will argue that matters are more complicated. Most of them accept that external and internal forces exist. However, they argue that people have free will because each individual is nevertheless able to choose his or her own behaviour.

The distinction between free will and determinism can be seen if we consider the following question: "Could an individual's behaviour in a given situation have been different if he or she had willed it?" Believers in free will answer that question "Yes". In contrast, advocates of determinism respond "No". Some of the main arguments for and against each of these positions are discussed next.

Determinism

Determinists argue that a proper science of human behaviour is only possible if psychologists adopt a deterministic account, according to which everything that happens has a definite cause. Free will, by definition, does not have a definite cause. If free will is taken into account, it becomes impossible to predict human behaviour with any precision. According to determinists, it is often possible with other sciences to make very accurate predictions from a deterministic position (e.g., forecasting planetary motion). If determinism is regarded as not applicable to psychology, then it is either a very different science from physics, chemistry, and so on, or it is not really a science at all.

Determinism in the physical sciences

These arguments were greatly weakened by the progress of science during the twentieth century. Precise prediction based on an understanding of the causal factors involved is

How might the notions of free will and determinism be important in a situation where doctors need to decide if a criminal is responsible for his or her own actions?

the exception rather than the rule even in physics and chemistry. For example, according to Heisenberg's uncertainty principle (1927), you cannot determine both the position and the velocity of a subatomic particle simultaneously because when you undertake to measure one or the other, you change the other measurement. Chaos theory (Hilborn, 1994) goes even further. Very small changes in initial conditions can result in major changes later. For example, theoretically the flap of a butterfly wing might ultimately change a whole weather system (called "the butterfly effect"). Such a chain of events doesn't lend itself to prediction. These views challenge the determinism that underlies science.

Behaviourist and Freudian approaches

Determinism is espoused by more approaches in psychology than is free will. The behaviourists believed especially strongly in determinism. Skinner argued that virtually all of our behaviour is determined by environmental factors. He proposed that we repeat behaviour that is rewarded, and we do not repeat behaviour that is not rewarded. Other behaviourists argued that we can predict how someone will respond given knowledge of the current stimulus situation and that individual's previous conditioning history. However, Bandura, a neo-behaviourist, proposed the principle of **reciprocal determinism** which was less determinist than traditional behaviourism (see page 425).

Freud was also a strong believer in determinism. He even argued that trivial phenomena, such as missing an appointment, calling someone by the wrong name, or humming a particular tune had definite causes within the individual's motivational system. For example, Freud (1971, p.157) suggested that in cases of failure to meet others as agreed, "the motive is an unusually large amount of contempt for other people".

Think of a time when you have called someone by the wrong name. Can you think of any underlying reason why you may have made this mistake?

Soft determinism

Many psychologists favour a position that was labelled **soft determinism** by William James. According to this position, there is a valid distinction between behaviour that is highly constrained by the situation (and so appears involuntary) and behaviour that is

---

Where do the main approaches in psychology stand on determinism?

The biological approach takes the view that behaviour is determined by internal, biological systems. This is **physiological determinism**. Up to a point physiological determinism is a valid argument. Clearly physiological factors provide explanations of behaviour but do they offer a complete explanation? They may be more applicable to non-human animals where learning has less influence on behaviour. Non-human animals also lack the ability to be self-reflective, as demonstrated by their lack of self-awareness, which is associated with the concept of "will". Without self-awareness and consciousness, can an organism be said to have a will?

The behaviourist approach proposes that all behaviour is learned and can be explained solely in terms of external (environmental) factors. This is **environmental determinism**. Skinner said that freedom was an illusion, maintained only because we are unaware of the environmental causes of behaviour. This gives us an answer to the our dilemma: "But I have a personal sense of free will"—the response from behaviourists is that what you experience is an illusion.

The cognitive approach is mechanistic, and any mechanistic explanation is determinist because it suggests that a particular action will result in a predictable result.

The psychoanalytic approach suggests that adult behaviour or personality is predetermined by events in early childhood. This is called **psychic determinism** because the causes of our behaviour are psychological and not freely chosen. Freud, like Skinner, believed that free will was an illusion. Freud believed this was because the actual causes of our behaviour are unconscious and therefore hidden from us.

However, Freud also believed that people have some potential for free will—psychoanalysis is based on the principle that people can change. Freud proposed the principle of "overdetermination", that behaviour has multiple causes some of which are conscious and these would be subject to free will.

The evolutionary approach is highly deterministic. A fundamental assumption of the evolutionary approach (**genetic determinism**) is that physical and psychological characteristics are inherited. This must be so because it is only inherited characteristics that can be naturally selected and passed on to the next generation. This means that the evolutionary approach is a highly deterministic one, though this may be less true as one moves up the evolutionary scale and cultural evolution has a greater effect on behaviour.

The humanistic approach embraces free will. Rogers believed that humans have an innate drive towards positive growth and self-actualisation. Individuals who deny aspects of themselves are unable to do this. If one disowns a part of one's behaviour ("That's not like me to do such a thing") then that behaviour is not part of one's self-concept and therefore cannot be controlled. Your behaviour is then not self-determined. Healthy psychological development and adjustment depend on "owning" all of your behaviour. In this way you are exercising free will, and are able to reach your full potential. In addition to this, the humanistic approach stresses the responsibility each of us has for our own actions. Rather than seeking explanations for our behaviour in terms of other influences, each of us must accept the moral responsibility for our actions. This is a fundamental issue for questions of adult legal responsibilities.

ly modestly constrained by the situation (and so appears voluntary). For example, a
ild may apologise for swearing because he or she will be punished if an apology is not
rthcoming (highly constrained behaviour) or because he or she is genuinely upset at
using offence (modestly constrained behaviour). Behaviour is determined in both
ses. However, the underlying causes are more obvious when behaviour is highly
nstrained by situational forces.

Evidence consistent with the views of William James was reported by Westcott (1982).
nadian students indicated how free they felt in various situations. They felt most free
situations involving an absence of responsibility or release from unpleasant stimulation
g., a nagging headache). In contrast, they felt least free in situations in which they had
recognise that there were limits on their behaviour (e.g., when they had to curtail their
sires to fit their abilities).

This view of soft determinism suggests that determinism is not an all-or-nothing
uation, but must be related to the circumstances in which a behaviour occurred.

How is determinism related to the situation in which a behaviour occurs? Is the behaviour still determined by forces outside our will?

stability

e major problem with determinism (whether soft or not) is that it is not really possible
submit it to a proper test. If it were, then the issue of free will versus determinism would
ve been settled, and so would no longer exist as an issue! If all behaviour is determined
internal and external forces, then in principle it should be possible to predict behaviour
m a knowledge of these causal factors. In fact, we usually only have very limited
owledge of the internal and external forces that might be influencing an individual's
naviour. As a result, it remains no more than an article of faith that human behaviour
l eventually be predicted accurately.

ree Will

st people feel that they possess free will, in the sense
t they can freely choose what to do from a number of
ions. As Dr Samuel Johnson (1709–1784) said to
swell, "We know our will is free, and there's an end
t." Most people also have feelings of personal
ponsibility, presumably because they feel that they are
t least partial control of their behaviour.

Determinism vs. free will	
Determinism	**Free will**
Behaviourism	Humanistic approach
Freudian psychodynamics	

Do you think the cognitive psychologists fit into one or other of these lists? Can you explain your answer?

umanistic approach

manistic psychologists such as Carl Rogers and Abraham Maslow are among those
o believe in free will. They argued that people exercise choice in their behaviour, and
y denied that people's behaviour is at the mercy of outside forces. Rogers' client-centred
rapy is based on the assumption that the client has free will. The therapist is called a
cilitator" precisely because his or her role is to make it easier for the client to exercise
e will in such a way as to maximise the rewardingness of the client's life. Humanistic
chologists argue that regarding human behaviour as being determined by external
:es is "de-humanising" and incorrect.

usality

ose who believe in free will have to confront two major problems. First, it is hard to
vide a precise account of what is meant by free will. Determinism is based on the
umption that all behaviour has one or more causes, and it could be argued that free
l implies that behaviour is random and has no cause. However, very few people would
it to argue for such an extreme position. Anyone whose behaviour seemed to be
dom would probably be classified as mentally ill or very stupid. If free will does not
ly that behaviour has no cause, then we need to know how free will plays a part in
sing behaviour.

Second, most sciences are based on the assumption of determinism. It is possible th
determinism applies to the natural world but does not apply to humans. If that is tl
case, then there are enormous implications for psychology that have hardly bee
addressed as yet.

Conclusions

The issue of free will versus determinism has created more heat than light for vario
reasons. First, it is not clear that it makes much sense to talk about "free will", becau
this assumes there is an agent (i.e., the will) that may or may not operate in an unrestrain
way. As the philosopher John Locke (1632–1704) pointed out, "We may as properly s
that the singing faculty sings and the dancing faculty dances as that the will chooses

Second, the issue is philosophical rather than scientific, as it is impossible to desi
an experiment to decide whether or not free will influences human behaviour. As Willia
James (1890, p.323) put it, "the fact is that the question of free will is insoluble on stric
psychological grounds". In other words, we can never know whether an individua
behaviour in a given situation could have been different if he or she had so willed it.

Third, although those who believe in determinism or free will often seem to ha
radically different views, there is more common ground between them than is genera
realised. Regardless of their position on the issue of free will versus determinism, mc
psychologists accept that heredity, past experience, and the present environment
influence our behaviour. Although some of these factors (such as the environment) a
external to the individual, others are internal. Most of these internal factors (such
character or personality) are the results of causal sequences stretching back into the pa
The dispute then narrows to the issue of whether a solitary internal factor (variously call
free will or self) is somehow immune from the influence of the past.

Fourth, and most important, we can go a step further and argue that there is no r
incompatibility between determinism and free will at all. According to determinists, i
possible in principle to show that an individual's actions are caused by a sequence
physical activities in the brain. If free will (e.g., conscious thinking and decision makir
forms part of that sequence, it is possible to believe in free will and human responsibil
at the same time as holding to a deterministic position. This would not be the case if fr
will is regarded as an intruder forcing its way into
sequence of physical activities in the brain, but there
no good grounds for adopting this position. In other wor
the entire controversy between determinism and free v
may be artificial and of less concern to psychologists th
has generally been supposed.

■ Activity: In small groups, think of some important decisions you have made or will probably make in the future. Discuss the extent to which they are made using free will. It might be useful to think of them on a scale from 1 to 10, where 1 is free choice and 10 is fully predetermined.

The issue of free will versus determinism was considered in detail by Valentine (199
In spite of the various criticisms of the deterministic position, she came to the followi
conclusion: "Determinism seems to have the edge in this difficult debate."

Reductionism

What is the difference between basic disciplines and more basic principles?

According to Reber (1995), **reductionism** is "the philosophical point of view that comp
phenomena are best understood by a componential analysis which breaks the phenome
down into their fundamental, elementary aspects", or "the analysis of complex thir
into simple constituents" (*Oxford Concise Dictionary*). Within the context of psycholc
the term has been used to refer to two rather different theoretical approaches. First, th
is the belief that the phenomena of psychology can potentially be accounted for wit
the framework of more basic sciences or disciplines (such as physiology). Second, th
is the assumption that complex forms of behaviour can be explained in terms of sim
principles. For example, the behaviourists argued that complex forms of behaviour co
be regarded as consisting of a set of simple stimulus–response associations.

Reductionism: the analysis of complex things into simple constituents.

Reductionism Across Scientific Disciplines

Psychology is related to several other scientific disciplines. It involves trying to understand people's behaviour, and this is influenced in part by basic internal processes of interest to physiologists. This is an example of one scientific discipline, one that might be regarded as rather simple.

As people are social animals, their behaviour is also affected by various social processes (e.g., conformity; the desire to impress others). This represents another kind of scientific discipline, one that is at a higher level than the physiological. The multidisciplinary nature of psychology has led many psychologists to focus on the ways in which it is related to other sciences.

Scientific disciplines can be regarded as being organised in a hierarchical way, with the sciences that take a more global perspective at the top, and the more narrowly focused sciences at the bottom. One could construct a hierarchy including psychology looking like this:

Sociology: the science of groups and societies.
Psychology: the science of human and animal behaviour.
Physiology: the science of the functional working of the healthy body.
Biochemistry: the science of the chemistry of the living organism.

Reductionists argue that the sciences towards the top of the hierarchy will at some point be replaced by those towards the bottom. In the case of psychology, this implies that it would ultimately be possible to explain psychological phenomena in physiological or biochemical terms. However, it should be noted that other hierarchical orderings are possible. For example, Putnam (1973) favoured the following ordering: social groups; multicellular living things; cells; molecules; atoms; and elementary particles.

> ### Physiological and psychological explanations
> Neurology and biochemistry underlie all behaviour. What happens when a person sees a sunset? The physiological explanation would be that light reflected from the landscape forms an image on the retina, which is converted into a neural signal and transmitted to the brain, and so on. No one disputes that this is true, and the process is absolutely essential, but does it give a full and adequate explanation of what is going on? A psychological explanation would probably include the personal and social relevance of the experience, which many would argue are of equal value.

Advantages of reductionism

The reductionist approach has an immediate appeal. Biochemistry, physiology, psychology, and sociology are all concerned with human functioning, so there is some overlap in their subject matter. As a result, it would seem that much could be gained from research co-operation among these disciplines. There might be an increased understanding of psychology resulting from taking full account of the relevant contributions of other sciences. Over time, this might lead to a *theoretical unification* in which the theories put forward by psychologists, physiologists, and biochemists became increasingly similar.

Biochemistry and physiology can be regarded as more developed and "scientific" than psychology or sociology. For example, it is probably true that there are more well-established facts and theories in biochemistry and physiology than in psychology or sociology. These arguments provide grounds for preferring biochemical or physiological explanations of behaviour to those offered by psychology, and thus for making use of a reductionist approach.

Even those who are not fully convinced of the benefits of reductionism generally accept that psychological theories should be consistent or *compatible* with physiological findings. For example, research by Zeki (1993) has shown that in brain studies of visual perception, different processes take place in different areas of the brain (see Section 8 Perceptual Processes and Development). Future theories of visual perception put forward by psychologists will need to take those findings into account.

Disadvantages of reductionism

In spite of its attractions, there are strong arguments against reductionism. Much human behaviour cannot be understood solely in terms of basic biological and physiological processes. As Putnam (1973, p.141) pointed out:

> *Psychology is as under-determined by biology as it is by elementary particle physics, and ... people's psychology is partly a reflection of deeply entrenched societal beliefs.*

Putnam's position can be illustrated by considering a simple example. Suppose a psychologist wants to predict how a group of people will vote in a forthcoming election. No one in their right mind would argue that a detailed biochemical and physiological examination of their brains would be of much value! Voting behaviour is determined by social attitudes, group pressures, and so on, rather than directly by underlying biochemical and physiological processes. However, it is reasonable to assume that some issues within psychology do lend themselves to the reductionist perspective. Thus, the usefulness of the reductionist approach may depend very much on the specific questions we are asking.

Can you think of some issues within psychology that might lend themselves to a reductionist approach?

Further problems for the reductionist approach can be seen if we consider the relationship between psychology and physiology. As Valentine (1992) pointed out, psychology typically describes the *processes* involved in performing some activity (e.g., visual perception), whereas physiology focuses more on the *structures* that are involved. In other words, psychologists tend to be interested in *how* questions, whereas physiologists are interested in *where* questions. These differences pose formidable obstacles to any attempt to reduce psychology to physiology.

Another obvious problem with reductionism is that it has not worked very well in practice. It is hard to think of many examples of psychological phenomena that have been

---

Where do the main approaches in psychology stand on reductionism?

The biological approach. Reductionism is often equated with **physiological reductionism,** offering explanations of behaviour in terms of physiological mechanisms. The evolutionary approach uses evolutionary reductionism when reducing behaviour to the effects of genes, as in some explanations of altruism or atypical behaviour.

The behaviourist approach uses a very reductionist vocabulary: stimulus, response, reinforcement, and punishment. These concepts alone are used to explain all behaviour. This is called environmental reductionism because it explains behaviour in terms of simple environmental factors. Behaviourists reduce the concept of the mind to behavioural components, i.e., stimulus–response links.

The cognitive approach uses the principle of **machine reductionism**. Information-processing approaches use the analogy of machine systems, and the simple components of such machines, as a means to describe and explain behaviour. More recent computer innovations, such as the Internet and connectionist networks can be described as holist because the network behaves differently from the individual parts that go to make it up. Wundt's early work in the areas of

perception and thinking was reductionist, in its attempt to reduce human thought to elementary sensations. In the same way that the chemical elements such as hydrogen and oxygen combine to form complex compounds, the same might be true for sensations and mental processes. The whole appears to be greater than the sum of its parts

The psychoanalytic approach is reductionist in so far as it relies on a basic set of structures that attempt to simplify a very complex picture. On the other hand, and to complicate things a little (!), Freud used idiographic techniques that aim to preserve the richness of human experience rather than teasing out simple strands of behaviour.

The humanistic approach emerged as a reaction against those dehumanising psychological perspectives that attempted to reduce behaviour to a set of simple elements. Humanistic, or third force psychologists, feel that holism is the only valid approach to the complete understanding of mind and behaviour.

We should also include experimental reductionism, the use of controlled laboratory studies to gain understanding of similar behaviours in the natural environment. This approach inevitably must reduce a complex behaviour to a simple set of variables that offer the possibility of identifying a cause and an effect.

explained completely in physiological or biochemical terms. This suggests that the psychodynamic, behaviourist, and humanistic psychologists may have been well advised to avoid the assumption that psychology could be reduced to physiology or biochemistry.

A final problem with reductionism is that lower-level explanations (such as those provided by physiologists) often contain many irrelevant details from the perspective of psychology. This can make it very hard to distinguish between what is relevant and what is irrelevant in a physiological account. This problem may have struck you if you have ever looked through a textbook of physiological psychology.

Simplifying Complex Issues

Reductionism in a different sense is involved when theorists try to reduce complex phenomena to separate simple parts. This approach often involves ignoring the findings from other sciences when developing theories. The behaviourists were reductionists in this sense.

What was the first "sense" of reductionism?

The behaviourist approach

As was mentioned earlier, behaviourists argued that the simple stimulus–response association was the appropriate unit of analysis in psychology. According to the behaviourists, we can explain complex forms of behaviour (e.g., use of language; problem solving; reasoning) by assuming that they involve the use of numerous stimulus–response units, and by assigning key importance to reward or reinforcement. The behaviourists tended not to be interested in physiological processes, arguing that what was important was to focus on observable stimuli and responses.

An example of the ways in which the behaviourists tried to simplify matters was Skinner's (1957) attempt to explain the complexities of language acquisition. He argued that children produce words and sentences that are rewarded or reinforced (see Section , Language and Thought). However, language acquisition cannot be accounted for in such simple terms (Chomsky, 1959).

Some of the problems of this type of reductionist position can be seen if we consider the chemistry of water (H_2O). It is possible to reduce water to hydrogen (H) and oxygen (O). Hydrogen burns and oxygen is necessary for burning, but water lacks both of those attributes. Here is a case where a reductionist approach confuses rather than clarifies.

Most phenomena in psychology are usually better explained in terms of various factors operating at different levels of complexity than in terms of a range of simple factors. For example, a full account of the ways in which children acquire language requires the combined expertise of developmental, social, and cognitive psychologists, as well as that of psycholinguists.

The reductionist position of the behaviourists is also rather limited in terms of its application to behaviour therapy as a form of treatment for mental disorders (see Section 18, Treating Mental Disorders). According to the behaviourist approach, patients have acquired certain symptoms or responses through faulty learning, and therapy should involve changing those responses into more useful ones. Some of the limitations of this approach can be seen if we consider panic disorder, a condition in which patients experience numerous panic attacks (see Section 17, Psychopathology). It proved hard to devise forms of behaviour therapy for panic disorder patients, in part because their problems cannot be regarded simply as faulty responses. In essence, panic patients exaggerate the threat posed by their own bodily symptoms, and it is this, rather than their actual physiological activity, that is the problem needing treatment.

In sum, reductionism is not a detailed theory in the sense of producing testable hypotheses. What it does is provide a set of assumptions that can be used to guide theory and research. As such, it is hard to know whether or not reductionism will prove of value in the future. However, the evidence available so far does not really support the reductionist emphasis on simplicity.

Alternatives to Reductionism

The humanistic approach discussed elsewhere provides one alternative to reductionism. As we have seen, humanistic psychologists such as Maslow (see page 211) and Rogers (see page 686) attached great importance to the self-concept, and to the efforts by humans to realise their potential by means of self-actualisation. Within this approach, there is no systematic attempt to divide the self up into smaller units, or to identify the physiological processes associated with the self-concept.

Many psychologists argue that the humanistic approach to reductionism is too limited. The refusal of humanistic psychologists to consider any kind of reductionism suggests that they do not regard physiological and biological factors as having any real significance. It may be true that each individual's conscious experience is of importance in understanding his or her behaviour. However, it is likely that other factors also need to be taken into account.

Another alternative to reductionism is what could be called the **eclectic approach**, in which relevant information is gathered together from various sources and disciplines. Consider, for example, research on the causes of schizophrenia (a serious condition involving hallucinations and loss of contact with reality, see pages 627–635). There is evidence that genetic factors are involved. At the biochemical level, some studies have suggested that schizophrenics tend to be unduly sensitive to the neurotransmitter dopamine (see Davison & Neale, 2000). Other evidence reviewed by Davison and Neale indicates that poor social relationships and adverse life events also play a part in producing schizophrenia (see Section 17, Psychopathology).

Reductionists might be tempted to produce a biochemical theory of schizophrenia. However, such an approach would involve ignoring environmental factors such as life events. According to the eclectic approach, a full understanding of schizophrenia involves considering all the relevant factors and the ways in which they combine.

The main problem with the eclectic approach is that it is very hard to combine information from different disciplines into a single theory. For example, it is not very clear how the concepts of biochemistry can be combined with those of life-event research. However, psychology should not ignore potentially valuable information from other disciplines. This can be seen clearly in recent studies on the brain by cognitive neuroscientists (see Section 4, Brain and Behaviour). Observation of physiological processes in the brain by means of MRI and PET scans is increasing our knowledge of human cognition.

Psychology as Science

■ Activity: Objectivity

Which of the following would you describe as objective, and why? Discuss your answers in small groups.

- It will probably rain, now that it is spring.
- The life expectancy of a cat is about 15 to 20 years.
- Deciduous trees all lose their leaves in winter.
- If you eat all that chocolate, you will definitely be sick.

The Nature of "Science"

The appropriate starting point for a discussion of whether psychology is a science is to consider the definition of science. This is hard to do, because views on the nature of science changed during the course of the twentieth century. According to the traditional view, science has the following features (Eysenck & Keane, 1990):

1. It is objective.
2. This objectivity is ensured by careful observation and experimentation.
3. The knowledge obtained by scientists is turned into law-like generalisations.

The behaviourists were much influenced by a version of this traditional view known as logical positivism. Logical positivists such as Ayer and Carnap argued that the theoretical constructs used in science are meaningful only to the extent that they can be observed. This was very much the position adopted by behaviourists such as Watson and Skinner.

s a result, some important concepts within psychology ere discarded. For example, Skinner argued as follows: "here is no place in a scientific analysis of behaviour for mind or self."

It is now generally accepted that there are major roblems with the traditional view of science held by the ehaviourists and others. As is discussed in more detail ortly, the notion that behaviour can be observed bjectively has been vigorously attacked. Writers such as uhn (1970) have argued that the scientific enterprise has mportant social and subjective aspects to it. This view was ken to extremes by Feyerabend (1975). He argued that ience progresses by a sort of "who-shouts-the-loudest" ategy, in which publicity and visibility count for more an the quality of the research. According to this position, bjectivity is essentially irrelevant to the conduct of ence.

Law-like generalisations are not always true.

What about the view that science involves forming law-like generalisations? Suppose e test a given hypothesis several times, and the findings consistently support the pothesis. Does that prove that the hypothesis is correct? Popper (1969) argued that it es not. Generalisations based on what has been found to be in the past may not hold ue in the future. Consider Bertrand Russell's example of a turkey forming the neralisation, "Each day I am fed", because for all of its life that has been true. This neralisation provides no certainty that the turkey will be fed tomorrow, and if tomorrow Christmas Eve it is likely to be proved false!

New Definition for Science

view of the fact that the traditional definition of science is inadequate, it is clear that a w definition is needed. This is easier said than done. As Eysenck and Keane (1990, p.5) inted out, the views of Feyerabend and other twentieth-century philosophers of science ave established the point that the division between science and non-science is by no eans as clear cut as used to be believed". However, there is probably reasonable reement that the following are key features of science:

Objectivity: even if total objectivity is impossible, it is still important for data to be collected in a way as close to objectivity as possible.
Falsifiability: the notion that scientific theories can potentially be disproved by evidence.
Paradigm: there is a generally accepted theoretical orientation within a science.
Replicability: the findings obtained by researchers need to be replicable or repeatable; it would be hard (or impossible) to base a science on inconsistent findings.

bjectivity

· have already referred to the importance of data collection or scientific observation as vay of testing hypotheses. According to the traditional view of science, scientific servations are entirely **objective**. However, Popper (1969, 1972) argued that scientific servations are theory-driven rather than objective. His famous lecture demonstration olved telling the audience, "Observe!" Their obvious and immediate retort was, bserve what?" This demonstration makes the point that no one ever observes without ne idea of what they are looking for. In other words, scientific observation is always ven by hypotheses and theories, and what you observe depends in part on what you ect to see.

Goals of science

What are the goals of science? According to Allport (1947), science has the aims of "understanding, prediction and control above the levels achieved by unaided common sense". Thus, three of the main goals of science are as follows;

1. Prediction.
2. Understanding.
3. Control.

As we will see shortly, psychologists differ among themselves as to the relative importance of these three goals.

Prediction

Scientists put forward theories, which are general explanations or accounts of certain findings or data. These theories can then be used to generate various hypotheses, which are predictions or expectations of what will happen in given situations. One of the best known theories in psychology is Thorndike's (1911) law of effect (see Section 13, Determinants of Animal Behaviour), according to which acts that are rewarded or reinforced are "stamped in", whereas those that are punished are "stamped out". This theory has generated numerous hypotheses including, for example, the predicted behaviour of rats that are rewarded for lever pressing or the behaviour of pigeons rewarded for pecking at a disc. The success or otherwise of predictions stemming from a theory is of great importance. Any theory that generates numerous incorrect predictions is seriously flawed.

Understanding

Even if a theory generates a number of accurate predictions, it does not necessarily follow that this will give us a good understanding of what is happening. For example, Craik and Lockhart's (1972) levels-of-processing theory led to the prediction that memory will be better for material that has been processed in terms of its meaning than for material that has not. This prediction has been confirmed experimentally numerous times (as discussed in your AS level studies). However, the precise reasons why it is beneficial to process meaning still remain unclear.

Control

After prediction and understanding have been achieved, it is sometimes possible to move on to control. For example, Thorndike, Skinner, and others predicted (and found) that people tend to repeat behaviour that is followed by reward or positive reinforcement, and the principles of operant conditioning were put forward in an attempt to understand what is going on. It is possible to use reinforcement to control human behaviour, as when parents persuade their children to behave well in return for sweets. Skinner (1948), in his utopian novel *Walden Two*, went further, and argued that it would be possible to create an ideal society by arranging matters so that only socially desirable behaviour was rewarded or reinforced.

If Skinner and Thorndike's theories are correct, then punishment should always be a deterrent, but this is not always true. What could be the reason for this?

Popper argues that we all see the world from our own particular viewpoints or biases. This influences the topic we choose to look at. How can scientists try to avoid bias in their work?

We can make this argument more concrete by taking a specific example. There have been thousands of experiments carried out in the Skinner box, in which the number of lever presses produced by a rat in a given period of time is the key behavioural measure. In most studies, the equipment is designed so that each lever press is recorded automatically. This procedure is less objective than might be thought. Lever presses with the rat's right paw, with its left paw, and even with its nose or tail are all recorded as a single lever press, even though the rat's actual behaviour differs considerably. Furthermore, the rat sometimes presses the lever too gently to activate the mechanism and this is not counted as a lever press at all.

A more sweeping attack on the notion that data in psychology are objective has been made by social constructionists such as Gergen (1985) and Harré and Secord (1972). Sem (1995, p.545) described their key assumptions as follows:

> In their view, there are no such things as pure observations. All observations require a prior viewpoint, irrespective of whether these stem from a theoretical perspective, or are due to learning … Thus data are socially "manufactured", irrespective of which form these data take.

Wallach and Wallach (1994) agreed that perfect objectivity cannot be achieved, and that it is not possible to be certain that the interpretation of someone's behaviour is correct. However, they pointed out that we can be more confident in our interpretation of behaviour if it is supported by other evidence. According to Wallach and Wallach (1994, p.234):

When a [participant] presses a lever that ostensibly [apparently] delivers shocks to another [participant], it may be far from certain that he or she intends to harm this other [participant]. If the [participant] also asserts that this was his or her intention, or it happens that on the experimenter's declaration that the experiment is over, the [participant] proceeds to punch the other [participant] in the nose, then, all else being equal, it seems likely that harm was intended.

Falsifiability

An extremely influential view of what distinguishes science from non-science was put forward by Popper (1969). He argued that the hallmark of science is **falsifiability** rather than generalisation from positive instances or findings. Scientists should form theories and hypotheses that can potentially be shown to be untrue by experimental tests. According to Popper, the possibility of falsification is what separates science from religions and pseudo-sciences such as psychoanalysis and Marxism.

> ### Hypothesis testing and falsifiability
>
> Any scientific hypothesis must be open to the possibility of being disproved, i.e. it must be falsifiable. An example that is often quoted is the assertion that "All ravens are black". To test this hypothesis fully, one would have to catch and examine every raven in the world, and even then an albino raven may be on the point of hatching out. Although it may be true that in most people's experience, ravens are all black, it would only take one albino bird for the whole hypothesis to be shown to be false.

Some theories in psychology are falsifiable, whereas others are not. For example, H.J. Eysenck (1967) put forward a theory, according to which those high in neuroticism (anxiety and depression) should be more physiologically responsive than those low in neuroticism. Numerous studies have tested this theory, with the great majority failing to support it (Fahrenberg, 1992). In other words, the theory has been falsified.

Another example of a theory that is falsifiable is Broadbent's (1958) filter theory of attention. If two messages are presented at the same time, the filter only allows one of them to be processed thoroughly. As a result, the other message receives only minimal processing. This clear prediction of the theory has been disproved or falsified several times (see Section 7, Attention and Pattern Recognition).

In contrast, Freud's notion that the mind consists of three parts (ego, superego, and id) is unfalsifiable. It is not possible to imagine any findings that would disprove such a vague and poorly specified theoretical position. In similar fashion, it is hard to test or to falsify Maslow's (1954) theory of motivation based on a hierarchy of needs. This theory assumes that there are five types of needs arranged in a hierarchical way, from need for survival at the bottom to need for self-actualisation at the top (see Section 6, Motivation and Emotion). The problems associated with falsifying this theory may explain why relatively few studies have tested it.

Paradigm: Kuhn's approach

According to Thomas Kuhn (1962, 1970, 1977), the most essential ingredient in a science is what he called a **paradigm**. This is a general theoretical orientation that is accepted by the great majority of workers in that field of study. With the advance of knowledge, the dominant paradigm in any science will gradually become less adequate. When there is very strong evidence against the current paradigm, it is eventually replaced by another paradigm.

These considerations led Kuhn (1970) to argue that there are three distinct stages in the development of a science:

- *Pre-science*: there is no generally accepted paradigm, and there is a wide range of opinion about the best theoretical approach to adopt.
- *Normal science*: there is a generally accepted paradigm, and it accounts for the phenomena that are regarded as being central to the field. This paradigm influences the experiments that are carried

> ■ Activity: Causes of schizophrenia
>
> The competing theories that exist for the causes of schizophrenia could be indicative of a pre-scientific stage in the psychology of mental disorders. Using other sources, research the dominant paradigms that exist in this area, and compare them with other less adequate explanations for schizophrenia. Can we say that psychologists have established a generally accepted explanation for the causes of certain forms of schizophrenia? If so, are these explanations proof of a scientific approach? What do you think are the chances of a competing explanation resulting in a paradigm shift, for example to environmental and/or social causes?

out, and how the findings are explained. A classic example of normal science is the use of Newtonian mechanics by physicists until the emergence of relativity theory.

3. *Revolutionary science*: when the evidence against the old paradigm reaches a certain point, there is what is known as a paradigm shift. This involves the old paradigm being replaced by a new one. An example of a paradigm shift is the Copernican revolution, in which the old view that the planets and the sun revolve around the earth was replaced by our present view that the earth and the other planets revolve around the sun.

The replacement of an old paradigm by a new one does not usually happen in an orderly way. Scientists who support the old paradigm often ignore conflicting evidence, or dismiss it as of little importance. Adherents of the old paradigm resist change for as long as possible, until they can no longer hold out against the onslaught. In other words, social and other pressures lead scientists to stick with paradigms that are clearly inadequate.

Which scientists are most likely to favour the new paradigm? Sulloway (1994) considered the views of hundreds of scientists writing during periods of scientific revolution. Scientists who were first-born children were much less likely to adopt the new scientific paradigm than were those who were later-born. Presumably later-born children have had more experience of rebellion through their childhood experiences with older siblings, and this helps them to reject the previous paradigm.

Before Copernicus showed that the planets, including the earth, revolved around the sun, all astronomical theories had been based on the paradigm that the earth was the centre of the universe. The complete change in science post-Copernicus is an example of a paradigm shift.

Where does psychology fit in?

It is time to return to Kuhn's three stages to consider where psychology fits in. Kuhn (1962) argued that psychology has failed to develop a paradigm, and so remains at the pre-science stage. Various arguments support this point of view. First, there are several general theoretical approaches within psychology (e.g., psychodynamic; behaviourist; humanist; cognitive). As a result, it cannot really be argued that most psychologists support the same paradigm.

Second, psychology is an unusually fragmented discipline. It has connections with several other disciplines, including biology, physiology, biochemistry, neurology, and sociology. Psychologists studying, for example, biochemistry have very little in common with those studying social factors within society. The fragmentation and diversity make it unlikely that agreement can be reached on a common paradigm or general theoretical orientation.

Valentine (1982, 1992) argued for a different position. She claimed that behaviourism can be regarded as at least coming close to being a paradigm. As she pointed out, behaviourism has had a massive influence on psychology through its insistence that psychology is the study of behaviour, and that behaviour should be observed in controlled experiments. It also had a great influence (but one that has declined considerably in recent decades) through its theoretical assumptions that the study of learning is of fundamental importance to psychology, and that learning can be understood in terms of conditioning principles.

It is not clear that behaviourism is a paradigm. Behaviourism's greatest impact on psychology has been at the methodological level, with its emphasis on studying behaviour. However, a paradigm in Kuhn's sense is more concerned with a general theoretical orientation rather than with methodological issues. Thus, behaviourism does not seem to be a paradigm, and Kuhn (1962) was probably correct to place psychology at the pre-science stage. This may not make psychology as different from other sciences as is often assumed. Kuhn's view of normal science, in which nearly all scientists within a discipline are working in harmony using the same paradigm, seems to exaggerate the similarity of perspective found among researchers in physics, chemistry, biology, and so on.

Replicability

It was indicated earlier that **replicability** or repeatability of findings is an important requirement for a subject to be considered as a science. Replicability of findings in psychology varies enormously as a function of the area and type of study being carried out. Replicability tends to be greatest when experiments are conducted in a carefully controlled way, and it tends to be lowest when the experimenter is unable to manipulate the variable or variables of interest.

What are the main obstacles to replicability in human psychology?

Clear evidence of replicability is available from studies of operant conditioning. There are characteristic patterns of responding that are found when animals are put into a Skinner box and rewarded on various schedules of reinforcement (see Section 13, Determinants of Animal Behaviour). For example, there is the fixed interval schedule, in which the animal is rewarded with food for the first response after a given interval of time (e.g., 30 seconds). What nearly always happens is that the animal stops responding immediately after receiving food, because it has learned that no additional food is available at that time. The animal starts to respond again more and more rapidly as the time at which reward will be available approaches.

Replicability tends to be lower when studies are carried out in social psychology, but often remains high when the situation is under good experimental control. For example, there is the Asch situation, in which there is one genuine participant and several participants who are confederates of the experimenter. They are given the task of deciding which of three lines is the same length as another line. The key condition is one in which all the confederates of the experimenter provide the same incorrect decision. Convincing evidence of conformity by the genuine participant has been found in numerous studies in several countries.

Laboratory experiments

Laboratory experiments permit high control and good replicability. In order for psychology to be regarded as a science, we must have confidence in laboratory (and other) experiments as a way of obtaining valid information about human behaviour. But not all psychologists respect the experimental approach as a means to investigate human behaviour. For example, at one extreme Boring (1957) argued as follows: "The application of the experimental method to the problem of mind is the great outstanding event in the history of the study of mind, an event to which no other is comparable." In contrast, Nick Heather (1976) was very dismissive of laboratory experiments. He argued that they are very artificial, and that all that can be learned from them is how strangers interact in an unusual situation.

Some of the strengths and weaknesses of laboratory research can be made clearer by looking at two kinds of validity. **Internal validity** refers to the validity of research within the context in which it is carried out. For example, if the same experiment is carried out time after time, and the same findings are obtained each time, this would indicate high internal validity. Experiments that can be repeated in this way are said to be high in replicability. **External validity** refers to the validity of the research outside the research situation. Many laboratory experiments are rather low in external validity, meaning that we cannot be confident that what is true in the laboratory is also true of everyday life. The term **ecological validity** is often used to refer to the extent to which experimental findings can be generalised to everyday settings.

Many laboratory-based experiments in psychology show low external validity—that is, their findings do not translate reliably to behaviour outside the laboratory.

Much psychological research on humans lacks external validity or ecological validity to a greater or lesser extent. We spend most of our time actively dealing with our environment, deciding in which situations to put ourselves, and then responding to those situations as seems appropriate. Much of that dynamic interaction is lacking in laboratory research. The experimenter (rather than the participant) determines the situation in which

■ Activity: Construct a brief outline for each of the following:

• An experiment that should show high internal validity.
• An experiment that will be unlikely to show high internal validity.
• An experiment that is unlikely to show high ecological validity.

the participant is placed, and what is of interest is the participant's response to that situation. This led Silverman (1977) to argue that the findings obtained from laboratory studies are only likely to generalise to institutions such as prisons, hospitals, or schools.

Non-scientific Approaches to Psychology

As we have seen, the behaviourists firmly believed that psychology should be a science, and they tried hard to achieve this. However, there are other approaches to psychology in which there is much less emphasis on the notion of psychology as a science. The humanistic psychologists and social constructionists agreed strongly that psychology should not be a science, and the social constructionists went further and argued that it cannot be a science.

Humanistic approaches

The humanistic psychologists such as Maslow and Rogers favoured the use of **phenomenology**, in which individuals report their conscious experiences in as pure and undistorted a way as possible. This approach was justified in the following terms by Rogers (1959):

> *This personal, phenomenological type of study—especially when one reads all of the responses—is far more valuable than the traditional "hard-headed" empirical approach. This kind of study, often scorned by psychologists as being "merely self-reports", actually gives the deepest insight into what the experience has meant.*

It will be remembered that three of the major aims of science are understanding, prediction, and control. The humanistic psychologists emphasised the goal of understanding. However, their approach failed to be scientific in part because they attached much less importance to the other two aims of prediction and control.

Social constructionist approaches

What response might a physicist give to the social constructionist view?

Those psychologists who favour **social constructionism** argue that there are no objective data, and that our "knowledge" of ourselves and of the world is based on social constructions. In other words, "What we call facts are simply versions of events which, for various reasons, are presently enjoying wide currency" (Burr, 1997, p.8). Social constructionists have attacked the "so-called objectivity of the 'scientist', disengaged from the cultural and historical circumstances" (Semin, 1995, p.545). According to them, the observations made by psychologists, and the ways in which those observations are interpreted, are determined in large measure by the cultural and historical forces influencing them. Thus, for example, teachers beating disruptive schoolchildren are now regarded as behaving violently and unacceptably, but the same behaviour was generally tolerated 40 or 50 years ago.

The importance of historical forces was emphasised by Gergen (1973, p.318). According to him, "We must think in terms of a *continuum of historical durability*, with phenomena highly susceptible to historical influence at one extreme and the more stable processes at the other." Behaviourists and other psychologists who favour the scientific approach tend to assume that the historical durability of phenomena is high, whereas social constructionists assume that it is often very low.

It follows from what has been said so far that social constructionists believe that psychology cannot be a science.

Phenomenology vs. empiricism

A simplistic example of the difference between the phenomenological school of thought and that of the empiricists (see next Unit) might be approaches to the personality changes that tend to take place during adolescence. Whereas the empiricists would observe and record the reactions (verbal and nonverbal) to a given stimulus such as a list of questions, a phenomenological approach would make observations within the context of the individual adolescent's personal profile, e.g. early childhood memories. The humanist would concentrate on the changes occurring against a backdrop of the whole self. The empiricist would concentrate on the stage of development reached.

How do they think that psychologists should proceed? According to Burr (1997, p.8), "Since there is no ultimate knowledge of human beings that we can call a final truth, what we must do instead is to try to understand where our current ways of understanding have come from." One of the ways in which that can be done is by means of **discourse analysis**, which involves focusing on analysing people's use of language in order to understand how they perceive the world.

Wetherell and Potter (1988) carried out discourse analysis on interviews conducted with white New Zealanders. These interviews dealt with the issue of the teaching of Maori culture in schools. What emerged from this discourse analysis was that many white New Zealanders had racist views, even though they claimed not be racist. They argued in favour of encouraging Maori culture, but emphasised the importance of togetherness (all New Zealanders working co-operatively) and of pragmatic realism (being in touch with the modern world). The hidden message was that fostering Maori culture would have adverse effects on togetherness and pragmatic realism, and so should not be done.

SCHOOL IN THE LAST CENTURY.

"TAKE DOWN HIS BREECHES."

In the past, physical punishment of disobedient children was generally accepted as appropriate. Psychologists today would view it differently, as the social view of physical punishment has undergone drastic changes.

Evaluation

There is some validity in the social constructionist position. However, many psychologists regard it as making exaggerated claims. For example, suppose that several people saw a policeman hitting a student hard with a long stick. Regardless of their beliefs, they would probably be able to agree on the basic facts of what had happened. However, there would be much disagreement as to whether the policeman's action was justified or unjustified. In other words, our beliefs may colour our *interpretation* of an action, but they are less likely to influence our *description* of that action.

Summary and Conclusions

It is hard to decide whether psychology should be regarded as a science. In general terms, psychology possesses many of the features of a science. However, it tends to possess them less clearly and less strongly than other sciences such as physics or chemistry.

On the positive side, some theoretical approaches in psychology have been successful in achieving the goals of prediction, understanding, and control. Many psychological theories fulfil Popper's criterion of falsifiability, as they have been disproved by experimental studies. The findings of numerous experiments in psychology have been replicated successfully, which is another criterion of a science. However, psychology is very variable with respect to falsifiability and replicability. As we have seen, some theories in psychology are not sufficiently precisely expressed to be falsifiable, and many findings are not replicable.

On the negative side, there are some doubts about the objectivity of the data collected by psychologists. At least some of the data obtained seem to be influenced by the experimenter's biases, which are determined by his or her social and cultural background. Many of the findings obtained from psychological research lack external or ecological validity, because they have been obtained under the artificial conditions of the laboratory. Finally, Kuhn (1970) is probably correct in arguing that psychology is a pre-science, because it lacks a generally accepted paradigm.

The issue of whether psychology is or is not a science can have important implications for research funding. The reason is that subjects regarded as sciences generally receive more research funding than those not so regarded. At the end of the 1970s, the main provider of research funding for psychology in Britain was the Social Science Research Council. However, the Conservative government under Margaret Thatcher was not convinced that psychology, economics, and the other disciplines funded by the Social

Science Research Council were really sciences, and it was nearly closed down altogether. What actually happened was that it was re-named the Economic and Social Research Council, and it received less money than before.

In sum, there are good reasons for arguing that psychology is on the way to becoming a science. At present, however, it should probably be regarded as having only some of the features of a science rather than being a fully fledged science.

Nature–Nurture

The so-called "**nature–nurture debate**" in psychology has a long history, stretching back into philosophical debate about the nature of humankind. The term "nature" refers to behaviour that is determined by inherited factors. "Nurture" is the influence of any environmental factors including learning. The debate is sometimes called heredity versus environment.

History of the Nature–Nurture Debate

Philosophers have long recognised that aspects of behaviour were inherited. This was long before the discovery of genes by Mendel in the late nineteenth century (see page 499). Plato, the Greek philosopher, talked about things being inborn or native to an individual, as contrasting with those characteristics that were acquired through experience. This view of inherited characteristics was referred to as **nativism**.

The opposing philosophical orientation was called **empiricism**. It was John Locke, in the seventeenth century, who first outlined the view that all newborn babies are alike. They are born with a mind that is like a blank slate (*tabula rasa*) and experience records itself in such a way that each individual becomes a unique being. We inherit nothing and all behaviour is acquired as a consequence of experience. The term "empiricism" is derived from "empirical" meaning to discover something through one's own senses.

There were, and are, a number of implications arising from this divergence of opinion. If behaviour is entirely due to heredity then intervention would have little effect on the development of children. Whereas, if all behaviour is learned through experience then the child's experiences during development are crucial.

Rousseau was an eighteenth-century French philosopher whose work had a major influence on education. He held the view that children were noble savages who should be given freedom to follow their innate and positive inclinations. In contrast the empiricist philosophy suggested that children should be trained in socially acceptable ways. This was the basis for behaviourism and took the view of the child as a passive recipient of his or her learning.

Nature or Nurture

Consider any area in psychology that you have studied. In what way is this behaviour caused by nature or by nurture?

The use of the term "debate" suggests that one must choose between these two opposing views. The nativists and empiricists certainly staunchly supported their different positions but philosophers and psychologists have come to recognise that it is not an either/or question. There are a number of arguments that demonstrate this, and it can be best seen in the context of understanding the development of intelligence (see also Section 10, Cognitive Development).

Phenylketonuria

There is an inherited metabolic disorder called phenylketonuria (PKU), where certain proteins are not processed properly, leaving a poisonous substance in the blood that causes brain damage. If the condition is detected early (and all newborns are tested) then the particular proteins can be eliminated from the child's diet and there is no brain damage. The question is whether intellectual impairment, should it occur, would be considered as due to nature or nurture. If the child's environment doesn't contain the proteins, no damage will occur. Therefore there is an interaction between nature and nurture.

Diathesis–stress model

The **diathesis–stress model** is based on a similar argument (see AS studies and Section 17, Psychopathology). The diathesis–stress model proposes that a complete explanation of any mental disorder is likely to involve both a predisposition to the disorder (an inherited susceptibility to become ill) and a stressor that triggers the appearance of the symptoms. This can be seen to apply to eating disorders, schizophrenia, and other mental disorders where there is clear evidence of a genetic link from studies of twins, yet we have seen that not everyone with the gene becomes ill. For example, Holland et al. (1988) studied anorexia in identical and non-identical twins. The concordance rate for identical twins was 56% compared with 5% for non-identical twins (who are genetically less similar). This indicates a high inherited factor, but it is not 100%. We can explain this in terms of the psychological factors that trigger the disorder, such as troubled families or stressful life events. This is an example of nature and nurture interacting.

In the case of anorexia nervosa, can we say whether nature or nurture is the cause of the disorder?

Genotype and phenotype

Those who believe in the importance of heredity draw a distinction between the **genotype** and the **phenotype**. The genotype is an individual's genetic constitution, as determined by the particular set of genes the individual possesses. Your genotype is your biological or genetic *potential* to become what you might become. The phenotype is the observable characteristics of an individual, which result from interaction between the genes he/she possesses (i.e., the individual's genotype) and the environment. Your phenotype is what you actually become as a consequence of the interaction between your biology/genetic make-up and the environment. An example would be hair colour. Your genes determine the colour of your hair, but the fact that you live in a sunny country may mean that your brown hair is bleached in the sun and this produces your blonde phenotype: your observable hair colour, which results from your genetic make-up, and an environmental influence.

As far as intelligence is concerned, we cannot access the genotype. All that can be done is to assess the phenotype by means of administering an intelligence test. This means we never assess inherited abilities except in the context of their environmental expression. There is no such thing as "pure nature".

The concept of nature presumes that we can isolate an individual who has had no interaction with the environment. People often talk of abilities being present at birth but at this time the human infant has already had 9 months-worth of environmental experience. Even before conception the state of the infant is not all "nature", as illustrated by something called the **transgenerational effect**: if a woman has a poor diet during pregnancy her foetus suffers. Perhaps more importantly, if the foetus is female the foetus's eggs for her own children, which are already formed, will be adversely affected. Therefore the next generation will be underdeveloped because of its *grandmother's* poor environment. What may appear to be inherited is in fact environmentally caused.

This all illustrates the practical difficulties in separating nature from nurture. Hebb (1949) suggested that asking the question of "nature or nurture" is like asking whether a field's area is determined more by its length or by its width. Of course, its area depends equally on both length and width. In similar fashion, Hebb argued, intelligence depends equally on both heredity and environment. However, we have earlier (see page 386) argued that, while this line of reasoning is valid, we can still reasonably ask whether the areas of different fields vary more because of differences in their lengths or in terms of their widths. In the same way, we can ask whether individual differences in intelligence depend *more* on differences in genetic endowment or on environmental differences. The question is not nature *or* nurture, but which one may contribute more. We will consider research methods shortly.

The form of interaction

There is no doubt that heredity and environment interact. Plomin et al. (1977) identified three different kinds of interaction that can help understand the different ways that a child may be affected by his or her environment:

1. *Passive heredity–environment interaction*. A child's parents shape the environment in which the child grows up. Intelligent, well-educated parents are likely to have a house full of books and prefer to watch certain programmes on television. This environment is related to the parents' genetic make-up and thus the parents' genes are transmitted passively to the child via the environment that the parents create.

2. *Reactive heredity–environment interaction*. Research has shown that adults do not behave in the same way to a beautiful child as to a "plain" one (Burns &

Where do the main approaches in psychology stand on nature–nurture?

The *biological approach* by definition takes a nature position though, as in the case of phenylketonuria, the environment clearly influences behaviour.

The *behaviourist approach* is entirely on the side of nurture, though the potential for learning is innate.

The *cognitive approach* similarly makes no special claims for nature except in so far as the structure of the mental system is innate. Its development, however, is a response to experience.

The *psychoanalytic approach* combines both nature and nurture in the view that innate, sexual forces are modified by experience to produce adult personality.

The *evolutionary approach* is clearly nativist.

The *humanistic approach* emphasises nurture but holds certain views about the nature of humankind—that it is positive, inclined towards psychological good health, and has the potential for self-actualisation.

The *social constructionist approach* is an example of the nurture approach. We are shaped by social forces.

Farina, 1992), and that they find it easier to form a relationship with a child who has an easy temperament than with a child who has a difficult one (Thomas & Chess, 1977). The child's inherited characteristics (physical attractiveness or temperament) create a reaction in others that leads to differences in the child's environment. In this way the child's genetic make-up affects the child's environment.

3. *Active heredity–environment interaction.* As each child interacts with his/her environment the environment is altered and this in turn affects the behaviour of the individual. Bandura called this **reciprocal determinism** (see page 425).

Researching Nature and Nurture

There is no true experimental evidence in nature–nurture research. Nature–nurture studies compare individuals with the same or different genetic make-up to determine the relative contributions of nature and nurture. Identical twins are genetically the same because they come from a single egg—one zygote. Therefore they are called monozygotic. Non-identical twins come from two zygotes—dizygotic. They are genetically as similar as any siblings, except they share a more similar environment than siblings do right from conception.

Twin studies are a form of natural experiment because the independent variable (genetic relatedness) is not directly controlled by the experimenter, and participants are not randomly allocated to conditions. It has become clear that, even though identical twins are genetically the same, there are differences from the very moment of conception. This makes it impossible to ever truly investigate the influences of nature versus nurture.

Although identical twins are genetically the same, there are still some differences between them.

The non-identical nature of identical twins

Recent understanding of genetics has shown us that even cloning will never result in two identical individuals. There are two reasons for this. First of all, due to cell mutation all the cells in a person's body are not identical. Monozygotic twins may start out as identical cells but as these cells divide and multiply to form the living organism, there is some faulty replication, and this leads to minor but possibly significant differences.

Second, small variations in inherited characteristics and in behaviour create different **micro-environments**. This was the view of Bandura in his concept of reciprocal determinism and is the stance taken by the behavioural geneticist Robert Plomin (1994). In his view each child creates his or her own environment in terms of how they react to others, how they select interactions, what they attend to and so on.

Twins who are reared apart

In order to conduct research comparing the effects of nature and nurture in identical twins, studies look at the differences between twins who are reared together or apart. In the case of Shields' (1962) classic study of twins reared together and apart, it was found that the concordance in IQ scores was 0.76 when they were reared together, and 0.77 when reared apart. This suggests that there was very little environmental influence because both groups of twins were as similar regardless of their environment. However, Kamin (1977) noted that, in reality the twins had often spent a substantial amount of time together before being separated and a number were raised by relatives, some even going to the same school.

Why do you think that adoption agencies try to match adoptive with natural homes?

The same problem occurs with adoption studies because adoption agencies tend to place children in homes that are similar to their natural homes. This makes it very difficult to separate the effects of nature and nurture.

Shared and non-shared environments

Harris (1995) raises the question about why siblings and twins, who are raised in the same environments and who have significant genetic similarity, can turn out so differently. Research indicates that about 50% of the variation in most adult characteristics is due to genetic factors. The rest must be environmental, but this cannot be the shared environment because otherwise twins and siblings would be more similar. Furthermore adopted siblings, who share the same environment, would be more similar than they turn out to be—by adulthood there is minimal resemblance between adopted siblings (Maccoby & Martin, 1983).

What is the "non-shared environment"? It cannot be the micro-environment of the child because this too is related to genetic factors, such as physical looks and temperament. The non-shared environment must be influences outside the child's home. This would explain the fact that twins reared together and twins reared apart show similar correlations in behaviour. The remaining influences are not in the home, i.e., are non-shared, such as peer influences.

How do your peers influence your development?

Resolving the Nature–Nurture Controversy

The best solution to the nature–nurture controversy may lie in Gottesman's (1963) concept of a **reaction range**, similar to the concept of susceptibility in the diathesis–stress model. Our genetic make-up limits the range of our potential development in terms of all characteristics: height, intelligence, mental illness, and so on. Actual development is related to our environmental opportunities, or lack of them. This is the concept of potential (genotype) versus realised potential (phenotype).

Racial differences

When we consider the question of whether intelligence is more determined by nature or more determined by nurture, there is one particularly significant issue that arises. This is the question of whether certain groups of people ("races") are genetically more intelligent than others. Jensen (1969) produced evidence to demonstrate that, in the United States, black people on average were less intelligent than white people by about 15 points (see page 393). One should note, however, that this is an average and about 20% of black people have a higher IQ than that of the average white person.

The difficulty with Jensen's argument is that between-group differences are environmental and not genetic. In other words the differences between two different genetic pools (black and white) are due to environmental and not genetic differences. Consider the following example. If you plant a seed in good soil and provide plenty of sunshine, warmth and food, it thrives. If you plant the identical seed in poor soil with little nourishment it will grow less well. If you plant genetically different seeds in the same soil there will be differences; in this case they are due to nature whereas in the first example the differences are due to nurture. If we compare genetically different groups of people (different racial groups) we must be certain they are

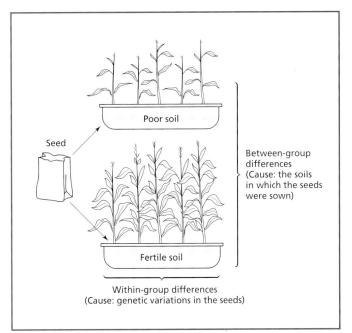

If the same seeds are planted in two different environments there will be large differences in growth between the groups, probably due to rich or poor soil. Within each group there are also differences, and as all the seeds in each group share the same environment, the within-group differences must be due to genetic variation.

sharing the same environment before we attribute the differences to nature, otherwise the differences must be at least in part due to nurture.

Practical and political consequences

The nature–nurture debate has important practical consequences, as suggested earlier. The interactionist view is that intervention is important. For example, if intelligence is entirely inherited then we should test children as early as possible and place them in suitable schools, and occupations, according to their fixed intellect. If intelligence is influenced by environmental factors, then it is critical that children are given enriching experiences wherever possible to enhance their ability. Operation Headstart (see page 392) is an example of the latter kind of programme, whereas psychologists such as Herrnstein and Murray (1994), the authors of *The Bell Curve*, have argued that individual and group differences in intelligence can never be overcome by interventionist programmes, and therefore it makes economic sense to avoid doing this. Furthermore, they argued that the downward spiral in IQ in the United States could be explained by government subsidies for low-income (low-IQ) mothers.

The political element in the nature–nurture issue should not be ignored. In the UK Cyril Burt's flawed IQ studies were one of the key sources of evidence used to argue in favour of the 11-plus examination and selective placement in secondary schools. (The data were flawed in so far as it later transpired that some of the participants had been invented, see for example Joynson, 1989.) The IQ data suggested that a child's IQ was a fixed quantity and the educational needs of individuals were better served by having two educational streams: one for brighter pupils and one for less academic pupils. The self-fulfilling prophecy tells us that such division will serve to create inequalities even where none existed previously.

The concept of the self-fulfilling prophecy suggests that expectations can affect development. How is this related to our understanding of nature and nurture?

SECTION SUMMARY

Free Will and Determinism

❖ One way to consider the debate of determinism versus free will is to consider the following question: "Could an individual's behaviour in a given situation have been different if he or she had willed it?"

❖ Determinists argue that all human behaviour has a definite cause. The scientific approach is a deterministic one and it used to be thought that, if we allow for free will, then psychology is not really a science at all. However, even in the physical sciences uncertainty and chaos are now recognised principles. More psychologists believe in determinism than in free will. The behaviourists are determinists, though social learning theory (neo-behaviourism) invoked some reciprocal determinism. The psychoanalytic, biological, cognitive, and evolutionary approaches are all determinist.

❖ According to those who favour soft determinism, some behaviour is highly constrained by the situation, whereas other behaviour is not. This permits some adaptability in the definition of determinism. The major problem with determinism is that it is not possible to submit it to a proper experimental test.

❖ Most people feel that they possess free will, because they feel able to choose freely what to do in many situations. Humanistic psychologists believe in free will, which is the basis for client-centred therapy. The belief in free will creates two problems: it is hard to provide a precise account of what is meant by free will, and most successful sciences are based on the assumption of determinism even if one recognises that uncertainty principles may operate.

❖ If free will does not imply that behaviour has no cause (and thus is random), then we need to know how free will helps to cause behaviour. The debate is largely a philosophical one because it cannot be subjected to testing. In fact, most psychologists accept that heredity, past experience, and the present environment all influence behaviour, and so the key issue is whether there is an internal factor known as free will which also influences behaviour. Moreover the debate may simply be artificial; if free will forms part of physical activities of the brain, it is possible to believe in free will at the same time as holding to a deterministic position.

Reductionism

❖ Reductionism refers to two rather different theoretical approaches: the belief that the phenomena of psychology can be explained within the framework of the basic sciences (such as physiology), and the belief that we can explain psychology in terms of simple principles, such as simple stimulus–response associations.

❖ Reductionism can be considered in terms of the basic sciences. We can see that the sciences can be organised in a hierarchy, with the more general sciences at the top and the more narrowly focused ones at the bottom. Higher-level sciences are progressively explained by those at the bottom. Reductionism has potential advantages: different sciences have overlapping interests; sciences differ in the narrowness of their focus; and theoretical unification could increase the explanatory power of psychology. Even those who are not fully convinced of the benefits of reductionism accept that psychological theories should be consistent with physiological findings.

❖ Reductionism has several disadvantages. Many psychological phenomena cannot be reduced to physiological or biological terms. The usefulness of the reductionist approach may depend very much on the specific questions. Psychology is concerned with processes, whereas physiology is concerned with structure. Reductionism has not worked very well in practice and lower-level explanations often contain many irrelevant details.

❖ Reductionism can also be considered in terms of reducing complex phenomena to separate simple parts, as in behaviourism. However this approach has been shown to be lacking, for example when using behaviourist principles to explain language acquisition or the causes of mental disorders. In fact, most phenomena in psychology are best explained in terms of factors operating at different levels of complexity. Reductionism can provide a set of assumptions that can be used to guide research, but the evidence does not support the reductionist emphasis on simplicity.

❖ The humanistic approach is an alternative to reductionism. It may be true that conscious experience is important but it is also likely that other factors need to be taken into account. According to the eclectic approach, psychologists should gather significant and relevant information together from various sources and disciplines, as exemplified by explanations of schizophrenia, rather than trying to produce a single theory.

Psychology as Science

❖ According to the traditional view, science involves the collection of objective data and the drawing of generalisations. This view has been challenged. At the opposite extreme some psychologists suggest that objectivity is irrelevant to successful science. Popper argued that the fundamental scientific belief in testing hypotheses as a means of demonstrating facts does not hold up, as in the example of the turkey. It may be possible to define science as possessing the following features: relatively objective data; falsifiability; use of a paradigm; and replicable findings.

❖ Science aims to be objective, yet all observations inevitably are influenced by what you expect to see. According to social constructionists, the observations made by psychologists, and their interpretations of those observations, are determined by cultural forces.

❖ Popper argued that the hallmark of science is falsifiability. Not all theories in psychology are falsifiable. Broadbent's filter theory of attention is falsifiable, while Freud's theory of psychoanalysis is not.

❖ Kuhn described three stages in the development of science: pre-science, normal science, and revolutionary science. Kuhn claimed psychology has failed to develop a paradigm and remains in the pre-science stage. This is supported by the variety of theoretical approaches within psychology and the fragmented nature of the subject. Some approaches within psychology, such as behaviourism, may be paradigms. However, behaviourism is largely methodological (concerned with studying behaviour) rather than a general theoretical orientation. However, other sciences may also be at a pre-science stage.

❖ Replicability is a key criterion of science. Laboratory studies in psychology are often well controlled and possess internal validity. This is more true of behaviourist research than of, for example, some studies in social psychology. Not all psychologists feel that this is the best route to investigating human behaviour. High internal validity often involves a sacrifice of external or ecological validity.

❖ Humanistic psychologists argue that psychology should not be a science, and social constructionists suggest it cannot be a science. Phenomenology is an alternative research approach which provides deep insights through self-reporting. Social constructionists suggest that the historical durability of phenomena is low and thus research, and understanding, is best served by qualitative research methods such as discourse analysis.

❖ Psychology has some features of a science (falsifiability; replicability) but does not fully possess other features (paradigm; objectivity). There are important implications for the funding of research.

Nature–Nurture

❖ Nature refers to inherited characteristics and nurture is the product of experience (environmental influences and learning). Historically, the nativist position was promoted by Plato and supported by Mendel's discovery of genetic inheritance. Empiricism was advocated by philosophers such as Locke, who claimed that at birth we are like a blank slate. We inherit nothing and all behaviour is acquired as a consequence of experience.

❖ Nature and nurture interact rather than one or the other determining behaviour. The cases of phenylketonuria and the diathesis–stress model illustrate this. The distinction made between genotype and phenotype shows us that we can never actually access the genotype and therefore are always assessing nature and nurture jointly. This can be seen in the transgenerational effect. There is no such thing as "pure nature". The interaction between heredity and environment can be passive, active, and/or reactive.

❖ Nature–nurture influences are often researched using twin studies, and comparing monozygotic and dizygotic twins. However, we now realise that monozygotic twins are not exactly identical, partly because of small genetic differences and also because they create their own micro-environments. The fact that twins who are reared apart often have similar environments further confounds the data. The non-shared rather than the shared environment has the greater influence.

❖ The concept of a "reaction range" may be one way of conceptualising the nature–nurture interaction. The debate has real-life implications in our understanding of racial differences in IQ. These cannot be due to genetic factors because the different groups do not share the same environment, therefore differences must be largely due to environment. The contribution of nature and nurture has important practical and political implications for interventionist programmes or schemes that separate individuals on the basis of their innate potential.

FURTHER READING

The topics in this Section are covered in greater depth by A. Bell (2001) *Debates in psychology* (London: Routledge), written specifically for the AQA A specification. Debates are also discussed in the classic book by E.R. Valentine (1992) *Conceptual issues in psychology (2nd Edn.)* (London: Routledge), and in M.W. Eysenck (1994) *Perspectives on psychology* (Hove, UK: Psychology Press). A useful account of some of the more difficult areas of the nature–nurture debate is provided by R. Plomin (1989) *Nature and nurture: An introduction to human behavioural genetics* (Pacific Grove, CA: Brooks/Cole).

Example Examination Questions

You should spend 40 minutes on each of the questions below, which aim to test the material in this Section. Unlike questions from Unit 4 of the examination, covered in Parts 1–5 of this book, the questions on Perspectives (Unit 5 examination) are marked out of 30 and an additional criterion is used in assessment: synopticity. "Synopticity" is defined as your "understanding and critical appreciation of the breadth and range of different theoretical perspectives and/or methodological approaches relevant to any question" (AQA specification).

1. Describe and critically assess the arguments for and against the existence of determinism in psychology. (30 marks)

2. Describe and analyse how theoretical approaches in psychology have addressed the free will–determinism issue. (30 marks)

3. (a) Examine reductionist approaches in different areas of psychology. (15 marks)
    (b) Critically assess the appropriateness of the reductionist approach in these areas of psychology. (15 marks)

4. Discuss the extent to which reductionism has helped to explain human behaviour. (30 marks)

5. "We might ask whether psychology is a science. We might also ask whether psychologists regard science as an appropriate goal for psychology."
    Discuss the view that psychology is a science. (30 marks)

6. Discuss the extent to which psychology fits into definitions of science. (30 marks)

7. Discuss the nature–nurture debate in psychology. (30 marks)

8. Critically consider the different views regarding the relationship between nature and nurture in psychology. (30 marks)

Examination Tips

Question 1. In order to attract good marks in this question you must ensure that you offer equal amounts of description and evaluation. For AO1 you must describe arguments both for and against determinism, using examples across the specification to illustrate the arguments (making your answer synoptic). For AO2 you must consider both the strengths and limitations of each argument (as required by the injunction "critically"), and might use different kinds of arguments in this assessment, such as those regarding ethics, practicality, research evidence and so on.

Question 2. This question makes it easy to include synopticity in the answer because you are required to look at different approaches in psychology in terms of how they address the free will–determinism debate. You are not required to describe the theoretical approaches as such, except in so far as to enable you to explain the stance taken by the approach on the debate. For the analysis (AO2) you might consider the implications of the debate within each approach/perspective or you might consider how some approaches have offered means to resolve the debate, such as Bandura's reciprocal determinism. "Analysis" requires breaking the topic down into its constituent parts in order to achieve a greater understanding.

Question 3. In part (a) you should describe different examples of reductionism in psychology, providing a good balance between both breadth and depth in your answer. For part (b) you are required to make a critical assessment (strengths and limitations) of whether such reductionist explanations are appropriate. You are restricted to discussing only those areas mentioned in the first part of your answer.

Question 4.   The AO1 element of the essay will be descriptions of reductionism in psychology. The AO2 element is the consideration of how much such explanations have enhanced our understanding of human behaviour. It might be useful to include non-reductionist examples by way of contrast; this will also increase the synoptic content.

Question 5.   It is not required that you address the quotation in this question but it is there to give you some ideas of what to discuss. You are invited to debate the question of whether psychology is a science. This requires some consideration of what science is (AO1) and in what way psychology is a science (AO1) followed by an evaluation of whether this is sufficient for psychology to be counted as science and perhaps a further consideration of alternative means of data collection. The AO2 element lies in determining the value of any views presented and/or considering contrasting views. You should endeavour to forge links across the specification as far as possible.

Question 6.   A good starting point would be to examine (describe) definitions of science and then assess the extent that psychology can fit in with the criteria identified. You should present arguments both for and against psychology as a science. You might offer further commentary in terms of the question of whether the aims of science are even appropriate for the study of human behaviour and/or non-human animal behaviour. You could also consider the implications of this discussion, for example for research funding.

Question 7.   "Discuss" is an AO1 and AO2 term, so you should both describe and evaluate the nature–nurture debate. One problem is likely to be the amount of the material that you could include and therefore selectivity will be important. In order to achieve the right amount of detail and give yourself time for thorough evaluation, you must limit the examples of the debate that you consider. You may approach the essay by considering particular examples of nature and nurture, such as with respect to perception and intelligence, or by considering more general issues such as different kinds of gene–environment interaction.

Question 8.   In this essay you should describe contrasting views of nature and nurture, and consider the strengths and weaknesses of these differing views. An example of a strength would be support from research studies or useful practical applications. An example of a weakness would be a logically flawed argument or a socially sensitive issue. Synopticity will be achieved through the breadth of differing views that you consider but you need to restrict this to some extent otherwise you will have insufficient detail in your response.

WEB SITES

http://www.espirituality.com/psychology/maslow.shtml
Some background information about Abraham Maslow.

http://www.crispian.demon.co.uk/q05.htm
Quotations from the nature–nurture debate.

www.a-levelpsychology.co.uk/websites.html
A continually updated list of useful links, including those printed in this book, may be found at the Psychology Press A level psychology site.

21

Approaches in Psychology

What is an approach in psychology? An "approach" is a way of addressing the problem of explaining behaviour. Different psychologists prefer different approaches in the same way that you may be politically liberal whereas someone else is politically conservative. We all find that different things make sense. In terms of psychology, the situation is not as straightforward as in politics, as most people might favour one kind of approach when explaining, say, aggression, whereas they might favour another approach when offering an account of why some individuals develop mental disorders.

No single explanation is "right" and no one explanation is right for every behaviour. Each of them is appropriate in different contexts and many of them can be used together. They form part of the psychologist's "toolkit". You must choose the psychological explanations that make best sense to you.

All of the approaches in this Section have been discussed elsewhere in this book, so here we will present an overview of the major approaches. You may not be equally familiar with all of these and may therefore just want to concentrate on three or four of them.

"I just love this view of the Firth—does it make you feel as exhilarated?" When psychologists view human behaviour they each have their own perspective.

In the examination you will be required to demonstrate your understanding of each approach by using it to explain a particular behaviour. In order to assist you, we have structured the text for each approach in the following way:

- A description of the approach, including some examples of the approach.
- An evaluation of the approach.
- An example of how the approaches question might be answered in the examination. The same target behaviour is taken for all seven approaches. It is one provided in the AQA A specimen material:

Lottery addict children

"Britain is producing a generation of child gamblers hooked on the Lottery and fruit machines. Disturbing new research by two eminent academics shows that hundreds of thousands of children—some as young as 11—are now addicted despite the supposed legal restrictions. The findings will fuel warnings from lottery critics that the country is storing up social problems and is likely to trigger pressure for a uniform age limit of 18 on all gambling."

(a) Describe how **two** approaches might try to explain (reference to the behaviour which is the focus of the stimulus material).   **(6 marks + 6 marks)**

(b) Assess **one** of these explanations of this phenomenon in terms of its strengths and limitations.   **(6 marks)**

(c) Analyse how **one** of these approaches might investigate this phenomenon.   **(6 marks)**

(d) Evaluate the use of this method of investigation on this phenomenon.   **(6 marks)**

Total for this question: 30 marks

The Biological Approach

A Description of the Biological Approach

Biology refers to the study of living organisms. Included within the biological approach are physiological psychology (Part 2), which is concerned with the functioning of the body; the nativist approach, which is concerned with an individual's genetic nature; and the medical approach, which is a term used to describe how mental disorders are explained in the same way that the medical profession explains physical illnesses.

The two key assumptions of this approach are that all behaviour can be explained and understood at the level of the functioning of biological systems, and that both behaviour and experience can be reduced to the functioning of biological systems.

The physiological approach

A **physiological** explanation is one that refers to bodily activity. There are physiological theories about dreaming that are based solely on brain activities, i.e., the functioning of the central nervous system. It is claimed, using the physiological perspective, that dreams are simply the random electrical activity of the brain during sleep upon which the mind imposes some sense (see page 189). Other physiological explanations make reference to **neurotransmitters** and **synapses**, such as explanations of depression (see page 638).

A further example of a physiological account could be of stress, which would focus on how your heart rate and breathing increase when in the presence of a stressor.

Explanations of how the body responds to stress were considered as part of your AS studies. Activity in the autonomic nervous system and endocrine system lead to the production of **hormones** which govern the stress response.

The nativist approach

In the Unit on nature and nurture we saw that Plato talked about things being inborn or native to an individual, as contrasted with those characteristics that were acquired through experience. The nativist approach to understanding behaviour is based on the idea that all behaviour is inherited. The unit of communication between one generation and the next is the **gene** (see Section 13, Determinants of Animal Behaviour).

The medical approach

The biological or somatic approach to the treatment of mental disorders (see Section 18, Treating Mental Disorders) suggests that psychological problems can be treated in the same way as physical problems. The medical model of mental illness assumes that all mental disorders have a physical cause (micro-organisms, genetics, biochemistry, or neuroanatomy). It also assumes that mental illnesses can be described in terms of clusters of symptoms; and symptoms can be identified, leading to the diagnosis of an illness. Finally diagnosis leads to appropriate physical treatments.

Can psychological problems be treated in the same way as physical problems?

Examples of the biological approach

The biological approach underlies the whole of Part 2 on physiological psychology. You might especially consider how psychologists use the biological approach to explain biological rhythms, sleep and dreaming, motivation, and emotion. You should also contrast such biological explanations with alternative ones such as Freud's account of the purpose of dreams, or the humanistic approach to understanding motivation.

Chomsky's account of language acquisition, given in Section 9, Language and Thought, is a biological (nativist) explanation. A number of explanations within developmental psychology are grounded in biology. Piaget's account of cognitive development relies on the notion of maturation or biologically determined stages in development (see Section 10, Cognitive Development). This also applies to Piaget's theory of moral development and to some theories of gender development (see Section 11, Social and Personality Development).

The evolutionary approach to explaining behaviour (see Part 5, Comparative Psychology, and also pages 774–776 in this Section) is also biological.

Finally, in your AS studies the study of individual differences included a consideration of the biological (medical) model of abnormality. This is continued in Part 6 of this book, (Individual Differences) which considers biological explanations of multiple personality disorder, culture-bound syndromes, schizophrenia, depression and anxiety disorders, as well as biological therapies that are used in the treatment of mental disorder.

An Evaluation of the Biological Approach

Strengths

The objective, reductionist nature of physiological explanations facilitates experimental research. For example, it is possible to investigate cause and effect relationships by observing the effects of certain drugs on behaviour.

Biological explanations have proved valuable in terms of practical applications; for example, using drug therapies to treat mental disorders. In certain circumstances these have proved highly effective, such as with schizophrenics, and this supports the biological explanations. More recently, genetic counselling for prospective parents is an outcome of our understanding of the links between genes and behaviour. For some parents this is an enormous relief where, for example, they carry a genetic susceptibility for a fatal disease. However genetic counselling raises many ethical problems in relation to the concept of "designer babies".

Weaknesses

Biological explanations offer a determinist, reductionist, and mechanistic (machine-like) explanation of behaviour, which is oversimplistic. However, there are positive aspects to this oversimplification, such as increased control in experiments and clear explanations of causal relationships. On the negative side such deterministic relationships may de-emphasise personal responsibility and free will.

The biological approach overlooks the experiential aspect of behaviour. It ignores past experience in our environment as an influence on behaviour.

Biological explanations are more appropriate for some kinds of behaviour (such as vision) than other kinds where higher-order thinking is involved (e.g., emotion). However, even vision involves some higher-order mental activity. Therefore biological explanations on their own are usually inadequate.

Answering the approaches question

Using the biological approach to explain a behaviour

"Lottery addict children

Britain is producing a generation of child gamblers hooked on the Lottery and fruit machines. Disturbing new research by two eminent academics shows that hundreds of thousands of children—some as young as 11— are now addicted despite the supposed legal restrictions. The findings will fuel warnings from lottery critics that the country is storing up social problems and is likely to trigger pressure for a uniform age limit of 18 on all gambling." (Reproduced from AQA A specimen material.)

In the A level examination you will be required to explain a target behaviour using any approach. The aim of this activity is to offer you, the candidate, the opportunity to express your true understanding of the approach by your ability to use it in a novel situation.

How would you explain lottery addiction in terms of the biological approach? The currency of the biological explanation is brain activity or brain anatomy, nervous impulses and neurotransmitters, hormones, and various organs in the body. A possible explanation could be as follows:

(a) *Why are young people hooked on the lottery and fruit machines? A psychologist might use the biological approach to explain this behaviour. Such a psychologist would explain the behaviour in terms of brain activity and the action of the central and autonomic nervous systems. The psychologist might also mention hormones.*

An answer like this would attract relatively few marks as it does little more than sketch out the possible elements of a biological explanation and has not demonstrated a true understanding of the approach. In order to do this you really need to try to put together an explanation of the target behaviour.

(a) *An explanation of lottery addiction using the biological approach would focus on how biological systems can be used to explain and understand this behaviour. When an individual stands in front of a fruit machine the flashing lights are physiologically arousing, creating a sense of excitement and probably pleasure. Physiological arousal causes the body to produce certain hormones that prepare the person for fight or flight. We can also understand the individual's behaviour in terms of nervous impulses. The eyes watch the pictures on the fruit machine go round and send impulses to the brain where they are interpreted and further messages sent to the hands to press a button at an appropriate moment to stop the machine.*

In the A level examination you will be given an opportunity to evaluate one of your explanations so you can take the opportunity, as below, to indicate in what way the explanation offered in the first part of the question is lacking. This highlights the fact that your explanations may not be satisfactory! They simply need to demonstrate your understanding of the named approach.

(b) *The problem with the biological approach is that for many aspects of behaviour it ignores some of the key elements of behaviour. In this case it is largely a description of what is happening at the level of nerves and hormones and doesn't actually explain anything, for example why the individual is playing the fruit machine or why the individual wants to repeat the behaviour. The behaviourist approach would offer a better account because we can use the idea of reinforcement and partial rewards.*

A suitable methodology for the biological approach

In the examination you will be further asked to analyse how one approach might investigate this phenomenon, and evaluate the use of this method of investigating this phenomenon. As already mentioned the biological approach lends itself to laboratory experiments. Therefore a further response would be to analyse the use of this method. The process of analysis involves identifying the constituent parts of a problem and discussing them. A good student answer might be:

(c) *The biological approach is particularly suitable for experiments because it reduces behaviours to simple components. If we were to conduct an experiment into gambling behaviour we might assess the stress experienced by individuals when playing the fruit machine by using a galvanic skin response. This registers the amount of sweat being produced during an activity and thus is indicative of autonomic arousal because when one is in a state of physiological arousal sweating increases. There are other signs of ANS arousal as well, such as pupil dilation. We might also consider reaction time and see whether this was enhanced during high ANS arousal.*

(d) *The investigation described above could be conducted in a laboratory where conditions are more highly controlled. Or it might be conducted in the field where behaviour might be more naturalistic but, on the negative side, participants' behaviour might be affected by other things in the environment rather than just the fruit machine activity (for example a noisy atmosphere in the pub). Field experiments increase ecological validity at a loss of internal validity for the experiment.*

The Behavioural Approach

A Description of the Behavioural Approach

The essence of the behavioural approach is the assumption that all behaviour is learned and that when we are born we are like a blank slate, or *tabula rasa*. Experience and interactions with the environment make us what we are. We become what we become as a result of forming stimulus–response units of behaviour in reaction to the environment. This perspective has been called **environmental determinism** because it suggests that we are determined by the environments in which we exist.

The second assumption is that all behaviour can be explained in terms of **conditioning theory**: stimulus and response (S–R) links that build up to produce more complex behaviours. Conditioning theory is explained in detail in Section 13, Determinants of Animal Behaviour. In essence, conditioning refers to changing behaviour in the absence of conscious thought, as in saying "I am conditioned to behave in that way".

The third main assumption is that we need look no further than the behaviours we can observe in order to understand and explain how humans and non-human animals operate. This is why of course it is called "behaviourism"—because the focus is solely on observable behaviour. There is no need to look at what goes on inside the "black box" of the mind (e.g., perception, attention, language, memory, thinking and so on), it is sufficient to be concerned only with external and observable behaviour.

A further assumption of the behavioural approach is that humans and non-human animals are only *quantitatively* different, i.e., they differ in terms of having more or less of something rather than differing qualitatively. This is supported by the theory of evolution which suggests that all animals have evolved from a common ancestor and are "built" from the same units (called stimulus–response units by the behaviourists). This means that behaviourists can generalise from non-human animals (such as rats and pigeons) to human behaviour. Much behaviourist research is conducted with non-human animals.

Do we really only differ quantitatively from animals?

It is important to recognise the contrasting perspectives within behaviourism:

- **Methodological behaviourism**: the view that that all perspectives use some behaviourist concepts to explain behaviour. This is a mild view of behaviourism—it is the view that the perspective is not a "stand-alone" approach but is part of all explanations.
- **Radical behaviourism**: the view that all behaviour is learned. Skinner was a radical behaviourist but most behaviourists nowadays would take a less radical view.
- **Neo-behaviourism**: this is a newer development and an extension of behaviourism. The best known example is **social learning theory** which was an attempt by Albert Bandura to reformulate learning theory to include a role for cognitive factors. The principle of social learning theory is that we learn through indirect (vicarious) rewards (which requires some cognitive activity) *as well as* through direct rewards.

Examples of the behavioural approach

Throughout your AS studies and in this A2 book there have been constant references to behaviourist approaches, learning theory, and social learning theory. We will identify some of the main examples here. At AS level we considered learning theory as an explanation of attachment and also discussed behavioural models of abnormality. At A2, we further considered behavioural explanations of mental disorder and behavioural methods of treatment (see Part 6, Individual Differences).

Learning theory was mentioned in Section 2, Relationships, when considering the reinforcement theory of interpersonal attraction, and again in Section 3, Pro- and

Anti-social Behaviour, as an explanation for aggression. Social learning theory is especially carefully explained in Section 3.

In Section 6, Motivation and Emotion, learning theory and the concept of reinforcement are also used as explanations for motivation (as part of drive-reduction theory). Section 9, Language and Thought, considers the acquisition of language, including Skinner's behaviourist explanation.

Both learning theory and social learning theory are important in developmental explanations (Part 4, Developmental Psychology) such as with respect to moral development (Section 10, Cognitive Development) and gender development (Section 11, Social and Personality Development).

An Evaluation of the Behavioural Approach

Behaviourism has had enormous influence through its emphasis on behaviour rather than introspection, and its insistence on studying behaviour in controlled conditions. However, the theory of behaviour put forward by the behaviourists has been rejected by most psychologists.

Strengths

Classic learning theory has had a major influence on all branches of psychology. This is described as methodological behaviourism. There is no doubt that conditioning, both classical and operant, is a fundamental part of psychological explanations. The argument arises over the extent to which such explanations can provide a full account. In the case of non-human animals it may be correct to suggest that learning theory can account for much of their behaviour because thinking clearly has a smaller, if not non-existent, role to play. On the other hand, the behaviour of lower-order animals may arguably be due even more to nature rather than nurture, i.e., can be explained in terms of the principles of evolution.

A second strength of the behaviourist approach is the large number of successful applications derived from this theory. For example behaviour therapy is clearly successful for target mental disorders, such as phobias (see Section 18, Treating Mental Disorders). Social skills training is also related to learning theory and may be the only way to teach some individuals how to acquire certain skills, such as teaching an autistic child some basic self-care. Learning theory has also been applied to education. Skinner advocated **programmed learning**, a method of teaching whereby the task is broken down into individual "frames" or very small steps. A correct response acts as a reward. The system may be linear (a list of questions) or branching (the programme can "respond" to a student's needs by offering special help with a question the student got wrong). This concept lends itself to computer-mediated learning.

A third strength of the behavioural approach is that it lends itself to scientific research. It focuses on observable and measurable behaviours, things that can be quantified and controlled in an experimental setting. Broadbent (1961) argued that behaviourism is the best method for rational advance in psychology.

Weaknesses

There are a raft of negative criticisms that are levelled at the behavioural approach. It is a mechanistic (machine-like) approach which ignores consciousness, subjective experience, and emotions. It is deterministic in so far as behaviour is seen as being determined by the environment though this may be an exaggeration. Bandura (1977) expressed this point very neatly: "If actions were determined solely by external rewards and punishments, people would behave like weather vanes, constantly shifting in radically different directions to conform to the whims of others." Much of our behaviour is relatively consistent, because it is under the control of various internal goals. This criticism is not true of social learning theory which portrays the individual as a more active

Consistent behaviour is dependent on internal goals, not just rewards.

participant in his/her experiences, using the concept of **reciprocal determinism**. Classic and operant conditioning, however, very much portray humans as passive.

The behavioural approach is also reductionist, reducing complex behaviour to stimulus–response links. However all these "weaknesses" (mechanistic, deterministic, and reductionist) are also strengths because they enable behaviourism to be highly appropriate for experimental research. Such reductionist and deterministic explanations may be appropriate for some non-human animal behaviour.

The behaviourists de-emphasised the influence of internal factors such as motivation and knowledge. The behaviourists also denied the role of innate factors, but we should remember that the nativist approach is equally determinist and reductionist. However there is clear evidence, for example in language acquisition (see Section 9, Language and Thought), that such nativist explanations are correct and this leads us to conclude that radical behaviourism must be rejected.

Behaviourism also excludes the role of cognitive (mental) factors, except for social learning theory, a neo-behaviourist perspective, which will be discussed later. Like the nativist position, the role of cognitive factors has been supported by much research evidence. For example, even non-human animals show evidence of cognition in their problem-solving abilities (see Section 13, Determinants of Animal Behaviour).

The behaviourists assumed that conditioning principles apply in very similar ways in different species. In so doing, they drastically underestimated the differences between species. For example, the fact that humans possess language transforms our learning ability. Rats who have learned to press a lever for food reward will keep pressing for a long time after food has stopped being provided. In contrast, most people will stop immediately if they are told that no more rewards will be given.

The behaviourists assumed that reward or reinforcement has a major impact on learning. In fact, however, reinforcement typically has more effect on performance than on learning. For example, suppose you were offered £1 every time you said, "The earth is flat." This might lead you to say it several hundred times. However, although the reward would have influenced your performance or behaviour, it would not have affected your knowledge or learning to the extent that you started to believe the earth was actually flat.

Many of the early behaviourist theories were very oversimplified. For example, Watson argued that thinking is merely sub-vocal speech. This led the philosopher Herbert Feigl to remark wittily that Watson "made up his windpipe that he had no mind". Watson's position was disproved in a dangerous study (Smith et al., 1947). Smith was given a drug that paralysed his entire musculature, and he had to be kept alive by a respirator. He was unable to engage in sub-vocal speech or any other bodily movement, and so, according to Watson's argument, he should have been unable to observe what was going on around him, to understand what people were saying, and to think about these events while in the paralysed state. In fact, Smith reported that he was able to do all of these things, indicating that thinking is possible in the absence of sub-vocal speech.

Finally, we should reflect on the fact that the use of behaviourist principles to control others (as in some prisons and psychiatric institutions using reward and punishment) could be considered unethical. Two notable behaviourists, Watson and Skinner, wished to use their principles to produce a better society.

Gamblers will keep playing so long as they think there is money to be won.

What other methods of investigation might be suitable for the behavioural approach?

Answering the approaches question

Using the behavioural approach to explain a behaviour

"Lottery addict children

Britain is producing a generation of child gamblers hooked on the Lottery and fruit machines. Disturbing new research by two eminent academics shows that hundreds of thousands of children—some as young as 11—are now addicted despite the supposed legal restrictions. The findings will fuel warnings from lottery critics that the country is storing up social problems and is likely to trigger pressure for a uniform age limit of 18 on all gambling." (Reproduced from AQA A specimen material.)

In the A level examination you will be required to explain a target behaviour using any approach. The aim of this activity is to offer you, the candidate, the opportunity to express your true understanding of the approach by your ability to use it in a novel situation.

How would you explain lottery addiction in terms of the behavioural approach? Any behavioural explanation should involve terms and concepts such as reinforcement, reward, and punishment. You could include social learning theory within your explanation and thus use concepts such as observational learning and vicarious reinforcement. An astute candidate will increase the amount of appropriate material by

continued overleaf

Answering the approaches question (continued)

extending their behavioural explanation to neo-behaviourist accounts, as in the case given here.

(a) *The most likely explanation for gambling behaviour would use the behavioural approach. Behaviourists would argue that the individual who plays the fruit machine experiences some rewards for the behaviour in the form of occasional small amounts of money or even the odd jackpot. Behaviourists have shown that partial reinforcement schedules, as used by fruit machines, create a greater likelihood that a behaviour will be increased than when reinforcement occurs on every trial. It is unlikely that the individual would experience any punishment so the behaviour will not be "stamped out". Such explanations cannot account for lottery addiction because most players never win anything, thus receiving no direct reinforcement. However, the concept of vicarious reinforcement can explain this as put forward by neo-behaviourists—still a behaviourist explanation. The idea of vicarious reinforcement is that, through seeing someone else receiving a reward, this increases the likelihood that you too will repeat the behaviour.*

This is a clear answer which uses behaviourist and neo-behaviourist concepts to explain the target behaviour, thus demonstrating the candidate's understanding of the behavioural approach in psychology. In the examination the candidate might go on to evaluate this approach and should again ensure that the evaluation is related to this particular context and not to behaviourism in general. For example, one might consider in what way this is a rather reductionist explanation of gambling behaviour. One should not overlook the fact that evaluation can consider the strengths of an explanation and the behaviourist account of why people gamble is relatively successful.

A suitable methodology for the biological approach

In the examination you will be further asked to analyse how one approach might investigate this phenomenon, and evaluate the use of this method of investigating this phenomenon. The process of analysis involves identifying the constituent parts of a problem and discussing these. A good student answer might be:

(c) *A behaviourist would be likely to test his or her explanation through the use of laboratory experiments because behaviourists believe that only observable behaviours count, and because they feel it is possible to reduce behaviour to simple cause and effect relationships. A behaviourist might investigate the effectiveness of reinforcement schedules by seeing which kind of reinforcement schedule led participants to rate a game more highly. They might also investigate whether people were more likely to play the lottery when there were very large jackpots or rather more jackpots that were smaller.*

The final part of the A level question requires an evaluation of this investigative approach. For example the candidate might write:

(d) *The advantages of the experimental approach are that one can demonstrate cause and effect relationships under highly controlled conditions. This is important in order to be able to exclude any extraneous variables from the investigation. On the negative side, laboratory experiments are low in ecological validity, in other words the results often cannot be generalised to other people and other situations than those used in the experiment. This limits their relevance. A further drawback of the experimental approach is that it focuses on a rather narrow set of factors and therefore may appear to account for a behaviour while in fact it only explains one aspect of this behaviour.*

The main drawback to this evaluation is that it only minimally relates to the target behaviour (gambling) and therefore the creditworthiness is significantly reduced. A few extra comments relating the criticisms (both positive and negative) to the target behaviour would significantly enhance the value of the response.

The Psychodynamic Approach

A Description of the Psychodynamic Approach

The term "psychodynamic" refers to any explanation that emphasises the processes of change and development, i.e., the dynamics of behaviour or the forces that drive an individual to behave as he or she does. "Dynamics" are the things that *drive* us or a machine to behave in particular ways. The best known example of a psychodynamic theory is Freud's account of the development of personality. This theory is covered in detail in Section 11 (Social and Personality Development) as well as in Section 10 (Cognitive Development) and Section 18 (Treating Mental Disorders).

Freud's theory and his method of therapy are both called psychoanalysis. The psychoanalytic perspective seeks to explain human development in terms of an interaction between innate drives and early experience. The basic assumption of Freud's approach is that early experience drives us to behave in predictable ways in later life. Childhood is a critical period of development. Infants are born with innate biological drives, e.g. for oral satisfaction. Such drives have a physical (sexual) basis. If these drives are not satisfied this can lead to personality or behavioural problems later in life, because our physical energies (libido) remain attached to these earlier stages and therefore the individual will regress to that stage when experiencing anxiety.

A further key assumption is that unconscious forces motivate much of our behaviour. At any time if drives are thwarted or not satisfied, the ego copes by using ego defence mechanisms such as sublimation, repression, and denial. Thoughts and feelings are redirected and placed beyond conscious awareness. An individual may express such feelings in dreams and unconsciously motivated behaviours such as Freudian slips.

Freud described personality dynamics in terms of various structures and stages. He wrote that your ego is the conscious and intellectual part of your personality which regulates the id. The id is the primitive, innate part of your personality, and the ego mediates between the id and the superego. The superego is the moral part which is learned from parents and society. These parts are hypothetical entities (i.e., they don't physically exist). They develop through the stages of childhood: oral, anal, phallic, latency, and genital.

A "neo-Freudian" psychologist basically agrees with the principles of psychoanalysis but has further adapted the theory. Neo-Freudians produced psychoanalytic theories that placed less emphasis on biological forces and more on the influences of social and cultural factors. For example, Erik Erikson proposed a stage theory of social development where each stage is marked by a crisis which must be confronted and resolved with the help of other people or else the individual cannot move on (see Section 11, Social and Personality Development, and Section 12, Adulthood). Erikson's stages started at age 1 and went through to old age. His perspective maintained some elements of classic psychodynamic theory—the unconscious and the components of personality—but placed greater emphasis on social influences and lifelong development.

Examples of the psychodynamic approach

Freud's psychodynamic approach was referred to in your AS studies as an explanation for attachment, and also as a model of abnormality and an explanation for eating disorders. The psychoanalytic perspective was also used to explain obedience—the authoritarian personality represses conflicting thoughts.

In this book the psychoanalytic perspective was used to explain prejudice (see Section 1, Social Cognition) and aggression (Section 3, Pro- and Anti-social Behaviour). Freud's theory of dreams was described in Section 5, Biological Rhythms. We have already noted Freud's contributions to our understanding of moral development (Section 10, Cognitive Development). In addition Section 11, Social and Personality Development, includes psychodynamic perspectives on gender development and adolescence. Gould's theory of adult consciousness also has a Freudian basis (see Section 12, Adulthood).

Using psychoanalysis to understand why we love monsters

Any approach in psychology can be used to help us understand different behaviours. Here is an example of how the psychoanalytic approach can be used to explain why people appear to be universally drawn to the idea of monsters. Tales of monsters and horror are to be found in a huge range of cultures. There are also instances of remarkable similarity between the legends of otherwise quite distinct cultures. For example, some form of "undead" are to be found in the folklore of cultures as diverse as Haiti (zombies) and central Europe (vampires). This suggests that the idea of monstrous undead must serve a psychological purpose. A psychoanalytic psychologist might suggest that monsters represent the human fear of death and, in overcoming the monsters we can overcome our fear. From a Freudian viewpoint, battling and overcoming monsters may represent the Oedipus complex, in which a monster—symbolising the same-sex parent—attacks but is vanquished (Minsky, 1998).

By considering the historical context of certain films we can see how films may express the anxieties of the time, and help people deal with their, possibly repressed, anxieties. Following the First World War, a number of films such as The Hunchback of Notre Dame and The Phantom of the Opera featured disfigured heroes. According to Skal (1993) these may have represented society's coming to terms with the mass disfigurement resulting from the war. With the rise of Hitler and the Third Reich, wolves and werewolves became particularly popular monsters, symbolising the marauding, predatory nature of the Nazi threat.

Following the war, with American and European politics dominated by the Cold War, film horror was dominated by alien invasion, symbolic of the threat of war with Russia. Meanwhile horror comics became dominated by images of corpses returning for revenge on the living. Skal draws a link between this and society's collective guilt following the death of 40,000,000 people in the Second World War. Godzilla, produced in Japan in 1954, involved a radiation-mutated monster rampaging through Japan burning all in its path, and possibly relates to the devastation caused by the atomic bombs.

In the late 1960s and throughout the 1970s, a major theme in horror was of demonic children. Examples included Village of the Damned, The Omen series, Rosemary's Baby, and It Lives. Skal suggested that these films represented society's anxiety following the sexual revolution, and perhaps the horror following the revelation of the effects of Thalidomide, the anti-morning sickness drug that caused babies to be born with missing limbs. More recent trends in horror can also be linked to the anxieties of society. In the 1990s there were a number of films involving computer domination, for example Terminator.

From M. Jarvis, (2000) Theoretical approaches in psychology. London: Routledge Modular Series.

Part 6 on Individual Differences refers to Freud's ideas in the explanations of mental disorders (Section 16, Issues in Classification and Diagnosis of Psychological Abnormality, and Section 17, Psychopathology) and psychoanalysis as a therapy (Section 18, Treating Mental Disorders).

An Evaluation of the Psychodynamic Approach

Strengths

In studying psychology it is important to try to take an unbiased view and reach an informed opinion. There is a tendency to be overcritical about Freud's theories, but it is worth remembering that the theory was constructed during a different epoch from ours and his concepts were quite revolutionary for their time. His ideas have endured—and not just in psychology. They appear in literature and art and everyday life. This testifies to the fact that there must be some important meanings in the theory. Many of these meanings have become such a part of commonplace knowledge that you are not even aware that they are Freudian. For example, when a person says something that appears to have hidden meaning, you might say "That's an unconscious slip". Hall and Lindzey (1970) suggested that the durability of the theory is due to Freud's fine literary style, a conception of human beings that is broad and deep, and one that combines the world of reality with make-believe.

Freud is responsible for introducing certain key concepts to early psychology, namely the recognition that childhood is a critical period of development, and that unconscious sexual (physical) desires influence behaviour. Neither of these was recognised in the Victorian society of his formative period. Williams (1987) introduced a chapter on Freud with the remark that "psychoanalysis has been society's most influential theory of human behaviour … it profoundly altered Western ideas about human nature and changed the way we viewed ourselves and our experience". Freud founded developmental psychology, proposed one of the first systematic theories of personality, and devised a form of therapy that was unsurpassed for over 80 years. Psychoanalysis has been widely used and adapted, though it tends to be suitable only for literate and wealthy people because of the time and expense involved.

Jarvis (2000) identifies the most significant feature of Freudian theory as the notion that the human personality has more than one aspect: "we reveal this when we say things like 'part of me wants to do it, but part of me is afraid to …'." Freud's introduction of the unconscious permits us to explain how one can be both rational and irrational, and this can account for many aspects of our behaviour, such as the fact that people often predict they will behave one way and actually do something quite different.

Freud focused on the individual, observing particular "cases" in fine detail, an **idiographic approach**. This has the advantage of providing unique insights into behaviour because of the depth of information collected. However, it may not be justifiable to use such unique observations to formulate general theories about human behaviour.

It has been suggested that Freud may have overemphasised sex because he developed his theory at a historical time of great sexual repression. Understandably this may have caused sex to be something that was repressed in many minds (Banyard & Hayes, 1994). There are a number of neo-Freudians who have adapted Freud's explanation and incorporated more social rather than sexual influences.

Freud's concepts were quite revolutionary for his time.

Weaknesses

Probably the most significant criticism concerns the empirical support for the theory. Freud based the theory on his case histories (see for example pages 418 and 651). These were mainly of middle-class Viennese women suffering from neurotic disorders. That he used these case studies to construct a theory of *normal* development is clearly questionable. He recorded only one case history of a child (Little Hans) and this study was largely second-hand. The data were retrospectively collected and interpreted by Freud, who is likely to have been biased by his own theoretical beliefs.

The theory of psychoanalysis lacks **falsifiability**. That is, it is difficult to prove his theory wrong because his arguments can be made to fit any behaviour. For instance, psychoanalysis depends heavily on the therapist's interpretation of what the client says. How, for example, does the therapist know that a girl dreaming about riding a horse is actually thinking about having sex rather than simply about horse-riding? Freud argued that the acid test was the client's reaction to the therapist's proposed interpretation. However, if the client accepts the accuracy of the interpretation, then it is probably correct. If the client vehemently rejects the therapist's interpretation of a dream, that may simply be resistance by the client's conscious mind to an unacceptable but entirely accurate interpretation. There is a problem here. The therapist can use either the client's acceptance or denial of the reasonableness of a dream interpretation as supporting evidence that the interpretation is correct! The therapist's interpretation is unfalsifiable.

The main evidence for Freud's theory consists of *correlations* between certain childhood experiences and type of adult personality. Correlations cannot prove causes, and so these correlations cannot show that adult personality has been caused by childhood experiences. Those parts of the theory of psychosexual development that can be tested have mostly been found to be incorrect. Freud argued that fear plays an important part in the development of identification in boys. It follows that boys whose fathers are threatening and hostile should show more identification than boys whose fathers are supportive. In fact, however, the evidence indicates that what happens is exactly the opposite (Mussen & Rutherford, 1963). There is also very little evidence for the existence of the Oedipus complex or penis envy (Kline, 1981).

Freud's theory is also highly determinist because it suggests that infant behaviour is determined by innate forces and adult behaviour is determined by childhood experiences. The theory reduces human activity to a basic set of structures, which are reifications (abstract concepts that are presented as if they are real things). The original theory probably lays too much emphasis on innate biological forces.

Answering the approaches question

Using the psychodynamic approach to explain a behaviour

"Lottery addict children

Britain is producing a generation of child gamblers hooked on the Lottery and fruit machines. Disturbing new research by two eminent academics shows that hundreds of thousands of children—some as young as 11—are now addicted despite the supposed legal restrictions. The findings will fuel warnings from lottery critics that the country is storing up social problems and is likely to trigger pressure for a uniform age limit of 18 on all gambling." (Reproduced from AQA A specimen material.)

In the A level examination you will be required to explain a target behaviour using any approach. The aim of this activity is to offer you, the candidate, the opportunity to express your true understanding of the approach by your ability to use it in a novel situation.

How would you explain lottery addiction in terms of the psychodynamic approach? Your response is likely to revolve around unconscious motivations that may be related to early childhood conflicts, and on how the id is motivated by the pleasure principle whereas the ego must restrain the id, leading to inevitable conflict and ego defences. In addition the superego acts as the moral voice. A possible explanation could be as follows:

(a) *The Freudian approach would suggest that gambling behaviour is in some way the expression of unconscious wish fulfilment. The unconscious motivations of the id are regulated by the ego through the reality principle. The conflicts that arise between the id and ego lead to ego defences so that the ego may repress*

unpleasant thoughts. The superego may also be involved, acting as the moral voice of reason.

Such an answer would attract relatively few marks as it does little more than identify features of Freud's theory without suggesting in what way these could be used to explain the target behaviour. This suggests that the candidate does not fully understand the psychoanalytic explanation of behaviour because he or she has been unable to use it to actually offer a coherent explanation. A better attempt would be:

(a) *The psychodynamic approach to explaining behaviour takes the view that our behaviour is motivated by unconscious influences of which we are not aware. According to Freud the personality consists of three aspects, the id, which wants immediate satisfaction, the superego that is based on morality and urges restraint, and the ego that has access to reality and can balance the influences of the id and superego. Gambling can be seen as the interaction of the three personality parts. The id wants the prize, the superego says you can't have it as you haven't earned it, so the ego compromises by saying you can gamble for it and have it if you win.*

The psychodynamic approach might further focus on adolescence as a time of identity crisis and this might help explain why gambling becomes a problem at that time. An adolescent might especially need parental attention during this period and, if both parents are at work, perhaps adolescents are getting less support than they used to so they are more likely to go off the rails.

continued overleaf

Answering the approaches question *(continued)*

In the A level examination you will be given an opportunity to evaluate one of your explanations.

(b) *The drawback to psychodynamic explanations is that they lack falsifiability. In other words it would be difficult to test whether this explanation is actually any better than any other explanation. The influence of the id, ego and superego is a hypothetical concept since none of these actually exist. They only provide a means of conceptualising the problem. However, the idea of unconscious influences has some validity as demonstrated by behaviours such as Freudian slips. Therefore it is possible that gambling is in some way expressing an unconscious desire for more attention especially at this vulnerable time of adolescent identity formation.*

A suitable methodology for the psychodynamic approach

In the examination you will be further asked to analyse how one approach might investigate this phenomenon, and evaluate the use of this method of investigating this phenomenon. The process of analysis involves identifying the constituent parts of a problem and discussing these. A good student answer might be:

(c) *It is likely that a psychoanalytic psychologist would investigate the behaviour described by using the case study approach. This is where one individual is studied intensively over a period of time. Retrospective accounts of their early life are analysed as a means of explaining their current gambling behaviour. A psychoanalytic psychologist would focus on experiences in early life that might have been repressed or led to conflicts. The psychiatrist would do this through free association where the patient just talks about whatever comes into their mind and the psychiatrist encourages their recall. The psychiatrist might also use dream interpretation as a way of understanding the repressed thoughts of the individual. Ultimately the case study could then be used to formulate an explanation for gambling behaviour because the psychiatrist would be able to suggest what past experiences were associated with the current pathological behaviour.*

The final part of the A level question requires the candidate to evaluate the use of this method, again in the context of the target behaviour. The danger, as in the above answers, is omitting to mention gambling behaviour and simply offering an evaluation of the method used in part (c).

The Cognitive Approach

A Description of the Cognitive Approach

The cognitive approach is in some ways at the opposite end of the spectrum to behaviourism. Where behaviourism emphasises external observable events only, the cognitive approach looks at internal, mental explanations of behaviour. The word "cognitive" comes from the Latin word *cognitio* meaning "to apprehend, understand, or know". These are all internal processes which involve the mind (brain processes)—processes such as those involved in perception, attention, language, memory, and thinking.

The cognitive approach is based on three main assumptions:

- That behaviour can largely be explained in terms of how the mind operates.
- That the mind works in a manner that is similar to a computer: inputting, storing, and retrieving data. Cognitive psychologists assume that there is an information-processing system in which information is altered or transformed.
- That psychology is a pure science, based mainly on laboratory experiments.

As you can see, the cognitive approach may be the opposite to behaviourism in some ways, but there are also similarities. Both approaches are quite reductionist and experimental. The cognitive approach is reductionist in its use of computer analogies, and experimental in its attitudes towards research.

Historical development

Psychology developed properly as a science towards the end of the nineteenth century when Wilhelm Wundt founded the first psychological laboratory at the University of Leipzig in Germany. Wundt was a cognitive psychologist. He studied mental processes and wanted to make such research more systematic. Instead of just developing his own ideas (like philosophers), he devised experiments to try to find evidence to support his theories. In this way he made psychology more scientific (seeking objective data on which to formulate theories).

Wundt argued that conscious mental states could be scientifically studied using **introspection**. Wundt's introspection was not a casual affair but a highly practised form

Wilhelm Wundt, 1832–1920.

of self-examination. He trained psychology students to make observations that were not biased by personal interpretation or previous experience, and used the results to develop a theory of conscious thought. Wundt did not believe that this perspective could be applied to all aspects of human psychology, but he did think that he could identify the elementary sensations and their interrelations, and thus identify the way that human thought was structured.

John B. Watson, the father of behaviourism, felt that such methods were not sufficiently scientific and proposed that psychology should adopt the experimental methods that had proved so successful within the physical sciences such as physics and chemistry. For many years cognitive psychology took a back seat to the domination of psychology by behaviourism.

The advent of the computer age gave cognitive psychology a new metaphor, and the 1950s and 1960s saw a tremendous rise in cognitive psychology research and the use of cognitive concepts in other areas of psychology, such as social cognition and cognitive-developmental theories. If machines could produce behaviours that were analogous to animal behaviours then psychologists might be able to use information-processing concepts to explain the behaviour of living things. Or, to put it another way, cognitive psychologists could explain behaviour using computer concepts to explain how animals process information.

The kind of concepts we are talking about are input, output, storage, retrieval, parallel processing, networking, schemas, filters, top-down and bottom-up processing, and so on. If you look at Part 3 (Cognitive Psychology) you will find these terms scattered everywhere. The cognitive perspective relies on the computer metaphor or analogy as a means of describing and explaining behaviour.

However, the cognitive perspective involves more than the information-processing metaphor. It is a perspective that focuses on the way that mental or cognitive processes work. In this way any explanation that incorporates mental concepts is using a cognitive perspective. For example, in social psychology (where the relationships between individuals are studied) there is a branch called "social cognition" which focuses on how one's thinking affects social behaviour. In developmental psychology, theorists such as Piaget explained behaviour in terms of mental operations and schemas.

Schemas

The concept of **schemas** (or sometimes "schemata") must arguably be the single most important concept introduced by cognitive psychology. It is the basic unit of our mental processes and is used throughout this book. What is a schema?

A schema is a cognitive structure that contains knowledge about a thing, including its attributes and the relations among its attributes (Fiske & Taylor, 1991).

Why are schemas so important? The concept of a schema (the schema of a schema) incorporates a number of critical features of our thought processes:

* A schema does not consist of a single dimension but of a cluster of interrelated concepts.
* A schema is derived from an individual's past experience and does not directly represent reality. Thus we can use schemas to explain how people distort information along the lines of their past experience.
* Schemas are also socially determined. They are learned and refined through social exchanges (conversations with other people and from the media).
* There are many different kinds of schema. Schemas about events are called **scripts**. These schemas guide us when performing commonplace activities, such as going to the cinema or to a football match. Role schemas tell us about different roles, and self-schemas embody our self-concept.
* Schemas are an obvious outcome of our cognitive processes. We need to categorise and summarise the large amounts of information processed in order to generate future behaviour. We are "cognitive misers".

You will find the concept of schemas used in Part 1 (Social Psychology), Part 3 (Cognitive Psychology), and Part 4 (Developmental Psychology). For example, Kelley's causal schemata theory of attribution (page 19), Sellen and Norman's schema theory of action slips (page 253), and Martin and Halverson's gender-schema theory (page 433).

An Evaluation of the Cognitive Approach

Strengths

The advent of computers encouraged a rebirth of cognitive psychology and a new legitimacy for the concept of mental processes (cognitions), moving psychology away from the dominance of behaviourism. The irony is that cognitive psychology today is rather similar to behaviourism in so far as it excludes certain other internal factors, such as the influences of motivation and emotion. The cognitive approach is seen as overly reductionist and mechanistic. However, cognitive psychology did bring mental states back to psychology, including their use in social learning theory. Some more recent developments in cognitive psychology have aimed to focus less on reductionist explanations (see later).

The approach has numerous useful applications, ranging from advice about the validity of eyewitness testimony, to suggestions about how to improve your memory (useful for examination candidates), how to improve performance in situations requiring close attention (such as air-traffic control and shift workers controlling nuclear power stations), and numerous successful therapies for psychological problems, such as Meichenbaum's stress inoculation treatment.

The cognitive approach has been applied within many other areas of psychology, such as social cognition. In fact it is as pervasive an approach as behaviourism.

Weaknesses

As we have noted, the cognitive perspective has been criticised as being overly mechanistic and ignoring social, motivational, and emotional factors. It is mechanistic because cognitive explanations themselves are based on the behaviour of machines. This inevitably de-emphasises the importance of emotion. However, this is changing. For example Bem and Keijzer (1996) argue that cognitive psychology is turning away from the dominant view of the mind as an isolated entity, separate from the body, and now sees the mind more as an activity in both a whole body and external environment. Nevertheless the cognitive perspective, as you have largely encountered it, still appears highly mechanistic and reductionist.

Much of the work in cognitive psychology is experimental and based in laboratories, looking at behaviours that are highly idealised and lack ecological validity. For example, the main body of research into memory focused on a particular kind of memory, called episodic memory or memory for facts, whereas there are many different kinds of memory.

Answering the approaches question

Using the cognitive approach to explain a behaviour

"Lottery addict children

Britain is producing a generation of child gamblers hooked on the Lottery and fruit machines. Disturbing new research by two eminent academics shows that hundreds of thousands of children—some as young as 11—are now addicted despite the supposed legal restrictions. The findings will fuel warnings from lottery critics that the country is storing up social problems and is likely to trigger pressure for a uniform age limit of 18 on all gambling." (Reproduced from AQA A specimen material.)

In the A level examination you will be required to explain a target behaviour using any approach. The aim of this activity is to offer you, the candidate, the opportunity to express your true understanding of the approach by your ability to use it in a novel situation.

How would you explain lottery addiction in terms of the cognitive approach? The key elements of the cognitive approach are that explanations focus on what is going on inside the mind and how cognitions, such as schemas and processing of data, can be used to explain behaviour. Such explanations de-emphasise emotion. A possible explanation could be as follows:

(a) *Addiction can be understood in terms of various theories of cognitive activity. Attribution theory offers one explanation. Addicts typically think of their behaviour as being governed by craving and beyond their voluntary control. However, if they can learn to associate their addiction with situational cues (such as the amusement arcade) then they can stop attributing the behaviour to*

Answering the approaches question (continued)

their internal disposition (I am a gambler) and overcome their addiction.

The cognitive approach might also use the idea of schemas to explain how we all acquire scripts about behaving in certain situations in certain ways. When you go into an amusement arcade you have a script that tells you what to do. You acquire such scripts from watching things on TV. Without a script you wouldn't know what to do in certain situations, which is why one often feels lost in a foreign city.

This answer is a tricky one for the examiner because the candidate clearly knows something about how attribution theory can explain addiction and has used this knowledge well. It does show an understanding of attribution theory, an example of a cognitive approach. The problem is that in this question you must demonstrate your understanding of the cognitive approach, rather than material you have learned when studying cognitive psychology (i.e., attribution theory). The second paragraph is in some ways better in terms of demonstrating an understanding of the cognitive approach though perhaps not as successful as the first. It at least illustrates an attempt to marry understanding of schemas and scripts to gambling addiction rather than just describing a known explanation, as with attribution theory.

A suitable methodology for the cognitive approach

In the examination you will be further asked to analyse how one approach might investigate this phenomenon, and evaluate the use of this method of investigating this phenomenon. The process of analysis involves identifying the constituent parts of a problem and discussing these. A good student answer might be:

(c) *If one wanted to investigate the kind of scripts that adolescents have one might interview people of this age group and ask them to describe what they do when they go into an amusement arcade. It is likely that you would use a fairly unstructured interview technique in order to find out as much as possible. You would start with a set of fixed questions and develop these as you went along in response to the answers that were given. At the end you would have a large amount of data to analyse and this could be done by identifying certain themes that occurred in the different accounts. Your aim would be to synthesise and summarise the data so that you could draw conclusions about the kind of behaviours that typically surrounded gambling addiction in young people.*

This is a reasonable attempt to explain how a cognitive psychologist might investigate gambling behaviour. The description is related to the target behaviour and the candidate has shown an understanding of various aspects of interviewing technique and the qualitative approach to research. The last part of the question requires the candidate to evaluate this methodology again with reference to the target behaviour:

(d) *The advantage of the unstructured interview is that one is able to collect a lot of data and some of this data may be unexpected because the material collected is not restricted by previous expectations about what people think about gambling addiction. One limitation of this method is that the data collected may be biased by the kind of questions the interviewer asks since they make some of the questions up on the spot. This might be a special problem when interviewing teenagers. A further limitation lies in the analysis, which again involves subjective decisions. Objectivity can be increased by triangulating the findings with findings from other research studies as a means of confirming the outcome.*

The Humanistic Approach

A Description of the Humanistic Approach

Since the 1950s the humanistic perspective has been welcomed as a counterpoint to the other orientations in psychology because it is neither scientific nor deterministic. Abraham Maslow, a humanistic psychologist, called it the "third force in psychology", regarding behaviourism and psychoanalyisis as the other two forces. Some might argue about the status of humanistic psychology, but there is no doubt that humanistic psychology is *a* major force representing the case for free will, the uniqueness of the individual, the striving to reach one's potential, and the inappropriateness of objective research into personal experience.

Humanistic perspectives are a reflection of modern society in the same way that both psychoanalysis and behaviourism were in their time. Perhaps because of its relative recency it is rather less well defined than the other perspectives. This lack of definition may also be related to the less scientific nature of the approach.

Having said that it is a recent approach, there are elements of the perspective that are not that recent. The *Encyclopaedia Britannica* traces the roots of **humanism** back to the fourteenth-century writings of Petrarch. Humanistic *psychology* is derived from these wider principles of humanism, described therein as "value systems that emphasise the personal worth of each individual but do not include a belief in God", in other words it is a kind of religion but one that does not invoke a divine being, instead it is based on a shared belief in human worth. The antecedents of psychological humanism go back to nineteenth-century **phenomenological** philosophers such as Kierkegaard who founded the existentialist movement, arguing that subjectivity is truth.

Humanistic psychologists reject behaviourist and psychodynamic perspectives as being reductionist and determinist. They feel that each individual has personal responsibility and is in control rather than controlled by external forces. Humanistic psychologists also suggest that most other perspectives in psychology overlook a key factor—that of experience. Descriptions of behaviour are often external rather than including important elements of experience, such as emotion.

This perspective is also at odds with the objective, empirical perspective to research that may produce statistically significant facts but ones that are humanly insignificant, lacking real-life validity. Humanistic psychologists have pioneered many alternative research methods such as observation, the Q-sort technique, and discourse analysis (see page 778).

Carl Rogers and counselling

Carl Rogers, the founder of the counselling movement, is a classic example of a humanistic psychologist. His view of human development was that personal growth was only possible with unconditional positive regard from significant others (such as your parents). This frees individuals from striving for social approval so that they can seek self-actualisation. Conditional love from a significant other leads to maladjustment because the self and ideal self within the individual are in conflict. Rogers, as all humanistic psychologists, values the uniqueness of each individual and the potential each person has for self-determination and self-actualisation.

Rogers' approach is also a psychodynamic approach because he describes the dynamics of adult personality, as illustrated in the box below.

The Q-sort method

One way of assessing the self-concept and the ideal self is to use the Q-sort method:

1. An individual is presented with a pile of cards, each of which contains a personal statement (e.g., "I am a friendly person"; "I am tense most of the time").
2. The individual decides which statements best describe his or her own self, which statements are the next best, and so on, right down to those statements that are the least descriptive.
3. The same procedure is followed with respect to the ideal self.
4. The experimenter works out the size of the gap between the statements selected as descriptive of the self and the ideal self.

There are three problems with using the Q-sort method or any similar method to assess the self-concept and the ideal self. First, such methods cannot shed any light on those

---

A humanistic perspective of personality development—a psychodynamic approach

In 1951 Carl Rogers published *Client-centred therapy*, a book outlining his approach to therapy and his theory of personality that is summarised here.

He began from the assumption that each individual is the centre of his or her world of experience. The sensations and thoughts of this private world can only ever truly be known by the individual and cannot be represented by external measurement. There is no need to have a concept of a "true" reality. Reality for each individual is what they perceive. The best vantage point for understanding behaviour is from the internal frame of reference of the individual him/herself.

The individual reacts as an organised whole, rather than as a set of stimulus–response (S–R) links. The individual has one basic tendency and striving—to actualise, maintain, and enhance their lives. People have a self-righting tendency—an urge for independence, the desire to be self-determined, and to strive towards socialised maturity.

As a child grows up he or she learns to differentiate what is "me" (the conscious concept of self) from the rest of the world. This self-concept is formed as a result of interaction with the environment. The values attached to the self-concept (i.e., self-esteem) are derived either from direct experience or from what other people tell you about yourself.

Through life the individual can assimilate experience in one of three ways: (a) organise it into the self-concept, (b) ignore it entirely as being irrelevant, or (c) distort the experience because it is inconsistent with self. Assimilation into the self-concept is most usual and most healthy. When a person does something that is apparently inconsistent with their self-concept they will disown it, for example by saying "I was not myself". In many cases of psychological maladjustment individuals say "I don't know why I do it" or "I'm just not myself when I do those things". Rogers points out that the problem here is that their behaviour has not been incorporated into their self-concept and therefore cannot be controlled. When they can accept themselves, then they are able to grow psychologically.

aspects of the self about which there is no conscious awareness. Second, there are obvious possibilities of deliberate distortion. For example, it is more desirable to be a friendly rather than an unfriendly person, and so many unfriendly people may pretend to be friendly for the purposes of the test. Third, people may possess a number of self-concepts, but the Q-sort method is designed to assess a single self-concept.

Abraham Maslow

Maslow (1970) pointed out that theories of motivation had focused mainly on basic physiological needs, or on our needs to reduce anxiety and to avoid pain. He assumed that human motivation is actually much broader than that. He proposed a **hierarchy of needs** consisting of seven levels (see Section 6, Motivation and Emotion). Physiological needs (such as those for food and water) are at the bottom of the hierarchy. Next come security and safety needs, followed by needs for love and belongingness. Moving further up the hierarchy, we come to esteem needs, then cognitive needs (such as curiosity and the need for understanding) and aesthetic (artistic) needs. Finally, there is the need for **self-actualisation**, which involves fulfilling one's potential in the broadest sense.

Self-actualised individuals are characterised by an acceptance of themselves, spontaneity, the need for privacy, resistance to cultural influences, empathy, profound interpersonal relationships, a democratic character structure, creativeness, and a philosophical sense of humour. Maslow (1954) identified Abraham Lincoln and Albert Einstein as famous people who were self-actualised.

Maslow characterised Abraham Lincoln as a famous individual who demonstrated "self-actualisation" —including characteristics such as self-acceptance, resistance to cultural influences, empathy and creativeness.

Assumptions of the humanistic perspective

The key assumptions of this approach are that each individual is unique. What matters is each person's subjective view rather than some objective reality. Reality is defined by the individual's perspective based on their own unique experiences in life. Each individual strives to maximise their potential (self-actualisation) and should be responsible for their lives (free will). The humanistic approach also assumes that human nature is inherently good and self-righting.

Examples of the humanistic approach

The humanistic approach is not well represented in this book. In Section 6 on motivation there is a consideration of Maslow's theory (see page 211) and humanistic therapy is discussed in Section 18, Treating Mental Disorders. Humanistic views on free will are included in Section 19, Issues.

An Evaluation of the Humanistic Approach

Strengths

This approach has encouraged psychologists in general to accept the view that there is more to behaviour than objectively discoverable facts (see also the social constructionist approach described in a later Unit). Humanistic psychology promotes a positive approach to human behaviour and one that emphasises individual responsibility.

Client-centred therapy is a major contribution of the humanistic approach. Counselling has become a huge "industry" underpinning self-help groups, and telephone helplines as well as trained therapists. The fundamental element of humanistic psychotherapy is unconditional positive regard and the power of each individual for self-healing.

Weaknesses

In spite of the various contributions of the humanistic approach, there are some criticisms that can be made of it. First, humanistic psychology is concerned only with those thoughts of which we have conscious awareness. As a result, it ignores all the important processes going on below the level of conscious awareness. Another problem with reliance on an individual's conscious experiences is that his or her report of those experiences may be systematically distorted (e.g., to create a good impression).

The humanistic perspective is vague, unscientific, and untestable. The theories are not set out in a way that lends itself to empirical verification but this is at least partly because humanist psychologists do not strive for this confirmation. The more recent, qualitative research approaches, such as discourse analysis, have developed methods that are more suitable, but it is still not clear to what extent such new approaches can generate a useful body of knowledge. In addition humanistic theories lack falsifiability, in other words they can neither be proved right nor wrong, and this too prevents our advance of understanding (see page 741).

For many individuals free will is not a reality. There are too many things in their lives that dictate how they must behave. Free will may be a luxury of the middle classes in the Western world. The assumption that everyone is born with the potential to become a self-actualiser provided their basic needs are met is dubious at best. The fact that a small percentage of people are self-actualised does not show that everyone could be. The main explanation for self-actualisation may simply be that self-actualised people tend to be more intelligent, talented, well educated, and motivated than the rest of us.

Free will is also a burden. Sartre, an existentialist philosopher, said that we are "condemned to be free". Freedom is as much a burden as a boon, and much of humanity may prefer to view their lives as being pre-determined.

The Evolutionary Approach

A Description of the Evolutionary Approach

Evolution is a fact—to evolve is to change over time. There is clear evidence that groups of animals have changed over time (see Section 13, Determinants of Animal Behaviour). Charles Darwin's theory of evolution and natural selection is an attempt to offer an explanation for this process of change. The essential principles of this theory are:

- Environments are always changing, or animals move to new environments. Environmental change requires new adaptations in order for species to survive.
- Living things are constantly changing. This happens partly because of sexual reproduction where two parents create a new individual by combining their **genes** (although Darwin wasn't aware that there were such things as genes, he knew that the information was transmitted in some way). It also happens through chance **mutations** of the genes. In both cases new traits are produced.
- Competition between individuals for limited resources (such as access to food and/or mates) means that those individuals who possess traits that are best adapted or suited to the changing environment are more likely to survive to reproduce (it is reproduction rather than survival that matters). Or, to put it another way, those individuals who best "fit" their environment survive (survival of the *fittest*). Or, to put it yet another way, the *genes* of the individuals with these traits are naturally selected. No one "selects" these individuals with useful traits, they are *naturally* selected.

Selective breeding is an artificial way of ensuring that good genes get passed to the next generation.

In order to understand the concept of **natural selection** consider this example. A cattle or sheep farmer chooses which male and female stock animals have the best characteristics for milk production or for increased reproduction (e.g., giving birth to lots of twins), and mates these individuals. This is selective breeding or artificial selection. In nature, no one does the selecting—it is natural pressures that do it, hence "natural selection".

The end result is that those individuals who possess the physical characteristics and behaviours that are **adaptive**, i.e., help the individual to better fit its environment, are the ones that survive. Those traits that are non-adaptive disappear, as do the individuals with those traits. It should be emphasised that it is not the individual, but their genes, that disappear. Natural selection takes place at the level of the genes. A classic example of this is the tendency for parents to risk their lives to save their offspring, which can be seen in altruistic behaviour. If altruistic behaviour is inherited then it must in some way promote survival and reproduction. But one would think this cannot be true, because an altruistic act involves a risk to the altruist's life. However, if the altruist is risking its life to save a genetic relative then the altruistic behaviour enhances the survival of the individual's genes. See Section 13, Determinants of Animal Behaviour, for a more detailed explanation of this and other altruistic behaviours.

Sociobiology

The concept that altruistic behaviour is adaptive because it promotes the survival of kin was not one of Darwin's ideas. In fact, for him, altruism was a paradox. It was sociobiologists such as Hamilton (1964) and Dawkins (1976) who suggested that in addition to natural selection there was **kin selection**. The principle of kin selection is that any behaviour that promotes the survival of kin will be selected. Darwin's theory of evolution focused on individual fitness. The sociobiologists extended this to include genetic relatives, thus kin selection *includes* the survival of any relatives sharing your genes (**inclusive fitness**).

Assumptions of the evolutionary perspective

The evolutionary approach assumes that all behaviour can be explained in terms of genetic determination. **Ethologists** study behaviour in order to ascertain what the function of the behaviour is for the individual. They argue that any behaviour must be adaptive in some way (or neutral) otherwise it would not remain in the individual's gene pool. This argument is applied, for example, to mental illnesses (see Section 15, Evolutionary Explanations of Human Behaviour). If the genes for mental disorders did not have some adaptive significance, why would they still be with us? This of course assumes that mental disorders have some genetic basis, but twin studies suggest that they do.

The second assumption of the evolutionary approach is that genetically determined traits evolve through natural and kin selection. A behaviour that promotes survival and reproduction of a genetic line will be "selected" and the genes for that trait survive. As the environment changes (or an individual moves to a new environment) new traits are needed to ensure survival. Environmental change and competition exert selective pressure. New genetic combinations produce adaptation and the individual and/or genes who best "fits" the environmental niche will survive (survival of the fittest).

Examples of the evolutionary approach

Part 5, Comparative Psychology, focuses on evolutionary explanations. In Section 13, Determinants of Animal Behaviour, evolutionary explanations of animal behaviour are discussed at length, and social learning explanations are also related to adaptive behaviour. Section 14, Animal Cognition, also uses evolutionary explanations to discuss animal navigation, communication, and language. Section 15, Evolutionary Explanations of Human Behaviour, focuses on how evolutionary explanations can be used to understand human reproductive behaviour, the existence of mental disorders, and the evolution of intelligence.

In your AS studies, Bowlby's theory of attachment was an example of the evolutionary approach to explaining behaviour. The adaptive nature of stress was also considered.

In this book, in Section 2, Relationships, sociobiology is used as an explanation for the formation of relationships. It is also important in understanding pro- and anti-social behaviour (Section 3, Pro- and Anti-social Behaviour) and in moral development (Section 10, Cognitive Development) and gender development (Section 11, Social and Personality Development). In Section 5, Biological Rhythms, an evolutionary theory of sleep is discussed.

An Evaluation of the Evolutionary Approach

Strengths

There is no doubt that aspects of our behaviour are determined by genetic factors and the pressures of natural selection. There are useful and powerful applications of this approach, such as genetic engineering: genetically modified crops, selective breeding of farm animals, and genetic counselling for prospective parents. However, there are many ethical problems associated with genetic engineering.

Weaknesses

The theory of evolution offers mainly *ex post facto* (after the fact) evidence. It is hard to know whether a behaviour is actually beneficial, and that is why it remained in a gene pool, or whether it was simply neutral and was never selected against, and thus survived. The fact that studies are often natural experiments means we cannot truly claim to have identified cause and effect relationships.

Evolutionary explanations are highly deterministic. What would we do if we discovered that the tendency to behave aggressively was a necessary and inherited behaviour in certain individuals? Would we lock up such individuals, or would we prevent them reproducing? Recent attempts to justify rape in terms evolutionary theory have met with strenuous objections from men and women (see page 573). Thornhill et al. (2000) argue that this kind of understanding could help us deal better with the problem. However, one must remember that many other approaches in psychology are equally as deterministic as the evolutionary one (such as the biological or behavioural approaches). In fact science itself is highly deterministic, so we should not simply view determinism as a bad thing.

In terms of non-human animal behaviour, evolutionary explanations may be more appropriate because behaviour is less governed by experience (the behavioural approach), and less by conscious thought. In humans it is highly questionable to what extent our behaviour really is determined in this way. Nevertheless the evidence presented can be quite convincing.

One might also ask why we continue to behave in a manner that may have been adaptive in our evolutionary past but is no longer so today. This is a valid criticism and evolutionary psychologists refer to the **environment of evolutionary adaptation** (EEA)— the period in human evolution during which our genes were shaped and naturally selected to solve survival problems operating then. This was roughly between 35,000 and 3 million years ago. The stress response is an example of a behaviour that was adaptive at that time, but today's stressors are not dealt with by increased physiological arousal and "fight or flight". Why, then, do such behaviours persist? The explanation is "genome lag"; the genes that we possess may not be especially adaptive but they are also not especially maladaptive, and therefore they have not been eliminated from our behavioural repertoire by **natural selection**.

Social Constructionism

A Description of the Social Constructionist Approach

Social constructionism, like humanistic psychology, is another source of change in the attitudes of psychologists to research (theory and study). The essence of the approach is that the quest for an objective reality is misleading. It is a mistake to think that there is an objective reality. Bartlett (1932) said "all human life is effort after meaning". In other words it is the *significance* that we place on experience that is critical not the experience itself. We can see this if we consider any physical event, such as death. The experience of death varies from individual to individual, and from culture to culture. The physical reality is the same, but the way we experience it is related to what we bring to the event. And our "baggage" is given to us through culture and language.

It is also a mistake to think that we can collect unbiased data, because our perceptions are inevitably affected by our expectations, and these expectations are related to culture and language. Social constructionists propose that once you accept that purportedly objective data, like the kind of data collected in an experiment, are actually as subjective as the most subjective kind of research, then one can move forward and establish new methods for making qualitative analyses more rigorous.

Social representations

A core concept within the social constructionist approach is that of social representations. Moscovici (1981) first described social representations as shared beliefs within a social/cultural group that are used to explain social events. Such explanations evolve through, for example, everyday conversations and media reports, eventually becoming regarded as "facts".

It is important to note the dual way that social representations are social: they are the way that we represent *social* knowledge and they also emphasise how this knowledge is unconsciously shaped by *social* groups.

The concept of social representations can be applied to scientific knowledge as well as more everyday knowledge. Moscovici (1961) used the idea of social representations to explain how psychoanalysis moved from a scientific theory to a broader explanation of why society is like it is. The first, scientific phase is when scientists use the theory. Second, the ideas become more widely known, and finally, in the ideological phase, the concepts are applied to society in general. Social representations and the influence of split-brain research is considered on page 156.

Conducting qualitative research

Many psychologists refute social constructionism on the basis of its subjective approach to research. However it is possible to make the methods more rigorous. The favoured approach of social constructionists is discourse analysis, where written or spoken conversations (discourses) are analysed. The focus is on the language used. It is argued that such discourses can reveal a great deal about the behaviour, feelings, thoughts, and attitudes of the individuals engaged in the discourse. And thus the discourse can inform us about the culture in which it takes place, because it reveals social attitudes and beliefs (social representations) of the participants. And the discourse also reveals the facts.

The technique itself involves collecting data, coding them (putting them into manageable chunks), and then analysing them. This process of analysis gains objectivity through being repeated (replication). There are no regular procedures advocated for such analyses because, if there were, one might fall back into the trap of closed rather than open-ended research, and preclude uncovering the unexpected.

Although it is not desirable or possible to replicate the findings of such studies, it is possible to use the findings of other studies as a means of confirming the results. This process is called **triangulation**, a term taken from mathematics that describes how a point can be accurately located by taking sightings from at least two different positions (a "trig point" is a triangulation point used for constructing maps). There are three types of triangulation:

1. *Between-methods*, as just described, where the results from several different studies, each using different methods, are compared.
2. *Within-method triangulation*, where one qualitative study uses several different methods during the course of the investigation.
3. *Investigator triangulation*, where two different qualitative researchers can conduct independent analyses of the same qualitative data, and then compare their findings, a kind of "inter-investigator" reliability.

An example of a discourse analysis

Burns (1998) used discourse analysis to unpack some of the implications of the lyrics to Aqua's song *Barbie Girl*, which reached Number 1 in the UK charts in November 1997. Verses 2, 3, and 4 are shown below.

[Barbie]

I'm a blonde bimbo girl
In a fantasy world
Dress me up
Make it tight
I'm your doll.

[Ken]

You're my doll
Rock n'roll
Feel the glamour and pain
Kiss me there
Touch me there
Hanky panky

[Barbie]

You can touch
You can play
If you say
I'm always yours

You may think, at first glance, that these lyrics are little more than light-hearted fun. Burns, however, suggested that the words actually express some important attitudes about male–female relationships. First, here is a discourse in which love, sex, and ownership are tied together. Barbie is constructed as a self-confessed blonde bimbo who describes herself as "your dolly", thus reducing herself to something less than a person and as the property of Ken. She offers herself as a sexual plaything (you can touch, you can play), on the condition that Ken gives a lasting commitment to her (if you say I'm always yours). Ken on the other hand is constructed as relatively unemotional. He makes no declarations of love, but instead demands sexual services (kiss me there, touch me there). Here is a representation of relationships in which women want love and men want sex, in which men swap love for sex and women give sex in exchange for love.

You can see that a very unhealthily stereotypical and sad account of human relationships is being played out here. You might say "so what, it's just a song?" However, to a social constructionist people construct their perceptions of relationships from the discourse concerning relationships that they hear. This means that songs like *Barbie Girl* may perpetuate unhealthy stereotypes of what men and women want from relationships.

Using this as an example of discourse analysis you can see some of the difficulties with the technique. It is highly subjective, i.e., different psychologists might analyse the same lyrics and come up with different interpretations. Furthermore, we don't know just from analysing the lyrics what the song-writer intended people to get from the song, or how it was perceived by fans. Was it in fact intended to be taken literally, or was the writer being sarcastic about stereotypical views on relationships?

Despite these difficulties, discourse analysis can be immensely helpful in understanding how unhealthy and undesirable perceptions of the world are maintained by our use of language.

Adapted from M. Jarvis et al. (2000) *Angles on psychology*.
Cheltenham, UK: Stanley Thornes.

Examples of the social constructionist approach

Within this book there has been very little reference to this approach in psychology, partly because of the nature of the topics studied and partly because it is a relatively new approach in psychology and therefore explanations in many areas of traditional research are not yet developed. Social representations are discussed in Section 1, Social Cognition, and social constructionist explanations for aggression are presented in Section 3, Pro- and Anti-social Behaviour. Multiple personality disorder (Section 16, Issues in Classification and Diagnosis of Psychological Abnormality) is considered as a possible social construction.

In Section 19, Issues, there is a discussion of social constructionism in relation to the issue of gender bias, and in Section 20, Debates, social constructionism is considered as an alternative view to psychology as a science (see page 744).

An Evaluation of the Social Constructionist Approach

Strengths

The social constructionist approach has certainly challenged psychologists to take a closer look at their notions of subjectivity and objectivity. It has also offered psychology new investigative techniques and new ways of looking at human behaviour, ways that emphasise the role of social influences in creating our world and also that emphasise the importance of experience. Discourses tell us what individuals are experiencing rather than allowing someone else to infer our feelings from observing our behaviour.

Weaknesses

It is difficult to criticise the approach properly as it has not really had time to establish itself. Clearly the main criticism comes from those psychologists who fundamentally disagree with the nature of discourse analysis as a means for discovering truths about human behaviour. They would argue that even flawed methodology has provided us with useful information about human behaviour. One can certainly point to a vast array of research stretching from studies of day-care and obedience, to sleep and emotion, and mental disorder, all based on traditional research approaches in psychology. It remains to be seen whether discourse analysis can become equally useful.

It may be that the place for social constructionism is ultimately as a means of questioning our knowledge but not generating it. "Social constructionists would make a good opposition but a poor government" (Humphreys, 2000).

SECTION SUMMARY

The Biological Approach

❖ The key assumptions of this approach is that all behaviour can be explained in terms of the functioning of biological systems.

❖ Physiological psychology explains behaviour in terms of bodily activity, making reference to brain activity (e.g., some theories of dreaming), neurotransmitters (e.g., explaining depression), and hormones (e.g., stress). The nativist approach offers explanations in terms of genes and heredity. The medical model of mental illness assumes that all psychological illnesses can be explained in terms of physical causes and that diseases can be diagnosed from symptoms, and suitable treatments prescribed.

❖ The strengths of the approach include its objective, reductionist nature, which facilitates experimental research, and a host of practical applications such as drug therapy for mental illness. The determinist, reductionist, and mechanistic nature of biological explanations can also be seen as a weakness because they oversimplify complex behaviours and de-emphasise personal responsibility. The biological approach overlooks the experiential aspect of behaviour and ignores past experience. Biological explanations are more appropriate for some kinds of behaviour.

The Behavioural Approach

❖ The assumptions of the behavioural approach include the belief that all behaviour is learned and can be explained in terms of conditioning theory, that the focus of explanation should be on observable behaviour, and that humans differ quantitatively but not qualitatively from non-human animals. We should recognise the varieties of behaviourism: methodological and radical behaviourism, and neo-behaviourism (social learning theory).

❖ The strengths of the approach lie in the ability to use it with respect to most behaviours. Learning theory and social learning theory underpin many explanations in psychology including attachment, aggression, language acquisition, and gender development. However, such explanations may be more applicable to non-human animals where cognitive activity has less influence, though genetic influences may be even stronger. A second strength is the successful applications derived from this approach, such as behaviour therapy and programmed learning. The approach also lends itself to scientific research.

❖ Its weaknesses include the fact that it is a mechanistic approach which ignores consciousness, subjective experience, and emotions. It is deterministic and reductionist, and ignores the role of cognitive and innate factors. In many ways, the behaviourists put forward a theory of performance rather than of learning. The theory is an oversimplification of behaviour and, in terms of its use for social control, an ethically questionable one.

The Psychodynamic Approach

❖ A psychodynamic approach is one that explains the dynamics of behaviour. Freud's psychoanalytic theory identified the forces that motivate personality development and adult behaviour. Early experience interacts with innate drives, and this leads us to behave in predictable ways later in life. Unconscious forces motivate much of our behaviour, due to ego defences that aim to protect the ego from feelings of anxiety. Personality dynamics are related to personality structures (id, ego, and superego) and stages of development (oral, anal, phallic, latency, and genital). Neo-Freudians placed more emphasis on social and cultural, rather than biological, factors.

❖ The value of Freud's contribution can be seen in its durability and the way that many of the concepts have come into everyday use. Within psychology he changed our views on childhood and the unconscious. His theory manages to combine both the rational and irrational elements of behaviour. The use of case studies as a means of research has advantages and limitations. Freud's emphasis on sex may be understandable in terms of the period of history in which he lived. Neo-Freudians have emphasised more social influences.

❖ However, his approach was basically unscientific. His theory of normal development is based largely on case histories of neurotic women. The theory lacks falsifiability and much of his evidence is correlational and cannot demonstrate causes. Most of his testable ideas have been disproved. The theory is also deterministic and reductionist, which may oversimplify behaviour, and lays too much emphasis on innate, biological forces rather than free will.

The Cognitive Approach

❖ The cognitive approach focuses on internal, mental activity as a means of explaining behaviour. The approach assumes that behaviour can be explained and understood using information-processing analogies, and that experimental research is desirable. Wundt's early work used introspection as a means of objectively studying mental processes. This approach to research was rejected by the behaviourists as too subjective, but the advent of computers offered cognitive psychology a new vocabulary and set of concepts. Cognitive explanations are not all based in information processing but share a focus on mental activity.

❖ The word (and concept) "schema" is by now used throughout psychology. It is so pervasive because it is multi-dimensional, embodies the influence of expectations and social constructions, and expresses our tendency for cognitive economy.

❖ The cognitive approach reintroduced mental states into psychological explanations, although other internal states (e.g., emotion) continued to be excluded. Recent developments are addressing this issue. The cognitive approach has a large number of useful applications and has been used in many psychological theories, but it is largely mechanistic, reductionist, and deterministic. The reliance on data from laboratory experiments means that some research lacks ecological validity.

The Humanistic Approach

❖ Humanistic psychology has been called the third force in psychology in its emphasis on free will, the uniqueness of the individual, the individual's striving towards personal growth, and the inappropriateness of objective research. The humanistic approach has its roots in humanism, phenomenology, and existentialism. It emphasises personal responsibility rather than external control, and the importance of experience in understanding behaviour. Humanistic psychologists seek to investigate issues of human rather than statistical significance and therefore reject highly controlled, experimental techniques in favour of qualitative methods such as discourse analysis.

❖ Rogers and Maslow exemplify the humanistic approach in psychology. Rogers developed client-centred therapy, in which the therapist is unconditional in positive regard, genuine, and empathic. The Q-sort method is one way of assessing the self-concept. Maslow's approach to explaining motivation included self-actualisation. Humanistic psychology is a comprehensive approach which has influenced psychology in general, suggesting that there is more to understanding behaviour than scientifically observable facts. There have been successful applications in terms of counselling as a means of treating certain psychological problems.

❖ However, humanistic psychology suffers from focusing too much on conscious awareness, and being unscientific, which may prevent the advance of knowledge. Humanistic theories lack falsifiability. Free will and self-actualisation may not be a reality for many people, and may actually be a burden.

The Evolutionary Approach

❖ Darwin's theory of evolution is an explanation for the process of change in living things. The principles of this theory are: environmental change requires new adaptation; living things are constantly changing and thus there is the possibility of new characteristics that may be more adaptive; competition means that those best adapted are more likely to survive and reproduce. It is the genes for adaptive characteristics that are selected, and this selection takes place naturally. Altruistic behaviour is an example of selection at the level of the genes. This latter explanation is a sociobiological one.
❖ Sociobiologists extended evolutionary theory to include the concepts of kin selection and inclusive fitness. The two main assumptions of the evolutionary approach are that most behaviours serve some adaptive function and that these behaviours are retained through natural selection (selective pressure).
❖ Many aspects of animal behaviour can be explained by the evolutionary approach. There are useful and powerful applications. However, the evidence is largely *ex post facto* and cannot truly demonstrate cause and effect. Evolutionary explanations are highly deterministic, and may be less appropriate for human behaviour.

Social Constructionism

❖ Social constructionism offers an alternative to the objective scientific approach in psychology, suggesting that such beliefs are mistaken as there are no objective realities. There is only socially determined knowledge and the investigation of this can be made as objective as the purportedly objective sciences. Social representations are one way to study the social construction of knowledge. Discourse analysis can be made more rigorous through the use, for example, of triangulation.
❖ The strengths of the social constructionist approach are that it re-evaluates our concepts of objectivity and subjectivity, and aims to uncover what individuals are experiencing rather than simply inferring attitudes from external observation. At present it is difficult to evaluate this rather new approach in psychology. It has to compete with a long history of success and failure from other approaches.

F U R T H E R   R E A D I N G

The topics in this Section are covered in greater depth by M. Jarvis (2000) *Theoretical approaches in psychology* (London: Routledge), written specifically for the AQA A specification. Two useful general textbooks on approaches in psychology are W.E. Glassman (1998) *Approaches to psychology (2nd Edn.)* (Buckingham, UK: Open University Press), and C. Tavris and C. Wade (1997) *Psychology in perspective* (New York: Longman). For detailed material on particular approaches you might consult B.F. Skinner (1974) *About behaviourism* (London: Jonathan Cape), which offers some defence against his critics. A. Lemma-Wright (1995) *Invitation to psychodynamic psychology* (London: Whurr) presents a balanced account of psychodynamic ideas for the general reader, and V. Burr (1995) *An introduction to social constructionism* (London: Routledge) offers commentary on this relatively new area in psychology.

Example Examination Questions

The "approaches" question is different from all the others in the examination. You have about 40 minutes to answer this question and it is worth a total of 30 marks, divided into 5 units of 6 marks. This gives you the guidance of spending about 6–7 minutes on each Unit (6 minutes for each of the two approaches and 6 minutes for each other part of the question).

This question will be assessed on "synopticity" which is defined as your "understanding and critical appreciation of the breadth and range of different theoretical perspectives and/or methodological approaches relevant to any question" (AQA specification).

In your answer you must be sure that you engage with the stimulus material and do not merely describe and assess an approach and a method of investigation.

1. **A farmer's life for me**

"Joe grew up in a town but spent his summers staying with his grandfather on the farm. The summers were always the best times and he felt more at home there, helping his beloved grandfather look after the livestock and the crops. When he was asked about what he wanted to be when he grew up, he said 'a farmer'. This pleased the old man enormously, though he didn't really believe it. When Joe was old enough he moved out to the farm and eventually took it over."

How might a psychologist explain Joe's desire to become a farmer?

(a) Describe how **two** approaches might try to explain Joe's desire to become a farmer.   (6 marks + 6 marks)
(b) Assess **one** of these explanations of Joe's desire to become a farmer in terms of its strengths and limitations.   (6 marks)
(c) Analyse how **one** of these approaches might investigate Joe's desire to become a farmer.   (6 marks)
(d) Evaluate the use of this method of investigating Joe's desire to become a farmer.   (6 marks)

Total for this question: 30 marks

2. **A rock climber**

"Sylvia climbs mountains for a hobby. She doesn't walk up them but ropes herself up to ascend sheer faces of rock. It's a hobby that requires skill, patience and no fear of heights. If you are not a rock climber it is hard to imagine what drives some people to do it."

(a) Describe how **two** approaches might try to explain rock climbing.   (6 marks + 6 marks)
(b) Assess **one** of these explanations of rock climbing in terms of its strengths and limitations.   (6 marks)
(c) Analyse how **one** of these approaches might investigate the desire for rock climbing.   (6 marks)
(d) Evaluate the use of this method of investigating the desire for rock climbing.   (6 marks)

Total for this question: 30 marks

Examination Tips

The question on approaches in psychology is different from all the others set at A2 level. The question will always comprise a piece of stimulus material followed by the same set of four questions. The intention is to assess a candidate's understanding of the synoptic elements of the specification: the approaches and perspectives, the means by which psychologists evaluate their explanations, and the methodologies they use.

Knowledge enables you to solve problems. In mathematics you learn various strategies for solving mathematical problems. What is a "psychological problem"? It is one where you are asked to offer an explanation for a particular behaviour. Having offered an explanation, it is important to determine the value (both positive and negative) of that explanation. This is just what you are asked to do in the approaches question.

If you were asked to describe the behavioural approach, for example, you could list all sorts of facts that you have memorised. However, by asking you to use the approach to explain a novel behaviour, your real understanding is being assessed. Therefore it is important in this question that you actually engage with the stimulus material and use your knowledge, rather than just describing the behavioural approach and/or outlining theories that you have learned about. You will not receive credit for someone else's theory or study. It is a taxing question but ultimately the question in the study of psychology— given any behaviour, what explanations can we offer as psychologists?

WEB SITES

http://psychclassics.yorku.ca/
Large collection of articles and links on some of the most influential movements and theories throughout the history of psychology.

http://psychology.wadsworth.com/study_center/student/common/resources/links/links04.html
Biological psychology links.

http://psychology.about.com/science/psychology/msubindex_beh.htm
Behavioural psychology links.

http://ahpweb.org/
Association for Humanistic Psychology homepage.

http://cogweb.english.ucsb.edu/EP/
Evolutionary psychology information and links.

http://evolution.humb.univie.ac.at/jump.html
International Society for Human Ethology links page.

http://www.hud.ac.uk/hip/soccon/soccon.html
Social constructionism links.

www.a-levelpsychology.co.uk/websites.html
A continually updated list of useful links, including those printed in this book, may be found at the Psychology Press A level psychology site.

PART 8

Coursework

The AQA A2 examination is divided into three units. The last unit of the exam, Unit 6, is Coursework. You need to present one piece of coursework on a topic related to your examination studies. This Part of the book covers information that will help you in your coursework.

- Where does one start with the coursework report?
- What is the project brief and what does it look like?
- What is a psychological journal?
- What is "psychological literature"?
- How do other students present their introduction?
- How do I present the references?
- What items might I have forgotten to include in my report?
- How is the coursework marked?

22

The Coursework Report

Preparation: Design and Project Brief

Before beginning your study, you must fill in a project brief (see form on the next page). The mark from this project brief forms part of your final A level mark. The aim of the project brief is to enable your teacher to check that your work is realistically planned and does not breach ethical guidelines. You may draw up a rough version of the project brief first and ask your teacher to comment on it so that you can improve it and maximise your final marks.

It may also be an idea, before starting the study, to consider the contents of the final report. You might write parts of the report beforehand as they may affect some of your design decisions. For example, the literature review may give you additional ideas for design considerations and the choice of statistical test may also influence your choice of method. The details of the report are considered next. Statistical matters are covered in Section 23, Statistical Tests.

The Report

Once you have conducted your study, the final stage of the coursework is to write the report. The mark scheme for this report is outlined on page 795. It is the report that gets the marks, so it is especially important to do this carefully. You are again permitted to hand in a rough draft to your teacher and you should take his or her feedback into account when preparing the final draft. You do not have to use a word processor but it makes it much easier when preparing several drafts. It also assists in creating a good overall impression (and should improve your spelling).

The total length for the report should be approximately 2000 words, excluding tables, figures, graphs, and appendices. Reports that are too long will be penalised in sections C1 and H of the mark scheme. This maximum report length is partly for your own benefit (otherwise you might feel that you have to write a great deal to obtain high marks) and also because selectivity is an important skill to practise.

Psychological research

Psychologists publish their research in magazines that are called "journals". The intention of these journal reports is to inform other psychologists of new findings and to give an analysis of what these new findings mean. The journal reports must also provide sufficient detail of the research study so that other psychologists could, if they wanted to, replicate the study to confirm the validity of the findings. The report that you are going to write follows the format generally used in journal articles, also called "papers".

Your report should be divided into the sections outlined next. You can include a table of contents. The title should be long enough to give the reader a clear idea about the topic

<table>
<tr><td>

PSYCHOLOGY PROJECT BRIEF PROPOSAL FORM

| Candidate Name: | Centre Name | Centre Number |

Title of Work:

12 marks in total

PB1: Identify the aim of the research and state the experimental/alternative and null hypotheses.
(mark awarded in coursework)

PB2: Explain why a directional or a non-directional experimental/alternative hypothesis has been selected.
(1 mark)

PB3: Identify the chosen research method [laboratory experiment, field experiment, natural experiment, survey, observation or correlational research] and [if appropriate] the design chosen.
(1 mark)

PB4: Evaluate the advantages and disadvantages of the chosen research method.   *(2 marks)*

PB5: Identify potential sources of bias in the investigation and any possible confounding variables.
(2 marks)

Project Brief Form Continues Overleaf

</td><td>

PB6: Explain what procedures will be adopted to deal with these.   *(2 marks)*

PB7: Select an appropriate level of statistical significance to be reached before the experiment/alternative hypothesis will be retained.
(1 mark)

PB8: Identify any relevant ethical considerations and explain the steps to be taken to deal with these.
(3 marks)

Total Mark =

Candidates are reminded that in order to fulfil the requirements of the specification they must collect, pool, and analyse their data individually or in groups of 4 or fewer.

</td></tr>
</table>

The above Project Brief Proposal Form is a provisional document that may be changed before January 2002.

under study. "Gender and behaviour" may be rather too vague, whereas "A study to investigate gender differences in the ways that boys and girls behave on the playground, including pro- and anti-social behaviours" is too lengthy. A suitable title might be "Gender and playground behaviour in primary age children".

Abstract

Invariably a journal article begins with a summary of the main points of the research study. This enables a reader to tell, at a glance, whether the article will be of interest to them. Your abstract should be about 150 words in length (if it is too long you may be penalised on criterion B). You should write this summary in full sentences but stick firmly to the key points. This should begin with the study aims, which might include the hypothesis. Next might be a brief description of the method used in the study, to include the participants and setting, plus the kind of design that was used (e.g., experiment or observation, repeated or independent measures, and so on). If you used named psychological tests or questionnaires, these should be mentioned. The third area to report is the findings. You may describe the findings and/or outline the statistical treatment(s) used, and their significance. Finally record your conclusion, plus any limitations or implications identified.

An example of an abstract is given here:

Craik and Lockhart's level of processing theory predicts that the more deeply a word is processed, the more likely it is to be remembered. This study set out to test this prediction by giving participants material that required different levels of processing: shallow (processing words in terms of case), phonetic (processing words in terms of rhyming), and semantic (processing words in terms of meaning). The study was experimental and a repeated measures design. Twenty female participants completed the questionnaire in silence during a school lesson. Comparisons between semantic and shallow processing were analysed using the Wilcoxon test and found to be significant at the $p < 0.05$ level. This suggests that memory is enhanced by deeper processing, as predicted by levels of processing theory. The theory has useful applications to student revision.   **[130 words]**

Introduction, aims, and hypothesis

The purpose of this part of the report is to identify the background to your study. The introduction should be about 600 words. Your intention should be to describe background research in such a way that it leads seamlessly into the aims of your study!

The background information is often described as the "psychological *literature*". This refers to the fact that research is published in books and journals. Ideally your introduction should start at a relatively broad level and quickly narrow down to examine two or three particularly relevant pieces of research. Once these studies are described it should seem obvious what the aims of your study are going to be. If you have described research into levels of processing theory it would seem strange to then state that you intend to investigate short-term memory. This is not a logical progression. Equally, if you describe a study and also identify the limitations in the research methodology of that study, it doesn't make sense to say you are intending to follow the same procedures. It would, however, make sense to say that you are going to attempt to conduct a similar study having made certain adjustments in the light of the criticisms mentioned.

An example of an introduction is given here:

Memory is one of the earliest areas to be studied in psychology, starting with Ebbinghaus' (1985/1913) study of forgetting. Other early research focused on the capacity and duration of different memory stores: sensory memory (which is equivalent to the eyes and ears), short-term memory and long-term memory. Information comes to the sensory memory store through the senses and may either be forgotten or transferred to the STM. From there the memory may be forgotten, either because the memory trace disappears or because the material is displaced by newer material. Verbal rehearsal leads a memory to be transferred to long-term memory. This is called the multi-store model of memory as described by Atkinson and Shiffrin (1968).

Craik and Watkins (1973) found that when participants were asked to remember words from a list they could do this without verbal rehearsal. Instead if they elaborated the words this also led to enhanced recall. This led to levels of processing theory. Craik and Lockhart (1972) suggested that it is the kind of processes that are operating at the time of storing data that determine the extent to which something is remembered. They suggested that it is the depth of processing in terms of elaboration that creates a durable memory.

This theory was tested in an experiment by Craik and Tulving (1975). Participants were shown a list of words (five-letter concrete nouns such as "table"). and were asked a question for each word. For each question the answer was "yes" or "no". The questions were one of three types: case (shallow processing), such as "Is the word in capital letters?"; rhyme (phonemic processing), such as "Does the word rhyme with 'able'?"; or sentence (semantic or deep processing), such as "Would the word fit in the sentence 'They met a —— in the street'?" Craik and Tulving found that those words that had been processed semantically were recalled best and those processed phonemically were recalled second best.

Other research has further investigated how depth of processing can be achieved. For example organisation is a form of elaborative processing. Mandler (1967) showed that organisation alone led to durable memory. Participants were asked to sort 52 word cards into categories. When they had done this repeatedly they were given an unexpected test of memory and they were quite able to recall the words. The more categories they had used, the better their recall. This shows that deeper processing leads to long-term memory.

Another study showed that distinctiveness can also enhance memory. Eysenck and Eysenck (1980) arranged for participants to say words in a non-semantic, distinctive condition (e.g., pronouncing the "b" in "comb") or a non-semantic, non-distinctive condition (e.g., saying the word "comb" normally). There were also semantic distinctive and non-distinctive conditions where the words were also processed for meaning. Recall was almost as good in the non-semantic, distinctive condition as for the semantic conditions. This shows that distinctiveness can be as powerful as meaning in terms of enhancing memory for words.

continued overleaf

> The *aim of this study* is to replicate the original work by Craik and Tulving as a means of demonstrating the levels of processing theory. The same design will be followed as in the original study where all participants are given three conditions: case, phonemic, and semantic in order to see which condition leads to best recall. The original experiment involved an expected and unexpected test of recall as well, but these will not be included here.
>
> In line with the levels of processing theory, we would expect recall to be highest on the semantic condition and lowest on the case condition. Given the fact that previous research has found that the semantic condition is associated with higher memory, a directional hypothesis would be appropriate.
>
> **The hypothesis**
> * Experimental hypothesis 1: Participants recall more words in the semantic condition than in the case condition.
> * Null hypothesis: There is no difference in recall between semantic and case conditions.
> * Experimental hypothesis 2: Participants recall more words in the semantic condition than in the phonemic condition.
> * Null hypothesis: There is no difference in recall between semantic and phonemic conditions.
>
> **[660 words]**

One point that arises in this example is the issue of references. At the end of the report you are required to provide the full references for any studies cited in the report. The citation style given here is used throughout this textbook, i.e., name (date). It is, however, acceptable to use the following referencing system: name (as cited in Eysenck & Flanagan, 2001). If you use the latter style then, in the reference section, you need only list the full reference for Eysenck and Flanagan plus a list of all articles that you have referred to from this book. (See also page 792.)

A second point regards copying. It is tempting to use passages from a textbook or journal article when reporting the psychological literature. You may feel that the writer of the textbook manages to convey exactly what you want to say, and says it more clearly than you could express it. If you feel you cannot put it into your own words, present the material as a quotation from the textbook. Never copy chunks of material without due credit.

The aims must lead logically from the literature review and act like a buckle in joining the introduction to the hypothesis. The statement of the hypothesis must be clear, unambiguous, and operationalised. (See *Psychology for AS Level* for a discussion of hypotheses.)

Method

Here you are aiming to provide the reader with sufficient detail to replicate your study. This section should cover about 600 words and is typically subdivided into the following sections:

Design
Describe design decisions, such as your choice of method (e.g., experiment or observation, etc.). If it is an experiment then state whether it is a repeated or independent measures design, and the key variables. If it is an observation, you should carefully describe details of your observational techniques. If it is a correlational study, state the covariables.

Participants
State how many people were involved, plus any relevant demographic details such as age, educational background, and gender. Describe where the participants were tested or observed, and how the particular sample was selected (sampling techniques were described in *Psychology for AS Level*). Finally, where appropriate, you should explain how participants were allocated to conditions.

Apparatus/materials
Full details of any questionnaires or other materials should be placed in the appendix section of the report. You should name the measures that you used and say "See Appendix

I". If you include a questionnaire, make sure you also include the means of scoring the questionnaire.

If you designed the stimulus material yourself, then you should explain how you did this. For example "we selected a list of 20 four-letter words to use as the words to be remembered. We avoided any unusual or distinctive words. The order of the word list was determined randomly."

Standardised procedures

You may place standardised instructions in the appendix, but in the main body of the report describe clearly and succinctly what you did.

Controls and ethics

You might mention any important controls or ethical decisions that were taken, although some of these have already been included in the project brief.

Results

There are three ways to illustrate your results:

1. *Raw data* are the numbers prior to any analysis. These should be placed in the appendices but a summary might be included in the results section.
2. *Descriptive statistics*, such as the use of measures of central tendency (mean, median, and mode) and/or spread (range or standard deviation), plus graphical representation. Descriptive statistics are vital for getting a feel for the data but don't overdo this. Select suitable methods of displaying your data so that one can see, at a glance, what was found in the study. Ensure that all descriptive statistics are labelled carefully.
3. *Statistical tests*. These enable you to determine whether your findings are significant. You must (a) state what test you are going to use, (b) justify your choice of statistical test, (c) record some details of the test calculations in the appendix, and (d) state the outcome of the statistical test and thus your conclusion regarding the significance of your results. We look at statistical tests and significance in Section 23.

The AQA A mark scheme (E1) requires the use of appropriate methods. This includes both descriptive and/or statistical tests as appropriate. If statistical tests are not appropriate then you must justify your decision not to use them. The mark scheme (E2) rewards clarity of presentation.

Discussion

The intention of the discussion section is to interpret the findings in terms of previous research, as mentioned in the introduction or with reference to other research. In addition, this is where the researcher reflects on the strengths and limitations of the study. The discussion section is worth 25% of the overall marks, so spend time getting this right. About 600 words is the right length for this part of the report.

The AQA A mark scheme (F) highlights four areas to include in your discussion. It seems a good idea to follow these clearly by using them as subheadings.

Explanation of findings

You are required to do more than state the significance of your results, which should have been done in the results section. The emphasis here is on an *explanation* of what you found. You might do this by relating your findings to your original aims. You might also note any findings that you did not anticipate.

Relationship to background research

Relate your findings to previous research. This is a reverse of the process at the start where the introduction led logically into the aims. Now you want to link your findings back to previous research. You might refer to studies mentioned in the beginning, although you will get little credit if you simply repeat the same material a second time. You may also wish to mention other research, in the light of your findings. You can refer to theory and/or other research studies.

Limitations and modifications

Select two or three important limitations and state how you might modify the problems. The limitations might refer to sampling procedures, design, lack of controls, procedures, and/or statistical treatments. Ensure that you do more than just state the problem by also explaining in what way it was a problem in this study.

Implications and suggestions

Could your findings be put to any practical use? Are there are theoretical implications not mentioned earlier? One or two ideas will be sufficient, including suggestions for future research.

References

The reason for full references is to provide the reader with the details of the original article or book if they wish to research the study/theory further themselves. Any named studies or theories in your report must be listed with full details in the reference section of your report. You can follow the same style as used in the reference section of this textbook.

There is an alternative style that is acceptable. This is to state the details of a textbook, and list all the studies you have cited from this book. This means that anyone who would like to follow up one of your references is still able to locate the exact reference and the article.

What references did I use?

It saves a great deal of time if you keep a note of all the relevant details of all the literature you refer to, cite, or quote from. The information needed includes names and initials of authors and/or editors, title of article and journal (or chapter and book), page numbers, volume and issue (or edition) numbers, and date of publication. If you used a book, then you need to note the authors, date of publication, title, place of publication and name of publisher.

Page numbers of quotations are also useful. Try setting up a card-index file, or start a database on your computer, and build it up as you go along.

Appendices

You may include details of materials and/or questionnaires, standardised instructions, raw data, and statistical tests in the appendices. The material in the appendix is not included in the word length for the report.

SECTION SUMMARY

❖   You must conduct one research study, either on your own or in a small group (four or fewer). For the study you must individually present a project brief and write a report of not more than 2000 words (not including appendices). This report follows the format used in journal articles. It should contain the following sections:
  • *Abstract*, about 150 words including the basic details of the study: aims, methods, results, and conclusions.
  • The *introduction* should be about 600 words, and cover background theory and relevant research, leading logically into the study's aims. This should not be a general essay but must be relevant and selective.
  • In the *aims* you should explain your area of investigation and justify the direction of the hypothesis. *Hypotheses* should be stated unambiguously (operationalised) and in a way that permits them to be tested. Include both the alternative and null hypotheses.
  • The *method* section should again be about 600 words. The main intention is to provide sufficient detail to permit full replication of your study. You should cover design, participants, materials/apparatus, procedures, controls, and ethical considerations. (Stimulus materials, observation checklists, questionnaires, and standardised instructions should be placed in the appendices.)

- The *results* section should include a summary of the raw data, descriptive statistics, and the interpretation of a statistical test. (Any raw data and calculations should be placed in the appendices.)
- A *discussion* of your study, in about 600 words, to include an explanation of the findings, relationship to background research, limitations and modifications, and implications and suggestions.
- The report should also include *references* and *appendices*.

F U R T H E R   R E A D I N G

An example report is included in the *Teacher's Guide* published by AQA.

A checklist for your report

Done	**Abstract**	Drafted	Done
☐	1. Have you stated what you are studying?		
	2. Have you mentioned the aim/hypothesis?	☐	☐
	3. Have you described the essentials of the method?	☐	☐
	4. Have you given some details about the participants and where the research was conducted?	☐	☐
	5. What did you discover? Give a statement of your results.	☐	☐
	6. Who cares (seriously!)? What is the importance of your research?	☐	☐

Done	**Introduction**	Drafted	Done
☐	1. Have you referred to some theory?	☐	☐
	2. Have you described one or two relevant studies but no more than five?	☐	☐
	3. Is the literature logically linked to the aims?	☐	☐

Done	**Aims and hypothesis**	Drafted	Done
☐	1. Why have you studied this topic? Have you stated your aims?	☐	☐
	2. Have you justified the direction of the hypothesis?	☐	☐
	3. Have you stated an unambiguous alternate hypothesis?	☐	☐
	4. Have you stated whether the hypothesis is directional or non-directional?	☐	☐
	5. Have you stated a null hypothesis?	☐	☐
	6. Have you given the desired level of significance?	☐	☐

Done	**Method**	Drafted	Done
☐	1. Have you stated the research design?	☐	☐
	2. Have you explained why each design decision was chosen?	☐	☐
	3. If you are conducting an experiment, have you stated the experimental and control conditions?	☐	☐
	4. If you are conducting an observation, have you described the method you used?	☐	☐
	5. Have you stated the IV and DV, or covariables (for a correlational study)?	☐	☐
	6. Have you explained any controls you used? And why?	☐	☐
	7. Have you mentioned ethical considerations?	☐	☐

continued overleaf

Done	**Method** *continued*	Drafted	Done
☐	8. Have you mentioned all researchers involved?	☐	☐
	9. Have you described the participants and the population from which they were drawn?	☐	☐
	10. Have you stated how the participants were selected and allocated to conditions?	☐	☐
	11. Have you described the design of all apparatus and materials that you used (in the appendix)?	☐	☐
	12. Have you included specimens of apparatus and materials that you used (in the appendix)?	☐	☐
	13. Have you included the "mark schemes" for any tests or questionnaires?	☐	☐
	14. Have you described your exact procedures?	☐	☐
	15. Have you described or included standardised instructions given to subjects?	☐	☐
	16. Have you given sufficient detail for someone else to replicate your study?	☐	☐

Done	**Results**	Drafted	Done
☐	1. Have you given a summary table of raw data (in the appendix)?	☐	☐
	2. Have you provided descriptive statistics for your data (e.g., mean, bar chart, or scattergram)?	☐	☐
	3. Have you labelled axes on graphs, columns on data tables, and given clear titles?	☐	☐
	4. Have you justified your choice (or lack of) statistical test?	☐	☐
	5. Have you included any calculations (in the appendix)?	☐	☐
	6. Does your statement of conclusion contain details of the level of significance, the critical and observed values, degrees of freedom, whether the hypothesis was directional or non-directional, and whether it was accepted or rejected?	☐	☐
	7. Have you stated the conclusion in terms of the original hypothesis?	☐	☐

Done	**Discussion**	Drafted	Done
☐	1. Have you explained your results?	☐	☐
	2. Have you stated what your results mean in relation to your hypothesis?	☐	☐
	3. Do you refer back to your introduction?	☐	☐
	4. Have you compared your results with those of other studies?	☐	☐
	5. What was wrong (or right) about your design and methods?	☐	☐
	6. Are any of the criticisms presented without a good explanation?	☐	☐
	7. How would you improve the study if you were to do it again?	☐	☐
	8. Have you included any ideas for follow-up studies?	☐	☐

Done	**References**	Drafted	Done
☐	1. Have you included all references mentioned?	☐	☐
	2. Have you followed the correct form for presenting references?	☐	☐

Done	**Appendices**	Drafted	Done
☐	1. Are these clearly labelled and well set out?	☐	☐

Done	**Report style**	Drafted	Done
☐	1. Have you checked your spelling?	☐	☐
	2. Is your project in a folder that can be easily opened?	☐	☐
	3. Is your project shorter than 2000 words? If not, then cut it.	☐	☐

Summary of the coursework mark scheme

A1 Implementation: Candidate's contribution

3   By an individual. Original design/adaptation
2   By a small group
1   With teacher support
0   No student input

A2 Implementation: Design decisions

3   Appropriate and competent
2   Appropriate, minor exceptions
1   Weakly applied
0   Inappropriate

B   Abstract

3   Covers aims/methods/results/conclusions
2   Fair, lacking clarity or conciseness
1   Poor
0   None or inappropriate

C1 Psychological literature

5   Relevant, carefully selected
4   Relevant, carefully selected but some omissions
3   Lacking selectivity
2   Important omissions
1   Minimal support
0   No support

C2 Aims/hypothesis: Formulation

3   Clear, logical progression
2   Some logical progression
1   Partial/inadequate progression
0   No logical progression

C3 Aims/hypothesis: Statement

2   Easily testable, quite specific
1   Lacking clarity or difficult to test
0   Incorrect/missing

D   Reporting of method

4   Full replicatiion
3   Reasonable, sufficient detail for replication
2   Difficult, lacking detail
1   Very difficult, fundamental omissions
0   Replication extremely difficult, information lacking

E1 Results: Techniques

4   Appropriate, fully justified, significance given/explained
3   Substantially appropriate, justification doesn't refer to data
2   Partially appropriate/justified, significance given
1   Minimal use/justification, inappropriate significance
0   Inappropriate/absent

F2 Results: Presentation

4   Precise and clear
3   Precise and clear, with minor exceptions
2   Some deficiencies
1   Serious deficiencies
0   Irrelevant/incorrect

F1 Discussion: Explanation of findings

3   Appropriate, coherent
2   Appropriate, coherent with minor exceptions
1   Inappropriate/lacking coherence
0   None made/irrelevant

F2 Discussion: Background research/theory

3   Thorough discussion
2   Reasonably coherent
1   Limited
0   None/irrelevant/incorrect

F3 Discussion: Limitations and modifications

3   Most mentioned and appropriate
2   Some limitations and modifications
1   Occasional limitations/modifications
0   None/inappropriate

F4 Discussion: Implications and suggestions

3   Appropriate, discussed thoroughly
2   Some, discussed reasonably coherently
1   Occasional/limited
0   None/irrelevant

G   References

2   Full
1   Incomplete
0   None

H   Report style

3   Concisely written, logical, good quality of language
2   Scientific style and logical structure evident, adequate expression of ideas and language
1   Lacked logical structure and scientific basis, poor expression of ideas and language
0   Little psychological basis

Maximum total is 48 marks + 12 marks for the project brief = 60 marks

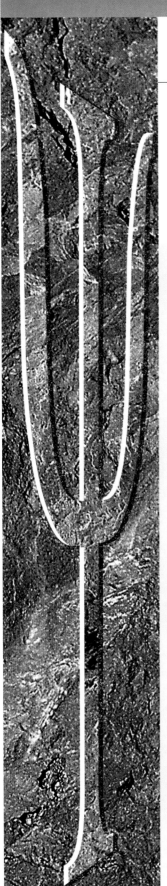

- What is the difference between descriptive statistics and statistical tests?

- How do I decide whether to use a one-tailed or two-tailed test?

- How do I know if my results are "significant"?

- When can you reject the null hypothesis?

- What level of significance is the most stringent?

- When do you use a test of difference?

- Which difference tests should be used?

- What test should I use if I am investigating an association or correlation between two sets of scores?

- How can I write a justification of this choice?

- What is the difference between the "observed value" and the "critical value"?

23

Statistical Tests

For your coursework you need to be able to know how to select and use statistical tests and interpret the results of these tests. There are just five tests you need to cover: Mann-Whitney, Wilcoxon, Sign, Chi-squared, and Spearman's tests. You will not be examined on this material in the AQA A examination.

Descriptive Statistics and Statistical Tests

Descriptive statistics give us convenient and easily understood summaries of what we have found. However, to have a clearer idea of what our findings mean, it is generally necessary to carry out one or more **statistical tests**.

Descriptive statistics are discussed in Psychology for AS Level *by the same authors.*

Test of difference, association, or correlation?

The first step in choosing an appropriate statistical test is to decide whether your data were obtained from an experiment in which some aspect of the situation (the independent variable) was manipulated in order to observe its effects on the dependent variable. If so, you need a **test of difference**. On the other hand, if you simply have two observations from each of your participants in a non-experimental design, then you need a **test of association** or **correlation**.

One-tailed or two-tailed test?

In using a statistical test, you need to take account of the experimental hypothesis. If you predicted the direction of any effects (e.g., loud noise will disrupt learning and memory), then you have a **directional hypothesis**, which should be evaluated by a one-tailed test. If you did not predict the direction of any effects (e.g., loud noise will affect learning and memory), then you have a **non-directional hypothesis**, which should be evaluated by a two-tailed test.

Level of precision

Another factor to consider when deciding which statistical test to use is the type of data you have obtained. There are four types of data, of increasing levels of precision:

- **Nominal**: the data consist of the numbers of participants falling into various categories (e.g., fat, thin; men, women).

> ■ Activity: Devising hypotheses
>
> Devise suitable null and experimental hypotheses for the following:
> - An investigator considers the effect of noise on students' ability to concentrate and complete a word-grid. One group only is subjected to the noise in the form of a distractor, i.e., a television programme.
> - An investigator explores the view that there might be a link between the amount of television children watch and their behaviour at school.

Nominal

Ordinal

Interval

Ratio

- **Ordinal**: the data can be ordered from lowest to highest (e.g., the finishing positions of athletes in a race).
- **Interval**: the data differ from ordinal data, because the units of measurement are fixed throughout the range; for example, there is the same "distance" between a height of 1.82 metres and 1.70 metres as between a height of 1.70 metres and one of 1.58 metres.
- **Ratio**: the data have the same characteristics as interval data, with the exception that they have a meaningful zero point; for example, time measurements provide ratio data because the notion of zero time is meaningful, and 10 seconds is twice as long as 5 seconds. The similarities between interval and ratio data are so great that they are sometimes combined and referred to as interval/ratio data.

Statistical Significance

So far we have discussed some of the issues that influence the choice of statistical test. Shortly we will consider how to conduct such tests, but first we should look at the meaning of **statistical significance**. What happens after we have chosen a statistical test, and analysed our data, and want to interpret our findings? We use the results of the test to choose between the following:

- Experimental hypothesis (e.g., loud noise disrupts learning).
- Null hypothesis, which asserts that there is no difference between conditions (e.g., loud noise has no effect on learning).

If the statistical test indicates that there is only a small probability of the difference between conditions (e.g., loud noise vs. no noise) having occurred *if the null hypothesis were true*, then we reject the null hypothesis in favour of the experimental hypothesis.

Why do we focus initially on the null hypothesis rather than the experimental hypothesis? The reason is that the experimental hypothesis is rather imprecise. It may state that loud noise will disrupt learning, but it does not indicate the *extent* of the disruption. This imprecision makes it hard to evaluate an experimental hypothesis directly. In contrast, a null hypothesis such as loud noise has no effect on learning *is* precise, and this precision allows us to use statistical tests to decide the probability that it is correct.

Psychologists generally use the 5% (0.05) level of statistical significance. What this means is that the null hypothesis is rejected (and the experimental hypothesis is accepted) if the probability that the results were due to chance alone is 5% or less. This is often expressed as $p = 0.05$, where p = the probability of the result if the null hypothesis is true. If the statistical test indicates that the findings do not reach the 5% (or $p = 0.05$) level of statistical significance, then we retain the null hypothesis, and reject the experimental hypothesis. The key decision is whether or not to reject the null hypothesis and that is why the 0.05 level of statistical significance is so important. However, our data sometimes indicate that the null hypothesis can be rejected with greater confidence, say, at the 1% (0.01) level. If the null hypothesis can be rejected at the 1% level, it is customary to state that the findings are highly significant. In general terms, you should state the precise level of statistical significance of your findings, whether it is the 5% level, the 1% level, or whatever.

These procedures may seem easy. In fact, there are two errors that may occur when reaching a conclusion on the basis of the results of a statistical test:

- **Type I error**: we may reject the null hypothesis in favour of the experimental hypothesis even though the findings are actually due to chance; the probability of this happening is given by the level of statistical significance that is selected.
- **Type II error**: we may retain the null hypothesis even though the experimental hypothesis is actually correct.

It would be possible to reduce the likelihood of a Type I error by using a more stringent level of significance. For example, if we used the 1% ($p = 0.01$) level of significance, this would greatly reduce the probability of a Type I error. However, use of a more stringent level of significance increases the probability of a Type II error. We could reduce the probability of a Type II error by using a less stringent level of significance, such as the 10% ($p = 0.10$) level. However, this would increase the probability of a Type I error. These considerations help to make it clear why most psychologists favour the 5% (or $p = 0.05$) level of significance: it allows the probabilities of both Type I and Type II errors to remain reasonably low.

From percentage to decimal		
10%	=	0.10
5%	=	0.05
1%	=	0.01
2.5%	=	0.025

To go from decimal to percentage, multiply by 100: move the decimal point two places to the right.

To go from percentage to decimal, divide by 100: move the decimal point two places to the left.

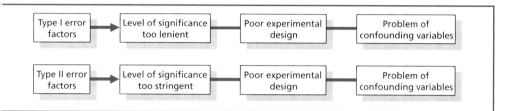

Psychologists generally use the 5% level of significance. However, they would use the 1% or even the 0.1% level of significance if it were very important to avoid making a Type I error. For example, clinical psychologists might require very strong evidence that a new form of therapy was more effective than existing forms of therapy before starting to use it on a regular basis. The 1% or 0.1% level of statistical significance is also used when the experimental hypothesis seems improbable. For example, very few people would accept that telepathy had been proved to exist on the basis of a single study in which the results were only just significant at the 5% level!

If you are familiar with Rosenhan's study "on being sane in insane places" (page 601), can you recall whether the psychiatrists initially made a Type I or Type II error?

Tests of Difference

Here, we will consider those statistical tests that are applicable when we are interested in deciding whether the differences between two conditions or groups are significant. As was discussed in your AS level studies, there are three kinds of design that can be used when we want to compare two conditions. First, there is the independent design, in which each participant is allocated at random to one and only one condition. Second, there is the repeated measures design, in which the same participants are used in both conditions. Third, there is the matched participants design, in which the participants in the two conditions are matched in terms of some variable or variables that might be relevant (e.g., intelligence, age).

When deciding which statistical test to use, it is very important to take account of the particular kind of experimental design that was used.

If the independent design has been used, then the Mann-Whitney U test is the appropriate test to use.
If the repeated measures or matched participants design has been used, then the sign test or the Wilcoxon matched pairs signed ranks test is the appropriate test to use.

Mann-Whitney U test

The Mann-Whitney U test can be used when an independent design has been used, and the data are either ordinal or interval. The worked example in the box overleaf shows how this test is calculated.

Suppose that we have two conditions. In both conditions, the participants have to fire arrows at a board, and the score obtained is recorded. There are 10 participants in condition A, in which no training is provided before their performance is assessed. There

Mann-Whitney U test: A worked example

Experimental hypothesis: Extensive training improves performance

Null hypothesis: Training has no effect on performance

Participant	Condition A	Rank	Participant	Condition B	Rank
1	4	2	1	21	15
2	10	9	2	26	18
3	12	11	3	20	14
4	28	20	4	22	16
5	7	5	5	32	22
6	13	13	6	5	3
7	12	11	7	12	11
8	2	1	8	6	4
9	9	7.5	9	8	6
10	27	19	10	24	17
			11	29	21
			12	9	7.5

Smaller sample = condition A
Sum of ranks in smaller sample (T) = 98.5
Number of participants in smaller sample (N_A) = 10
Number of participants in larger sample (N_B) = 12

Formula: $U = N_A N_B + \left(\dfrac{N_A(N_A + 1)}{2} \right) - T$

Example: $U = (10 \times 12) + \left(\dfrac{10(10 + 1)}{2} \right) - 98.5 = 76.5$

Formula for calculating U': $U' = N_A N_B - U$

Example: $U' = (10 \times 12) - 76.5 = 43.5$

Comparing U and U', U' is the smaller value. The calculated value of U' (43.5) is checked against the tabled value for a one-tailed test at 5%.

Table values

	$N_A = 10$
$N_B = 12$	34

Conclusion: As 43.5 is greater than 34, the null hypothesis should be retained—i.e., training has no effect on performance in this task.

The appropriate tables of significance for the Mann–Whitney test can be found on pages 816–817.

are 12 participants in condition B, and they receive extensive training before their performance is assessed. The experimental hypothesis is that extensive training would improve performance; in other words, the scores in condition B should be significantly higher than those in condition A.

The first step is to rank all of the scores from both groups together, with a rank of 1 being given to the smallest score, a rank of 2 to the second smallest score, and so on. If there are tied scores, then the mean of the ranks involved is given to each of the tied participants. For example, two participants were tied for the 7th and 8th ranks, and so they both received a rank of 7.5.

The second step is to work out the sum of the ranks in the smaller sample, which is condition A in our example. This value is known as T, and it is 98.5 in the example.

The third step is to calculate U from the formula, in which N_A is the number of participants in the smaller sample and N_B is the number in the larger sample:

$$U = N_A N_B + \left(\frac{N_A(N_A + 1)}{2} \right) - T$$

The fourth step is to calculate U' (U prime):

$$U' = N_A N_B - U$$

The fifth step is to compare U and U', selecting whichever is the smaller value provided that the results are in the correct direction. The smaller value (i.e., 43.5) is then looked up in Table 1 (see bottom table on page 817). Here, we have a one-tailed test, because the experimental hypothesis stated that extensive training would improve performance. With 10 participants in our first condition and 12 in our second condition, the tabled value for significance on a one-tailed test at 0.05 is 34. The observed value must be equal to, or smaller than, the tabled value in order to be significant. As our value of 43.5 is greater than 34, the conclusion is that we retain the null hypothesis. The presence of ties reduces the accuracy of the tables, but the effect is small unless there are several ties.

Sign test

The sign test can be used when a repeated measures or matched participants design has been used, and the data are ordinal. If the data are interval or ratio, then it would be more appropriate to use the Wilcoxon matched pairs signed ranks test. The worked example in the box below illustrates the way in which the sign test is calculated.

Suppose that there were 12 participants in an experiment. In condition A these participants were presented with 20 words to learn in a situation with no noise; learning was followed 5 minutes later by a test of free recall in which they wrote down as many words as they could remember in any order. Condition B involved presenting 20 different words to learn in a situation of loud noise; as in condition A, learning was followed 5 minutes later by a test of free recall. The experimenter predicted that free recall would be higher in the no-noise condition. Thus, there was a directional hypothesis.

In order to calculate the sign test it is necessary first of all to draw up a table like the one in the example, in which each participant's scores in condition A and in condition B are recorded. Each participant whose score in condition A is greater than his or her score in condition B is given a plus sign (+) in the sign column, and each participant whose score in condition B is greater than his or her score in condition A is given a minus sign

---

Sign test: A worked example

Experimental hypothesis: Free recall is better when learning takes place in the absence of noise than in its presence

Null hypothesis: Free recall is not affected by whether or not noise is present during learning

Participant	Condition A (no noise)	Condition B (loud noise)	Sign
1	12	8	+
2	10	10	0
3	7	8	−
4	12	11	+
5	8	3	+
6	10	10	0
7	13	7	+
8	8	9	−
9	14	10	+
10	11	9	+
11	15	12	+
12	11	10	+

Number of + signs = 8
Number of − signs = 2
Number of 0 signs = 2

Number of participants with differing scores (N) = 8 + 2 = 10
Number of participants with less frequent sign (S) = 2

Question: Is the value of S in this example the same as or lower than the tabled value for S?

Table values

	5%
N = 10	S = 1

Conclusion: In this experiment the value of S is higher than the tabled value, when N = 10. The null hypothesis (that noise has no effect on learning and memory) cannot be rejected.

The appropriate table of significance for the sign test can be found on page 818.

The sign test is ideal to use if the data are **nominal** or **ordinal** as it analyses at a very basic level, e.g., in a race it can tell you that "John beat Peter". It can also be used with **interval** or **ratio** data, but, as it only gives a crude analysis, this data would be better applied to the Wilcoxon test, which can give a more sophisticated analysis, e.g., "John beat Peter by 2 seconds."

(–) in the sign column. Each participant whose scores in both conditions are the same receives a 0 sign in the sign column. Such participants are ignored in the subsequent calculations, and they do not contribute to N (the number of paired scores), as they provide no evidence about the direction of any effect.

In the example, there are eight plus signs, two minus signs, and two participants had the same scores in both conditions. If we ignore the two participants with the same scores in both conditions, this gives us N = 10. Now all we need to do is to work out the number of these 10 participants having the less frequently occurring sign; this value is known as S. In terms of our example, S = 2. We can refer to the relevant table (Table 2, see page 818) with N = 10 and S = 2. The obtained value for S must be the same as or lower than the value for S given in the table. The tabled value for a one-tailed test is 1. Thus, our obtained S value of 2 is not significant at the 5% level on a one-tailed test. We therefore conclude that we cannot reject the null hypothesis that noise has no effect on learning and memory.

Compare this result with that gained from using the Wilcoxon test. How can you explain this contradiction?

Wilcoxon matched pairs signed ranks test

The Wilcoxon matched pairs signed ranks test can be used when a repeated measures or matched participants design has been used, and the data are at least ordinal. This test or the sign test can be used if the data are ordinal or interval. However, the Wilcoxon matched pairs signed ranks test uses more of the information obtained from a study, and so is usually more sensitive and useful than the sign test.

The worked example in the box below uses the data from the sign test. The first step is to place all the data in a table in which each participant's two scores are in the same row. The second step is to subtract the condition B score from the condition A score for each participant. The third step is to omit all the participants whose two scores are the

---

Wilcoxon matched pairs signed ranks test: A worked example

Experimental hypothesis: Free recall is better when learning takes place in the absence of noise than in its presence

Null hypothesis: Free recall is not affected by whether or not noise is present during learning

Participant	Condition A (no noise)	Condition B (loud noise)	Difference (d) (A – B)	Rank
1	12	8	4	7.5
2	10	10	0	—
3	7	8	–1	2.5
4	12	11	1	2.5
5	8	3	5	9
6	10	10	0	—
7	13	7	6	10
8	8	9	–1	2.5
9	14	10	4	7.5
10	11	9	2	5
11	15	12	3	6
12	11	10	1	2.5

Sum of positive ranks (7.5 + 2.5 + 9 + 10 + 7.5 + 5 + 6 + 2.5) = 50

Sum of negative ranks (2.5 + 2.5) = 5

Smaller value (5) = T

Number of participants who scored differently in condition A and B, N = 10

Question: For the results to be significant, the value of T must be the same as, or less than, the tabled value.

Table values

	5%	1%
N = 10	11	5

Conclusion: In this experiment T is less than the tabled value at the 5% level and the same as the tabled value at the 1% level of significance, so the null hypothesis is rejected in favour of the experimental hypothesis.

The appropriate table of significance for the Wilcoxon test can be found on page 818.

same, i.e., d = 0. The fourth step is to rank all the difference scores obtained in the second step from 1 for the smallest difference, to 2 for the second smallest difference, and so on. For this purpose, ignore the + and – signs, thus taking the absolute size of the difference. The fifth step is to add up the sum of the positive ranks (50 in the example) and separately to add up the sum of the negative ranks (5 in the example). The smaller of these values is T, which in this case is 5. The sixth step is to work out the number of participants whose two scores are not the same, i.e., d ≠ 0. In the example, N = 10.

The obtained value of T must be the same as, or less than, the tabled value (see Table 3 on page 818) in order for the results to be significant. The tabled value for a one-tailed test and N = 10 is 11 at the 5% level of statistical significance, and it is 5 at the 1% level. Thus, the findings are significant at the 1% level on a one-tailed test. The null hypothesis is rejected in favour of the experimental hypothesis that free recall is better when learning takes place in the absence of noise than in its presence ($p = 0.01$). The presence of ties means that the tables are not completely accurate, but this does not matter provided that there are only a few ties.

You may be wondering how it is possible for the same data to produce a significant finding on a Wilcoxon test but not on a sign test. Does this indicate that statistics are useless? Not at all. The sign test is insensitive (or lacking in power) because it takes no account of the *size* of each individual's difference in free recall in the two conditions. It is because this information is made use of in the Wilcoxon test that a significant result was obtained using that test. Thus, the Wilcoxon test has more power than the sign test to detect differences between two conditions.

A positive correlation: The taller the player, the higher the score.

Studies Using Correlational Analysis

In the case of studies using correlational analysis, the data are in the form of two measures of behaviour from each member of a single group of participants. What is often done is to present the data in the form of a **scattergraph** (also known as a scattergram). It is given this name, because it shows the ways in which the scores of individuals are scattered.

Spearman's rho

Suppose that we have scores on two variables from each of our participants, and we want to see whether there is an association or correlation between the two sets of scores. This can be done by using a test known as Spearman's rho, provided that the data are at least ordinal. Spearman's rho or r_s indicates the strength of the association. If r_s is +1.0, then there is a perfect positive correlation between the two variables. If r_s is –1.0, then there is a perfect negative correlation between the two variables. If r_s is 0.0, then there is generally no relationship between the two variables. The working of this test is shown in the box on the next page.

An experimenter collects information about the amount of television violence seen in the past month and about the amount of aggressive behaviour exhibited in the past month from 12 participants. She predicts that there will be a positive association between these two variables, i.e., those participants who have seen the most television violence (variable A) will tend to be the most aggressive (variable B). In other words, there is a directional hypothesis.

The first step is to draw up a table in which each participant's scores for the two variables are placed in the same row.

The second step is to rank all the scores for variable A. A rank of 1 is assigned to the smallest score, a rank of 2 to the second smallest score, and so on up to 12. What do we do if there are tied scores? In the example, participants 9 and 12 had the same score for variable A. The ranks that they are competing for are ranks 5 and 6. What is done is to take the average or mean of the ranks at issue: $(5 + 6)/2 = 5.5$.

The third step is to rank all the scores for variable B, with a rank of 1 being assigned to the smallest score. Participants 6, 7, 9, and 11 are all tied, with the ranks at issue being ranks 4, 5, 6, and 7. The mean rank will be $(4 + 5 + 6 + 7)/4 = 5.5$.

A negative correlation: The more time spent playing computer games, the less time spent studying.

No correlation: Where there is no relationship, variables are uncorrelated.

The appropriate table of significance for the Spearman's rho test can be found on page 819.

Spearman's rho: A worked example

Experimental hypothesis: There is a positive association between amount of television violence watched and aggressive behaviour

Null hypothesis: There is no association between amount of television violence watched and aggressive behaviour

Participant	TV violence seen (hours)	Aggressive behaviour (out of 10)	Rank A	Rank B	Difference d	Difference d^2
1	17	8	7.5	9	−1.50	2.25
2	6	3	2	2	0.00	0.00
3	23	9	10	10.5	−0.50	0.25
4	17	7	7.5	8	−0.50	0.25
5	2	2	1	1	0.00	0.00
6	20	6	9	5.5	+3.50	12.25
7	12	6	4	5.5	−1.50	2.25
8	31	10	12	12	0.00	0.00
9	14	6	5.5	5.5	0.00	0.00
10	26	9	11	10.5	+0.50	0.25
11	9	6	3	5.5	−2.50	6.25
12	14	4	5.5	3	+2.50	6.25

Sum of squared difference scores (Σd^2) = 30

Number of participants (N) = 12

Formula: $\text{rho} = 1 - \dfrac{(\Sigma d^2 \times 6)}{N(N^2 - 1)}$

Example: $1 - \dfrac{(30 \times 6)}{12(143)} = 1 - 0.105 = +0.895$

Is the value of rho (+0.895) as great as, or greater than the tabled value?

Table values

	0.05 level	0.01 level	0.005 level
N = 12	+0.503	+0.671	+0.727

Conclusion: Null hypothesis rejected in favour of experimental hypothesis, i.e., there is a positive correlation between the amount of television violence watched and aggressive behaviour ($p = 0.005$).

The fourth step is to calculate the difference between the two ranks obtained by each individual, with the rank for variable B being subtracted from the rank for variable A. This produces 12 difference (d) scores.

The fifth step is to square all of the d scores obtained in the fourth step. This produces 12 squared difference (d^2) scores.

The sixth step is to add up all of the d^2 scores in order to obtain the sum of the squared difference scores. This is known as Σd^2, and comes to 30 in the example.

The seventh step is to work out the number of participants. In the example, the number of participants (N) is 12.

The eighth step is to calculate rho from the following formula:

$$\text{rho} = 1 - \frac{(\Sigma d^2 \times 6)}{N(N^2 - 1)}$$

Note that the "6" in the equation is always present, and is a feature of the Spearman's rho formula.

In the example, this becomes

$$1 - \frac{(30 \times 6)}{12(143)} = 1 - 0.105 = +0.895$$

The ninth and final step is to work out the significance of the value of rho by referring the result to the table (see Table 4 on page 819). The obtained value must be as great as, or greater than, the tabled value. The tabled value for a one-tailed test with N = 12 is +0.503 at the 0.05 level; it is +0.671 at the 0.01 level; and it is +0.727 at the 0.005 level. Thus, it can be concluded that the null hypothesis should be rejected in favour of the experimental hypothesis that there is a positive correlation between the amount of television violence watched and aggressive behaviour ($p = 0.005$).

An important point about Spearman's rho is that the statistical significance of the obtained value of rho depends very heavily on the number of participants. For example, the tabled value for significance at the 0.05 level on a one-tailed test is +0.564 if there are 10 participants. However, it is only +0.306 if there are 30 participants. In practical terms, this means that it is very hard to obtain a significant correlation with Spearman's rho if the number of participants is low.

According to the American Psychological Association, numbers that can never be greater than one, as in the case of correlations, should never be written with a zero to the left of the decimal point. However, this convention has not been followed in this book.

Why is it a good idea to have a reasonable number of participants in a correlational study?

Test of association

The **chi-squared test** is a test of association. It is used when we have nominal data in the form of frequencies, and when each and every observation is independent of all the other observations. For example, suppose that we are interested in the association between eating patterns and cholesterol level. We could divide people into those having a healthy diet with relatively little fat and those having an unhealthy diet. We could also divide them into those having a fairly high level of cholesterol and those having a low level of cholesterol. In essence, the chi-squared test tells us whether membership of a given category on one dimension (e.g., unhealthy diet) is associated with membership of a given category on the other dimension (e.g., high cholesterol level).

In the worked example (see the box on the next page) we will assume that we have data from 186 individuals with an unhealthy diet, and from 128 individuals with a healthy diet. Of those with an unhealthy diet, 116 have a high cholesterol level and 70 have a low cholesterol level. Of those with a healthy diet, 41 have a high cholesterol level and 87 have a low cholesterol level. Our experimental hypothesis is that there is an association between healthiness of diet and low cholesterol level.

The first step is to arrange the frequency data in a 2 x 2 "contingency table" as in the example, with the row and column totals included. The second step is to work out what the four frequencies would be if there were no association at all between diet and cholesterol levels. The expected frequency (by chance alone) in each case is given by the following formula:

$$\text{expected frequency} = \frac{\text{row total} \times \text{column total}}{\text{overall total}}$$

For example, the expected frequency for the number of participants having a healthy diet and high cholesterol is 157- x 128 divided by 314, which comes to 64. The four expected frequencies (those expected by chance alone) are also shown in the worked example.

The third step is to apply the following formula to the observed (O) and expected (E) frequencies in each of the four categories:

$$\frac{(|O - E| - 1/2)^2}{E}$$

In the formula, $|O - E|$ means that the difference between the observed and the expected frequency should be taken, and it should then have a + sign put in front of it regardless of the direction of the difference. The correction factor (i.e., $-\frac{1}{2}$) is only used when there are two rows and two columns.

The fourth step is to add together the four values obtained in the third step in order to provide the chi-squared statistic, or X^2. This is $7.91 + 5.44 + 7.91 + 5.44 = 26.70$.

As vertical lines denote absolute values, "lO – El" is the difference between these values disregarding the sign. Whether it is 3 – 5 or 5 – 3, the difference is always a positive number, i.e., 2 in this case.

Test of association: Chi-squared test: A worked example

Experimental hypothesis: There is an association between healthiness of diet and low cholesterol level

Null hypothesis: There is no association between healthiness of diet and low cholesterol level

Contingency table:

	Healthy diet	Unhealthy diet	Row total
High cholesterol	41	116	157
Low cholesterol	87	70	157
Column total	128	186	314

Expected frequency if there were no association:

Formula: $\dfrac{\text{row total} \times \text{column total}}{\text{expected frequency}}$ = overall total

	Healthy diet	Unhealthy diet	Row total
High cholesterol	64	93	157
Low cholesterol	64	93	157
Column total	128	186	314

Calculating chi-squared statistic (χ^2):

Formula: $\chi^2 = \sum \dfrac{(IO - EI - 1/2)^2}{E} = 26.7$

Note: Correction factor ($-1/2$) is only used where there are two rows and two columns

Category	Observed	Expected	IO −EI	$\dfrac{(IO - EI - 1/2)^2}{E}$
Healthy, high cholesterol	41	64	23	7.91
Unhealthy, high cholesterol	116	93	23	5.44
Healthy, low cholesterol	87	64	23	7.91
Unhealthy, low cholesterol	70	93	23	5.44
				26.70

Calculating degrees of freedom:

Formula: (no. of rows − 1) × (no. of columns −1) = degrees of freedom (2 − 1) × (2 − 1) = 1

Compare chi-squared statistic with tabled values:

Table values

	0.025 level	0.005 level	0.0005 level
df = 1	3.84	6.64	10.83

Question: Is the observed chi-squared value of 26.70 and one degree of freedom the same as or greater than the tabled value?

Conclusion: The chi-squared value is greater than the tabled value, so the null hypothesis can be rejected, and the experimental hypothesis, that there is an association between healthiness of diet and cholesterol level, accepted.

The appropriate table of significance for the chi-squared test can be found on page 820.

The fifth step is to calculate the number of "degrees of freedom" (df). This is given by:

(the number of rows − 1) x (the number of columns − 1)

For this we need to refer back to the contingency table. In the example, this is 1 x 1 = 1 Why is there one degree of freedom? Once we know the row and column totals, then only one of the four observed values is free to vary. Thus, for example, knowing that the row totals are 157 and 157, the column totals are 128 and 186, and the number of participants having a healthy diet and high cholesterol is 41, we can complete the entire table. In other words, the number of degrees of freedom corresponds to the number of values that are free to vary.

The sixth step is to compare the tabled values in Table 5 (see page 820) with chi-square = 26.70 and one degree of freedom. The observed value needs to be the same as, or greater than, the tabled value for a one-tailed test in order for the results to be significant.

The tabled value for a one-tailed test with $df = 1$ is 3.84 at the 0.025 level, 6.64 at the 0.005 level, and 10.83 at the 0.0005 level. Thus, we can reject the null hypothesis, and conclude that there is an association between healthiness of diet and cholesterol level ($p = 0.0005$).

It is easy to use the chi-squared test wrongly. According to Robson (1994), "There are probably more inappropriate and incorrect uses of the chi-squared test than of all the other statistical tests put together." In order to avoid using the chi-squared test wrongly, it is important to make use of the following rules:

- Ensure that every observation is independent of every other observation; in other words, each individual should be counted only once and in only *one* category.
- Make sure that each observation is included in the appropriate category; it is not permitted to omit some of the observations (e.g., those from individuals with intermediate levels of cholesterol).
- The total sample should exceed 20; otherwise, the chi-squared test as described here is not applicable. More precisely, the minimum expected frequency should be at least 5 in every cell of the table.
- The significance level of a chi-squared test is assessed by consulting the one-tailed values in the Table 5 if a specific form of association has been predicted and that form was obtained. However, the two-tailed values should always be consulted if there are more than two categories on either dimension.
- Remember that showing there is an association is not the same as showing that there is a causal effect; for example, the association between a healthy diet and low cholesterol does not demonstrate that a healthy diet *causes* low cholesterol.

Using an Inferential Test for Your Coursework

Choosing a test

The table on the next page summarises the reasons for choosing each test, and thus gives you the necessary information for justifying your choice of test.

Justifying your choice of test

For the purposes of your coursework report you need to explain why you choose a particular test. For example, if you have conducted a study where you are seeking to determine whether there are differences between two independent groups of participants then you might state:

> *In order to assess the significance of these findings it was necessary to use a statistical test. In this study an appropriate test would be a Mann-Whitney U test because (1) a test of differences was required, (2) the design was independent measures, and (3) the data were at least at an ordinal level.*

Calculating the observed value

The next step is to perform the calculations. You may do this with a computer program or you may follow the instructions in this Section. Either way you must include some

<table>
<tr><td colspan="4">Selecting a suitable statistical test</td></tr>
<tr><td colspan="4">If you wish to see if there is a difference between one set of data and another, you need a test of difference. Your choice of test depends on the level of measurement; whether the data are measured at the nominal or ordinal/interval level, and whether the groups of data are independent or related.</td></tr>
<tr><td colspan="4">If you wish to find out whether pairs of variables are associated or correlated, then you need a test of correlation. The test you should use is Spearman's rho.</td></tr>
<tr><td></td><td colspan="2" align="center">Difference test</td><td>Correlational test</td></tr>
<tr><td>Level of measurement</td><td>Independent data</td><td>Related data</td><td></td></tr>
<tr><td>Nominal</td><td>Chi-squared test</td><td>Sign test</td><td></td></tr>
<tr><td>Ordinal and interval</td><td>Mann-Whitney U test</td><td>Wilcoxon matched pairs signed ranks</td><td>Spearman's rho</td></tr>
<tr><td colspan="4">Note: this chart deals only with the statistical tests described in Section 23, Statistical Tests, even though other tests do exist.</td></tr>
</table>

details of the calculations in an appendix of your coursework report. The outcome of a statistical test is a number, called the **observed value**.

Using a table of significance

In order to determine whether this observed value is significant we consult an appropriate table of significance. These are located in the Appendix, and include instructions about how to use each table. A comparison between the **critical value** in the table and your own observed value enables you decide whether you can accept or reject the null hypothesis.

Reporting the result

The final step is to record the outcome of this whole process. You should include the following information in your final statement: details of the level of significance, the critical and observed values, degrees of freedom, whether the hypothesis was directional or non-directional, and whether it was accepted or rejected. For example:

> *For 10 participants, the critical value for rho is 0.504 at the 5% level of significance ($p < 0.05$, one-tailed). As the observed value of rho is 0.703 this is greater than the critical value and so there is less than a 5% probability that the result is due to chance. The null hypothesis can be rejected and the alternate hypothesis accepted.*

S E C T I O N   S U M M A R Y

❖ When we have obtained scores from a group of participants, we can summarise our data using descriptive statistics. We also can determine the significance of the result(s) using a statistical test.

❖ A test of difference is used when data are obtained from a study in which an independent variable was manipulated to observe its effects. A test of correlation is used when the data from the study are in the form of scores on two response variables from every participant. If the experimental hypothesis predicts the direction of effects (a directional hypothesis), then a one-tailed test should be used. Otherwise, a two-tailed test should be used (for a non-directional hypothesis). There are four types of data of increasing levels of precision: nominal, ordinal, interval, and ratio.

❖ The meaningfulness of research findings is determined through statistical significance. If the statistical test indicates that there is only a small probability of the difference between conditions (e.g., loud noise vs. no noise) having occurred if the null hypothesis were true, then we reject the null hypothesis in favour of the experimental hypothesis. Psychologists generally use the 5% level of statistical significance. This produces fairly small probabilities of incorrectly rejecting the null hypothesis in favour of the experimental hypothesis (Type I error) or of incorrectly retaining the null hypothesis (Type II error).

❖ The Mann-Whitney U test is the appropriate test of difference if an independent design has been used. The sign test can be used when a repeated measures or matched participants design has been used and the data are nominal or ordinal. The same is true of the Wilcoxon matched pairs signed ranks test, except that the data must be at least ordinal.

❖ The correlation between two sets of scores can be calculated by means of Spearman's rho test, provided that the data are at least ordinal. The chi-squared test is a test of association. It is used when we have nominal data in the form of frequencies, and when each and every observation is independent of all the other observations. All the expected frequencies should be five or more. Finding an association is not the same as showing the existence of a causal effect.

❖ When using a statistical test in your coursework you must (1) select a suitable test, (2) justify the choice of test, (3) perform the necessary calculations, (4) consult a table of significance to determine if the observed value is significant, and (5) report the significance of your findings.

FURTHER READING

These topics are covered in greater depth by A. Searle (1999) *Introducing research and data in psychology* (London: Routledge), written specifically for AQA A students. There is detailed but user-friendly coverage of the topics discussed in this Section in H. Coolican (1999) *Research methods and statistics in psychology (3rd Edn.)* (London: Hodder & Stoughton). A shorter version of the Coolican textbook is H. Coolican (1995) *Introduction to research methods and statistics in psychology* (London: Hodder & Stoughton).

Ideas for a Laboratory Experiment

- Levels of processing
- Effects of arousal on emotion

Ideas for a Field Experiment

- Modelling pro-social behaviour

Ideas for a Survey and Correlational Study

- Type A behaviour

Ideas for an Observational Study

- Gender content in TV advertisements
- Attachments in dogs and their owners
- Non-human animal behaviour

24

Ideas for Coursework

Your choice of coursework will be related to the particular areas of psychology you have studied. The examples here are taken from AS and A2 specifications. They are all based on previous research studies but you should feel encouraged to make your own adaptations.

For AQA A you are required to conduct one study, either alone or with a small group of students (four or fewer). You are permitted to receive assistance from your teacher in the design of this study or to base your study on a previous piece of research. In such cases you would receive only 1 mark for section A1 of the coursework mark scheme (see page 795). We would argue that, for many students, this approach is worthwhile because it means you have the opportunity to devote your energies to conducting the study and writing the report, rather than designing the whole project. You may choose to adapt some features of a pre-existing design, which may be the best compromise between designing your own study entirely and "lifting" someone else's design.

Laboratory Experiment

Levels of processing
(Craik & Tulving, 1975)

Many of the studies of memory are especially suitable for coursework. This one is an example of a repeated measures design where all participants are given a list of words. They must answer yes or no to the questions: "Is the word in capital letters?" (case), "Does the word rhyme with 'able'?" (phonemic processing), or "Would the word fit in the sentence 'They met a —— in the street'?" (semantic).

You should select a suitable list of five-letter words, aiming to ensure that they are equally familiar. You might restrict your analysis to case and meaning only to avoid having multiple hypotheses.

The effects of arousal on emotion
(White et al., 1981)

This experiment demonstrated the cognitive labelling theory of emotion, which has also been used to explain love. Under certain circumstances an individual may misattribute their feelings of arousal to physical attraction.

Assemble a set of stimulus photographs (or videotapes), and arrange for them to be independently judged in terms of attractiveness. Select some attractive and some unattractive photographs. Randomly allocate participants to conditions. One group will

run on the spot for 120 seconds before rating the photographs, while the other might do nothing, or run for a much shorter period. Interview participants individually. You will need to give them some explanation for the experiment and might want to arrange for them to do other activities as well as the target activity so they do not guess the purpose of the experiment.

Field Experiment

Ethical considerations are important in field experiments when participants are not aware that they are taking part in psychological research. It is preferable to avoid such situations unless you feel that your intervention is in no way harmful.

Modelling pro-social behaviour (Bryan & Test, 1967)

In this study a confederate of the researcher was used to act as a model for pro-social behaviour. A Salvation Army kettle was held by the researcher, who observed whether donations increased when the confederate put money in the kettle.

You could arrange to collect money for charity. You can arrange two conditions, one where a confederate regularly passes by, placing money in the tin, and one with no confederate. This study is independent measures design.

Survey and Correlational Study

The task of drawing up your own questionnaire is a study in itself. It is preferable to use an existing questionnaire and test one or more hypotheses.

Type A behaviour (Rosenman et al., 1975)

The original study demonstrated that Type A behaviour was associated with congestive heart failure. You might choose to associate Type A behaviour with some other aspect of health, such as frequency of illness. In order to assess illness you will need to draw up your own questionnaire. Type A behaviour can be assessed using a free questionnaire available at the following web site www.queendom.com/typea.html

Observational Study

Gender content in TV advertisements (Manstead & McCullough, 1981)

Content analysis is a form of observation. This study looked at the way men and women were portrayed on television using the following categories: credibility basis of the central character (user, authority, other), role of central character (dependent autonomous, other), argument spoken by central character (factual, opinion, other) product type used by central character (food/drink, alcoholic drink, body, household other).

You should watch a representative sample of advertisements and record whether the central character is male or female and then record which of the categories the person belongs in. Research has consistently found gender differences.

Attachments in dogs and their owners (Topal et al., 1998)

A study in Hungary used a modified version of the Strange Situation to assess attachments between owners and their dogs. They found it was possible to classify the dogs as securely or insecurely attached. And why not, they argued, the dog's relationship to a human is analogous to the child–parent relationship because it involves trust.

You could replicate this controlled observation.

Non-human animal behaviour

Good observational studies require careful consideration of observation grids. Ethologists observe animal behaviour using ethograms. This is a record of the behavioural repertoire of a particular species of animal. You might use a pet animal to construct such an ethogram. Spend time observing the animal and record all kinds of behaviours. For example, in the case of a cat this would include: sleeping, stretching, rubbing nose against furniture, rubbing whole body against furniture, and so on.

Once you have developed the ethogram you can use it to test a hypothesis. For example, you might compare male and female cats.

FURTHER READING

Some useful sources for coursework ideas are C. Flanagan (1998) *Practicals for psychology* (London: Routledge), C. Flanagan (1996) *A resource pack for "A" level psychology* (Hartshill Press, available through London: Hodder & Stoughton), and McIlveen et al. (1992) *BPS manual of psychology practicals* (Exeter, UK: BPS).

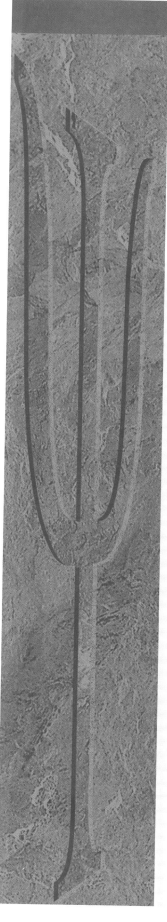

APPENDIX

Tables of Significance

Remember that decisions based on statistical tests are open to error, but if you follow the standard procedures outlined in the Section on Statistical Tests the potential for errors can be minimised. Try to be as unbiased as possible, and try not to assume too much about the results in advance.

How to Use the Tables

In the Mann-Whitney U test (on pages 816–817), use the smaller value of U and U' to look up the critical value of U for a one- or two-tailed test, as appropriate, at 0.05, initially (bottom and top tables, page 817). If the tabled value is equal to or less than your value at that level, the null hypothesis is retained; if it is greater than your value, it is rejected and your experimental hypothesis is proved.

In the sign test (on page 818), look up the critical value of S for a one- or two-tailed test, as appropriate, for N, the number of participants with differing scores, at 0.05, initially. If the tabled value is equal to or less than your value at that level, the null hypothesis is retained; if it is greater than your value, it is rejected and your experimental hypothesis is proved.

In the Wilcoxon test (on page 818), look up the critical value of T for a one- or two-tailed test, as appropriate, for N, the number of participants with differing scores, at 0.05, initially. If the tabled value is equal to or less than your value at that level, the null hypothesis is retained; if it is greater than your value, it is rejected and your experimental hypothesis is proved.

In the Spearman's rho test (on page 819), look up the critical value of r_s for a one- or two-tailed test, as appropriate, for N, the number of participants, at 0.05, initially. If the tabled value is greater than or equal to your value at that level, the null hypothesis is retained; if it is less than your value, it is rejected and your experimental hypothesis is proved.

In the chi-squared test (on page 820), look up the critical value of chi-squared (also shown as χ^2) for a one- or two-tailed test, as appropriate, for df, the degrees of freedom, at 0.05, initially. If the tabled value is greater than or equal to your value at that level, the null hypothesis is retained; if it is less than your value, it is rejected and your experimental hypothesis is proved.

815

Table 1: Mann-Whitney U test

Critical values of U for a one-tailed test at 0.005; two-tailed test at 0.01*

										N_A										
N_B	1	2	3	4	5	6	7	8	9	10	11	12	13	14	15	16	17	18	19	20
1	—	—	—	—	—	—	—	—	—	—	—	—	—	—	—	—	—	—	—	—
2	—	—	—	—	—	—	—	—	—	—	—	—	—	—	—	—	—	—	0	0
3	—	—	—	—	—	—	—	—	0	0	0	1	1	1	2	2	2	2	3	3
4	—	—	—	—	—	0	0	1	1	2	2	3	3	4	5	5	6	6	7	8
5	—	—	—	—	0	1	1	2	3	4	5	6	7	7	8	9	10	11	12	13
6	—	—	—	0	1	2	3	4	5	6	7	9	10	11	12	13	15	16	17	18
7	—	—	—	0	1	3	4	6	7	9	10	12	13	15	16	18	19	21	22	24
8	—	—	—	1	2	4	6	7	9	11	13	15	17	18	20	22	24	26	28	30
9	—	—	0	1	3	5	7	9	11	13	16	18	20	22	24	27	29	31	33	36
10	—	—	0	2	4	6	9	11	13	16	18	21	24	26	29	31	34	37	39	42
11	—	—	0	2	5	7	10	13	16	18	21	24	27	30	33	36	39	42	45	48
12	—	—	1	3	6	9	12	15	18	21	24	27	31	34	37	41	44	47	51	54
13	—	—	1	3	7	10	13	17	20	24	27	31	34	38	42	45	49	53	56	60
14	—	—	1	4	7	11	15	18	22	26	30	34	38	42	46	50	54	58	63	67
15	—	—	2	5	8	12	16	20	24	29	33	37	42	46	51	55	60	64	69	73
16	—	—	2	5	9	13	18	22	27	31	36	41	45	50	55	60	65	70	74	79
17	—	—	2	6	10	15	19	24	29	34	39	44	49	54	60	65	70	75	81	86
18	—	—	2	6	11	16	21	26	31	37	42	47	53	58	64	70	75	81	87	92
19	—	0	3	7	12	17	22	28	33	39	45	51	56	63	69	74	81	87	93	99
20	—	0	3	8	13	18	24	30	36	42	48	54	60	67	73	79	86	92	99	105

*Dashes in the body of the table indicate that no decision is possible at the stated level of significance.
For any N_A and N_B the observed value of U is significant at a given level of significance if it is *equal* to or *less* than the critical values shown.

Source: R. Runyon and A. Haber (1976), *Fundamentals of behavioural statistics (3rd Edn.)*. Reading, MA: McGraw-Hill, Inc. With the kind permission of the publisher.

Critical values of U for a one-tailed test at 0.01; two-tailed test at 0.02*

										N_A										
N_B	1	2	3	4	5	6	7	8	9	10	11	12	13	14	15	16	17	18	19	20
1	—	—	—	—	—	—	—	—	—	—	—	—	—	—	—	—	—	—	—	—
2	—	—	—	—	—	—	—	—	—	—	—	—	0	0	0	0	0	0	1	1
3	—	—	—	—	—	—	0	0	1	1	1	2	2	2	3	3	4	4	4	5
4	—	—	—	—	0	1	1	2	3	3	4	5	5	6	7	7	8	9	9	10
5	—	—	—	0	1	2	3	4	5	6	7	8	9	10	11	12	13	14	15	16
6	—	—	—	1	2	3	4	6	7	8	9	11	12	13	15	16	18	19	20	22
7	—	—	0	1	3	4	6	7	9	11	12	14	16	17	19	21	23	24	26	28
8	—	—	0	2	4	6	7	9	11	13	15	17	20	22	24	26	28	30	32	34
9	—	—	1	3	5	7	9	11	14	16	18	21	23	26	28	31	33	36	38	40
10	—	—	1	3	6	8	11	13	16	19	22	24	27	30	33	36	38	41	44	47
11	—	—	1	4	7	9	12	15	18	22	25	28	31	34	37	41	44	47	50	53
12	—	—	2	5	8	11	14	17	21	24	28	31	35	38	42	46	49	53	56	60
13	—	0	2	5	9	12	16	20	23	27	31	35	39	43	47	51	55	59	63	67
14	—	0	2	6	10	13	17	22	26	30	34	38	43	47	51	56	60	65	69	73
15	—	0	3	7	11	15	19	24	28	33	37	42	47	51	56	61	66	70	75	80
16	—	0	3	7	12	16	21	26	31	36	41	46	51	56	61	66	71	76	82	87
17	—	0	4	8	13	18	23	28	33	38	44	49	55	60	66	71	77	82	88	93
18	—	0	4	9	14	19	24	30	36	41	47	53	59	65	70	76	82	88	94	100
19	—	1	4	9	15	20	26	32	38	44	50	56	63	69	75	82	88	94	101	107
20	—	1	5	10	16	22	28	34	40	47	53	60	67	73	80	87	93	100	107	114

*Dashes in the body of the table indicate that no decision is possible at the stated level of significance.
For any N_A and N_B the observed value of U is significant at a given level of significance if it is *equal* to or *less* than the critical values shown.

Source: R. Runyon and A. Haber (1976), *Fundamentals of behavioural statistics (3rd Edn.)*. Reading, MA: McGraw-Hill, Inc. With the kind permission of the publisher.

Critical values of U for a one-tailed test at 0.025; two-tailed test at 0.05*

N_B \ N_A	1	2	3	4	5	6	7	8	9	10	11	12	13	14	15	16	17	18	19	20
1	—	—	—	—	—	—	—	—	—	—	—	—	—	—	—	—	—	—	—	—
2	—	—	—	—	—	—	—	0	0	0	0	1	1	1	1	1	2	2	2	2
3	—	—	—	—	0	1	1	2	2	3	3	4	4	5	5	6	6	7	7	8
4	—	—	—	0	1	2	3	4	4	5	6	7	8	9	10	11	11	12	13	13
5	—	—	0	1	2	3	5	6	7	8	9	11	12	13	14	15	17	18	19	20
6	—	—	1	2	3	5	6	8	10	11	13	14	16	17	19	21	22	24	25	27
7	—	—	1	3	5	6	8	10	12	14	16	18	20	22	24	26	28	30	32	34
8	—	0	2	4	6	8	10	13	15	17	19	22	24	26	29	31	34	36	38	41
9	—	0	2	4	7	10	12	15	17	20	23	26	28	31	34	37	39	42	45	48
10	—	0	3	5	8	11	14	17	20	23	26	29	33	36	39	42	45	48	52	55
11	—	0	3	6	9	13	16	19	23	26	30	33	37	40	44	47	51	55	58	62
12	—	1	4	7	11	14	18	22	26	29	33	37	41	45	49	53	57	61	65	69
13	—	1	4	8	12	16	20	24	28	33	37	41	45	50	54	59	63	67	72	76
14	—	1	5	9	13	17	22	26	31	36	40	45	50	55	59	64	67	74	78	83
15	—	1	5	10	14	19	24	29	34	39	44	49	54	59	64	70	75	80	85	90
16	—	1	6	11	15	21	26	31	37	42	47	53	59	64	70	75	81	86	92	98
17	—	2	6	11	17	22	28	34	39	45	51	57	63	67	75	81	87	93	99	105
18	—	2	7	12	18	24	30	36	42	48	55	61	67	74	80	86	93	99	106	112
19	—	2	7	13	19	25	32	38	45	52	58	65	72	78	85	92	99	106	113	119
20	—	2	8	13	20	27	34	41	48	55	62	69	76	83	90	98	105	112	119	127

*Dashes in the body of the table indicate that no decision is possible at the stated level of significance.
For any N_A and N_B the observed value of U is significant at a given level of significance if it is *equal* to or *less* than the critical values shown.

Source: R. Runyon and A. Haber (1976), *Fundamentals of behavioural statistics (3rd Edn.)*. Reading, MA: McGraw-Hill, Inc. With the kind permission of the publisher.

Critical values of U for a one-tailed test at 0.05; two-tailed test at 0.10*

N_B \ N_A	1	2	3	4	5	6	7	8	9	10	11	12	13	14	15	16	17	18	19	20
1	—	—	—	—	—	—	—	—	—	—	—	—	—	—	—	—	—	—	0	0
2	—	—	—	—	0	0	0	1	1	1	1	2	2	2	3	3	3	4	4	4
3	—	—	0	0	1	2	2	3	3	4	5	5	6	7	7	8	9	9	10	11
4	—	—	0	1	2	3	4	5	6	7	8	9	10	11	12	14	15	16	17	18
5	—	0	1	2	4	5	6	8	9	11	12	13	15	16	18	19	20	22	23	25
6	—	0	2	3	5	7	8	10	12	14	16	17	19	21	23	25	26	28	30	32
7	—	0	2	4	6	8	11	13	15	17	19	21	24	26	28	30	33	35	37	39
8	—	1	3	5	8	10	13	15	18	20	23	26	28	31	33	36	39	41	44	47
9	—	1	3	6	9	12	15	18	21	24	27	30	33	36	39	42	45	48	51	54
10	—	1	4	7	11	14	17	20	24	27	31	34	37	41	44	48	51	55	58	62
11	—	1	5	8	12	16	19	23	27	31	34	38	42	46	50	54	57	61	65	69
12	—	2	5	9	13	17	21	26	30	34	38	42	47	51	55	60	64	68	72	77
13	—	2	6	10	15	19	24	28	33	37	42	47	51	56	61	65	70	75	80	84
14	—	2	7	11	16	21	26	31	36	41	46	51	56	61	66	71	77	82	87	92
15	—	3	7	12	18	23	28	33	39	44	50	55	61	66	72	77	83	88	94	100
16	—	3	8	14	19	25	30	36	42	48	54	60	65	71	77	83	89	95	101	107
17	—	3	9	15	20	26	33	39	45	51	57	64	70	77	83	89	96	102	109	115
18	—	4	9	16	22	28	35	41	48	55	61	68	75	82	88	95	102	109	116	123
19	0	4	10	17	23	30	37	44	51	58	65	72	80	87	94	101	109	116	123	130
20	0	4	11	18	25	32	39	47	54	62	69	77	84	92	100	107	115	123	130	138

*Dashes in the body of the table indicate that no decision is possible at the stated level of significance.
For any N_A and N_B the observed value of U is significant at a given level of significance if it is *equal* to or *less* than the critical values shown.

Source: R. Runyon and A. Haber (1976), *Fundamentals of behavioural statistics (3rd Edn.)*. Reading, MA: McGraw-Hill, Inc. With the kind permission of the publisher.

Table 2: Sign test

N	Level of significance for one-tailed test				
	0.05	0.025	0.01	0.005	0.0005
	Level of significance for two-tailed test				
	0.10	0.05	0.02	0.01	0.001
5	0	—	—	—	—
6	0	0	—	—	—
7	0	0	0	—	—
8	1	0	0	0	—
9	1	1	0	0	—
10	1	1	0	0	—
11	2	1	1	0	0
12	2	2	1	1	0
13	3	2	1	1	0
14	3	2	2	1	0
15	3	3	2	2	1
16	4	3	2	2	1
17	4	4	3	2	1
18	5	4	3	3	1
19	5	4	4	3	2
20	5	5	4	3	2
25	7	7	6	5	4
30	10	9	8	7	5
35	12	11	10	9	7

Calculated S must be *equal* to or *less* than the table (critical) value for significance at the level shown.

Source: F. Clegg (1982), *Simple statistics*. Cambridge University Press. With the kind permission of the publisher.

Table 3: Wilcoxon signed ranks test

Sample size	Levels of significance			
	One-tailed test			
	0.05	0.025	0.01	0.001
	Two-tailed test			
	0.1	0.05	0.02	0.002
N = 5	T ≤ 0			
6	2	0		
7	3	2	0	
8	5	3	1	
9	8	5	3	
10	11	8	5	0
11	13	10	7	1
12	17	13	9	2
13	21	17	12	4
14	25	21	15	6
15	30	25	19	8
16	35	29	23	11
17	41	34	27	14
18	47	40	32	18
19	53	46	37	21
20	60	52	43	26
21	67	58	49	30
22	75	65	55	35
23	83	73	62	40
24	91	81	69	45
25	100	89	76	51
26	110	98	84	58
27	119	107	92	64
28	130	116	101	71
29	141	125	111	78
30	151	137	120	86
31	163	147	130	94
32	175	159	140	103
33	187	170	151	112

Calculated T must be *equal* to or *less* than the table (critical) value for significance at the level shown.

Source: R. Meddis (1975b), *Statistical handbook for non-statisticians*. London: McGraw-Hill. With the kind permission of the publisher.

Table 4: Spearman's rho test

	Level of significance for two-tailed test			
	0.10	0.05	0.02	0.01
	Level of significance for one-tailed test			
	0.05	0.025	0.01	0.005
N = 4	1.000			
5	0.900	1.000	1.000	
6	0.829	0.886	0.943	1.000
7	0.714	0.786	0.893	0.929
8	0.643	0.738	0.833	0.881
9	0.600	0.700	0.783	0.833
10	0.564	0.648	0.745	0.794
11	0.536	0.618	0.709	0.755
12	0.503	0.587	0.671	0.727
13	0.484	0.560	0.648	0.703
14	0.464	0.538	0.566	0.675
15	0.443	0.521	0.604	0.654
16	0.429	0.503	0.582	0.635
17	0.414	0.485	0.566	0.615
18	0.401	0.472	0.550	0.600
19	0.391	0.460	0.535	0.584
20	0.380	0.447	0.520	0.570
21	0.370	0.435	0.508	0.556
22	0.361	0.425	0.496	0.544
23	0.353	0.415	0.486	0.532
24	0.344	0.406	0.476	0.521
25	0.337	0.398	0.466	0.511
26	0.331	0.390	0.457	0.501
27	0.324	0.382	0.448	0.491
28	0.317	0.375	0.440	0.483
29	0.312	0.368	0.433	0.475
30	0.306	0.362	0.425	0.467

For n > 30, the significance of r_s can be tested by using the formula:

$$t = r_s \sqrt{\frac{n-2}{1-r_s^2}} \quad df = n - 2$$

and checking the value of t.

Calculated r_s must *equal* or *exceed* the table (critical) value for significance at the level shown.

Source: J.H. Zhar (1972), Significance testing of the Spearman rank correlation coefficient. *Journal of the American Statistical Association, 67*, 578–580. With the kind permission of the publisher.

Table 5: Chi-squared test

	Level of significance for one-tailed test					
	0.10	0.05	0.025	0.01	0.005	0.0005
	Level of significance for two-tailed test					
df	0.20	0.10	0.05	0.02	0.01	0.001
1	1.64	2.71	3.84	5.41	6.64	10.83
2	3.22	4.60	5.99	7.82	9.21	13.82
3	4.64	6.25	7.82	9.84	11.34	16.27
4	5.99	7.78	9.49	11.67	13.28	18.46
5	7.29	9.24	11.07	13.39	15.09	20.52
6	8.56	10.64	12.59	15.03	16.81	22.46
7	9.80	12.02	14.07	16.62	18.48	24.32
8	11.03	13.36	15.51	18.17	20.09	26.12
9	12.24	14.68	16.92	19.68	21.67	27.88
10	13.44	15.99	18.31	21.16	23.21	29.59
11	14.63	17.28	19.68	22.62	24.72	31.26
12	15.81	18.55	21.03	24.05	26.22	32.91
13	16.98	19.81	22.36	25.47	27.69	34.53
14	18.15	21.06	23.68	26.87	29.14	36.12
15	19.31	22.31	25.00	28.26	30.58	37.70
16	20.46	23.54	26.30	29.63	32.00	39.29
17	21.62	24.77	27.59	31.00	33.41	40.75
18	22.76	25.99	28.87	32.35	34.80	42.31
19	23.90	27.20	30.14	33.69	36.19	43.82
20	25.04	28.41	31.41	35.02	37.57	45.32
21	26.17	29.62	32.67	36.34	38.93	46.80
22	27.30	30.81	33.92	37.66	40.29	48.27
23	28.43	32.01	35.17	38.97	41.64	49.73
24	29.55	33.20	36.42	40.27	42.98	51.18
25	30.68	34.38	37.65	41.57	44.31	52.62
26	31.80	35.56	38.88	42.86	45.64	54.05
27	32.91	36.74	40.11	44.14	46.96	55.48
28	34.03	37.92	41.34	45.42	48.28	56.89
29	35.14	39.09	42.69	46.69	49.59	58.30
30	36.25	40.26	43.77	43.49	50.89	59.70
32	38.47	42.59	46.19	50.49	53.49	62.49
34	40.68	44.90	48.60	53.00	56.06	65.25
36	42.88	47.21	51.00	55.49	58.62	67.99
38	45.08	49.51	53.38	57.97	61.16	70.70
40	47.27	51.81	55.76	60.44	63.69	73.40
44	51.64	56.37	60.48	65.34	68.71	78.75
48	55.99	60.91	65.17	70.20	73.68	84.04
52	60.33	65.42	69.83	75.02	78.62	89.27
56	64.66	69.92	74.47	79.82	83.51	94.46
60	68.97	74.40	79.08	84.58	88.38	99.61

Calculated value of χ^2 must *equal* or *exceed* the table (critical) value for significance at the level shown.

Abridged from R.A. Fisher and F. Yates (1974), *Statistical tables for biological, agricultural and medical research (6th Edn.)*. Harlow, UK: Addison Wesley Longman.

References

Abeles, R.P. (1976). Relative deprivation, rising expectations and black militancy. *Journal of Social Issues, 32*, 119–137.

Abernethy, E.M. (1940). The effect of changed environmental conditions upon the results of college examinations. *Journal of Psychology, 10*, 293–301.

Abramowitz, E.S., Baker, A.H., & Fleischer, S.F. (1982). Onset of depressive psychiatric crises and the menstrual cycle. *American Journal of Psychiatry, 139*(4), 475–478.

Abramson, L.Y., Seligman, M.E., & Teasdale, J. (1978). Learned helplessness in humans: Critique and reformulation. *Journal of Abnormal Psychology, 87*, 49–74.

Adams, E.S., & Caldwell, R.L. (1990). Deceptive communications in asymmetric fights of the stomatopod crustacean, *Gonodactylus bredini*. *Animal Behaviour, 39*, 706–716.

Adolphs, R., Damasio, H., Tranel, D., & Damasio, A.R. (1996). Cortical systems for the recognition of emotion in facial expressions. *Journal of Neuroscience, 16*, 7678–7687.

Adorno, T.W., Frenkel-Brunswik, E., Levinson, D., & Sanford, R. (1950). *The authoritarian personality*. New York: Harper.

Aglioti, S., Goodale, M.A., & DeSouza, J.F.X. (1995). Size-contrast illusions deceive the eye but not the hand. *Current Biology, 5*, 679–685.

Ainsworth, M.D.S., & Bell, S.M. (1970). Attachment, exploration and separation: Illustrated by the behaviour of one-year-olds in a strange situation. *Child Development, 41*, 49–67.

Ainsworth, M.D.S., Blehar, M.C., Waters, E., & Wall, S. (1978). *Patterns of attachment: A psychological study of the strange situation*, Hillsdale, NJ: Lawrence Erlbaum Associates Inc.

Akerstedt, T. (1977). Inversion of the sleep wakefulness pattern: Effects on circadian variations in psychophysiological activation. *Ergonomics, 20*, 459–474.

Allen, M.G. (1976). Twin studies of affective illness. *Archives of General Psychiatry, 33*, 1476–1478.

Allison, A.C. (1954, February 6). Protection afforded by sickle cell trait against subtertian malarial infection. *British Medical Journal, 290–294*.

Allison, R.B., & Schwartz, T. (1980). *Minds in many pieces: The making of a very special doctor*. New York: Rawson, Wade.

Allison, T., & Cicchetti, D.V. (1976). Sleep in mammals: Ecological and constitutional correlates. *Science, 194*, 732–734.

Allport, D.A. (1989). Visual attention. In M.I. Posner (Ed.), *Foundations of cognitive science*. Cambridge, MA: MIT Press.

Allport, D.A. (1993). Attention and control: Have we been asking the wrong questions? A critical review of twenty-five years. In D.E. Meyer & S.M. Kornblum (Eds.), *Attention and performance, Vol. XIV*. London: MIT Press.

Allport, D.A., Antonis, B., & Reynolds, P. (1972). On the division of attention: A disproof of the single channel hypothesis. *Quarterly Journal of Experimental Psychology, 24*, 225–235.

Allport, G.W. (1947). *The use of personal documents in psychological science*. London: Holt, Rinehart, & Winston.

Allport, G.W. (1954). *The nature of prejudice*. Reading, MA: Addison-Wesley.

Allport, G.W., & Pettigrew, T.F. (1957). Cultural influences on the perception of movement: The trapezoidal illusion among Zulus. *Journal of Abnormal and Social Psychology, 55*, 104–113.

Altman, I., & Taylor, D.A. (1973). *Social penetration theory: The development of interpersonal relationships*. New York: Holt, Rinehart, & Winston.

Altmeyer, B. (1998). The other "authoritarian personality". In M.P. Zanna (Ed.), *Advances in experimental social psychology, Vol. 30*. San Diego, CA: Academic Press.

Amato, P.R., Loomis, L.S., & Booth, A. (1995). Parental divorce, marital conflict, and offspring well-being during early adulthood. *Social Forces, 73*(3), 895–915.

Amato, P.R., & Rogers, S.J. (1997). A longitudinal study of marital problems and subsequent divorce. *Journal of Marriage and the Family, 59*(3), 612–624.

Ames, G.J., & Murray, F.B. (1982). When two wrongs make a right: Promoting cognitive change by social conflict. *Developmental Psychology, 18*, 894–897.

Amir, Y., & Sharon, I. (1987). Are social-psychological laws cross-culturally valid? *Journal of Cross-Cultural Psychology, 18*(4), 383–470.

Anand, B.K., & Brobeck, J.R. (1951). Hypothalamic control of food intake in rats and cats. *Yale Journal of Biological Medicine, 24*, 123–140.

Andersen, S.N., & Klatsky, R.L. (1987). Traits and stereotypes: Levels of categorisation in person perception. *Journal of Personality and Social Psychology, 53*, 235–246.

Anderson, C.A. (1989). Temperature and aggression: Unbiquitous effects of heat on occurrence of human violence. *Psychological Bulletin, 106*, 74–96.

Anderson, J.L., Crawford, C.B., Nadeau, J., & Lindberg, T. (1992). Was the Duchess of Windsor right? A cross-cultural review of the socioecology of ideals of female body shape. *Ethology and Sociobiology, 13*, 197–227.

Andersson, M. (1982). Female choice selects for extreme tail length in a widow-bird. *Nature, 299*, 818–820.

Andreeva, G. (1984). Cognitive processes in developing groups. In L.H. Strickland (Ed.), *Directions in Soviet social psychology*. New York: Springer.

Annis, R.C., & Frost, B. (1973). Human visual ecology and orientation anisotropies in acuity. *Science, 182,* 729–741.

Archer, J. (1992). Childhood gender roles: Social context and organisation. In H. McGurk (Ed.), *Childhood social development: Contemporary perspectives.* Hove, UK: Psychology Press.

Archer, R.L. (1979). Role of personality and the social situation. In G.J. Chelune (Ed.), *Self-disclosure.* San Francisco: Jossey-Bass.

Archer, S. (1982). The lower age boundaries of identity development. *Child Development, 53,* 1551–1556.

Argyle, M. (1988). Social relationships. In M. Hewstone, W. Stroebe, J.-P. Codol, & G.M. Stephenson (Eds.), *Introduction to social psychology.* Oxford, UK: Blackwell.

Argyle, M. (1994). *The psychology of interpersonal behaviour* (5th Edn.). London: Penguin.

Argyle, M., & Furnham, A. (1983). Sources of satisfaction and conflict in long-term relationships. *Journal of Marriage and the Family, 45,* 481–493.

Argyle, M., & Henderson, M. (1984). The rules of friendship. *Journal of Social and Personal Relationships, 1,* 211–237.

Argyle, M., Henderson, M., Bond, M., Iizuka, Y., & Contarello, A. (1986). Cross-cultural variations in relationship rules. *International Journal of Psychology, 21,* 287–315.

Aronoff, J. (1967). *Psychological needs and cultural systems: A case study.* Princeton, NJ: Van Nostrand.

Aronson, E., & Osherow, N. (1980). Co-operation, prosocial behaviour, and academic performance: Experiments in the desegregated classroom. In L. Bickerman (Ed.), *Applied social psychology annual.* Beverly Hills, CA: Sage.

Aronson, E., Wilson, T.D., & Akert, R.M. (1998). *Social psychology.* New York: Longman.

Arterberry, M., Yonas, A., & Bensen, A.S. (1989). Self-produced locomotion and the development of responsiveness to linear perspective and texture gradients. *Developmental Psychology, 25,* 976–982.

Asch, S.E. (1946). Forming impressions of personality. *Journal of Abnormal and Social Psychology, 41,* 258–290.

Asch, S.E. (1951). Effects of group pressure on the modification and distortion of judgements. In H. Guetzkow (Ed.), *Groups, leadership and men.* Pittsburgh, PA: Carnegie.

Asch, S.E. (1955). Opinions and social pressure. *Scientific American, 193,* 31–35.

Asch, S.E. (1956). Studies of independence and conformity: A minority of one against a unanimous majority. *Psychological Monographs, 70* (Whole no. 416).

Aserinsky, E., & Kleitman, N. (1955). Two types of ocular motility occurring in sleep. *Journal of Applied Physiology, 8,* 1–10.

Asher, S.R., Hymel, S., & Renshaw, P.D. (1984). Loneliness in children. *Child Development, 55*(4), 1456–1464.

Atchley, R. (1977). *The sociology of retirement.* Cambridge, MA: Schenkman.

Atchley, R.C. (1982). The process of retirement: The female experience. In M. Szinovacz (Ed.), *Women's retirement.* Beverly Hills, CA: Sage Publications.

Atkinson, R.C., & Shiffrin, R.M. (1968). Human memory: A proposed system and its control processes. In K.W. Spence & J.T. Spence (Eds.), *The psychology of learning and motivation, Vol. 2.* London: Academic Press.

Atkinson, R.L., Atkinson, R.C., Smith, E.E., & Bem, D.J. (1993). *Introduction to psychology* (11th Edn.). New York: Harcourt Brace College Publishers.

Attwood, M.E., & Polson, P.G. (1976). A process model for water jug problems. *Memory and Cognition, 8,* 191–216.

Aubry, T., Tefft, B., & Kingsbury, N. (1990). Behavioural and psychological consequences of unemployment in blue-collar couples. *Journal of Community Psychology, 18,* 99–109.

Ax, A.F. (1953). The physiological differentiation between fear and anger in humans. *Psychosomatic Medicine, 15,* 433–442.

Axelrod, R. (1984). *The evolution of cooperation.* New York: Basic Books.

Axelrod, R., & Hamilton, W.D. (1981). The evolution of cooperation. *Science, 211,* 1390–1396.

Ayllon, T., & Azrin, N.H. (1968). *The token economy: A motivational system for therapy and rehabilitation.* New York: Appleton-Century-Crofts.

Baars, B.J. (1997). Consciousness versus attention, perception, and working memory. *Consciousness and Cognition, 5,* 363–371.

Baerends, G.P. (1941). Fortpflanzungsverhalten und orientierung der Grabwaspe *Ammophilia camperstris. Jur. Tijdscher. Ent. Deel., 84,* 268–275.

Baghdoyan, H.A., Spotts, J.L., & Snyder, S.G. (1993). Simultaneous pontine and basal forebrain microinjections of carbachol suppress REM sleep. *Journal of Neuroscience, 13,* 229–242.

Bagley, C., & Verma, G.K. (1979). *Racial prejudice: The individual and society.* Farnborough, UK: Saxon House.

Bahrick, H.P., Bahrick, P.O., & Wittinger, R.P. (1975). Fifty years of memory for names and faces: A cross-sectional approach. *Journal of Experimental Psychology: General, 104,* 54–75.

Baillargeon, R., & Graber, M. (1988). Evidence of location memory in 8-month-old infants in a nonsearch AB task. *Developmental Psychology, 24,* 502–511.

Baker, R.R. (1978). *The evolutionary ecology of animal migration.* New York: Holmes & Meier Publishers.

Baker, R.R. (1987). Human navigation and magnoreception: The Manchester experiments do replicate. *Animal Behaviour, 35,* 691–704.

Ball, P., Giles, H., & Hewstone, M. (1984). Second language acquisition: The intergroup theory with catastrophic dimensions. In H. Tajfel (Ed.), *The social dimension: European developments in social psychology, Vol. 2.* Cambridge, UK: Cambridge University Press.

Baltes, P.B., & Baltes, M.M. (Eds.). (1990). *Successful aging: Perspectives from the behavioural sciences.* Cambridge, UK: Cambridge University.

Bandura, A. (1965). Influences of models' reinforcement contingencies on the acquisition of initiative responses. *Journal of Personality and Social Psychology, 1,* 589–593.

Bandura, A. (1973). *Aggression: A social learning analysis.* Englewood Cliffs, NJ: Prentice-Hall.

Bandura, A. (1977). Self-efficacy: Toward a unifying theory of behavioural change. *Psychological Review, 84,* 191–215.

Bandura, A. (1986). *Social foundations of thought and action: A social cognitive theory.* Englewood Cliffs, NJ: Prentice-Hall.

Bandura, A., Blanchard, E., & Ritter, B. (1969) Relative efficacy of desensitization and modeling approaches for inducing behavioural, affective and attitudinal changes. *Journal of Personality and Social Psychology, 13,* 173–199.

Bandura, A., & Cervone, D. (1983). Self-evaluation and self-efficacy mechanisms governing the motivational effect of goal systems. *Journal of Personality and Social Psychology, 45,* 1017–1028.

Bandura, A., & McDonald, F.J. (1963). The influence of social reinforcement and the behaviour of models in shaping children's moral judgements. *Journal of Abnormal and Social Psychology, 67,* 274–281.

Bandura, A., Ross, D., & Ross, S.A. (1961). Transmission of aggression through imitation of aggressive models. *Journal of Abnormal and Social Psychology, 63,* 575–582.

Bandura, A., Ross, D., & Ross, S.A. (1963). Transmission of aggression through imitation of aggressive models. *Journal of Abnormal and Social Psychology, 66,* 3–11.

Banks, M.S., Aslin, R.N., & Weiskopf, S. (1975). Sensitive period for the development of human binocular vision. *Science, 190,* 675–677.

Banyard, P., & Hayes, N. (1994). *Psychology: Theory and application.* London: Chapman & Hall.

Baran, S.J. (1979). Television drama as a facilitator of pro-social behaviour. *Journal of Broadcasting, 23,* 277–285.

Barber, J.P., & DeRubeis, R.J. (1989). On second thought: Where the action is in cognitive therapy for depression. *Cognitive Therapy and Research, 13,* 441–457.

Bard, P. (1929). The central representation of the sympathetic system. *Archives of Neurology and Psychiatry, 22,* 230–246.

Barkley, R.A., Ullman, D.G., Otto, L., & Brecht, J.M. (1977). The effects of sex typing and sex appropriateness of modelled behaviour on children's imitation. *Child Development, 48,* 721–725.

Barlow, D.H., & Durand, V.M. (1995). *Abnormal psychology: An integrative approach.* New York: Brooks/Cole.

Barnier, G. (1989). L'effet-tuteur dans des situations mettant en jeu des rapports spatiaux chez des enfants de 7–8 ans en interactions dyadiques avec des pairs de 6 –7 ans. *European Journal of Psychology of Education, 4,* 385–399.

Baron, R.A. (1977). *Human aggression.* New York: Plenum.

Baron, R.A., & Bell, P.A. (1976). Aggression and heat: The influence of ambient temperature, negative affect, and a cooling drink on physical aggression. *Journal of Personality and Social Psychology, 33,* 245–255.

Baron, R.A., & Byrne, D. (1991). *Social psychology: Understanding human interaction* (6th Edn.). Boston: Allyn & Bacon.

Baron, R.A., & Ransberger, V.M. (1978). Ambient temperature and the occurrence of collective violence: The "long hot summer" revisited. *Journal of Personality and Social Psychology, 36,* 351–360.

Baron, R.A., & Richardson, D.R. (1993). *Human aggression* (2nd Edn.). New York: Plenum.

Baron-Cohen, S., Leslie, A.M., & Frith, U. (1985). Does the autistic child have a "theory of mind"? *Cognition, 21,* 37–46.

Barrett, J.E. (1979). The relationship of life events to the onset of neurotic disorders. In J.E. Barrett (Ed.), *Stress and mental disorder.* New York: Raven Press.

Barry, H., Bacon, M.K., & Child, I.L. (1957). A cross-cultural survey of some sex differences in socialisation. *Journal of Abnormal and Social Psychology, 55,* 327–332.

Bartlett, F.C. (1932). *Remembering: A study in experimental and social psychology.* Cambridge, UK: Cambridge University Press.

Bastion, J. (1967). The transmission of arbitrary environmental information between bottlenose dolphins. In R.G. Busnel (Ed.), *Animal sonar systems, Vol. II.* Jouy-en-Josas, France: Laboratoire de Physiologie Acoustique.

Bateson, G., Jackson, D.D., Haley, J., & Weakland, J. (1956). Toward a theory of schizophrenia. *Behavioral Science, 1,* 251–264.

Bateson, P. (1986). When to experiment on animals. *New Scientist, 109,* 30–32.

Batson, C.D. (1983). Sociobiology and the role of religion in promoting prosocial behaviour: An alternative view. *Journal of Personality and Social Psychology, 45,* 1380–1385.

Batson, C.D. (1987). Prosocial motivation: Is it ever truly altruistic? In L. Berkowitz (Ed.), *Advances in experimental social psychology, Vol. 20.* New York: Academic Press.

Batson, C.D., Batson, J.G., Slingsby, J.K., Harrell, K.L., Peekna, H.M., & Todd, R.M. (1991). Empathic joy and the empathy-altruism hypothesis. *Journal of Personality and Social Psychology, 61,* 413–426.

Batson, C.D., Cochrane, P.J., Biederman, M.F., Blosser, J.L., Ryan, M.J., & Vogt, B. (1978). Failure to help when in a hurry: Callousness or conflict? *Personality and Social Psychology Bulletin, 4,* 97–101.

Batson, C.D., Duncan, B.D., Ackerman, P., Buckley, T., & Birch, K. (1981). Is empathic emotion a source of altruistic motivation? *Journal of Personality and Social Psychology, 40,* 290–302.

Batson, C.D., Dyck, J.L., Brandt, J.R., Batson, J.G., Powell, A.L., McMaster, M.R., & Griffit, C. (1988). Five studies testing new egotistic alternatives to the empathy-altruism hypothesis. *Journal of Personality and Social Psychology, 55,* 52–77.

Batson, C.D., & Oleson, K.C. (1991). Current status of the empathy-altruism hypothesis. In M.S. Clark (Ed.), *Review of personality and social psychology, Vol. 12: Prosocial behaviour.* Newbury Park, CA: Sage.

Batson, C.D., O'Quinn, K., Fultz, J., Vanderplas, N., & Isen, A.M. (1983). Influence of self-reported distress and empathy on egoistic versus altruistic motivation to help. *Journal of Personality and Social Psychology, 45,* 706–718.

Beason, R.C. (1989). *Magnetic sensitivity and orientation in the bobolink.* Paper presented at the Royal Institute of Navigation.

Beck, A.T. (1967). *Depression: Clinical, experimental, and theoretical aspects.* New York: Hoeber.

Beck, A.T. (1976). *Cognitive therapy of the emotional disorders.* New York: New American Library.

Beck, A.T., & Clark, D.A. (1988). Anxiety and depression: An information processing perspective. *Anxiety Research, 1,* 23–36.

Beck, A.T., & Emery, G. (1985). *Anxiety disorders and phobias.* New York: Basic Books.

Beck, A.T., Rush, A.J., Shaw, B.F., & Emery, G. (1979). *Cognitive therapy of depression.* New York: Guilford Press.

Beck, A.T., & Ward, C.H. (1961). Dreams of depressed patients: Characteristic themes in manifest content. *Archives of General Psychiatry, 5,* 462–467.

Beck, A.T., & Weishaar, M.E. (1989). Cognitive therapy. In R.J. Corsini & D. Wedding (Eds.), *Current psychotherapies.* Itacca, IL: Peacock.

Beck, I.L., & Carpenter, P.A. (1986). Cognitive approaches to understanding reading. *American Psychologist, 41,* 1088–1105.

Bee, H. (1994). *Lifespan development.* New York: HarperCollins.

Bee, H. (1995). *The developing child* (7th Edn.). London: HarperCollins.

Bee, H.L., & Mitchell, S.K. (1984). *The developing person: A life-span approach* (2nd Edn.). New York: Harper & Row.

Behrend, D.A., Harris, L.L., & Cartwright, K.B. (1992). Morphological cues to verb meaning: Verb inflections and the initial mapping of verb meanings. *Journal of Child Language, 22,* 89–106.

Bellack, A.S., & Hersen, M. (1980). *Introduction to clinical psychology.* New York: Oxford University Press.

Bellrose, F.C. (1958). Celestial orientation in wild mallards. *Bird Banding, 29,* 75–90.

Bem, S., & Keijzer, F. (1996). Recent changes in the concept of cognition. *Theory and Psychology, 6*(3), 449–469.

Bem, S.L. (1974). The measurement of psychological androgyny. *Journal of Consulting and Clinical Psychology, 42,* 155–162.

Bem, S.L. (1993). Is there a place in psychology for a feminist analysis of the social context? *Feminism and Psychology, 3*(2), 230–234.

Bem, S.L. (1994, August 17). In a male-centered world, female differences are transformed into female disadvantages. *Chronicle of Higher Education,* B1–B3.

Benderly, B.L. (1980). The great ape debate. *Science, 174,* 1139–1141.

Bennett-Levy, J., & Marteau, T. (1984). Fear of animals: What is prepared? *British Journal of Psychology, 75,* 37–42.

Bentley, E. (2000). *Awareness.* London: Routledge.

Bergen, D.J., & Williams, J.E. (1991). Sex stereotypes in the United States revisited. *Sex Roles, 24*, 413–423.

Bergin, A.E. (1971). The evaluation of therapeutic outcomes. In A.E. Bergin & S.L. Garfield (Eds.), *Handbook of psychotherapy and behaviour change*. New York: Wiley.

Berk, L.E. (1994). Why children talk to themselves. *Scientific American, November*, 60–65.

Berko, J. (1958). The child's learning of English morphology. *Word, 14*, 150–177.

Berkowitz, L. (1968). Impulse, aggression and the gun. *Psychology Today*, September, 18–22.

Berkowitz, L. (1989). Frustration–aggression hypothesis: Examination and reformulation. *Psychological Bulletin, 106*, 59–73.

Berkowitz, L., & LePage, A. (1967). Weapons as aggression-eliciting stimuli. *Journal of Personality and Social Psychology, 7*, 202–207.

Bermond, B., Nieuwenhuyse, B., Fasotti, L., & Schwerman, J. (1991). Spinal cord lesions, peripheral feedback, and intensities of emotional feelings. *Cognition and Emotion, 5*, 201–220.

Berndt, R., & Sternberg, H. (1969). Alters und Geschlechtsunterschiede in der dispersion des Trauerschnappers *(Ficedula hypoleuca). Journal Ornithologie, 110*, 22–26.

Berndt, T.J. (1979). Developmental changes in conformity to peers and parents. *Developmental Psychology, 15*, 608–616.

Bernstein, B. (1961). Social class and linguistic development. In A.H. Halsey, J. Flaud, & C.A. Anderson (Eds.), *Education, economy and society*. London: Collier-Macmillan.

Bernstein, B. (1970). Social class, language and socialisation. In P.P. Giglioli (1972, Ed.), *Language and social context*. Harmondsworth, UK: Penguin Books.

Bernstein, B. (1973). *Class, codes and control*. London: Paladin.

Bernstein, R.L., & Gaw, A.C. (1990). Koro: Proposed classification for DSM-IV. *American Journal of Psychiatry, 147*(12), 1670–1674.

Berry, D.C., & Broadbent, D.E. (1984). On the relationship between task performance and associated verbalisable knowledge. *Quarterly Journal of Experimental Psychology, 36A*, 209–231.

Berry, D.T.R., & Webb, W.B. (1983). State measures and sleep stages. *Psychological Reports, 52*, 807–812.

Berry, J.W. (1969). On cross-cultural comparability. *International Journal of Psychology, 4*, 119–128.

Berry, J.W. (1974). Radical cultural relativism and the concept of intelligence. In J.W. Berry & P.R. Dasen (Eds.), *Culture and cognition: Readings in cross-cultural psychology*. London: Methuen.

Berry, J.W. (1997). Acculturation strategies. In A. Baum, S. Newman, J. Weinman, R. West, & C. McManus (Eds.), *Cambridge handbook of psychology, health, and medicine*. Cambridge, UK: Cambridge University Press.

Berry, J.W., Poortinga, Y.H., Segall, M.H., & Dasen, P.R. (1992). *Cross-cultural psychology*. Cambridge, UK: Cambridge University Press.

Bersheid, E., & Walster, E.H. (1978). *Interpersonal attraction* (2nd Edn.). Reading, MA: Addison-Wesley.

Bertelsen, B., Harvald, B., & Hauge, M. (1977). A Danish twin study of manic-depressive disorders. *British Journal of Psychiatry, 130*, 330–351.

Berthold, P., Wiltschko, W., Miltenberger, H., & Querner, W. (1990). Genetic transmission of migratory behaviour into a non-migrating population. *Experientia, 46*, 107–108.

Biederman, I. (1987). Recognition-by-components: A theory of human image understanding. *Psychological Review, 94*, 115–147.

Biederman, I., Glass, A.L., & Stacy, E.W. (1973). Searching for objects in real-world scenes. *Journal of Experimental Psychology, 97*, 22–27.

Biederman, I., Ju, G., & Clapper, J. (1985). *The perception of partial objects*. Unpublished manuscript, State University of New York at Buffalo.

Bifulco, A., Harris, T., & Brown, G.W. (1992). Mourning or early inadequate care? Re-examining the relationship of maternal loss in childhood with adult depression and anxiety. *Development and Psychopathology, 4*, 433–449.

Billig, M. (1976). *Social psychology and intergroup relations*. London: Academic Press.

Billig, M., & Tajfel, H. (1973). Social categorisation and similarity in intergroup behaviour. *European Journal of Social Psychology, 3*, 27–52.

Bingman, V.P., & Mench, J.A. (1990). Homing behaviour of hippocampus and parahippocampus lesioned pigeons following short-distance releases. *Behavioural Brain Research, 40*, 227–238.

Birch, H.G. (1945). The relationship of previous experience to insightful problem solving. *Journal of Comparative Psychology, 38*, 267–283.

Birren, J.E., Butler, R.N., Greenhouse, S.W., Sokoloff, L., & Yarrow, M.R. (Eds.). (1963). *Human ageing: A biological and behavioural study* [Publication number 71-9051]. London: Her Majesty's Stationery Office.

Blake, M.J.F. (1967). Time of day effects on performance on a range of tasks. *Psychonomic Science, 9*, 349–350.

Blake, W. (1973). The influence of race on diagnosis. *Smith College Studies in Social Work, 43*, 184–192.

Blakemore, C. (1988). *The mind machine*. London: BBC Publications.

Blakemore, C., & Cooper, G.F. (1970). Development of the brain depends on the visual environment. *Nature, 228*, 477–478.

Blasdel, G.G. (1992). Orientation selectivity, preference, and continuity in monkey striate cortex. *Journal of Neuroscience, 12*, 3139–3161.

Blasi, A. (1980). Bridging moral cognition and moral action: A critical review of the literature. *Psychological Bulletin, 88*, 1–45.

Bloom, J.W. (1998). The ethical practice of web counseling. *British Journal of Guidance and Counselling, 26*(1), 53–59.

Blumenthal, M., Kahn, R.L., Andrews, F.M., & Head, K.B. (1972). *Justifying violence: The attitudes of American men*. Ann Arbor, MI: Institute for Social Research.

Blumstein, P., & Schwartz, P. (1983). *American couples: Money, work, sex*. New York: Morrow.

Bodenhausen, G.V. (1988). Stereotypic biases in social decision making: Testing process models of stereotype use. *Journal of Personality and Social Psychology, 55*, 726–737.

Boesch, C. (1991). Teaching among wild chimpanzees. *Animal Behaviour, 41A*, 530–532.

Bohannon, J.N., & Warren-Leubecker, A. (1989). Theoretical approaches to language acquisition. In J.B. Gleason (Ed.), *The development of language*. Columbus, OH: Merrill.

Bohannon, P. (1970). *Divorce and after*. New York: Doubleday.

Bond, S., & Cash, T.F. (1992). Black beauty: Skin colour and body images among African-American college women. *Journal of Applied Social Psychology, 22*, 874–888.

Bonvillain, N. (1999). *Language, culture, and communication: The meaning of messages*. Engelwood Cliffs, NJ: Prentice-Hall.

Bootzin, R., Alloy, L.B., & Acocella, J.R. (1993). *Abnormal psychology: Current perspectives*. New York: McGraw-Hill.

Boring, E.G. (1957). *A history of experimental psychology* (2nd Edn.). New York: Appleton-Century-Crofts.

Bossard, J. (1932). Residential propinquity as a factor in marriage selection. *American Journal of Sociology, 38*, 219–224

Bouchard, T.J., Lykken, D.T., McGue, M., Segal, N.L., & Tellegen, A. (1990). Sources of human psychological differences: The Minnesota study of twins reared apart. *Science, 250,* 223–228.

Bouchard, T.J., & McGue, M. (1981). Familial studies of intelligence: A review. *Science, 212,* 1055–1059.

Bourhis, R.Y., & Giles, H. (1977). The language of intergroup distinctiveness. In H. Giles (Ed.), *Language, ethnicity and intergroup relations* (pp. 119–135). London: Academic Press.

Bourhis, R.Y., Giles, H., & Lambert, W.E. (1975). Social consequences of accommodating one's style of speech: A cross-national investigation. *International Journal of the Sociology of Language, 6,* 55–72.

Bourke, P.A., Duncan, J., & Nimmo-Smith, I. (1996). A general factor involved in dual-task performance decrement. *Quarterly Journal of Experimental Psychology, 49A,* 525–545.

Bower, T.G.R. (1966). The visual world of infants. *Scientific American, 215,* 80–92.

Bower, T.G.R. (1979). *Human development.* San Francisco: W.H. Freeman.

Bower, T.G.R. (1982). *Development in infancy* (2nd Edn.). San Francisco: W.H. Freeman.

Bower, T.G.R., Broughton, J.M., & Moore, M.K. (1970). The co-ordination of visual and tactual input in infants. *Perception and Psychophysics, 8,* 51–53.

Bower, T.G.R., & Wishart, J.G. (1972). The effects of motor skill on object permanence. *Cognition, 1,* 165–172.

Bowlby, J. (1969). *Attachment and love: Vol. 1. Attachment.* London: Hogarth.

Bowlby, J. (1973). *Attachment and loss: Vol. 3.* Harmondsworth, UK: Penguin.

Boycott, B.B. (1965). Learning in the octopus. *Scientific American, 212,* 42–50.

Bradbard, M.R., Martin, C.L., Endsley, R.C., & Halverson, C.F. (1986). Influence of sex stereotypes on children's exploration and memory: A competence versus performance distinction. *Developmental Psychology, 22,* 481–486.

Bradburn, N. (1969). *The structure of psychological well-being.* Chicago: Aldine.

Bradshaw, J.L., & Sherlock, D. (1982). Bugs and faces in the two visual fields: The analytic/holistic processing dichotomy and task sequencing. *Cortex, 18,* 211–226.

Bradshaw, J.L., & Wallace, G. (1971). Models for the processing and identification of faces. *Perception and Psychophysics, 9,* 443–448.

Braine, M.D.S. (1963). The ontogeny of English phrase structure: The first phase. *Language, 39,* 1–13.

Brainerd, C.J. (1983). Modifiability of cognitive development. In S. Meadows (Ed.), *Developing thinking: Approaches to children's cognitive development.* London: Methuen.

Brandsma, J.M., Maultsby, M.C., & Welsh, R. (1978). Self-help techniques in the treatment of alcoholism. Cited in G.T. Wilson & K.D. O'Leary, *Principles of behaviour therapy.* Englewood Cliffs, NJ: Prentice-Hall.

Breger, L., Hunter, I., & Lane, R.W. (1971). The effect of stress on dreams. *Psychological Issues, 7,* 1–213.

Brehm, S.S. (1992). *Intimate relationships* (2nd Edn.). New York: McGraw-Hill.

Breland, K., & Breland, M. (1961). The misbehaviour of organisms. *American Psychologist, 61,* 681–684.

Brewer, M.B., & Miller, N. (1984). Beyond the contact hypothesis: Theoretical perspectives on desegregation. In N. Miller & M.B. Brewer (Eds.), *Groups in contact: The psychology of desegregation.* Orlando, FL: Academic Press.

Brickman, P., Rabinowitz, V.C., Karuza, J., Coates, D., Cohn, E., & Kidder, L. (1982). Models of helping and coping. *American Psychologist, 37,* 368–384.

Brigham, J.C. (1971). Ethnic stereotypes. *Psychological Bulletin, 76,* 15–38.

Bright, M. (1984). *Animal language.* London: BBC Publications.

Brinkman, C. (1984). Supplementary motor area of the monkey's cerebral cortex: Short- and long-term deficits after unilateral ablation and the effects of subsequent callosal section. *Journal of Neuroscience, 4,* 918–929.

Broadbent, D.E. (1958). *Perception and communication.* Oxford, UK: Pergamon.

Broadbent, D.E. (1961). *Behaviour.* London: Eyre & Spottiswoode.

Broadbent, D.E. (1982). Task combination and selective intake of information. *Acta Psychologica, 50,* 253–290.

Broca, P. (1861). Remarques sur le siège de la faculté du langage articulé suiées d'une observation d'aphémie. *Bulletin de la Société Anatomique, 6,* 330–357.

Brodbar-Nemzer, J.Y. (1986). Divorce and group commitment: The case of the Jews. *Journal of Marriage and the Family, 48,* 329–340.

Brody, G.H., & Shaffer, D.R. (1982). Contributions of parents and peers to children's moral socialisation. *Developmental Review, 2,* 31–75.

Broverman, I.K., Broverman, D.M., Clarkson, F.E., Rosencrantz, P.S., & Vogel, S.R. (1981). Sex role stereotypes and clinical judgements of mental health. In E. Howell & M. Bayes (Eds.), *Women and mental health.* New York: Basic Books.

Brown, G.W. (1989). Depression. In G.W. Brown & T.O. Harris (Eds.), *Life events and illness.* New York: Guilford Press.

Brown, G.W., & Harris, T. (1978). *Social origins of depression.* London: Tavistock.

Brown, G.W., & Harris, T. (1982). Fall-off in the reporting of life events. *Social Psychiatry, 17,* 23.

Brown, J.S., & Burton, R.D. (1978). Diagnostic model for procedural bugs in basic mathematical skills. *Cognitive Science, 2,* 155–192.

Brown, R. (1973). *A first language: The early stages.* London: George Allen & Unwin.

Brown, R. (1978). Divided we fall: An analysis of relations between sections of a factory work-force. In H. Tajfel (Ed.), *Differentiation between social groups: Studies in the social psychology of intergroup relations.* London: Academic Press.

Brown, R. (1986). *Social psychology* (2nd Edn.). New York: The Free Press.

Brown, R. (1988). Intergroup relations. In M. Hewstone, W. Stroebe, J.P. Codol, & G.M. Stephenson (Eds.), *Introduction to social psychology.* Oxford, UK: Blackwell.

Brown, R. (1996). Intergroup relations. In M. Hewstone, W. Stroebe, & G.M. Stephenson (Eds.), *Introduction to social psychology* (2nd Edn.). Oxford, UK: Blackwell.

Brown, R., Cazden, C., & Bellugi, U. (1969). The child's grammar from I to III. In J.P. Hill (Ed.), *Minnesota symposium on child psychology, Vol. 2.* Minneapolis, MI: University of Minnesota Press.

Brown, R.C., & Tedeschi, J.T. (1976). Determinants of perceived aggression. *Journal of Social Psychology, 100,* 77–87.

Brown, R.J., & Wade, G.S. (1987). Superordinate goals and intergroup behaviour. In J.C. Turner & H. Giles (Eds.), *Intergroup behaviour.* Oxford, UK: Blackwell.

Bruce, M.L., Takeuchi, D.T., & Leaf, P.J. (1991). Poverty and psychiatric status: Longitudinal evidence from the New Haven Epidemiologic Catchment Area Study. *Archives of General Psychiatry, 48,* 470–474.

Bruce, V., Green, P.R., & Georgeson, M.A. (1996). *Visual perception: Physiology, psychology, and ecology* (3rd Edn.). Hove, UK: Psychology Press.

Bruce, V., & Valentine, T. (1986). Semantic priming of familiar faces. *Quarterly Journal of Experimental Psychology, 38A,* 125–150.

Bruce, V., & Valentine, T. (1988). When a nod's as good as a wink: The role of dynamic information in face recognition. In M.M. Gruneberg, P.E. Morris, & R.N. Sykes (Eds.), *Practical aspects of memory: Current research and issues (Vol. 1).* Chichester, UK: John Wiley.

Bruce, V., & Young, A.W. (1986). Understanding face recognition. *British Journal of Psychology, 77*, 305–327.

Bruner, J.S. (1983). *Child's talk*. New York: Norton.

Bruner, J.S., & Minturn, A.L. (1955). Perceptual identification and perceptual organisation. *Journal of General Psychology, 53*, 21–28.

Bruner, J.S., Olver, R.R., & Greenfield, P.M. (1966). *Studies in cognitive growth*. New York: Wiley.

Bruner, J.S., Postman, L., & Rodrigues, J. (1951). Expectations and the perception of colour. *American Journal of Psychology, 64*, 216–227.

Bruner, J.S., & Tagiuri, R. (1954). The perception of people. In G. Lindzey (Ed.), *Handbook of social psychology* (pp. 634–654). Reading, MA: Addision-Wesley.

Brunner, H.G., Nelen, M., Breakefield, X.O., Ropers, H.H., et al. (1993). Abnormal behavior associated with a point mutation in the structural gene for monoamine oxidase. *Science, 262*(5133), 578–580.

Bruno, N., & Cutting, J.E. (1988). Mini-modularity and the perception of layout. *Journal of Experimental Psychology: General, 117*, 161–170.

Bryan, J.H., & Test, M.A. (1967). Models and helping: Naturalistic studies inhelping behaviour. *Journal of Personality and Social Psychology, 6*, 400–407.

Buchsbaum, M.S., Kessler, R., King, A., Johnson, J., & Cappelletti, J. (1984). Simultaneous cerebral glucography with positron emission tomography and topographic electroencephalography. In G. Pfurtscheller, E.J. Jonkman, & F. H. Lopes da Silva (Eds.), *Brain ischemia: Quantitative EEG and imaging techniques*. Amsterdam: Elsevier.

Bugelski, B.R., & Alampay, D.A. (1961). The role of frequency in developing perceptual sets. *Canadian Journal of Psychology, 15*, 205–211.

Buhrmester, D. (1992). The developmental courses of sibling and peer relationships. In F. Boer & J. Dunn (Eds.), *Children's sibling relationships: Developmental and clinical issues*. Hillsdale, NJ: Lawrence Erlbaum Associates Inc.

Burgess, R.L., & Wallin, P. (1953). Marital happiness of parents and their children's attitudes to them. *American Sociological Review, 18*, 424–431.

Burghardt, G.M. (1970). Defining "communication". In J.W. Johnston, D.G. Moulton, & A. Turk (Eds.), *Communication by chemical signals*. New York: Appleton-Century-Crofts.

Burns, A. (1998). Pop psychology or Ken behaving badly. *The Psychologist, 11*(7), 360.

Burns, G.L., & Farina, A. (1992). The role of physical attractiveness in adjustment. *Genetic, Social, and General Psychology Monographs, 118*, 157–194.

Burns, J. (1993). Invisible women—women who have learning disabilities. *The Psychologist, 6*, 102–105.

Burns, R.B. (1966). Age and mental ability: Re-testing with thirty-three years' interval. *British Journal of Educational Psychology, 36*, 116.

Burnstein, E., Crandall, C., & Kitayama, S. (1994). Some neo-Darwinian roles for altruism: Weighing cues for inclusive fitness as function of the biological importance of the decision. *Journal of Personality and Social Psychology, 67*, 773–789.

Burr, V. (1997). Social constructionism and psychology. *The New Psychologist, April*, 7–12.

Burt, C. (1955). The evidence for the concept of intelligence. *British Journal of Psychology, 25*, 158–177.

Burt de Perera, T., & Guilford, T. (1999). The social transmission of spatial information in homing pigeons. *Animal Behaviour, 57*(3), 715–719.

Burton, A.M., & Bruce, V. (1993). Naming faces and naming names: Exploring an interactive activation model of person recognition. *Memory, 1*, 457–480.

Burton, R.V. (1976). Honesty and dishonesty. In T. Lickona (Ed.), *Moral development and behaviour*. New York: Holt, Rinehart & Winston.

Bury, M., & Holme, A. (1991). *Life after ninety*. London: Routledge.

Buss, D.M. (1989). Sex differences in human mate preferences: Evolutionary hypotheses tested in 37 cultures. *Behavioral and Brain Sciences, 12*, 1–49.

Buss, D.M., Larsen, R.J., Westen, D., & Semmelroth, J. (1992). Sex differences in jealousy: Evolution, physiology and psychology. *Psychological Science, 3*, 251–255.

Butterworth, G.E., & Cicchetti, D. (1978). Visual calibration of posture in normal and Down's syndrome infants. *Perception, 5*, 155–160.

Buunk, B.P. (1996). Affiliation, attraction and close relationships. In M. Hewstone, W. Stroebe, & G.M. Stephenson (Eds.), *Introduction to social psychology* (2nd Edn.). Oxford, UK: Blackwell.

Buunk, B.P., & VanYperen, N.W. (1991). Referential comparisons, relational comparisons and exchange orientation: Their relation to marital satisfaction. *Personality and Social Psychology Bulletin, 17*, 710–718.

Byrne, D. (1971). *The attraction paradigm*. New York: Academic Press.

Byrne, D., London, O., & Griffit, W. (1968). The effect of topic importance and attitude similarity–dissimilarity on attraction in an intrastranger design. *Psychonomic Science, 11*, 303–313.

Calhoun, J.B. (1962). Population density and social pathology. *Scientific American, February*, 206.

Campbell, S.S., & Murphy, P.J. (1998). Extraocular circadian phototransduction in humans. *Science, 279*(5349), 396–399.

Campfield, L.A., & Smith, F.J. (1990). Systemic factors in the control of food intake: Evidence for patterns as signals. In E.M. Stricker (Ed.), *Handbook of behavioral neurobiology: Vol. 10. Neurobiology of food and fluid intake*. New York: Plenum.

Campos, J.J., Hiatt, S., Ramsay, D., Henderson, C., & Svejda, M. (1978). The emergence of fear on the visual cliff. In M. Lewis & L.A. Rosenblum (Eds.), *The development of affect*. New York: Plenum Press.

Cannon, W.B. (1929). *Bodily changes in pain, hunger, fear and rage*. New York: Appleton-Century-Crofts.

Cannon, W.B., & Washburn, A.L. (1912). An explanation of hunger. *American Journal of Psychology, 29*, 441–454.

Capron, C., & Duyne, M. (1989). Assessment of effects of socio-economic status on IQ in a full cross-fostering study. *Nature, 340*, 552–554.

Carlson, N.R. (1994). *Physiology of behavior* (5th Edn.). Boston: Allyn & Bacon.

Carmichael, L.C., Hogan, H.P., & Walters, A.A. (1932). An experimental study of the effect of language on the reproduction of visually perceived form. *Journal of Experimental Psychology, 15*, 73–86.

Caro, T.M. (1980). Predatory behaviour in domestic cat mothers. *Behaviour, 74*, 128–148.

Caron, A.J., Caron, R.F., & Carlson, V.R. (1979). Infant perception of the invariant shape of objects varying in slant. *Child Development, 50*, 716–721.

Carpenter, R.H.S., & Blakemore, C. (1973). Interactions between orientations in human vision. *Experimental Brain Research, 18*, 287–303.

Carroll, B.J., Feinberg, M., Greden, J.F., Haskett, R.F., James, N.M., Steiner, M., & Tarika, J. (1980). Diagnosis of endogenous depression: Comparison of clinical, research, and neuroendocrine criteria. *Journal of Affective Disorders, 2*, 177–194.

Carroll, J.B., & Casagrande, J.B. (1958). The function of language classifications in behaviour. In E.E. Maccoby, T.M. Newcombe, & E. L. Hartley (Eds.), *Readings in social psychology* (3rd Edn.). Boston: Allyn & Bacon.

Cartwright, D.S. (1979). *Theories and models of personality*. Dubuque, IO: Brown Company.

Cartwright, J. (2000). *Evolution and human behaviour: Darwinian perspectives on human nature*. London: Macmillan.

Cartwright, J. (2001). *Evolutionary explanations of human behaviour*. London: Routledge.

Cartwright, R. (1984). Broken dreams: A study on the effects of divorce and separation on dream content. *Journal for the Study of Interpersonal Processes, 47*, 51–59.

Carugati, F. (1990). Everyday ideas, theoretical models and social representations: The case of intelligence and its development. In G.R. Semin & K.J. Gergen (Eds.), *Everyday understanding: Social and scientific implications*. London: Sage.

Case, R. (1974). Structures and strictures: Some functional limitations on the course of cognitive growth. *Cognitive Psychology, 6*, 544–573.

Case, R. (1985). *Intellectual development*. Orlando, FL: Academic Press.

Case, R. (1992). Neo-Piagetian theories of intellectual development. In H. Beilin & P.B. Pufall (Eds.), *Piaget's theory: Prospects and possibilities*. Hillsdale, NJ: Lawrence Erlbaum Associates Inc.

Cattell, R.B. (1963). Theory of fluid and crystallised intelligence: A critical experiment. *Journal of Educational Psychology, 54*, 1–22.

Cave, C.B., & Kosslyn, S.M. (1993). The role of parts and spatial relations in object identification. *Perception, 22*, 229–248.

Ceci, S.J. (1991). How much does schooling influence general intelligence and its cognitive components? A reassessment of the evidence. *Developmental Psychology, 27*, 703–722.

Ceci, S.J., Peters, D., & Plotkin, J. (1985). Human subjects review, personal values and the regulation of social science research. *American Psychologist, 40*, 994–1002.

Chadda, R.K., & Ahuja, N. (1990). Dhat syndrome: A sex neurosis of the Indian subcontinent. *British Journal of Psychiatry, 156*, 577–579.

Chapman, L.J. (1967). Illusory correlation in observational report. *Journal of Verbal Learning and Verbal Behaviour, 6*, 151–155.

Central Statistical Office. (1996). *Social trends*. London: Author.

Charlton, A. (1998, January 12). TV violence has little impact on children, study finds. *The Times*, p.5.

Cheney, D.L., & Seyfarth, R.M. (1990). *How monkeys see the world*. Chicago: University of Chicago Press.

Cheng, P.W. (1985). Restructuring versus automaticity: Alternative accounts of skills acquisition. *Psychological Review, 92*, 414–423.

Cherry, E.C. (1953). Some experiments on the recognition of speech with one and two ears. *Journal of the Acoustical Society of America, 25*, 975–979.

Chi, M.T. (1978). Knowledge, structure and memory development. In R.S. Siegler (Ed.), *Children's thinking. What develops?* Hillsdale, NJ: Lawrence Erbaum Associates Inc.

Chiara, C., Pompeiano, M., & Tononi, G. (1996). Neuronal gene expression in the waking state: A role for the locus coeruleus. *Science, 274*, 1211–1215.

Child, I.L. (1968). Personality in culture. In E.F. Borgatta & W.W. Lambert (Eds.), *Handbook of personality theory and research*. Chicago: Rand McNally.

Chodorow, N. (1978). *The reproduction of mothering*. Berkeley, CA: University of California Press.

Chomsky, N. (1959). Review of Skinner's "Verbal behaviour". *Language, 35*, 26–58.

Chomsky, N. (1965). *Aspects of the theory of syntax*. Cambridge, MA: MIT Press.

Chomsky, N. (1986). *Knowledge of language: Its nature, origin, and use*. New York: Praeger.

Chowdhury, A.N. (1998). Hundred years of koro: The history of a culture-bound syndrome. *International Journal of Social Psychiatry, 44*(3), 181–188.

Christensen-Szalanski, J.J., & Bushyhead, J.B. (1981). Physicians' use of probabilistic information in a real clinical setting. *Journal of Experimental Psychology: Human Perception and Performance, 7*, 928–935.

Cialdini, R.B., Borden, R.J., Thorne, A., Walker, M.R., Freeman, S., & Sloan, L.R. (1976). Basking in reflected glory: Three (football) field studies. *Journal of Personality and Social Psychology, 34*, 366–375.

Cialdini, R.B., Schaller, M., Houlihan, D., Arps, K., Fultz, J., & Beaman, A.L. (1987). Empathy-based helping: Is it selflessly or selfishly motivated? *Journal of Personality and Social Psychology, 52*, 749–758.

Clark, D.M. (1986). A cognitive approach to panic. *Behaviour Research and Therapy, 24*, 461–470.

Clark, D.M., Salkovskis, P.M., Gelder, M., Koehler, K., Martin, M., Anastasiades, P., Hackman, A., Middleton, H., & Jeavons, A. (1988). Tests of a cognitive theory of panic. In I. Hand & H.-U. Wittchen (Eds.), *Panic and phobias, Vol. 2.* Berlin: Springer.

Clark, M.S. (1984). Record keeping in two types of relationships. *Journal of Personality and Social Psychology, 47*, 549–557.

Clark, M.S., & Mills, J. (1979). Interpersonal attraction in exchange and communal relationships. *Journal of Personality and Social Psychology, 37*, 12–24.

Clark, R.D., & Hatfield, E. (1989). Gender differences in receptivity to sexual offers. *Journal of Psychology and Human Sexuality, 2*, 39–55.

Clegg, F. (1982). *Simple statistics*. Cambridge, UK: Cambridge University Press.

Cochrane, R. (1983). *The social creation of mental illness*. London: Longman.

Cochrane, R. (1988). Marriage, separation and divorce. In S. Fisher & J. Reason (Eds.), *Handbook of life stress, cognition and health*. Chichester, UK: Wiley.

Cochrane, R., & Sashidharan, S.P. (1995). *Mental health and ethnic minorities: A review of the literature and implications for services*. Paper presented to the Birmingham and Northern Birmingham Health Trust.

Cocker, J. (1998). Where Monarchs spend the winter. *Journal of the Association for Teaching Psychology, 7*, 2–20.

Cohen, C.E. (1981). Person categories and social perception: Testing some boundaries of the processing effects of prior knowledge. *Journal of Personality and Social Psychology, 40*, 441–452.

Colapinto, J. (2000). *As nature made him*. London: Quartet Books.

Colby, A., & Kohlberg, L. (1987). *The measurement of moral judgement*. Cambridge, UK: Cambridge University Press.

Colby, A., Kohlberg, L., Gibbs, J., & Lieberman, M. (1983). A longitudinal study of moral judgement. *Monographs of the Society for Research in Child Development, 48*(Nos. 1–2, Serial No. 200).

Cole, J.O., & Davis, J.M. (1975). Antidepressant drugs. In A.M. Freedman, H.I. Kaplan, & B.J. Saddock (Eds.), *Comprehensive textbook of psychiatry, Vol. 2.* Baltimore: Williams & Williams.

Cole, M., Gay, J., Glick, J., & Sharp, D.W. (1971). *The cultural context of learning and thinking*. New York: Basic Books.

Colebatch, J.G., Deiber, M.-P., Passingham, R.E., Friston, K.J., & Frackowiak, R.S.J. (1991). Regional cerebral blood flow during voluntary arm and hand movements in human subjects. *Journal of Neurophysiology, 65*, 1392–1401.

Coleman, J.C. (1974). *Relationships in adolescence*. London: Routledge & Kegan Paul.

Coleman, J.C., & Hendry, L. (1990). *The nature of adolescence*. London: Routledge.

Comstock, G., & Paik, H. (1991). *Television and the American child*. San Diego: Academic Press.

Condry, J., & Condry, S. (1976). Sex differences: A study in the eye of the beholder. *Child Development, 47*, 812–819.

Conley, J.J. (1984). The hierarchy of consistency: A review and model of longitudinal findings on adult individual differences in intelligence, personality and self-opinion. *Personality and Individual Differences, 5*, 11–25.

Conner, D.B., Knight, D.K., & Cross, D.R. (1997). Mothers' and fathers' scaffolding of their 2–year-olds during problem-solving and literary interactions. *British Journal of Developmental Psychology, 15*, 323–338.

Cooke, T.P., & Apolloni, T. (1976). Developing positive social-emotional behaviors: A study of training and generalization effects. *Journal of Applied Behavior Analysis, 9*(1), 65–78.

Cooper, A., & Sportolari, L. (1997). Romance in cyberspace: Understanding online attraction. *Journal of Sex Education and Therapy, 22*, 7–14.

Cooper, C. (1998). *Individual differences*. London: Arnold.

Cooper, J., & Mackie, D. (1986). Video games and aggression in children. *Journal of Applied Social Psychology, 16*(8), 726–744.

Coren, S., & Girgus, J.S. (1972). Visual spatial illusions: Many explanations. *Science, 179*, 503–504.

Cosmides, L. (1989). The logic of social exchange: Has natural selection shaped how humans reason? Studies with the Wason selection task. *Cognition, 31*, 187–276.

Cosmides, L., & Tooby, J. (1992). Cognitive adaptations for social exchange. In J.H. Barkow Jerome, L. Cosmides, & J. Tooby (Eds.), *The adapted mind: Evolutionary psychology and the generation of culture* (pp. 163–228). New York: Oxford University Press.

Costa, P.T., & McCrae, R.R. (1980). Influence of extraversion and neuroticism on subjective well-being: Happy and unhappy people. *Journal of Personality and Social Psychology, 38*, 668–678.

Costanzo, P.R., Coie, J.D., Grumet, J., & Famill, D. (1973). A re-examination of the effects of intent and consequence on the quality of child rearing. *Child Development, 57*, 362–374.

Costanzo, P.R., & Shaw, M.E. (1966). Conformity as a function of age level. *Child Development, 37*, 967–975.

Costello, T.W., Costello, J.T., & Holmes, D.A. (1995). *Abnormal psychology*. London: HarperCollins.

Cox, M.J., Owen, M.T., Lewis, J.M., & Henderson, K.V. (1989). Marriage, adult adjustment, and early parenting. *Child Development, 60*, 1015–1024.

Craik, F.I., & Watkins, M.J. (1973). The role of rehearsal in short-term memory. *Journal of Verbal Learning and Verbal Behavior, 12*(6), 599–607.

Craik, F.I.M., & Lockhart, R.S. (1972). Levels of processing: A framework for memory research. *Journal of Verbal Learning and Verbal Behavior, 11*, 671–684.

Craik, F.I.M., & Tulving, E. (1975). Depth of processing and the retention of words in episodic memory. *Journal of Experimental Psychology, 104*, 268–294.

Crick, F., & Mitchison, G. (1983). The function of dream sleep. *Nature, 304*, 111–114.

Crook, J.H. (1964). The evolution of social organisation and visual communication in the weaver birds (Ploceinae). *Behaviour Supplement, 10*, 1–178.

Crook, T., & Eliot, J. (1980). Parental death during childhood and adult depression: A critical review of the literature. *Psychological Bulletin, 87*, 252–259.

Crooks, R.L., & Stein, J. (1991). *Psychology: Science, behaviour and life* (2nd Edn.), London: Harcourt Brace Jovanovich.

Crossman, E.R.F.W., & Szafran, J. (1956). Changes with age in the speed of information intake and discrimination. *Experimentia Supplement, 4*, 128–135.

Crow, T.J. (1998). Sexual selection, timing and the descent of man: A theory of the genetic origins of language. *Current Psychology of Cognition, 17*(6), 1079–1114.

Crow, T.J. (2000). Schizophrenia as the price that homo sapiens pays for language: A resolution of the central paradox in the origin of the species. *Brain Research Reviews, 31*(2–3), 118–129.

Csikszentmihalyi, M., & Larson, R. (1984). *Being adolescent: Conflict and growth in the teenage years*. New York: Basic Books.

Cullen, E. (1957). Adaptations in the kittiwake to cliff-nesting. *Ibis, 99*, 275–302.

Cumberbatch, G. (1990). *Television advertising and sex role stereotyping: A content analysis* (working paper IV for the Broadcasting Standards Council). Communications Research Group, Aston University, Birmingham, UK.

Cumming, E. (1975). Engagement with an old theory. *International Journal of Ageing and Human Development, 6*, 187–191.

Cumming, E., & Henry, W.H. (1961). *Growing old*. New York: Basic Books.

Cunningham, J.D., & Antrill, J.K. (1995). Current trends in non-marital cohabitation: In search of the POSSLQ. In J.T. Wood & S. Duck (Eds.), *Understudied relationships: Off the beaten track*. Thousand Oaks, CA: Sage.

Cunningham, M.R. (1986). Measuring the physical in physical attractiveness: Quasi experiments on the sociobiology of female facial beauty. *Journal of Personality and Social Psychology, 50*, 925–935.

Curtiss, S. (1977). *Genie: A psycholinguistic study of a modern-day "wild child"*. London: Academic Press.

Cuthill, I. (1991). Field experiments in animal behaviour. *Animal Behaviour, 42*, 1007–1014.

Cutting, J.E., & Kozlowski, L.T. (1977). A biomechanical invariant for gait perception. *Journal of Experimental Psychology: Human Perception and Performance, 4*, 357–372.

Czeisler, C.A., Moore-Ede, M.C., & Coleman, R.M. (1982). Rotating shift work schedules that disrupt sleep are improved by applying circadian principles. *Science, 217*(4558), 460–463.

Damasio, H. (1989). Neuroimaging contributions to the understanding of aphasia. In F. Boller & J. Grafman (Eds.), *Handbook of neuropsychology, Vol. 2*. New York: Elsevier.

Damasio, H., Eslinger, P., & Adams, H.P. (1984). Aphasia following basal ganglia lesions: New evidence. *Seminars in Neurology, 4*, 151–161.

Dammann, E.J. (1997). "The myth of mental illness": Continuing controversies and their implications for mental health professionals. *Clinical Psychology Review, 17*, 733–756.

Damon, W., & Hart, D. (1988). *Self-understanding in childhood and adolescence*. Cambridge, UK: Cambridge University Press.

Dannemiller, J.L., & Stephens, B.R. (1988). A critical test of infant pattern preference models. *Child Development, 59*, 210–216.

Darley, J.M. (1991). Altruism and prosocial behaviour research: Reflections and prospects. In M.S. Clark (Ed.), *Prosocial behaviour: Review of personality and social psychology, Vol. 12*. Newbury Park, CA: Sage.

Darley, J.M., & Gross, P.H. (1983). A hypothesis-continuing bias in labelling effects. *Journal of Personality and Social Psychology, 44*, 20–33.

Darley, J.M., & Latané, B. (1968). Bystander intervention in emergencies: Diffusion of responsibility. *Journal of Personality and Social Psychology, 8*, 377–383.

Dartnall, H.J.A., Bowmaker, J.K., & Mollon, J.D. (1983). Microspectrophotometry of human photoreceptors. In J.D. Mollon & L.T. Sharpe (Eds.), *Colour vision: Physiology and psychophysics*. New York: Academic Press.

Darwin, C. (1859). *The origin of species*. London: Macmillan.

Darwin, C. (1871). *The descent of man and selection in relation to sex*. London: Murray.

Darwin, C. (1872). *The expression of the emotions in man and animals*. London: John Murray.

Davey, G.C.L. (1983). An associative view of human classical conditioning. In G.C.L. Davey (Ed.), *Animal models of human behaviour: Conceptual, evolutionary, and neurobiological perspectives*. Chichester, UK: Wiley.

Davidson, M., Keefe, R.S.E., Mohs, R.C., Siever, L.J., Losonczy, M.F., Horvath, T.B., & Davis, K.L. (1987). L-Dopa challenge and relapse in schizophrenia. *American Journal of Psychiatry, 144*, 934–938.

Davidson, R., Ekman, P., Saron, C.D., Senulis, J.A., & Friesen, W.V. (1990). Approach–withdrawal and cerebral asymmetry. *Journal of Personality and Social Psychology, 58*, 330–341.

Davies, I.R.L. (1998). A study of colour grouping in three languages: A test of the linguistic relativity hypothesis. *British Journal of Psychology, 89*, 433–452.

Davies, N.B., & Brooke, M. de L. (1988). Cuckoos versus reed warblers: Adaptations and counter-adaptations. *Animal Behaviour, 36*, 262–284.

Davies, N.B., & Lundberg, A. (1984). Food distribution and a variable mating system in the dunnock, *Prunella modularis*. *Journal of Animal Ecology, 53*, 895–913.

Davis, M.H. (1983). Empathic concern and the muscular dystrophy telethon: Empathy as a multidimensional construct. *Personality and Social Psychology Bulletin, 9*, 223–229.

Davis, M.H., & Harvey, J.C. (1992). Declines in major league batting performance as a function of game pressure: A drive theory analysis. *Journal of Applied Social Psychology, 22*(9), 714–735.

Davis, S. (1990). Men as success objects and women as sex objects: A study of personal advertisements. *Sex Roles, 23*, 43–50.

Davison, G.C., & Neale, J.M. (1996). *Abnormal psychology* (Rev. 6th Edn.). New York: Wiley.

Dawkins, R. (1976). *The selfish gene*. Oxford, UK: Oxford University Press.

Dawkins, R. (1998). *Unweaving the rainbow*. London: Penguin.

Dawkins, R., & Krebs, J.R. (1979). Arms races within and between species. *Proceedings of the Royal Society of London, B205*, 489–511.

Dawson, D., & Campbell, S.S. (1991). Time exposure to bright light improves sleep and alertness during simulated night shifts. *Sleep, 14*, 511–516.

Day, L.B., Crews, D., & Wilczynski, W. (1999). Spatial and reversal learning in congeneric lizards with different foraging strategies. *Animal Behaviour, 57*, 648–652.

Day, R., Nielsen, J.A., Korten, A., Ernberg, G., et al. (1987). Stressful life events preceding the acute onset of schizophrenia: A cross-national study from the World Health Organization. *Culture, Medicine and Psychiatry, 11*(2), 123–205.

Day, R., & Wong, S. (1996). Anomalous perceptual asymmetries for negative emotional stimuli in the psychopath. *Journal of Abnormal Psychology, 105*, 648–652.

De Boysson-Bardies, B., Sagart, L., & Durand, C. (1984). Discernible differences in the babbling of infants according to target language. *Journal of Child Language, 11*, 1–16.

DeGroot, A.D. (1965). *Thought and choice in chess*. The Hague, The Netherlands: Mouton.

De Haan, E.H.F., Young, A.W., & Newcombe, F. (1991). A dissociation between the sense of familiarity and access to semantic information concerning familiar people. *European Journal of Cognitive Psychology, 3*, 51–67.

Delgado, P.L., Charney, D.S., Price, L.H., Aghajanian, G.K., et al. (1990). Serotonin function and the mechanism of antidepressant action: Reversal of antidepressant-induced remission by rapid depletion of plasma tryptophan. *Archives of General Psychiatry, 47*(5), 411–418.

DeLucia, P.R., & Hochberg, J. (1991). Geometrical illusions in solid objects under ordinary viewing conditions. *Perception and Psychophysics, 50*, 547–554.

Dement, W.C. (1960). The effects of dream deprivation. *Science, 131*, 1705–1707.

Dement, W.C., & Kleitman, N. (1957). Cyclic variations in EEG during sleep and their relation to eye movements, body motility, and dreaming. *Clinical Neurophysiology, 9*, 673–690.

Dement, W.C., & Kleitman, N. (1957). The relation of eye movements during sleep to dream activity: An objective method for the study of dreaming. *Journal of Experimental Psychology, 53*, 339–346.

Deregowski, J., Muldrow, E.S., & Muldrow, W.F. (1972). Pictorial recognition in a remote Ethiopian population. *Perception, 1*, 417–425.

Deuel, N.R. (1996). Our passionate response to virtual reality. In S.C. Herring (Ed.), *Computer-mediated communication: Linguistic, social and cross-cultural perspectives* (pp. 129–146). Amsterdam: John Benjamins Publishing Company.

Deutsch, J.A., & Deutsch, D. (1963). Attention: Some theoretical considerations. *Psychological Review, 70*, 80–90.

Deutsch, J.A., & Deutsch, D. (1967). Comments on "Selective attention: Perception or response?". *Quarterly Journal of Experimental Psychology, 19*, 362–363.

Deutsch, J.A., & Gonzalez, M.F. (1980). Gastic nutrient content signals satiety. *Behavioral and Neural Biology, 30*, 113–116.

Deutsch, M., & Collins, M.E. (1951). *Inter-racial housing: A psychological evaluation of a social experiment*. Minneapolis, MN: University of Minneapolis Press.

DeValois, R.L., & DeValois, K.K. (1975). Neural coding of colour. In E.C. Carterette & M.P. Friedman (Eds.), *Handbook of perception, Vol. 5*. New York: Academic Press.

de Villiers, J.G., & de Villiers, P.A. (1973). A cross-sectional study of the acquisition of grammatic morphemes in child speech. *Journal of Psycholinguistic Research, 2*, 267–278.

Devine, P.A., & Fernald, P.S. (1973). Outcome effects of receiving a preferred, randomly assigned or non-preferred therapy. *Journal of Consulting and Clinical Psychology, 41*, 104–107.

Devine, P.G. (1995). Prejudice and out-group perception. In A. Tesser (Ed.), *Advanced social psychology*. New York: McGraw-Hill.

DiNardo, P.A., Guzy, L.T., Jenkins, J.A., Bak, R.M., Tomasi, S.F., & Copland, M. (1988). Aetiology and maintenance of dog fears. *Behaviour Research and Therapy, 26*, 241–244.

Dindia, K., & Allen, M. (1992). Sex differences in self-disclosure: A meta-analysis. *Psychological Bulletin, 112*, 106–124.

Dindia, K., & Baxter, L.A. (1987). Maintenance and repair strategies in marital relationships. *Journal of Social and Personal Relationships, 4*, 143–158.

Dobelle, W.H., Mladejovsky, M.G., & Girvin, J.P. (1974). Artificial vision for the blind: Electrical stimulation of visual cortex offers hope for a functional prosthesis. *Science, 183*, 440–444.

Dobson, K.S. (1989). A meta-analysis of the efficacy of cognitive therapy for depression. *Journal of Consulting and Clinical Psychology, 57*, 414–419.

Doise, W. (1976). *L'articulation psychosociologique et les relations entre groupes*. Brussels: de Boeck.

Doise, W., & Mugny, G. (1984). *The social development of the intellect*. Oxford, UK: Pergamon.

Doise, W., Rijsman, J.B., van Meel, J., Bressers, I., & Pinxten, L. (1981). Sociale markering en cognitieve ontwikkeling. *Pedagogische Studien, 58*, 241–248.

Dollard, J., Doob, L.W., Miller, N.E., Mowrer, O.H., & Sears, R.R. (1939). *Frustration and aggression*. New Haven, CT: Yale University Press.

Dollard, J., & Miller, N.E. (1950). *Personality and psychotherapy*. New York: McGraw-Hill.

Donaldson, M. (1978). *Children's minds*. London: Fontana.

Doob, L.W., & Sears, R.R. (1939). Factors determining substitute behaviour and the overt expression of aggression. *Journal of Abnormal and Social Psychology, 34*, 293–313.

Dorner, S., & Atwell, J.D. (1985). Family adjustment to the early loss of a baby born with spina bifida. *Developmental Medicine and Child Neurology, 27*(4), 461–466.

Douvan, E., & Adelson, J. (1966). *The adolescent experience*. New York: Wiley.

Dovidio, J.F., Piliavin, J.A., & Clark, R.D. (1991). The arousal-cost reward model and the process of intervention: A review of the evidence. In M.S. Clark (Ed.), *Review of personality and social psychology: Vol. 12. Prosocial behaviour*. New York: Academic Press.

Drever, J. (1964). *A dictionary of psychology*. Harmondsworth, UK: Penguin.

Driver, J., & Tipper, S.P. (1989). On the nonselectivity of "selective seeing": Contrast between interference and priming in selective attention. *Journal of Experimental Psychology: Human Perception and Performance, 15*, 448–456.

Duck, S. (1982). *Personal relationships: 4. Dissolving personal relationships*. London: Academic Press.

Duck, S. (1992). *Human relationships* (2nd Edn.). London: Sage.

Duck, S.W. (1994). *Meaningful relationships*. London: Sage.

Duck, S.W., & Pond, K. (1989). Friends, Romans, countrymen: Lend me your retrospective data: Rhetoric and reality in personal relationships. In C. Hendrick (Ed.), *Review of social psychology and personality: Vol. 10. Close relationships* (pp. 3–27). Newbury Park, CA: Sage.

Duck, S.W., & Wright, P. (1993). Reexamining gender differences in same-gender friendships: A close look at two kinds of data. *Sex Roles, 28*, 709–727.

Ducret, J.J. (1990). *Jean Piaget: Biographie et parcours intellectuel*. Lausanne, Switzerland: Editions Delachaux et Niestlé.

Dunbar, R. (1993). Coevolution of neocortical size, group size and language in humans. *Behavioural and Brain Sciences, 16*, 681–735.

Dunbar, R. (1996). *Grooming, gossip and the evolution of language*. London: Faber & Faber.

Duncan, J. (1979). Divided attention: The whole is more than the sum of its parts. *Journal of Experimental Psychology: Human Perception and Performance, 5*, 216–228.

Duncan, S.L. (1976). Differential social perception and attribution of intergroup violence: Testing the lower limits of stereotyping of blacks. *Journal of Personality and Social Psychology, 34*, 590–598.

Duncker, K. (1926). A qualitative (experimental and theoretical) study of productive thinking (solving comprehensible problems). *Journal of Genetic Psychology, 68*, 97–116.

Duncker, K. (1945). On problem solving. *Psychological Monographs, 58*(Whole No. 270).

Dunn, J., & Plomin, R. (1990). *Separate lives: Why siblings are so different*. New York: Basic Books.

Durkin, K. (1995). *Developmental social psychology: From infancy to old age*. Oxford, UK: Blackwell.

Durkin, K. (1997). *Developmental social psychology: From infancy to old age*. Oxford, UK: Blackwell.

Dutton, D.G., & Aron, A.P. (1974). Some evidence for heightened sexual attraction under conditions of high anxiety. *Journal of Personality and Social Psychology, 30*, 510–517.

Dweck, C.S. (1975). The role of expectations and attributions in the alleviation of learned helplessness. *Journal of Personality and Social Psychology, 31*, 674–685.

Dworetzsky, J.P. (1996). *Introduction to child development* (6th Edn.). New York: West Publishing Co.

Dwyer, D. (2001). *Interpersonal relations*. London: Routledge.

Eagly, A.H. (1978). Sex differences in influenceability. *Psychological Bulletin, 85*, 86–116.

Eagly, A.H., & Carli, L. (1981). Sex of researchers and sex-typed communications as determinants of sex differences in influenceability: A meta-analysis of social influence studies. *Psychological Bulletin, 90*, 1–20.

Eagly, A.H., & Crowley, M. (1986). Gender and helping behaviour: A meta-analytic review of the social psychological literature. *Psychological Bulletin, 100*, 283–308.

Ebbesen, E.B., Kjos, G.L., & Konecni, V.J. (1976). Spatial ecology: Its effects on the choice of friends and enemies. *Journal of Experimental Social Psychology, 12*, 505–518.

Ebbinghaus, H. (1913). *Memory* (H. Ruyer & C.E. Bussenius, Trans.). New York: Teachers College, Columbia University. (Original work published 1885)

Ebigno, P.O. (1986). A cross-sectional study of somatic complaints of Nigerian females using the Enugu Somatization Scale. *Culture, Medicine, and Psychiatry, 10*, 167–186.

Egan, D.W., & Greeno, J.G. (1974). Theories of rule induction: Knowledge acquired in concept learning, serial pattern learning and problem solving. In W.G. Gregg (Ed.), *Knowledge and cognition*. Hillsdale, NJ: Lawrence Erlbaum Associates Inc.

Egeland, B., Gerhard, D.S., Pauls, D.L., Sussex, J.N., Kidd, K.K., Allen, C.R., Hostetter, A.M., & Housman, D.E. (1987). Bipolar affective disorders linked to DNA markers on chromosome 11. *Nature, 325*, 783–787.

Eisdorfer, C., & Wilkie, F. (1977). Stress, disease, aging and behaviour. In J.E. Birren & K.W. Schaie (Eds.), *Handbook of the psychology of aging* (3rd Edn.). San Diego: Academic Press.

Eisenberg, N., Lennon, R., & Roth, K. (1983). Prosocial development: A longitudinal study. *Developmental Psychology, 19*, 846–855.

Eisenberg, N., Miller, P.A., Shell, R., McNalley, S., & Shea, C. (1991). Prosocial development in adolescence: A longitudinal study. *Developmental Psychology, 27*, 849–857.

Eisenberg, N., & Mussen, P.H. (1989). *The roots of prosocial behaviour in children*. Cambridge, UK: Cambridge University Press.

Eisenberg-Berg, N., & Hand, M. (1979). The relationship of preschoolers' reasoning about prosocial moral conflicts to prosocial behaviour. *Child Development, 50*, 356–363.

Elliott, J. (1990). *Discovery psychology* [PBS video series, program 20]. Washington, DC: Annenberg/CBS program.

Ellis, A. (1962). *Reason and emotion in psychotherapy*. Secaucus, NJ: Prentice-Hall.

Ellis, A. (1978). The basic clinical theory of rational emotive therapy. In A. Ellis & R. Grieger (Eds.), *Handbook of rational emotive therapy*. New York: Springer.

Ellis, S., & Gauvain, M. (1992). Social and cultural influences on children's collaborative interactions. In L.T. Winegar & J. Valsiner (Eds.), *Children's development within social context: Vol. 2. Research and methodology*. Hillsdale, NJ: Lawrence Erlbaum Associates Inc.

Emlen, J.M. (1966). The role of time and energy in food preference. *American Naturalist, 100*, 611–617.

Emlen, S.T., & Emlen, J.T. (1966). *Auk, 83*, 361–367.

Emlen, S.T. (1975). The stellar-orientation system of a migratory bird. *Scientific American, 233*(2), 102–111.

Emler, N. (1984). Differential involvement in delinquency: Toward an interpretation in terms of reputation management. In B.A. Maher & W.B. Maher (Eds.), *Progress in experimental personality research, Vol. 13.* New York: Academic Press.

Emler, N., & Reicher, S. (1995). Adolescence and delinquency: The collective management of reputation. *Social Psychology and Society, XIV.*

Emler, N., Reicher, S., & Ross, A. (1987). The social context of delinquent conduct. *Journal of Child Psychology and Psychiatry, 28,* 99–109.

Empson, J.A.C. (1989). *Sleep and dreaming.* London: Faber & Faber.

Engels, G.I., Garnefski, N., & Diekstra, R.F.W. (1993). Efficacy of rational-emotive therapy: A quantitative analysis. *Journal of Consulting and Clinical Psychology, 61,* 1083–1090.

Epstein, R., Lanza, R.P., & Skinner, B.F. (1981). "Self-awareness" in the pigeon. *Science, 212,* 695–696.

Eriksen, C.W. (1990). Attentional search of the visual field. In D. Brogan (Ed.), *Visual search.* London: Taylor & Francis.

Erikson, E.H. (1950). *Childhood and society.* New York: Norton.

Erikson, E.H. (1959). *Identity and life styles: Selected papers.* New York: International Universities Press.

Erikson, E.H. (1963). *Childhood and society* (2nd Edn.). New York: Norton.

Erikson, E.H. (1968). *Identity: Youth and crisis.* New York: Norton.

Erikson, E.H. (1969). *Gandhi's truth: On the origin of militant nonviolence.* New York: W.W. Norton.

Eron, L.D. (1982). Parent–child interaction, television violence, and aggression of children. *American Psychologist, 37,* 197–211.

Ervin-Tripp, S. (1964). An analysis of the interaction of language, topic and listener. *American Anthropologist, 66,* 94–100.

Estes, W.K. (1944). An experimental study of punishment. *Psychological Monographs: General & Applied, 54* (No. 263).

Etcoff, N.L., Ekman, P., Frank, M., Magee, J., & Torreano, L. (1992). *Detecting deception: Do aphasics have an advantage?* Paper presented at the Conference of International Society for Research on Emotions, Carnegie Mellon University, Pittsburgh, PA.

Eysenck, H.J. (1952). The effects of psychotherapy: An evaluation. *Journal of Consulting Psychology, 16,* 319–324.

Eysenck, H.J. (1967). *The biological basis of personality.* Springfield, IL: C.C. Thomas.

Eysenck H.J. (1981). *The intelligence controversy: H. J. Eysenck vs. Leon Kamin.* New York: Wiley.

Eysenck, H.J., & Broadhurst, P.L. (1964). Experiments with animals. In H.J. Eysenck (Ed.), *Experiments in motivation.* London: Pergamon Press.

Eysenck, H.J., & Eysenck, M.W. (1981). *Mindwatching.* London: Michael Joseph.

Eysenck, H.J., & Eysenck, M.W. (1989). *Mindwatching: Why we behave the way we do.* London: Prion.

Eysenck, M.W. (1984). *A handbook of cognitive psychology.* Hove, UK: Psychology Press.

Eysenck, M.W. (1982). *Attention and arousal: Cognition and performance.* Berlin: Springer.

Eysenck, M.W. (1990). *Happiness: Facts and myths.* Hove, UK: Psychology Press.

Eysenck, M.W. (1997). *Anxiety and cognition: A unified theory.* Hove, UK: Psychology Press.

Eysenck, M.W., & Eysenck, M.C. (1980). Effects of processing depth, distinctiveness, and word frequency on retention. *British Journal of Psychology, 71,* 263–274.

Eysenck, M.W., & Keane, M.T. (1990). *Cognitive psychology: A student's handbook* (2nd Edn.). Hove, UK: Psychology Press.

Eysenck, M.W., & Keane, M.T. (1995). *Cognitive psychology: A student's handbook* (3rd Edn.). Hove, UK: Psychology Press.

Eysenck, M.W., & Keane, M.T. (2000). *Cognitive psychology: A student's handbook* (4th Edn.). Hove, UK: Psychology Press.

Fabes, R.A., Fultz, J., Eisenberg, N., May-Plumlee, T., & Christopher, F.S. (1989). Effects of rewards on children's prosocial motivation: A socialisation study. *Developmental Psychology, 25,* 509–515.

Fagot, B.I. (1985). Beyond the reinforcement principle: Another step toward understanding sex-role development. *Developmental Psychology, 21,* 1097–1104.

Fagot, B.I., & Leinbach, M.D. (1989). The young child's gender schema: Environmental input, internal organisation. *Child Development, 60,* 663–672.

Fahrenberg, J. (1992). Psychophysiology of neuroticism and emotionality. In A. Gale & M.W. Eysenck (Eds.), *Handbook of individual differences: Biological perspectives.* Chichester, UK: Wiley.

Fairchild, H.H. (1988). Creating positive television images. *Applied Social Psychology Annual, 8,* 270–280.

Falek, A., & Moser, H.M. (1975). Classification on schizophrenia. *Archives of General Psychiatry, 32,* 59–67.

Fantz, R.L. (1961). The origin of form perception. *Scientific American, 204,* 66–72.

Fantz, R.L. (1966). Pattern discrimination and selective attention as determinants of perceptual development from birth. In A.H. Kidd & J.F. Rivoire (Eds.), *Perceptual development in children.* New York: International Universities Press.

Farah, M.J. (1994). Specialisation within visual object recognition: Clues from prosopagnosia and alexia. In M.J. Farah & G. Ratcliff (Eds.), *The neuropsychology of high-level vision: Collected tutorial essays.* Hillsdale, NJ: Lawrence Erlbaum Associates Inc.

Farr, J.L. (1976). Task characteristics, reward contingency, and intrinsic motivation. *Organizational Behavior and Human Performance, 16,* 294–307.

Fava, M., Copeland, P.M., Schweiger, U., & Herzog, D.B. (1989). Neurochemical abnormalities of anorexia and bulimia nervosa. *American Journal of Psychiatry, 47,* 213–219.

Fein, S., Hilton, J.L., & Miller, D.T. (1990). Suspicion of ulterior motivation and the correspondence bias. *Journal of Personality and Social Psychology, 58,* 753–764.

Fellner, C.H., & Marshall, J.R. (1981). Kidney donors revisited. In J.P. Rushton & R.M. Sorrentino (Eds.), *Altruism and helping behaviour.* Hillsdale, NJ: Lawrence Erlbaum Associates Inc.

Ferguson, C.A. (1959). Diglossia. *Word, 15,* 325–340.

Ferguson, T.J., & Rule, B.G. (1983). An attributional perspective on anger and aggression. In R. Green & E. Donnerstein (Eds.), *Aggression: Theoretical and empirical reviews: Vol. 1. Method and theory.* New York: Academic Press.

Ferris, C., & Branston, P. (1994). Quality of life in the elderly: A contribution to its understanding. *American Journal of Ageing, 13,* 120–123.

Festinger, L., Schachter, S., & Back, K. (1950). *Social pressures in informal groups: A study of a housing community.* New York: Harper.

Feyerabend, P. (1975). *Against method: Outline of an anarchist theory of knowledge.* London: New Left Books.

Field, D., & Minkler, M. (1988). Continuity and change in social support between young-old and old-old or very-old age. *Journal of Gerontology, 43,* 100–107.

Fijneman, Y.A., Willemsen, M.E., & Poortinga, Y.H. (1996). Individualism-collectivism: An empirical study of a conceptual issue. *Journal of Cross-Cultural Psychology, 27,* 381–402.

Fincham, F.D., & Bradbury, T.N. (1993). Marital satisfaction, depression, and attributions: A longitudinal analysis. *Journal of Personality and Social Psychology, 64*, 442–452.

Fink, M. (1985). Convulsive therapy: Fifty years of progress. *Convulsive Therapy, 1*, 204–216.

Finlay-Jones, R.A., & Brown, G.W. (1981). Types of stressful life events and the onset of anxiety and depressive disorders. *Psychological Medicine, 11*, 803–815.

Fischer, E.A. (1980). The relationship between mating system and simultaneous hermaphroditism in the coral reef fish, *Hypoplectrus nigricans. Animal Behaviour, 28*, 620–633.

Fisher, J., & Hinde, R.A. (1948). The opening of milk bottles by birds. *British Birds, 42*, 347–357.

Fisher, R.A. (1930). *The genetical theory of natural selection.* Oxford, UK: Clarendon Press.

Fisher, R.A., & Yates, F. (1974). *Statistical tables for biological, agricultural and medical research* (6th Edn.). Harlow, UK: Addison Wesley Longman.

Fiske, S.T. (1993). Social cognition and social perception. *Annual Review of Psychology, 44*, 155–194.

Fiske, S.T., & Taylor, S.E. (1991). *Social cognition* (2nd Edn.). New York: McGraw-Hill.

Fitts, P.M., & Posner, M.I. (1967). *Human performance.* Englewood Cliffs, NJ: Prentice-Hall.

Fitzgibbon, C.D., & Fanshaw, J.H. (1988). Stotting in Thompson's gazelles: An honest signal of condition. *Behavioral Ecology and Sociobiology, 23*, 69–74.

Flanagan, C. (1995). *Revise GCSE.* London: Letts Educational.

Flanagan, C. (1999). *Early socialisation: Sociability and attachment.* London: Routledge.

Flanagan, D. (1988). *Flanagan's version: A spectator's guide to science on the eve of the 21st century.* New York: Knopf.

Floody, O.R. (1968). Hormones and aggression in female animals. In B.B. Suare (Ed.), *Hormones and aggressive behaviour.* New York: Plenum Press.

Flynn, J.P. (1976). Neural basis of threat and attack. In R.G. Grenell & S. Gabay (Eds.), *Biological foundations of psychiatry.* New York: Raven.

Foa, U.G., & Foa, E.B. (1975). *Resource theory of social exchange.* Morristown, NJ: General Learning Press.

Fodor, J.A. (1983). *The modularity of mind.* Cambridge, MA: MIT Press.

Fodor, J.A., & Pylyshyn, Z.W. (1981). How direct is visual perception? Some reflections on Gibson's "ecological approach". *Cognition, 9*, 139–196.

Folkard, S. (1996, September 28). *Daily Express.*

Folkman, S., Bernstein, L., & Lazarus, R.S. (1987). Stress processes and the misuse of drugs in older adults. *Psychology and Aging, 2*, 366–374.

Ford, M.R., & Widiger, T.A. (1989). Sex bias in the diagnosis of histrionic and antisocial personality disorders. *Journal of Consulting and Clinical Psychology, 57*, 301–305.

Forman, E.A., & Cazden, C.B. (1985). Exploring Vygotskian perspectives in education: The cognitive value of peer interaction. In J.V. Wertsch (Ed.), *Culture, communication, and cognition: Vygotskian perspectives.* Cambridge, UK: Cambridge University Press.

Forsyth, D.R. (1987). *Social psychology.* Monterey, CA: Brooks-Cole.

Fouts, R.S. (1973). Acquisition and testing of gestural signs in four young chimpanzees. *Science, 180*, 978–980.

Fowler, W. (1990). Early stimulation and the development of verbal talents. In M.J.A. Howe (Ed.), *Encouraging the development of exceptional abilities and talents.* Leicester, UK: BPS Books.

Francolini, C.N., & Egeth, H.E.(1980). On the non-automaticity of automatic activation: Evidence of selective seeing. *Perception and Psychophysics, 27*, 331–342.

Frank, A. (1997). *The diary of a young girl* (O. Frank & M. Pressler, Eds.). London: Viking.

Frank, A. (1997). *Anne Frank: The diary of a young girl* (O. Frank & M. Pressler, Eds., S. Massotty, Trans.). Harmondsworth, UK: Penguin Books.

Franzoi, S.L. (1996). *Social psychology.* Madison: Brown & Benchmark.

Freedman, J.L. (1973). The effects of population density on humans. In J.T. Fawcett (Ed.), *Psychological perspectives on population.* New York: Basic Books.

Freeman, D. (1983). *Margaret Mead and Samoa: The making and unmaking of an anthropological myth.* Cambridge, MA: Harvard University Press.

Freud, S. (1900). *The interpretation of dreams* (J. Strachey, Trans.). London: Allen & Unwin.

Freud, S. (1910). The origin and development of psychoanalysis. *American Journal of Psychology, 21*, 181–218.

Freud, S. (1917). Introductory lectures on psychoanalysis. In J. Strachey (Ed.), *The complete psychological works, Vol. 16.* New York: Norton.

Freud, S. (1933). *New introductory lectures in psychoanalysis.* New York: Norton.

Freud, S. (1971). *The psychopathology of everyday life* (A. Tyson, Trans.). New York: W.W. Norton.

Freud, S., & Breuer, J. (1895). Studies on hysteria. In J. Strachey (Ed.), *The complete psychological works, Vol. 2.* New York: Norton.

Friedman, A. (1979). Framing pictures: The role of knowledge in automatised encoding and memory for gist. *Journal of Experimental Psychology: General, 108*, 316–355.

Friedman, M.I., Tordoff, M.G., & Ramirez, I. (1986). Integrated metabolic control of food intake. *Brain Research Bulletin, 17*, 855–859.

Friedrich, L.K., & Stein, A.H. (1973). Aggressive and pro-social television programmes and the natural behaviour of pre-school children. *Monographs of the Society for Research in Child Development, 38*, 1–64.

Frijda, N.H., Kuipers, P., & ter Schure, E. (1989). Relations among emotion, appraisal, and emotional action readiness. *Journal of Personality and Social Psychology, 57*, 212–228.

Frith, C.D. (1992). *The cognitive neuropsychology of schizophrenia.* Hove, UK: Psychology Press.

Fritz, J., & Kotrschal, K. (1999). Social learning in common ravens, *Corvus corax. Animal Behaviour, 57*, 785–793.

Frueh, T., & McGhee, P.E. (1975). Traditional sex-role development and the amount of time spent watching television. *Developmental Psychology, 11*, 109.

Fuligni, A.J., & Eccles, J.S. (1993). Perceived parent–child relationships and early adolescents' orientation toward peers. *Developmental Psychology, 29(4)*, 622–632.

Furnham, A., & Pinder, A. (1990). Young people's attitudes to experimentation on animals. *The Psychologist, 3*, 444–448.

Fuster, J.M. (1989). *The prefrontal cortex* (2nd Ed.). New York: Raven Press.

Fyer, A.J., Mannuzza, S., Chapman, T.F., Liebowitz, M.R., & Klein, D.F. (1993). A direct-interview family study of social phobia. *Archives of General Psychiatry, 50*, 286–293.

Fyer, A.J., Mannuzza, S., Gallops, M.S., Martin, L.Y., et al. (1990). Familial transmission of simple phobias and fears: A preliminary report. *Archives of General Psychiatry, 47(3)*, 252–256.

Gabrieli, J.D.E., Desmond, J.E., Demb, J.B., Wagner, A.D., Stone, M.V., Vaidyla, C.J., & Glover, G.H. (1996). Functional magnetic resonance imaging of semantic memory processes in the frontal lobes. *Psychological Science, 7*, 278–283.

Gaertner, S.L., & Dovidio, J.F. (1977). The subtlety of white racism, arousal, and helping behaviour. *Journal of Personality and Social Psychology, 35*, 691–707.

Gainotti, G. (1972). Emotional behaviour and hemispheric side of lesion. *Cortex, 8,* 41–55.

Galef, B.G., Jr., & Wigmore, S.W. (1983). Transfer of information concerning distant foods: A laboratory investigation of the "information-centre" hypothesis. *Animal Behaviour, 31,* 748–758.

Galli, I., & Nigro, G. (1987). The social representation of radioactivity among Italian children. *Social Science Information, 26,* 535–549.

Gallup, G. (1971). It's done with mirrors: Chimps and self-concept. *Psychology Today, 4*(10), 58–61.

Gallup, G.G. (1977). Self-recognition in primates. *American Psychologist, 32,* 329–338.

Garcia, J., Ervin, F.R., & Koelling, R. (1966). Learning with prolonged delay of reinforcement. *Psychonomic Science, 5,* 121–122.

Gardner, R.A., & Gardner, B.T. (1969). Teaching sign language to a chimpanzee. *Science, 165,* 664–672.

Gardner, R.A., & Gardner, B.T. (1978). Comparative psychology and language acquisition. *Annals of the New York Academy of Sciences, 309,* 37–76.

Gardner, R.C. (1979). Social aspects of second language acquisition. In H. Giles & R. St. Clair (Eds.), *Language and social psychology* (pp. 193–220). Oxford, UK: Blackwell.

Garfield, S.L. (1980). *Psychotherapy: An eclectic approach.* New York: Wiley.

Garland, H., Hardy, A., & Stephenson, L. (1975). Information search as affected by attribution type and response category. *Personality and Social Psychology Bulletin, 1,* 612–615.

Gaulin, S.J.C., & Fitzgerald, R.W. (1989). Sexual selection for spatial learning ability. *Animal Behaviour, 37,* 322–331.

Gavey, N. (1992). Technologies and effects of heterosexual coercion. *Feminism and Psychology, 2,* 325–351.

Gelder, M., Gath, D., & Mayon, R. (1989). *Oxford textbook of psychiatry* (2nd Edn.). Oxford, UK: Oxford University Press.

Gerbino, L., Oleshansky, M., & Gershon, S. (1978). Clinical use and mode of action of lithium. In M.A. Lipton, A. DiMascio, & F.K. Killam (Eds.), *Psychopharmacology: A generation of progress.* New York: Raven Press.

Gerbner, G., & Gross, L. (1976). The scary world of TV's heavy viewer. *Psychology Today, 9,* 41–45.

Gergen, K.J. (1973). Social psychology as history. *Journal of Personality and Social Psychology, 26,* 309–320.

Gergen, K.J. (1985). Social constructionist inquiry: Context and implications. In K.J. Gergen & K.E. Davis (Eds.), *The social construction of the person.* New York: Springer-Verlag.

Gergen, K.J. (1997). Social psychology as social construction: The emerging vision. In C. McGarty & A. Haslam (Eds.), *The message of social psychology.* Oxford, UK: Blackwell.

Gergen, K.J., Morse, S.J., & Gergen, M.M. (1980). Behaviour exchange in cross-cultural perspective. In H.C. Triandis & W.W. Lambert (Eds.), *Handbook of cross-cultural psychology: Vol. 5. Social psychology.* Boston: Allyn & Bacon.

Gerlsman, C., Emmelkamp, P.M.G., & Arrindell, W.A. (1990). Anxiety, depression, and perception of early parenting: A meta-analysis. *Clinical Psychology Review, 10,* 251–277.

Gershon, E.S. (1990). Genetics. In F.K. Goodwin & K.R. Jamison (Eds.), *Manic-depressive illness.* Oxford, UK: Oxford University Press.

Geschwind, N. (1979). *The brain.* San Francisco: Freeman.

Geschwind, N., & Galaburda, A.M. (1985). Cerebral lateralisation: Biological mechanisms, associations and pathology: I. A hypothesis and a program for research. *Archives of Neurology, 42,* 428–459.

Gibbs, J., Young, R.C., & Smith, G.P. (1973). Cholecystokinin decreases food intake in rats. *Journal of Comparative and Physiological Psychology, 84,* 488–495.

Gibson, E.J. (1969). *Principles of perceptual learning and development.* New York: Appleton-Century-Crofts.

Gibson, E.J., Gibson, J.J., Pick, A.D., & Osser, H.A. (1962). A developmental study of the discrimination of letter-like forms. *Journal of Comparative and Physiological Psychology, 55,* 897–906.

Gibson, E.J., & Spelke, E.S. (1983). The development of perception. In J.H. Flavell & E.M. Markman (Eds.), *Cognitive development: Vol. III. Handbook of child psychology.* Chichester, UK: Wiley.

Gibson, E.J., & Walk, R.D. (1960). The visual cliff. *Scientific American, 202,* 64–71.

Gibson, J.J. (1950). *The perception of the visual world.* Boston: Houghton Mifflin.

Gibson, J.J. (1966). *The senses considered as perceptual systems.* Boston: Houghton Mifflin.

Gibson, J.J. (1979). *The ecological approach to visual perception.* Boston: Houghton Mifflin.

Gick, M.L., & Holyoak, K.J. (1980). Analogical problem solving. *Cognitive Psychology, 12,* 306–355.

Giglioli, P.P. (Ed.). (1972). *Language and social context.* Harmondsworth, UK: Penguin Books.

Gilbert, D.T. (1995). Attribution and interpersonal perception. In A. Tesser (Ed.), *Advanced social psychology.* New York: McGraw-Hill.

Gilbert, D.T., Pelham, B.W., & Krull, D.S. (1988). On cognitive busyness: When person perceivers meet persons perceived. *Journal of Personality and Social Psychology, 54,* 733–740.

Gilbert, G.M. (1951). Stereotype persistence and change among college students. *Journal of Personality and Social Psychology, 46,* 245–254.

Giles, H. (Ed.). (1984). The dynamics of speech accommodation theory. *International Journal of the Sociology of Language, 46*(Whole No.).

Giles, H., & Johnson, P. (1981). The role of language in ethnic group relations. In J. Turner & H. Giles (Eds.), *Intergroup behaviour* (pp. 199–243). Oxford, UK: Blackwell.

Giles, H., & Powesland, P.F. (1975). *Speech style and social evaluation.* London: Academic Press.

Gilhooly, K.J. (1996). *Thinking: Directed, undirected and creative* (3rd Edn.). London: Academic Press.

Gilligan, C. (1977). In a different voice: Women's conceptions of the self and of morality. *Harvard Educational Review, 47,* 481–517.

Gilligan, C. (1982). *In a different voice: Psychological theory and women's development.* Cambridge, MA: Harvard University Press.

Gilligan, C., & Attanucci, J. (1988). Two moral orientations: Gender differences and similarities. *Merrill-Palmer Quarterly, 34,* 223–237.

Glass, D.C., Singer, J.E., & Friedman, L.W. (1969). Psychic cost of adaptation to an environmental stressor. *Journal of Personality and Social Psychology, 12,* 200–210.

Glassman, W.E. (1995). *Approaches to psychology* (2nd Edn.). Buckingham, UK: Open University Press.

Gleitman, H. (1986). *Psychology* (2nd Edn.). London: Norton.

Glenn, N.D., & McLanahan, S. (1982). Children and marital happiness: A further specification of the relationship. *Journal of Marriage and the Family, 44,* 63–72.

Goddard, H.H. (1913). *Feeble-mindedness: Its causes and consequences.* New York: Macmillan.

Goddard, S.J., & Cross, J. (1987). A social skills training approach to dealing with disruptive behaviour in a primary school. *Maladjustment and Therapeutic Education, 5*(3), 24–29.

Goldfried, M.R., & Davison, G.C. (1976). *Clinical behaviour therapy.* San Francisco: Holt, Rinehart & Winston.

Goldman, R.J., & Goldman, J.D.G. (1981). How children view old people and ageing: A developmental study of children in four countries. *Australian Journal of Psychology, 3*, 405–418.

Goldwyn, E. (1979, May 24). The fight to be male. *Listener*, 709–712.

Goodall, J. (1978). Chimp killings: Is it the man in them? *Science News, 113*, 276.

Goodwin, R. (1995). Personal relationships across cultures. *The Psychologist, 8*, 73–75.

Goodwin, R. (1999). *Social relationships across cultures*. London: Routledge.

Gopher, D. (1993). The skill of attentional control: Acquisition and execution of attentional strategies. In S. Kornblum & D.E. Meyer (Eds.), *Attention and performance, Vol. XIV*. Cambridge, MA: MIT Press.

Gordon, I.E. (1989). *Theories of visual perception*. Chichester, UK: Wiley.

Goren, C.C., Sarty, M., & Wu, P.Y.K. (1975). Visual following and pattern discrimination of face-like stimuli by newborn infants. *Pediatrics, 56*, 544–549.

Gottesman, I.I. (1963). Heritability of personality: A demonstration. *Psychological Monographs, 77*(Whole No. 572).

Gottesman, I.I. (1991). *Schizophrenia genesis: The origins of madness*. New York: W.H. Freeman.

Gottesman, I.I., & Bertelsen, A. (1989). Dual mating studies in psychiatry: Offspring of inpatients with examples from reactive (psychogenic) psychoses. *International Review of Psychiatry, 1*, 287–296.

Gottfried, A.W. (1984). Home environment and early cognitive development: Integration, meta-analyses, and conclusions. In A.W. Gottfried (Ed.), *Home environment and early cognitive development: Longitudinal research*. Orlando, FL: Academic Press.

Gould, J.L. (1987). Landmark learning by honeybees. *Animal Behaviour, 35*, 26–34.

Gould, J.L. (1992). Honey bee cognition. In C.R. Gallistel (Ed.), *Animal cognition*. Cambridge, MA: MIT Press.

Gould, R.L. (1978). *Transformations: Growth and change in adult life*. New York: Simon & Schuster.

Gould, R.L. (1980). Transformational tasks in adulthood. In S.I. Greenspan & G.H. Pollack (Eds.), *The course of everyday life: Psychoanalytic contributions toward understanding personality development: Vol. 3. Adulthood and the ageing process*. Washington, DC: National Institute for Mental Health.

Gould, S.J. (1981). *The mismeasure of man*. New York: Norton.

Gove, W.R. (1979). The relationship between sex roles, marital status and mental illness. *Social Forces, 51*, 34–44.

Graham, I.D., & Baker, P.M. (1989). Status, age and gender: Perceptions of old and young adults. *Psychology and Aging, 8*, 10–17.

Gray, J.A. (1985). A whole and its parts: Behaviour, the brain, cognition and emotion. *Bulletin of the British Psychological Society, 38*, 99–112.

Gray, J.A. (1991). On the morality of speciesism. *The Psychologist, 14*, 196–198.

Gray, J.A., & Wedderburn, A.A. (1960). Grouping strategies with simultaneous stimuli. *Quarterly Journal of Experimental Psychology, 12*, 180–184.

Gredler, M. (1992). *Learning and instruction theory into practice*. New York: Macmillan Publishing Company.

Green, J., & Hicks, C. (1984). *Basic cognitive processes*. Milton Keynes: Open University Press.

Green, S. (1975). Dialects in Japanese monkeys. *Zeitschrift für Tierpsychologie, 38*, 305–314.

Green, S. (1994). *Principles of biopsychology*. Hove, UK: Psychology Press.

Greenberg, J.H. (1963). Some universals of grammar with particular reference to the order of meaningful elements. In J.H. Greenberg (Ed.), *Universals of language*. Cambridge, MA: MIT Press.

Greene, J. (1975). *Thinking and language*. London: Methuen.

Greenfield, P.M. (1984). *Mind and media: The effect of television, video games and computers*. Aylesbury, UK: Fontana.

Gregor, A.J., & McPherson, D.A. (1965). A study of susceptibility to geometrical illusion among cultural subgroups of Australian aborigines. *Psychology in Africa, 11*, 1–13.

Gregory, R.L. (1972, June 24). Seeing as thinking. *Times Literary Supplement*.

Gregory, R.L. (1970). *The intelligent eye*. New York: McGraw-Hill.

Gregory, R.L. (1973). The confounded eye. In R.L. Gregory & E.H. Gombrich (Eds.), *Illusion in nature and art*. London: Duckworth.

Gregory, R.L. (1978). *Eye and brain* (3rd Edn.). London: Weidenfeld & Nicolson.

Gregory, R.L. (1980). Perceptions as hypotheses. *Philosophical Transactions of the Royal Society of London, Series B, 290*, 181–197.

Gregory, R.L., & Wallace, J. (1963). *Recovery from early blindness*. Cambridge, UK: Heffer.

Grier, J.W., & Burk, T. (1992). *Biology of animal behaviour*. Dubuque, IO: W.C. Brown.

Grier, J.W., & Burk, T. (1992). *Biology of animal behaviour* (2nd Edn.). Oxford, UK: W.C. Brown.

Griffin, D.R. (1955). Bird navigation. In A. Wolfson (Ed.), *Recent studies in avian biology*. Urbana, IL: University of Illinois Press.

Griffiths, M.D. (1999). All but connected (online relationships). *Psychology Post, 17*, 6–7.

Griffiths, M.D. (2000). Cyberaffairs. *Psychology Review, 7*(1), 28–31.

Griffiths, M.D., & Hunt, N. (1995). Computer game playing in adolescence: Prevalence and demographic indicators. *Journal of Community and Applied Psychology, 5*, 189–193.

Gross, R. (1996). *Psychology: The science of mind and behaviour* (3rd Edn.). London: Hodder & Stoughton.

Gross, R. (1999). *Key studies in psychology*. London: Hodder & Stoughton.

Gross, R., McIlveen, R., Coolican, H., Clamp, A., & Russell, J. (2000). *Psychology: A new introduction for A level* (2nd Ed.). London: Hodder & Stoughton.

Grudin, J.T. (1983). Error patterns in novice and skilled transcription typing. In W.E. Cooper (Ed.), *Cognitive aspects of skilled typewriting*. New York: Springer.

Guimond, S., Begin, G., & Palmer, D.L. (1989). Education and causal attributions: The development of "person-blame" and "system-blame" ideology. *Social Psychology Quarterly, 52*, 126–140.

Gunter, B., & McAleer, J.L. (1990). *Children and television: The one-eyed monster?* London: Routledge.

Guterman, L. (1998). Trail of dung spells disaster for roaches. *New Scientist, 2160*, 12.

Gwinner, E. (1986). Circannual rhythms in the control of avian rhythms. *Advances in the Study of Behaviour, 16*, 191–228.

Hagedorn, M., & Heiligenberg, W. (1985). Court and spark: Electric signals in the courtship and mating of gymnotoid fish. *Animal Behaviour, 33*, 254–265.

Hailman, J. (1992). The necessity of a "show-me" attitude in science. In J.W. Grier & T. Burk, *Biology of animal behaviour* (2nd Edn.). Dubuque, IO: W.C. Brown.

Hajek, P., & Belcher, M. (1991). Dreams of absent-minded transgression: An empirical study of a cognitive withdrawal symptom. *Journal of Abnormal Psychology, 100*, 487–491.

Halaas, J.L., Gajiwala, K.S., Maffei, M., Cohen, S.L., Chait, B.T., Rabinowitz, D., Lallone, R., Burley, S.K., & Friedman, J.M. (1995). Weight-reducing effects of the plasma protein encoded by the *obese* gene. *Science, 269,* 543–546.

Halbreich, U., Endicott, J., Schacht, S., & Nee, J. (1982). The diversity of premenstrual changes as reflected in the Premenstrual Assessment Form. *Acta Psychiatrica Scandinavica, 65*(1), 46–65.

Halgin, R.P., & Whitbourne, S.K. (1997). *Abnormal psychology: The human experience of psychological disorders.* Madison, WI: Brown & Benchmark.

Hall, C.S. (1953). A cognitive theory of dream symbols. *Journal of General Psychology, 48,* 169–186.

Hall, C.S., & Lindzey, G. (1970). *Theories of personality.* London: Wiley.

Hall, G.S. (1904). *Adolescence.* New York: Appleton-Century-Crofts.

Halliday, T., & Arnold, S.J. (1987). Multiple mating by females: A perspective from quantitative genetics. *Animal Behaviour, 35,* 939–941.

Hamilton, D.L. (1981). Illusory correlation and stereotyping. In D.L. Hamilton (Ed.), *Cognitive processes in stereotyping and intergroup behaviour.* Hillsdale, NJ: Lawrence Erlbaum Associates Inc.

Hamilton, D.L., & Gifford, R.K. (1976). Illusory correlation in interpersonal personal perception: A cognitive basis of stereotypic judgments. *Journal of Experimental Social Psychology, 12,* 392–407.

Hamilton, W.D. (1964). The genetical evolution of social behaviour: I and II. *Journal of Theoretical Biology, 7,* 1–52.

Hamilton, W.D., & Zuk, M. (1982). Heritable true fitness and bright birds: A role for parasites? *Science, 218,* 384–387.

Hammen, C.L. (1991). The generation of stress in the course of unipolar depression. *Journal of Abnormal Psychology, 100,* 555–561.

Hampson, P.J. (1989). Aspects of attention and cognitive science. *Irish Journal of Psychology, 10,* 261–275.

Hampson, S.E. (1988). *The construction of personality: An introduction* (2nd Edn.). London: Routledge.

Han, P.J., Feng, L.Y., & Kuo, P.T. (1972). Insulin sensitivity of pair-fed, hyperlipemic, hyperinsulinemic, obese hypothalamic rats. *American Journal of Physiology, 223,* 1206–1209.

Hardyck, C.D., & Petrinovich, L.F. (1970). Subvocal speech and comprehension level as a function of the difficulty level of reading material. *Journal of Verbal Learning and Verbal Behavior, 9,* 647–652.

Hare-Mustin, R.T., & Maracek, J. (1988). The meaning of difference: Gender theory, post-modernism and psychology. *American Psychologist, 43,* 455–464.

Hargreaves, D. (1967). *Social relations in a secondary school.* London: Routledge & Kegan Paul.

Harkness, A.R., DeBono, K.G., & Borgida, E. (1985). Personal involvement and strategies for making contingency judgments: A stake in the dating game makes a difference. *Journal of Personality and Social Psychology, 49,* 22–32.

Harley, T.A. (2001). *The psychology of language: From data to theory* (2nd Ed.). Hove, UK: Psychology Press.

Harlow, H.F. (1959). Love in infant monkeys. *Scientific American, 200,* 68–74.

Harlow, H.F., & Mears, C. (1979). *The human model: Primate perspectives.* Washington, DC: Winston.

Harlow, J.M. (1868). Dr Harlow's case of recovery from the passage of an iron bar through the head. *American Journal of the Medical Sciences, 19,* 13–22.

Harré, R., & Lamb, R. (Eds.). (1983). *The encyclopaedic dictionary of psychology.* London: Blackwell.

Harré, R., & Secord, P. (1972). *The explanation of social behaviour.* Oxford, UK: Basil Blackwell.

Harris, E.L., Noyes, R., Crowe, R.R., & Chaudhry, D.R. (1983). Family study of agoraphobia: Report of a pilot study. *Archives of General Psychiatry, 40,* 1061–1064.

Harris, M. (1990). Language and thought. In M.W. Eysenck (Ed.), *The Blackwell dictionary of cognitive psychology.* Oxford, UK: Blackwell.

Harris, M., Jones, D., Brookes, S., & Grant, J. (1986). Relations between the non-verbal context of maternal speech and rate of language development. *British Journal of Developmental Psychology, 4,* 261–268.

Harris, T.O. (1997). Adult attachment processes and psychotherapy: A commentary on Bartholomew and Birtschnell. *British Journal of Medical Psychology, 70,* 281–290.

Harris, W.H. (1995, June). *The opportunity for romantic love among hunter-gatherers.* Paper presented at the annual convention of the Human Behavior and Evolution Society, Santa Barbara, California.

Hart, B., & Risley, T. (1995). *Meaningful differences in everyday parenting and intellectual development in young American children.* Baltimore: Brookes.

Harter, S., & Monsour, A. (1992). Developmental analysis of conflict caused by opposing attributes in the adolescent self-portrait. *Developmental Psychology, 28,* 251–260.

Hartmann, E.L. (1973). *The functions of sleep.* New Haven, CT: Yale University Press.

Hartshorne, H., & May, M.S. (1928). *Studies in the nature of character: Vol. 1. Studies in deceit.* New York: Macmillan.

Harvey, L.O., Roberts, J.O., & Gervais, M.J. (1983). The spatial frequency basis of internal representations. In H.-G. Geissler, H.F.J.M. Buffart, E.L.J. Leeuwenberg, & V. Sarris (Eds.), *Modern issues in perception.* Rotterdam, The Netherlands: North-Holland.

Haskey, J.C. (1987). Divorce in the early years of marriage in England and Wales: Results from a prospective study using linked records. *Journal of Biosocial Science, 19*(3), 255–271.

Hasler, A.D. (1986). Review of R.J.F. Smith (1985). *Zeitschrift für Tierpsychologie, 70,* 168–169.

Hatfield, E., Utne, M.K., & Traupmann, J. (1979). Equity theory and intimate relationships. In R.L. Burgess & T.L. Huston (Eds.), *Exchange theory in developing relationships.* New York: Academic Press.

Hatfield, E., & Walster, G.W. (1981). *A new look at love.* Reading, MA: Addison-Wesley.

Hauser, M.D. (1988). Invention and social transmission: New data from wild vervet monkeys. In R. Byrne & A. Whiten (Eds.), *Machiavellian intelligence.* Oxford, UK: Clarendon Press.

Havighurst, R.J. (1964). Stages of vocational development. In H. Borrow (Ed.), *Man in a world of work.* Boston: Houghton Mifflin.

Havighurst, R.J., Neugarten, B.L.A., & Tobin, S.S.C. (1968). Disengagement and patterns of aging. In B.L. Neugarten (Ed.), *Middle age and aging.* Chicago: University of Chicago Press.

Hawkins, L.H., & Armstrong-Esther, C.A. (1978, May 4). Circadian rhythms and night shift working in nurses. *Nursing Times,* 49–52.

Hay, J.F., & Jacoby, L.L. (1996). Separating habit and recollection: Memory slips, process dissociations, and probability matching. *Journal of Experimental Psychology: Learning, Memory, and Cognition, 22,* 1323–1335.

Hayes, C. (1951). *The ape in our house.* New York: Harper.

Hazan, C., & Shaver, P.R. (1987). Romantic love conceptualised as an attachment process. *Journal of Personality and Social Psychology, 52,* 511–524.

Hearold, S. (1986). A synthesis of 1043 effects of television on social behaviour. In G. Comstock (Ed.), *Public communication and behaviour, Vol. 1*. Orlando, FL: Academic Press.

Heather, N. (1976). *Radical perspectives in psychology*. London: Methuen.

Hebb, D.O. (1958). *A textbook of psychology*. Philadelphia: W.B. Saunders.

Heckhausen, J. (1997). Developmental regulation across adulthood: Primary and secondary control of age-related challenges. *Developmental Psychology, 33*, 176–187.

Heider, E.R. (1972). Universals in colour naming and memory. *Journal of Experimental Psychology, 93*, 10–20.

Heider, F. (1958). *The psychology of interpersonal relations*. New York: Wiley.

Heinicke, C.H., & Guthrie, D. (1992). Stability and change in husband-wife adaptation and the development of the positive parent-child relationship. *Infant Behavior and Development, 15*, 109–127.

Heisenberg, W. (1927). Uber den anschlauchichen Inhalt der quantentheoretischen Kinetik und Mechanik. *Zeitschrift für Physik, 43*, 172–198.

Hennigan, K.M., Del Rosario, M.L., Cook, T.D., & Calder, B.J. (1982). Impact of the introduction of television on crime in the United States: Empirical findings and theoretical implications. *Journal of Personality and Social Psychology, 42*, 461–477.

Hering, E. (1878). *Outlines of a theory of the light sense* (L.M. Hurvich & D. Jameson, Trans.). Cambridge, MA: Harvard University Press.

Herman, D., & Green, J. (1991). *Madness: A study guide*. London: BBC Education.

Herman, L.M., Richards, D.G., & Wolz, J.P. (1984). Comprehension of sentences by bottlenosed dolphins. *Cognition, 16*, 129–219.

Herrnstein, R.J., & Murray, C.A. (1994). *The bell curve: Intelligence and class structure in American life*. New York: Free Press.

Herzlich, C. (1973). *Health and illness: A social-psychological analysis*. London: Academic Press.

Herzog, H.A. (1988). The moral status of mice. *American Psychologist, 43*, 473–474.

Hess, E.H. (1956). Space perception in the chick. *Scientific American, 227*, 71–80.

Hess, R.D., & Shipman, V. (1965). Early experience and the socialisation of cognitive modes in children. *Child Development, 36*, 860–886.

Hetherington, A.W., & Ranson, S.W. (1942). The relation of various hypothalamic lesions to adiposity in the rat. *Journal of Comparative Neurology, 76*, 475–499.

Hewstone, M., & Antaki, C. (1988). Attribution theory and social explanations. In M. Hewstone, W. Stroebe, J.-P. Codol, & G.M. Stephenson (Eds.), *Introduction to social psychology*. Oxford, UK: Blackwell.

Hewstone, M.R.C., & Brown, R.J. (1986). Contact is not enough: An intergroup perspective on the contact hypothesis. In M.R.C. Hewstone & R.J. Brown (Eds.), *Contact and conflict in intergroup encounters*. Oxford, UK: Blackwell.

Heyes, C.M. (1998). Theory of mind in non-human primates. *Behavioural and Brain Sciences, 21*(1), 103–134.

Hilgard, E.R. (1986). *Divided consciousness: Multiple controls in human thought and action* (Expanded Edn.). New York: Wiley.

Hilgard, E.R., & Marquis, D.G. (1961). *Conditioning and learning*. London: Methuen.

Hirt, E.R., Zillmann, D., Erickson, G.A., & Kennedy, C. (1992). Costs and benefits of allegiance: Changes in fans' self-ascribed competencies after team victory versus defeat. *Journal of Personality and Social Psychology, 63*, 724–738.

Hitchcock, C.L., & Sherry, D.F. (1990). Long-term memory for cache sites in the black-capped chickadee. *Animal Behaviour, 40*, 701–712.

Hobson, J.A. (1988). *The dreaming brain*. New York: Basic Books.

Hobson, J.A. (1994). Sleep and dreaming. In A.M. Colman (Ed.), *Companion encyclopedia of psychology, Vol. 1*. London: Routledge.

Hobson, J.A., & McCarley, R.W. (1977). The brain as a dream state generator: An activation-synthesis hypothesis of the dream process. *American Journal of Psychiatry, 134*, 1335–1348.

Hockett, C.F. (1960). The origin of speech. *Scientific American, 203*, 89–96.

Hodgkinson, S., Sherrington, R., Gurling, H., Marchbanks, R., et al. (1987). Molecular genetic evidence for heterogeneity in manic depression. *Nature, 325*(6107), 805–806.

Hoebel, B.G., & Teitelbaum, P. (1966). Weight regulation in normal and hypothalamic hyperphagic rats. *Journal of Comparative and Physiological Psychology, 61*, 189–193.

Hoffman, C., Lau, I., & Johnson, D.R. (1986). The linguistic relativity of person cognition. *Journal of Personality and Social Psychology, 51*, 1097–1105.

Hoffman, D.D., & Richards, W.A. (1984). Parts of recognition. *Cognition, 18*, 65–96.

Hoffman, M.L. (1970). Moral development. In P.H. Mussen (Ed.), *Carmichael's manual of child psychology, Vol. 2*. New York: Wiley.

Hoffman, M.L. (1975). Altruistic behaviour and the parent–child relationship. *Journal of Personality and Social Psychology, 31*, 937–943.

Hoffman, M.L. (1988). Moral development. In M.H. Bornstein & M. E. Lamb (Eds.), *Developmental psychology: An advanced textbook*. Hillsdale, NJ: Lawrence Erlbaum Associates Inc.

Hofling, C.K. (1974). *Textbook of psychiatry for medical practice*.

Hofstede, G. (1980). *Culture's consequences: International differences in work-related values*. Beverly Hills, CA: Sage.

Hogg, M.A. (1985). Masculine and feminine speech in dyads and groups: A study of speech style and gender salience. *Journal of Language and Social Psychology, 4*, 99–112.

Hogg, M.A., Joyce, N., & Abrams, D. (1984). Disglossia in Switzerland? A social identity analysis of speaker evaluations. *Journal of Language and Social Psychology, 3*, 185–196.

Hohmann, G.W. (1966). Some effects of spinal cord lesions on experienced emotional feelings. *Psychophysiology, 3*, 143–156.

Holland, A.J., Sicotte, N., & Treasure, J. (1988). Anorexia nervosa: Evidence for a genetic basis. *Journal of Psychosomatic Research, 32*, 561–572.

Holldobler, B. (1971). Communication between ants and their guests. *Scientific American, 224*, 85–93.

Holmes, T.H., & Rahe, R.H. (1967). The social readjustment rating scale. *Journal of Psychosomatic Research, 11*, 213–218.

Holmes, W.G., & Sherman, P.W. (1982). The ontogeny of kin recognition in two species of ground squirrels. *American Zoologist, 22*, 491–517.

Holway, A.F., & Boring, E.G. (1941). Determinants of apparent visual size with distance variant. *American Journal of Psychology, 54*, 21–37.

Hoogland, J.L. (1983). Nepotism and alarm calling in the black-tailed prairie dog (*Cynomys ludovicianus*). *Animal Behaviour, 31*, 472–479.

Hooley, J.M., Orley, J., & Teasdale, J.D. (1986). Levels of expressed emotion and relapse in depressed patients. *British Journal of Psychiatry, 148*, 642–647.

Horn, J.M. (1983). The Texas adoption project: Adopted children and their intellectual resemblance to biological and adoptive parents. *Child Development, 54*, 268–275.

Horne, J. (1988). *Why we sleep? The functions of sleep in humans and other mammals*. Oxford, UK: Oxford University Press.

Horne, J.A., & Minard, A. (1985). Sleep and sleepiness following a behaviourally "active" day. *Ergonomics, 28*, 567–575.

Hovland, C., & Sears, R. (1940). Minor studies in aggression: VI. Correlation of lynchings with economic indices. *Journal of Personality, 9*, 301–310.

Howard, J.A., Blumstein, P., & Schwartz, P. (1987). Social evolutionary theories? Some observations on preferences in human mate selection. *Journal of Personality and Social Psychology, 53*, 194–200.

Howe, C., Tolmie, A., & Rodgers, C. (1992). The acquisition of conceptual knowledge in science by primary school children: Group interaction and the understanding of motion down an incline. *British Journal of Developmental Psychology, 10*, 113–130.

Howitt, D., & Owusu-Bempah (1990). Racism in a British journal? *The Psychologist, 3*, 396–400.

Hsu, F. (1981). *Americans and Chinese: Passage to difference* (3rd Edn.). Honolulu: University Press of Honolulu.

Hubel, D.H., & Wiesel, T.N. (1962). Receptive fields, binocular interaction and functional architecture in the cat's visual cortex. *Journal of Physiology, 160*, 106–154.

Hubel, D.H., & Wiesel, T.N. (1979). Brain mechanisms of vision. *Scientific American, 249*, 150–162.

Hüber-Weidman, H. (1976). *Sleep, sleep disturbances and sleep deprivation.* Cologne, Germany: Kiepenheuser & Witsch.

Hudson, W. (1960). Pictorial depth perception in subcultural groups in Africa. *Journal of Social Psychology, 52*, 183–208.

Huesmann, L.R., & Eron, L.D. (1986). *Television and the aggressive child: A cross-national comparison.* Hillsdale, NJ: Lawrence Erlbaum Associates Inc.

Huesmann, L.R., Lagerspitz, K., & Eron, L.D. (1984). Intervening variables in the TV violence–aggression relation: Evidence from two countries. *Developmental Psychology, 20*, 746–775.

Hughes, M. (1975). *Egocentrism in preschool children.* Unpublished PhD thesis, University of Edinburgh, UK.

Hull, C.L. (1943). *Principles of behaviour.* New York: Appleton-Century-Crofts.

Hummel, J.E., & Biederman, I. (1992). Dynamic binding in a neural network for shape recognition. *Psychological Review, 99*, 480–517.

Hummel, J.E., & Holyoak, K.J. (1997). Distributed representations of structure: A theory of analogical access and mapping. *Psychological Review, 104*, 427–466.

Humphreys, P.W. (1999). Culture-bound syndromes. *Psychology Review, 6*(3), 14–18.

Hunt, E., & Agnoli, F. (1991). The Whorfian hypothesis: A cognitive psychological perspective. *Psychological Review, 98*, 377–389.

Hunter, M.L., & Krebs, J.R. (1979). Geographical variation in the song of the great tit (*Parus major*) in relation to ecological factors. *Journal of Animal Ecology, 48*, 759–785.

Huston, A.C. (1985). The development of sex typing: Themes from recent research. *Developmental Review, 5*, 1–17.

Huston, T.L., Ruggiero, M., Conner, R., & Geis, G. (1981). Bystander intervention into crime: A study based on naturally-occurring episodes. *Social Psychology Quarterly, 44*, 14–23.

Hyde, J.S., & Linn, M.C. (1988). Gender differences in verbal ability: A meta-analysis. *Psychological Bulletin, 104*, 53–69.

Imperato-McGinley, J., Guerro, L., Gautier, T., & Peterson, R.E. (1974). Steroid 5–reductase deficiency in man: An inherited form of male pseudohermaphroditism. *Science, 186*, 1213–1216.

Inhelder, B., & Piaget, J. (1958). *The growth of logical thinking from childhood to adolescence.* New York: Basic Books.

Irwin, A.R., & Gross, A.M. (1995). Cognitive tempo, violent video games, and aggressive behaviour in young boys. *Journal of Family Violence, 10*, 337–350.

Irwin, M., Lovitz, A., Marder, S.R., Mintz, J., Winslade, W.J., Van Putten, T., & Mills, M.J. (1985). Psychotic patients understanding of informed consent. *American Journal of Psychiatry, 142*, 1351–1354.

Ittelson, W.H. (1951). Size as a cue to distance: Static localisation. *American Journal of Psychology, 64*, 54–67.

Ittelson, W.H. (1952). *The Ames demonstrations in perception.* New York: Hafner.

Jacobs, P.A., Brunton, M., & Melville, M.M. (1965). Aggressive behaviour, mental abnormality and XXY male. *Nature, 208*, 1351–1352.

Jacobsen, C.F., Wolfe, J.B., & Jackson, T.A. (1935). An experimental analysis of the functions of the frontal association areas in primates. *Journal of Nervous and Mental Disorders, 82*, 1–14.

James, W. (1890). *Principles of psychology.* New York: Holt.

Janicak, P.G., Davis, J.M, Gibbons, R.D., Ericksen, S., Chang, S., & Gallagher, P. (1985). Efficacy of ECT: A meta-analysis. *American Journal of Psychiatry, 142*, 297–302.

Janik, V.M. (2000). Whistle matching in wild bottlenose dolphins (*Tursiops truncatus*). *Science, 289*, 1355–1357.

Jarrard, L.E. (1995). What does the hippocampus really do? *Behavioural Brain Research, 71*, 1–10.

Jarvis, M. (2000). *Theoretical approaches in psychology.* London: Routledge.

Jenkins, C.D., Hurst, M.W., & Rose, R.M. (1979). Life changes: Do people really remember? *Archives of General Psychiatry, 36*, 379–384.

Jens, K.S., & Evans, H.I. (1983). *The diagnosis and treatment of multiple personality clients.* Workshop presented at the Rocky Mountain Psychological Association, Snowbird, Utah. [Reported in D.L. Rosenhan and M.E.P. Seligman (1989). *Abnormal psychology* (2nd Edn.). London: Norton.]

Jensen, A.R. (1969). How much can we boost IQ and scholastic achievement? *Harvard Educational Review, 39*, 1-123.

Jodelet, D. (1991). Représentation sociale: Phénomenes, concept et théorie. In S. Moscovici (Ed.), *Psychologie sociale.* Paris: Presses Universitaires de France.

Johansson, G. (1973). Visual perception of biological motion and a model for its analysis. *Perception and Psychophysics, 14*, 201–211.

Johnson, S.C., Pinkston, J.B., Bigler, E.D., & Blatter, D.D. (1996). Corpus callosum morphology in normal controls and traumatic brain injury: Sex differences, mechanisms of injury, and neuropsychological correlates. *Neuropsychology, 10*, 408–415.

Johnston, J., & Ettema, J.S. (1982). *Positive image: Breaking stereotypes with children's television.* Beverly Hills, CA: Sage.

Johnston, W.A., & Dark, V.J. (1986). Selective attention. *Annual Review of Psychology, 37*, 43–75.

Johnston, J., & Ettema, J. (1986). Using television to best advantage: Research for prosocial television. In J. Bryant & D. Zillman (Eds.), *Perspectives on media effects.* Hillsdale, NJ: Lawrence Erlbaum Associates Inc.

Johnston, W.A., & Heinz, S.P. (1978). Flexibility and capacity demands of attention. *Journal of Experimental Psychology: General, 107*, 420–435.

Johnston, W.A., & Wilson, J. (1980). Perceptual processing of non-targets in an attention task. *Memory and Cognition, 8*, 372–377.

Johnstone, L. (1989). *Users and abusers of psychiatry: A critical look at traditional psychiatric practice.* London: Routledge.

Jolicoeur, P., & Landau, M.J. (1984). Effects of orientation on the identification of simple visual patterns. *Canadian Journal of Psychology, 38*, 80–93.

Jones, E.E., & Davis, K.E. (1965). From acts to dispositions: The attribution process in person perception. In L. Berkowitz (Ed.), *Advances in experimental social psychology, Vol. 2.* New York: Academic Press.

Jones, E.E., & Harris, V.A. (1967). The attribution of attitudes. *Journal of Experimental Social Psychology, 3*, 1–24.

Jones, E.E., & Nisbett, R.E. (1972). The actor and the observer: Divergent perceptions of the causes of behaviour. In E.E. Jones, D.E. Kanouse, H.H. Kelley, R.E. Nisbett, S. Valins, & B. Weiner (Eds.), *Attribution: Perceiving the causes of behaviour*. Morristown, NJ: General Learning Press.

Jones, M.C. (1925). A laboratory study of fear: The case of Peter. *Pedagogical Seminary, 31*, 308–315.

Josephson, W.L. (1987). Television violence and children's aggression: Testing the priming, social script, and disinhibition predictions. *Journal of Personality and Social Psychology, 53*, 882–890.

Jouvet, M. (1967). Mechanisms of the states of sleep: A neuropharmological approach. *Research Publications of the Association for the Research in Nervous and Mental Disorders, 45*, 86–126.

Joynson, R.B. (1989). *The Burt affair*. London: Routledge.

Juola, J.F., Bowhuis, D.G., Cooper, E.E., & Warner, C.B. (1991). Control of attention around the fovea. *Journal of Experimental Psychology: Human Perception and Performance, 15*, 315–330.

Kahneman, D., & Henik, A. (1979). Perceptual organisation and attention. In M. Kubovy & J.R. Pomerantz (Eds.), *Perceptual organisation*. Hillsdale, NJ: Lawrence Erlbaum Associates Inc.

Kahneman, D., & Tversky, A. (1972). Subjective probability: A judgment of representativeness. *Cognitive Psychology, 3*, 430–454.

Kahneman, D., & Tversky, A. (1973). On the psychology of prediction. *Psychological Review, 80*, 237–251.

Kahneman, D., & Tversky, A. (1984). Choices, values and frames. *American Psychologist, 39*, 341–350.

Kalat, J.W. (1998). *Biological psychology*. Pacific Grove, CA: Brooks/Cole Publishing Co.

Kamin, L. (1981). *The intelligence controversy: H.J. Eysenck vs. Leon Kamin*. New York: Wiley.

Kamin, L.J. (1969). Predictability, surprise, attention and conditioning. In R. Campbell & R. Church (Eds.), *Punishment and aversive behaviour*. New York: Appleton-Century-Crofts.

Kamin, L.J. (1977). *The science and politics of IQ*. Harmondsworth, UK: Penguin.

Kandel, D.B. (1978). Similarity in real-life adolescent friendship pairs. *Journal of Personality and Social Psychology, 36*, 306–312.

Kane, J., Honigfeld, G., Singer, J., & Meltzer, H.Y. (1988). Clozapine for the treatment resistant schizophrenic. *Archives of General Psychiatry, 45*, 789–796.

Kanizsa, G. (1976). Subjective contours. *Scientific American, 234*, 48–52.

Kanner, L. (1943). Autistic disturbances of affective contact. *Nervous Child, 2*, 217–250.

Karlins, M., Coffman, T.L., & Walters, G. (1969). On the fading of social stereotypes: Studies in three generations of college students. *Journal of Personality and Social Psychology, 13*, 1–16.

Karney, B.R., & Bradbury, T.N. (1995). The longitudinal course of marital quality and stability: A review of theory, method, and research. *Psychological Bulletin, 118*, 3–34.

Kashima, Y., & Triandis, H.C. (1986). The self-serving bias in attributions as a coping strategy: A cross-cultural study. *Journal of Cross-Cultural Psychology, 17*, 83–97.

Katz, D., & Braly, K.W. (1933). Racial stereotypes of one hundred college students. *Journal of Abnormal and Social Psychology, 28*, 280–290.

Kavanagh, D.J. (1992). Recent developments in expressed emotion and schizophrenia. *British Journal of Psychiatry, 160*, 601–620.

Kawai, M. (1965). Newly acquired pre-cultural behaviour of the natural troop of Japanese monkeys on Koshima Islet. *Primates, 6*, 1–30.

Keane, M.T., Ledgeway, T., & Duff, S. (1994). Constraints on analogical mapping: A comparison of three models. *Cognitive Science, 18*, 287–334.

Keeton, W.T. (1974). The mystery of pigeon homing. *Scientific American, 231*, 96–107.

Kekhy, S.R., & Sejnowski, T.J. (1988). Network model of shape-from-shading: Neural function arises from both receptive and projective fields. *Nature, 333*, 452–454.

Kelley, H.H. (1950). The warm–cold variable in first impressions of people. *Journal of Personality, 18*, 431–439.

Kelley, H.H. (1967). Attribution theory in social psychology. In D. Levine (Ed.), *Nebraska symposium on motivation*. Lincoln, NE: University of Nebraska Press.

Kelley, H.H. (1973). The processes of causal attribution. *American Psychologist, 28*, 107–128.

Kendall, P.C., & Hammen, C. (1995). *Abnormal psychology*. Boston: Houghton Mifflin.

Kendall, P.C., & Hammen, C. (1998). *Abnormal psychology* (2nd Edn.). Boston: Houghton Mifflin.

Kenrick, D.T., & Gutierres, S.E. (1980). Contrast effects in judgments of attractiveness: When beauty becomes a social problem. *Journal of Personality and Social Psychology, 38*, 131–140.

Kerckhoff, A.C., & Davis, K.E. (1962). Value consensus and need complementarity in mate selection. *American Sociological Review, 27*, 295–303.

Kessel, E.L. (1955). Mating activities of balloon flies. *Systematic Zoology, 4*, 97–104.

Kettlewell, H.B.D. (1955). Selection experiments on industrial melanism in the Lepidoptera. *Heredity, 9*, 323–342.

Kety, S.S. (1974). From rationalisation to reason. *American Journal of Psychiatry, 131*, 957–963.

Kety, S.S. (1975). Biochemistry of the major psychoses. In A. Freedman, H. Kaplan, & B. Sadock (Eds.), *Comprehensive textbook of psychiatry*. Baltimore: Williams & Wilkins.

Kety, S.S., Rosenthal, D., Wender, P.H., Schulsinger, F., & Jacobsen, B. (1978). The biological and adoptive families of adoptive individuals who become schizophrenic. In L.C. Wynne, R.L. Cromwell, & S. Matthysse (Eds.), *The nature of schizophrenia*. New York: John Wiley.

Keuthen, N. (1980). *Subjective probability estimation and somatic structures in phobic individuals*. Unpublished manuscript, State University of New York at Stony Brook.

Kimble, D.P., Robinson, T.S., & Moon, S. (1980). *Biological psychology*. New York: Holt, Reinhart, & Winston.

Kimmel, D.C. (1990). *Adulthood and ageing* (3rd Edn.). New York: John Wiley & Sons.

Kimura, D. (1979). Neuromotor mechanisms in the evolution of human communication. In H.E. Steklis & M.J. Raleigh (Eds.), *Neurobiology of social communication in primates*. New York: Academic Press.

Kimura, D. (1992). Sex differences in the brain. *Scientific American, 267*(3), 118–125.

Kimura, D., & Watson, N. (1989). The relation between oral movement control and speech. *Brain and Language, 37*, 565–590.

Kinchla, R.A., & Wolf, J.M. (1979). The order of visual processing: "Top-down," "bottom-up," or "middle-out." *Perception and Psychophysics, 25*, 225–231.

Kingston, A., & Gazzaniga, M.S. (1995). Subcortical transfer of higher order information: More illusory than real? *Neuropsychology, 9*, 321–328.

Kitzinger, C., & Coyle, A. (1995). Lesbian and gay couples: Speaking of difference. *The Psychologist, 8*, 64–69.

Klein, K.E., Wegman, H.M., & Hunt, B.I. (1972). Desynchronisation of body temperature and performance circadian rhythm as a result of outgoing and homegoing transmeridian flights. *Aerospace Medicine, 43,* 119–132.

Kleiner, L., & Marshall, W.L. (1987). The role of interpersonal problems in the development of agoraphobia with panic attacks. *Journal of Anxiety Disorders, 1,* 313–323.

Kleinman, A., & Cohen, A. (1997). Psychiatry's global challenge. *Scientific American,* March, 74–77.

Kleinmuntz, B. (1974). *Essentials of abnormal psychology.*

Kline, P. (1981). *Fact and fantasy in Freudian theory.* London: Methuen.

Kluger, M.J. (1991). Fever: Role of pyrogens and cryogens. *Physiological Reviews, 71,* 93–127.

Klüver, H., & Bucy, P.C. (1939). Preliminary analysis of functions of the temporal lobes in monkeys. *Archives of Neurology and Psychiatry, 42,* 979–1000.

Knecht, T. (1999). Amok and quasi-amok. *Schweizer Archiv fuer Neurologie und Psychiatrie, 150*(3), 142–148.

Knoblich, G., Ohlsson, S., Haider, H., & Rhenius, D. (1999). Constraint relaxation and chunk decomposition in insight. *Journal of Experimental Psychology: Learning, Memory and Cognition, 25,* 1534–1555.

Knox, J.V., Morgan, A.H., & Hilgard, E.R. (1974). Pain and suffering in ischemia: The paradox of hypnotically suggested anaesthesia as contradicted by reports from the "hidden-observer". *Archives of General Psychiatry, 30,* 840–847.

Koehler, J.J. (1996). The base rate fallacy reconsidered: Descriptive, normative, and methological challenges. *Behavioral and Brain Sciences, 19,* 1–53.

Koestner, R., & McClelland, D.C. (1990). Perspectives on competence motivation. In L.A. Pervin (Ed.), *Handbook of personality: Theory and research.* New York: Guilford.

Koffka, K. (1935). *Principles of Gestalt psychology.* New York: Harcourt Brace.

Kohlberg, L. (1963). Development of children's orientations toward a moral order. *Vita Humana, 6,* 11–36.

Kohlberg, L. (1966). A cognitive-development analysis of children's sex-role concepts and attitudes. In E.E. Maccoby (Ed.), *The development of sex differences.* Stanford, CA: Stanford University Press.

Kohlberg, L. (1969). Stage and sequence: The cognitive-developmental approach to socialisation. In D.A. Goslin (Ed.), *Handbook of socialisation theory and practice.* Skokie, IL: Rand McNally.

Kohlberg, L. (1975). The cognitive-developmental approach to moral education. *Phi Delta Kappan, June,* 670–677.

Kohlberg, L. (1976). Moral stages and moralization. In T. Likona (Ed.), *Moral development and behaviour.* New York: Holt, Rinehart & Winston.

Kohlberg, L. (1981). *Essays on moral development: Vol. 1. The philosophy of moral development.* San Francisco: Harper & Row.

Kohler, W. (1925). *The mentality of apes.* New York: Harcourt Brace & World.

Kolb, B., & Whishaw, I.Q. (1990). *Fundamentals of human neuropsychology* (3rd Edn.). New York: Freeman.

Kosslyn, S.M. (1988). Aspects of cognitive neuroscience of mental imagery. *Science, 240,* 1621–1626.

Kozlowski, L.T., & Cutting, J.E. (1978). Recognising the gender of walkers from point-lights mounted on ankles: Some second thoughts. *Perception and Psychophysics, 23,* 459.

Kramer, A.F., & Hahn, S. (1995). Splitting the beam: Distribution of attention over noncontiguous regions of the visual field. *Psychological Science, 6,* 381–386.

Kramer, G. (1953). Die Sonnenorientiering der Vogel. *Verh. Deut. Zool. Ges. Freiburg, 1952,* 72–84.

Krause, N., Jay, G., & Liang, J. (1991). Financial strain and psychological well-being among the American and Japanese elderly. *Psychology and Aging, 6,* 170–181.

Krebs, J.R., & Davies, N.B. (1993). *An introduction to behavioural ecology* (3rd Edn.). Oxford, UK: Blackwell.

Kübler-Ross, E. (1969). *On death and dying.* London: Tavistock/Routledge.

Kuhn, T.S. (1962). *The structure of scientific revolutions.* Chicago: Chicago University Press.

Kuhn, T.S. (1970). *The structure of scientific revolutions* (2nd Edn.). Chicago: Chicago University Press.

Kuhn, T.S. (1977). *The essential tension: Selected studies in scientific tradition and change.* Chicago: Chicago University Press.

Kunnapas, T.M. (1968). Distance perception as a function of available visual cues. *Journal of Experimental Psychology, 77,* 523–529.

Kuo-shu, Y., & Bond, M.H. (1990). Exploring implicit personality theories with indigenous or imported constructs: The Chinese case. *Journal of Personality and Social Psychology, 58,* 1087–1095.

Kurdek, L.A., & Schmitt, J.P. (1986). Relationship quality of partners in heterosexual married, heterosexual cohabiting, and gay and lesbian relationships. *Journal of Personality and Social Psychology, 51,* 711–720.

LaBerge, D. (1983). Spatial extent of attention to letters and words. *Journal of Experimental Psychology: Human Perception and Performance, 9,* 371–379.

LaBerge, S., Greenleaf, W., & Kedzierski, B. (1983). Physiological responses to dreamed sexual activity during lucid REM sleep. *Psychophysiology, 20,* 454–455.

Labov, W. (1969). The logic of nonstandard English. *Georgetown Monographs on Language and Linguistics, 22,* 1–22, 26–31.

Labov, W. (1972). *Language in the inner city: Studies in Black English vernacular.* Philadelphia: Falmer Press.

Lack, D. (1968). *Ecological adaptations for breeding in birds.* London: Methuen.

Lader, M.H., & Mathews, A. (1968). A physiological model of phobic anxiety and desensitisation. *Behaviour Research and Therapy, 6,* 411–421.

Laing, R.D. (1967). *The politics of experience.* New York: Ballantine.

Laird, J.D. (1974). Self-attribution of emotion: The effects of facial expression on the quality of emotional experience. *Journal of Personality and Social Psychology, 29,* 475–486.

Lalljee, M. (1981). Attribution theory and the analysis of explanations. In C. Antaki (Ed.), *The psychology of ordinary explanations of social behaviour.* London: Academic Press.

Land, E.H. (1977). The retinex theory of colour vision. *Scientific American, 237,* 108–128.

Langer, E.J., & Rodin, J. (1976). The effects of choice and enhanced personal responsibility for the aged. *Journal of Personality and Social Psychology, 34,* 191–198.

Larsen, A., & Bundesen, C. (1992). The efficiency of holistic template matching in the recognition of unconstrained handwritten digits. *Psychological Research, 54,* 187–193.

Larsen, A., & Bundesen, C. (1996). A template-matching pandemonium recognises unconstrained handwritten characters with high accuracy. *Memory and Cognition, 24,* 136–143.

Larsen, P. (1997). The impact of ageing on cognitive functioning: An 11-year follow-up study of four age cohorts. *Acta Neurologica Scandinavica, 96*(S172).

Larson, R.W., & Lampman-Petraitis, C. (1989). Daily emotional states as reported by children and adolescents. *Child Development, 60,* 1250–1260.

Larson, R.W., Richards, M.H., Moneta, G., Holmbeck, G., & Duckett, E. (1996). Changes in adolescents' daily interactions with their families from ages 10 to 18: Disengagement and transformation. *Developmental Psychology, 32,* 744–754.

Lashley, K. (1931). Mass action in cerebral function. *Science, 73,* 245–254.

Latané, B., & Darley, J.M. (1970). *The unresponsive bystander: Why doesn't he help?* Englewood Cliffs, NJ: Prentice-Hall.

Latham, G.P., & Yukl, G.A. (1975). Assigned versus participative goal setting with educated and uneducated woods workers. *Journal of Applied Psychology, 60,* 299–302.

Lazar, I., & Darlington, R. (1982). Lasting effects of early education: A report from the Consortium for Longitudinal Studies. *Monographs of the Society for Research in Child Development, 47*(195).

Lazarus, A.A., & Davison, G.C. (1971). Clinical innovation in research and practice. In A.E. Bergin & S.L. Garfield (Eds.), *Handbook of psychotherapy and behaviour change: An empirical analysis.* Chichester, UK: Wiley.

Lazarus, R.S. (1966). *Psychological stress and the coping process.* New York: McGraw-Hill.

Lazarus, R.S. (1982). Thoughts on the relations between emotion and cognition. *American Psychologist, 37,* 1019–1024.

Lazarus, R.S. (1991). *Emotion and adaptation.* Oxford, UK: Oxford University Press.

Lazarus, R.S., Opton, E.M., Jr., Nomikos, M.S., & Rankin, N.O. (1965). The principle of short-circuiting of threat: Further evidence. *Journal of Personality and Social Psychology, 33,* 622–635.

Lednore, A.J., & Walcott, C. (1983). Homing pigeons in navigation: The effects of in-flight exposure to a varying magnetic field. *Comparative Biochemistry and Physiology, 76,* 665–671.

LeDoux, J.E. (1989). Cognitive-emotional interactions in the brain. *Cognition and Emotion, 3,* 267–289.

LeDoux, J.E. (1995). Emotion: Clues from the brain. *Annual Review of Psychology, 46,* 209–235.

Lee, H. (1997). *Virginia Woolf.* London: Vintage.

Lee, J.A. (1973). *The colours of love: An exploration of the ways of loving.* Ontario, Canada: New Press.

Lee, L. (1984). Sequences in separation: A framework for investigating endings of the personal (romantic) relationship. *Journal of Social and Personal Relationships, 1,* 49–74.

Leibowitz, H., Brislin, R., Permutter, L., & Hennessy, R. (1969). Ponzo perspective illusions as a manifestation of space perception. *Science, 166,* 1174–1176.

Lemyre, L., & Smith, P.M. (1985). Intergroup discrimination and self-esteem in the minimal group paradigm. *Journal of Personality and Social Psychology, 49,* 660–670.

Lenneberg, E.H. (1967). *The biological foundations of language.* New York: Wiley.

Lenneberg, E.H., & Roberts, J.M. (1956). *The language of experience. Memoir 13.* University of Indiana, Publications in Anthropology and Linguistics.

Lepper, M.R., Greene, D., & Nisbett, R.E. (1973). Undermining children's intrinsic interest with extrinsic reward: A test of the overjustification hypothesis. *Journal of Personality and Social Psychology, 28,* 129–137.

Lerner, M.J., & Lichtman, R.R. (1968). Effects of perceived norms on attitudes and altruistic behaviour towards a dependent other. *Journal of Personality and Social Psychology, 9,* 226–232.

Lerner, R.M., & Galambos, N.L. (1985). The adolescent experience: A view of the issues. In R.M. Lerner & N.L. Galambos (Eds.), *Experiencing adolescents: A sourcebook for parents, teachers, and teens.* New York: Garland.

Lester, D. (1977). Multiple personality: A review. *Psychology, 14,* 54–59.

Levine, R., Sato, S., Hashimoto, T., & Verma, J. (1995). Love and marriage in eleven cultures. *Journal of Cross-Cultural Psychology, 26,* 554–571.

Levinger, G. (1976). A social psychological perspective on marital dissolution. *Journal of Social Issues, 32,* 21–47.

Levinger, G. (1980). Toward the analysis of close relationships. *Journal of Experimental Social Psychology, 16,* 510–544.

Levinger, G., & Clark, J. (1961). Emotional factors in the forgetting of word associations. *Journal of Abnormal and Social Psychology, 62,* 99–105.

Levinson, D.J. (1978). *The seasons of a man's life.* New York: Ballantine.

Levinson, D.J. (1986). A conception of adult development. *American Psychologist, 41,* 3–13.

Levy, J. (1969). Possible basis for the evolution of lateral specialisation of the human brain. *Nature, 224,* 614–615.

Levy, J., Heller, W., Banich, M.T., & Burton, L.A. (1983). Asymmetry of perception in free viewing of chimeric faces. *Brain and Cognition, 2,* 404–419.

Levy, J., Trevarthen, C., & Sperry, R.W. (1972). Perception of bilateral chimeric figures following hemispheric deconnection. *Brain, 95,* 61–78.

Lewinsohn, P.M. (1974). A behavioural approach to depression. In R.J. Friedman & M.M. Katz (Eds.), *The psychology of depression: Contemporary theory and research.* Washington, DC: Winston-Wiley.

Lewinsohn, P.M., Steimetz, J.L., Larsen, D.W., & Franklin, J. (1981). Depression related cognitions: Antecedent or consequences? *Journal of Abnormal Psychology, 90,* 213–219.

Lewis, M., & Brooks-Gunn, J. (1979). *Social cognition and the acquisition of self.* New York: Plenum.

Leyens, J.-P., Camino, L., Parke, R.D., & Berkowitz, L. (1975). Effects of movie violence on aggression in a field setting as a function of group dominance and cohesion. *Journal of Personality and Social Psychology, 32,* 346–360.

Lichtenstein, S., Slovic, P., Fischhoff, B., Layman, M., & Combs, B. (1978). Judged frequency of lethal events. *Journal of Experimental Psychology: Human Learning and Memory, 4,* 551–578.

Lick, J. (1975). Expectancy, false galvanic skin response feedback and systematic desensitisation in the modification of phobic behaviour. *Journal of Consulting and Clinical Psychology, 43,* 557–567.

Lieberman, M., & Coplan, A. (1970). Distance from death as a variable in the study of aging. *Developmental Psychology, 2,* 71–84.

Light, P., Buckingham, N., & Robbins, A.H. (1979). The conservation task as an interactional setting. *British Journal of Educational Psychology, 49,* 304–310.

Light, P., Littleton, K., Messer, D., & Joiner, R. (1994). Social and communicative processes in computer-based problem solving. *European Journal of Psychology of Education, 9,* 93–109.

Lilienfield, S., Lyn, S., Kirsch, T., Chaves, J., Sarbin, T., Gammaway, G., & Powell, R. (1999). Dissociative identity disorder and the sociocognitive model: Recalling the lessons of the past. *Psychological Bulletin, 125*(5), 507–523.

Lim, R.F., & Keh-Ming, L. (1996). Cultural formulation of psychiatric diagnosis: Case No. 03: Psychosis following qi-gong in a Chinese immigrant. *Culture, Medicine, and Psychiatry, 20,* 369–378.

Locke, E.A. (1968). Toward a theory of task motivation and incentives. *Organizational Behavior and Human Performance, 3,* 157–189.

Locke, E.A., Bryan, J.F., & Kendall, L.M. (1968). Goals and intention as mediators of the effects of monetary incentives on behaviour. *Journal of Applied Psychology, 52,* 104–121.

Locke, E.A., Shaw, K.N., Saari, L.M., & Latham, G.P. (1981). Goal setting and task performance: 1969–1980. *Psychological Bulletin, 90,* 125–152.

Loehlin, J.C., Horn, J.M., & Willerman, L. (1989). Modeling IQ change: Evidence from the Texas Adoption Project. *Child Development*, 60, 893–904.

Loehlin, J.C., & Nichols, R.C. (1976). *Heredity, environment and personality*. Austin, TX: University of Texas Press.

Logan, G.D. (1988). Toward an instance theory of automatisation. *Psychological Review*, 95, 492–527.

Loo, C.M. (1979). The effects of spatial density on the social behaviour of children. *Journal of Applied Social Research*, 2, 372–381.

Lopata, H.Z. (1979). Widowhood and husband sanctification. In L.A. Bugen (Ed.), *Death and dying: Theory, research, practice*. Dubuque, IO: W.C. Brown.

Lopes, L.L. (1987). Between hope and fear: The psychology of risk. In L. Berkowitz (Ed.), *Advances in experimental social psychology, Vol. 20*. San Diego, CA: Academic Press.

Lorenz, K.Z. (1966). *On aggression*. New York: Harcourt, Brace & World.

Lott, B.E. (1994). *Women's lives: Theories and variations in gender learning*. Pacific Grove, CA: Brooks Cole.

Lovaas, O.I., Freitas, L., Nelson, K., & Whalen, C. (1967). The establishment of imitation and its use for development of complex behaviour in schizophrenic children. *Behaviour Research and Therapy*, 5, 171–181.

Lovelace, V., & Huston, H.C. (1983). Can television teach prosocial behaviour? *Prevention in Human Services*, 2, 93–106.

Loveless, N.E. (1983). Event-related brain potentials and human performance. In A. Gale & J.A. Edwards (Eds.), *Physiological correlates of human behaviour: Vol. II. Attention and performance*. London: Academic Press.

Luborsky, L., & Spence, D.P. (1978). Quantitative research on psychoanalytic therapy. In S.L. Garfield & A.E. Bergin (Eds.), *Handbook of psychotherapy and behaviour change: An empirical analysis* (2nd Edn.). New York: Wiley.

Lucas, A., Morley, R., Cole, T.J., Lister, G., & Leeson, P.C. (1992). Breast milk and subsequent intelligence quotient in children born preterm. *Lancet*, 339(8788), 261–264.

Luce, G.G., & Segal, J. (1966). *Sleep*. New York: Coward, McCann & Geoghegan.

Luchins, A.S. (1957). Primacy-recency in impression formation. In C. Hovland (Ed.), *The order of presentation in persuasion*. New Haven, CT: Yale University Press.

Luchins, A.S., & Luchins, E.H. (1959). *Rigidity of behaviour*. Eugene, OR: University of Oregon Press.

Lucy, J., & Schweder, R. (1979). Whorf and his critics: Linguistic and non-linguistic influences on colour memory. *American Anthropologist*, 81, 581–615.

Ludwig, A.M. (1975). Sensory overload and psychopathology. *Diseases of the Nervous System*, 36, 357–360.

Luepnitz, R.R., Randolph, D.L., & Gutsch, K.U. (1982). Race and socioeconomic status as confounding variables in the accurate diagnosis of alcoholism. *Journal of Clinical Psychology*, 38, 665–669.

Lugaressi, E., Medori, R., Montagna, P., Baruzzi, A., Cortelli, P., Lugaressi, A., Tinuper, A., Zucconi, M., & Gambetti, P. (1986). Fatal familial insomnia and dysautonomia in the selective degeneration of thalamic nuclei. *New England Journal of Medicine*, 315, 997–1003.

Lund, M. (1985). The development of investment and commitment scales for predicting continuity of personal relationships. *Journal of Social and Personal Relationships*, 2, 3–23.

Lund, N. (2001). *Attention and pattern recognition*. London: Routledge.

Lynch, J.J. (1977). *The broken heart: The medical consequences of loneliness*. New York: Basic Books.

Lytton, H. (1977). Do parents create, or respond to, differences in twins? *Developmental Psychology*, 13, 456–459.

Lytton, H., & Romney, D.M. (1991). Parents' differential socialisation of boys and girls: A meta-analysis. *Psychological Bulletin*, 109, 267–296.

Ma, H.K. (1988). The Chinese perspective on moral judgement development. *International Journal of Psychology*, 23, 201–227.

MacArthur, R.H., & Pianka, E.R. (1966). On optimal use of a patchy environment. *American Naturalist*, 100, 603–609.

Maccoby, E.E., & Jacklin, C.N. (1974). *The psychology of sex differences*. Stanford, CA: Stanford University Press.

MacDonald, I.M.V. (1997). Field experiments on duration and precision of grey and red squirrel spatial memory. *Animal Behaviour*, 54, 879–891.

MacKay, D. (1987). Divided brains—divided minds. In C. Blakemore & S. Greenfield (Eds.), *Mindwaves: Thoughts on intelligence, identity and consciousness*. Oxford, UK: Blackwell.

MacKay, D.G. (1973). Aspects of the theory of comprehension, memory and attention. *Quarterly Journal of Experimental Psychology*, 25, 22–40.

Mackintosh, N.J. (1986). The biology of intelligence? *British Journal of Psychology*, 77, 1–18.

Mackintosh, N.J. (1994). Classical and operant conditioning. In A.M. Colman (Ed.), *Companion encyclopedia of psychology, Vol. 1*. London: Routledge.

MacLean, P.D. (1949). Psychosomatic disease and the "visceral brain": Recent developments bearing on the Papez theory of emotion. *Psychosomatic Medicine*, 11, 338–353.

MacLeod, A. (1998). Abnormal psychology. In M.W. Eysenck (Ed.), *Psychology: An integrated approach*. Harlow, UK: Addison Wesley Longman.

Macrae, C.N., Milne, A.B., & Bodenhausen, G.V. (1994). Stereotypes as energy-saving devices: A peek inside the cognitive toolbox. *Journal of Personality and Social Psychology*, 66, 37–47.

Maddox, G.L. (1970). Persistence of life style among the elderly. In E. Palmore (Ed.), *Normal aging*. Durham: Duke University Press.

Maguire, E., Frackowiak, R., & Frith, C.D. (1997). Recalling routes around London: Activation of the right hippocampus in taxi drivers. *Journal of Neuroscience*, 17, 7103–7110.

Maguire, E., Gadian, D., Johnsrude, I., Good, C., Ashburner, J., Frackowiak, R., & Frith, D. (2000). Navigation-related structural change in the hippocampi of taxi drivers. *Proceedings of the National Academy of Sciences*, 96, 10.1073/pnas 070039597, 14 March.

Maier, N.R.F. (1931). Reasoning in humans: II. The solution of a problem and its appearance in consciousness. *Journal of Comparative Psychology*, 12, 181–194.

Mair, K. (1992). The myth of therapist expertise. In W. Dryden & C. Feltham (Eds.), *Psychotherapy and its discontents*. Buckingham, UK: Open University Press.

Malim, T., Birch, A., & Wadeley, A. (1992). *Perspectives in psychology*. London: Macmillan.

Malone, D.R., Morris, H.H., Kay, M.C., & Levin, H.S. (1982). Prosopagnosia: A double dissociation between the recognition of familiar and unfamiliar faces. *Journal of Neurology, Neurosurgery and Psychiatry*, 45, 820–822.

Malott, R.W., Malott, M.K., & Pokrzywinski, J. (1967). The effects of outward pointing arrowheads on the Muller-Lyer illusion in pigeons. *Psychonomic Science*, 9, 55–56.

Malthus, T.R. (1798). *An essay on the principle of population*. Harmondsworth, UK: Penguin Books.

Mandler, G. (1967). Organisation and memory. In K.W. Spence & J.T. Spence (Eds.), *Advances in research and theory: Vol. 1. The psychology of learning and motivation*: London: Academic Press.

Manstead, A.R., & McCulloch, C. (1981). Sex-role stereotyping in British television advertisements. *British Journal of Social Psychology*, 20, 171–180.

Marañon, G. (1924). Contribution a l'étude de l'action emotive de l'adrenaline. *Révue Française d'Endocrinologie, 2*, 301–325.

Marcia, J. (1966). Development and validation of ego-identity status. *Journal of Personality and Social Psychology, 3*, 551–558.

Marcia, J. (1967). The case history of a construct: Ego identity status. *Journal of Personality and Social Psychology, 3*, 551–558.

Marcia, J. (1976). Identity six years after: A follow-up study. *Journal of Youth and Adolescence, 5*, 145–160.

Marcia, J. (1980). Identity in adolescence. In J. Adelson (Ed.), *Handbook of adolescent psychology*. New York: Wiley.

Markus, H.R., & Kitayama, S. (1991). Culture and the self: Implications for cognition, emotion, and motivation. *Psychological Review, 98*, 224–253.

Marler, P., & Mundinger, P. (1971). Vocal learning in birds. In H. Moltz (Ed.), *The ontogeny of vertebrate behaviour*. New York: Academic Press.

Marr, D. (1982). *Vision: A computational investigation into the human representation and processing of visual information*. San Francisco: W.H. Freeman.

Marr, D., & Nishihara, K. (1978). Representation and recognition of the spatial organisation of three-dimensional shapes. *Philosophical Transactions of the Royal Society (London), B200*, 269–294.

Marsh, H.W. (1989). Age and sex effects in multiple dimensions of self-concept: A replication and extension. *Australian Journal of Psychology, 37*, 197–204.

Marsh, P., Rosser, E., & Harré, R. (1978). *The rules of disorder*. London: Routledge & Kegan Paul.

Marshall, G.D., & Zimbardo, P.G. (1979). Affective consequences of inadequately explained physiological arousal. *Journal of Personality and Social Psychology, 37*, 970–988.

Martin, C.L., & Halverson, C.F. (1983). The effects of sex-typing schemas on young children's memory. *Child Development, 54*, 563–574.

Martin, C.L., & Halverson, C.F. (1987). The roles of cognition in sex role acquisition. In D.B. Carter (Ed.), *Current conceptions of sex roles and sex typing: Theory and research*. New York: Praeger.

Martin, R.A. (1989). Techniques for data acquisition and analysis in field investigations of stress. In R.W.J. Neufeld (Ed.), *Advances in the investigation of psychological stress*. New York: Wiley.

Maslow, A.H. (1954). *Motivation and personality*. New York: Harper.

Maslow, A.H. (1970). *Toward a psychology of being* (3rd Edn.). New York: Van Nostrand.

Masters, J.C., Ford, M.E., Arend, R., Grotevant, H.D., & Clark, L.V. (1979). Modelling and labelling as integrated determinants of children's sex-typed imitative behaviour. *Child Development, 50*, 364–371.

Mathes, E.W., Adams, H.E., & Davies, R.M. (1985). Jealousy: Loss of relationship rewards, loss of self-esteem, depression, anxiety, and anger. *Journal of Personality and Social Psychology, 48*, 1552–1561.

Matlin, M.W., & Foley, H.J. (1997). *Sensation and perception* (4th Edn.). Boston: Allyn & Bacon.

Matt, G.E., & Navarro, A.M. (1997). What meta-analyses have and have not taught us about psychotherapy effects: A review and future directions. *Clinical Psychology Review, 17*, 1–32.

Matthews, G.V.T. (1953). Navigation in the Manx shearwater. *Journal of Experimental Biology, 28*, 508–536.

Matthews, G.V.T. (1955). *Bird navigation*. Cambridge, UK: Cambridge University Press.

Maurer, D., & Salapatek, P. (1976). Developmental changes in the scanning of faces by young infants. *Child Development, 47*, 523–527.

Mayer, J. (1955). Regulation of energy intake and the body weight: The glucostatic theory and the lipostatic hypothesis. *Annals of the New York Academy of Sciences, 63*, 15–43.

Maynard Smith, J. (1964). Group selection and kin selection. *Nature, 201*, 1145–1147.

Maynard Smith, J. (1976). Group selection. *Quarterly Review of Biology, 51*, 277–283.

McArthur, L.Z. (1972). The how and what of why: Some determinants and consequences of causal attribution. *Journal of Personality and Social Psychology, 22*, 171–193.

McArthur, L.Z., & Friedman, S.A. (1980). Illusory correlation in impression formation: Variations in the shared distinctiveness effect as a function of the distinctive person's age, race, and sex. *Journal of Personality and Social Psychology, 39*, 615–624.

McArthur, L.Z., & Post, D.L. (1977). Figural emphasis and person perception. *Journal of Experimental Social Psychology, 13*, 520–535.

McCain, B., Gabrielli, W.F., Bentler, P.M., & Mednick, S.A. (1980). Rearing, social class, education, and criminality: A multiple indicator model. *Journal of Abnormal Psychology, 90*, 354–364.

McCauley, C., & Stitt, C.L. (1978). An individual and quantitative measure of stereotypes. *Journal of Personality and Social Psychology, 36*, 929–940.

McClelland, D.C., Atkinson, J.W., Clark, R.A., & Lowell, E.L. (1953). *The achievement motive*. New York: Appleton-Century-Crofts.

McClelland, J.L., & Rumelhart, D.A. (1985). Distributed memory and the representation of general and specific information. *Journal of Experimental Psychology: General, 114*, 159–188.

McClintock, C.G. (1971). Menstrual synchrony and suppression. *Nature, 229*, 244–245.

McConaghy, M.J. (1979). Gender permanence and the genital basis of gender: Stages in the development of constancy of gender identity. *Child Development, 50*, 1223–1226.

McCrae, R.R., & Costa, P.T. (1982). Aging, the life course, and models of personality. In T.M. Field, A. Huston, H.C. Quay, L. Troll, & G.E. Finley (Eds.), *Review of human development*. New York: Wiley.

McDonald, L. (1995). *Are old people egocentric? Performance of the elderly on the three mountains task*. Paper presented at the BPS conference.

McDougall, W. (1912). *Psychology: The study of behaviour*. London: Williams & Norgate.

McFarland, S.G., Ageyev, V.S., & Abalakina-Paap, M.A. (1992). Authoritarianism in the former Soviet Union. *Journal of Personality and Social Psychology, 63*, 1004–1010.

McGarrigle, J., & Donaldson, M. (1974). Conservation accidents. *Cognition, 3*, 341–350.

McGinnies, E. (1949). Emotionality and perceptual defence. *Psychological Review, 56*, 244–251.

McGlone, J. (1980). Sex differences in human brain asymmetry: A critical survey. *Behavioural and Brain Sciences, 3*(2), 215–263.

McGue, M., Brown, S., & Lykken, D.T. (1992). Personality stability and change in early adulthood: A behavioural genetic analysis. *Developmental Psychology, 29*, 96–109.

McGuigan, F.J. (1966). Covert oral behaviour and auditory hallucinations. *Psychophysiology, 3*, 421–428.

McIlveen, R., & Gross, R. (1996). *Biopsychology*. London: Hodder & Stoughton.

McIlveen, R., Higgins, L., & Wadeley, A. (1992). *BPS manual of psychology practicals*. Leicester, UK: BPS Books.

McKelvie, S.J. (1997). The availability heuristic: Effects of fame and gender on the estimated frequency of male and female names. *Journal of Social Psychology, 137*(1), 63–78.

McKenna, K., & Yael, A. (1999). The computers that bind: Relationship formation on the internet. *Dissertation Abstracts International Section A: Humanities and Social Sciences, 59*(7-A), 2236.

McLeod, P. (1977). A dual-task response modality effect: Support for multiprocessor models of attention. *Quarterly Journal of Experimental Psychology, 29*, 651–667.

McNeill, D. (1970). *The acquisition of language: The study of developmental psycholinguistics.* New York: Harper & Row.

Mead, M. (1928). *Coming of age in Samoa.* New York: Morrow.

Mead, M. (1935). *Sex and temperament in three primitive societies.* New York: Morrow.

Meadows, S. (1986). *Understanding child development.* London: Routledge.

Meadows, S. (1994). Cognitive development. In A.M. Colman (Ed.), *Companion encyclopedia of psychology, Vol. 2.* London: Routledge.

Meddis, R. (1975a). On the function of sleep. *Animal Behaviour, 23*, 676–691.

Meddis, R. (1975b). *Statistical handbook for non-statisticians.* London: McGraw-Hill.

Meddis, R. (1979). The evolution and function of sleep. In D.A. Oakley & H.C. Plotkin (Eds.), *Brain, behaviour and evolution.* London: Methuen.

Meddis, R., Pearson, A.J.D., & Langford, G. (1973). An extreme case of healthy insomnia. *Electroencephalography and Clinical Neurophysiology, 35*, 213–224.

Mednick, S.A., & Schulsinger, F. (1968). Some premorbid characteristics related to breakdown in children with schizophrenic mothers. *Journal of Psychiatric Research, 6*, 267–291.

Meichenbaum, D. (1985). *Stress inoculation training.* New York: Pergamon.

Meilman, P.W. (1979). Cross-sectional age changes in ego identity status during adolescence. *Developmental Psychology, 15*, 230–231.

Meltzoff, A.N. (1988). Imitation of televised models by infants. *Child Development, 59*, 1221–1229.

Menzel, E.W. (1971). Communication about the environment in a group of young chimpanzees. *Folia Primat, 15*, 220–232.

Menzel, E.W. (1978). Cognitive mapping in chimpanzees. In S.H. Hulse, F. Fowler, & W.K. Honig (Eds.), *Cognitive processes in animal behaviour.* Hillsdale, NJ: Lawrence Erlbaum Associates Inc.

Menzies, R.G., & Clarke, J.C. (1993). The aetiology of childhood water phobia. *Behaviour Research and Therapy, 31*, 499–501.

Menzies, R.G., & Clarke, J.C. (1994). Retrospective studies of the origins of phobias: A review. *Anxiety, Stress, and Coping, 7*, 305–318.

Merckelbach, H., de Jong, P.J., Muris, P., & van den Hout, M.A. (1996). The etiology of specific phobias: A review. *Clinical Psychology Review, 16*, 337–361.

Merriman, A. (1984). Social customs affecting the role of elderly women in Indian society. In D.B. Bromley (Ed.), *Gerontology: Social and behavioural perspectives.* London: Croom Helm.

Mersky, H. (1992). The manufacture of personalities: The production of multiple personality disorder. *British Journal of Psychiatry, 160*, 327–340.

Metter, E.J. (1991). Brain–behaviour relationships in aphasia studied by positron emission tomography. *Annals of the New York Academy of Sciences, 620*, 153–164.

Michaels, J.W., Acock, A.C., & Edwards, J.N. (1986). Social exchange and equity determinants of relationship commitment. *Journal of Social and Personal Relationships, 3*, 161–175.

Midlarsky, E., & Bryan, J.H. (1972). Affect expressions and children's imitative altruism. *Journal of Experimental Research in Personality, 6*, 195–203.

Miles, L.E.M., Raynal, D.M., & Wilson, M.A. (1977). Blind man living in normal society has circadian rhythms of 24.9 hours. *Science, 198*, 421–423.

Milgram, S. (1963). Behavioural study of obedience. *Journal of Abnormal and Social Psychology, 67*, 371–378.

Milgram, S. (1974). *Obedience to authority: An experimental view.* New York: Harper & Row.

Miller, D.T. (1976). Ego involvement and attributions for success and failure. *Journal of Personality and Social Psychology, 34*, 901–906.

Miller, D.T., & Ross, M. (1975). Self-serving bias in the attribution of causality: Fact or fiction? *Psychological Bulletin, 82*, 213–225.

Miller, G. (1996). Sexual selection in human evolution. In C. Crawford & D.L. Krebs (Eds.), *Evolution and human behaviour.* Mahwah, NJ: Lawrence Erlbaum Associates Inc.

Miller, G.A., & McNeill, D. (1969). Psycholinguistics. In G. Lindzey & E. Aronson (Eds.), *The handbook of social psychology, Vol. III.* Reading, MA: Addison-Wesley.

Miller, G.F. (1998). How mate choice shaped human nature: A review of sexual selection and human evolution. In C. Crawford (Ed.), *Handbook of evolutionary psychology.* Mahwah, NJ: Lawrence Erlbaum Associates Inc.

Miller, J.G. (1984). Culture and the development of everyday social explanation. *Journal of Personality and Social Psychology, 46*, 961–978.

Miller, J.G., Bersoff, D.M., & Harwood, R.L. (1990). Perception of social responsibilities in India and the United States: Moral imperatives or personal decisions? *Journal of Personality and Social Psychology, 58*, 33–47.

Miller, N.E. (1941). The frustration–aggression hypothesis. *Psychological Review, 48*, 337–342.

Miller, P.H. (1993). *Theories of developmental psychology (3rd Edn.).* New York: Freeman.

Milner, A.D., & Goodale, M.A. (1995). *The visual brain in action* (Oxford Psychology series, no. 27, p. xvii). Oxford, UK: Oxford University Press.

Milner, A.D., & Goodale, M.A. (1998). The visual brain in action. *Psyche, 4*, 1–14.

Mineka, S., Davidson, M., Cook, M., & Kuir, R. (1984). Observational conditioning of snake fear in rhesus monkeys. *Journal of Abnormal Psychology, 93*, 355–372.

Minsky, R. (1998). *Psychoanalysis and culture.* Cambridge, UK: Polity Press.

Mischel, W. (1968). *Personality and assessment.* New York: Wiley.

Mischel, W. (1970). Sex-typing and socialisation. In P.H. Mussen (Ed.), *Carmichael's manual of child psychology, Vol. 2.* New York: Wiley.

Mischel, W. (1993). *Introduction to personality (5th Edn.).* Fort Worth, TX: Harcourt Brace.

Mischel, W., & Peake, P.K. (1982). Beyond déjà vu in the search for cross-situational consistency. *Psychological Review, 89*, 730–755.

Mischler, E.G., & Waxler, N.E. (1968). Interaction in families: An experimental study of family processes and schizophrenia. In A. Smith (Ed.), *Childhood schizophrenia.* New York: Wiley.

Miyawaki, K., Strange, W., Verbrugge, R., Liberman, A.M., Jenkins, J.J., & Furjima, O. (1975). An effect of linguistic experience: The discrimination of [r] and [l] by native speakers of Japanese and English. *Perception and Psychophysics, 18*, 331–340.

Modestin, J. (1992). Multiple personality disorder in Switzerland. *American Journal of Psychiatry, 149*, 88–92.

Moghaddam, F.M., Taylor, D.M., & Wright, S.C. (1993). *Social psychology in cross-cultural perspective.* New York: W.H. Freeman.

Mogilner, A., Grossman, J.A., Ribary, U., Joliot, M., Volkman, J., Rapaport, D., Beasley, R.W., & Llinas, R.R. (1993). Somatosensory cortical plasticity in adult humans revealed by magnetoencephalography. *Proceedings of the National Academy of Sciences*, 90, 3593–3597.

Mohr, D.C. (1995). Negative outcome in psychotherapy: A critical review. *Clinical Psychology: Science and Practice*, 2, 1–27.

Møller, A.P. (1990). Effects of a haematophagous mite on the barn swallow *Hirundo rustica*: A test of the Hamilton and Zuk hypothesis. *Evolution*, 44, 771–784.

Money, J., & Ehrhardt, A.A. (1972). *Man and woman, boy and girl*. Baltimore: John Hopkins University Press.

Monk, T.H., & Folkard, S. (1983). Circadian rhythms and shiftwork. In R. Hockey (Ed.), *Stress and fatigue in human performance*. Chichester, UK: Wiley.

Monteith, M.J. (1993). Self-regulation of prejudiced responses: Implications for progress in prejudice-reduction efforts. *Journal of Personality and Social Psychology*, 65, 469–485.

Moore, B.R. (1973). The form of the auto-shaped response with food or water reinforcers. *Journal of the Experimental Analysis of Behavior*, 20, 163–181.

Moore, C., & Frye, D. (1986). The effect of the experimenter's intention on the child's understanding of conservation. *Cognition*, 22, 283–298.

Moore-Ede, M. (1993). *The 24-hour society*. Reading, MA: Addison-Wesley.

Moore-Ede, M., Sulzman, F., & Fuller, C. (1982). *The clocks that time us: Physiology of the circadian timing system*. Cambridge, MA: Harvard University Press.

Moray, N. (1959). Attention in dichotic listening: Affective cues and the influence of instructions. *Quarterly Journal of Experimental Psychology*, 11, 56–60.

Morgan, C.D., & Murray, H.A. (1935). A method of investigating fantasies: The thematic apperception test. *Archives of Neurological Psychiatry*, 34, 289–306.

Morgan, E. (1995). Measuring time with a biological clock. *Biological Sciences Review*, 7, 2–5.

Moruzzi, G., & Magoun, H.W. (1949). Brain stem reticular formation and activation of the EEG. *Electroencephalography and Clinical Neurophysiology*, 1, 455–473.

Moscovici, S. (1961). *La psychoanalyse: Son image et son public*. Paris: Presses Universitaires de France.

Moscovici, S. (1981). On social representations. In J.P. Forgas (Ed.), *Social cognition: Perspectives on everyday understanding*. London: Academic Press.

Moscovici, S. (1985). Social influence and conformity. In G. Lindzey & E. Aronson (Eds.), *Handbook of social psychology, Vol. 2*. New York: Random House.

Moscovici, S. (1988). Notes towards a description of social representations. *European Journal of Social Psychology*, 18, 211–250.

Moscovici, S., & Hewstone, M. (1983). Social representations and social explanations: From the "naive" to the "amateur" scientist. In M. Hewstone (Ed.), *Attribution theory: Social and functional extensions*. Oxford, UK: Basil Blackwell.

Moscovici, S., Lage, E., & Naffrenchoux, M. (1969). Influence of a consistent minority on the responses of a majority in a colour perception task. *Sociometry*, 32, 365–380.

Moser, K.A., Fox, A.J., & Jones, D.R. (1984). Unemployment and mortality in the OPCS longitudinal study. *Lancet*, 2, 1324–1329.

Moss, E. (1992). The socioaffective context of joint cognitive activity. In L.T. Winegar & J. Valsiner (Eds.), *Children's development within social context: Vol. 2. Research and methodology*. Hillsdale, NJ: Lawrence Erlbaum Associates Inc.

Motluck, A. (1999). When too much sex is exhausting. *New Scientist, 2181*, 8.

Mowrer, O.H. (1947). On the dual nature of learning: A re-interpretation of "conditioning" and "problem-solving". *Harvard Educational Review*, 17, 102–148.

Moynihan, M.H. (1970). Control, suppression, decay, disappearance and replacement of displays. *Journal of Theoretical Biology*, 29, 85–112.

Mulac, A., Bradac, J.J., & Mann, S.K. (1985). Male/female language differences and attributional consequences in children's television. *Human Communication Research*, 11(4), 481–506.

Mukerjee, M. (1997). Trends in animal research. *Scientific American*, February, 70–77.

Mullen, B., Brown, R., & Smith, C. (1992). Ingroup bias as a function of salience, relevance and status: An integration. *European Journal of Social Psychology*, 22, 103–122.

Mumford, D.B. (1996). The "Dhat syndrome": A culturally determined symptom of depression? *Acta Psychiatrica Scandinavica*, 94(3), 163–167.

Mumme, R.L. (1992). Do helpers increase reproductive success: An experimental analysis in the Florida scrub jay. *Behavioural Ecology and Sociobiology*, 31, 319–328.

Munro, G., & Adams, G.R. (1977). Mothers, infants and pointing: A study of gesture. In H.R. Schaffer (Ed.), *Studies in mother–infant interaction*. London: Academic Press.

Munroe, R.H., Shimmin, H.S., & Munroe, R.L. (1984). Gender understanding and sex-role preferences in four cultures. *Developmental Psychology*, 20, 673–682.

Murphy, H.B.M. (1982). Culture and schizophrenia. In I. Al-Issa (Ed.), *Culture and psychopathology* (pp. 221–249). Baltimore: University Park Press.

Murphy, R.G. (1989). *The development of magnetic compass orientation in children*. Paper presented at the Royal Institute of Navigation Conference.

Murray, H.A. (1938). *Explorations in personality*. Oxford, UK: Oxford University Press.

Murray, S.L., & Holmes, J.G. (1993). Seeing virtues in faults: Negativity and the transformation of interpersonal narratives in close relationships. *Journal of Personality and Social Psychology*, 65, 707–722.

Murstein, B.I. (1972). Physical attractiveness and marital choice. *Journal of Personality and Social Psychology*, 22, 8–12.

Murstein, B.I., & Christy, P. (1976). Physical attractiveness and marriage adjustment in middle-aged couples. *Journal of Personality and Social Psychology*, 34, 537–542.

Murstein, B.I., MacDonald, M.G., & Cerreto, M. (1977). A theory and investigation of the effects of exchange-orientation on marriage and friendship. *Journal of Marriage and the Family*, 39, 543–548.

Mussen, P.H., & Rutherford, E. (1963). Parent–child relations and parental personality in relation to young children's sex-role preferences. *Child Development*, 34, 589–607.

Myers, L.B., & Brewin, C.R. (1994). Recall of early experiences and the repressive coping style. *Journal of Abnormal Psychology*, 103, 288–292.

Nagell, K., Olguin, R.S., & Tomasello, M. (1993). Processes of social learning in the tool use of chimpanzees (*Pan troglodytes*) and human children (*Homo sapiens*). *Journal of Comparative Psychology*, 107, 174–186.

Naitoh, P. (1975). Sleep stage deprivation and total sleep loss: Effects on sleep behaviour. *Psychophysiology*, 12, 141–146.

Navon, D. (1977). Forest before trees: The precedence of global features in visual perception. *Cognitive Psychology*, 9, 353–383.

Neisser, U. (1964). Visual search. *Scientific American*, 210, 94–102.

Neisser, U. (1967). *Cognitive psychology*. New York: Appleton-Century-Crofts.

Neisser, U. (1976). *Cognition and reality*. San Francisco: W.H. Freeman.

Neisser, U., & Becklen, P. (1975). Selective looking: Attending to visually superimposed events. *Cognitive Psychology, 7*, 480–494.

Nelson, K. (1973). Structure and strategy in learning to talk. *Monographs of the Society for Research in Child Development, 38*(Serial no. 149).

Nesse, M., & Williams, C. (1995). *Evolution and healing: The new science of Darwinian medicine*. London: Weidenfeld & Nicolson.

Neugarten, B.L. (1975). Personality and aging. In J.E. Birren & K.W. Schaie (Eds.), *Handbook of the psychology of aging*. New York: Reinhold.

Newcomb, T.M. (1961). *The acquaintance process*. New York: Holt, Rinehart & Winston.

Newell, A., & Simon, H.A. (1963). GPS, a program that simulates human thought. In E.A. Feigenbaum & J. Feldman (Eds.), *Computers and thought*. New York: Wiley.

Newell, A., & Simon, H.A. (1972). *Human problem solving*. Englewood Cliffs, NJ: Prentice-Hall.

Newmark, C.S., Frerking, R.A., Cook, L., & Newmark, L. (1973). Endorsement of Ellis' irrational beliefs as a function of psychopathology. *Journal of Clinical Psychology, 29*, 300–302.

Newport, E.L. (1994). Maturational constraints on language learning. *Cognitive Science, 14*, 11–28.

Newson, J., & Newson, E. (1968). *Four years old in an urban community*. London: Allen & Unwin.

Nisbett, R.E. (1972). Hunger, obesity and the ventromedial hypothalamus. *Psychological Review, 79*, 433–453.

Nisbett, R.E., & Ross, L. (1980). *Human inference: Strategies and shortcomings of social judgment*. Englewood Cliffs, NJ: Prentice Hall.

Nobles, W.W. (1976). Extended self: Rethinking the so-called Negro self-concept. *Journal of Black Psychology, 2*, 99–105.

Nolen-Hoeksma, S. (1990). *Sex differences in depression*. Stanford, CA: Stanford University Press.

Nolen-Hoeksma, S., Girgus, J.S., & Seligman, M.E.P. (1992). Predictors and consequences of childhood depressive symptoms: A 5-year longitudinal study. *Journal of Abnormal Psychology, 101*, 405–422.

Norman, D.A., & Bobrow, D.G. (1975). On data-limited and resource-limited processes. *Cognitive Psychology, 7*, 44–64.

Norton, G.R., Dorward, J., & Cox, B.J. (1986). Factors associated with panic attacks in nonclinical subjects. *Behavior Therapy, 17*, 239–252.

Noyes, R., Crowe, R.R., Harris, E.L., Hamra, B.J., McChesney, C.M., & Chandry, D.R. (1986). Relationship between panic disorder and agoraphobia: A family study. *Archives of General Psychiatry, 43*, 227–232.

O'Connor, J. (1980). Intermediate-size transposition and children's operational level. *Developmental Psychology, 16*, 588–596.

Offer, D., Ostrov, E., Howard, K.I., & Atkinson, R. (1988). *The teenage world: Adolescents' self-image in ten countries*. New York: Plenum Press.

Ohbuchi, K., & Kambara, T. (1985). Attacker's intent and awareness of outcome, impression management, and retaliation. *Journal of Experimental Social Psychology, 21*, 321–330.

Ohlsson, S. (1992). Information processing explanations of insight and related phenomena. In M.T. Keane & K.J. Gilhooly (Eds.), *Advances in the psychology of thinking*. London: Harvester Wheatsheaf.

Ojemann, G.A. (1979). Individual variability in cortical localisation of language. *Journal of Neurosurgery, 50*, 164–169.

Olds, J., & Milner, P. (1954). Positive reinforcement produced by electrical stimulation of septal area and other regions of rat brain. *Journal of Comparative and Physiological Psychology, 47*, 419–427.

Olds, M.E., & Forbes, J.L. (1981). The central basis of motivation: Intracranial self-stimulation studies. *Annual Review of Psychology, 32*, 523–574.

Olson, D.R. (1980). *The social foundation of language and thought*. New York: W.W. Norton.

Ost, L.G. (1985). Mode of acquisition of phobias. *Acta Universitatis Uppsaliensis, 529*, 1–45.

Ost, L.G. (1989). *Blood phobia: A specific phobia subtype in DSM-IV*. Paper requested by the Simple Phobia subcommittee of the DSM-IV Anxiety Disorders Work Group.

Oswald, I. (1980). *Sleep* (4th Edn.). Harmondsworth, UK: Penguin Books.

Owusu-Bempah & Howitt, D. (1994). Racism and the psychological textbook. *The Psychologist, 7*, 163–166.

Packer, C. (1977). Reciprocal altruism in *Papio anubis*. *Nature, 265*, 441–443.

Packer, C., Gilbert, D.A., Pusey, A.E., & O'Brien, S.J. (1991). A molecular genetic analysis of kinship and cooperation in African lions. *Nature, 351*, 562–565.

Pahl, J.J., Swayze, V.W., & Andreasen, N.C. (1990). Diagnostic advances in anatomical and functional brain imaging in schizophrenia. In A. Kales, C.N. Stefanis, & J.A. Talbot (Eds.), *Recent advances in schizophrenia*. New York: Springer-Verlag.

Palincsar, A.S., & Brown, A.L. (1984). Reciprocal teaching of comprehension-fostering and comprehension-monitoring activities. *Cognition and Instruction, 1*, 117–175.

Palmer, P.H. (1997). The psychosocial consequences of sudden infant death syndrome. *Dissertation Abstracts International: Section B. The Sciences and Engineering, 57*(10-B), 6587.

Palmer, S.E. (1975). The effects of contextual scenes on the identification of objects. *Memory and Cognition, 3*, 519–526.

Palmonari, A., Pombeni, M.L., & Kirchler, E. (1989). Peer groups and evolution of the self-system in adolescence. *European Journal of Psychology of Education, 4*, 3–15.

Papez, J.W. (1937). A proposed mechanism of emotion. *Archives of Neurology and Psychiatry, 38*, 725–743.

Papi, F., Fiore, L., Fiaschi, V., & Benvenuti, S. (1972). Olfaction and homing in pigeons. *Monit. Zool. Ital., 6*, 85–95.

Park, R.J., Lawrie, J.M., & Freeman, C.P. (1995). Post-viral onset of anorexia nervosa. *British Journal of Psychology, 166*, 386–389.

Parke, R.D. (1977). Some effects of punishment on children's behaviour: Revisited. In E.M. Hetherington & R.D. Parke (Eds.), *Contemporary readings in child psychology*. New York: McGraw-Hill.

Parkes, C.M. (1986). *Bereavement: Studies in grief in adult life*. London: Tavistock.

Parkinson, B. (1994). Emotion. In A.M. Colman (Ed.), *Companion encyclopaedia of psychology, Vol. 2*. London: Routledge.

Parks, M.R., & Floyd, K. (1996). Making friends in cyberspace. *Journal of Communication, 46*(1), 80–97.

Pascual-Leone, J. (1984). Attentional, dialectic, and mental effort. In M.L. Commons, F.A. Richards, & C. Armon (Eds.), *Beyond formal operations*. New York: Plenum.

Pastore, N. (1952). The role of arbitrariness in the frustration–aggression hypothesis. *Journal of Abnormal and Social Psychology, 47*, 728–731.

Patterson, F.G. (1979). Conversations with a gorilla. *National Geographic, 154*, 438–465.

Patterson, G.R., DeBaryshe, B.D., & Ramsey, E. (1989). A developmental perspective on antisocial behaviour. *American Psychologist, 44*, 329–335.

Paul, G.L., & Lentz, R.J. (1977). *Psychosocial treatment of chronic mental patients: Milieu versus social learning programs*. Cambridge, MA: Harvard University Press.

Paykel, E.S. (1974). Life stress and psychiatric disorder: Applications of the clinical approach. In B.S. Dohrenwend & B.P. Dohrenwend (Eds.), *Stressful life events: Their nature and effects*. New York: Wiley.

Payne, J. (1976). Task complexity and contingent processing in decision making: An information search and protocol analysis. *Organizational Behavior and Human Performance, 16*, 366–387.

Payne, K., & Payne, R. (1985). Large scale changes over 19 years in songs of humpback whales in Bermuda. *Zeitschrift für Tierpsychologie, 68*, 89–114.

Penfield, W. (1969). Consciousness, memory, and man's conditioned reflexes. In K. Pribram (Ed.), *On the biology of learning*. New York: Harcourt, Brace, & World.

Penfield, W., & Boldrey, E. (1937). Somatic motor and sensory representations in cerebral cortex of man as studied by electrical stimulation. *Brain, 60*, 389–443.

Penfield, W., & Rasmussen, T. (1950). *The cerebral cortex of man*. New York: Macmillan.

Pengelley, E.T., & Fisher, K.C. (1957). Onset and cessation of hibernation under constant temperature and light in the golden-mantled ground squirrel, *Citellus lateralis*. *Nature, 180*, 1371–1372.

Pennington, D. (2000). *Social cognition*. Routledge: London.

Peplau, L.A. (1991). Lesbian and gay relationships. In J.C. Gonsiorek & J. Dweinrich (Eds.), *Homosexuality: Research implications for public policy*. Newbury Park, CA: Sage.

Perdeck, A.C. (1958). Two types of orientation in migrating starlings, *Sturnus vulgaris L.*, and chaffinches, *Fringilla coelbs L.*, as revealed by displacement experiments. *Ardea, 46*, 1–37.

Perez, S., Taylor, O., & Jander, R. (1977). A sun compass in Monarch butterflies. *Nature, 387*, 29.

Perrett, D.I., Burt, D.M., Penton-Voak, I.S., Lee, K.J., Rowland, D.A., & Edwards, R. (1999). Symmetry and human facial attractiveness. *Evolution and Human Behaviour, 20*(5), 295–307.

Perrett, D.I., Oram, M.W., Hietanen, J.K., & Benson, P.J. (1994). Issues of representation in object vision. In M.J. Farah & G. Ratcliff (Eds.), *The neuropsychology of higher vision: Collated tutorial essays*. Hillsdale, NJ: Lawrence Erlbaum Associates Inc.

Perrin, S., & Spencer, C. (1980). The Asch effect: A child of its time. *Bulletin of the British Psychological Society, 33*, 405–406.

Perry, D.G., & Bussey, K. (1979). The social learning theory of sex differences: Imitation is alive and well. *Journal of Personality and Social Psychology, 37*, 1699–1712.

Petersen, S.E., Fox, P.T., Mintun, M.A., Posner, M.I., & Raichle, M.E. (1989). Studies of the processing of single words using averaged positron emission tomographic measurements of cerebral blood flow change. *Journal of Cognitive Neuroscience, 1*, 153–170.

Peterson, C.C., Peterson, J.L., & Skevington, S. (1986). Heated argument and adolescent development. *Journal of Social and Personal Relationships, 3*, 229–240.

Peterson, W., Doty, R.M., & Winter, D.G. (1993). Authoritarianism and attitudes toward contemporary issues. *Personality and Social Psychology Bulletin, 19*(2), 174–184.

Pettigrew, T.F. (1959). Regional difference in anti-Negro prejudice. *Journal of Abnormal and Social Psychology, 59*, 28–56.

Pfungst, O. (1911). *Clever Hans: The horse of Mr von Osten*. New York: Holt.

Piaget, J. (1932). *The moral judgement of the child*. Harmondsworth, UK: Penguin.

Piaget, J. (1967). *The child's conception of the world*. Totowa, NJ: Littlefield, Adams.

Piaget, J. (1970). Piaget's theory. In J. Mussen (Ed.), *Carmichael's manual of child psychology, Vol. 1*. New York: Basic Books.

Piaget, J., & Szeminska, A. (1952). *The child's conception of number*. London: Routledge & Kegan Paul.

Piliavin, I.M., Rodin, J., & Piliavin, J.A. (1969). Good samaritarianism: An underground phenomenon? *Journal of Personality and Social Psychology, 13*, 289–299.

Piliavin, J.A., Dovidio, J.F., Gaertner, S.L., & Clark, R.D. (1981). *Emergency intervention*. New York: Academic Press.

Pilleri, G. (1979). The blind Indus dolphin, *Platanista indi*. *Endeavour, 3*, 48–56.

Pinel, J.P.J. (1997). *Biopsychology* (3rd Edn.). Boston: Allyn & Bacon.

Pinker, S. (1994). *The language instinct*. Harmondsworth, UK: Allen Lane.

Plomin, R. (1988). The nature and nurture of cognitive abilities. In R.J. Sternberg (Ed.), *Advances in the psychology of human intelligence, Vol. 4*. Hillsdale, NJ: Lawrence Erlbaum Associates Inc.

Plomin, R. (1990). The role of inheritance in behaviour. *Science, 248*, 183–188.

Plomin, R. (1994). *Genetics and experience: The interplay between nature and nurture*. Thousand Oaks, CA: Sage.

Plomin, R. (1997). DNA: Implications. *The Psychologist, 11*, 61–62.

Plomin, R., DeFries J.C., & Loehlin, J.C. (1977). Genotype–environment interaction and correlation in the analysis of human behavior. *Psychological Bulletin, 84*(2), 309–322.

Poincaré, H. (1913). Mathematical creation. In H. Poincaré, *The foundations of science*. New York: Science Press.

Pomerantz, J., & Garner, W.R. (1973). Stimulus configuration in selective attention tasks. *Perception and Psychophysics, 14*, 565–569.

Popper, K.R. (1969). *Conjectures and refutations*. London: Routledge & Kegan Paul.

Popper, K.R. (1972). *Objective knowledge*. Oxford, UK: Oxford University Press.

Posner, M.I., & Petersen, S.E. (1990). The attention system of the human brain. *Annual Review of Neuroscience, 13*, 25–42.

Pottiez, J.-M. (1986). *A walk with a white Bushman*. London: Chatto & Windus.

Povinelli, D.J., Nelson, K.E., & Boysen, S.T. (1992). Comprehension of role reversal in chimpanzees: Evidence of empathy? *Animal Behaviour, 43*, 269–281.

Premack, D., & Woodruff, G. (1978). Does the chimpanzee have a theory of mind? *Behavioural and Brain Sciences, 4*, 515–526.

Prioleau, L., Murdock, M., & Brody, N. (1983). An analysis of psychotherapy versus placebo studies. *Behavior and Brain Sciences, 6*, 273–310.

Pritchard, R.M. (1961). Stabilised images on the retina. *Scientific American*, June.

Pritchard, S. (1998, October 16). Triumph of mind over matter. *The Independent*.

Pucetti, R. (1977). Sperry on consciousness: A critical appreciation. *Journal of Medicine and Physiology, 2*, 127–146.

Putnam, F.W., Guroff, J.J., Silberman, E.K., et al. (1986). The clinical phenomenology of multiple personality disorder: Review of 100 recent cases. *Journal of Clinical Psychiatry, 47*(6), 285–293.

Putnam, H. (1973). Reductionism and the nature of psychology. *Cognition, 2*, 131–146.

Quattrone, G.A., & Jones, E.E. (1980). The perception of variability within ingroups and outgroups. *Journal of Personality and Social Psychology, 38*, 141–152.

Quay, L.C. (1971). Language, dialect, reinforcement, and the intelligence test performance of Negro children. *Child Development, 42*, 5–15.

Quinlan, P.T., & Wilton, R.N. (1998). Grouping by proximity or similarity? Competition between the Gestalt principles in vision. *Perception, 27*, 417–430.

Rabbie, J.M., & Horwitz, M. (1960). Arousal of ingroup–outgroup bias by a chance win or loss. *Journal of Personality and Social Psychology, 13*, 269–277.

Rabbie, J.M., Schot, J.C., & Visser, L. (1989). Social identity theory: A conceptual and empirical critique from the perspective of a behavioural interaction model. *European Journal of Social Psychology, 19*, 171–202.

Rachman, S.J. (1993). A critique of cognitive therapy for anxiety disorders. *Behaviour Research and Therapy, 24*, 274–288.

Rachman, S.J., & de Silva, P. (1978). Abnormal and normal obsessions. *Behaviour Research and Therapy, 16*, 233–238.

Raichle, M.E. (1994). Images of the mind: Studies with modern imaging techniques. *Annual Review of Psychology, 45*, 333–356.

Raine, A., Buchsbaum, M., & LaCasse, L. (1997). Brain abnormalities in murderers indicated by positron emission tomography. *Biological Psychiatry, 42*(6), 495–508.

Ramey, C.T. (1993). A rejoinder to Spitz's critique of the Abecedarian experiment. *Intelligence, 17*, 25–30.

Ramey, C.T., Campbell, F.A., & Ramey, S.L. (1999). Early intervention: Successful pathways to improving intellectual development. *Developmental Neuropsychology, 16*(3), 385–392.

Ramsay, R., & de Groot, W. (1977). A further look at bereavement: Paper presented at EATI conference, Uppsala. [Cited in P.E. Hodgkinson (1980, January 17). Treating abnormal grief in the bereaved. *Nursing Times*, pp. 126–128.]

Rasmussen, T., & Milner, B. (1975). Excision of Broca's area without persistent aphasia. In K.J. Zulch, O. Creutzfeldt, & G.C. Galbraith (Eds.), *Cerebral localisation*. New York: Springer.

Reason, J.T. (1979). Actions not as planned: The price of automatisation. In G. Underwood & R. Stevens (Eds.), *Aspects of consciousness: Vol. 1. Psychological issues*. London: Academic Press.

Reason, J.T. (1992). Cognitive underspecification: Its variety and consequences. In B.J. Baars (Ed.), *Experimental slips and human error: Exploring the architecture of volition*. New York: Plenum Press.

Reber, A.S. (1995). *Dictionary of psychology*. London: Penguin.

Rechtschaffen, A., Gilliland, M., Bergmann, B., & Winter, J. (1983). Physiological correlates of prolonged sleep deprivation in rats. *Science, 221*, 182–184.

Reibstein, J., & Richards, M. (1992). *Sexual arrangements: Marriage and affairs*. London: Heinemann.

Reichard, S., Livson, F., & Peterson, P.G. (1962). *Aging and personality: A study of 87 older men*. New York: Wiley.

Reicher, S., & Emler, N. (1986). The management of delinquent reputations. In H. Beloff (Ed.), *Getting into life*. London: Methuen.

Reinberg, R. (1967). *Eclairement et cycle menstruel de la femme*. Rapport au Colloque International du CRNS, la photorégulation de la reproduction chez les oiseaux et les mammifères. Montpelier, France.

Rescorla, R.A., & Wagner, A.R. (1972). A theory of Pavlovian conditioning: Variations in the effectiveness of reinforcement and nonreinforcement. In A.H. Black & W.F. Prokasy (Eds.), *Classical conditioning: II. Current research and theory*. New York: Appleton-Century-Crofts.

Richards, W. (1975). Visual space perception. In E.C. Carterette & M.P. Friedman (Eds.), *Handbook of perception*. New York: Academic Press.

Ridley, M. (1983). *The explanation of organic diversity*. Oxford, UK: Clarendon Press.

Ridley, M. (1986). *Animal behaviour: A concise introduction*. Oxford, UK: Blackwell Scientific Publications.

Ridley, M. (1993). *The red queen*. London: Viking.

Ridley, M. (1995). *Animal behaviour* (2nd Edn.). Oxford, UK: Blackwell.

Rieber, R.W. (1999). Hypnosis, false memory and multiple personality: A trinity of affinity. *History of Psychiatry, 10*(37, Pt. 1), 3–11.

Riesen, A.H. (1950). Arrested vision. *Scientific American, 408*, 16–19.

Risavy, C.F. (1996). Effects of gender, age, social class and relationship satisfaction on love styles. *Dissertation Abstracts International: Section A: Humanities and Social Science, 57*(2-A), 0591.

Ritter, S., & Taylor, J.S. (1990). Vagal sensory neurons are required for lipoprivic but not glucoprivic feeding in rats. *American Journal of Physiology, 258*, R1395–R1401.

Roberts, P., & Newton, P.M. (1987). Levinsonian studies of women's adult development. *Psychology and Aging, 2*, 154–163.

Robins, L.N., Helzer, J.E., Weissman, M.M., Orvaschel, H., Gruenberg, E., Burke, J.K., & Regier, D.A. (1984). Lifetime prevalence of specific psychiatric disorders in three cities. *Archives of General Psychiatry, 41*, 949–958.

Robson, C. (1994). *Experimental design and statistics in psychology* (3rd Edn.). Harmondsworth, UK: Penguin.

Rogers, C.R. (1951). *Client-centred therapy*. Boston: Houghton Mifflin.

Rogers, C.R. (1959). A theory of therapy, personality, and interpersonal relationships as developed in the client-centred framework. In S. Koch (Ed.), *Psychology: A study of a science*. New York: McGraw-Hill.

Rogers, C.R. (1986). Client-centred therapy. In I. Kutash & A. Wolf (Eds.), *Psychotherapist's casebook*. San Francisco: Jossey-Bass.

Rogers, P.J., & Blundell, J.E. (1980). Investigation of food selection and meal parameters during the development of dietary induced obesity. *Appetite, 1*, 85–88.

Rokeach, M. (1960). *The open and closed mind*. New York: Basic Books.

Roland, P.E. (1993). *Brain activation*. New York: Wiley-Liss.

Rolls, B.J., & Rolls, E.T. (1982). *Thirst*. Cambridge, UK: Cambridge University Press.

Rolls, B.J., Wood, R.J., & Rolls, R.M. (1980). Thirst: The initiation, maintenance, and termination of drinking. In J.M. Sprague & A.N. Epstein (Eds.), *Progress in psychology and physiological psychology*. New York: Academic Press.

Romer, A.S. (1962). *The vertebrate body*. PA: W.B. Saunders Co.

Rookes, P., & Willson, J. (2000). *Perception*. London: Routledge.

Rose, S.A., & Blank, M. (1974). The potency of context in children's cognition: An illustration through conservation. *Child Development, 45*, 499–502.

Rosekrans, M.A., & Hartup, W.W. (1967). Imitative influences of consistent and inconsistent response consequences to a model on aggressive behaviour in children. *Journal of Personality and Social Psychology, 7*, 429–434.

Rosenberg, M.J., Nelson, C., & Vivekanathan, P.S. (1968). A multidimensional approach to the structure of personality impression. *Journal of Personality and Social Psychology, 9*, 283–294.

Rosenberg, S., & Sedlak, A. (1972). Structural representations of implicit personality theory. In L. Berkowitz (Ed.), *Advances in experimental social psychology* (Vol. 6, pp. 235–297). New York: Academic Press.

Rosenfield, D., Stephan, W.G., & Lucker, G.W. (1981). Attraction to competent and incompetent members of cooperative and competitive groups. *Journal of Applied Social Psychology, 11*, 416–433.

Rosenhan, D.L. (1970). The natural socialisation of altruistic autonomy. In J. Macaulay & L. Berkowitz (Eds.), *The uncommon child*. New York: Plenum Press.

Rosenhan, D.L. (1973). On being sane in insane places. *Science, 179*, 250–258.

Rosenhan, D.L., & Seligman, M.E.P. (1989). *Abnormal psychology* (2nd Edn.). New York: Norton.

Rosenhan, D.L., & Seligman, M.E.P. (1995). *Abnormal psychology* (3rd Edn.). New York: Norton.

Rosenman, R.H., Brand, R.J., Jenkins, C.D., Friedman, M., Straus, R., & Wurm, M. (1975). Coronary heart disease in the Western Collaborative Group Study: Final follow-up experience of 8½ years. *Journal of the American Medical Association, 233*, 872–877.

Rosenthal, D. (1963). *The Genain quadruplets: A case study and theoretical analysis of heredity and environment in schizophrenia.* New York: Basic Books.

Rosenthal, R. (1966). *Experimenter effects in behavioural research.* New York: Appleton-Century-Crofts.

Rosenzweig, M.R. (1992). Psychological science around the world. *American Psychologist, 47*, 718–722.

Ross, L., Greene, D., & House, P. (1977). The false consensus phenomenon: An attributional bias in self-perception and social perception processes. *Journal of Experimental Social Psychology, 13*, 279–301.

Rubin, K.H., & Trotter, K.T. (1977). Kohlberg's moral judgement scale: Some methodological considerations. *Developmental Psychology, 13*, 535–536.

Rubin, Z. (1970). Measurement of romantic love. *Journal of Personality and Social Psychology, 16*, 265–273.

Rubin, Z. (1973). *Liking and loving: An invitation to social psychology.* New York: Holt, Rinehart & Winston.

Ruble, D.N., Balaban, T., & Cooper, J. (1981). Gender constancy and the effects of sex-typed televised toy commercials. *Child Development, 52*, 667–673.

Ruble, D.N., Fleming, A.S., Hackel, L.S., & Stangor, C. (1988). Changes in the marital relationship during the transition to first time motherhood: The effects of violated expectations concerning division of household labour. *Journal of Personality and Social Psychology, 55*, 78–87.

Rumbaugh, D.M., Savage-Rumbaugh, E.S., & Washburn, D.A. (1996). Toward a new look on primate learning and behaviour: Complex learning and emergent processes in comparative perspective. *Japanese Psychological Research, 38*, 113–125.

Runciman, W.G. (1966). *Relative deprivation and social justice.* London: Routledge & Kegan Paul.

Runyon, R., & Haber, A. (1976). *Fundamentals of behavioural statistics* (3rd Edn.). Reading, MA: McGraw-Hill.

Rusbult, C.E. (1980). Commitment and satisfaction in romantic associations: A test of the investment model. *Journal of Experimental Social Psychology, 16*, 172–186.

Rusbult, C.E., Zembrodt, I., & Iwaniszek, J. (1986). The impact of gender and sex-role orientation on responses to dissatisfaction in close relationships. *Sex Roles, 15*, 1–20.

Russek, M. (1971). Hepatic receptors and the neurophysiological mechanisms controlling feeding behaviour. In S. Ehrenpreis (Ed.), *Neurosciences Research, Vol. 4.* New York: Academic Press.

Russell, C.S. (1974). Transition to parenthood: Problems and gratifications. *Journal of Marriage and the Family, 36*, 294–302.

Russell, D.W., & Catrona, C.E. (1991). Social support, stress, and depressive symptoms among the elderly: Test of a process model. *Psychology and Aging, 6*, 190–201.

Russell, M.J., Switz, G.M., & Thompson, K. (1980). Olfactory influences on the human menstrual cycle. *Pharmacology, Biochemistry and Behaviour, 13*, 737–738.

Rutter, M., Graham, P., Chadwick, D.F.D., & Yule, W. (1976). Adolescent turmoil: Fact or fiction. *Journal of Child Psychology and Psychiatry, 17*, 35–56.

Rutter, M., & Rutter, M. (1992). *Developing minds: Challenge and continuity across the life-span.* Harmondsworth, UK: Penguin.

Ryan, R.M., & Lynch, J.H. (1989). Emotional autonomy versus detachment: Revisiting the vicissitudes of adolescence and young adulthood. *Child Development, 60*, 340–356.

Ryder, R. (1990). *Animal revolution: Changing attitudes towards speciesism.* Oxford, UK: Blackwell.

Ryder, R. (1991). Sentientism: A comment on Gray and Singer. *The Psychologist, 14*, 201.

Sachs, J., Bard, B., & Johnson, M.L. (1981). Language learning with restricted input: Case studies of two hearing children of deaf parents. *Applied Psycholinguistics, 2*, 33–54.

Sackheim, H.A., Nordlie, J.W., & Gur, R.C. (1993). Effects of stimulus intensity and electrode replacement on the efficacy of the effects of electroconvulsive therapy. *New England Journal of Medicine, 328*, 839–846.

Sacks, O. (1985). *The man who mistook his wife for a hat.* London: Picador.

Sacks, O. (1995). *An anthropologist on Mars.* London: Picador.

Sagotsky, G., Wood-Schneider, M., & Konop, M. (1981). Learning to co-operate: Effects of modelling and direct instructions. *Child Development, 52*, 1037–1042.

Salamon, S. (1977). Family bonds and friendship bonds: Japan and West Germany. *Journal of Marriage and the Family, 39*, 807–820.

Salley, R.D. (1988). Subpersonalities with dreaming functions in a patient with multiple personalities. *Journal of Nervous and Mental Disease, 176*, 112–115.

Salomon, G., & Globerson, T. (1989). When groups do not function the way they ought to. *International Journal of Educational Research, 13*, 89–99.

Salovey, P. (Ed.). (1991). *The psychology of jealousy and envy.* New York: Guilford Press.

Sameroff, A.J., Bartko, W.T., Baldwin, A., Baldwin, C., & Seifer, R. (1998). Family and social influences on the development of child competence. *Families, Risk, and Competence, 161*–185.

Sameroff, A.J., Seifer, R., Baldwin, A., & Baldwin, C. (1993). Stability of intelligence from preschool to adolescence: The influence of social and family risk factors. *Child Development, 64*, 80–97.

Sameroff, A.J., Seifer, R., Barocas, R., Zax, M., & Greenspan, S. (1987). Intelligence quotient scores of 4-year-old children: Social-environmental risk factors. *Paediatrics, 79*, 343–350.

Samuel, J., & Bryant, P. (1984). Asking only one question in the conservation experiment. *Journal of Child Psychology and Psychiatry, 25*(2), 315–318.

Santrock, J.W. (1975). Moral structure: The interrelations of moral behaviour, moral judgement, and moral affect. *Journal of Genetic Psychology, 127*, 201–213.

Santschi, F. (1911). Observations et remarques critiques sur le mechanisms de l'orientation. *Rev. suisse Zool., 62*, 250–259.

Sartorius, N., Jablensky, A., Korten, A., Ernberg, G., Anker, M., Cooper, J.E., & Day, R. (1986). Early manifestations and first-contact incidence of schizophrenia in different cultures. *Psychological Medicine, 16*, 909–928.

Sasse, G., Müller, H., Chakraborty, R., & Ott, J. (1994). Estimating the frequency of non-paternity in Switzerland. *Human Heredity, 44*(6), 337–342.

Savage-Rumbaugh, E.S. (1991). Language learning in the bonobo: How and why they learn . In N.A. Krasnegor, D.M. Rumbaugh, R.L. Schiefelbusch, & M. Studdert-Kennedy (Eds.), *Biological and behavioural determinants of language development.* Hillsdale, NJ: Lawrence Erlbaum Associates Inc.

Savage-Rumbaugh, E.S., & Lewin, R. (1994). *Kanzi: At the brink of the human mind.* New York: Wiley.

Savage-Rumbaugh, E.S., McDonald, K., Sevcik, R.A., Hopkins, W.D., & Rupert, E. (1986). Spontaneous symbol acquisition and communicative use by pygmy chimpanzees (*Pan paniscus*). *Journal of Experimental Psychology: General, 115*, 211–235.

Savin, H.B. (1973). Professors and psychological researchers: Conflicting values in conflicting roles. *Cognition, 2*, 147–149.

Scarr, S. (1988). Race and gender as psychological variables. *American Psychologist, 43*, 56–59.

Schachter, S., & Singer, J.E. (1962). Cognitive, social, and physiological determinants of an emotional state. *Psychological Review, 69*, 379–399.

Schachter, S., & Wheeler, L. (1962). Epinephrine, chlorpromazine and amusement. *Journal of Abnormal and Social Psychology, 65*, 121–128.

Schacter, D.L. (Ed.). (1999). The cognitive neuropsychology of false memories: A special issue of the journal Cognitive Neuropsychology. Hove, UK: Psychology Press Ltd.

Schafer, R., & Murphy, G. (1943). The role of autism in visual figure–ground relationship. *Journal of Experimental Psychology, 32*, 335–343.

Schaie, K.W. (Ed.). (1983). *Longitudinal studies of adult psychological development*. New York: Guilford Press.

Schank, R.C., & Abelson, R.P. (1977). *Scripts, plans, goals and understanding*. Hillsdale, NJ: Lawrence Erlbaum Associates Inc.

Schaller, G.B. (1972). *The Serengeti lion*. Chicago: University of Chicago Press.

Scheerer, M. (1963). Problem-solving. *Scientific American, 208*(4), 118–128.

Scheff, T.J. (1966). *Being mentally ill: A sociological theory*. Chicago: Aldine.

Schiffman, H.R. (1967). Size estimation of familiar objects under informative and reduced conditions of viewing. *American Journal of Psychology, 80*, 229–235.

Schneider, W., & Shiffrin, R.M. (1977). Controlled and automatic human information processing: I. Detection, search and attention. *Psychological Review, 84*, 1–66.

Schochat, T., Luboshitzky, R., & Lavie, P. (1997). Nocturnal melatonin onset is phase locked to the primary sleep gate. *American Journal of Physiology, 273*, R364–R370.

Schooler, J.W., & Engstler-Schooler, T.Y. (1990). Verbal overshadowing of visual memories: Some things are better left unsaid. *Cognitive Psychology, 22*, 36–71.

Schroeder, D.H., & Costa, D.T. (1984). Influence of life event stress on physical illness: Substantive effects or methodological flaws? *Journal of Personality and Social Psychology, 46*, 853–863.

Schultz, N.R., Kaye, D.B., & Hoyer, W.J. (1980). Intelligence and spontaneous flexibility in adulthood and old age. *Intelligence, 4*, 219–231.

Schuster, B., Fosterling, F., & Weiner, B. (1989). Perceiving the causes of success and failure: A cross-cultural examination of attributional concepts. *Journal of Cross-Cultural Psychology, 20*, 191–213.

Schuz, E. (1971). *Grundriss der Vogelzugskunde*. Berlin: Paul Parey.

Schwartz, G., Weinberger, C., & Singer, J. (1981). Cardiovascular differentiation of happiness, sadness, anger and fear following imagery and exercise. *Psychosomatic Medicine, 43*, 343–364.

Schwartz, S., Deutsch, C.P., & Weissmann, A. (1967). Language development in two groups of socially disadvantaged young children. *Psychological Reports, 21*(1), 169–178.

Schwartz, W., Recht, L., & Lew, R. (1995, October 29). Three time zones and you're out. *New Scientist*.

Schwarz, N., Groves, R.M., & Schuman, H. (1998). Survey methods. In D. Gilbert, S. Fiske, & G. Lindzey (Eds.), *The handbook of social psychology* (Vol. 1, 4th Edn., pp. 143–79). New York: Random House.

Schwarzer, R., & Leppin, A. (1992). Social support and mental health: A conceptual and empirical overview. In L. Montada, S.H. Filipp, & M.J. Lerner (Eds.), *Life crises and experience of loss in adulthood*. Hillsdale, NJ: Lawrence Erlbaum Associates Inc.

Scroppo, J., Weinberger, J., Drob, S., & Eagle, P. (1998). Identifying dissociative identity disorder: A self-report and projective study. *Journal of Abnormal Psychology, 92*, 272–284.

Segal, S.J., & Fusella, V. (1970). Influence of imaged pictures and sounds on detection of visual and auditory signals. *Journal of Experimental Psychology, 83*, 458–464.

Segall, M.H., Campbell, D.T., & Herskovits, M.J. (1963). Cultural differences in the perception of geometrical illusions. *Science, 139*, 769–771.

Seger, C.A. (1994). Implicit learning. *Psychological Bulletin, 115*, 163–196.

Seidman, L.J. (1983). Schizophrenia and brain dysfunction: An integration of recent neurodiagnostic findings. *Psychological Bulletin, 94*, 195–238.

Seitz, V. (1990). Intervention programs for impoverished children: A comparison of educational and family support models. *Annals of Child Development: A Research Annual, 7*, 73–103.

Sekuler, R., & Blake, R. (1994). *Perception* (3rd Edn.). New York: McGraw-Hill.

Selfridge, O.G. (1959). Pandemonium: A paradigm for learning. In *The mechanisms of thought processes*. London: Her Majesty's Stationery Office.

Seligman, M.E.P. (1970). On the generality of the laws of learning. *Psychological Review, 77*, 406–418.

Seligman, M.E.P. (1971). Phobias and preparedness. *Behavior Therapy, 2*, 307–320.

Seligman, M.E.P. (1975). *Helplessness: On depression, development and death*. San Francisco: W.H. Freeman.

Sellen, A.J., & Norman, D.A. (1992). The psychology of slips. In B.J. Baars (Ed.), *Experimental slips and human error: Exploring the architecture of volition*. New York: Plenum Press.

Semin, G.R. (1995). Social constructionism. In A.S.R. Manstead, M. Hewstone, S.T. Fiske, M.A. Hogg, H.T. Reis, & G.R. Semin (Eds.), *The Blackwell encyclopaedia of social psychology*. Oxford, UK: Blackwell.

Serpell, R.S. (1979). How specific are perceptual skills? A cross-cultural study of pattern reproduction. *British Journal of Psychology, 70*, 365–380.

Shaffer, D.R. (1993). *Developmental psychology: Childhood and adolescence* (3rd Edn.). Pacific Grove, CA: Brooks/Cole.

Shaffer, L.H. (1975). Multiple attention in continuous verbal tasks. In P.M.A. Rabbitt & S. Dornic (Eds.), *Attention and performance, Vol. V*. London: Academic Press.

Shapiro, C.M., Bortz, R., Mitchell, D., Bartel, P., & Jooste, P. (1981). Slow-wave sleep: A recovery period after exercise. *Science, 214*, 1253–1254.

Shapiro, J.P. (1991). Interviewing children about psychological issues associated with sexual abuse. *Psychotherapy, 28*, 55–65.

Shatz, M., & Gelman, R. (1973). The development of communication skills: Modifications in the speech of young children as a function of the listener. *Monographs of the Society for Research in Child Development, 38*.

Shaver, J.P., & Strong, W. (1976). *Facing value decisions: Rationale-building for teachers*. Belmont, CA: Wadsworth.

Sherif, M. (1966). *Group conflict and co-operation: Their social psychology*. London: Routledge & Kegan Paul.

Sherif, M., Harvey, O.J., White, B.J., Hood, W.R., & Sherif, C.W. (1961). *Intergroup conflict and co-operation: The robber's cave experiment*. Norman, OK: University of Oklahoma.

Sherry, D., Jacobs, L.F., & Gaulin, S.J.C. (1992). Spatial memory and adaptive specialisation of the hippocampus. *Trends in Neurosciences, 15*, 298–303.

Sherry, D.F., & Galef, B.G. (1984). Cultural transmission without imitation: Milk bottle opening by birds. *Animal Behaviour, 32*, 937–938.

Sherry, D.F., Krebs, J.R., & Cowie, R.J. (1981). Memory for the location of stored food in marsh tits. *Animal Behaviour, 29*(4), 1260–1266.

Shields, J. (1962). *Monozygotic twins*. Oxford, UK: Oxford University Press.

Sherman, P.W. (1977). Nepotism and the evolution of alarm calls. *Science, 197*, 1246–1253.

Shiffrin, R.M., & Schneider, W. (1977). Controlled and automatic human information processing: II. Perceptual learning, automatic attending, and a general theory. *Psychological Review, 84*, 127–190.

Short, R.V. (1994). Why sex. In R.V. Short & E. Balaban (Eds.), *The differences between the sexes*. Cambridge, UK: Cambridge University Press.

Shotland, R.L., & Straw, M.K. (1976). Bystander response to an assault: When a man attacks a woman. *Journal of Personality and Social Psychology, 34*, 990–999.

Shweder, R.A., Mahapatra, M., & Miller, J.G. (1990). Culture and moral development. In J. Stigler, R.A. Shweder, & G. Herdt (Eds.), *Cultural psychology: Essays in comparative human development* (pp. 130–204). New York: Cambridge University Press.

Sieber, J.E., & Stanley, B. (1988). Ethical and professional dimensions of socially sensitive research. *American Psychologist, 43*, 49–55.

Siffre, M. (1975). Six months alone in a cave. *National Geographic*, March, 426–435.

Siipola, E.M. (1935). A study of some effects of preparatory set. *Psychological Monographs, 46*(Serial No. 210), 27–39.

Silver, R., LeSauter, J., Tresco, P.A., & Lehman, M.N. (1996). A diffusible coupling signal from the transplanted suprachiasmatic nucleus controlling circadian locomotor rhythms. *Nature, 382*(6594), 810–813.

Silverman, I. (1977). *The human subject in the psychological laboratory*. Oxford, UK: Pergamon.

Silvern, S.B., & Williamson, P.A. (1987). The effects of video game play on young children's aggression, fantasy, and prosocial behavior. *Journal of Applied Developmental Psychology, 8*(4), 453–462.

Simmel, G. (1971). *On individuality and social forms*. Chicago: University of Chicago Press.

Simmons, J.V. (1981). *Project Sea Hunt: A report on prototype development and tests*, [Tech. Rep., No. 746]. San Diego, CA: Naval Ocean System Center.

Simmons, R.G., Burgeson, R., Carlton-Ford, S., & Blyth, D.A. (1987). The impact of cumulative changes in early adolescence. *Child Development, 58*, 1220–1234.

Simon, H.A. (1978). Rationality as process and product of thought. *American Economic Association, 68*, 1–16.

Simon, H.A., & Reed, S.K. (1976). Modelling strategy shifts on a problem solving task, *Cognitive Psychology, 8*, 86–97.

Sinclair-de-Zwart, H. (1969). Developmental psycholinguistics. In D. Elkind & J. Flavell (Eds.), *Studies in cognitive development*. Oxford, UK: Oxford University Press.

Singer, P. (1991). Speciesism, morality and biology: A response to Jeffrey Gray. *The Psychologist, 14*, 199–200.

Singer, P. (1998, June). Darwin for the Left. *Prospect Magazine*.

Singleton, J., & Newport, E. (1993). *When learners surpass their models: The acquisition of sign language from impoverished input*. Unpublished manuscript, Department of Psychology, University of Rochester.

Siqueland, E.R., & DeLucia, C.A. (1969). Visual reinforcement of non-nutritive sucking in human infants. *Science, 165*, 1144–1146.

Skal, D. (1993). *The monster show: A cultural history of horror*. London: Plexus.

Skinner, B.F. (1938). *The behaviour of organisms*. New York: Appleton-Century-Crofts.

Skinner, B.F. (1948). *Walden two*. New York: Macmillan.

Skinner, B.F. (1957). *Verbal behaviour*. New York: Appleton-Century-Crofts.

Skre, I., Onstad, S., Torgersen, S., Lygren, S., & Kringlen, E. (1993). A twin study of DSM-III-R anxiety disorders. *Acta Psychiatrica Scandinavica, 88*, 85–92.

Slaby, R.G., & Frey, K.S. (1975). Development of gender constancy and selective attention to same-sex models. *Child Development, 46*, 849–856.

Slater, A.M. (1990). Perceptual development. In M.W. Eysenck (Ed.), *The Blackwell dictionary of cognitive psychology*. Oxford, UK: Blackwell.

Slater, P.J.B. (1981). Chaffinch song repertoires: Observations, experiments and a discussion of their significance. *Zeitschrift für Tierpsychologie, 56*, 1–24.

Slavin, R.E. (1983). When does cooperative learning increase student achievement? *Psychological Bulletin, 94*, 429–445.

Sloane, R.B., Staples, F.R., Cristol, A.H., Yorkston, N.J., & Whipple, K. (1975). *Psychotherapy versus behaviour therapy*. Cambridge, MA: Harvard University Press.

Smetana, J.G. (1988). Adolescents' and parents' concepts of parental authority. *Child Development, 59*, 321–335.

Smith, E.A. (1998). Is Tibetan polyandry adaptive? Methodological and metatheoretical analyses. *Human Nature, 9*(3), 225–261.

Smith, K.A., Clifford, E.M., Hockney, R.A., & Clark, D.M. (1997). Effect of tryptophan depletion on mood in male and female volunteers: A pilot study. *Human Psychopharmacology, Clinical and Experimental, 12*(2), 111–117.

Smith, K.D., Keating, J.P., & Stotland, E. (1989). Altruism reconsidered: The effect of denying feedback on a victim's status to empathic witnesses. *Journal of Personality and Social Psychology, 57*, 641–650.

Smith, M.L., Glass, G.V., & Miller, T.I. (1980). *The benefits of psychotherapy*. Baltimore: John Hopkins Press.

Smith, N.V., & Tsimpli, I.-M. (1991). Linguistic modularity? A case-study of a "savant" linguist. *Lingua, 84*, 315–351.

Smith, P., & Bond, M.H. (1993). *Social psychology across cultures: Analysis and perspectives*. New York: Harvester Wheatsheaf.

Smith, R.L. (1984). Human sperm competition. In R.L. Smith (Ed.), *Sperm competition and the evolution of animal mating systems*. Orlando, FL: Academic Press.

Smith, S.M., Brown, H.O., Toman, J.E.P., & Goodman, L.S. (1947). Lack of cerebral effects of D-tubocurarine. *Anaesthesiology, 8*, 1–14.

Snarey, J.R. (1985). Cross-cultural universality of social-moral development: A critical review of Kohlbergian research. *Psychological Bulletin, 97*, 202–232.

Solomon, R.L., & Wynne, L.C. (1953). Traumatic avoidance learning: Acquisition in normal dogs. *Psychological Monographs, 67*, 1–19.

Spanos, N.P. (1989). Experimental research on hypnotic analgesia. In N.P. Spanos & J.F. Cahves (Eds.), *Hypnosis: The cognitive-behavioural perspective*. Buffalo, NY: Prometheus.

Spanos, N.P., Weekes, J.R., & Bertrand, L.D. (1985). Multiple personality: A social psychological perspective. *Journal of Abnormal Psychology, 94*, 362–376.

Speisman, J.C., Lazarus, R.S., Mordkoff, A., & Davison, L. (1964). Experimental reduction of stress based on ego-defence theory. *Journal of Abnormal and Social Psychology, 68*, 367–380.

Spelke, E.S., Hirst, W.C., & Neisser, U. (1976). Skills of divided attention. *Cognition, 4*, 215–230.

Sperry, R.W. (1968). Hemispheric disconnection and unity in conscious awareness. *American Psychologist, 23,* 723–733.

Sperry, R.W. (1985). Consciousness, personal identity, and the divided brain. In D.F. Benson & E. Zaidel (Eds.), *The dual brain: Hemispheric specialisation in humans.* New York: Guilford Press.

Spitzer, R.L., & Fleiss, J.L. (1974). A re-analysis of the reliability of psychiatric diagnosis. *British Journal of Psychiatry, 125,* 341–347.

Spitzer, R.L., Williams, J.B.W., Kass, F., & Davies, M. (1989). National field trial of the DSM-III-R diagnostic criteria for self-defeating personality disorder. *American Journal of Psychiatry, 146,* 1561–1567.

Sprafkin, J.N., Liebert, R.M., & Poulos, R.W. (1975). Effects of a pro-social televised example on children's helping. *Journal of Experimental Child Psychology, 20,* 119–126.

Sroufe, L.A., Bennett, C., Englund, M., & Urban, J. (1993). The significance of gender boundaries in preadolescence: Contemporary correlates and antecedents of boundary violation and maintenance. *Child Development, 64,* 455–466.

Stammbach, E. (1988). Group responses to specially skilled individuals in Macaca fascicularis group. *Behaviour, 107,* 241–266.

Stemberger, R.T., Turner, S.M., & Beidel, D.C. (1995). Social phobia: An analysis of possible developmental factors. *Journal of Abnormal Psychology, 104,* 526–531.

Stephan, W.G. (1987). The contact hypothesis in intergroup relations. In C. Hendrick (Ed.), *Review of personality and social psychology: Vol. 9. Group processes in intergroup relations.* Newbury Park, CA: Sage.

Stephan, W.G., & Stephan, C.W. (1989). Antecedents of intergroup anxiety in Oriental-Americans and Hispanics. *International Journal of Intercultural Communication, 13,* 203–219.

Stephens, T.W., Basinski, M., Bristow, P.K., Bue-Valleskey, J.M., Burgett, S.G., Craft, L., Hale, J., Hoffman, J., Hsiung, H.M., Kriauciunas, A., MacKellar, W., Rosteck, P.R., Jr., Schoner, B., Smith, D., Tinsley, F.C., Zhang, W.-Y., & Heiman, M. (1995). The role of neuropeptide Y in the antiobesity action of the *obese* gene product. *Nature, 377,* 530–532.

Stern, S.L., Rush, J., & Mendels, J. (1980). Toward a rational pharmacotherapy of depression. *American Journal of Psychiatry, 137,* 545–552.

Stern, W.C., & Morgane, P.J. (1974). Theoretical view of REM sleep function: Maintenance of catecholamine systems in the central nervous system. *Behavioural Biology, 11,* 1–32.

Sternberg, R.J. (1985). *Beyond IQ: A triarchic theory of human intelligence.* Cambridge, UK: Cambridge University Press.

Sternberg, R.J. (1986). A triangular theory of love. *Psychological Review, 93,* 119–135.

Sternberg, R.J. (1994). Intelligence and cognitive styles. In A.M. Colman (Ed.), *Companion encyclopedia of psychology, Vol. 1.* London: Routledge.

Sternberg, R.J. (1995). *In search of the human mind.* New York: Harcourt Brace.

Sternberg, R.J., & Grajek, S. (1984). The nature of love. *Journal of Personality and Social Psychology, 47,* 312–329.

Stevens, A., & Price, J. (1996). *Evolutionary psychiatry.* London: Routledge.

Stevens, J. (1987). Brief psychoses: Do they contribute to the good prognosis and equal prevalence of schizophrenia in developing countries? *British Journal of Psychiatry, 151,* 393–396.

Stevenson, M.R., & Black, K.N. (1988). Paternal absence and sex-role development: A meta-analysis. *Child Development, 59,* 793–814.

Stirling, J. (2000). *Cortical functions.* London: Routledge.

Stirling, J.D., & Hellewell, J.S.E. (1999). *Psychopathology.* London: Routledge.

Stopa, L., & Clark, D.M. (1993). Cognitive processes in social phobia. *Behaviour Research and Therapy, 31,* 255–267.

Storms, M.D. (1973). Videotape and the attribution process: Reversing actors' and observers' points of view. *Journal of Personality and Social Psychology, 27,* 165–175.

Strack, F., Martin, L.L., & Stepper, S. (1988). Inhibiting and facilitating conditions of facial expressions: A non-obtrusive test of the facial feedback hypothesis. *Journal of Personality and Social Psychology, 54,* 768–776.

Stratton, G.M. (1896). Some preliminary experiments on vision without inversion of the retinal image. *Psychological Review, 3,* 611–617.

Stroebe, M.S., Stroebe, W., & Hansson, R.O. (1993). Contemporary themes and controversies in bereavement research. In M.S. Stroebe, W. Stroebe, & R.O. Hansson (Eds.), *Handbook of bereavement: Theory, research and intervention.* New York: Cambridge University Press.

Strupp, H.H. (1996). The tripartite model and the Consumer Reports study. *American Psychologist, 51,* 1017–1024.

Stuart-Hamilton, I. (1994). *The psychology of ageing: An introduction* (2nd Edn.). London: Jessica Kingsley.

Suddath, R.L., Christison, G.W., Torrey, E.F., Casanova, M.F., & Weinberger, D.R. (1990). Anatomical abnormalities in the brains of monozygotic twins discordant for schizophrenia. *New England Journal of Medicine, 322,* 789–794.

Sue, D., Sue, D., & Sue, S. (1994). *Understanding abnormal behaviour.* Boston: Houghton Mifflin.

Sullivan, L. (1976). Selective attention and secondary message analysis: A reconsideration of Broadbent's filter model of selective attention. *Quarterly Journal of Experimental Psychology, 28,* 167–178.

Sulloway, E. (1994). *Born to rebel: Radical thinking in science and social thought.* Unpublished manuscript, Cambridge, MA: MIT Press.

Szasz, T.S. (1962). *The myth of mental illness: Foundation of a theory of personal conduct.* New York: Hoeber-Harper.

Szasz, T.S. (1974). *The age of madness: The history of involuntary hospitalisation.* New York: Jason Aronson.

Taguiri, R. (1969). Person perception. In G. Lindzey & E. Aronson (Eds.), *Handbook of social psychology, Vol. 3.* Reading, MA: Addison-Wesley.

Tajfel, H. (1970). Experiments in intergroup discrimination. *Scientific American, 223,* 96–102.

Tajfel, H. (1978). Intergroup behaviour. 1: Individualistic perspectives. In H. Tajfel, & C. Fraser (Eds.), *Introducing social psychology.* Harmondsworth, UK: Penguin.

Tajfel, H. (1981). *Human groups and social categories: Studies in social psychology.* Cambridge, UK: Cambridge University Press.

Tajfel, H. (1982). Social psychology of intergroup relations. *Annual Review of Psychology, 33,* 1–30.

Talland, G.A. (Ed.). (1968). *Human ageing and behaviour.* New York: Academic Press.

Tannen, D. (1990, June 24). Sex, lies, and conversation: Why is it so hard for men and women to talk to each other? *The Washington Post.*

Tannen, D. (1991). *You just don't understand.* London: Virago Press.

Taylor, A., Sluckin, W., Davies, D.R., Reason, J.T., Thomson, R., & Colman, A.M. (1982). *Introducing psychology* (2nd Edn.). Harmondsworth, UK: Penguin.

Taylor, S.E. (1981). The interface of cognitive and social psychology. In J. Harvey (Ed.), *Cognition, social behaviour, and the environment* (pp. 189–211). Hillsdale, NJ: Lawrence Erlbaum Associates Inc.

Teitelbaum, P. (1957). Random and food-directed activity in hyperphagic and normal rats. *Journal of Comparative and Physiological Psychology, 50,* 486–490.

Terman, M. (1988). On the question of mechanism in phototherapy for seasonal affective disorder: Considerations of clinical efficacy and epidemiology. *Journal of Biological Rhythms, 3,* 155–172.

Terrace, H.S. (1979). *Nim.* New York: Alfred Knopf.

Terrace, H.S., Petitto, L.A., Sanders, D.J., & Bever, T.G. (1979). On the grammatical capacities of apes. In K. Nelson (Ed.), *Children's language, Vol. 2.* New York: Gardner Press.

Tetlock, P.E. (1991). An alternative metaphor in the study of judgement and choice: People as politicians. *Theory and Psychology, 1,* 451–475.

Teuting, P., Rosen, S., & Hirschfeld, R. (1981). *Special report on depression research* [NIMH-DHHS Publication No. 81–1085]. Washington, DC.

Thibaut, J.W., & Kelley, H.H. (1959). *The social psychology of groups.* New York: Wiley.

Thigpen, C.H., & Cleckley, H. (1954). A case of multiple personality. *Journal of Abnormal and Social Psychology, 49,* 135–151.

Thoits, P.A. (1982). Direct, indirect, and moderating effects of social support on psychological distress and associated conditions. In H.B. Kaplan (Ed.), *Psychosocial stress: Trends in theory and research.* New York: Academic Press.

Thomas, A., & Chess, S. (1977). *Temperament and development.* New York: Brunner/Mazel.

Thomas, A., Chess, S., & Birch, H.G. (1970). The origin of personality. *Scientific American, 223,* 102–109.

Thomas, J., & Blackman, D. (1991). Are animal experiments on the way out? *The Psychologist, 4,* 208–212.

Thomas, M.H., Horton, R.W., Lippincott, E.C., & Drabman, R.S. (1977). Desensitisation to portrayals of real-life aggression as a function of exposure to television violence. *Journal of Personality and Social Psychology, 35,* 450–458.

Thompson, L.W., Gallagher-Thompson, D.G., & Futterman, A. (1991). The effects of late-life spousal bereavement over a 30-month internal. *Psychology and Aging, 6,* 434–441.

Thompson, W.C., Cowan, C.L., & Rosenhan, D.L. (1980). Focus of attention mediates the impact of negative affect on altruism. *Journal of Personality and Social Psychology, 38,* 291–300.

Thorndike, E.L. (1911). *Animal intelligence: Experimental studies.* New York: MacMillan.

Thornhill, R. (1980). Rape in *Panorpa* scorpionflies and a general rape hypothesis. *Animal Behaviour, 28,* 52–59.

Thornhill, R., Palmer, C.T., & Wilson, M. (2000). *A natural history of rape: Biological bases of sexual coercion.* Cambridge, MA: MIT Press.

Thornhill, R., & Thornhill, N. (1983). Human rape: An evolutionary analysis. *Ethology and Sociobiology, 4*(3), 137–173.

Tienari, P. (1991). Interaction between genetic vulnerability and family environment: The Finnish adoptive family study of schizophrenia. *Acta Psychiatrica Scandinavica, 84,* 460–465.

Timberlake, W., & Grant, D.L. (1975). Autoshaping in rats to the presentation of another rat predicting food. *Science, 190,* 690–692.

Tinbergen, N. (1951). *The study of instinct.* Oxford, UK: Oxford University Press.

Tinbergen, N. (1952). The curious behaviour of the stickleback. *Scientific American, 187*(6), 22–26.

Tizard, B., & Hughes, M. (1984). *Young children learning.* London: Fontana.

Tobin, J. (1996). A case of koro in a 20 year old Irish male. *Irish Journal of Psychological Medicine, 13*(2), 72–73.

Tolman, E.C. (1948). Cognitive maps in rats and men. *Psychological Review, 55,* 189–208.

Tolman, E.C., & Honzik, C.H. (1930). Introduction and removal of reward and maze learning in rats. *University of California Publications in Psychology, 4,* 257–275.

Tolstedt, B.E., & Stokes, J.P. (1984). Self-disclosure, intimacy, and the depenetration process. *Journal of Personality and Social Psychology, 46,* 84–90.

Tomarken, A.J., Mineka, S., & Cook, M. (1989). Fear-relevant associations and covariation bias. *Journal of Abnormal Psychology, 98,* 381–394.

Tomasello, M., & Call, J. (1997). *Primate cognition.* Oxford, UK: Oxford University Press.

Tomlinson-Keasey, C., Eisert, D.C., Kahle, L.R., Hardy-Brown, K., & Keasey, B. (1979). The structure of concrete-operational thought. *Child Development, 57,* 1454–1463.

Tomlinson-Keasey, C., & Keasey, C.B. (1974). The mediating role of cognitive development in moral judgement. *Child Development, 45,* 291–298.

Tompkins, C.A., & Mateer, C.A. (1985). Right hemisphere appreciation of intonational and linguistic indications of affect. *Brain and Language, 24,* 185–203.

Topal, J., Miklosi, A., Csanyi, V., & Doka, A. (1998). Antal attachment behavior in dogs (*Canis familiaris*): A new application of Ainsworth's (1969) Strange Situation Test. *Journal of Comparative Psychology, 112*(3), 219–229.

Torgersen, S. (1983). Genetic factors in anxiety disorders. *Archives of General Psychiatry, 40,* 1085–1089.

Tout, K. (1989). *Ageing in developing countries.* Oxford, UK: Oxford University Press.

Towhey, J.C. (1979). Sex-role stereotyping and individual differences in liking for the physically attractive. *Social Psychology Quarterly, 42,* 285–289.

Treisman, A.M. (1960). Verbal cues in selective listening. *Quarterly Journal of Experimental Psychology, 12,* 242–248.

Treisman, A.M. (1964). Verbal cues, language, and meaning in selective attention. *American Journal of Psychology, 77,* 206–219.

Treisman, A.M., & Geffen, G. (1967). Selective attention: Perception or response? *Quarterly Journal of Experimental Psychology, 19,* 1–18.

Treisman, A.M., & Gelade, G. (1980). A feature integration theory of attention. *Cognitive Psychology, 12,* 97–136.

Treisman, A.M., & Riley, J.G.A. (1969). Is selective attention selective perception or selective response: A further test. *Journal of Experimental Psychology, 79,* 27–34.

Treisman, A.M., & Sato, S. (1990). Conjunction search revisited. *Journal of Experimental Psychology: Human Perception and Performance, 16,* 459–478.

Treisman, A.M., & Schmidt, H. (1982). Illusory conjunctions in the perception of objects. *Cognitive Psychology, 14,* 107–141.

Tresilian, J.R. (1994). Two straw men stay silent when asked about the "direct" versus "inferential" controversy. *Behavioral and Brain Sciences, 17,* 335–336.

Triandis, H.C. (1994). *Culture and social behaviour.* New York: McGraw-Hill.

Triandis, H.C., & Vassiliou, V. (1967). A comparative analysis of subjective culture. In H.C. Triandis (Ed.), *The analysis of subjective culture.* New York: Wiley.

Trivers, R.L. (1971). The evolution of reciprocal altruism. *Quarterly Review of Biology, 46,* 35–57.

Trivers, R.L. (1972). Parental investment and sexual selection. In B. Campbell (Ed.), *Sexual selection and the descent of man, 1871–1971.* Chicago: Aldine.

Truax, C.B. (1966). Therapist empathy, genuineness, and warmth and patient therapeutic outcome. *Journal of Consulting Psychology, 30,* 395–401.

Tulving, E. (1979). Relation between encoding specificity and levels of processing. In L.S. Cermak & F.I.M. Craik (Eds.), *Levels of processing in human memory*. Hillsdale, NJ: Lawrence Erlbaum Associates Inc.

Tulving, E. (1989). Memory: Performance, knowledge, and experience. *European Journal of Cognitive Psychology, 1*, 3–26.

Tulving, E., & Gold, C. (1963). Stimulus information and contextual information as determinants of tachistoscopic recognition of words. *Journal of Experimental Psychology, 66*, 319–327.

Turnbull, C.M. (1961). *The forest people*. New York: Simon & Schuster.

Turnbull, C.M. (1989). *The mountain people*. London: Paladin.

Turner, J.S., & Helms, D.B. (1983). *Lifespan development* (2nd Edn.). New York: Holt, Rinehart & Winston.

Turner, R.J., & Wagonfeld, M.O. (1967). Occupational mobility and schizophrenia. *American Sociological Review, 32*, 104–113.

Tversky, A. (1972). Elimination by aspects: A theory of choice. *Psychological Review, 79*, 281–299.

Tversky, A., & Kahneman, D. (1973). Availability: A heuristic for judging frequency and probability. *Cognitive Psychology, 5*, 207–232.

Tversky, A., & Kahneman, D. (1980). Causal schemas in judgements under uncertainty. In M. Fishbein (Ed.), *Progress in social psychology*. Hillsdale, NJ: Lawrence Erlbaum Associates Inc.

Tversky, A., & Kahneman, D. (1983). Extensional versus intuitive reasoning: The conjunction fallacy in probability judgement. *Psychological Review, 90*, 293–315.

Tversky, A., & Kahneman, D. (1987). Rational choice and the framing of decisions. In R. Hogarth & M. Reder (Eds.), *Rational choice: The contrast between economics and psychology*. Chicago: University of Chicago Press.

Tversky, A., & Shafir, E. (1992). The disjunction effect in choice under uncertainty. *Psychological Science, 3*, 305–309.

Tyack, P. (1983). Differential response of humpback whales *Megaptera novaengliae* to playback of song or social sounds. *Behavioural Ecology, 13*(1), 49–55.

Tyerman, A., & Spencer, C. (1983). A critical test of the Sherifs' Robbers' Cave experiment: Intergroup competition and co-operation between groups of well-acquainted individuals. *Small Group Behaviour, 14*, 515–531.

Umbenhauer, S.L., & DeWitte, L.L. (1978). Patient race and social class: Attitudes and decisions among three groups of mental health professionals. *Comprehensive Psychiatry, 19*, 509–515.

Underwood, G. (1974). Moray vs. the rest: The effects of extended shadowing practice. *Quarterly Journal of Experimental Psychology, 26*, 368–372.

US Congress, Office of Technology Assessment. (1991). *Biological rhythms: Implications for the worker* [OTA-BA-463]. Washington, DC: US Government Printing Office.

Vaillant, C.O., & Vaillant, G.E. (1993). Is the U-curve of marital satisfaction an illusion? A 40-year study of marriage. *Journal of Marriage and the Family, 55*, 230–239.

Vaillant, G.E. (1977). *Adaptation to life: How the best and brightest come of age*. Boston: Little, Brown.

Valentine, E.R. (1982). *Conceptual issues in psychology*. London: Routledge.

Valentine, E.R. (1992). *Conceptual issues in psychology* (2nd Edn.). London: Routledge.

Valins, S. (1966). Cognitive effects of false heart-rate feedback. *Journal of Personality and Social Psychology, 4*, 400–408.

Vandereycken, W., & Hoek, H.W. (1992). Are eating disorders culture-bound syndromes? *American Psychopathological Association series*, 19–36.

Van Kammen, D.P., Docherty, J.P., & Bunney, W.E. (1982). Prediction of early relapse after pimozide discontinuation by response to d-amphetamine during pimozide treatment. *Biological Psychiatry, 17*, 223–242.

Van Kleeck, M.H., & Kosslyn, S.M. (1993). Visual information processing: A perspective. In D.E. Meyer & S. Kornblum (Eds.), *Attention and performance XIV: Synergies in experimental psychology, artificial intelligence, and cognitive neuroscience*. London: MIT Press.

Vanneman, R.D., & Pettigrew, T.F. (1972). Race and relative deprivation in the urban United States. *Race, 13*, 461–486.

van Oppen, P., de Haan, E., van Balkom, A.J.L.M., Spinhoven, P., Hoogduin, K., & van Dyck, R. (1995). Cognitive therapy and exposure in vivo in the treatment of obsessive-compulsive disorder. *Behaviour Research and Therapy, 33*, 379–390.

Veitch, R., & Griffitt, W. (1976). Good news, bad news: Affective and interpersonal effects. *Journal of Applied Social Psychology, 6*, 69–75.

Verburg, K., Griez, E., Meijer, J., & Pols, H. (1995). Respiratory disorders as a possible predisposing factor for panic disorder. *Journal of Affective Disorders, 33*, 129–134.

Virkkunen, M., Nuutila, A., Goodwin, F.K., & Linnoila, M. (1987). Cerebrospinal fluid monamine metabolite levels in male arsonists. *Archives of General Psychiatry, 44*, 241–247.

von Senden, M. (1932). *Space and sight*. London: Methuen.

Von Wright, J.M., Anderson, K., & Stenman, U. (1975). Generalisation of conditioned GSRs in dichotic listening. In P.M.A. Rabbitt & S. Dornic (Eds.), *Attention and performance, Vol. V*. London: Academic Press.

Vygotsky, L.S. (1962). *Thought and language*. Cambridge, MA: MIT Press.

Vygotsky, L.S. (1976). Play and its role in the mental development of the child. In J.S. Bruner, A. Jolly, & K. Sylva (Eds.), *Play*. Harmondsworth, UK: Penguin.

Vygotsky, L.S. (1978). *Mind in society: The development of higher psychological processes*. Cambridge, MA: MIT Press.

Vygotsky, L.S. (1981). The genesis of higher mental functions. In J.V. Wertsch (Ed.), *The concept of activity in Soviet psychology*. Armonk, NY: Sharpe.

Wade, C., & Tavris, C. (1993). *Psychology*. New York: Harper Collins.

Walcott, C., & Green, R.P. (1974). Orientation of homing pigeons altered by a change in the direction of an applied magnetic field. *Science, 184*, 180–182.

Walcott, C., & Schmidt-Koenig, K. (1971). The effect of anaesthesia during displacement on the homing performance of pigeons. *Auk, 90*, 281–286.

Walker, L.J. (1999). Seedy world: Sexual scandal is rife in the grain store. *New Scientist, 2181*, 12.

Walker, L.J., de Vries, B., & Trevethan, S.D. (1987). Moral stages and moral orientations in real-life and hypothetical dilemmas. *Child Development, 58*, 842–858.

Wallach, L., & Wallach, M.A. (1994). Gergen versus the mainstream: Are hypotheses in social psychology subject to empirical test? *Journal of Personality and Social Psychology, 67*, 233–242.

Wallas, G. (1926). *The art of thought*. London: Cape.

Walster, E. (1966). The assignment of responsibility for an accident. *Journal of Personality and Social Psychology, 3*, 73–79.

Walster, E., Aronson, V., Abrahams, D., & Rottman, L. (1966). The importance of physical attractiveness in dating behaviour. *Journal of Personality and Social Psychology, 4*, 508–516.

Walster, E., & Walster, G.W. (1969). *A new look at love*. Reading, MA: Addison Wesley.

Walster, E., Walster, G.W., & Berscheid, E. (1978). *Equity: Theory and research*. Boston: Allyn & Bacon.

Walters, R.H., & Thomas, L. (1963). Enhancement of punitiveness by visual and audiovisual displays. *Canadian Journal of Psychology, 16*, 244–255.

Wampold, B.E., Mondin, G.W., Moody, M., Stich, F., Benson, K., & Ahn, H. (1997). A meta-analysis of outcome studies comparing bona fide psychotherapies: Empirically, "All must have prizes". *Psychological Bulletin, 122*, 203–215.

Warden, C.J. (1951). Animal intelligence. *Scientific American, 184*(6), 64–68.

Warr, P.B. (1987). *Work, unemployment and mental health*. Oxford, UK: Clarendon Press

Warren, R.M., & Warren, R.P. (1970). Auditory illusions and confusions. *Scientific American, 223*, 30–36.

Warrington, E.K., & Taylor, A.M. (1978). Two categorical stages of object recognition. *Perception, 7*, 695–705.

Wason, P.C., & Shapiro, D. (1971). Natural and contrived experience in reasoning problems. *Quarterly Journal of Experimental Psychology, 23*, 63–71.

Waterman, A.S. (1982). Identity development from adolescence to adulthood: An extension of theory and review of research. *Developmental Psychology, 18*, 341–348.

Waterman, A.S. (1985). Identity in the context of adolescent psychology. *New directions for child development, 30*, 5–24.

Waterman, T.H. (1989). *Animal navigation*. New York: Scientific American Library.

Watson, J.B., & Rayner, R. (1920). Conditioned emotional reactions. *Journal of Experimental Psychology, 3*, 1–14.

Webb, W.B. (1982). Sleep and biological rhythms. In W.B. Webb (Ed.), *Biological rhythms, sleep and performance*. Chichester, UK: John Wiley & Sons.

Webb, W.B., & Bonnet, M.H. (1978). The sleep of "morning" and "evening" types. *Biological Psychology, 7*(1–2), 29–35.

Webb, W.B., & Cartwright, R.D. (1978). Sleep and dreams. *Annual Review of Psychology, 29*, 223–252.

Wechsler, D. (1955). *Manual for the Adult Intelligence Scale*. New York: The Psychological Corporation.

Weiner, B. (1980). *Human motivation*. New York: Holt, Rinehart & Winston.

Weiner, M.J., & Wright, F.E. (1973). Effects of underlying arbitrary discrimination upon subsequent attitudes toward a minority group. *Journal of Experimental Social Psychology, 3*, 94–102.

Weingarten, H.P., & Kulikovsky, O.T. (1989). Taste-to-postingestive consequence conditioning: Is the rise in sham feeding with repeated experience a learning phenomenon? *Physiology and Behavior, 45*, 471–476.

Weinreich, P. (1979). Ethnicity and adolescent identity conflicts. In S. Khan (Ed.), *Minority families in Britain*. London: Macmillan.

Weisberg, R.W. (1980). *Memory, thought and behaviour*. Oxford, UK: Oxford University Press.

Weisberg, R.W., & Sals, J. (1973). An information-processing model of Duncker's candle problem. *Cognitive Psychology, 4*, 255–276.

Weiskrantz, L., Warrington, E.K., Sanders, M.D., & Marshall, J. (1974). Visual capacity in the hemianopic field following a restricted occipital ablation. *Brain, 97*, 709–728.

Weissman, M.M., Klerman, G.L., & Paykel, E.S. (1971). Clinical evaluation of hostility in depression. *American Journal of Psychiatry, 39*, 1397–1403.

Weisstein, N., & Harris, C.S. (1974). Visual detection of line segments: An object-superiority effect. *Science, 186*, 752–755.

Weisz, J.R., Chaiyasit, W., Weiss, B., Eastman, K., & Jackson, E. (1995). A multimethod study of problem behaviour among Thai and American children in school: Teacher reports versus direct observations. *Child Development, 66*, 402–415.

Weisz, J.R., Suwanlert, S., Chaiyasit, W., & Walter, B.R. (1987). Over- and undercontrolled referral problems among children and adolescents from Thailand and the United States: The wat and wai of cultural differences. *Journal of Consulting and Clinical Psychology, 55*, 719–726.

Weltman, G., Smith, J.E., & Egstrom, G.H. (1971). Perceptual narrowing during simulated pressure-chamber exposure. *Human Factors, 13*, 99–107.

Wender, P.H., Kety, S.S., Rosenthal, D., Schulsinger, F., Ortmann, J., & Lunde, I. (1986). Psychiatric disorders in the biological and adoptive families of adopted individuals with affective disorders. *Archives of General Psychiatry, 43*, 923–929.

Werner, C., & Parmalee, P. (1979). Similarity of activity preferences among friends: Those who play together, stay together. *Social Psychology Quarterly, 42*, 62–66.

Wertheimer, M. (1912). Experimental studies on the seeing of motion (T. Shipley, Trans.). In *Classics in perception*. Princeton, NJ: Van Nostrand.

Wertsch, J.V., McNamee, G.D., Mclane, J.B., & Budwig, N.A. (1980). The adult–child dyad as a problem-solving system. *Child Development, 51*, 1215–1221.

Westcott, M.R. (1982). Quantitative and qualitative aspects of experienced freedom. *Journal of Mind and Behavior, 3*, 99–126.

Westen, D. (1996). *Psychology: Mind, brain, and culture*. New York: Wiley.

Westermeyer, J. (1973). Grenade amok in Laos: A psychosocial perspective. *International Journal of Psychosocial Psychiatry, 19*, 1–5.

Wetherell, M. (1982). Cross-cultural studies of minimal groups: Implications for the social identity theory of intergroup relations. In H. Tajfel (Ed.), *Social identity and intergroup relations*. Cambridge, UK: Cambridge University Press.

Wetherell, M., & Potter, J. (1988). Discourse analysis and the identification of interpretive repertoires. In C. Antaki (Ed.), *Analysing everyday explanation: A casebook of methods*. London: Sage.

Wever, R. (1979). *Circadian rhythms system of man: Results of experiments under temporal isolation*. New York: Springer.

Wharton, C.M., Grafman, J., Flitman, S.K., Hansen, E.K., Brauner, J., Marks, A., & Honda, M. (1998). The neuroanatomy of analogical reasoning. In K.J. Holyoak, D. Gentner, & B. Kekinar (Eds.), *Analogy 98*. Sofia, Bulgaria: New University of Bulgaria.

Wheatstone, C. (1838). Contributions to the physiology of vision. Part I: On some remarkable and hitherto unobserved phenomena of binocular vision. *Philosophical Transactions of the Royal Society of London, 128*, 371–394.

Wheeler, L.R. (1932). The intelligence of East Tennessee children. *Journal of Educational Psychology, 23*, 351–370.

Wheeler, L.R. (1942). A comparative study of the intelligence of East Tennessee mountain children. *Journal of Educational Psychology, 33*, 321–334.

Wheldall, K., & Poborca, B. (1980). Conservation without conversation: An alternative, non-verbal paradigm for assessing conservation of liquid quantity. *British Journal of Psychology, 71*, 117–134.

White, G.L., Fishbein, S., & Rutstein, J. (1981). Passionate love and the misattribution of arousal. *Journal of Personality and Social Psychology, 41*, 56–62.

Whiting, B.B., & Whiting, J.W. (1975). *Children of six countries: A psychological analysis*. Cambridge, MA: Harvard University Press.

Whorf, B.L. (1956). *Language, thought, and reality: Selected writings of Benajmain Lee Whorf*. New York: Wiley.

Wickens, C.D. (1984). Processing resources in attention. In R. Parasuraman & D.R. Davies (Eds.), *Varieties of attention*. London: Academic Press.

Wider, E., Johnsen, S., & Balser, E. (1999). Light show. *New Scientist, 2177*, 11.

Wiesel, T.N. (1982). Postnatal development of the visual cortex and the influence of environment. *Nature, 299*, 583–591.

Wiggins, D.A., & Morris, R.D. (1986). Criteria for female choice of mates: Courtship feeding and paternal care in the common tern. *American Naturalist, 128*, 126–129.

Wilder, D.A. (1984). Intergroup contact: The typical member and the exception to the rule. *Journal of Experimental Social Psychology, 20*, 177–194.

Wilkinson, G.S. (1984). Reciprocal food sharing in the vampire bat. *Nature, 308*, 181–184.

Wilkinson, R.T. (1969). Sleep deprivation: Performance tests for partial and selective sleep deprivation. In L.A. Abt & J.R. Reiss (Eds.), *Progress in clinical psychology*. New York: Grune & Stratton.

Willerman, L. (1979). *The psychology of individual and group differences*. San Francisco: W.H. Freeman.

Willerman, L., Schultz, R., Rutledge, J.N., & Bigler, E.D. (1991). *In vivo* brain size and intelligence. *Intelligence, 15*, 223–228.

Williams, J.E., & Best, D.L. (1982). *Measuring sex stereotypes: A thirty nations study*. London: Sage.

Williams, J.E., & Best, D.L. (1990). *Measuring sex stereotypes: A multination study*. Newbury Park, CA: Sage.

Williams, J.E., & Best, D.L. (1992). Psychological factors associated with cross-cultural differences in individualism-collectivism. In S. Iwawaki, Y. Kashima, and K. Leung (Eds.), *Innovations in cross-cultural psychology*. Amsterdam: Swets & Zeitlinger.

Williams, J.H. (1987). *Psychology of women* (3rd Edn.). London: W.W. Norton & Co.

Williams, L.M. (1994). Recall of childhood trauma: A prospective study of women's memories of child sexual abuse. *Journal of Consulting and Clinical Psychology, 62*, 1167–1176.

Williams, R.L. (1972). *The BITCH Test (Black Intelligence Test of Cultural Homogeneity)*. St. Louis, MI: Washington University.

Williams, T.M. (Ed.) (1986). *The impact of television: A national experiment in three communities*. New York: Academic Press.

Wilson, E.O. (1975). *Sociobiology: The new synthesis*. Cambridge, UK: Harvard University Press.

Wilson, E.O. (1978). *On human nature*. Cambridge, MA: Harvard University Press.

Wiltschko, W. (1972). The influence of magnetic total intensity and inclination on directions preferred by migrating European robins (*Erithacus rubecula*). In S.R. Galler (Ed.), *Animal orientation and navigation*. Science and Technical Information Office, NASA Special Publications, Washington, DC.

Wiltschko, W., & Wiltschko, R. (1988). Magnetic orientation in birds. *Current Ornithology, 5*, 67–121.

Wimmer, H., & Perner, J. (1983). Beliefs about beliefs: Representation and the constraining function of wrong beliefs in young children's understanding of deception. *Cognition, 13*, 103–128.

Winch, R.F. (1958). *Mate selections: A study of complementary needs*. New York: Harper.

Windgassen, K. (1992). Treatment with neuroleptics: The patient's perspective. *Acta Psychiatrica Scandinavica, 86*, 405–410.

Winson, H. (1997). The relationship of dissociative conditions to sleep and dreaming. In S. Krispner & S.M. Powers (Eds.), *Broken images, broken selves: Dissociative narratives in clinical practice*. Bristol, PA: Brunner/Mazel.

Witelson, S.F., & Pallie, W. (1973). Left hemisphere specialisation for language in the newborn: Neuroanatomical evidence of asymmetry. *Brain, 96*, 3418–3428.

Witkin, H.A., & Berry, J.W. (1975). Psychological differentiation in cross-cultural perspective. *Journal of Cross-Cultural Psychology, 6*, 4–87.

Wolpe, J. (1958). *Psychotherapy by reciprocal inhibition*. New York: Pergamon Press.

Wood, D.J., Bruner, J.S., & Ross, G. (1976). The role of tutoring in problem solving. *Journal of Child Psychology and Psychiatry, 17*, 89–100.

Wood, J.T., & Duck, S. (Eds.). (1995). *Understanding relationships: Off the beaten track*. Thousand Oaks, CA: Sage.

Wood, W., Wong, F.Y., & Chachere, J.G. (1991). Effects of media violence on viewers' aggression in unconstrained social interaction. *Psychological Bulletin, 109*, 371–383.

Woodworth, R.S. (1918). *Dynamic psychology*. New York: Columbia University Press.

Woodworth, R.S., & Schlosberg, H. (1954). *Experimental psychology* (2nd Edn.). New York: Holt, Rinehart, & Winston.

Worell, J., & Remer, P. (1992). *Feminist perspectives in therapy*. Chichester, UK: Wiley.

World Health Organisation. (1981). *International classification of diseases and related health problems*. Geneva: Author.

Wraga, M., Creem, S.H., & Proffitt, D.R. (2000). Perception-action dissociations of a walkable Müller-Lyer configuration. *Psychological Science, 11*, 239–243.

Wright, P.H. (1982). Men's friendships, women's friendships and the alleged inferiority of the latter. *Sex Roles, 8*, 1–20.

Wynne-Edwards, V.C. (1962). *Animal dispersion in relation to social behaviour*. Edinburgh, UK: Oliver & Boyd.

Yaguchi, K., Otsuka, T., Fujita, T., & Hatano, S. (1987). The relationships between the emotional status and physical activities of the Japanese elderly. *Journal of Human Development, 23*, 42–47.

Yaniv, I., & Meyer, D.E. (1987). Activation and metacognition of inaccessible information: Potential bases for incubation effects in problem solving. *Journal of Experimental Psychology: Learning, Memory and Cognition, 13*, 187–205.

Yap, P.M. (1969). The culture-bound reactive syndromes. In W. Caudill & T.-Y. Lin (Eds.), *Mental health research in Asia and the Pacific*. Honolulu, HI: East West Centre Press.

Yeates, K.O., MacPhee, D., Campbell, F.A., & Ramey, C.T. (1983). Maternal IQ and home environment as determinants of early childhood intellectual competence: A developmental analysis. *Developmental Psychology, 19*, 731–739.

Yelsma, P., & Athappily, K. (1988). Marital satisfaction and communication practices: Comparisons among Indian and American couples. *Journal of Comparative Family Studies, 19*, 37–54.

Yerkes, R.M., & Dodson, J.D. (1908). The relation of strength stimulus to rapidity of habit-formation. *Journal of Comparative Neurological Psychology, 18*, 459–482.

Yerkes, R.M., & Morgulis, S. (1909). The method of Pavlov in animal psychology. *Psychological Bulletin, 6*, 257–273.

Yin, R.K. (1969). Looking at upside-down faces. *Journal of Experimental Psychology, 81*, 141–145.

Young, A.W., Hay, D.C., & Ellis, A.W. (1985). The faces that launched a thousand slips: Everyday difficulties and errors in recognising people. *British Journal of Psychology, 76*, 495–523.

Young, A.W., Hellawell, D., & Hay, D.C. (1987). Configural information in face perception. *Perception, 16*, 747–759.

Young, A.W., McWeeny, K.H., Hay, D.C., & Ellis, A.W. (1986). Naming and categorisation latencies for faces and written names. *Quarterly Journal of Experimental Psychology, 38A*, 297–318.

Young, A.W., Newcombe, F., de Haan, E.H.F., Small, M., & Hay, D.C. (1993). Face perception after brain injury: Selective impairments affecting identity and expression. *Brain, 116*, 941–959.

Young, K. (1999). *Cyber-disorders: The mental illness concern for the millennium*. Paper presented at the 108th annual meeting of the American Psychological Association, Boston.

Young, W.C., Goy, R.W., & Phoenix, C.H. (1964). Hormones and sexual behaviour. *Science, 143*, 212–219.

Youniss, J. (1989). Parent–adolescent relationships. In W. Damon (Ed.), *Child development today and tomorrow*. San Francisco: Jossey-Bass.

Zach, R. (1979). Shell dropping: Decision making and optimal foraging in Northwestern crows. *Behaviour, 68*, 106–117.

Zahavi, A. (1977). The cost of honesty (further remarks on the handicap principle). *Journal of Theoretical Biology, 67*, 603–605.

Zahn-Waxler, C., Radke-Yarrow, M., & King, R.A. (1979). Child rearing and children's prosocial initiations toward victims of distress. *Child Development, 50*, 319–330.

Zajonc, R.B. (1980). Feeling and thinking: Preferences need no inferences. *American Psychologist, 35*, 151–175.

Zajonc, R.B. (1984). On the primacy of affect. *American Psychologist, 39*, 117–123.

Zeki, S. (1993). *A vision of the brain*. Oxford, UK: Blackwell.

Zhar, J.H. (1972). Significance testing of the Spearman rank correlation coefficient. *Journal of the American Statistical Association, 67*, 578–580.

Zigler, E., & Muenchow, S. (1992). *Head Start: The inside story of America's most successful educational experiment*. New York: Basic Books.

Zigler, E.F., Abelson, W.D., & Seitz, V. (1973). Motivational factors in the performance of economically disadvantaged children on the Peabody Picture Vocabulary Test. *Child Development, 44*, 294–303.

Zihl, J., von Cramon, D., & Mai, N. (1983). Selective disturbance of movement vision after bilateral brain damage. *Brain, 106*, 313–340.

Zillmann, D. (1979). *Hostility and aggression*. Hillsdale, NJ: Lawrence Erlbaum Associates Inc.

Zillmann, D., Johnson, R.C., & Day, K.D. (1974). Attribution of apparent arousal and proficiency of recovery from sympathetic activation affecting excitation transfer to aggressive behaviour. *Journal of Experimental Social Psychology, 10*, 503–515.

Zimbardo, P.G. (1973). On the ethics of intervention in human psychological research: With special reference to the Stanford prison experiment. *Cognition, 2*, 243–256.

Zuckerman, M. (1979). Attribution of success and failure revisited or the motivational bias is alive and well in attribution theory. *Journal of Personality, 47*, 245–287.

Glossary

Ablation: a surgical procedure in which brain tissue is systematically destroyed and often removed.

Abnormal or atypical psychology: the study of individuals who differ from the norm, such as those with mental disorders.

Absolute morality: this is based on the notion that the ends cannot justify the means; some acts are basically immoral regardless of the consequences they produce.

Accommodation: the process of adjusting the shape of the lens to ensure that images are focused on the retina.

Accommodation: in Piaget's theory, the process of changing existing schemas or creating new schemas because new information cannot be assimilated.

Acculturation strategy: the approach adopted by members of ethnic groups, involving decisions about preserving their own cultural identity and about contact with other cultural groups.

Action slips: actions that occur, but were not intended.

Active sleep: a term used to refer to REM sleep.

Actor–observer effect: the tendency for actors to attribute their actions to situational factors, whereas observers attribute them to internal/external dispositional factors.

Adaptive: the extent to which a behaviour increases the reproductive potential of an individual and survival of its genes.

Aetiology: the cause of a disease or disorder.

Affordances: in Gibson's theory, the possible uses of objects, which are claimed to be given directly in the sensory information provided by the stimulus.

Algorithms: step-by-step procedures that will definitely solve a problem (e.g., a knitting pattern).

Allele: one of the two (or more) forms of a gene. Chromosomes are paired and at the same position on each chromosome is a gene for a particular characteristic such as eye colour. These two genes are called alleles.

Alpha bias: the tendency to exaggerate differences between the sexes.

Altruism: a form of pro-social behaviour that is costly to the altruist, and which is motivated by the wish to help another individual.

Amnesia: partial loss of long-term memory, usually caused by brain damage.

Amygdalotomy: a form of psychosurgery where the amygdala, which is the part of the brain involved in anger, is destroyed using strong electrical currents.

Anaclitic depression: a severe and progressive depression resulting from prolonged separation from a caregiver.

Anchoring: forming social representations by relating new ideas closely to existing knowledge.

Androcentric bias: a bias in favour of males. An androcentric theory is based on research data on males and then applied to all human behaviour.

Anisogamy: sexual reproduction in which the gametes of the two sexes are dissimilar.

Anorexia nervosa: an eating disorder in which the individual is seriously underweight and has a fear of eating.

Anti-social behaviour: behaviour that harms or injures another person.

Apparent motion: the illusion of movement created when similar stationary stimuli are presented in rapid succession.

Arcuate fasciculus: a bundle of axons connecting Broca's area with Wernicke's area; damage to this bundle of axons can cause conduction aphasia.

Arousal/cost–reward model: Piliavin et al.'s view that whether a bystander helps a victim depends on his or her level of arousal, and on the rewards and costs of different possible actions.

Assimilation: in Piaget's theory, dealing with new environmental situations by using existing cognitive organisation.

Association areas: those parts of the cerebral cortex that are involved in higher-order processing; such as associations between sensory and motor activity as well as language.

Attributions: statements about the causes of behaviour.

Auditory cortex: the part of the cerebral cortex dedicated to hearing, located in the temporal lobes.

Augmenting principle: a heuristic for making attributions where explanations are selected if they appear to be "against the odds".

Authoritarian personality: an individual who holds rigid beliefs, hostility towards other groups, and submissive attitudes towards those in authority.

Automatic processes: processes that typically occur rapidly, do not require attention, and for which there is no conscious awareness.

Autonomic nervous system: that part of the nervous system that controls vital body functions, which is self-regulating and needs no conscious control (automatic).

Autonomous morality: a later stage of moral development, where the person's intentions are used as a basis for judgement. See Heteronomous morality.

Availability heuristic: a mental shortcut based on how quickly instances come to mind.

Aversion therapy: a form of treatment in which undesirable behaviour is eliminated by associating it with severe punishment (classical conditioning).

Avoidance learning: a form of operant conditioning where an animal learns to prevent an unpleasant or aversive situation by making a particular response to a stimulus. Usually the stimulus precedes the unpleasant situation.

Backward conditioning: the situation in which the unconditioned stimulus is presented just before the conditioned stimulus in classical conditioning.

Barbiturates: drugs that used to be widely used in the treatment of anxiety disorders

Basal ganglia: a group of subcortical structures (most importantly the caudate nucleus, the putamen, and the globus pallidus) with extensive interconnections with other areas of the brain. Involved in movement, language and emotion.

Behavioural model: a model of abnormality based on the behaviourist approach (behaviourism). Mental illness is explained in terms of classical and operant conditioning.

Behavioural therapy: forms of clinical therapy based on the learning principles associated with classical and operant conditioning.

Behaviourism: an approach in psychology based on learning theory that focuses only on observable behaviour and rejects reference to internal mental activity.

Beta bias: the tendency to minimise differences between the sexes.

Bilateral: when behavioural functions are equally represented in both cerebral hemispheres.

Binocular cues: visual cues about depth provided by information from both eyes.

Binocular disparity: the difference in the image of any given object on the two retinas.

Biological clock: a biological pacemaker that governs rhythms such as the sleep–wake cycle. In humans, this function is located in the suprachiasmatic nucleus.

Biological determinism: the view that behaviour is determined by internal biological systems, e.g., physiological or genetic mechanisms.

Blindsight: a phenomenon in which brain-damaged patients can perform simple visual tasks even though they have no conscious awareness of seeing.

Blob: the central portion of a module within the primary visual cortex that responds strongly to contrast and colour.

Blocking: the failure of a conditioned stimulus to produce a conditioned response because another conditioned stimulus already predicts the presentation of the unconditioned stimulus.

Bottom-up processing: gathering information directly from the external environment, as distinct from the effects of expectations (top-down processing).

Brood parasitism: when a parent animal rears offspring of another animal placed in the nest, as it if it were their own (cuckoos are the best known example).

CAT scan: a three-dimensional picture of a cross-section of the brain produced with the use of X-rays; CAT stands for computerised axial tomography.

Categorical differentiation: exaggerating the differences between two social categories in order to simplify and to organise our social worlds.

Centration: attending to only one aspect of a situation.

Cerebral cortex: the surface layer of the forebrain or cerebrum.

Chi-squared test: a statistical test of association that is used with nominal data in the form of frequencies.

Cingulotomy: a form of psychosurgery where the cingulate gyrus is destroyed using strong electrical currents to reduce aggressive behaviour.

Circadian rhythm: a biological rhythm that recurs approximately every 24 hours; "*circa*" and "*dies*" mean "around the day". The most obvious example is the sleep–wake cycle.

Circannual rhythm: a biological rhythm that recurs approximately once a year, such as annual migration.

Classical conditioning: a basic form of learning in which simple responses are associated with new stimuli.

Client-centred therapy: a form of humanistic therapy introduced by Rogers and designed to increase the client's self-esteem.

Clinical method: a form of unstructured interview where the interviewer starts with some predetermined set of questions, but as the interview proceeds these questions are adapted in line with the responses given. This kind of interview is used by clinicians when assessing mentally-ill patients.

Clock shifting: this involves changing an animal's internal daily rhythms relative to external time.

Cocktail party effect: the ability to be aware of the physical characteristics of a non-attended message when focused on another message or conversation and "tuning out" all other noise.

Coefficient of relatedness: the probability that an allele chosen at random from one individual will also be present in another individual.

Co-evolution: where two forms of behaviour, such as that of prey and predator, evolve in unison because changes in one behaviour act as a form of selective pressure on the other.

Cognitive-behavioural therapy: a development of cognitive therapy where some elements of behavioural therapy (such as a focus on behaviour change) have been added.

Cognitive biases: a predisposition to think in a certain way.

Cognitive labelling theory: a theory of emotion proposing that all emotional experiences are preceded by a generalised state of physiological arousal which is then "labelled" on the basis of situational cues and past experience.

Cognitive map: a mental representation of spatial relationships in an animal's immediate environment.

Cognitive model: a model of abnormality that emphasises the role of cognitive factors in mental disorders. The view is that thinking in a maladaptive way leads to disordered behaviour.

Cognitive neuropsychology: an area of research concerned with trying to understand the workings of the cognitive system by studying brain-damaged patients and the kinds of impairment associated with brain damage.

Cognitive neuroscience: using various techniques for the study of brain functioning (e.g., brain scans) to understand human cognition.

Cognitive priming: the idea that cues, e.g., violent TV programmes, lead to thoughts and feelings that produce aggression.

Cognitive therapy: a form of treatment involving attempts to change or restructure the client's thoughts and beliefs.

Cognitive triad: negative thoughts about the self, the world, and the future, found in depressed clients.

Cohort effect: when a group of individuals of similar age (a cohort) is unique because of historical events during development, such as those people who were children in the 1940s. If research is conducted with this group the results may not generalise to other groups due to the cohort effect.

Collectivist: a culture where individuals share tasks, belongings, and income. The people may live in large family groups and value interdependence.

Colour constancy: the tendency for an object to be perceived as having the same colour under varying viewing conditions.

Comorbidity: the presence of two or more disorders in a given individual at the same time.

Comparison level: the outcomes that people think they deserve from a relationship on the basis of past experience.

Concordance rate: if one twin has a disorder or condition, the likelihood that the other twin also has it.

Concrete operations stage: the third stage in Piaget's theory of cognitive development, from 7 to 11 years. The child can now use adult internally consistent logic but only when the problem is presented in a concrete way.

Conditioning theory: the view that all behaviour can be explained in terms of stimulus–response links.

Conduction aphasia: in this condition, patients can understand speech and speak fluently and meaningfully, but cannot repeat non-words or unfamiliar words; produced by damage to the arcuate fasciculus.

Cones: photoreceptors in the retina that are specialised for colour vision and sharpness of vision.

Confirmation bias: a preference for information that supports rather than disproves our predictions.

Conserve (conservation): to understand that quantity does not change even when a display is transformed, i.e., the quantity is conserved.

Conspecifics: members of the same species.

Contact hypothesis: the notion that contact between groups can reduce prejudice.

Context-dependent learning: Recall is better when it occurs in the same context as original learning. May result in learning that some behaviours are appropriate in some contexts and not in others.

Continuous reinforcement: schedule of operant conditioning when reinforcement is given after every response (as opposed to various forms of partial reinforcement).

Contralateral: when behavioural functions on one side of the body are controlled by the opposite cerebral hemisphere, as distinct from ipsilateral.

Core sleep: those aspects of sleep that are more essential to survival.

Cornea: a transparent membrane at the front of the eye.

Corpus callosum: a bundle of nerve fibres that connect the right and left hemispheres of the cerebral cortex.

Correlation: an association that is found between two variables.

Cortex: the outer part of an organ, as in the cerebral cortex (the outer layer of the brain) and the adrenal cortex.

Counterconditioning: in systematic desensitisation, substituting a relaxation response for a fear response to threatening stimuli.

Counter-stereotype: a positive stereotype, such as a lawyer in a wheelchair, used to counter the negative effects of stereotyping.

Critical value: numerical values found in statistical tables that are used to determine the significance of the observed value produced by a statistical test.

Cross-cultural psychology: an approach in which different cultures are studied and compared.

Cultural relativism: the notion that any behaviour can only be judged in relation to the culture in which it originates.

Cultural universality: the notion that a behaviour is unaffected by its cultural context, and that it is the same in every culture.

Culture: the rules, morals, and methods of interactions specific to a group of people.

Culture-bound syndromes: a locality-specific pattern of mental disorder.

Dark–light adaptation: the process by which the eyes rapidly adapt to changes in illumination.

Decentration: in Piaget's theory, the ability to focus on more than one aspect of a problem, overcoming the problem of centration.

Decision model: Latané and Darley's model for predicting when an individual will help in an emergency situation, based on a series of decisions to be taken.

Defence mechanisms: strategies used by the ego to defend itself against anxiety.

Deferred imitation: in Piaget's theory, the ability to imitate behaviour that was observed at an earlier time.

Deindividuation: losing a sense of personal identity that may occur, e.g., when in a crowd or wearing a mask.

Delayed reciprocal altruism: one individual performs a favour for another on the assumption that the favour will be returned later on (also known as reciprocity).

Demand characteristics: features of an experimental situation that help participants work out what is expected of them and "invite" them to behave in predictable ways.

Depenetration: deliberately reducing the amount of self-disclosure to someone else.

Derived etic: using a series of emic studies to build up a picture of a particular culture.

Desensitisation: the process of becoming less sensitive to stimuli the more they are encountered.

Determinism: the view that all behaviour is caused by factors other than one's own will.

Deviance amplification effect: the creation of unrealistic norms, for example that the world is more dangerous than it really is.

Diagnostic and Statistical Manual (DSM): a multiaxial system used for classifying and diagnosing over 200 mental disorders, published by the American Psychiatric Association.

Diathesis–stress model: the notion that psychological disorders occur when there is a genetically determined vulnerability (diathesis) and relevant stressful conditions.

Dichotic listening task: an attention task in which one auditory message is presented to one ear and a different message is presented to the other ear.

Diffusion of responsibility: if there are many observers of an incident, each person feels they bear only a small portion of the blame for not helping.

Dimorphism: the existence of two forms, such as male and female forms of the same species.

Direct fitness: fitness in terms of gene survival gained through production of offspring.

Directional hypothesis: a prediction that there will be a difference or correlation between the two variables *and* a statement of the direction of this difference.

Discounting principle: a heuristic for making attributions in which an observer attaches less importance to one potential cause of behaviour when other more obvious potential causes are also present.

Discourse analysis: qualitative analysis of spoken and written communications produced in fairly natural conditions; usually based on tape recordings.

Discrimination: in learning theory, the conditioned response to one conditioned stimulus is strengthened at the same time as that to a second conditioned stimulus is weakened.

Discrimination: in social psychology, the behaviour (usually negative) that results from prejudiced attitudes and which is directed at members of some particular group.

Disinhibition: loss of inhibitions.

Dispositional attributions: deciding that other people's actions are caused by their internal characteristics or dispositions.

Dissociative disorders: a group of mental illnesses where patients experience dissociation between areas of conscious behaviour, as in multiple personality disorder (dissociative identity disorder) and dissociative amnesia.

Dissociative identity disorder: a condition characterised by the existence of more than two identities that recurrently take control of an individual's behaviour and by the occurrence of episodes of lost recall, none of which can be explained by physical causes.

Distributed control: the concept that major functions are controlled by many different areas of the brain with diffuse interconnections, in contrast to the concept of localisation.

Dizygotic twins: fraternal twins derived from two fertilised ova.

Double-bind theory: an explanation for schizophrenia that suggests that the disorder is a learned response to mutually-exclusive demands being made on a child, which can be met or avoided.

Drives: the motivational forces that make individuals active and lead them to pursue certain goals.

Echoic response: a term used by Skinner to describe imitation of another's verbalisations; an aspect of the process of language acquisition.

Eclectic approach: any approach in psychology that draws on many different perspectives.

Ecological validity: the extent to which the findings of a study can be generalised to real-life settings.

Ego: the conscious, rational mind; one of the three main parts of the mind in Freud's theory.

Ego analysis: a form of therapy developed from psychoanalysis that focused on strengthening the ego.

Egocentric speech: a term used by Vygotsky to indicate that young children's speech is often self-centred and like inner speech.

Egocentrism: the sense of being the centre of everything and that one's view is the only view.

Elaborated code: in Bernstein's theory, complex and abstract language.

Electra complex: Jung's suggestion that girls experience something similar to the Oedipus complex, where a young girl desires her father and sees her mother as a rival.

Electrodes: a piece of metal or other material that conducts electricity from one place to another.

Electroencephalogram (EEG): electrical brain potentials recorded from the scalp.

Elementary mental functions: innate capacities, such as attention and sensation. Such functions are possessed by all animals and these will develop to a limited extent through experience.

Emic constructs: those that vary from one culture to another.

Empathic joy hypothesis: the notion that when people help a needy person they share that person's joy at being helped.

Empathy: the ability to understand someone else's point of view, and to share their emotions.

Empathy–altruism hypothesis: Batson's notion that altruism is largely motivated by empathy.

Empiricism: the view that all behaviour is the consequence of experience. The extreme "nurture" side of the nature–nurture debate.

Endocrine system: a system of a number of ductless glands located throughout the body which produce the body's chemical messengers, called hormones.

Endogenous: internally caused, as distinct from external causes (exogenous).

Endogenous depression: depression resulting from internal, biological causes, as distinct from reactive depression.

Entraining: synchronising two or more things.

Environment of evolutionary adaptation (EEA): the period in human evolution during which our genes were shaped and naturally selected to solve survival problems that were operating at that time (between 35,000 and 3 million years ago).

Environmental determinism: the view that all behaviour can be explained solely in terms of the effects of external (environmental) factors.

Equilibration: using the processes of accommodation and of assimilation to produce a state of equilibrium or balance.

Equipotentiality: the view that essentially any response can be conditioned to any stimulus.

Ethnic groups: cultural groups (e.g., those defined by race or religion) living within a larger society.

Ethnographics: making comparisons between cultures with a view to learning more about a target culture, in a similar way to how comparative psychology can enlighten us about human behaviour.

Ethology: the biological study of animal behaviour, which seeks to determine the functional value of behaviours and tends to rely on naturalistic observation.

Etic constructs: universal factors that hold across cultures.

Eurocentric: believing that European culture and behaviour is superior to, or more natural than, other cultures.

Evoked potentials: the average pattern in the EEG produced when a stimulus is presented several times.

Evolutionarily stable strategy: a behaviour or strategy that persists because it cannot be bettered.

Evolutionary: following the theory of evolution, that certain behaviours are adaptive otherwise they would not have survived the process of natural selection.

Evolutionary psychiatry: an application of the evolutionary approach to treating mental disorders through understanding the function of the behaviours involved in the disorder.

Evolutionary psychology: an approach that explains behaviour in terms of its function and adaptiveness (i.e., the extent to which a behaviour enhances survival and reproduction of the individual's genes).

Exogenous: based on factors external to the organism.

Expected utility: the anticipated value of each option's outcome.

Experimental extinction: in conditioning, the loss of a learned response. In classical conditioning this happens when the conditioned stimulus is no longer accompanied by the unconditioned stimulus. In operant conditioning it happens when the response is no longer reinforced.

Experts: people with greater knowledge. This can include peers.

Expiatory punishment: the view that the amount of punishment should match the badness of behaviour, but without the idea that the form of punishment should fit the crime.

Expressed emotion: a way of describing the behaviour of certain families. These behaviours include too much criticism, hostility, and emotional over-protectiveness.

External validity: the extent to which findings generalise across populations, locations, measures, and times.

Extrinsic: a feature that lies outside the organism, i.e., is external.

F (Fascism) Scale: a test of tendencies towards fascism.

Falsifiability: the notion that scientific theories can potentially be disproved by evidence; it is the hallmark of science, according to Popper.

Field dependence: a perceptual style in which perception is distorted by background or contextual factors.

Fixation: in Freud's theory, spending a long time at a given stage of development because of problems or excessive gratification.

Flooding: a form of behavioural therapy where a patient is given maximum exposure to a feared stimulus until their fear subsides, thus extinguishing a learned response.

Foraging: the various actions performed by animals in their attempts to find suitable food.

Foreclosure: an identity status during adolescence in which the individual has not focused on identity issues, but has nevertheless made definite future commitments.

Formal operations: the final stage in Piaget's theory of cognitive development, from 11 onwards. Thinking now involves formal internally consistent adult logic and abstract thinking.

Forward conditioning: a situation in which the conditioned stimulus is presented a short time before the unconditioned stimulus, and remains while the unconditioned stimulus is presented.

Framing effect: influence on decision produced by the phrasing or frame of a problem.

Free will: the notion that we are free to make decisions.

Frustration–aggression hypothesis: a social-psychological explanation for aggressive behaviour that states that frustration always leads to aggression and aggression is always caused by frustration.

Functional fixedness: the tendency to solve problems in a particular or fixed way.

Functional MRI (fMRI): using the MRI technology to study the brain in action.

Fundamental attribution error: the tendency when trying to identify the causes of a person's behaviour to overestimate the role of his or her personal characteristics and to underestimate the role of the situation.

Gender: the psychological characteristics associated with being male or female, i.e. masculinity and femininity.

Gender bias: the differential treatment or representation of men and women based on stereotypes rather than real differences.

Gender identity: one's concept of being male or female, a fundamental part of the self concept.

Gender role: those behaviours, attitudes, and interests that are considered appropriate for one gender and not the other.

Gender schema: organised set of beliefs about gender behaviour.

Gender stereotypes: the social perception of a man or a woman based on beliefs about gender roles.

Gene pool: the whole stock of different genes in a breeding population of any species.

Generalisation: the tendency of a conditioned response to occur in a weaker form to stimuli similar to the conditioned stimulus.

General Problem Solver (GPS): a computer program devised by Newell and Simon based on means–ends analysis.

Genes: units of inheritance that form part of a chromosome. Some characteristics are determined by one gene whereas for others many genes are involved.

Genetic determinism: the view that animal behaviour is caused by genetic influences; this view underpins evolutionary explanations.

Genome: the total genetic material of an individual organism.

Genotype: an individual's genetic potential.

Geons: in Biederman's theory, the basic three-dimensional shapes that combine to form patterns, shapes, and objects.

Glucostats: specialised neurons in the brain and liver that measure the level of blood glucose.

Goal-setting theory: a theory that suggests that motivation is raised by setting appropriate long-term incentives or goals.

Group selection theory: the notion that, if a group of animals possess more favourable characteristics, the group will be more likely to survive to reproduce.

Group socialisation theory: the view that children are socialised by groups outside the home, especially their peer groups, rather than the family.

Group-splitting hypothesis: an account of schizophrenia in which the schizophrenic individual acts as a leader to split a group that has become too large to function well.

Halo effect: the tendency for one outstanding trait to unduly influence an overall impression.

Handedness: an individual's preference to use one hand or side of the body for certain activities, such as writing or throwing a ball.

Handicapping theory: according to this theory, females select males who have a handicap because this suggests the male must be genetically robust. Symmetry may be a handicap because of its physiological cost.

Haplodiploidy: a mechanism for sex determination found in some species of insects, in which males are derived from unfertilised eggs, whereas females are derived from fertilised eggs.

Hello–goodbye effect: the observation that patients tend to exaggerate their unhappiness at the beginning of therapy in order to convince the therapist that they are in genuine need. In contrast, at the end of therapy the reverse may be true; the patient may exaggerate their well-being to show appreciation to therapist.

Hemispheres: the two halves of the forebrain or cerebrum.

Hemispheric asymmetry: an imbalance between the two cerebral hemispheres, where one is dominant for some behaviour.

Heritability estimate: an estimate of the importance of genetic factors which takes account of total variability in the population. It is calculated by working out the ratio between the genetic variability of the particular trait and total variability in the whole population.

Heteronomous morality: younger children base their judgements of right and wrong on the severity of outcome and/or externally imposed rules.

Heterosexual bias: the notion that heterosexuality is more natural than, and preferable to, homosexuality.

Heuristics: general guidelines or "rules of thumb" that may assist in problem solving or cognition generally, but do not guarantee a solution.

Hidden observer phenomenon: in hypnosis, a part of consciousness that is separate from the hypnotised self and remains more aware of what is happening.

Hierarchical model: a model where elements are organised in a hierarchy, suggesting some elements are more important/more developed or superior to others.

Hierarchy of needs: in Maslow's theory, a range of needs starting from physiological ones at the bottom of the hierarchy to self-actualisation at the top.

Higher mental functions: according to Vygotsky those mental abilities, such as problem solving, that develop from elementary mental functions largely as a consequence of cultural influences.

Holophrastic period: the first stage of language acquisition when children use holophrases—single words that express relatively complex meanings.

Homeostasis: the process of maintaining a reasonably constant internal environment.

Homeostatic drive theory: an explanation of motivation that proposes that animals are motivated to seek food or liquid in order to return their body to a steady state. Once this occurs the drive is reduced.

Homing: behaviour used by an animal to locate, for example, its home, point of origin, or food store.

Horizontal décalage: Piaget's concept that, at any stage of cognitive development, not all aspects of the stage will appear at the same time.

Hormones: chemical substances produced by endocrine glands, and circulated in the blood. They only affect target organs and are produced in large quantities but disappear very quickly.

"Hot house" children: children whose intellectual capabilities have been artificially "ripened" through intensive instruction or stimulation.

Humanism: a view of humanity based on shared belief in human worth, without reference to a "divine being" or god.

Humanistic model: a model of abnormality based on the humanistic approach that emphasises the uniqueness of each individual, a focus on the present rather than the past, the importance of subjective experience, and the drive of each individual to be self-righting and to self-actualise.

Hypnogogic state: a state sometimes experienced during the first stage of sleep, accompanied by hallucinatory images.

Hypothalamus: the part of the brain that integrates the activity of the autonomic nervous system. Involved with emotion, stress, motivation, and hunger.

Hypovolemic thirst: thirst created by low blood volume.

Iatrogenic: disorders that are produced by a physician or therapist unwittingly through selective attention and expectations.

Id: in Freudian theory, that part of the mind containing the sexual instinct.

Identification: to become associated with a person or a thing; this increases the likelihood of imitation.

Identity achievement: in adolescence an identity status in which the individual has focused on identity issues, and has made definite future commitments.

Identity crisis: the state of lacking a clear sense of what one is; it is most common in adolescence and early adulthood.

Identity diffusion: an identity status in which the individual has not focused on identity issues and has made no definite future commitments.

Idiographic approach: an approach that emphasises the uniqueness of the individual.

Illusion of outgroup homogeneity: the illusion that members of an outgroup are more alike than they really are.

Illusory correlation: the perception of a relationship between things where none exists in reality.

Imitation: in social learning theory, learning a complex set of behaviours from one's conspecifics.

Immanent justice: punishment should be fair; wrongdoing should always result in some punishment.

Implicit learning: complex learning that occurs without the learner being able to verbalise clearly what he or she has learned.

Imposed etic: the use of a technique developed in one culture to study another culture.

Inclusive fitness: fitness that includes the reproductive success of one's genetic relatives, as such success is beneficial at the level of the genes.

Incongruence: in Rogers' approach, the discrepancies between an individual's self-concept and his or her ideal self.

Incorrect comparison theory: the notion that our perception of visual illusions is influenced by parts of the figure that are not being judged.

Indirect fitness: increasing one's own fitness through helping genetic relations to survive and reproduce.

Individualist: a culture that emphasises individuality, individual needs, and independence. People tend to live in small nuclear families.

Informational social influence: yielding to group pressure because others are thought to possess more knowledge.

Information-processing framework: an approach to understanding cognitive processes by making analogies with computing and information technology.

Infradian rhythm: a biological rhythm that recurs in a cycle of more than 24 hours ("*infra*" and "*dies*" = below or lower frequency than a day); for example, the menstrual cycle.

Ingroups: the groups to which an individual belongs.

Insight: in Freudian theory, access to and understanding of emotional memories emerging from the unconscious; the goal of therapy.

Insight learning: a form of learning first identified by Gestalt psychologists, where a new behaviour is acquired simply through the process of insight rather than trial and error.

Instinct: an innate impulse or motive.

Instrumental aggression: harming another person in order to achieve some desired goal.

Instrumental learning: see Operant conditioning.

Intelligence quotient: a measure of general intellectual ability that can be calculated by dividing mental age by chronological age; abbreviated as IQ.

Inter-blob region: the region around the blob in the visual cortex that is sensitive to orientation, some movement and binocular disparity.

Inter-judge reliability: as applied to diagnoses, the level of agreement on patients' diagnoses among different psychiatrists or clinical psychologists.

Internal validity: the extent to which research findings are genuine and can be regarded as being caused by the independent variable.

International Classification of Diseases and Health Related Problems (ICD): a means of classifying mental disorders and providing basic health statistics, published by the World Health Organisation.

Intersexual selection: sexual selection based on the members of one sex (usually female) selecting or choosing opposite-sexed mates.

Intersubjectivity: a process by which two individuals with different views about a task adjust those views so they become more similar.

Interval data: data is measured using units of equal intervals; the intervals reflect a real difference.

Intrasexual selection: sexual selection based on competition for mates among the same-sexed (generally male) members of a species.

Intrinsic: a feature of an organism that is inherent in it, i.e., internal.

Introspection: examination and observation of one's own mental processes.

Invariants: in Gibson's theory, those aspects of the visual environment that remain the same as an observer moves.

Jigsaw classroom: an approach to reducing prejudice in which the teacher makes sure that all of the children can contribute to the achievement of classroom goals.

Kin selection: the view that the process of natural selection functions at the level of an individual's genes and thus any behaviour that promotes the survival and reproduction of all "kin" (genetic relatives) will also be selected.

Klüver-Bucy syndrome: a pattern of behaviour associated with removal of, damage to, or tumours in the temporal lobe leading to, e.g., reduced aggression and increased sexual behaviour.

Labelling theory: the notion that attaching a psychiatric label to a patient may worsen his or her condition, because he or she is then treated as someone who is mentally ill.

Language acquisition device: innate knowledge of grammatical structure, which is used to assist language learning.

Latent content: in Freud's theory, the underlying meaning of a dream.

Latent learning: learning that takes place in the absence of any observable behaviour, or with no apparent reinforcement.

Lateral inhibition: a process in which the firing of receptors inhibits the firing of adjacent receptors, thus causing contrast enhancement.

Lateralisation: the tendency for some neural functions to be located in one cerebral hemisphere rather than the other, as in the case of language.

Law of reinforcement: the probability of a given response being produced is increased if it is followed by reward or a positive reinforcer.

Leadership: a form of social influence where one member of a group alters the behaviour and/or thoughts of others with the aim of reaching a specific goal.

Learned helplessness: passive behaviour produced by the perception that punishment is unavoidable.

Learning: a relatively permanent change in behaviour, which is not due to maturation.

Lesion: a wound or injury. When brain lesions are produced surgically, the amount of tissue destroyed is typically less than with ablation.

Liberal humanism: the view that all people, e.g., gays, lesbians, and heterosexuals, are equal and the ways they conduct relationships are basically similar.

Libido: Freud's term for the psychological energy that is associated with sexual drives. At each stage of psychosexual development, the libido becomes focused on a part of the body.

Life cycle: in Levinson's theory of adult development, the sequence of different periods spanning adult life.

Life events: experiences that are common to most people and involve change from a steady state; they are a means of explaining why some people become ill.

Life structure: the underlying pattern of someone's life at a given time.

Limbic model: a physiological account of emotion identifying the brain structures involved (the limbic system).

Localisation: the view that certain areas of the cerebral cortex are associated with specific behavioural functions.

Loss aversion: greater sensitivity to losses than to gains.

Lucid dreams: a dream where the individual is aware that they are dreaming and can sometimes control the dream content.

Machiavellian intelligence: the capacity to intentionally deceive another individual.

Machine reductionism: explaining behaviour by analogy with rather simpler machine systems.

Mand: this refers to a word that is learned because its meaning is of significance in the child's life.

Manifest content: in Freud's theory, the actual or obvious content of a dream.

Manipulation: an animal is tricked or manipulated into behaving in an apparently altruistic way.

Map-compass hypothesis: the idea that navigation is achieved by using the sun as a compass in addition to knowledge of visual landmarks, which serve as a map. True navigation requires a map and a compass.

Mass action: the principle that the amount of material stored in the cerebral cortex is equivalent to the space it occupies. Thus the more cortex you remove, the more severe will be the likely resulting damage.

Matching hypothesis: the notion that we are attracted to those who are about as physically attractive as we are.

Means–ends analysis: a heuristic method of problem solving in which the difference between current and goal states is reduced using subgoals.

Medical model: a model of abnormality based on the medical approach to treating physical illness; the model assumes that all illnesses (physical and psychological) have an underlying biochemical or physiological basis.

Medulla oblongata: part of the reticular formation; it is involved in the control of breathing, digestion, and swallowing.

Melatonin: a hormone produced by the pineal gland that increases sleepiness.

Memory: refers to (1) the mental function of retaining information, (2) the storage system that holds that data, and (3) the data that are retained.

Mendelian genetics: an explanation for the mechanisms of inheritance based on single genes, named after Gregor Mendel.

Meta-analysis: an analysis in which all of the findings from many studies relating to a given hypothesis are combined for statistical testing.

Metacognitive knowledge: knowledge about the usefulness of various cognitive processes relevant to learning.

Methodological behaviourism: the view that all psychological perspectives use some behaviourist concepts to explain behaviour.

Micro-environment: the view that each individual to a certain extent creates his/her own environment through their behaviour and physical characteristics.

Micro-sleep: brief periods of relaxed wakefulness during the day when a person stares blankly into space and temporarily loses awareness. Such periods may permit some restorative functions to take place.

Migration: travel over long distances to specific locations.

Mirror test: a test of self-recognition using a mirror, in which a red mark is put on an animal's face.

Misapplied size-constancy theory: a theory proposed by Gregory, according to which the processes producing size constancy with three-dimensional objects are used inappropriately in the perception of two-dimensional objects.

Modelling: imitation; a form of learning or therapy based on observing a model and imitating that behaviour.

Monoamines: a group of neurotransmitters that are chemically similar, such as serotonin, dopamine, and noradrenaline. They are also called catecholamines.

Monocular cues: cues to depth that only require the use of one eye.

Monogamy: a mating system in which a male and a female remain together over a long period, with both of them generally contributing to parental care.

Monozygotic twins: identical twins derived from the same fertilised ovum.

Mood-state-dependent memory: memory is better when the mood at the time of retrieval matches the mood at the time of learning.

Morality: the principles used by individuals to distinguish between right and wrong.

Moratorium: an identity status in adolescence in which the individual has focused on identity issues, but has made no definite future commitments.

Motherese: a special style of speaking used by mothers when talking with children (also known as "parentese").

Motion parallax: a visual cue used to perceive motion and depth; things that are closer move faster in relation to things that are farther away.

Motor neuron: a single nerve cell that activates a muscle or gland.

MRI scans: three-dimensional pictures of the brain based on the detection of magnetic changes; MRI stands for magnetic resonance imaging.

Multiple personality disorder: see Dissociative identity disorder.

Mutation: a genetic change that can then be inherited by any offspring.

Mutualism: two individuals behaving in a co-operative or altruistic way towards each other at the same time.

Nativism: the view that people's characteristics are inherited.

Natural experiment: a type of experiment where use is made of some naturally-occurring independent variable (IV); it is a quasi-experiment because the IV is not directly manipulated.

Natural selection: the process by which certain traits (and the associated genes) are perpetuated because of the advantage they confer in terms of survival and increased reproduction.

Nature–nurture debate: the question of whether behaviour is determined by inherited factors or by experience (learning). Now increasingly recognised as more than just an either/or question.

Navigation: using a compass and a "map" to find an exact location. A compass alone provides orientation.

Negative-state relief model: Cialdini et al.'s view that someone who feels empathy for a victim will help that person to relieve the sadness produced by the empathy.

Neo-behaviourism: an extension of behaviourism to allow for some cognitive factors, e.g., Bandura's social learning theory.

Neo-dissociation theory: Hilgard's theory, according to which one part of the mind is separated off from other parts in the hypnotic state.

Neuroleptic drugs: drugs that reduce psychotic symptoms but can produce some of the symptoms of neurological diseases.

Neurotransmitter: a chemical substance that is released at the junction between neurons (a synapse) and which affects the transmission of messages in the nervous system.

Nominal data: data consisting of the numbers of participants falling into qualitatively different categories.

Nomothetic approach: an approach based on the attempt to establish general laws of behaviour.

Non-directional hypothesis: a prediction that there will be a difference or correlation between two variables, but no statement about the direction of the difference.

Non-mentalistic behaviour: behaviour involving no mental activity.

Norm of reciprocity: the cultural expectation that it is justified to treat others in the way they treat you.

Norm of self-disclosure reciprocity: the expectation that friends usually match how much they disclose about themselves, gradually increasing how much they mutually reveal.

Norm of social responsibility: the cultural expectation that help should be given to those in need of help.

Normative social influence: this occurs when someone conforms in order that others will like or respect him or her.

Object permanence: an awareness that objects continue to exist when they can no longer be seen.

Objectification: forming social representations by making abstract ideas more concrete.

Objective: dealing with facts in a way that is unaffected by feelings or opinions.

Observational learning: a form of learning based on imitating or copying the behaviour of others.

Observed value: the numerical value calculated when using a statistical test. The observed value is compared with the critical value to determine significance.

Oedipus complex: in Freudian theory, the notion that young boys desire their mother sexually and so experience rivalry with their father.

Operant conditioning: a form of learning in which behaviour is controlled by the giving of reward or reinforcement. An extension of Thorndike's "instrumental learning" theory.

Operational diagnostic criteria: a set of standards that can be used to judge whether someone is suffering from a particular mental illness.

Optic array: in Gibson's theory, the pattern of light reaching the eye.

Optic chiasm: the point at which the optic nerves from each eye cross over to the opposite side of the brain.

Optic flow patterns: perceptual effect in which the visual environment appears to move away from the point towards which a person is moving.

Optimal foraging theory: an explanation of foraging in terms of achieving a balance between costs and benefits.

Optimum level of arousal: an explanation of motivation that proposes that the animal has a drive to return to an optimum state—that of moderate arousal.

Ordinal data: data that can be ordered from smallest to largest.

Osmoreceptors: specialised neurons in the lateral preoptic area of the hypothalamus that detect changes in osmotic pressure.

Osmosis: the passage of a solution through a semi-permeable membrane into a more concentrated solution, i.e., one with higher osmotic pressure.

Osmotic thirst: thirst created as a consequence of increased solutes in the body. This increases the osmotic pressure outside the cells, thus creating intracellular water loss and changes in osmotic pressure that are detected by osmoreceptors.

Outcome measures: ways of assessing the consequences of different forms of therapy.

Outgroups: the groups to which an individual does not belong, often regarded unfavourably.

Over-extension: using words to apply to more objects than is strictly correct.

Over-regularisation: applying grammatical rules to situations in which they do not apply.

Panic disorder with agoraphobia: a disorder characterised by panic attacks and avoidance of open or public places.

Papez circuit: a brain circuit or loop involved in emotion, based on the hypothalamus, hippocampus, and thalamus.

Paradigm: according to Kuhn, a general theoretical orientation that is accepted by most scientists in a given discipline.

Paradox of altruism: the paradox that altruistic behaviour has been naturally selected (as evidenced by the fact that it exists) despite the fact that such behaviour would appear to reduce the altruist's own survival and reproduction.

Paradoxical sleep: a term used to describe REM sleep because of the behavioural contradictions (paradoxes): eye movement, heart rate, breathing, etc. are increased but the body is in a state of near paralysis and it is difficult to wake a person up.

Paralanguage: nonverbal signals, e.g., body language, eye contact.

Paralinguistics: the study of the subtext of communication, e.g., pauses, pitch, body language, etc.

Parasympathetic branch: the part of the autonomic nervous system that monitors the relaxed state, conserving resources, and promoting digestion and metabolism.

Parental investment: the time and effort devoted by a parent to rearing its offspring.

Pattern recognition: identifying two-dimensional patterns and three-dimensional objects in spite of variations in size and orientation.

Peer tutoring: teaching of one child by another, with the child doing the teaching generally being slightly older than the child being taught.

Permissive amine theory: the view that mood disorders result from low levels of serotonin leading to reduced control of noradrenaline levels, both of which are neurotransmitters in the amine group.

Perseverative search: mistakenly searching for an object in the place in which it was previously found, rather than the place in which it is currently hidden.

Personality: semi-permanent internal predispositions that make people behave consistently, but in ways that differ from those of other people.

Person-oriented aggression: aggression that has as its main goal harming another person.

Person variables: the ways that people differ, such as beliefs and cognitive abilities.

PET scan: a picture of brain activity based on radioactive glucose levels within the brain; PET stands for positron emission tomography.

Phenomenology: an approach that emphasises subjective experience as the basis for understanding the world, as opposed to objective, external reality.

Phenothiazines: neuroleptic drugs that reduce dopamine activity.

Phenotype: the observable characteristics of an individual, resulting from the interaction between genes and the environment.

Pheromones: chemical substances produced by the body and secreted into the air. They act on conspecifics by being absorbed into their bloodstream. The pheromones then work like hormones.

Phrenology: a pseudoscience which supposed that the bumps on the surface of the skull are related to function, the larger the bump the more developed the function.

Physiological: concerning the study of living organisms and their body parts.

Physiological determinism: the view that behaviour is determined by internal, bodily systems.

Physiological reductionism: explanations of complex behaviours in terms of simpler physiological (bodily) changes.

Pictorial cues: various monocular cues to depth used by artists to create a three-dimensional impression.

Pineal gland: a very small endocrine gland located in the brain that produces melatonin, and is involved in the circadian rhythm.

Placebo effect: positive responses to a drug or form of therapy based on the patient's beliefs that the drug or therapy will be effective, rather than on the actual make-up of the drug or therapy.

Planning fallacy: the tendency to underestimate how long a work task will take to complete in spite of evidence from similar tasks completed in the past.

Pleasure principle: the drive to do things that produce pleasure or gratification.

Polyandry: a mating system in which one female mates with many males.

Polygamy: a mating system in which one individual of one sex mates with many individuals of the other sex.

Polygenetic inheritance: behaviours, such as intelligence, that are inherited through more than one gene.

Polygynandry: a mating system in which many males mate with many females (also known as promiscuity).

Polygyny: a mating system in which a male mates with several females, but females usually mate with only one male; parental care is usually provided by the female.

Prejudice: an attitude, which is usually negative, towards the members of some group on the basis of their membership of that group.

Pre-operational stage: the second stage in Piaget's theory of cognitive development, from 2 to 7 years. The child can cope with symbols (such as using language) but cannot cope with adult internally consistent logic (operations).

Preparedness: the notion that each species finds some forms of learning more "natural" and easier than others.

Prefrontal leukotomy: a more precise form of psychosurgery than the prefrontal lobotomy, which involves drilling two holes in either side of the skull and inserting needles to sever specific nerve fibres, thus effecting a functional removal of areas of the frontal lobes.

Prefrontal lobotomy: a form of psychosurgery where the fibers running from the frontal lobes to other parts of the brain are cut. Lobotomies typically make patients calmer but there are side-effects include apathy, diminished intellectual powers, impaired judgements, and even coma and death.

Press: those environmental characteristics that are relevant to need-satisfaction.

Primacy effect: the high level of recall of the first items in a list in free recall; it depends mainly on extra rehearsal.

Primary motor cortex: a region located in the frontal lobe of the cerebral cortex that contains neurons that directly affect motor neurons. The areas of the body are topographically represented.

Primary reinforcers: rewarding stimuli that are needed to live (e.g., food; water).

Principle of equipotentiality: the view that all parts of the cerebral cortex have the same potential.

Proactive aggression: aggressive behaviour that is initiated by the individual in order to achieve some goal.

Problem space: an abstract view of all the possible states that can occur, when solving a problem, between the start and the solution.

Programmed learning: a type of learning devised by Skinner and based on operant conditioning, in which tasks are broken down into individual frames.

Promiscuity: See Polygynandry.

Pro-social behaviour: behaviour that is of benefit to others.

Prosopagnosia: a condition caused by brain damage in which the patient cannot recognise familiar faces, but can recognise familiar objects.

Protocol: the steps used by a participant while carrying out a cognitive task (e.g., solving a problem). Often recorded by asking the person to speak their thoughts out loud.

Prototype: a typical example of something.

Psychic determinism: the view that adult behaviour or personality is predetermined by events in early childhood—a mix of biological and experiential factors.

Psychoanalysis: Freud's set of theories about human behaviour; also the form of treatment for mental disorders he devised.

Psychodynamic model: a model of abnormality based on the psychodynamic (psychoanalytic) approach which emphasises the influence of early experiences and of repressed emotions that are expressed unconsciously.

Psychological altruism: altruistic behaviour resulting from cognitive rather than biological processes.

Psychopathology: this is an area of psychology in which the focus is on the nature of mental disorders and the factors that cause them to exist.

Psychosurgery: sections of the brain are removed or lesions are made to treat a psychological condition.

Punctuated equilibrium: the notion that long periods of relative stability for a species are punctuated by short-lived periods of rapid change.

Punishment training: a form of operant conditioning in which the probability of a response being made is reduced by following it with an unpleasant or aversive stimulus.

Qualitative change: change in how things are expressed, what it feels like, meanings or explanations; i.e., the quality.

Quantitative change: change in how much there is of something; i.e., the quantity.

Quiet sleep: a term used to refer to NREM (non-rapid eye movement) sleep.

Radical behaviourism: the view that all behaviour is learned. Skinner was a radical behaviourist.

Ratio data: as interval data, but with a meaningful zero point.

Rational-emotive therapy: a form of cognitive therapy developed by Ellis that aims to produce rational thinking by aggressively challenging irrational beliefs.

Reaction range: Gottesman's solution to the nature–nurture debate in which genetic make-up (genotype) sets some limit on the range of possible development. Actual development within this range (phenotype) is related to environmental opportunity.

Reactive aggression: aggressive behaviour that is produced in response to someone else's aggressive behaviour.

Reactive depression: depression resulting from external causes, as distinct from endogenous depression.

Reality principle: Freud's explanation for the motivating force of the ego; it is a drive to accommodate the demands of the environment in a realistic way.

Received pronunciation (RP): a form of spoken English used by educated, middle-class individuals in southern England.

Recency effect: good free recall of the last few items in a list based on information in the short-term store.

Reciprocal altruism: a form of mutual benefit where a selfless act is performed with the expectation that the favour will be returned at a later date. Such behaviour is adaptive as long as cheating doesn't occur.

Reciprocal determinism: Bandura's concept that what one learns is affected by one's characteristics (personality, beliefs, and cognitive abilities). Personality isn't simply determined by the environment, but the individual also shapes the environment.

Reciprocal punishment: the view that the form of punishment should fit the crime.

Reciprocity: altruistic behaviour by one animal towards a second, with the second returning the favour later.

Reductionism: the notion that psychology can ultimately be reduced to more basic sciences such as physiology or biochemistry.

Reflex: an innate and automatic response to a stimulus.

Regression: returning to earlier stages of development when severely stressed.

Reinforcement: a behaviour is more likely to re-occur because the response was agreeable. Both positive and negative reinforcement have agreeable consequences.

Relative deprivation: a gap between what we have done (and have) and what we expected to be able to do (and have).

Relative morality: this is based on the notion that the acceptability of any act depends in part on the benefits that it produces; in other words, the ends can justify the means.

Reliability: the extent to which a method of measurement or a research study produces consistent findings across situations or over time.

Replicability: a feature of research, in which the findings of an experiment can be repeated.

Representativeness heuristic: "rule of thumb" enabling judgements to be made on the basis of probability.

Repression: the process of forcing very threatening thoughts and memories out of the conscious mind in Freudian theory; motivated forgetting.

Resonance: Gibson's explanation for how we detect invariant sensory information; the information is there in the environment and one simply tunes into it.

Restricted code: in Bernstein's theory, concrete and descriptive language.

Ritualisation: the evolutionary process by means of which signals come to be more effective at communicating information to other animals; ritualised signals tend to be stereotyped, exaggerated, and repetitive.

Rods: photoreceptors in the retina that are specialised for vision in dim light and for detection of movement.

Role taking: the ability to watch the behaviour of another individual and understand their intentions.

Runaway process: Fisher's theory that some inherited characteristics become more and more exaggerated because females actively select mates with this feature. Also called "sexy sons hypothesis".

Salience: that aspect of a situation or behaviour that is especially prominent or conspicuous.

Scaffolding: the context provided by an adult or other knowledgeable person which helps the child to develop his or her cognitive skills.

Scattergraph: two-dimensional representation of all the participants' scores in a correlational study; also known as scattergram.

Schemas: organised packets of information stored in long-term memory.

Schizophrenia: a severe condition in which there is a loss of contact with reality, including distortions of thought, emotion, and behaviour.

Scripts: sets of schemas that guide people when performing commonplace activities, such as going to a restaurant or catching a bus.

Search image: a mental representation of an object that assists in recognition, for example, the visual features of a prey.

Seasonal affective disorder: a disorder that nearly always involves the sufferer experiencing severe depression during winter months.

Secondary reinforcer: a stimulus that is rewarding because it has been associated with a primary reinforcer; examples are money and praise.

Selective pressure: in evolutionary terms, the pressure of competition to reproduce successfully in the face of limited resources.

Self-actualisation: the need to discover and fulfil one's potential.

Self-disclosure: revealing personal information about oneself to someone else.

Self-discovery: an active approach to learning in which the child is encouraged to use his or her initiative in learning.

Self-efficacy: an individual's assessment of his or her ability to cope with given situations.

Self-regulation: a process of self-reward if an internal standard of performance is achieved, but with feelings of failure if it is not achieved.

Self-serving bias: the tendency to take the credit for one's successes, but not to accept blame for one's failures.

Sensori-motor stage: the first stage in Piaget's theory, at which children learn to co-ordinate their sensory and motor abilities.

Sensory buffer: an early part of the processing system, in which information stays for a short period of time before being attended to or disappearing from the system.

Separation anxiety: the sense of anxiety felt by a child when separated from their attachment figure.

Seriation: a child's ability to arrange objects in order on the basis of a single feature (e.g., height).

Serotonin: a neurotransmitter that is associated with lower arousal, sleepiness, and reduced anxiety.

Sex: the biological fact of being male or female as determined by a pair of chromosomes.

Sexual identity: maleness or femaleness based on biological factors.

Sexual selection: selection for characteristics that increase mating success.

Sexy sons hypothesis: the notion that females mate with the most attractive males so that their own sons will inherit these characteristics and thus be attractive to other females. Related to the runaway process.

Shadowing task: a task in which one auditory message is repeated back out loud while another auditory message is ignored.

Sham rage: a kind of cool aggression that was displayed in cats whose cerebral cortex had been ablated.

Shaping: a form of operant conditioning in which responses need to become closer and closer to what is desired in order to be rewarded.

Situational attributions: deciding that people's actions are caused by the situation in which they find themselves rather than by their personality.

Sneak copulation: mating by a non-dominant male when the dominant male is not looking.

Social causation hypothesis: the view that schizophrenia may be related to the greater stress experienced by members of the lower class, whereas middle classes have less stressful lives.

Social constructionism: an approach to psychology based on the assumption that our knowledge of ourselves and of others are social constructions, and thus there is no objective reality for research.

Social drift hypothesis: the view that more schizophrenics are members of the lower classes, not because of the social causation hypothesis, but because they drift into the lower classes due to their inability to cope.

Social facilitation: the enhancement of an individual's performance when working in the presence of other people.

Social identities: each of the groups with which we identify produces a social identity; our feelings about ourselves depend on how we feel about the groups with which we identify.

Social learning theory: the view that behaviour can be explained in terms of both direct and indirect (vicarious) reinforcement; indirect reinforcement and identification lead to imitation.

Social marking: conflict between an individual's cognitive understanding and a social rule.

Social norms: the standards or rules of behaviour for individuals expected by a given society or culture.

Social penetration theory: the theory that the development of a relationship involves increasing self-disclosure on both sides.

Social perception: how we use data from our environment to perceive our social world.

Social representations: knowledge about the world that is derived from social dialogues.

Social skills training: a form of therapy based on the behavioural approach that involves teaching appropriate social skills by using rewards, modelling and conditioning.

Socio-cognitive conflict: intellectual conflict produced by exposure to the differing views of others.

Sociobiologists: scientists who argue that the roots of social behaviour are to be found in biological and genetic factors.

Sociobiology: an approach to explaining social behaviour in terms of evolutionary processes; with special emphasis on the gene as the unit for natural selection.

Sociolinguists: scientists who argue that language functions in a social context and it is important to study it in this context.

Soft determinism: the notion that we should distinguish between behaviour that is very constrained by the situation (i.e., determined) and behaviour that is only modestly constrained (i.e., less exactly determined).

Somatic therapy: a form of treatment for mental illness involving manipulations of the body (e.g., drug treatment).

Somatosensory area: a region located in the parietal lobe of the cerebral cortex that receives information from various senses about temperature, pain, and pressure. The areas of the body are topographically represented.

Spatial memory: memory for the layout of one's environment.

Speciesism: discrimination and exploitation based on differences between species.

Speech accommodation theory: the theory that people modify the way they speak to suit the context.

Split-brain patients: individuals who have had the fibres connected the two cerebral hemispheres severed. This is done to reduce epileptic attacks in cases of severe epilepsy and involves severing the cerebral commisures that includes the corpus callosum.

Spontaneous recovery: the re-emergence of responses over time following experimental extinction.

Spontaneous remission: recovering from an illness (or experiencing reduced symptoms) as a consequence of the passage of time rather than any treatment.

Squid magnetometry: a technique for assessing the magnetic flux or field in the brain using a superconducting quantum interference device.

Standardised tests: psychological tests that have been used with large groups of individuals in order to establish a set of "standards" or norms.

Statistical significance: the level at which the decision is made to reject the null hypothesis in favour of the experimental hypothesis.

Statistical tests: various formulae that enable you to analyse and compare data produced in research studies. A statistical test produces a statistic that can then be assessed, using tables of significance, to see if the data fit or do not fit the hypothesis.

Stereotactic neurosurgery: a refined method of psychosurgery that requires only a small opening to be made in the patient's skull, under local anaesthesia.

Stereotaxic: being able to precisely locate areas of the brain, for example to enable an electrode to be placed there to record brain activity.

Stereotype: a social perception of an individual in terms of some readily available feature, such as skin colour or gender, rather than their actual personal attributes.

Stimulus enhancement: where an animal may notice a stimulus in their environment because of the behaviour of another animal.

Stimulus generalisation: see Generalisation.

Subcortical: those parts of the frontal region of the brain that are not part of the cerebral cortex. They lie "under" the cortex.

Superego: in Freudian theory, the part of the mind concerned with moral issues.

Suprachiasmatic nucleus: a small group of neurones in the hypothalamus that act as a biological clock and help regulate the circadian rhythm.

Sympathetic branch: the part of the autonomic nervous system that activates internal organs.

Symptom: an indicator of an underlying pathological condition.

Symptom substitution: when one symptom is eliminated, but the underlying problems lead to its replacement with another symptom.

Symptom–syndrome approach: dealing with illness (physical or psychological) by identifying symptoms, diagnosing a syndrome, and suggesting a suitable form of treatment.

Synapses: the extremely small gaps between adjacent neurons.

Syncretic thought: a kind of thinking where new experiences are assimilated into rather vague and global schema. Syncretic thought occurs because young children focus on two objects at a time, and find it hard to consider the characteristics of several objects at the same time. It is characteristic of the preoperational stage.

Syndrome: a set of symptoms that are generally found together.

Synopticity: a synopsis is a survey or outline that draws together common threads. The various approaches in psychology, such as behaviourism and the biological approach, and issues, such as reductionism and ethics, are common threads that run through the whole of psychology, i.e., they are synoptic.

Systematic desensitisation: a form of treatment for phobias, in which the fear response to threatening stimuli is replaced by a different response such as muscle relaxation.

Tact: a form of language learning in which saying a word almost correctly leads to a reward.

Telegraphic period: the second stage of language development, during which children use nouns and verbs in their speech, but tend to leave out other parts of speech.

Test of association: a type of statistical test where a calculation is made to see how closely pairs of data vary together, i.e., how closely they are associated or correlated.

Test of difference: a type of statistical test where two sets of data are compared to see if they differ significantly.

Testosterone: a male hormone.

Theory of Mind: having an understanding that others' thoughts and emotions are different from one's own.

Theory of naïve psychology: the theory that people behave like naïve scientists who relate observable behaviour to unobservable causes.

Top-down processing: processing that is affected by expectations and prior knowledge, as distinct from bottom-up processing, which is driven directly by the stimulus.

Transference: in psychoanalysis, the transfer of the patient's strong feelings for one or both parents onto the therapist.

Transformational grammar: Chomsky's concept of an innate set of rules for combining words to produce meaning.

Transgenerational effect: if a woman has, e.g., a poor diet during pregnancy, her foetus suffers and may be less able to reproduce future generations.

Transitivity: understanding the relation between elements, for example x is greater than y and y is greater than z, therefore x is greater than z.

Treatment aetiology fallacy: the mistaken belief that the effectiveness of a form of treatment indicates the cause of a disorder.

Trepanning: cutting holes in the skull so that the devils thought to cause mental illness can escape. It is still used to relieve pressure inside the cranial cavity.

Triangular theory of love: Sternberg's theory that love has three components: intimacy, passion, and decision/commitment.

Triangulation: a term borrowed from mathematics to describe the way in which research findings can be confirmed by looking at findings from other studies.

Tutorial training: a traditional approach in which the teacher imparts knowledge to fairly passive students.

Type I error: mistakenly rejecting the null hypothesis in favour of the experimental hypothesis when the results are actually due to chance.

Type II error: mistakenly retaining the null hypothesis when the experimental hypothesis is actually correct.

Ultradian rhythm: a biological rhythm that recurs in a cycle of less than a day ("*ultra*" and "*dies*" = above or higher frequency than a day); e.g., the sleep stages.

Under-extension: using words to apply to fewer objects than is strictly correct.

Uniformitarianism: the notion that biological and other processes operate in the same constant way over time.

Validity: the extent to which something is true. This may be applied to a measurement tool, such as a psychological test, or to the "trueness" of an experimental procedure both in terms of what goes on within the experiment (internal validity) and its relevance to other situations (external validity).

Verbal deprivation theory: Bernstein's theory that language development is determined by social environment, and this affects cognitive development.

Vicarious reinforcement: the concept in social learning theory that reinforcement can be received indirectly, by observing another person being reinforced.

Visual agnosia: a condition where individuals can see but fail to be able to recognise objects.

Visual constancies: an object's size, shape, colour, and so on, are perceived as remaining fairly constant or unchanging in spite of large variations in the retinal image.

Visual cortex: the part of the cerebral cortex dedicated to vision, located in the occipital lobes.

Visual search: a task in which a visual target or targets must be located as quickly as possible from among distractors.

Weapons effect: an increase in aggressive behaviour caused by the mere sight of weapons (e.g., guns).

Yerkes–Dodson law: the curvilinear relationship between arousal and performance; when arousal is very low or very high, performance is poor. Performance is highest at a medium level of arousal.

Zeitgeber: external events that partially determine biological rhythms.

Zone of proximal development: in Vygotsky's theory, capacities that are being developed but are not as yet functioning fully.

Zoom-lens model: the notion that visual attention is a spotlight with an adjustable beam.

Author Index

Wampold, B.E. 687
Ward, C.H. 641
Warden, C.J. 525
Warner, C.B. 239
Warr, P.B. 476
Warren, R.M. 298, 323, 474
Warren, R.P 298, 323, 474
Warren-Leubecker, A. 337
Warrington, E.K. 150, 152
Washburn, A.L. 200
Washburn, D.A. 584
Wason, P.C. 370, 371, 582
Waterman, A.S. 443, 447
Waterman, T.H. 534
Waters, E. 79
Watkins, M.J. 789
Watson, J.B. 318, 508, 579, 652, 763, 769
Watson, N. 162
Waxler, N.E. 634
Weakland, J. 634
Webb, W.B. 182, 185, 186, 193
Wechsler, D. 473
Wedderburn, A.A. 235
Weekes, J.R. 608, 609
Wegman, H.M. 176
Weinberger, C. 218, 219
Weinberger, D.R. 632
Weinberger, J. 612
Weiner, B. 21, 22
Weiner, M.J. 47, 50, 51
Weingarten, H.P. 203
Weinreich, P. 451
Weishaar, M.E. 681
Weiskopf, S. 307
Weiskrantz, L. 150
Weiss, B. 616
Weissman, M.M. 617, 641
Weissmann, A. 328
Weisstein, N. 256, 260
Weisz, J.R. 616
Welsh, R. 680
Weltman, G. 246
Wender, P.H. 631, 637
Werner, C. 62
Wernicke, C. 153
Wertheimer, M. 289, 291
Wertsch, J.V. 375
Westcott, M.R. 733
Westen, D. 75, 82, 83, 568, 573, 701, 702
Westermeyer, J. 613
Wetherell, M. 45, 745
Wever, R. 170, 171
Whalen, C. 677
Wharton, C.M. 347
Wheatstone, C. 293
Wheeler, L. 221
Wheeler, L.R. 391

Wheldall, K. 367
Whipple, K. 685, 688
Whishaw, I.Q. 162
Whitbourne, S.K. 620
White, B.J. 45, 46, 47, 49, 700
White, G.L. 218, 220, 811
Whiting, B.B. 120
Whiting, J.W. 120
Whorf, B.L. 318, 320
Wickens, C.D. 242
Wider, E. 495
Widiger, T.A. 618
Wiesel, T.N. 143, 149, 150, 258, 274, 306
Wiggins, D.A. 569
Wigmore, S.W. 520
Wilczynski, W. 554
Wilder, D.A. 50
Wilkie, F. 477
Wilkinson, G.S. 505
Wilkinson, R.T. 181
Willemsen, M.E. 120
Willerman, L. 390, 436, 585
Williams, C. 578, 580, 640
Williams, J.B.W. 597
Williams, J.E. 439, 440, 698
Williams, J.H. 421, 766
Williams, L.M. 421
Williams, R.L. 386, 395
Williams, T.M. 435
Williamson, P.A. 102
Willson, J. 280
Wilson, E.O. 541, 573
Wilson, J. 237
Wilson, M. 573, 776
Wilson, M.A. 172
Wilson, T.D. 18
Wilton, R.N. 290, 291
Wiltschko, R. 535
Wiltschko, W. 499, 534, 535
Winch, R.F. 63
Windgassen, K. 668
Winslade, W.J. 672
Winson, H. 191, 193
Winter, D.G. 41
Winter, J. 181
Wishart, J.G. 364
Witelson, S.F. 160
Witkin, H.A. 307
Wittinger, R.P. 264
Wolf, J.M. 290
Wolfe, J.B. 216
Wolpe, J. 675, 678
Wolz, J.P. 547
Wong, F.Y. 127
Wong, S. 216
Wood, J.T. 82, 374
Wood, R.J. 204, 206

Wood, W. 127
Wood-Schneider, M. 124
Woodruff, G. 523, 524
Woodworth, R.S. 207, 294, 295
Worell, J. 618
World Health Organisation 594, 615
Wraga, M. 298
Wright, F.E. 47, 50, 51
Wright, P. 86
Wright, P.H. 86
Wright, S.C. 82
Wrightsman, L.S. 29
Wu, P.Y.K. 263
Wu, S. 83
Wundt, W. 736, 768
Wurm, M. 812
Wynne, L.C. 513
Wynne-Edwards, V.C. 500

Yael, A. 90, 91
Yaguchi, K. 482
Yaniv, I. 341
Yap, P.M. 615
Yarrow, M.R. 474
Yates, F. 820
Yeates, K.O. 392
Yelsma, P. 83
Yerkes, R.M. 209, 507
Yin, R.K. 264
Yonas, A. 303
Yorkston, N.J. 685, 688
Young, A.W. 263, 264, 265, 266
Young, K. 92
Young, R.C. 202
Young, T. 276, 277
Young, W.C. 437
Youniss, J. 449
Yukl, G.A. 213
Yule, W. 441

Zach, R. 520
Zahavi, A. 565
Zahn-Waxler, C. 398, 409
Zajonc, R.B. 222
Zax, M. 393
Zeki, S. 278, 736
Zembrodt, I. 71
Zhang, W.-Y. 204
Zhar, J.H. 819
Zigler, E.F. 386, 392
Zihl, J. 291
Zillmann, D. 44, 104, 105
Zimbardo, P.G. 104, 105, 221, 707
Zucconi, M. 181
Zuckerman, M. 209
Zuk, M. 565

Subject Index

Illustration Credits

895

supplied by Bipinchandra J. Mistry. Page 220: Photofusion/David Montford.

PART 3

Page 233: Eliza Armstrong/Impact. Page 240: Photofusion/Louis Quail. Page 242: Popperfoto. Page 243: Popperfoto. Page 246: TRIP. Page 253: TRIP. Page 257 (top): Reproduced with permission from J. Green and C. Hicks (1984), *Basic cognitive processes*. Milton Keynes: Open University Press. Page 258: Adapted from I. Biederman (1987). Recognition-by-components: A theory of human image understanding. *Psychological Review, 94,* 115–147. Page 261: Adapted from B.R. Bugelski and D.A. Alampay (1961). The role of frequency in developing perceptual sets. *Canadian Journal of Psychology, 15,* 205–211. Page 262: Adapted from M.J. Farah (1994). Specialisation within visual object recognition: Clues from prosopagnosia and alexia. In M.J. Farah and G. Ratcliff (Eds.), *The neuropsychology of high-level vision: Collected tutorial essays.* Hillsdale, NJ: Lawrence Erlbaum Associates Inc. Page 263 (bottom): Reproduced with permission from C. Flanagan (1999). *Early socialisation: Sociability and attachment.* London: Routledge. Page 264: Photofusion/Crispin Hughes. Page 265 (bottom): Popperfoto. Page 278: From *Biological Psychology, 6 edition,* by J.W. Kalat © 1998. Reprinted with permission of Wadsworth, an imprint of the Wadsworth Group, a division of Thomson Learning. Fax 800 730-2215. Page 279 (top): Popperfoto. Page 279 (bottom): TRIP. Page 280 (top): From J.J. Gibson (1966). *The senses considered as perceptual systems.* Boston, MA: Houghton Mifflin. Copyright ©1966 by Houghton Mifflin Company. Reprinted with permission. Page 280 (middle): Adapted from P. Rookes and J. Wilson (2000). *Perception.* London: Routledge. Page 281: Photofusion/Steve Eason. Page 282: Weidenfeld & Nicolson. Page 283: Reproduced with permission from R. Schafer and G. Murphy (1943), The role of autism in visual figure–ground relationship. *Journal of Experimental Psychology, 32,* 335–343. Copyright © 1943 American Psychological Association. Page 284 (top right): TRIP. Page 286 (bottom, left): Photographed and supplied by Bipinchandra J. Mistry. Page 286 (bottom, right): Photographed and supplied by Bipinchandra J. Mistry. Page 288: Photographed and supplied by Bipinchandra J. Mistry. Page 290 (top): "Pintos" by Bev Doolittle Copyright © 2001, licensed courtesy of The Greenwich Workshop, Inc. www.greenwichworkshop.com. Page 291: Adapted from P.T. Quinlan and R.N. Wilton (1998). Grouping by proximity or similarity? Competition between the

Gestalt principles in vision. *Perception, 27,* 417–430. Page 293 (top): Popperfoto. Page 296 (top): Popperfoto. Page 297 (bottom): M.C. Escher's "Waterfall" © 2000 Cordon Art B.V., Baarn, Holland. All rights reserved. Page 300 (bottom left): Photograph by David Linton, in Scientific American. Reproduced with permission. Page 303: Adapted from E.J. Gibson, J.J. Gibson, A.D. Pick, and H.A. Osser (1962). A developmental study of the discrimination of letter-like forms. *Journal of Comparative and Physiological Psychology, 55,* 897–906. Page 304: Reprinted with permission from C. Blakemore and G.F. Cooper (1970). Development of the brain depends on the visual environment. *Nature, 228,* 477–478. Copyright © 1970 Macmillan Magazines Limited. Page 308 (bottom): TRIP. Page 309: From W. Hudson (1960). Pictorial depth perception in subcultural groups in Africa. *Journal of Social Psychology, 52,* 183–208. Reprinted with permission of the Helen Dwight Reid Educational Foundation. Published by Heldref Publications, 1319 Eighteenth St, NW, Washington, DC 20036-1802. Copyright © 1960. Page 318: Archives of the History of American Psychology/The University of Akron. Reproduced with permission. Page 324 (top): VinMag Archive. Page 324 (bottom): Popperfoto. Page 330: Photos by C. Trevarthen, reproduced with permission. From C. Trevarthen (1980). Development of interpersonal cooperative understanding in infants. In D. Olson (Ed.), *The social foundations of language and thought: Essays in honor of J.S. Bruner.* New York: W.W. Norton. Page 340 (top): Adapted from R.W. Weisberg and J. Suls (1973), An information-processing model of Duncker's candle problem. *Cognitive Psychology, 4,* 255–276. Page 341: Reproduced with permission from G. Knoblich, S. Ohlsson, H. Haider, and D. Rhenius (1999), Constraint relaxation and chunk decomposition in insight. *Journal of Experimental Psychology: Learning, Memory, and Cognition, 25,* 1534–1555. Copyright © 1999 American Psychological Association.

PART 4

Page 361: Reproduced with permission from J.J. Ducret (1990). *Jean Piaget: Biographie et parcours intellectuel.* Lausanne, Switzerland: Editions Delachaux et Niestlé. Page 362: Popperfoto. Page 364 (bottom): Photos by Peter Willatts. Reproduced with permission. Page 363 (top): Photofusion/Bob Watkins. Page 370 (top): Copyright © Hasbro International Inc. Mastermind is a Trademark of Invicta Toys and Games Ltd. Used with permission. Page 375 (bottom): Photofusion/Bob Watkins. Page 376: Popperfoto. Page 377 (bottom):

Popperfoto. Page 380: Photofusion/Christa Stadtler. Page 382 (top): Lupe Cunha Photographer and Picture Library. Page 382 (bottom): Photofusion/Ewa Ohlsson. Page 383: Photographed and supplied by Bipinchandra J. Mistry. Page 386 (top): Popperfoto/Reuters. Page 387 (bottom): Popperfoto. Page 393: Adapted from A.J. Sameroff, R. Seifer, A. Baldwin, and C. Baldwin (1993). Stability of intelligence from preschool to adolescence: The influence of social and family risk factors. *Child Development, 64,* 80–97. Page 394 (top): Photofusion/Crispin Hughes. Page 394 (bottom): Photofusion/Paul Mattsson. Page 397 (bottom): Popperfoto. Page 402: Photographed and supplied by Bipinchandra J. Mistry. Page 404: Adapted from A. Colby, L. Kohlberg, J. Gibbs, and M. Lieberman (1983). A longitudinal study of moral judgment. *Monographs of the Society for Research in Child Development, 48,* (Nos. 1–2, serial no. 200). Page 407: Popperfoto. Page 408: Photofusion/Paul Doyle. Page 409: Photofusion/Gina Glover. Page 418: Archives of the History of American Psychology/The University of Akron. Reproduced with permission. Page 422 (top): Popperfoto. Page 422 (bottom): Popperfoto. Page 424: TRIP. Page 425: Popperfoto. Page 426 (left): Photofusion/David Trainer. Page 426 (right): Photofusion/David Trainer. Page 430 (top): Popperfoto. Page 430 (bottom): Popperfoto. Page 432: Penny Tweedie/Panos Pictures. Page 434: TRIP. Page 435 (left): Photofusion/Helen Stone. Page 435 (right): Photofusion/David Montford. Page 439: Photofusion/Crispin Hughes. Page 448: Photofusion/Sam Turner. Page 451: Popperfoto. Page 454 (left): Photofusion/Bob Watkins. Page 454 (right): Photofusion/Paul Baldesare. Page 455 (left): Photofusion/David Montford. Page 455 (right): Photofusion/Tina Gue. Page 460: TRIP. Page 466: Reprinted from T. Holmes and R. Rahe (1967), The social readjustment rating scale. *Journal of Psychosomatic Research, 11,* 213–218. Copyright © 1967, with permission from Elsevier Science. Page 469 (top): Photofusion/Paul Doyle. Page 470: TRIP. Page 473: Popperfoto/Reuters. Page 472: Photofusion/Reen Pilkington. Page 476: Popperfoto/Reuters. Page 478: Popperfoto. Page 479: Photofusion/Paul Baldesare. Page 480: Photofusion/Sam Tanner. Page 482: Photofusion/Mark Campbell.

PART 5

Page 492 (middle): Heather Angel/Biofotos. Page 492 (bottom): Heather Angel/Biofotos. Page 493 (top left): Popperfoto. Page 493 (top right): Popperfoto. Page 493 (bottom): Popperfoto. Page 494 (top): Heather Angel/Biofotos. Page 494 (bottom): TRIP. Page 496: Popperfoto. Page 497: Heather Angel/Biofotos. Page 498 (left): Heather Angel/Biofotos. Page 498 (right): Heather Angel/Biofotos. Page 499: TRIP. Page 500 (bottom): TRIP. Page 502 (bottom): TRIP. Page 503 (top right): Brian Rogers/Biofotos. Page 503 (bottom): Heather Angel/Biofotos. Page 505: TRIP. Page 506: Archives of the History of American Psychology/The University of Akron. Reproduced with permission. Page 507: Adapted from R.M. Yerkes and S. Morgulis (1909). The method of Pavlov in animal psychology. *Psychological Bulletin, 6*, 257–273. Page 508: Archives of the History of American Psychology/The University of Akron. Reproduced with permission. Page 509: Heather Angel/Biofotos. Page 510 (bottom): Archives of the History of American Psychology/The University of Akron. Reproduced with permission. Page 511 (bottom): TRIP. Page 512 (top): Popperfoto. Page 512 (bottom): Popperfoto. Page 516: Reproduced by kind permission of Professor Albert Bandura. Page 522: Photos courtesy of Cognitive Evolution Group, University of Louisiana at Lafayette. Reproduced with permission. Page 525: Reprinted from H. Wimmer and J. Perner (1983). Beliefs about beliefs: Representation and the constraining function of wrong beliefs in young children's understanding of deception. *Cognition, 13*, 103–128. Copyright © 1983, with permission from Elsevier Science. Page 531: Adapted from R.R. Baker (1978). *The evolutionary ecology of animal migration*. New York: Holmes & Meier Publishers. Page 532: Adapted from A.C. Perdeck (1958). Two types of orientation in migrating starlings, *Sturnus vulgaris L.*, and chaffinches, *Fringilla coelbs L.*, as revealed by displacement experiments. *Ardea, 46*, 1–37. Page 535 (top): Reproduced with permission from R. Gross, R. McIlveen, H. Coolican, A. Clamp, and J. Russell (2000), *Psychology: A new introduction for A level (2nd Ed.)*. London: Hodder & Stoughton. Page 536 (top part of top figure): Adapted from G.V.T. Matthews (1955). *Bird navigation*. Cambridge: Cambridge University Press. Page 536 (bottom part of top figure): Adapted from W.T. Keeton (1974). The mystery of pigeon homing. *Scientific American, 231*, 96–107. Copyright Bunji Tagawa. Page 536 (bottom): Reproduced with permission from S.T. Emlen and J.T. Emlen (1966). *Auk, 83*, 361–367. Page 538: Adapted from N. Tinbergen (1951). *The study of instinct*. Oxford: Oxford University Press. Page 541: Adapted from E.O. Wilson (1975). *Sociobiology: The new synthesis*. Cambridge, MA: Harvard University Press. Page 542 (top): Brian

Rogers/Biofotos. Page 542 (bottom): Heather Angel/Biofotos. Page 547: Reprinted from C.M. Herman, D.G. Richards, and J.P. Wolz (1984). Comprehension of sentences by bottlenosed dolphins. *Cognition, 16*, 129–219. Copyright © 1984, with permission from Elsevier Science. Page 543 (top): Popperfoto. Page 546: TRIP. Page 548: Photo by April Ottey. Reproduced with permission of the Chimpanzee and Human Communication Institute, Central Washington University. Page 549: Reproduced from O. Pfungst (1911). *Clever Hans: The horse of Mr von Osten*. New York: Holt. Page 550: Photograph by Mike Nichols. Reproduced with permission. Page 551: Reproduced with permission from E.S. Savage-Rumbaugh and R. Lewin (1994). *Kanzi: At the brink of the human mind*. New York: Wiley. Copyright © 1994, reprinted by permission of John Wiley and Sons, Inc. Page 564 (top): Heather Angel/Biofotos. Page 564 (bottom): Francis Leroy, Biocosmos/Science Photo Library. Page 565: Popperfoto. Page 566: TRIP. Page 567: Photofusion/Bob Watkins. Page 568: Heather Angel/Biofotos. Page 569: Adapted with permission from N. Tinbergen (1952). The curious behaviour of the stickleback. *Scientific American, 187 (6)*, 22–26. Page 570: Popperfoto/Reuters. Page 571: TRIP. Page 572: Figure from "Human sperm competition" in *Sperm competition and the evolution of animal mating systems* by Robert L. Smith, copyright © 1984 by Academic Press, reproduced by permission of the publisher. Page 582: Adapted from L. Cosmides and J. Tooby (1992). Cognitive adaptations for social exchange. In J.H. Barkow Jerome, L. Cosmides, and J. Tooby (Eds.), *The adapted mind: Evolutionary psychology and the generation of culture*. New York: Oxford University Press. Page 584 (top): Adapted from J.M. Fuster (1989). *The prefrontal cortex (2nd Ed.)*. New York: Raven Press. Page 584 (bottom): Adapted from A.S. Romer (1962). *The vertebrate body*. PA: W.B. Saunders Co. Page 585: Reproduced with permission from *The Times*, London, June 18 1999. Copyright © Times Newspapers Limited, 29 July 1999.

PART 6
Page 603: Photofusion/David Montford. Page 604: VinMag Archive. Page 605: Popperfoto. Page 608 (left): Popperfoto. Page 608 (right): VinMag Archive. Page 617: Photofusion/Louis Quail. Page 619: Photofusion/Ingrid Gavshon. Page 628: Photofusion/Debbie Humphry. Page 630 (top): Photofusion/Linda Sole. Page 637: Popperfoto. Page 640: Photofusion/Steve Eason. Page 642: Photofusion/Crispin Hughes. Page 650: TRIP. Page 652:

Reproduced with the kind permission of Benjamin Harris, University of Wisconsin. Page 653: Popperfoto. Page 664: VinMag Archive. Page 665: Science Photo Library. Page 674: Popperfoto. Page 684: Popperfoto.

PART 7
Page 698: Anita Corbin/Impact. Page 699: Popperfoto. Page 701: TRIP. Page 708–709: *Ethical principles for conducting research with human participants* are Society guidelines, reproduced by kind permission of The British Psychological Society. Page 710: Reproduced with permission of P.G. Zimbardo Inc. Page 711: Popperfoto. Page 714 (top): Image supplied by the Commission for Racial Equality. Reproduced with permission. Page 714 (bottom): TRIP. Page 715: Photofusion/David Montford. Page 716: Photofusion/George Montgomery. Page 717: Popperfoto/Reuters. Page 718: TRIP. Page 720: Photographed and supplied by Bipinchandra J. Mistry. Page 721: Photo by April Ottey. Reproduced with permission of the Chimpanzee and Human Communication Institute, Central Washington University. Page 723: Text is based on the *British Psychological Society guidelines for research with animals*. The complete version of these guidelines is available on www.bps.org.uk/documents/Code.pdf. Page 724: Richard Day/Biofotos. Page 742: Science Photo Library. Page 743: Popperfoto. Page 745: Popperfoto. Page 749: Photofusion/Bob Watkins. Page 750: Reproduced with permission from A. Colby, L. Kohlberg, J. Gibbs, and M. Liebermann (1983). A longitudinal study of moral development, *Monographs of the Society for Research in Child Development, 48*, (Nos. 1–2, Serial No. 200). Page 757: TRIP. Page 758: Photofusion/Steve Eason. Page 768: Archives of the History of American Psychology/The University of Akron. Reproduced with permission. Page 769: Science Photo Library. Page 773: Popperfoto. Page 781: Science Photo Library.

PART 8
Page 788: Project Brief Proposal Form (draft version) for AQA specification has been reproduced by kind permission of the Assessment and Qualifications Alliance.

APPENDIX
Page 816–817: Critical values of U for the Mann-Whitney U test from R. Runyon and A. Haber (1976). *Fundamentals of behavioural statistics (3rd Ed.)*. Reading, MA: McGraw-Hill. Reproduced with permission. Page 818 (top): Sign test values from F. Clegg (1982). *Simple statistics*. Cambridge, UK: Cambridge

versity Press. Reproduced with mission. Page 818 (bottom): Wilcoxon ned ranks test values from R. Meddis 975). *Statistical handbook for non-atisticians*. London: McGraw-Hill. Reproduced with permission of the publisher. Page 819: Critical values of Spearman's rho from J.H. Zhar (1972).

Significance testing of the Spearman Rank Correlation Coefficient. *Journal of the American Statistical Association, 67*, 578–580. Reproduced with permission from *The Journal of the American Statistical Association*. Copyright ((1972) by the American Statistical Association. All rights reserved. Page 820: Critical values of chi-

squared abridged from R.A. Fisher and F. Yates (1974). *Statistical tables for biological, agricultural and medical research (6th Ed.)*. Harlow, UK: Addison Wesley Longman. Copyright © 1963 R.A. Fisher and F. Yates. Reprinted by permission of Addison Wesley Longman Limited. Reprinted by permission of Pearson Education Ltd.